Prepare, Apply, and Confirm

- **Enhanced eText**—The Pearson eText gives students access to their textbook anytime, anywhere. In addition to notetaking, highlighting, and bookmarking, the Pearson eText offers interactive and sharing features. Students actively read and learn, through embedded and auto-graded practice, animations, author videos, and more. Instructors can share comments or highlights, and students can add their own, for a tight community of learners in any class.

- **Dynamic Study Modules**—Work by continuously assessing student performance and activity, then using data and analytics to provide personalized content in real time to reinforce concepts that target each student's particular strengths and weaknesses.

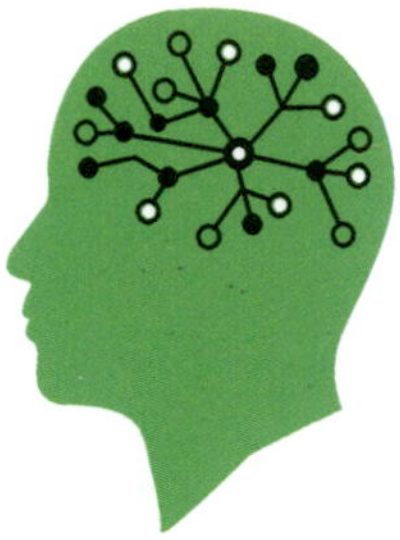

- **Hallmark Features**—Personalized Learning Aids, like Help Me Solve This, View an Example, and instant feedback are available for further practice and mastery when students need the help most!

- **Learning Catalytics**—Generates classroom discussion, guides lecture, and promotes peer-to-peer learning with real-time analytics. Now, students can use any device to interact in the classroom.

- **Adaptive Study Plan**—Assists students in monitoring their own progress by offering them a customized study plan powered by Knewton, based on Homework, Quiz, and Test results. Includes regenerated exercises with unlimited practice and the opportunity to prove mastery through quizzes on recommended learning objectives.

with MyFinanceLab™

- **Worked Solutions**—Provide step-by-step explanations on how to solve select problems using the exact numbers and data that were presented in the problem. Instructors will have access to the Worked Solutions in preview and review mode.

- **Algorithmic Test Bank**—Instructors have the ability to create multiple versions of a test or extra practice for students.

- **Financial Calculator**—The Financial Calculator is available as a smartphone application, as well as on a computer, and includes important functions such as cash flow, net present value, and internal rate of return. Fifteen helpful tutorial videos show the many ways to use the Financial Calculator in MyFinanceLab.

- **Reporting Dashboard**—View, analyze, and report learning outcomes clearly and easily. Available via the Gradebook and fully mobile-ready, the Reporting Dashboard presents student performance data at the class, section, and program levels in an accessible, visual manner.

- **LMS Integration**—Link from any LMS platform to access assignments, rosters, and resources, and synchronize MyLab grades with your LMS gradebook. For students, new direct, single sign-on provides access to all the personalized learning MyLab resources that make studying more efficient and effective.

- **Mobile Ready**—Students and instructors can access multimedia resources and complete assessments right at their fingertips, on any mobile device.

COMMON SYMBOLS AND NOTATION

A	market value of assets, premerger total value of acquirer
APR	annual percentage rate
B	risk-free investment in the replicating portfolio
C	cash flow, call option price
$Corr(R_i, R_j)$	correlation between returns of i and j
$Cov(R_i, R_j)$	covariance between returns of i and j
CPN	coupon payment
D	market value of debt
d	debt-to-value ratio
Div_t	dividends paid in year t
dis	discount from face value
E	market value of equity
EAR	effective annual rate
$EBIT$	earnings before interest and taxes
$EBITDA$	earnings before interest, taxes, depreciation, and amortization
EPS_t	earnings per share on date t
$E[R_i]$	expected return of security i
F, F_T	one-year and T-year forward exchange rate
FCF_t	free cash flow at date t
FV	future value, face value of a bond
g	growth rate
I	initial investment or initial capital committed to the project
Int_t	interest expense on date t
IRR	internal rate of return
K	strike price
k	interest coverage ratio, compounding periods per year
L	lease payment, market value of liabilities
ln	natural logarithm
MV_i	total market capitalization of security i
N	number of cash flows, terminal date, notational principal of a swap contract
N_i	number of shares outstanding of security i
$NPER$	annuity spreadsheet notation for the number of periods or dates of the last cash flow
NPV	net present value
P	price, initial principal or deposit, or equivalent present value, put option price
P_i	price of security i
P/E	price-earnings ratio
PMT	annuity spreadsheet notation for cash flow
PV	present value; annuity spreadsheet notation for the initial amount
q	dividend yield
p	risk-neutral probability
r	interest rate, discount rate of cost of capital
R_i	return of security i
R_{mkt}	return of the market portfolio
R_P	return on portfolio P
RATE	annuity spreadsheet notation for interest rate
r_E, r_D	equity and debt costs of capital
r_f	risk-free interest rate
r_i	required return or cost of capital of security i
r_U	unlevered cost of capital
r_{wacc}	weighted average cost of capital
S	stock price, spot exchange rate, value of all synergies
$SD(R_i)$	standard deviation (volatility) of return of security i
T	option expiration date, maturity date, market value of target
U	market value of unlevered equity
V_t	enterprise value on date t
$Var(R)$	variance of return R
x_i	portfolio weight of investment in i
YTC	yield to call on a callable bond
YTM	yield to maturity
α_i	alpha of security i
β_D, β_E	beta of debt or equity
β_i	beta of security i with respect to the market portfolio
β_s^P	beta of security i with respect to portfolio P
β_U	beta of unlevered firm
Δ	shares of stock in the replicating portfolio; sensitivity of option price to stock price
σ	volatility
τ	tax rate
τ_c	marginal corporate tax rate

CORPORATE FINANCE

FOURTH EDITION

JONATHAN BERK
STANFORD UNIVERSITY

PETER DEMARZO
STANFORD UNIVERSITY

Pearson

To Rebecca, Natasha, and Hannah, for the love and for being there —J. B.

To Kaui, Pono, Koa, and Kai, for all the love and laughter —P. D.

Vice President, Business Publishing: Donna Battista
Editor-in-Chief: Adrienne D'Ambrosio
Acquisitions Editor: Kate Fernandes
Editorial Assistant: Kathryn Brightney
Vice President, Product Marketing: Roxanne McCarley
Product Marketing Manager: Katie Rowland
Field Marketing Manager: Ramona Elmer
Product Marketing Assistant: Jessica Quazza
Team Lead, Program Management: Ashley Santora
Program Manager: Nancy Freihofer
Team Lead, Project Management: Jeff Holcomb
Project Manager: Meredith Gertz
Operations Specialist: Carol Melville
Creative Director: Blair Brown
Art Director: Jonathan Boylan
Vice President, Director of Digital Strategy and Assessment: Paul Gentile
Manager of Learning Applications: Paul DeLuca
Digital Editor: Brian Hyland
Director, Digital Studio: Sacha Laustsen
Digital Studio Manager: Diane Lombardo
Digital Studio Project Managers: Melissa Honig, Alana Coles, Robin Lazrus
Digital Content Team Lead: Noel Lotz
Digital Content Project Lead: Miguel Leonarte
Full-Service Project Management and Composition: SPi Global
Cover Designer: Jonathan Boylan
Cover Image: Chris Rayner Photos, Getty Images
Printer/Binder: LSC Communications
Cover Printer: LSC Communications

Library of Congress Cataloging-in-Publication Data
Names: Berk, Jonathan B., author. | DeMarzo, Peter M., author.
Title: Corporate finance / Jonathan Berk, Peter DeMarzo.
Description: 4th edition. | Boston : Pearson, 2017. | Includes bibliographical references and index.
Identifiers: LCCN 2016025490 | ISBN 9780134083278
Subjects: LCSH: Corporations—Finance.
Classification: LCC HG4026 .B46 2017 | DDC 658.15--dc23
LC record available at https://lccn.loc.gov/2016025490

Pearson www.pearsonhighered.com

ISBN 10: 0-13-408327-X
ISBN 13: 978-0-13-408327-8

The Pearson Series in Finance

Berk/DeMarzo
*Corporate Finance**
*Corporate Finance: The Core**

Berk/DeMarzo/Harford
*Fundamentals of Corporate Finance**

Brooks
*Financial Management: Core Concepts**

Copeland/Weston/Shastri
Financial Theory and Corporate Policy

Dorfman/Cather
Introduction to Risk Management and Insurance

Eakins/McNally
*Corporate Finance Online**

Eiteman/Stonehill/Moffett
*Multinational Business Finance**

Fabozzi
Bond Markets: Analysis and Strategies

Foerster
*Financial Management: Concepts and Applications**

Frasca
Personal Finance

Gitman/Zutter
*Principles of Managerial Finance**
*Principles of Managerial Finance—Brief Edition**

Haugen
The Inefficient Stock Market: What Pays Off and Why
Modern Investment Theory

Holden
Excel Modeling in Corporate Finance
Excel Modeling in Investments

Hughes/MacDonald
International Banking: Text and Cases

Hull
Fundamentals of Futures and Options Markets
Options, Futures, and Other Derivatives

Keown
*Personal Finance: Turning Money into Wealth**

Keown/Martin/Petty
*Foundations of Finance: The Logic and Practice of Financial Management**

Madura
*Personal Finance**

Marthinsen
Risk Takers: Uses and Abuses of Financial Derivatives

McDonald
Derivatives Markets
Fundamentals of Derivatives Markets

Mishkin/Eakins
Financial Markets and Institutions

Moffett/Stonehill/Eiteman
Fundamentals of Multinational Finance

Pennacchi
Theory of Asset Pricing

Rejda/McNamara
Principles of Risk Management and Insurance

Smart/Gitman/Joehnk
*Fundamentals of Investing**

Solnik/McLeavey
Global Investments

Titman/Keown/Martin
*Financial Management: Principles and Applications**

Titman/Martin
Valuation: The Art and Science of Corporate Investment Decisions

Weston/Mitchel/Mulherin
Takeovers, Restructuring, and Corporate Governance

Brief Contents

KV 11.28.2018 0744

Detailed Contents

PART 4 RISK AND RETURN

PART 10 SPECIAL TOPICS

Bridging Theory and Practice

Focus on the Financial Crisis and Sovereign Debt Crisis

Global Financial Crisis boxes reflect the reality of the recent financial crisis and ongoing sovereign debt crisis, noting lessons learned. Twenty-two boxes across the book illustrate and analyze key details.

GLOBAL FINANCIAL CRISIS European Sovereign Debt Yields: A Puzzle

Before the EMU created the euro as a single European currency, the yields of sovereign debt issued by European countries varied widely. These variations primarily reflected differences in inflation expectations and currency risk (see Figure 6.6). However, after the monetary union was put in place at the end of 1998, the yields all essentially converged to the yield on German government bonds. Investors seemed to conclude that there was little distinction between the debt of the European countries in the union—they seemed to feel that all countries in the union were essentially exposed to the same default, inflation and currency risk and thus equally "safe."

Presumably, investors believed that an outright default was unthinkable: They apparently believed that member countries would be fiscally responsible and manage their debt obligations to avoid default at all costs. But as illustrated by Figure 6.6, once the 2008 financial crisis revealed the folly of this assumption, debt yields once again diverged as investors acknowledged the likelihood that some countries (particularly Portugal and Ireland) might be unable to repay their debt and would be forced to default.

In retrospect, rather than bringing fiscal responsibility, the monetary union allowed the weaker member countries to borrow at dramatically lower rates. In response, these countries reacted by increasing their borrowing—and at least in Greece's case, borrowed to the point that default became inevitable.

The Law of One Price as the Unifying Valuation Framework

The Law of One Price framework reflects the modern idea that the absence of arbitrage is the unifying concept of valuation. This critical insight is introduced in Chapter 3, revisited in each part opener, and integrated throughout the text—motivating all major concepts and connecting theory to practice.

Study Aids with a Practical Focus

To be successful, students need to master the core concepts and learn to identify and solve problems that today's practitioners face.

Common Mistakes boxes alert students to frequently made mistakes stemming from misunderstanding core concepts and calculations—in the classroom and in the field.

COMMON MISTAKE Discounting One Too Many Times

The perpetuity formula assumes that the first payment occurs at the end of the first period (at date 1). Sometimes perpetuities have cash flows that start later in the future. In this case, we can adapt the perpetuity formula to compute the present value, but we need to do so carefully to avoid a common mistake.

To illustrate, consider the MBA graduation party described in Example 4.7. Rather than starting immediately, suppose that the first party will be held two years from today (for the current entering class). How would this delay change the amount of the donation required?

Now the timeline looks like this:

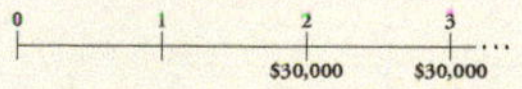

We need to determine the present value of these cash flows, as it tells us the amount of money in the bank needed today to finance the future parties. We cannot apply the perpetuity formula directly, however, because these cash flows are not *exactly* a perpetuity as we defined it. Specifically, the cash flow in the first period is "missing." But consider the situation on date 1—at that point, the first party is one period away and then the cash flows are periodic. From the perspective of date 1, this *is* a perpetuity, and we can apply the formula. From the preceding calculation, we know we need $375,000 on date 1 to have enough to start the parties on date 2. We rewrite the timeline as follows:

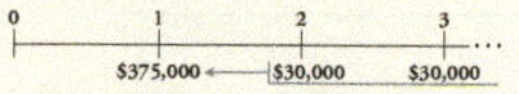

Our goal can now be restated more simply: How much do we need to invest today to have $375,000 in one year? This is a simple present value calculation:

$$PV = \$375{,}000/1.08 = \$347{,}222 \text{ today}$$

A common mistake is to discount the $375,000 twice because the first party is in two periods. *Remember—the present value formula for the perpetuity already discounts the cash flows to one period prior to the first cash flow.* Keep in mind that this common mistake may be made with perpetuities, annuities, and all of the other special cases discussed in this section. All of these formulas discount the cash flows to one period prior to the first cash flow.

Worked Examples accompany every important concept using a step-by-step procedure that guides students through the solution process. Clear labels make them easy to find for help with homework and studying.

EXAMPLE 4.14 Evaluating an Annuity with Monthly Cash Flows

Problem

You are about to purchase a new car and have two options to pay for it. You can pay $20,000 in cash immediately, or you can get a loan that requires you to pay $500 each month for the next 48 months (four years). If the monthly interest rate you earn on your cash is 0.5%, which option should you take?

Solution

Let's start by writing down the timeline of the loan payments:

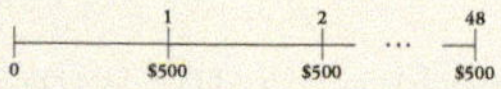

The timeline shows that the loan is a 48-period annuity. Using the annuity formula the present value is

$$PV(\text{48-period annuity of } \$500) = \$500 \times \frac{1}{0.005}\left(1 - \frac{1}{1.005^{48}}\right) = \$21{,}290$$

Alternatively, we may use the annuity spreadsheet to solve the problem:

	NPER	RATE	PV	PMT	FV	Excel Formula
Given	48	0.50%		500	0	
Solve for PV			(21,290)			=PV(0.005,48,500,0)

Thus, taking the loan is equivalent to paying $21,290 today, which is costlier than paying cash. You should pay cash for the car.

Applications that Reflect Real Practice

Corporate Finance features actual companies and leaders in the field.

Interviews with notable practitioners—six new for this edition—highlight leaders in the field and address the effects of the financial crisis.

INTERVIEW WITH **KEVIN M. WARSH**

Kevin M. Warsh, a lecturer at Stanford's Graduate School of Business and a distinguished visiting fellow at the Hoover Institution, was a Federal Reserve governor from 2006 to 2011, serving as chief liaison to the financial markets.

QUESTION: *What are the main policy instruments used by central banks to control the economy?*

ANSWER: The Federal Reserve (Fed) deploys several policy tools to achieve its goals of price stability, maximum sustainable employment, and financial stability. Lowering the federal funds short-term interest rate, the primary policy instrument, stimulates the economy. Raising the federal funds rate generally slows the economy. Buying and selling short-term U.S. Treasury securities through *open market operations* is standard practice. Prior to the 2007–2009 financial crisis, the Fed's balance sheet ranged from $700–$900 billion. But when the Fed was unable to lower interest rates further because rates were so close to zero already, it resorted to large-scale, longer-term open market operations to increase liquidity in the financial system in the hopes of stimulating the economy further, thus growing its balance sheet significantly. With *open mouth operations*, the Fed's announcements of its intent to buy or sell assets indicates its desired degree of future policy accommodation, often prompting markets to react ... interest rates immediately. The Fed's Lend... clarity and confidence in the financial wherewithal of each other. One effective, innovative tool, the *Term Auction Facility (TAF)*, stimulated the economy by providing cheap and readily available term funding to banks, large and small, on the front lines of the economy, thus encouraging them to extend credit to businesses and consumers. After reducing the policy rate to near zero to help revive the economy, the Fed instituted two *Quantitative Easing (QE)* programs—special purchases of government and agency securities—to increase money supply, promote lending, and according to some proponents, increase prices of riskier assets.

The Fed also addressed the global financial crisis by establishing temporary *central bank liquidity swap lines* with the European Central Bank and other major central banks. Using this facility, a foreign central bank is able to obtain dollar funding for its customers by swapping Euros for dollars or another currency and agreeing to reverse the swap at a later date. The Fed does not take exchange rate risk, but it is subject to the credit risk of its central bank counterparty.

QUESTION: *What tools is the European Central Bank (ECB) using to address the sovereign debt crisis? How does its approach comp... the 2007–2009*

General Interest boxes highlight timely material from financial publications that shed light on business problems and real-company practices.

Teaching Students to Think Finance

With a consistency in presentation and an innovative set of learning aids, *Corporate Finance* simultaneously meets the needs of both future financial managers and non-financial managers. This textbook truly shows every student how to "think finance."

Simplified Presentation of Mathematics

One of the hardest parts of learning finance is mastering the jargon, math, and non-standardized notation. *Corporate Finance* systematically uses:

Notation Boxes: Each chapter opens by defining the variables and acronyms used in the chapter as a "legend" for students' reference.

Timelines: Introduced in Chapter 4, timelines are emphasized as the important first step in solving *every* problem that involves cash flows.

Numbered and Labeled Equations: The first time a full equation is given in notation form it is numbered. Key equations are titled and revisited in the chapter summary.

Using Excel Boxes: Provide hands-on instruction of Excel techniques and include screenshots to serve as a guide for students.

Spreadsheet Tables: Select tables are available as Excel files, enabling students to change inputs and manipulate the underlying calculations.

USING EXCEL

Excel's IRR Function

Excel also has a built-in function, IRR, that will calculate the IRR of a stream of cash flows. Excel's IRR function has the format, IRR (values, guess), where "values" is the range containing the cash flows, and "guess" is an optional starting guess where Excel begins its search for an IRR. See the example below:

	A	B	C	D	E
1	Period	0	1	2	3
2	Cash Flow C_t	(1,000.0)	300.0	400.0	500.0
3	IRR	8.9%	=IRR(B2:E2)		

There are three things to note about the IRR function. First, the values given to the IRR function should include all of the cash flows of the project, including the one at date 0. In this sense, the IRR and NPV functions in Excel are inconsistent. Second, like the NPV function, the IRR ignores the period associated with any blank cells. Finally, as we will discuss in Chapter 7, in some settings the IRR function may fail to find a solution, or may give a different answer, depending on the initial guess.

TABLE 8.1 SPREADSHEET — HomeNet's Incremental Earnings Forecast

	Year	0	1	2	3	4	5
Incremental Earnings Forecast ($000s)							
1	Sales	—	26,000	26,000	26,000	26,000	—
2	Cost of Goods Sold	—	(11,000)	(11,000)	(11,000)	(11,000)	—
3	**Gross Profit**	—	15,000	15,000	15,000	15,000	—
4	Selling, General, and Administrative	—	(2,800)	(2,800)	(2,800)	(2,800)	—
5	Research and Development	(15,000)	—	—	—	—	
6	Depreciation	—	(1,500)	(1,500)	(1,500)	(1,500)	(1,500)
7	**EBIT**	(15,000)	10,700	10,700	10,700	10,700	(1,500)
8	Income Tax at 40%	6,000	(4,280)	(4,280)	(4,280)	(4,280)	600
9	**Unlevered Net Income**	**(9,000)**	**6,420**	**6,420**	**6,420**	**6,420**	**(900)**

Practice Finance to Learn Finance

Working problems is the proven way to cement and demonstrate an understanding of finance.

Concept Check questions at the end of each section enable students to test their understanding and target areas in which they need further review.

End-of-chapter problems written personally by Jonathan Berk and Peter DeMarzo offer instructors the opportunity to assign first-rate materials to students for homework and practice with the confidence that the problems are consistent with chapter content. Both the problems and solutions, which also were written by the authors, have been class-tested and accuracy-checked to ensure quality.

Data Cases present in-depth scenarios in a business setting with questions designed to guide students' analysis. Many questions involve the use of Internet resources and Excel techniques.

Data Case

This is your second interview with a prestigious brokerage firm for a job as an equity analyst. You survived the morning interviews with the department manager and the Vice President of Equity. Everything has gone so well that they want to test your ability as an analyst. You are seated in a room with a computer and a list with the names of two companies—Ford (F) and Microsoft (MSFT). You have 90 minutes to complete the following tasks:

1. Download the annual income statements, balance sheets, and cash flow statements for the last four fiscal years from MarketWatch (www.morningstar.com). Enter each company's stock symbol and then go to "financials." Export the statements to Excel by clicking the export button.
2. Find historical stock prices for each firm from Yahoo! Finance (finance.yahoo.com). Enter your stock symbol, click "Historical Prices" in the left column, and enter the proper date range to cover the last day of the month corresponding to the date of each financial statement. Use the closing stock prices (not the adjusted close). To calculate the firm's market capitalization at each date, multiply the number of shares outstanding (see "Basic" on the income statement under "Weighted Average Shares Outstanding") by the firm's historic stock price.
3. For each of the four years of statements, compute the following ratios for each firm:

Valuation Ratios
Price-Earnings Ratio (for EPS use Diluted EPS Total)
Market-to-Book Ratio
Enterprise Value-to-EBITDA
(For debt, include long-term and short-term debt; for cash, include marketable securities.)

Profitability Ratios
Operating Margin
Net Profit Margin

MyFinanceLab

Because practice with homework problems is crucial to learning finance, *Corporate Finance* is available with MyFinanceLab, a fully integrated homework and tutorial system. MyFinanceLab revolutionizes homework and practice with material written and developed by Jonathan Berk and Peter DeMarzo.

Online Assessment Using End-of-Chapter Problems

The seamless integration among the textbook, assessment materials, and online resources sets a new standard in corporate finance education.

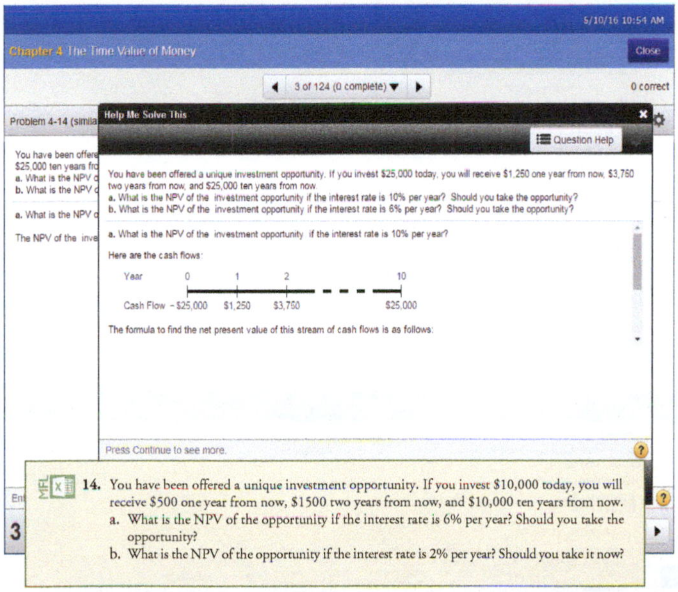

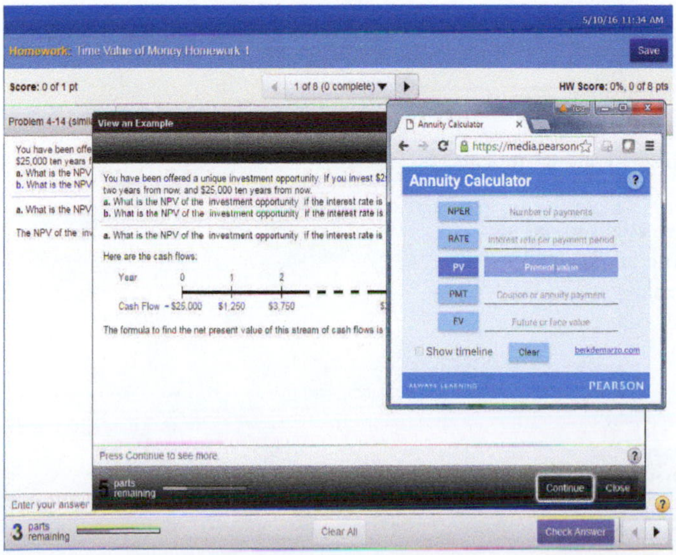

- **End-of-chapter problems**—every single one —appear online. The values in the problems are algorithmically generated, giving students many opportunities for practice and mastery. Problems can be assigned by professors and completed online by students.
- **Helpful tutorial tools**, along with the same pedagogical aids from the text, support students as they study. Links to the eText direct students right to the material they most need to review.
- **Interactive Figures**—Select in-text graphs and figures—covering topics such as bonds, stock valuation, NPV, and IRR—have been digitally enhanced to allow students to interact with variables to affect outcomes and bring concepts to life.

Additional Resources in MyFinanceLab

- **Video clips** profile high-profile firms such as Boeing, Cisco, Delta, and Intel through interviews and analysis. The videos focus on core topical areas, including capital budgeting, mergers and acquisitions, and risk and return.
- **Auto-Graded Excel Projects**—Using proven, field-tested technology, MyFinanceLab's new auto-graded Excel Projects allow instructors to seamlessly integrate Excel content into their course.
- **Finance in the News** provides weekly postings of a relevant and current article from a newspaper or journal article with discussion questions that are assignable in MyFinanceLab.
- Live **news and video feeds** from *The Financial Times* and ABC News provide real-time news updates.
- **Author Solution Videos** walk through the in-text examples using math, the financial calculator, and spreadsheets.

To learn more about MyFinanceLab, contact your local Pearson representative, www.pearsoneducation.com/replocator, or visit www.myfinancelab.com.

Hands-On Practice, Hands-Off Grading

Hands-On, Targeted Practice

Students can take pre-built Practice Tests for each chapter, and their test results will generate an individualized Study Plan. With the Study Plan, students learn to focus their energies on the topics they need to be successful in class, on exams, and, ultimately, in their careers.

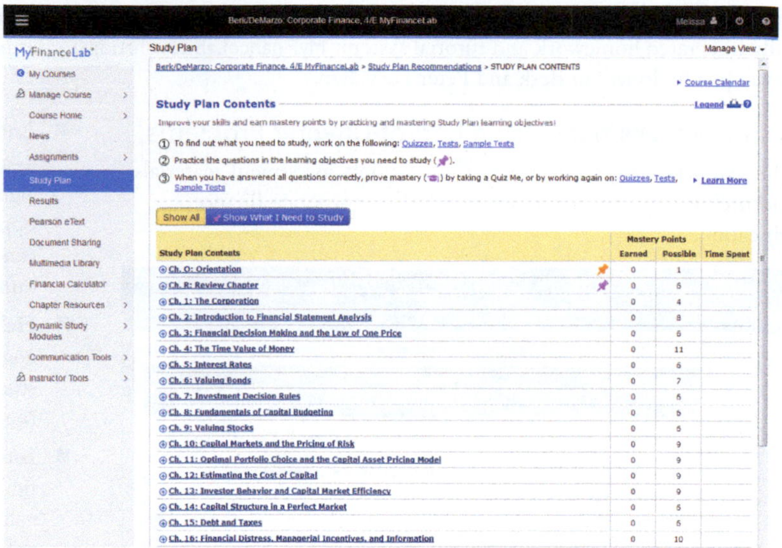

Powerful Instructor Tools

MyFinanceLab provides flexible tools that enable instructors to easily customize the online course materials to suit their needs.

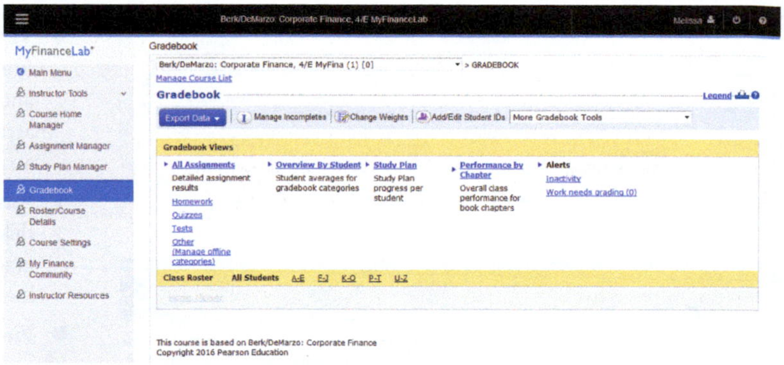

- **Easy-to-Use Homework Manager.** Instructors can easily create and assign tests, quizzes, or graded homework assignments. In addition to pre-built MyFinanceLab questions, the Test Bank is also available so that instructors have ample material with which to create assignments.
- **Flexible Gradebook.** MyFinanceLab saves time by automatically grading students' work and tracking results in an online Gradebook.
- **Downloadable Classroom Resources.** Instructors also have access to online versions of each instructor supplement, including the Instructor's Manual, Solutions Manual, PowerPoint Lecture Notes, and Test Bank.

To learn more about MyFinanceLab, contact your local Pearson representative, www.pearsoneducation.com/replocator, or visit www.myfinancelab.com.

About the Authors

Jonathan Berk is the A.P. Giannini Professor of Finance at the Graduate School of Business, Stanford University and is a Research Associate at the National Bureau of Economic Research. Before coming to Stanford, he was the Sylvan Coleman Professor of Finance at Haas School of Business at the University of California, Berkeley. Prior to earning his Ph.D., he worked as an Associate at Goldman Sachs (where his education in finance really began).

Professor Berk's research interests in finance include corporate valuation, capital structure, mutual funds, asset pricing, experimental economics, and labor economics. His work has won a number of research awards including the TIAA-CREF Paul A. Samuelson Award, the Smith Breeden Prize, Best Paper of the Year in *The Review of Financial Studies*, and the FAME Research Prize. His paper, "A Critique of Size-Related Anomalies," was selected as one of the two best papers ever published in *The Review of Financial Studies*. In recognition of his influence on the practice of finance he has received the Bernstein-Fabozzi/Jacobs Levy Award, the Graham and Dodd Award of Excellence, and the Roger F. Murray Prize. He served two terms as an Associate Editor of the *Journal of Finance*, and a term as a director of the American Finance Association, the Western Finance Association, and academic director of the Financial Management Association. He is a Fellow of the Financial Management Association and a member of the advisory board of the *Journal of Portfolio Management*.

Born in Johannesburg, South Africa, Professor Berk is married, with two daughters, and is an avid skier and biker.

Peter DeMarzo and Jonathan Berk

Peter DeMarzo is the Mizuho Financial Group Professor of Finance at the Graduate School of Business, Stanford University. He is the current Vice President of the American Finance Association and a Research Associate at the National Bureau of Economic Research. He teaches MBA and Ph.D. courses in Corporate Finance and Financial Modeling. In addition to his experience at the Stanford Graduate School of Business, Professor DeMarzo has taught at the Haas School of Business and the Kellogg Graduate School of Management, and he was a National Fellow at the Hoover Institution.

Professor DeMarzo received the Sloan Teaching Excellence Award at Stanford and the Earl F. Cheit Outstanding Teaching Award at U.C. Berkeley. Professor DeMarzo has served as an Associate Editor for *The Review of Financial Studies*, *Financial Management*, and the *B.E. Journals in Economic Analysis and Policy*, as well as a director of the American Finance Association. He has served as Vice President and President of the Western Finance Association. Professor DeMarzo's research is in the area of corporate finance, asset securitization, and contracting, as well as market structure and regulation. His recent work has examined issues of the optimal design of contracts and securities, leverage dynamics and the role of bank capital regulation, and the influence of information asymmetries on stock prices and corporate investment. He has received numerous awards including the Western Finance Association Corporate Finance Award and the Barclays Global Investors/Michael Brennan best-paper award from *The Review of Financial Studies*.

Professor DeMarzo was born in Whitestone, New York, and is married with three boys. He and his family enjoy hiking, biking, and skiing.

Preface

WE WERE MOTIVATED TO WRITE THIS TEXTBOOK BY A CENTRAL insight: The core concepts in finance are simple and intuitive. What makes the subject challenging is that it is often difficult for a novice to distinguish between these core ideas and other intuitively appealing approaches that, if used in financial decision making, will lead to incorrect decisions. De-emphasizing the core concepts that underlie finance strips students of the essential intellectual tools they need to differentiate between good and bad decision making.

We present corporate finance as an application of a set of simple, powerful ideas. At the heart is the principal of the absence of arbitrage opportunities, or Law of One Price—*in life, you don't get something for nothing*. This simple concept is a powerful and important tool in financial decision making. By relying on it, and the other core principles in this book, financial decision makers can avoid the bad decisions brought to light by the recent financial crisis. We use the Law of One Price as a compass; it keeps financial decision makers on the right track and is the backbone of the entire book.

New to This Edition

We have updated all text discussions and figures, tables, data cases, and facts to accurately reflect developments in the field in the last four years. Specific highlights include the following:

- Increased coverage of early stage financing in Chapter 23 (Raising Equity Capital), including a detailed explanation of angel financing, venture capital deal terms, and an expanded explanation of typical returns investors might earn.
- Addressed the implications of negative interest rates throughout the book.
- Expanded coverage of the European debt crisis in Chapter 6 (Valuing Bonds) including a case study on the Greek default.
- Added material throughout Part 5 (Capital Structure) that relates the capital structure to the current debate on bank leverage.
- Added coverage in Chapter 1 (The Corporation) describing the ongoing changes to how stocks are traded worldwide.
- Expanded the explanation of key financial ratios in Chapter 2 (Introduction to Financial Statement Analysis) and index arbitrage in Chapter 3 (Financial Decision Making and the Law of One Price).
- Redesigned sections of Chapter 22 (Real Options) with new examples to make the exposition clearer.
- Updated the coverage in Chapter 13 (Investor Behavior and Capital Market Efficiency) to reflect recent developments in asset pricing.
- Six new practitioner interviews incorporate timely perspectives from leaders in the field related to the recent financial crisis and ongoing European sovereign debt crisis.
- Added Nobel Prize boxes to reflect the recent Nobel Prizes awarded for material covered in the book.
- Added a new Case Study, two new Data Cases, new problems and refined many others, once again personally writing and solving each one. In addition, every single problem is available in MyFinanceLab, the groundbreaking homework and tutorial system that accompanies the book.

The Law of One Price as a Unifying Principle of Valuation

This book presents corporate finance as an application of a small set of simple core ideas. Modern finance theory and practice is grounded in the idea of the absence of arbitrage—or the Law of One Price—as the unifying concept in valuation. We introduce the Law of One Price concept as the basis for NPV and the time value of money in Chapter 3, *Financial Decision Making and the Law of One Price*. In the opening of each part and as pertinent throughout the remaining chapters, we relate major concepts to the Law of One Price, creating a framework to ground the student reader and connect theory to practice.

Table of Contents Overview

Corporate Finance offers coverage of the major topical areas for introductory-level MBA students as well as the depth required in a reference textbook for upper-division courses. Most professors customize their classes by selecting a subset of chapters reflecting the subject matter they consider most important. We designed this book from the outset with this need for flexibility in mind. Parts 2 through 6 are the core chapters in the book. We envision that most MBA programs will cover this material—yet even within these core chapters instructors can pick and choose.

Single quarter course: Cover Chapters 3–15; if time allows, or students are previously familiar with the time value of money, add on Chapters 16–19.

Semester-long course: Incorporate options (Chapters 20–22) and Part 10, *Special Topics*, chapters as desired.

Single mini-semester: Assign Chapters 3–10, 14, and 15 if time allows.

Chapter	Highlights and Changes
1 The Corporation	Introduces the corporation and its governance; updated the Dodd-Frank Act information; new interview with M. Hatheway, NASDAQ
2 Introduction to Financial Statement Analysis	Introduces key financial statements; coverage of financial ratios is centralized to prepare students to analyze financial statements holistically; new interview with Ruth Porat, Google
3 Financial Decision Making and the Law of One Price	Introduces the Law of One Price and net present value as the basis of the book's unifying framework; new box on dynamics of stock index arbitrage and high-frequency trading
4 The Time Value of Money	Introduces the mechanics of discounting with applications to personal finance; Using Excel boxes familiarizes students with spreadsheet functionality; new box on an annuity due
5 Interest Rates	Discusses key determinants of interest rates and their relation to the cost of capital; new Data Case on Florida's pension plan liability
6 Valuing Bonds	Analyzes bond prices and yields, as well as the risk of fixed-income securities as illustrated by the sovereign debt crisis; expanded Global Financial Crisis box on negative bond yields; new Case Study on Greek default
7 Investment Decision Rules	Introduces the NPV rule as the "golden rule" against which we evaluate other investment decision rules; new Data Case using NPV rule to choose between mortgage loans; introduces the use of Data Tables for sensitivity analysis
8 Fundamentals of Capital Budgeting	Provides a clear focus on the distinction between earnings and free cash flow, and shows how to build a financial model to assess the NPV of an investment decision; new Common Mistake box on the sunk cost fallacy

Chapter	Highlights and Changes
9 Valuing Stocks	Provides a unifying treatment of projects within the firm and the valuation of the firm as a whole
10 Capital Markets and the Pricing of Risk	Establishes the intuition for understanding risk and return, explains the distinction between diversifiable and systematic risk, and introduces beta and the CAPM; extensive data updates throughout to reflect current market conditions
11 Optimal Portfolio Choice and the Capital Asset Pricing Model	Presents the CAPM and develops the details of mean-variance portfolio optimization; updated examples and Data Case
12 Estimating the Cost of Capital	Demonstrates the practical details of estimating the cost of capital for equity, debt, or a project, and introduces asset betas, and the unlevered and weighted-average cost of capital; new Common Mistake box on using a single cost of capital in multi-divisional firms; new Using Excel box on estimating beta
13 Investor Behavior and Capital Market Efficiency	Examines the role of behavioral finance and ties investor behavior to the topic of market efficiency and alternative models of risk and return; expanded discussion of fund manager performance; updated interview with Jonathan Clements, former columnist at *WSJ*
14 Capital Structure in a Perfect Market	Presents Modigliani and Miller's results and introduces the market value balance sheet, discussion of important leverage fallacies with application to bank capital regulation
15 Debt and Taxes	Analyzes the tax benefits of leverage, including the debt tax shield and the after-tax WACC; new box on the repatriation tax controversy
16 Financial Distress, Managerial Incentives, and Information	Examines the role of asymmetric information and introduces the debt overhang and leverage ratchet effect
17 Payout Policy	Considers alternative payout policies including dividends and share repurchases; analyzes the role of market imperfections in determining the firm's payout policy; updated discussion of corporate cash retention
18 Capital Budgeting and Valuation with Leverage	Develops in depth the three main methods for capital budgeting with leverage and market imperfections: the weighted average cost of capital (WACC) method, the adjusted present value (APV) method, and the flow-to-equity (FTE) method; new interview with Zane Rowe, VMware; new appendix explaining the relation between DCF and residual income valuation methods
19 Valuation and Financial Modeling: A Case Study	Builds a financial model for a leveraged acquisition; new Using Excel box "Summarizing Model Outputs"
20 Financial Options	Introduces the concept of financial options, how they are used and exercised; demonstrates how corporate securities may be interpreted using options
21 Option Valuation	Develops the binomial, Black-Scholes, and risk-neutral pricing methods for option pricing
22 Real Options	Analyzes real options using decision tree and Black-Scholes methods, and considers the optimal staging of investment; expanded discussion of decision tree methodology with new examples
23 Raising Equity Capital	Overview of the stages of equity financing, from angel financing and venture capital to IPO to seasoned equity offerings; new expanded coverage of venture capital financing including common deal terms and protections as well as an illustration of typical funding patterns and success rates; new Common Mistake box on misinterpreting start-up valuations; new interview with Kevin Laws, AngelList

Chapter	Highlights and Changes
24 Debt Financing	Overview of debt financing, including a discussion of asset-backed securities and their role in the financial crisis; new box on Detroit's municipal bond default
25 Leasing	Introduces leasing as an alternative form of levered financing; update on new FASB rules for lease accounting; new interview with Mark S. Long, XOJet
26 Working Capital Management	Introduces the Cash Conversion Cycle and methods for managing working capital
27 Short-Term Financial Planning	Develops methods for forecasting and managing short-term cash needs; new box on the Ex-Im Bank controversy
28 Mergers and Acquisitions	Considers motives and methods for mergers and acquisitions, including leveraged buyouts; expanded discussion of valuation and premiums paid
29 Corporate Governance	Evaluates direct monitoring, compensation policies, and regulation as methods to manage agency conflicts within the firm; addresses impact of Dodd-Frank Act; new discussion of shareholder activism and its recent impact on corporate governance
30 Risk Management	Analyzes the methods and motives for the use of insurance, commodity futures, currency forwards and options, and interest rate swaps to hedge risk
31 International Corporate Finance	Analyzes the valuation of projects with foreign currency cash flows with integrated or segregated capital markets

A Complete Instructor and Student Support Package

MyFinanceLab

A critical component of the text, MyFinanceLab will give all students the practice and tutorial help they need to succeed. For more details, see pages xxi–xxii.

Instructor's Resource Center

This password-protected site, accessible at www.pearsonhighered.com/irc, hosts all of the instructor resources that follow. Instructors should click on the "IRC Help Center" link for easy-to-follow instructions on getting access or may contact their sales representative for further information.

Solutions Manual

- Prepared by Jonathan Berk and Peter DeMarzo.
- Provides detailed, accuracy-verified, class-tested solutions to every chapter Problem.
- See the Instructor's Resource Center for spreadsheet solutions to select chapter Problems and Data Cases.

Instructor's Manual

- Written by Janet Payne of Texas State University.
- Corresponding to each chapter, provides: chapter overview and outline correlated to the PowerPoint Lecture Notes; learning objectives; guide to fresh worked examples in the PowerPoint Lecture Notes; and listing of chapter problems with accompanying Excel spreadsheets.

Test Item File

- Revised by Janet Payne and William Chittenden of Texas State University.
- Provides a wide selection of multiple-choice, short answer, and essay questions qualified by difficulty level and skill type and correlated to chapter topics. Numerical-based Problems include step-by-step solutions.
- Available as Computerized Test Bank in TestGen.

PowerPoint Lecture Presentation

- Authored by William Chittenden of Texas State University.
- Offers outlines of each chapter with graphs, tables, key terms, and concepts from each chapter.
- Worked examples provide detailed, step-by-step solutions in the same format as the boxes from the text and correlated to parallel specific textbook examples.

Videos

- Profile well-known firms such as Boeing and Intel through interview and analysis.
- Focus on core topical areas such as capital budgeting and risk and return.
- Author Solution Videos that walk through the in-text examples using math, the financial calculator, and spreadsheets.
- Available in MyFinanceLab.

Acknowledgments

Looking back, it is hard to believe that this book is in its fourth edition. We are heartened by its success and impact on the profession through shaping future practitioners. As any textbook writer will tell you, achieving this level of success requires a substantial amount of help. First and foremost we thank Donna Battista, whose leadership, talent, and market savvy are imprinted on all aspects of the project and are central to its more than 10 years of success; Denise Clinton, a friend and a leader in fact not just in name, whose experience and knowledge were indispensable in the earliest stages; Rebecca Ferris-Caruso, for her unparalleled expertise in managing the complex writing, reviewing, and editing processes and patience in keeping us on track—it is impossible to imagine writing the first edition without her; Jami Minard, for spearheading marketing efforts; Kate Fernandes, for her energy and fresh perspective as our new editor; Miguel Leonarte, for his central role on MyFinanceLab; Gillian Hall for getting the book from draft pages into print; and Paul Corey for his insightful leadership and unwavering support of this fourth edition. We were blessed to be approached by the best publisher in the business and we are both truly thankful for the indispensable help provided by these and other professionals, including Kathryn Brightney, Dottie Dennis, Meredith Gertz, Nancy Freihofer, Melissa Honig, and Carol Melville.

Updating a textbook like ours requires a lot of painstaking work, and there are many who have provided insights and input along the way. We would especially like to call out Jared Stanfield for his important contributions and suggestions throughout. We're also appreciative of Marlene Bellamy's work conducting the lively interviews that provide a critically important perspective, and to the interviewees who graciously provided their time and insights.

Of course, this fourth edition text is built upon the shoulders of the first three, and we have many to thank for helping us make those early versions a reality. We remain forever grateful for Jennifer Koski's critical insights, belief in this project, and tireless effort, all of which were critical to the first edition. Many of the later, non-core chapters required specific detailed knowledge. Nigel Barradale, Reid Click, Jarrad Harford, and Marianne Plunkert ensured that this knowledge was effectively communicated. Joseph Vu and Vance P. Lesseig contributed their talents to the Concept Check questions and Data Cases, respectively.

Creating a truly error-free text is a challenge we could not have lived up to without our team of expert error checkers; we owe particular thanks to Sukarnen Suwanto, Siddharth Bellur, Robert James, Anand Goel, Ian Drummond Gow, Janet Payne, and Jared Stanfield. Thomas Gilbert and Miguel Palacios tirelessly worked examples and problems in the first edition, while providing numerous insights along the way.

A corporate finance textbook is the product of the talents and hard work of many talented colleagues. We are especially gratified with the work of those who updated the impressive array of supplements to accompany the book: Janet Payne and William Chittenden, for the Instructor's Manual, Test Item File, and PowerPoint; and Sukarnen Suwanto, for his accuracy review of the Solutions Manual.

As a colleague of both of us, Mark Rubinstein inspired us with his passion to get the history of finance right by correctly attributing the important ideas to the people who first enunciated them. We have used his book, *A History of the Theory of Investments: My Annotated Bibliography*, extensively in this text and we, as well as the profession as a whole, owe him a debt of gratitude for taking the time to write it all down.

We could not have written this text if we were not once ourselves students of finance. As any student knows, the key to success is having a great teacher. In our case we are lucky to have been taught and advised by the people who helped create modern finance: Ken Arrow, Darrell Duffie, Mordecai Kurz, Stephen Ross, and Richard Roll. It was from them that we learned the importance of the core principles of finance, including the Law of One Price, on which this book is based. The learning process does not end at graduation and like most people we have had especially influential colleagues and mentors from which we learned a great deal during our careers and we would like to recognize them explicitly here: Mike Fishman, Richard Green, Vasant Naik, Art Raviv, Mark Rubinstein, Joe Williams, and Jeff Zwiebel. The passing of Rick last year was a loss we will feel forever. We continue to learn from all of our colleagues and we are grateful to all of them. Finally, we would like to thank those with whom we have taught finance classes over the years: Anat Admati, Ming Huang, Dirk Jenter, Robert Korajczyk, Paul Pfleiderer, Sergio Rebelo, Richard Stanton, and Raman Uppal. Their ideas and teaching strategies have without a doubt influenced our own sense of pedagogy and found their way into this text.

Finally, and most importantly, we owe our biggest debt of gratitude to our spouses, Rebecca Schwartz and Kaui Chun DeMarzo. Little did we (or they) know how much this project would impact our lives, and without their continued love and support—and especially their patience and understanding—this text could not have been completed. We owe a special thanks to Kaui DeMarzo, for her inspiration and support at the start of this project, and for her willingness to be our in-house editor, contributor, advisor, and overall sounding-board throughout each stage of its development.

Jonathan Berk
Peter DeMarzo

Contributors

We are truly thankful to have had so many manuscript reviewers, class testers, and focus group participants. We list all of these contributors below, but Gordon Bodnar, James Conover, Anand Goel, James Linck, Evgeny Lyandres, Marianne Plunkert, Mark Simonson, and Andy Terry went so far beyond the call of duty that we would like to single them out.

We are very grateful for all comments—both informal and in written evaluations—from Third Edition users. We carefully weighed each reviewer suggestion as we sought to streamline the narrative to improve clarity and add relevant new material. The book has benefited enormously for this input.

Reviewers

Ashok B. Abbott, *West Virginia University*
Michael Adams, *Jacksonville University*
Ilan Adler, *University of California, Berkeley*
Ibrahim Affaneh, *Indiana University of Pennsylvania*
Kevin Ahlgrim, *Illinois State University*
Andres Almazan, *University of Texas, Austin*
Confidence Amadi, *Florida A&M University*
Christopher Anderson, *University of Kansas*
Tom Arnold, *University of Richmond*
John Banko, *University of Florida*
Nigel Barradale, *Copenhagen Business School*
Peter Basciano, *Augusta State University*
Thomas Bates, *University of Arizona*
Paul Bayes, *East Tennessee State University*
Omar Benkato, *Ball State University*
Gordon Bodnar, *Johns Hopkins University*
Stephen Borde, *University of Central Florida*
Waldo Born, *Eastern Illinois University*
Alex Boulatov, *Higher School of Economics, Moscow*
Tyrone Callahan, *University of Southern California*
Yingpin (George) Chang, *Grand Valley State University*
Engku Ngah S. Engku Chik, *University Utara Malaysia*
William G. Christie, *Vanderbilt University*
Ting-Heng Chu, *East Tennessee State University*
John H. Cochrane, *University of Chicago*
James Conover, *University of North Texas*
James Cordeiro, *SUNY Brockport*
Henrik Cronqvist, *Claremont McKenna College*
Maddur Daggar, *Citigroup*
Hazem Daouk, *Cornell University*
Theodore Day, *University of Texas at Dallas*
Daniel Deli, *DePaul University*
Andrea DeMaskey, *Villanova University*
B. Espen Eckbo, *Dartmouth College*
Larry Eisenberg, *University of Southern Mississippi*
Riza Emekter, *Robert Morris University*
T. Hanan Eytan, *Baruch College*
Andre Farber, *Universite Libre de Bruxelles*
Stephen Ferris, *University of Missouri–Columbia*
Eliezer Fich, *Drexel University*
Michael Fishman, *Northwestern University*
Fangjian Fu, *Singapore Management University*
Michael Gallmeyer, *University of Virginia*
Diego Garcia, *University of North Carolina*
Tom Geurts, *Marist College*
Frank Ghannadian, *University of Tampa*
Thomas Gilbert, *University of Washington*
Anand Goel, *DePaul University*
Marc Goergen, *Cardiff Business School*
David Goldenberg, *Rensselaer Polytechnic Institute*
Qing (Grace) Hao, *University of Missouri*
Milton Harris, *University of Chicago*
Christopher Hennessy, *London Business School*
J. Ronald Hoffmeister, *Arizona State University*
Vanessa Holmes, *Xavier University*
Wenli Huang, *Boston University School of Management*
Mark Hutchinson, *University College Cork*
Michael Hutchinson, *Wilmington University*
Stuart Hyde, *University of Manchester*
Ronen Israel, *IDC*
Robert James, *Boston College*
Keith Johnson, *University of Kentucky*
Jouko Karjalainen, *Helsinki University of Technology*
Ayla Kayhan, *Louisiana State University*
Doseong Kim, *University of Akron*
Kenneth Kim, *State University of New York—Buffalo*
Halil Kiymaz, *Rollins College*
Brian Kluger, *University of Cincinnati*
John Knopf, *University of Connecticut*
C.N.V. Krishnan, *Case Western Reserve University*
George Kutner, *Marquette University*
Vance P. Lesseig, *Texas State University*
Martin Lettau, *University of California, Berkeley*
Michel G. Levasseur, *Esa Universite de Lille 2*
Jose Liberti, *DePaul University*
James Linck, *University of Georgia*
David Lins, *University of Illinois at Urbana-Champaign*
Lan Liu, *California State University, Sacramento*
Michelle Lowry, *Pennsylvania State University*
Deborah Lucas, *Massachusetts Institute of Technology*
Peng (Peter) Liu, *Cornell University*
Evgeny Lyandres, *Boston University*
Balasundram Maniam, *Sam Houston State University*
Suren Mansinghka, *University of California, Irvine*
Daniel McConaughy, *California State University, Northridge*

Robert McDonald, *Northwestern University*
Mark McNabb, *University of Cincinnati*
Ilhan Meric, *Rider University*
Timothy Michael, *James Madison University*
Dag Michalsen, *Norwegian School of Management*
Todd Milbourn, *Washington University in St. Louis*
James Miles, *Penn State University*
Darius Miller, *Southern Methodist University*
Emmanuel Morales-Camargo, *University of New Mexico*
Helen Moser, *University of Minnesota*
Arjen Mulder, *Erasmus University*
Michael Muoghalu, *Pittsburg State University*
Jeryl Nelson, *Wayne State College*
Tom Nelson, *University of Colorado*
Chee Ng, *Fairleigh Dickinson University*
Ben Nunnally, *University of North Carolina, Charlotte*
Terrance Odean, *University of California, Berkeley*
Frank Ohara, *University of San Francisco*
Marcus Opp, *University of California, Berkeley*
Henry Oppenheimer, *University of Rhode Island*
Miguel Palacios, *Vanderbilt University*
Mitchell Petersen, *Northwestern University*
Marianne Plunkert, *University of Colorado at Denver*
Paul Povel, *University of Houston*
Eric A. Powers, *University of South Carolina*
Michael Provitera, *Barry University*
Brian Prucyk, *Marquette University*
Charu Raheja, *TriageLogic Management*
Latha Ramchand, *University of Houston*
Adriano Rampini, *Duke University*
P. Raghavendra Rau, *University of Cambridge*
S. Abraham Ravid, *Yeshiva University*
William A. Reese, Jr., *Tulane University*
Ali Reza, *San Jose State University*
Steven P. Rich, *Baylor University*
Antonio Rodriguez, *Texas A&M International University*
Bruce Rubin, *Old Dominion University*
Mark Rubinstein, *University of California, Berkeley*
Doriana Ruffino, *University of Minnesota*
Harley E. Ryan, Jr., *Georgia State University*
Jacob A. Sagi, *Vanderbilt University*
Harikumar Sankaran, *New Mexico State University*
Mukunthan Santhanakrishnan, *Idaho State University*
Frederik Schlingemann, *University of Pittsburgh*
Eduardo Schwartz, *University of California, Los Angeles*
Mark Seasholes, *Hong Kong University of Science and Technology*
Berk Sensoy, *Ohio State University*
Mark Shackleton, *Lancaster University*
Jay Shanken, *Emory University*
Dennis Sheehan, *Penn State University*
Anand Shetty, *Iona College*
Clemens Sialm, *University of Texas at Austin*
Mark Simonson, *Arizona State University*
Rajeev Singhal, *Oakland University*
Erik Stafford, *Harvard Business School*
David Stangeland, *University of Manitoba*
Richard H. Stanton, *University of California, Berkeley*
Mark Hoven Stohs, *California State University, Fullerton*
Ilya A. Strebulaev, *Stanford University*
Ryan Stever, *Bank for International Settlements*
John Strong, *College of William and Mary*
Diane Suhler, *Columbia College*
Lawrence Tai, *Zayed University*
Mark Taranto, *University of Maryland*
Amir Tavakkol, *Kansas State University*
Andy Terry, *University of Arkansas at Little Rock*
John Thornton, *Kent State University*
Alex Triantis, *University of Maryland*
Sorin Tuluca, *Fairleigh Dickinson University*
P. V. Viswanath, *Pace University*
Joe Walker, *University of Alabama at Birmingham*
Edward Waller, *University of Houston, Clear Lake*
Shelly Webb, *Xavier University*
Peihwang Wei, *University of New Orleans*
Peter Went, *Global Association of Risk Professionals (GARP)*
John White, *Georgia Southern University*
Michael E. Williams, *University of Denver*
Annie Wong, *Western Connecticut State University*
K. Matthew Wong, *International School of Management, Paris*
Bob Wood, Jr., *Tennessee Tech University*
Lifan (Frank) Wu, *California State University, Los Angeles*
Tzyy-Jeng Wu, *Pace University*
Jaime Zender, *University of Colorado*
Jeffrey H. Zwiebel, *Stanford University*

Chapter Class Testers

Jack Aber, *Boston University*
John Adams, *University of South Florida*
James Conover, *University of North Texas*
Lou Gingerella, *Rensselaer Polytechnic Institute*
Tom Geurts, *Marist College*
Keith Johnson, *University of Kentucky*
Gautum Kaul, *University of Michigan*
Doseong Kim, *University of Akron*

Jennifer Koski, *University of Washington*
George Kutner, *Marquette University*
Larry Lynch, *Roanoke College*
Vasil Mihov, *Texas Christian University*
Jeryl Nelson, *Wayne State College*
Chee Ng, *Fairleigh Dickinson University*
Ben Nunnally, *University of North Carolina, Charlotte*
Michael Proviteria, *Barry University*
Charu G. Raheja, *Vanderbilt University*
Bruce Rubin, *Old Dominion University*
Mark Seasholes, *University of California, Berkeley*
Dennis Sheehan, *Pennsylvania State University*
Ravi Shukla, *Syracuse University*
Mark Hoven Stohs, *California State University, Fullerton*
Andy Terry, *University of Arkansas*
Sorin Tuluca, *Fairleigh Dickinson University*
Joe Ueng, *University of Saint Thomas*
Bob Wood, *Tennessee Technological University*

End-of-Chapter Problems Class Testers

James Angel, *Georgetown University*
Ting-Heng Chu, *East Tennessee State University*
Robert Kravchuk, *Indiana University*
George Kutner, *Marquette University*
James Nelson, *East Carolina University*
Don Panton, *University of Texas at Arlington*
P. Raghavendra Rau, *Purdue University*
Carolyn Reichert, *University of Texas at Dallas*
Mark Simonson, *Arizona State University*
Diane Suhler, *Columbia College*

Focus Group Participants

Christopher Anderson, *University of Kansas*
Chenchu Bathala, *Cleveland State University*
Matthew T. Billett, *University of Iowa*
Andrea DeMaskey, *Villanova University*
Anand Desai, *Kansas State University*
Ako Doffou, *Sacred Heart University*
Shannon Donovan, *Bridgewater State University*
Ibrahim Elsaify, *Goldey-Beacom College*
Mark Holder, *Kent State University*
Steve Isberg, *University of Baltimore*
Arun Khanna, *Butler University*
Brian Kluger, *University of Cincinnati*
Greg La Blanc, *University of California, Berkeley*
Dima Leshchinskii, *Rensselaer Polytechnic University*
James S. Linck, *University of Georgia*
Larry Lynch, *Roanoke College*
David C. Mauer, *Southern Methodist University*
Alfred Mettler, *Georgia State University*
Stuart Michelson, *Stetson University*
Vassil Mihov, *Texas Christian University*
Jeryl Nelson, *Wayne State College*
Chee Ng, *Fairleigh Dickinson University*
Ben Nunnally, *University of North Carolina at Charlotte*
Sunny Onyiri, *Campbellsville University*
Janet Payne, *Texas State University*
Michael Provitera, *Barry University*
S. Abraham Ravid, *Rutgers University*
William A. Reese, Jr., *Tulane University*
Mario Reyes, *University of Idaho*
Hong Rim, *Shippensburg University*
Robert Ritchey, *Texas Tech University*
Antonio Rodriquez, *Texas A&M International University*
Dan Rogers, *Portland State University*
Harley E. Ryan, Jr., *Georgia State University*
Harikumar Sankaran, *New Mexico State University*
Sorin Sorescu, *Texas A&M University*
David Stangeland, *University of Manitoba*
Jonathan Stewart, *Abilene Christian University*
Mark Hoven Stohs, *California State University, Fullerton*
Tim Sullivan, *Bentley College*
Olie Thorp, *Babson College*
Harry Turtle, *Washington State University*
Joseph Vu, *DePaul University*
Joe Walker, *University of Alabama at Birmingham*
Jill Wetmore, *Saginaw Valley State University*
Jack Wolf, *Clemson University*
Bob Wood, Jr., *Tennessee Tech University*
Donald H. Wort, *California State University, East Bay*
Scott Wright, *Ohio University*
Tong Yao, *University of Arizona*

MyFinanceLab Contributors

Carlos Bazan, *San Diego State University*
Ting-Heng Chu, *East Tennessee State University*
Shannon Donovan, *Bridgewater State College*
Michael Woodworth

Introduction

PART 1

WHY STUDY CORPORATE FINANCE? No matter what your role in a corporation, an understanding of why and how financial decisions are made is essential. The focus of this book is how to make optimal corporate financial decisions. In this part of the book, we lay the foundation for our study of corporate finance. We begin, in Chapter 1, by introducing the corporation and related business forms. We then examine the role of financial managers and outside investors in decision making for the firm. To make optimal decisions, a decision maker needs information. As a result, in Chapter 2, we review an important source of information for corporate decision-making—the firm's financial statements.

We then introduce the most important idea in this book, the concept of *the absence of arbitrage* or *Law of One Price* in Chapter 3. The Law of One Price allows us to use market prices to determine the value of an investment opportunity to the firm. We will demonstrate that the Law of One Price is the one unifying principle that underlies all of financial economics and links all of the ideas throughout this book. We will return to this theme throughout our study of Corporate Finance.

CHAPTER 1

The Corporation

THE MODERN U.S. CORPORATION WAS BORN IN A COURTROOM in Washington, D.C., on February 2, 1819. On that day the U.S. Supreme Court established the legal precedent that the property of a corporation, like that of a person, is private and entitled to protection under the U.S. Constitution. Today, it is hard to entertain the possibility that a corporation's private property would not be protected under the Constitution. However, before the 1819 Supreme Court decision, the owners of a corporation were exposed to the possibility that the state could take their business. This concern was real enough to stop most businesses from incorporating and, indeed, in 1816 that concern was realized: The state seized Dartmouth College.

Dartmouth College was incorporated in 1769 as a private educational institution governed by a self-perpetuating board of trustees. Unhappy with the political leanings of the board, the state legislature effectively took control of Dartmouth by passing legislation in 1816 that established a governor-appointed board of overseers to run the school. The legislation had the effect of turning a private university under private control into a state university under state control. If such an act were constitutional, it implied that any state (or the federal government) could, at will, nationalize any corporation.

Dartmouth sued for its independence and the case made it to the Supreme Court under Chief Justice John Marshall in 1818. In a nearly unanimous 5–1 decision, the court struck down the New Hampshire law, ruling that a corporation was a "contract" and that, under Article 1 of the Constitution, "the state legislatures were forbidden to pass any law impairing the obligation of contracts."[1] The precedent was set: Owners of businesses could incorporate and still enjoy the protection of private property, as well as protection from seizure, both guaranteed by the U.S. Constitution. The modern business corporation was born.

[1]The full text of John Marshall's decision can be found at www.constitution.org/dwebster/dartmouth_decision.htm.

Today, the corporate structure is ubiquitous all over the world, and yet continues to evolve in the face of new forces. In 2008 the financial crisis once again transformed the financial landscape, bringing down giants like Bear Stearns, Lehman Brothers, and AIG and reshaping investment banks like Goldman Sachs into government-guaranteed commercial banks. Government bailouts have provoked challenging questions regarding the role of the federal government in the control and management of private corporations. In the wake of the crisis, significant reforms of the regulation and oversight of financial markets were passed into law. Understanding the principles of corporate finance has never been more important to the practice of business than it is now, during this time of great change.

The focus of this book is on how people in corporations make financial decisions. This chapter introduces the corporation and explains alternative business organizational forms. A key factor in the success of corporations is the ability to easily trade ownership shares, and so we will also explain the role of stock markets in facilitating trading among investors in a corporation and the implications that has for the ownership and control of corporations.

1.1 The Four Types of Firms

We begin our study of corporate finance by introducing the four major types of firms: *sole proprietorships*, *partnerships*, *limited liability companies*, and *corporations*. We explain each organizational form in turn, but our primary focus is on the most important form—the corporation. In addition to describing what a corporation is, we also provide an overview of why corporations are so successful.

Sole Proprietorships

A **sole proprietorship** is a business owned and run by one person. Sole proprietorships are usually very small with few, if any, employees. Although they do not account for much sales revenue in the economy, they are the most common type of firm in the world, as shown in Figure 1.1. Statistics indicate that nearly 72% of businesses in the United States are sole proprietorships, although they generate only 4% of the revenue.[2] Contrast this with corporations, which make up under 18% of firms but are responsible for 83% of U.S. revenue.

Sole proprietorships share the following key characteristics:

1. Sole proprietorships are straightforward to set up. Consequently, many new businesses use this organizational form.
2. The principal limitation of a sole proprietorship is that there is no separation between the firm and the owner—the firm can have only one owner. If there are other investors, they cannot hold an ownership stake in the firm.
3. The owner has unlimited personal liability for any of the firm's debts. That is, if the firm defaults on any debt payment, the lender can (and will) require the owner to repay the loan from personal assets. An owner who cannot afford to repay the loan must declare personal bankruptcy.

[2] www.irs.gov (www.irs.gov/uac/SOI-Tax-Stats-Integrated-Business-Data)

FIGURE 1.1

Types of U.S. Firms

There are four different types of firms in the United States. As (a) and (b) show, although the majority of U.S. firms are sole proprietorships, they generate only a small fraction of total revenue, in contrast to corporations.

Source: www.irs.gov

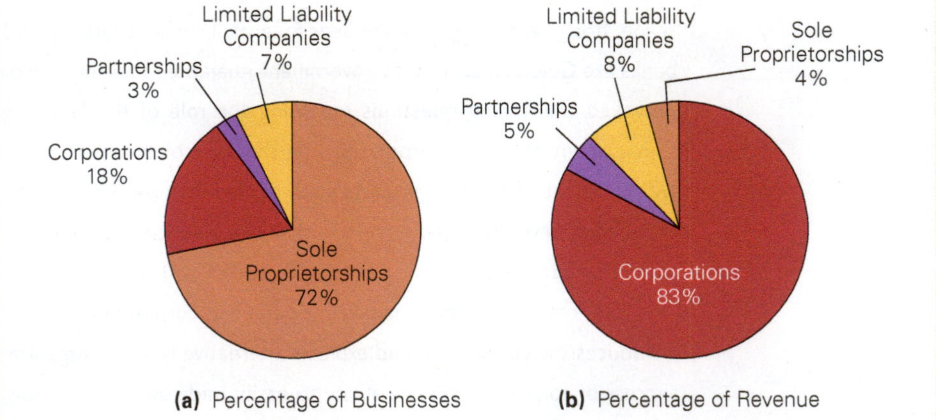

4. The life of a sole proprietorship is limited to the life of the owner. It is also difficult to transfer ownership of a sole proprietorship.

For most businesses, the disadvantages of a sole proprietorship outweigh the advantages. As soon as the firm reaches the point at which it can borrow without the owner agreeing to be personally liable, the owners typically convert the business into a form that limits the owner's liability.

Partnerships

A **partnership** is identical to a sole proprietorship except it has more than one owner. The following are key features of a partnership:

1. *All* partners are liable for the firm's debt. That is, a lender can require *any* partner to repay all the firm's outstanding debts.
2. The partnership ends on the death or withdrawal of any single partner, although partners can avoid liquidation if the partnership agreement provides for alternatives such as a buyout of a deceased or withdrawn partner.

Some old and established businesses remain partnerships or sole proprietorships. Often these firms are the types of businesses in which the owners' personal reputations are the basis for the businesses. For example, law firms, groups of doctors, and accounting firms are often organized as partnerships. For such enterprises, the partners' personal liability increases the confidence of the firm's clients that the partners will strive to maintain their reputation.

A **limited partnership** is a partnership with two kinds of owners, general partners and limited partners. General partners have the same rights and privileges as partners in a (general) partnership—they are personally liable for the firm's debt obligations. Limited partners, however, have **limited liability**—that is, their liability is limited to their investment. Their private property cannot be seized to pay off the firm's outstanding debts. Furthermore, the death or withdrawal of a limited partner does not dissolve the partnership, and a limited partner's interest is transferable. However, a limited partner has no management authority and cannot legally be involved in the managerial decision making for the business.

Private equity funds and venture capital funds are two examples of industries dominated by limited partnerships. In these firms, a few general partners contribute some of their own capital and raise additional capital from outside investors who are limited partners. The general partners control how all the capital is invested. Most often they will actively participate in running the businesses they choose to invest in. The outside investors play no active role in the partnership other than monitoring how their investments are performing.

Limited Liability Companies

A **limited liability company (LLC)** is a limited partnership without a general partner. That is, all the owners have limited liability, but unlike limited partners, they can also run the business.

The LLC is a relatively new phenomenon in the United States. The first state to pass a statute allowing the creation of an LLC was Wyoming in 1977; the last was Hawaii in 1997. Internationally, companies with limited liability are much older and established. LLCs rose to prominence first in Germany over 100 years ago as a *Gesellschaft mit beschränkter Haftung* (GmbH) and then in other European and Latin American countries. An LLC is known in France as a *Société à responsabilité limitée* (SARL), and by similar names in Italy (SRL) and Spain (SL).

Corporations

The distinguishing feature of a **corporation** is that it is a legally defined, artificial being (a judicial person or legal entity), separate from its owners. As such, it has many of the legal powers that people have. It can enter into contracts, acquire assets, incur obligations, and, as we have already established, it enjoys protection under the U.S. Constitution against the seizure of its property. Because a corporation is a legal entity separate and distinct from its owners, it is solely responsible for its own obligations. Consequently, the owners of a corporation (or its employees, customers, etc.) are not liable for any obligations the corporation enters into. Similarly, the corporation is not liable for any personal obligations of its owners.

Formation of a Corporation. Corporations must be legally formed, which means that the state in which it is incorporated must formally give its consent to the incorporation by chartering it. Setting up a corporation is therefore considerably more costly than setting up a sole proprietorship. Delaware has a particularly attractive legal environment for corporations, so many corporations choose to incorporate there. For jurisdictional purposes, a corporation is a citizen of the state in which it is incorporated. Most firms hire lawyers to create a corporate charter that includes formal articles of incorporation and a set of bylaws. The corporate charter specifies the initial rules that govern how the corporation is run.

Ownership of a Corporation. There is no limit on the number of owners a corporation can have. Because most corporations have many owners, each owner owns only a small fraction of the corporation. The entire ownership stake of a corporation is divided into shares known as **stock**. The collection of all the outstanding shares of a corporation is known as the **equity** of the corporation. An owner of a share of stock in the corporation is known as a **shareholder**, **stockholder**, or **equity holder** and is entitled to **dividend payments**, that is, payments made at the discretion of the corporation to its equity holders. Shareholders usually receive a share of the dividend payments that is proportional to the amount of stock they own. For example, a shareholder who owns 25% of the firm's shares will be entitled to 25% of the total dividend payment.

A unique feature of a corporation is that there is no limitation on who can own its stock. That is, an owner of a corporation need not have any special expertise or qualification. This feature allows free trade in the shares of the corporation and provides one of the most important advantages of organizing a firm as a corporation rather than as sole proprietorship, partnership, or LLC. Corporations can raise substantial amounts of capital because they can sell ownership shares to anonymous outside investors.

The availability of outside funding has enabled corporations to dominate the economy, as shown by Panel (b) of Figure 1.1. Let's take one of the world's largest firms, Wal-Mart Stores Inc. (brand name Walmart), as an example. Walmart had over 2 million employees, and reported annual revenue of $486 billion in 2014. Indeed, the top five companies by sales volume in 2014 (Walmart, Sinopec, Royal Dutch Shell, Exxon Mobile, and BP) had combined sales exceeding $2 trillion, an amount significantly larger than the total sales of the more than 22 million U.S. sole proprietorships.

Tax Implications for Corporate Entities

An important difference between the types of organizational forms is the way they are taxed. Because a corporation is a separate legal entity, a corporation's profits are subject to taxation separate from its owners' tax obligations. In effect, shareholders of a corporation pay taxes twice. First, the corporation pays tax on its profits, and then when the remaining profits are distributed to the shareholders, the shareholders pay their own personal income tax on this income. This system is sometimes referred to as double taxation.

EXAMPLE 1.1 Taxation of Corporate Earnings

Problem

You are a shareholder in a corporation. The corporation earns $5 per share before taxes. After it has paid taxes, it will distribute the rest of its earnings to you as a dividend. The dividend is income to you, so you will then pay taxes on these earnings. The corporate tax rate is 40% and your tax rate on dividend income is 15%. How much of the earnings remains after all taxes are paid?

Solution

First, the corporation pays taxes. It earned $5 per share, but must pay $0.40 \times \$5 = \$2$ to the government in corporate taxes. That leaves $3 to distribute. However, you must pay $0.15 \times \$3 = \$0.45$ in income taxes on this amount, leaving $\$3 - \$0.45 = \$2.55$ per share after all taxes are paid. As a shareholder you only end up with $2.55 of the original $5 in earnings; the remaining $\$2 + \$0.45 = \$2.45$ is paid as taxes. Thus, your total effective tax rate is $2.45/5 = 49\%$.

S Corporations. The corporate organizational structure is the only organizational structure subject to double taxation. However, the U.S. Internal Revenue Code allows an exemption from double taxation for **"S" corporations**, which are corporations that elect subchapter S tax treatment. Under these tax regulations, the firm's profits (and losses) are not subject to corporate taxes, but instead are allocated directly to shareholders based on their ownership share. The shareholders must include these profits as income on their individual tax returns (even if no money is distributed to them). However, after the shareholders have paid income taxes on these profits, no further tax is due.

Corporate Taxation Around the World

Most countries offer investors in corporations some relief from double taxation. Thirty countries make up the Organization for Economic Co-operation and Development (OECD), and of these countries, only Ireland offers no relief whatsoever. A few countries, including Australia, Canada, Chile, Mexico and New Zealand, give shareholders a tax credit for the amount of corporate taxes paid, while others, such as Estonia and Finland, fully or partially exempt dividend income from individual taxes. The United States offers partial relief by having a lower tax rate on dividend income than on other sources of income. As of 2015, for most investors qualified dividends are taxed at up to 20%, a rate significantly below their personal income tax rate. Despite this relief, the effective corporate tax rate in the U.S. is one of the highest in the world (and nearly 30% above the median for the OECD).*

*OECD Tax Database Table II.4

EXAMPLE 1.2 Taxation of S Corporation Earnings

Problem

Rework Example 1.1 assuming the corporation in that example has elected subchapter S treatment and your tax rate on non-dividend income is 30%.

Solution

In this case, the corporation pays no taxes. It earned \$5 per share. Whether or not the corporation chooses to distribute or retain this cash, you must pay $0.30 \times \$5 = \$1.50$ in income taxes, which is substantially lower than the \$2.45 paid in Example 1.1.

The government places strict limitations on the qualifications for subchapter S tax treatment. In particular, the shareholders of such corporations must be individuals who are U.S. citizens or residents, and there can be no more than 100 of them. Because most corporations have no restrictions on who owns their shares or the number of shareholders, they cannot qualify for subchapter S treatment. Thus most large corporations are **"C" corporations**, which are corporations subject to corporate taxes. S corporations account for less than one quarter of all corporate revenue.

CONCEPT CHECK

1. What is a limited liability company (LLC)? How does it differ from a limited partnership?
2. What are the advantages and disadvantages of organizing a business as a corporation?

1.2 Ownership Versus Control of Corporations

It is often not feasible for the owners of a corporation to have direct control of the firm because there are sometimes many owners, each of whom can freely trade his or her stock. That is, in a corporation, direct control and ownership are often separate. Rather than the owners, the *board of directors* and *chief executive officer* possess direct control of the corporation. In this section, we explain how the responsibilities for the corporation are divided between these two entities and how together they shape and execute the goals of the firm.

The Corporate Management Team

The shareholders of a corporation exercise their control by electing a **board of directors**, a group of people who have the ultimate decision-making authority in the corporation.

INTERVIEW WITH DAVID VINIAR

David Viniar is Chief Financial Officer and head of the Operations, Technology and Finance Division at Goldman Sachs—the last major investment bank to convert from a partnership to a corporation. As the firm's CFO, he played a leading role in the firm's conversion to a corporation in 1999 and charting the firm's course through the financial crisis of 2008–2009.

QUESTION: *What are the advantages of partnerships and corporations?*

ANSWER: We debated this question at length when we were deciding whether to go public or stay a private partnership in the mid-1990s. There were good arguments on both sides. Those in favor of going public argued we needed greater financial and strategic flexibility to achieve our aggressive growth and market leadership goals. As a public corporation, we would have a more stable equity base to support growth and disperse risk; increased access to large public debt markets; publicly traded securities with which to undertake acquisitions and reward and motivate our employees; and a simpler and more transparent structure with which to increase scale and global reach.

Those against going public argued our private partnership structure worked well and would enable us to achieve our financial and strategic goals. As a private partnership, we could generate enough capital internally and in the private placement markets to fund growth; take a longer-term view of returns on our investments with less focus on earnings volatility, which is not valued in public companies; and retain voting control and alignment of the partners and the firm.

A big perceived advantage of our private partnership was its sense of distinctiveness and mystique, which reinforced our culture of teamwork and excellence and helped differentiate us from our competitors. Many questioned whether the special qualities of our culture would survive if the firm went public.

QUESTION: *What was the driving force behind the conversion?*

ANSWER: We ultimately decided to go public for three main reasons: to secure permanent capital to grow; to be able to use publicly traded securities to finance strategic acquisitions; and to enhance the culture of ownership and gain compensation flexibility.

QUESTION: *Did the conversion achieve its goals?*

ANSWER: Yes. As a public company, we have a simpler, bigger and more permanent capital base, including enhanced long-term borrowing capacity in the public debt markets. We have drawn on substantial capital resources to serve clients, take advantage of new business opportunities, and better control our own destiny through changing economic and business conditions. We have been able to use stock to finance key acquisitions and support large strategic and financial investments. Given how the stakes in our industry changed, how capital demands grew, going public when we did fortunately positioned us to compete effectively through the cycle.

Our distinctive culture of teamwork and excellence has thrived in public form, and our equity compensation programs turned out better than we could have hoped. Making everyone at Goldman Sachs an owner, rather than just 221 partners, energized all our employees. The growing size and scope of our business—not the change to public form—has presented the greatest challenges to the positive aspects of our culture.

QUESTION: *What prompted Goldman's decision to become a bank holding company in Fall 2008?*

ANSWER: The market environment had become extraordinarily unstable following the collapse of Bear Stearns in March 2008. There was an increased focus on the SEC-supervised broker/dealer business model, and in September, market sentiment had become increasingly negative with growing concerns over Lehman Brothers' solvency. Following the bankruptcy of Lehman Brothers and the sale of Merrill Lynch in the middle of September, and notwithstanding the reporting of quite strong earnings by both Goldman Sachs and Morgan Stanley, it became clear to us that the market viewed oversight by the Federal Reserve and the ability to source insured bank deposits as offering a greater degree of safety and soundness. By changing our status, we gained all the benefits available to our commercial banking peers, including access to permanent liquidity and funding, without affecting our ability to operate or own any of our current businesses or investments.

In most corporations, each share of stock gives a shareholder one vote in the election of the board of directors, so investors with the most shares have the most influence. When one or two shareholders own a very large proportion of the outstanding stock, these shareholders may either be on the board of directors themselves, or they may have the right to appoint a number of directors.

The board of directors makes rules on how the corporation should be run (including how the top managers in the corporation are compensated), sets policy, and monitors the performance of the company. The board of directors delegates most decisions that involve day-to-day running of the corporation to its management. The **chief executive officer (CEO)** is charged with running the corporation by instituting the rules and policies set by the board of directors. The size of the rest of the management team varies from corporation to corporation. The separation of powers within corporations between the board of directors and the CEO is not always distinct. In fact, it is not uncommon for the CEO also to be the chairman of the board of directors. The most senior financial manager is the **chief financial officer (CFO)**, who often reports directly to the CEO. Figure 1.2 presents part of a typical organizational chart for a corporation, highlighting the key positions a financial manager may take.

The Financial Manager

Within the corporation, financial managers are responsible for three main tasks: making investment decisions, making financing decisions, and managing the firm's cash flows.

Investment Decisions. The financial manager's most important job is to make the firm's investment decisions. The financial manager must weigh the costs and benefits of all investments and projects and decide which of them qualify as good uses of the money stockholders have invested in the firm. These investment decisions fundamentally shape what the firm does and whether it will add value for its owners. In this book, we will develop the tools necessary to make these investment decisions.

FIGURE 1.2

Organizational Chart of a Typical Corporation

The board of directors, representing the stockholders, controls the corporation and hires the Chief Executive Officer who is then responsible for running the corporation. The Chief Financial Officer oversees the financial operations of the firm, with the Controller managing both tax and accounting functions, and the Treasurer responsible for capital budgeting, risk management, and credit management activities.

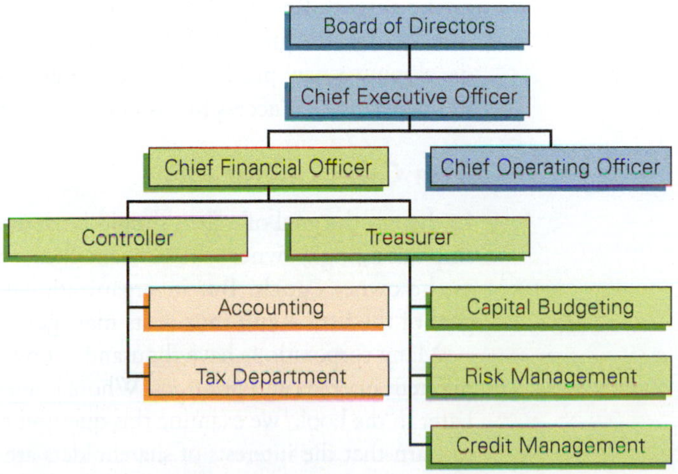

GLOBAL FINANCIAL CRISIS **The Dodd-Frank Act**

In response to the 2008 financial crisis, the U.S. federal government reevaluated its role in the control and management of financial institutions and private corporations. Signed into law on July 21, 2010, the **Dodd-Frank Wall Street Reform and Consumer Protection Act** brought a sweeping change to financial regulation in response to widespread calls for financial regulatory system reform after the near collapse of the world's financial system in the fall of 2008 and the ensuing global credit crisis. History indeed repeats itself: It was in the wake of the 1929 stock market crash and subsequent Great Depression that Congress passed the Glass-Steagall Act establishing the Federal Deposit Insurance Corporation (FDIC) and instituted significant bank reforms to regulate transactions between commercial banks and securities firms.

The Dodd-Frank Act aims to (i) promote U.S. financial stability by "improving accountability and transparency in the financial system," (ii) put an end to the notion of "too big to fail," (iii) "protect the American taxpayer by ending bailouts," and (iv) "protect consumers from abusive financial services practices." Time will tell whether the Act will actually achieve these important goals.

Implementing the wide-ranging financial reforms in the Dodd-Frank Act requires the work of many federal agencies, either through rulemaking or other regulatory actions. As of mid-2015, five years since Dodd-Frank's passage, 247 of the reforms have been finalized, providing a clear picture of the Dodd-Frank regulatory framework. But another 143 rules or actions await completion. While only two-thirds of the rules have been finalized, many of the core reforms have been or are nearing completion. For instance, the Volcker Rule, which bars banks that take government-insured deposits from making speculative investments took full effect in late July of 2015.

Financing Decisions. Once the financial manager has decided which investments to make, he or she also decides how to pay for them. Large investments may require the corporation to raise additional money. The financial manager must decide whether to raise more money from new and existing owners by selling more shares of stock (equity) or to borrow the money (debt). In this book, we will discuss the characteristics of each source of funds and how to decide which one to use in the context of the corporation's overall mix of debt and equity.

Cash Management. The financial manager must ensure that the firm has enough cash on hand to meet its day-to-day obligations. This job, also commonly known as managing working capital, may seem straightforward, but in a young or growing company, it can mean the difference between success and failure. Even companies with great products require significant amounts of money to develop and bring those products to market. Consider the $150 million Apple spent during its secretive development of the iPhone, or the costs to Boeing of producing the 787—the firm spent billions of dollars before the first 787 left the ground. A company typically burns through a significant amount of cash developing a new product before its sales generate income. The financial manager's job is to make sure that access to cash does not hinder the firm's success.

The Goal of the Firm

In theory, the goal of a firm should be determined by the firm's owners. A sole proprietorship has a single owner who runs the firm, so the goals of a sole proprietorship are the same as the owner's goals. But in organizational forms with multiple owners, the appropriate goal of the firm—and thus of its managers—is not as clear.

Many corporations have thousands of owners (shareholders). Each owner is likely to have different interests and priorities. Whose interests and priorities determine the goals of the firm? Later in the book, we examine this question in more detail. However, you might be surprised to learn that the interests of shareholders are aligned for many, if not most, important decisions. That is because, regardless of their own personal financial position and stage in life, all the shareholders will agree that they are better off if management makes decisions that increase the value of their shares. For example, by July 2015, Apple shares were worth over 120 times as much as they were in October 2001, when the first iPod was introduced. Clearly, regardless of their preferences and other differences, all investors who held shares of Apple stock over this period have benefited from the investment decisions Apple's managers have made.

The Firm and Society

Are decisions that increase the value of the firm's equity beneficial for society as a whole? Most often they are. While Apple's shareholders have become much richer since 2001, its customers also are better off with products like the iPod and iPhone that they might otherwise never have had. But even if the corporation only makes its shareholders better off, as long as nobody else is made worse off by its decisions, increasing the value of equity is good for society.

The problem occurs when increasing the value of equity comes at the expense of others. Consider a corporation that, in the course of business, pollutes the environment and does not pay the costs to clean up the pollution. Alternatively, a corporation may not itself pollute, but use of its products may harm the environment. In such cases, decisions that increase shareholder wealth can be costly for society as whole.

The 2008 financial crisis highlighted another example of decisions that can increase shareholder wealth but are costly for society. In the early part of the last decade, banks took on excessive risk. For a while, this strategy benefited the banks' shareholders. But when the bets went bad, the resulting financial crisis harmed the broader economy.

When the actions of the corporation impose harm on others in the economy, appropriate public policy and regulation is required to assure that corporate interests and societal interests remain aligned. Sound public policy should allow firms to continue to pursue the maximization of shareholder value in a way that benefits society overall.

Ethics and Incentives within Corporations

But even when all the owners of a corporation agree on the goals of the corporation, these goals must be implemented. In a simple organizational form like a sole proprietorship, the owner, who runs the firm, can ensure that the firm's goals match his or her own. But a corporation is run by a management team, separate from its owners, giving rise to conflicts of interest. How can the owners of a corporation ensure that the management team will implement their goals?

Agency Problems. Many people claim that because of the separation of ownership and control in a corporation, managers have little incentive to work in the interests of the shareholders when this means working against their own self-interest. Economists call this an **agency problem**—when managers, despite being hired as the agents of shareholders, put their own self-interest ahead of the interests of shareholders. Managers face the ethical dilemma of whether to adhere to their responsibility to put the interests of shareholders first, or to do what is in their own personal best interest.

This agency problem is commonly addressed in practice by minimizing the number of decisions managers must make for which their own self-interest substantially differs from the interests of the shareholders. For example, managers' compensation contracts are designed to ensure that most decisions in the shareholders' interest are also in the managers' interests; shareholders often tie the compensation of top managers to the corporation's profits or perhaps to its stock price. There is, however, a limitation to this strategy. By tying compensation too closely to performance, the shareholders might be asking managers to take on more risk than they are comfortable taking. As a result, managers may not make decisions that the shareholders want them to, or it might be hard to find talented managers

GLOBAL FINANCIAL CRISIS The Dodd-Frank Act on Corporate Compensation and Governance

Compensation is one of the most important conflicts of interest between corporate executives and shareholders. To limit senior corporate executives' influence over their own compensation and prevent excessive compensation, the Act directs the SEC to adopt new rules that:

- Mandate the independence of a firm's compensation committee and its advisers.
- Provide shareholders the opportunity to approve—in a non-binding, advisory vote—the compensation of executive officers at least once every three years (referred to as a "Say-on-Pay" vote).
- Require firm disclosure and shareholder approval of large bonus payments (so-called "golden parachutes") to ousted senior executives as the result of a takeover.
- Require disclosure of the relationship of executive pay to the company's performance, as well as the ratio between the CEO's total compensation and that of the median employee.
- Require disclosure of whether executives are permitted to hedge their stock or option holdings.
- Create "clawback" provisions that allow firms to recoup compensation paid based on erroneous financial results.

willing to accept the job. On the other hand, if compensation contracts reduce managers' risk by rewarding good performance but limiting the penalty associated with poor performance, managers may have an incentive to take excessive risk.

Further potential for conflicts of interest and ethical considerations arise when some stakeholders in the corporation benefit and others lose from a decision. Shareholders and managers are two stakeholders in the corporation, but others include the regular employees and the communities in which the company operates, for example. Managers may decide to take the interests of other stakeholders into account in their decisions, such as keeping a loss-generating factory open because it is the main provider of jobs in a small town, paying above-market wages to factory workers in a developing country, or operating a plant at a higher environmental standard than local law mandates.

In some cases, these actions that benefit other stakeholders also benefit the firm's shareholders by creating a more dedicated workforce, generating positive publicity with customers, or other indirect effects. In other instances, when these decisions benefit other stakeholders at shareholders' expense, they represent a form of corporate charity. Indeed, many if not most corporations explicitly donate (on behalf of their shareholders) to local and global charitable and political causes. For example, in 2013, Walmart gave $312 million in cash to charity (making it the largest corporate donor of cash in that year). These actions are costly and reduce shareholder wealth. Thus, while some shareholders might support such policies because they feel that they reflect their own moral and ethical priorities, it is unlikely that all shareholders will feel this way, leading to potential conflicts of interest amongst shareholders.

Citizens United v. Federal Election Commission

On January 21, 2010, the U.S. Supreme Court ruled on what some scholars have argued is the most important First Amendment case in many years. In *Citizens United v. Federal Election Commission* the Court held, in a controversial 5–4 decision, that the First Amendment allows corporations and unions to make political expenditures in support of a particular candidate. This ruling overturned existing restrictions on political campaigning by corporations. But because it is highly unlikely that all shareholders of a corporation would unanimously support a particular candidate, allowing such activities effectively guarantees a potential conflict of interest.

The CEO's Performance. Another way shareholders can encourage managers to work in the interests of shareholders is to discipline them if they don't. If shareholders are unhappy with a CEO's performance, they could, in principle, pressure the board to oust the CEO. Disney's Michael Eisner, Hewlett Packard's Carly Fiorina, and Barclay's Antony Jenkins were all reportedly forced to resign by their boards. Despite these high-profile examples, directors and top executives are rarely replaced through a grassroots shareholder uprising. Instead, dissatisfied investors often choose to sell their shares. Of course, somebody must be willing to buy the shares from the dissatisfied shareholders. If enough shareholders are dissatisfied, the only way to entice investors to buy (or hold on to) the shares is to offer them a low price. Similarly, investors who see a well-managed corporation will want to purchase shares, which drives the stock price up. Thus, the stock price of the corporation is a barometer for corporate leaders that continuously gives them feedback on their shareholders' opinion of their performance.

When the stock performs poorly, the board of directors might react by replacing the CEO. In some corporations, however, the senior executives are entrenched because boards of directors do not have the will to replace them. Often the reluctance to fire results because the board members are close friends of the CEO and lack objectivity. In corporations in which the CEO is entrenched and doing a poor job, the expectation of continued poor performance will decrease the stock price. Low stock prices create a profit opportunity. In a **hostile takeover**, an individual or organization—sometimes known as a corporate raider—can purchase a large fraction of the stock and acquire enough votes to replace the board of directors and the CEO. With a new superior management team, the stock is a much more attractive investment, which would likely result in a price rise and a profit for the corporate raider and the other shareholders. Although the words "hostile" and "raider" have negative connotations, corporate raiders themselves provide an important service to shareholders. The mere threat of being removed as a result of a hostile takeover is often enough to discipline bad managers and motivate boards of directors to make difficult decisions. Consequently, when a corporation's shares are publicly traded, a "market for corporate control" is created that encourages managers and boards of directors to act in the interests of their shareholders.

Corporate Bankruptcy. Ordinarily, a corporation is run on behalf of its shareholders. But when a corporation borrows money, the holders of the firm's debt also become investors in the corporation. While the debt holders do not normally exercise control over the firm, if the corporation fails to repay its debts, the debt holders are entitled to seize the assets of the corporation in compensation for the default. To prevent such a seizure, the firm may attempt to renegotiate with the debt holders, or file for bankruptcy protection in a federal court. (We describe the details of the bankruptcy process and its implications for corporate decisions in much more detail in Part 5 of the textbook.) Ultimately, however, if the firm is unable to repay or renegotiate with the debt holders, the control of the corporation's assets will be transferred to them.

Thus, when a firm fails to repay its debts, the end result is a change in ownership of the firm, with control passing from equity holders to debt holders. Importantly, bankruptcy need not result in a **liquidation** of the firm, which involves shutting down the business and selling off its assets. Even if control of the firm passes to the debt holders, it is in the debt holders' interest to run the firm in the most profitable way possible. Doing so often means keeping the business operating. For example, in 1990, Federated Department Stores declared bankruptcy. One of its best-known assets at the time was Bloomingdale's, a nationally recognized department store. Because Bloomingdale's was a profitable business,

Airlines in Bankruptcy

On December 9, 2002, United Airlines filed for bankruptcy protection following an unsuccessful attempt to convince the federal government to bail out the company's investors by providing loan guarantees. Although United remained in bankruptcy for the next three years, it continued to operate and fly passengers, and even expanded capacity in some markets. One of those expansions was "Ted," an ill-fated attempt by United to start a budget airline to compete directly with Southwest Airlines. In short, although United's original shareholders were wiped out, as far as customers were concerned it was business as usual. People continued to book tickets and United continued to fly and serve them.

It is tempting to think that when a firm files for bankruptcy, things are "over." But often, rather than liquidate the firm, bondholders and other creditors are better off allowing the firm to continue operating as a going concern. United was just one of many airlines to move in and out of bankruptcy since 2002; others include U.S. Airways, Air Canada, Hawaiian Airlines, Northwest Airlines, and Delta Airlines. In November 2011, American Airlines became the latest airline to declare bankruptcy. Like United in 2002, American continued to operate while it cut costs and reorganized, returning to profitability in mid-2012. American ultimately settled with creditors in December 2013 as part of a merger agreement with US Airways.

neither equity holders nor debt holders had any desire to shut it down, and it continued to operate in bankruptcy. In 1992, when Federated Department Stores was reorganized and emerged from bankruptcy, Federated's original equity holders had lost their stake in Bloomingdale's, but this flagship chain continued to perform well for its new owners, and its value as a business was not adversely affected by the bankruptcy.

Thus, a useful way to understand corporations is to think of there being two sets of investors with claims to its cash flows—debt holders and equity holders. As long as the corporation can satisfy the claims of the debt holders, ownership remains in the hands of the equity holders. If the corporation fails to satisfy debt holders' claims, debt holders may take control of the firm. Thus, a corporate bankruptcy is best thought of as a *change in ownership* of the corporation, and not necessarily as a failure of the underlying business.

CONCEPT CHECK

1. What are the three main tasks of a financial manager?
2. What is a principal-agent problem that may exist in a corporation?
3. How may a corporate bankruptcy filing affect the ownership of a corporation?

1.3 The Stock Market

As we have discussed, shareholders would like the firm's managers to maximize the value of their investment in the firm. The value of their investment is determined by the price of a share of the corporation's stock. Because **private companies** have a limited set of shareholders and their shares are not regularly traded, the value of their shares can be difficult to determine. But many corporations are **public companies**, whose shares trade on organized markets called a **stock market** (or **stock exchange**). Figure 1.3 shows the major exchanges worldwide, by total value of listed stocks and trading volume.

These markets provide *liquidity* and determine a market price for the company's shares. An investment is said to be **liquid** if it is possible to sell it quickly and easily for a price very close to the price at which you could contemporaneously buy it. This liquidity is attractive to outside investors, as it provides flexibility regarding the timing and duration of their investment in the firm. In addition, the research and trading of participants in these markets give rise to share prices that provide constant feedback to managers regarding investors' views of their decisions.

Primary and Secondary Stock Markets

When a corporation itself issues new shares of stock and sells them to investors, it does so on the **primary market**. After this initial transaction between the corporation and investors, the shares continue to trade in a **secondary market** between investors without the involvement of the corporation. For example, if you wish to buy 100 shares of Starbucks Coffee, you would place an order on a stock exchange, where Starbucks trades under the ticker symbol SBUX. You would buy your shares from someone who already held shares of Starbucks, not from Starbucks itself. Because firms only occasionally issue new shares, secondary market trading accounts for the vast majority of trading in the stock market.

Traditional Trading Venues

Historically, a firm would choose one stock exchange on which to list its stock, and almost all trade in the stock would occur on that exchange. In the U.S., the two most important exchanges are the New York Stock Exchange (NYSE) and the National Association of Security Dealers Automated Quotation (NASDAQ).

Prior to 2005, almost all trade on the NYSE took place on the exchange's trading floor in lower Manhattan. **Market makers** (known then on the NYSE as **specialists**) matched buyers and sellers. They posted two prices for every stock in which they made a market: the price at which they were willing to *buy* the stock (the **bid price**) and the price at which they were willing to *sell* the stock (the **ask price**). When a customer arrived and wanted to make a trade at these prices, the market maker would honor the posted prices (up to a limited number of shares) and make the trade even when they did not have another customer willing to take the other side of the trade. In this way, market makers provided **liquidity** by ensuring that market participants always had somebody to trade with.

FIGURE 1.3 Worldwide Stock Markets Ranked by Two Common Measures

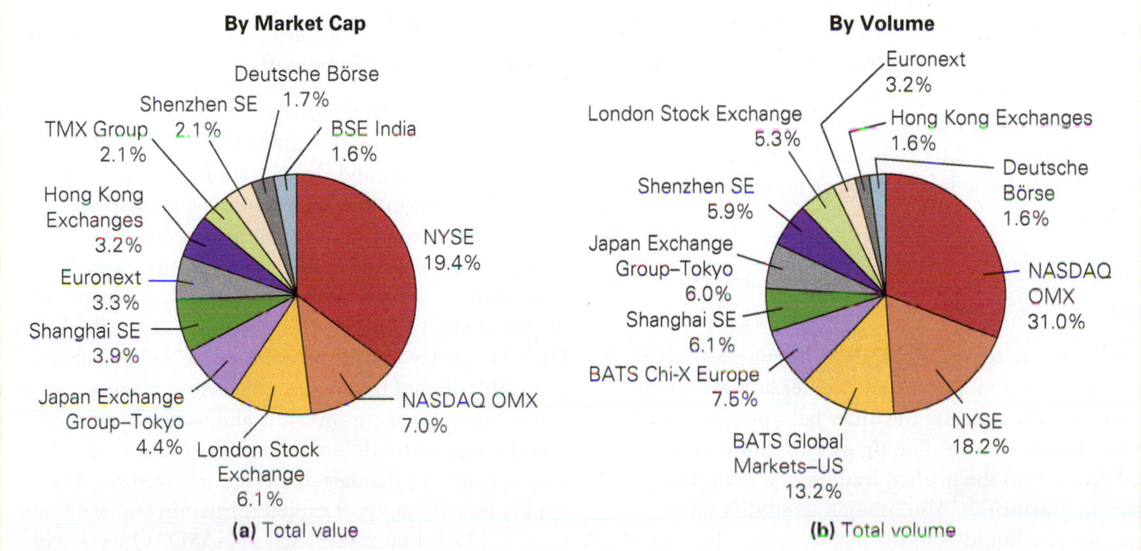

The 10 biggest stock markets in the world (a) by total value of all domestic corporations listed on the exchange at year-end 2014 and (b) by total volume of shares traded on the exchange in 2014.

Source: www.world-exchanges.org

INTERVIEW WITH
FRANK HATHEWAY

As Chief Economist and Senior Vice President for NASDAQ, Dr. Frank Hatheway leads a team of 20 professionals who serve as an internal consultancy for the NASDAQ markets. Their work includes designing new features, evaluating operations markets, and advising on strategic initiatives.

QUESTION: *Compared to 15 years ago, the number of potential trading venues for investors has changed dramatically. Who have these changes benefited?*

ANSWER: The number of trading venues has increased dramatically. In 2000 you placed an order on NASDAQ or the NYSE, and the majority of trading activity in that stock occurred on the same market as your order. That's not the case anymore. Your trade may be executed on the National Stock Exchange, BATS, or one of 10 other exchanges. To deal with the soaring number of venues, trading became highly automated and highly competitive, benefiting both individual and institutional investors. A fast retail trade in the 1980s took about three minutes and cost over $100 (in 1980s money). Now it's a mouse click, browser refresh, and maybe $20 (in 2016 money). Trading costs for individual investors are down over 90 percent since 2000. Institutional-size block orders are also cheaper and easier to trade today.

Automation has virtually removed traditional equity traders like the market makers, specialists, and floor brokers at the exchanges. As the head of the trading desk for a major firm quipped around 2006, "I used to have 100 traders and 10 IT guys. I now have 100 IT guys and 10 traders." The once bustling New York Stock Exchange floor is now essentially a TV studio.

QUESTION: *How have these changes affected market liquidity?*

ANSWER: Liquidity is very transitory. The computer algorithms controlling trading constantly enter orders into the market and remove orders if the order fails to trade or if market conditions change. The algorithms quickly re-enter removed orders into the market, leading to rapidly changing prices and quantities. Also, numerous studies show that there is more liquidity in the market today. To control an order 15 years ago, you phoned your broker with your instructions. Today, the algorithm you selected controls the order and can change the order almost instantly. Because computers have more control over orders than human traders did, there is less risk associated with placing an order. Consequently there are more orders and greater liquidity.

QUESTION: *How has NASDAQ been affected by these changes and what does the future hold?*

ANSWER: NASDAQ has become an innovative, technologically savvy company—much like the companies we list. Fifteen years ago we operated a single stock market in the United States. Thanks to increased technological efficiency, today we operate three stock markets, three listed-options markets, and a futures market. Operating these seven markets requires less than half the personnel required for a single market 15 years ago. To compete in this environment, NASDAQ had to develop a better trading system to handle our increased order volume. Order volume that took an entire day to process 15 years ago, today takes a few seconds. We've also transformed our culture from supporting an industry based on human traders to one based on algorithmic traders and the IT professionals who design those algorithms.

QUESTION: *Is High Frequency Trading a cause for concern in the market? Should it be limited?*

ANSWER: Specific concerns about High Frequency Trading are generally about market disruptions and manipulation, and cases center around the operation of trading algorithms. I believe market oversight is evolving to appropriately address disruptive or manipulative activity.

These days essentially every order in the United States is handled by a computer trading algorithm. Simply put, we are all High Frequency Traders. Consequently, limiting High Frequency Trading should not be a policy objective. What should be a policy objective is making sure that equity markets benefit investors and issuers by ensuring that the algorithms do not disrupt the markets and that they operate in a manner that is fair to investors. The market exists to support capital formation and economic growth. Market operators such as NASDAQ work with regulators and others to look after the interests of investors and issuers.

In contrast to the NYSE, the NASDAQ market never had a trading floor. Instead, all trades were completed over the phone or on a computer network. An important difference between the NYSE and NASDAQ was that on the NYSE, each stock had only one market maker. On the NASDAQ, stocks had multiple market makers who competed with one another. Each market maker posted bid and ask prices on the NASDAQ network that were viewed by all participants.

Market makers make money because ask prices are higher than bid prices. This difference is called the **bid-ask spread.** Customers always buy at the ask (the higher price) and sell at the bid (the lower price). The bid-ask spread is a **transaction cost** investors pay in order to trade. Because specialists on the NYSE took the other side of the trade from their customers, this cost accrued to them as a profit. This was the compensation they earned for providing a liquid market by standing ready to honor any quoted price. Investors also paid other forms of transactions costs like commissions.

New Competition and Market Changes

Stock markets have gone through enormous changes in the last decade. In 2005, the NYSE and NASDAQ exchanges accounted for over 75% of all trade in U.S. stocks. Since that time, however, they have faced increasing competition from new fully electronic exchanges, as well as alternative trading systems. Today, these new entrants handle more than 50% of all trades, as shown in Figure 1.4.

With this change in market structure, the role of an official market maker has largely disappeared. Because all transactions occur electronically with computers matching buy and sell orders, anyone can make a market in a stock by posting a **limit order**—an order to buy or sell a set amount at a fixed price. For example, a limit buy order might be an order to buy 100 shares of IBM at a price of $138/share. The bid-ask spread of a stock is determined

FIGURE 1.4

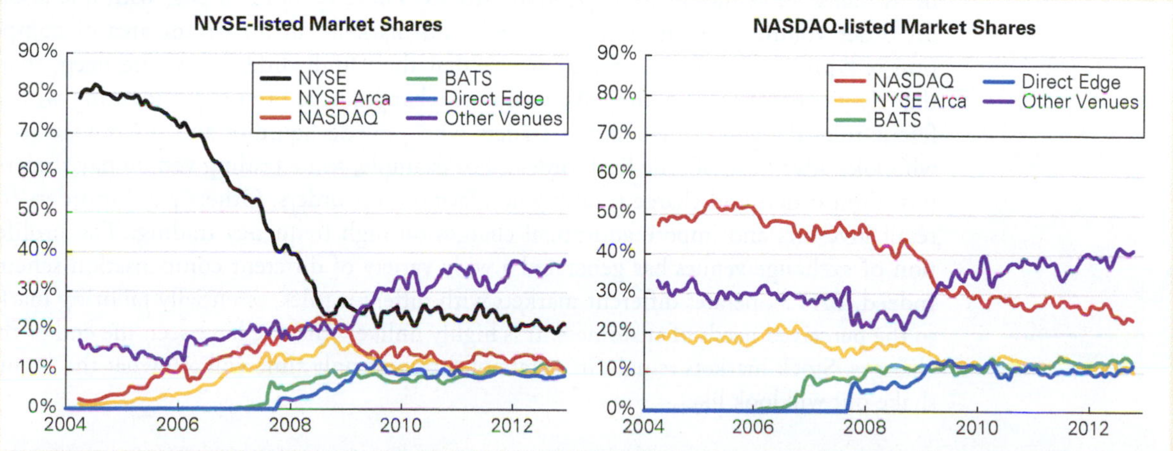

Distribution of trading volume for NYSE-listed shares (left panel) and NASDAQ-listed shares (right panel). NYSE-Arca is the electronic trading platform of the NYSE. BATS and Direct Edge merged in 2014; these new electronic exchanges now handle about 20% of all trades. Other venues, including internal dealer platforms and so called "dark pools," accounted for almost 40% of all trades in 2015.

Source: J. Angel, L. Harris, and C. Spatt, "Equity Trading in the 21st Century: An Update," *Quarterly Journal of Finance* 5 (2015): 1–39.

by the outstanding limit orders. The limit sell order with the lowest price is the ask price. The limit buy order with the highest price is the bid price. Traders make the market in the stock by posting limit buy and sell orders. The collection of all limit orders is known as the **limit order book.** Exchanges make their limit order books public so that investors (or their brokers) can see the best bid and ask prices when deciding where to trade.

Traders who post limit orders provide the market with liquidity. On the other hand, traders who place **market orders**—orders that trade immediately at the best outstanding limit order—are said to be "takers" of liquidity. Providers of liquidity earn the bid-ask spread, but in so doing they risk the possibility of their orders becoming stale: When news about a stock arrives that causes the price of that stock to move, smart traders will quickly take advantage of the existing limit orders by executing trades at the old prices. To protect themselves against this possibility, liquidity providers need to constantly monitor the market, cancelling old orders and posting new orders when appropriate. So-called **high frequency traders (HFTs)** are a class of traders who, with the aid of computers, will place, update, cancel, and execute trades many times per second in response to new information as well as other orders, profiting both by providing liquidity and by taking advantage of stale limit orders.

Dark Pools

When trading on an exchange, investors are guaranteed the opportunity to trade immediately at the current bid or ask price, and transactions are visible to all traders when they occur. In contrast, alternative trading systems called **dark pools** do not make their limit order books visible. Instead, these dark pools offer investors the ability to trade at a better price (for example, the average of the bid and ask, thus saving the bid-ask spread), with the tradeoff being that the order might not be filled if an excess of either buy or sell orders is received. Trading on a dark pool is therefore attractive to traders who do not want to reveal their demand and who are willing to sacrifice the guarantee of immediacy for a potentially better price.

When dark pools are included, researchers estimate that in the U.S. alone there could be as many 50 venues in which to trade stocks. These venues compete with one another for order volume. Because traders value liquid markets, an important area of competition is liquidity—exchanges try to ensure that their limit order books are deep, that is, that they contain many orders. As a result, exchanges have been experimenting with different rules designed to encourage traders who provide liquidity and discourage traders who take advantage of stale limit orders. For example, some trading venues pay traders to post limit orders and charge traders who place market orders. Others pay for orders from retail investors and impose additional charges on high frequency trading. The proliferation of exchange venues has generated a wide variety of different compensation schemes. Indeed, BATS operates different markets with different rules, essentially tailoring markets to the perceived needs of customers. It is highly unlikely that we have seen the end of these changes. Stock markets remain in a state of flux, and only time will tell what the eventual shake out will look like.

CONCEPT CHECK

1. What are the important changes that have occurred in stock markets over the last decade?
2. What is the limit order book?
3. Why are people who post limit orders termed "providers" of liquidity?

MyFinanceLab

Here is what you should know after reading this chapter. MyFinanceLab will help you identify what you know and where to go when you need to practice.

1.1 The Four Types of Firms

- There are four types of firms in the United States: sole proprietorships, partnerships, limited liability companies, and corporations.
- Firms with unlimited personal liability include sole proprietorships and partnerships.
- Firms with limited liability include limited partnerships, limited liability companies, and corporations.
- A corporation is a legally defined artificial being (a judicial person or legal entity) that has many of the same legal powers as people. It can enter into contracts, acquire assets, incur obligations, and, as we have already established, it enjoys the protection under the U.S. Constitution against the seizure of its property.
- The shareholders in a C corporation effectively must pay tax twice. The corporation pays tax once and then investors must pay personal tax on any funds that are distributed.
- S corporations are exempt from the corporate income tax.

1.2 Ownership Versus Control of Corporations

- The ownership of a corporation is divided into shares of stock collectively known as equity. Investors in these shares are called shareholders, stockholders, or equity holders.
- The ownership and control of a corporation are separated. Shareholders exercise their control indirectly through the board of directors.
- Financial managers within the firm are responsible for three main tasks: making investment decisions, making financing decisions, and managing the firm's cash flows.
- Good public policy should ensure that when firms take actions that benefit their shareholders, they are also benefiting society.
- While the firm's shareholders would like managers to make decisions that maximize the firm's share price, managers often must balance this objective with the desires of other stakeholders (including themselves).
- Corporate bankruptcy can be thought of as a change in ownership and control of the corporation. The equity holders give up their ownership and control to the debt holders.

1.3 The Stock Market

- The shares of public corporations are traded on stock markets. The shares of private corporations do not trade on a stock market.
- Traders provide liquidity in stock markets by posting limit orders.
- The bid-ask spread is determined by the best bid and offer prices in the limit order book.

Key Terms

agency problem *p. 11*
ask price *p. 15*
bid-ask spread *p. 17*
bid price *p. 15*
board of directors *p. 7*
"C" corporations *p. 7*
chief executive officer (CEO) *p. 9*
chief financial officer (CFO) *p. 9*
corporation *p. 5*
dark pools *p. 18*
dividend payments *p. 5*
Dodd-Frank Act *p. 10*
equity *p. 5*
equity holder *p. 5*
high frequency traders (HFTs) *p. 18*
hostile takeover *p. 13*
limit order *p. 17*
limit order book *p. 18*
limited liability *p. 4*
limited liability company (LLC) *p. 5*
limited partnership *p. 4*
liquid *p. 14*
liquidation *p. 13*
liquidity *p. 15*

market makers *p. 15*
market orders *p. 18*
partnership *p. 4*
primary market *p. 15*
private companies *p. 14*
public companies *p. 14*
"S" corporations *p. 6*
secondary market *p. 15*
shareholder *p. 5*
sole proprietorship *p. 3*
specialists *p. 15*
stock *p. 5*
stock market (or stock exchange) *p. 14*
stockholder *p. 5*
transaction cost *p. 17*

Further Reading

Readers interested in John Marshall's decision that led to the legal basis for the corporation can find a more detailed description of the decision in J. Smith, *John Marshall: Definer of a Nation* (Henry Holt, 1996): 433–38.

An informative discussion that describes the objective of a corporation can be found in M. Jensen, "Value Maximization, Stakeholder Theory, and the Corporate Objective Function," *Journal of Applied Corporate Finance* (Fall 2001): 8–21.

For background on what determines the goals of corporate managers and how they differ from shareholders' goals, read M. Jensen and W. Meckling, "Theory of the Firm: Managerial Behavior, Agency Costs and Ownership Structure," *Journal of Financial Economics* 3 (1976): 305–60; J. Core, W. Guay, and D. Larker, "Executive Equity Compensation and Incentives: A Survey," *Federal Reserve Bank of New York Economic Policy Review* 9 (April 2003): 27–50.

The following papers explain corporate governance and ownership around the world: F. Barca and M. Becht, *The Control of Corporate Europe* (Oxford University Press, 2001); D. Denis and J. McConnell, "International Corporate Governance," *Journal of Financial Quantitative Analysis* 38 (2003): 1–36; R. La Porta, F. Lopez-de-Silanes, and A. Shleifer, "Corporate Ownership Around the World," *Journal of Finance* 54 (1999): 471–517. Readers interested in a more detailed discussion of how taxes affect incorporation can consult J. MacKie-Mason and R. Gordon, "How Much Do Taxes Discourage Incorporation?" *Journal of Finance* 52 (1997): 477–505.

The following papers provide a summary of the recent changes in stock markets: J. Angel, L. Harris, and C. Spatt, "Equity Trading in the 21st Century: An Update," *Quarterly Journal of Finance* 5 (2015): 1–39 and M. O'Hara, "High frequency market microstructure," *Journal of Financial Economics* 116 (2015) 257–270.

Problems

All problems are available in MyFinanceLab.

The Four Types of Firms

1. What is the most important difference between a corporation and *all* other organizational forms?

2. What does the phrase *limited liability* mean in a corporate context?

3. Which organizational forms give their owners limited liability?

4. What are the main advantages and disadvantages of organizing a firm as a corporation?

5. Explain the difference between an S corporation and a C corporation.

6. You are a shareholder in a C corporation. The corporation earns $2 per share before taxes. Once it has paid taxes it will distribute the rest of its earnings to you as a dividend. The corporate tax rate is 40% and the personal tax rate on (both dividend and non-dividend) income is 30%. How much is left for you after all taxes are paid?

7. Repeat Problem 6 assuming the corporation is an S corporation.

Ownership Versus Control of Corporations

8. You have decided to form a new start-up company developing applications for the iPhone. Give examples of the three distinct types of financial decisions you will need to make.

9. When a pharmaceutical company develops a new drug, it often receives patent protection for that medication, allowing it to charge a higher price. Explain how this public policy of providing patent protection might help align the corporation's interests with society's interests.

10. Corporate managers work for the owners of the corporation. Consequently, they should make decisions that are in the interests of the owners, rather than their own. What strategies are available to shareholders to help ensure that managers are motivated to act this way?

11. Suppose you are considering renting an apartment. You, the renter, can be viewed as an agent while the company that owns the apartment can be viewed as the principal. What principal-agent conflicts do you anticipate? Suppose, instead, that you work for the apartment company. What features would you put into the lease agreement that would give the renter incentives to take good care of the apartment?

12. You are the CEO of a company and you are considering entering into an agreement to have your company buy another company. You think the price might be too high, but you will be the CEO of the combined, much larger company. You know that when the company gets bigger, your pay and prestige will increase. What is the nature of the agency conflict here and how is it related to ethical considerations?

13. Are hostile takeovers necessarily bad for firms or their investors? Explain.

The Stock Market

14. What is the difference between a public and a private corporation?

15. Describe the important changes that have occurred in stock markets over the last decade.

16. Explain why the bid-ask spread is a transaction cost.

17. Explain how the bid-ask spread is determined in most markets today.

18. The following quote on Yahoo! stock appeared on July 23, 2015, on Yahoo! Finance:

Yahoo! Inc. (YHOO) - NasdaqGS Add to Portfolio

39.55 ↑0.31(0.79%) 12:00PM EDT - Nasdaq Real Time Price

Prev Close:	39.24	Day's Range:	38.26 - 39.78
Open:	39.29	52wk Range:	35.04 - 52.62
Bid:	39.65 x 1200	Volume:	4,423,901
Ask:	39.66 x 2200	Avg Vol (3m):	13,765,100
1y Target Est:	51.85	Market Cap:	37.12B
Beta:	1.6	P/E (ttm):	5.40
Next Earnings Date:	N/A	EPS (ttm):	7.32
		Div & Yield:	N/A (N/A)

Quotes delayed, except where indicated otherwise. Currency in USD.

If you wanted to buy Yahoo!, what price would you pay? How much would you receive if you wanted to sell Yahoo!?

19. Suppose the following orders are received by an exchange for Cisco stock:

- Limit Order: Buy 200 shares at $25
- Limit Order: Sell 200 shares at $26
- Limit Order: Sell 100 shares at $25.50
- Limit Order: Buy 100 shares at $25.25

a. What are the best bid and ask prices for Cisco stock?
b. What is the current bid-ask spread for Cisco stock?
c. Suppose a market order arrives to buy 200 shares of Cisco. What average price will the buyer pay?
d. After the market order in (c) clears, what are the new best bid and ask prices, and what is the new bid-ask spread for Cisco?

Introduction to Financial Statement Analysis

CHAPTER 2

AS WE DISCUSSED IN CHAPTER 1, ONE OF THE GREAT ADVANTAGES of the corporate organizational form is that it places no restriction on who can own shares in the corporation. Anyone with money to invest is a potential investor. As a result, corporations are often widely held, with investors ranging from individuals who hold 100 shares to mutual funds and institutional investors who own millions of shares. For example, in 2012, International Business Machines Corporation (IBM) had about 980 million shares outstanding held by nearly 600,000 shareholders. Most shareholders were small. Warren Buffett's Berkshire Hathaway was the largest shareholder with about an 8% stake. Less than 1% of the company was owned by insiders (IBM executives).

Although the corporate organizational structure greatly facilitates the firm's access to investment capital, it also means that stock ownership is most investors' sole tie to the company. How, then, do investors learn enough about a company to know whether or not they should invest in it? How can financial managers assess the success of their own firm and compare it to the performance of competitors? One way firms evaluate their performance and communicate this information to investors is through their *financial statements*.

Firms issue financial statements regularly to communicate financial information to the investment community. A detailed description of the preparation and analysis of these statements is sufficiently complicated that to do it justice would require an entire book. Here, we briefly review the subject, emphasizing only the material that investors and corporate financial managers need in order to make the corporate-finance decisions we discuss in the text.

We review the four main types of financial statements, present examples of these statements for a firm, and discuss where an investor or manager might find various types of information about the company. We also discuss some of the financial ratios that investors and analysts use to assess a firm's performance and value. We close the chapter with a look at a few highly publicized financial reporting abuses.

2.1 Firms' Disclosure of Financial Information

Financial statements are accounting reports with past performance information that a firm issues periodically (usually quarterly and annually). U.S. public companies are required to file their financial statements with the U.S. Securities and Exchange Commission (SEC) on a quarterly basis on form **10-Q** and annually on form **10-K**. They must also send an **annual report** with their financial statements to their shareholders each year. Private companies often prepare financial statements as well, but they usually do not have to disclose these reports to the public. Financial statements are important tools through which investors, financial analysts, and other interested outside parties (such as creditors) obtain information about a corporation. They are also useful for managers within the firm as a source of information for corporate financial decisions. In this section, we examine the guidelines for preparing financial statements and introduce the types of financial statements.

Preparation of Financial Statements

Reports about a company's performance must be understandable and accurate. **Generally Accepted Accounting Principles (GAAP)** provide a common set of rules and a standard format for public companies to use when they prepare their reports. This standardization also makes it easier to compare the financial results of different firms.

Investors also need some assurance that the financial statements are prepared accurately. Corporations are required to hire a neutral third party, known as an **auditor**, to check the annual financial statements, to ensure that the annual financial statements are reliable and prepared according to GAAP.

International Financial Reporting Standards

Because Generally Accepted Accounting Principles (GAAP) differ among countries, companies operating internationally face tremendous accounting complexity. Investors also face difficulty interpreting financial statements of foreign companies, which is often considered a major barrier to international capital mobility. As companies and capital markets become more global, however, interest in harmonizing accounting standards across countries has increased.

The most important harmonization project began in 1973 when representatives of 10 countries (including the United States) established the International Accounting Standards Committee. This effort led to the creation of the International Accounting Standards Board (IASB) in 2001, with headquarters in London. Now the IASB has issued a set of International Financial Reporting Standards (IFRS).

The IFRS are taking root throughout the world. The European Union (EU) approved an accounting regulation in 2002 requiring all publicly traded EU companies to follow IFRS in their consolidated financial statements starting in 2005. As of 2012, over 120 jurisdictions either require or permit the use of IFRS, including the EU, Australia, Brazil, Canada, Russia, Hong Kong, Taiwan, and Singapore. China, India and Japan will soon follow suit. Indeed, currently all major stock exchanges around the world accept IFRS except the United States and Japan, which maintain their local GAAP.

The main difference between U.S. GAAP and IFRS is conceptual—U.S. GAAP are based primarily on accounting rules with specific guidance in applying them, whereas IFRS are based more on principles requiring professional judgment by accountants, and specific guidance in application is limited. Even so, some differences in rules also exist. For example, U.S. GAAP generally prohibit the upward revaluation of non-financial assets, whereas the IFRS allow the revaluation of some such assets to fair value. U.S. GAAP also rely more heavily on historical cost, as opposed to "fair value," to estimate the value of assets and liabilities.

Effort to achieve convergence between U.S. GAAP and IFRS was spurred by the Sarbanes-Oxley Act of 2002. It included a provision that U.S. accounting standards move toward international convergence on high-quality accounting standards. Currently SEC regulations still require public U.S. firms to report using U.S. GAAP. That said, modifications to both IFRS and U.S. GAAP have brought the two closer together, with the key remaining differences in the areas of impairment charges, leasing, insurance, and the treatment of financial instruments. As of mid-2015, the SEC looks likely to allow U.S. companies to use IFRS to provide supplemental information, but it will still require them to file their financials in accordance with U.S. GAAP.

INTERVIEW WITH RUTH PORAT

Ruth Porat is Senior Vice President and Chief Financial Officer of Alphabet and Google. Previously she spent 27 years at Morgan Stanley, where she last was Executive Vice President and Chief Financial Officer. As Morgan Stanley's Vice Chairman of Investment Banking and Global Head of the Financial Institutions Group, she advised the U.S. Treasury and the New York Federal Reserve Bank.

QUESTION: *What best practices do you recommend for financial managers?*

ANSWER:

1. *Maintain a tight financial control environment with respect to accounting controls and process.* Incorporate a strategic approach to IT architecture to ensure data integrity, consistency, and process controls while reducing reliance on human, manual processes—a source of risk and errors.
2. *Ensure a robust budgeting and capital allocation process built on a strong Financial Planning & Analysis team that is well integrated into the business.* Push data transparency to business leaders. They are best positioned to make difficult trade-offs in the budgeting process, but often lack data granularity to make those choices (and to see the imperative).
3. *Culture matters.* A culture of honest, frank debate that challenges the status quo and avoids homogeneity of thought makes the job more fun and leads to better results. A broad range of experience, and even some "battle scars," ensures the organization recognizes patterns to foresee emerging risks. In that regard, a diverse team with respect to gender, race, and socioeconomic background brings differentiated perspectives, contributing to effective risk management.
4. *Make tough calls early and, ideally, once.* Lead.

QUESTION: *How has the crisis shaped the role of the CFO, or your view of it?*

ANSWER: In financial services, it redefined the perception of a CFO. Beyond focusing on accounting and external reporting functions, the CFO is now also the firm's most senior global manager for guardianship and risk management. Guardianship includes accounting (the controller function) and overseeing a comprehensive approach to IT systems. Risk management requires identifying sources of vulnerability, stress testing, and planning against them. The CFO has become a trusted adviser to the CEO, board and business leaders, which includes budgeting, capital allocation, and sensitivity analyses. Finally, in certain industries the CFO is the point person with regulators.

QUESTION: *What key lessons did you take from the financial crisis? What advice would you give future CFOs?*

ANSWER: I have three key takeaways from the financial crisis, relevant in both good and bad markets as well as across industries:

1. *Understand your greatest sources of vulnerability and defend against them.* For financial services, liquidity (access to cash) was a weak spot. In that period, we often said, "Liquidity is oxygen for a financial system: without it, you choke." Without sufficient liquidity, banks were forced into a negative cycle of selling assets to raise cash. As Morgan Stanley's CFO, I managed liquidity with the maxim that it was sacrosanct. We invested substantially in the amount and durability of the company's liquidity reserve. Similarly, regulators coming out of the crisis appropriately demanded higher capital, lower leverage, better liquidity, more durable funding, and rigorous stress testing, which imposed transparency on the banks and exposed their weaknesses.
2. *Build a robust control infrastructure ahead of needs, including financial and risk management controls, systems, and processes.* Just as one shouldn't drive a car at 100 mph with mud on the windshield, business leaders must have visibility about their business from accurate, insightful, and timely data consistent with strong financial controls. Rapid growth industries need to invest in infrastructure early because the business requirements continue to grow so rapidly.
3. *Recognize that time is your enemy.* Treasury Secretary Paulson told me during the financial crisis that you must have the will and the means to solve problems; too often, by the time you have the will, you no longer have the means. He was talking about policy, but that rule applies to any decision maker. The glaring examples, in retrospect, were the clear signs of crisis in August 2007 and the March 2008 collapse of Bear Stearns, but reactions were slow or nonexistent. Even in good times, business leaders must focus on resource optimization to maximize the potential for highest returns on investment.

Types of Financial Statements

Every public company is required to produce four financial statements: the *balance sheet*, the *income statement*, the *statement of cash flows*, and the *statement of stockholders' equity*. These financial statements provide investors and creditors with an overview of the firm's financial performance. In the sections that follow, we take a close look at the content of these financial statements.

CONCEPT CHECK

1. What are the four financial statements that all public companies must produce?
2. What is the role of an auditor?

2.2 The Balance Sheet

The **balance sheet**, or **statement of financial position**,[1] lists the firm's *assets* and *liabilities*, providing a snapshot of the firm's financial position at a given point in time. Table 2.1 shows the balance sheet for a fictitious company, Global Conglomerate Corporation. Notice that the balance sheet is divided into two parts ("sides"), with the assets on the left side and the liabilities on the right. The **assets** list the cash, inventory, property, plant, and equipment, and other investments the company has made; the **liabilities** show the firm's obligations to creditors. Also shown with liabilities on the right side of the balance sheet is

TABLE 2.1 Global Conglomerate Corporation Balance Sheet

GLOBAL CONGLOMERATE CORPORATION

Consolidated Balance Sheet
Year Ended December 31 (in $ million)

Assets	2015	2014	Liabilities and Stockholders' Equity	2015	2014
Current Assets			**Current Liabilities**		
Cash	21.2	19.5	Accounts payable	29.2	24.5
Accounts receivable	18.5	13.2	Notes payable/short-term debt	3.5	3.2
Inventories	15.3	14.3	Current maturities of long-term debt	13.3	12.3
Other current assets	2.0	1.0	Other current liabilities	2.0	4.0
Total current assets	57.0	48.0	Total current liabilities	48.0	44.0
Long-Term Assets			**Long-Term Liabilities**		
Land	22.2	20.7	Long-term debt	99.9	76.3
Buildings	36.5	30.5	Capital lease obligations	—	—
Equipment	39.7	33.2	Total debt	99.9	76.3
Less accumulated depreciation	(18.7)	(17.5)	Deferred taxes	7.6	7.4
Net property, plant, and equipment	79.7	66.9	Other long-term liabilities	—	—
Goodwill and intangible assets	20.0	20.0	Total long-term liabilities	107.5	83.7
Other long-term assets	21.0	14.0	**Total Liabilities**	**155.5**	**127.7**
Total long-term assets	120.7	100.9	**Stockholders' Equity**	**22.2**	**21.2**
Total Assets	**177.7**	**148.9**	**Total Liabilities and Stockholders' Equity**	**177.7**	**148.9**

[1] In IFRS and recent U.S. GAAP pronouncements, the balance sheet is referred to as the *statement of financial position*.

the *stockholders' equity*. **Stockholders' equity**, the difference between the firm's assets and liabilities, is an accounting measure of the firm's net worth.

The assets on the left side show how the firm uses its capital (its investments), and the right side summarizes the sources of capital, or how a firm raises the money it needs. Because of the way stockholders' equity is calculated, the left and right sides must balance:

The Balance Sheet Identity

$$\text{Assets} = \text{Liabilities} + \text{Stockholders' Equity} \tag{2.1}$$

In Table 2.1, total assets for 2015 ($177.7 million) are equal to total liabilities ($155.5 million) plus stockholders' equity ($22.2 million).

Let's examine Global's assets, liabilities, and stockholders' equity in more detail.

Assets

In Table 2.1, Global's assets are divided into current and long-term assets. We discuss each in turn.

Current Assets. **Current assets** are either cash or assets that could be converted into cash within one year. This category includes the following:

1. Cash and other **marketable securities**, which are short-term, low-risk investments that can be easily sold and converted to cash (such as money market investments like government debt that matures within a year);
2. **Accounts receivable**, which are amounts owed to the firm by customers who have purchased goods or services on credit;
3. **Inventories**, which are composed of raw materials as well as work-in-progress and finished goods;
4. Other current assets, which is a catch-all category that includes items such as prepaid expenses (such as rent or insurance paid in advance).

Long-Term Assets. The first category of **long-term assets** is net property, plant, and equipment. These include assets such as real estate or machinery that produce tangible benefits for more than one year. If Global spends $2 million on new equipment, this $2 million will be included with property, plant, and equipment on the balance sheet. Because equipment tends to wear out or become obsolete over time, Global will reduce the value recorded for this equipment each year by deducting a **depreciation expense**. An asset's **accumulated depreciation** is the total amount deducted over its life. The firm reduces the value of fixed assets (other than land) over time according to a depreciation schedule that depends on the asset's life span. Depreciation is not an actual cash expense that the firm pays; it is a way of recognizing that buildings and equipment wear out and thus become less valuable the older they get. The **book value** of an asset, which is the value shown in the firm's financial statements, is equal to its acquisition cost less accumulated depreciation. Net property, plant, and equipment shows the book value of these assets.

When a firm acquires another company, it will acquire a set of tangible assets (such as inventory or property, plant, and equipment) that will then be included on its balance sheet. In many cases, however, the firm may pay more for the company than the total book value of the assets it acquires. In this case, the difference between the price paid for the company and the book value assigned to its tangible assets is recorded separately as **goodwill** and **intangible assets**. For example, Global paid $25 million in 2013 for a firm whose tangible assets had a book value of $5 million. The remaining $20 million appears as goodwill and intangible assets in Table 2.1. This entry in the balance sheet captures the value of other "intangibles" that the firm acquired through the acquisition (e.g., brand names and trademarks, patents, customer relationships, and employees). If the firm assesses that the value of these intangible assets declined over time, it will reduce the amount listed on the balance sheet by an **amortization** or **impairment charge** that captures the change in value of the acquired assets. Like depreciation, amortization is not an actual cash expense.

Other long-term assets can include such items as property not used in business operations, start-up costs in connection with a new business, investments in long-term securities, and property held for sale. The sum of all the firms' assets is the total assets at the bottom of the left side of the balance sheet in Table 2.1.

Liabilities

We now examine the liabilities shown on the right side of the balance sheet, which are divided into *current* and *long-term liabilities*.

Current Liabilities. Liabilities that will be satisfied within one year are known as **current liabilities**. They include the following:

1. **Accounts payable**, the amounts owed to suppliers for products or services purchased with credit;
2. **Short-term debt** or notes payable, and current maturities of *long-term debt*, which are all repayments of debt that will occur within the next year;
3. Items such as salary or taxes that are owed but have not yet been paid, and deferred or unearned revenue, which is revenue that has been received for products that have not yet been delivered.

The difference between current assets and current liabilities is the firm's **net working capital**, the capital available in the short term to run the business. For example, in 2015, Global's net working capital totaled $9 million ($57 million in current assets – $48 million in current liabilities). Firms with low (or negative) net working capital may face a shortage of funds unless they generate sufficient cash from their ongoing activities.

Long-Term Liabilities. Long-term liabilities are liabilities that extend beyond one year. We describe the main types as follows:

1. **Long-term debt** is any loan or debt obligation with a maturity of more than a year. When a firm needs to raise funds to purchase an asset or make an investment, it may borrow those funds through a long-term loan.
2. **Capital leases** are long-term lease contracts that obligate the firm to make regular lease payments in exchange for use of an asset.[2] They allow a firm to gain use of an asset by leasing it from the asset's owner. For example, a firm may lease a building to serve as its corporate headquarters.
3. **Deferred taxes** are taxes that are owed but have not yet been paid. Firms generally keep two sets of financial statements: one for financial reporting and one for tax purposes. Occasionally, the rules for the two types of statements differ. Deferred tax liabilities generally arise when the firm's financial income exceeds its income for tax purposes. Because deferred taxes will eventually be paid, they appear as a liability on the balance sheet.[3]

---

[2]See Chapter 25 for a precise definition of a capital lease.

[3]A firm may also have deferred tax assets related to tax credits it has earned that it will receive in the future.

Stockholders' Equity

The sum of the current liabilities and long-term liabilities is total liabilities. The difference between the firm's assets and liabilities is the stockholders' equity; it is also called the **book value of equity**. As we stated earlier, it is an accounting measure of the net worth of the firm.

Ideally, the balance sheet would provide us with an accurate assessment of the true value of the firm's equity. Unfortunately, this is unlikely to be the case. First, many of the assets listed on the balance sheet are valued based on their historical cost rather than their true value today. For example, an office building is listed on the balance sheet according to its historical cost net of depreciation. But the actual value of the office building today may be very different (and possibly much *more*) than the amount the firm paid for it years ago. The same is true for other property, plant, and equipment, as well as goodwill: The true value today of an asset may be very different from, and even exceed, its book value. A second, and probably more important, problem is that *many of the firm's valuable assets are not captured on the balance sheet.* Consider, for example, the expertise of the firm's employees, the firm's reputation in the marketplace, the relationships with customers and suppliers, the value of future research and development innovations, and the quality of the management team. These are all assets that add to the value of the firm that do not appear on the balance sheet.

Market Value Versus Book Value

For the reasons cited above, the book value of equity, while accurate from an accounting perspective, is an inaccurate assessment of the true value of the firm's equity. Successful firms are often able to borrow in excess of the book value of their assets because creditors recognize that the market value of the assets is far higher than the book value. Thus, it is not surprising that the book value of equity will often differ substantially from the amount investors are willing to pay for the equity. The total *market* value of a firm's equity equals the number of shares outstanding times the firm's market price per share:

$$\text{Market Value of Equity} = \text{Shares outstanding} \times \text{Market price per share} \tag{2.2}$$

The market value of equity is often referred to as the company's **market capitalization** (or "market cap"). The market value of a stock does not depend on the historical cost of the firm's assets; instead, it depends on what investors expect those assets to produce in the future.

EXAMPLE 2.1 Market Versus Book Value

Problem

If Global has 3.6 million shares outstanding, and these shares are trading for a price of $14 per share, what is Global's market capitalization? How does the market capitalization compare to Global's book value of equity in 2015?

Solution

Global's market capitalization is (3.6 million shares) × ($14/share) = $50.4 million. This market capitalization is significantly higher than Global's book value of equity of $22.2 million. Thus, investors are willing to pay 50.4/22.2 = 2.27 times the amount Global's shares are "worth" according to their book value.

Market-to-Book Ratio. In Example 2.1, we computed the **market-to-book ratio** (also called the **price-to-book [P/B] ratio**) for Global, which is the ratio of its market capitalization to the book value of stockholders' equity.

$$\text{Market-to-Book Ratio} = \frac{\text{Market Value of Equity}}{\text{Book Value of Equity}} \tag{2.3}$$

The market-to-book ratio for most successful firms substantially exceeds 1, indicating that the value of the firm's assets when put to use exceeds their historical cost. Variations in this ratio reflect differences in fundamental firm characteristics as well as the value added by management.

In Fall 2015, Citigroup (C) had a market-to-book ratio of 0.76, a reflection of investors' assessment that many of Citigroup's assets (such as some mortgage securities) were worth far less than their book value. At the same time, the average market-to-book ratio for major U.S. banks and financial firms was 1.9, and for all large U.S. firms it was 2.9. In contrast, Pepsico (PEP) had a market-to-book ratio of 8.3, and IBM had a market-to-book ratio of 11.3. Analysts often classify firms with low market-to-book ratios as **value stocks**, and those with high market-to-book ratios as **growth stocks**.

Enterprise Value

A firm's market capitalization measures the market value of the firm's equity, or the value that remains after the firm has paid its debts. But what is the value of the business itself? The **enterprise value** of a firm (also called the **total enterprise value** or **TEV**) assesses the value of the underlying business assets, unencumbered by debt and separate from any cash and marketable securities. We compute it as follows:

$$\text{Enterprise Value} = \text{Market Value of Equity} + \text{Debt} - \text{Cash} \tag{2.4}$$

From Example 2.1, Global's market capitalization in 2015 is \$50.4 million. Its debt is \$116.7 million (\$3.5 million of notes payable, \$13.3 million of current maturities of long-term debt, and remaining long-term debt of \$99.9 million). Therefore, given its cash balance of \$21.2 million, Global's enterprise value is $50.4 + 116.7 - 21.2 = \$145.9$ million. The enterprise value can be interpreted as the cost to take over the business. That is, it would cost $50.4 + 116.7 = \$167.1$ million to buy all of Global's equity and pay off its debts, but because we would acquire Global's \$21.2 million in cash, the net cost of the business is only $167.1 - 21.2 = \$145.9$ million.

CONCEPT CHECK

1. What is the balance sheet identity?
2. The book value of a company's assets usually does not equal the market value of those assets. What are some reasons for this difference?
3. What is a firm's enterprise value, and what does it measure?

2.3 The Income Statement

When you want somebody to get to the point, you might ask him or her for the "bottom line." This expression comes from the *income statement*. The **income statement** or **statement of financial performance**[4] lists the firm's revenues and expenses over a period of time. The last or "bottom" line of the income statement shows the firm's **net income**, which is a measure of its profitability during the period. The income statement is sometimes called a profit and loss, or "P&L" statement, and the net income is also referred to as the firm's **earnings**. In this section, we examine the components of the income statement in detail and introduce ratios we can use to analyze this data.

[4] In IFRS and recent U.S. GAAP pronouncements, the income statement is referred to as the *statement of financial performance*.

Earnings Calculations

Whereas the balance sheet shows the firm's assets and liabilities at a given point in time, the income statement shows the flow of revenues and expenses generated by those assets and liabilities between two dates. Table 2.2 shows Global's income statement for 2015. We examine each category on the statement.

Gross Profit. The first two lines of the income statement list the revenues from sales of products and the costs incurred to make and sell the products. Cost of sales shows costs directly related to producing the goods or services being sold, such as manufacturing costs. Other costs such as administrative expenses, research and development, and interest expenses are not included in the cost of sales. The third line is **gross profit**, which is the difference between sales revenues and the costs.

Operating Expenses. The next group of items is operating expenses. These are expenses from the ordinary course of running the business that are not directly related to producing the goods or services being sold. They include administrative expenses and overhead, salaries, marketing costs, and research and development expenses. The third type of operating expense, depreciation and amortization, is not an actual cash expense but represents an estimate of the costs that arise from wear and tear or obsolescence of the firm's assets.[5] The firm's gross profit net of operating expenses is called **operating income**.

TABLE 2.2 Global Conglomerate Corporation Income Statement Sheet

GLOBAL CONGLOMERATE CORPORATION
Income Statement
Year Ended December 31 (in $ million)

	2015	2014
Total sales	186.7	176.1
Cost of sales	(153.4)	(147.3)
Gross Profit	33.3	28.8
Selling, general, and administrative expenses	(13.5)	(13.0)
Research and development	(8.2)	(7.6)
Depreciation and amortization	(1.2)	(1.1)
Operating Income	10.4	7.1
Other income	—	—
Earnings Before Interest and Taxes (EBIT)	10.4	7.1
Interest income (expense)	(7.7)	(4.6)
Pretax Income	2.7	2.5
Taxes	(0.7)	(0.6)
Net Income	2.0	1.9
Earnings per share:	$0.556	$0.528
Diluted earnings per share:	$0.526	$0.500

[5]Only certain types of amortization are deductible as a pretax expense (e.g., amortization of the cost of an acquired patent). Also, firms often do not separately list depreciation and amortization on the income statement, but rather include them with the expenses by function (e.g., depreciation of R&D equipment would be included with R&D expenses). When depreciation and amortization has been separated in this way, practitioners often refer to the expense items as "clean" (e.g., "clean R&D" is R&D expenses excluding any depreciation or amortization).

Earnings before Interest and Taxes. We next include other sources of income or expenses that arise from activities that are not the central part of a company's business. Income from the firm's financial investments is one example of other income that would be listed here. After we have adjusted for other sources of income or expenses, we have the firm's earnings before interest and taxes, or **EBIT**.

Pretax and Net Income. From EBIT, we deduct the interest expense related to outstanding debt to compute Global's pretax income, and then we deduct corporate taxes to determine the firm's net income.

Net income represents the total earnings of the firm's equity holders. It is often reported on a per-share basis as the firm's **earnings per share (EPS)**, which we compute by dividing net income by the total number of shares outstanding:

$$\text{EPS} = \frac{\text{Net Income}}{\text{Shares Outstanding}} = \frac{\$2.0 \text{ Million}}{3.6 \text{ Million Shares}} = \$0.556 \text{ per Share} \tag{2.5}$$

Although Global has only 3.6 million shares outstanding as of the end of 2015, the number of shares outstanding may grow if Global compensates its employees or executives with **stock options** that give the holder the right to buy a certain number of shares by a specific date at a specific price. If the options are "exercised," the company issues new stock and the number of shares outstanding will grow. The number of shares may also grow if the firm issues **convertible bonds**, a form of debt that can be converted to shares. Because there will be more total shares to divide the same earnings, this growth in the number of shares is referred to as **dilution**. Firms disclose the potential for dilution by reporting **diluted EPS**, which represents earnings per share for the company calculated as though, for example, in-the-money stock options or other stock-based compensation had been exercised or dilutive convertible debt had been converted. For example, in 2014, Global awarded 200,000 shares of restricted stock to its key executives. While these are currently unvested, they will ultimately increase the number of shares outstanding, so Global's diluted EPS is \$2 million/3.8 million shares = \$0.526.[6]

CONCEPT CHECK

1. What it is the difference between a firm's gross profit and its net income?
2. What is the diluted earnings per share?

2.4 The Statement of Cash Flows

The income statement provides a measure of the firm's profit over a given time period. However, it does not indicate the amount of *cash* the firm has generated. There are two reasons that net income does not correspond to cash earned. First, there are non-cash entries on the income statement, such as depreciation and amortization. Second, certain uses of cash, such as the purchase of a building or expenditures on inventory, are not reported on the income statement. The firm's **statement of cash flows** utilizes the information

[6] In the case of stock options, the diluted share count is typically calculated using the *treasury stock method*, in which the number of shares added has the same value as the profit from exercising the option. For example, given Global's share price of \$14 per share, an option giving an employee the right to purchase a share for \$7 would add (\$14 − \$7)/\$14 = 0.5 shares to the diluted share count.

from the income statement and balance sheet to determine how much cash the firm has generated, and how that cash has been allocated, during a set period. As we will see, from the perspective of an investor attempting to value the firm, the statement of cash flows provides what may be the most important information of the four financial statements.

The statement of cash flows is divided into three sections: operating activities, investment activities, and financing activities. The first section, operating activity, starts with net income from the income statement. It then adjusts this number by adding back all non-cash entries related to the firm's operating activities. The next section, investment activity, lists the cash used for investment. The third section, financing activity, shows the flow of cash between the firm and its investors. Global Conglomerate's statement of cash flows is shown in Table 2.3. In this section, we take a close look at each component of the statement of cash flows.

Operating Activity

The first section of Global's statement of cash flows adjusts net income by all non-cash items related to operating activity. For instance, depreciation is deducted when computing net income, but it is not an actual cash outflow. Thus, we add it back to net income when determining the amount of cash the firm has generated. Similarly, we add back any other non-cash expenses (for example, deferred taxes or expenses related to stock-based compensation).

TABLE 2.3 **Global Conglomerate Corporation Statement of Cash Flows**

GLOBAL CONGLOMERATE CORPORATION
Statement of Cash Flows
Year Ended December 31 (in $ million)

	2015	2014
Operating activities		
Net income	2.0	1.9
Depreciation and amortization	1.2	1.1
Other non-cash items	(2.8)	(1.0)
Cash effect of changes in		
Accounts receivable	(5.3)	(0.3)
Accounts payable	4.7	(0.5)
Inventory	(1.0)	(1.0)
Cash from operating activities	**(1.2)**	**0.2**
Investment activities		
Capital expenditures	(14.0)	(4.0)
Acquisitions and other investing activity	(7.0)	(2.0)
Cash from investing activities	**(21.0)**	**(6.0)**
Financing activities		
Dividends paid	(1.0)	(1.0)
Sale (or purchase) of stock	—	—
Increase in borrowing	24.9	5.5
Cash from financing activities	**23.9**	**4.5**
Change in cash and cash equivalents	**1.7**	**(1.3)**

Next, we adjust for changes to net working capital that arise from changes to accounts receivable, accounts payable, or inventory. When a firm sells a product, it records the revenue as income even though it may not receive the cash from that sale immediately. Instead, it may grant the customer credit and let the customer pay in the future. The customer's obligation adds to the firm's accounts receivable. We use the following guidelines to adjust for changes in working capital:

1. *Accounts Receivable*: When a sale is recorded as part of net income, but the cash has not yet been received from the customer, we must adjust the cash flows by *deducting* the increases in accounts receivable. This increase represents additional lending by the firm to its customers, and it reduces the cash available to the firm.
2. *Accounts Payable*: Conversely, we *add* increases in accounts payable. Accounts payable represents borrowing by the firm from its suppliers. This borrowing increases the cash available to the firm.
3. *Inventory*: Finally, we *deduct* increases to inventory. Increases to inventory are not recorded as an expense and do not contribute to net income (the cost of the goods are only included in net income when the goods are actually sold). However, the cost of increasing inventory is a cash expense for the firm and must be deducted.

We can identify the changes in these working capital items from the balance sheet. For example, from Table 2.1, Global's accounts receivable increased from \$13.2 million in 2014 to \$18.5 million in 2015. We deduct the increase of $18.5 - 13.2 = \$5.3$ million on the statement of cash flows. Note that although Global showed positive net income on the income statement, it actually had a negative \$1.2 million cash flow from operating activity, in large part because of the increase in accounts receivable.

Investment Activity

The next section of the statement of cash flows shows the cash required for investment activities. Purchases of new property, plant, and equipment are referred to as **capital expenditures**. Recall that capital expenditures do not appear immediately as expenses on the income statement. Instead, firms recognize these expenditures over time as depreciation expenses. To determine the firm's cash flow, we already added back depreciation because it is not an actual cash outflow. Now, we subtract the actual capital expenditure that the firm made. Similarly, we also deduct other assets purchased or long-term investments made by the firm, such as acquisitions or purchases of marketable securities. In Table 2.3, we see that in 2015, Global spent \$21 million in cash on investing activities.

Financing Activity

The last section of the statement of cash flows shows the cash flows from financing activities. Dividends paid to shareholders are a cash outflow. Global paid \$1 million to its shareholders as dividends in 2015. The difference between a firm's net income and the amount it spends on dividends is referred to as the firm's **retained earnings** for that year:

$$\text{Retained Earnings} = \text{Net Income} - \text{Dividends} \tag{2.6}$$

Global retained \$2 million − \$1 million = \$1 million, or 50% of its earnings in 2015.

Also listed under financing activity is any cash the company received from the sale of its own stock, or cash spent buying (repurchasing) its own stock. Global did not issue or repurchase stock during this period. The last items to include in this section result from changes to Global's short-term and long-term borrowing. Global raised money by issuing debt, so the increases in borrowing represent cash inflows.

The final line of the statement of cash flows combines the cash flows from these three activities to calculate the overall change in the firm's cash balance over the period of the statement. In this case, Global had cash inflows of $1.7 million, which matches the change in cash from 2014 to 2015 shown earlier in the balance sheet. By looking at the statement in Table 2.3 as a whole, we can determine that Global chose to borrow to cover the cost of its investment and operating activities. Although the firm's cash balance has increased, Global's negative operating cash flows and relatively high expenditures on investment activities might give investors some reasons for concern. If that pattern continues, Global will need to raise capital, by continuing to borrow or issuing equity, to remain in business.

EXAMPLE 2.2 **The Impact of Depreciation on Cash Flow**

Problem

Suppose Global had an additional $1 million depreciation expense in 2015. If Global's tax rate on pretax income is 26%, what would be the impact of this expense on Global's earnings? How would it impact Global's cash balance at the end of the year?

Solution

Depreciation is an operating expense, so Global's operating income, EBIT, and pretax income would fall by $1 million. This decrease in pretax income would reduce Global's tax bill by $26\% \times \$1$ million $= \$0.26$ million. Therefore, net income would fall by $1 - 0.26 =$ $0.74 million.

On the statement of cash flows, net income would fall by $0.74 million, but we would add back the additional depreciation of $1 million because it is not a cash expense. Thus, cash from operating activities would rise by $-0.74 + 1 = \$0.26$ million. Thus, Global's cash balance at the end of the year would increase by $0.26 million, the amount of the tax savings that resulted from the additional depreciation expense.

CONCEPT CHECK

1. Why does a firm's net income not correspond to cash generated?
2. What are the components of the statement of cash flows?

2.5 Other Financial Statement Information

The most important elements of a firm's financial statements are the balance sheet, income statement, and the statement of cash flows, which we have already discussed. Several other pieces of information contained in the financial statements warrant brief mention: the statement of stockholders' equity, the management discussion and analysis, and notes to the financial statements.

Statement of Stockholders' Equity

The **statement of stockholders' equity** breaks down the stockholders' equity computed on the balance sheet into the amount that came from issuing shares (par value plus paid-in capital) versus retained earnings. Because the book value of stockholders' equity is not a useful assessment of value for financial purposes, financial managers use the statement of stockholders' equity infrequently (so we will skip the computational details here). We can, however, determine the change in stockholders' equity using information from the firm's other financial statements as follows:[7]

$$\begin{aligned}\text{Change in Stockholders' Equity} &= \text{Retained Earnings} + \text{Net sales of stock}\\ &= \text{Net Income} - \text{Dividends} +\\ &\quad \text{Sales of stock} - \text{Repurchases of stock} \qquad (2.7)\end{aligned}$$

For example, because Global had no stock sales or repurchases, its stockholders' equity increased by the amount of its retained earnings, or $1.0 million, in 2015. Note that this result matches the change in stockholders' equity shown earlier on Global's balance sheet.

Management Discussion and Analysis

The **management discussion and analysis (MD&A)** is a preface to the financial statements in which the company's management discusses the recent year (or quarter), providing a background on the company and any significant events that may have occurred. Management may also discuss the coming year, and outline goals, new projects, and future plans.

Management should also discuss any important risks that the firm faces or issues that may affect the firm's liquidity or resources. Management is also required to disclose any **off-balance sheet transactions**, which are transactions or arrangements that can have a material impact on the firm's future performance yet do not appear on the balance sheet. For example, if a firm has made guarantees that it will compensate a buyer for losses related to an asset purchased from the firm, these guarantees represent a potential future liability for the firm that must be disclosed as part of the MD&A.

Notes to the Financial Statements

In addition to the four financial statements, companies provide extensive notes with further details on the information provided in the statements. For example, the notes document important accounting assumptions that were used in preparing the statements. They often provide information specific to a firm's subsidiaries or its separate product lines. They show the details of the firm's stock-based compensation plans for employees and the different types of debt the firm has outstanding. Details of acquisitions, spin-offs, leases, taxes, debt repayment schedules, and risk management activities are also given. The information provided in the notes is often very important to interpret fully the firm's financial statements.

EXAMPLE 2.3 Sales by Product Category

Problem

In the Segment Results section of its financial statements, Hormel Foods Corp (HRL) reported the following sales revenues by reportable segment/product category ($ million):

	2014	2013
Grocery Products	$1,558	$1,518
Refrigerated Foods	4,644	4,252
Jennie-O Turkey Store	1,672	1,602
Specialty Foods	907	932
International & Other	534	448

Which category showed the highest percentage growth? If Hormel has the same percentage growth by category from 2014 to 2015, what will its total revenues be in 2015?

[7] Sales of stock would also include any stock-based compensation.

Solution

The percentage growth in the sales of grocery products was $1558/1518 - 1 = 2.6\%$. Similarly, growth in Refrigerated Foods was 9.2%, Jennie-O Turkey Store was 4.4%, Specialty Foods was −2.7%, and International and Other categories were 19.2%. Thus, International and Other categories showed the highest growth.

If these growth rates continue for another year, sales of Grocery Products will be $1558 \times 1.026 = \$1598$ million, and the other categories will be $5071 million, $1746 million, $883 million, and $637 million, respectively, for total revenues of $9.9 billion, a 6.7% increase over 2014.

CONCEPT CHECK

1. Where do off-balance sheet transactions appear in a firm's financial statements?
2. What information do the notes to financial statements provide?

2.6 Financial Statement Analysis

Investors often use accounting statements to evaluate a firm in one of two ways:

1. Compare the firm with itself by analyzing how the firm has changed over time.
2. Compare the firm to other similar firms using a common set of financial ratios.

In this section we will describe the most commonly used ratios—related to profitability, liquidity, working capital, interest coverage, leverage, valuation, and operating returns—and explain how each one is used in practice.

Profitability Ratios

The income statement provides very useful information regarding the profitability of a firm's business and how it relates to the value of the firm's shares. The **gross margin** of a firm is the ratio of gross profit to revenues (sales):

$$\text{Gross Margin} = \frac{\text{Gross Profit}}{\text{Sales}} \tag{2.8}$$

A firm's gross margin reflects its ability to sell a product for more than the cost of producing it. For example, in 2015, Global had gross margin of $33.3/186.7 = 17.8\%$.

Because there are additional expenses of operating a business beyond the direct costs of goods sold, another important profitability ratio is the **operating margin**, the ratio of operating income to revenues:

$$\text{Operating Margin} = \frac{\text{Operating Income}}{\text{Sales}} \tag{2.9}$$

The operating margin reveals how much a company earns before interest and taxes from each dollar of sales. In 2015, Global's operating margin was $10.4/186.7 = 5.57\%$, an increase from its 2014 operating margin of $7.1/176.1 = 4.03\%$. We can similarly compute a firm's **EBIT margin** = (EBIT/Sales).

By comparing operating or EBIT margins across firms within an industry, we can assess the relative efficiency of the firms' operations. For example, Figure 2.1 compares the EBIT margins of five major U.S. airlines from 2007 to 2012. Notice the impact on profitability from the financial crisis during 2008–2009, as well as the consistently low profits of the largest and oldest of the carriers, United-Continental (UAL), relative to its competitors.

FIGURE 2.1

EBIT Margins for Five U.S. Airlines

Annual (last twelve month) EBIT margins for five U.S. airlines: Alaska Airlines, Delta Airlines, JetBlue, Southwest, and United-Continental. Note the decline in profitability for all airlines in the wake of the 2008 financial crisis, followed by a recovery by mid-2010. Note also the consistently lower profitability of the legacy carrier, United-Continental, relative to its younger peers.

Source: Capital IQ

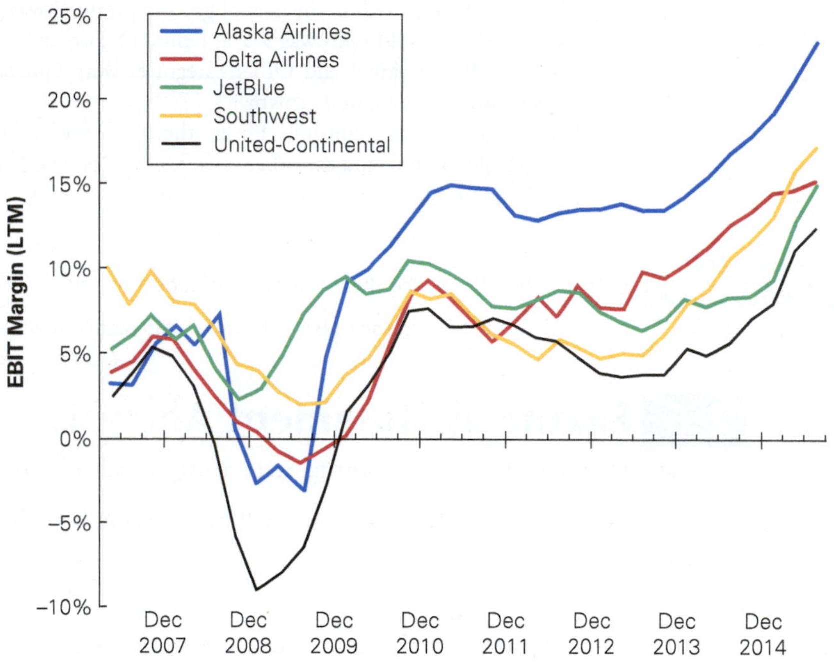

In addition to the efficiency of operations, differences in operating margins can result from corporate strategy. For example, in 2014, high-end retailer Nordstrom (JWN) had an operating margin of 9.8%; Wal-Mart Stores (WMT, brand name Walmart) had an operating margin of only 5.6%. In this case, Walmart's lower operating margin was not a result of its inefficiency. Rather, the low operating margin is part of Walmart's strategy of offering low prices to sell common products in high volume. Indeed, Walmart's sales were nearly 36 times higher than those of Nordstrom.

Finally, a firm's **net profit margin** is the ratio of net income to revenues:

$$\text{Net Profit Margin} = \frac{\text{Net Income}}{\text{Sales}} \tag{2.10}$$

The net profit margin shows the fraction of each dollar in revenues that is available to equity holders after the firm pays interest and taxes. In 2015, Global's net profit margin was 2.0/186.7 = 1.07%. One must be cautious when comparing net profit margins: While differences in net profit margins can be due to differences in efficiency, they can also result from differences in leverage, which determines the amount of interest expense, as well as differences in accounting assumptions.

Liquidity Ratios

Financial analysts often use the information in the firm's balance sheet to assess its financial solvency or liquidity. Specifically, creditors often compare a firm's current assets and current liabilities to assess whether the firm has sufficient working capital to meet its short-term needs. This comparison can be summarized in the firm's **current ratio**, the ratio of current assets to current liabilities:

$$\text{Current Ratio} = \frac{\text{Current Assets}}{\text{Current Liabilities}}$$

Notice that Global's current ratio increased from $48/44 = 1.09$ in 2014 to $57/48 = 1.19$ in 2015.

A more stringent test of the firm's liquidity is the **quick ratio**, which compares only cash and "near cash" assets, such as short-term investments and accounts receivable, to current liabilities. In 2015, Global's quick ratio was $(21.2 + 18.5)/48 = 0.83$. A higher current or quick ratio implies less risk of the firm experiencing a cash shortfall in the near future. A reason to exclude inventory is that it may not be that liquid; indeed an increase in the current ratio that results from an unusual increase in inventory could be an indicator that the firm is having difficulty selling its products.

Ultimately, firms need cash to pay employees and meet other obligations. Running out of cash can be very costly for a firm, so firms often gauge their cash position by calculating the **cash ratio**, which is the most stringent liquidity ratio:

$$\text{Cash Ratio} = \frac{\text{Cash}}{\text{Current Liabilities}}$$

Of course, all of these liquidity ratios are limited in that they only consider the firm's current assets. If the firm is able to generate significant cash quickly from its ongoing activities, it might be highly liquid even if these ratios are poor.

EXAMPLE 2.4 **Computing Liquidity Ratios**

Problem

Calculate Global's quick ratio and cash ratio. Based on these measures, how has its liquidity changed between 2014 and 2015?

Solution

In 2014, Global's quick ratio was $(19.5 + 13.2)/44 = 0.74$ and its cash ratio was $19.5/44 = 0.44$. In 2015, these ratios were 0.83 and $21.2/48 = 0.44$, respectively. Thus, Global's cash ratio remained stable over this period, while its quick ratio improved slightly. But although these liquidity measures have not deteriorated, a more worrisome indicator for investors regarding Global's liquidity might be its ongoing negative cash flow from operating and investing activities, shown in the statement of cash flows.

Working Capital Ratios

We can use the combined information in the firm's income statement and balance sheet to gauge how efficiently the firm is utilizing its net working capital. To evaluate the speed at which a company turns sales into cash, firms often compute the number of

accounts receivable days—that is, the number of days' worth of sales accounts receivable represents:[8]

$$\text{Accounts Receivable Days} = \frac{\text{Accounts Receivable}}{\text{Average Daily Sales}} \tag{2.11}$$

Given average daily sales of \$186.7 million/365 = \$0.51 million in 2015, Global's receivables of \$18.5 million represent 18.5/0.51 = 36 days' worth of sales. In other words, on average, Global takes a little over one month to collect payment from its customers. In 2014, Global's accounts receivable represented only 27 days' worth of sales. Although the number of receivable days can fluctuate seasonally, a significant unexplained increase could be a cause for concern (perhaps indicating the firm is doing a poor job of collecting from its customers or is trying to boost sales by offering generous credit terms).

There are similar ratios for accounts payable and inventory. For these items, it is natural to compare them to the firm's cost of sales, which should reflect the total amount paid to suppliers and inventory sold. Therefore, **accounts payable days** is defined as:

$$\text{Accounts Payable Days} = \frac{\text{Accounts Payable}}{\text{Average Daily Cost of Sales}} \tag{2.12}$$

Similarly, **inventory days** = (inventory/average daily cost of sales).[9]

Turnover ratios are an alternative way to measure working capital. We compute turnover ratios by expressing annual revenues or costs as a multiple of the corresponding working capital account. For example,

$$\text{Inventory Turnover} = \frac{\text{Annual Cost of Sales}}{\text{Inventory}} \tag{2.13}$$

Global's **inventory turnover** in 2015 is 153.4/15.3 = 10.0×, indicating that Global sold roughly 10 times its current stock of inventory during the year. Similarly, **accounts receivable turnover** = (annual sales/accounts receivable) and **accounts payable turnover** = (annual cost of sales/accounts payable). Note that higher turnover corresponds to shorter days, and thus a more efficient use of working capital.

While working capital ratios can be meaningfully compared over time or within an industry, there are wide differences across industries. While the average large U.S. firm had about 49 days' worth of receivables and 54 days' worth of inventory in 2015, airlines tend to have minimal accounts receivable or inventory, as their customers pay in advance and they sell a transportation service as opposed to a physical commodity. On the other hand, distillers and wine producers tend to have very large inventory (over 300 days on average), as their products are often aged prior to sale.

Interest Coverage Ratios

Lenders often assess a firm's ability to meet its interest obligations by comparing its earnings with its interest expenses using an **interest coverage ratio**. One common ratio to consider is the firm's EBIT as a multiple of its interest expenses. A high ratio indicates that the firm is earning much more than is necessary to meet its required interest payments.

---

[8]Accounts receivable days can also be calculated based on the *average* accounts receivable at the end of the current and prior year.

[9]As with accounts receivable days, these ratios can also be calculated using the average accounts payable or inventory balance from the current and prior year.

As a benchmark, creditors often look for an EBIT/Interest coverage ratio in excess of 5× for high-quality borrowers. When EBIT/Interest falls below 1.5, lenders may begin to question a company's ability to repay its debts.

Depreciation and amortization expenses are deducted when computing EBIT, but they are not actually cash expenses for the firm. Consequently, financial analysts often compute a firm's earnings before interest, taxes, depreciation, and amortization, or **EBITDA**, as a measure of the cash a firm generates from its operations and has available to make interest payments:[10]

$$\text{EBITDA} = \text{EBIT} + \text{Depreciation and Amortization} \tag{2.14}$$

We can similarly compute the firm's EBITDA/Interest coverage ratio.

EXAMPLE 2.5 **Computing Interest Coverage Ratios**

Problem

Assess Global's ability to meet its interest obligations by calculating interest coverage ratios using both EBIT and EBITDA.

Solution

In 2014 and 2015, Global had the following interest coverage ratios:

$$2014: \quad \frac{\text{EBIT}}{\text{Interest}} = \frac{7.1}{4.6} = 1.54 \quad \text{and} \quad \frac{\text{EBITDA}}{\text{Interest}} = \frac{7.1 + 1.1}{4.6} = 1.78$$

$$2015: \quad \frac{\text{EBIT}}{\text{Interest}} = \frac{10.4}{7.7} = 1.35 \quad \text{and} \quad \frac{\text{EBITDA}}{\text{Interest}} = \frac{10.4 + 1.2}{7.7} = 1.51$$

In this case Global's low—and declining—interest coverage could be a source of concern for its creditors.

Leverage Ratios

An important piece of information that we can learn from a firm's balance sheet is the firm's **leverage**, or the extent to which it relies on debt as a source of financing. The **debt-equity ratio** is a common ratio used to assess a firm's leverage. We calculate this ratio by dividing the total amount of short- and long-term debt (including current maturities) by the total stockholders' equity:

$$\text{Debt-Equity Ratio} = \frac{\text{Total Debt}}{\text{Total Equity}} \tag{2.15}$$

We can calculate the debt-equity ratio using either book or market values for equity and debt. From Table 2.1, Global's debt in 2015 includes notes payable ($3.5 million), current

[10]Because firms often do not separately list depreciation and amortization expenses on the income statement, EBITDA is generally calculated by combining EBIT from the income statement and depreciation and amortization from the statement of cash flows. Note also that because the firm may ultimately need to invest to replace depreciating assets, EBITDA is best viewed as a measure of the firm's *short-run* ability to meet interest payments.

maturities of long-term debt (\$13.3 million), and long-term debt (\$99.9 million), for a total of \$116.7 million. Therefore, its *book* debt-equity ratio is $116.7/22.2 = 5.3$, using the book value of equity. Note the increase from 2014, when the book debt-equity ratio was only $(3.2 + 12.3 + 76.3)/21.2 = 91.8/21.2 = 4.3$.

Because of the difficulty interpreting the book value of equity, the book debt-equity ratio is not especially useful. Indeed, the book value of equity might even be negative, making the ratio meaningless. For example, Domino's Pizza (DPZ) has, based on the strength of its cash flow, consistently borrowed in excess of the book value of its assets. In 2014, it had debt of \$1.8 billion, with a total book value of assets of only \$600 million and an equity book value of −\$1.2 billion!

It is therefore most informative to compare the firm's debt to the market value of its equity. Recall from Example 2.1 that in 2015, the total market value of Global's equity, its market capitalization, is 3.6 million shares × \$14/share = \$50.4 million. Therefore, Global's *market* debt-equity ratio in 2015 is $116.7/50.4 = 2.3$, which means Global's debt is a bit more than double the market value of its equity.[11] As we show later in the text, a firm's market debt-equity ratio has important consequences for the risk and return of its stock.

We can also calculate the fraction of the firm financed by debt in terms of its **debt-to-capital ratio**:

$$\text{Debt-to-Capital Ratio} = \frac{\text{Total Debt}}{\text{Total Equity} + \text{Total Debt}} \tag{2.16}$$

Again, this ratio can be computed using book or market values.

While leverage increases the risk to the firm's equity holders, firms may also hold cash reserves in order to reduce risk. Thus, another useful measure to consider is the firm's **net debt**, or debt in excess of its cash reserves:

$$\text{Net Debt} = \text{Total Debt} - \text{Excess Cash \& Short-term Investments} \tag{2.17}$$

To understand why net debt may be a more relevant measure of leverage, consider a firm with more cash than debt outstanding: Because such a firm could pay off its debts immediately using its available cash, it has not increased its risk and has no effective leverage.

Analogous to the debt-to-capital ratio, we can use the concept of net debt to compute the firm's **debt-to-enterprise value ratio**:

$$\begin{aligned}\text{Debt-to-Enterprise Value Ratio} &= \frac{\text{Net Debt}}{\text{Market Value of Equity} + \text{Net Debt}} \\ &= \frac{\text{Net Debt}}{\text{Enterprise Value}}\end{aligned} \tag{2.18}$$

Given Global's 2015 cash balance of \$21.2 million, and total long- and short-term debt of \$116.7 million, its net debt is $116.7 - 21.2 = \$95.5$ million.[12] Given its market value of equity of \$50.4 million, Global's enterprise value in 2015 is $50.4 + 95.5 = \$145.9$ million,

[11]In this calculation, we have compared the market value of equity to the book value of debt. Strictly speaking, it would be best to use the market value of debt. But because the market value of debt is generally not very different from its book value, this distinction is often ignored in practice.

[12]While net debt should ideally be calculated by deducting cash in excess of the firm's operating needs, absent additional information, it is typical in practice to deduct all cash on the balance sheet.

and thus its debt-to-enterprise value ratio is 95.5/145.9 = 65.5%. That is, 65.5% of Global's underlying business activity is financed via debt.

A final measure of leverage is a firm's **equity multiplier**, measured in book value terms as Total Assets/Book Value of Equity. As we will see shortly, this measure captures the amplification of the firm's accounting returns that results from leverage. The market value equity multiplier, which is generally measured as Enterprise Value/Market Value of Equity, indicates the amplification of shareholders' financial risk that results from leverage.

Valuation Ratios

Analysts use a number of ratios to gauge the market value of the firm. The most common is the firm's **price-earnings ratio (P/E)**:

$$\text{P/E Ratio} = \frac{\text{Market Capitalization}}{\text{Net Income}} = \frac{\text{Share Price}}{\text{Earnings per Share}} \tag{2.19}$$

That is, the P/E ratio is the ratio of the value of equity to the firm's earnings, either on a total basis or on a per-share basis. For example, Global's P/E ratio in 2015 was 50.4/2.0 = 14/0.556 = 25.2. In other words, investors are willing to pay over 25 times Global's earnings to purchase a share.

The P/E ratio is a simple measure that is used to assess whether a stock is over- or undervalued based on the idea that the value of a stock should be proportional to the level of earnings it can generate for its shareholders. P/E ratios can vary widely across industries and tend to be highest for industries with high expected growth rates. For example, in late 2015, the median large U.S. firm had a P/E ratio of about 21. But software firms, which tend to have above-average growth rates, had an average P/E ratio of 38, while automotive firms, which have experienced slower growth since the recession, had an average P/E ratio of about 15. The risk of the firm will also affect this ratio—all else equal, riskier firms have lower P/E ratios.

Because the P/E ratio considers the value of the firm's equity, it is sensitive to the firm's choice of leverage. The P/E ratio is therefore of limited usefulness when comparing firms with markedly different leverage. We can avoid this limitation by instead assessing the market value of the underlying business using valuation ratios based on the firm's enterprise value. Common ratios include the ratio of enterprise value to revenue, or enterprise value to operating income, EBIT, or EBITDA. These ratios compare the value of the business to its sales, operating profits, or cash flow. Like the P/E ratio, these ratios are used to make intra-industry comparisons of how firms are priced in the market.

COMMON MISTAKE Mismatched Ratios

When considering valuation (and other) ratios, be sure that the items you are comparing both represent amounts related to the entire firm or that both represent amounts related solely to equity holders. For example, a firm's share price and market capitalization are values associated with the firm's equity. Thus, it makes sense to compare them to the firm's earnings per share or net income, which are amounts to equity holders after interest has been paid to debt holders. We must be careful, however, if we compare a firm's market capitalization to its revenues, operating income, or EBITDA because these amounts are related to the whole firm, and both debt and equity holders have a claim to them. Thus, it is better to compare revenues, operating income, or EBITDA to the enterprise value of the firm, which includes both debt and equity.

EXAMPLE 2.6 Computing Profitability and Valuation Ratios

Problem

Consider the following data as of July 2015 for Walmart and Target Corporation (in $ billion):

	Walmart (WMT)	Target (TGT)
Sales	485.7	73.1
EBIT	26.6	4.5
Depreciation and Amortization	9.2	2.1
Net Income	16.2	2.5
Market Capitalization	235.6	52.9
Cash	9.1	2.2
Debt	48.8	12.8

Compare Walmart's and Target's EBIT margins, net profit margins, P/E ratios, and the ratio of enterprise value to sales, EBIT, and EBITDA.

Solution

Walmart had an EBIT Margin of $26.6/485.7 = 5.5\%$, a net profit margin of $16.2/485.7 = 3.3\%$, and a P/E ratio of $235.6/16.2 = 14.5$. Its enterprise value was $235.6 + 48.8 - 9.1 = 275.3$ billion, which has a ratio of $275.3/485.7 = 0.57$ to sales, $275.3/26.6 = 10.3$ to EBIT, and $275.3/(26.6 + 9.2) = 7.7$ to EBITDA.

Target had an EBIT margin of $4.5/73.3 = 6.2\%$, a net profit margin of $2.5/73.1 = 3.4\%$, and a P/E ratio of $52.9/2.5 = 21.2$. Its enterprise value was $52.9 = 12.8 - 2.2 = \$63.5$ billion, which has a ratio of $63.4/73.1 = 0.87$ to sales, $63.5/4.5 = 14.1$ to EBIT, and $63.5/(4.5 + 2.1) = 9.6$ to EBITDA.

Note that despite the large difference in the size of the two firms, Target trades at higher, though comparable, multiples.

The P/E ratio, or ratios to EBIT or EBITDA, are not meaningful if the firm's earnings are negative. In this case, it is common to look at the firm's enterprise value relative to sales. The risk in doing so, however, is that earnings might be negative because the firm's underlying business model is fundamentally flawed, as was the case for many Internet firms in the late 1990s.

Operating Returns

Analysts often evaluate the firm's return on investment by comparing its income to its investment using ratios such as the firm's **return on equity (ROE)**:[13]

$$\text{Return on Equity} = \frac{\text{Net Income}}{\text{Book Value of Equity}} \tag{2.20}$$

Global's ROE in 2015 was $2.0/22.2 = 9.0\%$. The ROE provides a measure of the return that the firm has earned on its past investments. A high ROE may indicate the firm is able to find investment opportunities that are very profitable.

[13] Because net income is measured over the year, the ROE can also be calculated based on the average book value of equity at the end of the current and prior year.

Another common measure is **return on assets (ROA)**, which we calculate as:[14]

$$\text{Return on Assets} = \frac{\text{Net Income} + \text{Interest Expense}}{\text{Book Value of Assets}} \tag{2.21}$$

The ROA calculation includes interest expense in the numerator because the assets in the denominator have been funded by both debt and equity investors.

As a performance measure, ROA has the benefit that it is less sensitive to leverage than ROE. However, it is sensitive to working capital—for example, an equal increase in the firm's receivables and payables will increase total assets and thus lower ROA. To avoid this problem, we can consider the firm's **return on invested capital (ROIC)**:

$$\text{Return on Invested Capital} = \frac{\text{EBIT}\ (1 - \text{tax rate})}{\text{Book Value of Equity} + \text{Net Debt}} \tag{2.22}$$

The return on invested capital measures the after-tax profit generated by the business itself, excluding any interest expenses (or interest income), and compares it to the capital raised from equity and debt holders that has already been deployed (i.e., is not held as cash). Of the three measures of operating returns, ROIC is the most useful in assessing the performance of the underlying business.

EXAMPLE 2.7 Computing Operating Returns

Problem

Assess how Global's ability to use its assets effectively has changed in the last year by computing the change in its return on assets and return on invested capital.

Solution

In 2015, Global's ROA was $(2.0 + 7.7)/177.7 = 5.5\%$, compared to an ROA in 2014 of $(1.9 + 4.6)/148.9 = 4.4\%$.

To compute the return on invested capital, we need to calculate after-tax EBIT, which requires an estimate of Global's tax rate. Because Net income = Pretax income × (1 − tax rate), we can estimate (1 − tax rate) = Net income/Pretax income. Thus, EBIT × (1 − tax rate) = $10.4 \times (2.0/2.7) = 7.7$ in 2015, and $7.1 \times (1.9/2.5) = 5.4$ in 2014.

To compute invested capital, note first that Global's net debt was $3.2 + 12.3 + 76.3 - 19.5 = 72.3$ in 2014 and $3.5 + 13.3 + 99.9 - 21.2 = 95.5$ in 2015. Thus, ROIC in 2015 was $7.7/(22.2 + 95.5) = 6.5\%$, compared with $5.4/(21.2 + 72.3) = 5.8\%$ in 2014.

The improvement in Global's ROA and ROIC from 2014 to 2015 suggests that Global was able to use its assets more effectively and increase its return over this period.

[14]ROA is sometimes calculated as Net Income/Assets, inappropriately ignoring the returns generated by the assets that are being used to support the firm's debt obligations (see also the box on Mismatched Ratios on page 43). Also, the interest expense that is added back is sometimes done on an after-tax basis in order to eliminate the benefit of the tax savings provided by debt. Finally, as with ROE, the *average* book value of assets at the beginning and end of the year may be used.

The DuPont Identity

We can gain further insight into a firm's ROE using a tool called the **DuPont Identity** (named for the company that popularized its use), which expresses the ROE in terms of the firm's profitability, asset efficiency, and leverage:

$$\text{ROE} = \underbrace{\left(\frac{\text{Net Income}}{\text{Sales}}\right)}_{\text{Net Profit Margin}} \times \underbrace{\left(\frac{\text{Sales}}{\text{Total Assets}}\right)}_{\text{Asset Turnover}} \times \underbrace{\left(\frac{\text{Total Assets}}{\text{Book Value of Equity}}\right)}_{\text{Equity Multiplier}} \quad (2.23)$$

The first term in the DuPont Identity is the firm's net profit margin, which measures its overall profitability. The second term is the firm's **asset turnover**, which measures how efficiently the firm is utilizing its assets to generate sales. Together, these terms determine the firm's return on assets. We compute ROE by multiplying by a measure of leverage called the equity multiplier, which indicates the value of assets held per dollar of shareholder equity. The greater the firm's reliance on debt financing, the higher the equity multiplier will be. Applying this identity to Global, we see that in 2015 its asset turnover is 186.7/177.7 = 1.05, with an equity multiplier of 177.7/22.2 = 8. Given its net profit margin of 1.07%, we can compute its ROE as

$$\text{ROE} = 9.0\% = 1.07\% \times 1.05 \times 8$$

EXAMPLE 2.8 Determinants of ROE

Problem

For the year ended January 2015, Walmart (WMT) had sales of $485.7 billion, net income of $16.2 billion, assets of $203.7 billion, and a book value of equity of $85.9 billion. For the same period, Target (TGT) had sales of $73.1 billion, net income of $2.5 billion, total assets of $41.4 billion, and a a book value of equity of $14 billion. Compare these firms' profitability, asset turnover, equity multipliers, and return on equity during this period. If Target had been able to match Walmart's asset turnover during this period, what would its ROE have been?

Solution

Walmart's net profit margin (from Example 2.6) was 16.2/485.7 = 3.34%, which was just below Target's net profit margin of 2.5/73.1 = 3.42%. On the other hand, Walmart used its assets more efficiently, with an asset turnover of 485.7/203.7 = 2.38, compared to only 73.1/41.4 = 1.77 for Target. Finally, Target had greater leverage (in terms of book value), with an equity multiplier of 41.4/14 = 2.96, relative to Walmart's equity multiplier of 203.7/85.9 = 2.37. Next, let's compute the ROE of each firm directly, and using the DuPont Identity:

$$\text{Walmart ROE} = \frac{16.2}{85.9} = 18.8\% = 3.34\% \times 2.38 \times 2.37$$

$$\text{Target ROE} = \frac{2.5}{14} = 17.9\% = 3.42\% \times 1.77 \times 2.96$$

Note that due to its lower asset turnover, Target had a lower ROE than Walmart despite its higher net profit margin and leverage. If Target had been able to match Walmart's asset turnover, its ROE would have been significantly higher: 3.42% × 2.38 × 2.96 = 24.1%.

To conclude our discussion of financial ratios, Table 2.4 presents the various measures of profitability, liquidity, working capital, interest coverage, leverage, valuation, and operating returns.

TABLE 2.4 **Key Financial Ratios for Large U.S. Firms, Fall 2015**

(Data shows quartiles [25%, median, 75%] for U.S. stocks with market capitalization over $1 billion)

Ratio	Quartiles [25%, median, 75%]	Formula
Profitability Ratios		
Gross Margin	[28%, 42%, 65%]	Gross Profit / Sales
Operating Margin	[7%, 13%, 22%]	Operating Income / Sales
EBIT Margin	[6%, 12%, 20%]	EBIT / Sales
Net Profit Margin	[2%, 7%, 14%]	Net Income / Sales
Liquidity Ratios		
Current Ratio	[1.2x, 1.8x, 2.9x]	Current Assets / Current Liabilities
Quick Ratio	[0.7x, 1.2x, 2.0x]	(Cash & Short-term Investments + Accounts Receivable) / Current Liabilities
Cash Ratio	[0.1x, 0.4x, 0.8x]	Cash / Current Liabilities
Working Capital Ratios		
Accounts Receivable Days	[32, 49, 67]	Accounts Receivable / Average Daily Sales
Accounts Payable Days	[25, 42, 62]	Accounts Payable / Average Daily Cost of Sales
Inventory Days	[24, 54, 92]	Inventory / Average Daily Cost of Sales
Interest Coverage Ratios		
EBIT/Interest Coverage	[2.9x, 6.7x, 15.8x]	EBIT / Interest Expense
EBITDA/Interest Coverage	[5.2x, 9.8x, 20.2x]	EBITDA / Interest Expense
Leverage Ratios		
Debt-Equity Ratio (book)	[21%, 60%, 121%]	Total Debt / Book Value of Equity
Debt-Equity Ratio (market)	[6%, 21%, 51%]	Total Debt / Market Value of Equity
Leverage Ratios (continued)		
Debt-to-Capital Ratio	[18%, 38%, 56%]	Total Debt / (Total Equity + Total Debt)
Debt-to-Enterprise Value Ratio	[−4%, 9%, 25%]	Net Debt / Enterprise Value
Equity Multiplier (book)	[1.7x, 2.5x, 4.0x]	Total Assets / Book Value of Equity
Equity Multiplier (market)	[1.0x, 1.1x, 1.5x]	Enterprise Value / Market Value of Equity
Valuation Ratios		
Market-to-Book Ratio	[1.6x, 2.9x, 5.5x]	Market Value of Equity / Book Value of Equity
Price-Earnings Ratio	[15.7x, 21.6x, 32.6x]	Share Price / Earnings per Share
Enterprise Value to Sales	[1.3x, 2.4x, 4.3x]	Enterprise Value / Sales
Enterprise Value to EBIT	[11.9x, 15.7x, 22.2x]	Enterprise Value / EBIT
Enterprise Value to EBITDA	[8.8x, 11.5x, 15.4x]	Enterprise Value / EBITDA
Operating Returns		
Asset Turnover	[0.3x, 0.6x, 1.1x]	Sales / Total Assets
Return on Equity (ROE)	[4%, 11%, 19%]	Net Income / Book Value of Equity
Return on Assets (ROA)	[−1%, 3%, 8%]	(Net Income + Interest Expense) / Book Value of Assets
Return on Invested Capital (ROIC)	[7%, 12%, 21%]	EBIT (1 − Tax Rate) / (Book Value of Equity + Net Debt)

CONCEPT CHECK

1. Why is EBITDA used to assess a firm's ability to meet its interest obligations?
2. What is the difference between a firm's book debt-equity ratio and its market debt-equity ratio?
3. To compare the valuations of firms with very different leverage, which valuation multiples would be most appropriate?
4. What is the DuPont Identity?

2.7 Financial Reporting in Practice

The various financial statements we have examined are of critical importance to investors and financial managers alike. Even with safeguards such as GAAP and auditors, though, financial reporting abuses unfortunately do take place. We now review two of the most infamous examples.

Enron

Enron was the most well known of the accounting scandals of the early 2000s. Enron started as an operator of natural-gas pipelines but evolved into a global trader dealing in a range of products including gas, oil, electricity, and even broadband Internet capacity. A series of events unfolded that, in December 2001, led Enron to file what was, at the time, the largest bankruptcy filing in U.S. history. By the end of that year, the market value of Enron's shares had fallen by over $60 billion.

Interestingly, throughout the 1990s and up to late 2001, Enron was touted as one of the most successful and profitable companies in America. *Fortune* rated Enron "The Most Innovative Company in America" for six straight years, from 1995 to 2000. But while many aspects of Enron's business were successful, subsequent investigations suggest that Enron executives had been manipulating Enron's financial statements to mislead investors and artificially inflate the price of Enron's stock and maintain its credit rating. In 2000, for example, 96% of Enron's reported earnings were the result of accounting manipulation.[15]

Although the accounting manipulations that Enron used were quite sophisticated, the essence of most of the deceptive transactions was surprisingly simple. Enron sold assets at inflated prices to other firms (or, in many cases, business entities that Enron's CFO Andrew Fastow had created), together with a promise to buy back those assets at an even higher future price. Thus, Enron was effectively borrowing money, receiving cash today in exchange for a promise to pay more cash in the future. But Enron recorded the incoming cash as revenue and then hid the promises to buy them back in a variety of ways.[16] In the end, much of Enron's revenue growth and profits in the late 1990s were the result of this type of manipulation.

WorldCom

Enron's record as the largest bankruptcy of all time lasted only until July 21, 2002, when WorldCom, which at its peak had a market capitalization of $120 billion, filed for bankruptcy. Again, a series of accounting manipulations beginning in 1998 hid the firm's financial problems from investors.

In WorldCom's case, the fraud was to reclassify $3.85 billion in operating expenses as long-term capital expenditures. The immediate impact of this change was to boost

---

[15] John R. Kroger, "Enron, Fraud and Securities Reform: An Enron Prosecutor's Perspective," *University of Colorado Law Review* (December 2009): pp. 57–138.

[16] In some cases, these promises were called "price risk management liabilities" and hidden with other trading activities; in other cases they were off-balance sheet transactions that were not fully disclosed.

WorldCom's reported earnings: Operating expenses are deducted from earnings immediately, whereas capital expenditures are depreciated slowly over time. Of course, this manipulation would not boost WorldCom's cash flows, because long-term investments must be deducted on the cash flow statement at the time they are made.

Some investors were concerned by WorldCom's excessive investment compared to the rest of the industry. As one investment advisor commented, "Red flags [were] things like big deviations between reported earnings and excess cash flow . . . [and] excessive capital expenditures for a long period of time. That was what got us out of WorldCom in 1999."[17]

Sarbanes-Oxley Act

The Enron and Worldcom scandals had an immediate and tangible impact on the accounting world. Both firms had been audited by the same accounting firm, Arthur Andersen, and accusations begin to emerge about their business practices in late 2001. By March 2002, Arthur Andersen was indicted on charges following from the Enron case, and it was convicted in June. With its reputation destroyed, the firm quickly collapsed, leaving its clients to find new auditors. These new auditors had a strong incentive to "clean house" and as a result new instances of errors and/or outright fraud were uncovered. Professors Alexander Dyck, Adair Morse, and Luigi Zingales used this event to estimate that nearly 15% of firms may have engaged in some form of financial misrepresentation, and that such fraud costs investors on average 22% of the firm's enterprise value.[18]

In an attempt to improve the reliability of financial reporting and corporate governance, Congress passed the Sarbanes-Oxley Act (SOX) in 2002. While SOX contains many provisions, the overall intent of the legislation was to improve the accuracy of information given to both boards and shareholders. SOX attempted to achieve this goal in three ways: (1) by overhauling incentives and the independence in the auditing process, (2) by stiffening penalties for providing false information, and (3) by forcing companies to validate their internal financial control processes.

Because auditors often have a long-standing relationship with their clients and receive lucrative auditing and consulting fees from them, their desire to continue earning these fees may make auditors less willing to challenge management. SOX addressed this concern by putting strict limits on the amount of non-audit fees (consulting or otherwise) that an accounting firm can earn from a company that it audits. It also required that audit partners rotate every five years to limit the likelihood that auditing relationships become too cozy over long periods of time. Finally, SOX called on the SEC to force companies to have audit committees that are dominated by outside directors, with at least one outside director having a financial background.

SOX also stiffened the criminal penalties for providing false information to shareholders (fines of up to $5 million and up to 20 years imprisonment), and required both the CEO and CFO to personally attest to the accuracy of the firm's financial statements. Furthermore, CEOs and CFOs must return bonuses or profits from the sale of stock that are later shown to be due to misstated financial reports.

Finally, Section 404 of SOX requires senior management and the boards of public companies to validate and certify the process through which funds are allocated and controlled, and outcomes are monitored. Section 404 has arguably garnered more attention than any other section in SOX because of the large potential compliance costs that it places on firms.

---

[17] Robert Olstein, as reported in the *Wall Street Journal*, August 23, 2002.

[18] See "How Pervasive Is Corporate Fraud?" Rotman School of Management Working Paper No. 2222608, 2013.

GLOBAL FINANCIAL CRISIS Bernard Madoff's Ponzi Scheme

"It's only when the tide goes out that you learn who's been swimming naked."
—*Warren Buffett*

On December 11, 2008, federal agents arrested Bernie Madoff, one of the largest and most successful hedge fund managers. It turned out that the $65 billion[19] fund he ran was in fact a fraud. His spectacular performance of the last 17 years, generating consistent annual returns between 10% and 15%, was actually a complete fabrication. Madoff had been running the world's largest Ponzi scheme: That is, he used the capital contributed by new investors to pay off old investors. His strategy was so successful that for more than a decade investors ranging from Steven Spielberg to New York University, as well as a number of large banks and investment advisors, lined up to invest with him. Indeed, Madoff quite likely would have been able to hide the fraud until his deathbed had not the global financial crisis spurred many investors to seek to withdraw funds from their Madoff accounts in order to raise cash and cover losses elsewhere in their portfolios. In addition, the financial crisis meant there were few new investors with both the cash and the willingness to invest. As a result, Madoff did not have enough new capital to pay off the investors who wanted to withdraw their capital, and the scheme finally collapsed.*

How was Madoff able to hide perhaps the largest fraud of all time for so long? Rather than simply manipulate his accounting statements, Madoff *made them up* with the assistance of a virtually unknown accounting firm with only one active accountant. Although many investors may have questioned why such a large fund, with $65 billion in assets, would choose an unknown and tiny audit firm, not enough of them recognized this choice as a potential red flag. In addition, because Madoff's firm was private, it was not subject to the strict regulatory requirements for public companies (such as the Sarbanes-Oxley Act) and so had weak reporting requirements. As this case makes clear, when making an investment decision, it is important not only to review the firm's financial statements, but also to consider the reliability and reputation of the auditors who prepared them.

*For reasons why fraud may be more likely to occur in booms, and then exposed in downturns, see P. Povel, R. Singh, and A. Winton, "Booms, Busts, and Fraud," *Review of Financial Studies* 20 (2007): 1219–1254.

These costs can be especially significant (in percentage terms) for small companies, and critics have argued that they are sufficiently onerous to cause some firms to avoid them by remaining privately held.[20]

Dodd-Frank Act

To mitigate the compliance burden on small firms, the Dodd-Frank Wall Street Reform and Consumer Protection Act passed in 2010 exempts firms with less than $75 million in publicly held shares from the SOX Section 404 requirements. It also requires the SEC to study how it might reduce cost for medium-sized firms with a public float of less than $250 million, and to assess whether such measures would encourage more firms to list on U.S. exchanges.

Dodd-Frank also broadened the whistleblower provisions of SOX, so that an individual who provides "information related to a possible violation of the federal securities laws (including any rules or regulations thereunder)" that results in penalties or recoveries by the SEC or agencies is eligible to receive from 10 to 30% of that penalty or recovery.

CONCEPT CHECK

1. Describe the transactions Enron used to increase its reported earnings.
2. What is the Sarbanes-Oxley Act, and how was it modified by the Dodd-Frank Act?

[19] $65 billion is the total amount Madoff had reported to his investors, including (fictitious) returns; investigators are still trying to determine the exact amount that investors had actually contributed to the fund, but it appears to be in excess of $17 billion (see www.madofftrustee.com).

[20] See Chapter 29 for a more detailed discussion of these and other corporate governance issues.

MyFinanceLab Here is what you should know after reading this chapter. MyFinanceLab will help you identify what you know and where to go when you need to practice.

2.1 Firms' Disclosure of Financial Information

- Financial statements are accounting reports that a firm issues periodically to describe its past performance.
- Investors, financial analysts, managers, and other interested parties such as creditors rely on financial statements to obtain reliable information about a corporation.
- The four required financial statements are the balance sheet, the income statement, the statement of cash flows, and the statement of stockholders' equity.

2.2 The Balance Sheet

- The balance sheet shows the current financial position (assets, liabilities, and stockholders' equity) of the firm at a single point in time.
- The two sides of the balance sheet must balance:

$$\text{Assets} = \text{Liabilities} + \text{Stockholders' Equity} \tag{2.1}$$

- The firm's net working capital, which is the capital available in the short term to run the business, is the difference between the firm's current assets and current liabilities. Excluding cash and debt, key components of net working capital are accounts receivable, inventory, and accounts payable.
- Many assets (such as property, plant, and equipment) are listed on the firm's balance sheet based on their historical cost rather than their current market value, whereas other assets (such as customer relationships) are not listed at all.
- Stockholders' equity is the book value of the firm's equity. It differs from market value of the firm's equity, its market capitalization, because of the way assets and liabilities are recorded for accounting purposes. A successful firm's market-to-book ratio typically exceeds 1.
- The enterprise value of a firm is the total value of its underlying business operations:

$$\text{Enterprise Value} = \text{Market Value of Equity} + \text{Debt} - \text{Cash} \tag{2.4}$$

2.3 The Income Statement

- The income statement reports the firm's revenues and expenses, and it computes the firm's bottom line of net income, or earnings, over a given time interval.
- The firm's operating income is equal to its revenues less its cost of goods sold and operating expenses. After adjusting for other, non-operating income or expenses, we have the firm's earnings before interest and taxes, or EBIT.
- Deducting interest and taxes from EBIT gives the firm's net income, which we can divide by the number of shares outstanding to calculate earnings per share (EPS).

2.4 The Statement of Cash Flows

- The statement of cash flows reports the sources and uses of the firm's cash during a given time period, and can be derived from the firm's income statement and the changes in the firm's balance sheet.
- The statement of cash flows shows the cash used (or provided) from operating, investing, and financing activities.

2.5 Other Financial Statement Information

- The change in stockholders' equity can be computed as retained earnings (net income less dividends) plus net sales of stock (new grants or issuances, net of repurchases).
- The management discussion and analysis section of the financial statements contains management's overview of the firm's performance, as well as disclosure of risks the firm faces, including those from off-balance sheet transactions.

- The notes to a firm's financial statements generally contain important details regarding the numbers used in the main statements.

2.6 Financial Statement Analysis

- Financial ratios allow us to (i) compare the firm's performance over time, and (ii) compare the firm to other similar firms.
- Key financial ratios measure the firm's profitability, liquidity, working capital, interest coverage, leverage, valuation, and operating returns. See Table 2.4 for a summary.
- EBITDA measures the cash a firm generates before capital investments:

$$\text{EBITDA} = \text{EBIT} + \text{Depreciation and Amortization} \tag{2.14}$$

- Net debt measures the firm's debt in excess of its cash reserves:

$$\text{Net Debt} = \text{Total Debt} - \text{Excess Cash \& Short-term Investments} \tag{2.17}$$

- The DuPont Identity expresses a firm's ROE in terms of its profitability, asset efficiency, and leverage:

$$\text{ROE} = \underbrace{\left(\frac{\text{Net Income}}{\text{Sales}}\right)}_{\text{Net Profit Margin}} \times \underbrace{\left(\frac{\text{Sales}}{\text{Total Assets}}\right)}_{\text{Asset Turnover}} \times \underbrace{\left(\frac{\text{Total Assets}}{\text{Book Value of Equity}}\right)}_{\text{Equity Multiplier}} \tag{2.23}$$

2.7 Financial Reporting in Practice

- Recent accounting scandals have drawn attention to the importance of financial statements. New legislation has increased the penalties for fraud and tightened the procedures firms must use to assure that statements are accurate.

Key Terms

Further Reading

For a basic primer on financial statements, see T. R. Ittelson, *Financial Statements: A Step-By-Step Guide to Understanding and Creating Financial Reports* (Career Press, 2009).

For additional information on financial accounting, there are many introductory, MBA-level financial accounting textbooks. See T. Dyckman, R. Magee, and G. Pfeiffer, *Financial Accounting* (Cambridge Business Publishers, 2010); and W. Harrison, C. Horngren, and C. W. Thomas, *Financial Accounting* (Prentice Hall, 2013).

For more on financial statement analysis, see J. Whalen, S. Baginski, and M. Bradshaw, *Financial Reporting, Financial Statement Analysis and Valuation: A Strategic Perspective* (South-Western College Pub, 2010); and L. Revsine, D. Collins, B. Johnson, F. Mittelstaedt, *Financial Reporting & Analysis* (McGraw-Hill/Irwin, 2011).

A great deal of public information is available regarding the alleged accounting abuses at Enron Corporation. A useful starting point is a report produced by a committee established by Enron's own board of directors: Report of the Special Investigative Committee of the Board of Directors of Enron (Powers Report), released February 2, 2002 (available online). Information regarding the resolution of Bernard Madoff's Ponzi scheme can be found on the site published by the Securities Investor Protection Act (SIPA) Trustee, www.madofftrustee.com.

For an estimate of the frequency and cost of accounting fraud, see A. Dyck, A. Morse, and L. Zingales, "How Pervasive Is Corporate Fraud?" Rotman School of Management Working Paper No. 2222608, 2013.

Problems

All problems are available in MyFinanceLab. *An asterisk (*) indicates problems with a higher level of difficulty.*

Firms' Disclosure of Financial Information

1. What four financial statements can be found in a firm's 10-K filing? What checks are there on the accuracy of these statements?
2. Who reads financial statements? List at least three different categories of people. For each category, provide an example of the type of information they might be interested in and discuss why.
3. Find the most recent financial statements for Starbucks Corporation (SBUX) using the following sources:
   a. From the company's Web page www.starbucks.com. (*Hint*: Search for "investor relations.")
   b. From the SEC Web site www.sec.gov. (*Hint*: Search for company filings in the EDGAR database.)

c. From the Yahoo! Finance Web site finance.yahoo.com.
d. From at least one other source. (*Hint*: Enter "SBUX 10K" at www.google.com.)

The Balance Sheet

4. Consider the following potential events that might have taken place at Global Conglomerate on December 30, 2015. For each one, indicate which line items in Global's balance sheet would be affected and by how much. Also indicate the change to Global's book value of equity. (In all cases, ignore any tax consequences for simplicity.)
a. Global used $20 million of its available cash to repay $20 million of its long-term debt.
b. A warehouse fire destroyed $5 million worth of uninsured inventory.
c. Global used $5 million in cash and $5 million in new long-term debt to purchase a $10 million building.
d. A large customer owing $3 million for products it already received declared bankruptcy, leaving no possibility that Global would ever receive payment.
e. Global's engineers discover a new manufacturing process that will cut the cost of its flagship product by over 50%.
f. A key competitor announces a radical new pricing policy that will drastically undercut Global's prices.

5. What was the change in Global Conglomerate's book value of equity from 2014 to 2015 according to Table 2.1? Does this imply that the market price of Global's shares increased in 2015? Explain.

6. Use EDGAR to find Qualcomm's 10K filing for 2015. From the balance sheet, answer the following questions:
a. How much did Qualcomm have in cash, cash equivalents, and marketable securities (short- and long-term)?
b. What were Qualcomm's total accounts receivable?
c. What were Qualcomm's total assets?
d. What were Qualcomm's total liabilities? How much of this was long-term debt?
e. What was the book value of Qualcomm's equity?

7. Find online the annual 10-K report for Costco Wholesale Corporation (COST) for fiscal year 2015 (filed in October 2015). Answer the following questions from their balance sheet:
a. How much cash did Costco have at the end of the fiscal year?
b. What were Costco's total assets?
c. What were Costco's total liabilities? How much debt did Costco have?
d. What was the book value of Costco equity?

8. In early 2012, General Electric (GE) had a book value of equity of $116 billion, 10.6 billion shares outstanding, and a market price of $17.00 per share. GE also had cash of $84 billion, and total debt of $410 billion. Three years later, in early 2015, GE had a book value of equity of $128 billion, 10.0 billion shares outstanding with a market price of $25 per share, cash of $85 billion, and total debt of $302 billion. Over this period, what was the change in GE's
a. market capitalization?
b. market-to-book ratio?
c. enterprise value?

9. In early-2015, Abercrombie & Fitch (ANF) had a book equity of $1390 million, a price per share of $25.52, and 69.35 million shares outstanding. At the same time, The Gap (GPS) had a book equity of $2983 million, a share price of $41.19, and 421 million shares outstanding.
a. What is the market-to-book ratio of each of these clothing retailers?
b. What conclusions can you draw by comparing the two ratios?

MFL **10.** See Table 2.5 showing financial statement data and stock price data for Mydeco Corp.
a. What is Mydeco's market capitalization at the end of each year?
b. What is Mydeco's market-to-book ratio at the end of each year?
c. What is Mydeco's enterprise value at the end of each year?

TABLE 2.5 **2012–2016 Financial Statement Data and Stock Price Data for Mydeco Corp.**

Mydeco Corp. 2012–2016	(All data as of fiscal year end; in $ million)				
Income Statement	**2012**	**2013**	**2014**	**2015**	**2016**
Revenue	404.3	363.8	424.6	510.7	604.1
Cost of Goods Sold	(188.3)	(173.8)	(206.2)	(246.8)	(293.4)
Gross Profit	216.0	190.0	218.4	263.9	310.7
Sales and Marketing	(66.7)	(66.4)	(82.8)	(102.1)	(120.8)
Administration	(60.6)	(59.1)	(59.4)	(66.4)	(78.5)
Depreciation & Amortization	(27.3)	(27.0)	(34.3)	(38.4)	(38.6)
EBIT	61.4	37.5	41.9	57.0	72.8
Interest Income (Expense)	(33.7)	(32.9)	(32.2)	(37.4)	(39.4)
Pretax Income	27.7	4.6	9.7	19.6	33.4
Income Tax	(9.7)	(1.6)	(3.4)	(6.9)	(11.7)
Net Income	18.0	3.0	6.3	12.7	21.7
Shares outstanding (millions)	55.0	55.0	55.0	55.0	55.0
Earnings per share	$0.33	$0.05	$0.11	$0.23	$0.39
Balance Sheet	**2012**	**2013**	**2014**	**2015**	**2016**
Assets					
Cash	48.8	68.9	86.3	77.5	85.0
Accounts Receivable	88.6	69.8	69.8	76.9	86.1
Inventory	33.7	30.9	28.4	31.7	35.3
Total Current Assets	171.1	169.6	184.5	186.1	206.4
Net Property, Plant & Equip.	245.3	243.3	309	345.6	347.0
Goodwill & Intangibles	361.7	361.7	361.7	361.7	361.7
Total Assets	778.1	774.6	855.2	893.4	915.1
Liabilities & Stockholders' Equity					
Accounts Payable	18.7	17.9	22.0	26.8	31.7
Accrued Compensation	6.7	6.4	7.0	8.1	9.7
Total Current Liabilities	25.4	24.3	29.0	34.9	41.4
Long-term Debt	500.0	500.0	575.0	600.0	600.0
Total Liabilities	525.4	524.3	604.0	634.9	641.4
Stockholders' Equity	252.7	250.3	251.2	258.5	273.7
Total Liabilities & Stockholders' Equity	778.1	774.6	855.2	893.4	915.1
Statement of Cash Flows	**2012**	**2013**	**2014**	**2015**	**2016**
Net Income	18.0	3.0	6.3	12.7	21.7
Depreciation & Amortization	27.3	27.0	34.3	38.4	38.6
Chg. in Accounts Receivable	3.9	18.8	(0.0)	(7.1)	(9.2)
Chg. in Inventory	(2.9)	2.8	2.5	(3.3)	(3.6)
Chg. in Payables & Accrued Comp.	2.2	(1.1)	4.7	5.9	6.5
Cash from Operations	48.5	50.5	47.8	46.6	54.0
Capital Expenditures	(25.0)	(25.0)	(100.0)	(75.0)	(40.0)
Cash from Investing Activities	(25.0)	(25.0)	(100.0)	(75.0)	(40.0)
Dividends Paid	(5.4)	(5.4)	(5.4)	(5.4)	(6.5)
Sale (or purchase) of stock	—	—	—	—	—
Debt Issuance (Pay Down)	—	—	75.0	25.0	—
Cash from Financing Activities	(5.4)	(5.4)	69.6	19.6	(6.5)
Change in Cash	18.1	20.1	17.4	(8.8)	7.5
Mydeco Stock Price	*$7.92*	*$3.30*	*$5.25*	*$8.71*	*$10.89*

The Income Statement

11. Suppose that in 2016, Global launches an aggressive marketing campaign that boosts sales by 15%. However, their operating margin falls from 5.57% to 4.50%. Suppose that they have no other income, interest expenses are unchanged, and taxes are the same percentage of pretax income as in 2015.

a. What is Global's EBIT in 2016?
b. What is Global's net income in 2016?
c. If Global's P/E ratio and number of shares outstanding remains unchanged, what is Global's share price in 2016?

12. Find online the annual 10-K report for Costco Wholesale Corporation (COST) for fiscal year 2015 (filed in October 2015). Answer the following questions from their income statement:

a. What were Costco's revenues for fiscal year 2015? By what percentage did revenues grow from the prior year?
b. What was Costco's operating income for the fiscal year?
c. What was Costco's average tax rate for the year?
d. What were Costco's diluted earnings per share in fiscal year 2015? What number of shares is this EPS based on?

13. See Table 2.5 showing financial statement data and stock price data for Mydeco Corp.

a. By what percentage did Mydeco's revenues grow each year from 2013–2016?
b. By what percentage did net income grow each year?
c. Why might the growth rates of revenues and net income differ?

14. See Table 2.5 showing financial statement data and stock price data for Mydeco Corp. Suppose Mydeco repurchases 2 million shares each year from 2013 to 2016. What would its earnings per share be in years 2013–2016? (Assume Mydeco pays for the shares using its available cash and that Mydeco earns no interest on its cash balances.)

15. See Table 2.5 showing financial statement data and stock price data for Mydeco Corp. Suppose Mydeco had purchased additional equipment for $12 million at the end of 2013, and this equipment was depreciated by $4 million per year in 2014, 2015, and 2016. Given Mydeco's tax rate of 35%, what impact would this additional purchase have had on Mydeco's net income in years 2013–2016? (Assume the equipment is paid for out of cash and that Mydeco earns no interest on its cash balances.)

16. See Table 2.5 showing financial statement data and stock price data for Mydeco Corp. Suppose Mydeco's costs and expenses had been the same fraction of revenues in 2013–2016 as they were in 2012. What would Mydeco's EPS have been each year in this case?

17. Suppose a firm's tax rate is 35%.

a. What effect would a $10 million operating expense have on this year's earnings? What effect would it have on next year's earnings?
b. What effect would a $10 million capital expense have on this year's earnings if the capital is depreciated at a rate of $2 million per year for five years? What effect would it have on next year's earnings?

***18.** Quisco Systems has 6.5 billion shares outstanding and a share price of $18. Quisco is considering developing a new networking product in house at a cost of $500 million. Alternatively, Quisco can acquire a firm that already has the technology for $900 million worth (at the current price) of Quisco stock. Suppose that absent the expense of the new technology, Quisco will have EPS of $0.80.

a. Suppose Quisco develops the product in house. What impact would the development cost have on Quisco's EPS? Assume all costs are incurred this year and are treated as an R&D expense, Quisco's tax rate is 35%, and the number of shares outstanding is unchanged.
b. Suppose Quisco does not develop the product in house but instead acquires the technology. What effect would the acquisition have on Quisco's EPS this year? (Note that acquisition expenses do not appear directly on the income statement. Assume the firm was acquired at the start of the year and has no revenues or expenses of its own, so that the only effect on EPS is due to the change in the number of shares outstanding.)

c. Which method of acquiring the technology has a smaller impact on earnings? Is this method cheaper? Explain.

The Statement of Cash Flows

19. Find online the annual 10-K report for Costco Wholesale Corporation (COST) for fiscal year 2015 (filed in October 2015). Answer the following questions from their cash flow statement:
a. How much cash did Costco generate from operating activities in fiscal year 2015?
b. What was Costco's total depreciation and amortization expense?
c. How much cash was invested in new property and equipment (net of any sales)?
d. How much did Costco raise from the sale of shares of its stock (net of any purchases)?

MFL **20.** See Table 2.5 showing financial statement data and stock price data for Mydeco Corp.
a. From 2012 to 2016, what was the total cash flow from operations that Mydeco generated?
b. What fraction of the total in (a) was spent on capital expenditures?
c. What fraction of the total in (a) was spent paying dividends to shareholders?
d. What was Mydeco's total retained earnings for this period?

21. See Table 2.5 showing financial statement data and stock price data for Mydeco Corp.
a. In what year was Mydeco's net income the lowest?
b. In what year did Mydeco need to reduce its cash reserves?
c. Why did Mydeco need to reduce its cash reserves in a year when net income was reasonably high?

22. See Table 2.5 showing financial statement data and stock price data for Mydeco Corp. Use the data from the balance sheet and cash flow statement in 2012 to determine the following:
a. How much cash did Mydeco have at the end of 2011?
b. What were Mydeco's accounts receivable and inventory at the end of 2011?
c. What were Mydeco's total liabilities at the end of 2011?
d. Assuming goodwill and intangibles were equal in 2011 and 2012, what was Mydeco's net property, plant, and equipment at the end of 2011?

23. Can a firm with positive net income run out of cash? Explain.

24. Suppose your firm receives a $5 million order on the last day of the year. You fill the order with $2 million worth of inventory. The customer picks up the entire order the same day and pays $1 million upfront in cash; you also issue a bill for the customer to pay the remaining balance of $4 million in 30 days. Suppose your firm's tax rate is 0% (i.e., ignore taxes). Determine the consequences of this transaction for each of the following:
a. Revenues b. Earnings c. Receivables d. Inventory e. Cash

25. Nokela Industries purchases a $40 million cyclo-converter. The cyclo-converter will be depreciated by $10 million per year over four years, starting this year. Suppose Nokela's tax rate is 40%.
a. What impact will the cost of the purchase have on earnings for each of the next four years?
b. What impact will the cost of the purchase have on the firm's cash flow for the next four years?

Other Financial Statement Information

26. See Table 2.5 showing financial statement data and stock price data for Mydeco Corp.
a. What were Mydeco's retained earnings each year?
b. Using the data from 2012, what was Mydeco's total stockholders' equity in 2011?

27. Find online the annual 10-K report for Costco Wholesale Corporation (COST) for fiscal year 2015 (filed in October 2015). Answer the following questions from the notes to their financial statements:
a. How many stores did Costco open outside of the U.S. in 2015?
b. What property does Costco lease? What are the minimum lease payments due in 2016?
c. What was Costco's worldwide member renewal rate for 2015? What proportion of Costco cardholders had Gold Star memberships in 2015?
d. What fraction of Costco's 2015 sales came from gas stations, pharmacy, food court, and optical? What fraction came from apparel and small appliances?

Financial Statement Analysis

28. See Table 2.5 showing financial statement data and stock price data for Mydeco Corp.
   a. What were Mydeco's gross margins each year?
   b. Comparing Mydeco's gross margin, EBIT margin, and net profit margin in 2012 to 2016, which margins improved?

29. For fiscal year end 2015, Wal-Mart Stores, Inc. (WMT, brand name Walmart) had revenues of $485.65 billion, gross profit of $120.57 billion, and net income of $16.36 billion. Costco Wholesale Corporation (COST) had revenue of $116.20 billion, gross profit of $15.13 billion, and net income of $2.38 billion.
   a. Compare the gross margins for Walmart and Costco.
   b. Compare the net profit margins for Walmart and Costco.
   c. Which firm was more profitable in 2015?

30. At the end of 2015, Apple had cash and short-term investments of $41.60 billion, accounts receivable of $35.89 billion, current assets of $89.38 billion, and current liabilities of $80.61 billion.
   a. What was Apple's current ratio?
   b. What was Apple's quick ratio?
   c. What was Apple's cash ratio?
   d. At the end of 2015, HPQ had a cash ratio of 0.35, a quick ratio of 0.73 and a current ratio of 1.15. What can you say about the asset liquidity of Apple relative to HPQ?

31. See Table 2.5 showing financial statement data and stock price data for Mydeco Corp.
   a. How did Mydeco's accounts receivable days change over this period?
   b. How did Mydeco's inventory days change over this period?
   c. Based on your analysis, has Mydeco improved its management of its working capital during this time period?

32. See Table 2.5 showing financial statement data and stock price data for Mydeco Corp.
   a. Compare Mydeco's accounts payable days in 2012 and 2016.
   b. Did this change in accounts payable days improve or worsen Mydeco's cash position in 2016?

33. See Table 2.5 showing financial statement data and stock price data for Mydeco Corp.
   a. By how much did Mydeco increase its debt from 2012 to 2016?
   b. What was Mydeco's EBITDA/Interest coverage ratio in 2012 and 2016? Did its coverage ratio ever fall below 2?
   c. Overall, did Mydeco's ability to meet its interest payments improve or decline over this period?

34. See Table 2.5 showing financial statement data and stock price data for Mydeco Corp.
   a. How did Mydeco's book debt-equity ratio change from 2012 to 2016?
   b. How did Mydeco's market debt-equity ratio change from 2012 to 2016?
   c. Compute Mydeco's debt-to-enterprise value ratio to assess how the fraction of its business that is debt financed has changed over the period.

35. Use the data in Problem 8 to determine the change, from 2012 to 2015, in GE's
   a. book debt-equity ratio.
   b. market debt-equity ratio.

36. You are analyzing the leverage of two firms and you note the following (all values in millions of dollars):

	Debt	Book Equity	Market Equity	EBIT	Interest Expense
Firm A	500	300	400	100	50
Firm B	80	35	40	8	7

   a. What is the market debt-to-equity ratio of each firm?
   b. What is the book debt-to-equity ratio of each firm?
   c. What is the EBIT/interest coverage ratio of each firm?
   d. Which firm may have more difficulty meeting its debt obligations? Explain.

37. See Table 2.5 showing financial statement data and stock price data for Mydeco Corp.

a. Compute Mydeco's PE ratio each year from 2012 to 2016. In which year was it the highest?

b. What was Mydeco's Enterprise Value to EBITDA ratio each year? In which year was it the highest?

c. What might explain the differing time pattern of the two valuation ratios?

38. In early-2015, United Airlines (UAL) had a market capitalization of $24.8 billion, debt of $12.8 billion, and cash of $5.5 billion. United also had annual revenues of $38.9 billion. Southwest Airlines (LUV) had a market capitalization of $28.8 billion, debt of $2.7 billion, cash of $2.9 billion, and annual revenues of $18.6 billion.

a. Compare the market capitalization-to-revenue ratio (also called the price-to-sales ratio) for United Airlines and Southwest Airlines.

b. Compare the enterprise value-to-revenue ratio for United Airlines and Southwest Airlines.

c. Which of these comparisons is more meaningful? Explain.

39. See Table 2.5 showing financial statement data and stock price data for Mydeco Corp.

a. Compute Mydeco's ROE each year from 2012 to 2016.

b. Compute Mydeco's ROA each year from 2012 to 2016.

c. Which return is more volatile? Why?

40. See Table 2.5 showing financial statement data and stock price data for Mydeco Corp. Was Mydeco able to improve its ROIC in 2016 relative to what it was in 2012?

41. For fiscal year 2015, Costco Wholesale Corporation (COST) had a net profit margin of 2.05%, asset turnover of 3.48, and a book equity multiplier of 3.15.

a. Use this data to compute Costco's ROE using the DuPont Identity.

b. If Costco's managers wanted to increase its ROE by one percentage point, how much higher would their asset turnover need to be?

c. If Costco's net profit margin fell by one percentage point, by how much would their asset turnover need to increase to maintain their ROE?

42. For fiscal year 2015, Wal-Mart Stores, Inc. (WMT) had total revenues of $485.65 billion, net income of $16.36 billion, total assets of $203.49 billion, and total shareholder's equity of $81.39 billion.

a. Calculate Walmart's ROE directly, and using the DuPont Identity.

b. Comparing with the data for Costco in Problem 41, use the DuPont Identity to understand the difference between the two firms' ROEs.

43. Consider a retailing firm with a net profit margin of 3.5%, a total asset turnover of 1.8, total assets of $44 million, and a book value of equity of $18 million.

a. What is the firm's current ROE?

b. If the firm increased its net profit margin to 4%, what would be its ROE?

c. If, in addition, the firm increased its revenues by 20% (while maintaining this higher profit margin and without changing its assets or liabilities), what would be its ROE?

Financial Reporting in Practice

44. Find online the annual 10-K report for Costco Wholesale Corporation (COST) for fiscal year 2015 (filed in October 2015).

a. Which auditing firm certified these financial statements?

b. Which officers of Costco certified the financial statements?

45. WorldCom reclassified $3.85 billion of operating expenses as capital expenditures. Explain the effect this reclassification would have on WorldCom's cash flows. (*Hint*: Consider taxes.) WorldCom's actions were illegal and clearly designed to deceive investors. But if a firm could legitimately choose how to classify an expense for tax purposes, which choice is truly better for the firm's investors?

Data Case

This is your second interview with a prestigious brokerage firm for a job as an equity analyst. You survived the morning interviews with the department manager and the Vice President of Equity. Everything has gone so well that they want to test your ability as an analyst. You are seated in a room with a computer and a list with the names of two companies—Ford (F) and Microsoft (MSFT). You have 90 minutes to complete the following tasks:

1. Download the annual income statements, balance sheets, and cash flow statements for the last four fiscal years from MarketWatch (www.morningstar.com). Enter each company's stock symbol and then go to "financials." Export the statements to Excel by clicking the export button.
2. Find historical stock prices for each firm from Yahoo! Finance (finance.yahoo.com). Enter your stock symbol, click "Historical Prices" in the left column, and enter the proper date range to cover the last day of the month corresponding to the date of each financial statement. Use the closing stock prices (not the adjusted close). To calculate the firm's market capitalization at each date, multiply the number of shares outstanding (see "Basic" on the income statement under "Weighted Average Shares Outstanding") by the firm's historic stock price.
3. For each of the four years of statements, compute the following ratios for each firm:

   Valuation Ratios
   Price-Earnings Ratio (for EPS use Diluted EPS Total)
   Market-to-Book Ratio
   Enterprise Value-to-EBITDA
   (For debt, include long-term and short-term debt; for cash, include marketable securities.)

   Profitability Ratios
   Operating Margin
   Net Profit Margin
   Return on Equity

   Financial Strength Ratios
   Current Ratio
   Book Debt-Equity Ratio
   Market Debt-Equity Ratio
   Interest Coverage Ratio (EBIT ÷ Interest Expense)
4. Obtain industry averages for each firm from Reuters.com (www.reuters.com/finance/stocks). Enter the stock symbol in the field under "Search Stocks," select the company from the list, and then click the "Financials" button.
   a. Compare each firm's ratios to the available industry ratios for the most recent year. (Ignore the "Company" column as your calculations will be different.)
   b. Analyze the performance of each firm versus the industry and comment on any trends in each individual firm's performance. Identify any strengths or weaknesses you find in each firm.
5. Examine the Market-to-Book ratios you calculated for each firm. Which, if any, of the two firms can be considered "growth firms" and which, if any, can be considered "value firms"?
6. Compare the valuation ratios across the two firms. How do you interpret the difference between them?
7. Consider the enterprise value of each firm for each of the four years. How have the values of each firm changed over the time period?

Note: Updates to this data case may be found at www.berkdemarzo.com.

CHAPTER

3

Financial Decision Making and the Law of One Price

NOTATION

NPV net present value

r_f risk-free interest rate

PV present value

IN MID-2007, MICROSOFT DECIDED TO ENTER A BIDDING WAR with competitors Google and Yahoo! for a stake in the fast-growing social networking site, Facebook. How did Microsoft's managers decide that this was a good decision?

Every decision has future consequences that will affect the value of the firm. These consequences will generally include both benefits and costs. For example, after raising its offer, Microsoft ultimately succeeded in buying a 1.6% stake in Facebook, along with the right to place banner ads on the Facebook Web site, for $240 million. In addition to the upfront cost of $240 million, Microsoft also incurred ongoing costs associated with software development for the platform, network infrastructure, and international marketing efforts to attract advertisers. The benefits of the deal to Microsoft included the revenues associated with the advertising sales, together with the appreciation of its 1.6% stake in Facebook. In the end, Microsoft's decision appeared to be a good one—in addition to advertising benefits, by the time of Facebook's IPO in May 2012, the value of Microsoft's 1.6% stake had grown to over $1 billion.

More generally, a decision is good for the firm's investors if it increases the firm's value by providing benefits whose value exceeds the costs. But comparing costs and benefits is often complicated because they occur at different points in time, may be in different currencies, or may have different risks associated with them. To make a valid comparison, we must use the tools of finance to express all costs and benefits in common terms. In this chapter, we introduce a central principle of finance, which we name the *Valuation Principle*, which states that we can use current market prices to determine the value today of the costs and benefits associated with a decision. This principle allows us to apply the concept of *net present value (NPV)* as a way to compare the costs and benefits of a project in terms of a common unit—namely, dollars today. We will then be able to evaluate a decision by answering this question: *Does the cash value today of its benefits exceed the cash value today of its costs?* In addition, we will see that the NPV indicates the net amount by which the decision will increase wealth.

We then turn to financial markets and apply these same tools to determine the prices of securities that trade in the market. We discuss strategies called *arbitrage*, which allow us to exploit situations in which the prices of publicly available investment opportunities do not conform to these values. Because investors trade rapidly to take advantage of arbitrage opportunities, we argue that equivalent investment opportunities trading simultaneously in competitive markets must have the same price. This *Law of One Price* is the unifying theme of valuation that we use throughout this text.

3.1 Valuing Decisions

A financial manager's job is to make decisions on behalf of the firm's investors. For example, when faced with an increase in demand for the firm's products, a manager may need to decide whether to raise prices or increase production. If the decision is to raise production and a new facility is required, is it better to rent or purchase the facility? If the facility will be purchased, should the firm pay cash or borrow the funds needed to pay for it?

In this book, our objective is to explain how to make decisions that increase the value of the firm to its investors. In principle, the idea is simple and intuitive: For good decisions, the benefits exceed the costs. Of course, real-world opportunities are usually complex and so the costs and benefits are often difficult to quantify. The analysis will often involve skills from other management disciplines, as in these examples:

Marketing: to forecast the increase in revenues resulting from an advertising campaign

Accounting: to estimate the tax savings from a restructuring

Economics: to determine the increase in demand from lowering the price of a product

Organizational Behavior: to estimate the productivity gains from a change in management structure

Strategy: to predict a competitor's response to a price increase

Operations: to estimate the cost savings from a plant modernization

Once the analysis of these other disciplines has been completed to quantify the costs and benefits associated with a decision, the financial manager must compare the costs and benefits and determine the best decision to make for the value of the firm.

Analyzing Costs and Benefits

The first step in decision making is to identify the costs and benefits of a decision. The next step is to quantify these costs and benefits. In order to compare the costs and benefits, we need to evaluate them in the same terms—cash today. Let's make this concrete with a simple example.

Suppose a jewelry manufacturer has the opportunity to trade 400 ounces of silver for 10 ounces of gold today. Because an ounce of gold differs in value from an ounce of silver, it is incorrect to compare 400 ounces to 10 ounces and conclude that the larger quantity is better. Instead, to compare the costs and benefits, we first need to quantify their values in equivalent terms.

Consider the silver. What is its cash value today? Suppose silver can be bought and sold for a current market price of \$15 per ounce. Then the 400 ounces of silver we give up has a cash value of[1]

$$(400 \text{ ounces of silver today}) \times (\$15/\text{ounce of silver today}) = \$6000 \text{ today}$$

If the current market price for gold is \$900 per ounce, then the 10 ounces of gold we receive has a cash value of

$$(10 \text{ ounces of gold today}) \times (\$900/\text{ounce of gold today}) = \$9000 \text{ today}$$

Now that we have quantified the costs and benefits in terms of a common measure of value, cash today, we can compare them. The jeweler's opportunity has a benefit of \$9000 today and a cost of \$6000 today, so the net value of the decision is \$9000 − \$6000 = \$3000 today. By accepting the trade, the jewelry firm will be richer by \$3000.

Using Market Prices to Determine Cash Values

In evaluating the jeweler's decision, we used the current market price to convert from ounces of silver or gold to dollars. We did not concern ourselves with whether the jeweler thought that the price was fair or whether the jeweler would use the silver or gold. Do such considerations matter? Suppose, for example, that the jeweler does not need the gold, or thinks the current price of gold is too high. Would he value the gold at less than \$9000? The answer is no—he can always sell the gold at the current market price and receive \$9000 right now. Similarly, he would not value the gold at more than \$9000, because even if he really needs the gold or thinks the current price of gold is too low, he can always buy 10 ounces of gold for \$9000. Thus, independent of his own views or preferences, the value of the gold to the jeweler is \$9000.

This example illustrates an important general principle: Whenever a good trades in a **competitive market**—by which we mean a market in which it can be bought *and* sold at the same price—that price determines the cash value of the good. As long as a competitive market exists, the value of the good will not depend on the views or preferences of the decision maker.

EXAMPLE 3.1 Competitive Market Prices Determine Value

Problem

You have just won a radio contest and are disappointed to find out that the prize is four tickets to the Def Leppard reunion tour (face value \$40 each). Not being a fan of 1980s power rock, you have no intention of going to the show. However, there is a second choice: two tickets to your favorite band's sold-out show (face value \$45 each). You notice that on eBay, tickets to the Def Leppard show are being bought and sold for \$30 apiece and tickets to your favorite band's show are being bought and sold at \$50 each. Which prize should you choose?

---

[1] You might worry about commissions or other transactions costs that are incurred when buying or selling gold, in addition to the market price. For now, we will ignore transactions costs, and discuss their effect in the appendix to this chapter.

Solution

Competitive market prices, not your personal preferences (nor the face value of the tickets), are relevant here:

Four Def Leppard tickets at \$30 apiece = \$120 market value

Two of your favorite band's tickets at \$50 apiece = \$100 market value

Instead of taking the tickets to your favorite band, you should accept the Def Leppard tickets, sell them on eBay, and use the proceeds to buy two tickets to your favorite band's show. You'll even have \$20 left over to buy a T-shirt.

Thus, by evaluating cost and benefits using competitive market prices, we can determine whether a decision will make the firm and its investors wealthier. This point is one of the central and most powerful ideas in finance, which we call the **Valuation Principle**:

The value of an asset to the firm or its investors is determined by its competitive market price. The benefits and costs of a decision should be evaluated using these market prices, and when the value of the benefits exceeds the value of the costs, the decision will increase the market value of the firm.

The Valuation Principle provides the basis for decision making throughout this text. In the remainder of this chapter, we first apply it to decisions whose costs and benefits occur at different points in time and develop the main tool of project evaluation, the *Net Present Value Rule*. We then consider its consequences for the prices of assets in the market and develop the concept of the *Law of One Price*.

EXAMPLE 3.2 Applying the Valuation Principle

Problem

You are the operations manager at your firm. Due to a pre-existing contract, you have the opportunity to acquire 200 barrels of oil and 3000 pounds of copper for a total of \$12,000. The current competitive market price of oil is \$50 per barrel and for copper is \$2 per pound. You are not sure you need all of the oil and copper, and are concerned that the value of both commodities may fall in the future. Should you take this opportunity?

Solution

To answer this question, you need to convert the costs and benefits to their cash values using market prices:

$$(200 \text{ barrels of oil}) \times (\$50/\text{barrel of oil today}) = \$10{,}000 \text{ today}$$

$$(3000 \text{ pounds of copper}) \times (\$2/\text{pound of copper today}) = \$6000 \text{ today}$$

The net value of the opportunity is \$10,000 + \$6000 − \$12,000 = \$4000 today. Because the net value is positive, you should take it. This value depends only on the *current* market prices for oil and copper. Even if you do not need all the oil or copper, or expect their values to fall, you can sell them at current market prices and obtain their value of \$16,000. Thus, the opportunity is a good one for the firm, and will increase its value by \$4000.

When Competitive Market Prices Are Not Available

Competitive market prices allow us to calculate the value of a decision without worrying about the tastes or opinions of the decision maker. When competitive prices are not available, we can no longer do this. Prices at retail stores, for example, are one sided: You can buy at the posted price, but you cannot sell the good to the store at that same price. We cannot use these one-sided prices to determine an exact cash value. They determine the maximum value of the good (since it can always be purchased at that price), but an individual may value it for much less depending on his or her preferences for the good.

Let's consider an example. It has long been common for banks to entice new depositors by offering free gifts for opening a new account. In 2014, RBC offered a free iPad mini for individuals opening a new account. At the time, the retail price of that model iPad was $399. But because there is no competitive market to trade iPads, the value of the iPad depends on whether you were going to buy one or not.

If you planned to buy the iPad anyway, then the value to you is $399, the price you would otherwise pay for it. But if you did not want or need the iPad, the value of the offer would depend on the price you could get for the iPad. For example, if you could sell the iPad for $300 to your friend, then RBC's offer is worth $300 to you. Thus, depending on your preferences, RBC's offer is worth somewhere between $300 (you don't want an iPad) and $399 (you definitely want one).

CONCEPT CHECK

1. In order to compare the costs and benefits of a decision, what must we determine?
2. If crude oil trades in a competitive market, would an oil refiner that has a use for the oil value it differently than another investor?

3.2 Interest Rates and the Time Value of Money

For most financial decisions, unlike in the examples presented so far, costs and benefits occur at different points in time. For example, typical investment projects incur costs upfront and provide benefits in the future. In this section, we show how to account for this time difference when evaluating a project.

The Time Value of Money

Consider an investment opportunity with the following certain cash flows:

Cost: $100,000 today

Benefit: $105,000 in one year

Because both are expressed in dollar terms, it might appear that the cost and benefit are directly comparable so that the project's net value is $105,000 − $100,000 = $5000. But this calculation ignores the timing of the costs and benefits, and it treats money today as equivalent to money in one year.

In general, a dollar today is worth more than a dollar in one year. If you have $1 today, you can invest it. For example, if you deposit it in a bank account paying 7% interest, you will have $1.07 at the end of one year. We call the difference in value between money today and money in the future the **time value of money**.

The Interest Rate: An Exchange Rate Across Time

By depositing money into a savings account, we can convert money today into money in the future with no risk. Similarly, by borrowing money from the bank, we can exchange money in the future for money today. The rate at which we can exchange money today for money in the future is determined by the current interest rate. In the same way that an exchange rate allows us to convert money from one currency to another, the interest rate allows us to convert money from one point in time to another. In essence, an interest rate is like an exchange rate across time. It tells us the market price today of money in the future.

Suppose the current annual interest rate is 7%. By investing or borrowing at this rate, we can exchange $1.07 in one year for each $1 today. More generally, we define the **risk-free interest rate**, r_f, for a given period as the interest rate at which money can be borrowed or lent without risk over that period. We can exchange $(1 + r_f)$ dollars in the future per dollar today, and vice versa, without risk. We refer to $(1 + r_f)$ as the **interest rate factor** for risk-free cash flows; it defines the exchange rate across time, and has units of "$ in one year/$ today."

As with other market prices, the risk-free interest rate depends on supply and demand. In particular, at the risk-free interest rate the supply of savings equals the demand for borrowing. After we know the risk-free interest rate, we can use it to evaluate other decisions in which costs and benefits are separated in time without knowing the investor's preferences.

Value of Investment in One Year. Let's reevaluate the investment we considered earlier, this time taking into account the time value of money. If the interest rate is 7%, then we can express our costs as

$$\begin{aligned} \text{Cost} &= (\$100{,}000 \text{ today}) \times (1.07 \text{ \$ in one year/\$ today}) \\ &= \$107{,}000 \text{ in one year} \end{aligned}$$

Think of this amount as the opportunity cost of spending $100,000 today: We give up the $107,000 we would have had in one year if we had left the money in the bank. Alternatively, if we were to borrow the $100,000, we would owe $107,000 in one year.

Both costs and benefits are now in terms of "dollars in one year," so we can compare them and compute the investment's net value:

$$\$105{,}000 - \$107{,}000 = -\$2000 \text{ in one year}$$

In other words, we could earn $2000 more in one year by putting our $100,000 in the bank rather than making this investment. We should reject the investment: If we took it, we would be $2000 poorer in one year than if we didn't.

Value of Investment Today. The previous calculation expressed the value of the costs and benefits in terms of dollars in one year. Alternatively, we can use the interest rate factor to convert to dollars today. Consider the benefit of $105,000 in one year. What is the equivalent amount in terms of dollars today? That is, how much would we need to have in the bank today so that we would end up with $105,000 in the bank in one year? We find this amount by dividing by the interest rate factor:

$$\begin{aligned} \text{Benefit} &= (\$105{,}000 \text{ in one year}) \div (1.07 \text{ \$ in one year/\$ today}) \\ &= \$105{,}000 \times \frac{1}{1.07} \text{ today} \\ &= \$98{,}130.84 \text{ today} \end{aligned}$$

This is also the amount the bank would lend to us today if we promised to repay $105,000 in one year.[2] Thus, it is the competitive market price at which we can "buy" or "sell" $105,000 in one year.

[2]We are assuming the bank will both borrow and lend at the risk-free interest rate. We discuss the case when these rates differ in "Arbitrage with Transactions Costs" in the appendix to this chapter.

Now we are ready to compute the net value of the investment:

$$\$98{,}130.84 - \$100{,}000 = -\$1869.16 \text{ today}$$

Once again, the negative result indicates that we should reject the investment. Taking the investment would make us $1869.16 poorer today because we have given up $100,000 for something worth only $98,130.84.

Present Versus Future Value. This calculation demonstrates that our decision is the same whether we express the value of the investment in terms of dollars in one year or dollars today: We should reject the investment. Indeed, if we convert from dollars today to dollars in one year,

$$(-\$1869.16 \text{ today}) \times (1.07 \text{ \$ in one year/\$ today}) = -\$2000 \text{ in one year}$$

we see that the two results are equivalent, but expressed as values at different points in time. When we express the value in terms of dollars today, we call it the **present value (PV)** of the investment. If we express it in terms of dollars in the future, we call it the **future value (FV)** of the investment.

Discount Factors and Rates. When computing a present value as in the preceding calculation, we can interpret the term

$$\frac{1}{1+r} = \frac{1}{1.07} = 0.93458 \text{ \$ today/\$ in one year}$$

as the *price* today of $1 in one year. Note that the value is less than $1—money in the future is worth less today, and so its price reflects a discount. Because it provides the discount at which we can purchase money in the future, the amount $\frac{1}{1+r}$ is called the one-year **discount factor**. The risk-free interest rate is also referred to as the **discount rate** for a risk-free investment.

EXAMPLE 3.3 Comparing Costs at Different Points in Time

Problem

The cost of rebuilding the San Francisco Bay Bridge to make it earthquake-safe was approximately $3 billion in 2004. At the time, engineers estimated that if the project were delayed to 2005, the cost would rise by 10%. If the interest rate were 2%, what would be the cost of a delay in terms of dollars in 2004?

Solution

If the project were delayed, it would cost $3 billion × 1.10 = $3.3 billion in 2005. To compare this amount to the cost of $3 billion in 2004, we must convert it using the interest rate of 2%:

$$\$3.3 \text{ billion in 2005} \div (\$1.02 \text{ in 2005/\$ in 2004}) = \$3.235 \text{ billion in 2004}$$

Therefore, the cost of a delay of one year was

$$\$3.235 \text{ billion} - \$3 \text{ billion} = \$235 \text{ million in 2004}$$

That is, delaying the project for one year was equivalent to giving up $235 million in cash.

FIGURE 3.1

Converting between Dollars Today and Gold, Euros, or Dollars in the Future

We can convert dollars today to different goods, currencies, or points in time by using the competitive market price, exchange rate, or interest rate.

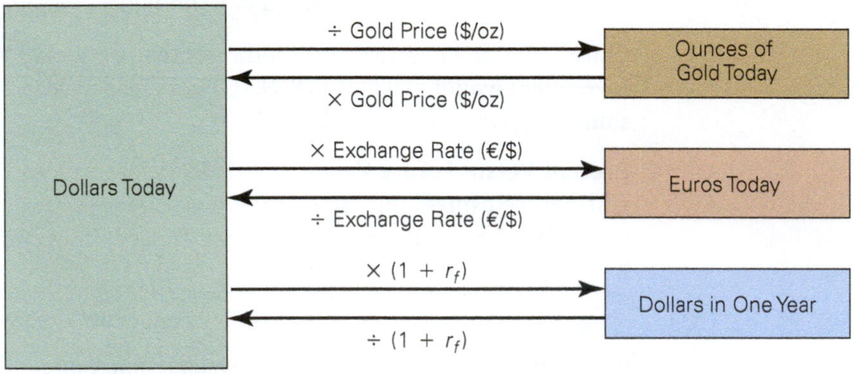

We can use the risk-free interest rate to determine values in the same way we used competitive market prices. Figure 3.1 illustrates how we use competitive market prices, exchange rates, and interest rates to convert between dollars today and other goods, currencies, or dollars in the future.

CONCEPT CHECK

1. How do you compare costs at different points in time?
2. If interest rates rise, what happens to the value today of a promise of money in one year?

3.3 Present Value and the NPV Decision Rule

In Section 3.2, we converted between cash today and cash in the future using the risk-free interest rate. As long as we convert costs and benefits to the same point in time, we can compare them to make a decision. In practice, however, most corporations prefer to measure values in terms of their present value—that is, in terms of cash today. In this section we apply the Valuation Principle to derive the concept of the *net present value*, or *NPV*, and define the "golden rule" of financial decision making, the *NPV Rule.*

Net Present Value

When we compute the value of a cost or benefit in terms of cash today, we refer to it as the present value (PV). Similarly, we define the **net present value (NPV)** of a project or investment as the difference between the present value of its benefits and the present value of its costs:

Net Present Value

$$NPV = PV(\text{Benefits}) - PV(\text{Costs}) \tag{3.1}$$

If we use positive cash flows to represent benefits and negative cash flows to represent costs, and calculate the present value of multiple cash flows as the sum of present values for individual cash flows, we can also write this definition as

$$NPV = PV(\text{All project cash flows}) \tag{3.2}$$

That is, the NPV is the total of the present values of all project cash flows.

Let's consider a simple example. Suppose your firm is offered the following investment opportunity: In exchange for \$500 today, you will receive \$550 in one year with certainty. If the risk-free interest rate is 8% per year then

$$\begin{aligned} PV(\text{Benefit}) &= (\$550 \text{ in one year}) \div (1.08 \text{ \$ in one year/\$ today}) \\ &= \$509.26 \text{ today} \end{aligned}$$

This PV is the amount we would need to put in the bank today to generate \$550 in one year (\$509.26 × 1.08 = \$550). In other words, *the present value is the cash cost today of "doing it yourself"—it is the amount you need to invest at the current interest rate to recreate the cash flow.*

Once the costs and benefits are in present value terms, we can compute the investment's NPV:

$$NPV = \$509.26 - \$500 = \$9.26 \text{ today}$$

But what if your firm doesn't have the \$500 needed to cover the initial cost of the project? Does the project still have the same value? Because we computed the value using competitive market prices, it should not depend on your tastes or the amount of cash your firm has in the bank. If your firm doesn't have the \$500, it could borrow \$509.26 from the bank at the 8% interest rate and then take the project. What are your cash flows in this case?

Today: \$509.26 (loan) − \$500 (invested in the project) = \$9.26
In one year: \$550 (from project) − \$509.26 × 1.08 (loan balance) = \$0

This transaction leaves you with exactly \$9.26 extra cash today and no future net obligations. So taking the project is like having an extra \$9.26 in cash up front. Thus, the NPV expresses the value of an investment decision as an amount of cash received today. *As long as the NPV is positive, the decision increases the value of the firm and is a good decision regardless of your current cash needs or preferences regarding when to spend the money.*

The NPV Decision Rule

Because NPV is expressed in terms of cash today, it simplifies decision making. As long as we have correctly captured all of the costs and benefits of the project, decisions with a positive NPV will increase the wealth of the firm and its investors. We capture this logic in the **NPV Decision Rule**:

> *When making an investment decision, take the alternative with the highest NPV. Choosing this alternative is equivalent to receiving its NPV in cash today.*

Accepting or Rejecting a Project. A common financial decision is whether to accept or reject a project. Because rejecting the project generally has NPV = 0 (there are no new costs or benefits from not doing the project), the NPV decision rule implies that we should

- Accept those projects with positive NPV because accepting them is equivalent to receiving their NPV in cash today, and
- Reject those projects with negative NPV; accepting them would reduce the wealth of investors, whereas not doing them has no cost (NPV = 0).

If the NPV is exactly zero, you will neither gain nor lose by accepting the project rather than rejecting it. It is not a bad project because it does not reduce firm value, but it does not increase value either.

EXAMPLE 3.4 The NPV Is Equivalent to Cash Today

Problem

Your firm needs to buy a new $9500 copier. As part of a promotion, the manufacturer has offered to let you pay $10,000 in one year, rather than pay cash today. Suppose the risk-free interest rate is 7% per year. Is this offer a good deal? Show that its NPV represents cash in your pocket.

Solution

If you take the offer, the benefit is that you won't have to pay $9500 today, which is already in PV terms. The cost, however, is $10,000 in one year. We therefore convert the cost to a present value at the risk-free interest rate:

$$PV(\text{Cost}) = (\$10{,}000 \text{ in one year}) \div (1.07 \text{ \$ in one year/\$ today}) = \$9345.79 \text{ today}$$

The NPV of the promotional offer is the difference between the benefits and the costs:

$$NPV = \$9500 - \$9345.79 = \$154.21 \text{ today}$$

The NPV is positive, so the investment is a good deal. It is equivalent to getting a cash discount today of $154.21, and only paying $9345.79 today for the copier. To confirm our calculation, suppose you take the offer and invest $9345.79 in a bank paying 7% interest. With interest, this amount will grow to $\$9345.79 \times 1.07 = \$10{,}000$ in one year, which you can use to pay for the copier.

Choosing among Alternatives. We can also use the NPV decision rule to choose among projects. To do so, we must compute the NPV of each alternative, and then select the one with the highest NPV. This alternative is the one that will lead to the largest increase in the value of the firm.

EXAMPLE 3.5 Choosing among Alternative Plans

Problem

Suppose you started a Web site hosting business and then decided to return to school. Now that you are back in school, you are considering selling the business within the next year. An investor has offered to buy the business for $200,000 whenever you are ready. If the interest rate is 10%, which of the following three alternatives is the best choice?

1. Sell the business now.
2. Scale back the business and continue running it while you are in school for one more year, and then sell the business (requiring you to spend $30,000 on expenses now, but generating $50,000 in profit at the end of the year).
3. Hire someone to manage the business while you are in school for one more year, and then sell the business (requiring you to spend $50,000 on expenses now, but generating $100,000 in profit at the end of the year).

Solution

The cash flows and NPVs for each alternative are calculated in Table 3.1. Faced with these three alternatives, the best choice is the one with highest NPV: Hire a manager and sell in one year. Choosing this alternative is equivalent to receiving $222,727 today.

TABLE 3.1 **Cash Flows and NPVs for Web Site Business Alternatives**

	Today	In One Year	NPV
Sell Now	\$200,000	0	\$200,000
Scale Back Operations	−\$30,000	\$50,000 \$200,000	$-\$30{,}000 + \frac{\$250{,}000}{1.10} = \$197{,}273$
Hire a Manager	−\$50,000	\$100,000 \$200,000	$-\$50{,}000 + \frac{\$300{,}000}{1.10} = \$222{,}727$

NPV and Cash Needs

When we compare projects with different patterns of present and future cash flows, we may have preferences regarding when to receive the cash. Some may need cash today; others may prefer to save for the future. In the Web site hosting business example, hiring a manager and selling in one year has the highest NPV. However, this option requires an initial outlay of \$50,000, as opposed to selling the business and receiving \$200,000 immediately. Suppose you also need \$60,000 in cash now to pay for school and other expenses. Would selling the business be a better choice in that case?

As was true for the jeweler considering trading silver for gold in Section 3.1, the answer is again no. As long as you can borrow and lend at the 10% interest rate, hiring a manager is the best choice whatever your preferences regarding the timing of the cash flows. To see why, suppose you borrow \$110,000 at the rate of 10% and hire the manager. Then you will owe $\$110{,}000 \times 1.10 = \$121{,}000$ in one year, for total cash flows shown in Table 3.2. Compare these cash flows with those from selling now, and investing the excess \$140,000 (which, at the rate of 10%, will grow to $\$140{,}000 \times 1.10 = \$154{,}000$ in one year). Both strategies provide \$60,000 in cash today, but the combination of hiring a manager and borrowing generates an additional $\$179{,}000 - \$154{,}000 = \$25{,}000$ in one year.[3] Thus, even if you need \$60,000 now, hiring the manager and selling in one year is still the best option.

TABLE 3.2 **Cash Flows of Hiring and Borrowing Versus Selling and Investing**

	Today	In One Year
Hire a Manager	−\$50,000	\$300,000
Borrow	\$110,000	−\$121,000
Total Cash Flow	\$60,000	\$179,000
Versus		
Sell Now	\$200,000	\$0
Invest	−\$140,000	\$154,000
Total Cash Flow	\$60,000	\$154,000

[3]Note also that the present value of this additional cash flow, $\$25{,}000 \div 1.10 = \$22{,}727$, is exactly the difference in NPVs between the two alternatives.

This example illustrates the following general principle:

Regardless of our preferences for cash today versus cash in the future, we should always maximize NPV first. We can then borrow or lend to shift cash flows through time and find our most preferred pattern of cash flows.

CONCEPT CHECK

1. What is the NPV decision rule?
2. Why doesn't the NPV decision rule depend on the investor's preferences?

3.4 Arbitrage and the Law of One Price

So far, we have emphasized the importance of using competitive market prices to compute the NPV. But is there always only one such price? What if the same good trades for different prices in different markets? Consider gold. Gold trades in many different markets, with the largest markets in New York and London. To value an ounce of gold we could look up the competitive price in either of these markets. But suppose gold is trading for \$850 per ounce in New York and \$900 per ounce in London. Which price should we use?

Fortunately, such situations do not arise, and it is easy to see why. Recall that these are competitive market prices at which you can both buy *and* sell. Thus, you can make money in this situation simply by buying gold for \$850 per ounce in New York and then immediately selling it for \$900 per ounce in London.[4] You will make \$900 − \$850 = \$50 per ounce for each ounce you buy and sell. Trading 1 million ounces at these prices, you would make \$50 million with no risk or investment! This is a case where that old adage, "Buy low, sell high," can be followed perfectly.

Of course, you will not be the only one making these trades. Everyone who sees these prices will want to trade as many ounces as possible. Within seconds, the market in New York would be flooded with buy orders, and the market in London would be flooded with sell orders. Although a few ounces (traded by the lucky individuals who spotted this opportunity first) might be exchanged at these prices, the price of gold in New York would quickly rise in response to all the orders, and the price in London would rapidly fall.[5] Prices would continue to change until they were equalized somewhere in the middle, such as \$875 per ounce.

Arbitrage

The practice of buying and selling equivalent goods in different markets to take advantage of a price difference is known as **arbitrage**. More generally, we refer to any situation in which it is possible to make a profit without taking any risk or making any investment as an **arbitrage opportunity**. Because an arbitrage opportunity has a positive NPV, whenever an arbitrage opportunity appears in financial markets, investors will race to take advantage

[4]There is no need to transport the gold from New York to London because investors in these markets trade ownership rights to gold that is stored securely elsewhere. For now, we ignore any further transactions costs, but discuss their effect in the appendix to this chapter.

[5]As economists would say, supply would not equal demand in these markets. In New York, demand would be infinite because everyone would want to buy. For equilibrium to be restored so that supply equals demand, the price in New York would have to rise. Similarly, in London there would be infinite supply until the price there fell.

of it. Those investors who spot the opportunity first and who can trade quickly will have the ability to exploit it. Once they place their trades, prices will respond, causing the arbitrage opportunity to evaporate.

Arbitrage opportunities are like money lying in the street; once spotted, they will quickly disappear. Thus the normal state of affairs in markets should be that no arbitrage opportunities exist. We call a competitive market in which there are no arbitrage opportunities a **normal market**.[6]

Law of One Price

In a normal market, the price of gold at any point in time will be the same in London and New York. The same logic applies more generally whenever equivalent investment opportunities trade in two different competitive markets. If the prices in the two markets differ, investors will profit immediately by buying in the market where it is cheap and selling in the market where it is expensive. In doing so, they will equalize the prices. As a result, prices will not differ (at least not for long). This important property is the **Law of One Price**:

> *If equivalent investment opportunities trade simultaneously in different competitive markets, then they must trade for the same price in all markets.*

One useful consequence of the Law of One Price is that when evaluating costs and benefits to compute a net present value, we can use any competitive price to determine a cash value, without checking the price in all possible markets.

CONCEPT CHECK

1. If the Law of One Price were violated, how could investors profit?
2. When investors exploit an arbitrage opportunity, how do their actions affect prices?

3.5 No-Arbitrage and Security Prices

An investment opportunity that trades in a financial market is known as a **financial security** (or, more simply, a **security**). The notions of arbitrage and the Law of One Price have important implications for security prices. We begin exploring its implications for the prices of individual securities as well as market interest rates. We then broaden our perspective to value a package of securities. Along the way, we will develop some important insights about firm decision making and firm value that will underpin our study throughout this textbook.

Valuing a Security with the Law of One Price

The Law of One Price tells us that the prices of equivalent investment opportunities should be the same. We can use this idea to value a security if we can find another equivalent investment whose price is already known. Consider a simple security that promises a one-time payment to its owner of $1000 in one year's time. Suppose there is no risk that the

---

[6]The term *efficient market* is also sometimes used to describe a market that, along with other properties, is without arbitrage opportunities. We avoid that term here because it is stronger than we require, as it also restricts the information held by market participants. We discuss notions of market efficiency in Chapter 9.

payment will not be made. One example of this type of security is a **bond**, a security sold by governments and corporations to raise money from investors today in exchange for the promised future payment. If the risk-free interest rate is 5%, what can we conclude about the price of this bond in a normal market?

To answer this question, consider an alternative investment that would generate the same cash flow as this bond. Suppose we invest money at the bank at the risk-free interest rate. How much do we need to invest today to receive \$1000 in one year? As we saw in Section 3.3, the cost today of recreating a future cash flow on our own is its present value:

$$PV(\$1000 \text{ in one year}) = (\$1000 \text{ in one year}) \div (1.05 \text{ \$ in one year/\$ today})$$
$$= \$952.38 \text{ today}$$

If we invest \$952.38 today at the 5% risk-free interest rate, we will have \$1000 in one year's time with no risk.

We now have two ways to receive the same cash flow: (1) buy the bond or (2) invest \$952.38 at the 5% risk-free interest rate. Because these transactions produce equivalent cash flows, the Law of One Price implies that, in a normal market, they must have the same price (or cost). Therefore,

$$\text{Price (Bond)} = \$952.38$$

Identifying Arbitrage Opportunities with Securities. Recall that the Law of One Price is based on the possibility of arbitrage: If the bond had a different price, there would be an arbitrage opportunity. For example, suppose the bond traded for a price of \$940. How could we profit in this situation?

In this case, we can buy the bond for \$940 and at the same time borrow \$952.38 from the bank. Given the 5% interest rate, we will owe the bank $\$952.38 \times 1.05 = \$1000$ in one year. Our overall cash flows from this pair of transactions are as shown in Table 3.3. Using this strategy we can earn \$12.38 in cash today for each bond that we buy, without taking any risk or paying any of our own money in the future. Of course, as we—and others who see the opportunity—start buying the bond, its price will quickly rise until it reaches \$952.38 and the arbitrage opportunity disappears.

A similar arbitrage opportunity arises if the bond price is higher than \$952.38. For example, suppose the bond is trading for \$960. In that case, we should sell the bond and invest \$952.38 at the bank. As shown in Table 3.4, we then earn \$7.62 in cash today, yet keep our future cash flows unchanged by replacing the \$1000 we would have received from the bond with the \$1000 we will receive from the bank. Once again, as people begin selling the bond to exploit this opportunity, the price will fall until it reaches \$952.38 and the arbitrage opportunity disappears.

TABLE 3.3 Net Cash Flows from Buying the Bond and Borrowing

	Today (\$)	In One Year (\$)
Buy the bond	−940.00	+1000.00
Borrow from the bank	+952.38	−1000.00
Net cash flow	+12.38	0.00

TABLE 3.4 Net Cash Flows from Selling the Bond and Investing

	Today ($)	In One Year ($)
Sell the bond	+960.00	−1000.00
Invest at the bank	−952.38	+1000.00
Net cash flow	+7.62	0.00

When the bond is overpriced, the arbitrage strategy involves selling the bond and investing some of the proceeds. But if the strategy involves selling the bond, does this mean that only the current owners of the bond can exploit it? The answer is no; in financial markets it is possible to sell a security you do not own by doing a *short sale*. In a **short sale**, the person who intends to sell the security first borrows it from someone who already owns it. Later, that person must either return the security by buying it back or pay the owner the cash flows he or she would have received. For example, we could short sell the bond in the example effectively promising to repay the current owner $1000 in one year. By executing a short sale, it is possible to exploit the arbitrage opportunity when the bond is overpriced even if you do not own it.

EXAMPLE 3.6 Computing the No-Arbitrage Price

Problem

Consider a security that pays its owner $100 today and $100 in one year, without any risk. Suppose the risk-free interest rate is 10%. What is the no-arbitrage price of the security today (before the first $100 is paid)? If the security is trading for $195, what arbitrage opportunity is available?

Solution

We need to compute the present value of the security's cash flows. In this case there are two cash flows: $100 today, which is already in present value terms, and $100 in one year. The present value of the second cash flow is

$$\$100 \text{ in one year} \div (1.10 \text{ \$ in one year/\$ today}) = \$90.91 \text{ today}$$

Therefore, the total present value of the cash flows is $100 + $90.91 = $190.91 today, which is the no-arbitrage price of the security.

If the security is trading for $195, we can exploit its overpricing by selling it for $195. We can then use $100 of the sale proceeds to replace the $100 we would have received from the security today and invest $90.91 of the sale proceeds at 10% to replace the $100 we would have received in one year. The remaining $195 − $100 − $90.91 = $4.09 is an arbitrage profit.

Determining the No-Arbitrage Price. We have shown that at any price other than $952.38, an arbitrage opportunity exists for our bond. Thus, in a normal market, the price of this bond must be $952.38. We call this price the **no-arbitrage price** for the bond.

By applying the reasoning for pricing the simple bond, we can outline a general process for pricing other securities:

1. Identify the cash flows that will be paid by the security.
2. Determine the "do-it-yourself" cost of replicating those cash flows on our own; that is, the present value of the security's cash flows.

Unless the price of the security equals this present value, there is an arbitrage opportunity. Thus, the general formula is

No-Arbitrage Price of a Security

$$\text{Price(Security)} = PV(\text{All cash flows paid by the security}) \tag{3.3}$$

Determining the Interest Rate from Bond Prices. Given the risk-free interest rate, the no-arbitrage price of a risk-free bond is determined by Eq. 3.3. The reverse is also true: If we know the price of a risk-free bond, we can use Eq. 3.3 to determine what the risk-free interest rate must be if there are no arbitrage opportunities.

For example, suppose a risk-free bond that pays \$1000 in one year is currently trading with a competitive market price of \$929.80 today. From Eq. 3.3, we know that the bond's price equals the present value of the \$1000 cash flow it will pay:

$$\$929.80 \text{ today} = (\$1000 \text{ in one year}) \div (1 + r_f)$$

We can rearrange this equation to determine the risk-free interest rate:

$$1 + r_f = \frac{\$1000 \text{ in one year}}{\$929.80 \text{ today}} = 1.0755 \ \$ \text{ in one year/\$ today}$$

That is, if there are no arbitrage opportunities, the risk-free interest rate must be 7.55%.

Interest rates are calculated by this method in practice. Financial news services report current interest rates by deriving these rates based on the current prices of risk-free government bonds trading in the market.

Note that the risk-free interest rate equals the percentage gain that you earn from investing in the bond, which is called the bond's **return**:

$$\text{Return} = \frac{\text{Gain at End of Year}}{\text{Initial Cost}}$$

$$= \frac{1000 - 929.80}{929.80} = \frac{1000}{929.80} - 1 = 7.55\% \tag{3.4}$$

Thus, if there is no arbitrage, the risk-free interest rate is equal to the return from investing in a risk-free bond. If the bond offered a higher return than the risk-free interest rate, then investors would earn a profit by borrowing at the risk-free interest rate and investing in the bond. If the bond had a lower return than the risk-free interest rate, investors would sell the bond and invest the proceeds at the risk-free interest rate. No arbitrage is therefore equivalent to the idea that *all risk-free investments should offer investors the same return.*

An Old Joke

There is an old joke that many finance professors enjoy telling their students. It goes like this:

A finance professor and a student are walking down a street. The student notices a $100 bill lying on the pavement and leans down to pick it up. The finance professor immediately intervenes and says, "Don't bother; there is no free lunch. If that were a real $100 bill lying there, somebody would already have picked it up!"

This joke invariably generates much laughter because it makes fun of the principle of no arbitrage in competitive markets. But once the laughter dies down, the professor then asks whether anyone has ever *actually* found a real $100 bill lying on the pavement. The ensuing silence is the real lesson behind the joke.

This joke sums up the point of focusing on markets in which no arbitrage opportunities exist. Free $100 bills lying on the pavement, like arbitrage opportunities, are extremely rare for two reasons: (1) Because $100 is a large amount of money, people are especially careful not to lose it, and (2) in the rare event when someone does inadvertently drop $100, the likelihood of your finding it before someone else does is extremely small.

The NPV of Trading Securities and Firm Decision Making

We have established that positive-NPV decisions increase the wealth of the firm and its investors. Think of buying a security as an investment decision. The cost of the decision is the price we pay for the security, and the benefit is the cash flows that we will receive from owning the security. When securities trade at no-arbitrage prices, what can we conclude about the value of trading them? From Eq. 3.3, the cost and benefit are equal in a normal market and so the NPV of buying a security is zero:

$$NPV\text{(Buy security)} = PV\text{(All cash flows paid by the security)} - \text{Price (Security)}$$
$$= 0$$

Similarly, if we sell a security, the price we receive is the benefit and the cost is the cash flows we give up. Again the NPV is zero:

$$NPV\text{(Sell security)} = \text{Price (Security)} - PV\text{(All cash flows paid by the security)}$$
$$= 0$$

Thus, the NPV of trading a security in a normal market is zero. This result is not surprising. If the NPV of buying a security were positive, then buying the security would be equivalent to receiving cash today—that is, it would present an arbitrage opportunity. Because arbitrage opportunities do not exist in normal markets, the NPV of all security trades must be zero.

Another way to understand this result is to remember that every trade has both a buyer and a seller. In a competitive market, if a trade offers a positive NPV to one party, it must give a negative NPV to the other party. But then one of the two parties would not agree to the trade. Because all trades are voluntary, they must occur at prices at which neither party is losing value, and therefore for which the trade is zero NPV.

The insight that security trading in a normal market is a zero-NPV transaction is a critical building block in our study of corporate finance. Trading securities in a normal market neither creates nor destroys value: Instead, value is created by the real investment projects in which the firm engages, such as developing new products, opening new stores, or creating more efficient production methods. Financial transactions are not sources of value but instead serve to adjust the timing and risk of the cash flows to best suit the needs of the firm or its investors.

An important consequence of this result is the idea that we can evaluate a decision by focusing on its real components, rather than its financial ones. That is, we can separate the firm's investment decision from its financing choice. We refer to this concept as the **Separation Principle**:

Security transactions in a normal market neither create nor destroy value on their own. Therefore, we can evaluate the NPV of an investment decision separately from the decision the firm makes regarding how to finance the investment or any other security transactions the firm is considering.

EXAMPLE 3.7 **Separating Investment and Financing**

Problem

Your firm is considering a project that will require an upfront investment of $10 million today and will produce $12 million in cash flow for the firm in one year without risk. Rather than pay for the $10 million investment entirely using its own cash, the firm is considering raising additional funds by issuing a security that will pay investors $5.5 million in one year. Suppose the risk-free interest rate is 10%. Is pursuing this project a good decision without issuing the new security? Is it a good decision with the new security?

Solution

Without the new security, the cost of the project is $10 million today and the benefit is $12 million in one year. Converting the benefit to a present value

$$\$12 \text{ million in one year} \div (1.10 \text{ \$ in one year/\$ today}) = \$10.91 \text{ million today}$$

we see that the project has an NPV of $10.91 million − $10 million = $0.91 million today.

Now suppose the firm issues the new security. In a normal market, the price of this security will be the present value of its future cash flow:

$$\text{Price(Security)} = \$5.5 \text{ million} \div 1.10 = \$5 \text{ million today}$$

Thus, after it raises $5 million by issuing the new security, the firm will only need to invest an additional $5 million to take the project.

To compute the project's NPV in this case, note that in one year the firm will receive the $12 million payout of the project, but owe $5.5 million to the investors in the new security, leaving $6.5 million for the firm. This amount has a present value of

$$\$6.5 \text{ million in one year} \div (1.10 \text{ \$ in one year/\$ today}) = \$5.91 \text{ million today}$$

Thus, the project has an NPV of $5.91 million − $5 million = $0.91 million today, as before.

In either case, we get the same result for the NPV. The separation principle indicates that we will get the same result for any choice of financing for the firm that occurs in a normal market. We can therefore evaluate the project without explicitly considering the different financing possibilities the firm might choose.

Valuing a Portfolio

So far, we have discussed the no-arbitrage price for individual securities. The Law of One Price also has implications for packages of securities. Consider two securities, A and B. Suppose a third security, C, has the same cash flows as A and B combined. In this case, security C is equivalent to a combination of the securities A and B. We use the term **portfolio** to describe a collection of securities. What can we conclude about the price of security C as compared to the prices of A and B?

Value Additivity. Because security C is equivalent to the portfolio of A and B, by the Law of One Price, they must have the same price. This idea leads to the relationship known as **value additivity**; that is, the price of C must equal the price of the portfolio, which is the combined price of A and B:

Value Additivity

$$\text{Price}(C) = \text{Price}(A + B) = \text{Price}(A) + \text{Price}(B) \tag{3.5}$$

Because security C has cash flows equal to the sum of A and B, its value or price must be the sum of the values of A and B. Otherwise, an obvious arbitrage opportunity would exist. For example, if the total price of A and B were lower than the price of C, then we could make a profit buying A and B and selling C. This arbitrage activity would quickly push prices until the price of security C equals the total price of A and B.

EXAMPLE 3.8 Valuing an Asset in a Portfolio

Problem

Holbrook Holdings is a publicly traded company with only two assets: It owns 60% of Harry's Hotcakes restaurant chain and an ice hockey team. Suppose the market value of Holbrook Holdings is \$160 million, and the market value of the entire Harry's Hotcakes chain (which is also publicly traded) is \$120 million. What is the market value of the hockey team?

Solution

We can think of Holbrook as a portfolio consisting of a 60% stake in Harry's Hotcakes and the hockey team. By value additivity, the sum of the value of the stake in Harry's Hotcakes and the hockey team must equal the \$160 million market value of Holbrook. Because the 60% stake in Harry's Hotcakes is worth 60% × \$120 million = \$72 million, the hockey team has a value of \$160 million − \$72 million = \$88 million.

GLOBAL FINANCIAL CRISIS Liquidity and the Informational Role of Prices

In the first half of 2008, as the extent and severity of the decline in the housing market became apparent, investors became increasingly worried about the value of securities that were backed by residential home mortgages. As a result, the volume of trade in the multi-trillion dollar market for mortgage-backed securities plummeted over 80% by August 2008. Over the next two months, trading in many of these securities ceased altogether, making the markets for these securities increasingly illiquid.

Competitive markets depend upon liquidity—there must be sufficient buyers and sellers of a security so that it is possible to trade at any time at the current market price. When markets become illiquid it may not be possible to trade at the posted price. As a consequence, we can no longer rely on market prices as a measure of value.

The collapse of the mortgage-backed securities market created two problems. First was the loss of trading opportunities, making it difficult for holders of these securities to sell them. But a potentially more significant problem was the loss of *information*. Without a liquid, competitive market for these securities, it became impossible to reliably value these securities. In addition, given that the value of the banks holding these securities was based on the sum of all projects and investments within them, investors could not value the banks either. Investors reacted to this uncertainty by selling both the mortgage-backed securities and securities of banks that held mortgage-backed securities. These actions further compounded the problem by driving down prices to seemingly unrealistically low levels and thereby threatening the solvency of the entire financial system.

The loss of information precipitated by the loss of liquidity played a key role in the breakdown of credit markets. As both investors and government regulators found it increasingly difficult to assess the solvency of the banks, banks found it difficult to raise new funds on their own and also shied away from lending to other banks because of their concerns about the financial viability of their competitors. The result was a breakdown in lending. Ultimately, the government was forced to step in and spend hundreds of billions of dollars in order to (1) provide new capital to support the banks and (2) provide liquidity by creating a market for the now "toxic" mortgage-backed securities.

Arbitrage in Markets

Value additively is the principle behind a type of trading activity known as stock index arbitrage. Common stock indices (such as the Dow Jones Industrial Average and the Standard and Poor's 500 (S&P 500)) represent portfolios of individual stocks. It is possible to trade the individual stocks that comprise an index on the New York Stock Exchange and NASDAQ. It is also possible to trade the entire index (as a single security) on the futures exchanges in Chicago, or as an exchange-traded fund (ETF) on the NYSE. When the price of the index security is below the total price of the individual stocks, traders buy the index and sell the stocks to capture the price difference. Similarly, when the price of the index security is above the total price of the individual stocks, traders sell the index and buy the individual stocks. It is not uncommon for 20% to 30% of the daily volume of trade on the NYSE to be due to index arbitrage activity via program trading.*

The traders that engage in stock index arbitrage automate the process by tracking prices and submitting (or cancelling) orders electronically. Over the years the competition to take advantage of these opportunities has caused traders to go to extraordinary lengths to reduce order execution time. One limiting factor is the time it takes to send an order from one exchange to another. For example, in 2010 Spread Networks paid $300 million for a new fiber optic line that reduced the communication time between New York and Chicago from 16 milliseconds to 13 milliseconds. Three milliseconds might not sound like a lot (it takes 400 milliseconds to blink), but it meant that Spread would be able to exploit mispricings that occurred between the NYSE and the Chicago futures exchange before any of its competitors, at least until one of its competitors constructed a faster line.

The evolution of how traders took advantage of these short-lived arbitrage opportunities provides a nice illustration of how competitive market forces act to remove profit-making opportunities. In a recent study, Professors Eric Budish, Peter Crampton, and John Shim** focused on the evolution of one particular arbitrage opportunity that resulted from differences in the price of the S&P 500 Futures Contract on the Chicago Mercantile Exchange and the price of the SPDR S&P 500 ETF traded on the New York Stock Exchange.

The left figure shows how the duration of arbitrage opportunities changed between 2005 and 2011. Each line shows, for the indicated year, the fraction of arbitrage opportunities that lasted longer than the amount of time indicated on the horizontal axis. So, for example, in 2005 about half of the arbitrage opportunities that existed lasted more than 100 milliseconds. By 2008, this number had dropped to 20 milliseconds, and by 2011, the number was under 10 milliseconds. Note also that in 2005 almost all opportunities lasted at least 20 milliseconds, but by 2011 the number of opportunities that lasted this long was less than 10% and hardly any persisted for more than 100 milliseconds.

What happened to the profits from exploiting these mispricings? You might have expected that the effect of this competition would be to decrease profits, but as the right figure shows, profits per opportunity remained relatively constant. Furthermore, the number of opportunities did not systematically decline over this period, implying that the aggregate profits from exploiting arbitrage opportunities did not diminish. In that sense, the competition between arbitrageurs has not reduced the magnitude or frequency of price deviations across these markets, but instead has reduced the amount of time that these deviations can persist.

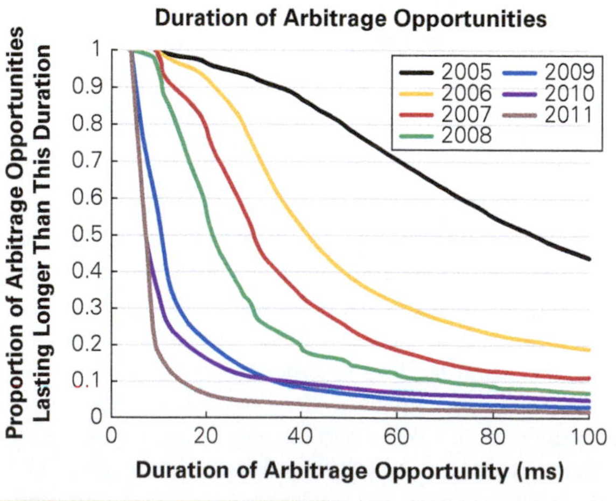

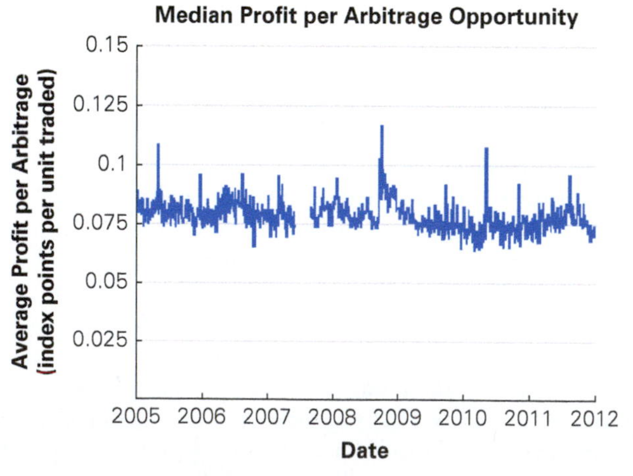

*See www.barrons.com/public/page/9_0210-nysepgtd.html

**"The High-Frequency Trading Arms Race: Frequent Batch Auctions as a Market Design Response," *Quarterly Journal of Economics* (2015): 1547–1621.

More generally, value additivity implies that the value of a portfolio is equal to the sum of the values of its parts. That is, the "à la carte" price and the package price must coincide.[7]

Value Additivity and Firm Value. Value additivity has an important consequence for the value of an entire firm. The cash flows of the firm are equal to the total cash flows of all projects and investments within the firm. Therefore, by value additivity, the price or value of the entire firm is equal to the sum of the values of all projects and investments within it. In other words, our NPV decision rule coincides with maximizing the value of the entire firm:

To maximize the value of the entire firm, managers should make decisions that maximize NPV. The NPV of the decision represents its contribution to the overall value of the firm.

Where Do We Go from Here?

The key concepts we have developed in this chapter—the Valuation Principle, Net Present Value, and the Law of One Price—provide the foundation for financial decision making. The Law of One Price allows us to determine the value of stocks, bonds, and other securities, based on their cash flows, and validates the optimality of the NPV decision rule in identifying projects and investments that create value. In the remainder of the text, we will build on this foundation and explore the details of applying these principles in practice.

For simplicity, we have focused in this chapter on projects that were not risky, and thus had known costs and benefits. The same fundamental tools of the Valuation Principle and the Law of One Price can be applied to analyze risky investments as well, and we will look in detail at methods to assess and value risk in Part 4 of the text. Those seeking some early insights and key foundations for this topic, however, are strongly encouraged to read the appendix to this chapter. There we introduce the idea that investors are risk averse, and then use the principle of no-arbitrage developed in this chapter to demonstrate two fundamental insights regarding the impact of risk on valuation:

1. When cash flows are risky, we must discount them at a rate equal to the risk-free interest rate plus an appropriate risk premium; and,
2. The appropriate risk premium will be higher the more the project's returns tend to vary with the overall risk in the economy.

Finally, the chapter appendix also addresses the important practical issue of transactions costs. There we show that when purchase and sale prices, or borrowing and lending rates differ, the Law of One Price will continue to hold, but only up to the level of transactions costs.

CONCEPT CHECK

1. If a firm makes an investment that has a positive NPV, how does the value of the firm change?
2. What is the separation principle?
3. In addition to trading opportunities, what else do liquid markets provide?

---

[7]This feature of financial markets does not hold in many other *noncompetitive* markets. For example, a round-trip airline ticket often costs much less than two separate one-way tickets. Of course, airline tickets are not sold in a competitive market—you cannot buy *and* sell the tickets at the listed prices. Only airlines can sell tickets, and they have strict rules against reselling tickets. Otherwise, you could make money buying round-trip tickets and selling them to people who need one-way tickets.

MyFinanceLab

Here is what you should know after reading this chapter. MyFinanceLab will help you identify what you know and where to go when you need to practice.

3.1 Valuing Decisions

- To evaluate a decision, we must value the incremental costs and benefits associated with that decision. A good decision is one for which the value of the benefits exceeds the value of the costs.
- To compare costs and benefits that occur at different points in time, in different currencies, or with different risks, we must put all costs and benefits in common terms. Typically, we convert costs and benefits into cash today.
- A competitive market is one in which a good can be bought and sold at the same price. We use prices from competitive markets to determine the cash value of a good.

3.2 Interest Rates and the Time Value of Money

- The time value of money is the difference in value between money today and money in the future. The rate at which we can exchange money today for money in the future by borrowing or investing is the current market interest rate. The risk-free interest rate, r_f, is the rate at which money can be borrowed or lent without risk.

3.3 Present Value and the NPV Decision Rule

- The present value (PV) of a cash flow is its value in terms of cash today.
- The net present value (NPV) of a project is

$$PV(\text{Benefits}) - PV(\text{Costs}) \tag{3.1}$$

- A good project is one with a positive net present value. The NPV Decision Rule states that when choosing from among a set of alternatives, choose the one with the highest NPV. The NPV of a project is equivalent to the cash value today of the project.
- Regardless of our preferences for cash today versus cash in the future, we should always first maximize NPV. We can then borrow or lend to shift cash flows through time and to find our most preferred pattern of cash flows.

3.4 Arbitrage and the Law of One Price

- Arbitrage is the process of trading to take advantage of equivalent goods that have different prices in different competitive markets.
- A normal market is a competitive market with no arbitrage opportunities.
- The Law of One Price states that if equivalent goods or securities trade simultaneously in different competitive markets, they will trade for the same price in each market. This law is equivalent to saying that no arbitrage opportunities should exist.

3.5 No-Arbitrage and Security Prices

- The No-Arbitrage Price of a Security is

$$PV(\text{All cash flows paid by the security}) \tag{3.3}$$

- No-arbitrage implies that all risk-free investments should offer the same return.
- The Separation Principle states that security transactions in a normal market neither create nor destroy value on their own. As a consequence, we can evaluate the NPV of an investment decision separately from the security transactions the firm is considering.
- To maximize the value of the entire firm, managers should make decisions that maximize the NPV. The NPV of the decision represents its contribution to the overall value of the firm.
- Value additivity implies that the value of a portfolio is equal to the sum of the values of its parts.

Key Terms

Further Reading

Many of the fundamental principles of this chapter were developed in the classic text by I. Fisher, *The Theory of Interest: As Determined by Impatience to Spend Income and Opportunity to Invest It* (Macmillan, 1930); reprinted (Augustus M. Kelley, 1955).

To learn more about the principle of no arbitrage and its importance as the foundation for modern finance theory, see S. Ross, *Neoclassical Finance* (Princeton University Press, 2004).

For a discussion of arbitrage and rational trading and their role in determining market prices, see M. Rubinstein, "Rational Markets: Yes or No? The Affirmative Case," *Financial Analysts Journal* (May/June 2001): 15–29.

For a discussion of some of the limitations to arbitrage that may arise in practice, see A. Shleifer and R. Vishny, "Limits of Arbitrage," *Journal of Finance* 52 (1997): 35–55.

Problems

All problems are available in MyFinanceLab.

Valuing Decisions

1. Honda Motor Company is considering offering a $2000 rebate on its minivan, lowering the vehicle's price from $30,000 to $28,000. The marketing group estimates that this rebate will increase sales over the next year from 40,000 to 55,000 vehicles. Suppose Honda's profit margin with the rebate is $6000 per vehicle. If the change in sales is the only consequence of this decision, what are its costs and benefits? Is it a good idea?

2. You are an international shrimp trader. A food producer in the Czech Republic offers to pay you 2 million Czech koruna today in exchange for a year's supply of frozen shrimp. Your Thai supplier will provide you with the same supply for 3 million Thai baht today. If the current competitive market exchange rates are 25.50 koruna per dollar and 41.25 baht per dollar, what is the value of this deal?

3. Suppose the current market price of corn is $3.75 per bushel. Your firm has a technology that can convert 1 bushel of corn to 3 gallons of ethanol. If the cost of conversion is $1.60 per bushel, at what market price of ethanol does conversion become attractive?

4. Suppose your employer offers you a choice between a $5000 bonus and 100 shares of the company stock. Whichever one you choose will be awarded today. The stock is currently trading for $63 per share.
   a. Suppose that if you receive the stock bonus, you are free to trade it. Which form of the bonus should you choose? What is its value?

b. Suppose that if you receive the stock bonus, you are required to hold it for at least one year. What can you say about the value of the stock bonus now? What will your decision depend on?

5. You have decided to take your daughter skiing in Utah. The best price you have been able to find for a roundtrip air ticket is $359. You notice that you have 20,000 frequent flier miles that are about to expire, but you need 25,000 miles to get her a free ticket. The airline offers to sell you 5000 additional miles for $0.03 per mile.

a. Suppose that if you don't use the miles for your daughter's ticket they will become worthless. What should you do?

b. What additional information would your decision depend on if the miles were not expiring? Why?

Interest Rates and the Time Value of Money

6. Suppose the risk-free interest rate is 4%.

a. Having $200 today is equivalent to having what amount in one year?

b. Having $200 in one year is equivalent to having what amount today?

c. Which would you prefer, $200 today or $200 in one year? Does your answer depend on when you need the money? Why or why not?

7. You have an investment opportunity in Japan. It requires an investment of $1 million today and will produce a cash flow of ¥114 million in one year with no risk. Suppose the risk-free interest rate in the United States is 4%, the risk-free interest rate in Japan is 2%, and the current competitive exchange rate is ¥110 per $1. What is the NPV of this investment? Is it a good opportunity?

8. Your firm has a risk-free investment opportunity where it can invest $160,000 today and receive $170,000 in one year. For what level of interest rates is this project attractive?

Present Value and the NPV Decision Rule

9. You run a construction firm. You have just won a contract to construct a government office building. It will take one year to construct it, requiring an investment of $10 million today and $5 million in one year. The government will pay you $20 million upon the building's completion. Suppose the cash flows and their times of payment are certain, and the risk-free interest rate is 10%.

a. What is the NPV of this opportunity?

b. How can your firm turn this NPV into cash today?

10. Your firm has identified three potential investment projects. The projects and their cash flows are shown here:

Project	Cash Flow Today ($)	Cash Flow in One Year ($)
A	−10	20
B	5	5
C	20	−10

Suppose all cash flows are certain and the risk-free interest rate is 10%.

a. What is the NPV of each project?

b. If the firm can choose only one of these projects, which should it choose?

c. If the firm can choose any two of these projects, which should it choose?

11. Your computer manufacturing firm must purchase 10,000 keyboards from a supplier. One supplier demands a payment of $100,000 today plus $10 per keyboard payable in one year. Another supplier will charge $21 per keyboard, also payable in one year. The risk-free interest rate is 6%.

a. What is the difference in their offers in terms of dollars today? Which offer should your firm take?

b. Suppose your firm does not want to spend cash today. How can it take the first offer and not spend $100,000 of its own cash today?

Arbitrage and the Law of One Price

12. Suppose Bank One offers a risk-free interest rate of 5.5% on both savings and loans, and Bank Enn offers a risk-free interest rate of 6% on both savings and loans.

a. What arbitrage opportunity is available?

b. Which bank would experience a surge in the demand for loans? Which bank would receive a surge in deposits?

c. What would you expect to happen to the interest rates the two banks are offering?

13. Throughout the 1990s, interest rates in Japan were lower than interest rates in the United States. As a result, many Japanese investors were tempted to borrow in Japan and invest the proceeds in the United States. Explain why this strategy does not represent an arbitrage opportunity.

14. An American Depositary Receipt (ADR) is security issued by a U.S. bank and traded on a U.S. stock exchange that represents a specific number of shares of a foreign stock. For example, Nokia Corporation trades as an ADR with symbol NOK on the NYSE. Each ADR represents one share of Nokia Corporation stock, which trades with symbol NOK1V on the Helsinki stock exchange. If the U.S. ADR for Nokia is trading for $6.74 per share, and Nokia stock is trading on the Helsinki exchange for 6.20 € per share, use the Law of One Price to determine the current $/€ exchange rate.

No-Arbitrage and Security Prices

MFL **15.** The promised cash flows of three securities are listed here. If the cash flows are risk-free, and the risk-free interest rate is 5%, determine the no-arbitrage price of each security before the first cash flow is paid.

Security	Cash Flow Today ($)	Cash Flow in One Year ($)
A	500	500
B	0	1000
C	1000	0

16. An Exchange-Traded Fund (ETF) is a security that represents a portfolio of individual stocks. Consider an ETF for which each share represents a portfolio of two shares of Hewlett-Packard (HPQ), one share of Sears (SHLD), and three shares of General Electric (GE). Suppose the current stock prices of each individual stock are as shown here:

Stock	Current Market Price
HPQ	$28
SHLD	$40
GE	$14

a. What is the price per share of the ETF in a normal market?
b. If the ETF currently trades for $120, what arbitrage opportunity is available? What trades would you make?
c. If the ETF currently trades for $150, what arbitrage opportunity is available? What trades would you make?

17. Consider two securities that pay risk-free cash flows over the next two years and that have the current market prices shown here:

Security	Price Today ($)	Cash Flow in One Year ($)	Cash Flow in Two Years ($)
B1	94	100	0
B2	85	0	100

a. What is the no-arbitrage price of a security that pays cash flows of $100 in one year and $100 in two years?
b. What is the no-arbitrage price of a security that pays cash flows of $100 in one year and $500 in two years?
c. Suppose a security with cash flows of $50 in one year and $100 in two years is trading for a price of $130. What arbitrage opportunity is available?

18. Suppose a security with a risk-free cash flow of $150 in one year trades for $140 today. If there are no arbitrage opportunities, what is the current risk-free interest rate?

19. Xia Corporation is a company whose sole assets are $100,000 in cash and three projects that it will undertake. The projects are risk-free and have the following cash flows:

Project	Cash Flow Today ($)	Cash Flow in One Year ($)
A	−20,000	30,000
B	−10,000	25,000
C	−60,000	80,000

Xia plans to invest any unused cash today at the risk-free interest rate of 10%. In one year, all cash will be paid to investors and the company will be shut down.
a. What is the NPV of each project? Which projects should Xia undertake and how much cash should it retain?
b. What is the total value of Xia's assets (projects and cash) today?
c. What cash flows will the investors in Xia receive? Based on these cash flows, what is the value of Xia today?
d. Suppose Xia pays any unused cash to investors today, rather than investing it. What are the cash flows to the investors in this case? What is the value of Xia now?
e. Explain the relationship in your answers to parts (b), (c), and (d).

CHAPTER 3 APPENDIX

The Price of Risk

NOTATION

r_s discount rate for security s

Thus far we have considered only cash flows that have no risk. But in many settings, cash flows are risky. In this section, we examine how to determine the present value of a risky cash flow.

Risky Versus Risk-Free Cash Flows

Suppose the risk-free interest rate is 4% and that over the next year the economy is equally likely to strengthen or weaken. Consider an investment in a risk-free bond, and one in the stock market index (a portfolio of all the stocks in the market). The risk-free bond has no risk and will pay $1100 whatever the state of the economy. The cash flow from an investment in the market index, however, depends on the strength of the economy. Let's assume that the market index will be worth $1400 if the economy is strong but only $800 if the economy is weak. Table 3A.1 summarizes these payoffs.

In Section 3.5, we saw that the no-arbitrage price of a security is equal to the present value of its cash flows. For example, the price of the risk-free bond corresponds to the 4% risk-free interest rate:

$$\begin{aligned}\text{Price (Risk-free Bond)} &= \text{PV (Cash Flows)}\\ &= (\$1100 \text{ in one year}) \div (1.04 \text{ \$ in one year/\$ today})\\ &= \$1058 \text{ today}\end{aligned}$$

Now consider the market index. An investor who buys it today can sell it in one year for a cash flow of either $800 or $1400, with an average payoff of $\frac{1}{2}(\$800) + \frac{1}{2}(\$1400) = \$1100$. Although this average payoff is the same as the risk-free bond, the market index has a lower price today. It pays $1100 *on average*, but its actual cash flow is risky, so investors are only willing to pay $1000 for it today rather than $1058. What accounts for this lower price?

Risk Aversion and the Risk Premium

Intuitively, investors pay less to receive $1100 on average than to receive $1100 with certainty because they don't like risk. In particular, it seems likely that for most individuals, *the personal cost of losing a dollar in bad times is greater than the benefit of an extra dollar in good times*. Thus, the benefit from receiving an extra $300 ($1400 versus $1100) when the economy is strong is less important than the loss of $300 ($800 versus $1100) when the economy is weak. As a result, investors prefer to receive $1100 with certainty.

The notion that investors prefer to have a safe income rather than a risky one of the same average amount is called **risk aversion**. It is an aspect of an investor's preferences, and different investors may have different degrees of risk aversion. The more risk averse

TABLE 3A.1 Cash Flows and Market Prices (in $) of a Risk-Free Bond and an Investment in the Market Portfolio

		Cash Flow in One Year	
Security	Market Price Today	Weak Economy	Strong Economy
Risk-free bond	1058	1100	1100
Market index	1000	800	1400

investors are, the lower the current price of the market index will be compared to a risk-free bond with the same average payoff.

Because investors care about risk, we cannot use the risk-free interest rate to compute the present value of a risky future cash flow. When investing in a risky project, investors will expect a return that appropriately compensates them for the risk. For example, investors who buy the market index for its current price of \$1000 receive \$1100 on average at the end of the year, which is an average gain of \$100, or a 10% return on their initial investment. When we compute the return of a security based on the payoff we expect to receive on average, we call it the **expected return**:

$$\text{Expected return of a risky investment} = \frac{\text{Expected gain at end of year}}{\text{Initial cost}} \tag{3A.1}$$

Of course, although the expected return of the market index is 10%, its *actual* return will be higher or lower. If the economy is strong, the market index will rise to 1400, which represents a return of

$$\text{Market return if economy is strong} = (1400 - 1000)/1000 = 40\%$$

If the economy is weak, the index will drop to 800, for a return of

$$\text{Market return if economy is weak} = (800 - 1000)/1000 = -20\%$$

We can also calculate the 10% expected return by computing the average of these actual returns:

$$\tfrac{1}{2}(40\%) + \tfrac{1}{2}(-20\%) = 10\%$$

Thus, investors in the market index earn an expected return of 10% rather than the risk-free interest rate of 4% on their investment. The difference of 6% between these returns is called the market index's **risk premium**. The risk premium of a security represents the additional return that investors expect to earn to compensate them for the security's risk. Because investors are risk averse, the price of a risky security cannot be calculated by simply discounting its expected cash flow at the risk-free interest rate. Rather,

When a cash flow is risky, to compute its present value we must discount the cash flow we expect on average at a rate that equals the risk-free interest rate plus an appropriate risk premium.

The No-Arbitrage Price of a Risky Security

The risk premium of the market index is determined by investors' preferences toward risk. And in the same way we used the risk-free interest rate to determine the no-arbitrage price of other risk-free securities, we can use the risk premium of the market index to value other risky securities. For example, suppose some security "A" will pay investors \$600 if the economy is strong and nothing if it is weak. Let's see how we can determine the market price of security A using the Law of One Price.

As shown in Table 3A.2, if we combine security A with a risk-free bond that pays \$800 in one year, the cash flows of the portfolio in one year are identical to the cash flows of the market index. By the Law of One Price, the total market value of the bond and security A must equal \$1000, the value of the market index. Given a risk-free interest rate of 4%, the market price of the bond is

$$(\$800 \text{ in one year}) \div (1.04 \text{ \$ in one year/\$ today}) = \$769 \text{ today}$$

TABLE 3A.2 **Determining the Market Price of Security A (cash flows in $)**

		Cash Flow in One Year	
Security	Market Price Today	Weak Economy	Strong Economy
Risk-free bond	769	800	800
Security A	?	0	600
Market index	1000	800	1400

Therefore, the initial market price of security A is $\$1000 - \$769 = \$231$. If the price of security A were higher or lower than $231, then the value of the portfolio of the bond and security A would differ from the value of the market index, violating the Law of One Price and creating an arbitrage opportunity.

Risk Premiums Depend on Risk

Given an initial price of $231 and an expected payoff of $\frac{1}{2}(0) + \frac{1}{2}(600) = 300$, security A has an expected return of

$$\text{Expected return of security A} = \frac{300 - 231}{231} = 30\%$$

Note that this expected return exceeds the 10% expected return of the market portfolio. Investors in security A earn a risk premium of $30\% - 4\% = 26\%$ over the risk-free interest rate, compared to a 6% risk premium for the market portfolio. Why are the risk premiums so different?

The reason for the difference becomes clear if we compare the actual returns for the two securities. When the economy is weak, investors in security A lose everything, for a return of -100%, and when the economy is strong, they earn a return of $(600 - 231)/231 = 160\%$. In contrast, the market index loses 20% in a weak economy and gains 40% in a strong economy. Given its much more variable returns, it is not surprising that security A must pay investors a higher risk premium.

Risk Is Relative to the Overall Market

The example of security A suggests that the risk premium of a security will depend on how variable its returns are. But before drawing any conclusions, it is worth considering one further example.

EXAMPLE 3A.1 **A Negative Risk Premium**

Problem

Suppose security B pays $600 if the economy is weak and $0 if the economy is strong. What are its no-arbitrage price, expected return, and risk premium?

Solution

If we combine the market index and security B together in a portfolio, we earn the same payoff as a risk-free bond that pays $1400, as shown in the following table (cash flows in $).

		Cash Flow in One Year	
Security	Market Price Today	Weak Economy	Strong Economy
Market index	1000	800	1400
Security B	?	600	0
Risk-free bond	1346	1400	1400

Because the market price of the risk-free bond is $\$1400 \div 1.04 = \$1346$ today, we can conclude from the Law of One Price that security B must have a market price of $\$1346 - 1000 = \$346$ today.

If the economy is weak, security B pays a return of $(600 - 346)/346 = 73.4\%$. If the economy is strong, security B pays nothing, for a return of -100%. The expected return of security B is therefore $\frac{1}{2}(73.4\%) + \frac{1}{2}(-100\%) = -13.3\%$. Its risk premium is $-13.3\% - 4\% = -17.3\%$; that is, security B pays investors 17.3% *less* on average than the risk-free interest rate.

The results for security B are quite striking. Looking at securities A and B in isolation, they seem very similar—both are equally likely to pay \$600 or \$0. Yet security A has a much lower market price than security B (\$231 versus \$346). In terms of returns, security A pays investors an expected return of 30%; security B pays -13.3%. Why are their prices and expected returns so different? And why would risk-averse investors be willing to buy a risky security with an expected return below the risk-free interest rate?

To understand this result, note that security A pays \$600 when the economy is strong, and B pays \$600 when the economy is weak. Recall that our definition of risk aversion is that investors value an extra dollar of income more in bad times than in good times. Thus, because security B pays \$600 when the economy is weak and the market index performs poorly, it pays off when investors' wealth is low and they value money the most. In fact, security B is not really "risky" from an investor's point of view; rather, security B is an insurance policy against an economic decline. By holding security B together with the market index, we can eliminate our risk from market fluctuations. Risk-averse investors are willing to pay for this insurance by accepting a return below the risk-free interest rate.

This result illustrates an extremely important principle. The risk of a security cannot be evaluated in isolation. Even when a security's returns are quite variable, if the returns vary in a way that offsets other risks investors are holding, the security will reduce rather than increase investors' risk. As a result, risk can only be assessed relative to the other risks that investors face; that is,

The risk of a security must be evaluated in relation to the fluctuations of other investments in the economy. A security's risk premium will be higher the more its returns tend to vary with the overall economy and the market index. If the security's returns vary in the opposite direction of the market index, it offers insurance and will have a negative risk premium.

Table 3A.3 compares the risk and risk premiums for the different securities we have considered thus far. For each security we compute the sensitivity of its return to the state of the economy by calculating the difference in its return when the economy is strong versus weak. Note that the risk premium for each security is proportional to this

TABLE 3A.3 **Risk and Risk Premiums for Different Securities**

	Returns				
Security	Weak Economy	Strong Economy	Expected Return	Sensitivity (Difference in Returns)	Risk Premium
Risk-free bond	4%	4%	4%	0%	0%
Market index	−20%	40%	10%	60%	6%
Security A	−100%	160%	30%	260%	26%
Security B	73%	−100%	−13.3%	−173%	−17.3%

sensitivity, and the risk premium is negative when the returns vary in the opposite direction of the market.[8]

Risk, Return, and Market Prices

We have shown that when cash flows are risky, we can use the Law of One Price to compute present values by constructing a portfolio that produces cash flows with identical risk. As shown in Figure 3A.1, computing prices in this way is equivalent to converting between cash flows today and the *expected* cash flows received in the future using a discount rate r_s that includes a risk premium appropriate for the investment's risk:

$$r_s = r_f + (\text{risk premium for investment } s) \tag{3A.2}$$

For the simple setting considered here with only a single source of risk (the strength of the economy), we have seen that the risk premium of an investment depends on how its returns vary with the overall economy. In Part 4 of the text, we show that this result holds for more general settings with many sources of risk and more than two possible states of the economy.

FIGURE 3A.1

Converting between Dollars Today and Dollars in One Year with Risk

When cash flows are risky, Eq. 3A.2 determines the expected return, r_s, that we can use to convert between prices or present values today and the expected cash flow in the future.

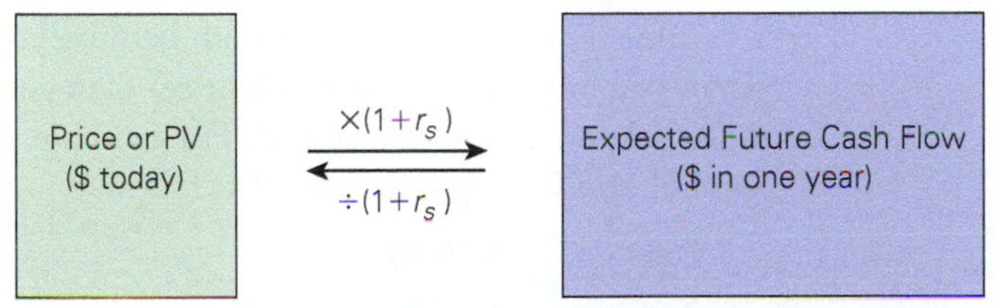

[8]You might notice that each security would have an expected return equal to the risk-free rate of 4% if the probability of the strong economy were 40% instead of 50%. The fact that risk aversion is equivalent to using a more pessimistic probability distribution is an important insight that we will revisit in Chapter 21.

EXAMPLE 3A.2 **Using the Risk Premium to Compute a Price**

Problem

Consider a risky bond with a cash flow of \$1100 when the economy is strong and \$1000 when the economy is weak. Suppose a 1% risk premium is appropriate for this bond. If the risk-free interest rate is 4%, what is the price of the bond today?

Solution

From Eq. 3A.2, the appropriate discount rate for the bond is

$$r_b = r_f + \text{(Risk Premium for the Bond)} = 4\% + 1\% = 5\%$$

The expected cash flow of the bond is $\frac{1}{2}(\$1100) + \frac{1}{2}(\$1000) = \$1050$ in one year. Thus, the price of the bond today is

$$\begin{aligned}\text{Bond Price} &= (\text{Average cash flow in one year}) \div (1 + r_b \text{ \$ in one year/\$ today})\\ &= (\$1050 \text{ in one year}) \div (1.05 \text{ \$ in one year/\$ today})\\ &= \$1000 \text{ today}\end{aligned}$$

Given this price, the bond's return is 10% when the economy is strong, and 0% when the economy is weak. (Note that the difference in the returns is 10%, which is 1/6 as variable as the market index; see Table 3A.3. Correspondingly, the risk premium of the bond is 1/6 that of the market index as well.)

CONCEPT CHECK

1. Why does the expected return of a risky security generally differ from the risk-free interest rate? What determines the size of its risk premium?
2. Explain why the risk of a security should not be evaluated in isolation.

Arbitrage with Transactions Costs

In our examples up to this point, we have ignored the costs of buying and selling goods or securities. In most markets, you must pay **transactions costs** to trade securities. As discussed in Chapter 1, when you trade securities in markets such as the NYSE and NASDAQ, you must pay two types of transactions costs. First, you must pay your broker a commission on the trade. Second, because you will generally pay a slightly higher price when you buy a security (the ask price) than you receive when you sell (the bid price), you will also pay the bid-ask spread. For example, a share of Intel Corporation stock (ticker symbol INTC) might be quoted as follows:

Bid:	\$28.50
Ask:	\$28.70

We can interpret these quotes as if the competitive price for INTC is \$28.60, but there is a transaction cost of \$0.10 per share when buying or selling.[9]

What consequence do these transactions costs have for no-arbitrage prices and the Law of One Price? Earlier we stated that the price of gold in New York and London must be identical in competitive markets. Suppose, however, that total transactions costs of \$5 per

[9]Any price in between the bid price and the ask price could be the competitive price, with differing transaction costs for buying and selling.

ounce are associated with buying gold in one market and selling it in the other. Then if the price of gold is \$1150 per ounce in New York and \$1152 per ounce in London, the "Buy low, sell high" strategy no longer works:

Cost:	\$1150 per ounce (buy gold in New York) + \$5 (transactions costs)
Benefit:	\$1152 per ounce (sell gold in London)
NPV:	\$1152 − \$1150 − \$5 = −\$3 per ounce

Indeed, there is no arbitrage opportunity in this case until the prices diverge by more than \$5, the amount of the transactions costs.

In general, we need to modify our previous conclusions about no-arbitrage prices by appending the phrase "up to transactions costs." In this example, there is only one competitive price for gold—up to a discrepancy of the \$5 transactions cost. The other conclusions of this chapter have the same qualifier. The package price should equal the à la carte price, up to the transactions costs associated with packaging and unpackaging. The price of a security should equal the present value of its cash flows, up to the transactions costs of trading the security and the cash flows.

Fortunately, for most financial markets, these costs are small. For example, in 2015, typical bid-ask spreads for large NYSE stocks were between 2 and 5 cents per share. As a first approximation we can ignore these spreads in our analysis. Only in situations in which the NPV is small (relative to the transactions costs) will any discrepancy matter. In that case, we will need to carefully account for all transactions costs to decide whether the NPV is positive or negative.

EXAMPLE 3A.3 The No-Arbitrage Price Range

Problem

Consider a bond that pays \$1000 at the end of the year. Suppose the market interest rate for deposits is 6%, but the market interest rate for borrowing is 6.5%. What is the no-arbitrage price *range* for the bond? That is, what is the highest and lowest price the bond could trade for without creating an arbitrage opportunity?

Solution

The no-arbitrage price for the bond equals the present value of the cash flows. In this case, however, the interest rate we should use depends on whether we are borrowing or lending. For example, the amount we would need to put in the bank today to receive \$1000 in one year is

$$(\$1000 \text{ in one year}) \div (1.06 \text{ \$ in one year/\$ today}) = \$943.40 \text{ today}$$

where we have used the 6% interest rate that we will earn on our deposit. The amount that we can borrow today if we plan to repay \$1000 in one year is

$$(\$1000 \text{ in one year}) \div (1.065 \text{ \$ in one year/\$ today}) = \$938.97 \text{ today}$$

where we have used the higher 6.5% rate that we will have to pay if we borrow.

Suppose the bond price P exceeded \$943.40. Then you could profit by selling the bond at its current price and investing \$943.40 of the proceeds at the 6% interest rate. You would still receive \$1000 at the end of the year, but you would get to keep the difference $\$(P - 943.40)$ today. This arbitrage opportunity will keep the price of the bond from going higher than \$943.40.

Alternatively, suppose the bond price P were less than \$938.97. Then you could borrow \$938.97 at 6.5% and use P of it to buy the bond. This would leave you with $\$(938.97 - P)$

today, and no obligation in the future because you can use the $1000 bond payoff to repay the loan. This arbitrage opportunity will keep the price of the bond from falling below $938.97.

If the bond price P is between $938.97 and $943.40, then both of the preceding strategies will lose money, and there is no arbitrage opportunity. Thus no arbitrage implies a narrow range of possible prices for the bond ($938.97 to $943.40), rather than an exact price.

To summarize, when there are transactions costs, arbitrage keeps prices of equivalent goods and securities close to each other. Prices can deviate, but not by more than the transactions costs of the arbitrage.

CONCEPT CHECK

1. In the presence of transactions costs, why might different investors disagree about the value of an investment opportunity?
2. By how much could this value differ?

MyFinanceLab

Here is what you should know after reading this chapter. MyFinanceLab will help you identify what you know and where to go when you need to practice.

- When cash flows are risky, we cannot use the risk-free interest rate to compute present values. Instead, we can determine the present value by constructing a portfolio that produces cash flows with identical risk, and then applying the Law of One Price. Alternatively, we can discount the expected cash flows using a discount rate that includes an appropriate risk premium.
- The risk of a security must be evaluated in relation to the fluctuations of other investments in the economy. A security's risk premium will be higher the more its returns tend to vary with the overall economy and the market index. If the security's returns vary in the opposite direction of the market index, it offers insurance and will have a negative risk premium.
- When there are transactions costs, the prices of equivalent securities can deviate from each other, but not by more than the transactions costs of the arbitrage.

Key Terms

expected return *p. 88*
risk aversion *p. 87*
risk premium *p. 88*
transactions costs *p. 92*

Problems

Problems are available in MyFinanceLab. An asterisk (*) indicates problems with a higher level of difficulty.

Risky Versus Risk-Free Cash Flows

A.1. The table here shows the no-arbitrage prices of securities A and B that we calculated.

		Cash Flow in One Year	
Security	Market Price Today	Weak Economy	Strong Economy
Security A	231	0	600
Security B	346	600	0

a. What are the payoffs of a portfolio of one share of security A and one share of security B?

b. What is the market price of this portfolio? What expected return will you earn from holding this portfolio?

A.2. Suppose security C has a payoff of \$600 when the economy is weak and \$1800 when the economy is strong. The risk-free interest rate is 4%.

a. Security C has the same payoffs as which portfolio of the securities A and B in Problem A.1?
b. What is the no-arbitrage price of security C?
c. What is the expected return of security C if both states are equally likely? What is its risk premium?
d. What is the difference between the return of security C when the economy is strong and when it is weak?
e. If security C had a risk premium of 10%, what arbitrage opportunity would be available?

***A.3.** You work for Innovation Partners and are considering creating a new security. This security would pay out \$1000 in one year if the last digit in the closing value of the Dow Jones Industrial index in one year is an even number and zero if it is odd. The one-year risk-free interest rate is 5%. Assume that all investors are averse to risk.

a. What can you say about the price of this security if it were traded today?
b. Say the security paid out \$1000 if the last digit of the Dow is odd and zero otherwise. Would your answer to part (a) change?
c. Assume both securities (the one that paid out on even digits and the one that paid out on odd digits) trade in the market today. Would that affect your answers?

***A.4.** Suppose a risky security pays an expected cash flow of \$80 in one year. The risk-free rate is 4%, and the expected return on the market index is 10%.

a. If the returns of this security are high when the economy is strong and low when the economy is weak, but the returns vary by only half as much as the market index, what risk premium is appropriate for this security?
b. What is the security's market price?

Arbitrage with Transactions Costs

A.5. Suppose Hewlett-Packard (HPQ) stock is currently trading on the NYSE with a bid price of \$28.00 and an ask price of \$28.10. At the same time, a NASDAQ dealer posts a bid price for HPQ of \$27.85 and an ask price of \$27.95.

a. Is there an arbitrage opportunity in this case? If so, how would you exploit it?
b. Suppose the NASDAQ dealer revises his quotes to a bid price of \$27.95 and an ask price of \$28.05. Is there an arbitrage opportunity now? If so, how would you exploit it?
c. What must be true of the highest bid price and the lowest ask price for no arbitrage opportunity to exist?

***A.6.** Consider a portfolio of two securities: one share of Johnson and Johnson (JNJ) stock and a bond that pays \$100 in one year. Suppose this portfolio is currently trading with a bid price of \$141.65 and an ask price of \$142.25, and the bond is trading with a bid price of \$91.75 and an ask price of \$91.95. In this case, what is the no-arbitrage price range for JNJ stock?

Time, Money, and Interest Rates

PART

2

THE LAW OF ONE PRICE CONNECTION. For a financial manager, evaluating financial decisions involves computing the value of future cash flows. In Chapter 4, we use the Law of One Price to derive a central concept in financial economics—the *time value of money*. We explain how to value a stream of future cash flows and derive a few useful shortcuts for computing the net present value of various types of cash flow patterns. Chapter 5 considers how to use market interest rates to determine the appropriate discount rate for a set of cash flows. We apply the Law of One Price to demonstrate that the discount rate will depend on the rate of return of investments with maturity and risk similar to the cash flows being valued. This observation leads to the important concept of the *cost of capital* of an investment decision.

Firms raise the capital they need for investment by issuing securities. The simplest security they can issue is a bond. In Chapter 6 use the tools we developed thus far to explain how to value bonds. We will see that the Law of One Price allows us to link bond prices and their yields to the term structure of market interest rates.

CHAPTER

4

The Time Value of Money

NOTATION

r	interest rate
C	cash flow
FV_n	future value on date n
PV	present value; annuity spreadsheet notation for the initial amount
C_n	cash flow at date n
N	date of the last cash flow in a stream of cash flows
NPV	net present value
P	initial principal or deposit, or equivalent present value
FV	future value; annuity spreadsheet notation for an extra final payment
g	growth rate
$NPER$	annuity spreadsheet notation for the number of periods or date of the last cash flow
$RATE$	annuity spreadsheet notation for interest rate
PMT	annuity spreadsheet notation for cash flow
IRR	internal rate of return
PV_n	present value on date n

AS DISCUSSED IN CHAPTER 3, TO EVALUATE A PROJECT, A FINANCIAL manager must compare its costs and benefits. In most cases, these costs and benefits are spread across time. For example, in September 2008, General Motors (GM) unveiled its plans to produce, starting in the 2011 model year, the Chevy Volt, an extended-range electric vehicle. GM's project involved significant upfront research and development costs, with revenues and expenses that will occur many years or even decades into the future. How can financial managers compare cost and benefits that occur over many years?

In order to evaluate a long-term project such as the Chevy Volt, we need tools that allow us to compare cash flows that occur at different points in time. We develop these tools in this chapter. The first tool is a visual method for representing a stream of cash flows: the timeline. After constructing a timeline, we establish three important rules for moving cash flows to different points in time. Using these rules, we show how to compute the present and future values of the costs and benefits of a general stream of cash flows. By converting all cash flows to a common point in time, these tools allow us to compare the costs and benefits of a long-term project, and thus assess its net present value, or NPV. The NPV expresses the net benefit of the project in terms of cash today.

While the general techniques developed in this chapter can be used to value any type of asset, certain types of assets have cash flows that follow a regular pattern. We develop shortcuts for valuing *annuities*, *perpetuities*, and other special cases of assets with cash flows that follow regular patterns.

4.1 The Timeline

We begin our look at valuing cash flows lasting several periods with some basic vocabulary and tools. We refer to a series of cash flows lasting several periods as a **stream of cash flows**. We can represent a stream of cash flows on a **timeline**, a linear representation of the timing of the expected cash flows. Timelines are an important first step in organizing and then solving a financial problem. We use them throughout this text.

To illustrate how to construct a timeline, assume that a friend owes you money. He has agreed to repay the loan by making two payments of $10,000 at the end of each of the next two years. We represent this information on a timeline as follows:

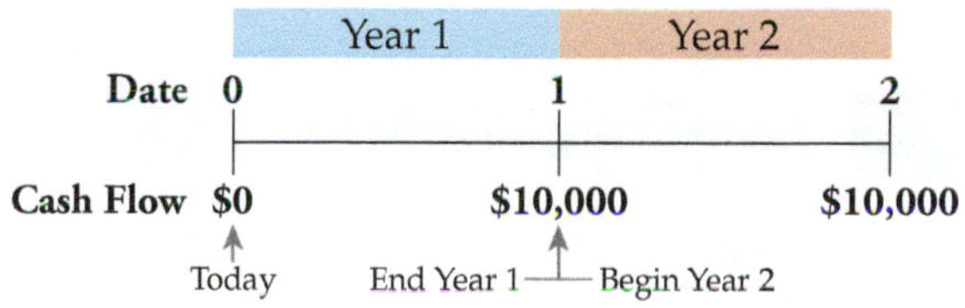

Date 0 represents the present. Date 1 is one year later and represents the end of the first year. The $10,000 cash flow below date 1 is the payment you will receive at the end of the first year. Date 2 is two years from now; it represents the end of the second year. The $10,000 cash flow below date 2 is the payment you will receive at the end of the second year.

To track cash flows on the timeline, interpret each point on the timeline as a specific date. The space between date 0 and date 1 then represents the time period between these dates—in this case, the first year of the loan. Date 0 is the beginning of the first year, and date 1 is the end of the first year. Similarly, date 1 is the beginning of the second year, and date 2 is the end of the second year. By denoting time in this way, date 1 signifies *both* the end of year 1 and the beginning of year 2, which makes sense since those dates are effectively the same point in time.[1]

In this example, both cash flows are inflows. In many cases, however, a financial decision will involve both inflows and outflows. To differentiate between the two types of cash flows, we assign a different sign to each: Inflows are positive cash flows, whereas outflows are negative cash flows.

To illustrate, suppose you're still feeling generous and have agreed to lend your brother $10,000 today. Your brother has agreed to repay this loan in two installments of $6000 at the end of each of the next two years. The timeline is as follows:

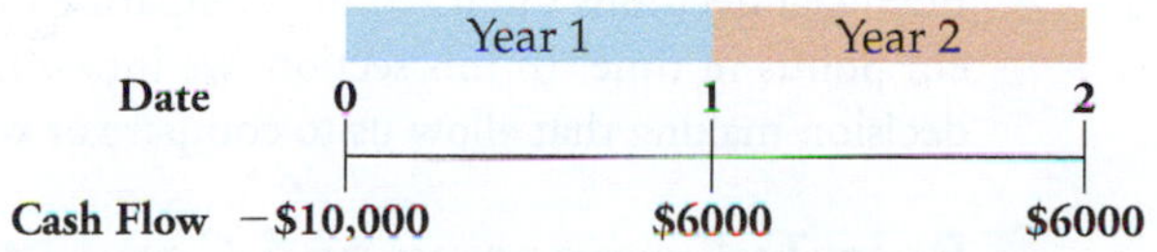

Notice that the first cash flow at date 0 (today) is represented as −$10,000 because it is an outflow. The subsequent cash flows of $6000 are positive because they are inflows.

[1]That is, there is no real time difference between a cash flow paid at 11:59 P.M. on December 31 and one paid at 12:01 A.M. on January 1, although there may be some other differences such as taxation that we overlook for now.

So far, we have used timelines to show the cash flows that occur at the end of each year. Actually, timelines can represent cash flows that take place at the end of any time period. For example, if you pay rent each month, you could use a timeline like the one in our first example to represent two rental payments, but you would replace the "year" label with "month."

Many of the timelines included in this chapter are very simple. Consequently, you may feel that it is not worth the time or trouble to construct them. As you progress to more difficult problems, however, you will find that timelines identify events in a transaction or investment that are easy to overlook. If you fail to recognize these cash flows, you will make flawed financial decisions. Therefore, we recommend that you approach *every* problem by drawing the timeline as we do in this chapter.

EXAMPLE 4.1 **Constructing a Timeline**

Problem

Suppose you must pay tuition of $10,000 per year for the next two years. Your tuition payments must be made in equal installments at the start of each semester. What is the timeline of your tuition payments?

Solution

Assuming today is the start of the first semester, your first payment occurs at date 0 (today). The remaining payments occur at semester intervals. Using one semester as the period length, we can construct a timeline as follows:

Date (Semesters)	0	1	2	3	4
Cash Flow	−$5000	−$5000	−$5000	−$5000	$0

CONCEPT CHECK

1. What are the key elements of a timeline?
2. How can you distinguish cash inflows from outflows on a timeline?

4.2 The Three Rules of Time Travel

Financial decisions often require comparing or combining cash flows that occur at different points in time. In this section, we introduce three important rules central to financial decision making that allow us to compare or combine values.

Rule 1: Comparing and Combining Values

Our first rule is that it is only possible to compare or combine values at the same point in time. This rule restates a conclusion introduced in Chapter 3: Only cash flows in the same units can be compared or combined. *A dollar today* and *a dollar in one year* are not equivalent. Having money now is more valuable than having money in the future; if you have the money today you can earn interest on it.

To compare or combine cash flows that occur at different points in time, you first need to convert the cash flows into the same units or *move* them to the same point in time. The next two rules show how to move the cash flows on the timeline.

Rule 2: Moving Cash Flows Forward in Time

Suppose we have \$1000 today, and we wish to determine the equivalent amount in one year's time. If the current market interest rate is 10%, we can use that rate as an exchange rate to move the cash flow forward in time. That is,

$$(\$1000 \text{ today}) \times (1.10 \text{ \$ in one year/\$ today}) = \$1100 \text{ in one year}$$

In general, if the market interest rate for the year is r, then we multiply by the interest rate factor, $(1 + r)$, to move the cash flow from the beginning to the end of the year. This process of moving a value or cash flow forward in time is known as **compounding**. *Our second rule stipulates that to move a cash flow forward in time, you must compound it.*

We can apply this rule repeatedly. Suppose we want to know how much the \$1000 is worth in two years' time. If the interest rate for year 2 is also 10%, then we convert as we just did:

$$(\$1100 \text{ in one year}) \times (1.10 \text{ \$ in two years/\$ in one year}) = \$1210 \text{ in two years}$$

Let's represent this calculation on a timeline as follows:

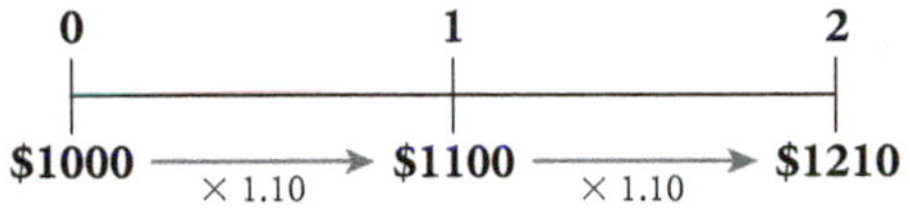

Given a 10% interest rate, all of the cash flows—\$1000 at date 0, \$1100 at date 1, and \$1210 at date 2—are equivalent. They have the same value but are expressed in different units (different points in time). An arrow that points to the right indicates that the value is being moved forward in time—that is, compounded.

The value of a cash flow that is moved forward in time is known as its future value. In the preceding example, \$1210 is the future value of \$1000 two years from today. Note that the value grows as we move the cash flow further in the future. The difference in value between money today and money in the future represents the **time value of money**, and it reflects the fact that by having money sooner, you can invest it and have more money later as a result. Note also that the equivalent value grows by \$100 the first year, but by \$110 the second year. In the second year we earn interest on our original \$1000, plus we earn interest on the \$100 interest we received in the first year. This effect of earning "interest on interest" is known as **compound interest.**

How does the future value change if we move the cash flow three years? Continuing with the same approach, we compound the cash flow a third time. Assuming the competitive market interest rate is fixed at 10%, we get

$$\$1000 \times (1.10) \times (1.10) \times (1.10) = \$1000 \times (1.10)^3 = \$1331$$

In general, to take a cash flow C forward n periods into the future, we must compound it by the n intervening interest rate factors. If the interest rate r is constant, then

Future Value of a Cash Flow

$$FV_n = C \times \underbrace{(1 + r) \times (1 + r) \times \cdots \times (1 + r)}_{n \text{ times}} = C \times (1 + r)^n \tag{4.1}$$

FIGURE 4.1

The Composition of Interest over Time

This graph shows the account balance and the composition of interest over time when an investor starts with an initial deposit of $1000, shown at bottom in red, in an account paying 10% annual interest. The green (middle) bars show the effect of **simple interest**, interest earned only on the initial deposit. The blue (top) bars show the effect of compound interest, where interest is also earned on prior interest payments. Over time, the effect of compounding is more pronounced, and by year 20, the total amount of simple interest earned is only $2000, whereas interest on interest is $3727.50

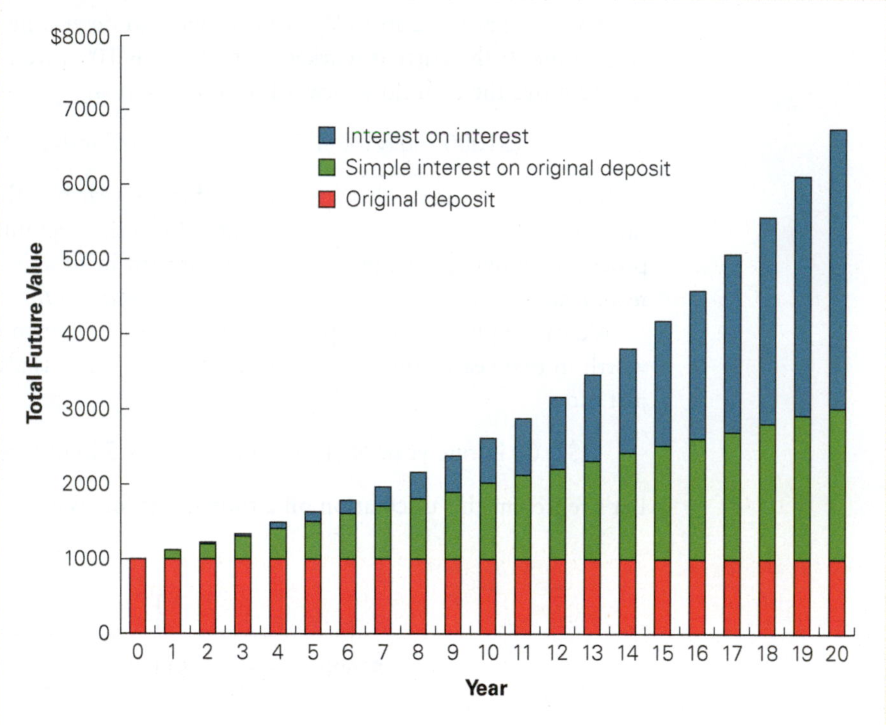

Figure 4.1 shows the importance of earning "interest on interest" in the growth of the account balance over time. The type of growth that results from compounding is called geometric or exponential growth. As Example 4.2 shows, over a long horizon, the effect of compounding can be quite dramatic.

EXAMPLE 4.2 **The Power of Compounding**

Problem

Suppose you invest $1000 in an account paying 10% interest per year. How much will you have in the account in 7 years? in 20 years? in 75 years?

Solution

You can apply Eq. 4.1 to calculate the future value in each case:

7 years:	$\$1000 \times (1.10)^7 = \$1948.72$
20 years:	$\$1000 \times (1.10)^{20} = \$6727.50$
75 years:	$\$1000 \times (1.10)^{75} = \$1,271,895.37$

Note that at 10% interest, your money will nearly double in 7 years. After 20 years, it will increase almost 7-fold. And if you invest for 75 years, you will be a millionaire!

Rule 3: Moving Cash Flows Back in Time

The third rule describes how to move cash flows backward in time. Suppose you would like to compute the value today of $1000 you anticipate receiving in one year. If the current

Rule of 72

Another way to think about the effect of compounding and discounting is to consider how long it will take your money to double given different interest rates. Suppose we want to know how many years it will take for \$1 to grow to a future value of \$2. We want the number of years, N, to solve

$$FV = \$1 \times (1 + r)^N = \$2$$

If you solve this formula for different interest rates, you will find the following approximation:

$$\text{Years to double} \approx 72 \div (\text{interest rate in percent})$$

This simple "Rule of 72" is fairly accurate (i.e., within one year of the exact doubling time) for interest rates higher than 2%. For example, if the interest rate is 9%, the doubling time should be about $72 \div 9 = 8$ years. Indeed, $1.09^8 = 1.99$! So, given a 9% interest rate, your money will approximately double every eight years.[2]

market interest rate is 10%, you can compute this value by converting units as we did in Chapter 3:

$$(\$1000 \text{ in one year}) \div (1.10 \text{ \$ in one year/\$ today}) = \$909.09 \text{ today}$$

That is, to move the cash flow backward in time, we divide it by the interest rate factor, $(1 + r)$, where r is the interest rate. This process of moving a value or cash flow backward in time—finding the equivalent value today of a future cash flow—is known as **discounting**. *Our third rule stipulates that to move a cash flow back in time, we must discount it.*

To illustrate, suppose that you anticipate receiving the \$1000 two years from today rather than in one year. If the interest rate for both years is 10%, we can prepare the following timeline:

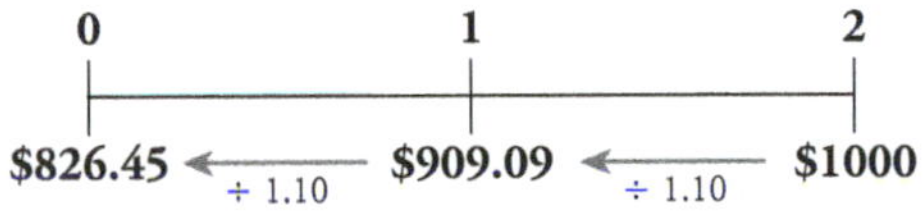

When the interest rate is 10%, all of the cash flows—\$826.45 at date 0, \$909.09 at date 1, and \$1000 at date 2—are equivalent. They represent the same value in different units (different points in time). The arrow points to the left to indicate that the value is being moved backward in time or discounted. Note that the value decreases as we move the cash flow further back.

The value of a future cash flow at an earlier point on the timeline is its present value at the earlier point in time. That is, \$826.45 is the present value at date 0 of \$1000 in two years. Recall from Chapter 3 that the present value is the "do-it-yourself" price to produce a future cash flow. Thus, if we invested \$826.45 today for two years at 10% interest, we would have a future value of \$1000, using the second rule of time travel:

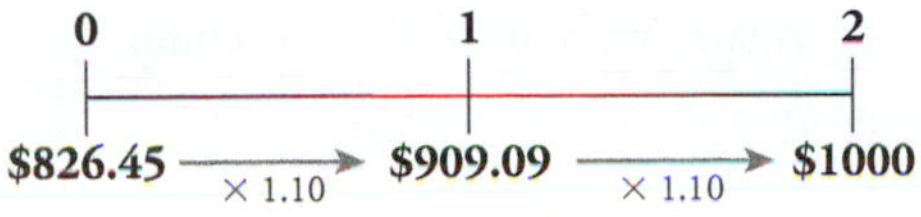

Suppose the \$1000 were three years away and you wanted to compute the present value. Again, if the interest rate is 10%, we have

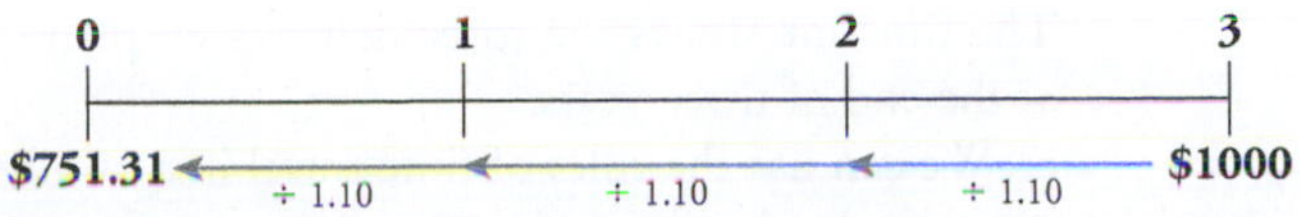

[2]See the appendix to this chapter for an explanation of how to calculate the exact doubling time.

That is, the present value today of a cash flow of $1000 in three years is given by

$$\$1000 \div (1.10) \div (1.10) \div (1.10) = \$1000 \div (1.10)^3 = \$751.31$$

In general, to move a cash flow C backward n periods, we must discount it by the n intervening interest rate factors. If the interest rate r is constant, then

Present Value of a Cash Flow

$$PV = C \div (1+r)^n = \frac{C}{(1+r)^n} \tag{4.2}$$

EXAMPLE 4.3 **Present Value of a Single Future Cash Flow**

Problem

You are considering investing in a savings bond that will pay $15,000 in 10 years. If the competitive market interest rate is fixed at 6% per year, what is the bond worth today?

Solution

The cash flows for this bond are represented by the following timeline:

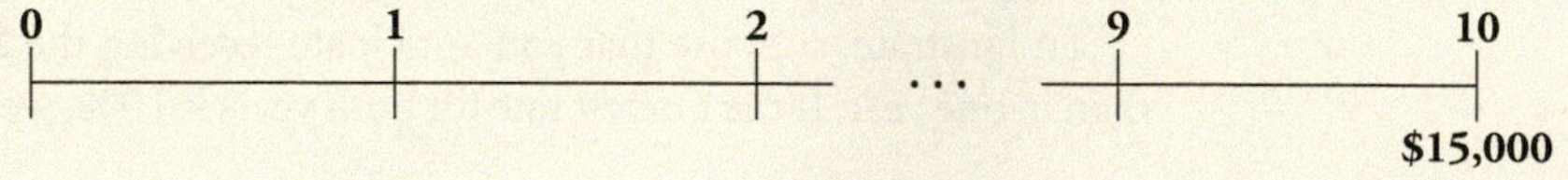

Thus, the bond is worth $15,000 in 10 years. To determine the value today, we compute the present value:

$$PV = \frac{15{,}000}{1.06^{10}} = \$8375.92 \text{ today}$$

The bond is worth much less today than its final payoff because of the time value of money.

Applying the Rules of Time Travel

The rules of time travel allow us to compare and combine cash flows that occur at different points in time. Suppose we plan to save $1000 today, and $1000 at the end of each of the next two years. If we earn a fixed 10% interest rate on our savings, how much will we have three years from today?

Again, we start with a timeline:

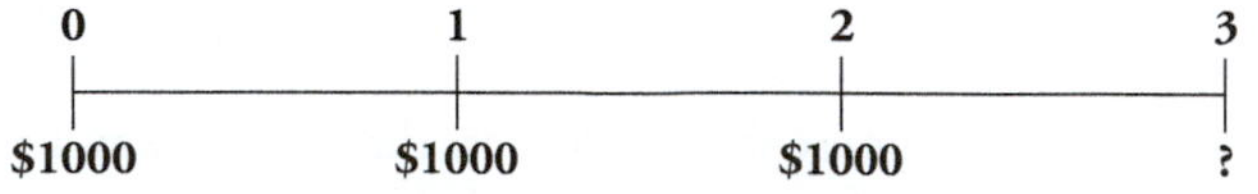

The timeline shows the three deposits we plan to make. We need to compute their value at the end of three years.

We can use the rules of time travel in a number of ways to solve this problem. First, we can take the deposit at date 0 and move it forward to date 1. Because it is then in the same time period as the date 1 deposit, we can combine the two amounts to find out the total in the bank on date 1:

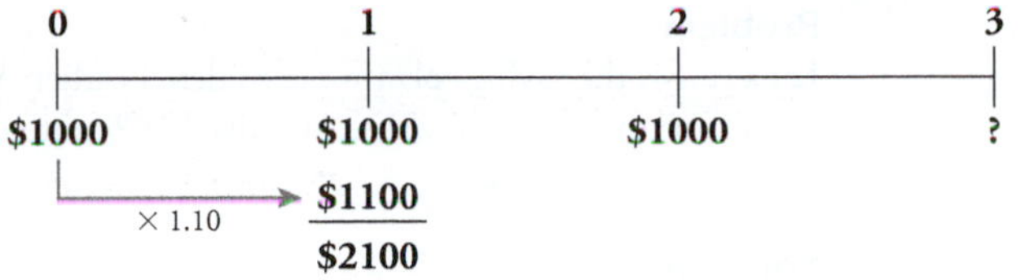

Using the first two rules of time travel, we find that our total savings on date 1 will be $2100. Continuing in this fashion, we can solve the problem as follows:

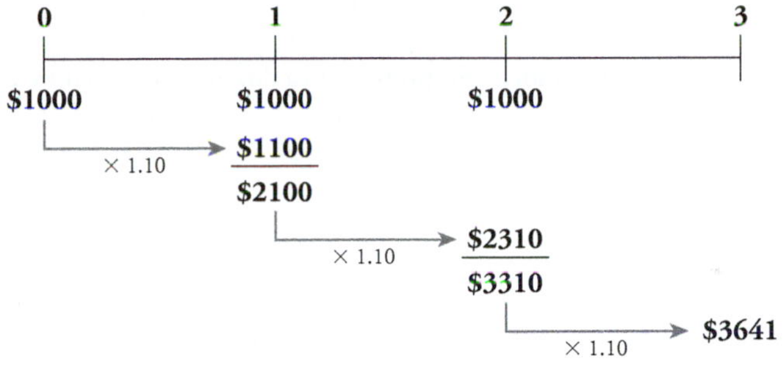

The total amount we will have in the bank at the end of three years is $3641. This amount is the future value of our $1000 savings deposits.

Another approach to the problem is to compute the future value in year 3 of each cash flow separately. Once all three amounts are in year 3 dollars, we can then combine them.

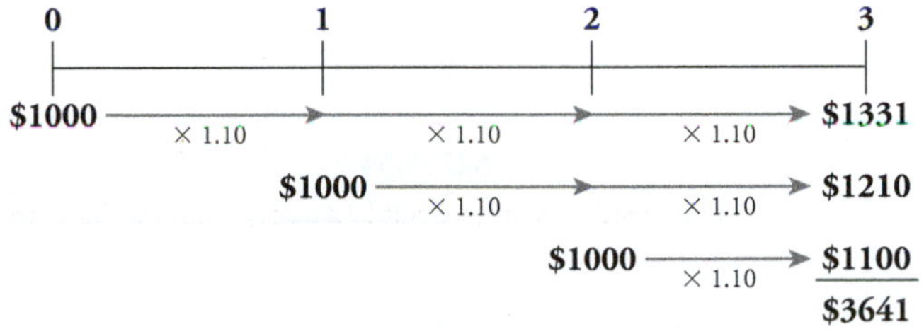

Both calculations give the same future value. As long as we follow the rules, we get the same result. The order in which we apply the rules does not matter. The calculation we choose depends on which is more convenient for the problem at hand. Table 4.1 summarizes the three rules of time travel and their associated formulas.

TABLE 4.1 The Three Rules of Time Travel

Rule 1	Only values at the same point in time can be compared or combined.	
Rule 2	To move a cash flow forward in time, you must compound it.	Future Value of a Cash Flow $FV_n = C \times (1 + r)^n$
Rule 3	To move a cash flow backward in time, you must discount it.	Present Value of a Cash Flow $PV = C \div (1 + r)^n = \dfrac{C}{(1 + r)^n}$

EXAMPLE 4.4 Computing the Future Value

Problem

Let's revisit the savings plan we considered earlier: We plan to save $1000 today and at the end of each of the next two years. At a fixed 10% interest rate, how much will we have in the bank three years from today?

Solution

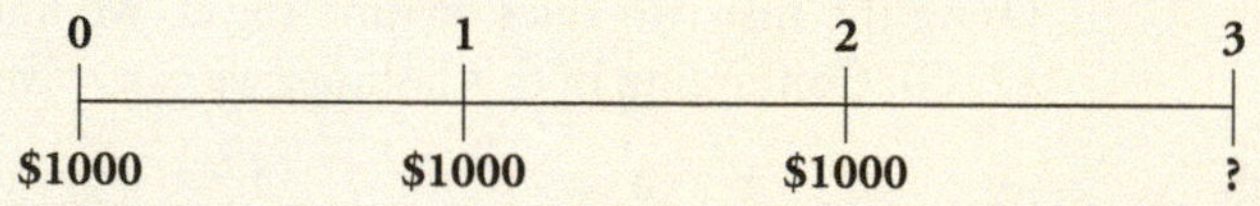

Let's solve this problem in a different way than we did earlier. First, compute the present value of the cash flows. There are several ways to perform this calculation. Here we treat each cash flow separately and then combine the present values.

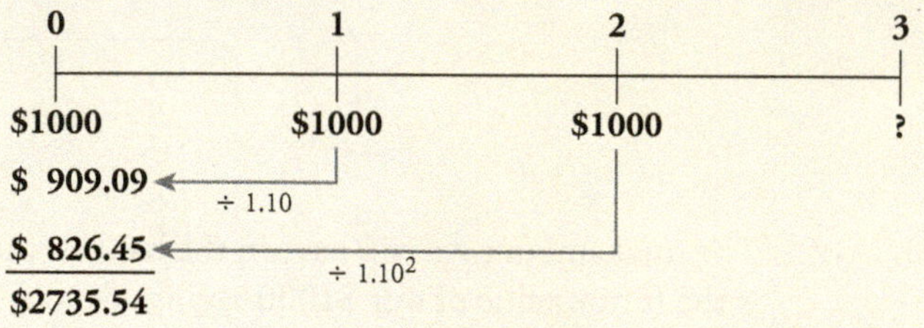

Saving $2735.54 today is equivalent to saving $1000 per year for three years. Now let's compute its future value in year 3:

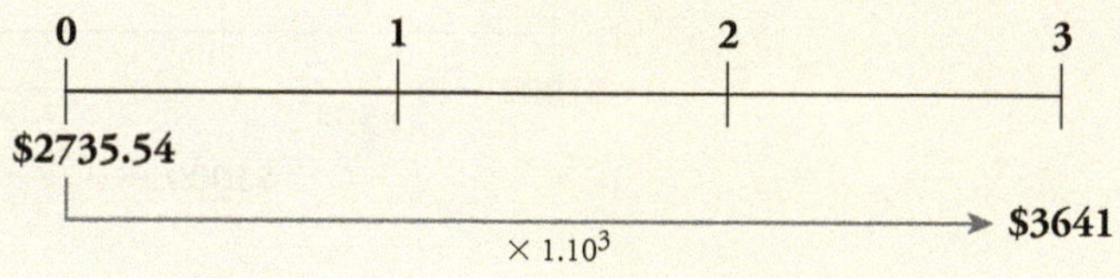

This answer of $3641 is precisely the same result we found earlier. As long as we apply the three rules of time travel, we will always get the correct answer.

CONCEPT CHECK

1. Can you compare or combine cash flows at different times?
2. What is compound interest?
3. How do you move a cash flow backward and forward in time?

4.3 Valuing a Stream of Cash Flows

Most investment opportunities have multiple cash flows that occur at different points in time. In Section 4.2, we applied the rules of time travel to value such cash flows. Now, we formalize this approach by deriving a general formula for valuing a stream of cash flows.

Consider a stream of cash flows: C_0 at date 0, C_1 at date 1, and so on, up to C_N at date N. We represent this cash flow stream on a timeline as follows:

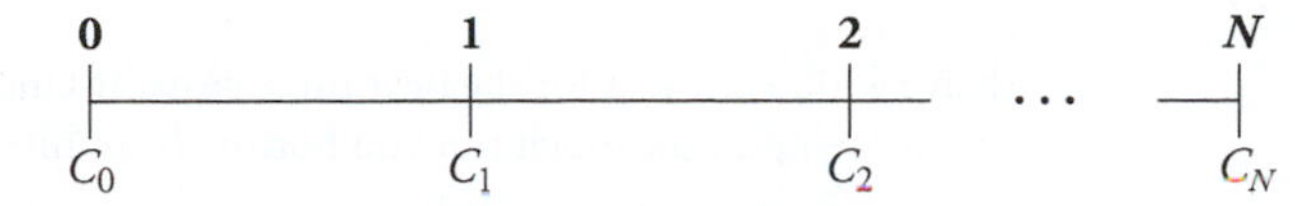

Using the time travel techniques, we compute the present value of this cash flow stream in two steps. First, we compute the present value of each individual cash flow. Then, once the cash flows are in common units of dollars today, we can combine them.

For a given interest rate r, we represent this process on the timeline as follows:

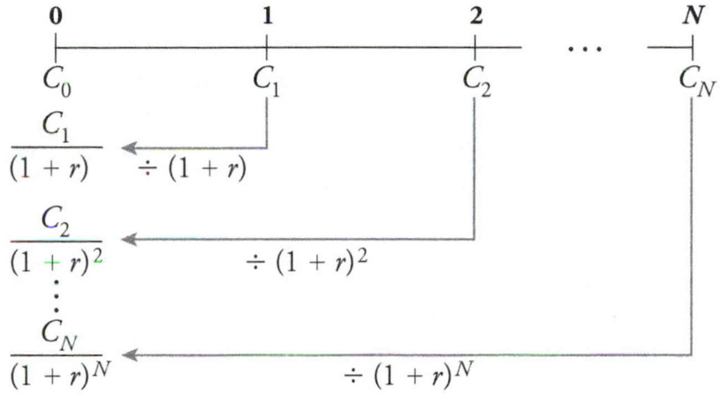

This timeline provides the general formula for the present value of a cash flow stream:

$$PV = C_0 + \frac{C_1}{(1+r)} + \frac{C_2}{(1+r)^2} + \cdots + \frac{C_N}{(1+r)^N} \tag{4.3}$$

We can also write this formula as a summation:

Present Value of a Cash Flow Stream

$$PV = \sum_{n=0}^{N} PV(C_n) = \sum_{n=0}^{N} \frac{C_n}{(1+r)^n} \tag{4.4}$$

The summation sign, Σ, means "sum the individual elements for each date n from 0 to N." Note that $(1 + r)^0 = 1$, so this shorthand matches precisely Eq. 4.3. That is, the present value of the cash flow stream is the sum of the present values of each cash flow. Recall from Chapter 3 how we defined the present value as the dollar amount you would need to invest today to produce the single cash flow in the future. The same idea holds in this context. The present value is the amount you need to invest today to generate the cash flow stream $C_0, C_1, \ldots, C_N$. That is, receiving those cash flows is equivalent to having their present value in the bank today.

EXAMPLE 4.5 Present Value of a Stream of Cash Flows

Problem

You have just graduated and need money to buy a new car. Your rich Uncle Henry will lend you the money so long as you agree to pay him back within four years, and you offer to pay him the rate of interest that he would otherwise get by putting his money in a savings account. Based on your earnings and living expenses, you think you will be able to pay him \$5000 in one year, and then \$8000 each year for the next three years. If Uncle Henry would otherwise earn 6% per year on his savings, how much can you borrow from him?

Solution

The cash flows you can promise Uncle Henry are as follows:

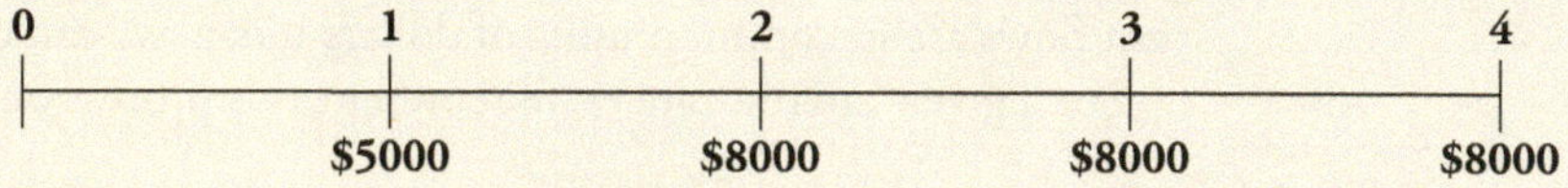

How much money should Uncle Henry be willing to give you today in return for your promise of these payments? He should be willing to give you an amount that is equivalent to these payments in present value terms. This is the amount of money that it would take him to produce these same cash flows, which we calculate as follows:

$$PV = \frac{5000}{1.06} + \frac{8000}{1.06^2} + \frac{8000}{1.06^3} + \frac{8000}{1.06^4}$$

$$= 4716.98 + 7119.97 + 6716.95 + 6336.75$$

$$= 24{,}890.65$$

Thus, Uncle Henry should be willing to lend you \$24,890.65 in exchange for your promised payments. This amount is less than the total you will pay him (\$5000+\$8000+\$8000+\$8000 = \$29,000) due to the time value of money.

Let's verify our answer. If your uncle kept his \$24,890.65 in the bank today earning 6% interest, in four years he would have

$$FV = \$24{,}890.65 \times (1.06)^4 = \$31{,}423.87 \text{ in four years}$$

Now suppose that Uncle Henry gives you the money, and then deposits your payments to him in the bank each year. How much will he have four years from now?

We need to compute the future value of the annual deposits. One way to do so is to compute the bank balance each year:

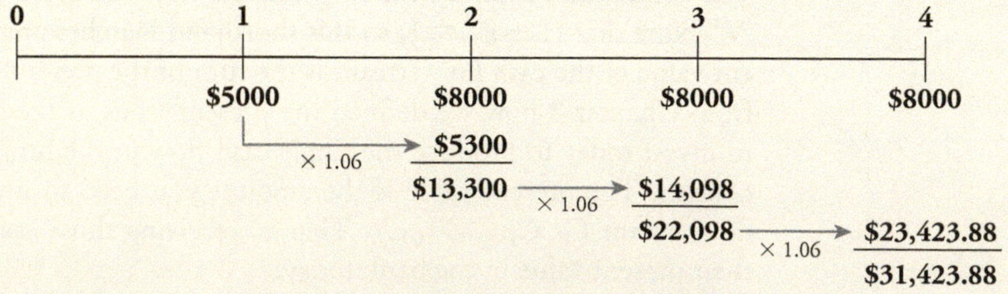

We get the same answer both ways (within a penny, which is because of rounding).

The last section of Example 4.5 illustrates a general point. If you want to compute the future value of a stream of cash flows, you can do it directly (the second approach used in Example 4.5), or you can first compute the present value and then move it to the future (the first approach). Because we obey the laws of time travel in both cases, we get the same result. This principle can be applied more generally to write the following formula for the future value in year n in terms of the present value of a set of cash flows:

Future Value of a Cash Flow Stream with a Present Value of PV

$$FV_n = PV \times (1 + r)^n \tag{4.5}$$

CONCEPT CHECK

1. How do you calculate the present value of a cash flow stream?
2. How do you calculate the future value of a cash flow stream?

4.4 Calculating the Net Present Value

Now that we have established the rules of time travel and determined how to compute present and future values, we are ready to address our central goal: comparing the costs and benefits of a project to evaluate a long-term investment decision. From our first rule of time travel, to compare cash flows we must value them at a common point in time. A convenient choice is to use present values. In particular, we define the **net present value (NPV)** of an investment decision as follows:

$$NPV = PV(\text{benefits}) - PV(\text{costs}) \tag{4.6}$$

In this context, the benefits are the cash inflows and the costs are the cash outflows. We can represent any investment decision on a timeline as a cash flow stream where the cash outflows (investments) are negative cash flows and the inflows are positive cash flows. Thus, the NPV of an investment opportunity is also the *present value* of the stream of cash flows of the opportunity:

$$NPV = PV(\text{benefits}) - PV(\text{costs}) = PV(\text{benefits} - \text{costs})$$

EXAMPLE 4.6 **Net Present Value of an Investment Opportunity**

Problem

You have been offered the following investment opportunity: If you invest \$1000 today, you will receive \$500 at the end of each of the next three years. If you could otherwise earn 10% per year on your money, should you undertake the investment opportunity?

Solution

As always, we start with a timeline. We denote the upfront investment as a negative cash flow (because it is money we need to spend) and the money we receive as a positive cash flow.

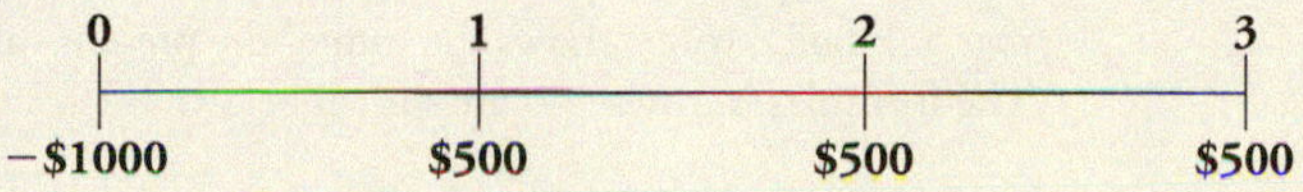

To decide whether we should accept this opportunity, we compute the NPV by computing the present value of the stream:

$$NPV = -1000 + \frac{500}{1.10} + \frac{500}{1.10^2} + \frac{500}{1.10^3} = \$243.43$$

Because the NPV is positive, the benefits exceed the costs and we should make the investment. Indeed, the NPV tells us that taking this opportunity is like getting an extra $243.43 that you can spend today. To illustrate, suppose you borrow $1000 to invest in the opportunity and an extra $243.43 to spend today. How much would you owe on the $1243.43 loan in three years? At 10% interest, the amount you would owe would be

$$FV = (\$1000 + \$243.43) \times (1.10)^3 = \$1655 \text{ in three years}$$

At the same time, the investment opportunity generates cash flows. If you put these cash flows into a bank account, how much will you have saved three years from now? The future value of the savings is

$$FV = (\$500 \times 1.10^2) + (\$500 \times 1.10) + \$500 = \$1655 \text{ in three years}$$

As you see, you can use your bank savings to repay the loan. Taking the opportunity therefore allows you to spend $243.43 today at no extra cost.

In principle, we have explained how to answer the question we posed at the beginning of the chapter: How should financial managers evaluate the cash flows from undertaking a multi-year project like the Chevy Volt? We have shown how to compute the NPV of an investment opportunity such as the Chevy Volt that lasts more than one period. In practice, when the number of cash flows exceeds four or five (as it most likely will), the calculations can become tedious. Fortunately, a number of special cases do not require us to treat each cash flow separately. We derive these shortcuts in Section 4.5.

USING EXCEL

Calculating Present Values in Excel

Calculating NPV

While present and future value calculations can be done with a calculator, it is often convenient to evaluate them using a spreadsheet program. For example, the following spreadsheet calculates the NPV in Example 4.6:

	A	B	C	D	E
1	Discount Rate	10.0%			
2	Period	0	1	2	3
3	Cash Flow C_t	(1,000.0)	500.0	500.0	500.0
4	Discount Factor	1.000	0.909	0.826	0.751
5	PV(C_t)	(1,000.0)	454.5	413.2	375.7
6	**NPV**	**243.43**			

Rows 1–3 provide the key data of the problem, the discount rate, and the cash flow timeline (note we use a blue font to indicate input data, and black for cells that are fixed or calculated). Row 4 then calculates the discount factor, $1/(1 + r)^n$, the present value of a dollar received in year n. We multiply each cash flow by the discount factor to convert it to a present value, shown in row 5. Finally, row 6 shows the sum of the present values of all the cash flows, which is the NPV. The formulas in rows 4–6 are shown below:

	A	B	C	D	E
4	Discount Factor	=1/(1+$B$1)^B2	=1/(1+$B$1)^C2	=1/(1+$B$1)^D2	=1/(1+$B$1)^E2
5	PV(C_t)	=B3*B4	=C3*C4	=D3*D4	=E3*E4
6	**NPV**	**=SUM(B5:E5)**			

Alternatively, we could have computed the entire NPV in one step, using a single (long) formula. We recommend as a best practice that you avoid that temptation and calculate the NPV step by step. Doing so facilitates error checking and makes clear the contribution of each cash flow to the overall NPV.

Excel's NPV Function

Excel also has a built-in NPV function. This function has the format *NPV* (rate, value1, value2, . . .), where "rate" is the interest rate per period used to discount the cash flows, and "value1", "value2", and so on are the cash flows (or ranges of cash flows). Unfortunately, however, the NPV function computes the present value of the cash flows *assuming the first cash flow occurs at date* 1. Therefore, if a project's first cash flow occurs at date 0, we must add it separately. For example, in the spreadsheet above, we would need the formula

$$= \text{B3} + NPV(\text{B1, C3:E3})$$

to calculate the NPV of the indicated cash flows.

Another pitfall with the NPV function is that cash flows that are left blank are treated differently from cash flows that are equal to zero. If the cash flow is left blank, *both the cash flow and the period are ignored*. For example, consider the example below in which the period 2 cash flow has been deleted:

	A	B	C	D	E
1	Discount Rate	10.0%			
2	Period	0	1	2	3
3	Cash Flow C_t	(1,000.0)	500.0		500.0
4	Discount Factor	1.000	0.909	0.826	0.751
5	PV(C_t)	(1,000.0)	454.5	-	375.7
6	**NPV**	**(169.80)**	=SUM(B5:E5)		
7	NPV function	(132.23)	=B3+NPV(B1,C3:E3)		

Our original method provides the correct solution in row 6, whereas the NPV function used in row 7 treats the cash flow in period 3 as though it occurred at period 2, which is clearly not what is intended and is incorrect.

CONCEPT CHECK

1. How do you calculate the net present value of a cash flow stream?
2. What benefit does a firm receive when it accepts a project with a positive NPV?

4.5 Perpetuities and Annuities

The formulas we have developed so far allow us to compute the present or future value of any cash flow stream. In this section, we consider two special types of cash flow streams, *perpetuities* and *annuities*, and we learn shortcuts for valuing them. These shortcuts are possible because the cash flows follow a regular pattern.

Perpetuities

A **perpetuity** is a stream of equal cash flows that occur at regular intervals and last forever. One example is the British government bond called a **consol** (or perpetual bond). Consol bonds promise the owner a fixed cash flow every year, forever.

Here is the timeline for a perpetuity:

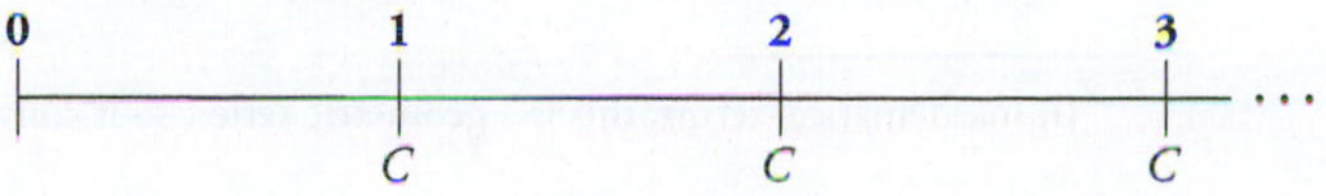

Note from the timeline that the first cash flow does not occur immediately; *it arrives at the end of the first period*. This timing is sometimes referred to as payment *in arrears* and is a standard convention that we adopt throughout this text.

Using the formula for the present value, the present value of a perpetuity with payment C and interest rate r is given by

$$PV = \frac{C}{(1+r)} + \frac{C}{(1+r)^2} + \frac{C}{(1+r)^3} + \cdots = \sum_{n=1}^{\infty} \frac{C}{(1+r)^n}$$

Notice that $C_n = C$ in the present value formula because the cash flow for a perpetuity is constant. Also, because the first cash flow is in one period, $C_0 = 0$.

To find the value of a perpetuity one cash flow at a time would take forever—literally! You might wonder how, even with a shortcut, the sum of an infinite number of positive terms could be finite. The answer is that the cash flows in the future are discounted for an ever-increasing number of periods, so their contribution to the sum eventually becomes negligible.[3]

To derive the shortcut, we calculate the value of a perpetuity by creating our own perpetuity. We can then calculate the present value of the perpetuity because, by the Law of One Price, the value of the perpetuity must be the same as the cost we would incur to create it ourselves. To illustrate, suppose you could invest \$100 in a bank account paying 5% interest per year forever. At the end of one year, you will have \$105 in the bank—your original \$100 plus \$5 in interest. Suppose you withdraw the \$5 interest and reinvest the \$100 for a second year. Again you will have \$105 after one year, and you can withdraw \$5 and reinvest \$100 for another year. By doing this year after year, you can withdraw \$5 every year in perpetuity:

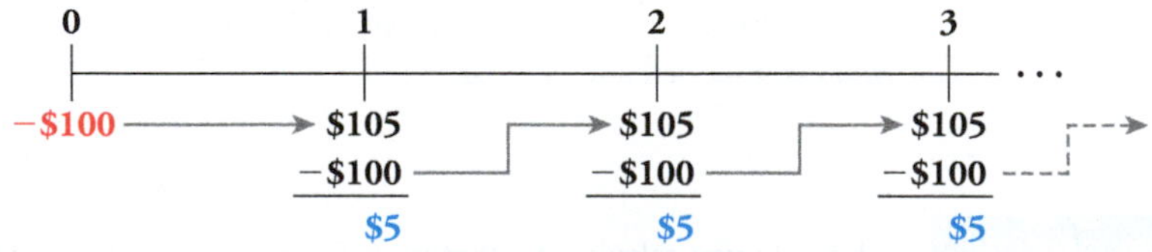

Historical Examples of Perpetuities

Companies sometimes issue bonds that they call perpetuities, but in fact are not really perpetuities. For example, in mid-2010, Europe's largest bank, HSBC, sold \$3.4 billion of "perpetual" bonds that promise investors a fixed amount each year with no maturity date. But while the bonds have no fixed maturity, they are not exactly true perpetuities as HSBC has the right to pay off the bonds after 5 1/2 years. Thus, the bond's payments might not last forever.

Perpetual bonds were some of the first bonds ever issued. The oldest perpetuities that are still making interest payments were issued in 1624 by the *Hoogheemraadschap Lekdijk Bovendams*, a seventeenth-century Dutch water board responsible for upkeep of the local dikes. To verify that these bonds continue to pay interest, two finance professors at Yale University, William Goetzmann and Geert Rouwenhorst, purchased one of these bonds in July 2003, and collected 26 years of back interest. On its issue date in 1648, this bond originally paid interest in Carolus guilders. Over the next 355 years, the currency of payment changed to Flemish pounds, Dutch guilders, and most recently euros. Currently, the bond pays interest of €11.34 annually.

Although the Dutch bonds are the oldest perpetuities still in existence, the first perpetuities date from much earlier times. For example, *cencus agreements* and *rentes*, which were forms of perpetuities and annuities, were issued in the twelfth century in Italy, France, and Spain. They were initially designed to circumvent the usury laws of the Catholic Church: Because they did not require the repayment of principal, in the eyes of the church they were not considered loans.

[3] In mathematical terms, this is a geometric series, so it converges if $r > 0$.

By investing \$100 in the bank today, you can, in effect, create a perpetuity paying \$5 per year. The Law of One Price tells us that the same good must have the same price in every market. Because the bank will "sell" us (allow us to create) the perpetuity for \$100, the present value of the \$5 per year in perpetuity is this "do-it-yourself" cost of \$100.

Now let's generalize this argument. Suppose we invest an amount P in the bank. Every year we can withdraw the interest we have earned, $C = r \times P$, leaving the principal, P, in the bank. The present value of receiving C in perpetuity is therefore the upfront cost $P = C/r$. Therefore,

Present Value of a Perpetuity

$$PV(C \text{ in perpetuity}) = \frac{C}{r} \tag{4.7}$$

In other words, by depositing the amount C/r today, we can withdraw interest of $(C/r) \times r = C$ each period in perpetuity. Thus, the present value of the perpetuity is C/r.

Note the logic of our argument. To determine the present value of a cash flow stream, we computed the "do-it-yourself" cost of creating those same cash flows at the bank. This is an extremely useful and powerful approach—and is much simpler and faster than summing those infinite terms![4]

EXAMPLE 4.7 **Endowing a Perpetuity**

Problem

You want to endow an annual MBA graduation party at your alma mater. You want the event to be a memorable one, so you budget \$30,000 per year forever for the party. If the university earns 8% per year on its investments, and if the first party is in one year's time, how much will you need to donate to endow the party?

Solution

The timeline of the cash flows you want to provide is

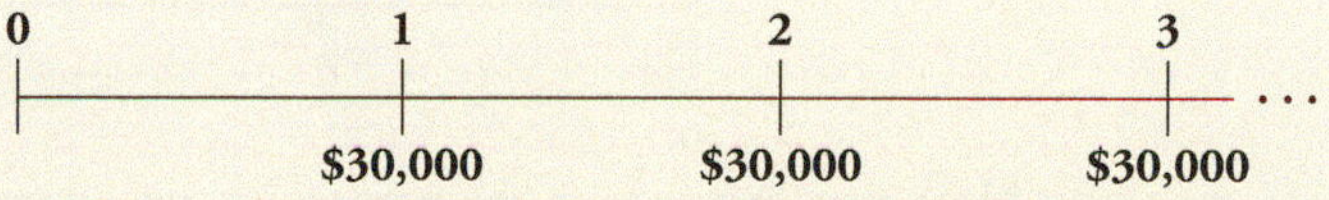

This is a standard perpetuity of \$30,000 per year. The funding you would need to give the university in perpetuity is the present value of this cash flow stream. From the formula,

$$PV = C/r = \$30{,}000/0.08 = \$375{,}000 \text{ today}$$

If you donate \$375,000 today, and if the university invests it at 8% per year forever, then the MBAs will have \$30,000 every year for their graduation party.

[4]Another mathematical derivation of this result exists (see online appendix at www.berkdemarzo.com), but it is less intuitive. This case is a good example of how the Law of One Price can be used to derive useful results.

COMMON MISTAKE Discounting One Too Many Times

The perpetuity formula assumes that the first payment occurs at the end of the first period (at date 1). Sometimes perpetuities have cash flows that start later in the future. In this case, we can adapt the perpetuity formula to compute the present value, but we need to do so carefully to avoid a common mistake.

To illustrate, consider the MBA graduation party described in Example 4.7. Rather than starting immediately, suppose that the first party will be held two years from today (for the current entering class). How would this delay change the amount of the donation required?

Now the timeline looks like this:

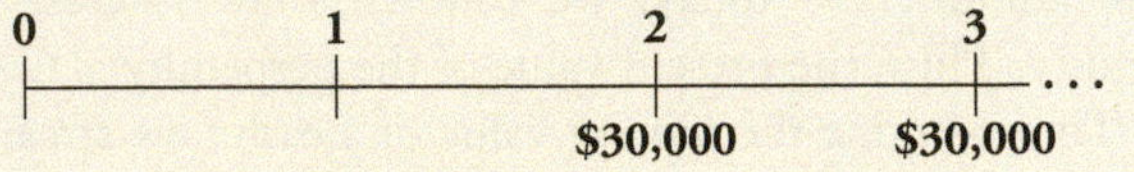

We need to determine the present value of these cash flows, as it tells us the amount of money in the bank needed today to finance the future parties. We cannot apply the perpetuity formula directly, however, because these cash flows are not *exactly* a perpetuity as we defined it. Specifically, the cash flow in the first period is "missing." But consider the situation on date 1—at that point, the first party is one period away and then the cash flows are periodic. From the perspective of date 1, this *is* a perpetuity, and we can apply the formula. From the preceding calculation, we know we need \$375,000 on date 1 to have enough to start the parties on date 2. We rewrite the timeline as follows:

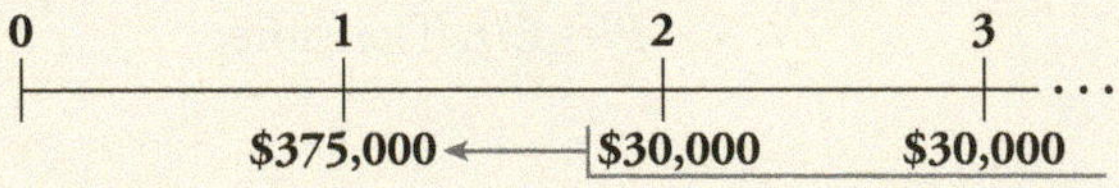

Our goal can now be restated more simply: How much do we need to invest today to have \$375,000 in one year? This is a simple present value calculation:

$$PV = \$375{,}000/1.08 = \$347{,}222 \text{ today}$$

A common mistake is to discount the \$375,000 twice because the first party is in two periods. *Remember—the present value formula for the perpetuity already discounts the cash flows to one period prior to the first cash flow.* Keep in mind that this common mistake may be made with perpetuities, annuities, and all of the other special cases discussed in this section. All of these formulas discount the cash flows to one period prior to the first cash flow.

Annuities

An **annuity** is a stream of N equal cash flows paid at regular intervals. The difference between an annuity and a perpetuity is that an annuity ends after some fixed number of payments. Most car loans, mortgages, and some bonds are annuities. We represent the cash flows of an annuity on a timeline as follows.

Note that just as with the perpetuity, we adopt the convention that the first payment takes place at date 1, one period from today. The present value of an N-period annuity with payment C and interest rate r is

$$PV = \frac{C}{(1+r)} + \frac{C}{(1+r)^2} + \frac{C}{(1+r)^3} + \cdots + \frac{C}{(1+r)^N} = \sum_{n=1}^{N} \frac{C}{(1+r)^n}$$

Present Value of an Annuity. To find a simpler formula, we use the same approach we followed with the perpetuity: find a way to create an annuity. To illustrate, suppose you invest \$100 in a bank account paying 5% interest. At the end of one year, you will have \$105 in the bank—your original \$100 plus \$5 in interest. Using the same strategy as for a perpetuity, suppose you withdraw the \$5 interest and reinvest the \$100 for a second year. Once again you will have \$105 after one year, and you can repeat the process, withdrawing \$5 and reinvesting \$100, every year. For a perpetuity, you left the principal in forever.

Alternatively, you might decide after 20 years to close the account and withdraw the principal. In that case, your cash flows will look like this:

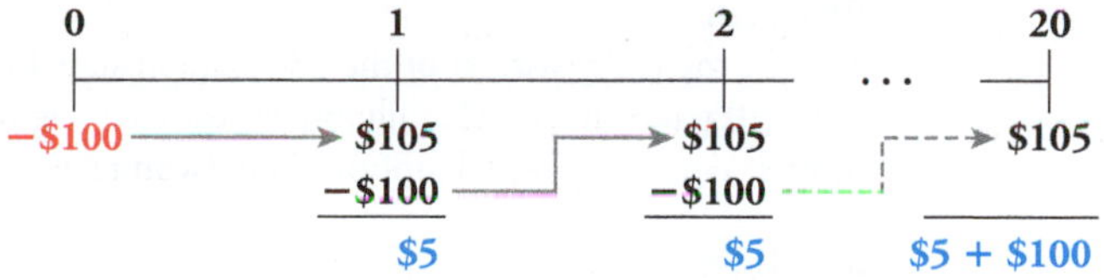

With your initial $100 investment, you have created a 20-year annuity of $5 per year, plus you will receive an extra $100 at the end of 20 years. By the Law of One Price, because it took an initial investment of $100 to create the cash flows on the timeline, the present value of these cash flows is $100, or

$$\$100 = PV(\text{20-year annuity of \$5 per year}) + PV(\$100 \text{ in 20 years})$$

Rearranging terms gives

$$\begin{aligned} PV(\text{20-year annuity of \$5 per year}) &= \$100 - PV(\$100 \text{ in 20 years}) \\ &= 100 - \frac{100}{(1.05)^{20}} = \$62.31 \end{aligned}$$

So the present value of $5 for 20 years is $62.31. Intuitively, the value of the annuity is the initial investment in the bank account minus the present value of the principal that will be left in the account after 20 years.

We can use the same idea to derive the general formula. First, we invest P in the bank, and withdraw only the interest $C = r \times P$ each period. After N periods, we close the account. Thus, for an initial investment of P, we will receive an N-period annuity of C per period, *plus* we will get back our original P at the end. P is the total present value of the two sets of cash flows, or

$$P = PV(\text{annuity of } C \text{ for } N \text{ periods}) + PV(P \text{ in period } N)$$

By rearranging terms, we compute the present value of the annuity:

$$\begin{aligned} PV(\text{annuity of } C \text{ for } N \text{ periods}) &= P - PV(P \text{ in period } N) \\ &= P - \frac{P}{(1+r)^N} = P\left(1 - \frac{1}{(1+r)^N}\right) \end{aligned} \tag{4.8}$$

Recall that the periodic payment C is the interest earned every period; that is, $C = r \times P$ or, equivalently, solving for P provides the upfront cost in terms of C,

$$P = C/r$$

Making this substitution for P, in Eq. 4.8, provides the formula for the present value of an annuity of C for N periods.

Present Value of an Annuity[5]

$$PV(\text{annuity of } C \text{ for } N \text{ periods with interest rate } r) = C \times \frac{1}{r}\left(1 - \frac{1}{(1+r)^N}\right) \tag{4.9}$$

[5] An early derivation of this formula is attributed to the astronomer Edmond Halley ("Of Compound Interest," published after Halley's death by Henry Sherwin, Sherwin's Mathematical Tables, London: W. and J. Mount, T. Page and Son, 1761).

EXAMPLE 4.8 Present Value of an Annuity Due

Problem

You are the lucky winner of the $30 million state lottery. You can take your prize money either as (a) 30 payments of $1 million per year (starting today), or (b) $15 million paid today. If the interest rate is 8%, which option should you take?

Solution

Option (a) provides $30 million of prize money but paid annually. In this case, the cash flows are an annuity in which the first payment begins immediately, sometimes called an **annuity due.**[6]

Because the first payment is paid today, the last payment will occur in 29 years (for a total of 30 payments). We can compute the present value of the final 29 payments as a standard annuity of $1 million per year using the annuity formula:

$$PV(29 \text{ yr annuity of } \$1 \text{ million/yr}) = \$1 \text{ million} \times \frac{1}{.08}\left(1 - \frac{1}{1.08^{29}}\right)$$

$$= \$11.16 \text{ million today}$$

Adding the $1 million we receive upfront, this option has a present value of $12.16 million:

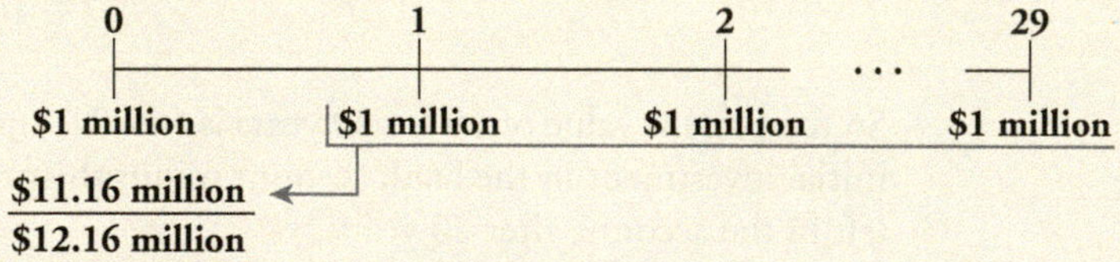

Therefore, the present value of option (a) is only $12.16 million, and so it is more valuable to take option (b) and receive $15 million upfront—even though we receive only half the total cash amount. The difference, of course, is due to the time value of money. To see that (b) really is better, if you have the $15 million today, you can use $1 million immediately and invest the remaining $14 million at an 8% interest rate. This strategy will give you $14 million × 8% = $1.12 million per year in perpetuity! Alternatively, you can spend $15 million − $11.16 million = $3.84 million today, and invest the remaining $11.16 million, which will still allow you to withdraw $1 million each year for the next 29 years before your account is depleted.

Future Value of an Annuity. Now that we have derived a simple formula for the present value of an annuity, it is easy to find a simple formula for the future value. If we want to know the value N years in the future, we move the present value N periods forward on the timeline; that is, we compound the present value for N periods at interest rate r:

Future Value of an Annuity

$$FV(\text{annuity}) = PV \times (1 + r)^N$$

$$= \frac{C}{r}\left(1 - \frac{1}{(1 + r)^N}\right) \times (1 + r)^N$$

$$= C \times \frac{1}{r}\left((1 + r)^N - 1\right) \quad (4.10)$$

This formula is useful if we want to know how a savings account will grow over time. Let's apply this result to evaluate a retirement savings plan.

[6]Throughout the text, we will always use the term "annuity" on its own to mean one that is paid in arrears, starting at the end of the first period.

Formula for an Annuity Due

Although it is straightforward to calculate the value of an annuity due as we did in Example 4.8, it is not uncommon for practitioners to use the following equivalent formula:

PV(annuity due of C for N periods) =

$$C \times \frac{1}{r}\left(1 - \frac{1}{(1+r)^N}\right)(1+r)$$

To understand where this formula comes from, note that one can think of an annuity due as the future value of a regular annuity in one year. To illustrate, compute the present value of the regular annuity in Example 4.8:

PV(30 yr annuity of \$1 million/yr) =

$$\$1 \text{ million} \times \frac{1}{.08}\left(1 - \frac{1}{1.08^{30}}\right) = \$11.26 \text{ million}$$

Then compute the future value in a year: \$11.26 million × 1.08 = \$12.16 million. On a timeline it looks like this:

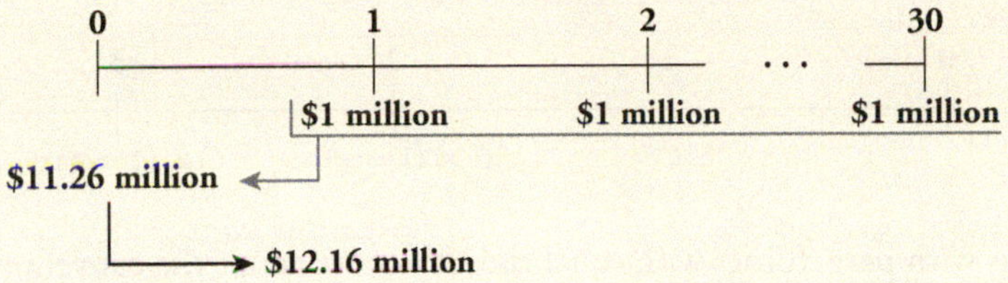

EXAMPLE 4.9 Retirement Savings Plan Annuity

Problem

Ellen is 35 years old, and she has decided it is time to plan seriously for her retirement. At the end of each year until she is 65, she will save \$10,000 in a retirement account. If the account earns 10% per year, how much will Ellen have saved at age 65?

Solution

As always, we begin with a timeline. In this case, it is helpful to keep track of both the dates and Ellen's age:

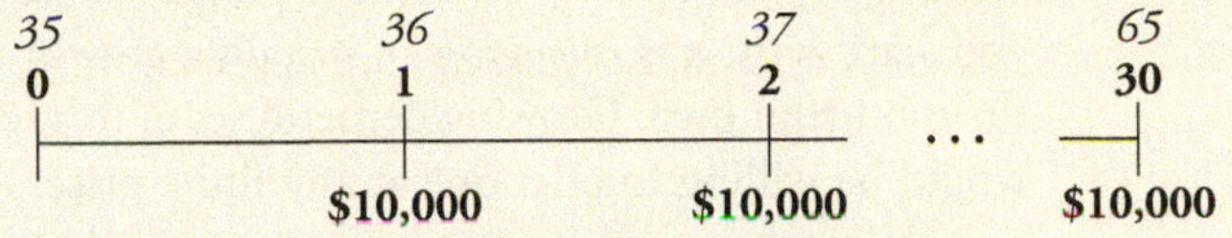

Ellen's savings plan looks like an annuity of \$10,000 per year for 30 years. (*Hint*: It is easy to become confused when you just look at age, rather than at both dates and age. A common error is to think there are only 65 − 36 = 29 payments. Writing down both dates and age avoids this problem.)

To determine the amount Ellen will have in the bank at age 65, we compute the future value of this annuity:

$$FV = \$10{,}000 \times \frac{1}{0.10}(1.10^{30} - 1)$$

$$= \$10{,}000 \times 164.49$$

$$= \$1.645 \text{ million at age 65}$$

Growing Cash Flows

So far, we have considered only cash flow streams that have the same cash flow every period. If, instead, the cash flows are expected to grow at a constant rate in each period, we can also derive a simple formula for the present value of the future stream.

Growing Perpetuity. A **growing perpetuity** is a stream of cash flows that occur at regular intervals and grow at a constant rate forever. For example, a growing perpetuity with a first payment of $100 that grows at a rate of 3% has the following timeline:

0	1	2	3	4	...
	$100	$100 × 1.03 = $103	$103 × 1.03 = $106.09	$106.09 × 1.03 = $109.27	

In general, a growing perpetuity with a first payment C and a growth rate g will have the following series of cash flows:

0	1	2	3	4	...
	C	$C \times (1+g)$	$C \times (1+g)^2$	$C \times (1+g)^3$	

As with perpetuities with equal cash flows, we adopt the convention that the first payment occurs at date 1. Note a second important convention: *The first payment does not include growth.* That is, the first payment is C, even though it is one period away. Similarly, the cash flow in period n undergoes only $n - 1$ periods of growth. Substituting the cash flows from the preceding timeline into the general formula for the present value of a cash flow stream gives

$$PV = \frac{C}{(1+r)} + \frac{C(1+g)}{(1+r)^2} + \frac{C(1+g)^2}{(1+r)^3} + \cdots = \sum_{n=1}^{\infty} \frac{C(1+g)^{n-1}}{(1+r)^n}$$

Suppose $g \geq r$. Then the cash flows grow even faster than they are discounted; each term in the sum gets larger, rather than smaller. In this case, the sum is infinite! What does an infinite present value mean? Remember that the present value is the "do-it-yourself" cost of creating the cash flows. An infinite present value means that no matter how much money you start with, it is *impossible* to sustain a growth rate of g *forever* and reproduce those cash flows on your own. Growing perpetuities of this sort cannot exist in practice because no one would be willing to offer one at any finite price. A promise to pay an amount that forever grew faster than the interest rate is also unlikely to be kept (or believed by any savvy buyer).

The only viable growing perpetuities are those where the perpetual growth rate is less than the interest rate, so that each successive term in the sum is less than the previous term and the overall sum is finite. Consequently, we assume that $g < r$ for a growing perpetuity.

To derive the formula for the present value of a growing perpetuity, we follow the same logic used for a regular perpetuity: Compute the amount you would need to deposit today to create the perpetuity yourself. In the case of a regular perpetuity, we created a constant payment forever by withdrawing the interest earned each year and reinvesting the principal. To increase the amount we can withdraw each year, the principal that we reinvest each year must grow. Therefore, we withdraw less than the full amount of interest earned each period, using the remaining interest to increase our principal.

Let's consider a specific case. Suppose you want to create a perpetuity with cash flows that grow by 2% per year, and you invest $100 in a bank account that pays 5% interest. At the end of one year, you will have $105 in the bank—your original $100 plus $5 in interest. If you withdraw only $3, you will have $102 to reinvest—2% more than the amount you had initially. This amount will then grow to $102 × 1.05 = $107.10 in the following year, and you can withdraw $3 × 1.02 = $3.06, which will leave you with principal of \$107.10 − \$3.06 = \$104.04. Note that \$102 × 1.02 = \$104.04. That is, both the amount you withdraw and the principal you reinvest grow by 2% each year. On a timeline, these cash flows look like this:

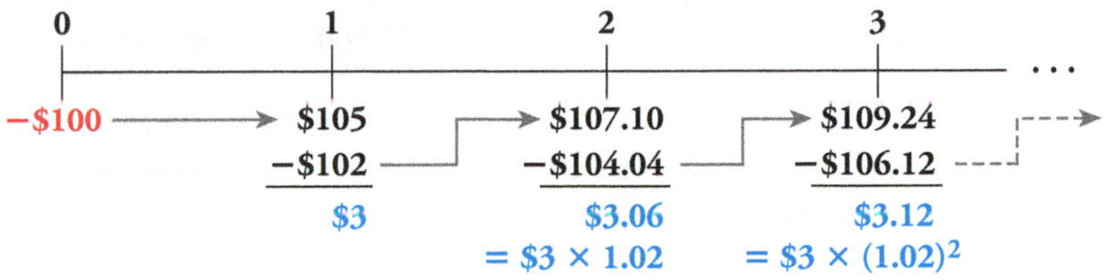

By following this strategy, you have created a growing perpetuity that starts at \$3 and grows 2% per year. This growing perpetuity must have a present value equal to the cost of \$100.

We can generalize this argument. In the case of an equal-payment perpetuity, we deposited an amount P in the bank and withdrew the interest each year. Because we always left the principal P in the bank, we could maintain this pattern forever. If we want to increase the amount we withdraw from the bank each year by g, then the principal in the bank will have to grow by the same factor g. So, instead of withdrawing all of the interest rP, we leave gP in the bank in addition to our original principal P, and only withdraw $C = (r - g)P$. Solving this last equation for P, the initial amount deposited in the bank account, gives the present value of a growing perpetuity with initial cash flow C:

Present Value of a Growing Perpetuity

$$PV(\text{growing perpetuity}) = \frac{C}{r - g} \tag{4.11}$$

To understand the formula for a growing perpetuity intuitively, start with the formula for a perpetuity. In the earlier case, you had to put enough money in the bank to ensure that the interest earned matched the cash flows of the regular perpetuity. In the case of a growing perpetuity, you need to put more than that amount in the bank because you have to finance the growth in the cash flows. How much more? If the bank pays interest at a rate of 5%, then all that is left to take out if you want to make sure the principal grows 2% per year is the difference: 5% − 2% = 3%. So instead of the present value of the perpetuity being the first cash flow divided by the interest rate, it is now the first cash flow divided by the *difference* between the interest rate and the growth rate.

EXAMPLE 4.10 Endowing a Growing Perpetuity

Problem

In Example 4.7, you planned to donate money to your alma mater to fund an annual \$30,000 MBA graduation party. Given an interest rate of 8% per year, the required donation was the present value of

$$PV = \$30{,}000/0.08 = \$375{,}000 \text{ today}$$

Before accepting the money, however, the MBA student association has asked that you increase the donation to account for the effect of inflation on the cost of the party in future years. Although \$30,000 is adequate for next year's party, the students estimate that the party's cost will rise by 4% per year thereafter. To satisfy their request, how much do you need to donate now?

Solution

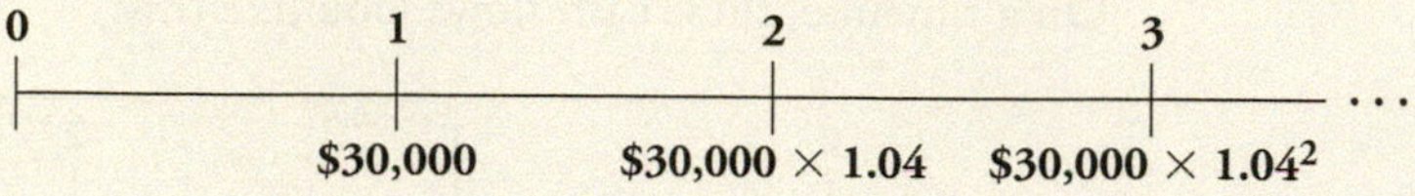

The cost of the party next year is \$30,000, and the cost then increases 4% per year forever. From the timeline, we recognize the form of a growing perpetuity. To finance the growing cost, you need to provide the present value today of

$$PV = \$30{,}000/(0.08 - 0.04) = \$750{,}000 \text{ today}$$

You need to double the size of your gift!

Growing Annuity. A **growing annuity** is a stream of N growing cash flows, paid at regular intervals. It is a growing perpetuity that eventually comes to an end. The following timeline shows a growing annuity with initial cash flow C, growing at rate g every period until period N:

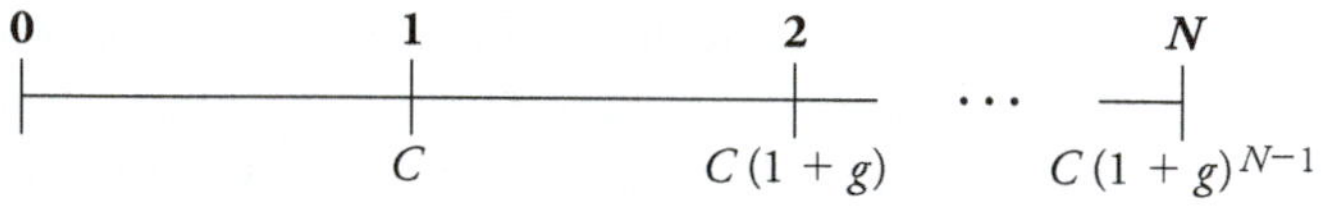

The conventions used earlier still apply: (1) The first cash flow arrives at the end of the first period, and (2) the first cash flow does not grow. The last cash flow therefore reflects only $N - 1$ periods of growth.

The present value of an N-period growing annuity with initial cash flow C, growth rate g, and interest rate r is given by

Present Value of a Growing Annuity

$$PV = C \times \frac{1}{r-g}\left(1 - \left(\frac{1+g}{1+r}\right)^{N}\right) \tag{4.12}$$

Because the annuity has only a finite number of terms, Eq. 4.12 also works when $g > r$.[7] The process of deriving this simple expression for the present value of a growing annuity is the same as for a regular annuity. Interested readers may consult the online appendix at www.berkdemarzo.com for details.

EXAMPLE 4.11 Retirement Savings with a Growing Annuity

Problem

In Example 4.9, Ellen considered saving \$10,000 per year for her retirement. Although \$10,000 is the most she can save in the first year, she expects her salary to increase each year so that she will be able to increase her savings by 5% per year. With this plan, if she earns 10% per year on her savings, how much will Ellen have saved at age 65?

Solution

Her new savings plan is represented by the following timeline:

---

[7] Eq. 4.12 does not work for $g = r$. But in that case, growth and discounting cancel out, and the present value is equivalent to receiving all the cash flows at date 1: $PV = C \times N/(1 + r)$

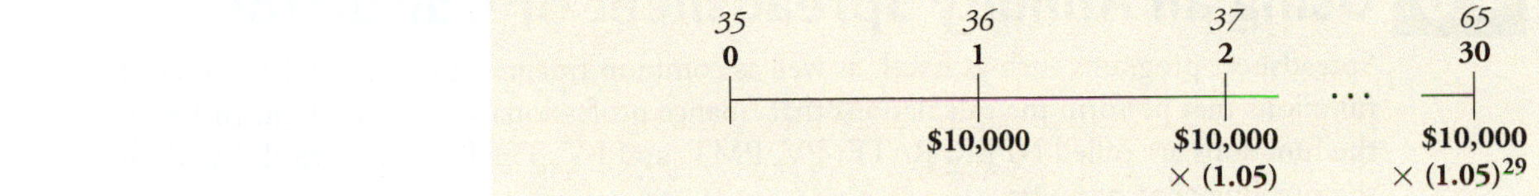

This example involves a 30-year growing annuity, with a growth rate of 5%, and an initial cash flow of $10,000. The present value of this growing annuity is given by

$$PV = \$10{,}000 \times \frac{1}{0.10 - 0.05}\left(1 - \left(\frac{1.05}{1.10}\right)^{30}\right)$$
$$= \$10{,}000 \times 15.0463$$
$$= \$150{,}463 \text{ today}$$

Ellen's proposed savings plan is equivalent to having $150,463 in the bank *today*. To determine the amount she will have at age 65, we need to move this amount forward 30 years:

$$FV = \$150{,}463 \times 1.10^{30}$$
$$= \$2.625 \text{ million in 30 years}$$

Ellen will have saved $2.625 million at age 65 using the new savings plan. This sum is almost $1 million more than she had without the additional annual increases in savings.

The formula for the growing annuity encompasses all of the other formulas in this section. To see how to derive the other formulas from this one, first consider a growing perpetuity. It is a growing annuity with $N = \infty$. If $g < r$, then

$$\frac{1+g}{1+r} < 1,$$

and so

$$\left(\frac{1+g}{1+r}\right)^N \to 0 \quad \text{as} \quad N \to \infty .$$

The formula for a growing annuity when $N = \infty$ therefore becomes

$$PV = \frac{C}{r-g}\left(1 - \left(\frac{1+g}{1+r}\right)^N\right) = \frac{C}{r-g}(1-0) = \frac{C}{r-g},$$

which is the formula for a growing perpetuity. The formulas for a regular annuity and perpetuity also follow from the formula if we let the growth rate $g = 0$. So, if you remember the growing annuity formula, you've got them all!

CONCEPT CHECK

1. How do you calculate the present value of a
   a. Perpetuity?
   b. Annuity?
   c. Growing perpetuity?
   d. Growing annuity?
2. How are the formulas for the present value of a perpetuity, annuity, growing perpetuity, and growing annuity related?

4.6 Using an Annuity Spreadsheet or Calculator

Spreadsheet programs such as Excel, as well as common financial calculators, have a set of functions that perform the calculations that finance professionals do most often. In Excel, the functions are called NPER, RATE, PV, PMT, and FV. The functions are all based on the timeline of an annuity:

The interest rate used to discount these cash flows is denoted by *RATE*. Thus, there are a total of five variables: *NPER*, *RATE*, *PV*, *PMT*, and *FV*. Each function takes four of these variables as inputs and returns the value of the fifth one that ensures that the NPV of the cash flows is zero. That is, the functions all solve the problem

$$NPV = PV + PMT \times \frac{1}{RATE}\left(1 - \frac{1}{(1 + RATE)^{NPER}}\right) + \frac{FV}{(1 + RATE)^{NPER}} = 0 \quad (4.13)$$

In words, the present value of the annuity payments *PMT*, plus the present value of the final payment *FV*, plus the initial amount *PV*, has a net present value of zero. Let's tackle a few examples.

EXAMPLE 4.12 Computing the Future Value in Excel

Problem

Suppose you plan to invest $20,000 in an account paying 8% interest. How much will you have in the account in 15 years?

Solution

We represent this problem with the following timeline:

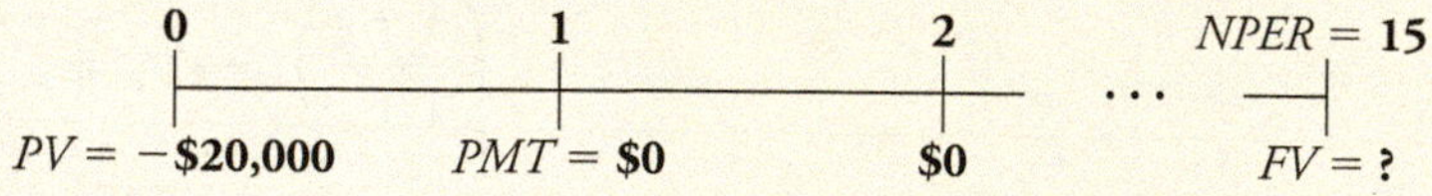

To compute the solution, we enter the four variables we know ($NPER = 15$, $RATE = 8\%$, $PV = -20{,}000$, $PMT = 0$) and solve for the one we want to determine (FV) using the Excel function *FV(RATE, NPER, PMT, PV)*. The spreadsheet here calculates a future value of $63,443.

	NPER	RATE	PV	PMT	FV	Excel Formula
Given	15	8.00%	−20,000	0		
Solve for FV					63,443	=FV(0.08,15,0,−20000)

Note that we entered *PV* as a negative number (the amount we are putting *into* the bank), and *FV* is shown as a positive number (the amount we can take *out* of the bank). It is important to use signs correctly to indicate the direction in which the money is flowing when using the spreadsheet functions.

To check the result, we can solve this problem directly:

$$FV = \$20{,}000 \times 1.08^{15} = \$63{,}443$$

The Excel spreadsheet in Example 4.12, which is available from MyFinanceLab or from www.berkdemarzo.com, is set up to allow you to compute any one of the five variables. We refer to this spreadsheet as the **annuity spreadsheet.** You simply enter the four input variables on the top line and leave the variable you want to compute blank. The spreadsheet computes the fifth variable and displays the answer on the bottom line. The spreadsheet also displays the Excel function that is used to get the answers. Let's work through a more complicated example that illustrates the convenience of the annuity spreadsheet.

EXAMPLE 4.13 Using the Annuity Spreadsheet

Problem

Suppose that you invest $20,000 in an account paying 8% interest. You plan to withdraw $2000 at the end of each year for 15 years. How much money will be left in the account after 15 years?

Solution

Again, we start with the timeline showing our initial deposit and subsequent withdrawals:

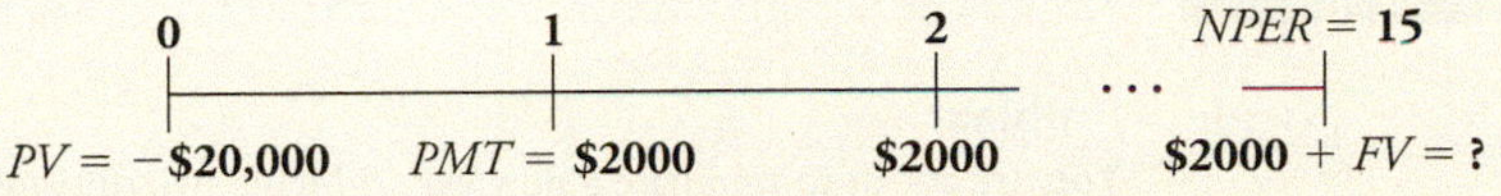

Note that *PV* is negative (money *into* the bank), while *PMT* is positive (money *out* of the bank). We solve for the final balance in the account, *FV*, using the annuity spreadsheet:

	NPER	RATE	PV	PMT	FV	Excel Formula
Given	15	8.00%	−20,000	2000		
Solve for FV					**9139**	=FV(0.08,15,2000,−20000)

We will have $9139 left in the bank after 15 years.

We can also compute this solution directly. One approach is to think of the deposit and the withdrawals as being separate accounts. In the account with the $20,000 deposit, our savings will grow to $63,443 in 15 years, as we computed in Example 4.12. Using the formula for the future value of an annuity, if we borrow $2000 per year for 15 years at 8%, at the end our debt will have grown to

$$\$2000 \times \frac{1}{0.08}(1.08^{15} - 1) = \$54,304$$

After paying off our debt, we will have $63,443 − $54,304 = $9139 remaining after 15 years.

You can also use a handheld financial calculator to do the same calculations. The calculators work in much the same way as the annuity spreadsheet. You enter any four of the five variables, and the calculator calculates the fifth variable.

CONCEPT CHECK

1. What tools can you use to simplify the calculation of present values?
2. What is the process for using the annuity spreadsheet?

4.7 Non-Annual Cash Flows

Until now, we have only considered cash flow streams that occur at annual intervals. Do the same tools apply if the cash flows occur at another interval, say monthly? The answer is yes: Everything we have learned about annual cash flow streams applies to monthly cash flow streams so long as:

1. The interest rate is specified as a monthly rate.
2. The number of periods is expressed in months.

For example, suppose you have a credit card that charges 2% interest per month. If you have a $1000 balance on the card today, and make no payments for six months, your future balance after six months will be

$$FV = C \times (1 + r)^n = \$1000 \times (1.02)^6 = \$1126.16$$

We apply the future value formula exactly as before, but with r equal to the *monthly* interest rate and n equal to the number of *months*.

The same logic applies to annuities, as in the following example.

EXAMPLE 4.14 Evaluating an Annuity with Monthly Cash Flows

Problem

You are about to purchase a new car and have two options to pay for it. You can pay $20,000 in cash immediately, or you can get a loan that requires you to pay $500 each month for the next 48 months (four years). If the monthly interest rate you earn on your cash is 0.5%, which option should you take?

Solution

Let's start by writing down the timeline of the loan payments:

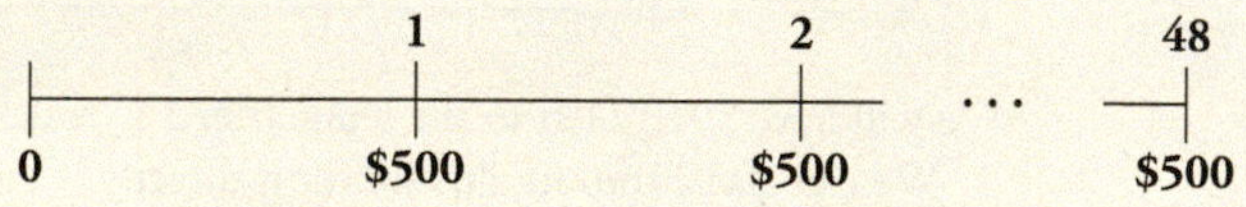

The timeline shows that the loan is a 48-period annuity. Using the annuity formula the present value is

$$PV(\text{48-period annuity of } \$500) = \$500 \times \frac{1}{0.005}\left(1 - \frac{1}{1.005^{48}}\right)$$
$$= \$21{,}290$$

Alternatively, we may use the annuity spreadsheet to solve the problem:

	NPER	RATE	PV	PMT	FV	Excel Formula
Given	48	0.50%		500	0	
Solve for PV			(21,290)			=PV(0.005,48,500,0)

Thus, taking the loan is equivalent to paying $21,290 today, which is costlier than paying cash. You should pay cash for the car.

CONCEPT CHECK

1. Do the present and future value formulas depend upon the cash flows occurring at annual intervals?
2. When cash flows occur at a non-annual interval, what interest rate must you use? What number of periods must you use?

4.8 Solving for the Cash Payments

So far, we have calculated the present value or future value of a stream of cash flows. Sometimes, however, we know the present value or future value, but do not know the cash flows. The best example is a loan—you know how much you want to borrow (the present value) and you know the interest rate, but you do not know how much you need to repay each year. Suppose you are opening a business that requires an initial investment of $100,000. Your bank manager has agreed to lend you this money. The terms of the loan state that you will make equal annual payments for the next 10 years and will pay an interest rate of 8% with the first payment due one year from today. What is your annual payment?

From the bank's perspective, the timeline looks like this:

The bank will give you $100,000 today in exchange for 10 equal payments over the next decade. You need to determine the size of the payment C that the bank will require. For the bank to be willing to lend you $100,000, the loan cash flows must have a present value of $100,000 when evaluated at the bank's interest rate of 8%. That is,

$$100{,}000 = PV(\text{10-year annuity of } C \text{ per year, evaluated at the loan rate})$$

Using the formula for the present value of an annuity,

$$100{,}000 = C \times \frac{1}{0.08}\left(1 - \frac{1}{1.08^{10}}\right) = C \times 6.71$$

Solving this equation for C gives

$$C = \frac{100{,}000}{6.71} = \$14{,}903$$

You will be required to make 10 annual payments of $14,903 in exchange for $100,000 today.

We can also solve this problem with the annuity spreadsheet:

	NPER	RATE	PV	PMT	FV	Excel Formula
Given	10	8.00%	100,000		0	
Solve for PMT				−14,903		=PMT(0.08,10,100000,0)

In general, when solving for a loan payment, think of the amount borrowed (the loan principal) as the present value of the payments when evaluated at the loan rate. If the payments of the loan are an annuity, we can solve for the payment of the loan by inverting the annuity formula. Writing this procedure formally, we begin with the timeline (from the bank's perspective) for a loan with principal P, requiring N periodic payments of C and interest rate r:

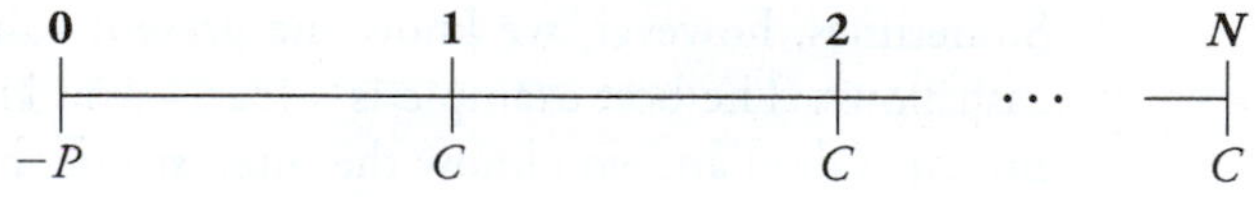

Setting the present value of the payments equal to the principal,

$$P = PV(\text{annuity of } C \text{ for } N \text{ periods}) = C \times \frac{1}{r}\left(1 - \frac{1}{(1+r)^N}\right)$$

Solving this equation for C gives the general formula for the loan payment in terms of the outstanding principal (amount borrowed), P; interest rate, r; and number of payments, N:

Loan or Annuity Payment

$$C = \frac{P}{\frac{1}{r}\left(1 - \frac{1}{(1+r)^N}\right)} \tag{4.14}$$

Note that the cash flow for a perpetuity is simply $C = rP$. Rewriting (4.14) as $C = rP/(1 - 1/(1+r)^N)$, we can see that the payment for an annuity always exceeds the payment of the equivalent value perpetuity, which makes sense because the annuity will eventually end.

EXAMPLE 4.15 Computing a Loan Payment

Problem

Your biotech firm plans to buy a new DNA sequencer for \$500,000. The seller requires that you pay 20% of the purchase price as a down payment, but is willing to finance the remainder by offering a 48-month loan with equal monthly payments and an interest rate of 0.5% per month. What is the monthly loan payment?

Solution

Given a down payment of 20% × \$500,000 = \$100,000, your loan amount is \$400,000. We start with the timeline (from the seller's perspective), where each period represents one month:

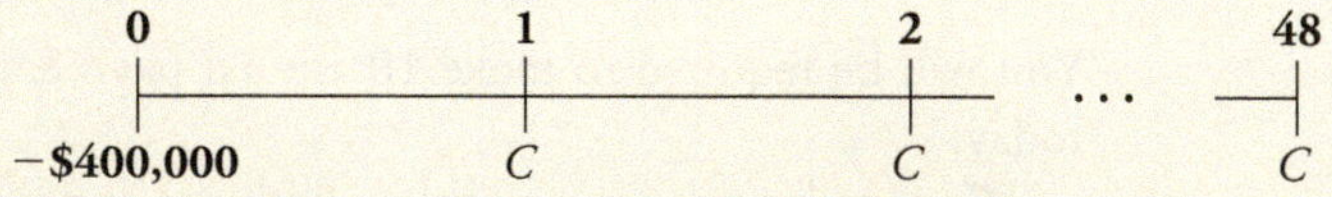

Using Eq. 4.14, we can solve for the loan payment, C, as follows:

$$C = \frac{P}{\frac{1}{r}\left(1 - \frac{1}{(1+r)^N}\right)} = \frac{400{,}000}{\frac{1}{0.005}\left(1 - \frac{1}{(1.005)^{48}}\right)}$$

$$= \$9394$$

Using the annuity spreadsheet:

	NPER	RATE	PV	PMT	FV	Excel Formula
Given	48	0.50%	–400,000		0	
Solve for PMT				**9,394**		=PMT(0.005,48,–400000,0)

Your firm will need to pay $9394 each month to repay the loan.

We can use this same idea to solve for the cash flows when we know the future value rather than the present value. As an example, suppose you have just had a child. You decide to be prudent and start saving this year for her college education. You would like to have $60,000 saved by the time your daughter is 18 years old. If you can earn 7% per year on your savings, how much do you need to save each year to meet your goal?

The timeline for this example is

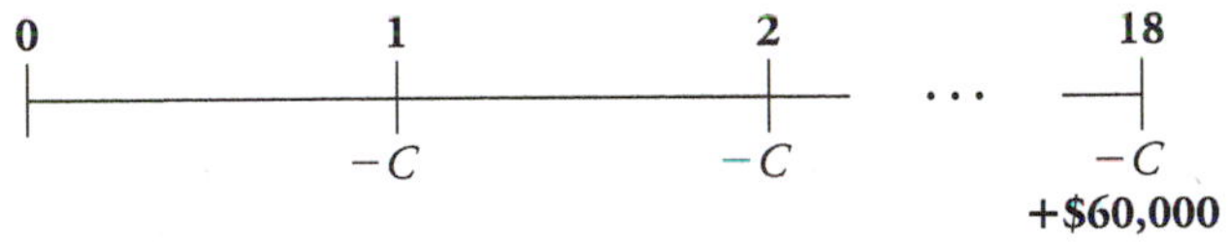

That is, you plan to save some amount C per year, and then withdraw $60,000 from the bank in 18 years. Therefore, we need to find the annuity payment that has a future value of $60,000 in 18 years. Using the formula for the future value of an annuity from Eq. 4.10,

$$60{,}000 = FV(\text{annuity}) = C \times \frac{1}{0.07}(1.07^{18} - 1) = C \times 34$$

Therefore, $C = \dfrac{60{,}000}{34} = \$1765$. So you need to save $1765 per year. If you do, then at a 7% interest rate, your savings will grow to $60,000 by the time your child is 18 years old.

Now let's solve this problem with the annuity spreadsheet:

	NPER	RATE	PV	PMT	FV	Excel Formula
Given	18	7.00%	0		60,000	
Solve for PMT				**−1765**		=PMT(0.07,18,0,60000)

Once again, we find that we need to save $1765 for 18 years to accumulate $60,000.

CONCEPT CHECK

1. How can we solve for the required annuity payment for a loan?
2. How can we determine the required amount to save each year to reach a savings goal?

4.9 The Internal Rate of Return

In some situations, you know the present value and cash flows of an investment opportunity but you do not know the interest rate that equates them. This interest rate is called the **internal rate of return (IRR)**, defined as the interest rate that sets the net present value of the cash flows equal to zero.

For example, suppose that you have an investment opportunity that requires a $1000 investment today and will have a $2000 payoff in six years. On a timeline,

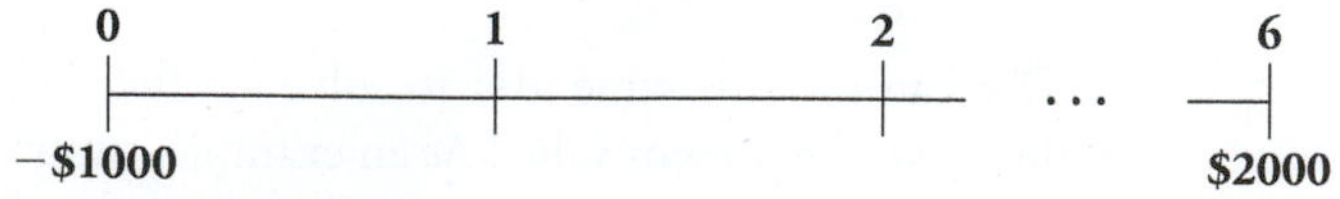

One way to analyze this investment is to ask the question: What interest rate, r, would you need so that the NPV of this investment is zero?

$$NPV = -1000 + \frac{2000}{(1+r)^6} = 0$$

Rearranging gives

$$1000 \times (1+r)^6 = 2000$$

That is, r is the interest rate you would need to earn on your $1000 to have a future value of $2000 in six years. We can solve for r as follows:

$$1 + r = \left(\frac{2000}{1000}\right)^{1/6} = 1.1225$$

or $r = 12.25\%$. This rate is the IRR of this investment opportunity. Making this investment is like earning 12.25% per year on your money for six years.

When there are just two cash flows, as in the preceding example, it is easy to compute the IRR. Consider the general case in which you invest an amount P today, and receive FV in N years. Then the IRR satisfies the equation $P \times (1 + IRR)^N = FV$, which implies

$$IRR \text{ with two cash flows} = (FV/P)^{1/N} - 1 \tag{4.15}$$

Note in the formula that we take the total return of the investment over N years, FV/P, and convert it to an equivalent one-year return by raising it to the power $1/N$. Because we are just comparing two cashflows, the IRR calculation in Equation 4.15 is equivalent to computing the **compound annual growth rate** (or **CAGR**) of the cash flow.

Another case for which the IRR is easy to calculate is a perpetuity, as we demonstrate in the next example.

EXAMPLE 4.16 Computing the IRR for a Perpetuity

Problem

Jessica has just graduated with her MBA. Rather than take the job she was offered at a prestigious investment bank—Baker, Bellingham, and Botts—she has decided to go into business for herself. She believes that her business will require an initial investment of $1 million. After that, it will generate a cash flow of $100,000 at the end of one year, and this amount will grow by 4% per year thereafter. What is the IRR of this investment opportunity?

Solution

The timeline is

0	1	2	...
−\$1,000,000	\$100,000	\$100,000 × 1.04	

The timeline shows that the future cash flows are a growing perpetuity with a growth rate of 4%. Recall from Eq. 4.11 that the PV of a growing perpetuity is $C/(r - g)$. Thus, the NPV of this investment would equal zero if

$$1{,}000{,}000 = \frac{100{,}000}{r - 0.04}$$

We can solve this equation for r

$$r = \frac{100{,}000}{1{,}000{,}000} + 0.04 = 0.14$$

So, the IRR on this investment is 14%.

More generally, if we invest P and receive a perpetuity with initial cash flow C and growth rate g, we can use the growing perpetuity formula to determine

$$IRR \text{ of growing perpetuity} = (C/P) + g \tag{4.16}$$

Now let's consider a more sophisticated example. Suppose your firm needs to purchase a new forklift. The dealer gives you two options: (1) a price for the forklift if you pay cash and (2) the annual payments if you take out a loan from the dealer. To evaluate the loan that the dealer is offering you, you will want to compare the rate on the loan with the rate that your bank is willing to offer you. Given the loan payment that the dealer quotes, how do you compute the interest rate charged by the dealer?

In this case, we need to compute the IRR of the dealer's loan. Suppose the cash price of the forklift is \$40,000, and the dealer offers financing with no down payment and four annual payments of \$15,000. This loan has the following timeline:

0	1	2	3	4
\$40,000	−\$15,000	−\$15,000	−\$15,000	−\$15,000

From the timeline it is clear that the loan is a four-year annuity with a payment of \$15,000 per year and a present value of \$40,000. Setting the NPV of the cash flows equal to zero requires that the present value of the payments equals the purchase price:

$$40{,}000 = 15{,}000 \times \frac{1}{r}\left(1 - \frac{1}{(1 + r)^4}\right)$$

The value of r that solves this equation, the IRR, is the interest rate charged on the loan. Unfortunately, in this case, there is no simple way to solve for the interest rate r.[8] The only way to solve this equation is to guess values of r until you find the right one.

Start by guessing $r = 10\%$. In this case, the value of the annuity is

$$15{,}000 \times \frac{1}{0.10}\left(1 - \frac{1}{(1.10)^4}\right) = 47{,}548$$

The present value of the payments is too large. To lower it, we need to use a higher interest rate. We guess 20% this time:

$$15{,}000 \times \frac{1}{0.20}\left(1 - \frac{1}{(1.20)^4}\right) = 38{,}831$$

Now the present value of the payments is too low, so we must pick a rate between 10% and 20%. We continue to guess until we find the right rate. Let us try 18.45%:

$$15{,}000 \times \frac{1}{0.1845}\left(1 - \frac{1}{(1.1845)^4}\right) = 40{,}000$$

The interest rate charged by the dealer is 18.45%.

An easier solution than guessing the IRR and manually calculating values is to use a spreadsheet or calculator to automate the guessing process. When the cash flows are an annuity, as in this example, we can use the annuity spreadsheet in Excel to compute the IRR. Recall that the annuity spreadsheet solves Eq. 4.13. It ensures that the NPV of investing in the annuity is zero. When the unknown variable is the interest rate, it will solve for the interest rate that sets the NPV equal to zero—that is, the IRR. For this case,

	NPER	RATE	PV	PMT	FV	Excel Formula
Given	4		40,000	−15,000	0	
Solve for Rate		**18.45%**				=RATE(4,−15000,40000,0)

The annuity spreadsheet correctly computes an IRR of 18.45%.

EXAMPLE 4.17 Computing the Internal Rate of Return for an Annuity

Problem

Baker, Bellingham, and Botts, was so impressed with Jessica that it has decided to fund her business. In return for providing the initial capital of $1 million, Jessica has agreed to pay them $125,000 at the end of each year for the next 30 years. What is the internal rate of return on Baker, Bellingham, and Botts's investment in Jessica's company, assuming she fulfills her commitment?

Solution

Here is the timeline (from Baker, Bellingham, and Botts's perspective):

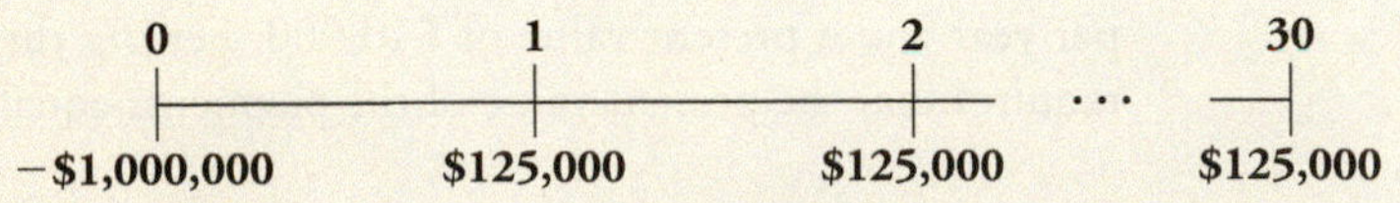

[8] With five or more periods and general cash flows, there is *no* general formula to solve for r; trial and error (by hand or computer) is the *only* way to compute the IRR.

The timeline shows that the future cash flows are a 30-year annuity. Setting the NPV equal to zero requires

$$1{,}000{,}000 = 125{,}000 \times \frac{1}{r}\left(1 - \frac{1}{(1+r)^{30}}\right)$$

Using the annuity spreadsheet to solve for r,

	NPER	RATE	PV	PMT	FV	Excel Formula
Given	30		−1,000,000	125,000	0	
Solve for Rate		**12.09%**				=RATE(30,125000,−1000000,0)

The IRR on this investment is 12.09%. In this case, we can interpret the IRR of 12.09% as the effective interest rate of the loan.

In this chapter, we developed the tools a financial manager needs to apply the NPV rule when cash flows occur at different points in time. As we have seen, the interest rate we use to discount or compound the cash flows is a critical input to any of our present or future value calculations. Throughout the chapter, we have taken the interest rate as given. What determines the interest rate that we should use when discounting cash flows? The Law of One Price implies that we must rely on market information to assess the value of cash flows across time. In Chapter 5, we learn the drivers of market interest rates as well as how they are quoted. Understanding interest rate quoting conventions will also allow us to extend the tools we developed in this chapter to situations where the cash flows are paid, and interest is compounded, more than once per year.

CONCEPT CHECK

1. What is the internal rate of return?
2. In what two cases is the internal rate of return easy to calculate?

USING EXCEL

Excel's IRR Function

Excel also has a built-in function, IRR, that will calculate the IRR of a stream of cash flows. Excel's IRR function has the format, IRR (values, guess), where "values" is the range containing the cash flows, and "guess" is an optional starting guess where Excel begins its search for an IRR. See the example below:

	A	B	C	D	E
1	Period	0	1	2	3
2	Cash Flow C_t	(1,000.0)	300.0	400.0	500.0
3	IRR	8.9%	=IRR(B2:E2)		

There are three things to note about the IRR function. First, the values given to the IRR function should include all of the cash flows of the project, including the one at date 0. In this sense, the IRR and NPV functions in Excel are inconsistent. Second, like the NPV function, the IRR ignores the period associated with any blank cells. Finally, as we will discuss in Chapter 7, in some settings the IRR function may fail to find a solution, or may give a different answer, depending on the initial guess.

MyFinanceLab Here is what you should know after reading this chapter. MyFinanceLab will help you identify what you know and where to go when you need to practice.

4.1 The Timeline

- Timelines are a critical first step in organizing the cash flows in a financial problem.

4.2 The Three Rules of Time Travel

- There are three rules of time travel:
  - Only cash flows that occur at the same point in time can be compared or combined.
  - To move a cash flow forward in time, you must compound it.
  - To move a cash flow backward in time, you must discount it.
- The future value in n years of a cash flow C today is

$$C \times (1 + r)^n \tag{4.1}$$

- The number of years it will take for an investment to double in value is approximately equal to 72 divided by the interest rate earned.
- The present value today of a cash flow C received in n years is

$$C \div (1 + r)^n \tag{4.2}$$

4.3 Valuing a Stream of Cash Flows

- The present value of a cash flow stream is

$$PV = \sum_{n=0}^{N} \frac{C_n}{(1 + r)^n} \tag{4.4}$$

- The present value equals the amount you would need in the bank today to recreate the cash flow stream.
- The future value on date n of a cash flow stream with a present value of PV is

$$FV_n = PV \times (1 + r)^n \tag{4.5}$$

4.4 Calculating the Net Present Value

- The net present value (NPV) of an investment opportunity is PV(benefits – costs). The NPV is the net benefit of the investment in terms of an equivalent amount of cash today.

4.5 Perpetuities and Annuities

- A perpetuity is a constant cash flow C paid every period, forever. The present value of a perpetuity is

$$\frac{C}{r} \tag{4.7}$$

- An annuity is a constant cash flow C paid every period for N periods. The present value of an annuity is

$$C \times \frac{1}{r}\left(1 - \frac{1}{(1 + r)^N}\right) \tag{4.9}$$

The future value of an annuity at the end of the annuity is

$$C \times \frac{1}{r}\left((1 + r)^N - 1\right) \tag{4.10}$$

- In a growing perpetuity or annuity, the cash flows grow at a constant rate g each period. The present value of a growing perpetuity is

$$\frac{C}{r-g} \tag{4.11}$$

The present value of a growing annuity is

$$C \times \frac{1}{r-g}\left(1-\left(\frac{1+g}{1+r}\right)^{N}\right) \tag{4.12}$$

4.6 Using an Annuity Spreadsheet or Calculator

- Present and future values can be easily calculated using a spreadsheet program. Most programs have built-in formulas for evaluating annuities.

4.7 Non-Annual Cash Flows

- Monthly cash flow streams (or any other period length) can be evaluated in exactly the same way as annual cash flow streams so long as the interest rate and number of periods are expressed in monthly terms.

4.8 Solving for the Cash Payments

- The annuity and perpetuity formulas can be used to solve for the annuity payments when either the present value or the future value is known. The periodic payment on an N-period loan with principal P and interest rate r is

$$C = \frac{P}{\frac{1}{r}\left(1-\frac{1}{(1+r)^{N}}\right)} \tag{4.14}$$

4.9 The Internal Rate of Return

- The internal rate of return (IRR) of an investment opportunity is the interest rate that sets the NPV of the investment opportunity equal to zero.
- When there are only two cash flows, the IRR can be calculated as:

$$IRR \text{ with two cash flows} = (FV/P)^{1/N} - 1 \tag{4.15}$$

- When the cash flows are a growing perpetuity with a starting cash flow of C with growth rate g, the IRR can be calculated as:

$$IRR \text{ of growing perpetuity} = (C/P) + g \tag{4.16}$$

Key Terms

annuity *p. 114*
annuity spreadsheet *p. 123*
compound annual growth rate (CAGR) *p. 128*
compound interest *p. 101*
compounding *p. 101*
consol *p. 111*
discounting *p. 103*
growing annuity *p. 120*
growing perpetuity *p. 118*
internal rate of return (IRR) *p. 128*
net present value (NPV) *p. 109*
perpetuity *p. 111*
simple interest *p. 102*
stream of cash flows *p. 99*
time value of money *p. 101*
timeline *p. 99*

Further Reading

The earliest known published work that introduces the ideas in this chapter was in 1202 by the famous Italian mathematician Fibonacci (or Leonardo of Pisa) in Liber Abaci (recently translated into English by Laurence Sigler, *Fibonacci's Liber Abaci, A Translation into Modern English of Leonardo Pisano's Book of Calculation*, Springer-Verlag, 2002). In this book, Fibonacci provides examples demonstrating the rules of time travel for cash flows.

Students who are interested in the early origins of finance and the historical development of the annuity formula will be interested in reading M. Rubinstein, *A History of the Theory of Investments: My Annotated Bibliography* (John Wiley and Sons, 2006) and W. Goetzmann and K. Rouwenhorst, eds., *Origins of Value: Innovations in the History of Finance* (Oxford University Press, 2005).

The material in this chapter should provide the foundation you need to understand the time value of money. For assistance using Excel, other spreadsheet programs, or financial calculators to compute present values, consult available help files and user manuals for additional information and examples.

Students in the lucky position of having to decide how to receive lottery winnings may consult A. Atkins and E. Dyl, "The Lotto Jackpot: The Lump Sum versus the Annuity," *Financial Practice and Education* (Fall/Winter 1995): 107–111.

Problems

All problems are available in MyFinanceLab. *An asterisk (*) indicates problems with a higher level of difficulty.*

The Timeline

1. You have just taken out a five-year loan from a bank to buy an engagement ring. The ring costs $5000. You plan to put down $1000 and borrow $4000. You will need to make annual payments of $1000 at the end of each year. Show the timeline of the loan from your perspective. How would the timeline differ if you created it from the bank's perspective?

2. You currently have a four-year-old mortgage outstanding on your house. You make monthly payments of $1500. You have just made a payment. The mortgage has 26 years to go (i.e., it had an original term of 30 years). Show the timeline from your perspective. How would the timeline differ if you created it from the bank's perspective?

The Three Rules of Time Travel

3. Calculate the future value of $2000 in
  a. Five years at an interest rate of 5% per year.
  b. Ten years at an interest rate of 5% per year.
  c. Five years at an interest rate of 10% per year.
  d. Why is the amount of interest earned in part (a) less than half the amount of interest earned in part (b)?

4. What is the present value of $10,000 received
  a. Twelve years from today when the interest rate is 4% per year?
  b. Twenty years from today when the interest rate is 8% per year?
  c. Six years from today when the interest rate is 2% per year?

5. Your brother has offered to give you either $5000 today or $10,000 in 10 years. If the interest rate is 7% per year, which option is preferable?

6. Consider the following alternatives:
  i. $100 received in one year
  ii. $200 received in five years
  iii. $300 received in ten years

a. Rank the alternatives from most valuable to least valuable if the interest rate is 10% per year.
b. What is your ranking if the interest rate is only 5% per year?
c. What is your ranking if the interest rate is 20% per year?

7. Suppose you invest $1000 in an account paying 8% interest per year.
a. What is the balance in the account after 3 years? How much of this balance corresponds to "interest on interest"?
b. What is the balance in the account after 25 years? How much of this balance corresponds to interest on interest?

8. Your daughter is currently eight years old. You anticipate that she will be going to college in 10 years. You would like to have $100,000 in a savings account to fund her education at that time. If the account promises to pay a fixed interest rate of 3% per year, how much money do you need to put into the account today to ensure that you will have $100,000 in 10 years?

9. You are thinking of retiring. Your retirement plan will pay you either $250,000 immediately on retirement or $350,000 five years after the date of your retirement. Which alternative should you choose if the interest rate is
a. 0% per year?
b. 8% per year?
c. 20% per year?

10. Your grandfather put some money in an account for you on the day you were born. You are now 18 years old and are allowed to withdraw the money for the first time. The account currently has $3996 in it and pays an 8% interest rate.
a. How much money would be in the account if you left the money there until your 25th birthday?
b. What if you left the money until your 65th birthday?
c. How much money did your grandfather originally put in the account?

Valuing a Stream of Cash Flows

11. Suppose you receive $100 at the end of each year for the next three years.
a. If the interest rate is 8%, what is the present value of these cash flows?
b. What is the future value in three years of the present value you computed in (a)?
c. Suppose you deposit the cash flows in a bank account that pays 8% interest per year. What is the balance in the account at the end of each of the next three years (after your deposit is made)? How does the final bank balance compare with your answer in (b)?

MFL **12.** You have just received a windfall from an investment you made in a friend's business. He will be paying you $10,000 at the end of this year, $20,000 at the end of the following year, and $30,000 at the end of the year after that (three years from today). The interest rate is 3.5% per year.
a. What is the present value of your windfall?
b. What is the future value of your windfall in three years (on the date of the last payment)?

MFL **13.** You have a loan outstanding. It requires making three annual payments at the end of the next three years of $1000 each. Your bank has offered to restructure the loan so that instead of making the three payments as originally agreed, you will make only one final payment at the end of the loan in three years. If the interest rate on the loan is 5%, what final payment will the bank require you to make so that it is indifferent between the two forms of payment?

Calculating the Net Present Value

MFL **14.** You have been offered a unique investment opportunity. If you invest $10,000 today, you will receive $500 one year from now, $1500 two years from now, and $10,000 ten years from now.
a. What is the NPV of the opportunity if the interest rate is 6% per year? Should you take the opportunity?
b. What is the NPV of the opportunity if the interest rate is 2% per year? Should you take it now?

15. Marian Plunket owns her own business and is considering an investment. If she undertakes the investment, it will pay $4000 at the end of each of the next three years. The opportunity requires an initial investment of $1000 plus an additional investment at the end of the second year of $5000. What is the NPV of this opportunity if the interest rate is 2% per year? Should Marian take it?

Perpetuities and Annuities

16. Your buddy in mechanical engineering has invented a money machine. The main drawback of the machine is that it is slow. It takes one year to manufacture $100. However, once built, the machine will last forever and will require no maintenance. The machine can be built immediately, but it will cost $1000 to build. Your buddy wants to know if he should invest the money to construct it. If the interest rate is 9.5% per year, what should your buddy do?

17. How would your answer to Problem 16 change if the machine takes one year to build?

18. The British government has a consol bond outstanding paying £100 per year forever. Assume the current interest rate is 4% per year.

a. What is the value of the bond immediately after a payment is made?
b. What is the value of the bond immediately before a payment is made?

19. What is the present value of $1000 paid at the end of each of the next 100 years if the interest rate is 7% per year?

***20.** You are head of the Schwartz Family Endowment for the Arts. You have decided to fund an arts school in the San Francisco Bay area in perpetuity. Every five years, you will give the school $1 million. The first payment will occur five years from today. If the interest rate is 8% per year, what is the present value of your gift?

***21.** When you purchased your house, you took out a 30-year annual-payment mortgage with an interest rate of 6% per year. The annual payment on the mortgage is $12,000. You have just made a payment and have now decided to pay the mortgage off by repaying the outstanding balance. What is the payoff amount if

a. You have lived in the house for 12 years (so there are 18 years left on the mortgage)?
b. You have lived in the house for 20 years (so there are 10 years left on the mortgage)?
c. You have lived in the house for 12 years (so there are 18 years left on the mortgage) and you decide to pay off the mortgage immediately *before* the twelfth payment is due?

22. You are 25 years old and decide to start saving for your retirement. You plan to save $5000 at the end of each year (so the first deposit will be one year from now), and will make the last deposit when you retire at age 65. Suppose you earn 8% per year on your retirement savings.

a. How much will you have saved for retirement?
b. How much will you have saved if you wait until age 35 to start saving (again, with your first deposit at the end of the year)?

23. Your grandmother has been putting $1000 into a savings account on every birthday since your first (that is, when you turned 1). The account pays an interest rate of 3%. How much money will be in the account on your 18th birthday immediately after your grandmother makes the deposit on that birthday?

24. A rich relative has bequeathed you a growing perpetuity. The first payment will occur in a year and will be $1000. Each year after that, on the anniversary of the last payment you will receive a payment that is 8% larger than the last payment. This pattern of payments will go on forever. If the interest rate is 12% per year,

a. What is today's value of the bequest?
b. What is the value of the bequest immediately after the first payment is made?

***25.** You are thinking of building a new machine that will save you $1000 in the first year. The machine will then begin to wear out so that the savings *decline* at a rate of 2% per year forever. What is the present value of the savings if the interest rate is 5% per year?

26. You work for a pharmaceutical company that has developed a new drug. The patent on the drug will last 17 years. You expect that the drug's profits will be \$2 million in its first year and that this amount will grow at a rate of 5% per year for the next 17 years. Once the patent expires, other pharmaceutical companies will be able to produce the same drug and competition will likely drive profits to zero. What is the present value of the new drug if the interest rate is 10% per year?

27. Your oldest daughter is about to start kindergarten at a private school. Tuition is \$10,000 per year, payable at the *beginning* of the school year. You expect to keep your daughter in private school through high school. You expect tuition to increase at a rate of 5% per year over the 13 years of her schooling. What is the present value of the tuition payments if the interest rate is 5% per year? How much would you need to have in the bank now to fund all 13 years of tuition?

28. A rich aunt has promised you \$5000 one year from today. In addition, each year after that, she has promised you a payment (on the anniversary of the last payment) that is 5% larger than the last payment. She will continue to show this generosity for 20 years, giving a total of 20 payments. If the interest rate is 5%, what is her promise worth today?

29. You are running a hot Internet company. Analysts predict that its earnings will grow at 30% per year for the next five years. After that, as competition increases, earnings growth is expected to slow to 2% per year and continue at that level forever. Your company has just announced earnings of \$1,000,000. What is the present value of all future earnings if the interest rate is 8%? (Assume all cash flows occur at the end of the year.)

***30.** Ten years ago Diana Torres wrote what has become the leading Tort textbook. She has been receiving royalties based on revenues reported by the publisher. These revenues started at \$1 million in the first year, and grew steadily by 5% per year. Her royalty rate is 15% of revenue. Recently, she hired an auditor who discovered that the publisher had been underreporting revenues. The book had actually earned 10% more in revenues than had been reported on her royalty statements.

a. Assuming the publisher pays an interest rate of 4% on missed payments, how much money does the publisher owe Diana?

b. The publisher is short of cash, so instead of paying Diana what is owed, the publisher is offering to increase her royalty rate on future book sales. Assume the book will generate revenues for an additional 20 years and that the current revenue growth will continue. If Diana would otherwise put the money into a bank account paying interest of 3%, what royalty rate would make her indifferent between accepting an increase in the future royalty rate and receiving the cash owed today.

***31.** Your brother has offered to give you \$100, starting next year, and after that growing at 3% for the next 20 years. You would like to calculate the value of this offer by calculating how much money you would need to deposit in the local bank so that the account will generate the same cash flows as he is offering you. Your local bank will guarantee a 6% annual interest rate so long as you have money in the account.

a. How much money will you need to deposit into the account today?

b. Using an Excel spreadsheet, show explicitly that you can deposit this amount of money into the account, and every year withdraw what your brother has promised, leaving the account with nothing after the last withdrawal.

Non-Annual Cash Flows

32. Suppose you currently have \$5000 in your savings account, and your bank pays interest at a rate of 0.5% per month. If you make no further deposits or withdrawals, how much will you have in the account in five years?

33. Your firm spends \$5000 every month on printing and mailing costs, sending statements to customers. If the interest rate is 0.5% per month, what is the present value of eliminating this cost by sending the statements electronically?

34. You have just entered an MBA program and have decided to pay for your living expenses using a credit card that has no minimum monthly payment. You intend to charge $1000 per month on the card for the next 21 months. The card carries a monthly interest rate of 1%. How much money will you owe on the card 22 months from now, when you receive your first statement post-graduation?

***35.** Your credit card charges an interest rate of 2% per month. You have a current balance of $1000, and want to pay it off. Suppose you can afford to pay off $100 per month. What will your balance be at the end of one year?

Solving for the Cash Payments

36. You have decided to buy a perpetuity. The bond makes one payment at the end of every year forever and has an interest rate of 5%. If you initially put $1000 into the bond, what is the payment every year?

37. You are thinking of purchasing a house. The house costs $350,000. You have $50,000 in cash that you can use as a down payment on the house, but you need to borrow the rest of the purchase price. The bank is offering a 30-year mortgage that requires annual payments and has an interest rate of 7% per year. What will your annual payment be if you sign up for this mortgage?

***38.** You would like to buy the house and take the mortgage described in Problem 37. You can afford to pay only $23,500 per year. The bank agrees to allow you to pay this amount each year, yet still borrow $300,000. At the end of the mortgage (in 30 years), you must make a *balloon* payment; that is, you must repay the remaining balance on the mortgage. How much will this balloon payment be?

39. You have just made an offer on a new home and are seeking a mortgage. You need to borrow $600,000.

a. The bank offers a 30-year mortgage with fixed monthly payments and an interest rate of 0.5% per month. What is the amount of your monthly payment if you take this loan?

b. Alternatively, you can get a 15-year mortgage with fixed monthly payments and an interest rate of 0.4% per month. How much would your monthly payments be if you take this loan instead?

40. Suppose you take the 30-year mortgage described in Problem 39, part (a). How much will you still owe on the mortgage after 15 years?

***41.** You are thinking about buying a piece of art that costs $50,000. The art dealer is proposing the following deal: He will lend you the money, and you will repay the loan by making the same payment every two years for the next 20 years (i.e., a total of 10 payments). If the interest rate is 4% per year, how much will you have to pay every two years?

42. You are saving for retirement. To live comfortably, you decide you will need to save $2 million by the time you are 65. Today is your 30th birthday, and you decide, starting today and continuing on every birthday up to and including your 65th birthday, that you will put the same amount into a savings account. If the interest rate is 5%, how much must you set aside each year to make sure that you will have $2 million in the account on your 65th birthday?

***43.** You realize that the plan in Problem 42 has a flaw. Because your income will increase over your lifetime, it would be more realistic to save less now and more later. Instead of putting the same amount aside each year, you decide to let the amount that you set aside grow by 3% per year. Under this plan, how much will you put into the account today? (Recall that you are planning to make the first contribution to the account today.)

***44.** You are 35 years old, and decide to save $5000 each year (with the first deposit one year from now), in an account paying 8% interest per year. You will make your last deposit 30 years from now when you retire at age 65. During retirement, you plan to withdraw funds from the account at the end of each year (so your first withdrawal is at age 66). What constant amount will you be able to withdraw each year if you want the funds to last until you are 90?

***45.** You have just turned 30 years old, have just received your MBA, and have accepted your first job. Now you must decide how much money to put into your retirement plan. The plan works as follows: Every dollar in the plan earns 7% per year. You cannot make withdrawals until you retire on your sixty-fifth birthday. After that point, you can make withdrawals as you see fit. You decide that you will plan to live to 100 and work until you turn 65. You estimate that to live comfortably in retirement, you will need $100,000 per year starting at the end of the first year of retirement and ending on your 100th birthday. You will contribute the same amount to the plan at the end of every year that you work. How much do you need to contribute each year to fund your retirement?

***46.** Problem 45 is not very realistic because most retirement plans do not allow you to specify a fixed amount to contribute every year. Instead, you are required to specify a fixed percentage of your salary that you want to contribute. Assume that your starting salary is $75,000 per year and it will grow 2% per year until you retire. Assuming everything else stays the same as in Problem 45, what percentage of your income do you need to contribute to the plan every year to fund the same retirement income

The Internal Rate of Return

47. You have an investment opportunity that requires an initial investment of $5000 today and will pay $6000 in one year. What is the IRR of this opportunity?

48. Suppose you invest $2000 today and receive $10,000 in five years.
- a. What is the IRR of this opportunity?
- b. Suppose another investment opportunity also requires $2000 upfront, but pays an equal amount at the end of each year for the next five years. If this investment has the same IRR as the first one, what is the amount you will receive each year?

49. You are shopping for a car and read the following advertisement in the newspaper: "Own a new Spitfire! No money down. Four annual payments of just $10,000." You have shopped around and know that you can buy a Spitfire for cash for $32,500. What is the interest rate the dealer is advertising (what is the IRR of the loan in the advertisement)? Assume that you must make the annual payments at the end of each year.

50. A local bank is running the following advertisement in the newspaper: "For just $1000 we will pay you $100 forever!" The fine print in the ad says that for a $1000 deposit, the bank will pay $100 every year in perpetuity, starting one year after the deposit is made. What interest rate is the bank advertising (what is the IRR of this investment)?

51. You are considering purchasing a warehouse. The cost to purchase the warehouse is $500,000. Renting the equivalent space costs $20,000 per year. If the annual interest rate is 6%, at what rate must rental cost increase each year to make the cost of renting comparable to purchasing?

***52.** The Tillamook County Creamery Association manufactures Tillamook Cheddar Cheese. It markets this cheese in four varieties: aged 2 months, 9 months, 15 months, and 2 years. At the shop in the dairy, it sells 2 pounds of each variety for the following prices: $7.95, $9.49, $10.95, and $11.95, respectively. Consider the cheese maker's decision whether to continue to age a particular 2-pound block of cheese. At 2 months, he can either sell the cheese immediately or let it age further. If he sells it now, he will receive $7.95 immediately. If he ages the cheese, he must give up the $7.95 today to receive a higher amount in the future. What is the IRR (expressed in percent per month) of the investment of giving up $79.50 today by choosing to store 20 pounds of cheese that is currently 2 months old and instead selling 10 pounds of this cheese when it has aged 9 months, 6 pounds when it has aged 15 months, and the remaining 4 pounds when it has aged 2 years?

Data Case

Assume today is March 16, 2016. Natasha Kingery is 30 years old and has a Bachelor of Science degree in computer science. She is currently employed as a Tier 2 field service representative for a telephony corporation located in Seattle, Washington, and earns $38,000 a year that she anticipates will grow at 3% per year. Natasha hopes to retire at age 65 and has just begun to think about the future.

Natasha has $75,000 that she recently inherited from her aunt. She invested this money in 30-year Treasury Bonds. She is considering whether she should further her education and would use her inheritance to pay for it.[9]

She has investigated a couple of options and is asking for your help as a financial planning intern to determine the financial consequences associated with each option. Natasha has already been accepted to both of these programs, and could start either one soon.

One alternative that Natasha is considering is attaining a certification in network design. This certification would automatically promote her to a Tier 3 field service representative in her company. The base salary for a Tier 3 representative is $10,000 more than what she currently earns and she anticipates that this salary differential will grow at a rate of 3% a year as long as she keeps working. The certification program requires the completion of 20 Web-based courses and a score of 80% or better on an exam at the end of the course work. She has learned that the average amount of time necessary to finish the program is one year. The total cost of the program is $5000, due when she enrolls in the program. Because she will do all the work for the certification on her own time, Natasha does not expect to lose any income during the certification.

Another option is going back to school for an MBA degree. With an MBA degree, Natasha expects to be promoted to a managerial position in her current firm. The managerial position pays $20,000 a year more than her current position. She expects that this salary differential will also grow at a rate of 3% per year for as long as she keeps working. The evening program, which will take three years to complete, costs $25,000 per year, due at the beginning of each of her three years in school. Because she will attend classes in the evening, Natasha doesn't expect to lose any income while she is earning her MBA if she chooses to undertake the MBA.

1. Determine the interest rate she is currently earning on her inheritance by going to Yahoo! Finance (finance.yahoo.com) and typing the word "Treasury" in the search field and picking the 30 year yield (ticker: ^TYX) off the dynamic menu that appears. Then go to "Historical Prices" (located in the left column) and enter the appropriate date, March 16, 2016 to obtain the closing yield or interest rate that she is earning. Use this interest rate as the discount rate for the remainder of this problem.
2. Create a timeline in Excel for her current situation, as well as the certification program and MBA degree options, using the following assumptions:
   - Salaries for the year are paid only once, at the end of the year.
   - The salary increase becomes effective immediately upon graduating from the MBA program or being certified. That is, because the increases become effective immediately but salaries are paid at the end of the year, the first salary increase will be paid exactly one year after graduation or certification.
3. Calculate the present value of the salary differential for completing the certification program. Subtract the cost of the program to get the NPV of undertaking the certification program.
4. Calculate the present value of the salary differential for completing the MBA degree. Calculate the present value of the cost of the MBA program. Based on your calculations, determine the NPV of undertaking the MBA.
5. Based on your answers to Questions 3 and 4, what advice would you give to Natasha? What if the two programs are mutually exclusive? That is, if Natasha undertakes one of the programs there is no further benefit to undertaking the other program. Would your advice be different?

Note: Updates to this data case may be found at www.berkdemarzo.com.

[9]If Natasha lacked the cash to pay for her tuition up front, she could borrow the money. More intriguingly, she could sell a fraction of her future earnings, an idea that has received attention from researchers and entrepreneurs; see M. Palacios, *Investing in Human Capital: A Capital Markets Approach to Student Funding*, Cambridge University Press, 2004.

CHAPTER 4 APPENDIX

Solving for the Number of Periods

In addition to solving for cash flows or the interest rate, we can solve for the amount of time it will take a sum of money to grow to a known value. In this case, the interest rate, present value, and future value are all known. We need to compute how long it will take for the present value to grow to the future value.

Suppose we invest \$10,000 in an account paying 10% interest, and we want to know how long it will take for the amount to grow to \$20,000.

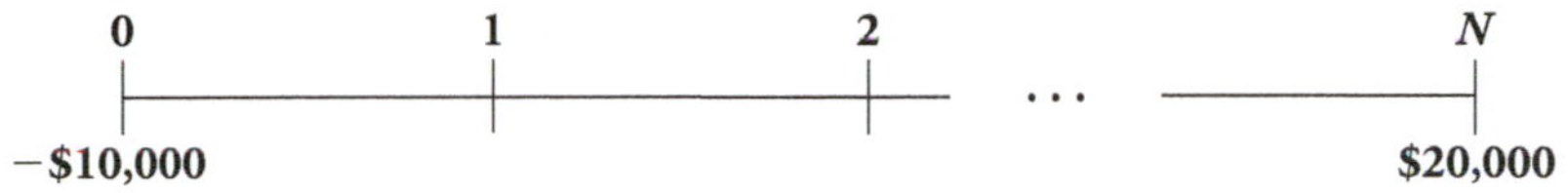

We want to determine N.

In terms of our formulas, we need to find N so that the future value of our investment equals \$20,000:

$$FV = \$10{,}000 \times 1.10^N = \$20{,}000 \quad (4A.1)$$

One approach is to use trial and error to find N, as with the IRR. For example, with $N = 7$ years, $FV = \$19{,}487$, so it will take longer than seven years. With $N = 8$ years, $FV = \$21{,}436$, so it will take between seven and eight years. Alternatively, this problem can be solved on the annuity spreadsheet. In this case, we solve for N:

	NPER	RATE	PV	PMT	FV	Excel Formula
Given		10.00%	−10,000	0	20,000	
Solve for NPER	7.27					=NPER(0.10,0,−10000,20000)

It will take about 7.3 years for our savings to grow to \$20,000.

Finally, this problem can be solved mathematically. Dividing both sides of Eq. 4A.1 by \$10,000, we have

$$1.10^N = 20{,}000/10{,}000 = 2$$

To solve for an exponent, we take the logarithm of both sides, and use the fact that $\ln(x^y) = y\ln(x)$:

$$N \ln(1.10) = \ln(2)$$

$$N = \ln(2)/\ln(1.10) = 0.6931/0.0953 \approx 7.3 \text{ years}$$

EXAMPLE 4A.1 Solving for the Number of Periods in a Savings Plan

Problem

You are saving for a down payment on a house. You have \$10,050 saved already, and you can afford to save an additional \$5000 per year at the end of each year. If you earn 7.25% per year on your savings, how long will it take you to save \$60,000?

Solution

The timeline for this problem is

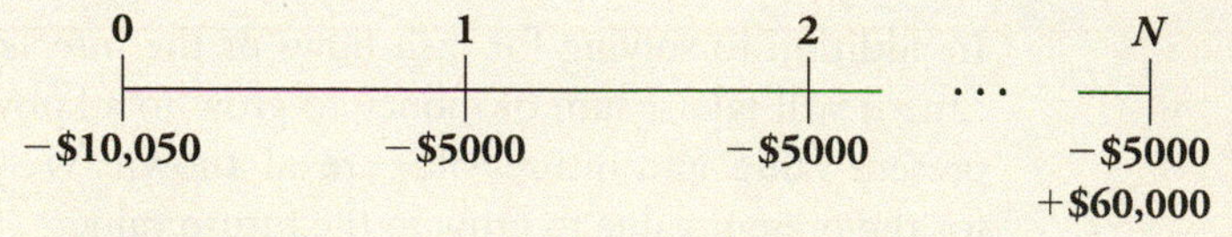

We need to find N so that the future value of our current savings plus the future value of our planned additional savings (which is an annuity) equals our desired amount:

$$10{,}050 \times 1.0725^N + 5000 \times \frac{1}{0.0725}(1.0725^N - 1) = 60{,}000$$

To solve mathematically, rearrange the equation to

$$1.0725^N = \frac{60{,}000 \times 0.0725 + 5000}{10{,}050 \times 0.0725 + 5000} = 1.632$$

We can then solve for N:

$$N = \frac{\ln(1.632)}{\ln(1.0725)} = 7.0 \text{ years}$$

It will take seven years to save the down payment. We can also solve this problem using the annuity spreadsheet:

	NPER	RATE	PV	PMT	FV	Excel Formula
Given		7.25%	−10,050	−5000	60,000	
Solve for N	7.00					=NPER(0.0725,−5000,−10050,60000)

Problems

All problems are available in MyFinanceLab. *An asterisk (*) indicates problems with a higher level of difficulty.*

***A.1.** Your grandmother bought an annuity from Rock Solid Life Insurance Company for $200,000 when she retired. In exchange for the $200,000, Rock Solid will pay her $25,000 per year until she dies. The interest rate is 5%. How long must she live after the day she retired to come out ahead (that is, to get more in *value* than what she paid in)?

***A.2.** You are thinking of making an investment in a new plant. The plant will generate revenues of $1 million per year for as long as you maintain it. You expect that the maintenance cost will start at $50,000 per year and will increase 5% per year thereafter. Assume that all revenue and maintenance costs occur at the end of the year. You intend to run the plant as long as it continues to make a positive cash flow (as long as the cash generated by the plant exceeds the maintenance costs). The plant can be built and become operational immediately. If the plant costs $10 million to build, and the interest rate is 6% per year, should you invest in the plant?

CHAPTER

5

Interest Rates

IN CHAPTER 4, WE EXPLORED THE MECHANICS OF COMPUTING present values and future values given a market interest rate. But how do we determine that interest rate? In practice, interest is paid and interest rates are quoted in different ways. For example, in mid-2012, Metropolitan National Bank offered savings accounts with an interest rate of 1.65% paid at the end of each year, while AIG Bank offered an annual interest rate of only 1.60%, but paid on a daily basis. Interest rates can also differ depending on the investment horizon. In July 2015, investors earned around 0.25% on one-year risk-free U.S. Treasury Bills, but could earn more than 2.9% on twenty-year Treasuries. Interest rates can also vary due to risk or tax consequences: The U.S. government is able to borrow at a lower interest rate than Johnson & Johnson, which in turn can borrow at a lower rate than American Airlines.

In this chapter, we consider the factors that affect interest rates and discuss how to determine the appropriate discount rate for a set of cash flows. We begin by looking at the way interest is paid and interest rates are quoted, and we show how to calculate the effective interest paid in one year given different quoting conventions. We then consider some of the main determinants of interest rates—namely, inflation and government policy. Because interest rates tend to change over time, investors will demand different interest rates for different investment horizons based on their expectations. Finally, we examine the role of risk in determining interest rates and show how to adjust interest rates to determine the effective amount received (or paid) after accounting for taxes.

NOTATION

EAR	effective annual rate
r	interest rate or discount rate
PV	present value
FV	future value
C	cash flow
APR	annual percentage rate
k	number of compounding periods per year
r_r	real interest rate
i	rate of inflation
NPV	net present value
C_n	cash flow that arrives in period n
n	number of periods
r_n	interest rate or discount rate for an n-year term
τ	tax rate

5.1 Interest Rate Quotes and Adjustments

Interest rates are quoted in a variety of ways. While generally stated as an annual rate, the interest payments themselves may occur at different intervals, such as monthly or semiannually. When evaluating cash flows, however, we must use a *discount rate* that matches the time period of our cash flows; this discount rate should reflect the actual return we could earn over that time period. In this section, we explore the mechanics of interpreting and adjusting the interest rate to determine the correct discount rate.

The Effective Annual Rate

Interest rates are often stated as an **effective annual rate (EAR)**, which indicates the actual amount of interest that will be earned at the end of one year.[1] This method of quoting the interest rate is the one we have used thus far in this textbook: in Chapter 4, we used the EAR as the discount rate r in our time value of money calculations. For example, with an EAR of 5%, a \$100,000 investment grows to

$$\$100{,}000 \times (1 + r) = \$100{,}000 \times (1.05) = \$105{,}000$$

in one year. After two years it will grow to

$$\$100{,}000 \times (1 + r)^2 = \$100{,}000 \times (1.05)^2 = \$110{,}250$$

Adjusting the Discount Rate to Different Time Periods. The preceding example shows that earning an effective annual rate of 5% for two years is equivalent to earning 10.25% in total interest over the entire period:

$$\$100{,}000 \times (1.05)^2 = \$100{,}000 \times 1.1025 = \$110{,}250$$

In general, by raising the interest rate factor $(1 + r)$ to the appropriate power, we can compute an equivalent interest rate for a longer time period.

We can use the same method to find the equivalent interest rate for periods shorter than one year. In this case, we raise the interest rate factor $(1 + r)$ to the appropriate fractional power. For example, earning 5% interest in one year is equivalent to receiving

$$(1 + r)^{1/2} = (1.05)^{1/2} = \$1.0247$$

for each \$1 invested every half year, or equivalently, every six months. That is, a 5% effective annual rate is equivalent to an interest rate of approximately 2.47% earned every six months. We can verify this result by computing the interest we would earn in one year by investing for two six-month periods at this rate:

$$(1 + r_{6\text{mo}})^2 = (1.0247)^2 = 1.05 = 1 + r_{1\text{yr}}$$

General Equation for Discount Rate Period Conversion. In general, we can convert a discount rate of r for one period to an equivalent discount rate for n periods using the following formula:

$$\text{Equivalent } n\text{-Period Discount Rate} = (1 + r)^n - 1 \tag{5.1}$$

In this formula, n can be larger than 1 (to compute a rate over more than one period) or smaller than 1 (to compute a rate over a fraction of a period). When computing present

[1] The effective annual rate is often referred to as the *effective annual yield* (EAY) or the *annual percentage yield* (APY).

or future values, it is convenient to adjust the discount rate to match the time period of the cash flows. This adjustment is *necessary* to apply the perpetuity or annuity formulas, as shown in Example 5.1.

EXAMPLE 5.1 Valuing Monthly Cash Flows

Problem

Suppose your bank account pays interest monthly with the interest rate quoted as an effective annual rate (EAR) of 6%. What amount of interest will you earn each month? If you have no money in the bank today, how much will you need to save at the end of each month to accumulate $100,000 in 10 years?

Solution

From Eq. 5.1, a 6% EAR is equivalent to earning $(1.06)^{1/12} - 1 = 0.4868\%$ per month. We can write the timeline for our savings plan using *monthly* periods as follows:

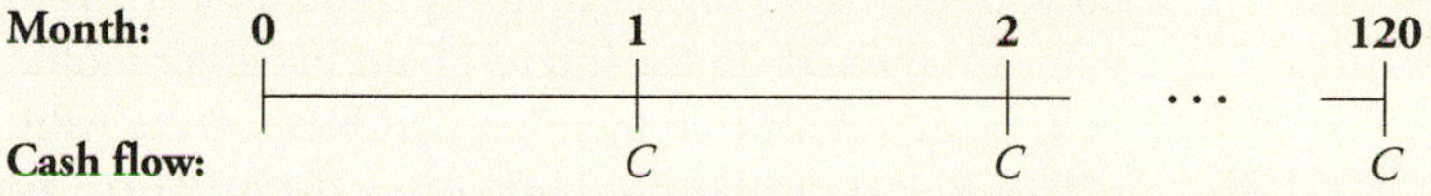

That is, we can view the savings plan as a monthly annuity with $10 \times 12 = 120$ monthly payments. We can calculate the total amount saved as the future value of this annuity, using Eq. 4.10:

$$FV(\text{annuity}) = C \times \frac{1}{r}[(1+r)^n - 1]$$

We can solve for the *monthly* payment C using the equivalent *monthly* interest rate $r = 0.4868\%$, and $n = 120$ months:

$$C = \frac{FV(\text{annuity})}{\frac{1}{r}[(1+r)^n - 1]} = \frac{\$100{,}000}{\frac{1}{0.004868}[(1.004868)^{120} - 1]} = \$615.47 \text{ per month}$$

We can also compute this result using the annuity spreadsheet:

	NPER	RATE	PV	PMT	FV	Excel Formula
Given	120	0.4868%	0		100,000	
Solve for PMT				**−615.47**		=PMT(0.004868,120,0,100000)

Thus, if we save $615.47 per month and we earn interest monthly at an effective annual rate of 6%, we will have $100,000 in 10 years.

COMMON MISTAKE Using the Wrong Discount Rate in the Annuity Formula

The discount rate period must match the periodicity of the cash flows in the annuity formula. In Example 5.1, because the cash flows were monthly, we first must convert the EAR into a monthly discount rate. A common mistake in this case is to treat the annuity as a 10-year annual annuity with a discount rate equal to the EAR of 6%. Doing so, we get

$$C = \frac{\$100{,}000}{\frac{1}{0.06}[(1.06)^{10} - 1]} = \$7586.80$$

which is the amount you would need to invest *per year*, not per month. Note also that if we try to convert this to a monthly amount by dividing by 12, we get $7586.80/12 = 632.23$, a higher amount than we need according to Example 5.1. The reason we can save less is that by depositing the cash monthly rather than at the end of each year, we will earn interest on our deposits throughout the year.

Annual Percentage Rates

Banks also quote interest rates in terms of an **annual percentage rate (APR)**, which indicates the amount of simple interest earned in one year, that is, the amount of interest earned *without* the effect of compounding. Because it does not include the effect of compounding, the APR quote is typically less than the actual amount of interest that you will earn. To compute the actual amount that you will earn in one year, we must first convert the APR to an effective annual rate.

For example, suppose Granite Bank advertises savings accounts with an interest rate of "6% APR with monthly compounding." In this case, you will earn 6%/12 = 0.5% every month. So an APR with monthly compounding is actually a way of quoting a *monthly* interest rate, rather than an annual interest rate. Because the interest compounds each month, you will earn

$$\$1 \times (1.005)^{12} = \$1.061678$$

at the end of one year, for an effective annual rate of 6.1678%. The 6.1678% that you earn on your deposit is higher than the quoted 6% APR due to compounding: In later months, you earn interest on the interest paid in earlier months.

It is important to remember that because the APR does not reflect the true amount you will earn over one year, *we cannot use the APR itself as a discount rate.* Instead, the APR with k compounding periods is a way of quoting the actual interest earned each compounding period:

$$\text{Interest Rate per Compounding Period} = \frac{APR}{k \text{ periods/year}} \tag{5.2}$$

Once we have computed the interest earned per compounding period from Eq. 5.2, we can compute the effective annual rate by compounding using Eq. 5.1. Thus the effective annual rate corresponding to an APR with k compounding periods per year is given by the following conversion formula:

Converting an APR to an EAR

$$1 + EAR = \left(1 + \frac{APR}{k}\right)^k \tag{5.3}$$

Table 5.1 shows the effective annual rates that correspond to an APR of 6% with different compounding intervals. The EAR increases with the frequency of compounding because of the ability to earn interest on interest sooner. Investments can compound even more frequently than daily. In principle, the compounding interval could be hourly or every second. In the limit we approach the idea of **continuous compounding**, in which we

TABLE 5.1 **Effective Annual Rates for a 6% APR with Different Compounding Periods**

Compounding Interval	Effective Annual Rate
Annual	$(1 + 0.06/1)^1 - 1 = 6\%$
Semiannual	$(1 + 0.06/2)^2 - 1 = 6.09\%$
Monthly	$(1 + 0.06/12)^{12} - 1 = 6.1678\%$
Daily	$(1 + 0.06/365)^{365} - 1 = 6.1831\%$

compound the interest every instant.[2] As a practical matter, compounding more frequently than daily has a negligible impact on the effective annual rate and is rarely observed.

Remember, when working with APRs we must

1. Divide the APR by the number of compounding periods per year to determine the actual interest rate per compounding period (Eq. 5.2).

Then, if the cash flows occur at a different interval than the compounding period,

2. Compute the appropriate discount rate by compounding (Eq. 5.1).

Once you have completed these steps, you can then use the discount rate to evaluate the present or future value of a set of cash flows.

EXAMPLE 5.2 Converting the APR to a Discount Rate

Problem

Your firm is purchasing a new telephone system, which will last for four years. You can purchase the system for an upfront cost of $150,000, or you can lease the system from the manufacturer for $4000 paid at the end of each month.[3] Your firm can borrow at an interest rate of 5% APR with semiannual compounding. Should you purchase the system outright or pay $4000 per month?

Solution

The cost of leasing the system is a 48-month annuity of $4000 per month:

Month:	0	1	2	. . .	48
Payment:		$4000	$4000		$4000

We can compute the present value of the lease cash flows using the annuity formula, but first we need to compute the discount rate that corresponds to a period length of one month. To do so, we convert the borrowing cost of 5% APR with semiannual compounding to a monthly discount rate. Using Eq. 5.2, the APR corresponds to a six-month discount rate of 5%/2 = 2.5%. To convert a six-month discount rate into a one-month discount rate, we compound the six-month rate by 1/6 using Eq. 5.1:

$$(1.025)^{1/6} - 1 = 0.4124\% \text{ per month}$$

(Alternatively, we could first use Eq. 5.3 to convert the APR to an EAR: $1 + EAR = (1 + 0.05/2)^2 = 1.050625$. Then we can convert the EAR to a monthly rate using Eq. 5.1: $(1.050625)^{1/12} - 1 = 0.4124\%$ per month.)

Given this discount rate, we can use the annuity formula (Eq. 4.9) to compute the present value of the 48 monthly payments:

$$PV = 4000 \times \frac{1}{0.004124}\left(1 - \frac{1}{1.004124^{48}}\right) = \$173{,}867$$

We can also use the annuity spreadsheet:

	NPER	RATE	PV	PMT	FV	Excel Formula
Given	48	0.4124%		−4,000	0	
Solve for PV			**173,867**			=PV(0.004124,48,−4000,0)

[2]A 6% APR with continuous compounding results in an EAR of approximately 6.1837%, which is almost the same as daily compounding. See the appendix for further discussion of continuous compounding.

[3]In addition to these cash flows, there may be tax and accounting considerations when comparing a purchase with a lease. We ignore these complications in this example, but will consider leases in detail in Chapter 25.

Thus, paying \$4000 per month for 48 months is equivalent to paying a present value of \$173,867 today. This cost is \$173,867 − \$150,000 = \$23,867 higher than the cost of purchasing the system, so it is better to pay \$150,000 for the system rather than lease it. We can interpret this result as meaning that at a 5% APR with semiannual compounding, by promising to repay \$4000 per month, your firm can borrow \$173,867 today. With this loan it could purchase the phone system and have an additional \$23,867 to use for other purposes.

CONCEPT CHECK

1. What is the difference between an EAR and an APR quote?
2. Why can't the APR itself be used as a discount rate?

5.2 Application: Discount Rates and Loans

Now that we have explained how to compute the discount rate from an interest rate quote, let's apply the concept to solve two common financial problems: calculating a loan payment and calculating the remaining balance on a loan.

Computing Loan Payments. To calculate a loan payment, we equate the outstanding loan balance with the present value of the loan payments using the discount rate from the quoted interest rate of the loan, and then solve for the loan payment.

Many loans, such as mortgages and car loans, are **amortizing loans**, which means that each month you pay interest on the loan plus some part of the loan balance. Usually, each monthly payment is the same, and the loan is fully repaid with the final payment. Typical terms for a new car loan might be "6.75% APR for 60 months." When the compounding interval for the APR is not stated explicitly, it is equal to the interval between the payments, or one month in this case. Thus, this quote means that the loan will be repaid with 60 equal monthly payments, computed using a 6.75% APR with monthly compounding. Consider the timeline for a \$30,000 car loan with these terms:

Month:	0	1	2	...	60
Cash flow:	\$30,000	$-C$	$-C$		$-C$

The payment, C, is set so that the present value of the cash flows, evaluated using the loan interest rate, equals the original principal amount of \$30,000. In this case, the 6.75% APR with monthly compounding corresponds to a one-month discount rate of 6.75%/12 = 0.5625%. So, using the annuity formula to compute the present value of the loan payments, the payment C must satisfy

$$C \times \frac{1}{0.005625}\left(1 - \frac{1}{1.005625^{60}}\right) = 30{,}000$$

and therefore,

$$C = \frac{30{,}000}{\frac{1}{0.005625}\left(1 - \frac{1}{1.005625^{60}}\right)} = \$590.50$$

Alternatively, we can solve for the payment C using the annuity spreadsheet:

	NPER	RATE	PV	PMT	FV	Excel Formula
Given	60	0.5625%	30,000		0	
Solve for PMT				**−590.50**		=PMT(0.005625,60,30000,0)

Computing the Outstanding Loan Balance. The outstanding balance on a loan, also called the outstanding principal, is equal to the present value of the remaining future loan payments, again evaluated using the loan interest rate.

EXAMPLE 5.3 Computing the Outstanding Loan Balance

Problem

Two years ago your firm took out a 30-year amortizing loan to purchase a small office building. The loan has a 4.80% APR with monthly payments of \$2623.33. How much do you owe on the loan today? How much interest did the firm pay on the loan in the past year?

Solution

After 2 years, the loan has 28 years, or 336 months, remaining:

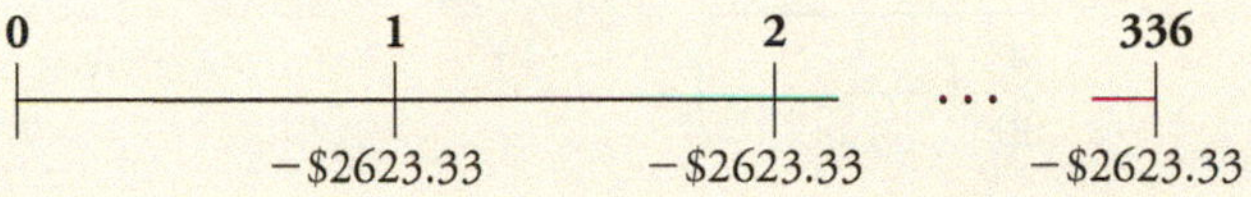

The remaining balance on the loan is the present value of these remaining payments, using the loan rate of 4.8%/12 = 0.4% per month:

$$\text{Balance after 2 years} = \$2623.33 \times \frac{1}{0.004}\left(1 - \frac{1}{1.004^{336}}\right) = \$484{,}332$$

During the past year, your firm made total payments of \$2623.33 × 12 = \$31,480 on the loan. To determine the amount that was interest, it is easiest to first determine the amount that was used to repay the principal. Your loan balance one year ago, with 29 years (348 months) remaining, was

$$\text{Balance after 1 year} = \$2623.33 \times \frac{1}{0.004}\left(1 - \frac{1}{1.004^{348}}\right) = \$492{,}354$$

Therefore, the balance declined by \$492,354 − \$484,332 = \$8022 in the past year. Of the total payments made, \$8022 was used to repay the principal and the remaining \$31,480 − \$8022 = \$23,458 was used to pay interest.

CONCEPT CHECK

1. How can you compute the outstanding balance on a loan?
2. What is an amortizing loan?

5.3 The Determinants of Interest Rates

How are interest rates determined? Fundamentally, interest rates are determined in the market based on individuals' willingness to borrow and lend. In this section, we look at some of the factors that may influence interest rates, such as inflation, government policy, and expectations of future growth.

GLOBAL FINANCIAL CRISIS — Teaser Rates and Subprime Loans

Some loans, such as **adjustable rate mortgages (ARMs)**, have interest rates that are not constant over the life of the loan. When the interest rate on such a loan changes, the loan payments are recalculated based on the loan's current outstanding balance, the new interest rate, and the remaining life of the loan.

Adjustable rate mortgages were the most common type of so-called "subprime" loans made to homebuyers with poor credit histories. These loans often featured low initial rates, aptly named *teaser rates*. After a short period (often 2 to 5 years) the interest rate would jump to a higher rate, implying that the monthly payment would also jump. For example, suppose the rate on the 30-year loan in Example 5.3 was a teaser rate, and that after 2 years the rate increased from 4.8% to 7.2%. Given the remaining balance after two years of \$484,332, with the higher interest rate of 7.2%/12 = 0.6% per month, the monthly payment will increase from \$2623.33 to

$$\text{New monthly payment} = \frac{\$484{,}332}{\frac{1}{.006}\left(1 - \frac{1}{1.006^{336}}\right)} = \$3355.62$$

While the loan might have been affordable at the initial teaser rate, many subprime borrowers could not afford the higher payments that were required after the loan rate adjusted. Prior to 2007, while interest rates remained low and home prices were high (and increasing), such borrowers were able to avoid default simply by refinancing their loans into new loans that also featured low initial teaser rates. In this way, they were able to keep their payments low. But as mortgage rates increased and housing prices began to decline in 2007, this strategy for keeping their loan payments low was no longer possible. In many cases the outstanding loan balance exceeded the market value of the home, making lenders unwilling to refinance the loans. Stuck with a loan at a now unaffordable interest rate, many homeowners defaulted, and the rate of foreclosure on subprime loans skyrocketed.

To prevent future lenders from using teaser rates to get borrowers into loans they might not ultimately be able to afford, the Dodd-Frank Act requires lenders to verify that borrowers have sufficient income to repay their loans even after the teaser rate expires.

Inflation and Real Versus Nominal Rates

The interest rates that are quoted by banks and other financial institutions, and that we have used for discounting cash flows, are **nominal interest rates**, which indicate the rate at which your money will grow if invested for a certain period. Of course, if prices in the economy are also growing due to inflation, the nominal interest rate does not represent the increase in purchasing power that will result from investing. The rate of growth of your purchasing power, after adjusting for inflation, is determined by the **real interest rate**, which we denote by r_r. If r is the nominal interest rate and i is the rate of inflation, we can calculate the rate of growth of purchasing power as follows:

$$\text{Growth in Purchasing Power} = 1 + r_r = \frac{1 + r}{1 + i} = \frac{\text{Growth of Money}}{\text{Growth of Prices}} \tag{5.4}$$

We can rearrange Eq. 5.4 to find the following formula for the real interest rate, together with a convenient approximation for the real interest rate when inflation rates are low:

The Real Interest Rate

$$r_r = \frac{r - i}{1 + i} \approx r - i \tag{5.5}$$

That is, the real interest rate is approximately equal to the nominal interest rate less the rate of inflation.[4]

---

[4]The real interest rate should not be used as a discount rate for future cash flows. It can only be used if the cash flows have been adjusted to remove the effect of inflation (in that case, we say the cash flows are in *real terms*). This approach is error prone, however, so throughout this book we will always forecast actual cash flows including any growth due to inflation, and discount using nominal interest rates.

EXAMPLE 5.4 Calculating the Real Interest Rate

Problem

At the start of 2011, one-year U.S. government bond rates were about 0.3%, while the rate of inflation that year was 3.0%. In May of 2014, one-year interest rates were about 0.1%, and inflation over the following year was around −0.05% (deflation). What was the real interest rate in 2011 and in May 2014?

Solution

Using Eq. 5.5, the real interest rate in 2011 was $(0.3\% - 3.0\%)/(1.03) = -2.62\%$. In May 2014, the real interest rate was $(0.1\% + 0.05\%)/(0.9995) = 0.15\%$. Note that the real interest rate was negative in 2011, indicating that interest rates were insufficient to keep up with inflation: Investors in U.S. government bonds were able to buy less at the end of the year than they could have purchased at the start of the year. On the other hand, prices actually decreased (deflation) in the year following May 2014, and so the real interest rate earned slighly above the nominal interest rate.

Figure 5.1 shows the history of U.S. nominal interest rates and inflation rates since 1960. Note that the nominal interest rate tends to move with inflation. Intuitively, individuals' willingness to save will depend on the growth in purchasing power they can expect (given by the real interest rate). Thus, when the inflation rate is high, a higher nominal interest rate is generally needed to induce individuals to save. Note, however, that by historical standards, the last few years have been somewhat exceptional: nominal interest rates have been extremely low, leading to negative real interest rates.

Investment and Interest Rate Policy

Interest rates also affect firms' incentive to raise capital and invest. Consider a risk-free investment opportunity that requires an upfront investment of $10 million and generates

FIGURE 5.1 U.S. Interest Rates and Inflation Rates, 1962–2012

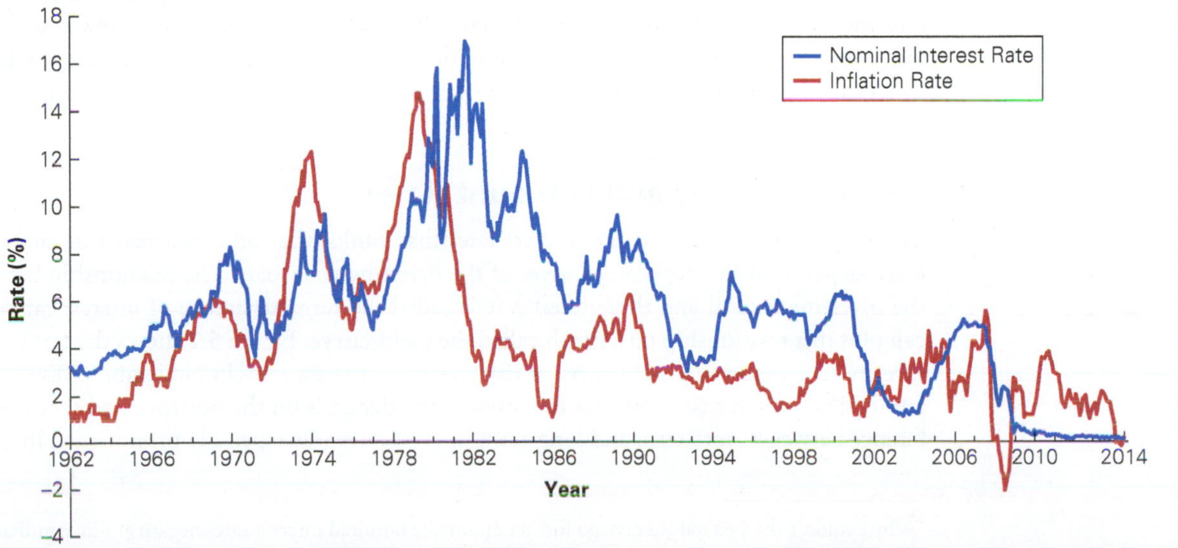

Interest rates are one-year Treasury rates, and inflation rates are the increase in the U.S. Bureau of Labor Statistics' consumer price index over the coming year, with both series computed on a monthly basis The difference between them thus reflects the approximate real interest rate earned by holding Treasuries. Note that interest rates tend to be high when inflation is high.

a cash flow of $3 million per year for four years. If the risk-free interest rate is 5%, this investment has an NPV of

$$NPV = -10 + \frac{3}{1.05} + \frac{3}{1.05^2} + \frac{3}{1.05^3} + \frac{3}{1.05^4} = \$0.638 \text{ million}$$

If the interest rate is 9%, the NPV falls to

$$NPV = -10 + \frac{3}{1.09} + \frac{3}{1.09^2} + \frac{3}{1.09^3} + \frac{3}{1.09^4} = -\$0.281 \text{ million}$$

and the investment is no longer profitable. The reason, of course, is that we are discounting the positive cash flows at a higher rate, which reduces their present value. The cost of $10 million occurs today, however, so its present value is independent of the discount rate.

More generally, when the costs of an investment precede the benefits, an increase in the interest rate will decrease the investment's NPV. All else equal, higher interest rates will therefore tend to shrink the set of positive-NPV investments available to firms. The Federal Reserve in the United States and central banks in other countries use this relationship between interest rates and investment to try to guide the economy. They can raise interest rates to reduce investment if the economy is "overheating" and inflation is on the rise, and they can lower interest rates to stimulate investment if the economy is slowing or in recession.

Monetary Policy, Deflation, and the 2008 Financial Crisis. When the 2008 financial crisis struck the economy, the U.S. Federal Reserve responded quickly to mitigate its impact on the broader economy by cutting its short-term interest rate target to 0% by year's end. But while this use of monetary policy is generally quite effective, because consumer prices were falling in late 2008, the inflation rate was negative, and so even with a 0% nominal interest rate the real interest rate remained positive initially. The consequence of this deflation, and the risk that it might continue, meant that the Federal Reserve was "out of ammunition" with regard to its usual weapon against an economic slowdown—it could not lower rates further.[5] This problem was one of the reasons the U.S. and other governments began to consider other measures, such as increased government spending and investment, to stimulate their economies. Former Federal Reserve Governor Kevin Warsh further discusses monetary policy responses to the economic crisis in both the U.S. and Europe in the interview box on page 156.

The Yield Curve and Discount Rates

You may have noticed that the interest rates that banks offer on investments or charge on loans depend on the horizon, or *term*, of the investment or loan. The relationship between the investment term and the interest rate is called the **term structure** of interest rates. We can plot this relationship on a graph called the **yield curve**. Figure 5.2 shows the term structure and corresponding yield curve of risk-free U.S. interest rates in November 2006, 2007, and 2008. In each case, note that the interest rate depends on the horizon, and that the difference between short-term and long-term interest rates was especially pronounced in 2008.

[5]Why couldn't the Federal Reserve go further and make nominal interest rates negative? Since individuals can always hold cash (or put their money in a savings account) and earn at least a zero return, the nominal interest rate can never be *significantly* negative. But because storing cash is costly, and because investors viewed many banks as unsafe, short-term U.S. Treasury interest rates were actually slightly negative (down to −0.05%) at several points throughout this period! (See Chapter 6 for further discussion.)

FIGURE 5.2 **Term Structure of Risk-Free U.S. Interest Rates, November 2006, 2007, and 2008**

Term (years)	Date		
	Nov-06	Nov-07	Nov-08
0.5	5.23%	3.32%	0.47%
1	4.99%	3.16%	0.91%
2	4.80%	3.16%	0.98%
3	4.72%	3.12%	1.26%
4	4.63%	3.34%	1.69%
5	4.64%	3.48%	2.01%
6	4.65%	3.63%	2.49%
7	4.66%	3.79%	2.90%
8	4.69%	3.96%	3.21%
9	4.70%	4.00%	3.38%
10	4.73%	4.18%	3.41%
15	4.89%	4.44%	3.86%
20	4.87%	4.45%	3.87%

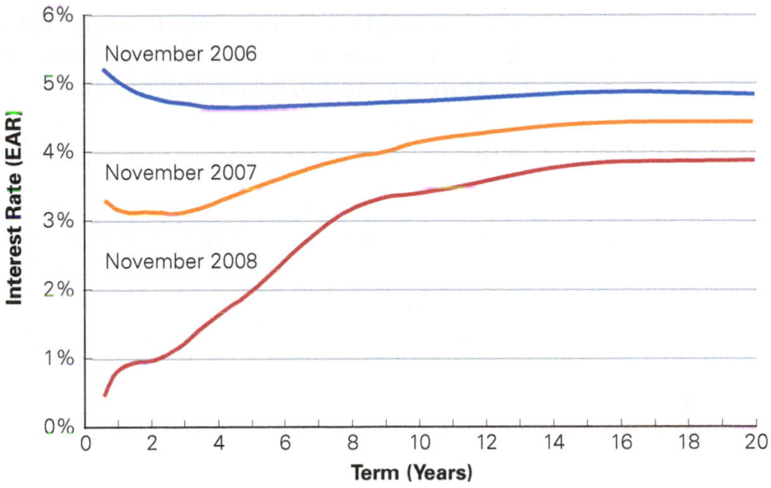

The figure shows the interest rate available from investing in risk-free U.S. Treasury securities with different investment terms. In each case, the interest rates differ depending on the horizon. (Data from U.S. Treasury STRIPS.)

We can use the term structure to compute the present and future values of a risk-free cash flow over different investment horizons. For example, $100 invested for one year at the one-year interest rate in November 2008 would grow to a future value of

$$\$100 \times 1.0091 = \$100.91$$

at the end of one year, and $100 invested for ten years at the ten-year interest rate in November 2008 would grow to[6]

$$\$100 \times (1.0341)^{10} = \$139.84$$

We can apply the same logic when computing the present value of cash flows with different maturities. A risk-free cash flow received in two years should be discounted at the two-year interest rate, and a cash flow received in ten years should be discounted at the ten-year interest rate. In general, a risk-free cash flow of C_n received in n years has present value

$$PV = \frac{C_n}{(1 + r_n)^n} \tag{5.6}$$

where r_n is the risk-free interest rate (expressed as an EAR) for an n-year term. In other words, when computing a present value we must match the term of the cash flow and term of the discount rate.

Combining Eq. 5.6 for cash flows in different years leads to the general formula for the present value of a cash flow stream:

Present Value of a Cash Flow Stream Using a Term Structure of Discount Rates

$$PV = \frac{C_1}{1 + r_1} + \frac{C_2}{(1 + r_2)^2} + \cdots + \frac{C_N}{(1 + r_N)^N} = \sum_{n=1}^{N} \frac{C_n}{(1 + r_n)^n} \tag{5.7}$$

[6] We could also invest for 10 years by investing at the one-year interest rate for 10 years in a row. However, because we do not know what future interest rates will be, our ultimate payoff would not be risk free.

Note the difference between Eq. 5.7 and Eq. 4.4. Here, we use a different discount rate for each cash flow, based on the rate from the yield curve with the same term. When the yield curve is relatively flat, as it was in November 2006, this distinction is relatively minor and is often ignored by discounting using a single "average" interest rate r. But when short-term and long-term interest rates vary widely, as they did in November 2008, Eq. 5.7 should be used.

Warning: All of our shortcuts for computing present values (annuity and perpetuity formulas, the annuity spreadsheet) are based on discounting all of the cash flows *at the same rate*. They *cannot* be used in situations in which cash flows need to be discounted at different rates.

EXAMPLE 5.5 **Using the Term Structure to Compute Present Values**

Problem

Compute the present value in November 2008 of a risk-free five-year annuity of $1000 per year, given the yield curve for November 2008 in Figure 5.2.

Solution

To compute the present value, we discount each cash flow by the corresponding interest rate:

$$PV = \frac{1000}{1.0091} + \frac{1000}{1.0098^2} + \frac{1000}{1.0126^3} + \frac{1000}{1.0169^4} + \frac{1000}{1.0201^5} = \$4775.25$$

Note that we cannot use the annuity formula here because the discount rates differ for each cash flow.

The Yield Curve and the Economy

Figure 5.3 shows the gap between short-term and long-term interest rate historically. Note how sometimes, short-term rates are close to long-term rates, and at other times they may be very different. What accounts for the changing shape of the yield curve?

Interest Rate Determination. The Federal Reserve determines very short-term interest rates through its influence on the **federal funds rate**, which is the rate at which banks can borrow cash reserves on an overnight basis. All other interest rates on the yield curve are set in the market and are adjusted until the supply of lending matches the demand for borrowing at each loan term. As we will see, expectations of future interest rate changes have a major effect on investors' willingness to lend or borrow for longer terms and, therefore, on the shape of the yield curve.

COMMON MISTAKE **Using the Annuity Formula When Discount Rates Vary by Maturity**

When computing the present value of an annuity, a common mistake is to use the annuity formula with a single interest rate even though interest rates vary with the investment horizon. For example, we *cannot* compute the present value of the five-year annuity in Example 5.5 using the five-year interest rate from November 2008:

$$PV \neq \$1000 \times \frac{1}{0.0201}\left(1 - \frac{1}{1.0201^5}\right) = \$4712.09$$

To find the single interest rate that we could use to value the annuity, we must first compute the present value of the annuity using Eq. 5.7 and then solve for its IRR. For the annuity in Example 5.5, we use the annuity spreadsheet below to find its IRR of 1.55%. The IRR of the annuity is always between the highest and lowest discount rates used to calculate its present value, as is the case in the example below.

	NPER	RATE	PV	PMT	FV	Excel Formula
Given	5		−4,775.25	1000	0	
Solve for Rate		1.55%				=RATE(5,1000,−4775.25,0)

FIGURE 5.3 **Short-Term Versus Long-Term U.S. Interest Rates and Recessions**

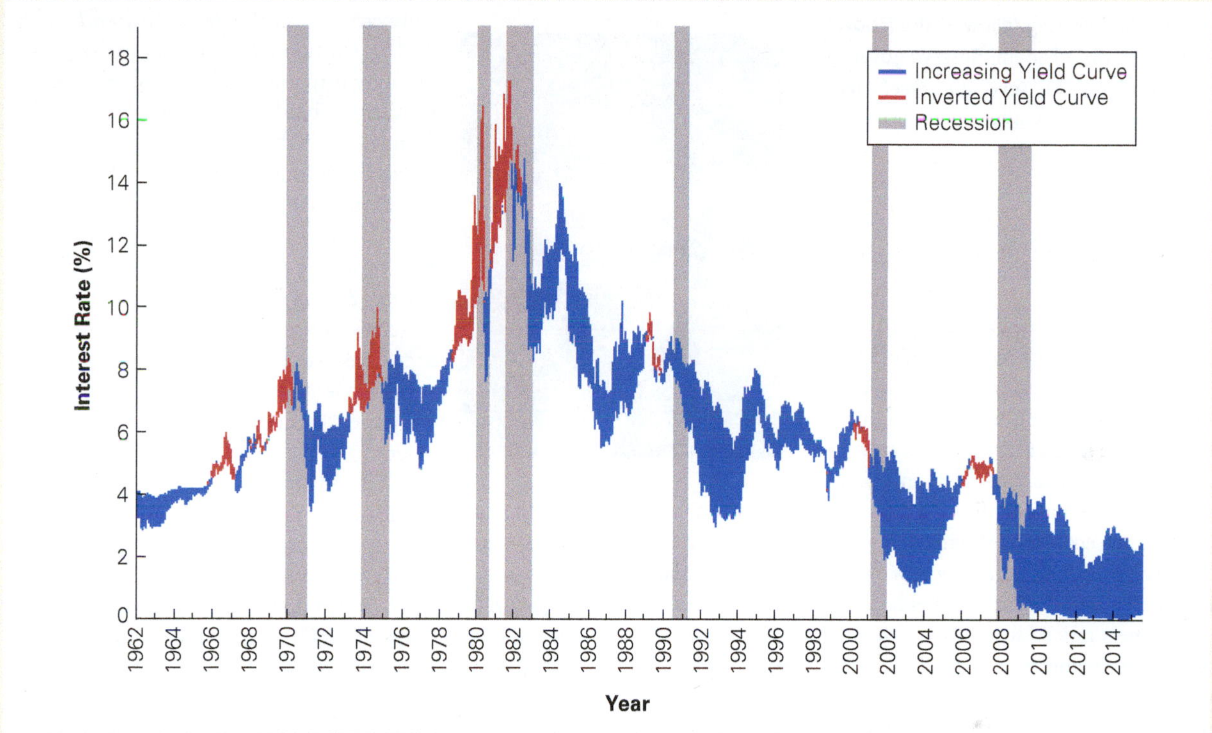

One-year and ten-year U.S. Treasury rates are plotted, with the spread between them shaded in blue if the shape of the yield curve is increasing (the one-year rate is below the ten-year rate) and in red if the yield curve is inverted (the one-year rate exceeds the ten-year rate). Gray bars show the dates of U.S. recessions as determined by the National Bureau of Economic Research. Note that inverted yield curves tend to precede recessions by 12–18 months. In recessions, interest rates tend to fall, with short-term rates dropping further. As a result, the yield curve tends to be steep coming out of a recession.

Interest Rate Expectations. Suppose short-term interest rates are equal to long-term interest rates. If investors expect interest rates to rise in the future, they would not want to make long-term investments. Instead, they could do better by investing on a short-term basis and then reinvesting after interest rates rose. Thus, if interest rates are expected to rise, long-term interest rates will tend to be higher than short-term rates to attract investors.

Similarly, if interest rates are expected to fall in the future, then borrowers would not wish to borrow at long-term rates that are equal to short-term rates. They would do better by borrowing on a short-term basis, and then taking out a new loan after rates fall. So, if interest rates are expected to fall, long-term rates will tend to be lower than short-term rates to attract borrowers.

These arguments imply that the shape of the yield curve will be strongly influenced by interest rate expectations. A sharply increasing (*steep*) yield curve, with long-term rates much higher than short-term rates, generally indicates that interest rates are expected to rise in the future (see the yield curve for November 2008 shown in Figure 5.2). A decreasing (*inverted*) yield curve, with long-term rates lower than short-term rates, generally signals an expected decline in future interest rates (see the yield curve for November 2006 shown in Figure 5.2). Because interest rates tend to drop in response to a slowdown in the economy, an inverted yield curve is often interpreted as a negative forecast for economic growth. Indeed, as Figure 5.3 illustrates, each of the last seven recessions in the United States was preceded by a

INTERVIEW WITH

KEVIN M. WARSH

Kevin M. Warsh, a lecturer at Stanford's Graduate School of Business and a distinguished visiting fellow at the Hoover Institution, was a Federal Reserve governor from 2006 to 2011, serving as chief liaison to the financial markets.

QUESTION: *What are the main policy instruments used by central banks to control the economy?*

ANSWER: The Federal Reserve (Fed) deploys several policy tools to achieve its goals of price stability, maximum sustainable employment, and financial stability. Lowering the federal funds short-term interest rate, the primary policy instrument, stimulates the economy. Raising the federal funds rate generally slows the economy. Buying and selling short-term U.S. Treasury securities through *open market operations* is standard practice. Prior to the 2007–2009 financial crisis, the Fed's balance sheet ranged from \$700–\$900 billion. But when the Fed was unable to lower interest rates further because rates were so close to zero already, it resorted to large-scale, longer-term open market operations to increase liquidity in the financial system in the hopes of stimulating the economy further, thus growing its balance sheet significantly. With *open mouth operations*, the Fed's announcements of its intent to buy or sell assets indicates its desired degree of future policy accommodation, often prompting markets to react by adjusting interest rates immediately. The Fed's Lender-of-Last-Resort authority allows it to lend money against good collateral to troubled institutions under certain conditions.

QUESTION: *What factors limit the effectiveness of Fed policy?*

ANSWER: Monetary policy does not act in isolation. Fiscal (taxing and spending), trade, and regulatory policies have huge consequence on the state of economic and financial conditions. In the short term, monetary policy can help buy time for an economy to improve, but it cannot cure structural failings of an economy in isolation or compensate for the country's growing indebtedness.

QUESTION: *What tools did the Fed create to address the 2007–2009 financial crisis?*

ANSWER: During the darkest days of the crisis, markets did not operate effectively, prices for securities did not clear, and banks and other financial institutions lacked clarity and confidence in the financial wherewithal of each other. One effective, innovative tool, the *Term Auction Facility (TAF)*, stimulated the economy by providing cheap and readily available term funding to banks, large and small, on the front lines of the economy, thus encouraging them to extend credit to businesses and consumers. After reducing the policy rate to near zero to help revive the economy, the Fed instituted two *Quantitative Easing (QE)* programs—special purchases of government and agency securities—to increase money supply, promote lending, and according to some proponents, increase prices of riskier assets.

The Fed also addressed the global financial crisis by establishing temporary *central bank liquidity swap lines* with the European Central Bank and other major central banks. Using this facility, a foreign central bank is able to obtain dollar funding for its customers by swapping Euros for dollars or another currency and agreeing to reverse the swap at a later date. The Fed does not take exchange rate risk, but it is subject to the credit risk of its central bank counterparty.

QUESTION: *What tools is the European Central Bank (ECB) using to address the sovereign debt crisis? How does its approach compare to the Fed's approach to the 2007–2009 financial crisis?*

ANSWER: As a novel economic federation, the ECB finds itself in a more difficult position than the Fed. The underlying economies and competitiveness are markedly different across the Eurozone—in Germany versus Greece, for example. From 2007 until mid-2010, many European financiers and policymakers believed that global financial crisis was largely American-made, with some strains exported to the continent. By mid-2010, however, they recognized that it was indeed a global crisis. The ECB is formally charged with a single mandate of ensuring price stability, rather than the broader mandate of the Fed. Still, its actions ultimately mirrored many of those undertaken by the Fed: lowering the effective policy rate to record lows, providing direct liquidity to the Eurozone's financial institutions to avoid a potential run on the banking system, and instituting the Security Market Purchase program (buying sovereign credit of some of its distressed countries).

period in which the yield curve was inverted. Conversely, the yield curve tends to be steep as the economy comes out of a recession and interest rates are expected to rise.[7]

Clearly, the yield curve provides extremely important information for a business manager. In addition to specifying the discount rates for risk-free cash flows that occur at different horizons, it is also a potential leading indicator of future economic growth.

EXAMPLE 5.6 **Comparing Short- and Long-Term Interest Rates**

Problem

Suppose the current one-year interest rate is 1%. If it is known with certainty that the one-year interest rate will be 2% next year and 4% the following year, what will the interest rates r_1, r_2, and r_3 of the yield curve be today? Is the yield curve flat, increasing, or inverted?

Solution

We are told already that the one-year rate $r_1 = 1\%$. To find the two-year rate, note that if we invest \$1 for one year at the current one-year rate and then reinvest next year at the new one-year rate, after two years we will earn

$$\$1 \times (1.01) \times (1.02) = \$1.0302$$

We should earn the same payoff if we invest for two years at the current two-year rate r_2:

$$\$1 \times (1 + r_2)^2 = \$1.0302$$

Otherwise, there would be an arbitrage opportunity: If investing at the two-year rate led to a higher payoff, investors could invest for two years and borrow each year at the one-year rate. If investing at the two-year rate led to a lower payoff, investors could invest each year at the one-year rate and borrow at the two-year rate.

Solving for r_2, we find that

$$r_2 = (1.0302)^{1/2} - 1 = 1.499\%$$

Similarly, investing for three years at the one-year rates should have the same payoff as investing at the current three-year rate:

$$(1.01) \times (1.02) \times (1.04) = 1.0714 = (1 + r_3)^3$$

We can solve for $r_3 = (1.0714)^{1/3} - 1 = 2.326\%$. Therefore, the current yield curve has $r_1 = 1\%$, $r_2 = 1.499\%$, and $r_3 = 2.326\%$. The yield curve is increasing as a result of the anticipated higher interest rates in the future.

CONCEPT CHECK

1. What is the difference between a nominal and real interest rate?
2. How do investors' expectations of future short-term interest rates affect the shape of the current yield curve?

5.4 Risk and Taxes

In this section, we discuss two other factors that are important when evaluating interest rates: risk and taxes.

---

[7] Other factors besides interest rate expectations—most notably risk—can have an impact on the shape of the yield curve. See Chapter 6 for further discussion.

Risk and Interest Rates

We have already seen that interest rates vary with the investment horizon. Interest rates also vary based on the identity of the borrower. For example, Figure 5.4 shows the interest rates required by investors for five-year loans to a number of different borrowers in mid-2015.

Why do these interest rates vary so widely? The lowest interest rate is the rate paid on U.S. Treasury notes. U.S. Treasury securities are widely regarded to be risk free because there is virtually no chance the government will fail to pay the interest and default on these loans. Thus, when we refer to the "risk-free interest rate," we mean the rate on U.S. Treasuries.

All other borrowers have some risk of default. For these loans, the stated interest rate is the *maximum* amount that investors will receive. Investors may receive less if the company has financial difficulties and is unable to fully repay the loan. To compensate for the risk that they will receive less if the firm defaults, investors demand a higher interest rate than the rate on U.S. Treasuries. The difference between the interest rate of the loan and the Treasury rate will depend on investors' assessment of the likelihood that the firm will default.

Later, we will develop tools to evaluate the risk of different investments and determine the interest rate or discount rate that appropriately compensates investors for the level of risk they are taking. For now, remember that when discounting future cash flows, it is important to use a discount rate that matches both the horizon and the risk of the cash flows. Specifically, *the right discount rate for a cash flow is the rate of return available in the market on other investments of comparable risk and term.*

FIGURE 5.4

Interest Rates on Five-Year Loans for Various Borrowers, December 2015

Interest rates shown based on yields of 5-year bonds for each issuer. Note the variation in interest rates based on the riskiness of the borrower.

Source: FINRA.org

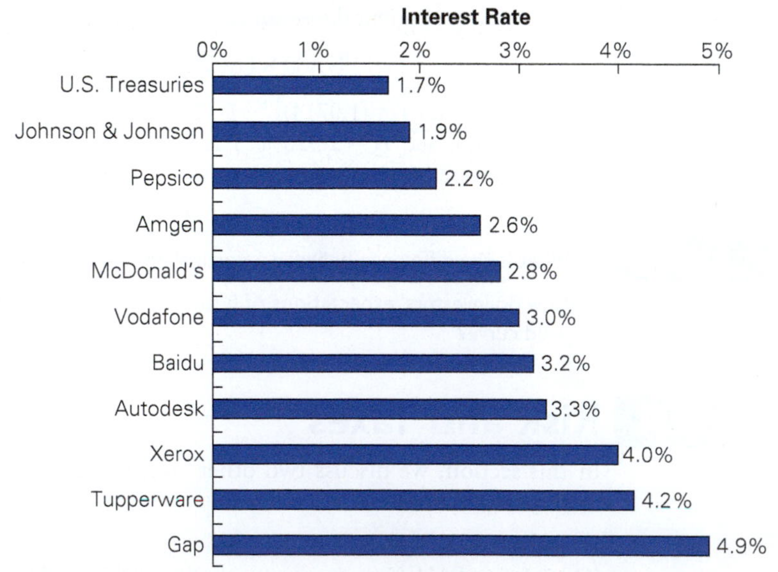

EXAMPLE 5.7 **Discounting Risky Cash Flows**

Problem

Suppose the U.S. government owes your firm \$1000, to be paid in five years. Based on the interest rates in Figure 5.4, what is the present value of this cash flow? Suppose instead Gap Inc. owes your firm \$1000. Estimate the present value in this case.

Solution

Assuming we can regard the government's obligation as risk free (there is no chance you won't be paid), then we discount the cash flow using the risk-free Treasury interest rate of 1.7%:

$$PV = \$1000 \div (1.017)^5 = \$919.17$$

The obligation from Gap is not risk-free. There is no guarantee that Gap will not have financial difficulties and fail to pay the \$1000. Because the risk of this obligation is likely to be comparable to the five-year bond quoted in Figure 5.4, the 4.9% interest rate of the loan is a more appropriate discount rate to use to compute the present value in this case:

$$PV = \$1000 \div (1.049)^5 = \$787.27$$

Note the substantially lower present value of Gap's debt compared to the government debt due to Gap's higher risk of default.

After-Tax Interest Rates

If the cash flows from an investment are taxed, the investor's actual cash flow will be reduced by the amount of the tax payments. We will discuss the taxation of corporate investments in detail in later chapters. Here, we consider the effect of taxes on the interest earned on savings (or paid on borrowing). Taxes reduce the amount of interest the investor can keep, and we refer to this reduced amount as the **after-tax interest rate**.

Consider an investment that pays 8% interest (EAR) for one year. If you invest \$100 at the start of the year, you will earn $8\% \times \$100 = \$8$ in interest at year-end. This interest may be taxable as income.[8] If you are in a 40% tax bracket, you will owe

$$(40\% \text{ income tax rate}) \times (\$8 \text{ interest}) = \$3.20 \text{ tax liability}$$

Thus, you will receive only $\$8 - \$3.20 = \$4.80$ after paying taxes. This amount is equivalent to earning 4.80% interest and not paying any taxes, so the after-tax interest rate is 4.80%.

In general, if the interest rate is r and the tax rate is τ, then for each \$1 invested you will earn interest equal to r and owe tax of $\tau \times r$ on the interest. The equivalent after-tax interest rate is therefore

After-Tax Interest Rate

$$r - (\tau \times r) = r(1 - \tau) \tag{5.8}$$

Applying this formula to our previous example of an 8% interest rate and a 40% tax rate, we find the interest rate is $8\% \times (1 - 0.40) = 4.80\%$ after taxes.

---

[8] In the United States, interest income for individuals is taxable as income unless the investment is held in a tax-sheltered retirement account or the investment is from tax-exempt securities (such as municipal bonds). Interest from U.S. Treasury securities is exempt from state and local taxes. Interest income earned by a corporation is also taxed at the corporate tax rate.

We can apply the same calculation to loans. In some cases, the interest on loans is tax deductible.[9] In that case, the cost of paying interest on the loan is offset by the benefit of the tax deduction. The net effect is that when interest on a loan is tax deductible, the effective after-tax interest rate is $r(1 - \tau)$. In other words, the ability to deduct the interest expense lowers the effective after-tax interest rate paid on the loan.

EXAMPLE 5.8 **Comparing After-Tax Interest Rates**

Problem

Suppose you have a credit card with a 14% APR with monthly compounding, a bank savings account paying 5% EAR, and a home equity loan with a 7% APR with monthly compounding. Your income tax rate is 40%. The interest on the savings account is taxable, and the interest on the home equity loan is tax deductible. What is the effective after-tax interest rate of each instrument, expressed as an EAR? Suppose you are purchasing a new car and are offered a car loan with a 4.8% APR and monthly compounding (which is not tax deductible). Should you take the car loan?

Solution

Because taxes are typically paid annually, we first convert each interest rate to an EAR to determine the actual amount of interest earned or paid during the year. The savings account has a 5% EAR. Using Eq. 5.3, the EAR of the credit card is $(1 + 0.14/12)^{12} - 1 = 14.93\%$, and the EAR of the home equity loan is $(1 + 0.07/12)^{12} - 1 = 7.23\%$.

Next, we compute the after-tax interest rate for each. Because the credit card interest is not tax deductible, its after-tax interest rate is the same as its pre-tax interest rate, 14.93%. The after-tax interest rate on the home equity loan, which is tax deductible, is $7.23\% \times (1 - 0.40) = 4.34\%$. The after-tax interest rate that we will earn on the savings account is $5\% \times (1 - 0.40) = 3\%$.

Now consider the car loan. Its EAR is $(1 + 0.048/12)^{12} - 1 = 4.91\%$. It is not tax deductible, so this rate is also its after-tax interest rate. Therefore, the car loan is not our cheapest source of funds. It would be best to use savings, which has an opportunity cost of foregone after-tax interest of 3%. If we don't have sufficient savings, we should use the home equity loan, which has an after-tax cost of 4.34%. And we should certainly not borrow using the credit card!

CONCEPT CHECK

1. Why do corporations pay higher interest rates on their loans than the U.S. government?
2. How do taxes affect the interest earned on an investment? What about the interest paid on a loan?

5.5 The Opportunity Cost of Capital

As we have seen in this chapter, the interest rates we observe in the market will vary based on quoting conventions, the term of the investment, and risk. The actual return kept by an investor will also depend on how the interest is taxed. In this chapter, we have developed

[9]In the United States, interest is tax deductible for individuals only for home mortgages or home equity loans (up to certain limits), some student loans, and loans made to purchase securities. Interest on other forms of consumer debt is not tax deductible. Interest on debt is tax deductible for corporations.

COMMON MISTAKE **States Dig a $3 Trillion Hole by Discounting at the Wrong Rate**

Almost all states in the United States offer their employees a defined benefit pension plan guaranteeing a retirement income based on the duration of their employment with the state and their final salary. These promised payments are the plan's liabilities—and because the payouts are guaranteed, they are comparable to a risk-free bond. To meet these liabilities, states put aside funds and invest them in risky assets like stocks and corporate bonds.

Unfortunately, states make a critical, but common, mistake when determining their funding requirements: They compute the present value of the liabilities using an arbitrary discount rate (typically 8%) that is unrelated to the riskiness of the plan's liabilities.

Because of their guaranteed nature, the risk-free rate, which is currently well below 8%, is the correct discount rate for plan liabilities.[10] This error has led states to grossly underestimate the value of their liabilities—and underfunded pension plans impose a potential future obligation on taxpayers. How large is this obligation? Professors Robert Novy-Marx and Joshua Rauh[11] found that total state pension underfunding in 2008 amounted to at least $3 *trillion*. They also estimated that there is less than a 5% probability that, over the next 15 years, states will be able to meet their pension obligations without turning to taxpayers. Worse still, states are most likely to need the money in market downturns, precisely when taxpayers are least able to pay.

the tools to account for these differences and gained some insights into how interest rates are determined.

In Chapter 3, we argued that the "market interest rate" provides the exchange rate that we need to compute present values and evaluate an investment opportunity. But with so many interest rates to choose from, the term "market interest rate" is inherently ambiguous. Therefore, going forward, we will base the discount rate that we use to evaluate cash flows on the investor's **opportunity cost of capital** (or more simply, the **cost of capital**), which is *the best available expected return offered in the market on an investment of comparable risk and term to the cash flow being discounted.*

The cost of capital is clearly relevant for a firm seeking to raise capital from outside investors. In order to attract funds, the firm must offer an expected return comparable to what investors could earn elsewhere with the same risk and horizon. The same logic applies when a firm considers a project it can fund internally. Because any funds invested in a new project could be returned to shareholders to invest elsewhere, the new project should be taken only if it offers a better return than shareholders' other opportunities.

Thus, the opportunity cost of capital provides the benchmark against which the cash flows of the new investment should be evaluated. For a risk-free project, it will typically correspond to the interest rate on U.S. Treasury securities with a similar term. The cost of capital for risky projects will often exceed this amount, depending on the nature and magnitude of the risk. We will develop tools for estimating the cost of capital for risky projects in Part IV.

CONCEPT CHECK

1. What is the opportunity cost of capital?
2. Why do different interest rates exist, even in a competitive market?

---

[10] States often justify the 8% rate as the return they expect to earn on their investments. But the risks of their investments and of their liabilities are not comparable (for example, the return on stocks is not guaranteed), so this argument is fundamentally flawed.

[11] R. Novy-Marx and J. Rau, The Liabilities and Risks of State-Sponsored Pension Plans, *Journal of Economic Perspectives* (Fall 2009) Vol. 23, No. 4.

5.1 Interest Rate Quotes and Adjustments

- The effective annual rate (EAR) indicates the actual amount of interest earned in one year. The EAR can be used as a discount rate for annual cash flows.
- Given an EAR, r, the equivalent discount rate for an n-year time interval, where n may be a fraction, is

$$(1 + r)^n - 1 \tag{5.1}$$

- An annual percentage rate (APR) indicates the total amount of interest earned in one year without considering the effect of compounding. APRs cannot be used as discount rates.
- Given an APR with k compounding intervals per year, the interest earned per compounding interval is APR/k.
- Given an APR with k compounding intervals per year, the EAR is given by:

$$1 + EAR = \left(1 + \frac{APR}{k}\right)^k \tag{5.3}$$

- For a given APR, the EAR increases with the compounding frequency.

5.2 Application: Discount Rates and Loans

- Loan rates are typically stated as APRs, with the compounding interval of the APR equal to the payment frequency.
- The outstanding balance of a loan is equal to the present value of the loan payments, when evaluated using the effective interest rate per payment interval based on the loan rate.

5.3 The Determinants of Interest Rates

- Quoted interest rates are nominal interest rates, which indicate the rate of growth of the money invested. The real interest rate indicates the rate of growth of one's purchasing power after adjusting for inflation.
- Given a nominal interest rate r and an inflation rate i, the real interest rate is

$$r_r = \frac{r - i}{1 + i} \approx r - i \tag{5.5}$$

- Nominal interest rates tend to be high when inflation is high and low when inflation is low.
- Higher interest rates tend to reduce the NPV of typical investment projects. The U.S. Federal Reserve raises interest rates to moderate investment and combat inflation and lowers interest rates to stimulate investment and economic growth.
- Interest rates differ with the investment horizon according to the term structure of interest rates. The graph plotting interest rates as a function of the horizon is called the yield curve.
- Cash flows should be discounted using the discount rate that is appropriate for their horizon. Thus the PV of a cash flow stream is

$$PV = \frac{C_1}{1 + r_1} + \frac{C_2}{(1 + r_2)^2} + \cdots + \frac{C_N}{(1 + r_N)^N} = \sum_{n=1}^{N} \frac{C_n}{(1 + r_n)^n} \tag{5.7}$$

- Annuity and perpetuity formulas cannot be applied when discount rates vary with the horizon.
- The shape of the yield curve tends to vary with investors' expectations of future economic growth and interest rates. It tends to be inverted prior to recessions and to be steep coming out of a recession.

5.4 Risk and Taxes

- U.S. government Treasury rates are regarded as risk-free interest rates. Because other borrowers may default, they will pay higher interest rates on their loans.

- The correct discount rate for a cash flow is the expected return available in the market on other investments of comparable risk and term.
- If the interest on an investment is taxed at rate τ, or if the interest on a loan is tax deductible, then the effective after-tax interest rate is

$$r(1 - \tau) \tag{5.8}$$

5.5 The Opportunity Cost of Capital

- The opportunity cost of capital is the best available expected return offered in the market on an investment of comparable risk and term.
- The opportunity cost of capital provides the benchmark against which the cash flows of a new investment should be evaluated.

Key Terms

adjustable rate mortgages (ARMs) *p. 150*
after-tax interest rate *p. 159*
amortizing loan *p. 148*
annual percentage rate (APR) *p. 146*
continuous compounding *p. 146*
cost of capital *p. 161*
effective annual rate (EAR) *p. 144*
federal funds rate *p. 154*
mid-year convention *p. 171*
nominal interest rate *p. 150*
opportunity cost of capital *p. 161*
real interest rate *p. 150*
term structure *p. 152*
yield curve *p. 152*

Further Reading

For an interesting account of the history of interest rates over the past four millennia, see S. Homer and R. Sylla, *A History of Interest Rates* (John Wiley & Sons, 2005).

For a deeper understanding of interest rates, how they behave with changing market conditions, and how risk can be managed, see J. C. Van Horne, *Financial Market Rates and Flows* (Prentice Hall, 2000).

For further insights into the relationship between interest rates, inflation, and economic growth, see a macroeconomics text such as A. Abel, B. Bernanke, and D. Croushore, *Macroeconomics* (Prentice Hall, 2010).

For further analysis of the yield curve and how it is measured and modeled, see M. Choudhry, *Analyzing and Interpreting the Yield Curve* (John Wiley & Sons, 2004).

Problems

All problems are available in MyFinanceLab. *An asterisk (*) indicates problems with a higher level of difficulty.*

Interest Rate Quotes and Adjustments

1. Your bank is offering you an account that will pay 20% interest in total for a two-year deposit. Determine the equivalent discount rate for a period length of
   a. Six months. b. One year. c. One month.

MFL X

2. Which do you prefer: a bank account that pays 5% per year (EAR) for three years or
   a. An account that pays 2½% every six months for three years?
   b. An account that pays 7½% every 18 months for three years?
   c. An account that pays ½% per month for three years?

3. Many academic institutions offer a sabbatical policy. Every seven years a professor is given a year free of teaching and other administrative responsibilities at full pay. For a professor earning $70,000 per year who works for a total of 42 years, what is the present value of the amount she will earn while on sabbatical if the interest rate is 6% (EAR)?

4. You have found three investment choices for a one-year deposit: 10% APR compounded monthly, 10% APR compounded annually, and 9% APR compounded daily. Compute the EAR for each investment choice. (Assume that there are 365 days in the year.)

5. You are considering moving your money to a new bank offering a one-year CD that pays an 8% APR with monthly compounding. Your current bank's manager offers to match the rate you have been offered. The account at your current bank would pay interest every six months. How much interest will you need to earn every six months to match the CD?

6. Your bank account pays interest with an EAR of 5%. What is the APR quote for this account based on semiannual compounding? What is the APR with monthly compounding?

7. Suppose the interest rate is 8% APR with monthly compounding. What is the present value of an annuity that pays $100 every six months for five years?

8. You can earn $50 in interest on a $1000 deposit for eight months. If the EAR is the same regardless of the length of the investment, determine how much interest you will earn on a $1000 deposit for

a. 6 months. b. 1 year. c. 1½ years.

9. Suppose you invest $100 in a bank account, and five years later it has grown to $134.39.

a. What APR did you receive, if the interest was compounded semiannually?

b. What APR did you receive if the interest was compounded monthly?

10. Your son has been accepted into college. This college guarantees that your son's tuition will not increase for the four years he attends college. The first $10,000 tuition payment is due in six months. After that, the same payment is due every six months until you have made a total of eight payments. The college offers a bank account that allows you to withdraw money every six months and has a fixed APR of 4% (semiannual) guaranteed to remain the same over the next four years. How much money must you deposit today if you intend to make no further deposits and would like to make all the tuition payments from this account, leaving the account empty when the last payment is made?

11. You make monthly payments on your mortgage. It has a quoted APR of 5% (monthly compounding). What percentage of the outstanding principal do you pay in interest each month?

Application: Discount Rates and Loans

12. Capital One is advertising a 60-month, 5.99% APR motorcycle loan. If you need to borrow $8000 to purchase your dream Harley Davidson, what will your monthly payment be?

13. Oppenheimer Bank is offering a 30-year mortgage with an EAR of 5⅜%. If you plan to borrow $150,000, what will your monthly payment be?

14. You have decided to refinance your mortgage. You plan to borrow whatever is outstanding on your current mortgage. The current monthly payment is $2356 and you have made every payment on time. The original term of the mortgage was 30 years, and the mortgage is exactly four years and eight months old. You have just made your monthly payment. The mortgage interest rate is 6⅜% (APR). How much do you owe on the mortgage today?

15. You have just sold your house for $1,000,000 in cash. Your mortgage was originally a 30-year mortgage with monthly payments and an initial balance of $800,000. The mortgage is currently exactly 18½ years old, and you have just made a payment. If the interest rate on the mortgage is 5.25% (APR), how much cash will you have from the sale once you pay off the mortgage?

16. You have just purchased a home and taken out a $500,000 mortgage. The mortgage has a 30-year term with monthly payments and an APR of 6%.

a. How much will you pay in interest, and how much will you pay in principal, during the first year?

b. How much will you pay in interest, and how much will you pay in principal, during the 20th year (i.e., between 19 and 20 years from now)?

17. Your mortgage has 25 years left, and has an APR of 7.625% with monthly payments of $1449.

a. What is the outstanding balance?

b. Suppose you cannot make the mortgage payment and you are in danger of losing your house to foreclosure. The bank has offered to renegotiate your loan. The bank expects to get $150,000 for the house if it forecloses. They will lower your payment as long as they will receive at least this amount (in present value terms). If current 25-year mortgage interest rates have dropped to 5% (APR), what is the lowest monthly payment you could make for the remaining life of your loan that would be attractive to the bank?

MFL ***18.** You have an outstanding student loan with required payments of $500 per month for the next four years. The interest rate on the loan is 9% APR (monthly). You are considering making an extra payment of $100 today (that is, you will pay an extra $100 that you are not required to pay). If you are required to continue to make payments of $500 per month until the loan is paid off, what is the amount of your final payment? What effective rate of return (expressed as an APR with monthly compounding) have you earned on the $100?

MFL ***19.** Consider again the setting of Problem 18. Now that you realize your best investment is to prepay your student loan, you decide to prepay as much as you can each month. Looking at your budget, you can afford to pay an extra $250 per month in addition to your required monthly payments of $500, or $750 in total each month. How long will it take you to pay off the loan?

***20.** Oppenheimer Bank is offering a 30-year mortgage with an APR of 5.25% based on monthly compounding. With this mortgage your monthly payments would be $2,000 per month. In addition, Oppenheimer Bank offers you the following deal: Instead of making the monthly payment of $2,000 every month, you can make half the payment every two weeks (so that you will make $52/2 = 26$ payments per year). With this plan, how long will it take to pay off the mortgage if the EAR of the loan is unchanged?

MFL ***21.** Your friend tells you he has a very simple trick for shortening the time it takes to repay your mortgage by one-third: Use your holiday bonus to make an extra payment on January 1 of each year (that is, pay your monthly payment due on that day twice). Assume that the mortgage has an original term of 30 years and an APR of 12%.

a. If you take out your mortgage on January 1 (so that your first payment is due on February 1), and you make your first extra payment at the end of the first year, in what year will you finish repaying your mortgage?

b. If you take out your mortgage on July 1 (so the first payment is on August 1), and you make the extra payment each January, in how many *months* will you pay off your mortgage?

c. How will the amount of time it takes to pay off the loan given this strategy vary with the interest rate on the loan?

MFL **22.** You need a new car and the dealer has offered you a price of $20,000, with the following payment options: (a) pay cash and receive a $2000 rebate, or (b) pay a $5000 down payment and finance the rest with a 0% APR loan over 30 months. But having just quit your job and started an MBA program, you are in debt and you expect to be in debt for at least the next 2½ years. You plan to use credit cards to pay your expenses; luckily you have one with a low (fixed) rate of 15% APR (monthly). Which payment option is best for you?

23. The mortgage on your house is five years old. It required monthly payments of $1402, had an original term of 30 years, and had an interest rate of 10% (APR). In the intervening five years, interest rates have fallen and so you have decided to refinance—that is, you will roll over the outstanding balance into a new mortgage. The new mortgage has a 30-year term, requires monthly payments, and has an interest rate of 6⅝% (APR).

a. What monthly repayments will be required with the new loan?
b. If you still want to pay off the mortgage in 25 years, what monthly payment should you make after you refinance?
c. Suppose you are willing to continue making monthly payments of $1402. How long will it take you to pay off the mortgage after refinancing?
d. Suppose you are willing to continue making monthly payments of $1402, and want to pay off the mortgage in 25 years. How much additional cash can you borrow today as part of the refinancing?

24. You have credit card debt of $25,000 that has an APR (monthly compounding) of 15%. Each month you pay the minimum monthly payment only. You are required to pay only the outstanding interest. You have received an offer in the mail for an otherwise identical credit card with an APR of 12%. After considering all your alternatives, you decide to switch cards, roll over the outstanding balance on the old card into the new card, and borrow additional money as well. How much can you borrow today on the new card without changing the minimum monthly payment you will be required to pay?

The Determinants of Interest Rates

25. In 1975, interest rates were 7.85% and the rate of inflation was 12.3% in the United States. What was the real interest rate in 1975? How would the purchasing power of your savings have changed over the year?

26. If the rate of inflation is 5%, what nominal interest rate is necessary for you to earn a 3% real interest rate on your investment?

27. Can the nominal interest rate available to an investor be significantly negative? (*Hint*: Consider the interest rate earned from saving cash "under the mattress.") Can the real interest rate be negative? Explain.

28. Consider a project that requires an initial investment of $100,000 and will produce a single cash flow of $150,000 in five years.

a. What is the NPV of this project if the five-year interest rate is 5% (EAR)?
b. What is the NPV of this project if the five-year interest rate is 10% (EAR)?
c. What is the highest five-year interest rate such that this project is still profitable?

MFL **29.** Suppose the term structure of risk-free interest rates is as shown below:

Term	1 year	2 years	3 years	5 years	7 years	10 years	20 years
Rate (EAR, %)	1.99	2.41	2.74	3.32	3.76	4.13	4.93

a. Calculate the present value of an investment that pays $1000 in two years and $2000 in five years for certain.
b. Calculate the present value of receiving $500 per year, with certainty, at the end of the next five years. To find the rates for the missing years in the table, linearly interpolate between the years for which you do know the rates. (For example, the rate in year 4 would be the average of the rate in year 3 and year 5.)
*c. Calculate the present value of receiving $2300 per year, with certainty, for the next 20 years. Infer rates for the missing years using linear interpolation. (*Hint*: Use a spreadsheet.)

MFL **30.** Using the term structure in Problem 29, what is the present value of an investment that pays $100 at the end of each of years 1, 2, and 3? If you wanted to value this investment correctly using the annuity formula, which discount rate should you use?

MFL **31.** What is the shape of the yield curve given the term structure in Problem 29? What expectations are investors likely to have about future interest rates?

MFL **32.** Suppose the current one-year interest rate is 6%. One year from now, you believe the economy will start to slow and the one-year interest rate will fall to 5%. In two years, you expect the economy to be in the midst of a recession, causing the Federal Reserve to cut interest rates drastically and the one-year interest rate to fall to 2%. The one-year interest rate will then rise to 3% the following year, and continue to rise by 1% per year until it returns to 6%, where it will remain from then on.

a. If you were certain regarding these future interest rate changes, what two-year interest rate would be consistent with these expectations?

b. What current term structure of interest rates, for terms of 1 to 10 years, would be consistent with these expectations?

c. Plot the yield curve in this case. How does the one-year interest rate compare to the 10-year interest rate?

Risk and Taxes

33. Figure 5.4 shows that Johnson and Johnson's five-year borrowing rate is 1.9% and Xerox's is 4.0%. Which would you prefer? $500 from Johnson and Johnson paid today or a promise that the firm will pay you $575 in five years? Which would you choose if Xerox offered you the same alternative?

34. Your best taxable investment opportunity has an EAR of 4%. Your best tax-free investment opportunity has an EAR of 3%. If your tax rate is 30%, which opportunity provides the higher after-tax interest rate?

35. Your uncle Fred just purchased a new boat. He brags to you about the low 7% interest rate (APR, monthly compounding) he obtained from the dealer. The rate is even lower than the rate he could have obtained on his home equity loan (8% APR, monthly compounding). If his tax rate is 25% and the interest on the home equity loan is tax deductible, which loan is truly cheaper?

36. You are enrolling in an MBA program. To pay your tuition, you can either take out a standard student loan (so the interest payments are not tax deductible) with an EAR of 5½% or you can use a tax-deductible home equity loan with an APR (monthly) of 6%. You anticipate being in a very low tax bracket, so your tax rate will be only 15%. Which loan should you use?

37. Your best friend consults you for investment advice. You learn that his tax rate is 35%, and he has the following current investments and debts:

- A car loan with an outstanding balance of $5000 and a 4.8% APR (monthly compounding)
- Credit cards with an outstanding balance of $10,000 and a 14.9% APR (monthly compounding)
- A regular savings account with a $30,000 balance, paying a 5.50% EAR
- A money market savings account with a $100,000 balance, paying a 5.25% APR (daily compounding)
- A tax-deductible home equity loan with an outstanding balance of $25,000 and a 5.0% APR (monthly compounding)

a. Which savings account pays a higher after-tax interest rate?

b. Should your friend use his savings to pay off any of his outstanding debts? Explain.

38. Suppose you have outstanding debt with an 8% interest rate that can be repaid any time, and the interest rate on U.S. Treasuries is only 5%. You plan to repay your debt using any cash that you don't invest elsewhere. Until your debt is repaid, what cost of capital should you use when evaluating a new risk-free investment opportunity? Why?

The Opportunity Cost of Capital

39. In the summer of 2008, at Heathrow Airport in London, Bestofthebest (BB), a private company, offered a lottery to win a Ferrari or 90,000 British pounds, equivalent at the time to about \$180,000. Both the Ferrari and the money, in 100-pound notes, were on display. If the U.K. interest rate was 5% per year, and the dollar interest rate was 2% per year (EARs), how much did it cost the company in dollars each month to keep the cash on display? That is, what was the opportunity cost of keeping it on display rather than in a bank account? (Ignore taxes.)

40. Your firm is considering the purchase of a new office phone system. You can either pay \$32,000 now, or \$1000 per month for 36 months.

a. Suppose your firm currently borrows at a rate of 6% per year (APR with monthly compounding). Which payment plan is more attractive?

b. Suppose your firm currently borrows at a rate of 18% per year (APR with monthly compounding). Which payment plan would be more attractive in this case?

41. After reading the Novy-Marx and Rauh article (see the Common Mistake Box on page 161), you decide to compute the total obligation of the state you live in. After some research you determine that your state's promised pension payments amount to \$1 billion annually, and you expect this obligation to grow at 2% per year. You determine that the riskiness of this obligation is the same as the riskiness of the state's debt. Based on the pricing of that debt you determine that the correct discount rate for the fund's liabilities is 3% per annum. Currently, based on actuarial calculations using 8% as the discount rate, the plan is neither over- nor underfunded—the value of the liabilities exactly matches the value of the assets. What is the extent of the true unfunded liability?

Data Case

Florida's Pension Plan Liability

You have been hired as a consultant by CARE (Conservatives Are REsponsible), a political action committee focusing on fiscal responsibility. The Florida chapter has become increasingly worried about the state's indebtedness. In an effort to assess the extent of the problem, you have been hired to estimate by how much the state pension plan is underfunded. Luckily for you, Florida publishes an annual financial report on the status of the state's pension plan.

1. Download the latest financial report by going to the Florida State Auditor General's Web site: www.myflorida.com/audgen/ and clicking on the Auditor General Released Reports: by Fiscal Year (located on the far left).
2. Choose the latest year the report is available. (In 2015 it was called "Florida Retirement System Pension Plan and Other State-Administered Systems—Financial Audit" and was listed as report number 2016-097 in the 2015–2016 fiscal year.)
3. Search for the place in the report listing the fund's future liabilities—its promised payments to existing empoyees. (In 2015 this information was listed on p. 102 in graphical format only. The Internet site WebPlotDigitizer—arohatgi.info/WebPlotDigitizer/—provides a convenient way to digitize information that is provided in graphical format. Alternatively, you can just eyeball the data.)
4. Because these pension payments are a legal obligation for the state, you assess their risk to be similar to other state debt, and therefore the cost of capital should be similar to Florida's current borrowing rate. Begin by first searching for the State of Florida's bond rating. Once you know the rating, go to FMSBonds Inc. (www.fmsbonds.com/market-yields/) to find out what Florida bonds at different maturities with this rating are currently yielding.
5. Using these yields to approximate the cost of capital, estimate the present value of Florida's pension liabilities.

6. Calculate the level of underfunding by finding the value of the pension fund's assets (in 2015, this information was on p. 19 of the report) and subtracting the present value of the liabilities. Express the underfunding as the value of the assets as a percentage of the present value of the pension liabilities.

7. Compare your estimate of the actual level of underfunding to what the report calculates using GAAP accounting. (In 2015, this information was on p. 61 of the report.) Explain the difference between your result and theirs.

8. Find the current level of the State of Florida indebtedness by going to the following Web site: www.usgovernmentspending.com/compare_state_spending_2015bH0d

9. In percentage terms, how much would the stated level of the indebtedness of the State of Florida increase if the level of underfunding in the state's pension plan is included in overall state indebtedness?

Note: Updates to this data case may be found at www.berkdemarzo.com.

CHAPTER 5 APPENDIX

Continuous Rates and Cash Flows

NOTATION

e 2.71828...

ln natural logarithm

r_{cc} continuously compounded discount rate

g_{cc} continuously compounded growth rate

$\overline{C}_1$ total cash flows received in first year

In this appendix, we consider how to discount cash flows when interest is paid, or cash flows are received, on a continuous basis.

Discount Rates for a Continuously Compounded APR

Some investments compound more frequently than daily. As we move from daily to hourly ($k = 24 \times 365$) to compounding every second ($k = 60 \times 60 \times 24 \times 365$), we approach the limit of continuous compounding, in which we compound every instant ($k = \infty$). Eq. 5.3 cannot be used to compute the discount rate from an APR quote based on continuous compounding. In this case, the discount rate for a period length of one year—that is, the EAR—is given by Eq. 5A.1:

The EAR for a Continuously Compounded APR

$$(1 + EAR) = e^{APR} \tag{5A.1}$$

where the mathematical constant[12] $e = 2.71828\ldots$. Once you know the EAR, you can compute the discount rate for any compounding period length using Eq. 5.1.

Alternatively, if we know the EAR and want to find the corresponding continuously compounded APR, we can invert Eq. 5A.1 by taking the natural logarithm (ln) of both sides:[13]

The Continuously Compounded APR for an EAR

$$APR = \ln(1 + EAR) \tag{5A.2}$$

Continuously compounded rates are not often used in practice. Sometimes, banks offer them as a marketing gimmick, but there is little actual difference between daily and continuous compounding. For example, with a 6% APR, daily compounding provides an EAR of $(1 + 0.06/365)^{365} - 1 = 6.18313\%$, whereas with continuous compounding the EAR is $e^{0.06} - 1 = 6.18365\%$.

Continuously Arriving Cash Flows

How can we compute the present value of an investment whose cash flows arrive continuously? For example, consider the cash flows of an online book retailer. Suppose the firm forecasts cash flows of \$10 million per year. The \$10 million will be received throughout each year, not at year-end; that is, the \$10 million is paid *continuously* throughout the year.

We can compute the present value of cash flows that arrive continuously using a version of the growing perpetuity formula. If cash flows arrive, starting immediately, at an initial

[12] The constant e raised to a power is also written as the function *exp*. That is, $e^{APR} = exp(APR)$. This function is built into most spreadsheets and calculators.

[13] Recall that $\ln(e^x) = x$

rate of $C per year, and if the cash flows grow at rate g per year, then given a discount rate (expressed as an EAR) of r per year, the present value of the cash flows is

Present Value of a Continuously Growing Perpetuity[14]

$$PV = \frac{C}{r_{cc} - g_{cc}} \tag{5A.3}$$

where $r_{cc} = \ln(1 + r)$ and $g_{cc} = \ln(1 + g)$ are the discount and growth rates expressed as continuously compounded APRs, respectively.

There is another, approximate method for dealing with continuously arriving cash flows. Let $\overline{C}_1$ be the total cash flows that arrive during the first year. Because the cash flows arrive throughout the year, we can think of them arriving "on average" in the middle of the year. In that case, we should discount the cash flows by ½ year less:

$$\frac{C}{r_{cc} - g_{cc}} \approx \frac{\overline{C}_1}{r - g} \times (1 + r)^{1/2} \tag{5A.4}$$

In practice, the approximation in Eq. 5A.4 works quite well. More generally, it implies that when cash flows arrive continuously, we can compute present values reasonably accurately by following a "**mid-year convention**" in which we pretend that all of the cash flows for the year arrive in the middle of the year.

EXAMPLE 5A.1 **Valuing Projects with Continuous Cash Flows**

Problem

Your firm is considering buying an oil rig. The rig will initially produce oil at a rate of 30 million barrels per year. You have a long-term contract that allows you to sell the oil at a profit of $1.25 per barrel. If the rate of oil production from the rig declines by 3% over the year and the discount rate is 10% per year (EAR), how much would you be willing to pay for the rig?

Solution

According to the estimates, the rig will generate profits at an initial rate of (30 million barrels per year) × ($1.25/barrel) = $37.5 million per year. The 10% discount rate is equivalent to a continuously compounded APR of $r_{cc} = \ln(1 + 0.10) = 9.531\%$; similarly, the growth rate has an APR of $g_{cc} = \ln(1 - 0.03) = -3.046\%$. From Eq. 5A.3, the present value of the profits from the rig is

$$PV(\text{profits}) = 37.5/(r_{cc} - g_{cc}) = 37.5/(0.09531 + 0.03046) = \$298.16 \text{ million}$$

Alternatively, we can closely approximate the present value as follows. The initial profit rate of the rig is $37.5 million per year. By the end of the year, the profit rate will have declined by 3% to 37.5 × (1 − 0.03) = $36.375 million per year. Therefore, the average profit rate during the year is approximately (37.5 + 36.375)/2 = $36.938 million. Valuing the cash flows as though they occur at the middle of each year, we have

$$\begin{aligned} PV(\text{profits}) &= [36.938/(r - g)] \times (1 + r)^{1/2} \\ &= [36.938/(0.10 + 0.03)] \times (1.10)^{1/2} = \$298.01 \text{ million} \end{aligned}$$

Note that both methods produce very similar results.

[14]Given the perpetuity formula, we can value an annuity as the difference between two perpetuities.

CHAPTER

6

Valuing Bonds

NOTATION

CPN	coupon payment on a bond
n	number of periods
y, *YTM*	yield to maturity
P	initial price of a bond
FV	face value of a bond
YTM_n	yield to maturity on a zero-coupon bond with *n* periods to maturity
r_n	interest rate or discount rate for a cash flow that arrives in period *n*
PV	present value
NPER	annuity spreadsheet notation for the number of periods or date of the last cash flow
RATE	annuity spreadsheet notation for interest rate
PMT	annuity spreadsheet notation for cash flow
APR	annual percentage rate

AFTER A FOUR-YEAR HIATUS, THE U.S. GOVERNMENT BEGAN ISSUING 30-year Treasury bonds again in August 2005. While the move was due in part to the government's need to borrow to fund record budget deficits, the decision to issue 30-year bonds was also a response to investor demand for long-term, risk-free securities backed by the U.S. government. These 30-year Treasury bonds are part of a much larger market for publicly traded bonds. As of January 2015, the value of traded U.S. Treasury debt was approximately $12.5 trillion, $4.5 trillion more than the value of all publicly traded U.S. corporate bonds. If we include bonds issued by municipalities, government agencies, and other issuers, investors had over $39 trillion invested in U.S. bond markets, compared with just over $26 trillion in U.S. equity markets.[1]

In this chapter, we look at the basic types of bonds and consider their valuation. Understanding bonds and their pricing is useful for several reasons. First, the prices of risk-free government bonds can be used to determine the risk-free interest rates that produce the yield curve discussed in Chapter 5. As we saw there, the yield curve provides important information for valuing risk-free cash flows and assessing expectations of inflation and economic growth. Second, firms often issue bonds to fund their own investments, and the returns investors receive on those bonds is one factor determining a firm's cost of capital. Finally, bonds provide an opportunity to begin our study of how securities are priced in a competitive market. The ideas we develop in this chapter will be helpful when we turn to the topic of valuing stocks in Chapter 9.

We begin the chapter by evaluating the promised cash flows for different types of bonds. Given a bond's cash flows, we can use the Law of One Price to directly relate the bond's return, or yield, and its price. We also describe how bond prices change dynamically over time and examine the relationship between the prices and yields of different bonds. Finally, we consider bonds for which there is a risk of default, so that their cash flows are not known with certainty. As an important application, we look at the behavior of corporate and sovereign bonds during the recent economic crisis.

[1] *Source:* Securities Industry and Financial Markets Association, www.sifma.org, and the World Bank, data.worldbank.org.

6.1 Bond Cash Flows, Prices, and Yields

In this section, we look at how bonds are defined and then study the basic relationship between bond prices and their yield to maturity.

Bond Terminology

Recall from Chapter 3 that a bond is a security sold by governments and corporations to raise money from investors today in exchange for promised future payments. The terms of the bond are described as part of the **bond certificate**, which indicates the amounts and dates of all payments to be made. These payments are made until a final repayment date, called the **maturity date** of the bond. The time remaining until the repayment date is known as the **term** of the bond.

Bonds typically make two types of payments to their holders. The promised interest payments of a bond are called **coupons**. The bond certificate typically specifies that the coupons will be paid periodically (e.g., semiannually) until the maturity date of the bond. The principal or **face value** of a bond is the notional amount we use to compute the interest payments. Usually, the face value is repaid at maturity. It is generally denominated in standard increments such as $1000. A bond with a $1000 face value, for example, is often referred to as a "$1000 bond."

The amount of each coupon payment is determined by the **coupon rate** of the bond. This coupon rate is set by the issuer and stated on the bond certificate. By convention, the coupon rate is expressed as an APR, so the amount of each coupon payment, *CPN*, is

Coupon Payment

$$CPN = \frac{\text{Coupon Rate} \times \text{Face Value}}{\text{Number of Coupon Payments per Year}} \tag{6.1}$$

For example, a "$1000 bond with a 10% coupon rate and semiannual payments" will pay coupon payments of $\$1000 \times 10\%/2 = \$50$ every six months.

Zero-Coupon Bonds

The simplest type of bond is a **zero-coupon bond**, which does not make coupon payments. The only cash payment the investor receives is the face value of the bond on the maturity date. **Treasury bills**, which are U.S. government bonds with a maturity of up to one year, are zero-coupon bonds. Recall from Chapter 4 that the present value of a future cash flow is less than the cash flow itself. As a result, prior to its maturity date, the price of a zero-coupon bond is less than its face value. That is, zero-coupon bonds trade at a **discount** (a price lower than the face value), so they are also called **pure discount bonds**.

Suppose that a one-year, risk-free, zero-coupon bond with a $100,000 face value has an initial price of $96,618.36. If you purchased this bond and held it to maturity, you would have the following cash flows:

0	1
−$96,618.36	$100,000

Although the bond pays no "interest" directly, as an investor you are compensated for the time value of your money by purchasing the bond at a discount to its face value.

Yield to Maturity. Recall that the IRR of an investment opportunity is the discount rate at which the NPV of the cash flows of the investment opportunity is equal to zero. So, the IRR of an investment in a zero-coupon bond is the rate of return that investors will earn on their money if they buy the bond at its current price and hold it to maturity. The IRR of an investment in a bond is given a special name, the **yield to maturity (YTM)** or just the *yield*:

The yield to maturity of a bond is the discount rate that sets the present value of the promised bond payments equal to the current market price of the bond.

Intuitively, the yield to maturity for a zero-coupon bond is the return you will earn as an investor from holding the bond to maturity and receiving the promised face value payment.

Let's determine the yield to maturity of the one-year zero-coupon bond discussed earlier. According to the definition, the yield to maturity of the one-year bond solves the following equation:

$$96{,}618.36 = \frac{100{,}000}{1 + YTM_1}$$

In this case,

$$1 + YTM_1 = \frac{100{,}000}{96{,}618.36} = 1.035$$

That is, the yield to maturity for this bond is 3.5%. Because the bond is risk free, investing in this bond and holding it to maturity is like earning 3.5% interest on your initial investment. Thus, by the Law of One Price, the competitive market risk-free interest rate is 3.5%, meaning all one-year risk-free investments must earn 3.5%.

Similarly, the yield to maturity for a zero-coupon bond with n periods to maturity, current price P, and face value FV solves[2]

$$P = \frac{FV}{(1 + YTM_n)^n} \tag{6.2}$$

Rearranging this expression, we get

Yield to Maturity of an n-Year Zero-Coupon Bond

$$YTM_n = \left(\frac{FV}{P}\right)^{1/n} - 1 \tag{6.3}$$

The yield to maturity (YTM_n) in Eq. 6.3 is the per-period rate of return for holding the bond from today until maturity on date n.

Risk-Free Interest Rates. In earlier chapters, we discussed the competitive market interest rate r_n available from today until date n for risk-free cash flows; we used this interest rate as the cost of capital for a risk-free cash flow that occurs on date n. Because a default-free zero-coupon bond that matures on date n provides a risk-free return over the same period, the Law of One Price guarantees that the risk-free interest rate equals the yield to maturity on such a bond.

Risk-Free Interest Rate with Maturity n

$$r_n = YTM_n \tag{6.4}$$

Consequently, we will often refer to the yield to maturity of the appropriate maturity, zero-coupon risk-free bond as *the* risk-free interest rate. Some financial professionals also use the term **spot interest rates** to refer to these default-free, zero-coupon yields.

---

[2]In Chapter 4, we used the notation FV_n for the future value on date n of a cash flow. Conveniently, for a zero-coupon bond, the future value is also its face value, so the abbreviation FV continues to apply.

In Chapter 5, we introduced the yield curve, which plots the risk-free interest rate for different maturities. These risk-free interest rates correspond to the yields of risk-free zero-coupon bonds. Thus, the yield curve we introduced in Chapter 5 is also referred to as the **zero-coupon yield curve.**

EXAMPLE 6.1 Yields for Different Maturities

Problem

Suppose the following zero-coupon bonds are trading at the prices shown below per $100 face value. Determine the corresponding spot interest rates that determine the zero coupon yield curve.

Maturity	1 Year	2 Years	3 Years	4 Years
Price	$96.62	$92.45	$87.63	$83.06

Solution

Using Eq. 6.3, we have

$$r_1 = YTM_1 = (100/96.62) - 1 = 3.50\%$$

$$r_2 = YTM_2 = (100/92.45)^{1/2} - 1 = 4.00\%$$

$$r_3 = YTM_3 = (100/87.63)^{1/3} - 1 = 4.50\%$$

$$r_4 = YTM_4 = (100/83.06)^{1/4} - 1 = 4.75\%$$

GLOBAL FINANCIAL CRISIS Negative Bond Yields

On December 9, 2008, in the midst of one of the worst financial crises in history, the unthinkable happened: For the first time since the Great Depression, U.S. Treasury Bills traded at a negative yield. That is, these risk-free pure discount bonds traded at premium. As Bloomberg.com reported: "If you invested $1 million in three-month bills at today's negative discount rate of 0.01%, for a price of 100.002556, at maturity you would receive the par value for a loss of $25.56."

A negative yield on a Treasury bill implies that investors have an arbitrage opportunity: By *selling* the bill, and holding the proceeds in cash, they would have a risk-free *profit* of $25.56. Why did investors not rush to take advantage of the arbitrage opportunity and thereby eliminate it?

Well, first, the negative yields did not last very long, suggesting that, in fact, investors did rush to take advantage of this opportunity. But second, after closer consideration, the opportunity might not have been a sure risk-free arbitrage. When selling a Treasury security, the investor must choose where to invest, or at least hold, the proceeds. In normal times investors would be happy to deposit the proceeds with a bank, and consider this deposit to be risk free. But these were not normal times—many investors had great concerns about the financial stability of banks and other financial intermediaries. Perhaps investors shied away from this "arbitrage" opportunity because they were worried that the cash they would receive could not be held safely *anywhere* (even putting it "under the mattress" has a risk of theft!). Thus, we can view the $25.56 as the price investors were willing to pay to have the U.S. Treasury hold their money safely for them at a time when no other investments seemed truly safe.

This phenomenon repeated itself in Europe starting in mid-2012. In this case, negative yields emerged due to a concern about both the safety of European banks as well as the stability of the euro as a currency. As investors in Greece or other countries began to worry their economies might depart from the euro, they were willing to hold German and Swiss government bonds even at negative yields as a way to protect themselves against the Eurozone unraveling. By mid-2015, almost 25% of European government bonds had negative yields, with some Swiss bonds having yields close to −1%!

The persistence of such large negative yields are challenging to explain. Most of the holders of these bonds are institutions and pension funds who are restricted to hold very safe assets. And while they could hold currency instead, obtaining, storing, and securing large quantities of cash would also be very costly. (Indeed, Swiss banks have reportedly refused large currency withdrawals by hedge funds attempting to exploit the arbitrage opportunity.) Bonds are also much easier to trade, and use as collateral, than giant vaults of cash. Together, the safety and convenience of these bonds must be worth the nearly 1% per year these investors are willing to sacrifice.

Coupon Bonds

Like zero-coupon bonds, **coupon bonds** pay investors their face value at maturity. In addition, these bonds make regular coupon interest payments. Two types of U.S. Treasury coupon securities are currently traded in financial markets: **Treasury notes**, which have original maturities from one to 10 years, and **Treasury bonds**, which have original maturities of more than 10 years.

EXAMPLE 6.2 The Cash Flows of a Coupon Bond

Problem

The U.S. Treasury has just issued a five-year, $1000 bond with a 5% coupon rate and semiannual coupons. What cash flows will you receive if you hold this bond until maturity?

Solution

The face value of this bond is $1000. Because this bond pays coupons semiannually, from Eq. 6.1, you will receive a coupon payment every six months of CPN = $1000 × 5%/2 = $25. Here is the timeline, based on a six-month period:

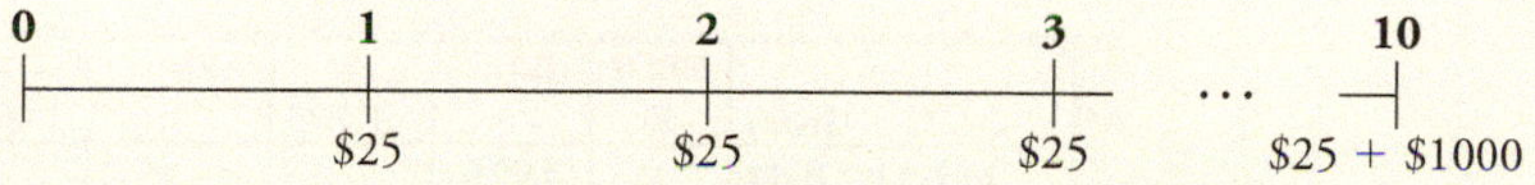

Note that the last payment occurs five years (10 six-month periods) from now and is composed of both a coupon payment of $25 and the face value payment of $1000.

We can also compute the yield to maturity of a coupon bond. Recall that the yield to maturity for a bond is the IRR of investing in the bond and holding it to maturity; it is the *single* discount rate that equates the present value of the bond's remaining cash flows to its current price, shown in the following timeline:

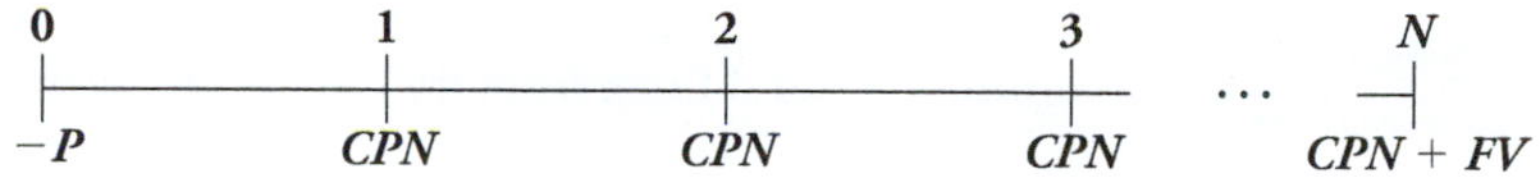

Because the coupon payments represent an annuity, the yield to maturity is the interest rate y that solves the following equation:[3]

Yield to Maturity of a Coupon Bond

$$P = CPN \times \frac{1}{y}\left(1 - \frac{1}{(1+y)^N}\right) + \frac{FV}{(1+y)^N} \tag{6.5}$$

Unfortunately, unlike in the case of zero-coupon bonds, there is no simple formula to solve for the yield to maturity directly. Instead, we need to use either trial-and-error or the annuity spreadsheet we introduced in Chapter 4 (or Excel's IRR function).

---

[3]In Eq. 6.5, we have assumed that the first cash coupon will be paid one period from now. If the first coupon is less than one period away, the cash price of the bond can be found by adjusting the price in Eq. 6.5 by multiplying by $(1 + y)^f$, where f is the fraction of the coupon interval that has already elapsed. (Also, bond prices are often quoted in terms of the *clean price*, which is calculated by deducting from the cash price P an amount, called *accrued interest*, equal to $f \times CPN$. See the box on "Clean and Dirty" bond prices on page 183.)

When we calculate a bond's yield to maturity by solving Eq. 6.5, the yield we compute will be a rate *per coupon interval.* This yield is typically stated as an annual rate by multiplying it by the number of coupons per year, thereby converting it to an APR with the same compounding interval as the coupon rate.

EXAMPLE 6.3 Computing the Yield to Maturity of a Coupon Bond

Problem

Consider the five-year, $1000 bond with a 5% coupon rate and semiannual coupons described in Example 6.2. If this bond is currently trading for a price of $957.35, what is the bond's yield to maturity?

Solution

Because the bond has 10 remaining coupon payments, we compute its yield y by solving:

$$957.35 = 25 \times \frac{1}{y}\left(1 - \frac{1}{(1+y)^{10}}\right) + \frac{1000}{(1+y)^{10}}$$

We can solve it by trial-and-error or by using the annuity spreadsheet:

	NPER	RATE	PV	PMT	FV	Excel Formula
Given	10		−957.35	25	1,000	
Solve for Rate		3.00%				=RATE(10,25,−957.35,1000)

Therefore, $y = 3\%$. Because the bond pays coupons semiannually, this yield is for a six-month period. We convert it to an APR by multiplying by the number of coupon payments per year. Thus the bond has a yield to maturity equal to a 6% APR with semiannual compounding.

We can also use Eq. 6.5 to compute a bond's price based on its yield to maturity. We simply discount the cash flows using the yield, as shown in Example 6.4.

EXAMPLE 6.4 Computing a Bond Price from Its Yield to Maturity

Problem

Consider again the five-year, $1000 bond with a 5% coupon rate and semiannual coupons presented in Example 6.3. Suppose you are told that its yield to maturity has increased to 6.30% (expressed as an APR with semiannual compounding). What price is the bond trading for now?

Solution

Given the yield, we can compute the price using Eq. 6.5. First, note that a 6.30% APR is equivalent to a semiannual rate of 3.15%. Therefore, the bond price is

$$P = 25 \times \frac{1}{0.0315}\left(1 - \frac{1}{1.0315^{10}}\right) + \frac{1000}{1.0315^{10}} = \$944.98$$

We can also use the annuity spreadsheet:

	NPER	RATE	PV	PMT	FV	Excel Formula
Given	10	3.15%		25	1,000	
Solve for PV			−944.98			=PV(0.0315,10,25,1000)

Because we can convert any price into a yield, and vice versa, prices and yields are often used interchangeably. For example, the bond in Example 6.4 could be quoted as having a yield of 6.30% or a price of $944.98 per $1000 face value. Indeed, bond traders generally quote bond yields rather than bond prices. One advantage of quoting the yield to maturity rather than the price is that the yield is independent of the face value of the bond. When prices are quoted in the bond market, they are conventionally quoted as a percentage of their face value. Thus, the bond in Example 6.4 would be quoted as having a price of 94.498, which would imply an actual price of $944.98 given the $1000 face value of the bond.

CONCEPT CHECK

1. What is the relationship between a bond's price and its yield to maturity?
2. The risk-free interest rate for a maturity of *n*-years can be determined from the yield of what type of bond?

6.2 Dynamic Behavior of Bond Prices

As we mentioned earlier, zero-coupon bonds trade at a discount—that is, prior to maturity, their price is less than their face value. Coupon bonds may trade at a discount, at a **premium** (a price greater than their face value), or at **par** (a price equal to their face value). In this section, we identify when a bond will trade at a discount or premium as well as how the bond's price will change due to the passage of time and fluctuations in interest rates.

Discounts and Premiums

If the bond trades at a discount, an investor who buys the bond will earn a return both from receiving the coupons *and* from receiving a face value that exceeds the price paid for the bond. As a result, if a bond trades at a discount, its yield to maturity will exceed its coupon rate. Given the relationship between bond prices and yields, the reverse is clearly also true: If a coupon bond's yield to maturity exceeds its coupon rate, the present value of its cash flows at the yield to maturity will be less than its face value, and the bond will trade at a discount.

A bond that pays a coupon can also trade at a premium to its face value. In this case, an investor's return from the coupons is diminished by receiving a face value less than the price paid for the bond. Thus, a bond trades at a premium whenever its yield to maturity is less than its coupon rate.

When a bond trades at a price equal to its face value, it is said to trade at par. A bond trades at par when its coupon rate is equal to its yield to maturity. A bond that trades at a discount is also said to trade below par, and a bond that trades at a premium is said to trade above par.

Table 6.1 summarizes these properties of coupon bond prices.

TABLE 6.1 Bond Prices Immediately After a Coupon Payment

When the bond price is	We say the bond trades	This occurs when
greater than the face value	"above par" or "at a premium"	Coupon Rate > Yield to Maturity
equal to the face value	"at par"	Coupon Rate = Yield to Maturity
less than the face value	"below par" or "at a discount"	Coupon Rate < Yield to Maturity

EXAMPLE 6.5 **Determining the Discount or Premium of a Coupon Bond**

Problem

Consider three 30-year bonds with annual coupon payments. One bond has a 10% coupon rate, one has a 5% coupon rate, and one has a 3% coupon rate. If the yield to maturity of each bond is 5%, what is the price of each bond per $100 face value? Which bond trades at a premium, which trades at a discount, and which trades at par?

Solution

We can compute the price of each bond using Eq. 6.5. Therefore, the bond prices are

$$P(10\%\text{ coupon}) = 10 \times \frac{1}{0.05}\left(1 - \frac{1}{1.05^{30}}\right) + \frac{100}{1.05^{30}} = \$176.86 \quad \text{(trades at a premium)}$$

$$P(5\%\text{ coupon}) = 5 \times \frac{1}{0.05}\left(1 - \frac{1}{1.05^{30}}\right) + \frac{100}{1.05^{30}} = \$100.00 \quad \text{(trades at par)}$$

$$P(3\%\text{ coupon}) = 3 \times \frac{1}{0.05}\left(1 - \frac{1}{1.05^{30}}\right) + \frac{100}{1.05^{30}} = \$69.26 \quad \text{(trades at a discount)}$$

Most issuers of coupon bonds choose a coupon rate so that the bonds will *initially* trade at, or very close to, par (i.e., at face value). For example, the U.S. Treasury sets the coupon rates on its notes and bonds in this way. After the issue date, the market price of a bond generally changes over time for two reasons. First, as time passes, the bond gets closer to its maturity date. Holding fixed the bond's yield to maturity, the present value of the bond's remaining cash flows changes as the time to maturity decreases. Second, at any point in time, changes in market interest rates affect the bond's yield to maturity and its price (the present value of the remaining cash flows). We explore these two effects in the remainder of this section.

Time and Bond Prices

Let's consider the effect of time on the price of a bond. Suppose you purchase a 30-year, zero-coupon bond with a yield to maturity of 5%. For a face value of $100, the bond will initially trade for

$$P(30\text{ years to maturity}) = \frac{100}{1.05^{30}} = \$23.14$$

Now let's consider the price of this bond five years later, when it has 25 years remaining until maturity. If the bond's yield to maturity remains at 5%, the bond price in five years will be

$$P(25\text{ years to maturity}) = \frac{100}{1.05^{25}} = \$29.53$$

Note that the bond price is higher, and hence the discount from its face value is smaller, when there is less time to maturity. The discount shrinks because the yield has not changed, but there is less time until the face value will be received. If you purchased the bond for $23.14 and then sold it after five years for $29.53, the IRR of your investment would be

$$\left(\frac{29.53}{23.14}\right)^{1/5} - 1 = 5.0\%$$

That is, your return is the same as the yield to maturity of the bond. This example illustrates a more general property for bonds: *If a bond's yield to maturity has not changed, then the IRR of an investment in the bond equals its yield to maturity even if you sell the bond early.*

These results also hold for coupon bonds. The pattern of price changes over time is a bit more complicated for coupon bonds, however, because as time passes, most of the cash flows get closer but some of the cash flows disappear as the coupons get paid. Example 6.6 illustrates these effects.

EXAMPLE 6.6 The Effect of Time on the Price of a Coupon Bond

Problem

Consider a 30-year bond with a 10% coupon rate (annual payments) and a $100 face value. What is the initial price of this bond if it has a 5% yield to maturity? If the yield to maturity is unchanged, what will the price be immediately before and after the first coupon is paid?

Solution

We computed the price of this bond with 30 years to maturity in Example 6.5:

$$P = 10 \times \frac{1}{0.05}\left(1 - \frac{1}{1.05^{30}}\right) + \frac{100}{1.05^{30}} = \$176.86$$

Now consider the cash flows of this bond in one year, immediately before the first coupon is paid. The bond now has 29 years until it matures, and the timeline is as follows:

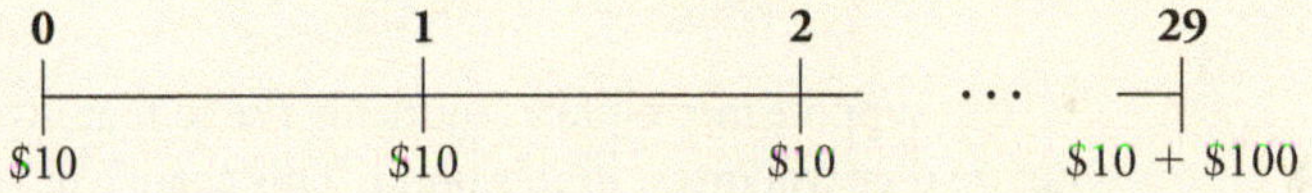

Again, we compute the price by discounting the cash flows by the yield to maturity. Note that there is a cash flow of $10 at date zero, the coupon that is about to be paid. In this case, we can treat the first coupon separately and value the remaining cash flows as in Eq. 6.5:

$$P(\text{just before first coupon}) = 10 + 10 \times \frac{1}{0.05}\left(1 - \frac{1}{1.05^{29}}\right) + \frac{100}{1.05^{29}} = \$185.71$$

Note that the bond price is higher than it was initially. It will make the same total number of coupon payments, but an investor does not need to wait as long to receive the first one. We could also compute the price by noting that because the yield to maturity remains at 5% for the bond, investors in the bond should earn a return of 5% over the year: $176.86 × 1.05 = $185.71.

What happens to the price of the bond just after the first coupon is paid? The timeline is the same as that given earlier, except the new owner of the bond will not receive the coupon at date zero. Thus, just after the coupon is paid, the price of the bond (given the same yield to maturity) will be

$$P(\text{just after first coupon}) = 10 \times \frac{1}{0.05}\left(1 - \frac{1}{1.05^{29}}\right) + \frac{100}{1.05^{29}} = \$175.71$$

The price of the bond will drop by the amount of the coupon ($10) immediately after the coupon is paid, reflecting the fact that the owner will no longer receive the coupon. In this case, the price is lower than the initial price of the bond. Because there are fewer coupon payments remaining, the premium investors will pay for the bond declines. Still, an investor who buys the bond initially, receives the first coupon, and then sells it earns a 5% return if the bond's yield does not change: (10 + 175.71)/176.86 = 1.05.

Figure 6.1 illustrates the effect of time on bond prices, assuming the yield to maturity remains constant. Between coupon payments, the prices of all bonds rise at a rate equal to the yield to maturity as the remaining cash flows of the bond become closer. But as each coupon is paid, the price of a bond drops by the amount of the coupon. When the bond is trading at a premium, the price drop when a coupon is paid will be larger than the price increase between coupons, so the bond's premium will tend to decline as time passes. If the bond is trading at a discount, the price increase between coupons will exceed the drop when a coupon is paid, so the bond's price will rise and its discount will decline as time passes. Ultimately, the prices of all bonds approach the bonds' face value when the bonds mature and their last coupon is paid.

For each of the bonds illustrated in Figure 6.1, if the yield to maturity remains at 5%, investors will earn a 5% return on their investment. For the zero-coupon bond, this return is earned solely due to the price appreciation of the bond. For the 10% coupon bond, this return comes from the combination of coupon payments and price depreciation over time.

Interest Rate Changes and Bond Prices

As interest rates in the economy fluctuate, the yields that investors demand to invest in bonds will also change. Let's evaluate the effect of fluctuations in a bond's yield to maturity on its price.

Consider again a 30-year, zero-coupon bond with a yield to maturity of 5%. For a face value of $100, the bond will initially trade for

$$P(5\% \text{ yield to maturity}) = \frac{100}{1.05^{30}} = \$23.14$$

But suppose interest rates suddenly rise so that investors now demand a 6% yield to maturity before they will invest in this bond. This change in yield implies that the bond price will fall to

$$P(6\% \text{ yield to maturity}) = \frac{100}{1.06^{30}} = \$17.41$$

FIGURE 6.1

The Effect of Time on Bond Prices

The graph illustrates the effects of the passage of time on bond prices when the yield remains constant. The price of a zero-coupon bond rises smoothly. The price of a coupon bond also rises between coupon payments, but tumbles on the coupon date, reflecting the amount of the coupon payment. For each coupon bond, the gray line shows the trend of the bond price just after each coupon is paid.

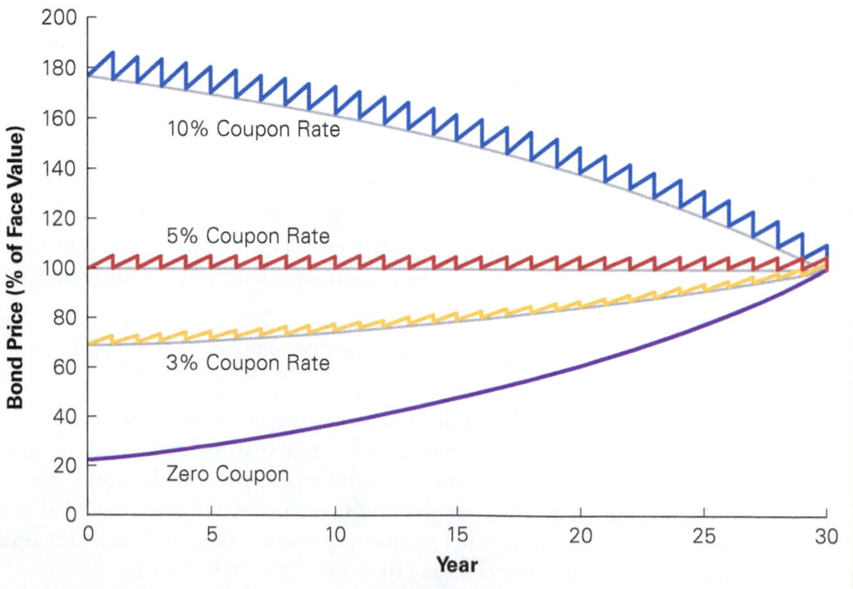

Clean and Dirty Prices for Coupon Bonds

As Figure 6.1 illustrates, coupon bond prices fluctuate around the time of each coupon payment in a sawtooth pattern: The value of the coupon bond rises as the next coupon payment gets closer and then drops after it has been paid. This fluctuation occurs even if there is no change in the bond's yield to maturity.

Because bond traders are more concerned about changes in the bond's price that arise due to changes in the bond's yield, rather than these predictable patterns around coupon payments, they often do not quote the price of a bond in terms of its actual cash price, which is also called the **dirty price** or **invoice price** of the bond. Instead, bonds are often quoted in terms of a **clean price**, which is the bond's cash price less an adjustment for accrued interest, the amount of the next coupon payment that has already accrued:

$$\text{Clean price} = \text{Cash (dirty) price} - \text{Accrued interest}$$

$$\text{Accrued interest} = \text{Coupon amount} \times \left(\frac{\text{Days since last coupon payment}}{\text{Days in current coupon period}}\right)$$

Note that immediately before a coupon payment is made, the accrued interest will equal the full amount of the coupon, whereas immediately after the coupon payment is made, the accrued interest will be zero. Thus, accrued interest will rise and fall in a sawtooth pattern as each coupon payment passes:

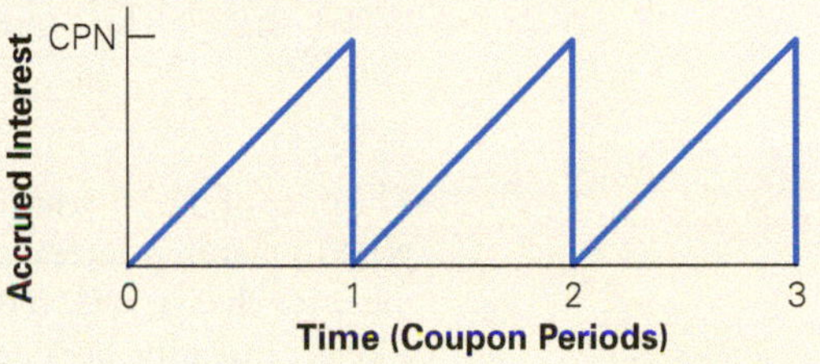

As Figure 6.1 demonstrates, the bonds cash price also has a sawtooth pattern. So if we subtract accrued interest from the bond's cash price and compute the clean price, the sawtooth pattern of the cash price is eliminated. Thus, absent changes in the bond's yield to maturity, its clean price converges smoothly over time to the bond's face value, as shown in the gray lines in Figure 6.1.

Relative to the initial price, the bond price changes by $(17.41 - 23.14)/23.14 = -24.8\%$, a substantial price drop.

This example illustrates a general phenomenon. A higher yield to maturity implies a higher discount rate for a bond's remaining cash flows, reducing their present value and hence the bond's price. Therefore, *as interest rates and bond yields rise, bond prices will fall, and vice versa.*

The sensitivity of a bond's price to changes in interest rates depends on the timing of its cash flows. Because it is discounted over a shorter period, the present value of a cash flow that will be received in the near future is less dramatically affected by interest rates than a cash flow in the distant future. Thus, shorter-maturity zero-coupon bonds are less sensitive to changes in interest rates than are longer-term zero-coupon bonds. Similarly, bonds with higher coupon rates—because they pay higher cash flows upfront—are less sensitive to interest rate changes than otherwise identical bonds with lower coupon rates. The sensitivity of a bond's price to changes in interest rates is measured by the bond's **duration.**[4] Bonds with high durations are highly sensitive to interest rate changes.

EXAMPLE 6.7 The Interest Rate Sensitivity of Bonds

Problem

Consider a 15-year zero-coupon bond and a 30-year coupon bond with 10% annual coupons. By what percentage will the price of each bond change if its yield to maturity increases from 5% to 6%?

[4] We define duration formally and discuss this concept more thoroughly in Chapter 30.

Solution

First, we compute the price of each bond for each yield to maturity:

Yield to Maturity	15-Year, Zero-Coupon Bond	30-Year, 10% Annual Coupon Bond
5%	$\frac{100}{1.05^{15}} = \$48.10$	$10 \times \frac{1}{0.05}\left(1 - \frac{1}{1.05^{30}}\right) + \frac{100}{1.05^{30}} = \$176.86$
6%	$\frac{100}{1.06^{15}} = \$41.73$	$10 \times \frac{1}{0.06}\left(1 - \frac{1}{1.06^{30}}\right) + \frac{100}{1.06^{30}} = \$155.06$

The price of the 15-year zero-coupon bond changes by $(41.73 - 48.10)/48.10 = -13.2\%$ if its yield to maturity increases from 5% to 6%. For the 30-year bond with 10% annual coupons, the price change is $(155.06 - 176.86)/176.86 = -12.3\%$. Even though the 30-year bond has a longer maturity, because of its high coupon rate, its sensitivity to a change in yield is actually less than that of the 15-year zero coupon bond.

In actuality, bond prices are subject to the effects of both the passage of time and changes in interest rates. Bond prices converge to the bond's face value due to the time effect, but simultaneously move up and down due to unpredictable changes in bond yields. Figure 6.2 illustrates

FIGURE 6.2

Yield to Maturity and Bond Price Fluctuations over Time

The graphs illustrate changes in price and yield for a 30-year zero-coupon bond over its life. The top graph illustrates the changes in the bond's yield to maturity over its life. In the bottom graph, the actual bond price is shown in blue. Because the yield to maturity does not remain constant over the bond's life, the bond's price fluctuates as it converges to the face value over time. Also shown is the price if the yield to maturity remained fixed at 4%, 5%, or 6%.

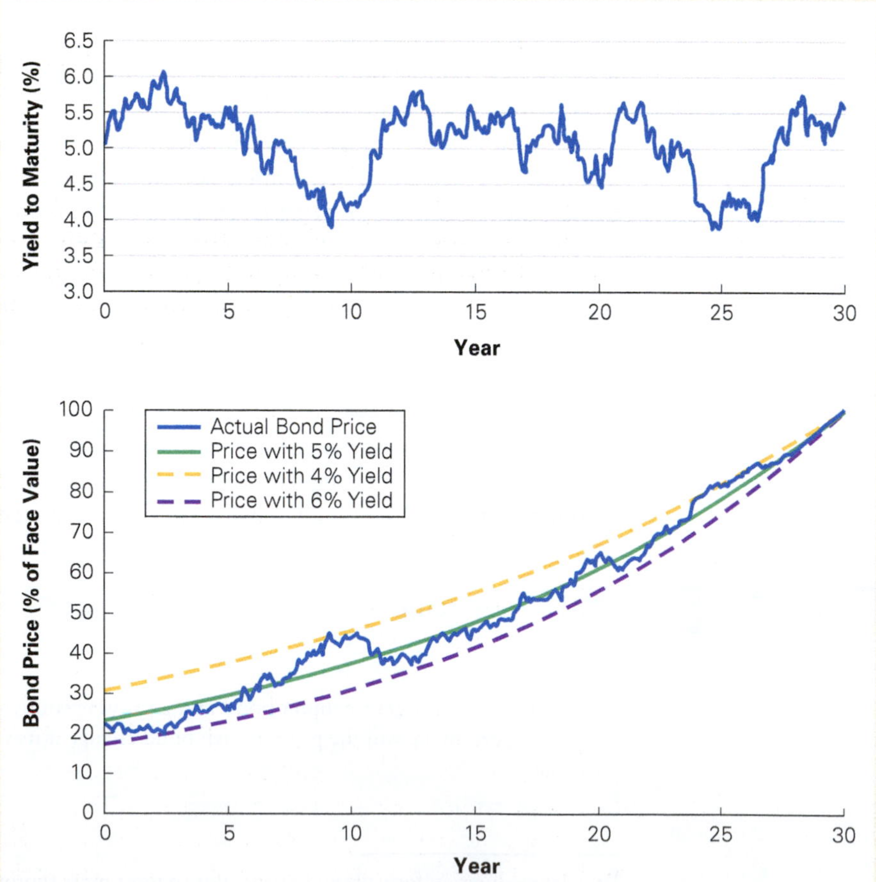

this behavior by demonstrating how the price of the 30-year, zero-coupon bond might change over its life. Note that the bond price tends to converge to the face value as the bond approaches the maturity date, but also moves higher when its yield falls and lower when its yield rises.

As Figure 6.2 demonstrates, prior to maturity the bond is exposed to interest rate risk. If an investor chooses to sell and the bond's yield to maturity has decreased, then the investor will receive a high price and earn a high return. If the yield to maturity has increased, the bond price is low at the time of sale and the investor will earn a low return. In the appendix to this chapter, we discuss one way corporations manage this type of risk.

CONCEPT CHECK

1. If a bond's yield to maturity does not change, how does its cash price change between coupon payments?
2. What risk does an investor in a default-free bond face if he or she plans to sell the bond prior to maturity?
3. How does a bond's coupon rate affect its duration—the bond price's sensitivity to interest rate changes?

6.3 The Yield Curve and Bond Arbitrage

Thus far, we have focused on the relationship between the price of an individual bond and its yield to maturity. In this section, we explore the relationship between the prices and yields of different bonds. Using the Law of One Price, we show that given the spot interest rates, which are the yields of default-free zero-coupon bonds, we can determine the price and yield of any other default-free bond. As a result, the yield curve provides sufficient information to evaluate all such bonds.

Replicating a Coupon Bond

Because it is possible to replicate the cash flows of a coupon bond using zero-coupon bonds, we can use the Law of One Price to compute the price of a coupon bond from the prices of zero-coupon bonds. For example, we can replicate a three-year, $1000 bond that pays 10% annual coupons using three zero-coupon bonds as follows:

	0	1	2	3
Coupon bond:		$100	$100	$1100
1-year zero:		$100		
2-year zero:			$100	
3-year zero:				$1100
Zero-coupon Bond portfolio:		$100	$100	$1100

We match each coupon payment to a zero-coupon bond with a face value equal to the coupon payment and a term equal to the time remaining to the coupon date. Similarly, we match the final bond payment (final coupon plus return of face value) in three years to a three-year, zero-coupon bond with a corresponding face value of $1100. Because the coupon bond cash flows are identical to the cash flows of the portfolio of zero-coupon bonds, the Law of One Price states that the price of the portfolio of zero-coupon bonds must be the same as the price of the coupon bond.

TABLE 6.2 **Yields and Prices (per $100 Face Value) for Zero-Coupon Bonds**

Maturity	1 year	2 years	3 years	4 years
YTM	3.50%	4.00%	4.50%	4.75%
Price	$96.62	$92.45	$87.63	$83.06

To illustrate, assume that current zero-coupon bond yields and prices are as shown in Table 6.2 (they are the same as in Example 6.1). We can calculate the cost of the zero-coupon bond portfolio that replicates the three-year coupon bond as follows:

Zero-Coupon Bond	Face Value Required		Cost
1 year	100		96.62
2 years	100		92.45
3 years	1100		$11 \times 87.63 = 963.93$
		Total Cost:	$1153.00

By the Law of One Price, the three-year coupon bond must trade for a price of $1153. If the price of the coupon bond were higher, you could earn an arbitrage profit by selling the coupon bond and buying the zero-coupon bond portfolio. If the price of the coupon bond were lower, you could earn an arbitrage profit by buying the coupon bond and short selling the zero-coupon bonds.

Valuing a Coupon Bond Using Zero-Coupon Yields

To this point, we have used the zero-coupon bond *prices* to derive the price of the coupon bond. Alternatively, we can use the zero-coupon bond *yields*. Recall that the yield to maturity of a zero-coupon bond is the competitive market interest rate for a risk-free investment with a term equal to the term of the zero-coupon bond. Therefore, the price of a coupon bond must equal the present value of its coupon payments and face value discounted at the competitive market interest rates (see Eq. 5.7 in Chapter 5):

Price of a Coupon Bond

$$P = PV(\text{Bond Cash Flows})$$
$$= \frac{CPN}{1 + YTM_1} + \frac{CPN}{(1 + YTM_2)^2} + \cdots + \frac{CPN + FV}{(1 + YTM_n)^n} \tag{6.6}$$

where CPN is the bond coupon payment, YTM_n is the yield to maturity of a *zero-coupon* bond that matures at the same time as the nth coupon payment, and FV is the face value of the bond. For the three-year, $1000 bond with 10% annual coupons considered earlier, we can use Eq. 6.6 to calculate its price using the zero-coupon yields in Table 6.2:

$$P = \frac{100}{1.035} + \frac{100}{1.04^2} + \frac{100 + 1000}{1.045^3} = \$1153$$

This price is identical to the price we computed earlier by replicating the bond. Thus, we can determine the no-arbitrage price of a coupon bond by discounting its cash flows using the zero-coupon yields. In other words, the information in the zero-coupon yield curve is sufficient to price all other risk-free bonds.

Coupon Bond Yields

Given the yields for zero-coupon bonds, we can use Eq. 6.6 to price a coupon bond. In Section 6.1, we saw how to compute the yield to maturity of a coupon bond from its price. Combining these results, we can determine the relationship between the yields of zero-coupon bonds and coupon-paying bonds.

Consider again the three-year, \$1000 bond with 10% annual coupons. Given the zero-coupon yields in Table 6.2, we calculate a price for this bond of \$1153. From Eq. 6.5, the yield to maturity of this bond is the rate y that satisfies

$$P = 1153 = \frac{100}{(1+y)} + \frac{100}{(1+y)^2} + \frac{100 + 1000}{(1+y)^3}$$

We can solve for the yield by using the annuity spreadsheet:

	NPER	RATE	PV	PMT	FV	Excel Formula
Given	3		−1,153	100	1,000	
Solve for Rate		**4.44%**				=RATE(3,100,−1153,1000)

Therefore, the yield to maturity of the bond is 4.44%. We can check this result directly as follows:

$$P = \frac{100}{1.0444} + \frac{100}{1.0444^2} + \frac{100 + 1000}{1.0444^3} = \$1153$$

Because the coupon bond provides cash flows at different points in time, the yield to maturity of a coupon bond is a weighted average of the yields of the zero-coupon bonds of equal and shorter maturities. The weights depend (in a complex way) on the magnitude of the cash flows each period. In this example, the zero-coupon bonds' yields were 3.5%, 4.0%, and 4.5%. For this coupon bond, most of the value in the present value calculation comes from the present value of the third cash flow because it includes the principal, so the yield is closest to the three-year, zero-coupon yield of 4.5%.

EXAMPLE 6.8 Yields on Bonds with the Same Maturity

Problem

Given the following zero-coupon yields, compare the yield to maturity for a three-year, zero-coupon bond; a three-year coupon bond with 4% annual coupons; and a three-year coupon bond with 10% annual coupons. All of these bonds are default free.

Maturity	1 year	2 years	3 years	4 years
Zero-coupon YTM	3.50%	4.00%	4.50%	4.75%

Solution

From the information provided, the yield to maturity of the three-year, zero-coupon bond is 4.50%. Also, because the yields match those in Table 6.2, we already calculated the yield to maturity for the 10% coupon bond as 4.44%. To compute the yield for the 4% coupon bond, we first need to calculate its price. Using Eq. 6.6, we have

$$P = \frac{40}{1.035} + \frac{40}{1.04^2} + \frac{40 + 1000}{1.045^3} = \$986.98$$

The price of the bond with a 4% coupon is \$986.98. From Eq. 6.5, its yield to maturity solves the following equation:

$$\$986.98 = \frac{40}{(1+y)} + \frac{40}{(1+y)^2} + \frac{40+1000}{(1+y)^3}$$

We can calculate the yield to maturity using the annuity spreadsheet:

	NPER	RATE	PV	PMT	FV	Excel Formula
Given	3		−986.98	40	1,000	
Solve for Rate		4.47%				=RATE(3,40,−986.98,1000)

To summarize, for the three-year bonds considered

Coupon rate	0%	4%	10%
YTM	4.50%	4.47%	4.44%

Example 6.8 shows that coupon bonds with the same maturity can have different yields depending on their coupon rates. As the coupon increases, earlier cash flows become relatively more important than later cash flows in the calculation of the present value. If the yield curve is upward sloping (as it is for the yields in Example 6.8), the resulting yield to maturity decreases with the coupon rate of the bond. Alternatively, when the zero-coupon yield curve is downward sloping, the yield to maturity will increase with the coupon rate. When the yield curve is flat, all zero-coupon and coupon-paying bonds will have the same yield, independent of their maturities and coupon rates.

Treasury Yield Curves

As we have shown in this section, we can use the zero-coupon yield curve to determine the price and yield to maturity of other risk-free bonds. The plot of the yields of coupon bonds of different maturities is called the **coupon-paying yield curve**. When U.S. bond traders refer to "the yield curve," they are often referring to the coupon-paying Treasury yield curve. As we showed in Example 6.8, two coupon-paying bonds with the same maturity may have different yields. By convention, practitioners always plot the yield of the most recently issued bonds, termed the **on-the-run bonds**. Using similar methods to those employed in this section, we can apply the Law of One Price to determine the zero-coupon bond yields using the coupon-paying yield curve (see Problem 25). Thus, either type of yield curve provides enough information to value all other risk-free bonds.

CONCEPT CHECK

1. How do you calculate the price of a coupon bond from the prices of zero-coupon bonds?
2. How do you calculate the price of a coupon bond from the yields of zero-coupon bonds?
3. Explain why two coupon bonds with the same maturity may each have a different yield to maturity.

6.4 Corporate Bonds

So far in this chapter, we have focused on default-free bonds such as U.S. Treasury securities, for which the cash flows are known with certainty. For other bonds such as **corporate bonds** (bonds issued by corporations), the issuer may default—that is, it might not pay back the full amount promised in the bond prospectus. This risk of default, which is known as the **credit risk** of the bond, means that the bond's cash flows are not known with certainty.

Corporate Bond Yields

How does credit risk affect bond prices and yields? Because the cash flows promised by the bond are the most that bondholders can hope to receive, the cash flows that a purchaser of a bond with credit risk *expects* to receive may be less than that amount. As a result, investors pay less for bonds with credit risk than they would for an otherwise identical default-free bond. Because the yield to maturity for a bond is calculated using the *promised* cash flows, the yield of bonds with credit risk will be higher than that of otherwise identical default-free bonds. Let's illustrate the effect of credit risk on bond yields and investor returns by comparing different cases.

No Default. Suppose that the one-year, zero-coupon Treasury bill has a yield to maturity of 4%. What are the price and yield of a one-year, $1000, zero-coupon bond issued by Avant Corporation? First, suppose that all investors agree that there is *no* possibility that Avant will default within the next year. In that case, investors will receive $1000 in one year for certain, as promised by the bond. Because this bond is risk free, the Law of One Price guarantees that it must have the same yield as the one-year, zero-coupon Treasury bill. The price of the bond will therefore be

$$P = \frac{1000}{1 + YTM_1} = \frac{1000}{1.04} = \$961.54$$

Certain Default. Now suppose that investors believe that Avant will default with certainty at the end of one year and will be able to pay only 90% of its outstanding obligations. Then, even though the bond promises $1000 at year-end, bondholders know they will receive only $900. Investors can predict this shortfall perfectly, so the $900 payment is risk free, and the bond is still a one-year risk-free investment. Therefore, we compute the price of the bond by discounting this cash flow using the risk-free interest rate as the cost of capital:

$$P = \frac{900}{1 + YTM_1} = \frac{900}{1.04} = \$865.38$$

The prospect of default lowers the cash flow investors expect to receive and hence the price they are willing to pay.

Are Treasuries Really Default-Free Securities?

Most investors treat U.S. Treasury securities as risk free, meaning that they believe there is no chance of default (a convention we follow in this book). But are Treasuries really risk free? The answer depends on what you mean by "risk free."

No one can be certain that the U.S. government will never default on its bonds—but most people believe the probability of such an event is very small. More importantly, the default probability is smaller than for any other bond. So saying that the yield on a U.S. Treasury security is risk free really means that the Treasury security is the lowest-risk investment denominated in U.S. dollars in the world.

That said, there have been occasions in the past where Treasury holders did not receive exactly what they were promised: In 1790, Treasury Secretary Alexander Hamilton lowered the interest rate on outstanding debt and in 1933 President Franklin Roosevelt suspended bondholders' right to be paid in gold rather than currency.

A new risk emerged in mid-2011 when a series of large budget deficits brought the United States up against the **debt ceiling**, a constraint imposed by Congress limiting the overall amount of debt the government can incur. An act of Congress was required by August 2011 for the Treasury to meet its obligations and avoid a default. In response to the political uncertainty about whether Congress would raise the ceiling in time, Standard & Poor's downgraded its rating of U.S. Government bonds. Congress ultimately raised the debt ceiling and no default occurred. Given persistent budget deficits, however, similar debt ceiling debates recurred in 2013 and 2015. These incidents serve as a reminder that perhaps no investment is truly "risk free."

Given the bond's price, we can compute the bond's yield to maturity. When computing this yield, we use the *promised* rather than the *actual* cash flows. Thus,

$$YTM = \frac{FV}{P} - 1 = \frac{1000}{865.38} - 1 = 15.56\%$$

The 15.56% yield to maturity of Avant's bond is much higher than the yield to maturity of the default-free Treasury bill. But this result does not mean that investors who buy the bond will earn a 15.56% return. Because Avant will default, the expected return of the bond equals its 4% cost of capital:

$$\frac{900}{865.38} = 1.04$$

Note that *the yield to maturity of a defaultable bond exceeds the expected return of investing in the bond.* Because we calculate the yield to maturity using the promised cash flows rather than the expected cash flows, the yield will always be higher than the expected return of investing in the bond.

Risk of Default. The two Avant examples were extreme cases, of course. In the first case, we assumed the probability of default was zero; in the second case, we assumed Avant would definitely default. In reality, the chance that Avant will default lies somewhere in between these two extremes (and for most firms, is probably much closer to zero).

To illustrate, again consider the one-year, $1000, zero-coupon bond issued by Avant. This time, assume that the bond payoffs are uncertain. In particular, there is a 50% chance that the bond will repay its face value in full and a 50% chance that the bond will default and you will receive $900. Thus, on average, you will receive $950.

To determine the price of this bond, we must discount this expected cash flow using a cost of capital equal to the expected return of other securities with equivalent risk. If, like most firms, Avant is more likely to default if the economy is weak than if the economy is strong, then—as we demonstrated in Chapter 3—investors will demand a risk premium to invest in this bond. That is, Avant's debt cost of capital, which is the expected return Avant's debt holders will require to compensate them for the risk of the bond's cash flows, will be higher than the 4% risk-free interest rate.

Let's suppose investors demand a risk premium of 1.1% for this bond, so that the appropriate cost of capital is 5.1%.[5] Then the present value of the bond's cash flow is

$$P = \frac{950}{1.051} = \$903.90$$

Consequently, in this case the bond's yield to maturity is 10.63%:

$$YTM = \frac{FV}{P} - 1 = \frac{1000}{903.90} - 1 = 10.63\%$$

Of course, the 10.63% promised yield is the most investors will receive. If Avant defaults, they will receive only $900, for a return of $900/903.90 - 1 = -0.43\%$. The average return is $0.50(10.63\%) + 0.50(-0.43\%) = 5.1\%$, the bond's cost of capital.

Table 6.3 summarizes the prices, expected return, and yield to maturity of the Avant bond under the various default assumptions. Note that the bond's price decreases, and its yield to maturity increases, with a greater likelihood of default. Conversely, *the bond's expected return, which is equal to the firm's debt cost of capital, is less than the yield to maturity*

[5]We will develop methods for estimating the appropriate risk premium for risky bonds in Chapter 12.

TABLE 6.3 Bond Price, Yield, and Return with Different Likelihoods of Default

Avant Bond (1-year, zero-coupon)	Bond Price	Yield to Maturity	Expected Return
Default Free	$961.54	4.00%	4%
50% Chance of Default	$903.90	10.63%	5.1%
Certain Default	$865.38	15.56%	4%

if there is a risk of default. Moreover, a higher yield to maturity does not necessarily imply that a bond's expected return is higher.

Bond Ratings

It would be both difficult and inefficient for every investor to privately investigate the default risk of every bond. Consequently, several companies rate the creditworthiness of bonds and make this information available to investors. The two best-known bond-rating companies are Standard & Poor's and Moody's. Table 6.4 summarizes the rating classes each company uses. Bonds with the highest rating are judged to be least likely to default. By consulting

TABLE 6.4 Bond Ratings

Rating*	Description (Moody's)
Investment Grade Debt	
Aaa/AAA	Judged to be of the best quality. They carry the smallest degree of investment risk and are generally referred to as "gilt edged." Interest payments are protected by a large or an exceptionally stable margin and principal is secure. While the various protective elements are likely to change, such changes as can be visualized are most unlikely to impair the fundamentally strong position of such issues.
Aa/AA	Judged to be of high quality by all standards. Together with the Aaa group, they constitute what are generally known as high-grade bonds. They are rated lower than the best bonds because margins of protection may not be as large as in Aaa securities or fluctuation of protective elements may be of greater amplitude or there may be other elements present that make the long-term risk appear somewhat larger than the Aaa securities.
A/A	Possess many favorable investment attributes and are considered as upper-medium-grade obligations. Factors giving security to principal and interest are considered adequate, but elements may be present that suggest a susceptibility to impairment some time in the future.
Baa/BBB	Are considered as medium-grade obligations (i.e., they are neither highly protected nor poorly secured). Interest payments and principal security appear adequate for the present but certain protective elements may be lacking or may be characteristically unreliable over any great length of time. Such bonds lack outstanding investment characteristics and, in fact, have speculative characteristics as well.
Speculative Bonds	
Ba/BB	Judged to have speculative elements; their future cannot be considered as well assured. Often the protection of interest and principal payments may be very moderate, and thereby not well safeguarded during both good and bad times over the future. Uncertainty of position characterizes bonds in this class.
B/B	Generally lack characteristics of the desirable investment. Assurance of interest and principal payments of maintenance of other terms of the contract over any long period of time may be small.
Caa/CCC	Are of poor standing. Such issues may be in default or there may be present elements of danger with respect to principal or interest.
Ca/CC	Are speculative in a high degree. Such issues are often in default or have other marked shortcomings.
C/C, D	Lowest-rated class of bonds, and issues so rated can be regarded as having extremely poor prospects of ever attaining any real investment standing.

*Ratings: Moody's/Standard & Poor's

Source: www.moodys.com

FIGURE 6.3

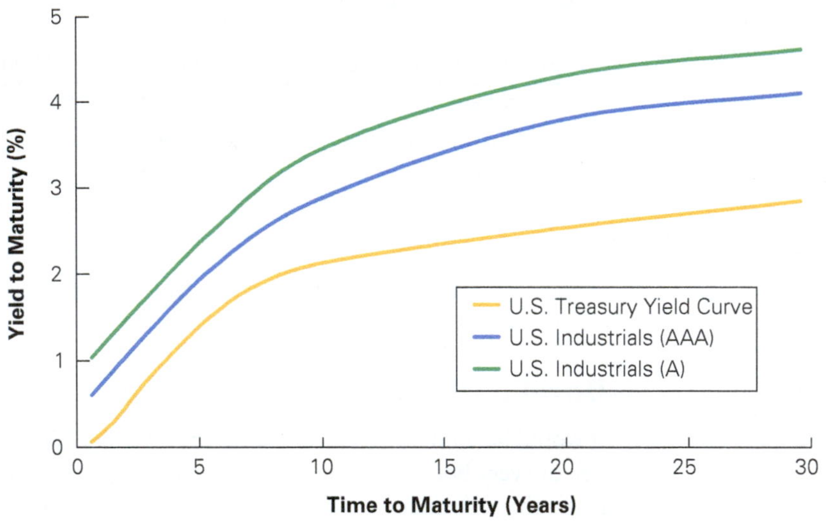

Corporate Yield Curves for Various Ratings, August 2015

This figure shows the yield curve for U.S. Treasury securities and yield curves for corporate securities with different ratings. Note how the yield to maturity is higher for lower rated bonds, which have a higher probability of default.

Source: Yahoo! Finance

these ratings, investors can assess the creditworthiness of a particular bond issue. The ratings therefore encourage widespread investor participation and relatively liquid markets.

Bonds in the top four categories are often referred to as **investment-grade bonds** because of their low default risk. Bonds in the bottom five categories are often called **speculative bonds**, **junk bonds**, or **high-yield bonds** because their likelihood of default is high. The rating depends on the risk of bankruptcy as well as the bondholders' ability to lay claim to the firm's assets in the event of such a bankruptcy. Thus, debt issues with a low-priority claim in bankruptcy will have a lower rating than issues from the same company that have a high-priority claim in bankruptcy or that are backed by a specific asset such as a building or a plant.

Corporate Yield Curves

Just as we can construct a yield curve from risk-free Treasury securities, we can plot a similar yield curve for corporate bonds. Figure 6.3 shows the average yields of U.S. corporate coupon bonds rated AAA or A, as well as the U.S. (coupon-paying) Treasury yield curve. We refer to the difference between the yields of the corporate bonds and the Treasury yields as the **default spread** or **credit spread**. Credit spreads fluctuate as perceptions regarding the probability of default change. Note that the credit spread is high for bonds with low ratings and therefore a greater likelihood of default.

CONCEPT CHECK

1. There are two reasons the yield of a defaultable bond exceeds the yield of an otherwise identical default-free bond. What are they?
2. What is a bond rating?

6.5 Sovereign Bonds

Sovereign bonds are bonds issued by national governments. We have, of course, already encountered an example of a sovereign bond—U.S. Treasury securities. But while U.S. Treasuries are generally considered to be default free, the same cannot be said for bonds issued by many other countries. Until recently, sovereign bond default was considered

GLOBAL FINANCIAL CRISIS — The Credit Crisis and Bond Yields

The financial crisis that engulfed the world's economies in 2008 originated as a credit crisis that first emerged in August 2007. At that time, problems in the mortgage market had led to the bankruptcy of several large mortgage lenders. The default of these firms, and the downgrading of many of the bonds backed by mortgages these firms had originated, caused investors to reassess the risk of other bonds in their portfolios. As perceptions of risk increased and investors attempted to move into safer U.S. Treasury securities, the prices of corporate bonds fell and so their credit spreads rose relative to Treasuries, as shown in Figure 6.4. Panel A of the figure shows the yield spreads for long-term corporate bonds, where we can see that spreads of even the highest-rated Aaa bonds increased dramatically, from a typical level of 0.5% to over 2% by the fall of 2008. Panel B shows a similar pattern for the rate banks had to pay on short-term loans compared to the yields of short-term Treasury bills. This increase in borrowing costs made it more costly for firms to raise the capital needed for new investment, slowing economic growth. The decline in these spreads in early 2009 was viewed by many as an important first step in mitigating the ongoing impact of the financial crisis on the rest of the economy. Note, however, the 2012 increase in spreads in the wake of the European debt crisis and consequent economic uncertainty.

FIGURE 6.4

Yield Spreads and the Financial Crisis

Panel A shows the yield spread between long-term (30-year) U.S. corporate and Treasury bonds. Panel B shows the yield spread of short-term loans to major international banks (LIBOR) and U.S. Treasury bills (also referred to as the Treasury-Eurodollar or "TED" spread). Note the dramatic increase in these spreads beginning in August 2007 and again in September 2008, before beginning to decline in early 2009. While spreads returned to pre-crisis levels by mid-2011, note the increase in spreads in 2012 in response to the European debt crisis. Spreads began rising again in 2015, partly in response to a surge in corporate borrowing, as well as declining demand from banks facing tighter regulation of their trading activities.

Source: www.Bloomberg.com

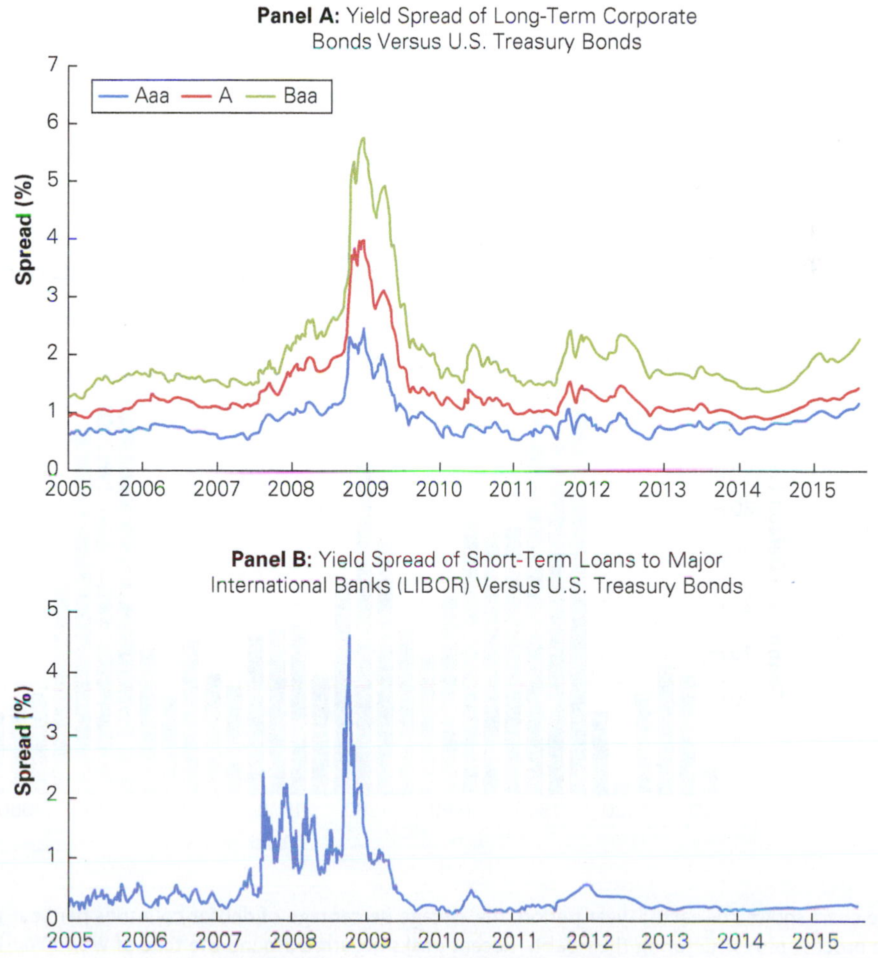

an emerging market phenomenon. The experience with Greek government bonds served as a wake-up call to investors that governments in the developed world can also default. In 2012, Greece defaulted and wrote off over $100 billion, or about 50%, of its outstanding debt, in the largest sovereign debt restructuring in world history (analyzed in the data case at the end of this chapter). Unfortunately, the restructuring did not solve the problem. Three years later, in 2015, Greece became the first developed country to default on an IMF loan when it failed to make a $1.7 billion payment. Later that year, Greece narrowly averted another default (this time to the European Central Bank) when its Eurozone partners put together an €86 billion bailout package that provided the funds to make the required bond payments. And Greece is far from unique—as Figure 6.5 shows, there have been periods when more than one-third of all debtor nations were either in default or restructuring their debt.

Because most sovereign debt is risky, the prices and yields of sovereign debt behave much like corporate debt: The bonds issued by countries with high probabilities of default have high yields and low prices. That said, there is a key difference between sovereign default and corporate default.

Unlike a corporation, a country facing difficulty meeting its financial obligations typically has the option to print additional currency to pay its debts. Of course, doing so is likely to lead to high inflation and a sharp devaluation of the currency. Consequently, debt holders carefully consider inflation expectations when determining the yield they are willing to accept because they understand that they may be repaid in money that is worth less than it was when the bonds were issued.

For most countries, the option to "inflate away" the debt is politically preferable to an outright default. That said, defaults do occur, either because the necessary inflation/

FIGURE 6.5 **Percent of Debtor Countries in Default or Restructuring Debt, 1800–2006**

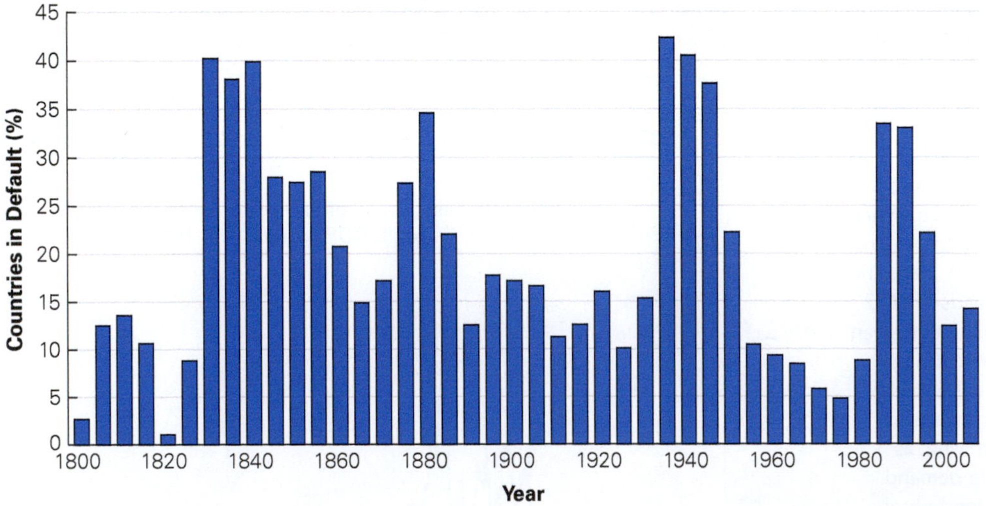

The chart shows, for each 5-year period, the average percentage of debtor countries per year that were either in default or in the process of restructuring their debt. Recent peaks occurred around the time of World War II and the Latin American, Asian, and Russian debt crises in the 1980s and 90s.

Source: Data from *This Time Is Different*, Carmen Reinhart and Kenneth Rogoff, Princeton University Press, 2009.

GLOBAL FINANCIAL CRISIS European Sovereign Debt Yields: A Puzzle

Before the EMU created the euro as a single European currency, the yields of sovereign debt issued by European countries varied widely. These variations primarily reflected differences in inflation expectations and currency risk (see Figure 6.6). However, after the monetary union was put in place at the end of 1998, the yields all essentially converged to the yield on German government bonds. Investors seemed to conclude that there was little distinction between the debt of the European countries in the union—they seemed to feel that all countries in the union were essentially exposed to the same default, inflation and currency risk and thus equally "safe."

Presumably, investors believed that an outright default was unthinkable: They apparently believed that member countries would be fiscally responsible and manage their debt obligations to avoid default at all costs. But as illustrated by Figure 6.6, once the 2008 financial crisis revealed the folly of this assumption, debt yields once again diverged as investors acknowledged the likelihood that some countries (particularly Portugal and Ireland) might be unable to repay their debt and would be forced to default.

In retrospect, rather than bringing fiscal responsibility, the monetary union allowed the weaker member countries to borrow at dramatically lower rates. In response, these countries reacted by increasing their borrowing—and at least in Greece's case, borrowed to the point that default became inevitable.

FIGURE 6.6 European Government Bond Yields, 1976–2015

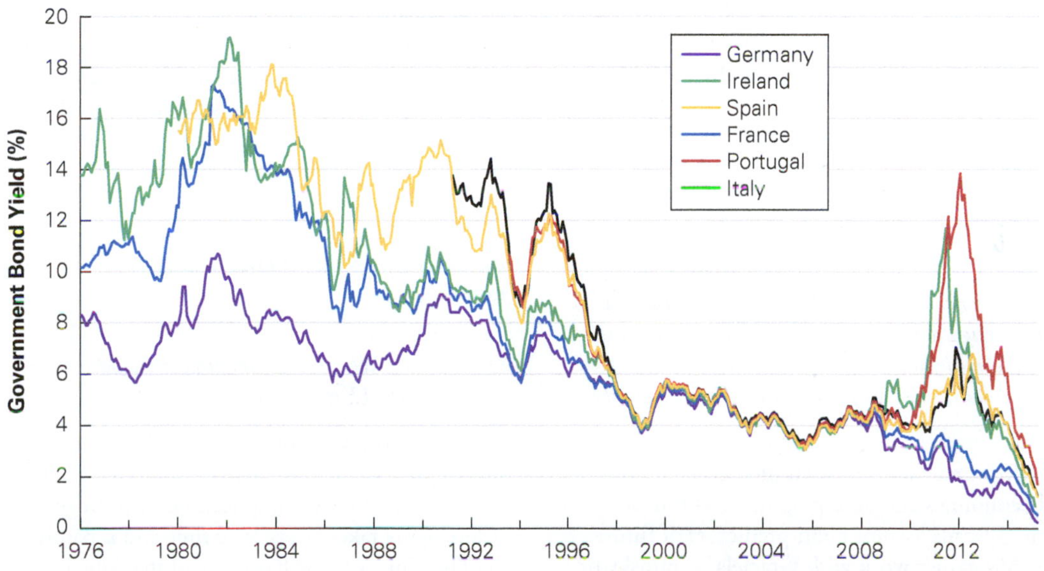

The plot shows the yield on government debt issued by six countries in the European Currency Union. Prior to the euro's introduction in 1999, yields varied in accordance with differing inflation expectations and currency risk. Yields converged once the euro was introduced, but diverged again after the 2008 financial crisis as investors recognized the possibility of default.

Source: Federal Reserve Economic Data, research.stlouisfed.org/fred2

devaluation would be too extreme, or sometimes because of a change in political regime (for example, Russian Tsarist debt became worthless paper after the 1917 revolution).

European sovereign debt is an interesting special case. Member states of the European Economic and Monetary Union (EMU) all share a common currency, the euro, and so have ceded control of their money supply to the European Central Bank (ECB). As a result, no individual

INTERVIEW WITH CARMEN M. REINHART

Carmen M. Reinhart is the Minos A. Zombanakis Professor of the International Financial System at the John F. Kennedy School of Government, Harvard University. She is co-author of the award- winning book *This Time Is Different: Eight Centuries of Financial Folly*, which documents the striking similarities of the recurring booms and busts characterizing financial history.

QUESTION: *Is Europe's sovereign debt crisis an anomaly in the developed world?*

ANSWER: There is a long history of sovereign debt crises in the developed world. Each time prior to the crisis people justified their actions with "this time is different." Two years ago no one thought Greece could default because it was in Europe. In fact, Greece has been in default 48% of the time since 1830. Before World War II, defaults, restructurings, and forced conversions among advanced economies were not rare. Post-World War II, sovereign debt defaults and restructurings have been largely confined to emerging markets such as Chile, Argentina, Peru, Nigeria, and Indonesia, leading people to the false assumption that debt crises were a developing market phenomena.

QUESTION: *Prior to the 2008/9 financial crisis, the yield spreads on sovereign debt issued by Eurozone countries were very narrow, seeming to indicate that investors believed that the debt was equally safe. Why would investors come to this conclusion?*

ANSWER: Economic and financial indicators in both advanced economies and emerging markets indicate that interest rate spreads are not good predictors of future debt rates. My earlier work with Graciela Kaminsky of early warnings supported this conclusion. Often public and private debt builds up but the spreads do not reflect the added risk. During the boom period, Eurozone countries had very low spreads and very strong credit ratings. Yet the underlying domestic fundamentals did not support these signals of financial health. People convinced themselves that the world was different.

Also, looking exclusively at rising sovereign debt levels can be deceptive. History has shown that private debts before a crisis become public afterwards. In the early 1980s, Chile had a fiscal surplus and still it had a massive debt crisis. In Ireland and Spain in the late 2000s, public debt was under control, but private sector debt, which carried an implicit guarantee, was skyrocketing.

QUESTION: *Since the financial crisis these yields have diverged. What has changed and why?*

ANSWER: People found out that the world was not different; that is, the countries in Europe were not equally risky. Financial crises adversely affect public finances—what starts as a financial crisis morphs into banking and sovereign debt crises. Financial crises related to recessions are deeper and more protracted than normal recessions, creating enormous problems because, even after fiscal stimulus, revenues collapse. In addition, governments take on private debt to circumvent a financial meltdown. In the U.S., FNMA and Freddie Mac moved from the private sector balance sheet before the crisis to the public sector balance sheet afterwards. In Ireland and Spain, public debt became bloated as the governments took on the debts of banks. In the aftermath of the 2007–2008 crisis, the slew of simultaneous crises in advanced economies limited opportunities to grow out of crisis (for example, by increasing exports).

QUESTION: *What's next for Europe? Could the same thing happen in the United States?*

ANSWER: I think Europe's prospects will remain fairly dismal for a while. Europe has been moving very slowly, if at all, to address the implications of its huge debt—deleveraging takes a very long time and is painful.

The United States has many of the same issues. While a U.S. Treasury default is unlikely, I do not believe that the currently low Treasury debt yields imply that the U.S. fundamentals are good. Treasury debt yields are low because of massive official intervention—the Fed and other central banks are buying Treasuries to prevent their currencies from appreciating and to keep their borrowing rates low. This kind of government intervention following a crisis is common. It is why recovery takes so long. Historically, lackluster GDP growth lasts 23 years on average following a financial crisis, and is a dark cloud over U.S. growth prospects.

country can simply print money to make debt payments. Furthermore, when the ECB does print money to help pay one country's debt, the subsequent inflation affects all citizens in the union, effectively forcing citizens in one country to shoulder the debt burden of another country. Because individual countries do not have discretion to inflate away their debt, default is a real possibility within the EMU. This risk became tangible in 2012 and again in 2015 with Greece's multiple defaults.

CONCEPT CHECK

1. Why do sovereign debt yields differ across countries?
2. What options does a country have if it decides it cannot meet its debt obligations?

MyFinanceLab

Here is what you should know after reading this chapter. **MyFinanceLab** will help you identify what you know and where to go when you need to practice.

6.1 Bond Cash Flows, Prices, and Yields

- Bonds pay both coupon and principal or face value payments to investors. By convention, the coupon rate of a bond is expressed as an APR, so the amount of each coupon payment, *CPN*, is

$$CPN = \frac{\text{Coupon Rate} \times \text{Face Value}}{\text{Number of Coupon Payments per Year}} \tag{6.1}$$

- Zero-coupon bonds make no coupon payments, so investors receive only the bond's face value.
- The internal rate of return of a bond is called its yield to maturity (or yield). The yield to maturity of a bond is the discount rate that sets the present value of the promised bond payments equal to the current market price of the bond.
- The yield to maturity for a zero-coupon bond is given by

$$YTM_n = \left(\frac{FV}{P}\right)^{1/n} - 1 \tag{6.3}$$

- The risk-free interest rate for an investment until date n equals the yield to maturity of a risk-free zero-coupon bond that matures on date n. A plot of these rates against maturity is called the zero-coupon yield curve.
- The yield to maturity for a coupon bond is the discount rate, y, that equates the present value of the bond's future cash flows with its price:

$$P = CPN \times \frac{1}{y}\left(1 - \frac{1}{(1+y)^N}\right) + \frac{FV}{(1+y)^N} \tag{6.5}$$

6.2 Dynamic Behavior of Bond Prices

- A bond will trade at a premium if its coupon rate exceeds its yield to maturity. It will trade at a discount if its coupon rate is less than its yield to maturity. If a bond's coupon rate equals its yield to maturity, it trades at par.
- As a bond approaches maturity, the price of the bond approaches its face value.
- If the bond's yield to maturity has not changed, then the IRR of an investment in a bond equals its yield to maturity even if you sell the bond early.

- Bond prices change as interest rates change. When interest rates rise, bond prices fall, and vice versa.
  - Long-term zero-coupon bonds are more sensitive to changes in interest rates than are short-term zero-coupon bonds.
  - Bonds with low coupon rates are more sensitive to changes in interest rates than similar maturity bonds with high coupon rates.
  - The duration of a bond measures the sensitivity of its price to changes in interest rates.

6.3 The Yield Curve and Bond Arbitrage

- Because we can replicate a coupon-paying bond using a portfolio of zero-coupon bonds, the price of a coupon-paying bond can be determined based on the zero-coupon yield curve using the Law of One Price:

$$P = PV(\text{Bond Cash Flows}) = \frac{CPN}{1 + YTM_1} + \frac{CPN}{(1 + YTM_2)^2} + \cdots + \frac{CPN + FV}{(1 + YTM_n)^n} \tag{6.6}$$

- When the yield curve is not flat, bonds with the same maturity but different coupon rates will have different yields to maturity.

6.4 Corporate Bonds

- When a bond issuer does not make a bond payment in full, the issuer has defaulted.
  - The risk that default can occur is called default or credit risk.
  - U.S. Treasury securities are generally considered free of default risk.
- The expected return of a corporate bond, which is the firm's debt cost of capital, equals the risk-free rate of interest plus a risk premium. The expected return is less than the bond's yield to maturity because the yield to maturity of a bond is calculated using the promised cash flows, not the expected cash flows.
- Bond ratings summarize the creditworthiness of bonds for investors.
- The difference between yields on Treasury securities and yields on corporate bonds is called the credit spread or default spread. The credit spread compensates investors for the difference between promised and expected cash flows and for the risk of default.

6.5 Sovereign Bonds

- Sovereign bonds are issued by national governments.
- Sovereign bond yields reflect investor expectations of inflation, currency, and default risk.
- Countries may repay their debt by printing additional currency, which generally leads to a rise in inflation and a sharp currency devaluation.
- When "inflating away" the debt is infeasible or politically unattractive, countries may choose to default on their debt.

Key Terms

bond certificate *p. 174*
clean price *p. 183*
corporate bonds *p. 188*
coupon bonds *p. 177*
coupon-paying yield curve *p. 188*
coupon rate *p. 174*
coupons *p. 174*
credit risk *p. 189*
debt ceiling *p. 189*
default (credit) spread *p. 192*
dirty price *p. 183*
discount *p. 174*
duration *p. 183*
face value *p. 174*
high-yield bonds *p. 192*
investment-grade bonds *p. 192*
invoice price *p. 183*
junk bonds *p. 192*

maturity date *p. 174*
on-the-run bonds *p. 188*
par *p. 179*
premium *p. 179*
pure discount bond *p. 174*
sovereign bonds *p. 192*
speculative bonds *p. 192*
spot interest rates *p. 175*
term *p. 174*
Treasury bills *p. 174*
Treasury bonds *p. 177*
Treasury notes *p. 177*
yield to maturity (YTM) *p. 175*
zero-coupon bond *p. 174*
zero-coupon yield curve *p. 176*

Further Reading

For readers interested in more details about the bond market, the following texts will prove useful: Z. Bodie, A. Kane, and A. Marcus, *Investments* (McGraw-Hill/Irwin, 2004); F. Fabozzi, *The Handbook of Fixed Income Securities* (McGraw-Hill, 2005); W. Sharpe, G. Alexander, and J. Bailey, *Investments* (Prentice-Hall, 1998); and B. Tuckman, *Fixed Income Securities: Tools for Today's Markets* (John Wiley & Sons, Inc., 2002). C. Reinhart and K. Rogoff, *This Time Is Different* (Princeton University Press, 2010), provides a historical perspective and an excellent discussion of the risk of sovereign debt. For details related to the 2012 Greek default, see "The Greek Debt Restructuring: An Autopsy," J. Zettelmeyer, C. Trebesch, and M. Gulati, *Economic Policy* (July 2013): 513–563.

Problems

All problems are available in MyFinanceLab. An asterisk (*) indicates problems with a higher level of difficulty.

Bond Cash Flows, Prices, and Yields

1. A 30-year bond with a face value of $1000 has a coupon rate of 5.5%, with semiannual payments.
   a. What is the coupon payment for this bond?
   b. Draw the cash flows for the bond on a timeline.

2. Assume that a bond will make payments every six months as shown on the following timeline (using six-month periods):

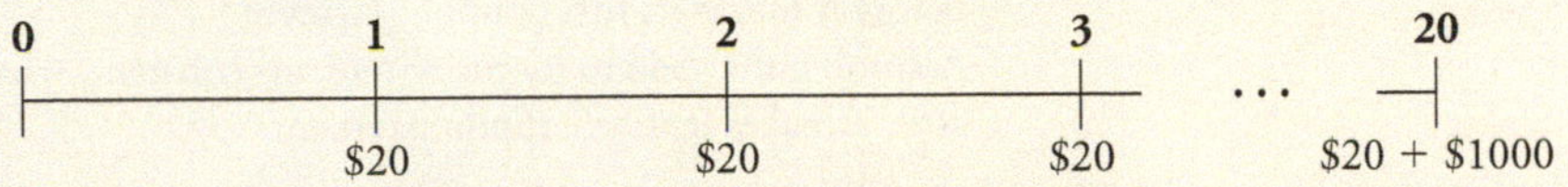

   a. What is the maturity of the bond (in years)?
   b. What is the coupon rate (in percent)?
   c. What is the face value?

3. The following table summarizes prices of various default-free, zero-coupon bonds (expressed as a percentage of face value):

Maturity (years)	1	2	3	4	5
Price (per $100 face value)	$95.51	$91.05	$86.38	$81.65	$76.51

   a. Compute the yield to maturity for each bond.
   b. Plot the zero-coupon yield curve (for the first five years).
   c. Is the yield curve upward sloping, downward sloping, or flat?

4. Suppose the current zero-coupon yield curve for risk-free bonds is as follows:

Maturity (years)	1	2	3	4	5
YTM	5.00%	5.50%	5.75%	5.95%	6.05%

a. What is the price per $100 face value of a two-year, zero-coupon, risk-free bond?
b. What is the price per $100 face value of a four-year, zero-coupon, risk-free bond?
c. What is the risk-free interest rate for a five-year maturity?

5. In the Global Financial Crisis box in Section 6.1, www.Bloomberg.com reported that the three-month Treasury bill sold for a price of $100.002556 per $100 face value. What is the yield to maturity of this bond, expressed as an EAR?

6. Suppose a 10-year, $1000 bond with an 8% coupon rate and semiannual coupons is trading for a price of $1034.74.
a. What is the bond's yield to maturity (expressed as an APR with semiannual compounding)?
b. If the bond's yield to maturity changes to 9% APR, what will the bond's price be?

7. Suppose a five-year, $1000 bond with annual coupons has a price of $900 and a yield to maturity of 6%. What is the bond's coupon rate?

Dynamic Behavior of Bond Prices

8. The prices of several bonds with face values of $1000 are summarized in the following table:

Bond	A	B	C	D
Price	$972.50	$1040.75	$1150.00	$1000.00

For each bond, state whether it trades at a discount, at par, or at a premium.

9. Explain why the yield of a bond that trades at a discount exceeds the bond's coupon rate.

10. Suppose a seven-year, $1000 bond with an 8% coupon rate and semiannual coupons is trading with a yield to maturity of 6.75%.
a. Is this bond currently trading at a discount, at par, or at a premium? Explain.
b. If the yield to maturity of the bond rises to 7% (APR with semiannual compounding), what price will the bond trade for?

11. Suppose that Ally Financial Inc. issued a bond with 10 years until maturity, a face value of $1000, and a coupon rate of 7% (annual payments). The yield to maturity on this bond when it was issued was 6%.
a. What was the price of this bond when it was issued?
b. Assuming the yield to maturity remains constant, what is the price of the bond immediately before it makes its first coupon payment?
c. Assuming the yield to maturity remains constant, what is the price of the bond immediately after it makes its first coupon payment?

12. Suppose you purchase a 10-year bond with 6% annual coupons. You hold the bond for four years, and sell it immediately after receiving the fourth coupon. If the bond's yield to maturity was 5% when you purchased and sold the bond,
a. What cash flows will you pay and receive from your investment in the bond per $100 face value?
b. What is the internal rate of return of your investment?

MFL **13.** Consider the following bonds:

Bond	Coupon Rate (annual payments)	Maturity (years)
A	0%	15
B	0%	10
C	4%	15
D	8%	10

a. What is the percentage change in the price of each bond if its yield to maturity falls from 6% to 5%?
b. Which of the bonds A–D is most sensitive to a 1% drop in interest rates from 6% to 5% and why? Which bond is least sensitive? Provide an intuitive explanation for your answer.

14. Suppose you purchase a 30-year, zero-coupon bond with a yield to maturity of 6%. You hold the bond for five years before selling it.
   a. If the bond's yield to maturity is 6% when you sell it, what is the internal rate of return of your investment?
   b. If the bond's yield to maturity is 7% when you sell it, what is the internal rate of return of your investment?
   c. If the bond's yield to maturity is 5% when you sell it, what is the internal rate of return of your investment?
   d. Even if a bond has no chance of default, is your investment risk free if you plan to sell it before it matures? Explain.

15. Suppose you purchase a 30-year Treasury bond with a 5% annual coupon, initially trading at par. In 10 years' time, the bond's yield to maturity has risen to 7% (EAR).
   a. If you sell the bond now, what internal rate of return will you have earned on your investment in the bond?
   b. If instead you hold the bond to maturity, what internal rate of return will you earn on your investment in the bond?
   c. Is comparing the IRRs in (a) versus (b) a useful way to evaluate the decision to sell the bond? Explain.

16. Suppose the current yield on a one-year, zero coupon bond is 3%, while the yield on a five-year, zero coupon bond is 5%. Neither bond has any risk of default. Suppose you plan to invest for one year. You will earn more over the year by investing in the five-year bond as long as its yield does not rise above what level?

The Yield Curve and Bond Arbitrage

For Problems 17–22, assume zero-coupon yields on default-free securities are as summarized in the following table:

Maturity (years)	1	2	3	4	5
Zero-coupon YTM	4.00%	4.30%	4.50%	4.70%	4.80%

17. What is the price today of a two-year, default-free security with a face value of $1000 and an annual coupon rate of 6%? Does this bond trade at a discount, at par, or at a premium?

18. What is the price of a five-year, zero-coupon, default-free security with a face value of $1000?

19. What is the price of a three-year, default-free security with a face value of $1000 and an annual coupon rate of 4%? What is the yield to maturity for this bond?

20. What is the maturity of a default-free security with annual coupon payments and a yield to maturity of 4%? Why?

*21. Consider a four-year, default-free security with annual coupon payments and a face value of $1000 that is issued at par. What is the coupon rate of this bond?

22. Consider a five-year, default-free bond with annual coupons of 5% and a face value of $1000.
   a. Without doing any calculations, determine whether this bond is trading at a premium or at a discount. Explain.
   b. What is the yield to maturity on this bond?
   c. If the yield to maturity on this bond increased to 5.2%, what would the new price be?

*23. Prices of zero-coupon, default-free securities with face values of $1000 are summarized in the following table:

Maturity (years)	1	2	3
Price (per $1000 face value)	$970.87	$938.95	$904.56

Suppose you observe that a three-year, default-free security with an annual coupon rate of 10% and a face value of $1000 has a price today of $1183.50. Is there an arbitrage opportunity? If so, show specifically how you would take advantage of this opportunity. If not, why not?

***24.** Assume there are four default-free bonds with the following prices and future cash flows:

		Cash Flows		
Bond	**Price Today**	**Year 1**	**Year 2**	**Year 3**
A	$934.58	1000	0	0
B	881.66	0	1000	0
C	1,118.21	100	100	1100
D	839.62	0	0	1000

Do these bonds present an arbitrage opportunity? If so, how would you take advantage of this opportunity? If not, why not?

***25.** Suppose you are given the following information about the default-free, coupon-paying yield curve:

Maturity (years)	1	2	3	4
Coupon rate (annual payments)	0.00%	10.00%	6.00%	12.00%
YTM	2.000%	3.908%	5.840%	5.783%

a. Use arbitrage to determine the yield to maturity of a two-year, zero-coupon bond.
b. What is the zero-coupon yield curve for years 1 through 4?

Corporate Bonds

26. Explain why the expected return of a corporate bond does not equal its yield to maturity.

27. In the Data Case in Chapter 5, we suggested using the yield on Florida Sate bonds to estimate the State of Florida's cost of capital. Why might this estimate overstate the actual cost of capital?

28. Grummon Corporation has issued zero-coupon corporate bonds with a five-year maturity. Investors believe there is a 20% chance that Grummon will default on these bonds. If Grummon does default, investors expect to receive only 50 cents per dollar they are owed. If investors require a 6% expected return on their investment in these bonds, what will be the price and yield to maturity on these bonds?

29. The following table summarizes the yields to maturity on several one-year, zero-coupon securities:

Security	Yield (%)
Treasury	3.1
AAA corporate	3.2
BBB corporate	4.2
B corporate	4.9

a. What is the price (expressed as a percentage of the face value) of a one-year, zero-coupon corporate bond with a AAA rating?
b. What is the credit spread on AAA-rated corporate bonds?
c. What is the credit spread on B-rated corporate bonds?
d. How does the credit spread change with the bond rating? Why?

30. Andrew Industries is contemplating issuing a 30-year bond with a coupon rate of 7% (annual coupon payments) and a face value of $1000. Andrew believes it can get a rating of A from Standard and Poor's. However, due to recent financial difficulties at the company, Standard and

Poor's is warning that it may downgrade Andrew Industries bonds to BBB. Yields on A-rated, long-term bonds are currently 6.5%, and yields on BBB-rated bonds are 6.9%.

a. What is the price of the bond if Andrew maintains the A rating for the bond issue?
b. What will the price of the bond be if it is downgraded?

MFL X **31.** HMK Enterprises would like to raise $10 million to invest in capital expenditures. The company plans to issue five-year bonds with a face value of $1000 and a coupon rate of 6.5% (annual payments). The following table summarizes the yield to maturity for five-year (annual-pay) coupon corporate bonds of various ratings:

Rating	AAA	AA	A	BBB	BB
YTM	6.20%	6.30%	6.50%	6.90%	7.50%

a. Assuming the bonds will be rated AA, what will the price of the bonds be?
b. How much total principal amount of these bonds must HMK issue to raise $10 million today, assuming the bonds are AA rated? (Because HMK cannot issue a fraction of a bond, assume that all fractions are rounded to the nearest whole number.)
c. What must the rating of the bonds be for them to sell at par?
d. Suppose that when the bonds are issued, the price of each bond is $959.54. What is the likely rating of the bonds? Are they junk bonds?

32. A BBB-rated corporate bond has a yield to maturity of 8.2%. A U.S. Treasury security has a yield to maturity of 6.5%. These yields are quoted as APRs with semiannual compounding. Both bonds pay semiannual coupons at a rate of 7% and have five years to maturity.

a. What is the price (expressed as a percentage of the face value) of the Treasury bond?
b. What is the price (expressed as a percentage of the face value) of the BBB-rated corporate bond?
c. What is the credit spread on the BBB bonds?

33. The Isabelle Corporation rents prom dresses in its stores across the southern United States. It has just issued a five-year, zero-coupon corporate bond at a price of $74. You have purchased this bond and intend to hold it until maturity.

a. What is the yield to maturity of the bond?
b. What is the expected return on your investment (expressed as an EAR) if there is no chance of default?
c. What is the expected return (expressed as an EAR) if there is a 100% probability of default and you will recover 90% of the face value?
d. What is the expected return (expressed as an EAR) if the probability of default is 50%, the likelihood of default is higher in bad times than good times, and, in the case of default, you will recover 90% of the face value?
e. For parts (b–d), what can you say about the five-year, risk-free interest rate in each case?

Sovereign Bonds

34. What does it mean for a country to "inflate away" its debt? Why might this be costly for investors even if the country does not default?

35. Suppose the yield on German government bonds is 1%, while the yield on Spanish government bonds is 6%. Both bonds are denominated in euros. Which country do investors believe is more likely to default? How can you tell?

Data Case

You are an intern with Sirius XM Radio in their corporate finance division. The firm is planning to issue $50 million of 6% annual coupon bonds with a 10-year maturity. The firm anticipates an increase in its bond rating. Your boss wants you to determine the gain in the proceeds of the new issue if the issue is rated above the firm's current bond rating. To prepare this information, you will have to determine Sirius's current debt rating and the yield curve for their particular rating.

1. Begin by finding the current U.S. Treasury yield curve. At the Treasury Web site (www.treas.gov), search using the term "yield curve" and select "Historic Yield Data." Click on "View Text Version of Treasury Yield Curve." The correct link is likely to be the first link on the page. Download that table into Excel by right clicking with the cursor in the table and selecting "Export to Microsoft Excel."
2. Find the current yield spreads for the various bond ratings. Unfortunately, the current spreads are available only for a fee, so you will use old ones. Go to BondsOnline (www.bondsonline.com) and click "Today's Market." Next, click "Corporate Bond Spreads." Download this table to Excel and copy and paste it to the same file as the Treasury yields.
3. Find the current bond rating for Sirius. Go to Standard & Poor's Web site (www.standardandpoors.com). Select "Find a Rating" from the list at the left of the page, then select "Credit Ratings Search." At this point, you will have to register (it's free) or enter the username and password provided by your instructor. Next, you will be able to search by Organization Name—enter Sirius and select Sirius XM Radio. Use the credit rating for the organization, not the specific issue ratings.
4. Return to Excel and create a timeline with the cash flows and discount rates you will need to value the new bond issue.
   a. To create the required spot rates for Sirius' issue, add the appropriate spread to the Treasury yield of the same maturity.
   b. The yield curve and spread rates you have found do not cover every year that you will need for the new bonds. Fill these in by linearly interpolating the given yields and spreads. For example, the four-year spot rate and spread will be the average of the three- and five-year rates.
   c. To compute the spot rates for Sirius' current debt rating, add the yield spread to the Treasury rate for each maturity. However, note that the spread is in basis points, which are 1/100th of a percentage point.
   d. Compute the cash flows that would be paid to bondholders each year and add them to the timeline.
5. Use the spot rates to calculate the present value of each cash flow paid to the bondholders.
6. Compute the issue price of the bond and its initial yield to maturity.
7. Repeat Steps 4–6 based on the assumption that Sirius is able to raise its bond rating by one level. Compute the new yield based on the higher rating and the new bond price that would result.
8. Compute the additional cash proceeds that could be raised from the issue if the rating were improved.

Note: Updates to this data case may be found at www.berkdemarzo.com.

Case Study

The 2012 Greek Default and Subsequent Debt Restructuring[6]

In March and April 2012 Greece defaulted on its debt by swapping its outstanding obligations for new obligations of much lesser face value. For each euro of face value outstanding, a holder of Greek debt was given the following securities with an issue date of 12 March 2012.

- Two European Financial Stability Fund (EFSF) notes. Each note had a face value of 7.5¢. The first note paid an annual coupon (on the anniversary of the issue date) of 0.4% and matured on 12 March 2013. The second note paid an annual coupon of 1% and matured on 12 March 2014.
- A series of bonds issued by the Greek government with a combined face value of 31.5¢. The simplest way to characterize these bonds is as a single bond paying an annual coupon

[6] This case is based on information and analysis published in "The Greek Debt Restruturing: An Autopsy," J. Zettelmeyer, C. Trebesch, and M. Gulati, *Economic Policy* (July 2013) 513–563. For pedagogical reasons, some details of the bond issues were changed marginally to simplify the calculations.

(on December 12 of each year) of 2% for years 2012–2015, 3% for years 2016–2020, 3.65% for 2021, and 4.3% thereafter. Principal is repaid in 20 equal installments (that is, 5% of face value) in December in the years 2023–2042.

- Other securities that were worth little.

An important feature of this swap is that the same deal was offered to all investors, regardless of which bonds they were holding. That meant that the loss to different investors was not the same. To understand why, begin by calculating the present value of what every investor received. For simplicity, assume that the coupons on the EFSF notes were issued at market rates so they traded at par. Next, put all the promised payments of the bond series on a timeline. Figure 6.7 shows the imputed yields on Greek debt that prevailed *after the debt swap* was announced. Assume the yields in Figure 6.7 are yields on zero coupon bonds maturing in the 23 years following the debt swap, and use them to calculate the present value of all promised payments on March 12, 2012.

Next, consider 2 different bonds that were outstanding before the default (there were a total of 117 different securities).

- A Greek government bond maturing on March 12, 2012
- A Greek government 4.7% annual coupon bond maturing on March 12, 2024.

Using the yields in Figure 6.7, calculate the value of each existing bond as a fraction of face value. Bondholders of both existing bonds received the same package of new bonds in exchange for their existing bonds. In each case calculate the haircut, that is, the amount of the loss (as a fraction of the original bonds' face value) that was sustained when the existing bonds were replaced with the new bonds. Which investors took a larger haircut, long-term or short-term bondholders?

Assume that participation in the swap was voluntary (as was claimed at the time), so that on the announcement the price of the existing bonds equaled the value of the new bonds. Using this equivalence, calculate the yield to maturity of the existing bond that matured in 2024. What might explain the difference between this yield and the yields in Figure 6.7?

FIGURE 6.7 **Imputed Greek Government Yield Curve on March 12, 2012**

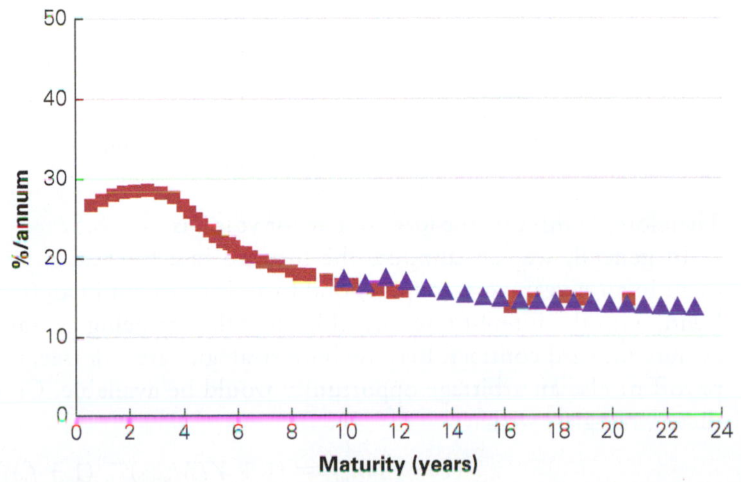

Source: "The Greek Debt Restructuring: An Autopsy," J. Zettelmeyer, C. Trebesch, and M. Gulati.

CHAPTER 6 APPENDIX

Forward Interest Rates

NOTATION

f_n one-year forward rate for year n

Given the risk associated with interest rate changes, corporate managers require tools to help manage this risk. One of the most important is the interest rate forward contract, which is a type of swap contract. An **interest rate forward contract** (also called a **forward rate agreement**) is a contract today that fixes the interest rate for a loan or investment in the future. In this appendix, we explain how to derive forward interest rates from zero-coupon yields.

Computing Forward Rates

A **forward interest rate** (or **forward rate**) is an interest rate that we can guarantee today for a loan or investment that will occur in the future. Throughout this section, we will consider interest rate forward contracts for one-year investments; thus, when we refer to the forward rate for year 5, we mean the rate available *today* on a one-year investment that begins four years from today and is repaid five years from today.

We can use the Law of One Price to calculate the forward rate from the zero-coupon yield curve. The forward rate for year 1 is the rate on an investment that starts today and is repaid in one year; it is equivalent to an investment in a one-year, zero-coupon bond. Therefore, by the Law of One Price, these rates must coincide:

$$f_1 = YTM_1 \tag{6A.1}$$

Now consider the two-year forward rate. Suppose the one-year, zero-coupon yield is 5.5% and the two-year, zero-coupon yield is 7%. There are two ways to invest money risk free for two years. First, we can invest in the two-year, zero-coupon bond at rate of 7% and earn $\$(1.07)^2$ after two years per dollar invested. Second, we can invest in the one-year bond at a rate of 5.5%, which will pay \$1.055 at the end of one year, and simultaneously guarantee the interest rate we will earn by reinvesting the \$1.055 for the second year by entering into an interest rate forward contract for year 2 at rate f_2. In that case, we will earn $\$(1.055)(1 + f_2)$ at the end of two years. Because both strategies are risk free, by the Law of One Price, they must have the same return:

$$(1.07)^2 = (1.055)(1 + f_2)$$

Rearranging, we have

$$(1 + f_2) = \frac{1.07^2}{1.055} = 1.0852$$

Therefore, in this case the forward rate for year 2 is $f_2 = 8.52\%$.

In general, we can compute the forward rate for year n by comparing an investment in an n-year, zero-coupon bond to an investment in an $(n - 1)$ year, zero-coupon bond, with the interest rate earned in the nth year being guaranteed through an interest rate forward contract. Because both strategies are risk free, they must have the same payoff or else an arbitrage opportunity would be available. Comparing the payoffs of these strategies, we have

$$(1 + YTM_n)^n = (1 + YTM_{n-1})^{n-1}(1 + f_n)$$

We can rearrange this equation to find the general formula for the forward interest rate:

$$f_n = \frac{(1 + YTM_n)^n}{(1 + YTM_{n-1})^{n-1}} - 1 \quad (6A.2)$$

EXAMPLE 6A.1 **Computing Forward Rates**

Problem

Calculate the forward rates for years 1 through 5 from the following zero-coupon yields:

Maturity	1	2	3	4
YTM	5.00%	6.00%	6.00%	5.75%

Solution

Using Eqs. 6A.1 and 6A.2:

$$f_1 = YTM_1 = 5.00\%$$

$$f_2 = \frac{(1 + YTM_2)^2}{(1 + YTM_1)} - 1 = \frac{1.06^2}{1.05} - 1 = 7.01\%$$

$$f_3 = \frac{(1 + YTM_3)^3}{(1 + YTM_2)^2} - 1 = \frac{1.06^3}{1.06^2} - 1 = 6.00\%$$

$$f_4 = \frac{(1 + YTM_4)^4}{(1 + YTM_3)^3} - 1 = \frac{1.0575^4}{1.06^3} - 1 = 5.00\%$$

Note that when the yield curve is increasing in year n (that is, when $YTM_n > YTM_{n-1}$), the forward rate is higher than the zero-coupon yield, $f_n > YTM_n$. Similarly, when the yield curve is decreasing, the forward rate is less than the zero-coupon yield. When the yield curve is flat, the forward rate equals the zero-coupon yield.

Computing Bond Yields from Forward Rates

Eq. 6A.2 computes the forward interest rate using the zero-coupon yields. It is also possible to compute the zero-coupon yields from the forward interest rates. To see this, note that if we use interest rate forward contracts to lock in an interest rate for an investment in year 1, year 2, and so on through year n, we can create an n-year, risk-free investment. The return from this strategy must match the return from an n-year, zero-coupon bond. Therefore,

$$(1 + f_1) \times (1 + f_2) \times \cdots \times (1 + f_n) = (1 + YTM_n)^n \quad (6A.3)$$

For example, using the forward rates from Example 6A.1, we can compute the four-year zero-coupon yield:

$$\begin{aligned} 1 + YTM_4 &= [(1 + f_1)(1 + f_2)(1 + f_3)(1 + f_4)]^{1/4} \\ &= [(1.05)(1.0701)(1.06)(1.05)]^{1/4} \\ &= 1.0575 \end{aligned}$$

Forward Rates and Future Interest Rates

A forward rate is the rate that you contract for today for an investment in the future. How does this rate compare to the interest rate that will actually prevail in the future? It is tempting to believe that the forward interest rate should be a good predictor of future interest rates. In reality, this will generally not be the case. Instead, it is a good predictor only when investors do not care about risk.

EXAMPLE 6A.2 Forward Rates and Future Spot Rates

Problem

JoAnne Wilford is corporate treasurer for Wafer Thin Semiconductor. She must invest some of the cash on hand for two years in risk-free bonds. The current one-year, zero-coupon yield is 5%. The one-year forward rate is 6%. She is trying to decide between three possible strategies: (1) buy a two-year bond, (2) buy a one-year bond and enter into an interest rate forward contract to guarantee the rate in the second year, or (3) buy a one-year bond and forgo the forward contract, reinvesting at whatever rate prevails next year. Under what scenarios would she be better off following the risky strategy?

Solution

From Eq. 6A.3, both strategies (1) and (2) lead to the same risk-free return of $(1 + YTM_2)^2 = (1 + YTM_1)(1 + f_2) = (1.05)(1.06)$. The third strategy returns $(1.05)(1 + r)$, where r is the one-year interest rate next year. If the future interest rate turns out to be 6%, then the two strategies will offer the same return. Otherwise Wafer Thin Semiconductor is better off with strategy (3) if the interest rate next year is greater than the forward rate—6%—and worse off if the interest rate is lower than 6%.

As Example 6A.2 makes clear, we can think of the forward rate as a break-even rate. If this rate actually prevails in the future, investors will be indifferent between investing in a two-year bond and investing in a one-year bond and rolling over the money in one year. If investors did not care about risk, then they would be indifferent between the two strategies whenever the expected one-year spot rate equals the current forward rate. However, investors *do* generally care about risk. If the expected returns of both strategies were the same, investors would prefer one strategy or the other depending on whether they want to be exposed to future interest rate risk fluctuations. In general, the expected future spot interest rate will reflect investors' preferences toward the risk of future interest rate fluctuations. Thus,

$$\text{Expected Future Spot Interest Rate} = \text{Forward Interest Rate} + \text{Risk Premium} \quad (6A.4)$$

This risk premium can be either positive or negative depending on investors' preferences.[7] As a result, forward rates tend not to be ideal predictors of future spot rates.

[7]Empirical research suggests that the risk premium tends to be negative when the yield curve is upward sloping, and positive when it is downward sloping. See E. Fama and R. Bliss, "The Information in Long-Maturity Forward Rates," *American Economic Review* 77(4) (1987): 680–692; and J. Campbell and R. Shiller, "Yield Spreads and Interest Rate Movements: A Bird's Eye View," *Review of Economic Studies* 58(3) (1991): 495–514.

Key Terms

forward interest rate (forward rate) *p. 206*
forward rate agreement *p. 206*
interest rate forward contract *p. 206*

Problems

All problems are available in MyFinanceLab. *An asterisk (*) indicates problems with a higher level of difficulty.*

Problems A.1–A.4 refer to the following table:

Maturity (years)	1	2	3	4	5
Zero-coupon YTM	4.0%	5.5%	5.5%	5.0%	4.5%

A.1. What is the forward rate for year 2 (the forward rate quoted today for an investment that begins in one year and matures in two years)?

A.2. What is the forward rate for year 3 (the forward rate quoted today for an investment that begins in two years and matures in three years)? What can you conclude about forward rates when the yield curve is flat?

A.3. What is the forward rate for year 5 (the forward rate quoted today for an investment that begins in four years and matures in five years)?

***A.4.** Suppose you wanted to lock in an interest rate for an investment that begins in one year and matures in five years. What rate would you obtain if there are no arbitrage opportunities?

***A.5.** Suppose the yield on a one-year, zero-coupon bond is 5%. The forward rate for year 2 is 4%, and the forward rate for year 3 is 3%. What is the yield to maturity of a zero-coupon bond that matures in three years?

Valuing Projects and Firms

PART 3

THE LAW OF ONE PRICE CONNECTION. Now that the basic tools for financial decision making are in place, we can begin to apply them. One of the most important decisions facing a financial manager is the choice of which investments the corporation should make. In Chapter 7, we compare the net present value rule to other investment rules that firms sometimes use and explain why the net present value rule is superior. The process of allocating the firm's capital for investment is known as capital budgeting, and in Chapter 8, we outline the discounted cash flow method for making such decisions. Both chapters provide a practical demonstration of the power of the tools that were introduced in Part 2.

Many firms raise the capital they need to make investments by issuing stock to investors. How do investors determine the price they are willing to pay for this stock? And how do managers' investment decisions affect this value? In Chapter 9, Valuing Stocks, we show how the Law of One Price leads to several alternative methods for valuing a firm's equity by considering its future dividends, its free cash flows, or how it compares to similar, publicly traded companies.

CHAPTER

7

Investment Decision Rules

NOTATION

r	discount rate
NPV	net present value
IRR	internal rate of return
PV	present value
NPER	annuity spreadsheet notation for the number of periods or dates of the last cash flow
RATE	annuity spreadsheet notation for interest rate
PMT	annuity spreadsheet notation for cash flow

IN 2000, TOSHIBA AND SONY BEGAN EXPERIMENTING WITH new DVD technology, leading to Sony's development of Blu-ray High Definition DVD players and Toshiba's introduction of the HD-DVD player. So began an eight-year format war that ended in February 2008 when Toshiba decided to stop producing HD-DVD players and abandon the format. How did Toshiba and Sony managers arrive at the decision to invest in new DVD formats? And how did Toshiba managers conclude that the best decision was to stop producing HD-DVD? In both cases, the managers made decisions they believed would maximize the value of their firms.

As we will see in this chapter, the NPV investment rule is the decision rule that managers should use to maximize firm value. Nevertheless, some firms use other techniques to evaluate investments and decide which projects to pursue. In this chapter, we explain several commonly used techniques—namely, the *payback rule* and the *internal rate of return rule*. We then compare decisions based on these rules to decisions based on the NPV rule and illustrate the circumstances in which the alternative rules are likely to lead to bad investment decisions. After establishing these rules in the context of a single, stand-alone project, we broaden our perspective to include deciding among alternative investment opportunities. We conclude with a look at project selection when the firm faces capital or other resource constraints.

7.1 NPV and Stand-Alone Projects

We begin our discussion of investment decision rules by considering a take-it-or-leave-it decision involving a single, stand-alone project. By undertaking this project, the firm does not constrain its ability to take other projects. To analyze such a decision, recall the NPV rule:

NPV Investment Rule: *When making an investment decision, take the alternative with the highest NPV. Choosing this alternative is equivalent to receiving its NPV in cash today.*

In the case of a stand-alone project, we must choose between accepting or rejecting the project. The NPV rule then says we should compare the project's NPV to zero (the NPV of doing nothing) and accept the project if its NPV is positive.

Applying the NPV Rule

Researchers at Fredrick's Feed and Farm have made a breakthrough. They believe that they can produce a new, environmentally friendly fertilizer at a substantial cost savings over the company's existing line of fertilizer. The fertilizer will require a new plant that can be built immediately at a cost of $250 million. Financial managers estimate that the benefits of the new fertilizer will be $35 million per year, starting at the end of the first year and lasting forever, as shown by the following timeline:

0	1	2	3	...
−$250	$35	$35	$35	

As we explained in Chapter 4, the NPV of this perpetual cash flow stream, given a discount rate r, is

$$NPV = -250 + \frac{35}{r} \tag{7.1}$$

The financial managers responsible for this project estimate a cost of capital of 10% per year. Using this cost of capital in Eq. 7.1, the NPV is $100 million, which is positive. The NPV investment rule indicates that by making the investment, the value of the firm will increase by $100 million today, so Fredrick's should undertake this project.

The NPV Profile and IRR

The NPV of the project depends on the appropriate cost of capital. Often, there may be some uncertainty regarding the project's cost of capital. In that case, it is helpful to compute an **NPV profile**: a graph of the project's NPV over a range of discount rates. Figure 7.1 plots the NPV of the fertilizer project as a function of the discount rate, r.

Notice that the NPV is positive only for discount rates that are less than 14%. When $r = 14\%$, the NPV is zero. Recall from Chapter 4 that the internal rate of return (IRR) of an investment is the discount rate that sets the NPV of the project's cash flows equal to zero. Thus, the fertilizer project has an IRR of 14%.

The IRR of a project provides useful information regarding the sensitivity of the project's NPV to errors in the estimate of its cost of capital. For the fertilizer project, if the cost of capital estimate is more than the 14% IRR, the NPV will be negative, as shown in

FIGURE 7.1

NPV of Fredrick's Fertilizer Project

The graph shows the NPV as a function of the discount rate. The NPV is positive only for discount rates that are less than 14%, the internal rate of return (IRR). Given the cost of capital of 10%, the project has a positive NPV of $100 million.

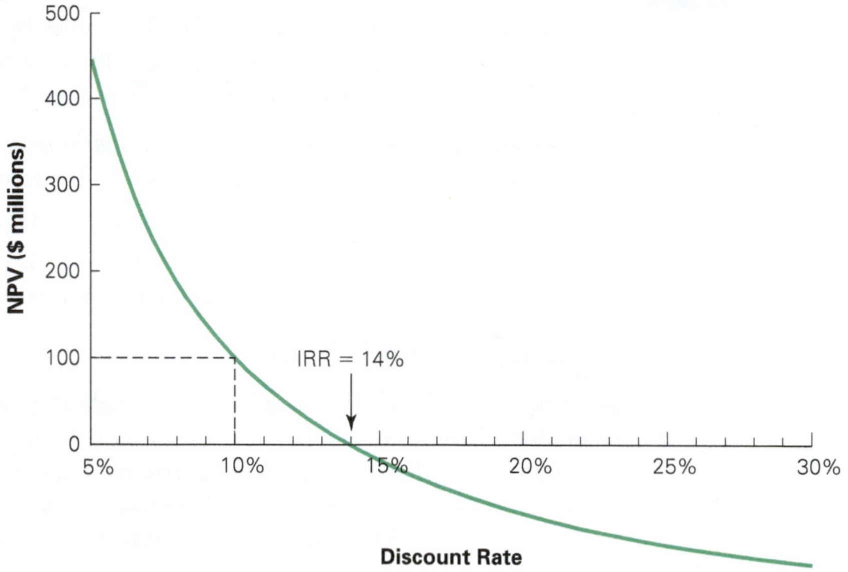

Figure 7.1. Therefore, the decision to accept the project is correct as long as our estimate of 10% is within 4% of the true cost of capital. In general, *the difference between the cost of capital and the IRR is the maximum estimation error in the cost of capital that can exist without altering the original decision.*

Alternative Rules Versus the NPV Rule

Although the NPV rule is the most accurate and reliable decision rule, in practice a wide variety of tools are applied, often in tandem with the NPV rule. In a 2001 study, 75% of the firms John Graham and Campbell Harvey[1] surveyed used the NPV rule for making investment decisions. This result is substantially different from that found in a similar study in 1977 by L. J. Gitman and J. R. Forrester,[2] who found that only 10% of firms used the NPV rule. MBA students in recent years must have been listening to their finance professors! Even so, Graham and Harvey's study indicates that one-fourth of U.S. corporations do not use the NPV rule. Exactly why other capital budgeting techniques are used in practice is not always clear. However, because you may encounter these techniques in the business world, you should know what they are, how they are used, and how they compare to NPV.

As we evaluate alternative rules for project selection in subsequent sections, keep in mind that sometimes other investment rules may give the same answer as the NPV rule, but at other times they may disagree. When the rules conflict, following the alternative rule means that we are either taking a negative NPV investment or turning down a positive NPV investment. In these cases, the alternative rules lead to bad decisions that reduce wealth.

[1] "The Theory and Practice of Corporate Finance: Evidence from the Field," *Journal of Financial Economics* 60 (2001): 187–243.

[2] "A Survey of Capital Budgeting Techniques Used by Major U.S. Firms," *Financial Management* 6 (1977): 66–71.

CONCEPT CHECK

1. Explain the NPV rule for stand-alone projects.
2. What does the difference between the cost of capital and the IRR indicate?

INTERVIEW WITH DICK GRANNIS

Dick Grannis is Senior Vice President and Treasurer of QUALCOMM Incorporated, a world leader in digital wireless communications technology and semiconductors, headquartered in San Diego. He joined the company in 1991 and oversees the company's $10 billion cash investment portfolio. He works primarily on investment banking, capital structure, and international finance.

QUESTION: *QUALCOMM has a wide variety of products in different business lines. How does your capital budgeting process for new products work?*

ANSWER: QUALCOMM evaluates new projects (such as new products, equipment, technologies, research and development, acquisitions, and strategic investments) by using traditional financial measurements including discounted cash flow/NPV models, IRR levels, peak funding requirements, the time needed to reach cumulative positive cash flows, and the short-term impact of the investment on our reported net earnings. For strategic investments, we consider the possible value of financial, competitive, technology and/or market value enhancements to our core businesses—even if those benefits cannot be quantified. Overall, we make capital budgeting decisions based on a combination of objective analyses and our own business judgment.

We do not engage in capital budgeting and analysis if the project represents an immediate and necessary requirement for our business operations. One example is new software or production equipment to start a project that has already received approval.

We are also mindful of the opportunity costs of allocating our internal engineering resources on one project vs. another project. We view this as a constantly challenging but worthwhile exercise, because we have many attractive opportunities but limited resources to pursue them.

QUESTION: *How often does QUALCOMM evaluate its hurdle rates and what factors does it consider in setting them? How do you allocate capital across areas and regions and assess the risk of non-U.S. investments?*

ANSWER: QUALCOMM encourages its financial planners to utilize hurdle (or discount) rates that vary according to the risk of the particular project. We expect a rate of return commensurate with the project's risk. Our finance staff considers a wide range of discount rates and chooses one that fits the project's expected risk profile and time horizon. The range can be from 6% to 8% for relatively safe investments in the domestic market to 50% or more for equity investments in foreign markets that may be illiquid and difficult to predict. We re-evaluate our hurdle rates at least every year.

We analyze key factors including: (1) market adoption risk (whether or not customers will buy the new product or service at the price and volume we expect), (2) technology development risk (whether or not we can develop and patent the new product or service as expected), (3) execution risk (whether we can launch the new product or service cost effectively and on time), and (4) dedicated asset risk (the amount of resources that must be consumed to complete the work).

QUESTION: *How are projects categorized and how are the hurdle rates for new projects determined? What would happen if QUALCOMM simply evaluated all new projects against the same hurdle rate?*

ANSWER: We primarily categorize projects by risk level, but we also categorize projects by the expected time horizon. We consider short-term and long-term projects to balance our needs and achieve our objectives. For example, immediate projects and opportunities may demand a great amount of attention, but we also stay focused on long-term projects because they often create greater long-term value for stockholders.

If we were to evaluate all new projects against the same hurdle rate, then our business planners would, by default, consistently choose to invest in the highest risk projects because those projects would appear to have the greatest expected returns in DCF models or IRR analyses. That approach would probably not work well for very long.

7.2 The Internal Rate of Return Rule

One interpretation of the internal rate of return is the average return earned by taking on the investment opportunity. The **internal rate of return (IRR) investment rule** is based on this idea: If the average return on the investment opportunity (i.e., the IRR) is greater than the return on other alternatives in the market with equivalent risk and maturity (i.e., the project's cost of capital), you should undertake the investment opportunity. We state the rule formally as follows:

IRR Investment Rule: *Take any investment opportunity where the IRR exceeds the opportunity cost of capital. Turn down any opportunity whose IRR is less than the opportunity cost of capital.*

Applying the IRR Rule

Like the NPV rule, the internal rate of return investment rule is applied to single, stand-alone projects within the firm. The IRR investment rule will give the correct answer (that is, the same answer as the NPV rule) in many—but not all—situations. For instance, it gives the correct answer for Fredrick's fertilizer opportunity. Looking again at Figure 7.1, whenever the cost of capital is below the IRR (14%), the project has a positive NPV and you should undertake the investment.

In the Fredrick fertilizer example, the NPV rule and the IRR rule coincide, so the IRR rule gives the correct answer. This need not always be the case, however. In fact, *the IRR rule is only guaranteed to work for a stand-alone project if all of the project's negative cash flows precede its positive cash flows.* If this is not the case, the IRR rule can lead to incorrect decisions. Let's examine several situations in which the IRR fails.

Pitfall #1: Delayed Investments

John Star, the founder of SuperTech, the most successful company in the last 20 years, has just retired as CEO. A major publisher has offered to pay Star \$1 million upfront if he agrees to write a book about his experiences. He estimates that it will take him three years to write the book. The time that he spends writing will cause him to forgo alternative sources of income amounting to \$500,000 per year. Considering the risk of his alternative income sources and available investment opportunities, Star estimates his opportunity cost of capital to be 10%. The timeline of Star's investment opportunity is

0	1	2	3
\$1,000,000	−\$500,000	−\$500,000	−\$500,000

The NPV of Star's investment opportunity is

$$NPV = 1{,}000{,}000 - \frac{500{,}000}{1 + r} - \frac{500{,}000}{(1 + r)^2} - \frac{500{,}000}{(1 + r)^3}$$

By setting the NPV equal to zero and solving for r, we find the IRR. Using the annuity spreadsheet:

	NPER	RATE	PV	PMT	FV	Excel Formula
Given	3		1,000,000	−500,000	0	
Solve for I		23.38%				=RATE(3,−500000,1000000, 0)

The 23.38% IRR is larger than the 10% opportunity cost of capital. According to the IRR rule, Star should sign the deal. But what does the NPV rule say?

$$NPV = 1{,}000{,}000 - \frac{500{,}000}{1.1} - \frac{500{,}000}{1.1^2} - \frac{500{,}000}{1.1^3} = -\$243{,}426$$

At a 10% discount rate, the NPV is negative, so signing the deal would reduce Star's wealth. He should not sign the book deal.

To understand why the IRR rule fails, Figure 7.2 shows the NPV profile of the book deal. No matter what the cost of capital is, the IRR rule and the NPV rule will give exactly opposite recommendations. That is, the NPV is positive only when the opportunity cost of capital is *above* 23.38% (the IRR). In fact, Star should accept the investment only when the opportunity cost of capital is greater than the IRR, the opposite of what the IRR rule recommends.

Figure 7.2 also illustrates the problem with using the IRR rule in this case. For most investment opportunities, expenses occur initially and cash is received later. In this case, Star gets cash *upfront* and incurs the costs of producing the book *later*. It is as if Star borrowed money—receiving cash today in exchange for a future liability—and when you borrow money you prefer as *low* a rate as possible. In this case the IRR is best interpreted as the rate Star is paying rather than earning, and so Star's optimal rule is to borrow money so long as this rate is *less* than his cost of capital.

Even though the IRR rule fails to give the correct answer in this case, the IRR itself still provides useful information *in conjunction* with the NPV rule. As mentioned earlier, IRR indicates how sensitive the investment decision is to uncertainty in the cost of capital estimate. In this case, the difference between the cost of capital and the IRR is large—13.38%. Star would have to have underestimated the cost of capital by 13.38% to make the NPV positive.

Pitfall #2: Multiple IRRs

Star has informed the publisher that it needs to sweeten the deal before he will accept it. In response, the publisher offers to give him a royalty payment when the book is published in exchange for taking a smaller upfront payment. Specifically, Star will receive $1 million when the book is published and sold four years from now, together with an upfront payment of $550,000. Should he accept or reject the new offer?

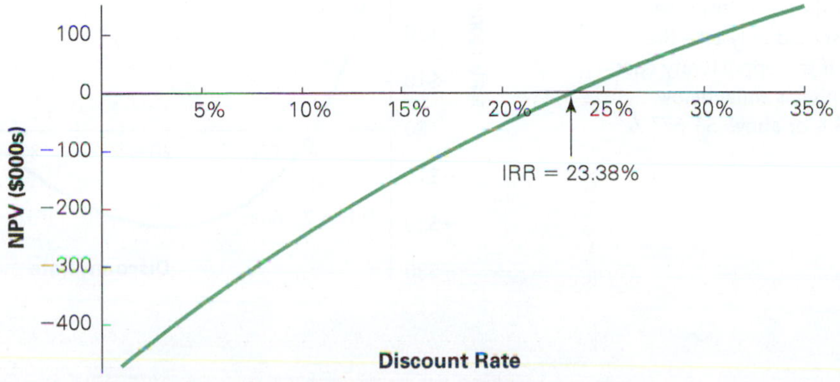

FIGURE 7.2

NPV of Star's $1 Million Book Deal

When the benefits of an investment occur before the costs, the NPV is an *increasing* function of the discount rate, and the IRR rule fails.

We begin with the new timeline:

0	1	2	3	4
\$550,000	−\$500,000	−\$500,000	−\$500,000	\$1,000,000

The NPV of Star's new offer is

$$NPV = 550{,}000 - \frac{500{,}000}{1 + r} - \frac{500{,}000}{(1 + r)^2} - \frac{500{,}000}{(1 + r)^3} + \frac{1{,}000{,}000}{(1 + r)^4}$$

By setting the NPV equal to zero and solving for r, we find the IRR. In this case, there are *two* IRRs—that is, there are two values of r that set the NPV equal to zero. You can verify this fact by substituting IRRs of 7.164% and 33.673% into the equation. Because there is more than one IRR, we cannot apply the IRR rule.

For guidance, let's turn to the NPV rule. Figure 7.3 shows the NPV profile of the new offer. If the cost of capital is *either* below 7.164% or above 33.673%, Star should undertake the opportunity. Otherwise, he should turn it down. Notice that even though the IRR rule fails in this case, the two IRRs are still useful as bounds on the cost of capital. If the cost of capital estimate is wrong, and it is actually smaller than 7.164% or larger than 33.673%, the decision not to pursue the project will change. Even if Star is uncertain whether his actual cost of capital is 10%, as long as he believes it is within these bounds, he can have a high degree of confidence in his decision to reject the deal.

There is no easy fix for the IRR rule when there are multiple IRRs. Although the NPV is negative between the IRRs in this example, the reverse is also possible. Furthermore, there are situations in which more than two IRRs exist.[3] When multiple IRRs exist, our only choice is to rely on the NPV rule.

FIGURE 7.3

NPV of Star's Book Deal with Royalties

In this case, there is more than one IRR, invalidating the IRR rule. In this case, Star should only take the offer if the opportunity cost of capital is *either* below 7.164% or above 33.673%.

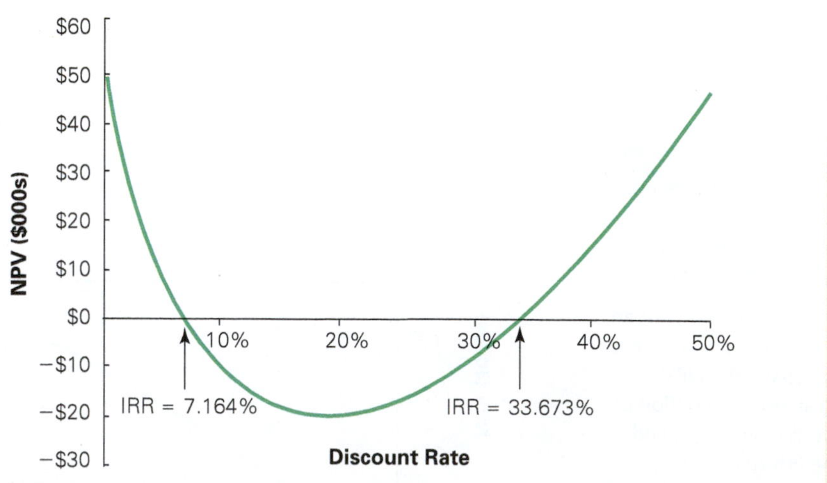

[3]In general, there can be as many IRRs as the number of times the project's cash flows change sign over time.

COMMON MISTAKE **IRR Versus the IRR Rule**

The examples in this section illustrate the potential shortcomings of the IRR rule when choosing to accept or reject a stand-alone project. As we said at the outset, we can only avoid these problems if all of the negative cash flows of the project precede the positive cash flows. Otherwise, we cannot rely on the IRR rule. However, even in that case, the IRR itself remains a very useful tool. The IRR measures the average return over the life of an investment and indicates the sensitivity of the NPV to estimation error in the cost of capital. Thus, knowing the IRR can be very useful, but relying on it alone to make investment decisions can be hazardous.

Pitfall #3: Nonexistent IRR

After protracted negotiations, Star is able to get the publisher to increase his initial payment to $750,000, in addition to his $1 million royalty payment when the book is published in four years. With these cash flows, no IRR exists; that is, there is no discount rate that makes the NPV equal to zero. Thus, the IRR rule provides no guidance whatsoever. To evaluate this final offer, let's again look at the NPV profile, shown in Figure 7.4. There we can see that the NPV is positive for any discount rate, and so the offer is attractive. But don't be fooled into thinking the NPV is always positive when the IRR does not exist—it can just as well be negative.

FIGURE 7.4

NPV of Star's Final Offer

In this case, the NPV is positive for every discount rate, and so there is no IRR. Thus, we cannot use the IRR rule.

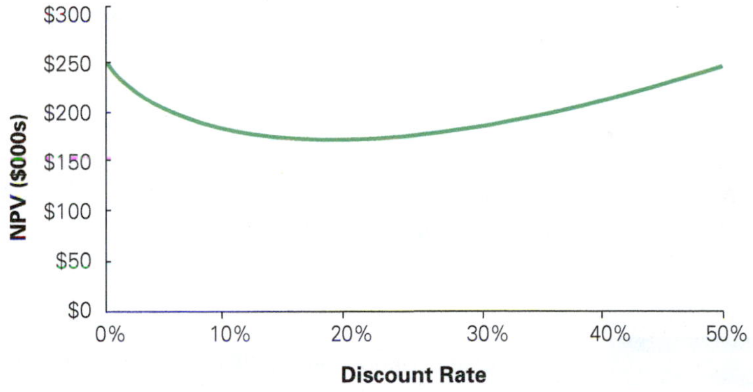

EXAMPLE 7.1 **Problems with the IRR Rule**

Problem

Consider projects with the following cash flows:

Project	0	1	2
A	−375	−300	900
B	−22,222	50,000	−28,000
C	400	400	−1,056
D	−4,300	10,000	−6,000

Which of these projects have an IRR close to 20%? For which of these projects is the IRR rule valid?

Solution

We plot the NPV profile for each project below. From the NPV profiles, we can see that projects A, B, and C each have an IRR of approximately 20%, while project D has no IRR. Note also that project B has another IRR of 5%.

The IRR rule is valid only if the project has a positive NPV for every discount rate below the IRR. Thus, the IRR rule is only valid for project A. This project is the only one for which all the negative cash flows precede the positive ones.

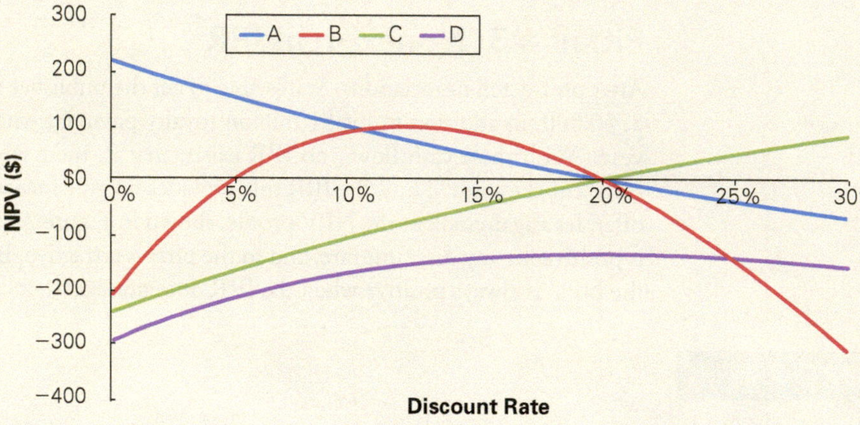

As the previous examples demonstrate, if a project has positive cash flows that precede negative ones, it is important to look at the project's NPV profile in order to interpret the IRR. See the appendix to this chapter for a simple approach to calculating the NPV profile in Excel.

CONCEPT CHECK

1. Under what conditions do the IRR rule and the NPV rule coincide for a stand-alone project?
2. If the IRR rule and the NPV rule lead to different decisions for a stand-alone project, which should you follow? Why?

7.3 The Payback Rule

In this section, we examine the *payback rule as an* alternative decision rule for single, stand-alone projects within the firm. The **payback investment rule** states that you should only accept a project if its cash flows pay back its initial investment within a prespecified period. To apply the payback rule, you first calculate the amount of time it takes to pay back the initial investment, called the **payback period**. Then you accept the project if the payback period is less than a prespecified length of time—usually a few years. Otherwise, you reject the project. For example, a firm might adopt any project with a payback period of less than two years.

Applying the Payback Rule

To illustrate the payback rule, we return to the Fredrick's Feed and Farm example.

EXAMPLE 7.2 **The Payback Rule**

Problem

Assume Fredrick's requires all projects to have a payback period of five years or less. Would the firm undertake the fertilizer project under this rule?

Solution

Recall that the project requires an initial investment of \$250 million, and will generate \$35 million per year. The sum of the cash flows from year 1 to year 5 is $\$35 \times 5 = \$175$ million, which will not cover the initial investment of \$250 million. In fact, it will not be until year 8 that the initial investment will be paid back ($\$35 \times 8 = \$280$ million). Because the payback period for this project exceeds five years, Fredrick's will reject the project.

Relying on the payback rule analysis in Example 7.2, Fredrick's will reject the project. However, as we saw earlier, with a cost of capital of 10%, the NPV is \$100 million. Following the payback rule would be a mistake because Fredrick's would pass up a project worth \$100 million.

Payback Rule Pitfalls in Practice

The payback rule is not as reliable as the NPV rule because it (1) ignores the project's cost of capital and the time value of money, (2) ignores cash flows after the payback period, and (3) relies on an ad hoc decision criterion (what is the right number of years to require for the payback period?).[4] Despite these failings, about 57% of the firms Graham and Harvey surveyed reported using the payback rule as part of the decision-making process.

Why do some companies consider the payback rule? The answer probably relates to its simplicity. This rule is typically used for small investment decisions—for example, whether to purchase a new copy machine or to service the old one. In such cases, the cost of making an incorrect decision might not be large enough to justify the time required to calculate the NPV. The payback rule also provides budgeting information regarding the length of time capital will be committed to a project. Some firms are unwilling to commit capital to long-term investments without greater scrutiny. Also, if the required payback period is short (one or two years), then most projects that satisfy the payback rule will have a positive NPV. So firms might save effort by first applying the payback rule, and only if it fails take the time to compute NPV.

CONCEPT CHECK

1. Can the payback rule reject projects that have positive NPV? Can it accept projects that have negative NPV?
2. If the payback rule does not give the same answer as the NPV rule, which rule should you follow? Why?

[4] Some companies address the first failing by computing the payback period using discounted cash flows (called discounted payback).

Why Do Rules Other Than the NPV Rule Persist?

Professors Graham and Harvey found that a sizable minority of firms (25%) in their study do not use the NPV rule at all. In addition, more than half of firms surveyed used the payback rule. Furthermore, it appears that most firms use *both* the NPV rule and the IRR rule. Why do firms use rules other than NPV if they can lead to erroneous decisions?

One possible explanation for this phenomenon is that Graham and Harvey's survey results might be misleading. Managers may use the payback rule for budgeting purposes or as a shortcut to get a quick sense of the project before calculating NPV. Similarly, CFOs who were using the IRR as a sensitivity measure in conjunction with the NPV rule might have checked both the IRR box and the NPV box on the survey. Nevertheless, a significant minority of managers surveyed replied that they used only the IRR rule, so this explanation cannot be the whole story.

Managers may use the IRR rule exclusively because you do not need to know the opportunity cost of capital to calculate the IRR. But this benefit is superficial: While you may not need to know the cost of capital to *calculate* the IRR, you certainly need to know the cost of capital when you *apply* the IRR rule. Consequently, the opportunity cost of capital is as important to the IRR rule as it is to the NPV rule.

Nonetheless, part of the appeal of the IRR rule is that the IRR seems to sum up the attractiveness of an investment without requiring an assumption about the cost of capital. However, a more useful summary is the project's NPV profile, showing the NPV as a function of the discount rate. The NPV profile also does not require knowing the cost of capital, but it has the distinct advantage of being much more informative and reliable.

7.4 Choosing Between Projects

Thus far, we have considered only decisions where the choice is either to accept or to reject a single, stand-alone project. Sometimes, however, a firm must choose just one project from among several possible projects, that is, the choices are mutually exclusive. For example, a manager may be evaluating alternative package designs for a new product. When choosing any one project excludes us from taking the others, we are facing mutually exclusive investments.

NPV Rule and Mutually Exclusive Investments

When projects are mutually exclusive, we need to determine which projects have a positive NPV and then rank the projects to identify the best one. In this situation, the NPV rule provides a straightforward answer: *Pick the project with the highest NPV.* Because the NPV expresses the value of the project in terms of cash today, picking the project with the highest NPV leads to the greatest increase in wealth.

EXAMPLE 7.3 NPV and Mutually Exclusive Projects

Problem

A small commercial property is for sale near your university. Given its location, you believe a student-oriented business would be very successful there. You have researched several possibilities and come up with the following cash flow estimates (including the cost of purchasing the property). Which investment should you choose?

Project	Initial Investment	First-Year Cash Flow	Growth Rate	Cost of Capital
Book Store	$300,000	$63,000	3.0%	8%
Coffee Shop	$400,000	$80,000	3.0%	8%
Music Store	$400,000	$104,000	0.0%	8%
Electronics Store	$400,000	$100,000	3.0%	11%

Solution

Assuming each business lasts indefinitely, we can compute the present value of the cash flows from each as a constant growth perpetuity. The NPV of each project is

$$NPV(\text{Book Store}) = -300{,}000 + \frac{63{,}000}{8\% - 3\%} = \$960{,}000$$

$$NPV(\text{Coffee Shop}) = -400{,}000 + \frac{80{,}000}{8\% - 3\%} = \$1{,}200{,}000$$

$$NPV(\text{Music Store}) = -400{,}000 + \frac{104{,}000}{8\%} = \$900{,}000$$

$$NPV(\text{Electronics Store}) = -400{,}000 + \frac{100{,}000}{11\% - 3\%} = \$850{,}000$$

Thus, all of the alternatives have a positive NPV. But, because we can only choose one, the coffee shop is the best alternative.

IRR Rule and Mutually Exclusive Investments

Because the IRR is a measure of the expected return of investing in the project, you might be tempted to extend the IRR investment rule to the case of mutually exclusive projects by picking the project with the highest IRR. Unfortunately, picking one project over another simply because it has a larger IRR can lead to mistakes. In particular, *when projects differ in their scale of investment, the timing of their cash flows, or their riskiness, then their IRRs cannot be meaningfully compared.*

Differences in Scale. Would you prefer a 500% return on \$1, or a 20% return on \$1 million? While a 500% return certainly sounds impressive, at the end of the day you will only make \$5. The latter return sounds much more mundane, but you will make \$200,000. This comparison illustrates an important shortcoming of IRR: Because it is a return, you cannot tell how much value will actually be created without knowing the scale of the investment.

If a project has a positive NPV, then if we can double its size, its NPV will double: By the Law of One Price, doubling the cash flows of an investment opportunity must make it worth twice as much. However, the IRR rule does not have this property—it is unaffected by the scale of the investment opportunity because the IRR measures the average return of the investment. Hence, we cannot use the IRR rule to compare projects of different scales.

As an illustration of this situation, consider the investment in the book store versus the coffee shop in Example 7.3. We can compute the IRR of each as follows:

$$\text{Book Store:} \quad -300{,}000 + \frac{63{,}000}{IRR - 3\%} = 0 \Rightarrow IRR = 24\%$$

$$\text{Coffee Shop:} \quad -400{,}000 + \frac{80{,}000}{IRR - 3\%} = 0 \Rightarrow IRR = 23\%$$

Both projects have IRRs that exceed their cost of capital of 8%. But although the coffee shop has a lower IRR, because it is on a larger scale of investment (\$400,000 versus \$300,000), it generates a higher NPV (\$1.2 million versus \$960,000) and thus is more valuable.

Differences in Timing. Even when projects have the same scale, the IRR may lead you to rank them incorrectly due to differences in the timing of the cash flows. The IRR is expressed as a return, but the dollar value of earning a given return—and therefore its NPV—depends on how long the return is earned. Earning a very high annual return is much more valuable if you earn it for several years than if you earn it for only a few days.

As an example, consider the following short-term and long-term projects:

Year	0	1	2	3	4	5
Short-Term Project	-100	150				
Long-Term Project	-100					$100 \times 1.50^5 = 759.375$

Both projects have an IRR of 50%, but one lasts for one year, while the other has a five-year horizon. If the cost of capital for both projects is 10%, the short-term project has an NPV of $-100 + 150/1.10 = \$36.36$, whereas the long-term project has an NPV of $-100 + 759.375/1.10^5 = \$371.51$. Notice that despite having the same IRR, the long-term project is more than 10 times as valuable as the short-term project.

Even when projects have the same horizon, the pattern of cash flows over time will often differ. Consider again the coffee shop and music store investment alternatives in Example 7.3. Both of these investments have the same initial scale, and the same horizon (infinite). The IRR of the music store investment is

$$\text{Music Store:} \quad -400{,}000 + \frac{104{,}000}{IRR} = 0 \Rightarrow IRR = 26\%$$

But although the music store has a higher IRR than the coffee shop (26% versus 23%), it has a lower NPV (\$900,000 versus \$1.2 million). The reason the coffee shop has a higher NPV despite having a lower IRR is its higher growth rate. The coffee shop has lower initial cash flows but higher long-run cash flows than the music store. The fact that its cash flows are relatively delayed makes the coffee shop effectively a longer-term investment.

Differences in Risk. To know whether the IRR of a project is attractive, we must compare it to the project's cost of capital, which is determined by the project's risk. Thus, an IRR that is attractive for a safe project need not be attractive for a risky project. As a simple example, while you might be quite pleased to earn a 10% return on a risk-free investment opportunity, you might be much less satisfied to earn a 10% expected return on an investment in a risky start-up company. Ranking projects by their IRRs ignores risk differences.

Looking again at Example 7.3, consider the investment in the electronics store. The IRR of the electronics store is

$$\text{Electronics Store:} \quad -400{,}000 + \frac{100{,}000}{IRR - 3\%} = 0 \Rightarrow IRR = 28\%$$

This IRR is higher than those of all the other investment opportunities. Yet the electronics store has the lowest NPV. In this case, the investment in the electronics store is riskier, as evidenced by its higher cost of capital. Despite having a higher IRR, it is not sufficiently profitable to be as attractive as the safer alternatives.

The Incremental IRR

When choosing between two projects, an alternative to comparing their IRRs is to compute the **incremental IRR**, which is the IRR of the incremental cash flows that would result from replacing one project with the other. The incremental IRR tells us the discount rate

When Can Returns Be Compared?

In this chapter, we have highlighted the many pitfalls that arise when attempting to compare the IRRs of different projects. But there are many situations in which it is quite reasonable to compare returns. For example, if we were thinking of saving money in a savings account for the next year, we would likely compare the effective annual rates associated with different accounts and choose the highest option.

When is it reasonable to compare returns in this way? Remember, *we can only compare returns if the investments (1) have the same scale, (2) have the same timing, and (3) have the same risk.* While one or more of these conditions are typically violated when we compare two investment projects, they are much more likely to be met when one of the investments is an investment in publicly traded securities or with a bank. When we invest with a bank or in traded securities, we can usually choose the scale of our investment, as well as our investment horizon, so that the opportunities match. In this case, as long as we are comparing opportunities with the same risk, comparing returns is meaningful. (Indeed, this condition was the basis for our definition of the cost of capital in Chapter 5.)

at which it becomes profitable to switch from one project to the other. Then, rather than compare the projects directly, we can evaluate the decision to switch from one to the other using the IRR rule, as in the following example.

EXAMPLE 7.4 Using the Incremental IRR to Compare Alternatives

Problem

Your firm is considering overhauling its production plant. The engineering team has come up with two proposals, one for a minor overhaul and one for a major overhaul. The two options have the following cash flows (in millions of dollars):

Proposal	0	1	2	3
Minor Overhaul	−10	6	6	6
Major Overhaul	−50	25	25	25

What is the IRR of each proposal? What is the incremental IRR? If the cost of capital for both of these projects is 12%, what should your firm do?

Solution

We can compute the IRR of each proposal using the annuity calculator. For the minor overhaul, the IRR is 36.3%:

	NPER	RATE	PV	PMT	FV	Excel Formula
Given	3		−10	6	0	
Solve for Rate		36.3%				=RATE(3,6,−10,0)

For the major overhaul, the IRR is 23.4%:

	NPER	RATE	PV	PMT	FV	Excel Formula
Given	3		−50	25	0	
Solve for Rate		23.4%				=RATE(3,25,−50,0)

Which project is best? Because the projects have different scales, we cannot compare their IRRs directly. To compute the incremental IRR of switching from the minor overhaul to the major overhaul, we first compute the incremental cash flows:

Proposal	0	1	2	3
Major Overhaul	−50	25	25	25
Less: Minor Overhaul	−(−10)	−6	−6	−6
Incremental Cash Flow	−40	19	19	19

These cash flows have an IRR of 20.0%:

	NPER	RATE	PV	PMT	FV	Excel Formula
Given	3		−40	19	0	
Solve for Rate		**20.0%**				=RATE(3,19,−40,0)

Because the incremental IRR exceeds the 12% cost of capital, switching to the major overhaul looks attractive (i.e., its larger scale is sufficient to make up for its lower IRR). We can check this result using Figure 7.5, which shows the NPV profiles for each project. At the 12% cost of capital, the NPV of the major overhaul does indeed exceed that of the minor overhaul, despite its lower IRR. Note also that the incremental IRR determines the crossover point of the NPV profiles, the discount rate for which the best project choice switches from the major overhaul to the minor one.

FIGURE 7.5

Comparison of Minor and Major Overhauls

Comparing the NPV profiles of the minor and major overhauls in Example 7.4, we can see that despite its lower IRR, the major overhaul has a higher NPV at the cost of capital of 12%. Note also that the incremental IRR of 20% determines the crossover point or discount rate at which the optimal decision changes.

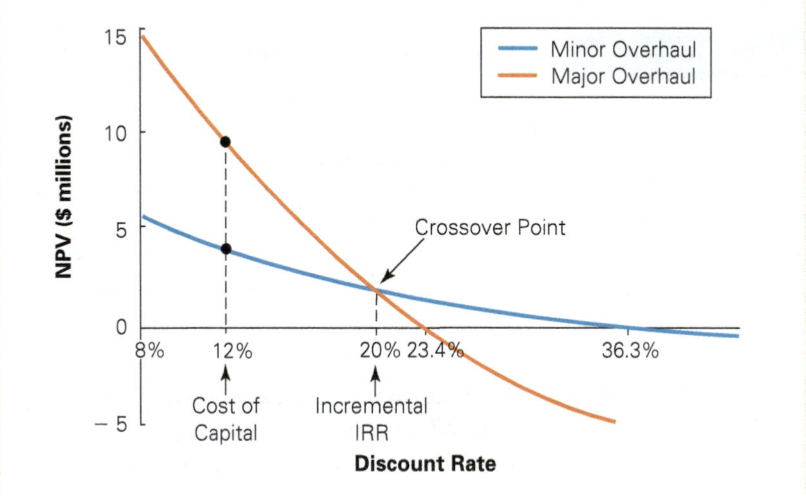

As we saw in Example 7.4, the incremental IRR identifies the discount rate at which the optimal decision changes. However, when using the incremental IRR to choose between projects, we encounter all of the same problems that arose with the IRR rule:

- Even if the negative cash flows precede the positive ones for the individual projects, it need not be true for the incremental cash flows. If not, the incremental IRR is difficult to interpret, and may not exist or may not be unique.
- The incremental IRR can indicate whether it is profitable to switch from one project to another, but it does not indicate whether either project has a positive NPV on its own.
- When the individual projects have different costs of capital, it is not obvious what cost of capital the incremental IRR should be compared to. In this case only the NPV rule, which allows each project to be discounted at its own cost of capital, will give a reliable answer.

COMMON MISTAKE **IRR and Project Financing**

Because the IRR is not itself a measure of value, it is easy to manipulate by restructuring the project's cash flows. In particular, it is easy to increase the IRR of a project by financing a portion of the initial investment. A common mistake in practice is to regard this higher IRR as an indication that the financing is attractive. For example, consider an investment in new equipment that will have the following cash flows:

0	1
−100	130

This investment has an IRR of 30%. Now suppose that seller of the equipment offers to lend us \$80, so that we only need to pay \$20 initially. In exchange, we must pay \$100 in one year. By financing the project in this way, the cash flows become

0	1
−20	30

The project's IRR is now $(30/20) - 1 = 50\%$. Does this higher IRR mean that the project is now more attractive? In other words, is the financing a good deal?

The answer is no. Remember, we cannot compare IRRs, so a 50% IRR is not necessarily better than a 30% IRR. In this case, the project with financing is a much smaller scale investment than without financing. In addition, borrowing money is likely to increase the risk to shareholders from undertaking the project. (We'll see explicitly the effect of leverage on risk and shareholders' required return in Parts 4 and 5 of the book.)

In this particular example, note that we borrowed \$80 initially in exchange for paying \$100 in one year. The IRR of this loan is $(100/80) - 1 = 25\%$ (this is also the incremental IRR of rejecting the financing). This rate is probably much higher than our firm's borrowing cost if it borrowed through other means. If so, including this financing with the project would be a mistake, despite the higher IRR.

In summary, although the incremental IRR provides useful information by telling us the discount rate at which our optimal project choice would change, using it as a decision rule is difficult and error prone. It is much simpler to use the NPV rule.

CONCEPT CHECK

1. For mutually exclusive projects, explain why picking one project over another because it has a larger IRR can lead to mistakes.
2. What is the incremental IRR and what are its shortcomings as a decision rule?

7.5 Project Selection with Resource Constraints

In principle, the firm should take on all positive-NPV investments it can identify. In practice, there are often limitations on the number of projects the firm can undertake. For example, when projects are mutually exclusive, the firm can only take on one of the projects even if many of them are attractive. Often this limitation is due to resource constraints—for example, there is only one property available in which to open either a coffee shop, or book store, and so on. Thus far, we have assumed that the different projects the firm is considering have the same resource requirements (in Example 7.3, each project would use 100% of the property). In this section, we develop an approach for situations where the choices have differing resource needs.

Evaluating Projects with Different Resource Requirements

In some situations, different projects will demand different amounts of a particular scarce resource. For example, different products may consume different proportions of a firm's production capacity, or might demand different amounts of managerial time and attention.

If there is a fixed supply of the resource so that you cannot undertake all possible opportunities, then the firm must choose the best *set* of investments it can make given the resources it has available.

Often, individual managers work within a budget constraint that limits the amount of capital they may invest in a given period. In this case, the manager's goal is to choose the projects that maximize the total NPV while staying within her budget. Suppose you are considering the three projects shown in Table 7.1. Absent any budget constraint, you would invest in all of these positive-NPV projects. Suppose, however, that you have a budget of at most $100 million to invest. While Project I has the highest NPV, it uses up the entire budget. Projects II and III can both be undertaken (together they also take up the entire budget), and their combined NPV exceeds the NPV of Project I. Thus, with a budget of $100 million, the best choice is to take Projects II and III for a combined NPV of $130 million, compared to just $110 million for Project I alone.

Profitability Index

Note that in the last column of Table 7.1 we included the ratio of the project's NPV to its initial investment. This ratio tells us that for every dollar invested in Project I, we will generate $1.10 in value (over and above the dollar invested).[5] Both Projects II and III generate higher NPVs per dollar invested than Project I, which indicates that they will use the available budget more efficiently.

In this simple example, identifying the optimal combination of projects to undertake is straightforward. In actual situations replete with many projects and resources, finding the optimal combination can be difficult. Practitioners often use the **profitability index** to identify the optimal combination of projects to undertake in such situations:

Profitability Index

$$\text{Profitability Index} = \frac{\text{Value Created}}{\text{Resource Consumed}} = \frac{NPV}{\text{Resource Consumed}} \tag{7.2}$$

The profitability index measures the "bang for your buck"—that is, the value created in terms of NPV per unit of resource consumed. After computing the profitability index, we can rank projects based on it. Starting with the project with the highest index, we move down the ranking, taking all projects until the resource is consumed. In Table 7.1, the ratio we computed in the last column is the profitability index when investment dollars

TABLE 7.1 **Possible Projects for a $100 Million Budget**

Project	NPV ($ millions)	Initial Investment ($ millions)	Profitability Index NPV/Investment
I	110	100	1.1
II	70	50	1.4
III	60	50	1.2

[5]Practitioners sometimes add 1 to this ratio to include the dollar invested (i.e., Project I generates a total of $2.10 per dollar invested, generating $1.10 in new value). Leaving out the 1 and just considering the *net* present value allows the ratio to be applied to other resources besides cash budgets, as shown in Example 7.5.

are the scarce resource. Note how the "profitability index rule" would correctly select Projects II and III. We can also apply this rule when other resources are scarce, as shown in Example 7.5.

EXAMPLE 7.5 Profitability Index with a Human Resource Constraint

Problem

Your division at NetIt, a large networking company, has put together a project proposal to develop a new home networking router. The expected NPV of the project is $17.7 million, and the project will require 50 software engineers. NetIt has a total of 190 engineers available, and the router project must compete with the following other projects for these engineers:

Project	NPV ($ millions)	Engineering Headcount
Router	17.7	50
Project A	22.7	47
Project B	8.1	44
Project C	14.0	40
Project D	11.5	61
Project E	20.6	58
Project F	12.9	32
Total	107.5	332

How should NetIt prioritize these projects?

Solution

The goal is to maximize the total NPV we can create with 190 engineers (at most). We compute the profitability index for each project, using Engineering Headcount in the denominator, and then sort projects based on the index:

Project	NPV ($ millions)	Engineering Headcount (EHC)	Profitability Index (NPV per EHC)	Cumulative EHC Required
Project A	22.7	47	0.483	47
Project F	12.9	32	0.403	79
Project E	20.6	58	0.355	137
Router	17.7	50	0.354	187
Project C	14.0	40	0.350	
Project D	11.5	61	0.189	
Project B	8.1	44	0.184	

We now assign the resource to the projects in descending order according to the profitability index. The final column shows the cumulative use of the resource as each project is taken on until the resource is used up. To maximize NPV within the constraint of 190 engineers, NetIt should choose the first four projects on the list. There is no other combination of projects that will create more value without using more engineers than we have. Note, however, that the resource constraint forces NetIt to forgo three otherwise valuable projects (C, D, and B) with a total NPV of $33.6 million.

Note that in the above examples, the firm's resource constraints cause it to pass up positive-NPV projects. The highest profitability index available from these remaining projects provides useful information regarding the value of that resource to the firm. In Example 7.5, for example, Project C would generate $350,000 in NPV per engineer. If the firm could recruit and train new engineers at a cost of less than $350,000 per engineer, it would be worthwhile to do so in order to undertake Project C. Alternatively, if engineering headcount has been allocated to another division of the firm for projects with a profitability index of less than $350,000 per engineer, it would be worthwhile to reallocate that headcount to this division to undertake Project C.

Shortcomings of the Profitability Index

Although the profitability index is simple to compute and use, for it to be completely reliable, two conditions must be satisfied:

1. The set of projects taken following the profitability index ranking completely exhausts the available resource.
2. There is only a single relevant resource constraint.

To see why the first condition is needed, suppose in Example 7.5 that NetIt has an additional small project with an NPV of only $120,000 that requires three engineers. The profitability index in this case is $0.12/3 = 0.04$, so this project would appear at the bottom of the ranking. However, notice that three of the 190 employees are not being used after the first four projects are selected. As a result, it would make sense to take on this project even though it would be ranked last. This shortcoming can also affect highly ranked projects. For example, in Table 7.1, suppose Project III had an NPV of only $25 million, making it significantly worse than the other projects. Then the best choice would be Project I even though Project II has a higher profitability index.

In many cases, the firm may face multiple resource constraints. For instance, there may be a budget limit as well as a headcount constraint. If more than one resource constraint is binding, then there is no simple index that can be used to rank projects. Instead, linear and integer programming techniques have been developed specifically to tackle this kind of problem. Even if the set of alternatives is large, by using these techniques on a computer we can readily calculate the set of projects that will maximize the total NPV while satisfying multiple constraints (see Further Reading for references).

CONCEPT CHECK

1. Explain why ranking projects according to their NPV might not be optimal when you evaluate projects with different resource requirements.
2. How can the profitability index be used to identify attractive projects when there are resource constraints?

MyFinanceLab Here is what you should know after reading this chapter. MyFinanceLab will help you identify what you know and where to go when you need to practice.

7.1 NPV and Stand-Alone Projects

- If your objective is to maximize wealth, the NPV rule always gives the correct answer.
- The difference between the cost of capital and the IRR is the maximum amount of estimation error that can exist in the cost of capital estimate without altering the original decision.

7.2 The Internal Rate of Return Rule

- IRR investment rule: Take any investment opportunity whose IRR exceeds the opportunity cost of capital. Turn down any opportunity whose IRR is less than the opportunity cost of capital.
- Unless all of the negative cash flows of the project precede the positive ones, the IRR rule may give the wrong answer and should not be used. Furthermore, there may be multiple IRRs or the IRR may not exist.

7.3 The Payback Rule

- Payback investment rule: Calculate the amount of time it takes to pay back the initial investment (the payback period). If the payback period is less than a prespecified length of time, accept the project. Otherwise, turn it down.
- The payback rule is simple, and favors short-term investments. But it is often incorrect.

7.4 Choosing Between Projects

- When choosing among mutually exclusive investment opportunities, pick the opportunity with the highest NPV.
- We cannot use the IRR to compare investment opportunities unless the investments have the same scale, timing, and risk.
- Incremental IRR: When comparing two mutually exclusive opportunities, the incremental IRR is the IRR of the difference between the cash flows of the two alternatives. The incremental IRR indicates the discount rate at which the optimal project choice changes.

7.5 Project Selection with Resource Constraints

- When choosing among projects competing for the same resource, rank the projects by their profitability indices and pick the set of projects with the highest profitability indices that can still be undertaken given the limited resource.

$$\text{Profitability Index} = \frac{\text{Value Created}}{\text{Resource Consumed}} = \frac{NPV}{\text{Resource Consumed}} \tag{7.2}$$

- The profitability index is only completely reliable if the set of projects taken following the profitability index ranking completely exhausts the available resource and there is only a single relevant resource constraint.

Key Terms

Data Table *p. 238*
incremental IRR *p. 224*
internal rate of return (IRR) investment rule *p. 216*
NPV profile *p. 213*
payback investment rule *p. 220*
payback period *p. 220*
profitability index *p. 228*

Further Reading

Readers who would like to know more about what managers actually do should consult J. Graham and C. Harvey, "How CFOs Make Capital Budgeting and Capital Structure Decisions," *Journal of Applied Corporate Finance* 15(1) (2002): 8–23; S. H. Kim, T. Crick, and S. H. Kim, "Do Executives Practice What Academics Preach?" *Management Accounting* 68 (November 1986): 49–52; and P. Ryan and G. Ryan, "Capital Budgeting Practices of the Fortune 1000: How Have Things Changed?" *Journal of Business and Management* 8(4) (2002): 355–364.

For readers interested in how to select among projects competing for the same set of resources, the following references will be helpful: M. Vanhoucke, E. Demeulemeester, and W. Herroelen, "On Maximizing the Net Present Value of a Project Under Renewable Resource Constraints," *Management Science* 47(8) (2001): 1113–1121; and H. M. Weingartner, *Mathematical Programming and the Analysis of Capital Budgeting Problems* (Englewood Cliffs, NJ: Prentice-Hall, 1963).

Problems

All problems are available in MyFinanceLab. *An asterisk (*) indicates problems with a higher level of difficulty.*

NPV and Stand-Alone Projects

1. Your brother wants to borrow $10,000 from you. He has offered to pay you back $12,000 in a year. If the cost of capital of this investment opportunity is 10%, what is its NPV? Should you undertake the investment opportunity? Calculate the IRR and use it to determine the maximum deviation allowable in the cost of capital estimate to leave the decision unchanged.

2. You are considering investing in a start-up company. The founder asked you for $200,000 today and you expect to get $1,000,000 in nine years. Given the riskiness of the investment opportunity, your cost of capital is 20%. What is the NPV of the investment opportunity? Should you undertake the investment opportunity? Calculate the IRR and use it to determine the maximum deviation allowable in the cost of capital estimate to leave the decision unchanged.

3. You are considering opening a new plant. The plant will cost $100 million upfront. After that, it is expected to produce profits of $30 million at the end of every year. The cash flows are expected to last forever. Calculate the NPV of this investment opportunity if your cost of capital is 8%. Should you make the investment? Calculate the IRR and use it to determine the maximum deviation allowable in the cost of capital estimate to leave the decision unchanged.

4. Your firm is considering the launch of a new product, the XJ5. The upfront development cost is $10 million, and you expect to earn a cash flow of $3 million per year for the next five years. Plot the NPV profile for this project for discount rates ranging from 0% to 30%. For what range of discount rates is the project attractive?

5. Bill Clinton reportedly was paid $15 million to write his book *My Life*. Suppose the book took three years to write. In the time he spent writing, Clinton could have been paid to make speeches. Given his popularity, assume that he could earn $8 million per year (paid at the end of the year) speaking instead of writing. Assume his cost of capital is 10% per year.

a. What is the NPV of agreeing to write the book (ignoring any royalty payments)?

b. Assume that, once the book is finished, it is expected to generate royalties of $5 million in the first year (paid at the end of the year) and these royalties are expected to decrease at a rate of 30% per year in perpetuity. What is the NPV of the book with the royalty payments?

***6.** FastTrack Bikes, Inc. is thinking of developing a new composite road bike. Development will take six years and the cost is $200,000 per year. Once in production, the bike is expected to make $300,000 per year for 10 years. Assume the cost of capital is 10%.

a. Calculate the NPV of this investment opportunity, assuming all cash flows occur at the end of each year. Should the company make the investment?

b. By how much must the cost of capital estimate deviate to change the decision? (*Hint*: Use Excel to calculate the IRR.)

c. What is the NPV of the investment if the cost of capital is 14%?

7. OpenSeas, Inc. is evaluating the purchase of a new cruise ship. The ship would cost $500 million, and would operate for 20 years. OpenSeas expects annual cash flows from operating the ship to be $70 million (at the end of each year) and its cost of capital is 12%.

a. Prepare an NPV profile of the purchase.

b. Estimate the IRR (to the nearest 1%) from the graph.

c. Is the purchase attractive based on these estimates?

d. How far off could OpenSeas' cost of capital be (to the nearest 1%) before your purchase decision would change?

8. You are CEO of Rivet Networks, maker of ultra-high performance network cards for gaming computers, and you are considering whether to launch a new product. The product, the Killer X3000, will cost $900,000 to develop up front (year 0), and you expect revenues the first year of $800,000, growing to $1.5 million the second year, and then declining by 40% per year for the next 3 years before the product is fully obsolete. In years 1 through 5, you will have fixed costs associated with the product of $100,000 per year, and variable costs equal to 50% of revenues.

a. What are the cash flows for the project in years 0 through 5?

b. Plot the NPV profile for this investment using discount rates from 0% to 40% in 10% increments.

c. What is the project's NPV if the project's cost of capital is 10%?

d. Use the NPV profile to estimate the cost of capital at which the project would become unprofitable; that is, estimate the project's IRR.

The Internal Rate of Return Rule

(Note: In most cases you will find it helpful to use Excel to compute the IRR.)

9. You are considering an investment in a clothes distributor. The company needs $100,000 today and expects to repay you $120,000 in a year from now. What is the IRR of this investment opportunity? Given the riskiness of the investment opportunity, your cost of capital is 20%. What does the IRR rule say about whether you should invest?

10. You have been offered a very long term investment opportunity to increase your money one hundredfold. You can invest $1000 today and expect to receive $100,000 in 40 years. Your cost of capital for this (very risky) opportunity is 25%. What does the IRR rule say about whether the investment should be undertaken? What about the NPV rule? Do they agree?

11. Does the IRR rule agree with the NPV rule in Problem 3? Explain.

12. How many IRRs are there in part (a) of Problem 5? Does the IRR rule give the right answer in this case? How many IRRs are there in part (b) of Problem 5? Does the IRR rule work in this case?

13. Professor Wendy Smith has been offered the following deal: A law firm would like to retain her for an upfront payment of $50,000. In return, for the next year the firm would have access to 8 hours of her time every month. Smith's rate is $550 per hour and her opportunity cost of capital is 15% (EAR). What does the IRR rule advise regarding this opportunity? What about the NPV rule?

14. Innovation Company is thinking about marketing a new software product. Upfront costs to market and develop the product are $5 million. The product is expected to generate profits of $1 million per year for 10 years. The company will have to provide product support expected to cost $100,000 per year in perpetuity. Assume all profits and expenses occur at the end of the year.

a. What is the NPV of this investment if the cost of capital is 6%? Should the firm undertake the project? Repeat the analysis for discount rates of 2% and 12%.

b. How many IRRs does this investment opportunity have?

c. Can the IRR rule be used to evaluate this investment? Explain.

15. You have 3 projects with the following cash flows:

Year	0	1	2	3	4
Project 1	−150	20	40	60	80
Project 2	−825	0	0	7000	−6500
Project 3	20	40	60	80	−245

a. For which of these projects is the IRR rule reliable?

b. Estimate the IRR for each project (to the nearest 1%).

c. What is the NPV of each project if the cost of capital is 5%? 20%? 50%?

***16.** You own a coal mining company and are considering opening a new mine. The mine itself will cost $120 million to open. If this money is spent immediately, the mine will generate $20 million for the next 10 years. After that, the coal will run out and the site must be cleaned and maintained at environmental standards. The cleaning and maintenance are expected to cost $2 million per year in perpetuity. What does the IRR rule say about whether you should accept this opportunity? If the cost of capital is 8%, what does the NPV rule say?

17. Your firm spends $500,000 per year in regular maintenance of its equipment. Due to the economic downturn, the firm considers forgoing these maintenance expenses for the next three years. If it does so, it expects it will need to spend $2 million in year 4 replacing failed equipment.

a. What is the IRR of the decision to forgo maintenance of the equipment?

b. Does the IRR rule work for this decision?

c. For what costs of capital is forgoing maintenance a good decision?

*18. You are considering investing in a new gold mine in South Africa. Gold in South Africa is buried very deep, so the mine will require an initial investment of $250 million. Once this investment is made, the mine is expected to produce revenues of $30 million per year for the next 20 years. It will cost $10 million per year to operate the mine. After 20 years, the gold will be depleted. The mine must then be stabilized on an ongoing basis, which will cost $5 million per year in perpetuity. Calculate the IRR of this investment. (*Hint*: Plot the NPV as a function of the discount rate.)

19. Your firm has been hired to develop new software for the university's class registration system. Under the contract, you will receive $500,000 as an upfront payment. You expect the development costs to be $450,000 per year for the next three years. Once the new system is in place, you will receive a final payment of $900,000 from the university four years from now.
    a. What are the IRRs of this opportunity?
    b. If your cost of capital is 10%, is the opportunity attractive?
    Suppose you are able to renegotiate the terms of the contract so that your final payment in year 4 will be $1 million.
    c. What is the IRR of the opportunity now?
    d. Is it attractive at these terms?

20. You are considering constructing a new plant in a remote wilderness area to process the ore from a planned mining operation. You anticipate that the plant will take a year to build and cost $100 million upfront. Once built, it will generate cash flows of $15 million at the end of every year over the life of the plant. The plant will be useless 20 years after its completion once the mine runs out of ore. At that point you expect to pay $200 million to shut the plant down and restore the area to its pristine state. Using a cost of capital of 12%,
    a. What is the NPV of the project?
    b. Is using the IRR rule reliable for this project? Explain.
    c. What are the IRRs of this project?

The Payback Rule

21. You are a real estate agent thinking of placing a sign advertising your services at a local bus stop. The sign will cost $5000 and will be posted for one year. You expect that it will generate additional revenue of $500 per month. What is the payback period?

22. You are considering making a movie. The movie is expected to cost $10 million upfront and take a year to make. After that, it is expected to make $5 million in the first year it is released and $2 million per year for the following four years. What is the payback period of this investment? If you require a payback period of two years, will you make the movie? Does the movie have positive NPV if the cost of capital is 10%?

Choosing Between Projects

23. You are deciding between two mutually exclusive investment opportunities. Both require the same initial investment of $10 million. Investment A will generate $2 million per year (starting at the end of the first year) in perpetuity. Investment B will generate $1.5 million at the end of the first year and its revenues will grow at 2% per year for every year after that.
    a. Which investment has the higher IRR?
    b. Which investment has the higher NPV when the cost of capital is 7%?
    c. In this case, for what values of the cost of capital does picking the higher IRR give the correct answer as to which investment is the best opportunity?

24. You have just started your summer internship, and your boss asks you to review a recent analysis that was done to compare three alternative proposals to enhance the firm's manufacturing facility. You find that the prior analysis ranked the proposals according to their IRR, and recommended the highest IRR option, Proposal A. You are concerned and decide to redo the analysis using NPV to determine whether this recommendation was appropriate. But while you are confident the IRRs were computed correctly, it seems that some of the underlying data regarding the cash flows that were estimated for each proposal was not included in the report. For Proposal B, you cannot find information regarding the total initial investment that was required

in year 0. And for Proposal C, you cannot find the data regarding additional salvage value that will be recovered in year 3. Here is the information you have:

Proposal	IRR	Year 0	Year 1	Year 2	Year 3
A	60.0%	−100	30	153	88
B	55.0%	?	0	206	95
C	50.0%	−100	37	0	204 +?

Suppose the appropriate cost of capital for each alternative is 10%. Using this information, determine the NPV of each project. Which project should the firm choose?

Why is ranking the projects by their IRR not valid in this situation?

25. Use the incremental IRR rule to correctly choose between the investments in Problem 23 when the cost of capital is 7%. At what cost of capital would your decision change?

26. You work for an outdoor play structure manufacturing company and are trying to decide between two projects:

	Year-End Cash Flows ($ thousands)			
Project	**0**	**1**	**2**	**IRR**
Playhouse	−30	15	20	10.4%
Fort	−80	39	52	8.6%

You can undertake only one project. If your cost of capital is 8%, use the incremental IRR rule to make the correct decision.

***27.** You are evaluating the following two projects:

	Year-End Cash Flows ($ thousands)		
Project	**0**	**1**	**2**
X	−30	20	20
Y	−80	40	60

Use the incremental IRR to determine the range of discount rates for which each project is optimal to undertake. Note that you should also include the range in which it does not make sense to take either project.

28. Consider two investment projects, both of which require an upfront investment of $10 million and pay a constant positive amount each year for the next 10 years. Under what conditions can you rank these projects by comparing their IRRs?

29. You are considering a safe investment opportunity that requires a $1000 investment today, and will pay $500 two years from now and another $750 five years from now.

a. What is the IRR of this investment?

b. If you are choosing between this investment and putting your money in a safe bank account that pays an EAR of 5% per year for any horizon, can you make the decision by simply comparing this EAR with the IRR of the investment? Explain.

30. Facebook is considering two proposals to overhaul its network infrastructure. They have received two bids. The first bid, from Huawei, will require a $20 million upfront investment and will generate $20 million in savings for Facebook each year for the next three years. The second bid, from Cisco, requires a $100 million upfront investment and will generate $60 million in savings each year for the next three years.

a. What is the IRR for Facebook associated with each bid?

b. If the cost of capital for this investment is 12%, what is the NPV for Facebook of each bid? Suppose Cisco modifies its bid by offering a lease contract instead. Under the terms of the lease, Facebook will pay $20 million upfront, and $35 million per year for the next three years. Facebook's savings will be the same as with Cisco's original bid.

c. Including its savings, what are Facebook's net cash flows under the lease contract? What is the IRR of the Cisco bid now?

d. Is this new bid a better deal for Facebook than Cisco's original bid? Explain.

Project Selection with Resource Constraints

31. Natasha's Flowers, a local florist, purchases fresh flowers each day at the local flower market. The buyer has a budget of $1000 per day to spend. Different flowers have different profit margins, and also a maximum amount the shop can sell. Based on past experience, the shop has estimated the following NPV of purchasing each type:

	NPV per Bunch	Cost per Bunch	Max. Bunches
Roses	$ 3	$20	25
Lilies	8	30	10
Pansies	4	30	10
Orchids	20	80	5

What combination of flowers should the shop purchase each day?

32. You own a car dealership and are trying to decide how to configure the showroom floor. The floor has 2000 square feet of usable space. You have hired an analyst and asked her to estimate the NPV of putting a particular model on the floor and how much space each model requires:

Model	NPV	Space Requirement (sq. ft.)
MB345	$3000	200
MC237	5000	250
MY456	4000	240
MG231	1000	150
MT347	6000	450
MF302	4000	200
MG201	1500	150

In addition, the showroom also requires office space. The analyst has estimated that office space generates an NPV of $14 per square foot. What models should be displayed on the floor and how many square feet should be devoted to office space?

33. Kaimalino Properties (KP) is evaluating six real estate investments. Management plans to buy the properties today and sell them five years from today. The following table summarizes the initial cost and the expected sale price for each property, as well as the appropriate discount rate based on the risk of each venture.

Project	Cost Today	Discount Rate	Expected Sale Price in Year 5
Mountain Ridge	$ 3,000,000	15%	$18,000,000
Ocean Park Estates	15,000,000	15%	75,500,000
Lakeview	9,000,000	15%	50,000,000
Seabreeze	6,000,000	8%	35,500,000
Green Hills	3,000,000	8%	10,000,000
West Ranch	9,000,000	8%	46,500,000

KP has a total capital budget of $18,000,000 to invest in properties.

a. What is the IRR of each investment?

b. What is the NPV of each investment?

c. Given its budget of $18,000,000, which properties should KP choose?

d. Explain why the profitably index method could not be used if KP's budget were $12,000,000 instead. Which properties should KP choose in this case?

***34.** Orchid Biotech Company is evaluating several development projects for experimental drugs. Although the cash flows are difficult to forecast, the company has come up with the following estimates of the initial capital requirements and NPVs for the projects. Given a wide variety of staffing needs, the company has also estimated the number of research scientists required for each development project (all cost values are given in millions of dollars).

Project Number	Initial Capital	Number of Research Scientists	NPV
I	\$10	2	\$10.1
II	15	3	19.0
III	15	4	22.0
IV	20	3	25.0
V	30	12	60.2

a. Suppose that Orchid has a total capital budget of \$60 million. How should it prioritize these projects?

b. Suppose in addition that Orchid currently has only 12 research scientists and does not anticipate being able to hire any more in the near future. How should Orchid prioritize these projects?

c. If instead, Orchid had 15 research scientists available, explain why the profitability index ranking cannot be used to prioritize projects. Which projects should it choose now?

Data Case

Your success in business thus far has put you in a position to purchase a home for \$500,000 located close to the university you attend. You plan to pay a 20% down payment of \$100,000 and borrow the remaining \$400,000. You need to decide on a mortgage, and realize you can apply the skills you have acquired in the last several chapters to evaluate your choices. To find the available options, go to www.bankrate.com. Select "Mortgages," then "Mortgage Rates." For location, choose the nearest large city; for mortgage type, choose purchase (not refinance). Consider 30-year fixed rate mortgages with 20% down, and assume your credit score is the highest possible.

Consider all the options by selecting loans with "All points." Update rates and sort by "Rate" to find the loan with the lowest rate (not APR). Record the rate, points, fees, "APR," and monthly payment for this loan.

Next consider only loans with "0 points" and find the loan with the lowest fees. Again, record the rate, points, fees, "APR," and monthly payment for this loan.

First, use the annuity formula or PMT function in Excel to verify the monthly payment for each loan. (Note that to convert the "Rate" to a monthly interest rate you must divide by 12. Your result may differ slightly due to rounding.)

Next, calculate the actual amount you will receive from each loan after both fees and points. (Note that fees are a fixed dollar amount; points are also paid up front and are calculated as a % of the loan amount.) Using this net amount as the amount you will receive (rather than \$400,000), show that the quoted "APR" of the loan is the effective IRR of the loan once all fees are included (you may use the Rate function in Excel, or calculate the NPV at the quoted "APR").

Compare the loans, assuming you will keep them for 30 years, as follows:

1. Compute the incremental cash flows of the lower rate loan; that is, determine how much more you will pay in fees, and how much you will save on your monthly payment.
2. What is the payback period of the lower rate loan? That is, how many years of lower monthly payments will it take to save an amount equal to the higher fees?
3. What is the IRR associated with paying the higher fees for the lower rate loan? (Again, the RATE function can be used.)
4. Plot the NPV profile of the decision to pay points for the lower rate loan. Do the NPV rule and the IRR rule coincide?

Next, compare the loans assuming you expect to keep them for only 5 years:

5. Compute the final payment you will need to make to pay off each loan at the end of 5 years (*Hint*: the FV function in Excel can be used). Which loan will be more expensive to repay?
6. Including the incremental cost to repay the loan after 5 years, what is the IRR and NPV profile associated with paying points now?

Create a data table showing the NPV of paying points for different horizons (1 to 30 years) and different discount rates (0% to the IRR in (3) above). What can you conclude about whether it is a good idea to pay points?

Suppose the bank gives you the option to increase either loan amount so that for either loan, you will receive \$400,000 today after all fees and points are paid. How would this affect your decision to pay points?

Note: Updates to this data case may be found at www.berkdemarzo.com.

CHAPTER 7 APPENDIX

Computing the NPV Profile Using Excel's Data Table Function

As the examples in this chapter demonstrate, interpreting the IRR can be difficult without seeing an investment's full NPV profile. Calculating the NPV for each discount rate can be tedious, however. Here we show an easy method to do so using Excel's **Data Table** functionality.

	A	B	C	D	E	F	G	H	I
1	Discount Rate	5.0%							NPV
2	Period	0	1	2	3	4		*r*	11.08
3	Cash Flow C_t	550.0	(500.0)	(500.0)	(500.0)	1,000.0		0%	50.00
4	Discount Factor	1.000	0.952	0.907	0.864	0.823		5%	11.08
5	PV(C_t)	550.0	(476.2)	(453.5)	(431.9)	822.7		10%	(10.41)
6	**NPV**	**11.08**	=SUM(B5:F5)					15%	(19.86)
7								20%	(20.99)
8	IRR	7.2%	=IRR(B3:F3,0%)					25%	(16.40)
9	IRR	33.7%	=IRR(B3:F3,20%)					30%	(7.93)
10								35%	3.13
11								40%	15.85
12								45%	29.57
13								50%	43.83

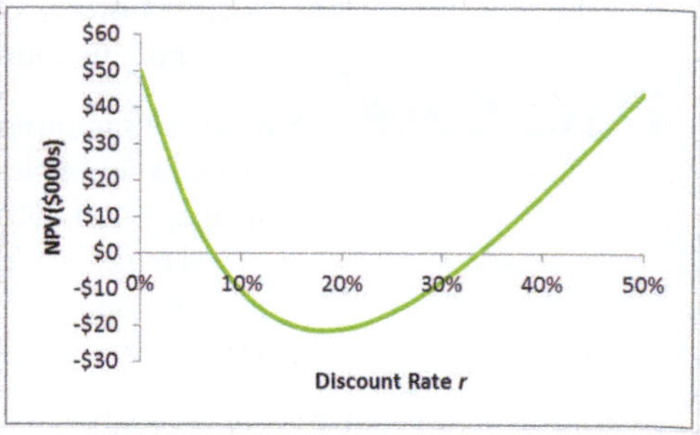

Consider the NPV and IRR calculations associated with Figure 7.3. As shown in cell B6, the investment has a positive NPV of 11.08 at a 5% discount rate. The project also has two IRRs, shown in cells B8:B9, which we can find by using Excel's IRR function with different initial guesses.

The NPV profile of the project—which shows the NPV for a range of discount rates from 0% to 50%—is shown in cells H2:I13, and corresponds to the data plotted in Figure 7.3. We could construct the NPV profile by plugging each discount rate into cell B1 and recording the resultant NPV from cell B6. Fortunately, Excel automates this "what-if" analysis using a data table. To build the data table, we first enter a column (or row) of data with the discount rates we would like to try, as shown in cells H3:H13. The top of the next column, in cell I2, is a formula whose output we would like to record. In this case the formula in I2 is simply "=B6", the NPV we calculated. To build the data table, we then select cells H2:I13 as shown below, and bring up the Data Table window (from the Data > What-If Analysis menu, or keyboard shortcut Alt-D-T). There we enter B1 as the "column input cell" to indicate that each entry in the column of discount rates should be substituted into cell B1. Upon clicking "OK," Excel will try each discount rate and record the resulting NPV in the table, generating the NPV profile. Moreover, the data table will automatically update should we change any of the project cash flows.

	H	I	J	K
1		NPV		
2	*r*	11.08		
3	0%			
4	5%			
5	10%			
6	15%			
7	20%			
8	25%			
9	30%			
10	35%			
11	40%			
12	45%			
13	50%			

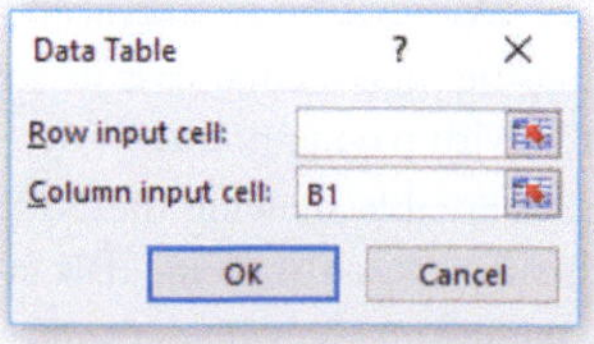

	H	I	J
1		NPV	
2	*r*	11.08	
3	0%	50.00	
4	5%	11.08	
5	10%	(10.41)	
6	15%	(19.86)	
7	20%	(20.99)	
8	25%	(16.40)	
9	30%	(7.93)	
10	35%	3.13	
11	40%	15.85	
12	45%	29.57	
13	50%	43.83	

CHAPTER

8

Fundamentals of Capital Budgeting

IN EARLY 2008, MCDONALD'S CORP., THE WORLD'S LEADING fast food restaurant, announced that it would add cappuccinos, lattes, and mochas to its menu of nearly 14,000 U.S. locations over the next two years. John Betts, vice president of national beverage strategy, described the introduction as "the biggest endeavor for McDonald's since our introduction of breakfast 35 years ago." Betts added that McDonald's menu enhancements could add up to $1 billion in sales. The decision by McDonald's to introduce "high-end" coffee options to its menu represents a classic capital budgeting decision. To make such decisions, McDonald's relies primarily on the NPV rule. But how can managers quantify the cost and benefits of a project like this one to compute its NPV?

An important responsibility of corporate financial managers is determining which projects or investments a firm should undertake. *Capital budgeting,* the focus of this chapter, is the process of analyzing investment opportunities and deciding which ones to accept. As we learned in Chapter 7, the NPV rule is the most accurate and reliable method for allocating the firm's resources so as to maximize its value. To implement the NPV rule, we must compute the NPV of our projects and only accept those for which the NPV is positive. The first step in this process is to forecast the project's revenues and costs, and from them estimate the project's expected future cash flows. In this chapter, we will consider in detail the process of estimating a project's expected cash flows, which are crucial inputs in the investment decision process. Using these cash flows, we can then compute the project's NPV—its contribution to shareholder value. Finally, because the cash flow forecasts almost always contain uncertainty, we demonstrate how to compute the sensitivity of the NPV to the uncertainty in the forecasts.

NOTATION

IRR	internal rate of return
$EBIT$	earnings before interest and taxes
τ_c	marginal corporate tax rate
NPV	net present value
NWC_t	net working capital in year t
ΔNWC_t	increase in net working capital between year t and year $t-1$
$CapEx$	capital expenditures
FCF_t	free cash flow in year t
PV	present value
r	projected cost of capital

8.1 Forecasting Earnings

A **capital budget** lists the projects and investments that a company plans to undertake during the coming year. To determine this list, firms analyze alternative projects and decide which ones to accept through a process called **capital budgeting**. This process begins with forecasts of the project's future consequences for the firm. Some of these consequences will affect the firm's revenues; others will affect its costs. Our ultimate goal is to determine the effect of the decision on the firm's cash flows, and evaluate the NPV of these cash flows to assess the consequences of the decision for the firm's value.

As we emphasized in Chapter 2, *earnings are not actual cash flows*. However, as a practical matter, to derive the forecasted cash flows of a project, financial managers often begin by forecasting earnings. Thus, we *begin* by determining the **incremental earnings** of a project—that is, the amount by which the firm's earnings are expected to change as a result of the investment decision. Then, in Section 8.2, we demonstrate how to use the incremental earnings to forecast the *cash flows* of the project.

Let's consider a hypothetical capital budgeting decision faced by managers of the router division of Cisco Systems, a maker of networking hardware. Cisco is considering the development of a wireless home networking appliance, called HomeNet, that will provide both the hardware and the software necessary to run an entire home from any Internet connection. In addition to connecting computers and smartphones, HomeNet will control Internet-based telepresence and phone systems, home entertainment systems, heating and air-conditioning units, major appliances, security systems, office equipment, and so on. Cisco has already conducted an intensive, $300,000 feasibility study to assess the attractiveness of the new product.

Revenue and Cost Estimates

We begin by reviewing the revenue and cost estimates for HomeNet. HomeNet's target market is upscale residential "smart" homes and home offices. Based on extensive marketing surveys, the sales forecast for HomeNet is 100,000 units per year. Given the pace of technological change, Cisco expects the product will have a four-year life. It will be sold through high-end electronics stores for a retail price of $375, with an expected wholesale price of $260.

Developing the new hardware will be relatively inexpensive, as existing technologies can be simply repackaged in a newly designed, home-friendly box. Industrial design teams will make the box and its packaging aesthetically pleasing to the residential market. Cisco expects total engineering and design costs to amount to $5 million. Once the design is finalized, actual production will be outsourced at a cost (including packaging) of $110 per unit.

In addition to the hardware requirements, Cisco must build a new software application to allow virtual control of the home from the Web. This software development project requires coordination with each of the Web appliance manufacturers and is expected to take a dedicated team of 50 software engineers a full year to complete. The cost of a software engineer (including benefits and related costs) is $200,000 per year. To verify the compatibility of new consumer Internet-ready appliances with the HomeNet system as they become available, Cisco must also install new equipment that will require an upfront investment of $7.5 million.

The software and hardware design will be completed, and the new equipment will be operational, at the end of one year. At that time, HomeNet will be ready to ship. Cisco expects to spend $2.8 million per year on marketing and support for this product.

Incremental Earnings Forecast

Given the revenue and cost estimates, we can forecast HomeNet's incremental earnings, as shown in the spreadsheet in Table 8.1. After the product is developed in year 0, it will generate sales of 100,000 units × \$260/unit = \$26 million each year for the next four years. The cost of producing these units is 100,000 units × \$110/unit = \$11 million per year. Thus, HomeNet will produce a gross profit of \$26 million − \$11 million = \$15 million per year, as shown in line 3 of Table 8.1. Note that while revenues and costs occur throughout the year, we adopt the standard convention of listing revenues and costs at the end of the year in which they occur.[1]

The project's operating expenses include \$2.8 million per year in marketing and support costs, which are listed as selling, general, and administrative expenses. In year 0, Cisco will spend \$5 million on design and engineering, together with 50 × \$200,000 = \$10 million on software, for a total of \$15 million in research and development expenditures.

Capital Expenditures and Depreciation. HomeNet also requires \$7.5 million in equipment that will be required to allow third-party manufacturers to upload the specifications and verify the compatibility of any new Internet-ready appliances that they might produce. To encourage the development of compatible products and provide service for existing customers, Cisco expects to continue to operate this equipment even after they phase out the current version of the product. Recall from Chapter 2 that while investments in plant, property, and equipment are a cash expense, they are not directly listed as expenses when calculating *earnings*. Instead, the firm deducts a fraction of the cost of these items each year as depreciation. Several different methods are used to compute depreciation. The simplest method is **straight-line depreciation**, in which the asset's cost (less any expected salvage value) is divided equally over its estimated useful life (we discuss other methods in Section 8.4). If we assume the equipment is purchased at the end of year 0, and then use straight-line depreciation over a five-year life for the new equipment, HomeNet's depreciation expense is \$1.5 million per year in years 1 through 5.[2] Deducting

TABLE 8.1 SPREADSHEET HomeNet's Incremental Earnings Forecast

	Year	0	1	2	3	4	5
Incremental Earnings Forecast (\$000s)							
1	Sales	—	26,000	26,000	26,000	26,000	—
2	Cost of Goods Sold	—	(11,000)	(11,000)	(11,000)	(11,000)	—
3	**Gross Profit**	—	15,000	15,000	15,000	15,000	—
4	Selling, General, and Administrative	—	(2,800)	(2,800)	(2,800)	(2,800)	—
5	Research and Development	(15,000)	—	—	—	—	
6	Depreciation	—	(1,500)	(1,500)	(1,500)	(1,500)	(1,500)
7	**EBIT**	(15,000)	10,700	10,700	10,700	10,700	(1,500)
8	Income Tax at 40%	6,000	(4,280)	(4,280)	(4,280)	(4,280)	600
9	**Unlevered Net Income**	**(9,000)**	**6,420**	**6,420**	**6,420**	**6,420**	**(900)**

[1]As a result, cash flows that occur at the end of one year will be listed in a different column than those that occur at the start of the next year, even though they may occur only weeks apart. When additional precision is required, cash flows are often estimated on a quarterly or monthly basis. (See also the appendix to Chapter 5 for a method of converting continuously arriving cash flows to annual ones.)

[2]Recall that although new product sales have ceased, the equipment will remain in use in year 5. Note also that as in Chapter 2, we list depreciation expenses separately rather than include them with other expenses (i.e., COGS, SG&A, and R&D are "clean" and do not include non-cash expenses. Using clean expenses is preferred in financial models.)

these depreciation expenses leads to the forecast for HomeNet's earnings before interest and taxes (EBIT) shown in line 7 of Table 8.1. This treatment of capital expenditures is one of the key reasons why earnings are not an accurate representation of cash flows.

Interest Expenses. In Chapter 2, we saw that to compute a firm's net income, we must first deduct interest expenses from EBIT. When evaluating a capital budgeting decision like the HomeNet project, however, we generally *do not include interest expenses*. Any incremental interest expenses will be related to the firm's decision regarding how to finance the project. Here we wish to evaluate the project on its own, separate from the financing decision.[3] Thus, we evaluate the HomeNet project *as if* Cisco will not use any debt to finance it (whether or not that is actually the case), and we postpone the consideration of alternative financing choices until Part 5 of the book. For this reason, we refer to the net income we compute in the spreadsheet in Table 8.1 as the **unlevered net income** of the project, to indicate that it does not include any interest expenses associated with debt.

Taxes. The final expense we must account for is corporate taxes. The correct tax rate to use is the firm's **marginal corporate tax rate**, which is the tax rate it will pay on an *incremental* dollar of pre-tax income. In Table 8.1, we assume the marginal corporate tax rate for the HomeNet project is 40% each year. The incremental income tax expense is calculated in line 8 as

$$\text{Income Tax} = EBIT \times \tau_c \tag{8.1}$$

where τ_c is the firm's marginal corporate tax rate.

In year 1, HomeNet will contribute an additional \$10.7 million to Cisco's EBIT, which will result in an additional \$10.7 million × 40% = \$4.28 million in corporate tax that Cisco will owe. We deduct this amount to determine HomeNet's after-tax contribution to net income.

In year 0, however, HomeNet's EBIT is negative. Are taxes relevant in this case? Yes. HomeNet will reduce Cisco's taxable income in year 0 by \$15 million. As long as Cisco earns taxable income elsewhere in year 0 against which it can offset HomeNet's losses, Cisco will owe \$15 million × 40% = \$6 million *less* in taxes in year 0. The firm should credit this tax savings to the HomeNet project. A similar credit applies in year 5, when the firm claims its final depreciation expense for the equipment.

EXAMPLE 8.1 Taxing Losses for Projects in Profitable Companies

Problem

Kellogg Company plans to launch a new line of high-fiber, gluten-free breakfast pastries. The heavy advertising expenses associated with the new product launch will generate operating losses of \$15 million next year for the product. Kellogg expects to earn pretax income of \$460 million from operations other than the new pastries next year. If Kellogg pays a 40% tax rate on its pretax income, what will it owe in taxes next year without the new pastry product? What will it owe with the new pastries?

[3]This approach is motivated by the Separation Principle (see Chapter 3): When securities are fairly priced, the net present value of a fixed set of cash flows is independent of how those cash flows are financed. Later in the text, we will consider cases in which financing may influence the project's value, and we will extend our capital budgeting techniques accordingly in Chapter 18.

Solution

Without the new pastries, Kellogg will owe \$460 million × 40% = \$184 million in corporate taxes next year. With the new pastries, Kellogg's pretax income next year will be only \$460 million − \$15 million = \$445 million, and it will owe \$445 million × 40% = \$178 million in tax. Thus, launching the new product reduces Kellogg's taxes next year by \$184 million − \$178 million = \$6 million.

Unlevered Net Income Calculation. We can express the calculation in the Table 8.1 spreadsheet as the following shorthand formula for unlevered net income:

$$\begin{aligned}\text{Unlevered Net Income} &= EBIT \times (1 - \tau_c)\\ &= (\text{Revenues} - \text{Costs} - \text{Depreciation}) \times (1 - \tau_c) \qquad (8.2)\end{aligned}$$

That is, a project's unlevered net income is equal to its incremental revenues less costs and depreciation, evaluated on an after-tax basis.[4]

Indirect Effects on Incremental Earnings

When computing the incremental earnings of an investment decision, we should include *all* changes between the firm's earnings with the project versus without the project. Thus far, we have analyzed only the direct effects of the HomeNet project. But HomeNet may have indirect consequences for other operations within Cisco. Because these indirect effects will also affect Cisco's earnings, we must include them in our analysis.

Opportunity Costs. Many projects use a resource that the company already owns. Because the firm does not need to pay cash to acquire this resource for a new project, it is tempting to assume that the resource is available for free. However, in many cases the resource could provide value for the firm in another opportunity or project. The **opportunity cost** of using a resource is the value it could have provided in its best alternative use.[5] Because this value is lost when the resource is used by another project, we should include the opportunity cost as an incremental cost of the project. In the case of the HomeNet project, suppose the project will require space for a new lab. Even though the lab will be housed in an existing facility, we must include the opportunity cost of not using the space in an alternative way.

EXAMPLE 8.2 **The Opportunity Cost of HomeNet's Lab Space**

Problem

Suppose HomeNet's new lab will be housed in warehouse space that the company would have otherwise rented out for \$200,000 per year during years 1–4. How does this opportunity cost affect HomeNet's incremental earnings?

Solution

In this case, the opportunity cost of the warehouse space is the forgone rent. This cost would reduce HomeNet's incremental earnings during years 1–4 by \$200,000 × (1 − 40%) = \$120,000, the after-tax benefit of renting out the warehouse space.

---

[4]Unlevered net income is sometimes also referred to as net operating profit after tax (NOPAT).

[5]In Chapter 5, we defined the opportunity cost of capital as the rate you could earn on an alternative investment with equivalent risk. We similarly define the opportunity cost of using an existing asset in a project as the cash flow generated by the next-best alternative use for the asset.

COMMON MISTAKE **The Opportunity Cost of an Idle Asset**

A common mistake is to conclude that if an asset is currently idle, its opportunity cost is zero. For example, the firm might have a warehouse that is currently empty or a machine that is not being used. Often, the asset may have been idled in anticipation of taking on the new project, and would have otherwise been put to use by the firm. Even if the firm has no alternative use for the asset, the firm could choose to sell or rent the asset. The value obtained from the asset's alternative use, sale, or rental represents an opportunity cost that must be included as part of the incremental cash flows.

Project Externalities. **Project externalities** are indirect effects of the project that may increase or decrease the profits of other business activities of the firm. For instance, in the McDonald's example in the chapter introduction, some cappuccino purchasers would otherwise have bought an alternative beverage, like a soft drink. When sales of a new product displace sales of an existing product, the situation is often referred to as **cannibalization.** Suppose that approximately 25% of HomeNet's sales come from customers who would have purchased an existing Cisco wireless router if HomeNet were not available. If this reduction in sales of the existing wireless router is a consequence of the decision to develop HomeNet, then we must include it when calculating HomeNet's incremental earnings.

The spreadsheet in Table 8.2 recalculates HomeNet's incremental earnings forecast including the opportunity cost of the lab space and the expected cannibalization of the existing product. The opportunity cost of the lab space in Example 8.2 increases selling, general, and administrative expenses from \$2.8 million to \$3.0 million. For the cannibalization, suppose that the existing router wholesales for \$100 so the expected loss in sales is

$$\$25\% \times 100{,}000 \text{ units} \times \$100/\text{unit} = \$2.5 \text{ million}$$

Compared to Table 8.1, the sales forecast falls from \$26 million to \$23.5 million. In addition, suppose the cost of the existing router is \$60 per unit. Then, because Cisco will no longer need to produce as many of its existing wireless routers, the incremental cost of goods sold for the HomeNet project is reduced by

$$25\% \times 100{,}000 \text{ units} \times (\$60 \text{ cost per unit}) = \$1.5 \text{ million}$$

from \$11 million to \$9.5 million. HomeNet's incremental gross profit therefore declines by \$2.5 million − \$1.5 million = \$1 million once we account for this externality.

Thus, comparing the spreadsheets in Table 8.1 and Table 8.2, our forecast for HomeNet's unlevered net income in years 1–4 declines from \$6.42 million to \$5.7 million due to the lost rent of the lab space and the lost sales of the existing router.

TABLE 8.2 SPREADSHEET **HomeNet's Incremental Earnings Forecast (Including Cannibalization and Lost Rent)**

	Year	0	1	2	3	4	5
Incremental Earnings Forecast ($000s)							
1	Sales	—	23,500	23,500	23,500	23,500	—
2	Cost of Goods Sold	—	(9,500)	(9,500)	(9,500)	(9,500)	—
3	**Gross Profit**	—	14,000	14,000	14,000	14,000	—
4	Selling, General, and Administrative	—	(3,000)	(3,000)	(3,000)	(3,000)	—
5	Research and Development	(15,000)	—	—	—	—	—
6	Depreciation	—	(1,500)	(1,500)	(1,500)	(1,500)	(1,500)
7	**EBIT**	(15,000)	9,500	9,500	9,500	9,500	(1,500)
8	Income Tax at 40%	6,000	(3,800)	(3,800)	(3,800)	(3,800)	600
9	**Unlevered Net Income**	**(9,000)**	**5,700**	**5,700**	**5,700**	**5,700**	**(900)**

Sunk Costs and Incremental Earnings

A **sunk cost** is any unrecoverable cost for which the firm is already liable. Sunk costs have been or will be paid regardless of the decision about whether or not to proceed with the project. Therefore, they are not incremental with respect to the current decision and should not be included in its analysis. For this reason, we did not include in our analysis the $300,000 already expended on the marketing and feasibility studies for HomeNet. Because this $300,000 has already been spent, it is a sunk cost. A good rule to remember is that *if our decision does not affect the cash flow, then the cash flow should not affect our decision*. Below are some common examples of sunk costs you may encounter.

Fixed Overhead Expenses. Overhead expenses are associated with activities that are not directly attributable to a single business activity but instead affect many different areas of the corporation. These expenses are often allocated to the different business activities for accounting purposes. To the extent that these overhead costs are fixed and will be incurred in any case, they are not incremental to the project and should not be included. Only include as incremental expenses the *additional* overhead expenses that arise because of the decision to take on the project.

Past Research and Development Expenditures. When a firm has already devoted significant resources to develop a new product, there may be a tendency to continue investing in the product even if market conditions have changed and the product is unlikely to be viable. The rationale sometimes given is that if the product is abandoned, the money that has already been invested will be "wasted." In other cases, a decision is made to abandon a project because it cannot possibly be successful enough to recoup the investment that has already been made. In fact, neither argument is correct: Any money that has already been spent is a sunk cost and therefore irrelevant. The decision to continue or abandon should be based only on the incremental costs and benefits of the product going forward.

Unavoidable Competitive Effects. When developing a new product, firms often worry about the cannibalization of their existing products. But if sales are likely to decline in any case as a result of new products introduced by competitors, then these lost sales are a sunk cost and we should not include them in our projections.

COMMON MISTAKE The Sunk Cost Fallacy

Sunk cost fallacy is a term used to describe the tendency of people to be influenced by sunk costs and to "throw good money after bad." That is, people sometimes continue to invest in a project that has a negative NPV because they have already invested a large amount in the project and feel that by not continuing it, the prior investment will be wasted. The sunk cost fallacy is also sometimes called the "Concorde effect," a term that refers to the British and French governments' decision to continue funding the joint development of the Concorde aircraft even after it was clear that sales of the plane would fall far short of what was necessary to justify the cost of continuing its development. Although the project was viewed by the British government as a commercial and financial disaster, the political implications of halting the project—and thereby publicly admitting that all past expenses on the project would result in nothing—ultimately prevented either government from abandoning the project.

It is important to note that sunk costs need not always be in the past. Any cash flows, even future ones, that will not be affected by the decision at hand are effectively sunk, and should not be included in our incremental forecast. For example, if Cisco believes it will lose some sales on its other products whether or not it launches HomeNet, these lost sales are a sunk cost that should not be included as part of the cannibalization adjustments in Table 8.2.

Real-World Complexities

We have simplified the HomeNet example in an effort to focus on the types of effects that financial managers consider when estimating a project's incremental earnings. For a real project, however, the estimates of these revenues and costs are likely to be much more complicated. For instance, our assumption that the same number of HomeNet units will be sold each year is probably unrealistic. A new product typically has lower sales initially, as customers gradually become aware of the product. Sales will then accelerate, plateau, and ultimately decline as the product nears obsolescence or faces increased competition.

Similarly, the average selling price of a product and its cost of production will generally change over time. Prices and costs tend to rise with the general level of inflation in the economy. The prices of technology products, however, often fall over time as newer, superior technologies emerge and production costs decline. For most industries, competition tends to reduce profit margins over time. These factors should be considered when estimating a project's revenues and costs.

EXAMPLE 8.3 Product Adoption and Price Changes

Problem

Suppose sales of HomeNet were expected to be 100,000 units in year 1, 125,000 units in years 2 and 3, and 50,000 units in year 4. Suppose also that HomeNet's sale price and manufacturing cost are expected to decline by 10% per year, as with other networking products. By contrast, selling, general, and administrative expenses are expected to rise with inflation by 4% per year. Update the incremental earnings forecast in the spreadsheet in Table 8.2 to account for these effects.

Solution

HomeNet's incremental earnings with these new assumptions are shown in the spreadsheet below:

	Year	0	1	2	3	4	5
Incremental Earnings Forecast ($000s)							
1	Sales	—	23,500	26,438	23,794	8,566	—
2	Cost of Goods Sold	—	(9,500)	(10,688)	(9,619)	(3,463)	—
3	**Gross Profit**	—	14,000	15,750	14,175	5,103	—
4	Selling, General, and Administrative	—	(3,000)	(3,120)	(3,245)	(3,375)	—
5	Research and Development	(15,000)	—	—	—	—	—
6	Depreciation	—	(1,500)	(1,500)	(1,500)	(1,500)	(1,500)
7	**EBIT**	(15,000)	9,500	11,130	9,430	228	(1,500)
8	Income Tax at 40%	6,000	(3,800)	(4,452)	(3,772)	(91)	600
9	**Unlevered Net Income**	**(9,000)**	**5,700**	**6,678**	**5,658**	**137**	**(900)**

For example, sale prices in year 2 will be $\$260 \times 0.90 = \$234$ per unit for HomeNet, and $\$100 \times 0.90 = \$90$ per unit for the cannibalized product. Thus, incremental sales in year 2 are equal to 125,000 units $\times$ (\$234 per unit) $-$ 31,250 cannibalized units $\times$ (\$90 per unit) $=$ \$26.438 million.

CONCEPT CHECK

1. How do we forecast unlevered net income?
2. Should we include sunk costs in the cash flow forecasts of a project? Why or why not?
3. Explain why you must include the opportunity cost of using a resource as an incremental cost of a project.

8.2 Determining Free Cash Flow and NPV

As discussed in Chapter 2, earnings are an accounting measure of the firm's performance. They do not represent real profits: The firm cannot use its earnings to buy goods, pay employees, fund new investments, or pay dividends to shareholders. To do those things, a firm needs cash. Thus, to evaluate a capital budgeting decision, we must determine its consequences for the firm's available cash. The incremental effect of a project on the firm's available cash, separate from any financing decisions, is the project's **free cash flow**.

In this section, we forecast the free cash flow of the HomeNet project using the earnings forecasts we developed in Section 8.1. We then use this forecast to calculate the NPV of the project.

Calculating Free Cash Flow from Earnings

As discussed in Chapter 2, there are important differences between earnings and cash flow. Earnings include non-cash charges, such as depreciation, but do not include the cost of capital investment. To determine HomeNet's free cash flow from its incremental earnings, we must adjust for these differences.

Capital Expenditures and Depreciation. Depreciation is not a cash expense that is paid by the firm. Rather, it is a method used for accounting and tax purposes to allocate the original purchase cost of the asset over its life. Because depreciation is not a cash flow, we do not include it in the cash flow forecast. Instead, we include the actual cash cost of the asset when it is purchased.

To compute HomeNet's free cash flow, we must add back to earnings the depreciation expense for the new equipment (a non-cash charge) and subtract the actual capital expenditure of $7.5 million that will be paid for the equipment in year 0. We show these adjustments in lines 10 and 11 of the spreadsheet in Table 8.3 (which is based on the incremental earnings forecast of Table 8.2).

TABLE 8.3 SPREADSHEET Calculation of HomeNet's Free Cash Flow (Including Cannibalization and Lost Rent)

	Year	0	1	2	3	4	5
Incremental Earnings Forecast ($000s)							
1	Sales	—	23,500	23,500	23,500	23,500	—
2	Cost of Goods Sold	—	(9,500)	(9,500)	(9,500)	(9,500)	—
3	**Gross Profit**	—	14,000	14,000	14,000	14,000	—
4	Selling, General, and Administrative	—	(3,000)	(3,000)	(3,000)	(3,000)	—
5	Research and Development	(15,000)	—	—	—	—	—
6	Depreciation	—	(1,500)	(1,500)	(1,500)	(1,500)	(1,500)
7	**EBIT**	(15,000)	9,500	9,500	9,500	9,500	(1,500)
8	Income Tax at 40%	6,000	(3,800)	(3,800)	(3,800)	(3,800)	600
9	**Unlevered Net Income**	**(9,000)**	**5,700**	**5,700**	**5,700**	**5,700**	**(900)**
Free Cash Flow ($000s)							
10	Plus: Depreciation	—	1,500	1,500	1,500	1,500	1,500
11	Less: Capital Expenditures	(7,500)	—	—	—	—	—
12	Less: Increases in NWC	—	(2,100)	—	—	—	2,100
13	**Free Cash Flow**	**(16,500)**	**5,100**	**7,200**	**7,200**	**7,200**	**2,700**

Net Working Capital (NWC). In Chapter 2, we defined net working capital as the difference between current assets and current liabilities. The main components of net working capital are cash, inventory, receivables, and payables:

$$\text{Net Working Capital} = \text{Current Assets} - \text{Current Liabilities}$$
$$= \text{Cash} + \text{Inventory} + \text{Receivables} - \text{Payables} \quad (8.3)$$

Most projects will require the firm to invest in net working capital. Firms may need to maintain a minimum cash balance[6] to meet unexpected expenditures, and inventories of raw materials and finished product to accommodate production uncertainties and demand fluctuations. Also, customers may not pay for the goods they purchase immediately. While sales are immediately counted as part of earnings, the firm does not receive any cash until the customers actually pay. In the interim, the firm includes the amount that customers owe in its receivables. Thus, the firm's receivables measure the total credit that the firm has extended to its customers. In the same way, payables measure the credit the firm has received from its suppliers. The difference between receivables and payables is the net amount of the firm's capital that is consumed as a result of these credit transactions, known as **trade credit.**

Suppose that HomeNet will have no incremental cash or inventory requirements (products will be shipped directly from the contract manufacturer to customers). However, receivables related to HomeNet are expected to account for 15% of annual sales, and payables are expected to be 15% of the annual cost of goods sold (COGS).[7] HomeNet's net working capital requirements are shown in the spreadsheet in Table 8.4.

Table 8.4 shows that the HomeNet project will require no net working capital in year 0, \$2.1 million in net working capital in years 1–4, and no net working capital in year 5. How does this requirement affect the project's free cash flow? Any increases in net working capital represent an investment that reduces the cash available to the firm and so reduces free cash flow. We define the increase in net working capital in year *t* as

$$\Delta NWC_t = NWC_t - NWC_{t-1} \quad (8.4)$$

TABLE 8.4 SPREADSHEET HomeNet's Net Working Capital Requirements

	Year	0	1	2	3	4	5
	Net Working Capital Forecast ($000s)						
1	Cash Requirements	—	—	—	—	—	—
2	Inventory	—	—	—	—	—	—
3	Receivables (15% of Sales)	—	3,525	3,525	3,525	3,525	—
4	Payables (15% of COGS)	—	(1,425)	(1,425)	(1,425)	(1,425)	—
5	**Net Working Capital**	**—**	**2,100**	**2,100**	**2,100**	**2,100**	**—**

[6]The cash included in net working capital is cash that is *not* invested to earn a market rate of return. It includes non-invested cash held in the firm's checking account, in a company safe or cash box, in cash registers (for retail stores), and other sites, which is needed to run the business.

[7]If customers take N days to pay, then accounts receivable will consist of those sales that occurred in the last N days. If sales are evenly distributed throughout the year, receivables will equal $(N/365)$ times annual sales. Thus, receivables equal to 15% of sales corresponds to an average payment period of $N = 15\% \times 365 = 55$ accounts receivable days. The same is true for payables. (See also Eq. 2.11 in Chapter 2.)

We can use our forecast of HomeNet's net working capital requirements to complete our estimate of HomeNet's free cash flow in Table 8.3. In year 1, net working capital increases by $2.1 million. This increase represents a cost to the firm as shown in line 12 of Table 8.3. This reduction of free cash flow corresponds to the fact that $3.525 million of the firm's sales in year 1 and $1.425 million of its costs have not yet been paid.

In years 2–4, net working capital does not change, so no further contributions are needed. In year 5, after the project is shut down, net working capital falls by $2.1 million as the payments of the last customers are received and the final bills are paid. We add this $2.1 million to free cash flow in year 5, as shown in line 12 of Table 8.3.

Now that we have adjusted HomeNet's unlevered net income for depreciation, capital expenditures, and increases to net working capital, we compute HomeNet's free cash flow as shown in line 13 of the spreadsheet in Table 8.3. Note that in the first two years, free cash flow is lower than unlevered net income, reflecting the upfront investment in equipment and net working capital required by the project. In later years, free cash flow exceeds unlevered net income because depreciation is not a cash expense. In the last year, the firm ultimately recovers the investment in net working capital, further boosting the free cash flow.

EXAMPLE 8.4 **Net Working Capital with Changing Sales**

Problem

Forecast the required investment in net working capital for HomeNet under the scenario in Example 8.3.

Solution

Required investments in net working capital are shown below:

	Year	0	1	2	3	4	5
Net Working Capital Forecast ($000s)							
1	Receivables (15% of Sales)	—	3,525	3,966	3,569	1,285	—
2	Payables (15% of COGS)	—	(1,425)	(1,603)	(1,443)	(519)	—
3	**Net Working Capital**	—	2,100	2,363	2,126	765	—
4	**Increases in NWC**	—	**2,100**	**263**	**(237)**	**(1,361)**	**(765)**

In this case, working capital changes each year. A large initial investment in working capital is required in year 1, followed by a small investment in year 2 as sales continue to grow. Working capital is recovered in years 3–5 as sales decline.

Calculating Free Cash Flow Directly

As we noted at the outset of this chapter, because practitioners usually begin the capital budgeting process by first forecasting earnings, we have chosen to do the same. However, we could have calculated the HomeNet's free cash flow directly by using the following shorthand formula:

Free Cash Flow

$$\text{Free Cash Flow} = \overbrace{(\text{Revenues} - \text{Costs} - \text{Depreciation}) \times (1 - \tau_c)}^{\text{Unlevered Net Income}} + \text{Depreciation} - \text{CapEx} - \Delta NWC \quad (8.5)$$

Note that we first deduct depreciation when computing the project's incremental earnings, and then add it back (because it is a non-cash expense) when computing free cash flow.

Thus, the only effect of depreciation is to reduce the firm's taxable income. Indeed, we can rewrite Eq. 8.5 as

$$\text{Free Cash Flow} = (\text{Revenues} - \text{Costs}) \times (1 - \tau_c) - \text{CapEx} - \Delta NWC + \tau_c \times \text{Depreciation} \tag{8.6}$$

The last term in Eq. 8.6, $\tau_c \times$ Depreciation, is called the **depreciation tax shield**. It is the tax savings that results from the ability to deduct depreciation. As a consequence, depreciation expenses have a *positive* impact on free cash flow. Firms often report a different depreciation expense for accounting and for tax purposes. Because only the tax consequences of depreciation are relevant for free cash flow, we should use the depreciation expense that the firm will use for tax purposes in our forecast.

Calculating the NPV

To compute HomeNet's NPV, we must discount its free cash flow at the appropriate cost of capital.[8] As discussed in Chapter 5, the cost of capital for a project is the expected return that investors could earn on their best alternative investment with similar risk and maturity. We will develop the techniques needed to estimate the cost of capital in Part 4. For now, we assume that Cisco's managers believe that the HomeNet project will have similar risk to other projects within Cisco's router division, and that the appropriate cost of capital for these projects is 12%.

Given this cost of capital, we compute the present value of each free cash flow in the future. As explained in Chapter 4, if the cost of capital $r = 12\%$, the present value of the free cash flow in year t (or FCF_t) is

$$PV(FCF_t) = \frac{FCF_t}{(1+r)^t} = FCF_t \times \underbrace{\frac{1}{(1+r)^t}}_{t\text{-year discount factor}} \tag{8.7}$$

We compute the NPV of the HomeNet project in the spreadsheet in Table 8.5. Line 3 calculates the discount factor, and line 4 multiplies the free cash flow by the discount factor to get the present value. The NPV of the project is the sum of the present values of each free cash flow, reported on line 5:[9]

$$NPV = -16{,}500 + 4554 + 5740 + 5125 + 4576 + 1532 = 5027$$

TABLE 8.5 SPREADSHEET Computing HomeNet's NPV

		Year	0	1	2	3	4	5
Net Present Value ($000s)								
1	**Free Cash Flow**		(16,500)	5,100	7,200	7,200	7,200	2,700
2	Project Cost of Capital	12%						
3	Discount Factor		1.000	0.893	0.797	0.712	0.636	0.567
4	**PV of Free Cash Flow**		(16,500)	4,554	5,740	5,125	4,576	1,532
5	**NPV**		**5,027**					

[8]Rather than draw a separate timeline for these cash flows, we can interpret the final line of the spreadsheet in Table 8.3 as the timeline.

[9]We can also compute the NPV using the Excel NPV function to calculate the present value of the cash flows in year 1 through 5, and then add the cash flow in year 0 (i.e., "$=NPV(r, FCF_1{:}FCF_5)+FCF_0$").

USING EXCEL

Capital Budgeting Using a Spreadsheet Program

Capital budgeting forecasts and analysis are most easily performed in a spreadsheet program. Here we highlight a few best practices when developing your own capital budgets.

Create a Project Dashboard

All capital budgeting analyses begin with a set of assumptions regarding future revenues and costs associated with the investment. Centralize these assumptions within your spreadsheet in a project dashboard so they are easy to locate, review, and potentially modify. Here we show an example for the HomeNet project.

	A–C	D	E	F	G	H	I
1	**HomeNet Capital Budget**						
2	***Key Assumptions***	**Year 0**	**Year 1**	**Year 2**	**Year 3**	**Year 4**	**Year 5**
3	*Revenues & Costs*						
4	HomeNet Units Sold	-	100	100	100	100	-
8	HomeNet Ave. Price/Unit	-	$260.00	$260.00	$260.00	$260.00	-
9	HomeNet Cost/Unit	-	$110.00	$110.00	$110.00	$110.00	-
10	Cannibalization Rate	-	25%	25%	25%	25%	-
11	Old Product Ave. Price/Unit	-	$100.00	$100.00	$100.00	$100.00	-
12	Old Product Cost/Unit	-	$60.00	$60.00	$60.00	$60.00	-
13	*Operating Expenses*						
14	Marketing & Support	-	(2,800)	(2,800)	(2,800)	(2,800)	-
15	Lost Rent	-	(200)	(200)	(200)	(200)	-
16	Hardware R&D	(5,000)	-	-	-	-	-
17	Software R&D	(10,000)	-	-	-	-	-
18	Lab Equipment	(7,500)	-	-	-	-	-
19	*Other Assumptions*						
20	*depreciation schedule*	*0.0%*	*20.0%*	*20.0%*	*20.0%*	*20.0%*	*20.0%*
21	*corporate tax rate*	*40.0%*	*40.0%*	*40.0%*	*40.0%*	*40.0%*	*40.0%*
22	*receivables (% sales)*	*15.0%*	*15.0%*	*15.0%*	*15.0%*	*15.0%*	*15.0%*
23	*payables (% cogs)*	*15.0%*	*15.0%*	*15.0%*	*15.0%*	*15.0%*	*15.0%*

Color Code for Clarity

In spreadsheet models, use a blue font color to distinguish numerical assumptions from formulas. For example, HomeNet's revenue and cost estimates are set to a numerical value in year 1, whereas estimates in later years are set to equal to the year 1 estimates. It is therefore clear which cells contain the main assumptions, should we wish to change them at a later date.

Maintain Flexibility

In the HomeNet dashboard, note that we state all assumptions on an annual basis even if we expect them to remain constant. For example, we specify HomeNet's unit volume and average sale price for each year. We can then calculate HomeNet revenues each year based on the corresponding annual assumptions. Doing so provides flexibility if we later determine that HomeNet's adoption rate might vary over time or if we expect prices to follow a trend, as in Example 8.3.

Never Hardcode

So that your assumptions are clear and easy to modify, reference any numerical values you need to develop your projections in the project dashboard. Never "hardcode," or enter numerical values directly into formulas. For example, in the computation of taxes in cell E34 below, we use the formula "=−E21*E33" rather than "=−0.40*E33". While the latter formula would compute the same answer, because the tax rate is hardcoded it would be difficult to update the model if the forecast for the tax rate were to change.

	A–C	D	E	F	G	H	I
26	***Incremental Earnings Forecast***	**Year 0**	**Year 1**	**Year 2**	**Year 3**	**Year 4**	**Year 5**
33	**EBIT**	(15,000)	9,500	9,500	9,500	9,500	(1,500)
34	**Taxes**	6,000	=-E21*E33	(3,800)	(3,800)	(3,800)	600
35	**Unlevered Net Income**	(9,000)	5,700	5,700	5,700	5,700	(900)

Based on our estimates, HomeNet's NPV is $5.027 million. While HomeNet's upfront cost is $16.5 million, the present value of the additional free cash flow that Cisco will receive from the project is $21.5 million. Thus, taking the HomeNet project is equivalent to Cisco having an extra $5 million in the bank today.

CONCEPT CHECK

1. What adjustments must you make to a project's unlevered net income to determine its free cash flows?
2. What is the depreciation tax shield?

8.3 Choosing Among Alternatives

Thus far, we have considered the capital budgeting decision to launch the HomeNet product line. To analyze the decision, we computed the project's free cash flow and calculated the NPV. Because *not* launching HomeNet produces an additional NPV of zero for the firm, launching HomeNet is the best decision for the firm if its NPV is positive. In many situations, however, we must compare mutually exclusive alternatives, each of which has consequences for the firm's cash flows. As we explained in Chapter 7, in such cases we can make the best decision by first computing the free cash flow associated with each alternative and then choosing the alternative with the highest NPV.

Evaluating Manufacturing Alternatives

Suppose Cisco is considering an alternative manufacturing plan for the HomeNet product. The current plan is to fully outsource production at a cost of $110 per unit. Alternatively, Cisco could assemble the product in-house at a cost of $95 per unit. However, the latter option will require $5 million in upfront operating expenses to reorganize the assembly facility, and starting in year 1 Cisco will need to maintain inventory equal to one month's production.

To choose between these two alternatives, we compute the free cash flow associated with each choice and compare their NPVs to see which is most advantageous for the firm. When comparing alternatives, we need to compare only those cash flows that differ between them. We can ignore any cash flows that are the same under either scenario (e.g., HomeNet's revenues).

The spreadsheet in Table 8.6 compares the two assembly options, computing the NPV of the cash costs for each. The difference in EBIT results from the upfront cost of setting up the in-house facility in year 0, and the differing assembly costs: $110/unit $\times$ 100,000 units/yr = $11 million/yr outsourced, versus $95/unit $\times$ 100,000 units/yr = $9.5 million/yr in-house. Adjusting for taxes, we see the consequences for unlevered net income on lines 3 and 9.

Because the options do not differ in terms of capital expenditures (there are none associated with assembly), to compare the free cash flow for each, we only need to adjust for their different net working capital requirements. If assembly is outsourced, payables account for 15% of the cost of goods, or 15% $\times$ $11 million = $1.65 million. This amount is the credit Cisco will receive from its supplier in year 1 and will maintain until year 5. Because Cisco will borrow this amount from its supplier, net working capital *falls* by $1.65 million in year 1, adding to Cisco's free cash flow. In year 5, Cisco's net working capital will increase as Cisco pays its suppliers, and free cash flow will fall by an equal amount.

TABLE 8.6 SPREADSHEET NPV Cost of Outsourced Versus In-House Assembly of HomeNet

	Year	0	1	2	3	4	5
Outsourced Assembly ($000s)							
1	**EBIT**	—	(11,000)	(11,000)	(11,000)	(11,000)	—
2	Income Tax at 40%	—	4,400	4,400	4,400	4,400	—
3	**Unlevered Net Income**	—	(6,600)	(6,600)	(6,600)	(6,600)	—
4	Less: Increases in NWC	—	1,650	—	—	—	(1,650)
5	**Free Cash Flow**	**—**	**(4,950)**	**(6,600)**	**(6,600)**	**(6,600)**	**(1,650)**
6	**NPV at 12%**	**(19,510)**					

	Year	0	1	2	3	4	5
In-House Assembly ($000s)							
7	**EBIT**	(5,000)	(9,500)	(9,500)	(9,500)	(9,500)	—
8	Income Tax at 40%	2,000	3,800	3,800	3,800	3,800	—
9	**Unlevered Net Income**	(3,000)	(5,700)	(5,700)	(5,700)	(5,700)	—
10	Less: Increases in NWC	—	633	—	—	—	(633)
11	**Free Cash Flow**	**(3,000)**	**(5,067)**	**(5,700)**	**(5,700)**	**(5,700)**	**(633)**
12	**NPV at 12%**	**(20,107)**					

If assembly is done in-house, payables are $15\% \times \$9.5$ million = $1.425 million. However, Cisco will need to maintain inventory equal to one month's production, which has cost of $\$9.5$ million $\div 12 = \$0.792$ million. Thus, Cisco's net working capital will decrease by $1.425 million − $0.792 million = $0.633 million in year 1 and will increase by the same amount in year 5.

Comparing Free Cash Flows for Cisco's Alternatives

Adjusting for increases to net working capital, we compare the free cash flow of each alternative on lines 5 and 11 and compute their NPVs using the project's 12% cost of capital.[10] In each case, the NPV is negative, as we are evaluating only the costs of production. Outsourcing, however, is somewhat cheaper, with a present value cost of $19.5 million versus $20.1 million if the units are produced in-house.[11]

CONCEPT CHECK

1. How do you choose between mutually exclusive capital budgeting decisions?
2. When choosing between alternatives, what cash flows can be ignored?

[10] While we assume it is not the case here, in some settings the risks of these options might differ from the risk of the project overall or from each other, requiring a different cost of capital for each case.

[11] It is also possible to compare these two cases in a single spreadsheet in which we compute the difference in the free cash flows directly, rather than compute the free cash flows separately for each option. We prefer to do them separately, as it is clearer and generalizes to the case when there are more than two options.

8.4 Further Adjustments to Free Cash Flow

In this section, we consider a number of complications that can arise when estimating a project's free cash flow, such as non-cash charges, alternative depreciation methods, liquidation or continuation values, and tax loss carryforwards.

Other Non-Cash Items. In general, other non-cash items that appear as part of incremental earnings should not be included in the project's free cash flow. The firm should include only actual cash revenues or expenses. For example, the firm adds back any amortization of intangible assets (such as patents) to unlevered net income when calculating free cash flow.

Timing of Cash Flows. For simplicity, we have treated the cash flows for HomeNet as if they occur at the end of each year. In reality, cash flows will be spread throughout the year. We can forecast free cash flow on a quarterly, monthly, or even continuous basis when greater accuracy is required.

Accelerated Depreciation. Because depreciation contributes positively to the firm's cash flow through the depreciation tax shield, it is in the firm's best interest to use the most accelerated method of depreciation that is allowable for tax purposes. By doing so, the firm will accelerate its tax savings and increase their present value. In the United States, the most accelerated depreciation method allowed by the IRS is MACRS (Modified Accelerated Cost Recovery System) depreciation. With **MACRS depreciation**, the firm first categorizes assets according to their recovery period. Based on the recovery period, MACRS depreciation tables assign a fraction of the purchase price that the firm can recover each year. We provide MACRS tables and recovery periods for common assets in the appendix.

EXAMPLE 8.5 Computing Accelerated Depreciation

Problem

What depreciation deduction would be allowed for HomeNet's equipment using the MACRS method, assuming the equipment is put into use by the end of year 0 and designated to have a five-year recovery period?

Solution

Table 8A.1 in the appendix provides the percentage of the cost that can be depreciated each year. Based on the table, the allowable depreciation expense for the lab equipment is shown below (in thousands of dollars):

	Year	0	1	2	3	4	5
MACRS Depreciation							
1	Lab Equipment Cost	(7,500)					
2	MACRS Depreciation Rate	20.00%	32.00%	19.20%	11.52%	11.52%	5.76%
3	Depreciation Expense	(1,500)	(2,400)	(1,440)	(864)	(864)	(432)

As long as the equipment is put into use by the end of year 0, the tax code allows us to take our first depreciation expense in the same year. Compared with straight-line depreciation, the MACRS method allows for larger depreciation deductions earlier in the asset's life, which increases the present value of the depreciation tax shield and so will raise the project's NPV. In the case of HomeNet, MACRS depreciation increases NPV by over $300,000 to $5.34 million.

Liquidation or Salvage Value. Assets that are no longer needed often have a resale value, or some salvage value if the parts are sold for scrap. Some assets may have a negative liquidation value. For example, it may cost money to remove and dispose of the used equipment.

In the calculation of free cash flow, we include the liquidation value of any assets that are no longer needed and may be disposed of. When an asset is liquidated, any gain on sale is taxed. We calculate the gain on sale as the difference between the sale price and the book value of the asset:

$$\text{Gain on Sale} = \text{Sale Price} - \text{Book Value} \tag{8.8}$$

The book value is equal to the asset's original cost less the amount it has already been depreciated for tax purposes:

$$\text{Book Value} = \text{Purchase Price} - \text{Accumulated Depreciation} \tag{8.9}$$

We must adjust the project's free cash flow to account for the after-tax cash flow that would result from an asset sale:[12]

$$\text{After-Tax Cash Flow from Asset Sale} = \text{Sale Price} - (\tau_c \times \text{Gain on Sale}) \tag{8.10}$$

EXAMPLE 8.6 Adding Salvage Value to Free Cash Flow

Problem

Suppose that in addition to the $7.5 million in new equipment required for HomeNet, some equipment will be transferred to the lab from another Cisco facility. This equipment has a resale value of $2 million and a book value of $1 million. If the equipment is kept rather than sold, its remaining book value can be depreciated next year. When the lab is shut down in year 5, the equipment will have a salvage value of $800,000. What adjustments must we make to HomeNet's free cash flow in this case?

Solution

The existing equipment could have been sold for $2 million. The after-tax proceeds from this sale are an opportunity cost of using the equipment in the HomeNet lab. Thus, we must reduce HomeNet's free cash flow in year 0 by the sale price less any taxes that would have been owed had the sale occurred: $2 million − 40% × ($2 million − $1 million) = $1.6 million.

In year 1, the remaining $1 million book value of the equipment can be depreciated, creating a depreciation tax shield of 40% × $1 million = $400,000. In year 5, the firm will sell the equipment for a salvage value of $800,000. Because the equipment will be fully depreciated at that time, the entire amount will be taxable as a capital gain, so the after-tax cash flow from the sale is $800,000 × (1 − 40%) = $480,000.

The spreadsheet below shows these adjustments to the free cash flow from the spreadsheet in Table 8.3 and recalculates HomeNet's free cash flow and NPV in this case.

	Year	0	1	2	3	4	5
	Free Cash Flow and NPV ($000s)						
1	Free Cash Flow w/o equipment	(16,500)	5,100	7,200	7,200	7,200	2,700
	Adjustments for use of existing equipment						
2	After-Tax Salvage Value	(1,600)	—	—	—	—	480
3	Depreciation Tax Shield	—	400	—	—	—	—
4	**Free Cash Flow with equipment**	**(18,100)**	**5,500**	**7,200**	**7,200**	**7,200**	**3,180**
5	**NPV at 12%**	**4,055**					

[12]When the sale price is less than the original purchase price of the asset, the gain on sale is treated as a recapture of depreciation and taxed as ordinary income. If the sale price exceeds the original purchase price, then this portion of the gain on sale is considered a capital gain, and in some cases may be taxed at a lower capital gains tax rate.

Terminal or Continuation Value. Sometimes the firm explicitly forecasts free cash flow over a shorter horizon than the full horizon of the project or investment. This is necessarily true for investments with an indefinite life, such as an expansion of the firm. In this case, we estimate the value of the remaining free cash flow beyond the forecast horizon by including an additional, one-time cash flow at the end of the forecast horizon called the **terminal** or **continuation value** of the project. This amount represents the market value (as of the last forecast period) of the free cash flow from the project at all future dates.

Depending on the setting, we use different methods for estimating the continuation value of an investment. For example, when analyzing investments with long lives, it is common to explicitly calculate free cash flow over a short horizon, and then assume that cash flows grow at some constant rate beyond the forecast horizon.

EXAMPLE 8.7 Continuation Value with Perpetual Growth

Problem

Base Hardware is considering opening a set of new retail stores. The free cash flow projections for the new stores are shown below (in millions of dollars):

0	1	2	3	4	5	6	...
−\$10.5	−\$5.5	\$0.8	\$1.2	\$1.3	\$1.3 × 1.05	\$1.3 × (1.05)^2	

After year 4, Base Hardware expects free cash flow from the stores to increase at a rate of 5% per year. If the appropriate cost of capital for this investment is 10%, what continuation value in year 4 captures the value of future free cash flows in year 5 and beyond? What is the NPV of the new stores?

Solution

Because the future free cash flow beyond year 4 is expected to grow at 5% per year, the continuation value in year 4 of the free cash flow in year 5 and beyond can be calculated as a constant growth perpetuity:

$$\text{Continuation Value in Year 4} = PV(\text{FCF in Year 5 and Beyond})$$

$$= \frac{FCF_4 \times (1+g)}{r-g} = \$1.30 \text{ million} \times \frac{1.05}{0.10 - 0.05}$$

$$= \$1.30 \text{ million} \times 21 = \$27.3 \text{ million}$$

Notice that under the assumption of constant growth, we can compute the continuation value as a multiple of the project's final free cash flow.

We can restate the free cash flows of the investment as follows (in thousands of dollars):

Year	0	1	2	3	4
Free Cash Flow (Years 0–4)	(10,500)	(5,500)	800	1,200	1,300
Continuation Value					27,300
Free Cash Flow	(10,500)	(5,500)	800	1,200	28,600

The NPV of the investment in the new stores is

$$NPV = -10{,}500 - \frac{5500}{1.10} + \frac{800}{1.10^2} + \frac{1200}{1.10^3} + \frac{28{,}600}{1.10^4} = \$5597$$

or \$5.597 million.

Tax Carryforwards. A firm generally identifies its marginal tax rate by determining the tax bracket that it falls into based on its overall level of pretax income. Two additional features of the tax code, called **tax loss carryforwards and carrybacks**, allow corporations to take losses during a current year and offset them against gains in nearby years. Since 1997, companies can "carry back" losses for two years and "carry forward" losses for 20 years. This tax rule means that the firm can offset losses during one year against income for the last two years, or save the losses to be offset against income during the next 20 years. When a firm can carry back losses, it receives a refund for back taxes in the current year. Otherwise, the firm must carry forward the loss and use it to offset future taxable income. When a firm has tax loss carryforwards well in excess of its current pretax income, then additional income it earns today will not increase the taxes it owes until after it exhausts its carryforwards. This delay reduces the present value of the tax liability.

EXAMPLE 8.8 Tax Loss Carryforwards

Problem

Verian Industries has outstanding tax loss carryforwards of $100 million from losses over the past six years. If Verian earns $30 million per year in pretax income from now on, when will it first pay taxes? If Verian earns an extra $5 million this coming year, in which year will its taxes increase?

Solution

With pretax income of $30 million per year, Verian will be able to use its tax loss carryforwards to avoid paying taxes until year 4 (in millions of dollars):

Year	1	2	3	4	5
Pretax Income	30	30	30	30	30
Tax Loss Carryforward	−30	−30	−30	−10	
Taxable Income	0	0	0	20	30

If Verian earns an additional $5 million the first year, it will owe taxes on an extra $5 million in year 4:

Year	1	2	3	4	5
Pretax Income	35	30	30	30	30
Tax Loss Carryforward	−35	−30	−30	−5	
Taxable Income	0	0	0	25	30

Thus, when a firm has tax loss carryforwards, the tax impact of current earnings will be delayed until the carryforwards are exhausted. This delay reduces the present value of the tax impact, and firms sometimes approximate the effect of tax loss carryforwards by using a lower marginal tax rate.

CONCEPT CHECK

1. Explain why it is advantageous for a firm to use the most accelerated depreciation schedule possible for tax purposes.
2. What is the continuation or terminal value of a project?

GLOBAL FINANCIAL CRISIS **The American Recovery and Reinvestment Act of 2009**

On February 17, 2009, President Obama signed into law the American Recovery and Reinvestment Act. The Act, like the earlier Economic Stimulus Act of 2008, included a number of tax changes designed to help businesses and stimulate investment:

Bonus Depreciation. The Act extended a temporary rule (first passed as part of the Economic Stimulus Act of 2008) allowing additional first-year depreciation of 50% of the cost of the asset. By further accelerating the depreciation allowance, this measure increases the present value of the depreciation tax shields associated with new capital expenditures, raising the NPV of such investment.

Increased Section 179 Expensing of Capital Expenditures. Section 179 of the tax code allows small- and medium-sized businesses to immediately deduct the full purchase price of capital equipment rather than depreciate it over time. Congress doubled the limit for this deduction to a maximum of $250,000 in 2008, and this higher limit was extended by the Act through 2009. Again, being able to receive the tax deductions for such expenses immediately increases their present value and makes investment more attractive.

Extended Loss Carrybacks for Small Businesses. Under the Act, small businesses could carry back losses incurred in 2008 for up to five years, rather than two years. While this extension did not directly affect the NPV of new investments, it meant struggling businesses were more likely to receive refunds of taxes already paid, providing much-needed cash in the midst of the financial crisis.

8.5 Analyzing the Project

When evaluating a capital budgeting project, financial managers should make the decision that maximizes NPV. As we have discussed, to compute the NPV for a project, you need to estimate the incremental cash flows and choose a discount rate. Given these inputs, the NPV calculation is relatively straightforward. The most difficult part of capital budgeting is deciding how to estimate the cash flows and cost of capital. These estimates are often subject to significant uncertainty. In this section, we look at methods that assess the importance of this uncertainty and identify the drivers of value in the project.

Break-Even Analysis

When we are uncertain regarding the input to a capital budgeting decision, it is often useful to determine the **break-even** level of that input, which is the level for which the investment has an NPV of zero. One example of a break-even level that we have already considered is the calculation of the internal rate of return (IRR). Recall from Chapter 7 that the IRR of a project tells you the maximal error in the cost of capital before the optimal investment decision would change. Using the Excel function IRR, the spreadsheet in Table 8.7 calculates an IRR of 24.1% for the free cash flow of the HomeNet project.[13] Hence, the true cost of capital can be as high as 24.1% and the project will still have a positive NPV.

TABLE 8.7 SPREADSHEET **HomeNet IRR Calculation**

	Year	0	1	2	3	4	5
NPV ($000s) and IRR							
1 **Free Cash Flow**		(16,500)	5,100	7,200	7,200	7,200	2,700
2 **NPV at 12%**		**5,027**					
3 **IRR**		24.1%					

[13] The format in Excel is = IRR(FCF0:FCF5).

TABLE 8.8 Break-Even Levels for HomeNet

Parameter	Break-Even Level
Units sold	79,759 units per year
Wholesale price	$232 per unit
Cost of goods	$138 per unit
Cost of capital	24.1%

There is no reason to limit our attention to the uncertainty in the cost of capital estimate. In a **break-even analysis**, for each parameter, we calculate the value at which the NPV of the project is zero.[14] Table 8.8 shows the break-even level for several key parameters. For example, based on the initial assumptions, the HomeNet project will break even with a sales level of just under 80,000 units per year. Alternatively, at a sales level of 100,000 units per year, the project will break even with a sales price of $232 per unit.

We have examined the break-even levels in terms of the project's NPV, which is the most useful perspective for decision making. Other accounting notions of break-even are sometimes considered, however. For example, we could compute the **EBIT break-even** for sales, which is the level of sales for which the project's EBIT is zero. While HomeNet's EBIT break-even level of sales is only about 32,000 units per year, given the large upfront investment required in HomeNet, its NPV is −$11.8 million at that sales level.

Sensitivity Analysis

Another important capital budgeting tool is sensitivity analysis. **Sensitivity analysis** breaks the NPV calculation into its component assumptions and shows how the NPV varies as the underlying assumptions change. In this way, sensitivity analysis allows us to explore the effects of errors in our NPV estimates for the project. By conducting a sensitivity analysis, we learn which assumptions are the most important; we can then invest further resources and effort to refine these assumptions. Such an analysis also reveals which aspects of the project are most critical when we are actually managing the project.

To illustrate, consider the assumptions underlying the calculation of HomeNet's NPV. There is likely to be significant uncertainty surrounding each revenue and cost assumption. Table 8.9 shows the base-case assumptions, together with the best and worst cases, for several key aspects of the project.

TABLE 8.9 Best- and Worst-Case Parameter Assumptions for HomeNet

Parameter	Initial Assumption	Worst Case	Best Case
Units sold (thousands)	100	70	130
Sale price ($/unit)	260	240	280
Cost of goods ($/unit)	110	120	100
NWC ($ thousands)	2100	3000	1600
Cannibalization	25%	40%	10%
Cost of capital	12%	15%	10%

[14]These break-even levels can be calculated by simple trial and error within Excel, or using the Excel goal seek or solver tools.

To determine the importance of this uncertainty, we recalculate the NPV of the HomeNet project under the best- and worst-case assumptions for each parameter. For example, if the number of units sold is only 70,000 per year, the NPV of the project falls to −\$2.4 million. We repeat this calculation for each parameter. The result is shown in Figure 8.1, which reveals that the most important parameter assumptions are the number of units sold and the sale price per unit. These assumptions deserve the greatest scrutiny during the estimation process. In addition, as the most important drivers of the project's value, these factors deserve close attention when managing the project.

EXAMPLE 8.9 Sensitivity to Marketing and Support Costs

Problem

The current forecast for HomeNet's marketing and support costs is \$3 million per year during years 1–4. Suppose the marketing and support costs may be as high as \$4 million per year. What is HomeNet's NPV in this case?

Solution

We can answer this question by changing the selling, general, and administrative expense to \$4 million in the spreadsheet in Table 8.3 and computing the NPV of the resulting free cash flow. We can also calculate the impact of this change as follows: A \$1 million increase in marketing and support costs will reduce EBIT by \$1 million and will, therefore, decrease HomeNet's free cash flow by an after-tax amount of \$1 million × (1 − 40%) = \$0.6 million per year. The present value of this decrease is

$$PV = \frac{-0.6}{1.12} + \frac{-0.6}{1.12^2} + \frac{-0.6}{1.12^3} + \frac{-0.6}{1.12^4} = -\$1.8 \text{ million}$$

HomeNet's NPV would fall to \$5.0 million − \$1.8 million = \$3.2 million.

FIGURE 8.1

HomeNet's NPV Under Best-and Worst-Case Parameter Assumptions

Green bars show the change in NPV under the best-case assumption for each parameter; red bars show the change under the worst-case assumption. Also shown are the break-even levels for each parameter. Under the initial assumptions, HomeNet's NPV is \$5.0 million.

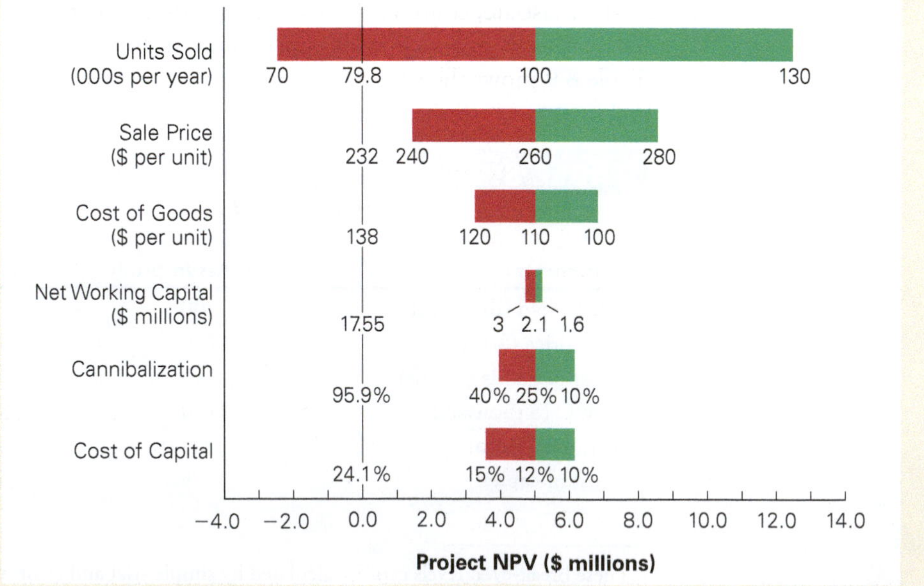

INTERVIEW WITH DAVID HOLLAND

David Holland, Senior Vice President and Treasurer of Cisco, is responsible for managing all funding, risk, and capital market activities related to the firm's $50 billion balance sheet.

QUESTION: *What is the importance of considering free cash flow, as opposed to just the earnings implications of a financial decision?*

ANSWER: There is an adage saying, "Cash flow is a fact and earnings are an opinion." Earnings use an accounting framework and are governed by many rules, making it hard to know what earnings tell the investor. The economics of cash flow are clear: We can't dispute whether cash has come in or gone out. Cisco's investment decisions are based primarily on cash flow models because they take project risk into account and show the impact on value creation for owners of the business.

QUESTION: *What key financial metrics does Cisco use to make investment decisions?*

ANSWER: Cisco focuses primarily on net present value (NPV) for investment decisions. Robust NPV analysis goes beyond simply accepting projects with positive NPVs and rejecting those with negative NPVs. It identifies the key drivers that affect project success and demonstrates the interplay between factors that affect cash flow. For example, running a model using a lower margin approach shows us the impact on revenue growth and on operating cost structures. We can compare that to a higher margin (premium pricing) approach. The business unit manager learns how to control aspects of the business model to alleviate risk or accelerate the upside potential.

We prefer NPV to internal rate of return (IRR), which may return multiple answers or give false signals as to an investment's profitability, depending on the organization of cash flows. An attraction of IRR analysis is the ease of comparing percentage returns. However, this method hides the scope of a project. A project with a 25% return may generate $1 million in shareholder value, while another with a 13% IRR might produce $1 billion. NPV captures the size of the return in dollar terms and shows a project's impact on share price. NPV also creates an ownership framework for employees whose compensation package includes some form of stock ownership, directly tying the decision-making criteria to stock price.

QUESTION: *When developing a model to analyze a new investment, how do you deal with the uncertainty surrounding estimates, especially for new technologies?*

ANSWER: Cisco relies on strong financial modeling for the thousands of investment decisions we make every year. Our 2500 finance people worldwide work with the internal client—the business lead—to understand the assumptions in the model and to check the model's result against alternative assumptions. Evaluating the cash flows for technology projects, especially new technology, is difficult. When you buy an oil refinery, you can see the throughput and the cash flows. Identifying the relevant savings from a component technology for a larger router or switch product or a strategic move into a new area is more complex and intangible. Scenario and sensitivity analyses and game theory help us control risk by adjusting our strategy. We also look at the qualitative aspects, such as how the strategy fits into the customer sector and the directions customers are moving with their tech platforms.

QUESTION: *How does Cisco adjust for risk?*

ANSWER: To stay competitive in the technology space, we must be prepared to take some level of risk, even in down markets. We apply the same discount rate to all projects in a category, based on their market risk (i.e., sensitivity to market conditions). We do not adjust the discount rate to account for project-specific risks, because our required return has not changed and that would distort the true value of the company. To assess a project's unique risks, we model the upside or downside of cash flows with scenario and sensitivity analysis. We might analyze the sensitivity of a project's NPV to a 1% change in both revenue growth and operating costs. Then we run the model with other assumptions, developing base, optimistic, and bearish cases. We discuss these models with the business lead and rerun the models based on their input. This process improves our potential outcome and project profitability.

Scenario Analysis

In the analysis thus far, we have considered the consequences of varying only one parameter at a time. In reality, certain factors may affect more than one parameter. **Scenario analysis** considers the effect on the NPV of changing multiple project parameters. For example, lowering HomeNet's price may increase the number of units sold. We can use scenario analysis to evaluate alternative pricing strategies for the HomeNet product in Table 8.10. In this case, the current strategy is optimal. Figure 8.2 shows the combinations of price and volume that lead to the same NPV of $5 million for HomeNet as the current strategy. Only strategies with price and volume combinations above the line will lead to a higher NPV.

TABLE 8.10 Scenario Analysis of Alternative Pricing Strategies

Strategy	Sale Price ($/unit)	Expected Units Sold (thousands)	NPV ($ thousands)
Current strategy	260	100	5027
Price reduction	245	110	4582
Price Increase	275	90	4937

FIGURE 8.2

Price and Volume Combinations for HomeNet with Equivalent NPV

The graph shows alternative price per unit and annual volume combinations that lead to an NPV of $5.0 million. Pricing strategies with combinations above this line will lead to a higher NPV and are superior.

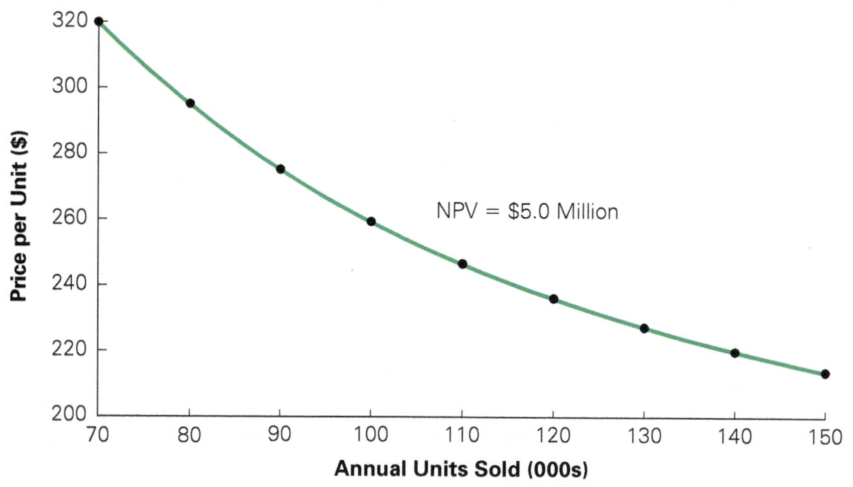

CONCEPT CHECK

1. What is sensitivity analysis?
2. How does scenario analysis differ from sensitivity analysis?

USING EXCEL

Project Analysis Using Excel

Here we describe several useful Excel tools that assist with project analysis.

Goal Seek for Break-Even Analysis

Excel's goal seek function determines the break-even point for key assumptions in our model. For example, to determine the break-even level of units for annual sales, use the Goal Seek window (see the Data > What-If Analysis menu, or keyboard shortcut Alt-A-W-G). The set cell is the cell in which we calculated NPV (cell D51). To set its value to 0 (break-even), we change the average sale price (cell E8). Excel will then use trial and error to find the sale price at which the project's NPV is zero—in this case $231.66.

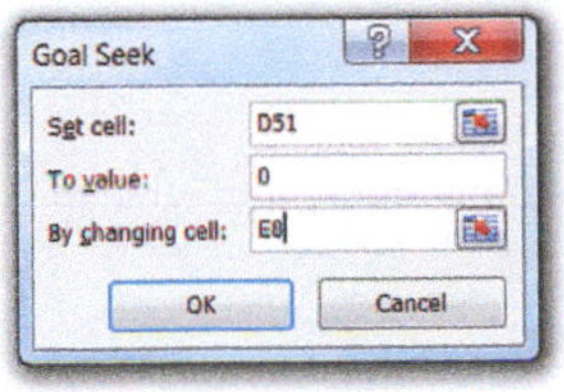

	A	B	C	D	E	F	G	H	I
1	HomeNet Capital Budget								
2	*Key Assumptions*			Year 0	Year 1	Year 2	Year 3	Year 4	Year 5
8		HomeNet Ave. Price/Unit		-	$260.00	$260.00	$260.00	$260.00	-
51	NPV			5,026					

Data Tables for Sensitivity Analysis

Data tables, which we introduced in the appendix of Chapter 7 to construct the NPV profile, allow us to compute the sensitivity of NPV to any other input variable in our financial model. Excel can also compute a two-dimensional data table showing the sensitivity of NPV to two inputs simultaneously. For example, the data table below shows NPVs for different combinations of the Hardware R&D budget and HomeNet's manufacturing costs.

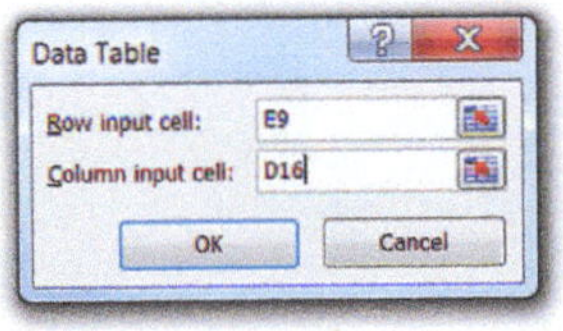

	C	D	E	F	G	H
55	NPV		HomeNet Cost / Unit			
56	Hardware R&D Expense	5,026	$110	$105	$100	$95
57		(5,000)	5,026	5,913	6,800	7,686
58		(5,500)	4,726	5,613	6,500	7,386
59		(6,000)	4,426	5,313	6,200	7,086
60		(6,500)	4,126	5,013	5,900	6,786
61		(7,000)	3,826	4,713	5,600	6,486
62		(7,500)	3,526	4,413	5,300	6,186
63		(8,000)	3,226	4,113	5,000	5,886
64		(8,500)	2,926	3,813	4,700	5,586
65		(9,000)	2,626	3,513	4,400	5,286
66		(9,500)	2,326	3,213	4,100	4,986
67		(10,000)	2,026	2,913	3,800	4,686

To construct this data table, put the values of each input along the sides of the table (shown in blue), and a formula for the value we want to compute in the upper left corner (cell D56, which in this case is just a link to the cell in which we computed the NPV). Select the entire table (D56:H67), bring up the Data Table window (see the Data > What-If Analysis menu or keyboard shortcut Alt-D-T), and input the locations in our project dashboard (see page 251) of the cost assumption (row input cell E9) and hardware budget (column input cell D16). The data table shows, for example, that NPV increases if we lower our manufacturing cost to $100 per unit by increasing the hardware budget to $7.5 million.

Scenarios in the Project Dashboard

The project dashboard on page 251 only shows our base-case assumptions. We can build multiple scenarios into our project dashboard by adding additional rows with alternative assumptions, and then using Excel's index function to select the scenario we would like to use in our analysis. For example, rows 5–7 below show alternative annual sales assumptions for HomeNet. We then select the scenario to analyze by entering the appropriate number (in this case 1, 2 or 3) in the highlighted cell (C4), and use the index function to pull the appropriate data into row 4.

	A	B	C	D	E	F	G	H
2	**Key Assumptions**			**Year 0**	**Year 1**	**Year 2**	**Year 3**	**Year 4**
3		*Revenues & Costs*						
4		HomeNet Units Sold	1	-	100	100	100	=INDEX(H5:H7,$C$4)
5		*Base Case*	*1*	-	*100*	*100*	*100*	*100*
6		*Fast Adoption*	*2*	-	*125*	*150*	*200*	*125*
7		*Slow Adoption*	*3*	-	*50*	*75*	*100*	*100*

We can then analyze the consequences for each scenario using the one-dimensional data table in C70:D73 below, with column input cell C4.

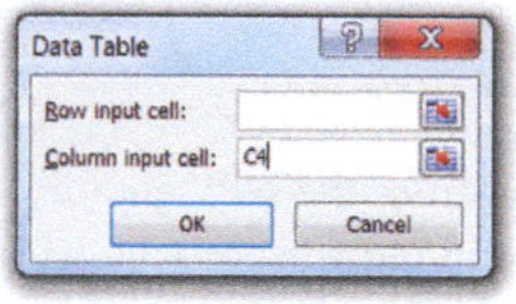

	A	B	C	D	E
69				NPV	
70		HomeNet Units Sold		5,026	
71		*Base Case*	*1*	5,026	
72		*Fast Adoption*	*2*	17,227	
73		*Slow Adoption*	*3*	(253)	

MyFinanceLab Here is what you should know after reading this chapter. MyFinanceLab will help you identify what you know and where to go when you need to practice.

8.1 Forecasting Earnings

- Capital budgeting is the process of analyzing investment opportunities and deciding which ones to accept. A capital budget is a list of all projects that a company plans to undertake during the next period.
- We use the NPV rule to evaluate capital budgeting decisions, making decisions that maximize NPV. When deciding to accept or reject a project, we accept projects with a positive NPV.
- The incremental earnings of a project comprise the amount by which the project is expected to change the firm's earnings.
- Incremental earnings should include all incremental revenues and costs associated with the project, including project externalities and opportunity costs, but excluding sunk costs and interest expenses.
    - Project externalities are cash flows that occur when a project affects other areas of the company's business.
    - An opportunity cost is the cost of using an existing asset, measured by the value the asset would have provided in its best alternative use.
    - A sunk cost is an unrecoverable cost that has already been incurred.
    - Interest and other financing-related expenses are excluded to determine the project's unlevered net income.
- We estimate taxes using the marginal tax rate, based on the net income generated by the rest of the firm's operations, as well as any tax loss carrybacks or carryforwards.

- When evaluating a capital budgeting decision, we first consider the project on its own, separate from the decision regarding how to finance the project. Thus, we ignore interest expenses and compute the unlevered net income contribution of the project:

$$\text{Unlevered Net Income} = EBIT \times (1 - \tau_c)$$
$$= (\text{Revenues} - \text{Costs} - \text{Depreciation}) \times (1 - \tau_c) \quad (8.2)$$

8.2 Determining Free Cash Flow and NPV

- We compute free cash flow from incremental earnings by eliminating all non-cash expenses and including all capital investment.
  - Depreciation is not a cash expense, so it is added back.
  - Actual capital expenditures are deducted.
  - Increases in net working capital are deducted. Net working capital is defined as

$$\text{Cash} + \text{Inventory} + \text{Receivables} - \text{Payables} \quad (8.3)$$

- The basic calculation for free cash flow is

$$\text{Free Cash Flow} = \overbrace{(\text{Revenues} - \text{Costs} - \text{Depreciation}) \times (1 - \tau_c)}^{\text{Unlevered Net Income}}$$
$$+ \text{Depreciation} - \text{CapEx} - \Delta NWC \quad (8.5)$$

- The discount rate for a project is its cost of capital: The expected return of securities with comparable risk and horizon.

8.3 Choosing Among Alternatives

- When choosing between mutual exclusive investment opportunities, pick the opportunity with the highest NPV.
- When choosing between alternatives, we only need to include those components of free cash flow that differ among the alternatives.

8.4 Further Adjustments to Free Cash Flow

- Depreciation expenses affect free cash flow only through the depreciation tax shield. The firm should generally use the most accelerated depreciation schedule that is allowable for tax purposes.
- Free cash flow should also include the (after-tax) liquidation or salvage value of any assets that are disposed of. It may also include a terminal (continuation) value if the project continues beyond the forecast horizon.
- When an asset is sold, tax is due on the difference between the sale price and the asset's book value net of depreciation.
- Terminal or continuation values should reflect the present value of the project's future cash flows beyond the forecast horizon.

8.5 Analyzing the Project

- Break-even analysis computes the level of a parameter that makes the project's NPV equal zero.
- Sensitivity analysis breaks the NPV calculation down into its component assumptions, showing how the NPV varies as the values of the underlying assumptions change.
- Scenario analysis considers the effect of changing multiple parameters simultaneously.

Key Terms

break-even *p. 258*
break-even analysis *p. 259*
cannibalization *p. 244*
capital budget *p. 240*
capital budgeting *p. 240*
depreciation tax shield *p. 250*
EBIT break-even *p. 259*
free cash flow *p. 247*
incremental earnings *p. 240*
MACRS depreciation *p. 254*
marginal corporate tax rate *p. 242*
opportunity cost *p. 243*
overhead expenses *p. 245*
project externalities *p. 244*
scenario analysis *p. 262*
sensitivity analysis *p. 259*
straight-line depreciation *p. 241*
sunk cost *p. 245*
tax loss carryforwards and carrybacks *p. 257*
terminal (continuation) value *p. 256*
trade credit *p. 248*
unlevered net income *p. 242*

Further Reading

For an excellent overview of the history of the concept of present value and its use in capital budgeting, see M. Rubinstein, "Great Moments in Financial Economics: I. Present Value," *Journal of Investment Management* (First Quarter 2003).

Irving Fisher was one of the first to apply the Law of One Price to propose that any capital project should be evaluated in terms of its present value; see I. Fisher, *The Rate of Interest: Its Nature, Determination and Relation to Economic Phenomena* (Macmillan, 1907). I. Fisher, *The Theory of Interest: As Determined by Impatience to Spend Income and Opportunity to Invest It* (Macmillan, 1930); reprinted (Augustus M. Kelley, 1955).

The use of this approach for capital budgeting was later popularized in the following book: J. Dean, *Capital Budgeting* (Columbia University Press, 1951).

We will revisit the topics of this chapter in Part 6. Additional readings for more advanced topics will be provided there.

Problems

All problems are available in MyFinanceLab. *An asterisk (*) indicates problems with a higher level of difficulty.*

Forecasting Earnings

1. Pisa Pizza, a seller of frozen pizza, is considering introducing a healthier version of its pizza that will be low in cholesterol and contain no trans fats. The firm expects that sales of the new pizza will be $20 million per year. While many of these sales will be to new customers, Pisa Pizza estimates that 40% will come from customers who switch to the new, healthier pizza instead of buying the original version.

a. Assume customers will spend the same amount on either version. What level of incremental sales is associated with introducing the new pizza?

b. Suppose that 50% of the customers who will switch from Pisa Pizza's original pizza to its healthier pizza will switch to another brand if Pisa Pizza does not introduce a healthier pizza. What level of incremental sales is associated with introducing the new pizza in this case?

2. Kokomochi is considering the launch of an advertising campaign for its latest dessert product, the Mini Mochi Munch. Kokomochi plans to spend $5 million on TV, radio, and print advertising this year for the campaign. The ads are expected to boost sales of the Mini Mochi Munch by $9 million this year and by $7 million next year. In addition, the company expects that new consumers who try the Mini Mochi Munch will be more likely to try Kokomochi's other products. As a result, sales of other products are expected to rise by $2 million each year.

Kokomochi's gross profit margin for the Mini Mochi Munch is 35%, and its gross profit margin averages 25% for all other products. The company's marginal corporate tax rate is 35% both this year and next year. What are the incremental earnings associated with the advertising campaign?

3. Home Builder Supply, a retailer in the home improvement industry, currently operates seven retail outlets in Georgia and South Carolina. Management is contemplating building an eighth retail store across town from its most successful retail outlet. The company already owns the land for this store, which currently has an abandoned warehouse located on it. Last month, the marketing department spent $10,000 on market research to determine the extent of customer demand for the new store. Now Home Builder Supply must decide whether to build and open the new store.

   Which of the following should be included as part of the incremental earnings for the proposed new retail store?
   a. The cost of the land where the store will be located.
   b. The cost of demolishing the abandoned warehouse and clearing the lot.
   c. The loss of sales in the existing retail outlet, if customers who previously drove across town to shop at the existing outlet become customers of the new store instead.
   d. The $10,000 in market research spent to evaluate customer demand.
   e. Construction costs for the new store.
   f. The value of the land if sold.
   g. Interest expense on the debt borrowed to pay the construction costs.

4. Hyperion, Inc. currently sells its latest high-speed color printer, the Hyper 500, for $350. It plans to lower the price to $300 next year. Its cost of goods sold for the Hyper 500 is $200 per unit, and this year's sales are expected to be 20,000 units.
   a. Suppose that if Hyperion drops the price to $300 immediately, it can increase this year's sales by 25% to 25,000 units. What would be the incremental impact on this year's EBIT of such a price drop?
   b. Suppose that for each printer sold, Hyperion expects additional sales of $75 per year on ink cartridges for the next three years, and Hyperion has a gross profit margin of 70% on ink cartridges. What is the incremental impact on EBIT for the next three years of a price drop this year?

5. After looking at the projections of the HomeNet project, you decide that they are not realistic. It is unlikely that sales will be constant over the four-year life of the project. Furthermore, other companies are likely to offer competing products, so the assumption that the sales price will remain constant is also likely to be optimistic. Finally, as production ramps up, you anticipate lower per unit production costs resulting from economies of scale. Therefore, you decide to redo the projections under the following assumptions: Sales of 50,000 units in year 1 increasing by 50,000 units per year over the life of the project, a year 1 sales price of $260/unit, decreasing by 10% annually and a year 1 cost of $120/unit decreasing by 20% annually. In addition, new tax laws allow you to depreciate the equipment over three rather than five years using straight-line depreciation.
   a. Keeping the other assumptions that underlie Table 8.1 the same, recalculate unlevered net income (that is, reproduce Table 8.1 under the new assumptions, and note that we are ignoring cannibalization and lost rent).
   b. Recalculate unlevered net income assuming, in addition, that each year 20% of sales comes from customers who would have purchased an existing Cisco router for $100/unit and that this router costs $60/unit to manufacture.

Determining Free Cash Flow and NPV

6. Cellular Access, Inc. is a cellular telephone service provider that reported net income of $250 million for the most recent fiscal year. The firm had depreciation expenses of $100 million, capital expenditures of $200 million, and no interest expenses. Working capital increased by $10 million. Calculate the free cash flow for Cellular Access for the most recent fiscal year.

7. Castle View Games would like to invest in a division to develop software for video games. To evaluate this decision, the firm first attempts to project the working capital needs for this

operation. Its chief financial officer has developed the following estimates (in millions of dollars):

	Year 1	Year 2	Year 3	Year 4	Year 5
Cash	6	12	15	15	15
Accounts Receivable	21	22	24	24	24
Inventory	5	7	10	12	13
Accounts Payable	18	22	24	25	30

Assuming that Castle View currently does not have any working capital invested in this division, calculate the cash flows associated with changes in working capital for the first five years of this investment.

8. Mersey Chemicals manufactures polypropylene that it ships to its customers via tank car. Currently, it plans to add two additional tank cars to its fleet four years from now. However, a proposed plant expansion will require Mersey's transport division to add these two additional tank cars in two years' time rather than in four years. The current cost of a tank car is $2 million, and this cost is expected to remain constant. Also, while tank cars will last indefinitely, they will be depreciated straight-line over a five-year life for tax purposes. Suppose Mersey's tax rate is 40%. When evaluating the proposed expansion, what incremental free cash flows should be included to account for the need to accelerate the purchase of the tank cars?

9. Elmdale Enterprises is deciding whether to expand its production facilities. Although long-term cash flows are difficult to estimate, management has projected the following cash flows for the first two years (in millions of dollars):

	Year 1	Year 2
Revenues	125	160
Costs of goods sold and operating expenses other than depreciation	40	60
Depreciation	25	36
Increase in net working capital	5	8
Capital expenditures	30	40
Marginal corporate tax rate	35%	35%

a. What are the incremental earnings for this project for years 1 and 2?
b. What are the free cash flows for this project for the first two years?

MFL **10.** You are a manager at Percolated Fiber, which is considering expanding its operations in synthetic fiber manufacturing. Your boss comes into your office, drops a consultant's report on your desk, and complains, "We owe these consultants $1 million for this report, and I am not sure their analysis makes sense. Before we spend the $25 million on new equipment needed for this project, look it over and give me your opinion." You open the report and find the following estimates (in thousands of dollars):

	Project Year				
	1	2	. . .	9	10
Sales revenue	30,000	30,000		30,000	30,000
− Cost of goods sold	18,000	18,000		18,000	18,000
= Gross profit	12,000	12,000		12,000	12,000
− General, sales, and administrative expenses	2,000	2,000		2,000	2,000
− Depreciation	2,500	2,500		2,500	2,500
= Net operating income	7,500	7,500		7,500	7,500
− Income tax	2,625	2,625		2,625	2,625
Net Income	4,875	4,875		4,875	4,875

All of the estimates in the report seem correct. You note that the consultants used straight-line depreciation for the new equipment that will be purchased today (year 0), which is what the accounting department recommended. The report concludes that because the project will increase earnings by $4.875 million per year for 10 years, the project is worth $48.75 million. You think back to your halcyon days in finance class and realize there is more work to be done!

First, you note that the consultants have not factored in that the project will require $10 million in working capital upfront (year 0), which will be fully recovered in year 10. Next, you see they have attributed $2 million of selling, general and administrative expenses to the project, but you know that $1 million of this amount is overhead that will be incurred even if the project is not accepted. Finally, you know that accounting earnings are not the right thing to focus on!

a. Given the available information, what are the free cash flows in years 0 through 10 that should be used to evaluate the proposed project?
b. If the cost of capital for this project is 14%, what is your estimate of the value of the new project?

11. Using the assumptions in part (a) of Problem 5 (assuming there is no cannibalization),
a. Calculate HomeNet's net working capital requirements (that is, reproduce Table 8.4 under the assumptions in Problem 5(a)).
b. Calculate HomeNet's FCF (that is, reproduce Table 8.3 under the same assumptions as in (a)).

Choosing Among Alternatives

12. A bicycle manufacturer currently produces 300,000 units a year and expects output levels to remain steady in the future. It buys chains from an outside supplier at a price of $2 a chain. The plant manager believes that it would be cheaper to make these chains rather than buy them. Direct in-house production costs are estimated to be only $1.50 per chain. The necessary machinery would cost $250,000 and would be obsolete after 10 years. This investment could be depreciated to zero for tax purposes using a 10-year straight-line depreciation schedule. The plant manager estimates that the operation would require $50,000 of inventory and other working capital upfront (year 0), but argues that this sum can be ignored since it is recoverable at the end of the 10 years. Expected proceeds from scrapping the machinery after 10 years are $20,000.

If the company pays tax at a rate of 35% and the opportunity cost of capital is 15%, what is the net present value of the decision to produce the chains in-house instead of purchasing them from the supplier?

13. Consider again the choice between outsourcing and in-house assembly of HomeNet discussed in Section 8.3 and analyzed in Table 8.6. Suppose, however, that the upfront cost to set up for in-house production is $6 million rather than $5 million, and the cost per unit for in-house production is expected to be $92 rather than $95.
a. Suppose the outside supplier decides to raise its price above $110/unit. At what cost per unit for the outsourced units would Cisco be indifferent between outsourcing and in-house assembly?
b. Alternatively, suppose the cost for outsourcing remains $110/unit, but expected demand increases above 100,000 units per year. At what level of annual sales, in terms of units sold, would Cisco be indifferent between these two options?

14. One year ago, your company purchased a machine used in manufacturing for $110,000. You have learned that a new machine is available that offers many advantages; you can purchase it for $150,000 today. It will be depreciated on a straight-line basis over 10 years, after which it has no salvage value. You expect that the new machine will produce EBITDA (earning before interest, taxes, depreciation, and amortization) of $40,000 per year for the next 10 years. The current machine is expected to produce EBITDA of $20,000 per year.

The current machine is being depreciated on a straight-line basis over a useful life of 11 years, after which it will have no salvage value, so depreciation expense for the current machine is $10,000 per year. All other expenses of the two machines are identical. The market value today of the current machine is $50,000. Your company's tax rate is 45%, and the opportunity cost of capital for this type of equipment is 10%. Is it profitable to replace the year-old machine?

15. Beryl's Iced Tea currently rents a bottling machine for $50,000 per year, including all maintenance expenses. It is considering purchasing a machine instead, and is comparing two options:

a. Purchase the machine it is currently renting for $150,000. This machine will require $20,000 per year in ongoing maintenance expenses.

b. Purchase a new, more advanced machine for $250,000. This machine will require $15,000 per year in ongoing maintenance expenses and will lower bottling costs by $10,000 per year. Also, $35,000 will be spent upfront in training the new operators of the machine.

Suppose the appropriate discount rate is 8% per year and the machine is purchased today. Maintenance and bottling costs are paid at the end of each year, as is the rental of the machine. Assume also that the machines will be depreciated via the straight-line method over seven years and that they have a 10-year life with a negligible salvage value. The marginal corporate tax rate is 35%. Should Beryl's Iced Tea continue to rent, purchase its current machine, or purchase the advanced machine?

Further Adjustments to Free Cash Flow

16. Markov Manufacturing recently spent $15 million to purchase some equipment used in the manufacture of disk drives. The firm expects that this equipment will have a useful life of five years, and its marginal corporate tax rate is 35%. The company plans to use straight-line depreciation.

a. What is the annual depreciation expense associated with this equipment?

b. What is the annual depreciation tax shield?

c. Rather than straight-line depreciation, suppose Markov will use the MACRS depreciation method for five-year property. Calculate the depreciation tax shield each year for this equipment under this accelerated depreciation schedule.

d. If Markov has a choice between straight-line and MACRS depreciation schedules, and its marginal corporate tax rate is expected to remain constant, which should it choose? Why?

e. How might your answer to part (d) change if Markov anticipates that its marginal corporate tax rate will increase substantially over the next five years?

17. Your firm is considering a project that would require purchasing $7.5 million worth of new equipment. Determine the present value of the depreciation tax shield associated with this equipment if the firm's tax rate is 40%, the appropriate cost of capital is 8%, and the equipment can be depreciated

a. Straight-line over a 10-year period, with the first deduction starting in one year.

b. Straight-line over a five-year period, with the first deduction starting in one year.

c. Using MACRS depreciation with a five-year recovery period and starting immediately.

d. Fully as an immediate deduction.

18. Arnold Inc. is considering a proposal to manufacture high-end protein bars used as food supplements by body builders. The project requires use of an existing warehouse, which the firm acquired three years ago for $1 million and which it currently rents out for $120,000. Rental rates are not expected to change going forward. In addition to using the warehouse, the project requires an upfront investment into machines and other equipment of $1.4 million. This investment can be fully depreciated straight-line over the next 10 years for tax purposes. However, Arnold Inc. expects to terminate the project at the end of eight years and to sell the machines and equipment for $500,000. Finally, the project requires an initial investment into net working capital equal to 10% of predicted first-year sales. Subsequently, net working capital is 10% of the predicted sales over the following year. Sales of protein bars are expected to be $4.8 million in the first year and to stay constant for eight years. Total manufacturing costs and operating expenses (excluding depreciation) are 80% of sales, and profits are taxed at 30%.

a. What are the free cash flows of the project?

b. If the cost of capital is 15%, what is the NPV of the project?

19. Bay Properties is considering starting a commercial real estate division. It has prepared the following four-year forecast of free cash flows for this division:

	Year 1	Year 2	Year 3	Year 4
Free Cash Flow	−$185,000	$12,000	$99,000	$240,000

Assume cash flows after year 4 will grow at 3% per year, forever. If the cost of capital for this division is 14%, what is the continuation value in year 4 for cash flows after year 4? What is the value today of this division?

20. Your firm would like to evaluate a proposed new operating division. You have forecasted cash flows for this division for the next five years, and have estimated that the cost of capital is 12%. You would like to estimate a continuation value. You have made the following forecasts for the last year of your five-year forecasting horizon (in millions of dollars):

	Year 5
Revenues	1200
Operating income	100
Net income	50
Free cash flows	110
Book value of equity	400

a. You forecast that future free cash flows after year 5 will grow at 2% per year, forever. Estimate the continuation value in year 5, using the perpetuity with growth formula.

b. You have identified several firms in the same industry as your operating division. The average P/E ratio for these firms is 30. Estimate the continuation value assuming the P/E ratio for your division in year 5 will be the same as the average P/E ratio for the comparable firms today.

c. The average market/book ratio for the comparable firms is 4.0. Estimate the continuation value using the market/book ratio.

21. In September 2008, the IRS changed tax laws to allow banks to utilize the tax loss carryforwards of banks they acquire to shield their future income from taxes (prior law restricted the ability of acquirers to use these credits). Suppose Fargo Bank acquires Covia Bank and with it acquires $74 billion in tax loss carryforwards. If Fargo Bank is expected to generate taxable income of 10 billion per year in the future, and its tax rate is 30%, what is the present value of these acquired tax loss carryforwards given a cost of capital of 8%?

Analyzing the Project

22. Using the FCF projections in part (b) of Problem 11, calculate the NPV of the HomeNet project assuming a cost of capital of

a. 10%.

b. 12%.

c. 14%.

What is the IRR of the project in this case?

23. For the assumptions in part (a) of Problem 5, assuming a cost of capital of 12%, calculate the following:

a. The break-even annual sales price decline.

b. The break-even annual unit sales increase.

24. Bauer Industries is an automobile manufacturer. Management is currently evaluating a proposal to build a plant that will manufacture lightweight trucks. Bauer plans to use a cost of capital of 12% to evaluate this project. Based on extensive research, it has prepared the following incremental free cash flow projections (in millions of dollars):

	Year 0	Years 1–9	Year 10
Revenues		100.0	100.0
− Manufacturing expenses (other than depreciation)		−35.0	−35.0
− Marketing expenses		−10.0	−10.0
− Depreciation		−15.0	−15.0
= EBIT		40.0	40.0
− Taxes (35%)		−14.0	−14.0
= Unlevered net income		26.0	26.0
+ Depreciation		+15.0	+15.0
− Increases in net working capital		−5.0	−5.0
− Capital expenditures	−150.0		
+ Continuation value			+12.0
= Free cash flow	−150.0	36.0	48.0

a. For this base-case scenario, what is the NPV of the plant to manufacture lightweight trucks?

b. Based on input from the marketing department, Bauer is uncertain about its revenue forecast. In particular, management would like to examine the sensitivity of the NPV to the revenue assumptions. What is the NPV of this project if revenues are 10% higher than forecast? What is the NPV if revenues are 10% lower than forecast?

c. Rather than assuming that cash flows for this project are constant, management would like to explore the sensitivity of its analysis to possible growth in revenues and operating expenses. Specifically, management would like to assume that revenues, manufacturing expenses, and marketing expenses are as given in the table for year 1 and grow by 2% per year every year starting in year 2. Management also plans to assume that the initial capital expenditures (and therefore depreciation), additions to working capital, and continuation value remain as initially specified in the table. What is the NPV of this project under these alternative assumptions? How does the NPV change if the revenues and operating expenses grow by 5% per year rather than by 2%?

d. To examine the sensitivity of this project to the discount rate, management would like to compute the NPV for different discount rates. Create a graph, with the discount rate on the x-axis and the NPV on the y-axis, for discount rates ranging from 5% to 30%. For what ranges of discount rates does the project have a positive NPV?

***25.** Billingham Packaging is considering expanding its production capacity by purchasing a new machine, the XC-750. The cost of the XC-750 is $2.75 million. Unfortunately, installing this machine will take several months and will partially disrupt production. The firm has just completed a $50,000 feasibility study to analyze the decision to buy the XC-750, resulting in the following estimates:

- *Marketing*: Once the XC-750 is operating next year, the extra capacity is expected to generate $10 million per year in additional sales, which will continue for the 10-year life of the machine.

- *Operations*: The disruption caused by the installation will decrease sales by $5 million this year. Once the machine is operating next year, the cost of goods for the products produced by the XC-750 is expected to be 70% of their sale price. The increased production will require additional inventory on hand of $1 million to be added in year 0 and depleted in year 10.
- *Human Resources*: The expansion will require additional sales and administrative personnel at a cost of $2 million per year.
- *Accounting*: The XC-750 will be depreciated via the straight-line method over the 10-year life of the machine. The firm expects receivables from the new sales to be 15% of revenues and payables to be 10% of the cost of goods sold. Billingham's marginal corporate tax rate is 35%.

a. Determine the incremental earnings from the purchase of the XC-750.

b. Determine the free cash flow from the purchase of the XC-750.

c. If the appropriate cost of capital for the expansion is 10%, compute the NPV of the purchase.

d. While the expected new sales will be $10 million per year from the expansion, estimates range from $8 million to $12 million. What is the NPV in the worst case? In the best case?

e. What is the break-even level of new sales from the expansion? What is the break-even level for the cost of goods sold?

f. Billingham could instead purchase the XC-900, which offers even greater capacity. The cost of the XC-900 is $4 million. The extra capacity would not be useful in the first two years of operation, but would allow for additional sales in years 3–10. What level of additional sales (above the $10 million expected for the XC-750) per year in those years would justify purchasing the larger machine?

Data Case

You have just been hired by Internal Business Machines Corporation (IBM) in their capital budgeting division. Your first assignment is to determine the free cash flows and NPV of a proposed new type of tablet computer similar in size to an iPad but with the operating power of a high-end desktop system.

Development of the new system will initially require an initial capital expenditure equal to 10% of IBM's Property, Plant, and Equipment (PPE) at the end of fiscal year 2014. The project will then require an additional investment equal to 10% of the initial investment after the first year of the project, a 5% increase after the second year, and a 1% increase after the third, fourth, and fifth years. The product is expected to have a life of five years. First-year revenues for the new product are expected to be 3% of IBM's total revenue for the fiscal year 2014. The new product's revenues are expected to grow at 15% for the second year then 10% for the third and 5% annually for the final two years of the expected life of the project. Your job is to determine the rest of the cash flows associated with this project. Your boss has indicated that the operating costs and net working capital requirements are similar to the rest of the company and that depreciation is straight-line for capital budgeting purposes. Since your boss hasn't been much help (welcome to the "real world"!), here are some tips to guide your analysis:

1. Obtain IBM's financial statements. (If you *really* worked for IBM you would already have this data, but at least you won't get fired if your analysis is off target.) Download the annual income statements, balance sheets, and cash flow statements for the last four fiscal years from Yahoo! Finance (finance.yahoo.com). Enter IBM's ticker symbol and then go to "financials."
2. You are now ready to estimate the Free Cash Flow for the new product. Compute the Free Cash Flow for each year using Eq. 8.5:

$$\text{Free Cash Flow} = \overbrace{(\text{Revenues} - \text{Costs} - \text{Depreciation}) \times (1 - \tau_c)}^{\text{Unlevered Net Income}} + \text{Depreciation} - \text{CapEx} - \Delta NWC$$

Set up the timeline and computation of free cash flow in separate, contiguous columns for each year of the project life. Be sure to make outflows negative and inflows positive.

a. Assume that the project's profitability will be similar to IBM's existing projects in 2014 and estimate (revenues − costs) each year by using the 2014 EBITDA/Sales profit margin. Calculate EBITDA as EBIT + Depreciation expense from the cash flow statement.
b. Determine the annual depreciation by assuming IBM depreciates these assets by the straight-line method over a 5-year life.
c. Determine IBM's tax rate by using the income tax rate in 2014.
d. Calculate the net working capital required each year by assuming that the level of NWC will be a constant percentage of the project's sales. Use IBM's 2014 NWC/Sales to estimate the required percentage. (Use only accounts receivable, accounts payable, and inventory to measure working capital. Other components of current assets and liabilities are harder to interpret and not necessarily reflective of the project's required NWC—for example, IBM's cash holdings.)
e. To determine the free cash flow, deduct the additional capital investment and the *change* in net working capital each year.

3. Use Excel to determine the NPV of the project with a 12% cost of capital. Also calculate the IRR of the project using Excel's IRR function.

4. Perform a sensitivity analysis by varying the project forecasts as follows:

a. Suppose first year sales will equal 2%–4% of IBM's revenues.
b. Suppose the cost of capital is 10%–15%.
c. Suppose revenue growth is constant after the first year at a rate of 0%–10%.

Note: Updates to this data case may be found at www.berkdemarzo.com.

CHAPTER 8 APPENDIX

MACRS Depreciation

The U.S. tax code allows for accelerated depreciation of most assets. The depreciation method that you use for any particular asset is determined by the tax rules in effect at the time you place the asset into service. (Congress has changed the depreciation rules many times over the years, so many firms that have held property for a long time may have to use several depreciation methods simultaneously.)

For most business property placed in service after 1986, the IRS allows firms to depreciate the asset using the MACRS (Modified Accelerated Cost Recovery System) method. Under this method, you categorize each business asset into a recovery class that determines the time period over which you can write off the cost of the asset. The most commonly used items are classified as shown below:

- *3-year property*: Tractor units, racehorses over 2 years old, and horses over 12 years old.
- *5-year property*: Automobiles, buses, trucks, computers and peripheral equipment, office machinery, and any property used in research and experimentation. Also includes breeding and dairy cattle.
- *7-year property*: Office furniture and fixtures, and any property that has not been designated as belonging to another class.
- *10-year property*: Water transportation equipment, single-purpose agricultural or horticultural structures, and trees or vines bearing fruit or nuts.
- *15-year property*: Depreciable improvements to land such as fences, roads, and bridges.
- *20-year property*: Farm buildings that are not agricultural or horticultural structures.
- *27.5-year property*: Residential rental property.
- *39-year property*: Nonresidential real estate, including home offices. (Note that the value of land may not be depreciated.)

Generally speaking, residential and nonresidential real estate is depreciated via the straight-line method, but other classes can be depreciated more rapidly in early years. Table 8A.1 shows the standard depreciation rates for assets in the other recovery classes; refinements of this table can be applied depending on the month that the asset was placed into service (consult IRS guidelines). The table indicates the percentage of the asset's cost that may be depreciated each year, with year 1 indicating the year the asset was first put into use.

The lower amount in year 1 reflects a "half-year convention" in which the asset is presumed to be in use (and this depreciated) for half of the first year, no matter when it was actually put into use. After year 1, it is assumed that the asset depreciates more rapidly in earlier years.

TABLE 8A.1 **MACRS Depreciation Table Showing the Percentage of the Asset's Cost That May Be Depreciated Each Year Based on Its Recovery Period**

	Depreciation Rate for Recovery Period					
Year	3 Years	5 Years	7 Years	10 Years	15 Years	20 Years
1	33.33	20.00	14.29	10.00	5.00	3.750
2	44.45	32.00	24.49	18.00	9.50	7.219
3	14.81	19.20	17.49	14.40	8.55	6.677
4	7.41	11.52	12.49	11.52	7.70	6.177
5		11.52	8.93	9.22	6.93	5.713
6		5.76	8.92	7.37	6.23	5.285
7			8.93	6.55	5.90	4.888
8			4.46	6.55	5.90	4.522
9				6.56	5.91	4.462
10				6.55	5.90	4.461
11				3.28	5.91	4.462
12					5.90	4.461
13					5.91	4.462
14					5.90	4.461
15					5.91	4.462
16					2.95	4.461
17						4.462
18						4.461
19						4.462
20						4.461
21						2.231

CHAPTER

9

Valuing Stocks

ON JANUARY 16, 2006, FOOTWEAR AND APPAREL MAKER KENNETH Cole Productions, Inc., announced that its president, Paul Blum, had resigned to pursue "other opportunities." The price of the company's stock had already dropped more than 16% over the prior two years, and the firm was in the midst of a major undertaking to restructure its brand. News that its president, who had been with the company for more than 15 years, was now resigning was taken as a bad sign by many investors. The next day, Kenneth Cole's stock price dropped by more than 6% on the New York Stock Exchange to $26.75, with over 300,000 shares traded, more than twice its average daily volume. How might an investor decide whether to buy or sell a stock such as Kenneth Cole at this price? Why would the stock suddenly be worth 6% less on the announcement of this news? What actions can Kenneth Cole's managers take to increase the stock price?

To answer these questions, we turn to the Law of One Price, which implies that the price of a security should equal the present value of the expected cash flows an investor will receive from owning it. In this chapter, we apply this idea to stocks. Thus, to value a stock, we need to know the expected cash flows an investor will receive and the appropriate cost of capital with which to discount those cash flows. Both of these quantities can be challenging to estimate, and many of the details needed to do so will be developed throughout the remainder of the text. In this chapter, we will begin our study of stock valuation by identifying the relevant cash flows and developing the main tools that practitioners use to evaluate them.

Our analysis begins with a consideration of the dividends and capital gains received by investors who hold the stock for different periods, from which we develop the *dividend-discount model* of stock valuation. Next, we apply Chapter 8's tools to value stocks based on the free cash flows generated by the firm. Having developed these stock valuation methods based on discounted cash flows, we then relate them to the

NOTATION

P_t	stock price at the end of year t
r_E	equity cost of capital
N	terminal date or forecast horizon
g	expected dividend growth rate
Div_t	dividends paid in year t
EPS_t	earnings per share on date t
PV	present value
$EBIT$	earnings before interest and taxes
FCF_t	free cash flow on date t
V_t	enterprise value on date t
τ_c	corporate tax rate
r_{wacc}	weighted average cost of capital
g_{FCF}	expected free cash flow growth rate
$EBITDA$	earnings before interest, taxes, depreciation, and amortization

practice of using valuation multiples based on comparable firms. We conclude the chapter by discussing the role of competition in determining the information contained in stock prices, as well as its implications for investors and corporate managers.

9.1 The Dividend-Discount Model

The Law of One Price implies that to value any security, we must determine the expected cash flows an investor will receive from owning it. Thus, we begin our analysis of stock valuation by considering the cash flows for an investor with a one-year investment horizon. We then consider the perspective of investors with longer investment horizons. We show that if investors have the same beliefs, their valuation of the stock will not depend on their investment horizon. Using this result, we then derive the first method to value a stock: the *dividend-discount model.*

A One-Year Investor

There are two potential sources of cash flows from owning a stock. First, the firm might pay out cash to its shareholders in the form of a dividend. Second, the investor might generate cash by choosing to sell the shares at some future date. The total amount received in dividends and from selling the stock will depend on the investor's investment horizon. Let's begin by considering the perspective of a one-year investor.

When an investor buys a stock, she will pay the current market price for a share, P_0. While she continues to hold the stock, she will be entitled to any dividends the stock pays. Let Div_1 be the total dividends paid per share of the stock during the year. At the end of the year, the investor will sell her share at the new market price, P_1. Assuming for simplicity that all dividends are paid at the end of the year, we have the following timeline for this investment:

0	1
$-P_0$	$Div_1 + P_1$

Of course, the future dividend payment and stock price in the timeline above are not known with certainty; rather, these values are based on the investor's expectations at the time the stock is purchased. Given these expectations, the investor will be willing to buy the stock at today's price as long as the NPV of the transaction is not negative—that is, as long as the current price does not exceed the present value of the expected future dividend and sale price. Because these cash flows are risky, we cannot compute their present value using the risk-free interest rate. Instead, we must discount them based on the **equity cost of capital**, r_E, for the stock, which is the expected return of other investments available in the market with equivalent risk to the firm's shares. Doing so leads to the following condition under which an investor would be willing to buy the stock:

$$P_0 \leq \frac{Div_1 + P_1}{1 + r_E}$$

Similarly, for an investor to be willing to sell the stock, she must receive at least as much today as the present value she would receive if she waited to sell next year:

$$P_0 \geq \frac{Div_1 + P_1}{1 + r_E}$$

But because for every buyer of the stock there must be a seller, *both* equations must hold, and therefore the stock price should satisfy

$$P_0 = \frac{Div_1 + P_1}{1 + r_E} \tag{9.1}$$

In other words, as we discovered in Chapter 3, in a competitive market, buying or selling a share of stock must be a zero-NPV investment opportunity.

Dividend Yields, Capital Gains, and Total Returns

We can reinterpret Eq. 9.1 if we multiply by $(1 + r_E)$, divide by P_0, and subtract 1 from both sides:

Total Return

$$r_E = \frac{Div_1 + P_1}{P_0} - 1 = \underbrace{\frac{Div_1}{P_0}}_{\text{Dividend Yield}} + \underbrace{\frac{P_1 - P_0}{P_0}}_{\text{Capital Gain Rate}} \tag{9.2}$$

The first term on the right side of Eq. 9.2 is the stock's **dividend yield**, which is the expected annual dividend of the stock divided by its current price. The dividend yield is the percentage return the investor expects to earn from the dividend paid by the stock. The second term on the right side of Eq. 9.2 reflects the **capital gain** the investor will earn on the stock, which is the difference between the expected sale price and purchase price for the stock, $P_1 - P_0$. We divide the capital gain by the current stock price to express the capital gain as a percentage return, called the **capital gain rate**.

The sum of the dividend yield and the capital gain rate is called the **total return** of the stock. The total return is the expected return that the investor will earn for a one-year investment in the stock. Thus, Eq. 9.2 states that the stock's total return should equal the equity cost of capital. In other words, *the expected total return of the stock should equal the expected return of other investments available in the market with equivalent risk.*

EXAMPLE 9.1 Stock Prices and Returns

Problem

Suppose you expect Walgreen Company (a drugstore chain) to pay dividends of \$1.40 per share and trade for \$80 per share at the end of the year. If investments with equivalent risk to Walgreen's stock have an expected return of 8.5%, what is the most you would pay today for Walgreen's stock? What dividend yield and capital gain rate would you expect at this price?

Solution

Using Eq. 9.1, we have

$$P_0 = \frac{Div_1 + P_1}{1 + r_E} = \frac{1.40 + 80.00}{1.085} = \$75.02$$

At this price, Walgreen's dividend yield is $Div_1/P_0 = 1.40/75.02 = 1.87\%$. The expected capital gain is $\$80.00 - \$75.02 = \$4.98$ per share, for a capital gain rate of $4.98/75.02 = 6.63\%$. Therefore, at this price, Walgreen's expected total return is $1.87\% + 6.63\% = 8.5\%$, which is equal to its equity cost of capital.

The Mechanics of a Short Sale

If a stock's expected total return is below that of other investments with comparable risk, investors who own the stock will choose to sell it and invest elsewhere. But what if you don't own the stock—can you profit in this situation?

The answer is yes, by short selling the stock. To short sell a stock, you must contact your broker, who will try to borrow the stock from someone who currently owns it.* Suppose John Doe holds the stock in a brokerage account. Your broker can lend you shares from his account so that you can sell them in the market at the current stock price. Of course, at some point you must close the short sale by buying the shares in the market and returning them to Doe's account. In the meantime, so that John Doe is not made worse off by lending his shares to you, you must pay him any dividends the stock pays.**

The following table compares the cash flows from buying with those from short-selling a stock:

	Date 0	Date t	Date 1
Cash flows from buying a stock	$-P_0$	$+Div_t$	$+P_1$
Cash flows from short-selling a stock	$+P_0$	$-Div_t$	$-P_1$

When you short sell a stock, first you receive the current share price. Then, while your short position remains open, you must pay any dividends made. Finally, you must pay the future stock price to close your position. These cash flows are exactly the reverse of those from buying a stock.

Because the cash flows are reversed, if you short sell a stock, rather than receiving its return, you must *pay* its return to the person you borrowed the stock from. But if this return is less than you expect to earn by investing your money in an alternative investment with equivalent risk, the strategy has a positive NPV and is attractive.† (We will discuss such strategies further in Chapter 11.)

In practice, short sales typically reflect a desire of some investors to bet against the stock. For example, in July 2008, Washington Mutual stood on the verge of bankruptcy as a result of its exposure to subprime mortgages. Even though its stock price had fallen by more than 90% in the prior year, many investors apparently felt the stock was still not attractive—the **short interest** (number of shares sold short) in Washington Mutual exceeded 500 million, representing more than 50% of Washington Mutual's outstanding shares.

The Cash Flows Associated with a Short Sale

P_0 is the initial price of the stock, P_1 is the price of the stock when the short sale is closed, and Div_t are dividends paid by the stock at any date t between 0 and 1.

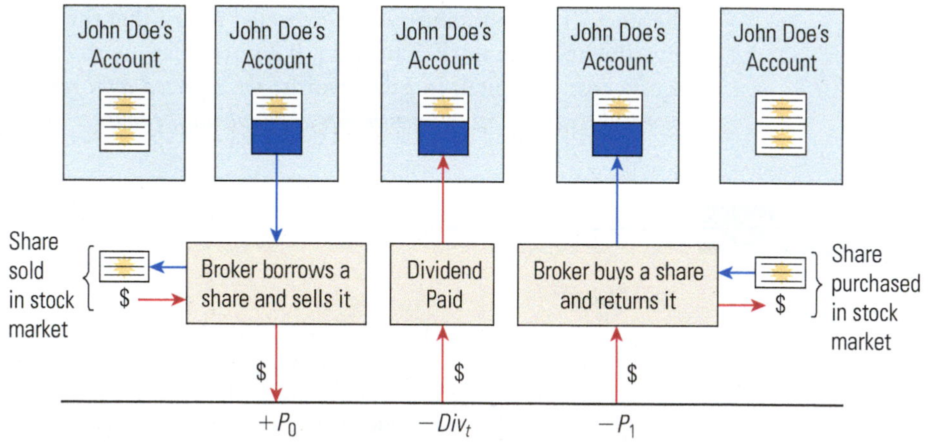

*Selling a stock without first locating a share to borrow is known as a *naked short sale*, and is prohibited by the SEC.

**In practice, John Doe need not know you borrowed his shares. He continues to receive dividends, and if he needs the shares, the broker will replace them either by (1) borrowing shares from someone else or (2) forcing the short-seller to close his position and buy the shares in the market.

†Typically, the broker will charge a fee for finding the shares to borrow, and require the short-seller to deposit collateral guaranteeing the short-seller's ability to buy the stock later. These costs of shorting tend to be small except in unusual circumstances.

The result in Eq. 9.2 is what we should expect: The firm must pay its shareholders a return commensurate with the return they can earn elsewhere while taking the same risk. If the stock offered a higher return than other securities with the same risk, investors would sell those other investments and buy the stock instead. This activity would drive up the stock's current price, lowering its dividend yield and capital gain rate until Eq. 9.2 holds true. If the stock offered a lower expected return, investors would sell the stock and drive down its current price until Eq. 9.2 was again satisfied.

A Multiyear Investor

Eq. 9.1 depends upon the expected stock price in one year, P_1. But suppose we planned to hold the stock for two years. Then we would receive dividends in both year 1 and year 2 before selling the stock, as shown in the following timeline:

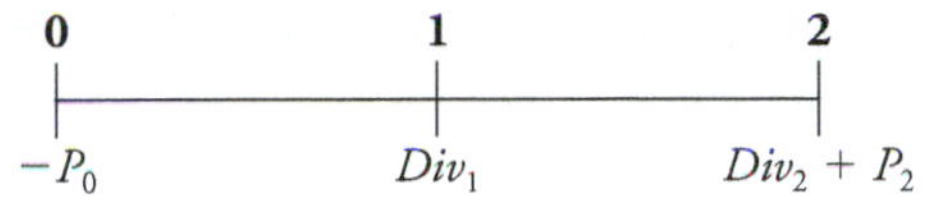

Setting the stock price equal to the present value of the future cash flows in this case implies[1]

$$P_0 = \frac{Div_1}{1 + r_E} + \frac{Div_2 + P_2}{(1 + r_E)^2} \tag{9.3}$$

Eqs. 9.1 and 9.3 are different: As a two-year investor we care about the dividend and stock price in year 2, but these terms do not appear in Eq. 9.1. Does this difference imply that a two-year investor will value the stock differently than a one-year investor?

The answer to this question is no. While a one-year investor does not care about the dividend and stock price in year 2 directly, she will care about them indirectly because they will affect the price for which she can sell the stock at the end of year 1. For example, suppose the investor sells the stock to another one-year investor with the same beliefs. The new investor will expect to receive the dividend and stock price at the end of year 2, so he will be willing to pay

$$P_1 = \frac{Div_2 + P_2}{1 + r_E}$$

for the stock. Substituting this expression for P_1 into Eq. 9.1, we get the same result as shown in Eq. 9.3:

$$\begin{aligned} P_0 &= \frac{Div_1 + P_1}{1 + r_E} = \frac{Div_1}{1 + r_E} + \frac{1}{1 + r_E}\overbrace{\left(\frac{Div_2 + P_2}{1 + r_E}\right)}^{P_1} \\ &= \frac{Div_1}{1 + r_E} + \frac{Div_2 + P_2}{(1 + r_E)^2} \end{aligned}$$

[1]By using the same equity cost of capital for both periods, we are assuming that the equity cost of capital does not depend on the term of the cash flows. Otherwise, we would need to adjust for the term structure of the equity cost of capital (as we did with the yield curve for risk-free cash flows in Chapter 5). This step would complicate the analysis but would not change the results.

Thus, the formula for the stock price for a two-year investor is the same as the one for a sequence of two one-year investors.

The Dividend-Discount Model Equation

We can continue this process for any number of years by replacing the final stock price with the value that the next holder of the stock would be willing to pay. Doing so leads to the general **dividend-discount model** for the stock price, where the horizon N is arbitrary:

Dividend-Discount Model

$$P_0 = \frac{Div_1}{1 + r_E} + \frac{Div_2}{(1 + r_E)^2} + \cdots + \frac{Div_N}{(1 + r_E)^N} + \frac{P_N}{(1 + r_E)^N} \tag{9.4}$$

Eq. 9.4 applies to a single N-year investor, who will collect dividends for N years and then sell the stock, or to a series of investors who hold the stock for shorter periods and then resell it. Note that Eq. 9.4 holds for *any* horizon N. Thus, all investors (with the same beliefs) will attach the same value to the stock, independent of their investment horizons. How long they intend to hold the stock and whether they collect their return in the form of dividends or capital gains is irrelevant. For the special case in which the firm eventually pays dividends and is never acquired, it is possible to hold the shares forever. Consequently, we can let N go to infinity in Eq. 9.4 and write it as follows:

$$P_0 = \frac{Div_1}{1 + r_E} + \frac{Div_2}{(1 + r_E)^2} + \frac{Div_3}{(1 + r_E)^3} + \cdots = \sum_{n=1}^{\infty} \frac{Div_n}{(1 + r_E)^n} \tag{9.5}$$

That is, *the price of the stock is equal to the present value of the expected future dividends it will pay.*

CONCEPT CHECK

1. How do you calculate the total return of a stock?
2. What discount rate do you use to discount the future cash flows of a stock?
3. Why will a short-term and long-term investor with the same beliefs be willing to pay the same price for a stock?

9.2 Applying the Dividend-Discount Model

Eq. 9.5 expresses the value of the stock in terms of the expected future dividends the firm will pay. Of course, estimating these dividends—especially for the distant future—is difficult. A common approximation is to assume that in the long run, dividends will grow at a constant rate. In this section, we will consider the implications of this assumption for stock prices and explore the trade-off between dividends and growth.

Constant Dividend Growth

The simplest forecast for the firm's future dividends states that they will grow at a constant rate, g, forever. That case yields the following timeline for the cash flows for an investor who buys the stock today and holds it:

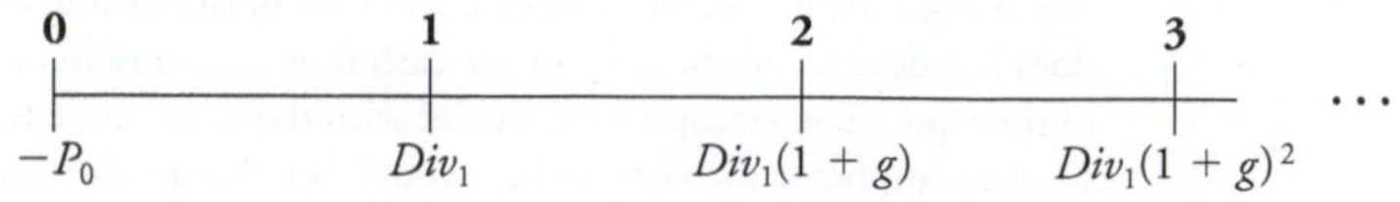

Because the expected dividends are a constant growth perpetuity, we can use Eq. 4.11 to calculate their present value. We then obtain the following simple formula for the stock price:[2]

Constant Dividend Growth Model

$$P_0 = \frac{Div_1}{r_E - g} \tag{9.6}$$

According to the **constant dividend growth model**, the value of the firm depends on the dividend level for the coming year, divided by the equity cost of capital adjusted by the expected growth rate of dividends.

EXAMPLE 9.2 **Valuing a Firm with Constant Dividend Growth**

Problem

Consolidated Edison, Inc. (Con Edison), is a regulated utility company that services the New York City area. Suppose Con Edison plans to pay \$2.60 per share in dividends in the coming year. If its equity cost of capital is 6% and dividends are expected to grow by 2% per year in the future, estimate the value of Con Edison's stock.

Solution

If dividends are expected to grow perpetually at a rate of 2% per year, we can use Eq. 9.6 to calculate the price of a share of Con Edison stock:

$$P_0 = \frac{Div_1}{r_E - g} = \frac{\$2.60}{0.06 - 0.02} = \$65$$

For another interpretation of Eq. 9.6, note that we can rearrange it as follows:

$$r_E = \frac{Div_1}{P_0} + g \tag{9.7}$$

Comparing Eq. 9.7 with Eq. 9.2, we see that g equals the expected capital gain rate. In other words, with constant expected dividend growth, the expected growth rate of the share price matches the growth rate of dividends.

Dividends Versus Investment and Growth

In Eq. 9.6, the firm's share price increases with the current dividend level, Div_1, and the expected growth rate, g. To maximize its share price, a firm would like to increase both these quantities. Often, however, the firm faces a trade-off: Increasing growth may require investment, and money spent on investment cannot be used to pay dividends. We can use the constant dividend growth model to gain insight into this trade-off.

[2]As we discussed in Chapter 4, this formula requires that $g < r_E$. Otherwise, the present value of the growing perpetuity is infinite. The implication here is that it is impossible for a stock's dividends to grow at a rate $g > r_E$ *forever*. If the growth rate exceeds r_E, it must be temporary, and the constant growth model does not apply.

John Burr Williams' *Theory of Investment Value*

The first formal derivation of the dividend-discount model appeared in the *Theory of Investment Value*, written by John Burr Williams in 1938. The book was an important landmark in the history of corporate finance, because Williams demonstrated for the first time that corporate finance relied on certain principles that could be derived using formal analytical methods. As Williams wrote in the preface:

> *The truth is that the mathematical method is a new tool of great power whose use promises to lead to notable advances in Investment Analysis. Always it has been the rule in the history of science that the invention of new tools is the key to new discoveries, and we may expect the same rule to hold true in this branch of Economics as well.*

Williams's book was not widely appreciated in its day—indeed, legend has it there was a lively debate at Harvard over whether it was acceptable as his Ph.D. dissertation. But Williams went on to become a very successful investor, and by the time he died in 1989, the importance of the mathematical method in corporate finance was indisputable, and the discoveries that resulted from this "new" tool had fundamentally changed its practice. Today, Williams is regarded as the founder of fundamental analysis, and his book pioneered the use of *pro forma* modeling of financial statements and cash flows for valuation purposes, as well as many other ideas now central to modern finance (see Chapter 14 for further contributions).

A Simple Model of Growth. What determines the rate of growth of a firm's dividends? If we define a firm's **dividend payout rate** as the fraction of its earnings that the firm pays as dividends each year, then we can write the firm's dividend per share at date t as follows:

$$Div_t = \underbrace{\frac{\text{Earnings}_t}{\text{Shares Outstanding}_t}}_{EPS_t} \times \text{Dividend Payout Rate}_t \tag{9.8}$$

That is, the dividend each year is the firm's earnings per share (EPS) multiplied by its dividend payout rate. Thus the firm can increase its dividend in three ways:

1. It can increase its earnings (net income).
2. It can increase its dividend payout rate.
3. It can decrease its shares outstanding.

Let's suppose for now that the firm does not issue new shares (or buy back its existing shares), so that the number of shares outstanding is fixed, and explore the potential tradeoff between options 1 and 2.

A firm can do one of two things with its earnings: It can pay them out to investors, or it can retain and reinvest them. By investing more today, a firm can increase its future earnings and dividends. For simplicity, let's assume that if no investment is made, the firm does not grow, so the current level of earnings generated by the firm remains constant. If all increases in future earnings result exclusively from new investment made with retained earnings, then

$$\text{Change in Earnings} = \text{New Investment} \times \text{Return on New Investment} \tag{9.9}$$

New investment equals earnings multiplied by the firm's **retention rate**, the fraction of current earnings that the firm retains:

$$\text{New Investment} = \text{Earnings} \times \text{Retention Rate} \tag{9.10}$$

Substituting Eq. 9.10 into Eq. 9.9 and dividing by earnings gives an expression for the growth rate of earnings:

$$\text{Earnings Growth Rate} = \frac{\text{Change in Earnings}}{\text{Earnings}}$$
$$= \text{Retention Rate} \times \text{Return on New Investment} \quad (9.11)$$

If the firm chooses to keep its dividend payout rate constant, then the growth in dividends will equal growth of earnings:

$$g = \text{Retention Rate} \times \text{Return on New Investment} \quad (9.12)$$

This growth rate is sometimes referred to as the firm's **sustainable growth rate**, the rate at which it can grow using only retained earnings.

Profitable Growth. Eq. 9.12 shows that a firm can increase its growth rate by retaining more of its earnings. However, if the firm retains more earnings, it will be able to pay out less of those earnings and, according to Eq. 9.8, will have to reduce its dividend. If a firm wants to increase its share price, should it cut its dividend and invest more, or should it cut investment and increase its dividend? Not surprisingly, the answer will depend on the profitability of the firm's investments. Let's consider an example.

EXAMPLE 9.3 Cutting Dividends for Profitable Growth

Problem

Crane Sporting Goods expects to have earnings per share of \$6 in the coming year. Rather than reinvest these earnings and grow, the firm plans to pay out all of its earnings as a dividend. With these expectations of no growth, Crane's current share price is \$60.

Suppose Crane could cut its dividend payout rate to 75% for the foreseeable future and use the retained earnings to open new stores. The return on its investment in these stores is expected to be 12%. Assuming its equity cost of capital is unchanged, what effect would this new policy have on Crane's stock price?

Solution

First, let's estimate Crane's equity cost of capital. Currently, Crane plans to pay a dividend equal to its earnings of \$6 per share. Given a share price of \$60, Crane's dividend yield is \$6/\$60 = 10%. With no expected growth ($g = 0$), we can use Eq. 9.7 to estimate r_E:

$$r_E = \frac{Div_1}{P_0} + g = 10\% + 0\% = 10\%$$

In other words, to justify Crane's stock price under its current policy, the expected return of other stocks in the market with equivalent risk must be 10%.

Next, we consider the consequences of the new policy. If Crane reduces its dividend payout rate to 75%, then from Eq. 9.8 its dividend this coming year will fall to $Div_1 = EPS_1 \times 75\% = \$6 \times 75\% = \$4.50$. At the same time, because the firm will now retain 25% of its earnings to invest in new stores, from Eq. 9.12 its growth rate will increase to

$$g = \text{Retention Rate} \times \text{Return on New Investment} = 25\% \times 12\% = 3\%$$

Assuming Crane can continue to grow at this rate, we can compute its share price under the new policy using the constant dividend growth model of Eq. 9.6:

$$P_0 = \frac{Div_1}{r_E - g} = \frac{\$4.50}{0.10 - 0.03} = \$64.29$$

Thus, Crane's share price should rise from \$60 to \$64.29 if it cuts its dividend to invest in projects that offer a return (12%) greater than their cost of capital (which we assume remains 10%). These projects are positive NPV, and so by taking them Crane has created value for its shareholders.

In Example 9.3, cutting the firm's dividend in favor of growth raised the firm's stock price. But this is not always the case, as the next example demonstrates.

EXAMPLE 9.4 Unprofitable Growth

Problem

Suppose Crane Sporting Goods decides to cut its dividend payout rate to 75% to invest in new stores, as in Example 9.3. But now suppose that the return on these new investments is 8%, rather than 12%. Given its expected earnings per share this year of \$6 and its equity cost of capital of 10%, what will happen to Crane's current share price in this case?

Solution

Just as in Example 9.3, Crane's dividend will fall to $\$6 \times 75\% = \$4.50$. Its growth rate under the new policy, given the lower return on new investment, will now be $g = 25\% \times 8\% = 2\%$. The new share price is therefore

$$P_0 = \frac{Div_1}{r_E - g} = \frac{\$4.50}{0.10 - 0.02} = \$56.25$$

Thus, even though Crane will grow under the new policy, the new investments have negative NPV. Crane's share price will fall if it cuts its dividend to make new investments with a return of only 8% when its investors can earn 10% on other investments with comparable risk.

Comparing Example 9.3 with Example 9.4, we see that the effect of cutting the firm's dividend to grow crucially depends on the return on new investment. In Example 9.3, the return on new investment of 12% exceeds the firm's equity cost of capital of 10%, so the investment has a positive NPV. In Example 9.4, the return on new investment is only 8%, so the new investment has a negative NPV (even though it will lead to earnings growth). Thus, *cutting the firm's dividend to increase investment will raise the stock price if, and only if, the new investments have a positive NPV.*

Changing Growth Rates

Successful young firms often have very high initial earnings growth rates. During this period of high growth, firms often retain 100% of their earnings to exploit profitable investment opportunities. As they mature, their growth slows to rates more typical of established companies. At that point, their earnings exceed their investment needs and they begin to pay dividends.

We cannot use the constant dividend growth model to value the stock of such a firm, for several reasons. First, these firms often pay *no* dividends when they are young. Second, their growth rate continues to change over time until they mature. However, we can use the general form of the dividend-discount model to value such a firm by applying the constant growth model to calculate the future share price of the stock P_N once the firm matures and its expected growth rate stabilizes:

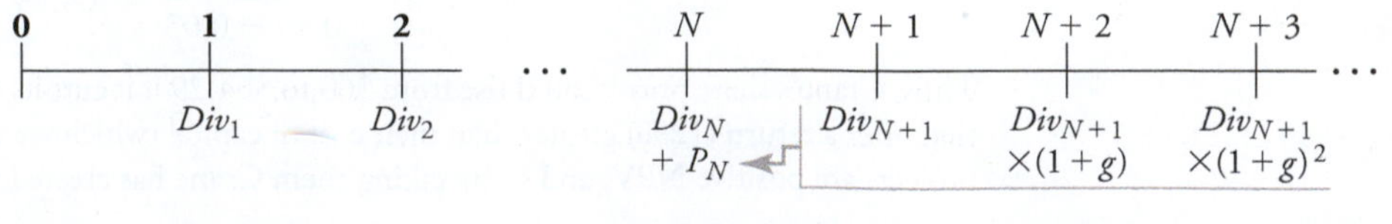

Specifically, if the firm is expected to grow at a long-term rate g after year $N+1$, then from the constant dividend growth model:

$$P_N = \frac{Div_{N+1}}{r_E - g} \tag{9.13}$$

We can then use this estimate of P_N as a terminal (continuation) value in the dividend-discount model. Combining Eq. 9.4 with Eq. 9.13, we have

Dividend-Discount Model with Constant Long-Term Growth

$$P_0 = \frac{Div_1}{1 + r_E} + \frac{Div_2}{(1 + r_E)^2} + \cdots + \frac{Div_N}{(1 + r_E)^N} + \frac{1}{(1 + r_E)^N}\left(\frac{Div_{N+1}}{r_E - g}\right) \tag{9.14}$$

EXAMPLE 9.5 Valuing a Firm with Two Different Growth Rates

Problem

Small Fry, Inc., has just invented a potato chip that looks and tastes like a french fry. Given the phenomenal market response to this product, Small Fry is reinvesting all of its earnings to expand its operations. Earnings were \$2 per share this past year and are expected to grow at a rate of 20% per year until the end of year 4. At that point, other companies are likely to bring out competing products. Analysts project that at the end of year 4, Small Fry will cut investment and begin paying 60% of its earnings as dividends and its growth will slow to a long-run rate of 4%. If Small Fry's equity cost of capital is 8%, what is the value of a share today?

Solution

We can use Small Fry's projected earnings growth rate and payout rate to forecast its future earnings and dividends as shown in the following spreadsheet:

Year	0	1	2	3	4	5	6
Earnings							
1 EPS Growth Rate (versus prior year)		20%	20%	20%	20%	4%	4%
2 EPS	\$2.00	\$2.40	\$2.88	\$3.46	\$4.15	\$4.31	\$4.49
Dividends							
3 Dividend Payout Rate		0%	0%	0%	60%	60%	60%
4 Dividend		\$ —	\$ —	\$ —	\$2.49	\$2.59	\$2.69

Starting from \$2.00 in year 0, EPS grows by 20% per year until year 4, after which growth slows to 4%. Small Fry's dividend payout rate is zero until year 4, when competition reduces its investment opportunities and its payout rate rises to 60%. Multiplying EPS by the dividend payout ratio, we project Small Fry's future dividends in line 4.

From year 4 onward, Small Fry's dividends will grow at the expected long-run rate of 4% per year. Thus, we can use the constant dividend growth model to project Small Fry's share price at the end of year 3. Given its equity cost of capital of 8%,

$$P_3 = \frac{Div_4}{r_E - g} = \frac{\$2.49}{0.08 - 0.04} = \$62.25$$

We then apply the dividend-discount model (Eq. 9.4) with this terminal value:

$$P_0 = \frac{Div_1}{1 + r_E} + \frac{Div_2}{(1 + r_E)^2} + \frac{Div_3}{(1 + r_E)^3} + \frac{P_3}{(1 + r_E)^3} = \frac{\$62.25}{(1.08)^3} = \$49.42$$

As this example illustrates, the dividend-discount model is flexible enough to handle any forecasted pattern of dividends.

Limitations of the Dividend-Discount Model

The dividend-discount model values the stock based on a forecast of the future dividends paid to shareholders. But unlike a Treasury bond, whose cash flows are known with virtual certainty, a tremendous amount of uncertainty is associated with any forecast of a firm's future dividends.

Let's consider the example of Kenneth Cole Productions (KCP), mentioned in the introduction to this chapter. In early 2006, KCP paid annual dividends of \$0.72. With an equity cost of capital of 11% and expected dividend growth of 8%, the constant dividend growth model implies a share price for KCP of

$$P_0 = \frac{Div_1}{r_E - g} = \frac{\$0.72}{0.11 - 0.08} = \$24$$

which is reasonably close to the \$26.75 share price the stock had at the time. With a 10% dividend growth rate, however, this estimate would rise to \$72 per share; with a 5% dividend growth rate, the estimate falls to \$12 per share. As we see, even small changes in the assumed dividend growth rate can lead to large changes in the estimated stock price.

Furthermore, it is difficult to know which estimate of the dividend growth rate is more reasonable. KCP more than doubled its dividend between 2003 and 2005, but earnings remained relatively flat during that time. Consequently, this rapid rate of dividend growth was not likely to be sustained. Forecasting dividends requires forecasting the firm's earnings, dividend payout rate, and future share count. But future earnings depend on interest expenses (which in turn depend on how much the firm borrows), and the firm's share count and dividend payout rate depend on whether the firm uses a portion of its earnings to repurchase shares. Because borrowing and repurchase decisions are at management's discretion, they can be difficult to forecast reliably.[3] We look at two alternative methods that avoid some of these difficulties in the next section.

CONCEPT CHECK

1. In what three ways can a firm increase its future dividend per share?
2. Under what circumstances can a firm increase its share price by cutting its dividend and investing more?

9.3 Total Payout and Free Cash Flow Valuation Models

In this section, we outline two alternative approaches to valuing the firm's shares that avoid some of the difficulties of the dividend-discount model. First, we consider the *total payout model*, which allows us to ignore the firm's choice between dividends and share repurchases. Then, we consider the *discounted free cash flow model*, which focuses on the cash flows to all of the firm's investors, both debt and equity holders, allowing us to avoid estimating the impact of the firm's borrowing decisions on earnings.

Share Repurchases and the Total Payout Model

In our discussion of the dividend-discount model, we implicitly assumed that any cash paid out by the firm to shareholders takes the form of a dividend. However, in recent years, an increasing number of firms have replaced dividend payouts with *share repurchases*. In a

[3] We discuss management's decision to borrow funds or repurchase shares in Part 5.

share repurchase, the firm uses excess cash to buy back its own stock. Share repurchases have two consequences for the dividend-discount model. First, the more cash the firm uses to repurchase shares, the less it has available to pay dividends. Second, by repurchasing shares, the firm decreases its share count, which increases its earnings and dividends on a per-share basis.

In the dividend-discount model, we valued a share from the perspective of a single shareholder, discounting the dividends the shareholder will receive:

$$P_0 = PV(\text{Future Dividends per Share}) \tag{9.15}$$

An alternative method that may be more reliable when a firm repurchases shares is the **total payout model**, which values *all* of the firm's equity, rather than a single share. To do so, we discount the total payouts that the firm makes to shareholders, which is the total amount spent on both dividends *and* share repurchases.[4] Then, we divide by the current number of shares outstanding to determine the share price.

Total Payout Model

$$P_0 = \frac{PV(\text{Future Total Dividends and Repurchases})}{\text{Shares Outstanding}_0} \tag{9.16}$$

We can apply the same simplifications that we obtained by assuming constant growth in Section 9.2 to the total payout method. The only change is that *we discount total dividends and share repurchases and use the growth rate of total earnings (rather than earnings per share) when forecasting the growth of the firm's total payouts*. This method can be more reliable and easier to apply when the firm uses share repurchases.

EXAMPLE 9.6 Valuation with Share Repurchases

Problem

Titan Industries has 217 million shares outstanding and expects earnings at the end of this year of $860 million. Titan plans to pay out 50% of its earnings in total, paying 30% as a dividend and using 20% to repurchase shares. If Titan's earnings are expected to grow by 7.5% per year and these payout rates remain constant, determine Titan's share price assuming an equity cost of capital of 10%.

Solution

Titan will have total payouts this year of 50% × $860 million = $430 million. Based on the equity cost of capital of 10% and an expected earnings growth rate of 7.5%, the present value of Titan's future payouts can be computed as a constant growth perpetuity:

$$PV(\text{Future Total Dividends and Repurchases}) = \frac{\$430 \text{ million}}{0.10 - 0.075} = \$17.2 \text{ billion}$$

This present value represents the total value of Titan's equity (i.e., its market capitalization). To compute the share price, we divide by the current number of shares outstanding:

$$P_0 = \frac{\$17.2 \text{ billion}}{217 \text{ million shares}} = \$79.26 \text{ per share}$$

[4]Think of the total payouts as the amount you would receive if you owned 100% of the firm's shares: You would receive all of the dividends, plus the proceeds from selling shares back to the firm in the share repurchase.

Using the total payout method, we did not need to know the firm's split between dividends and share repurchases. To compare this method with the dividend-discount model, note that Titan will pay a dividend of 30% × \$860 million/(217 million shares) = \$1.19 per share, for a dividend yield of 1.19/79.26 = 1.50%. From Eq. 9.7, Titan's expected EPS, dividend, and share price growth rate is $g = r_E - Div_1/P_0 = 8.50\%$. These "per share" growth rates exceed the 7.5% growth rate of total earnings because Titan's share count will decline over time due to share repurchases.[5]

The Discounted Free Cash Flow Model

In the total payout model, we first value the firm's equity, rather than just a single share. The **discounted free cash flow model** goes one step further and begins by determining the total value of the firm to all investors—both equity *and* debt holders. That is, we begin by estimating the firm's enterprise value, which we defined in Chapter 2 as[6]

$$\text{Enterprise Value} = \text{Market Value of Equity} + \text{Debt} - \text{Cash} \tag{9.17}$$

The enterprise value is the value of the firm's underlying business, unencumbered by debt and separate from any cash or marketable securities. We can interpret the enterprise value as the net cost of acquiring the firm's equity, taking its cash, paying off all debt, and thus owning the unlevered business. The advantage of the discounted free cash flow model is that it allows us to value a firm without explicitly forecasting its dividends, share repurchases, or its use of debt.

Valuing the Enterprise. How can we estimate a firm's enterprise value? To estimate the value of the firm's equity, we computed the present value of the firm's total payouts to equity holders. Likewise, to estimate a firm's enterprise value, we compute the present value of the *free cash flow* (FCF) that the firm has available to pay all investors, both debt and equity holders. We saw how to compute the free cash flow for a project in Chapter 8; we now perform the same calculation for the entire firm:

$$\text{Free Cash Flow} = \overbrace{EBIT \times (1 - \tau_c)}^{\text{Unlevered Net Income}} + \text{Depreciation}$$
$$- \text{Capital Expenditures} - \text{Increases in Net Working Capital} \tag{9.18}$$

When we are looking at the entire firm, it is natural to define the firm's **net investment** as its capital expenditures in excess of depreciation:

$$\text{Net Investment} = \text{Capital Expenditures} - \text{Depreciation} \tag{9.19}$$

We can loosely interpret net investment as investment intended to support the firm's growth, above and beyond the level needed to maintain the firm's existing capital. With that definition, we can also write the free cash flow formula as

[5] The difference in the per share and total earnings growth rate results from Titan's "repurchase yield" of (20% × \$860 million/217 million shares)/(\$79.26/share) = 1%. Indeed, given an expected share price of \$79.26 × 1.085 = \$86.00 next year, Titan will repurchase 20% × \$860 million ÷ (\$86 per share) = 2 million shares next year. With the decline in the number of shares from 217 million to 215 million, EPS grows by a factor of 1.075 × (217/215) = 1.085 or 8.5%.

[6] To be precise, by cash we are referring to the firm's cash in excess of its working capital needs, which is the amount of cash it has invested at a competitive market interest rate.

$$\text{Free Cash Flow} = EBIT \times (1 - \tau_c) - \text{Net Investment}$$
$$- \text{Increases in Net Working Capital} \tag{9.20}$$

Free cash flow measures the cash generated by the firm before any payments to debt or equity holders are considered.

Thus, just as we determine the value of a project by calculating the NPV of the project's free cash flow, we estimate a firm's current enterprise value V_0 by computing the present value of the firm's free cash flow:

Discounted Free Cash Flow Model

$$V_0 = PV(\text{Future Free Cash Flow of Firm}) \tag{9.21}$$

Given the enterprise value, we can estimate the share price by using Eq. 9.17 to solve for the value of equity and then divide by the total number of shares outstanding:

$$P_0 = \frac{V_0 + \text{Cash}_0 - \text{Debt}_0}{\text{Shares Outstanding}_0} \tag{9.22}$$

Intuitively, the difference between the discounted free cash flow model and the dividend-discount model is that in the dividend-discount model, the firm's cash and debt are included indirectly through the effect of interest income and expenses on earnings. In the discounted free cash flow model, we ignore interest income and expenses (free cash flow is based on EBIT), but then adjust for cash and debt directly in Eq. 9.22.

Implementing the Model. A key difference between the discounted free cash flow model and the earlier models we have considered is the discount rate. In previous calculations we used the firm's equity cost of capital, r_E, because we were discounting the cash flows to equity holders. Here we are discounting the free cash flow that will be paid to both debt and equity holders. Thus, we should use the firm's **weighted average cost of capital (WACC)**, denoted by r_{wacc}, which is the average cost of capital the firm must pay to all of its investors, both debt and equity holders. If the firm has no debt, then $r_{wacc} = r_E$. But when a firm has debt, r_{wacc} is an average of the firm's debt and equity cost of capital. In that case, because debt is generally less risky than equity, r_{wacc} is generally less than r_E. We can also interpret the WACC as reflecting the average risk of all of the firm's investments. We'll develop methods to calculate the WACC explicitly in Parts 4 and 5.

Given the firm's weighted average cost of capital, we implement the discounted free cash flow model in much the same way as we did the dividend-discount model. That is, we forecast the firm's free cash flow up to some horizon, together with a terminal (continuation) value of the enterprise:

$$V_0 = \frac{FCF_1}{1 + r_{wacc}} + \frac{FCF_2}{(1 + r_{wacc})^2} + \cdots + \frac{FCF_N + V_N}{(1 + r_{wacc})^N} \tag{9.23}$$

Often, the terminal value is estimated by assuming a constant long-run growth rate g_{FCF} for free cash flows beyond year N, so that

$$V_N = \frac{FCF_{N+1}}{r_{wacc} - g_{FCF}} = \left(\frac{1 + g_{FCF}}{r_{wacc} - g_{FCF}}\right) \times FCF_N \tag{9.24}$$

The long-run growth rate g_{FCF} is typically based on the expected long-run growth rate of the firm's revenues.

EXAMPLE 9.7 Valuing Kenneth Cole Using Free Cash Flow

Problem

Kenneth Cole (KCP) had sales of $518 million in 2005. Suppose you expect its sales to grow at a 9% rate in 2006, but that this growth rate will slow by 1% per year to a long-run growth rate for the apparel industry of 4% by 2011. Based on KCP's past profitability and investment needs, you expect EBIT to be 9% of sales, increases in net working capital requirements to be 10% of any increase in sales, and net investment (capital expenditures in excess of depreciation) to be 8% of any increase in sales. If KCP has $100 million in cash, $3 million in debt, 21 million shares outstanding, a tax rate of 37%, and a weighted average cost of capital of 11%, what is your estimate of the value of KCP's stock in early 2006?

Solution

Using Eq. 9.20, we can estimate KCP's future free cash flow based on the estimates above as follows:

	Year	2005	2006	2007	2008	2009	2010	2011
	FCF Forecast ($ millions)							
1	Sales	518.0	564.6	609.8	652.5	691.6	726.2	755.3
2	*Growth versus Prior Year*		*9.0%*	*8.0%*	*7.0%*	*6.0%*	*5.0%*	*4.0%*
3	**EBIT** (9% of sales)		50.8	54.9	58.7	62.2	65.4	68.0
4	Less: Income Tax (37% EBIT)		(18.8)	(20.3)	(21.7)	(23.0)	(24.2)	(25.1)
5	Less: Net Investment (8% ΔSales)		(3.7)	(3.6)	(3.4)	(3.1)	(2.8)	(2.3)
6	Less: Inc. in NWC (10% ΔSales)		(4.7)	(4.5)	(4.3)	(3.9)	(3.5)	(2.9)
7	**Free Cash Flow**		23.6	26.4	29.3	32.2	35.0	37.6

Because we expect KCP's free cash flow to grow at a constant rate after 2011, we can use Eq. 9.24 to compute a terminal enterprise value:

$$V_{2011} = \left(\frac{1 + g_{FCF}}{r_{wacc} - g_{FCF}}\right) \times FCF_{2011} = \left(\frac{1.04}{0.11 - 0.04}\right) \times 37.6 = \$558.6 \text{ million}$$

From Eq. 9.23, KCP's current enterprise value is the present value of its free cash flows plus the terminal enterprise value:

$$V_0 = \frac{23.6}{1.11} + \frac{26.4}{1.11^2} + \frac{29.3}{1.11^3} + \frac{32.2}{1.11^4} + \frac{35.0}{1.11^5} + \frac{37.6 + 558.6}{1.11^6} = \$424.8 \text{ million}$$

We can now estimate the value of a share of KCP's stock using Eq. 9.22:

$$P_0 = \frac{424.8 + 100 - 3}{21} = \$24.85$$

Connection to Capital Budgeting. There is an important connection between the discounted free cash flow model and the NPV rule for capital budgeting that we developed in Chapter 8. Because the firm's free cash flow is equal to the sum of the free cash flows from the firm's current and future investments, we can interpret the firm's enterprise value as the total NPV that the firm will earn from continuing its existing projects and initiating new ones. Hence, the NPV of any individual project represents its contribution to the firm's enterprise value. To maximize the firm's share price, we should accept projects that have a positive NPV.

Recall also from Chapter 8 that many forecasts and estimates were necessary to estimate the free cash flows of a project. The same is true for the firm: We must forecast future sales, operating expenses, taxes, capital requirements, and other factors. On the one hand, estimating free cash flow in this way gives us flexibility to incorporate many specific details about the future prospects of the firm. On the other hand, some uncertainty inevitably surrounds each assumption. It is therefore important to conduct a sensitivity analysis, as we described in Chapter 8, to translate this uncertainty into a range of potential values for the stock.

EXAMPLE 9.8 Sensitivity Analysis for Stock Valuation

Problem

In Example 9.7, KCP's revenue growth rate was assumed to be 9% in 2006, slowing to a long-term growth rate of 4%. How would your estimate of the stock's value change if you expected revenue growth of 4% from 2006 on? How would it change if in addition you expected EBIT to be 7% of sales, rather than 9%?

Solution

With 4% revenue growth and a 9% EBIT margin, KCP will have 2006 revenues of $518 \times 1.04 = \$538.7$ million, and EBIT of $9\%(538.7) = \$48.5$ million. Given the increase in sales of $538.7 - 518.0 = \$20.7$ million, we expect net investment of $8\%(20.7) = \$1.7$ million and additional net working capital of $10\%(20.7) = \$2.1$ million. Thus, KCP's expected FCF in 2006 is

$$FCF_{06} = 48.5\,(1 - .37) - 1.7 - 2.1 = \$26.8 \text{ million}$$

Because growth is expected to remain constant at 4%, we can estimate KCP's enterprise value as a growing perpetuity:

$$V_0 = \$26.8/(0.11 - 0.04) = \$383 \text{ million}$$

for an initial share value of $P_0 = (383 + 100 - 3)/21 = \$22.86$. Thus, comparing this result with that of Example 9.7, we see that a higher initial revenue growth of 9% versus 4% contributes about \$2 to the value of KCP's stock.

If, in addition, we expect KCP's EBIT margin to be only 7%, our FCF estimate would decline to

$$FCF_{06} = (.07 \times 538.7)(1 - .37) - 1.7 - 2.1 = \$20.0 \text{ million}$$

for an enterprise value of $V_0 = \$20/(0.11 - 0.04) = \$286$ million and a share value of $P_0 = (286 + 100 - 3)/21 = \$18.24$. Thus, we can see that maintaining an EBIT margin of 9% versus 7% contributes more than \$4.50 to KCP's stock value in this scenario.

Figure 9.1 summarizes the different valuation methods we have discussed thus far. The value of the stock is determined by the present value of its future dividends. We can estimate the total market capitalization of the firm's equity from the present value of the firm's total payouts, which includes dividends and share repurchases. Finally, the present value

FIGURE 9.1 A Comparison of Discounted Cash Flow Models of Stock Valuation

By computing the present value of the firm's dividends, total payouts or free cash flows, we can estimate the value of the stock, the total value of the firm's equity, or the firm's enterprise value.

Present Value of ...	Determines the ...
Dividend Payments	Stock Price
Total Payouts (All dividends and repurchases)	Equity Value
Free Cash Flow (Cash available to pay all security holders)	Enterprise Value

of the firm's free cash flow, which is the cash the firm has available to make payments to equity or debt holders, determines the firm's enterprise value.

CONCEPT CHECK

1. How does the growth rate used in the total payout model differ from the growth rate used in the dividend-discount model?
2. What is the enterprise value of the firm?
3. How can you estimate a firm's stock price based on its projected free cash flows?

9.4 Valuation Based on Comparable Firms

Thus far, we have valued a firm or its stock by considering the expected future cash flows it will provide to its owner. The Law of One Price then tells us that its value is the present value of its future cash flows, because the present value is the amount we would need to invest elsewhere in the market to replicate the cash flows with the same risk.

Another application of the Law of One Price is the method of comparables. In the **method of comparables** (or "comps"), rather than value the firm's cash flows directly, we estimate the value of the firm based on the value of other, comparable firms or investments that we expect will generate very similar cash flows in the future. For example, consider the case of a new firm that is *identical* to an existing publicly traded company. If these firms will generate identical cash flows, the Law of One Price implies that we can use the value of the existing company to determine the value of the new firm.

Of course, identical companies do not exist. Although they may be similar in many respects, even two firms in the same industry selling the same types of products are likely to be of a different size or scale. In this section, we consider ways to adjust for scale differences to use comparables to value firms with similar business, and then discuss the strengths and weaknesses of this approach.

Valuation Multiples

We can adjust for differences in scale between firms by expressing their value in terms of a **valuation multiple**, which is a ratio of the value to some measure of the firm's scale. As an analogy, consider valuing an office building. A natural measure to consider would be the price per square foot for other buildings recently sold in the area. Multiplying the size of the office building under consideration by the average price per square foot would typically provide a reasonable estimate of the building's value. We can apply this same idea to stocks, replacing square footage with some more appropriate measure of the firm's scale.

The Price-Earnings Ratio. The most common valuation multiple is the price-earnings (P/E) ratio, which we introduced in Chapter 2. A firm's P/E ratio is equal to the share price divided by its earnings per share. The intuition behind its use is that when you buy a stock, you are in a sense buying the rights to the firm's future earnings. Because differences in the scale of firms' earnings are likely to persist, you should be willing to pay proportionally more for a stock with higher current earnings. Thus, we can estimate the value of a firm's share by multiplying its current earnings per share by the average P/E ratio of comparable firms.

To interpret the P/E multiple, consider the stock price formula we derived in Eq. 9.6 for the case of constant dividend growth: $P_0 = Div_1/(r_E - g)$. If we divide both sides of this equation by EPS_1, we have the following formula:

$$\text{Forward P/E} = \frac{P_0}{EPS_1} = \frac{Div_1/EPS_1}{r_E - g} = \frac{\text{Dividend Payout Rate}}{r_E - g} \tag{9.25}$$

Eq. 9.25 provides a formula for the firm's **forward P/E**, which is the P/E multiple computed based on its **forward earnings** (expected earnings over the next twelve months). We can also compute a firm's **trailing P/E** ratio using **trailing earnings** (earnings over the prior 12 months).[7] For valuation purposes, the forward P/E is generally preferred, as we are most concerned about future earnings.[8]

Eq. 9.25 implies that if two stocks have the same payout and EPS growth rates, as well as equivalent risk (and therefore the same equity cost of capital), then they should have the same P/E. It also shows that firms and industries with high growth rates, and that generate cash well in excess of their investment needs so that they can maintain high payout rates, should have high P/E multiples.

EXAMPLE 9.9 Valuation Using the Price-Earnings Ratio

Problem

Suppose furniture manufacturer Herman Miller, Inc., has earnings per share of $1.38. If the average P/E of comparable furniture stocks is 21.3, estimate a value for Herman Miller using the P/E as a valuation multiple. What are the assumptions underlying this estimate?

Solution

We estimate a share price for Herman Miller by multiplying its EPS by the P/E of comparable firms. Thus, $P_0 = \$1.38 \times 21.3 = \$29.39$. This estimate assumes that Herman Miller will have similar future risk, payout rates, and growth rates to comparable firms in the industry.

Enterprise Value Multiples. It is also common practice to use valuation multiples based on the firm's enterprise value. As we discussed in Section 9.3, because it represents the total value of the firm's underlying business rather than just the value of equity, using the enterprise value is advantageous if we want to compare firms with different amounts of leverage.

Because the enterprise value represents the entire value of the firm before the firm pays its debt, to form an appropriate multiple, we divide it by a measure of earnings or cash flows before interest payments are made. Common multiples to consider are enterprise value to EBIT, EBITDA (earnings before interest, taxes, depreciation, and amortization), and free cash flow. However, because capital expenditures can vary substantially from period to period (e.g., a firm may need to add capacity and build a new plant one year, but then not need to expand further for many years), most practitioners rely on enterprise value to EBITDA multiples. From Eq. 9.24, if expected free cash flow growth is constant, then

$$\frac{V_0}{EBITDA_1} = \frac{FCF_1 / EBITDA_1}{r_{wacc} - g_{FCF}} \tag{9.26}$$

As with the P/E multiple, this multiple is higher for firms with high growth rates and low capital requirements (so that free cash flow is high in proportion to EBITDA).

---

[7]Assuming EPS grows at rate g_0 between date 0 and 1,

$$\text{Trailing P/E} = P_0/EPS_0 = (1 + g_0)\,P_0/EPS_1 = (1 + g_0)\,(\text{Forward P/E})$$

so trailing multiples tend to be higher for growing firms. Thus, when comparing multiples, be sure to be consistent in the use of either trailing or forward multiples across firms.

[8]Because we are interested in the persistent components of the firm's earnings, it is also common practice to exclude extraordinary items that will not be repeated when calculating a P/E ratio for valuation purposes.

EXAMPLE 9.10 **Valuation Using an Enterprise Value Multiple**

Problem

Suppose Rocky Shoes and Boots (RCKY) has earnings per share of $2.30 and EBITDA of $30.7 million. RCKY also has 5.4 million shares outstanding and debt of $125 million (net of cash). You believe Deckers Outdoor Corporation is comparable to RCKY in terms of its underlying business, but Deckers has little debt. If Deckers has a P/E of 13.3 and an enterprise value to EBITDA multiple of 7.4, estimate the value of RCKY's shares using both multiples. Which estimate is likely to be more accurate?

Solution

Using Decker's P/E, we would estimate a share price for RCKY of $P_0 = \$2.30 \times 13.3 = \$30.59$. Using the enterprise value to EBITDA multiple, we would estimate RCKY's enterprise value to be $V_0 = \$30.7$ million $\times\ 7.4 = \$227.2$ million. We then subtract debt and divide by the number of shares to estimate RCKY's share price: $P_0 = (227.2 - 125)/5.4 = \$18.93$. Because of the large difference in leverage between the firms, we would expect the second estimate, which is based on enterprise value, to be more reliable.

Other Multiples. Many other valuation multiples are possible. Looking at enterprise value as a multiple of sales can be useful if it is reasonable to assume that the firms will maintain similar margins in the future. For firms with substantial tangible assets, the ratio of price to book value of equity per share is sometimes used. Some multiples are specific to an industry. In the cable TV industry, for example, it is natural to consider enterprise value per subscriber.

Limitations of Multiples

If comparable firms were identical, their multiples would match precisely. Of course, firms are not identical. Thus, the usefulness of a valuation multiple will depend on the nature of the differences between firms and the sensitivity of the multiples to these differences.

Table 9.1 lists several valuation multiples for Kenneth Cole as well as for other firms in the footwear industry as of January 2006. Also shown is the average for each multiple, together with the range around the average (in percentage terms). Comparing Kenneth Cole with the industry averages, KCP looks somewhat overvalued according to its P/E (i.e., it trades at a higher P/E multiple), and somewhat undervalued according to the other multiples shown. For all of the multiples, however, a significant amount of dispersion across the industry is apparent. While the enterprise value to EBITDA multiple shows the smallest variation, even with it we cannot expect to obtain a precise estimate of value.

The differences in these multiples are most likely due to differences in their expected future growth rates, profitability, risk (and therefore costs of capital), and, in the case of Puma, differences in accounting conventions between the United States and Germany. Investors in the market understand that these differences exist, so the stocks are priced accordingly. But when valuing a firm using multiples, there is no clear guidance about how to adjust for these differences other than by narrowing the set of comparables used.

Thus, a key shortcoming of the comparables approach is that it does not take into account the important differences among firms. One firm might have an exceptional management team, another might have developed an efficient manufacturing process, or secured a patent on a new technology. Such differences are ignored when we apply a valuation multiple.

TABLE 9.1 Stock Prices and Multiples for the Footwear Industry, January 2006

Ticker	Name	Stock Price ($)	Market Capitalization ($ millions)	Enterprise Value ($ millions)	P/E	Price/ Book	Enterprise Value/ Sales	Enterprise Value/ EBITDA
KCP	Kenneth Cole Productions	26.75	562	465	16.21	2.22	0.90	8.36
NKE	NIKE, Inc.	84.20	21,830	20,518	16.64	3.59	1.43	8.75
PMMAY	Puma AG	312.05	5,088	4,593	14.99	5.02	2.19	9.02
RBK	Reebok International	58.72	3,514	3,451	14.91	2.41	0.90	8.58
WWW	Wolverine World Wide	22.10	1,257	1,253	17.42	2.71	1.20	9.53
BWS	Brown Shoe Company	43.36	800	1,019	22.62	1.91	0.47	9.09
SKX	Skechers U.S.A.	17.09	683	614	17.63	2.02	0.62	6.88
SRR	Stride Rite Corp.	13.70	497	524	20.72	1.87	0.89	9.28
DECK	Deckers Outdoor Corp.	30.05	373	367	13.32	2.29	1.48	7.44
WEYS	Weyco Group	19.90	230	226	11.97	1.75	1.06	6.66
RCKY	Rocky Shoes & Boots	19.96	106	232	8.66	1.12	0.92	7.55
DFZ	R.G. Barry Corp.	6.83	68	92	9.20	8.11	0.87	10.75
BOOT	LaCrosse Footwear	10.40	62	75	12.09	1.28	0.76	8.30
			Average (excl. KCP)		**15.01**	**2.84**	**1.06**	**8.49**
			Max (relative to Avg.)		+51%	+186%	+106%	+27%
			Min (relative to Avg.)		−42%	−61%	−56%	−22%

Another limitation of comparables is that they only provide information regarding the value of the firm *relative to* the other firms in the comparison set. Using multiples will not help us determine if an entire industry is overvalued, for example. This issue became especially important during the Internet boom of the late 1990s. Because many of these firms did not have positive cash flows or earnings, new multiples were created to value them (e.g., price to "page views"). While these multiples could justify the value of these firms in relation to one another, it was much more difficult to justify the stock prices of many of these firms using a realistic estimate of cash flows and the discounted free cash flow approach.

Comparison with Discounted Cash Flow Methods

Using a valuation multiple based on comparables is best viewed as a "shortcut" to the discounted cash flow methods of valuation. Rather than separately estimate the firm's cost of capital and future earnings or free cash flows, we rely on the market's assessment of the value of other firms with similar future prospects. In addition to its simplicity, the multiples approach has the advantage of being based on actual prices of real firms, rather than what may be unrealistic forecasts of future cash flows.

On the other hand, discounted cash flow (DCF) methods have the advantage that they allow us to incorporate specific information about the firm's profitability, cost of capital, or future growth potential, as well as perform sensitivity analysis. Because the true driver of value for any firm is its ability to generate cash flows for its investors, the discounted cash flow methods have the potential to be more accurate and insightful than the use of a valuation multiple. In particular, DCF methods make explicit the future performance the firm must achieve in order to justify its current value.

Stock Valuation Techniques: The Final Word

In the end, no single technique provides a final answer regarding a stock's true value. All approaches require assumptions or forecasts that are too uncertain to provide a definitive assessment of the firm's value. Most real-world practitioners use a combination of these approaches and gain confidence if the results are consistent across a variety of methods.

Figure 9.2 compares the ranges of values for Kenneth Cole Productions using the different valuation methods that we have discussed in this chapter.[9] Kenneth Cole's stock price of $26.75 in January 2006 is within the range estimated by all of these methods. Hence, based on this evidence alone we would not conclude that the stock is obviously under- or overpriced.

FIGURE 9.2 **Range of Valuations for KCP Stock Using Alternative Valuation Methods**

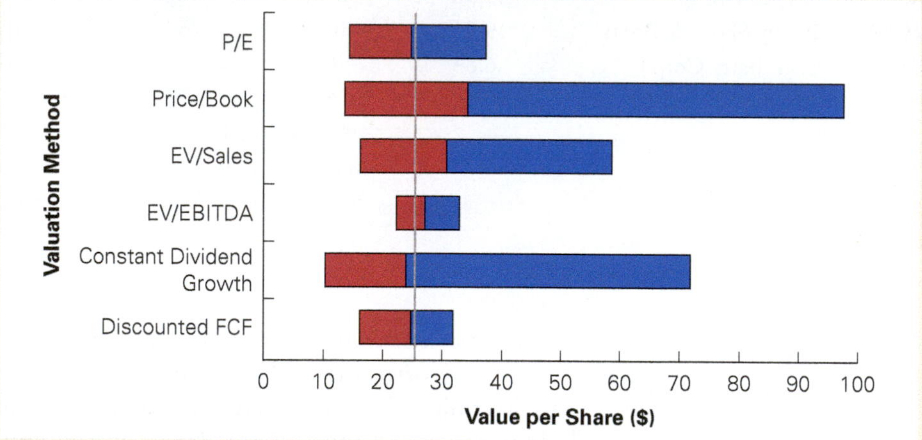

Valuations from multiples are based on the low, high, and average values of the comparable firms from Table 9.1 (see Problems 25 and 26 at the end of the chapter). The constant dividend growth model is based on an 11% equity cost of capital and 4%, 8%, and 10% dividend growth rates, as discussed at the end of Section 9.2. The discounted free cash flow model is based on Example 9.7 with the range of parameters in Problem 22. (Midpoints are based on average multiples or base case assumptions. Red and blue regions show the variation between the lowest-multiple/worst-case scenario and the highest-multiple/best-case scenario. KCP's actual share price of $26.75 is indicated by the gray line.)

CONCEPT CHECK

1. What are some common valuation multiples?
2. What implicit assumptions are made when valuing a firm using multiples based on comparable firms?

[9] A chart such as this one, showing the range of values produced by each valuation method, is often referred to as a valuation "football field chart" by practitioners.

INTERVIEW WITH DOUGLAS KEHRING

Since 2005, Douglas Kehring has been Senior Vice President of Oracle Corporation's Corporate Development and Strategic Planning group, providing planning, advisory, execution, and integration management services to Oracle on mergers and acquisitions and related transactions.

QUESTION: *How does Oracle target companies to acquire?*

ANSWER: Oracle uses an ongoing strategic planning process to identify potential acquisition targets. Top-down, the corporate development group works with the CEO's office looking for large, game-changing acquisitions. We also work bottom-up with engineering executives who sponsor potential acquisitions to fill customer needs and product gaps. Together we identify prospects, engage with targets, perform due diligence, develop business plans, and proceed with feasible transactions. Our group also provides the CEO's office with objective opinions of sponsor proposals, based on Oracle's overall needs and priorities. The CEO's office approves all transactions.

We see about 300 to 400 opportunities a year and show all to the appropriate product group executives, including those from venture capital firms and investment bankers. Typically, they express an interest in about 20 to 40, and we sign confidentiality agreements to proceed with a thorough analysis. About 12 of those reach the letter of intent stage, where we issue a term sheet and an exclusivity period to complete the transaction.

QUESTION: *Once you decide to try to acquire a company, how do you determine how much to pay for it?*

ANSWER: The pricing occurs after due diligence but before the letter of intent. From a practical standpoint, we negotiate the price point with the seller—that's where the art comes into play. Our DCF analysis is the most important part in justifying the value. We take into account what we believe we can do with the business from an income statement perspective, to determine the breakeven valuation at the chosen hurdle rate. If we pay less, we'll earn a higher rate of return, and vice versa.

QUESTION: *Discuss the role of both discounted cash flow and comparables analysis in determining the price to pay.*

ANSWER: We use 5-year DCFs, because it takes that long to get to a steady state and predicting beyond that is difficult. The hardest part is determining the income statement inputs. The fifth-year numbers dominate value. Getting to that point depends on how fast you grow the business and how profitable it is. Assumptions are the key. We take a conservative approach, leveraging available information. Overly aggressive sponsor assumptions lead to extreme valuations, creating an acquirer's biggest problems.

The hurdle rate for a project varies. We might use cost of equity or the WACC. Then we ask, "What is right risk/return profile for this transaction?" and adjust the rate accordingly—for example, possibly requiring a higher return for a smaller, more volatile company.

Oracle's 80 completed transactions give us actual experience on which to base more realistic assumptions. We look at variables and attributes—was it a product line, a specific feature, a stand-alone acquisition?—and assess how well we did based on our models, to improve our cash flow analysis for future acquisitions. Then we benchmark using common valuation multiples based on comparable publicly traded companies and similar M&A transactions.

QUESTION: *How does your analysis differ for private versus public companies?*

ANSWER: The basic DCF analysis is no different: We perform the same due diligence for private and public companies and receive the same types of information. Typically, the larger the public company's revenues, the more stable it is and the more professional its orientation and systems. We feel more confident in our risk attributes and the information we receive. In acquiring a public company, we prepare a pro forma statement for the combined entity to determine whether it will increase or decrease our earnings per share.

Of greater concern to us is the target's size. A $2 billion company, whether public or private, has multiple product lines and larger installed bases, reducing its risk profile. A $100 million company may have only one product line and thus, higher risk and volatility. On the other hand, the small company may grow faster than a large one.

9.5 Information, Competition, and Stock Prices

As shown in Figure 9.3, the models described in this chapter link the firm's expected future cash flows, its cost of capital (determined by its risk), and the value of its shares. But what conclusions should we draw if the actual market price of a stock doesn't appear to be consistent with our estimate of its value? Is it more likely that the stock is mispriced or that we made a mistake in our risk and future cash flow estimates? We close this chapter with a consideration of this question and the implications for corporate managers.

Information in Stock Prices

Consider the following situation. You are a new junior analyst assigned to research Kenneth Cole Productions' stock and assess its value. You scrutinize the company's recent financial statements, look at the trends in the industry, and forecast the firm's future earnings, dividends, and free cash flows. You carefully run the numbers and estimate the stock's value at $30 per share. On your way to present your analysis to your boss, you run into a slightly more experienced colleague in the elevator. It turns out your colleague has been researching the same stock and has different beliefs. According to her analysis, the value of the stock is only $20 per share. What would you do?

Most of us in this situation would reconsider our own analysis. The fact that someone else who has carefully studied the stock has come to a very different conclusion is powerful evidence that we might have missed something. In the face of this information from our colleague, we would probably reconsider our analysis and adjust our assessment of the stock's value downward. Of course, our colleague might also revise her opinion based on our assessment. After sharing our analyses, we would likely end up with a consensus estimate somewhere between $20 and $30 per share. That is, at the end of this process our beliefs would be similar.

This type of encounter happens millions of times every day in the stock market. When a buyer seeks to buy a stock, the willingness of other parties to sell the same stock suggests that they value the stock differently, as the NPV of buying and selling the stock cannot *both* be positive. Thus, the information that others are willing to trade should lead buyers and sellers to revise their valuations. Ultimately, investors trade until they reach a consensus regarding the value of the stock. In this way, stock markets aggregate the information and views of many different investors.

FIGURE 9.3 **The Valuation Triad**

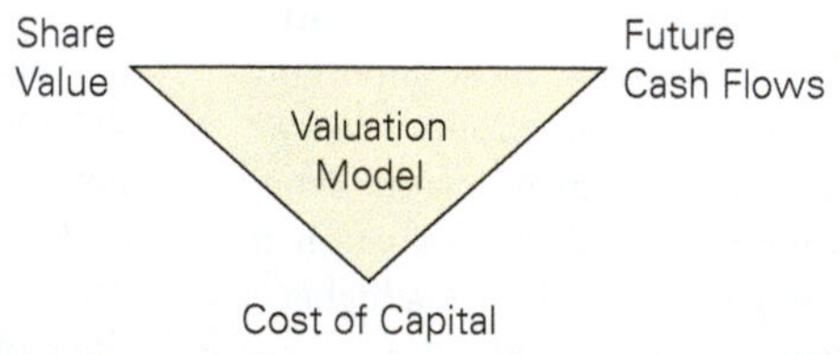

Valuation models determine the relationship among the firm's future cash flows, its cost of capital, and the value of its shares. The stock's expected cash flows and cost of capital can be used to assess its market price. Conversely, the market price can be used to assess the firm's future cash flows or cost of capital.

Thus, if your valuation model suggests a stock is worth \$30 per share when it is trading for \$20 per share in the market, the discrepancy is equivalent to knowing that thousands of investors—many of them professionals who have access to the best information—disagree with your assessment. This knowledge should make you reconsider your original analysis. You would need a very compelling reason to trust your own estimate in the face of such contrary opinions.

What conclusion can we draw from this discussion? Recall Figure 9.3, in which a valuation model links the firm's future cash flows, its cost of capital, and its share price. In other words, given accurate information about any two of these variables, a valuation model allows us to make inferences about the third variable. Thus, the way we use a valuation model will depend on the quality of our information: The model will tell us the most about the variable for which our prior information is the least reliable.

For a publicly traded firm, its market price should already provide very accurate information, aggregated from a multitude of investors, regarding the true value of its shares. Therefore, in most situations, a valuation model is best applied to tell us something about the firm's future cash flows or cost of capital, based on its current stock price. Only in the relatively rare case in which we have some superior information that other investors lack regarding the firm's cash flows and cost of capital would it make sense to second-guess the stock price.

EXAMPLE 9.11 **Using the Information in Market Prices**

Problem

Suppose Tecnor Industries will pay a dividend this year of \$5 per share. Its equity cost of capital is 10%, and you expect its dividends to grow at a rate of about 4% per year, though you are somewhat unsure of the precise growth rate. If Tecnor's stock is currently trading for \$76.92 per share, how would you update your beliefs about its dividend growth rate?

Solution

If we apply the constant dividend growth model based on a 4% growth rate, we would estimate a stock price of $P_0 = 5/(0.10 - 0.04) = \$83.33$ per share. The market price of \$76.92, however, implies that most investors expect dividends to grow at a somewhat slower rate. If we continue to assume a constant growth rate, we can solve for the growth rate consistent with the current market price using Eq. 9.7:

$$g = r_E - Div_1/P_0 = 10\% - 5/76.92 = 3.5\%$$

Thus, given this market price for the stock, we should lower our expectations for the dividend growth rate unless we have very strong reasons to trust our own estimate.

Competition and Efficient Markets

The idea that markets aggregate the information of many investors, and that this information is reflected in security prices, is a natural consequence of investor competition. If information were available that indicated that buying a stock had a positive NPV, investors with that information would choose to buy the stock; their attempts to purchase it would then drive up the stock's price. By a similar logic, investors with information that selling a stock had a positive NPV would sell it and the stock's price would fall.

The idea that competition among investors works to eliminate *all* positive-NPV trading opportunities is referred to as the **efficient markets hypothesis**. It implies that securities will be fairly priced, based on their future cash flows, given all information that is available to investors.

The underlying rationale for the efficient markets hypothesis is the presence of competition. What if new information becomes available that affects the firm's value? The degree of competition, and therefore the accuracy of the efficient markets hypothesis, will depend on the number of investors who possess this information. Let's consider two important cases.

Public, Easily Interpretable Information. Information that is available to all investors includes information in news reports, financial statements, corporate press releases, or in other public data sources. If the impact of this information on the firm's future cash flows can be readily ascertained, then all investors can determine the effect of this information on the firm's value.

In this situation, we expect competition between investors to be fierce and the stock price to react nearly instantaneously to such news. A few lucky investors might be able to trade a small quantity of shares before the price fully adjusts. But most investors would find that the stock price already reflected the new information before they were able to trade on it. In other words, we expect the efficient markets hypothesis to hold very well with respect to this type of information.

EXAMPLE 9.12 Stock Price Reactions to Public Information

Problem

Myox Labs announces that due to potential side effects, it is pulling one of its leading drugs from the market. As a result, its future expected free cash flow will decline by $85 million per year for the next 10 years. Myox has 50 million shares outstanding, no debt, and an equity cost of capital of 8%. If this news came as a complete surprise to investors, what should happen to Myox's stock price upon the announcement?

Solution

In this case, we can use the discounted free cash flow method. With no debt, $r_{wacc} = r_E = 8\%$. Using the annuity formula, the decline in expected free cash flow will reduce Myox's enterprise value by

$$\$85 \text{ million} \times \frac{1}{0.08}\left(1 - \frac{1}{1.08^{10}}\right) = \$570 \text{ million}$$

Thus, the share price should fall by $570/50 = $11.40 per share. Because this news is public and its effect on the firm's expected free cash flow is clear, we would expect the stock price to drop by this amount nearly instantaneously.

Private or Difficult-to-Interpret Information. Some information is not publicly available. For example, an analyst might spend time and effort gathering information from a firm's employees, competitors, suppliers, or customers that is relevant to the firm's future cash flows. This information is not available to other investors who have not devoted a similar effort to gathering it.

Even when information is publicly available, it may be difficult to interpret. Nonexperts in the field may find it difficult to evaluate research reports on new technologies, for example. It may take a great deal of legal and accounting expertise and effort to understand the full consequences of a highly complicated business transaction. Certain consulting experts may have greater insight into consumer tastes and the likelihood of a product's acceptance. In these cases, while the fundamental information may be public, the interpretation of how that information will affect the firm's future cash flows is itself private information.

When private information is relegated to the hands of a relatively small number of investors, these investors may be able to profit by trading on their information.[10] In this case, the efficient markets hypothesis will not hold in the strict sense. However, as these informed traders begin to trade, they will tend to move prices, so over time prices will begin to reflect their information as well.

If the profit opportunities from having this type of information are large, other individuals will attempt to gain the expertise and devote the resources needed to acquire it. As more individuals become better informed, competition to exploit this information will increase. Thus, in the long run, we should expect that the degree of "inefficiency" in the market will be limited by the costs of obtaining the information.

EXAMPLE 9.13 **Stock Price Reactions to Private Information**

Problem

Phenyx Pharmaceuticals has just announced the development of a new drug for which the company is seeking approval from the Food and Drug Administration (FDA). If approved, the future profits from the new drug will increase Phenyx's market value by \$750 million, or \$15 per share given its 50 million shares outstanding. If the development of this drug was a surprise to investors, and if the average likelihood of FDA approval is 10%, what do you expect will happen to Phenyx's stock price when this news is announced? What may happen to the stock price over time?

Solution

Because many investors are likely to know that the chance of FDA approval is 10%, competition should lead to an immediate jump in the stock price of $10\% \times \$15 = \$1.50$ per share. Over time, however, analysts and experts in the field are likely to do their own assessments of the probable efficacy of the drug. If they conclude that the drug looks more promising than average, they will begin to trade on their private information and buy the stock, and the price will tend to drift higher over time. If the experts conclude that the drug looks less promising than average, they will tend to sell the stock, and its price will drift lower over time. Examples of possible price paths are shown in Figure 9.4. While these experts may be able to trade on their superior information and earn a profit, for uninformed investors who do not know which outcome will occur, the stock may rise or fall and so appears fairly priced at the announcement.

Lessons for Investors and Corporate Managers

The effect of competition based on information about stock prices has important consequences for both investors and corporate managers.

Consequences for Investors. As in other markets, investors should be able to identify positive-NPV trading opportunities in securities markets only if some barrier or restriction to free competition exists. An investor's competitive advantage may take several forms.

---

[10]Even with private information, informed investors may find it difficult to profit from that information, because they must find others who are willing to trade with them; that is, the market for the stock must be sufficiently *liquid*. A liquid market requires that other investors in the market have alternative motives to trade (e.g., selling shares of a stock to purchase a house) and so be willing to trade even when facing the risk that other traders may be better informed. See Chapter 13 for more details.

FIGURE 9.4

Possible Stock Price Paths for Example 9.13

Phenyx's stock price jumps on the announcement based on the average likelihood of approval. The stock price then drifts up (green path) or down (gold path) as informed traders trade on their more accurate assessment of the drug's likelihood of approval. Because an uninformed investor does not know which outcome will occur, the stock is fairly priced at the announcement, even though it will appear under- or overpriced ex post.

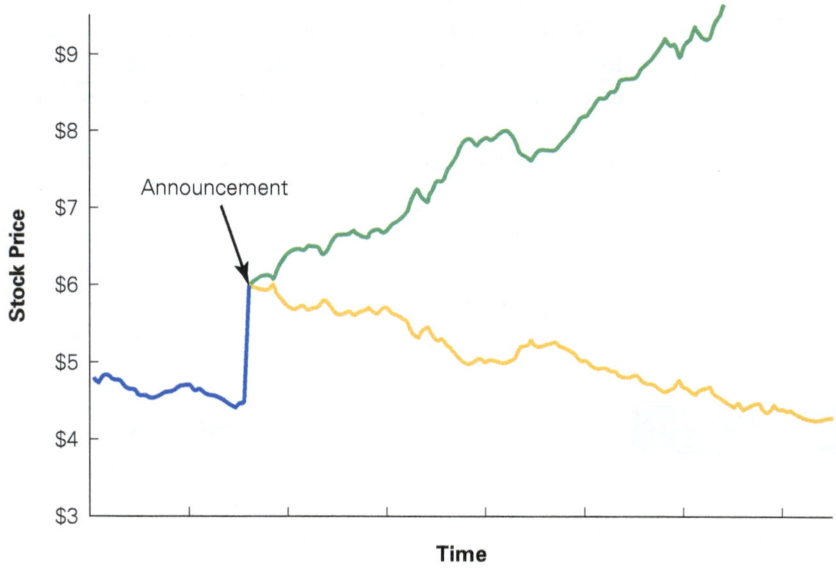

The investor may have expertise or access to information that is known to only a few people. Alternatively, the investor may have lower trading costs than other market participants and so can exploit opportunities that others would find unprofitable. In all cases, however, the source of the positive-NPV trading opportunity must be something that is hard to replicate; otherwise, any gains would be competed away.

While the fact that positive-NPV trading opportunities are hard to come by may be disappointing, there is some good news as well. If stocks are fairly priced according to our valuation models, then investors who buy stocks can expect to receive future cash flows that fairly compensate them for the risk of their investment. Thus, in such cases the average investor can invest with confidence, even if he is not fully informed.

Implications for Corporate Managers. If stocks are fairly valued according to the models we have described, then the value of the firm is determined by the cash flows that it can pay to its investors. This result has several key implications for corporate managers:

- *Focus on NPV and free cash flow.* A manager seeking to boost the price of her firm's stock should make investments that increase the present value of the firm's free cash flow. Thus, the capital budgeting methods outlined in Chapter 8 are fully consistent with the objective of maximizing the firm's share price.
- *Avoid accounting illusions.* Many managers make the mistake of focusing on accounting earnings as opposed to free cash flows. With efficient markets, the accounting consequences of a decision do not directly affect the value of the firm and should not drive decision making.
- *Use financial transactions to support investment.* With efficient markets, the firm can sell its shares at a fair price to new investors. Thus, the firm should not be constrained from raising capital to fund positive NPV investment opportunities.

Kenneth Cole Productions—What Happened?

The biggest challenge in valuing a stock is forecasting the future. Events will often arise that cause the company's performance to exceed or fall short of analysts' expectations. Often these events are specific to the company itself. But other times the events are beyond the company's control. For example, no one could have predicted the severity of the economic collapse that would ensue in 2008–2009, and the impact it would have on retailers worldwide. Consider what actually happened to Kenneth Cole Productions.

Unanticipated problems within the company meant that the remainder of 2006 was challenging for KCP. Despite strong revenue growth in its wholesale division, its retail stores suffered an unexpected large same-store sales decline of 13%. Overall, KCP revenues grew only 3.6% in 2006, well below analysts' forecasts. Losses in the retail division caused KCP's EBIT margin to drop below 7%.

After the departure of its president, KCP also struggled to find new leadership. As both Chairman and CEO, founder Kenneth Cole was able to spend less time on the creative aspects of the brand, and its image suffered. Sales declined 4.8% in 2007, and its EBIT margin fell to 1%. However there was some cause for optimism—in Spring 2008, KCP hired Jill Granoff, a former Liz Claiborne executive, as its new CEO.

The optimism was short-lived. Like many other retailers, in Fall 2008, KCP was hit hard by the effects of the financial crisis. It found itself saddled with large inventories, and had to aggressively cut prices. By year end, sales had fallen by 3.6%. Worse, KCP reported operating losses, with an EBIT margin of −2%. Analysts forecast that 2009 would be KCP's most difficult year yet, with sales declines exceeding 8% and EBIT margins falling below −4%.

Reflecting its poor performance, KCP cut its dividend in half at the start of 2008 and suspended dividend payments altogether at the start of 2009. The chart below shows KCP's stock price performance—clearly, investors in KCP did not do well over this period, with the stock losing more than 70% of its value by early 2009, with more than half of that loss occurring in the wake of the financial crisis.

As the economy recovered in 2010, KCP returned to profitability, and sales experienced double digit growth. In early 2012, the company's founder, Kenneth Cole, offered to buy the firm from its shareholders. The deal closed on September 25, 2012 for a price $15.25/share, still well under its early 2006 value.

It is important to recognize, however, that while we know *now* that KCP was overpriced in 2006, that does not mean that the market for KCP stock was "inefficient" at that time. Indeed, as we saw earlier, KCP may have been appropriately priced based on reasonable expectations for its future growth that investors had at the time. Unfortunately, due to problems both within KCP and with the broader economy, those expectations were not realized.

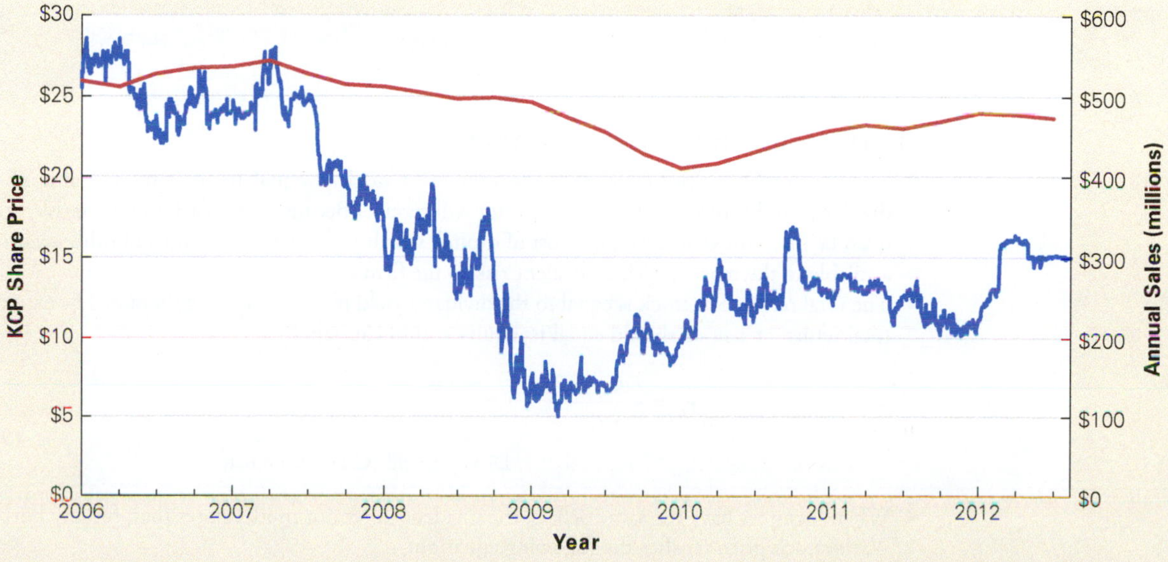

The Efficient Markets Hypothesis Versus No Arbitrage

We can draw an important distinction between the efficient markets hypothesis and the notion of a normal market that we introduced in Chapter 3, which is based on the idea of arbitrage. An arbitrage opportunity is a situation in which two securities (or portfolios) with *identical* cash flows have different prices. Because anyone can earn a sure profit in this situation by buying the low-priced security and selling the high-priced one, we expect that investors will immediately exploit and eliminate these opportunities. Thus, in a normal market, arbitrage opportunities will not be found.

The efficient markets hypothesis, that the NPV of investing is zero, is best expressed in terms of returns, as in Eq. 9.2. When the NPV of investing is zero, the price of every security equals the present value of its expected cash flows when discounted at a cost of capital that reflects its risk. So the efficient markets hypothesis implies that securities with *equivalent risk* should have the same *expected return*. The efficient markets hypothesis is therefore incomplete without a definition of "equivalent risk." Furthermore, because investors must *forecast* the riskiness of securities, and may do so differently, there is no reason to expect the efficient markets hypothesis to hold perfectly; it is best viewed as an idealized approximation for highly competitive markets.

To test the validity of the efficient markets hypothesis and, more importantly, to implement the discounted cash flow methods of stock valuation introduced in this chapter, we need a theory of how investors can estimate the risk of investing in a security and how this risk determines the security's expected return. Developing such a theory is the topic of Part 4, which we turn to next.

CONCEPT CHECK

1. State the efficient market hypothesis.
2. What are the implications of the efficient market hypothesis for corporate managers?

MyFinanceLab Here is what you should know after reading this chapter. MyFinanceLab will help you identify what you know and where to go when you need to practice.

9.1 The Dividend-Discount Model

- The Law of One Price states that the value of a stock is equal to the present value of the dividends and future sale price the investor will receive. Because these cash flows are risky, they must be discounted at the equity cost of capital, which is the expected return of other securities available in the market with equivalent risk to the firm's equity.
- The total return of a stock is equal to the dividend yield plus the capital gain rate. The expected total return of a stock should equal its equity cost of capital:

$$r_E = \frac{Div_1 + P_1}{P_0} - 1 = \underbrace{\frac{Div_1}{P_0}}_{\text{Dividend Yield}} + \underbrace{\frac{P_1 - P_0}{P_0}}_{\text{Capital Gain Rate}} \tag{9.2}$$

- When investors have the same beliefs, the dividend-discount model states that, for any horizon N, the stock price satisfies the following equation:

$$P_0 = \frac{Div_1}{1 + r_E} + \frac{Div_2}{(1 + r_E)^2} + \cdots + \frac{Div_N}{(1 + r_E)^N} + \frac{P_N}{(1 + r_E)^N} \tag{9.4}$$

- If the stock eventually pays dividends and is never acquired, the dividend-discount model implies that the stock price equals the present value of all future dividends.

9.2 Applying the Dividend-Discount Model

- The constant dividend growth model assumes that dividends grow at a constant expected rate g. In that case, g is also the expected capital gain rate, and

$$P_0 = \frac{Div_1}{r_E - g} \tag{9.6}$$

- Future dividends depend on earnings, shares outstanding, and the dividend payout rate:

$$Div_t = \underbrace{\frac{\text{Earnings}_t}{\text{Shares Outstanding}_t}}_{EPS_t} \times \text{Dividend Payout Rate}_t \tag{9.8}$$

- If the dividend payout rate and the number of shares outstanding is constant, and if earnings change only as a result of new investment from retained earnings, then the growth rate of the firm's earnings, dividends, and share price is calculated as follows:

$$g = \text{Retention Rate} \times \text{Return on New Investment} \tag{9.12}$$

- Cutting the firm's dividend to increase investment will raise the stock price if, and only if, the new investments have a positive NPV.
- If the firm has a long-term growth rate of g after the period $N + 1$, then we can apply the dividend-discount model and use the constant dividend growth formula to estimate the terminal stock value P_N.
- The dividend-discount model is sensitive to the dividend growth rate, which is difficult to estimate accurately.

9.3 Total Payout and Free Cash Flow Valuation Models

- If the firm undertakes share repurchases, it is more reliable to use the total payout model to value the firm. In this model, the value of equity equals the present value of future total dividends and repurchases. To determine the stock price, we divide the equity value by the initial number of shares outstanding of the firm:

$$P_0 = \frac{PV(\text{Future Total Dividends and Repurchases})}{\text{Shares Outstanding}_0} \tag{9.16}$$

- The growth rate of the firm's total payout is governed by the growth rate of earnings, not earnings per share.
- When a firm has leverage, it is more reliable to use the discounted free cash flow model. In this model,
  - We can estimate the firm's future free cash flow as

$$\begin{aligned}\text{Free Cash Flow} = EBIT \times (1 - \tau_c) &- \text{Net Investment}\\ &- \text{Increases in Net Working Capital}\end{aligned} \tag{9.20}$$

    where Net Investment equals the firm's capital expenditures in excess of depreciation.
  - The firm's enterprise value (the market value of equity plus debt, less excess cash) equals the present value of the firm's future free cash flow:

$$V_0 = PV(\text{Future Free Cash Flow of Firm}) \tag{9.21}$$

  - We discount cash flows using the weighted average cost of capital, which is the expected return the firm must pay to investors to compensate them for the risk of holding the firm's debt and equity together.
  - We can estimate a terminal enterprise value by assuming free cash flow grows at a constant rate (typically equal to the rate of long-run revenue growth).

- We determine the stock price by subtracting debt and adding cash to the enterprise value, and then dividing by the initial number of shares outstanding of the firm:

$$P_0 = \frac{V_0 + \text{Cash}_0 - \text{Debt}_0}{\text{Shares Outstanding}_0} \tag{9.22}$$

9.4 Valuation Based on Comparable Firms

- We can also value stocks by using valuation multiples based on comparable firms. Multiples commonly used for this purpose include the P/E ratio and the ratio of enterprise value to EBITDA. Using multiples assumes that comparable firms have the same risk and future growth as the firm being valued.
- No valuation model provides a definitive value for the stock. It is best to use several methods to identify a reasonable range for the value.

9.5 Information, Competition, and Stock Prices

- Stock prices aggregate the information of many investors. Therefore, if our valuation disagrees with the stock's market price, it is most likely an indication that our assumptions about the firm's cash flows are wrong.
- Competition between investors tends to eliminate positive-NPV trading opportunities. Competition will be strongest when information is public and easy to interpret. Privately informed traders may be able to profit from their information, which is reflected in prices only gradually.
- The efficient markets hypothesis states that competition eliminates all positive-NPV trades, which is equivalent to stating that securities with equivalent risk have the same expected returns.
- In an efficient market, investors will not find positive-NPV trading opportunities without some source of competitive advantage. By contrast, the average investor will earn a fair return on his or her investment.
- In an efficient market, to raise the stock price corporate managers should focus on maximizing the present value of the free cash flow from the firm's investments, rather than accounting consequences or financial policy.

Key Terms

capital gain *p. 279*
capital gain rate *p. 279*
constant dividend growth model *p. 283*
discounted free cash flow model *p. 290*
dividend-discount model *p. 282*
dividend payout rate *p. 284*
dividend yield *p. 279*
efficient markets hypothesis *p. 301*
equity cost of capital *p. 278*
forward earnings *p. 295*
forward P/E *p. 295*
method of comparables *p. 294*
net investment *p. 290*
retention rate *p. 284*
share repurchase *p. 289*
short interest *p. 280*
sustainable growth rate *p. 285*
total payout model *p. 289*
total return *p. 279*
trailing earnings *p. 295*
trailing P/E *p. 295*
valuation multiple *p. 294*
weighted average cost of capital (WACC) *p. 291*

Further Reading

For a more thorough discussion of different stock valuation methods, see T. Copeland, T. Koller, and J. Murrin, *Valuation: Measuring and Managing the Value of Companies* (John Wiley & Sons, 2001).

For a comparison of the discounted free cash flow model and the method of comparables for a sample of 51 highly leveraged transactions, see S. Kaplan and R. Ruback "The Valuation of Cash Flow Forecasts: An Empirical Analysis," *Journal of Finance* 50 (1995): 1059–1093.

An entertaining introduction to efficient markets can be found in B. Malkiel's popular book, *A Random Walk Down Wall Street: Completely Revised and Updated Eighth Edition* (W. W. Norton, 2003).

For a classic discussion of market efficiency, the arguments that support it, and important empirical tests, see E. F. Fama, "Efficient Capital Markets: A Review of Theory and Empirical Work," *Journal of Finance* 25 (1970): 383–417, and "Efficient Capital Markets: II," *The Journal of Finance* 46(5) (1991): 1575–1617. Another review of the literature and apparent anomalies can be found in R. Ball, "The Development, Accomplishments and Limitations of the Theory of Stock Market Efficiency," *Managerial Finance* 20(2,3) (1994): 3–48.

For two sides of the debate of whether the price of Internet companies in the late 1990s could be justified by a valuation model, see: L. Pástor and P. Veronesi, "Was There a Nasdaq Bubble in the Late 1990s?" *Journal of Financial Economics* 81(2006): 61–100; M. Richardson and E. Ofek, "DotCom Mania: The Rise and Fall of Internet Stock Prices," *Journal of Finance* 58 (2003): 1113–1138.

For a survey of how private equity investors value firms see: P. Gompers, S. Kaplan, and V. Mukharlyamov, "What Do Private Equity Firms Say They Do?," *Journal of Financial Economics* (2016) forthcoming.

Problems

All problems are available in MyFinanceLab. *An asterisk (*) indicates problems with a higher level of difficulty.*

The Dividend-Discount Model

1. Assume Evco, Inc., has a current price of $50 and will pay a $2 dividend in one year, and its equity cost of capital is 15%. What price must you expect it to sell for right after paying the dividend in one year in order to justify its current price?
2. Anle Corporation has a current price of $20, is expected to pay a dividend of $1 in one year, and its expected price right after paying that dividend is $22.
   a. What is Anle's expected dividend yield?
   b. What is Anle's expected capital gain rate?
   c. What is Anle's equity cost of capital?
3. Suppose Acap Corporation will pay a dividend of $2.80 per share at the end of this year and $3 per share next year. You expect Acap's stock price to be $52 in two years. If Acap's equity cost of capital is 10%:
   a. What price would you be willing to pay for a share of Acap stock today, if you planned to hold the stock for two years?
   b. Suppose instead you plan to hold the stock for one year. What price would you expect to be able to sell a share of Acap stock for in one year?
   c. Given your answer in part (b), what price would you be willing to pay for a share of Acap stock today, if you planned to hold the stock for one year? How does this compare to your answer in part (a)?
4. Krell Industries has a share price of $22 today. If Krell is expected to pay a dividend of $0.88 this year, and its stock price is expected to grow to $23.54 at the end of the year, what is Krell's dividend yield and equity cost of capital?

Applying the Dividend-Discount Model

5. NoGrowth Corporation currently pays a dividend of $2 per year, and it will continue to pay this dividend forever. What is the price per share if its equity cost of capital is 15% per year?
6. Summit Systems will pay a dividend of $1.50 this year. If you expect Summit's dividend to grow by 6% per year, what is its price per share if its equity cost of capital is 11%?

7. Dorpac Corporation has a dividend yield of 1.5%. Dorpac's equity cost of capital is 8%, and its dividends are expected to grow at a constant rate.
   a. What is the expected growth rate of Dorpac's dividends?
   b. What is the expected growth rate of Dorpac's share price?

8. Canadian-based mining company El Dorado Gold (EGO) suspended its dividend in March 2016 as a result of declining gold prices and delays in obtaining permits for its mines in Greece. Suppose you expect EGO to resume paying annual dividends in two years time, with a dividend of $0.25 per share, growing by 2% per year. If EGO's equity cost of capital is 10%, what is the value of a share of EGO today?

9. In 2006 and 2007, Kenneth Cole Productions (KCP) paid annual dividends of $0.72. In 2008, KCP paid an annual dividend of $0.36, and then paid no further dividends through 2012. KCP was acquired at the end of 2012 for $15.25 per share.
   a. What would an investor with perfect foresight of the above been willing to pay for KCP at the start of 2006? (*Note*: Because an investor with perfect foresight bears no risk, use a risk-free equity cost of capital of 5%.)
   b. Does your answer to (a) imply that the market for KCP stock was inefficient in 2006?

10. DFB, Inc., expects earnings at the end of this year of $5 per share, and it plans to pay a $3 dividend at that time. DFB will retain $2 per share of its earnings to reinvest in new projects with an expected return of 15% per year. Suppose DFB will maintain the same dividend payout rate, retention rate, and return on new investments in the future and will not change its number of outstanding shares.
   a. What growth rate of earnings would you forecast for DFB?
   b. If DFB's equity cost of capital is 12%, what price would you estimate for DFB stock today?
   c. Suppose DFB instead paid a dividend of $4 per share at the end of this year and retained only $1 per share in earnings. If DFB maintains this higher payout rate in the future, what stock price would you estimate now? Should DFB raise its dividend?

11. Cooperton Mining just announced it will cut its dividend from $4 to $2.50 per share and use the extra funds to expand. Prior to the announcement, Cooperton's dividends were expected to grow at a 3% rate, and its share price was $50. With the new expansion, Cooperton's dividends are expected to grow at a 5% rate. What share price would you expect after the announcement? (Assume Cooperton's risk is unchanged by the new expansion.) Is the expansion a positive NPV investment?

12. Procter and Gamble (PG) paid an annual dividend of $1.72 in 2009. You expect PG to increase its dividends by 8% per year for the next five years (through 2014), and thereafter by 3% per year. If the appropriate equity cost of capital for Procter and Gamble is 8% per year, use the dividend-discount model to estimate its value per share at the end of 2009.

13. Colgate-Palmolive Company has just paid an annual dividend of $1.50. Analysts are predicting dividends to grow by $0.12 per year over the next five years. After then, Colgate's earnings are expected to grow 6% per year, and its dividend payout rate will remain constant. If Colgate's equity cost of capital is 8.5% per year, what price does the dividend-discount model predict Colgate stock should sell for today?

14. What is the value of a firm with initial dividend *Div*, growing for n years (i.e., until year $n + 1$) at rate g_1 and after that at rate g_2 forever, when the equity cost of capital is r?

15. Halliford Corporation expects to have earnings this coming year of $3 per share. Halliford plans to retain all of its earnings for the next two years. For the subsequent two years, the firm will retain 50% of its earnings. It will then retain 20% of its earnings from that point onward. Each year, retained earnings will be invested in new projects with an expected return of 25% per year. Any earnings that are not retained will be paid out as dividends. Assume Halliford's share count remains constant and all earnings growth comes from the investment of retained earnings. If Halliford's equity cost of capital is 10%, what price would you estimate for Halliford stock?

Total Payout and Free Cash Flow Valuation Models

16. Suppose Amazon.com Inc. pays no dividends but spent \$3 billion on share repurchases last year. If Amazon's equity cost of capital is 8%, and if the amount spent on repurchases is expected to grow by 6.5% per year, estimate Amazon's market capitalization. If Amazon has 450 million shares outstanding, what stock price does this correspond to?

17. Maynard Steel plans to pay a dividend of \$3 this year. The company has an expected earnings growth rate of 4% per year and an equity cost of capital of 10%.

a. Assuming Maynard's dividend payout rate and expected growth rate remains constant, and Maynard does not issue or repurchase shares, estimate Maynard's share price.

b. Suppose Maynard decides to pay a dividend of \$1 this year and use the remaining \$2 per share to repurchase shares. If Maynard's total payout rate remains constant, estimate Maynard's share price.

c. If Maynard maintains the same split between dividends and repurchases, and the same payout rate, as in part (b), at what rate are Maynard's dividends, earnings per share, and share price expected to grow in the future?

18. Benchmark Metrics, Inc. (BMI), an all-equity financed firm, reported EPS of \$5.00 in 2008. Despite the economic downturn, BMI is confident regarding its current investment opportunities. But due to the financial crisis, BMI does not wish to fund these investments externally. The Board has therefore decided to suspend its stock repurchase plan and cut its dividend to \$1 per share (vs. almost \$2 per share in 2007), and retain these funds instead. The firm has just paid the 2008 dividend, and BMI plans to keep its dividend at \$1 per share in 2009 as well. In subsequent years, it expects its growth opportunities to slow, and it will still be able to fund its growth internally with a target 40% dividend payout ratio, and reinitiating its stock repurchase plan for a total payout rate of 60%. (All dividends and repurchases occur at the end of each year.)

Suppose BMI's existing operations will continue to generate the current level of earnings per share in the future. Assume further that the return on new investment is 15%, and that reinvestments will account for all future earnings growth (if any). Finally, assume BMI's equity cost of capital is 10%.

a. Estimate BMI's EPS in 2009 and 2010 (before any share repurchases).

b. What is the value of a share of BMI at the start of 2009?

19. Heavy Metal Corporation is expected to generate the following free cash flows over the next five years:

Year	1	2	3	4	5
FCF (\$ millions)	53	68	78	75	82

After then, the free cash flows are expected to grow at the industry average of 4% per year. Using the discounted free cash flow model and a weighted average cost of capital of 14%:

a. Estimate the enterprise value of Heavy Metal.

b. If Heavy Metal has no excess cash, debt of \$300 million, and 40 million shares outstanding, estimate its share price.

20. IDX Technologies is a privately held developer of advanced security systems based in Chicago. As part of your business development strategy, in late 2008 you initiate discussions with IDX's founder about the possibility of acquiring the business at the end of 2008. Estimate the value of IDX per share using a discounted FCF approach and the following data:

- Debt: \$30 million
- Excess cash: \$110 million
- Shares outstanding: 50 million
- Expected FCF in 2009: \$45 million
- Expected FCF in 2010: \$50 million
- Future FCF growth rate beyond 2010: 5%
- Weighted-average cost of capital: 9.4%

21. Sora Industries has 60 million outstanding shares, $120 million in debt, $40 million in cash, and the following projected free cash flow for the next four years:

		Year	0	1	2	3	4
Earnings and FCF Forecast ($ millions)							
1	Sales		433.0	468.0	516.0	547.0	574.3
2	*Growth versus Prior Year*			*8.1%*	*10.3%*	*6.0%*	*5.0%*
3	Cost of Goods Sold			(313.6)	(345.7)	(366.5)	(384.8)
4	**Gross Profit**			154.4	170.3	180.5	189.5
5	Selling, General, and Administrative			(93.6)	(103.2)	(109.4)	(114.9)
6	Depreciation			(7.0)	(7.5)	(9.0)	(9.5)
7	**EBIT**			53.8	59.6	62.1	65.2
8	Less: Income Tax at 40%			(21.5)	(23.8)	(24.8)	(26.1)
9	Plus: Depreciation			7.0	7.5	9.0	9.5
10	Less: Capital Expenditures			(7.7)	(10.0)	(9.9)	(10.4)
11	Less: Increase in NWC			(6.3)	(8.6)	(5.6)	(4.9)
12	**Free Cash Flow**			**25.3**	**24.6**	**30.8**	**33.3**

a. Suppose Sora's revenue and free cash flow are expected to grow at a 5% rate beyond year 4. If Sora's weighted average cost of capital is 10%, what is the value of Sora's stock based on this information?

b. Sora's cost of goods sold was assumed to be 67% of sales. If its cost of goods sold is actually 70% of sales, how would the estimate of the stock's value change?

c. Let's return to the assumptions of part (a) and suppose Sora can maintain its cost of goods sold at 67% of sales. However, now suppose Sora reduces its selling, general, and administrative expenses from 20% of sales to 16% of sales. What stock price would you estimate now? (Assume no other expenses, except taxes, are affected.)

*d. Sora's net working capital needs were estimated to be 18% of sales (which is their current level in year 0). If Sora can reduce this requirement to 12% of sales starting in year 1, but all other assumptions remain as in part (a), what stock price do you estimate for Sora? (*Hint*: This change will have the largest impact on Sora's free cash flow in year 1.)

22. Consider the valuation of Kenneth Cole Productions in Example 9.7.

a. Suppose you believe KCP's initial revenue growth rate will be between 4% and 11% (with growth slowing in equal steps to 4% by year 2011). What range of share prices for KCP is consistent with these forecasts?

b. Suppose you believe KCP's EBIT margin will be between 7% and 10% of sales. What range of share prices for KCP is consistent with these forecasts (keeping KCP's initial revenue growth at 9%)?

c. Suppose you believe KCP's weighted average cost of capital is between 10% and 12%. What range of share prices for KCP is consistent with these forecasts (keeping KCP's initial revenue growth and EBIT margin at 9%)?

d. What range of share prices is consistent if you vary the estimates as in parts (a), (b), and (c) simultaneously?

23. Kenneth Cole Productions (KCP) was acquired in 2012 for a purchase price of $15.25 per share. KCP has 18.5 million shares outstanding, $45 million in cash, and no debt at the time of the acquisition.

a. Given a weighted average cost of capital of 11%, and assuming no future growth, what level of annual free cash flow would justify this acquisition price?

b. If KCP's current annual sales are $480 million, assuming no net capital expenditures or increases in net working capital, and a tax rate of 35%, what EBIT margin does your answer in part (a) require?

Valuation Based on Comparable Firms

24. You notice that PepsiCo (PEP) has a stock price of $72.62 and EPS of $3.80. Its competitor, the Coca-Cola Company (KO), has EPS of $1.89. Estimate the value of a share of Coca-Cola stock using only this data.

25. Suppose that in January 2006, Kenneth Cole Productions had EPS of $1.65 and a book value of equity of $12.05 per share.
    a. Using the average P/E multiple in Table 9.1, estimate KCP's share price.
    b. What range of share prices do you estimate based on the highest and lowest P/E multiples in Table 9.1?
    c. Using the average price to book value multiple in Table 9.1, estimate KCP's share price.
    d. What range of share prices do you estimate based on the highest and lowest price to book value multiples in Table 9.1?

26. Suppose that in January 2006, Kenneth Cole Productions had sales of $518 million, EBITDA of $55.6 million, excess cash of $100 million, $3 million of debt, and 21 million shares outstanding.
    a. Using the average enterprise value to sales multiple in Table 9.1, estimate KCP's share price.
    b. What range of share prices do you estimate based on the highest and lowest enterprise value to sales multiples in Table 9.1?
    c. Using the average enterprise value to EBITDA multiple in Table 9.1, estimate KCP's share price.
    d. What range of share prices do you estimate based on the highest and lowest enterprise value to EBITDA multiples in Table 9.1?

27. In addition to footwear, Kenneth Cole Productions designs and sells handbags, apparel, and other accessories. You decide, therefore, to consider comparables for KCP outside the footwear industry.
    a. Suppose that Fossil, Inc., has an enterprise value to EBITDA multiple of 9.73 and a P/E multiple of 18.4. What share price would you estimate for KCP using each of these multiples, based on the data for KCP in Problems 25 and 26?
    b. Suppose that Tommy Hilfiger Corporation has an enterprise value to EBITDA multiple of 7.19 and a P/E multiple of 17.2. What share price would you estimate for KCP using each of these multiples, based on the data for KCP in Problems 25 and 26?

28. Consider the following data for the airline industry for December 2015 (EV = enterprise value, Book = equity book value). Discuss the potential challenges of using multiples to value an airline.

Company Name	Market Capitalization	Enterprise Value (EV)	EV/Sales	EV/EBITDA	EV/EBIT	P/E	P/Book
Delta Air Lines (DAL)	40,857	45,846	1.1x	6.0x	7.6x	15.0x	4.0x
American Airlines (AAL)	27,249	38,937	0.9x	4.5x	5.5x	6.2x	7.5x
United Continental (UAL)	22,000	28,522	0.7x	4.2x	5.6x	3.4x	2.6x
Southwest Airlines (LUV)	28,499	28,125	1.5x	6.0x	7.4x	16.1x	4.1x
Alaska Air (ALK)	10,396	9,870	1.8x	6.3x	7.9x	13.4x	4.4x
JetBlue Airways (JBLU)	7,338	8,189	1.3x	6.1x	7.9x	13.8x	2.4x
SkyWest (SKYW)	1,039	2,590	0.8x	5.2x	11.1x	21.2x	0.7x
Hawaiian (HA)	1,974	2,281	1.0x	5.3x	6.9x	15.1x	5.3x

Source: Capital IQ and Yahoo! Finance

MFL **29.** Suppose Hawaiian Airlines (HA) has 53 million shares outstanding. Estimate Hawaiian's share value using each of the five valuation multiples in Problem 28, based on the median valuation multiple of the other seven airlines shown.

Information, Competition, and Stock Prices

30. You read in the paper that Summit Systems from Problem 6 has revised its growth prospects and now expects its dividends to grow at 3% per year forever.

a. What is the new value of a share of Summit Systems stock based on this information?

b. If you tried to sell your Summit Systems stock after reading this news, what price would you be likely to get and why?

31. In mid-2015, Coca-Cola Company (KO) had a share price of $41, and had paid a dividend of $1.32 for the prior year. Suppose you expect Coca-Cola to raise this dividend by approximately 7% per year in perpetuity.

a. If Coca-Cola's equity cost of capital is 8%, what share price would you expect based on your estimate of the dividend growth rate?

b. Given Coca-Cola's share price, what would you conclude about your assessment of Coca-Cola's future dividend growth?

32. Roybus, Inc., a manufacturer of flash memory, just reported that its main production facility in Taiwan was destroyed in a fire. While the plant was fully insured, the loss of production will decrease Roybus' free cash flow by $180 million at the end of this year and by $60 million at the end of next year.

a. If Roybus has 35 million shares outstanding and a weighted average cost of capital of 13%, what change in Roybus' stock price would you expect upon this announcement? (Assume the value of Roybus' debt is not affected by the event.)

b. Would you expect to be able to sell Roybus' stock on hearing this announcement and make a profit? Explain.

33. Apnex, Inc., is a biotechnology firm that is about to announce the results of its clinical trials of a potential new cancer drug. If the trials were successful, Apnex stock will be worth $70 per share. If the trials were unsuccessful, Apnex stock will be worth $18 per share. Suppose that the morning before the announcement is scheduled, Apnex shares are trading for $55 per share.

a. Based on the current share price, what sort of expectations do investors seem to have about the success of the trials?

b. Suppose hedge fund manager Paul Kliner has hired several prominent research scientists to examine the public data on the drug and make their own assessment of the drug's promise. Would Kliner's fund be likely to profit by trading the stock in the hours prior to the announcement?

c. What would limit the fund's ability to profit on its information?

Data Case

As a new analyst for a large brokerage firm, you are anxious to demonstrate the skills you learned in your MBA program and prove that you are worth your attractive salary. Your first assignment is to analyze the stock of the General Electric Corporation. Your boss recommends determining prices based on both the dividend-discount model and discounted free cash flow valuation methods. GE uses a cost of equity of 10.5% and an after-tax weighted average cost of capital of 7.5%. The expected return on new investments is 12%. However, you are a little concerned because your finance professor has told you that these two methods can result in widely differing estimates when applied to real data. You are really hoping that the two methods will reach similar prices. Good luck with that!

1. Go to Yahoo! Finance (finance.yahoo.com) and enter the symbol for General Electric (GE). From the main page for GE, gather the following information and enter it onto a spreadsheet:

   a. The current stock price (last trade) at the top of the page.

   b. The current dividend amount, found at the bottom right of the stock quote table.

2. Next, click "Key Statistics" from the left side of the page. From the Key Statistics page, find the total number of shares outstanding.

3. Next, click "Analyst Estimates" from the left side of the page. From the Analyst Estimates page, find the expected growth rate for the next five years and enter it onto your spreadsheet. It will be near the very bottom of the page.

4. Next, click "Income Statement" near the bottom of the menu on the left. Copy and paste the entire three years of income statements into a new worksheet in your existing Excel file. (*Note*: if you are using IE as your browser, you can place the cursor in the middle of the statement, right-click, and select "Export to Microsoft Excel" to download an Excel version.) Repeat this process for both the balance sheet and cash flow statement for General Electric. Keep all the different statements in the same Excel worksheet.

5. Finally, go to Morningstar (www.morningstar.com) and enter the symbol for General Electric (GE). From the main page, click on the "Key Ratios" tab and calculate the average payout ratio from the prior five fiscal years.

6. To determine the stock value based on the dividend-discount model:
   a. Create a timeline in Excel for five years.
   b. Use the dividend obtained from Yahoo! Finance as the current dividend to forecast the next five annual dividends based on the five-year growth rate.
   c. Determine the long-term growth rate based on GE's payout ratio (which is one minus the retention ratio) using Eq. 9.12.
   d. Use the long-term growth rate to determine the stock price for year five using Eq. 9.13.
   e. Determine the current stock price using Eq. 9.14.

7. To determine the stock value based on the discounted free cash flow method:
   a. Forecast the free cash flows using the historic data from the financial statements downloaded from Yahoo! to compute the three-year average of the following ratios:
      i. EBIT/Sales
      ii. Tax Rate (Income Tax Expense/Income Before Tax)
      iii. Property Plant and Equipment/Sales
      iv. Depreciation/Property Plant and Equipment
      v. Net Working Capital/Sales
   b. Create a timeline for the next seven years.
   c. Forecast future sales based on the most recent year's total revenue growing at the five-year growth rate from Yahoo! for the first five years and the long-term growth rate for years 6 and 7.
   d. Use the average ratios computed in part (a) to forecast EBIT, property, plant and equipment, depreciation, and net working capital for the next seven years.
   e. Forecast the free cash flow for the next seven years using Eq. 9.18.
   f. Determine the horizon enterprise value for year 5 using Eq. 9.24.
   g. Determine the enterprise value of the firm as the present value of the free cash flows.
   h. Determine the stock price using Eq. 9.22.

8. Compare the stock prices from the two methods to the actual stock price. What recommendations can you make as to whether clients should buy or sell GE stock based on your price estimates?

9. Explain to your boss why the estimates from the two valuation methods differ. Specifically, address the assumptions implicit in the models themselves as well as those you made in preparing your analysis. Why do these estimates differ from the actual stock price of GE?

Note: Updates to this data case may be found at www.berkdemarzo.com.

Risk and Return

PART 4

THE LAW OF ONE PRICE CONNECTION. To apply the Law of One Price correctly requires comparing investment opportunities of equivalent risk. In this part of the book, we explain how to measure and compare risks across investment opportunities. Chapter 10 introduces the key insight that investors only demand a risk premium for risk they cannot costlessly eliminate by diversifying their portfolios. Hence, only non-diversifiable market risk will matter when comparing investment opportunities. Intuitively, this insight suggests that an investment's risk premium will depend on its sensitivity to market risk. In Chapter 11, we quantify these ideas and derive investors' optimal investment portfolio choices. We then consider the implications of assuming *all* investors choose their portfolio of risky investments optimally. This assumption leads to the *Capital Asset Pricing Model* (CAPM), the central model in financial economics that quantifies the notion of "equivalent risk" and thereby provides the relation between risk and return. In Chapter 12, we apply these ideas and consider the practicalities of estimating the cost of capital for a firm and for an individual investment project. Chapter 13 takes a closer look at the behavior of individual, as well as professional, investors. Doing so reveals some strengths and weaknesses of the CAPM, as well as ways we can combine the CAPM with the principle of no arbitrage for a more general model of risk and return.

CHAPTER

10

Capital Markets and the Pricing of Risk

NOTATION

p_R	probability of return R
$Var(R)$	variance of return R
$SD(R)$	standard deviation of return R
$E[R]$	expectation of return R
Div_t	dividend paid on date t
P_t	price on date t
R_t	realized or total return of a security from date $t-1$ to t
$\overline{R}$	average return
β_s	beta of security s
r	cost of capital of an investment opportunity

OVER THE TEN-YEAR PERIOD 2006 THROUGH 2015, INVESTORS IN household product maker Procter & Gamble earned an average return of 7% per year. Within this period, there was some variation, with the annual return ranging from −14% in 2008 to 24% in 2013. Over the same period, investors in auctioneer Sotheby's earned an average return of 27% per year. These investors, however, lost over 75% in 2008 and gained nearly 160% in 2009. Finally, investors in three-month U.S. Treasury bills earned an average annual return of 1.1% during the period, with a high of 4.7% in 2006 and a low of 0.02% in 2014. Clearly, these three investments offered returns that were very different in terms of their average level and their variability. What accounts for these differences?

In this chapter, we will consider why these differences exist. Our goal is to develop a theory that explains the relationship between average returns and the variability of returns and thereby derive the risk premium that investors require to hold different securities and investments. We then use this theory to explain how to determine the cost of capital for an investment opportunity.

We begin our investigation of the relationship between risk and return by examining historical data for publicly traded securities. We will see, for example, that while stocks are riskier investments than bonds, they have also earned higher average returns. We can interpret the higher average return on stocks as compensation to investors for the greater risk they are taking.

But we will also find that not all risk needs to be compensated. By holding a portfolio containing many different investments, investors can eliminate risks that are specific to individual securities. Only those risks that cannot be eliminated by holding a large portfolio determine the risk premium required by investors. These observations will allow us to refine our definition of what risk is, how we can measure it, and thus, how to determine the cost of capital.

10.1 Risk and Return: Insights from 89 Years of Investor History

We begin our look at risk and return by illustrating how risk affects investor decisions and returns. Suppose your great-grandparents invested $100 on your behalf at the end of 1925. They instructed their broker to reinvest any dividends or interest earned in the account until the beginning of 2015. How would that $100 have grown if it were placed in one of the following investments?

1. Standard & Poor's 500 (S&P 500): A portfolio, constructed by Standard and Poor's, comprising 90 U.S. stocks up to 1957 and 500 U.S. stocks after that. The firms represented are leaders in their respective industries and are among the largest firms, in terms of market value, traded on U.S. markets.
2. Small Stocks: A portfolio, updated quarterly, of U.S. stocks traded on the NYSE with market capitalizations in the bottom 20%.
3. World Portfolio: A portfolio of international stocks from all of the world's major stock markets in North America, Europe, and Asia.[1]
4. Corporate Bonds: A portfolio of long-term, AAA-rated U.S. corporate bonds with maturities of approximately 20 years.[2]
5. Treasury Bills: An investment in one-month U.S. Treasury bills.

Figure 10.1 shows the result, through the start of 2015, of investing $100 at the end of 1925 in each of these five investment portfolios, ignoring transactions costs. During this 89-year period in the United States, small stocks experienced the highest long-term return, followed by the large stocks in the S&P 500, the international stocks in the world portfolio, corporate bonds, and finally Treasury bills. All of the investments grew faster than inflation, as measured by the consumer price index (CPI).

At first glance the graph is striking—had your great-grandparents invested $100 in the small stock portfolio, the investment would be worth more than $4.6 million at the beginning of 2015! By contrast, if they had invested in Treasury bills, the investment would be worth only about $2,000. Given this wide difference, why invest in anything other than small stocks?

But first impressions can be misleading. While over the full horizon stocks (especially small stocks) did outperform the other investments, they also endured periods of significant losses. Had your great-grandparents put the $100 in a small stock portfolio during the Depression era of the 1930s, it would have grown to $181 in 1928, but then fallen to only $15 by 1932. Indeed, it would take until World War II for stock investments to outperform corporate bonds.

Even more importantly, your great-grandparents would have sustained losses at a time when they likely needed their savings the most—in the depths of the Great Depression. A similar story held during the 2008 financial crisis: All of the stock portfolios declined by more than 50%, with the small stock portfolio declining by almost 70% (over $1.5 million!) from its peak in 2007 to its lowest point in 2009. Again, many investors faced a double whammy: an increased risk of being unemployed (as firms started laying off employees)

[1]Based on a World Market Index constructed by Global Financial Data, with approximate initial weights of 44% North America, 44% Europe, and 12% Asia, Africa, and Australia.

[2]Based on Global Financial Data's Corporate Bond Index.

FIGURE 10.1 **Value of $100 Invested in 1925 in Stocks, Bonds, or Bills**

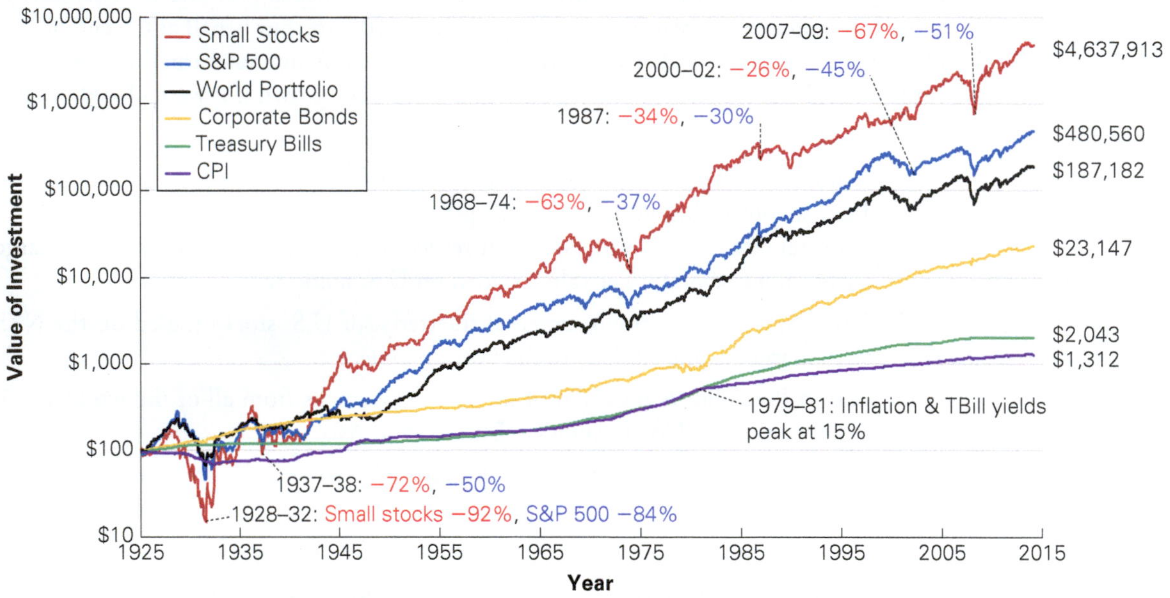

The chart shows the growth in value of $100 invested in 1925 if it were invested in U.S. large stocks, small stocks, world stocks, corporate bonds, or Treasury bills, with the level of the consumer price index (CPI) shown as a reference. Returns were calculated at year-end assuming all dividends and interest are reinvested and excluding transactions costs. Note that while stocks have generally outperformed bonds and bills, they have also endured periods of significant losses (numbers shown represent peak to trough decline, with the decline in small stocks in red and the S&P 500 in blue).

Source: Chicago Center for Research in Security Prices, Standard and Poor's, MSCI, and Global Financial Data.

precisely when the value of their savings eroded. Thus, while the stock portfolios had the best performance over this 89-year period, that performance came at a cost—the risk of large losses in a downturn. On the other hand, Treasury bills enjoyed steady—albeit modest—gains each year.

Few people ever make an investment for 89 years, as depicted in Figure 10.1. To gain additional perspective on the risk and return of these investments, Figure 10.2 shows the results for more realistic investment horizons and different initial investment dates. Panel (a), for example, shows the value of each investment after one year and illustrates that if we rank the investments by the volatility of their annual increases and decreases in value, we obtain the same ranking we observed with regard to performance: Small stocks had the most variable returns, followed by the S&P 500, the world portfolio, corporate bonds, and finally Treasury bills.

Panels (b), (c), and (d) of Figure 10.2 show the results for 5-, 10-, and 20-year investment horizons, respectively. Note that as the horizon lengthens, the relative performance of the stock portfolios improves. That said, even with a 10-year horizon there were periods during which stocks underperformed Treasuries. And while investors in small stocks most often came out ahead, this was not assured even with a 20-year horizon: For investors in

FIGURE 10.2 **Value of $100 Invested in Alternative Assets for Differing Horizons**

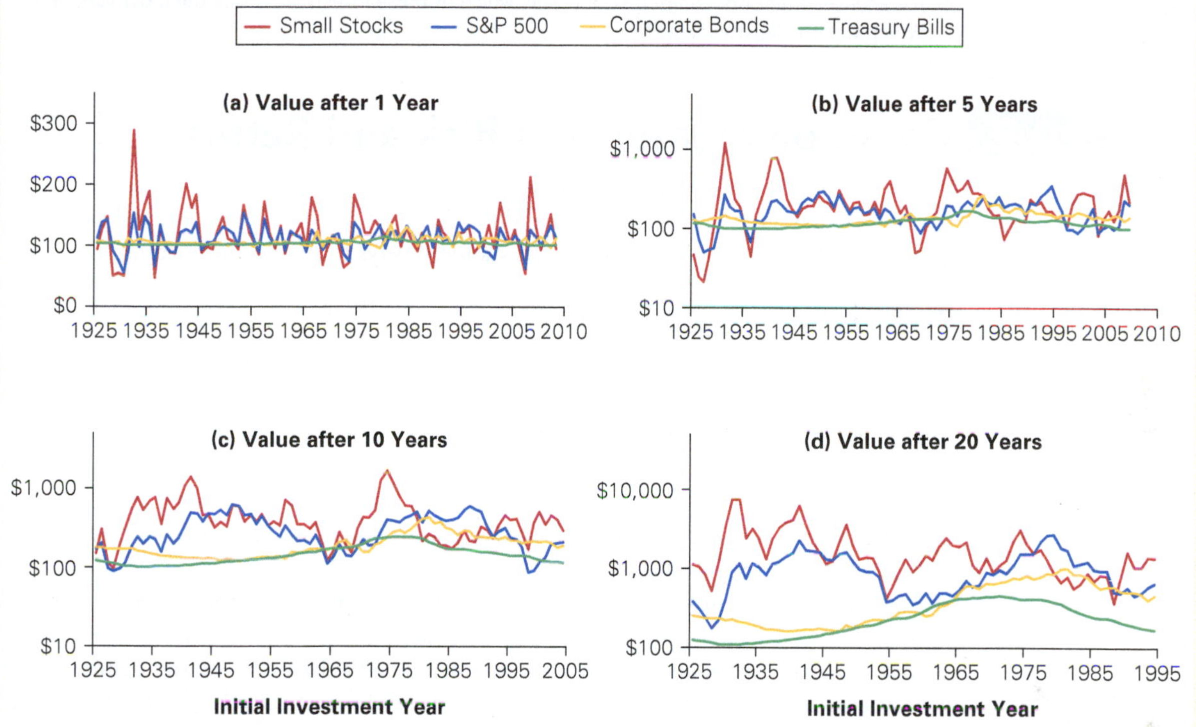

Each panel shows the result of investing $100 at the end of the initial investment year, in each investment opportunity, for horizons of 1, 5, 10, or 20 years. That is, each point on the plot is the result of an investment over the specified horizon, plotted as a function of the initial investment date. Dividends and interest are reinvested and transaction costs are excluded. Note that small stocks show the greatest variation in performance at the one-year horizon, followed by large stocks and then corporate bonds. For longer horizons, the relative performance of stocks improved, but they remained riskier.

Source Data: Chicago Center for Research in Security Prices, Standard and Poor's, MSCI, and Global Financial Data.

the early 1980s, small stocks did worse than both the S&P 500 *and* corporate bonds over the subsequent 20 years. Finally, stock investors with long potential horizons might find themselves in need of cash in intervening years, and be forced to liquidate at a loss relative to safer alternatives.

In Chapter 3, we explained why investors are averse to fluctuations in the value of their investments, and that investments that are more likely to suffer losses in downturns must compensate investors for this risk with higher expected returns. Figures 10.1 and 10.2 provide compelling historical evidence of this relationship between risk and return, just as we should expect in an efficient market. But while it is clear that investors do not like risk and thus demand a risk premium to bear it, our goal in this chapter is to quantify this relationship. We want to explain *how much* investors demand (in terms of a higher expected return) to bear a given level of risk. To do so, we must first develop tools that will allow us to measure risk and return—the objective of the next section.

CONCEPT CHECK

1. For an investment horizon from 1926 to 2012, which of the following investments had the highest return: the S&P 500, small stocks, world portfolio, corporate bonds, or Treasury bills? Which had the lowest return?
2. For an investment horizon of just one year, which of these investments was the most variable? Which was the least variable?

10.2 Common Measures of Risk and Return

When a manager makes an investment decision or an investor purchases a security, they have some view as to the risk involved and the likely return the investment will earn. Thus, we begin our discussion by reviewing the standard ways to define and measure risks.

Probability Distributions

Different securities have different initial prices, pay different cash flows, and sell for different future amounts. To make them comparable, we express their performance in terms of their returns. The return indicates the percentage increase in the value of an investment per dollar initially invested in the security. When an investment is risky, there are different returns it may earn. Each possible return has some likelihood of occurring. We summarize this information with a **probability distribution**, which assigns a probability, p_R, that each possible return, R, will occur.

Let's consider a simple example. Suppose BFI stock currently trades for $100 per share. You believe that in one year there is a 25% chance the share price will be $140, a 50% chance it will be $110, and a 25% chance it will be $80. BFI pays no dividends, so these payoffs correspond to returns of 40%, 10%, and −20%, respectively. Table 10.1 summarizes the probability distribution for BFI's returns.

We can also represent the probability distribution with a histogram, as shown in Figure 10.3.

Expected Return

Given the probability distribution of returns, we can compute the expected return. We calculate the **expected** (or **mean**) **return** as a weighted average of the possible returns, where the weights correspond to the probabilities.[3]

Expected (Mean) Return

$$\text{Expected Return} = E[R] = \sum_R p_R \times R \tag{10.1}$$

TABLE 10.1 Probability Distribution of Returns for BFI

		Probability Distribution	
Current Stock Price ($)	Stock Price in One Year ($)	Return, R	Probability, p_R
	140	0.40	25%
100	110	0.10	50%
	80	−0.20	25%

[3]The notation Σ_R means that we calculate the sum of the expression (in this case, $p_R \times R$) over all possible returns R.

FIGURE 10.3

Probability Distribution of Returns for BFI

The height of a bar in the histogram indicates the likelihood of the associated outcome.

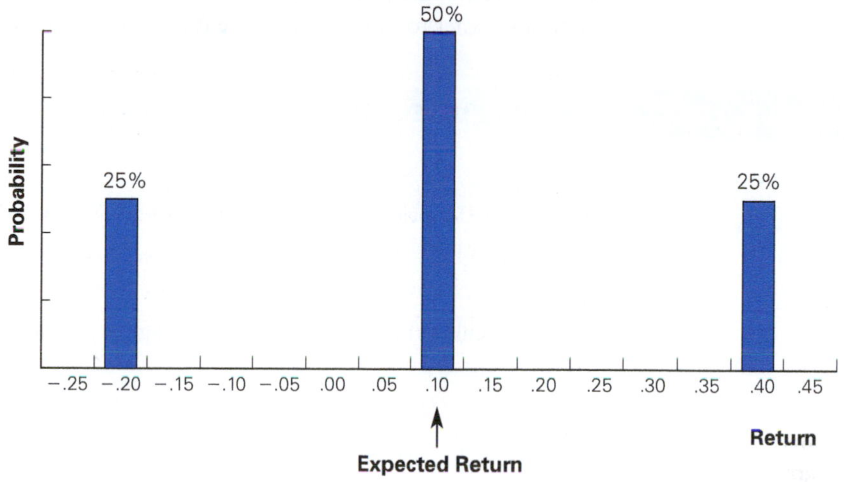

The expected return is the return we would earn on average if we could repeat the investment many times, drawing the return from the same distribution each time. In terms of the histogram, the expected return is the "balancing point" of the distribution, if we think of the probabilities as weights. The expected return for BFI is

$$E[R_{BFI}] = 25\%(-0.20) + 50\%(0.10) + 25\%(0.40) = 10\%$$

This expected return corresponds to the balancing point in Figure 10.3.

Variance and Standard Deviation

Two common measures of the risk of a probability distribution are its *variance* and *standard deviation*. The **variance** is the expected squared deviation from the mean, and the **standard deviation** is the square root of the variance.

Variance and Standard Deviation of the Return Distribution

$$Var(R) = E[(R - E[R])^2] = \sum_R p_R \times (R - E[R])^2$$

$$SD(R) = \sqrt{Var(R)} \tag{10.2}$$

If the return is risk-free and never deviates from its mean, the variance is zero. Otherwise, the variance increases with the magnitude of the deviations from the mean. Therefore, the variance is a measure of how "spread out" the distribution of the return is. The variance of BFI's return is

$$Var(R_{BFI}) = 25\% \times (-0.20-0.10)^2 + 50\% \times (0.10-0.10)^2 + 25\% \times (0.40-0.10)^2$$
$$= 0.045$$

The standard deviation of the return is the square root of the variance, so for BFI,

$$SD(R) = \sqrt{Var(R)} = \sqrt{0.045} = 21.2\% \tag{10.3}$$

In finance, we refer to the standard deviation of a return as its **volatility**. While the variance and the standard deviation both measure the variability of the returns, the standard deviation is easier to interpret because it is in the same units as the returns themselves.[4]

EXAMPLE 10.1 Calculating the Expected Return and Volatility

Problem

Suppose AMC stock is equally likely to have a 45% return or a −25% return. What are its expected return and volatility?

Solution

First, we calculate the expected return by taking the probability-weighted average of the possible returns:

$$E[R] = \sum_R p_R \times R = 50\% \times 0.45 + 50\% \times (-0.25) = 10.0\%$$

To compute the volatility, we first determine the variance:

$$Var(R) = \sum_R p_R \times (R - E[R])^2 = 50\% \times (0.45 - 0.10)^2 + 50\% \times (-0.25 - 0.10)^2$$
$$= 0.1225$$

Then, the volatility or standard deviation is the square root of the variance:

$$SD(R) = \sqrt{Var(R)} = \sqrt{0.1225} = 35\%$$

Note that both AMC and BFI have the same expected return, 10%. However, the returns for AMC are more spread out than those for BFI—the high returns are higher and the low returns are lower, as shown by the histogram in Figure 10.4. As a result, AMC has a higher variance and volatility than BFI.

FIGURE 10.4

Probability Distribution for BFI and AMC Returns

While both stocks have the same expected return, AMC's return has a higher variance and standard deviation.

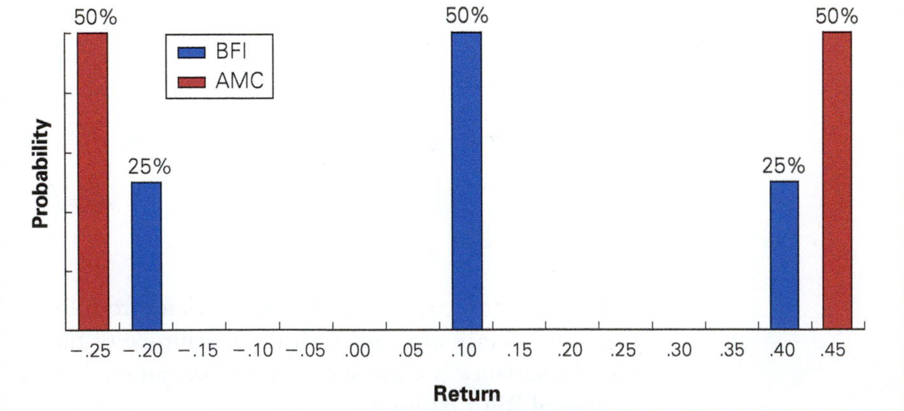

[4]While variance and standard deviation are the most common measures of risk, they do not differentiate upside and downside risk. Alternative measures that focus on downside risk include the semivariance (variance of the losses only) and the expected tail loss (the expected loss in the worst x% of outcomes). Because they often produce the same ranking (as in Example 10.1, or if returns are normally distributed) but are more complicated to apply, these alternative measures tend to be used only in special applications.

If we could observe the probability distributions that investors anticipate for different securities, we could compute their expected returns and volatilities and explore the relationship between them. Of course, in most situations we do not know the explicit probability distribution, as we did for BFI. Without that information, how can we estimate and compare risk and return? A popular approach is to extrapolate from historical data, which is a sensible strategy if we are in a stable environment and believe that the distribution of future returns should mirror that of past returns. Let's look at the historical returns of stocks and bonds, to see what they reveal about the relationship between risk and return.

CONCEPT CHECK

1. How do we calculate the expected return of a stock?
2. What are the two most common measures of risk, and how are they related to each other?

10.3 Historical Returns of Stocks and Bonds

In this section, we explain how to compute average returns and volatilities using historical stock market data. The distribution of past returns can be helpful when we seek to estimate the distribution of returns investors may expect in the future. We begin by first explaining how to compute historical returns.

Computing Historical Returns

Of all the possible returns, the **realized return** is the return that actually occurs over a particular time period. How do we measure the realized return for a stock? Suppose you invest in a stock on date t for price P_t. If the stock pays a dividend, Div_{t+1}, on date $t + 1$, and you sell the stock at that time for price P_{t+1}, then the realized return from your investment in the stock from t to $t + 1$ is

$$R_{t+1} = \frac{Div_{t+1} + P_{t+1}}{P_t} - 1 = \frac{Div_{t+1}}{P_t} + \frac{P_{t+1} - P_t}{P_t}$$
$$= \text{Dividend Yield} + \text{Capital Gain Rate} \qquad (10.4)$$

That is, as we discussed in Chapter 9, the realized return, R_{t+1}, is the total return we earn from dividends and capital gains, expressed as a percentage of the initial stock price.[5]

Calculating Realized Annual Returns. If you hold the stock beyond the date of the first dividend, then to compute your return you must specify how you invest any dividends you receive in the interim. To focus on the returns of a single security, let's assume that *you reinvest all dividends immediately and use them to purchase additional shares of the same stock or security*. In this case, we can use Eq. 10.4 to compute the stock's return between dividend payments, and then compound the returns from each dividend interval to compute the return over a longer horizon. For example, if a stock pays dividends at the end of each quarter, with realized returns $R_{Q1}, \ldots, R_{Q4}$ each quarter, then its annual realized return, R_{annual}, is

$$1 + R_{\text{annual}} = (1 + R_{Q1})(1 + R_{Q2})(1 + R_{Q3})(1 + R_{Q4}) \qquad (10.5)$$

[5]We can compute the realized return for any security in the same way, by replacing the dividend payments with any cash flows paid by the security (e.g., with a bond, coupon payments would replace dividends).

EXAMPLE 10.2 Realized Returns for Microsoft Stock

Problem

What were the realized annual returns for Microsoft stock in 2004 and 2008?

Solution

When we compute Microsoft's annual return, we assume that the proceeds from the dividend payment were immediately reinvested in Microsoft stock. That way, the return corresponds to remaining fully invested in Microsoft over the entire period. To do that we look up Microsoft stock price data at the start and end of the year, as well as at any dividend dates (Yahoo!Finance is a good source for such data; see also MyFinanceLab or www.berkdemarzo.com for additional sources). From these data, we can construct the following table (prices and dividends in \$/share):

Date	Price	Dividend	Return	Date	Price	Dividend	Return
12/31/03	27.37			12/31/07	35.60		
8/23/04	27.24	0.08	−0.18%	2/19/08	28.17	0.11	−20.56%
11/15/04[6]	27.39	3.08	11.86%	5/13/08	29.78	0.11	6.11%
12/31/04	26.72		−2.45%	8/19/08	27.32	0.11	−7.89%
				11/18/08	19.62	0.13	−27.71%
				12/31/08	19.44		−0.92%

The return from December 31, 2003, until August 23, 2004, is equal to

$$\frac{0.08 + 27.24}{27.37} - 1 = -0.18\%$$

The rest of the returns in the table are computed similarly. We then calculate the annual returns using Eq. 10.5:

$$R_{2004} = (0.9982)(1.1186)(0.9755) - 1 = 8.92\%$$

$$R_{2008} = (0.7944)(1.0611)(0.9211)(0.7229)(0.9908) - 1 = -44.39\%$$

Example 10.2 illustrates two features of the returns from holding a stock like Microsoft. First, both dividends and capital gains contribute to the total realized return—ignoring either one would give a very misleading impression of Microsoft's performance. Second, the returns are risky. In years like 2004 the returns are positive, but in other years like 2008 they are negative, meaning Microsoft's shareholders lost money over the year.

We can compute realized returns in this same way for any investment. We can also compute the realized returns for an entire portfolio, by keeping track of the interest and dividend payments paid by the portfolio during the year, as well as the change in the market value of the portfolio. For example, the realized returns for the S&P 500 index are shown in Table 10.2, which for comparison purposes also lists the returns for Microsoft and for three-month Treasury bills.

[6]The large dividend in November 2004 included a \$3 special dividend which Microsoft used to reduce its accumulating cash balance and disburse \$32 billion in cash to its investors, in the largest aggregate dividend payment in history.

TABLE 10.2 **Realized Return for the S&P 500, Microsoft, and Treasury Bills, 2002–2014**

Year End	S&P 500 Index	Dividends Paid*	S&P 500 Realized Return	Microsoft Realized Return	1-Month T-Bill Return
2001	1148.08				
2002	879.82	14.53	−22.1%	−22.0%	1.6%
2003	1111.92	20.80	28.7%	6.8%	1.0%
2004	1211.92	20.98	10.9%	8.9%	1.2%
2005	1248.29	23.15	4.9%	−0.9%	3.0%
2006	1418.30	27.16	15.8%	15.8%	4.8%
2007	1468.36	27.86	5.5%	20.8%	4.7%
2008	903.25	21.85	−37.0%	−44.4%	1.5%
2009	1115.10	27.19	26.5%	60.5%	0.1%
2010	1257.64	25.44	15.1%	−6.5%	0.1%
2011	1257.60	26.59	2.1%	−4.5%	0.0%
2012	1426.19	32.67	16.0%	5.8%	0.1%
2013	1848.36	39.75	32.4%	44.2%	0.0%
2014	2058.90	42.47	13.7%	27.5%	0.0%

*Total dividends paid by the 500 stocks in the portfolio, based on the number of shares of each stock in the index, adjusted until the end of the year, assuming they were reinvested when paid.

Source: Standard & Poor's, Microsoft and U.S. Treasury Data

Comparing Realized Annual Returns. Once we have calculated the realized annual returns, we can compare them to see which investments performed better in a given year. From Table 10.2, we can see that Microsoft stock outperformed the S&P 500 and Treasuries in 2007, 2009, 2013, and 2014. On the other hand, in 2002 and 2008, Treasury bills performed better than both Microsoft stock and the S&P 500. Note also the overall tendency for Microsoft's return to move in the same direction as the S&P 500, which it did in ten out of the thirteen years.

Over any particular period we observe only one draw from the probability distribution of returns. However, if the probability distribution remains the same, we can observe multiple draws by observing the realized return over multiple periods. By counting the number of times the realized return falls within a particular range, we can estimate the underlying probability distribution. Let's illustrate this process with the data in Figure 10.1.

Figure 10.5 plots the annual returns for each U.S. investment in Figure 10.1 in a histogram. The height of each bar represents the number of years that the annual returns were in each range indicated on the x-axis. When we plot the probability distribution in this way using historical data, we refer to it as the **empirical distribution** of the returns.

Average Annual Returns

The **average annual return** of an investment during some historical period is simply the average of the realized returns for each year. That is, if R_t is the realized return of a security in year t, then the average annual return for years 1 through T is

Average Annual Return of a Security

$$\bar{R} = \frac{1}{T}(R_1 + R_2 + \cdots + R_T) = \frac{1}{T}\sum_{t=1}^{T} R_t \tag{10.6}$$

Notice that the average annual return is the balancing point of the empirical distribution—in this case, the probability of a return occurring in a particular range is measured by the number of times the realized return falls in that range. Therefore, if the probability

FIGURE 10.5

The Empirical Distribution of Annual Returns for U.S. Large Stocks (S&P 500), Small Stocks, Corporate Bonds, and Treasury Bills, 1926–2014.

The height of each bar represents the number of years that the annual returns were in each 5% range. Note the greater variability of stock returns (especially small stocks) compared to the returns of corporate bonds or Treasury bills.

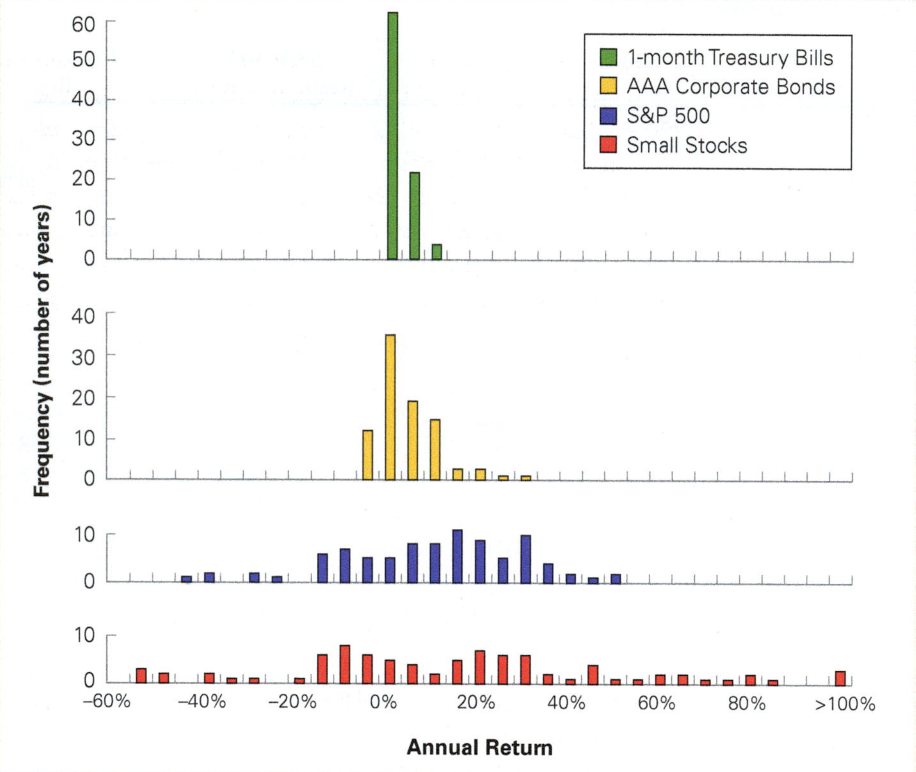

distribution of the returns is the same over time, the average return provides an estimate of the expected return.

Using the data from Table 10.2, the average return for the S&P 500 for the years 2002–2014 is

$$\bar{R} = \frac{1}{13}(-0.221 + 0.287 + 0.109 + 0.049 + 0.158$$

$$+ 0.055 - 0.37 + 0.265 + 0.151 + 0.021 + 0.160 + 0.324 + 0.137) = 8.7\%$$

The average Treasury bill return from 2002–2014 was 1.4%. Therefore, investors earned 7.3% more on average holding the S&P 500 rather than investing in Treasury bills over this period. Table 10.3 provides the average returns for different U.S. investments from 1926–2014.

TABLE 10.3 **Average Annual Returns for U.S. Small Stocks, Large Stocks (S&P 500), Corporate Bonds, and Treasury Bills, 1926–2014**

Investment	Average Annual Return
Small stocks	18.8%
S&P 500	12.0%
Corporate bonds	6.5%
Treasury bills	3.5%

The Variance and Volatility of Returns

Looking at Figure 10.5, we can see that the variability of the returns is very different for each investment. The distribution of small stocks' returns shows the widest spread. The large stocks of the S&P 500 have returns that vary less than those of small stocks, but much more than the returns of corporate bonds or Treasury bills.

To quantify this difference in variability, we can estimate the standard deviation of the probability distribution. As before, we will use the empirical distribution to derive this estimate. Using the same logic as we did with the mean, we estimate the variance by computing the average squared deviation from the mean. We do not actually know the mean, so instead we use the best estimate of the mean—the average realized return.[7]

Variance Estimate Using Realized Returns

$$Var(R) = \frac{1}{T-1}\sum_{t=1}^{T}(R_t - \overline{R})^2 \qquad (10.7)$$

We estimate the standard deviation or volatility as the square root of the variance.[8]

EXAMPLE 10.3 **Computing a Historical Volatility**

Problem

Using the data from Table 10.2, what are the variance and volatility of the S&P 500's returns for the years 2002–2014?

Solution

Earlier, we calculated the average annual return of the S&P 500 during this period to be 8.7%. Therefore,

$$Var(R) = \frac{1}{T-1}\sum_t (R_t - \overline{R})^2$$

$$= \frac{1}{13-1}[(-0.221 - 0.087)^2 + (0.287 - 0.087)^2 + \cdots + (0.137 - 0.087)^2]$$

$$= 0.038$$

The volatility or standard deviation is therefore $SD(R) = \sqrt{Var(R)} = \sqrt{0.038} = 19.5\%$

We can compute the standard deviation of the returns to quantify the differences in the variability of the distributions that we observed in Figure 10.5. These results are shown in Table 10.4.

Comparing the volatilities in Table 10.4 we see that, as expected, small stocks have had the most variable historical returns, followed by large stocks. The returns of corporate bonds and Treasury bills are much less variable than stocks, with Treasury bills being the least volatile investment category.

---

[7]Why do we divide by $T-1$ rather than by T here? It is because we do not know the true expected return, and so must compute deviations from the estimated average return $\overline{R}$. But in calculating the average return from the data, we lose a degree of freedom (in essence, we "use up" one of the data points), so that effectively we only have $T-1$ remaining data points to estimate the variance.

[8]If the returns used in Eq. 10.7 are not annual returns, the variance is typically converted to annual terms by multiplying the number of periods per year. For example, when using monthly returns, we multiply the variance by 12 and, equivalently, the standard deviation by $\sqrt{12}$.

TABLE 10.4 Volatility of U.S. Small Stocks, Large Stocks (S&P 500), Corporate Bonds, and Treasury Bills, 1926–2014

Investment	Return Volatility (Standard Deviation)
Small stocks	38.8%
S&P 500	20.1%
Corporate bonds	7.0%
Treasury bills	3.1%

Estimation Error: Using Past Returns to Predict the Future

To estimate the cost of capital for an investment, we need to determine the expected return that investors will require to compensate them for that investment's risk. If the distribution of past returns and the distribution of future returns are the same, we could look at the return investors expected to earn in the past on the same or similar investments, and assume they will require the same return in the future. However, there are two difficulties with this approach. First,

> *We do not know what investors expected in the past; we can only observe the actual returns that were realized.*

In 2008, for example, investors lost 37% investing in the S&P 500, which is surely not what they expected at the beginning of the year (or they would have invested in Treasury Bills instead!).

If we believe that investors are neither overly optimistic nor pessimistic on average, then over time, the average realized return should match investors' expected return. Armed with this assumption, we can use a security's historical average return to infer its expected return. But now we encounter the second difficulty:

> *The average return is just an estimate of the true expected return, and is subject to estimation error.*

Given the volatility of stock returns, this estimation error can be large even with many years of data, as we will see next.

Standard Error. We measure the estimation error of a statistical estimate by its *standard error*. The **standard error** is the standard deviation of the estimated value of the mean of the actual distribution around its true value; that is, it is the standard deviation of the average return. The standard error provides an indication of how far the sample average might deviate from the expected return. If the distribution of a stock's return is identical each year, and each year's return is independent of prior years' returns,[9] then we calculate the standard error of the estimate of the expected return as follows:

Standard Error of the Estimate of the Expected Return

$$SD\,(\text{Average of Independent, Identical Risks}) = \frac{SD\,(\text{Individual Risk})}{\sqrt{\text{Number of Observations}}} \tag{10.8}$$

[9]Saying that returns are independent and identically distributed (IID) means that the likelihood that the return has a given outcome is the same each year and does not depend on past returns (in the same way that the odds of a coin coming up heads do not depend on past flips). It turns out to be a reasonable first approximation for stock returns.

Because the average return will be within two standard errors of the true expected return approximately 95% of the time,[10] we can use the standard error to determine a reasonable range for the true expected value. The **95% confidence interval** for the expected return is

$$\text{Historical Average Return} \pm (2 \times \text{Standard Error}) \tag{10.9}$$

For example, from 1926 to 2014 the average return of the S&P 500 was 12.0% with a volatility of 20.1%. Assuming its returns are drawn from an independent and identical distribution (IID) each year, the 95% confidence interval for the expected return of the S&P 500 during this period is

$$12.0\% \pm 2\left(\frac{20.1\%}{\sqrt{89}}\right) = 12.0\% \pm 4.3\%$$

or a range from 7.7% to 16.3%. Thus, even with 89 years of data, we cannot estimate the expected return of the S&P 500 very accurately. If we believe the distribution may have changed over time and we can use only more recent data to estimate the expected return, then the estimate will be even less accurate.

Limitations of Expected Return Estimates. Individual stocks tend to be even more volatile than large portfolios, and many have been in existence for only a few years, providing little data with which to estimate returns. Because of the relatively large estimation error in such cases, the average return investors earned in the past is not a reliable estimate of a security's expected return. Instead, we need to derive a different method to estimate the expected return that relies on more reliable statistical estimates. In the remainder of this chapter, we will pursue the following alternative strategy: First we will consider how to measure a security's risk, and then we will use the relationship between risk and return—which we must still determine—to estimate its expected return.

EXAMPLE 10.4 The Accuracy of Expected Return Estimates

Problem

Using the returns for the S&P 500 from 2002–2014 only (see Table 10.2), what is the 95% confidence interval you would estimate for the S&P 500's expected return?

Solution

Earlier, we calculated the average return for the S&P 500 during this period to be 8.7%, with a volatility of 19.5% (see Example 10.3). The standard error of our estimate of the expected return is $19.5\% \div \sqrt{13} = 5.4\%$, and the 95% confidence interval is $8.7\% \pm (2 \times 5.4\%)$, or from -2.1% to 19.5%. As this example shows, with only a few years of data, we cannot reliably estimate expected returns for stocks—or even whether they are positive or negative!

CONCEPT CHECK

1. How do we estimate the average annual return of an investment?
2. We have 89 years of data on the S&P 500 returns, yet we cannot estimate the expected return of the S&P 500 very accurately. Why?

[10] If returns are independent and from a normal distribution, then the estimated mean will be within two standard errors of the true mean 95.44% of the time. Even if returns are not normally distributed, this formula is approximately correct with a sufficient number of independent observations.

Arithmetic Average Returns Versus Compound Annual Returns

We compute average annual returns by calculating an *arithmetic* average. An alternative is the compound annual return (also called the compound annual growth rate, or CAGR), which is computed as the *geometric* average of the annual returns $R_1, \ldots, R_T$:

$$\text{Compound Annual Return} = [(1+R_1) \times (1+R_2) \times \ldots \times (1+R_T)]^{1/T} - 1$$

It is equivalent to the IRR of the investment over the period:

$$(\text{Final Value/Initial Investment})^{1/T} - 1$$

For example, using the data in Figure 10.1, the compound annual return of the S&P 500 from 1926–2014 was

$$(480{,}560/100)^{1/89} - 1 = 9.99\%$$

That is, investing in the S&P 500 from 1926 to 2015 was equivalent to earning 9.99% per year over that time period. Similarly, the compound annual return for small stocks was 12.8%, for corporate bonds was 6.3%, and for Treasury bills was 3.4%.

In each case, the compound annual return is below the average annual return shown in Table 10.3. This difference reflects the fact that returns are volatile. To see the effect of volatility, suppose an investment has annual returns of +20% one year and −20% the next year. The average annual return is $\frac{1}{2}(20\% - 20\%) = 0\%$, but the value of $1 invested after two years is

$$\$1 \times (1.20) \times (0.80) = \$0.96$$

That is, an investor would have lost money. Why? Because the 20% gain happens on a $1 investment, whereas the 20% loss happens on a larger investment of $1.20. In this case, the compound annual return is

$$(0.96)^{1/2} - 1 = -2.02\%$$

This logic implies that the compound annual return will always be below the average return, and the difference grows with the volatility of the annual returns. (Typically, the difference is about half of the variance of the returns.)

Which is a better description of an investment's return? The compound annual return is a better description of the long-run *historical* performance of an investment. It describes the equivalent risk-free return that would be required to duplicate the investment's performance over the same time period. The ranking of the long-run performance of different investments coincides with the ranking of their compound annual returns. Thus, the compound annual return is the return that is most often used for comparison purposes. For example, mutual funds generally report their compound annual returns over the last five or ten years.

Conversely, we should use the arithmetic average return when we are trying to estimate an investment's *expected* return over a *future* horizon based on its past performance. If we view past returns as independent draws from the same distribution, then the arithmetic average return provides an unbiased estimate of the true expected return.*

For example, if the investment mentioned above is equally likely to have annual returns of +20% and −20% in the future, then if we observe many two-year periods, a $1 investment will be equally likely to grow to

$$(1.20)(1.20) = \$1.44,$$
$$(1.20)(0.80) = \$0.96,$$
$$(0.80)(1.20) = \$0.96,$$
$$\text{or} \quad (0.80)(0.80) = \$0.64.$$

Thus, the average value in two years will be (1.44 + 0.96 + 0.96 + 0.64)/4 = $1, so that the expected annual and two-year returns will both be 0%.

*For this result to hold we must compute the historical returns using the same time interval as the expected return we are estimating; that is, we use the average of past monthly returns to estimate the future monthly return, or the average of past annual returns to estimate the future annual return. Because of estimation error the estimate for different time intervals will generally differ from the result one would get by simply compounding the average annual return. With enough data, however, the results will converge.

10.4 The Historical Trade-Off Between Risk and Return

In Chapter 3, we discussed the idea that investors are risk averse: The benefit they receive from an increase in income is smaller than the personal cost of an equivalent decrease in income. This idea suggests that investors would not choose to hold a portfolio that is more volatile unless they expected to earn a higher return. In this section, we quantify the historical relationship between volatility and average returns.

The Returns of Large Portfolios

In Tables 10.3 and 10.4, we computed the historical average returns and volatilities for several different types of investments. We combine those data in Table 10.5, which lists the volatility and *excess return* for each investment. The **excess return** is the difference between the average return for the investment and the average return for Treasury bills, a risk-free investment, and measures the average risk premium investors earned for bearing the risk of the investment.

In Figure 10.6, we plot the average return versus the volatility of different investments. In addition to the ones we have already considered, we also include data for a large portfolio of mid-cap stocks, or stocks of median size in the U.S. market. Note the positive relationship: The investments with higher volatility have rewarded investors with higher average returns. Both Table 10.5 and Figure 10.6 are consistent with our view that investors are risk averse. Riskier investments must offer investors higher average returns to compensate them for the extra risk they are taking on.

TABLE 10.5 Volatility Versus Excess Return of U.S. Small Stocks, Large Stocks (S&P 500), Corporate Bonds, and Treasury Bills, 1926–2014

Investment	Return Volatility (Standard Deviation)	Excess Return (Average Return in Excess of Treasury Bills)
Small stocks	38.8%	15.3%
S&P 500	20.1%	8.5%
Corporate bonds	7.0%	3.0%
Treasury bills (30-day)	3.1%	0.0%

FIGURE 10.6

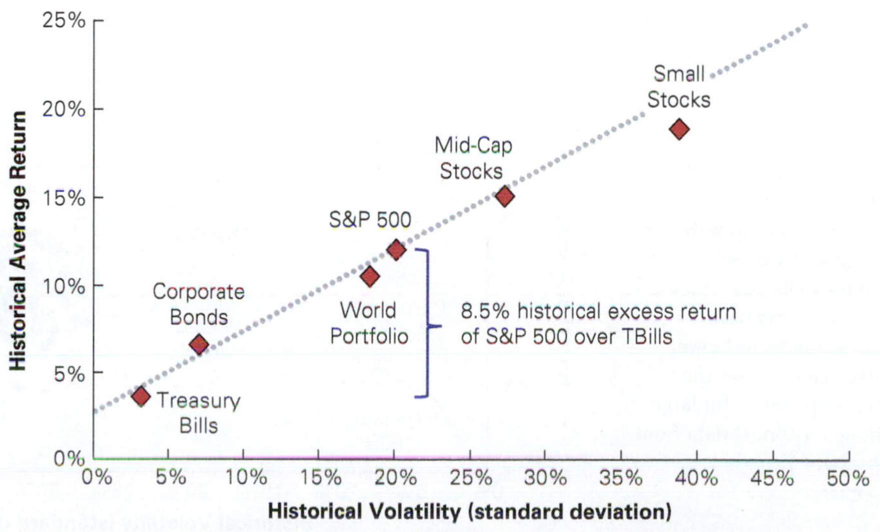

The Historical Trade-Off Between Risk and Return in Large Portfolios

Note the general increasing relationship between historical volatility and average return for these large portfolios. In addition to the portfolios in Figure 10.1, also included is a mid-cap portfolio composed of the 10% of U.S. stocks whose size is just above the median of all U.S. stocks. (Data from 1926–2014.)

Source: CRSP, Morgan Stanley Capital International

The Returns of Individual Stocks

Figure 10.6 suggests the following simple model of the risk premium: Investments with higher volatility should have a higher risk premium and therefore higher returns. Indeed, looking at Figure 10.6 it is tempting to draw a line through the portfolios and conclude that all investments should lie on or near this line—that is, expected return should rise proportionately with volatility. This conclusion appears to be approximately true for the large portfolios we have looked at so far. Is it correct? Does it apply to individual stocks?

Unfortunately, the answer to both questions is no. Figure 10.7 shows that, if we look at the volatility and return of individual stocks, we do not see any clear relationship between them. Each point represents the volatility and average return from investing in the Nth largest stock traded in the United States (updated quarterly) for $N = 1$ to 500.

We can make several important observations from these data. First, there is a relationship between size and risk: Larger stocks have lower volatility overall. Second, even the largest stocks are typically more volatile than a portfolio of large stocks, the S&P 500. Finally, there is no clear relationship between volatility and return. While the smallest stocks have a slightly higher average return, many stocks have higher volatility and lower average returns than other stocks. And all stocks seem to have higher risk and lower returns than we would have predicted from a simple extrapolation of our data from large portfolios.

Thus, while volatility is perhaps a reasonable measure of risk when evaluating a large portfolio, it is not adequate to explain the returns of individual securities. Why wouldn't investors demand a higher return from stocks with a higher volatility? And how is it that the S&P 500—a portfolio of the 500 largest stocks—is so much less risky than all of the 500 stocks individually? To answer these questions, we need to think more carefully about how to measure risk for an investor.

FIGURE 10.7

Historical Volatility and Return for 500 Individual Stocks, Ranked Annually by Size

Unlike the case for large portfolios, there is no precise relationship between volatility and average return for individual stocks. Individual stocks have higher volatility and lower average returns than the relationship shown for large portfolios. (Annual data from 1926–2014.)

Source: CRSP

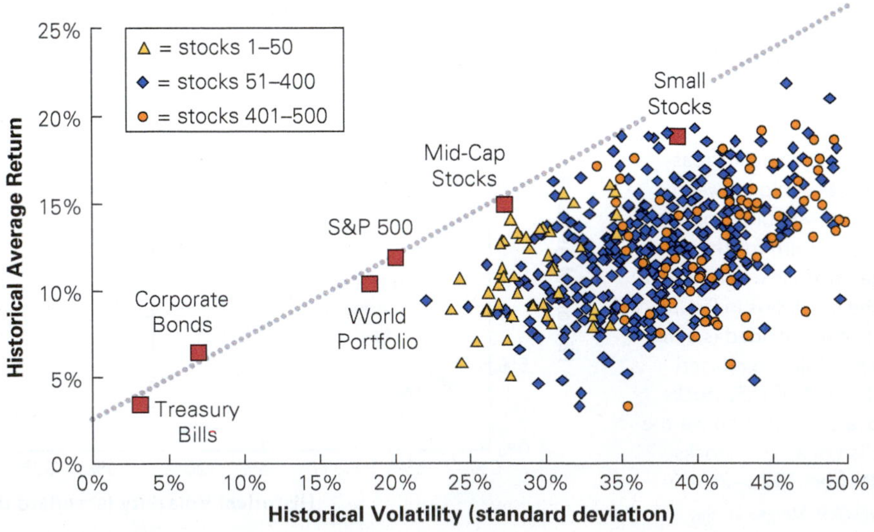

CONCEPT CHECK

1. What is the excess return?
2. Do expected returns of well-diversified large portfolios of stocks appear to increase with volatility?
3. Do expected returns for individual stocks appear to increase with volatility?

10.5 Common Versus Independent Risk

In this section, we explain why the risk of an individual security differs from the risk of a portfolio composed of similar securities. We begin with an example from the insurance industry.

Theft Versus Earthquake Insurance: An Example

Consider two types of home insurance: theft insurance and earthquake insurance. Let us assume, for the purpose of illustration, that the risk of each of these two hazards is similar for a given home in the San Francisco area. Each year there is about a 1% chance that the home will be robbed and a 1% chance that the home will be damaged by an earthquake. So, the chance the insurance company will pay a claim for a single home is the same for both types of insurance policies. Suppose an insurance company writes 100,000 policies of each type for homeowners in San Francisco. We know that the risks of the individual policies are similar, but are the risks of the portfolios of policies similar?

First, consider theft insurance. Because the chance of a theft in any given home is 1%, we would expect about 1% of the 100,000 homes to experience a robbery. Thus, the number of theft claims will be about 1000 per year. The actual number of claims may be a bit higher or lower each year, but not by much. We can estimate the likelihood that the insurance company will receive different numbers of claims, assuming that instances of theft are independent of one another (that is, the fact that one house is robbed does not change the odds of other houses being robbed). The number of claims will almost always be between 875 and 1125 (0.875% and 1.125% of the number of policies written). In this case, if the insurance company holds reserves sufficient to cover 1200 claims, it will almost certainly have enough to meet its obligations on its theft insurance policies.

Now consider earthquake insurance. Most years, an earthquake will not occur. But because the homes are in the same city, if an earthquake does occur, all homes are likely to be affected and the insurance company can expect as many as 100,000 claims. As a result, the insurance company will have to hold reserves sufficient to cover claims on all 100,000 policies it wrote to meet its obligations if an earthquake occurs.

Thus, although the expected numbers of claims may be the same, earthquake and theft insurance lead to portfolios with very different risk characteristics. For earthquake insurance, the number of claims is very risky. It will most likely be zero, but there is a 1% chance that the insurance company will have to pay claims on *all* the policies it wrote. In this case, the risk of the portfolio of insurance policies is no different from the risk of any single policy—it is still all or nothing. Conversely, for theft insurance, the number of claims in a given year is quite predictable. Year in and year out, it will be very close to 1% of the total number of policies, or 1000 claims. The portfolio of theft insurance policies has almost no risk![11]

[11] In the case of insurance, this difference in risk—and therefore in required reserves—can lead to a significant difference in the cost of the insurance. Indeed, earthquake insurance is generally thought to be much more expensive to purchase, even though the risk to an individual household may be similar to other risks, such as theft or fire.

Types of Risk. Why are the portfolios of insurance policies so different when the individual policies themselves are quite similar? Intuitively, the key difference between them is that an earthquake affects all houses simultaneously, so the risk is perfectly correlated across homes. We call risk that is perfectly correlated **common risk**. In contrast, because thefts in different houses are not related to each other, the risk of theft is uncorrelated and independent across homes. We call risks that share no correlation **independent risks**. When risks are independent, some individual homeowners are unlucky and others are lucky, but overall the number of claims is quite predictable. The averaging out of independent risks in a large portfolio is called **diversification**.

The Role of Diversification

We can quantify this difference in terms of the standard deviation of the percentage of claims. First, consider the standard deviation for an individual homeowner. At the beginning of the year, the homeowner expects a 1% chance of placing a claim for either type of insurance. But at the end of the year, the homeowner will have filed a claim (100%) or not (0%). Using Eq. 10.2, the standard deviation is

$$\begin{aligned} SD\text{ (Claim)} &= \sqrt{Var\text{(Claim)}} \\ &= \sqrt{0.99 \times (0 - 0.01)^2 + 0.01 \times (1 - 0.01)^2} = 9.95\% \end{aligned}$$

For the homeowner, this standard deviation is the same for a loss from earthquake or theft.

Now consider the standard deviation of the percentage of claims for the insurance company. In the case of earthquake insurance, because the risk is common, the percentage of claims is either 100% or 0%, just as it was for the homeowner. Thus, the percentage of claims received by the earthquake insurer is also 1% on average, with a 9.95% standard deviation.

While the theft insurer also receives 1% of claims on average, because the risk of theft is independent across households, the portfolio is much less risky. To quantify this difference, let's calculate the standard deviation of the average claim using Eq. 10.8. Recall that when risks are independent and identical, the standard deviation of the average is known as the standard error, which declines with the square root of the number of observations. Therefore,

$$\begin{aligned} SD\text{ (Percentage Theft Claims)} &= \frac{SD\text{ (Individual Claim)}}{\sqrt{\text{Number of Observations}}} \\ &= \frac{9.95\%}{\sqrt{100{,}000}} = 0.03\% \end{aligned}$$

Thus, there is almost *no* risk for the theft insurer.

The principle of diversification is used routinely in the insurance industry. In addition to theft insurance, many other forms of insurance (e.g., life, health, auto) rely on the fact that the number of claims is relatively predictable in a large portfolio. Even in the case of earthquake insurance, insurers can achieve some diversification by selling policies in different geographical regions or by combining different types of policies. Diversification reduces risk in many other settings. For example, farmers often diversify the types of crops they plant to reduce the risk from the failure of any individual crop. Similarly, firms may diversify their supply chains or product lines to reduce the risk from supply disruptions or demand shocks.

EXAMPLE 10.5 Diversification and Gambling

Problem

Roulette wheels are typically marked with the numbers 1 through 36 plus 0 and 00. Each of these outcomes is equally likely every time the wheel is spun. If you place a bet on any one number and are correct, the payoff is 35:1; that is, if you bet \$1, you will receive \$36 if you win (\$35 plus your original \$1) and nothing if you lose. Suppose you place a \$1 bet on your favorite number. What is the casino's expected profit? What is the standard deviation of this profit for a single bet? Suppose 9 million similar bets are placed throughout the casino in a typical month. What is the standard deviation of the casino's average revenues per dollar bet each month?

Solution

Because there are 38 numbers on the wheel, the odds of winning are 1/38. The casino loses \$35 if you win, and makes \$1 if you lose. Therefore, using Eq. 10.1, the casino's expected profit is

$$E[\text{Payoff}] = (1/38) \times (-\$35) + (37/38) \times (\$1) = \$0.0526$$

That is, for each dollar bet, the casino earns 5.26 cents on average. For a single bet, we calculate the standard deviation of this profit using Eq. 10.2 as

$$SD(\text{Payoff}) = \sqrt{(1/38) \times (-35 - 0.0526)^2 + (37/38) \times (1 - 0.0526)^2} = \$5.76$$

This standard deviation is quite large relative to the magnitude of the profits. But if many such bets are placed, the risk will be diversified. Using Eq. 10.8, the standard deviation of the casino's average revenues per dollar bet (i.e., the standard error of their payoff) is only

$$SD(\text{Average Payoff}) = \frac{\$5.76}{\sqrt{9{,}000{,}000}} = \$0.0019$$

In other words, by the same logic as Eq. 10.9, there is roughly 95% chance the casino's profit per dollar bet will be in the interval \$0.0526 ± (2 × 0.0019) = \$0.0488 to \$0.0564. Given \$9 million in bets placed, the casino's monthly profits will almost always be between \$439,000 and \$508,000, which is very little risk. The key assumption, of course, is that each bet is separate so that their outcomes are independent of each other. If the \$9 million were placed in a single bet, the casino's risk would be large—losing 35 × \$9 million = \$315 million if the bet wins. For this reason, casinos often impose limits on the amount of any individual bet.

CONCEPT CHECK

1. What is the difference between common risk and independent risk?
2. Under what circumstances will risk be diversified in a large portfolio of insurance contracts?

10.6 Diversification in Stock Portfolios

As the insurance example indicates, the risk of a portfolio of insurance contracts depends on whether the individual risks within it are common or independent. Independent risks are diversified in a large portfolio, whereas common risks are not. Let's consider the implication of this distinction for the risk of stock portfolios.[12]

[12]Harry Markowitz was the first to formalize the role of diversification in forming an optimal stock market portfolio. See H. Markowitz, "Portfolio Selection," *Journal of Finance* 7 (1952): 77–91.

Firm-Specific Versus Systematic Risk

Over any given time period, the risk of holding a stock is that the dividends plus the final stock price will be higher or lower than expected, which makes the realized return risky. What causes dividends or stock prices, and therefore returns, to be higher or lower than we expect? Usually, stock prices and dividends fluctuate due to two types of news:

1. *Firm-specific news* is good or bad news about the company itself. For example, a firm might announce that it has been successful in gaining market share within its industry.
2. *Market-wide news* is news about the economy as a whole and therefore affects all stocks. For instance, the Federal Reserve might announce that it will lower interest rates to boost the economy.

Fluctuations of a stock's return that are due to firm-specific news are independent risks. Like theft across homes, these risks are unrelated across stocks. This type of risk is also referred to as **firm-specific**, **idiosyncratic**, **unique**, or **diversifiable risk**.

Fluctuations of a stock's return that are due to market-wide news represent common risk. As with earthquakes, all stocks are affected simultaneously by the news. This type of risk is also called **systematic**, **undiversifiable**, or **market risk**.

When we combine many stocks in a large portfolio, the firm-specific risks for each stock will average out and be diversified. Good news will affect some stocks, and bad news will affect others, but the amount of good or bad news overall will be relatively constant. The systematic risk, however, will affect all firms—and therefore the entire portfolio—and will not be diversified.

Let's consider an example. Suppose type S firms are affected *only* by the strength of the economy, which has a 50–50 chance of being either strong or weak. If the economy is strong, type S stocks will earn a return of 40%; if the economy is weak, their return will be −20%. Because these firms face systematic risk (the strength of the economy), holding a large portfolio of type S firms will not diversify the risk. When the economy is strong, the portfolio will have the same return of 40% as each type S firm; when the economy is weak, the portfolio will also have a return of −20%.

Now consider type I firms, which are affected only by idiosyncratic, firm-specific risks. Their returns are equally likely to be 35% or −25%, based on factors specific to each firm's local market. Because these risks are firm specific, if we hold a portfolio of the stocks of many type I firms, the risk is diversified. About half of the firms will have returns of 35%, and half will have returns of −25%, so that the return of the portfolio will be close to the average return of $0.5\ (35\%) + 0.5\ (-25\%) = 5\%$.

Figure 10.8 illustrates how volatility declines with the size of the portfolio for type S and I firms. Type S firms have only systematic risk. As with earthquake insurance, the volatility of the portfolio does not change as the number of firms increases. Type I firms have only idiosyncratic risk. As with theft insurance, the risk is diversified as the number of firms increases, and volatility declines. As is evident from Figure 10.8, with a large number of firms, the risk is essentially eliminated.

Of course, actual firms are not like type S or I firms. Firms are affected by both systematic, market-wide risks and firm-specific risks. Figure 10.8 also shows how the volatility changes with the size of a portfolio containing the stocks of typical firms. When firms carry both types of risk, only the firm-specific risk will be diversified when we combine many firms' stocks into a portfolio. The volatility will therefore decline until only the systematic risk, which affects all firms, remains.

FIGURE 10.8

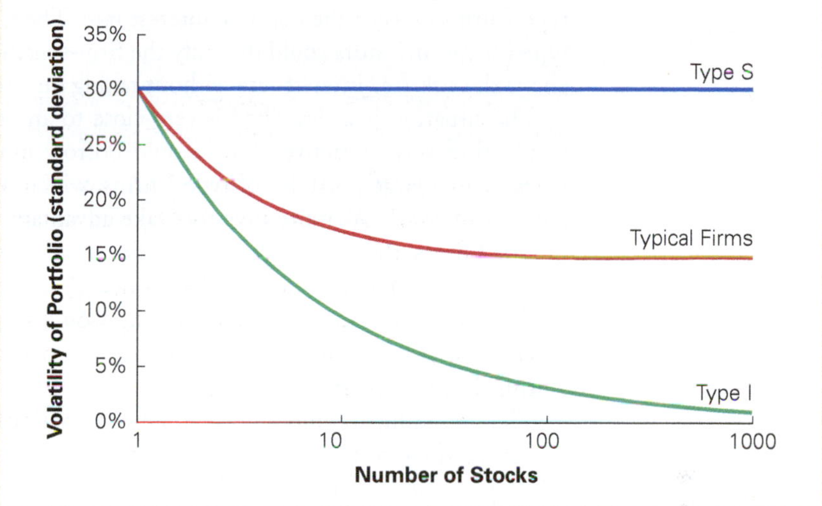

Volatility of Portfolios of Type S and I Stocks

Because type S firms have only systematic risk, the volatility of the portfolio does not change. Type I firms have only idiosyncratic risk, which is diversified and eliminated as the number of firms in the portfolio increases. Typical stocks carry a mix of both types of risk, so that the risk of the portfolio declines as idiosyncratic risk is diversified away, but systematic risk still remains.

This example explains one of the puzzles shown in Figure 10.7. There we saw that the S&P 500 had much lower volatility than any of the individual stocks. Now we can see why: The individual stocks each contain firm-specific risk, which is eliminated when we combine them into a large portfolio. Thus, the portfolio as a whole can have lower volatility than each of the stocks within it.

EXAMPLE 10.6 **Portfolio Volatility**

Problem

What is the volatility of the average return of ten type S firms? What is the volatility of the average return of ten type I firms?

Solution

Type S firms have equally likely returns of 40% or −20%. Their expected return is $\frac{1}{2}(40\%) + \frac{1}{2}(-20\%) = 10\%$, so

$$SD(R_S) = \sqrt{\tfrac{1}{2}(0.40 - 0.10)^2 + \tfrac{1}{2}(-0.20 - 0.10)^2} = 30\%$$

Because all type S firms have high or low returns at the same time, the average return of ten type S firms is also 40% or −20%. Thus, it has the same volatility of 30%, as shown in Figure 10.8.

Type I firms have equally likely returns of 35% or −25%. Their expected return is $\frac{1}{2}(35\%) + \frac{1}{2}(-25\%) = 5\%$, so

$$SD(R_I) = \sqrt{\tfrac{1}{2}(0.35 - 0.05)^2 + \tfrac{1}{2}(-0.25 - 0.05)^2} = 30\%$$

Because the returns of type I firms are independent, using Eq. 10.8, the average return of 10 type I firms has volatility of $30\% \div \sqrt{10} = 9.5\%$, as shown in Figure 10.8.

No Arbitrage and the Risk Premium

Consider again type I firms, which are affected only by firm-specific risk. Because each individual type I firm is risky, should investors expect to earn a risk premium when investing in type I firms?

In a competitive market, the answer is no. To see why, suppose the expected return of type I firms exceeds the risk-free interest rate. Then, by holding a large portfolio of many type I firms, investors could diversify the firm-specific risk of these firms and earn a return above the risk-free interest rate without taking on any significant risk.

The situation just described is very close to an arbitrage opportunity, which investors would find very attractive. They would borrow money at the risk-free interest rate and invest it in a large portfolio of type I firms, which offers a higher return with only a tiny amount of risk.[13] As more investors take advantage of this situation and purchase shares of type I firms, the current share prices for type I firms would rise, lowering their expected return—recall that the current share price P_t is the denominator when computing the stock's return as in Eq. 10.4. This trading would stop only after the return of type I firms equaled the risk-free interest rate. Competition between investors drives the return of type I firms down to the risk-free return.

The preceding argument is essentially an application of the Law of One Price: Because a large portfolio of type I firms has no risk, it must earn the risk-free interest rate. This no-arbitrage argument suggests the following more general principle:

The risk premium for diversifiable risk is zero, so investors are not compensated for holding firm-specific risk.

We can apply this principle to all stocks and securities. It implies that the risk premium of a stock is not affected by its diversifiable, firm-specific risk. If the diversifiable risk of stocks were compensated with an additional risk premium, then investors could buy the stocks, earn the additional premium, and simultaneously diversify and eliminate the risk. By doing so, investors could earn an additional premium without taking on additional risk. This opportunity to earn something for nothing would quickly be exploited and eliminated.[14]

Because investors can eliminate firm-specific risk "for free" by diversifying their portfolios, they will not require a reward or risk premium for holding it. However, diversification does not reduce systematic risk: Even holding a large portfolio, an investor will be exposed to risks that affect the entire economy and therefore affect all securities. Because investors are risk averse, they will demand a risk premium to hold systematic risk; otherwise they would be better off selling their stocks and investing in risk-free bonds. Because investors can eliminate firm-specific risk for free by diversifying, whereas systematic risk can be eliminated only by sacrificing expected returns, it is a security's systematic risk that determines the risk premium investors require to hold it. This fact leads to a second key principle:

The risk premium of a security is determined by its systematic risk and does not depend on its diversifiable risk.

This principle implies that a stock's volatility, which is a measure of total risk (that is, systematic risk plus diversifiable risk), is not especially useful in determining the risk premium that investors will earn. For example, consider again type S and I firms. As calculated in Example 10.6, the volatility of a single type S or I firm is 30%. Although both types of firms have the same volatility, type S firms have an expected return of 10% and type I firms have an expected return of 5%. The difference in expected returns derives from the difference in the kind of risk each firm bears. Type I firms have only firm-specific risk, which does not require a risk premium, so the expected return of 5% for type I firms equals the

---

[13]If investors could actually hold a large enough portfolio and completely diversify all the risk, then this would be a true arbitrage opportunity.

[14]The main thrust of this argument can be found in S. Ross, "The Arbitrage Theory of Capital Asset Pricing," *Journal of Economic Theory* 13 (December 1976): 341–360.

GLOBAL FINANCIAL CRISIS Diversification Benefits During Market Crashes

The figure below illustrates the benefits of diversification over the last 40 years. The blue graph shows the historical volatility of the S&P 500 portfolio (annualized based on daily returns each quarter). The pink graph is the average volatility of the individual stocks in the portfolio (weighted according to the size of each stock). Thus, the pink shaded area is idiosyncratic risk—risk that has been diversified away by holding the portfolio. The blue area is market risk which cannot be diversified.

Market volatility clearly varies, increasing dramatically during times of crisis. But notice also that the fraction of risk that can be diversified away also varies, and seems to decline during times of crisis. For example, since 1970, on average about 50% of the volatility of individual stocks is diversifiable (i.e., the pink area is about 50% of the total). But as the figure demonstrates, during the 1987 stock market crash, the 2008 financial crisis, and the recent Eurozone debt crisis, this fraction fell dramatically, so that only about 20% of the volatility of individual stocks could be diversified. The combined effect of increased volatility and reduced diversification during the 2008 financial crisis was so severe that the risk that investors care about—market risk—increased *seven*-fold, from 10% to 70%, between 2006 and the last quarter of 2008.

Although you are always better off diversifying, it is important to keep in mind that the benefits of diversification depend on economic conditions. In times of extreme crisis, the benefits may go down, making downturns in the market particularly painful for investors.

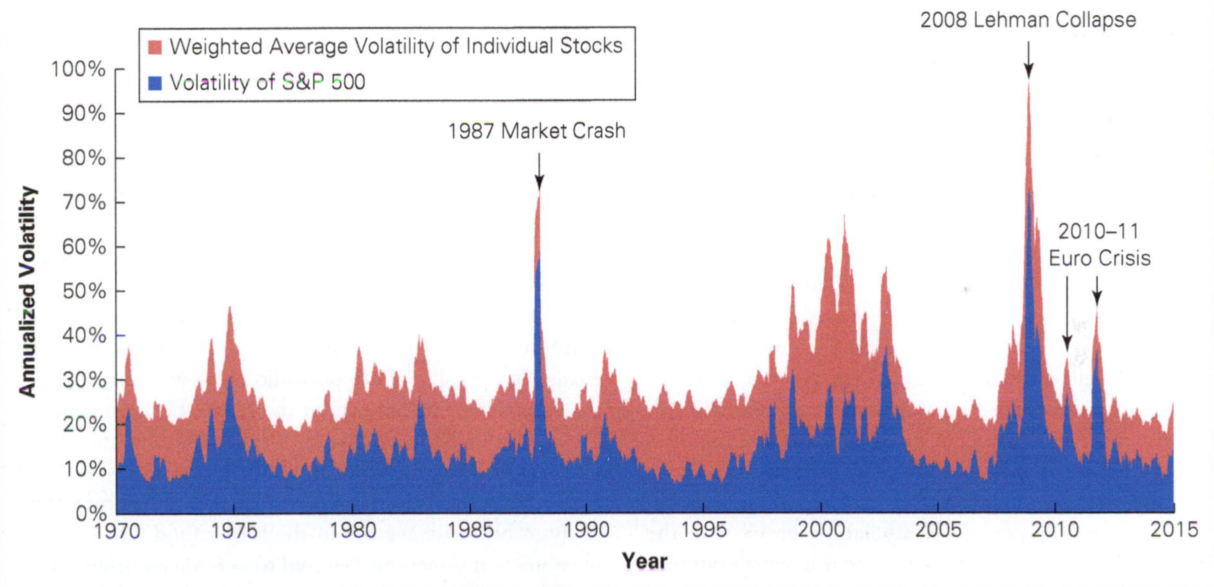

risk-free interest rate. Type S firms have only systematic risk. Because investors will require compensation for taking on this risk, the expected return of 10% for type S firms provides investors with a 5% risk premium above the risk-free interest rate.

We now have an explanation for the second puzzle of Figure 10.7. While volatility might be a reasonable measure of risk for a well-diversified portfolio, it is not an appropriate metric for an individual security. Thus, there should be no clear relationship between volatility and average returns for individual securities. Consequently, to estimate a security's expected return, we need to find a measure of a security's systematic risk.

In Chapter 3, we argued that an investment's risk premium depends on how its returns move in relation to the overall economy. In particular, risk-averse investors will demand a premium to invest in securities that will do poorly in bad times (recall, for example, the performance of small stocks in Figure 10.1 during the Great Depression). This idea coincides with the notion of systematic risk we have defined in this chapter. Economy-wide risk—that is, the risk of recessions and booms—is systematic risk that cannot be diversified. Therefore an asset that moves with the economy contains systematic risk and so requires a risk premium.

EXAMPLE 10.7 Diversifiable Versus Systematic Risk

Problem

Which of the following risks of a stock are likely to be firm-specific, diversifiable risks, and which are likely to be systematic risks? Which risks will affect the risk premium that investors will demand?

a. The risk that the founder and CEO retires
b. The risk that oil prices rise, increasing production costs
c. The risk that a product design is faulty and the product must be recalled
d. The risk that the economy slows, reducing demand for the firm's products

Solution

Because oil prices and the health of the economy affect all stocks, risks (b) and (d) are systematic risks. These risks are not diversified in a large portfolio, and so will affect the risk premium that investors require to invest in a stock. Risks (a) and (c) are firm-specific risks, and so are diversifiable. While these risks should be considered when estimating a firm's future cash flows, they will not affect the risk premium that investors will require and, therefore, will not affect a firm's cost of capital.

COMMON MISTAKE A Fallacy of Long-Run Diversification

We have seen that investors can greatly reduce their risk by dividing their investment dollars over many different investments, eliminating the diversifiable risk in their portfolios. Does the same logic apply over time? That is, by investing for many years, can we also diversify the risk we face during any particular year? In the long run, does risk still matter?

Eq. 10.8 tells us that if returns each year are independent, the volatility of the average annual return declines with the number of years that we invest. Of course, as long-term investors, we don't care about the volatility of our *average* return; instead, we care about the volatility of our *cumulative* return over the period. This volatility grows with the investment horizon, as illustrated in the following example.

In 1925, large U.S. stocks increased in value by about 30%. In fact, a \$77 investment at the start of 1925 would have grown to $\$77 \times 1.30 = \$100$ by the end of the year. Notice from Figure 10.1 that a \$100 investment in the S&P 500 from 1926 onward would have grown to about \$480,560 by the start of 2015. But suppose instead stocks had dropped by 35% in 1925. Then, the initial \$77 invested would be worth only $\$77 \times (1 - 35\%) = \$50$ at the beginning of 1926. If returns from then on were unchanged, the investment would be worth half as much in 2015, or \$240,280. Thus, despite the long horizon, the difference in the first year's return still has a significant effect on the final payoff.

The financial crisis in 2008 brought home the reality of this fallacy to many investors. Consider for example, a long-term investor who invested \$100 in small stocks in 1925. If her investment horizon was 81 years (end of 2006), she would have a little over \$2 million. If instead her investment horizon was 83 years (end of 2008) her portfolio would have dropped by over 50% to just \$1 million. Again, having a longer horizon did not reduce risk!

More generally, if returns are independent over time so that future returns are not affected by past returns, then any change in the value of our portfolio today will translate into the same percentage change in the value of our portfolio in the future, and there is no diversification over time. The only way the length of the time horizon can reduce risk is if a below-average return today implies that returns are more likely to be above average in the future (and vice versa), a phenomenon sometimes referred to as ***mean reversion***. Mean reversion implies that past low returns can be used to predict future high returns in the stock market.

For short horizons of a few years, there is no evidence of mean reversion in the stock market. For longer horizons, there is some evidence of mean reversion historically, but it is not clear how reliable this evidence is (there are not enough decades of accurate stock market data available) or whether the pattern will continue. Even if there is long-run mean reversion in stock returns, a buy-and-hold diversification strategy is still not optimal: Because mean reversion implies that past returns can be used to predict future returns, you should invest more in stocks when returns are predicted to be high, and invest less when they are predicted to be low. This strategy is very different from the diversification we achieve by holding many stocks, where we cannot predict which stocks will have good or bad firm-specific shocks.

CONCEPT CHECK

1. Explain why the risk premium of diversifiable risk is zero.
2. Why is the risk premium of a security determined only by its systematic risk?

10.7 Measuring Systematic Risk

As we have discussed, investors can eliminate the firm-specific risk in their investments by diversifying their portfolio. Thus, when evaluating the risk of an investment, an investor will care about its systematic risk, which cannot be eliminated through diversification. In exchange for bearing systematic risk, investors want to be compensated by earning a higher return. So, to determine the additional return, or risk premium, investors will require to undertake an investment, we first need to measure the investment's systematic risk.

Identifying Systematic Risk: The Market Portfolio

To measure the systematic risk of a stock, we must determine how much of the variability of its return is due to systematic, market-wide risks versus diversifiable, firm-specific risks. That is, we would like to know how sensitive the stock is to systematic shocks that affect the economy as a whole.

To determine how sensitive a stock's return is to interest rate changes, for example, we would look at how much the return tends to change on average for each 1% change in interest rates. Similarly, to determine how sensitive a stock's return is to oil prices, we would examine the average change in the return for each 1% change in oil prices. In the same way, to determine how sensitive a stock is to systematic risk, we can look at the average change in its return for each 1% change in the return of *a portfolio that fluctuates solely due to systematic risk*.

Thus, the first step to measuring systematic risk is finding a portfolio that contains *only* systematic risk. Changes in the price of this portfolio will correspond to systematic shocks to the economy. We call such a portfolio an **efficient portfolio**. An efficient portfolio cannot be diversified further—that is, there is no way to reduce the risk of the portfolio without lowering its expected return. How can we identify such a portfolio?

As we will see over the next few chapters, the best way to identify an efficient portfolio is one of the key questions in modern finance. Because diversification improves with the number of stocks held in a portfolio, an efficient portfolio should be a large portfolio containing many different stocks. Thus, a natural candidate for an efficient portfolio is the **market portfolio**, which is a portfolio of all stocks and securities traded in the capital markets. Because it is difficult to find data for the returns of many bonds and small stocks, it is common in practice to use the S&P 500 portfolio as an approximation for the market portfolio, under the assumption that the S&P 500 is large enough to be essentially fully diversified.

Sensitivity to Systematic Risk: Beta

If we assume that the market portfolio (or the S&P 500) is efficient, then changes in the value of the market portfolio represent systematic shocks to the economy. We can then measure the systematic risk of a security by calculating the sensitivity of the security's return to the return of the market portfolio, known as the **beta** (β) of the security. More precisely,

> *The beta of a security is the expected % change in its return given a 1% change in the return of the market portfolio.*

EXAMPLE 10.8 Estimating Beta

Problem

Suppose the market portfolio tends to increase by 47% when the economy is strong and decline by 25% when the economy is weak. What is the beta of a type S firm whose return is 40% on average when the economy is strong and −20% when the economy is weak? What is the beta of a type I firm that bears only idiosyncratic, firm-specific risk?

Solution

The systematic risk of the strength of the economy produces a 47% − (−25%) = 72% change in the return of the market portfolio. The type S firm's return changes by 40% − (−20%) = 60% on average. Thus the firm's beta is $\beta_S = 60\%/72\% = 0.833$. That is, each 1% change in the return of the market portfolio leads to a 0.833% change in the type S firm's return on average.

The return of a type I firm has only firm-specific risk, however, and so is not affected by the strength of the economy. Its return is affected only by factors specific to the firm. Because it will have the same expected return, whether the economy is strong or weak, $\beta_I = 0\%/72\% = 0$.

Real-Firm Betas. We will look at statistical techniques for estimating beta from historical stock returns in Chapter 12. There we will see that we can estimate beta reasonably accurately using just a few years of data (which was not the case for expected returns, as we saw in Example 10.4). Using the S&P 500 to represent the market's return, Table 10.6 shows the betas of several stocks during 2010–2015. As shown in the table, each 1% change in the return of the market during this period led, on average, to a 1.21% change in the return for Yahoo! but only a 0.52% change in the return for Coca-Cola.

Interpreting Betas. Beta measures the sensitivity of a security to market-wide risk factors. For a stock, this value is related to how sensitive its underlying revenues and cash flows are to general economic conditions. The average beta of a stock in the market is about 1; that is, the average stock price tends to move about 1% for each 1% move in the overall market. Stocks in cyclical industries, in which revenues and profits vary greatly over the business cycle, are likely to be more sensitive to systematic risk and have betas that exceed 1, whereas stocks of non-cyclical firms tend to have betas that are less than 1.

For example, notice the relatively low betas of PG&E (a utility company), Johnson & Johnson (pharmaceuticals), General Mills and Hershey (food processing), and Amgen (biotechnology). Utilities tend to be stable and highly regulated, and thus are insensitive to fluctuations in the overall market. Drug and food companies are also very insensitive—the demand for their products appears to be unrelated to the booms and busts of the economy as a whole.

At the other extreme, technology stocks tend to have higher betas; consider Oracle, Hewlett-Packard, Netgear, Autodesk, and Advanced Micro Devices. Shocks in the economy have an amplified impact on these stocks: When the market as a whole is up, Advanced Micro Devices' (AMD)'s stock tends to rise more than twice as much; but when the market stumbles, it tends to fall more than twice as far. Note also the high beta of luxury retailers Coach and Tiffany & Co., compared with the much lower beta of Walmart; presumably their sales respond very differently to economic booms and busts. Finally, we see that highly levered firms in cyclical industries, such as General Motors and U.S. Steel, tend to have high betas reflecting their sensitivity to economic conditions.

CONCEPT CHECK

1. What is the market portfolio?
2. Define the beta of a security.

TABLE 10.6 **Betas with Respect to the S&P 500 for Individual Stocks (based on monthly data for 2010–2015)**

Company	Ticker	Industry	Equity Beta
PG&E	PGE	Utilities	0.26
General Mills	GIS	Packaged Foods	0.30
Newmont Mining	NEM	Gold	0.32
The Hershey Company	HSY	Packaged Foods	0.33
McDonald's	MCD	Restaurants	0.39
Clorox	CLX	Household Products	0.40
Pepsico	PEP	Soft Drinks	0.42
Wal-Mart Stores	WMT	Superstores	0.49
Procter & Gamble	PG	Household Products	0.52
Coca-Cola	KO	Soft Drinks	0.52
Altria Group	MO	Tobacco	0.54
Amgen	AMGN	Biotechnology	0.64
Johnson & Johnson	JNJ	Pharmaceuticals	0.65
Nike	NKE	Footwear	0.67
Southwest Airlines	LUV	Airlines	0.80
Kroger	KR	Food Retail	0.80
Starbucks	SBUX	Restaurants	0.80
Whole Foods Market	WFM	Food Retail	0.83
Intel	INTC	Semiconductors	0.87
Microsoft	MSFT	Systems Software	0.89
Pfizer	PFE	Pharmaceuticals	0.89
Apple	AAPL	Computer Hardware	0.92
Amazon.com	AMZN	Internet Retail	0.94
Macy's	M	Department Stores	0.95
Foot Locker	FL	Apparel Retail	0.99
Alphabet (Google)	GOOG	Internet Software and Services	0.99
Molson Coors Brewing	TAP	Brewers	0.99
Harley-Davidson	HOG	Motorcycle Manufacturers	1.14
Yahoo!	YHOO	Internet Software and Services	1.21
salesforce.com	CRM	Application Software	1.22
Marriott International	MAR	Hotels and Resorts	1.24
Walt Disney	DIS	Movies and Entertainment	1.25
Coach	COH	Apparel and Luxury Goods	1.25
Cisco Systems	CSCO	Communications Equipment	1.27
Williams-Sonoma	WSM	Home Furnishing Retail	1.27
Staples	SPLS	Specialty Stores	1.36
Oracle	ORCL	Systems Software	1.42
Hewlett-Packard	HPQ	Computer Hardware	1.52
J. C. Penney	JCP	Department Stores	1.52
Wynn Resorts Ltd.	WYNN	Casinos and Gaming	1.59
Ryland Group	RYL	Homebuilding	1.60
Caterpillar	CAT	Construction Machinery	1.62
United States Steel	X	Steel	1.62
General Motors	GM	Automobile Manufacturers	1.66
Netgear	NTGR	Communications Equipment	1.91
Tiffany & Co.	TIF	Apparel and Luxury Goods	1.92
Autodesk	ADSK	Application Software	1.96
Ethan Allen Interiors	ETH	Home Furnishings	2.04
Advanced Micro Devices	AMD	Semiconductors	2.23
Sotheby's	BID	Auction Services	2.48

Source: CapitalIQ

10.8 Beta and the Cost of Capital

Throughout this text, we have emphasized that financial managers should evaluate an investment opportunity based on its cost of capital, which is the expected return available on alternative investments in the market with comparable risk and term. For risky investments, this cost of capital corresponds to the risk-free interest rate, plus an appropriate risk premium. Now that we can measure the systematic risk of an investment according to its beta, we are in a position to estimate the risk premium investors will require.

Estimating the Risk Premium

Before we can estimate the risk premium of an individual stock, we need a way to assess investors' appetite for risk. The size of the risk premium investors will require to make a risky investment depends upon their risk aversion. Rather than attempt to measure this risk aversion directly, we can measure it indirectly by looking at the risk premium investors' demand for investing in systematic, or market, risk.

The Market Risk Premium. We can calibrate investors' appetite for market risk from the market portfolio. The risk premium investors earn by holding market risk is the difference between the market portfolio's expected return and the risk-free interest rate:

$$\text{Market Risk Premium} = E[R_{Mkt}] - r_f \tag{10.10}$$

For example, if the risk-free rate is 5% and the expected return of the market portfolio is 11%, the market risk premium is 6%. In the same way that the market interest rate reflects investors' patience and determines the time value of money, the market risk premium reflects investors' risk tolerance and determines the market price of risk in the economy.

Adjusting for Beta. The market risk premium is the reward investors expect to earn for holding a portfolio with a beta of 1—the market portfolio itself. Consider an investment opportunity with a beta of 2. This investment carries twice as much systematic risk as an investment in the market portfolio. That is, for each dollar we invest in the opportunity, we could invest twice that amount in the market portfolio and be exposed to exactly the same amount of systematic risk. Because it has twice as much systematic risk, investors will require twice the risk premium to invest in an opportunity with a beta of 2.

COMMON MISTAKE **Beta Versus Volatility**

Recall that beta differs from volatility. Volatility measures total risk—that is, both market and firm-specific risks—so that there is no necessary relationship between volatility and beta. For example, from 2010 to 2015, the stocks of Vertex Pharmaceuticals and networking equipment maker Netgear had similar volatility (about 12% per month). Vertex, however, had a much lower beta (0.6 versus about 2 for Netgear). While drug companies face a great deal of risk related to the development and approval of new drugs, this risk is unrelated to the rest of the economy. And though health care expenditures do vary a little with the state of the economy, they vary much less than expenditures on technology. Thus, while their volatilities are similar, much more of the risk of Vertex's stock is diversifiable risk, whereas Netgear's stock has a much greater proportion of systematic risk.

To summarize, we can use the beta of the investment to determine the scale of the investment in the market portfolio that has equivalent systematic risk. Thus, to compensate investors for the time value of their money as well as the systematic risk they are bearing, the cost of capital r_I for an investment with beta β_I should satisfy the following formula:

Estimating the Cost of Capital of an Investment from Its Beta

$$r_I = \text{Risk-Free Interest Rate} + \beta_I \times \text{Market Risk Premium}$$

$$= r_f + \beta_I \times (E[R_{Mkt}] - r_f) \tag{10.11}$$

As an example, let's consider Sotheby's (BID) and Procter & Gamble (PG) stocks, using the beta estimates in Table 10.6. According to Eq. 10.11, if the market risk premium is 6% and the risk-free interest rate is 5%, the equity cost of capital for each of these firms is

$$r_{BID} = 5\% + 2.48 \times 6\% = 19.9\%$$

$$r_{PG} = 5\% + 0.52 \times 6\% = 8.1\%$$

Thus, the difference in the average returns of these two stocks that we reported in the introduction of this chapter is not so surprising. Investors in Sotheby's require a much higher return on average to compensate them for Sotheby's much higher systematic risk.

EXAMPLE 10.9 Expected Returns and Beta

Problem

Suppose the risk-free rate is 5% and the economy is equally likely to be strong or weak. Use Eq. 10.11 to determine the cost of capital for the type S firms considered in Example 10.8. How does this cost of capital compare with the expected return for these firms?

Solution

If the economy is equally likely to be strong or weak, the expected return of the market is $E[R_{Mkt}] = \frac{1}{2}(0.47) + \frac{1}{2}(-0.25) = 11\%$, and the market risk premium is $E[R_{Mkt}] - r_f = 11\% - 5\% = 6\%$. Given the beta of 0.833 for type S firms that we calculated in Example 10.8, the estimate of the cost of capital for type S firms from Eq. 10.11 is

$$r_s = r_f + \beta_s \times (E[R_{Mkt}] - r_f) = 5\% + 0.833 \times (11\% - 5\%) = 10\%$$

This matches their expected return: $\frac{1}{2}(40\%) + \frac{1}{2}(-20\%) = 10\%$. Thus, investors who hold these stocks can expect a return that appropriately compensates them for the systematic risk they are bearing by holding them (as we should expect in a competitive market).

What happens if a stock has a negative beta? According to Eq. 10.11, such a stock would have a negative risk premium—it would have an expected return below the risk-free rate. While this might seem unreasonable at first, note that stock with a negative beta will tend to do well when times are bad, so owning it will provide insurance against the systematic risk of other stocks in the portfolio. (For an example of such a security, see Example 3A.1 in Chapter 3.) Risk-averse investors are willing to pay for this insurance by accepting a return below the risk-free interest rate.

The Capital Asset Pricing Model

Equation 10.11, for estimating the cost of capital, is often referred to as the **Capital Asset Pricing Model (CAPM)**,[15] the most important method for estimating the cost of capital that is used in practice. In this chapter, we have provided an intuitive justification of the CAPM, and its use of the market portfolio as the benchmark for systematic risk. We provide a more complete development of the model and its assumptions in Chapter 11, where we also detail the portfolio optimization process used by professional fund managers. Then, in Chapter 12, we look at the practicalities of implementing the CAPM, and develop statistical tools for estimating the betas of individual stocks, together with methods for estimating the beta and cost of capital of projects within these firms. Finally, in Chapter 13 we look at the empirical evidence for (and against) the CAPM, both as a model of investor behavior and as forecast of expected returns, and introduce some proposed extensions to the CAPM.

CONCEPT CHECK

1. How can you use a security's beta to estimate its cost of capital?
2. If a risky investment has a beta of zero, what should its cost of capital be according to the CAPM? How can you justify this?

MyFinanceLab

Here is what you should know after reading this chapter. MyFinanceLab will help you identify what you know and where to go when you need to practice.

10.1 Risk and Return: Insights from 89 Years of Investor History

- Historically, over long horizons, investments in stocks have outperformed investments in bonds.
- Investing in stocks has also been much riskier than investing in bonds historically. Even over a horizon of 5 years, there have been many occasions in the past that stocks have substantially underperformed bonds.

10.2 Common Measures of Risk and Return

- A probability distribution summarizes information about possible different returns and their likelihood of occurring.
  - The expected, or mean, return is the return we expect to earn on average:

$$\text{Expected Return} = E[R] = \sum_R p_R \times R \tag{10.1}$$

  - The variance or standard deviation measures the variability of the returns:

$$Var(R) = E[(R - E[R])^2] = \sum_R p_R \times (R - E[R])^2$$

$$SD(R) = \sqrt{Var(R)} \tag{10.2}$$

  - The standard deviation of a return is also called its volatility.

[15]The CAPM was first developed independently by William Sharpe, Jack Treynor, John Lintner, and Jan Mossin. See J. Lintner "The Valuation of Risk Assets and the Selection of Risky Investments in Stock Portfolios and Capital Budgets," *Review of Economics and Statistics* 47 (1965): 13–37; W. Sharpe, "Capital Asset Prices: A Theory of Market Equilibrium Under Conditions of Risk," *Journal of Finance* 19 (1964): 425–442; J. Treynor, "Toward a Theory of the Market Value of Risky Assets" (1961); and J. Mossin "Equilibrium in a Capital Asset Market," *Econometrica*, 34 (1966): 768–783.

10.3 Historical Returns of Stocks and Bonds

- The realized or total return for an investment is the total of the dividend yield and the capital gain rate.
  - Using the empirical distribution of realized returns, we can estimate the expected return and variance of the distribution of returns by calculating the average annual return and variance of realized returns:

$$\overline{R} = \frac{1}{T}(R_1 + R_2 + \cdots + R_T) = \frac{1}{T}\sum_{t=1}^{T} R_t \tag{10.6}$$

$$Var(R) = \frac{1}{T-1}\sum_{t=1}^{T}(R_t - \overline{R})^2 \tag{10.7}$$

  - The square root of the estimated variance is an estimate of the volatility of returns.
  - Because a security's historical average return is only an estimate of its true expected return, we use the standard error of the estimate to gauge the amount of estimation error:

$$SD\text{ (Average of Independent, Identical Risks)} = \frac{SD\text{ (Individual Risk)}}{\sqrt{\text{Number of Observations}}} \tag{10.8}$$

10.4 The Historical Trade-Off Between Risk and Return

- Comparing historical data for large portfolios, small stocks have had higher volatility and higher average returns than large stocks, which have had higher volatility and higher average returns than bonds.
- There is no clear relationship between the volatility and return of individual stocks.
  - Larger stocks tend to have lower overall volatility, but even the largest stocks are typically more risky than a portfolio of large stocks.
  - All stocks seem to have higher risk and lower returns than would be predicted based on extrapolation of data for large portfolios.

10.5 Common Versus Independent Risk

- The total risk of a security represents both idiosyncratic risk and systematic risk.
  - Variation in a stock's return due to firm-specific news is called idiosyncratic risk. This type of risk is also called firm-specific, unique, or diversifiable risk. It is risk that is independent of other shocks in the economy.
  - Systematic risk, also called market or undiversifiable risk, is risk due to market-wide news that affects all stocks simultaneously. It is risk that is common to all stocks.

10.6 Diversification in Stock Portfolios

- Diversification eliminates idiosyncratic risk but does not eliminate systematic risk.
  - Because investors can eliminate idiosyncratic risk, they do not require a risk premium for taking it on.
  - Because investors cannot eliminate systematic risk, they must be compensated for holding it. As a consequence, the risk premium for a stock depends on the amount of its systematic risk rather than its total risk.

10.7 Measuring Systematic Risk

- An efficient portfolio contains only systematic risk and cannot be diversified further—that is, there is no way to reduce the risk of the portfolio without lowering its expected return.
- The market portfolio contains all shares of all stocks and securities in the market. The market portfolio is often assumed to be efficient.
- If the market portfolio is efficient, we can measure the systematic risk of a security by its beta (β). The beta of a security is the sensitivity of the security's return to the return of the overall market.

10.8 Beta and the Cost of Capital

- The market risk premium is the expected excess return of the market portfolio:

$$\text{Market Risk Premium} = E[R_{Mkt}] - r_f \tag{10.10}$$

  It reflects investors' overall risk tolerance and represents the market price of risk in the economy.
- The cost of capital for a risky investment equals the risk-free rate plus a risk premium. The Capital Asset Pricing Model (CAPM) states that the risk premium equals the investment's beta times the market risk premium:

$$r_I = r_f + \beta_I \times (E[R_{Mkt}] - r_f) \tag{10.11}$$

Key Terms

95% confidence interval *p. 331*
average annual return *p. 327*
beta (β) *p. 343*
Capital Asset Pricing Model (CAPM) *p. 348*
common risk *p. 336*
diversification *p. 336*
efficient portfolio *p. 343*
empirical distribution *p. 327*
excess return *p. 333*
expected (mean) return *p. 322*
firm-specific, idiosyncratic, unique, or diversifiable risk *p. 338*
independent risk *p. 336*
market portfolio *p. 343*
probability distribution *p. 322*
realized return *p. 325*
standard deviation *p. 323*
standard error *p. 330*
systematic, undiversifiable, or market risk *p. 338*
variance *p. 323*
volatility *p. 324*

Further Reading

The original work on diversification was developed in the following papers: H. Markowitz, "Portfolio Selection," *Journal of Finance* 7 (1952): 77–91; A. Roy, "Safety First and the Holding of Assets," *Econometrica* 20 (July 1952): 431–449; and, in the context of insurance, B. de Finetti, "Il problema de pieni," *Giornale dell'Instituto Italiano degli Attuari*, 11 (1940): 1–88.

For information on historical returns of different types of assets, see: E. Dimson, P. Marsh, and M. Staunton, *Triumph of the Optimist: 101 Years of Global Equity Returns* (Princeton University Press, 2002); and Ibbotson Associates, Inc., *Stocks, Bonds, Bills, and Inflation* (Ibbotson Associates, 2009).

Many books address the topics of this chapter in more depth: E. Elton, M. Gruber, S. Brown, and W. Goetzmann, *Modern Portfolio Theory and Investment Analysis* (John Wiley & Sons, 2006); J. Francis, *Investments: Analysis and Management* (McGraw-Hill, 1991); R. Radcliffe, *Investment: Concepts, Analysis, and Strategy* (Harper-Collins, 1994); F. Reilly and K. Brown, *Investment Analysis and Portfolio Management* (Dryden Press, 1996); and Z. Bodie, A. Kane, and A. Marcus, *Investments* (McGraw-Hill/Irwin, 2008).

Problems

All problems are available in MyFinanceLab. *An asterisk (*) indicates problems with a higher level of difficulty.*

Common Measures of Risk and Return

1. The figure on page 351 shows the one-year return distribution for RCS stock. Calculate
   a. The expected return.
   b. The standard deviation of the return.

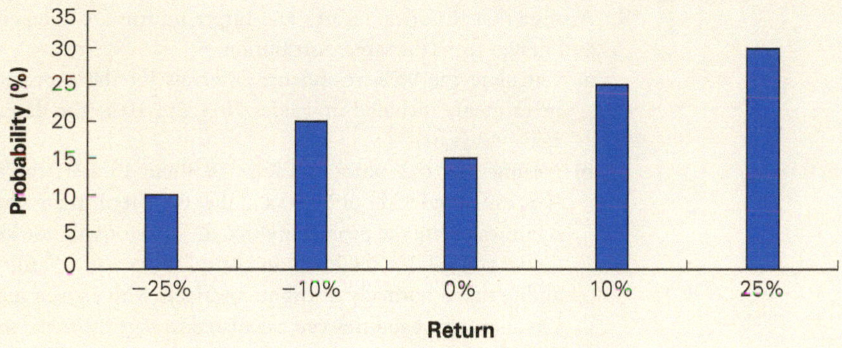

2. The following table shows the one-year return distribution of Startup, Inc. Calculate
   a. The expected return.
   b. The standard deviation of the return.

Probability	40%	20%	20%	10%	10%
Return	−100%	−75%	−50%	−25%	1000%

3. Characterize the difference between the two stocks in Problems 1 and 2. What trade-offs would you face in choosing one to hold?

Historical Returns of Stocks and Bonds

4. You bought a stock one year ago for $50 per share and sold it today for $55 per share. It paid a $1 per share dividend today.
   a. What was your realized return?
   b. How much of the return came from dividend yield and how much came from capital gain?
5. Repeat Problem 4 assuming that the stock fell $5 to $45 instead.
   a. Is your capital gain different? Why or why not?
   b. Is your dividend yield different? Why or why not?
6. Using the data in the following table, calculate the return for investing in Boeing stock (BA) from January 2, 2008, to January 2, 2009, and also from January 3, 2011, to January 3, 2012, assuming all dividends are reinvested in the stock immediately.

Historical Stock and Dividend Data for Boeing

Date	Price	Dividend	Date	Price	Dividend
1/2/2008	86.62		1/3/2011	66.40	
2/6/2008	79.91	0.40	2/9/2011	72.63	0.42
5/7/2008	84.55	0.40	5/11/2011	79.08	0.42
8/6/2008	65.40	0.40	8/10/2011	57.41	0.42
11/5/2008	49.55	0.40	11/8/2011	66.65	0.42
1/2/2009	45.25		1/3/2012	74.22	

7. The last four years of returns for a stock are as follows:

Year	1	2	3	4
Return	−4%	+28%	+12%	+4%

   a. What is the average annual return?
   b. What is the variance of the stock's returns?
   c. What is the standard deviation of the stock's returns?

***8.** Assume that historical returns and future returns are independently and identically distributed and drawn from the same distribution.

a. Calculate the 95% confidence intervals for the expected annual return of four different investments included in Tables 10.3 and 10.4 (the dates are inclusive, so the time period spans 86 years).

b. Assume that the values in Tables 10.3 and 10.4 are the true expected return and volatility (i.e., estimated without error) and that these returns are normally distributed. For each investment, calculate the probability that an investor will not lose more than 5% in the next year. (*Hint*: you can use the function normdist (*x*,mean,volatility,1) in Excel to compute the probability that a normally distributed variable with a given mean and volatility will fall below *x*.)

c. Do all the probabilities you calculated in part (b) make sense? If so, explain. If not, can you identify the reason?

9. Using the data in Table 10.2,

a. What was the average annual return of Microsoft stock from 2002–2014?

b. What was the annual volatility for Microsoft stock from 2002–2014?

10. Using the data in Table 10.2,

a. What was the average dividend yield for the SP500 from 2002–2014?

b. What was the volatility of the dividend yield?

c. What was the average annual return of the SP500 from 2002–2014 excluding dividends (i.e., from capital gains only)?

d. What was the volatility of the S&P 500 returns from capital gains?

e. Were dividends or capital gains a more important component of the S&P 500's average returns during this period? Which were the more important source of volatility?

11. Consider an investment with the following returns over four years:

Year	1	2	3	4
Return	10%	20%	−5%	15%

a. What is the compound annual growth rate (CAGR) for this investment over the four years?

b. What is the average annual return of the investment over the four years?

c. Which is a better measure of the investment's past performance?

d. If the investment's returns are independent and identically distributed, which is a better measure of the investment's expected return next year?

12. Download the spreadsheet from MyFinanceLab that contains historical monthly prices and dividends (paid at the end of the month) for Ford Motor Company stock (Ticker: F) from August 1994 to August 1998. Calculate the realized return over this period, expressing your answer in percent per month (i.e., what monthly return would have led to the same cumulative performance as an investment in Ford stock over this period).

13. Using the same data as in Problem 12, compute the

a. Average monthly return over this period.

b. Monthly volatility (or standard deviation) over this period.

14. Explain the difference between the average return you calculated in Problem 13(a) and the realized return you calculated in Problem 12. Are both numbers useful? If so, explain why.

15. Compute the 95% confidence interval of the estimate of the average monthly return you calculated in Problem 13(a).

The Historical Trade-Off Between Risk and Return

16. How does the relationship between the average return and the historical volatility of individual stocks differ from the relationship between the average return and the historical volatility of large, well-diversified portfolios?

17. Download the spreadsheet from MyFinanceLab containing the data for Figure 10.1.
a. Compute the average return for each of the assets from 1929 to 1940 (The Great Depression).
b. Compute the variance and standard deviation for each of the assets from 1929 to 1940.
c. Which asset was riskiest during the Great Depression? How does that fit with your intuition?

18. Using the data from Problem 17, repeat your analysis over the 1990s.
a. Which asset was riskiest?
b. Compare the standard deviations of the assets in the 1990s to their standard deviations in the Great Depression. Which had the greatest difference between the two periods?
c. If you only had information about the 1990s, what would you conclude about the relative risk of investing in small stocks?

19. What if the last two and a half decades had been "normal"? Download the spreadsheet from MyFinanceLab containing the data for Figure 10.1.
a. Calculate the arithmetic average return on the S&P 500 from 1926 to 1989.
b. Assuming that the S&P 500 had simply continued to earn the average return from (a), calculate the amount that $100 invested at the end of 1925 would have grown to by the end of 2014.
c. Do the same for small stocks.

Common Versus Independent Risk

20. Consider two local banks. Bank A has 100 loans outstanding, each for $1 million, that it expects will be repaid today. Each loan has a 5% probability of default, in which case the bank is not repaid anything. The chance of default is independent across all the loans. Bank B has only one loan of $100 million outstanding, which it also expects will be repaid today. It also has a 5% probability of not being repaid. Explain the difference between the type of risk each bank faces. Which bank faces less risk? Why?

***21.** Using the data in Problem 20, calculate
a. The expected overall payoff of each bank.
b. The standard deviation of the overall payoff of each bank.

Diversification in Stock Portfolios

22. Consider the following two, completely separate, economies. The expected return and volatility of all stocks in both economies is the same. In the first economy, all stocks move together—in good times all prices rise together and in bad times they all fall together. In the second economy, stock returns are independent—one stock increasing in price has no effect on the prices of other stocks. Assuming you are risk-averse and you could choose one of the two economies in which to invest, which one would you choose? Explain.

23. Consider an economy with two types of firms, S and I. S firms all move together. I firms move independently. For both types of firms, there is a 60% probability that the firms will have a 15% return and a 40% probability that the firms will have a −10% return. What is the volatility (standard deviation) of a portfolio that consists of an equal investment in 20 firms of (a) type S, and (b) type I?

***24.** Using the data in Problem 23, plot the volatility as a function of the number of firms in the two portfolios.

25. Explain why the risk premium of a stock does not depend on its diversifiable risk.

26. Identify each of the following risks as most likely to be systematic risk or diversifiable risk:
a. The risk that your main production plant is shut down due to a tornado.
b. The risk that the economy slows, decreasing demand for your firm's products.
c. The risk that your best employees will be hired away.
d. The risk that the new product you expect your R&D division to produce will not materialize.

27. Suppose the risk-free interest rate is 5%, and the stock market will return either 40% or −20% each year, with each outcome equally likely. Compare the following two investment strategies: (1) invest for one year in the risk-free investment, and one year in the market, or (2) invest for both years in the market.
   a. Which strategy has the highest expected final payoff?
   b. Which strategy has the highest standard deviation for the final payoff?
   c. Does holding stocks for a longer period decrease your risk?

28. Download the spreadsheet from MyFinanceLab containing the realized return of the S&P 500 from 1929–2008. Starting in 1929, divide the sample into four periods of 20 years each. For each 20-year period, calculate the final amount an investor would have earned given a $1000 initial investment. Also express your answer as an annualized return. If risk were eliminated by holding stocks for 20 years, what would you expect to find? What can you conclude about long-run diversification?

Measuring Systematic Risk

29. What is an efficient portfolio?

30. What does the beta of a stock measure?

31. You turn on the news and find out the stock market has gone up 10%. Based on the data in Table 10.6, by how much do you expect each of the following stocks to have gone up or down: (1) Starbucks, (2) Tiffany & Co., (3) Hershey, and (4) McDonald's.

32. Based on the data in Table 10.6, estimate which of the following investments you expect to lose the most in the event of a severe market down turn: (1) A $2000 investment in Hershey, (2) a $1500 investment in Macy's, or (3) a $1000 investment in Caterpillar.

33. Suppose the market portfolio is equally likely to increase by 30% or decrease by 10%.
   a. Calculate the beta of a firm that goes up on average by 43% when the market goes *up* and goes down by 17% when the market goes *down*.
   b. Calculate the beta of a firm that goes up on average by 18% when the market goes *down* and goes down by 22% when the market goes *up*.
   c. Calculate the beta of a firm that is expected to go up by 4% *independently* of the market.

Beta and the Cost of Capital

34. Suppose the risk-free interest rate is 4%.
   a. i. Use the beta you calculated for the stock in Problem 33(a) to estimate its expected return.
      ii. How does this compare with the stock's actual expected return?
   b. i. Use the beta you calculated for the stock in Problem 33(b) to estimate its expected return.
      ii. How does this compare with the stock's actual expected return?

35. Suppose the market risk premium is 5% and the risk-free interest rate is 4%. Using the data in Table 10.6, calculate the expected return of investing in
   a. Starbucks' stock.
   b. Hershey's stock.
   c. Autodesk's stock.

36. Given the results to Problem 35, why don't all investors hold Autodesk's stock rather than Hershey's stock?

37. Suppose the market risk premium is 6.5% and the risk-free interest rate is 5%. Calculate the cost of capital of investing in a project with a beta of 1.2.

38. State whether each of the following is inconsistent with an efficient capital market, the CAPM, or both:
   a. A security with only diversifiable risk has an expected return that exceeds the risk-free interest rate.

b. A security with a beta of 1 had a return last year of 15% when the market had a return of 9%.
c. Small stocks with a beta of 1.5 tend to have higher returns on average than large stocks with a beta of 1.5.

Data Case

Today is April 30, 2015, and you have just started your new job with a financial planning firm. In addition to studying for all your license exams, you have been asked to review a portion of a client's stock portfolio to determine the risk/return profiles of 12 stocks in the portfolio. Unfortunately, your small firm cannot afford the expensive databases that would provide all this information with a few simple keystrokes, but that's why they hired you. Specifically, you have been asked to determine the monthly average returns and standard deviations for the 12 stocks for the past five years. In the following chapters, you will be asked to do more extensive analyses on these same stocks.

The stocks (with their symbols in parentheses) are:

Archer Daniels Midland (ADM)
Boeing (BA)
Caterpillar (CAT)
Deere & Co. (DE)
General Mills, Inc. (GIS)
eBay (EBAY)
Hershey (HSY)
International Business Machines Corporation (IBM)
JPMorgan Chase & Co. (JPM)
Microsoft (MSFT)
Procter and Gamble (PG)
Walmart (WMT)

1. Collect price information for each stock from Yahoo! Finance (finance.yahoo.com) as follows:
   a. Enter the stock symbol. On the page for that stock, click "Historical Prices" on the left side of the page.
   b. Enter the "start date" as April 30, 2010 and the "end date" as April 30, 2015 to cover the five-year period. Make sure you click "monthly" next to the date; the closing prices reported by Yahoo! will then be for the last day of each month.
   c. After hitting "Get Prices," scroll to the bottom of the first page and click "Download to Spreadsheet." If you are asked if you want to open or save the file, click open.
   d. Copy the entire spreadsheet, open Excel, and paste the Web data into a spreadsheet. Delete all the columns except the date and the adjusted close (the first and last columns).
   e. Keep the Excel file open and go back to the Yahoo! Finance Web page and hit the back button. If you are asked if you want to save the data, click no.
   f. When you return to the prices page, enter the next stock symbol and hit "Get Prices" again. Do not change the dates or frequency, but make sure you have the same dates for all the stocks you will download. Again, click "Download to Spreadsheet" and then open the file. Copy the last column, "Adj. Close," paste it into the Excel file and change "Adj. Close" to the stock symbol. Make sure that the first and last prices are in the same rows as the first stock.
   g. Repeat these steps for the remaining 10 stocks, pasting each closing price right next to the other stocks, again making sure that the correct prices on the correct dates all appear on the same rows.
2. Convert these prices to monthly returns as the percentage change in the monthly prices. (*Hint*: Create a separate worksheet within the Excel file.) Note that to compute a return for each month, you need a beginning and ending price, so you will not be able to compute the return for the first month.
3. Compute the mean monthly returns and standard deviations for the monthly returns of each of the stocks.[16] Convert the monthly statistics to annual statistics for easier interpretation (multiply the mean monthly return by 12, and multiply the monthly standard deviation by $\sqrt{12}$).

[16]In Eq. 10.4, we showed how to compute returns with stock price and dividend data. The "adjusted close" series from Yahoo! Finance is already adjusted for dividends and splits, so we may compute returns based on the percentage change in monthly adjusted prices.

4. Add a column in your Excel worksheet with the average return across stocks for each month. This is the monthly return to an equally weighted portfolio of these 12 stocks. Compute the mean and standard deviation of monthly returns for the equally weighted portfolio. Double check that the average return on this equally weighted portfolio is equal to the average return of all of the individual stocks. Convert these monthly statistics to annual statistics (as described in Step 3) for interpretation.

5. Using the annual statistics, create an Excel plot with standard deviation (volatility) on the *x*-axis and average return on the *y*-axis as follows:

a. Create three columns on your spreadsheet with the statistics you created in Questions 3 and 4 for each of the individual stocks and the equally weighted portfolio. The first column will have the ticker, the second will have annual standard deviation, and the third will have the annual mean return.

b. Highlight the data in the last two columns (standard deviation and mean), choose Insert>Chart>XY Scatter Plot. Complete the chart wizard to finish the plot.

6. What do you notice about the average of the volatilities of the individual stocks, compared to the volatility of the equally weighted portfolio?

Note: Updates to this data case may be found at www.berkdemarzo.com.

Optimal Portfolio Choice and the Capital Asset Pricing Model

CHAPTER

11

IN THIS CHAPTER, WE BUILD ON THE IDEAS WE INTRODUCED IN Chapter 10 to explain how an investor can choose an efficient portfolio. In particular, we will demonstrate how to find the optimal portfolio for an investor who wants to earn the highest possible return given the level of volatility he or she is willing to accept by developing the statistical techniques of *mean-variance portfolio optimization*. Both elegant and practical, these techniques are used routinely by professional investors, money managers, and financial institutions. We then introduce the assumptions of the Capital Asset Pricing Model (CAPM), the most important model of the relationship between risk and return. Under these assumptions, the efficient portfolio is the market portfolio of all stocks and securities. As a result, the expected return of any security depends upon its beta with the market portfolio.

In Chapter 10, we explained how to calculate the expected return and volatility of a single stock. To find the efficient portfolio, we must understand how to do the same thing for a portfolio of stocks. We begin this chapter by explaining how to calculate the expected return and volatility of a portfolio. With these statistical tools in hand, we then describe how an investor can create an efficient portfolio out of individual stocks, and consider the implications, if all investors attempt to do so, for an investment's expected return and cost of capital.

In our exploration of these concepts, we take the perspective of a stock market investor. These concepts, however, are also important for a corporate financial manager. After all, financial managers are also investors, investing money on behalf of their shareholders. When a company makes a new investment, financial managers must ensure that the investment has a positive NPV. Doing so requires knowing the cost of capital of the investment opportunity and, as we shall see in the next chapter, the CAPM is the main method used by most major corporations to calculate the cost of capital.

NOTATION

R_i	return of security (or investment) i
x_i	fraction invested in security i
$E[R_i]$	expected return
r_f	risk-free interest rate
$\overline{R}_i$	average return of security (or investment)
$Corr(R_i, R_j)$	correlation between returns of i and j
$Cov(R_i, R_j)$	covariance between returns of i and j
$SD(R)$	standard deviation (volatility) of return R
$Var(R)$	variance of return R
n	number of securities in a portfolio
R_{xP}	return of portfolio with fraction x invested in portfolio P and $(1 - x)$ invested in the risk-free security
β_i^P	beta or sensitivity of the investment i to the fluctuations of the portfolio P
β_i	beta of security i with respect to the market portfolio
r_i	required return or cost of capital of security i

11.1 The Expected Return of a Portfolio

To find an optimal portfolio, we need a method to define a portfolio and analyze its return. We can describe a portfolio by its **portfolio weights**, the fraction of the total investment in the portfolio held in each individual investment in the portfolio:

$$x_i = \frac{\text{Value of investment } i}{\text{Total value of portfolio}} \tag{11.1}$$

These portfolio weights add up to 1 (that is, $\Sigma_i x_i = 1$), so that they represent the way we have divided our money between the different individual investments in the portfolio.

As an example, consider a portfolio with 200 shares of Dolby Laboratories worth \$30 per share and 100 shares of Coca-Cola worth \$40 per share. The total value of the portfolio is $200 \times \$30 + 100 \times \$40 = \$10{,}000$, and the corresponding portfolio weights x_D and x_C are

$$x_D = \frac{200 \times \$30}{\$10{,}000} = 60\%, \qquad x_C = \frac{100 \times \$40}{\$10{,}000} = 40\%$$

Given the portfolio weights, we can calculate the return on the portfolio. Suppose $x_1, \ldots, x_n$ are the portfolio weights of the n investments in a portfolio, and these investments have returns $R_1, \ldots, R_n$. Then the return on the portfolio, R_P, is the weighted average of the returns on the investments in the portfolio, where the weights correspond to portfolio weights:

$$R_P = x_1 R_1 + x_2 R_2 + \cdots + x_n R_n = \sum_i x_i R_i \tag{11.2}$$

The return of a portfolio is straightforward to compute if we know the returns of the individual stocks and the portfolio weights.

EXAMPLE 11.1 Calculating Portfolio Returns

Problem

Suppose you buy 200 shares of Dolby Laboratories at \$30 per share and 100 shares of Coca-Cola stock at \$40 per share. If Dolby's share price goes up to \$36 and Coca-Cola's falls to \$38, what is the new value of the portfolio, and what return did it earn? Show that Eq. 11.2 holds. After the price change, what are the new portfolio weights?

Solution

The new value of the portfolio is $200 \times \$36 + 100 \times \$38 = \$11{,}000$, for a gain of \$1000 or a 10% return on your \$10,000 investment. Dolby's return was $36/30 - 1 = 20\%$, and Coca-Cola's was $38/40 - 1 = -5\%$. Given the initial portfolio weights of 60% Dolby's and 40% Coca-Cola, we can also compute the portfolio's return from Eq. 11.2:

$$R_P = x_D R_D + x_C R_C = 0.6 \times (20\%) + 0.4 \times (-5\%) = 10\%$$

After the price change, the new portfolio weights are

$$x_D = \frac{200 \times \$36}{\$11{,}000} = 65.45\%, \qquad x_C = \frac{100 \times \$38}{\$11{,}000} = 34.55\%$$

Without trading, the weights increase for those stocks whose returns exceed the portfolio's return.

Equation 11.2 also allows us to compute the expected return of a portfolio. Using the facts that the expectation of a sum is just the sum of the expectations and that the expectation of a known multiple is just the multiple of its expectation, we arrive at the following formula for a portfolio's expected return:

$$E[R_P] = E\left[\sum_i x_i R_i\right] = \sum_i E[x_i R_i] = \sum_i x_i E[R_i] \tag{11.3}$$

That is, the expected return of a portfolio is simply the weighted average of the expected returns of the investments within it, using the portfolio weights.

EXAMPLE 11.2 **Portfolio Expected Return**

Problem

Suppose you invest \$10,000 in Ford stock, and \$30,000 in Tyco International stock. You expect a return of 10% for Ford and 16% for Tyco. What is your portfolio's expected return?

Solution

You invested \$40,000 in total, so your portfolio weights are 10,000/40,000 = 0.25 in Ford and 30,000/40,000 = 0.75 in Tyco. Therefore, your portfolio's expected return is

$$E[R_P] = x_F E[R_F] + x_T E[R_T] = 0.25 \times 10\% + 0.75 \times 16\% = 14.5\%$$

CONCEPT CHECK

1. What is a portfolio weight?
2. How do we calculate the return on a portfolio?

11.2 The Volatility of a Two-Stock Portfolio

As we explained in Chapter 10, combining stocks in a portfolio eliminates some of their risk through diversification. The amount of risk that will remain depends on the degree to which the stocks are exposed to common risks. In this section, we describe the statistical tools that we can use to quantify the risk stocks have in common and determine the volatility of a portfolio.

Combining Risks

Let's begin with a simple example of how risk changes when stocks are combined in a portfolio. Table 11.1 shows returns for three hypothetical stocks, along with their average returns and volatilities. While the three stocks have the same volatility and average return,

TABLE 11.1 **Returns for Three Stocks, and Portfolios of Pairs of Stocks**

	Stock Returns			Portfolio Returns	
Year	North Air	West Air	Tex Oil	$1/2R_N + 1/2R_W$	$1/2R_W + 1/2R_T$
2010	21%	9%	−2%	15.0%	3.5%
2011	30%	21%	−5%	25.5%	8.0%
2012	7%	7%	9%	7.0%	8.0%
2013	−5%	−2%	21%	−3.5%	9.5%
2014	−2%	−5%	30%	−3.5%	12.5%
2015	9%	30%	7%	19.5%	18.5%
Average Return	10.0%	10.0%	10.0%	10.0%	10.0%
Volatility	13.4%	13.4%	13.4%	12.1%	5.1%

the pattern of their returns differs. When the airline stocks performed well, the oil stock tended to do poorly (see 2010–2011), and when the airlines did poorly, the oil stock tended to do well (2013–2014).

Table 11.1 also shows the returns for two portfolios of the stocks. The first portfolio consists of equal investments in the two airlines, North Air and West Air. The second portfolio includes equal investments in West Air and Tex Oil. The average return of both portfolios is equal to the average return of the stocks, consistent with Eq. 11.3. However, their volatilities—12.1% and 5.1%—are very different from the individual stocks *and* from each other.

This example demonstrates two important phenomena. First, by combining stocks into a portfolio, we reduce risk through diversification. Because the prices of the stocks do not move identically, some of the risk is averaged out in a portfolio. As a result, both portfolios have lower risk than the individual stocks. Second, the amount of risk that is eliminated in a portfolio depends on the degree to which the stocks face common risks and their prices move together. Because the two airline stocks tend to perform well or poorly at the same time, the portfolio of airline stocks has a volatility that is only slightly lower than that of the individual stocks. The airline and oil stocks, by contrast, do not move together; indeed, they tend to move in opposite directions. As a result, additional risk is canceled out, making that portfolio much less risky. This benefit of diversification is obtained costlessly—without any reduction in the average return.

Determining Covariance and Correlation

To find the risk of a portfolio, we need to know more than the risk and return of the component stocks: We need to know the degree to which the stocks face common risks and their returns move together. In this section, we introduce two statistical measures, *covariance* and *correlation*, that allow us to measure the co-movement of returns.

Covariance. **Covariance** is the expected product of the deviations of two returns from their means. The covariance between returns R_i and R_j is:

Covariance between Returns R_i and R_j

$$Cov(R_i, R_j) = E[(R_i - E[R_i])(R_j - E[R_j])] \tag{11.4}$$

When estimating the covariance from historical data, we use the formula[1]

Estimate of the Covariance from Historical Data

$$Cov(R_i, R_j) = \frac{1}{T-1}\sum_t (R_{i,t} - \overline{R}_i)(R_{j,t} - \overline{R}_j) \tag{11.5}$$

Intuitively, if two stocks move together, their returns will tend to be above or below average at the same time, and the covariance will be positive. If the stocks move in opposite directions, one will tend to be above average when the other is below average, and the covariance will be negative.

Correlation. While the sign of the covariance is easy to interpret, its magnitude is not. It will be larger if the stocks are more volatile (and so have larger deviations from their expected returns), and it will be larger the more closely the stocks move in relation to each

[1] As with Eq. 10.7 for historical volatility, we divide by $T - 1$ rather than by T to make up for the fact that we have used the data to compute the average returns $\overline{R}$, eliminating a degree of freedom.

FIGURE 11.1 **Correlation**

Correlation measures how returns move in relation to each other. It is between +1 (returns always move together) and −1 (returns always move oppositely). Independent risks have no tendency to move together and have zero correlation.

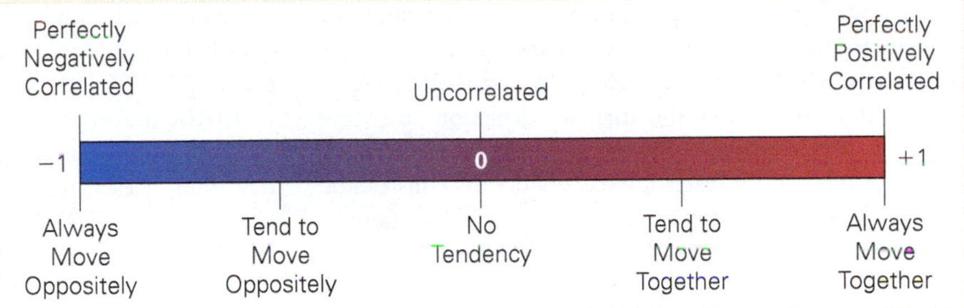

other. In order to control for the volatility of each stock and quantify the strength of the relationship between them, we can calculate the **correlation** between two stock returns, defined as the covariance of the returns divided by the standard deviation of each return:

$$Corr(R_i, R_j) = \frac{Cov(R_i, R_j)}{SD(R_i)\, SD(R_j)} \tag{11.6}$$

The correlation between two stocks has the same sign as their covariance, so it has a similar interpretation. Dividing by the volatilities ensures that correlation is always between −1 and +1, which allows us to gauge the strength of the relationship between the stocks. As Figure 11.1 shows, correlation is a barometer of the degree to which the returns share common risk and tend to move together. The closer the correlation is to +1, the more the returns tend to move together as a result of common risk. When the correlation (and thus the covariance) equals 0, the returns are *uncorrelated*; that is, they have no tendency to move either together or in opposition to one another. Independent risks are uncorrelated. Finally, the closer the correlation is to −1, the more the returns tend to move in opposite directions.

EXAMPLE 11.3 **The Covariance and Correlation of a Stock with Itself**

Problem

What are the covariance and the correlation of a stock's return with itself?

Solution

Let R_s be the stock's return. From the definition of the covariance,

$$\begin{aligned} Cov(R_s, R_s) &= E[(R_s - E[R_s])(R_s - E[R_s])] = E[(R_s - E[R_s])^2] \\ &= Var(R_s) \end{aligned}$$

where the last equation follows from the definition of the variance. That is, the covariance of a stock with itself is simply its variance. Then,

$$Corr(R_s, R_s) = \frac{Cov(R_s, R_s)}{SD(R_s)\, SD(R_s)} = \frac{Var(R_s)}{SD(R_s)^2} = 1$$

where the last equation follows from the definition of the standard deviation. That is, a stock's return is perfectly positively correlated with itself, as it always moves together with itself in perfect synchrony.

COMMON MISTAKE — Computing Variance, Covariance, and Correlation in Excel

The computer spreadsheet program Excel does not compute the standard deviation, variance, covariance, and correlation consistently. The Excel functions STDEV and VAR correctly use Eq. 10.7 to estimate the standard deviation and variance from historical data. But the Excel function COVAR does *not* use Eq. 11.5; instead, Excel divides by T instead of $T - 1$. Therefore, to estimate the covariance from a sample of historical returns using COVAR, you must correct the inconsistency by multiplying by the number of data points and dividing by the number of data points minus one; i.e., COVAR*$T/(T - 1)$. Alternatively, you can use the function CORREL to compute the correlation, and then estimate the covariance by multiplying the correlation by the standard deviation of each return. Finally, Excel 2010 introduced a new function, COVARIANCE.S, that correctly estimates the covariance from a historical sample.

EXAMPLE 11.4 — Computing the Covariance and Correlation

Problem

Using the data in Table 11.1, what are the covariance and the correlation between North Air and West Air? Between West Air and Tex Oil?

Solution

Given the returns in Table 11.1, we deduct the mean return (10%) from each and compute the product of these deviations between the pairs of stocks. We then sum them and divide by $T - 1 = 5$ to compute the covariance, as in Table 11.2.

From the table, we see that North Air and West Air have a positive covariance, indicating a tendency to move together, whereas West Air and Tex Oil have a negative covariance, indicating a tendency to move oppositely. We can assess the strength of these tendencies from the correlation, obtained by dividing the covariance by the standard deviation of each stock (13.4%). The correlation for North Air and West Air is 62.4%; the correlation for West Air and Tex Oil is −71.3%.

TABLE 11.2 Computing the Covariance and Correlation between Pairs of Stocks

	Deviation from Mean			North Air and West Air	West Air and Tex Oil
Year	$(R_N - \bar{R}_N)$	$(R_W - \bar{R}_W)$	$(R_T - \bar{R}_T)$	$(R_N - \bar{R}_N)(R_W - \bar{R}_W)$	$(R_W - \bar{R}_W)(R_T - \bar{R}_T)$
2010	11%	−1%	−12%	−0.0011	0.0012
2011	20%	11%	−15%	0.0220	−0.0165
2012	−3%	−3%	−1%	0.0009	0.0003
2013	−15%	−12%	11%	0.0180	−0.0132
2014	−12%	−15%	20%	0.0180	−0.0300
2015	−1%	20%	−3%	−0.0020	−0.0060
			$\text{Sum} = \sum_t (R_{i,t} - \bar{R}_i)(R_{j,t} - \bar{R}_j) =$	0.0558	−0.0642
Covariance:			$Cov(R_i, R_j) = \frac{1}{T-1}\text{Sum} =$	0.0112	−0.0128
Correlation:			$Corr(R_i, R_j) = \frac{Cov(R_i, R_j)}{SD(R_i)SD(R_j)} =$	0.624	−0.713

TABLE 11.3 **Historical Annual Volatilities and Correlations for Selected Stocks (based on monthly returns, 1996–2014)**

	Microsoft	HP	Alaska Air	Southwest Airlines	Ford Motor	Kellogg	General Mills
Volatility (Standard Deviation)	33%	37%	37%	31%	50%	20%	17%
Correlation with							
Microsoft	1.00	0.39	0.21	0.24	0.27	0.05	0.08
HP	0.39	1.00	0.28	0.35	0.27	0.11	0.06
Alaska Air	0.21	0.28	1.00	0.39	0.15	0.15	0.20
Southwest Airlines	0.24	0.35	0.39	1.00	0.30	0.15	0.22
Ford Motor	0.27	0.27	0.15	0.30	1.00	0.18	0.06
Kellogg	0.05	0.11	0.15	0.15	0.18	1.00	0.54
General Mills	0.08	0.06	0.20	0.22	0.06	0.54	1.00

When will stock returns be highly correlated with each other? Stock returns will tend to move together if they are affected similarly by economic events. Thus, stocks in the same industry tend to have more highly correlated returns than stocks in different industries. This tendency is illustrated in Table 11.3, which shows the volatility of individual stock returns and the correlation between them for several common stocks. Consider, for example, Microsoft and Hewlett-Packard. The returns of these two technology stocks have a higher correlation with each other (39%) than with any of the non-technology stocks (35% or lower). The same pattern holds for the airline and food-processing stocks—their returns are most highly correlated with the other firm in their industry, and much less correlated with those outside their industry. General Mills and Kellogg have the lowest correlation with each of the other stocks; indeed, Kellogg and Microsoft have a correlation of only 5%, suggesting that these two firms are subject to essentially uncorrelated risks. Note, however, that all of the correlations are positive, illustrating the general tendency of stocks to move together.

EXAMPLE 11.5 **Computing the Covariance from the Correlation**

Problem

Using the data from Table 11.3, what is the covariance between Microsoft and HP?

Solution

We can rewrite Eq. 11.6 to solve for the covariance:

$$\begin{aligned} Cov(R_M, R_{HP}) &= Corr(R_M, R_{HP}) SD(R_M) SD(R_{HP}) \\ &= (0.39)(0.33)(0.37) = 0.0476 \end{aligned}$$

Computing a Portfolio's Variance and Volatility

We now have the tools to compute the variance of a portfolio. For a two-stock portfolio with $R_P = x_1 R_1 + x_2 R_2$,

$$\begin{aligned} Var(R_P) &= Cov(R_P, R_P) \\ &= Cov(x_1 R_1 + x_2 R_2, x_1 R_1 + x_2 R_2) \\ &= x_1 x_1 Cov(R_1, R_1) + x_1 x_2 Cov(R_1, R_2) + x_2 x_1 Cov(R_2, R_1) + x_2 x_2 Cov(R_2, R_2) \quad (11.7) \end{aligned}$$

In the last line of Eq. 11.7, we use the fact that, as with expectations, we can change the order of the covariance with sums and multiples.[2] By combining terms and recognizing, from Example 11.4, that $Cov(R_i, R_i) = Var(R_i)$, we arrive at our main result of this section:

The Variance of a Two-Stock Portfolio

$$Var(R_P) = x_1^2 Var(R_1) + x_2^2 Var(R_2) + 2x_1 x_2 Cov(R_1,R_2) \tag{11.8}$$

As always, the volatility is the square root of the variance, $SD(R_P) = \sqrt{Var(R_P)}$.

Let's check this formula for the airline and oil stocks in Table 11.1. Consider the portfolio containing shares of West Air and Tex Oil. The variance of each stock is equal to the square of its volatility, $0.134^2 = 0.018$. From Example 11.3, the covariance between the stocks is -0.0128. Therefore, the variance of a portfolio with 50% invested in each stock is

$$\begin{aligned} Var\left(\tfrac{1}{2}R_W + \tfrac{1}{2}R_T\right) &= x_W^2 Var(R_W) + x_T^2 Var(R_T) + 2x_W x_T Cov(R_W, R_T) \\ &= \left(\tfrac{1}{2}\right)^2 (0.018) + \left(\tfrac{1}{2}\right)^2 (0.018) + 2\left(\tfrac{1}{2}\right)\left(\tfrac{1}{2}\right)(-0.0128) \\ &= 0.0026 \end{aligned}$$

The volatility of the portfolio is $\sqrt{0.0026} = 5.1\%$, which corresponds to the calculation in Table 11.1. For the North Air and West Air portfolio, the calculation is the same except for the stocks' higher covariance of 0.0112, resulting in a higher volatility of 12.1%.

Equation 11.8 shows that the variance of the portfolio depends on the variance of the individual stocks *and* on the covariance between them. We can also rewrite Eq. 11.8 by calculating the covariance from the correlation (as in Example 11.5):

$$Var(R_P) = x_1^2 SD(R_1)^2 + x_2^2 SD(R_2)^2 + 2x_1 x_2 Corr(R_1,R_2) SD(R_1) SD(R_2) \tag{11.9}$$

Equations 11.8 and 11.9 demonstrate that with a positive amount invested in each stock, the more the stocks move together and the higher their covariance or correlation, the more variable the portfolio will be. The portfolio will have the greatest variance if the stocks have a perfect positive correlation of +1.

EXAMPLE 11.6 Computing the Volatility of a Two-Stock Portfolio

Problem

Using the data from Table 11.3, what is the volatility of a portfolio with equal amounts invested in Microsoft and Hewlett-Packard stock? What is the volatility of a portfolio with equal amounts invested in Microsoft and Alaska Air stock?

Solution

With portfolio weights of 50% each in Microsoft and Hewlett-Packard stock, from Eq. 11.9, the portfolio's variance is

$$\begin{aligned} Var(R_P) &= x_M^2 SD(R_M)^2 + x_{HP}^2 SD(R_{HP})^2 + 2x_M x_{HP} Corr(R_M,R_{HP}) SD(R_M) SD(R_{HP}) \\ &= (0.50)^2(0.33)^2 + (0.50)^2(0.37)^2 + 2(0.50)(0.50)(0.39)(0.33)(0.37) \\ &= 0.0853 \end{aligned}$$

[2] That is, $Cov(A + B, C) = Cov(A, C) + Cov(B, C)$ and $Cov(mA, B) = m\, Cov(A, B)$.

The volatility is therefore $SD(R) = \sqrt{Var(R)} = \sqrt{0.0853} = 29.2\%$.

For the portfolio of Microsoft and Alaska Air stock,

$$\begin{aligned} Var(R_P) &= x_M^2 SD(R_M)^2 + x_A^2 SD(R_A)^2 + 2x_M x_A Corr(R_M, R_A) SD(R_M) SD(R_A) \\ &= (0.50)^2(0.33)^2 + (0.50)^2(0.37)^2 + 2(0.50)(0.50)(0.21)(0.33)(0.37) \\ &= 0.0743 \end{aligned}$$

The volatility in this case is $SD(R) = \sqrt{Var(R)} = \sqrt{0.0743} = 27.3\%$.

Note that the portfolio of Microsoft and Alaska Air stock is less volatile than either of the individual stocks. It is also less volatile than the portfolio of Microsoft and Hewlett-Packard stock. Even though Alaska Air's stock returns are as volatile as Hewlett-Packard's, its lower correlation with Microsoft's returns leads to greater diversification in the portfolio.

CONCEPT CHECK

1. What does the correlation measure?
2. How does the correlation between the stocks in a portfolio affect the portfolio's volatility?

11.3 The Volatility of a Large Portfolio

We can gain additional benefits of diversification by holding more than two stocks in our portfolio. While these calculations are best done on a computer, by understanding them we can obtain important intuition regarding the amount of diversification that is possible if we hold many stocks.

Large Portfolio Variance

Recall that the return on a portfolio of n stocks is simply the weighted average of the returns of the stocks in the portfolio:

$$R_P = x_1 R_1 + x_2 R_2 + \cdots + x_n R_n = \sum_i x_i R_i$$

Using the properties of the covariance, we can write the variance of a portfolio as follows:

$$Var(R_P) = Cov(R_P, R_P) = Cov(\Sigma_i x_i R_i, R_P) = \sum_i x_i \, Cov(R_i, R_P) \qquad (11.10)$$

This equation indicates that the *variance of a portfolio is equal to the weighted average covariance of each stock with the portfolio*. This expression reveals that the risk of a portfolio depends on how each stock's return moves in relation to it.

We can reduce the formula even further by replacing the second R_P with a weighted average and simplifying:

$$\begin{aligned} Var(R_P) &= \sum_i x_i \, Cov(R_i, R_P) = \sum_i x_i \, Cov(R_i, \Sigma_j x_j R_j) \\ &= \sum_i \sum_j x_i x_j \, Cov(R_i, R_j) \end{aligned} \qquad (11.11)$$

This formula says that the variance of a portfolio is equal to the sum of the covariances of the returns of all pairs of stocks in the portfolio multiplied by each of their portfolio weights.[3] That is, the overall variability of the portfolio depends on the total co-movement of the stocks within it.

[3] Looking back, we can see that Eq. 11.11 generalizes the case of two stocks in Eq. 11.7.

Diversification with an Equally Weighted Portfolio

We can use Eq. 11.11 to calculate the variance of an **equally weighted portfolio**, a portfolio in which the same amount is invested in each stock. An equally weighted portfolio consisting of n stocks has portfolio weights $x_i = 1/n$. In this case, we have the following formula:[4]

Variance of an Equally Weighted Portfolio of *n* Stocks

$$Var(R_P) = \frac{1}{n}(\text{Average Variance of the Individual Stocks}) + \left(1 - \frac{1}{n}\right)(\text{Average Covariance between the Stocks}) \tag{11.12}$$

Equation 11.12 demonstrates that as the number of stocks, n, grows large, the variance of the portfolio is determined primarily by the average covariance among the stocks. As an example, consider a portfolio of stocks selected randomly from the stock market. The historical volatility of the return of a typical large firm in the stock market is about 40%, and the typical correlation between the returns of large firms is about 25%. Using Eq. 11.12, and calculating the covariance from the correlation as in Example 11.5, the volatility of an equally weighted portfolio varies with the number of stocks, n, as follows:

$$SD(R_P) = \sqrt{\frac{1}{n}(0.40^2) + \left(1 - \frac{1}{n}\right)(0.25 \times 0.40 \times 0.40)}$$

We graph the volatility for different numbers of stocks in Figure 11.2. Note that the volatility declines as the number of stocks in the portfolio grows. In fact, nearly half of the volatility

FIGURE 11.2

Volatility of an Equally Weighted Portfolio Versus the Number of Stocks

The volatility declines as the number of stocks in the portfolio increases. Even in a very large portfolio, however, market risk remains.

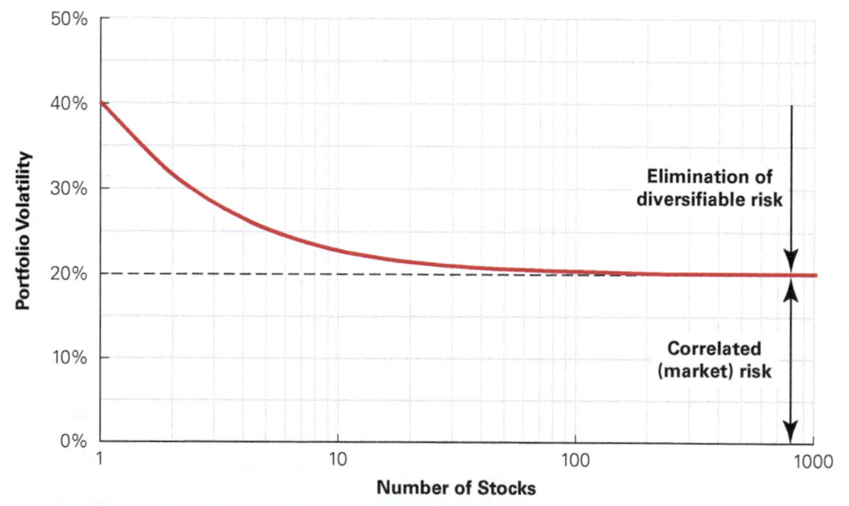

[4] For an n-stock portfolio, there are n variance terms (any time $i = j$ in Eq. 11.11) with weight $x_i^2 = 1/n^2$ on each, which implies a weight of $n/n^2 = 1/n$ on the average variance. There are $n^2 - n$ covariance terms (all the $n \times n$ pairs minus the n variance terms) with weight $x_i x_j = 1/n^2$ on each, which implies a weight of $(n^2 - n)/n^2 = 1 - 1/n$ on the average covariance.

of the individual stocks is eliminated in a large portfolio as the result of diversification. The benefit of diversification is most dramatic initially: The decrease in volatility when going from one to two stocks is much larger than the decrease when going from 100 to 101 stocks—indeed, almost all of the benefit of diversification can be achieved with about 30 stocks. Even for a very large portfolio, however, we cannot eliminate all of the risk. The variance of the portfolio converges to the average covariance, so the volatility declines to $\sqrt{0.25 \times 0.4 \times 0.4} = 20\%$.[5]

EXAMPLE 11.7 **Diversification Using Different Types of Stocks**

Problem

Stocks within a single industry tend to have a higher correlation than stocks in different industries. Likewise, stocks in different countries have lower correlation on average than stocks within the United States. What is the volatility of a very large portfolio of stocks within an industry in which the stocks have a volatility of 40% and a correlation of 60%? What is the volatility of a very large portfolio of international stocks with a volatility of 40% and a correlation of 10%?

Solution

From Eq. 11.12, the volatility of the industry portfolio as $n \longrightarrow \infty$ is given by

$$\sqrt{\text{Average Covariance}} = \sqrt{0.60 \times 0.40 \times 0.40} = 31.0\%$$

This volatility is higher than when using stocks from different industries as in Figure 11.2. Combining stocks from the same industry that are more highly correlated therefore provides less diversification. We can achieve superior diversification using international stocks. In this case,

$$\sqrt{\text{Average Covariance}} = \sqrt{0.10 \times 0.40 \times 0.40} = 12.6\%$$

We can also use Eq. 11.12 to derive one of the key results that we discussed in Chapter 10: When risks are independent, we can diversify all of the risk by holding a large portfolio.

EXAMPLE 11.8 **Volatility When Risks Are Independent**

Problem

What is the volatility of an equally weighted average of n independent, identical risks?

Solution

If risks are independent, they are uncorrelated and their covariance is zero. Using Eq. 11.12, the volatility of an equally weighted portfolio of the risks is

$$SD(R_P) = \sqrt{Var(R_P)} = \sqrt{\frac{1}{n} Var(\text{Individual Risk})} = \frac{SD(\text{Individual Risk})}{\sqrt{n}}$$

This result coincides with Eq. 10.8, which we used earlier to evaluate independent risks. Note that as $n \longrightarrow \infty$, the volatility goes to 0—that is, a very large portfolio will have *no* risk. In this case, we can eliminate all risk because there is no common risk.

[5] You might wonder what happens if the average covariance is negative. It turns out that while the covariance between a pair of stocks can be negative, as the portfolio grows large, the average covariance cannot be negative because the returns of all stocks cannot move in opposite directions simultaneously.

INTERVIEW WITH JOHN POWERS

John F. Powers was president and chief executive officer of the Stanford Management Company from 2006–2015, responsible for managing Stanford University's $22 billion endowment. Prior to joining Stanford, he served as managing director and the director of research at Offit Hall Capital Management, an investment advisory firm.

QUESTION: *Describe how you manage Stanford's $16.5 billion endowment.*

ANSWER: Our objective is to grow the endowment's value after meeting our 5% annual payout obligation to Stanford University. We begin with the return we think will exceed 5%, account for inflation, and grow modestly, creating a portfolio that combines liquid and private (illiquid) strategies. We run a modified mean-variance optimization model using forward-looking assumptions of return and volatility of our asset classes, to find that place on the efficient frontier that meets our long-term objectives. Once we have our asset allocation strategy, we outsource money to a select group of third-party managers, to capture their expertise, gain access to the higher returns from illiquid assets, and increase diversification. We retain a relatively small portion in market replication instruments, including ETFs, so that we can modify our asset allocation quickly in response to pricing dislocations we perceive in the market.

QUESTION: *You hold assets with very different expected returns. If your goal is to maximize the value of Stanford's endowment, why not just hold those with the highest expected returns?*

ANSWER: Illiquid assets provide us the highest returns. If they dominated our portfolio, we would expose the university to their greater volatility and risk. As an operating business, Stanford requires some predictability of payout now and for future planning. Without diversification and a balanced portfolio, we'd create extreme risks of both spikes and crashes in portfolio value.

We also consider consequences across multiple time periods and in correlation to other assets. Increasing diversification may yield better portfolio performance with lower risk levels. For example, real assets—commodities and real estate—typically have very low correlation with equity markets. However, during the 2008–2009 financial crisis, these assets became highly correlated to credits and equities—they all behaved the same way under pressure, creating a "correlation storm." Ultimately, that led to a reshaping of the portfolio.

QUESTION: *Historically, university endowments have performed extremely well compared to public markets. Why do you think this is?*

ANSWER: Endowment managers recognized early the power of diversification. Their willingness to invest in alternative assets such as private equity funds yielded extraordinary returns. In addition, the declining interest rate environment over the past 25 years rewarded strategies that explicitly or implicitly employ leverage. Our ability to access premier money managers, acquire private assets, and use leveraged strategies like buyouts boosted our returns. From 2001–2011, Stanford's annualized return was 9.3%, compared to 2.7% for the S&P 500 and 5.7% for the U.S. bond market.

QUESTION: *During the financial crisis, did the portfolio achieve the benefits of diversification that you had expected? Has your strategy changed since the financial crisis?*

ANSWER: Because of the above-mentioned "correlation storm," we did not get the expected benefit of diversification. We were nervous about the pricing of investment-grade bonds, which were several standard deviations away from previous levels, and so we substantially reduced our exposure to corporate debt. This created cash and liquidity for us to redeploy funds into attractively priced assets.

Going forward, we expect ongoing episodes of heightened market volatility. Our strategy is to increase the diversification of our portfolio as much as possible. We are working with money managers who buy value-based assets, looking for long-term price appreciation, and increasing exposure to more arbitrage-oriented strategies (less based on fundamentals of equity and corporate credit markets). When markets are under pressure, our goal is to be positioned to be able to acquire stressed assets priced at significant discounts.

Diversification with General Portfolios

The results in the last section depend on the portfolio being equally weighted. For a portfolio with arbitrary weights, we can rewrite Eq. 11.10 in terms of the correlation as follows:

$$Var(R_P) = \sum_i x_i Cov(R_i, R_P) = \sum_i x_i SD(R_i) SD(R_P) Corr(R_i, R_P)$$

Dividing both sides of this equation by the standard deviation of the portfolio yields the following important decomposition of the volatility of a portfolio:

Volatility of a Portfolio with Arbitrary Weights

$$SD(R_P) = \sum_i \overbrace{\underset{\substack{\uparrow \\ \text{Amount} \\ \text{of } i \text{ held}}}{x_i} \times \underset{\substack{\uparrow \\ \text{Total} \\ \text{risk of } i}}{SD(R_i)} \times \underset{\substack{\uparrow \\ \text{Fraction of } i\text{'s} \\ \text{risk that is} \\ \text{common to } P}}{Corr(R_i, R_P)}}^{\text{Security } i\text{'s contribution to the volatility of the portfolio}} \tag{11.13}$$

Equation 11.13 states that each security contributes to the volatility of the portfolio according to its volatility, or total risk, scaled by its correlation with the portfolio, which adjusts for the fraction of the total risk that is common to the portfolio. Therefore, when combining stocks into a portfolio that puts positive weight on each stock, unless all of the stocks have a perfect positive correlation of +1 with the portfolio (and thus with one another), the risk of the portfolio will be lower than the weighted average volatility of the individual stocks:

$$SD(R_P) = \sum_i x_i SD(R_i)\, Corr(R_i, R_P) < \sum_i x_i SD(R_i) \tag{11.14}$$

Contrast Eq. 11.14 with Eq. 11.3 for the expected return. The expected return of a portfolio is equal to the weighted average expected return, but the volatility of a portfolio is *less than* the weighted average volatility: We can eliminate some volatility by diversifying.

CONCEPT CHECK

1. How does the volatility of an equally weighted portfolio change as more stocks are added to it?
2. How does the volatility of a portfolio compare with the weighted average volatility of the stocks within it?

11.4 Risk Versus Return: Choosing an Efficient Portfolio

Now that we understand how to calculate the expected return and volatility of a portfolio, we can return to the main goal of the chapter: Determine how an investor can create an efficient portfolio.[6] Let's start with the simplest case—an investor who can choose between only two stocks.

[6]The techniques of portfolio optimization were developed in a 1952 paper by Harry Markowitz, as well as in related work by Andrew Roy (1952) and Bruno de Finetti (1940) (see Further Reading).

Efficient Portfolios with Two Stocks

Consider a portfolio of Intel and Coca-Cola stock. Suppose an investor believes these stocks are uncorrelated and will perform as follows:

Stock	Expected Return	Volatility
Intel	26%	50%
Coca-Cola	6%	25%

How should the investor choose a portfolio of these two stocks? Are some portfolios preferable to others?

Let's compute the expected return and volatility for different combinations of the stocks. Consider a portfolio with 40% invested in Intel stock and 60% invested in Coca-Cola stock. We can compute the expected return from Eq. 11.3 as

$$E[R_{40\text{-}60}] = x_I E[R_I] + x_C E[R_C] = 0.40(26\%) + 0.60(6\%) = 14\%$$

We can compute the variance using Eq. 11.9,

$$\begin{aligned} Var(R_{40\text{-}60}) &= x_I^2 SD(R_I)^2 + x_C^2 SD(R_C)^2 + 2x_I x_C Corr(R_I, R_C) SD(R_I) SD(R_C) \\ &= 0.40^2(0.50)^2 + 0.60^2(0.25)^2 + 2(0.40)(0.60)(0)(0.50)(0.25) = 0.0625 \end{aligned}$$

so that the volatility is $SD(R_{40\text{-}60}) = \sqrt{0.0625} = 25\%$. Table 11.4 shows the results for different portfolio weights.

Due to diversification, it is possible to find a portfolio with even lower volatility than either stock: Investing 20% in Intel stock and 80% in Coca-Cola stock, for example, has a volatility of only 22.3%. But knowing that investors care about volatility *and* expected return, we must consider both simultaneously. To do so, we plot the volatility and expected return of each portfolio in Figure 11.3. We labeled the portfolios from Table 11.4 with the portfolio weights. The curve (a hyperbola) represents the set of portfolios that we can create using arbitrary weights.

Faced with the choices in Figure 11.3, which ones make sense for an investor who is concerned with both the expected return and the volatility of her portfolio? Suppose the investor considers investing 100% in Coca-Cola stock. As we can see from Figure 11.3, other portfolios—such as the portfolio with 20% in Intel stock and 80% in Coca-Cola stock—make the investor better off in *both* ways: (1) They have a higher expected return, and (2) they have lower volatility. As a result, investing solely in Coca-Cola stock is not a good idea.

TABLE 11.4 **Expected Returns and Volatility for Different Portfolios of Two Stocks**

Portfolio Weights		Expected Return (%)	Volatility (%)
x_I	x_C	$E[R_P]$	$SD[R_P]$
1.00	0.00	26.0	50.0
0.80	0.20	22.0	40.3
0.60	0.40	18.0	31.6
0.40	0.60	14.0	25.0
0.20	0.80	10.0	22.4
0.00	1.00	6.0	25.0

FIGURE 11.3

Volatility Versus Expected Return for Portfolios of Intel and Coca-Cola Stock

Labels indicate portfolio weights (x_I, x_C) for Intel and Coca-Cola stocks. Portfolios on the red portion of the curve, with at least 20% invested in Intel stock, are efficient. Those on the blue portion of the curve, with less than 20% invested in Intel stock, are inefficient—an investor can earn a higher expected return with lower risk by choosing an alternative portfolio.

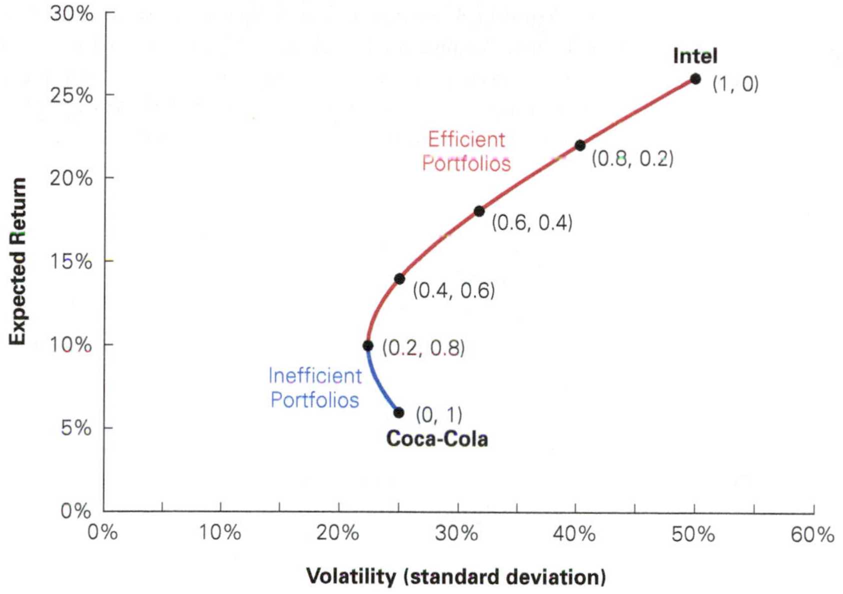

Identifying Inefficient Portfolios. More generally, we say a portfolio is an **inefficient portfolio** whenever it is possible to find another portfolio that is better in terms of both expected return and volatility. Looking at Figure 11.3, a portfolio is inefficient if there are other portfolios above and to the left—that is, to the northwest—of it. Investing solely in Coca-Cola stock is inefficient, and the same is true of all portfolios with more than 80% in Coca-Cola stock (the blue part of the curve). Inefficient portfolios are not optimal for an investor seeking high returns and low volatility.

Identifying Efficient Portfolios. By contrast, portfolios with at least 20% in Intel stock are efficient (the red part of the curve): There is no other portfolio of the two stocks that offers a higher expected return with lower volatility. But while we can rule out inefficient portfolios as inferior investment choices, we cannot easily rank the efficient ones—investors will choose among them based on their own preferences for return versus risk. For example, an extremely conservative investor who cares only about minimizing risk would choose the lowest-volatility portfolio (20% Intel, 80% Coca-Cola). An aggressive investor might choose to invest 100% in Intel stock—even though that approach is riskier, the investor may be willing to take that chance to earn a higher expected return.

EXAMPLE 11.9 **Improving Returns with an Efficient Portfolio**

Problem

Sally Ferson has invested 100% of her money in Coca-Cola stock and is seeking investment advice. She would like to earn the highest expected return possible without increasing her volatility. Which portfolio would you recommend?

Solution

In Figure 11.3, we can see that Sally can invest up to 40% in Intel stock without increasing her volatility. Because Intel stock has a higher expected return than Coca-Cola stock, she will earn higher expected returns by putting more money in Intel stock. Therefore, you should recommend that Sally put 40% of her money in Intel stock, leaving 60% in Coca-Cola stock. This portfolio has the same volatility of 25%, but an expected return of 14% rather than the 6% she has now.

The Effect of Correlation

In Figure 11.3, we assumed that the returns of Intel and Coca-Cola stocks are uncorrelated. Let's consider how the risk and return combinations would change if the correlations were different.

Correlation has no effect on the expected return of a portfolio. For example, a 40–60 portfolio will still have an expected return of 14%. However, the volatility of the portfolio will differ depending on the correlation, as we saw in Section 11.2. In particular, the lower the correlation, the lower the volatility we can obtain. In terms of Figure 11.3, as we lower the correlation and therefore the volatility of the portfolios, the curve showing the portfolios will bend to the left to a greater degree, as illustrated in Figure 11.4.

When the stocks are perfectly positively correlated, we can identify the set of portfolios by the straight line between them. In this extreme case (the red line in Figure 11.4), the volatility of the portfolio is equal to the weighted average volatility of the two stocks—there is no diversification. When the correlation is less than 1, however, the volatility of the portfolios is reduced due to diversification, and the curve bends to the left. The reduction in risk (and the bending of the curve) becomes greater as the correlation decreases. At the other extreme of perfect negative correlation (blue line), the line again becomes straight,

FIGURE 11.4

Effect on Volatility and Expected Return of Changing the Correlation between Intel and Coca-Cola Stock

This figure illustrates correlations of 1, 0.5, 0, −0.5 and −1 The lower the correlation, the lower the risk of the portfolios.

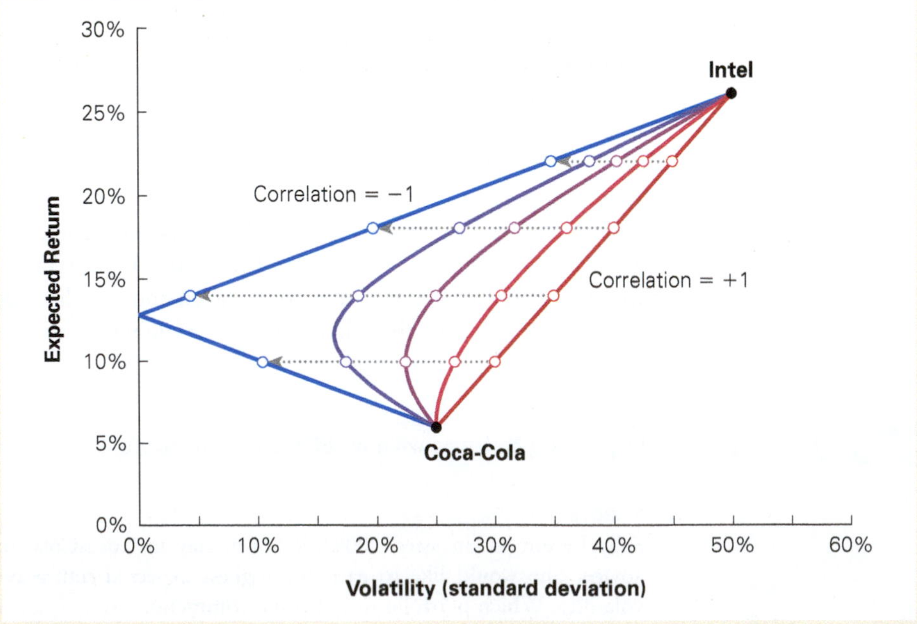

this time reflecting off the vertical axis. In particular, when the two stocks are perfectly negatively correlated, it becomes possible to hold a portfolio that bears absolutely no risk.

Short Sales

Thus far, we have considered only portfolios in which we invest a positive amount in each stock. We refer to a positive investment in a security as a **long position** in the security. But it is also possible to invest a *negative* amount in a stock, called a **short position**, by engaging in a short sale, a transaction in which you sell a stock today that you do not own, with the obligation to buy it back in the future. (For the mechanics of a short sale, see the box on page 280 in Chapter 9). As the next example demonstrates, we can include a short position as part of a portfolio by assigning that stock a negative portfolio weight.

EXAMPLE 11.10 Expected Return and Volatility with a Short Sale

Problem

Suppose you have \$20,000 in cash to invest. You decide to short sell \$10,000 worth of Coca-Cola stock and invest the proceeds from your short sale, plus your \$20,000, in Intel. What is the expected return and volatility of your portfolio?

Solution

We can think of our short sale as a negative investment of −\$10,000 in Coca-Cola stock. In addition, we invested +\$30,000 in Intel stock, for a total net investment of \$30,000 − \$10,000 = \$20,000 cash. The corresponding portfolio weights are

$$x_I = \frac{\text{Value of investment in Intel}}{\text{Total value of portfolio}} = \frac{30{,}000}{20{,}000} = 150\%$$

$$x_C = \frac{\text{Value of investment in Coca-Cola}}{\text{Total value of portfolio}} = \frac{-10{,}000}{20{,}000} = -50\%$$

Note that the portfolio weights still add up to 100%. Using these portfolio weights, we can calculate the expected return and volatility of the portfolio using Eq. 11.3 and Eq. 11.8 as before:

$$E[R_P] = x_I E[R_I] + x_C E[R_C] = 1.50 \times 26\% + (-0.50) \times 6\% = 36\%$$

$$SD(R_P) = \sqrt{Var(R_P)} = \sqrt{x_I^2 Var(R_I) + x_C^2 Var(R_C) + 2x_I x_C Cov(R_I, R_C)}$$

$$= \sqrt{1.5^2 \times 0.50^2 + (-0.5)^2 \times 0.25^2 + 2(1.5)(-0.5)(0)} = 76.0\%$$

Note that in this case, short selling increases the expected return of your portfolio, but also its volatility, above those of the individual stocks.

Short selling is profitable if you expect a stock's price to decline in the future. Recall that when you borrow a stock to short sell it, you are obligated to buy and return it in the future. So when the stock price declines, you receive more upfront for the shares than the cost to replace them in the future. But as the preceding example shows, short selling can be advantageous even if you expect the stock's price to rise, as long as you invest the proceeds in another stock with an even higher expected return. That said, and as the example also shows, short selling can greatly increase the risk of the portfolio.

In Figure 11.5, we show the effect on the investor's choice set when we allow for short sales. Short selling Intel to invest in Coca-Cola is not efficient (blue dashed curve)—other portfolios exist that have a higher expected return *and* a lower volatility. However, because Intel is expected to outperform Coca-Cola, short selling Coca-Cola to invest in Intel is efficient in this case. While such a strategy leads to a higher volatility, it also provides the investor with a higher expected return. This strategy could be attractive to an aggressive investor.

Efficient Portfolios with Many Stocks

Recall from Section 11.3 that adding more stocks to a portfolio reduces risk through diversification. Let's consider the effect of adding to our portfolio a third stock, Bore Industries, which is uncorrelated with Intel and Coca-Cola but is expected to have a very low return of 2%, and the same volatility as Coca-Cola (25%). Figure 11.6 illustrates the portfolios that we can construct using these three stocks.

Because Bore stock is inferior to Coca-Cola stock—it has the same volatility but a lower return—you might guess that no investor would want to hold a long position in Bore. However, that conclusion ignores the diversification opportunities that Bore provides. Figure 11.6 shows the results of combining Bore with Coca-Cola or with Intel (light blue curves), or combining Bore with a 50–50 portfolio of Coca-Cola and Intel (dark blue curve).[7] Notice that some of the portfolios we obtained by combining only Intel and Coca-Cola (black curve) are inferior to these new possibilities.

FIGURE 11.5

Portfolios of Intel and Coca-Cola Allowing for Short Sales

Labels indicate portfolio weights (X_I, X_C) for Intel and Coca-Cola stocks. Red indicates efficient portfolios, blue indicates inefficient portfolios. The dashed curves indicate positions that require shorting either Coca-Cola (red) or Intel (blue). Shorting Intel to invest in Coca-Cola is inefficient. Shorting Coca-Cola to invest in Intel is efficient and might be attractive to an aggressive investor who is seeking high expected returns.

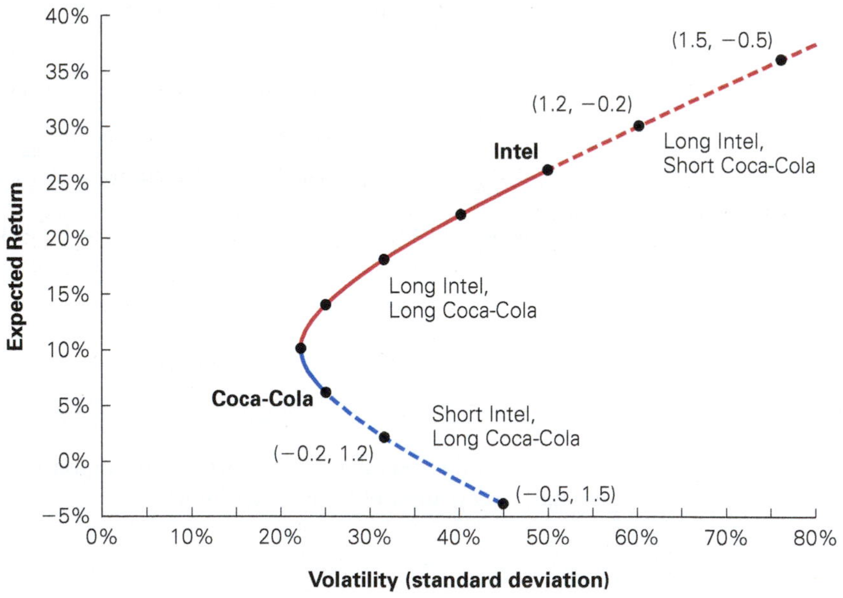

[7]When a portfolio includes another portfolio, we can compute the weight of each stock by multiplying the portfolio weights. For example, a portfolio with 30% in Bore stock and 70% in the *portfolio* of (50% Intel, 50% Coca-Cola) has 30% in Bore stock, 70% × 50% = 35% in Intel stock, and 70% × 50% = 35% in Coca-Cola stock.

FIGURE 11.6

Expected Return and Volatility for Selected Portfolios of Intel, Coca-Cola, and Bore Industries Stocks

By combining Bore (B) with Intel (I), Coca-Cola (C), and portfolios of Intel and Coca-Cola, we introduce new risk and return possibilities. We can also do better than with just Coca-Cola and Intel alone (the black curve). Portfolios of Bore and Coca-Cola (B + C) and Bore and Intel (B + I) are shown in light blue in the figure. The dark blue curve is a combination of Bore with a portfolio of Intel and Coca-Cola.

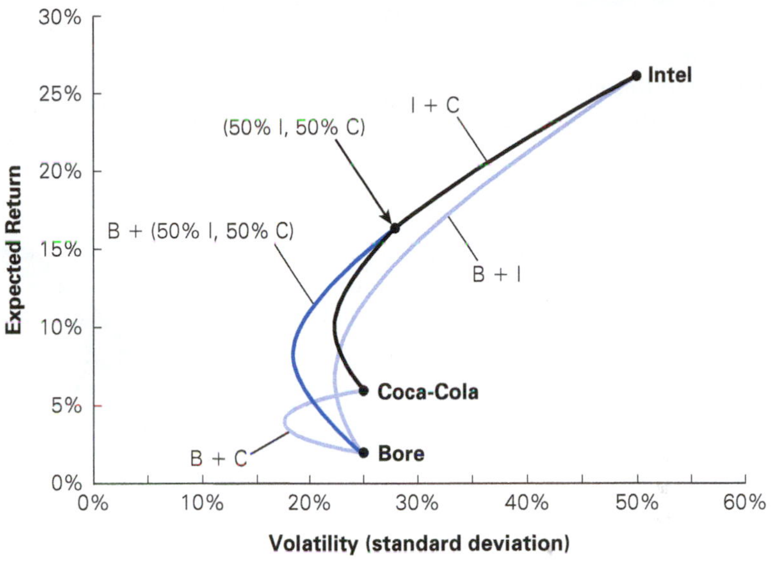

NOBEL PRIZES Harry Markowitz and James Tobin

The techniques of mean-variance portfolio optimization, which allow an investor to find the portfolio with the highest expected return for any level of variance (or volatility), were developed in an article, "Portfolio Selection," published in the *Journal of Finance* in 1952 by Harry Markowitz. Markowitz's approach has evolved into one of the main methods of portfolio optimization used on Wall Street. In recognition for his contribution to the field, Markowitz was awarded the Nobel Prize for economics in 1990.

Markowitz's work made clear that it is a security's covariance with an investor's portfolio that determines its incremental risk, and thus an investment's risk cannot be evaluated in isolation. He also demonstrated that diversification provided a "free lunch"—the opportunity to reduce risk without sacrificing expected return. In later work Markowitz went on to develop numerical algorithms to compute the efficient frontier for a set of securities.

Many of these same ideas were developed concurrently by Andrew Roy in "Safety First and the Holding of Assets" published in *Econometrica* in the same year. After winning the Nobel Prize, Markowitz graciously wrote "I am often called the father of modern portfolio theory, but Roy can claim an equal share of this honor."* Interestingly, Mark Rubinstein discovered many of these ideas in an earlier 1940 article by Bruno de Finetti in the Italian journal *Giornale dell'Instituto Italiano degli Attuari*, but the work remained in obscurity until its recent translation in 2004.**

While Markowitz assumed that investors might choose any portfolio on the efficient frontier of risky investments, James Tobin furthered this theory by considering the implications of allowing investors to combine risky securities with a risk-free investment. As we will show in Section 11.5, in that case we can identify a *unique* optimal portfolio of risky securities that does not depend on an investor's tolerance for risk. In his article "Liquidity Preference as Behavior Toward Risk" published in the *Review of Economic Studies* in 1958, Tobin proved a "Separation Theorem," which applied Markowitz's techniques to find this optimal risky portfolio. The Separation Theorem showed that investors could choose their ideal exposure to risk by varying their investments in the optimal portfolio and the risk-free investment. Tobin was awarded the Nobel Prize for economics in 1981 for his contributions to finance and economics.

*H. Markowitz, "The Early History of Portfolio Theory: 1600–1960," *Financial Analysts Journal* 55 (1999): 5–16.

**M. Rubinstein, "Bruno de Finetti and Mean-Variance Portfolio Selection," *Journal of Investment Management* 4 (2006) 3–4; the issue also contains a translation of de Finetti's work and comments by Harry Markowitz.

FIGURE 11.7

The Volatility and Expected Return for All Portfolios of Intel, Coca-Cola, and Bore Stock

Portfolios of all three stocks are shown, with the dark blue area showing portfolios without short sales, and the light blue area showing portfolios that include short sales. The best risk–return combinations are on the efficient frontier (red curve). The efficient frontier improves (has a higher return for each level of risk) when we move from two to three stocks.

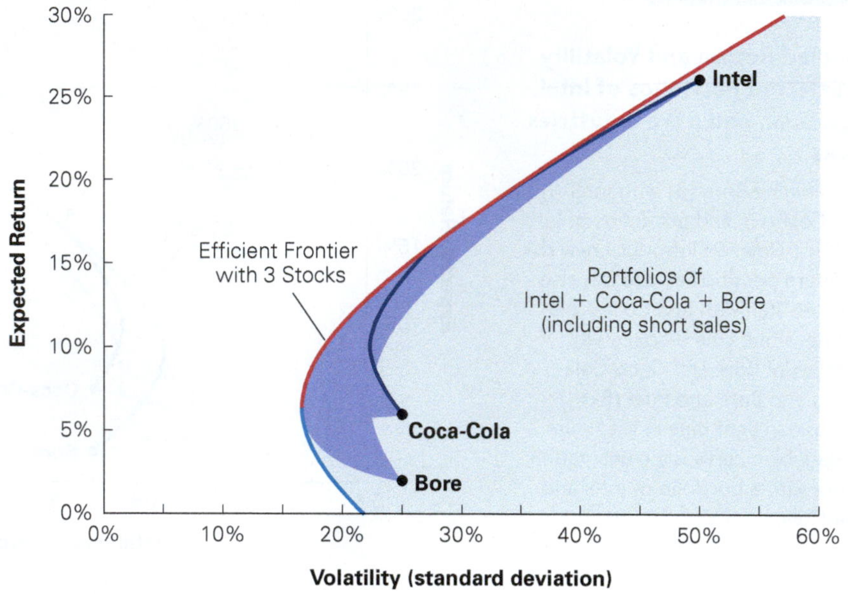

When we combine Bore stock with every portfolio of Intel and Coca-Cola, and allow for short sales as well, we get an entire region of risk and return possibilities rather than just a single curve. This region is shown in the shaded area in Figure 11.7. But note that most of these portfolios are inefficient. The efficient portfolios—those offering the highest possible expected return for a given level of volatility—are those on the northwest edge of the shaded region, which we call the **efficient frontier** for these three stocks. In this case none of the stocks, on its own, is on the efficient frontier, so it would not be efficient to put all our money in a single stock.

When the set of investment opportunities increases from two to three stocks, the efficient frontier improves. Visually, the old frontier with any two stocks is located inside the new frontier. In general, adding new investment opportunities allows for greater diversification and improves the efficient frontier. Figure 11.8 uses historical data to show the effect of increasing the set from three stocks (Amazon, GE, and McDonald's) to ten stocks. Even though the added stocks appear to offer inferior risk–return combinations on their own, because they allow for additional diversification, the efficient frontier improves with their inclusion. Thus, to arrive at the best possible set of risk and return opportunities, we should keep adding stocks until all investment opportunities are represented. Ultimately, based on our estimates of returns, volatilities, and correlations, we can construct the efficient frontier for *all* available risky investments showing the best possible risk and return combinations that we can obtain by optimal diversification.

CONCEPT CHECK

1. How does the correlation between two stocks affect the risk and return of portfolios that combine them?
2. What is the efficient frontier?
3. How does the efficient frontier change when we use more stocks to construct portfolios?

FIGURE 11.8

Efficient Frontier with Three Stocks Versus Ten Stocks

The efficient frontier expands as new investments are added. (Volatilities and correlations based on monthly returns, 2005–2015, expected returns based on forecasts.)

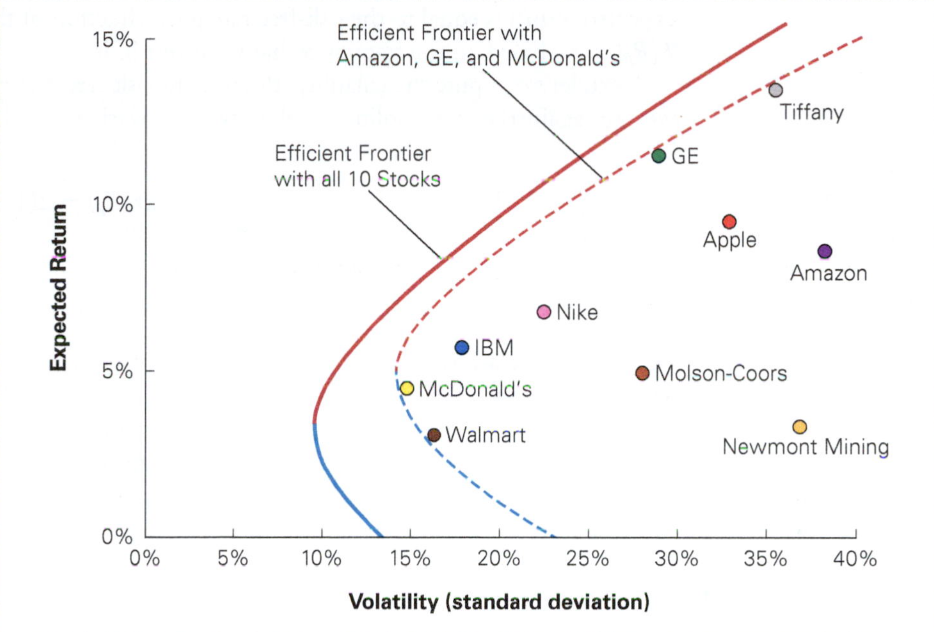

11.5 Risk-Free Saving and Borrowing

Thus far, we have considered the risk and return possibilities that result from combining risky investments into portfolios. By including all risky investments in the construction of the efficient frontier, we achieve maximum diversification.

There is another way besides diversification to reduce risk that we have not yet considered: We can keep some of our money in a safe, no-risk investment like Treasury bills. Of course, doing so will reduce our expected return. Conversely, if we are an aggressive investor who is seeking high expected returns, we might decide to borrow money to invest even more in the stock market. In this section we will see that the ability to choose the amount to invest in risky versus risk-free securities allows us to determine the *optimal portfolio* of risky securities for an investor.

Investing in Risk-Free Securities

Consider an arbitrary risky portfolio with returns R_P. Let's look at the effect on risk and return of putting a fraction x of our money in the portfolio, while leaving the remaining fraction $(1 - x)$ in risk-free Treasury bills with a yield of r_f.

Using Eq. 11.3 and Eq. 11.8, we calculate the expected return and variance of this portfolio, whose return we will denote by R_{xP}. First, the expected return is

$$\begin{aligned} E[R_{xP}] &= (1 - x)r_f + xE[R_P] \\ &= r_f + x(E[R_P] - r_f) \end{aligned} \tag{11.15}$$

The first equation simply states that the expected return is the weighted average of the expected returns of Treasury bills and the portfolio. (Because we know up front the current interest rate paid on Treasury bills, we do not need to compute an expected return for them.) The second equation rearranges the first to give a useful interpretation: Our expected return is equal to the risk-free rate plus a fraction of the portfolio's risk premium, $E[R_P] - r_f$, based on the fraction x that we invest in it.

Next, let's compute the volatility. Because the risk-free rate r_f is fixed and does not move with (or against) our portfolio, its volatility and covariance with the portfolio are both zero. Thus,

$$\begin{aligned} SD(R_{xP}) &= \sqrt{(1-x)^2 Var(r_f) + x^2 Var(R_P) + 2(1-x)x Cov(r_f, R_P)} \quad (Var(r_f) = Cov(r_f, R_P) = 0) \\ &= \sqrt{x^2 Var(R_P)} \\ &= x SD(R_P) \end{aligned} \tag{11.16}$$

That is, the volatility is only a fraction of the volatility of the portfolio, based on the amount we invest in it.

The blue line in Figure 11.9 illustrates combinations of volatility and expected return for different choices of x. Looking at Eq. 11.15 and Eq. 11.16, as we increase the fraction x invested in P, we increase both our risk and our risk premium proportionally. Hence the line is *straight* from the risk-free investment through P.

Borrowing and Buying Stocks on Margin

As we increase the fraction x invested in the portfolio P from 0 to 100%, we move along the line in Figure 11.9 from the risk-free investment to P. If we increase x beyond 100%, we get points beyond P in the graph. In this case, we are short selling the risk-free investment, so we must pay the risk-free return; in other words, we are borrowing money at the risk-free interest rate.

Borrowing money to invest in stocks is referred to as **buying stocks on margin** or using leverage. A portfolio that consists of a short position in the risk-free investment is known

FIGURE 11.9

The Risk–Return Combinations from Combining a Risk-Free Investment and a Risky Portfolio

Given a risk-free rate of 5%, the point with 0% volatility and an expected return of 5% represents the risk-free investment. The blue line shows the portfolios we obtained by investing x in portfolio P and $(1 - x)$ in the risk-free investment. Investments with weight ($x > 100\%$) in portfolio P require borrowing at the risk-free interest rate.

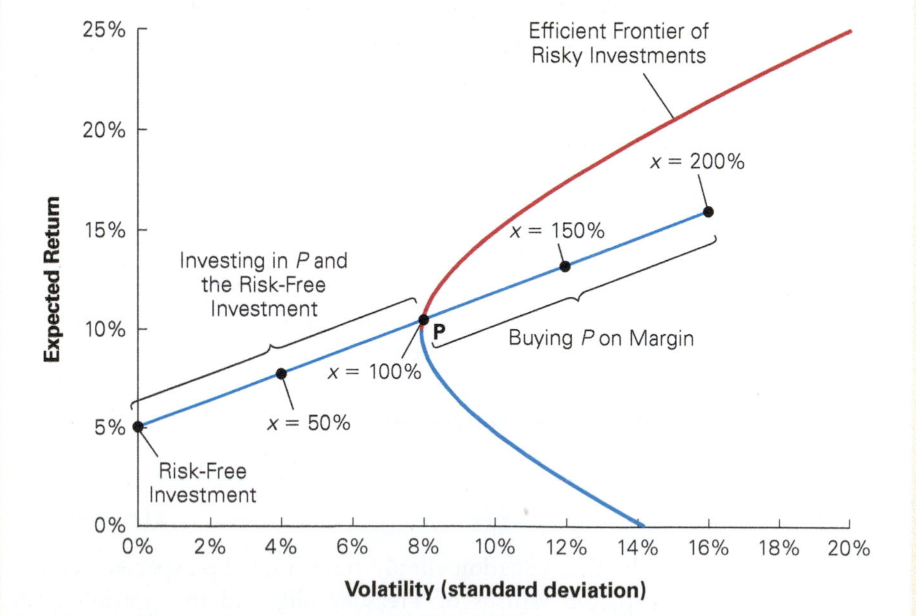

as a *levered* portfolio. As you might expect, margin investing is a risky investment strategy. Note that the region of the blue line in Figure 11.9 with $x > 100\%$ has higher risk than the portfolio P itself. At the same time, margin investing can provide higher expected returns than investing in P using only the funds we have available.

EXAMPLE 11.11 **Margin Investing**

Problem

Suppose you have \$10,000 in cash, and you decide to borrow another \$10,000 at a 5% interest rate in order to invest \$20,000 in portfolio Q, which has a 10% expected return and a 20% volatility. What is the expected return and volatility of your investment? What is your realized return if Q goes up 30% over the year? What if Q falls by 10%?

Solution

You have doubled your investment in Q using margin, so $x = 200\%$. From Eq. 11.15 and Eq. 11.16, we see that you have increased both your expected return and your risk relative to the portfolio Q:

$$E(R_{xQ}) = r_f + x(E[R_Q] - r_f) = 5\% + 2 \times (10\% - 5\%) = 15\%$$

$$SD(R_{xQ}) = xSD(R_Q) = 2 \times (20\%) = 40\%$$

If Q goes up 30%, your investment will be worth \$26,000, but you will owe \$10,000 × 1.05 = \$10,500 on your loan, for a net payoff of \$15,500 or a 55% return on your \$10,000 initial investment. If Q drops by 10%, you are left with \$18,000 − \$10,500 = \$7500, and your return is −25%. Thus the use of margin doubled the range of your returns (55% − (−25%) = 80% versus 30% − (−10%) = 40%), corresponding to the doubling of the volatility of the portfolio.

Identifying the Tangent Portfolio

Looking back at Figure 11.9, we can see that portfolio P is not the best portfolio to combine with the risk-free investment. By combining the risk-free asset with a portfolio somewhat higher on the efficient frontier than portfolio P, we will get a line that is steeper than the line through P. If the line is steeper, then for any level of volatility, we will earn a higher expected return.

To earn the highest possible expected return for any level of volatility we must find the portfolio that generates the steepest possible line when combined with the risk-free investment. The slope of the line through a given portfolio P is often referred to as the **Sharpe ratio** of the portfolio:

$$\text{Sharpe Ratio} = \frac{\text{Portfolio Excess Return}}{\text{Portfolio Volatility}} = \frac{E[R_P] - r_f}{SD(R_P)} \tag{11.17}$$

The Sharpe ratio measures the ratio of reward-to-volatility provided by a portfolio.[8] The optimal portfolio to combine with the risk-free asset will be the one with the highest Sharpe ratio, where the line with the risk-free investment just touches, and so is tangent to, the efficient frontier of risky investments, as shown in Figure 11.10. The portfolio that

[8]The Sharpe ratio was first introduced by William Sharpe as a measure to compare the performance of mutual funds. See W. Sharpe, "Mutual Fund Performance," *Journal of Business* 39 (1966): 119–138.

generates this tangent line is known as the **tangent portfolio**. All other portfolios of risky assets lie below this line. Because the tangent portfolio has the highest Sharpe ratio of any portfolio in the economy, the tangent portfolio provides the biggest reward per unit of volatility of any portfolio available.[9]

As is evident from Figure 11.10, combinations of the risk-free asset and the tangent portfolio provide the best risk and return trade-off available to an investor. This observation has a striking consequence: The tangent portfolio is efficient and, once we include the risk-free investment, all efficient portfolios are combinations of the risk-free investment and the tangent portfolio. Therefore, the optimal portfolio of *risky* investments no longer depends on how conservative or aggressive the investor is; every investor should invest in the tangent portfolio *independent of his or her taste for risk*. The investor's preferences will determine only how much to invest in the tangent portfolio versus the risk-free investment. Conservative investors will invest a small amount, choosing a portfolio on the line near the risk-free investment. Aggressive investors will invest more, choosing a portfolio that is near the tangent portfolio or even beyond it by buying stocks on margin. But both types of investors will choose to hold the *same* portfolio of risky assets, the tangent portfolio.

We have achieved one of the primary goals of this chapter and explained how to identify *the* efficient portfolio of risky assets. The **efficient portfolio** is the tangent portfolio, the portfolio with the highest Sharpe ratio in the economy. By combining it with the risk-free investment, an investor will earn the highest possible expected return for any level of volatility he or she is willing to bear.

FIGURE 11.10

The Tangent or Efficient Portfolio

The tangent portfolio is the portfolio with the highest Sharpe ratio. Investments on the green line connecting the risk-free investment and the tangent portfolio provide the best risk and return trade-off available to an investor. As a result, we also refer to the tangent portfolio as *the* efficient portfolio.

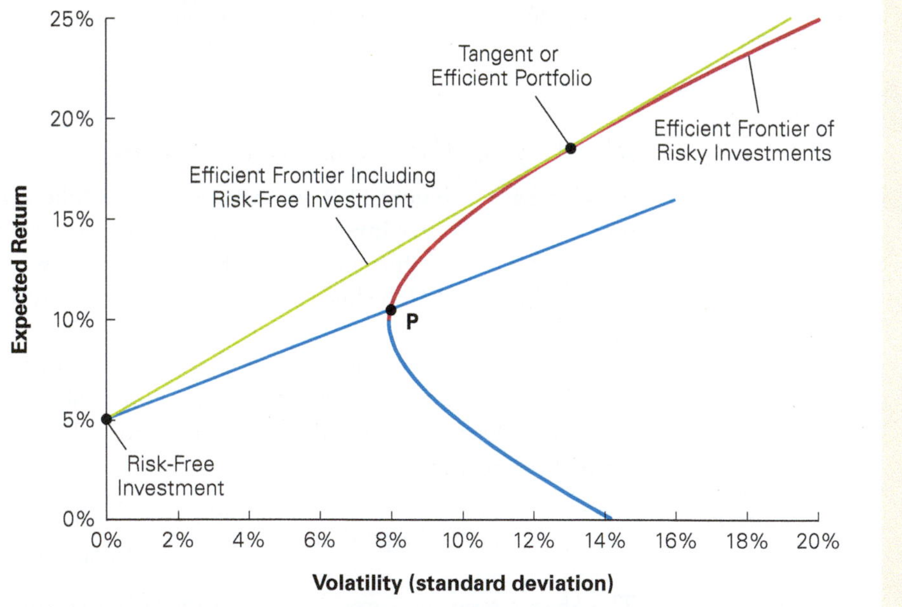

[9]The Sharpe ratio can also be interpreted as the number of standard deviations the portfolio's return must fall to underperform the risk-free investment. Thus, if returns are normally distributed, the tangent portfolio is the portfolio with the greatest chance of earning a return above the risk-free rate.

EXAMPLE 11.12 **Optimal Portfolio Choice**

Problem

Your uncle asks for investment advice. Currently, he has \$100,000 invested in portfolio P in Figure 11.10, which has an expected return of 10.5% and a volatility of 8%. Suppose the risk-free rate is 5%, and the tangent portfolio has an expected return of 18.5% and a volatility of 13%. To maximize his expected return without increasing his volatility, which portfolio would you recommend? If your uncle prefers to keep his expected return the same but minimize his risk, which portfolio would you recommend?

Solution

In either case the best portfolios are combinations of the risk-free investment and the tangent portfolio. If we invest an amount x in the tangent portfolio T, using Eq. 11.15 and Eq. 11.16, the expected return and volatility are

$$E[R_{xT}] = r_f + x(E[R_T] - r_f) = 5\% + x(18.5\% - 5\%)$$

$$SD(R_{xT}) = x\,SD(R_T) = x(13\%)$$

So, to maintain the volatility at 8%, $x = 8\%/13\% = 61.5\%$. In this case, your uncle should invest \$61,500 in the tangent portfolio, and the remaining \$38,500 in the risk-free investment. His expected return will then be 5% + (61.5%)(13.5%) = 13.3%, the highest possible given his level of risk.

Alternatively, to keep the expected return equal to the current value of 10.5%, x must satisfy $5\% + x(13.5\%) = 10.5\%$, so $x = 40.7\%$. Now your uncle should invest \$40,700 in the tangent portfolio and \$59,300 in the risk-free investment, lowering his volatility level to (40.7%)(13%) = 5.29%, the lowest possible given his expected return.

CONCEPT CHECK

1. What do we know about the Sharpe ratio of the efficient portfolio?
2. If investors are holding optimal portfolios, how will the portfolios of a conservative and an aggressive investor differ?

11.6 The Efficient Portfolio and Required Returns

Thus far, we have evaluated the optimal portfolio choice for an investor, and concluded that the tangent or efficient portfolio in Figure 11.10 offers the highest Sharpe ratio and therefore the best risk-return trade-off available. We now turn to the implications of this result for a firm's cost of capital. After all, if a firm wants to raise new capital, investors must find it attractive to increase their investment in it. In this section we derive a condition to determine whether we can improve a portfolio by adding more of a given security, and use it to calculate an investor's required return for holding an investment.

Portfolio Improvement: Beta and the Required Return

Take an arbitrary portfolio P, and let's consider whether we could raise its Sharpe ratio by selling some of our risk-free assets (or borrowing money) and investing the proceeds in an investment i. If we do so, there are two consequences:

1. Expected return: Because we are giving up the risk-free return and replacing it with i's return, our expected return will increase by i's excess return, $E[R_i] - r_f$.

2. Volatility: We will add the risk that i has in common with our portfolio (the rest of i's risk will be diversified). From Eq. 11.13, incremental risk is measured by i's volatility multiplied by its correlation with P: $SD(R_i) \times Corr(R_i, R_P)$.

Is the gain in return from investing in i adequate to make up for the increase in risk? Another way we could have increased our risk would have been to invest more in portfolio P itself. In that case, P's Sharpe ratio,

$$\frac{E[R_P] - r_f}{SD(R_P)},$$

tells us how much the return would increase for a given increase in risk. Because the investment in i increases risk by $SD(R_i) \times Corr(R_i, R_P)$, it offers a larger increase in return than we could have gotten from P alone if[10]

$$\underbrace{E[R_i] - r_f}_{\substack{\text{Additional return}\\ \text{from investment } i}} > \overbrace{\underbrace{SD(R_i) \times Corr(R_i, R_P)}_{\substack{\text{Incremental volatility}\\ \text{from investment } i}} \times \underbrace{\frac{E[R_P] - r_f}{SD(R_P)}}_{\substack{\text{Return per unit of volatility}\\ \text{available from portfolio } P}}}^{\text{Additional return from taking the same risk investing in } P} \tag{11.18}$$

To provide a further interpretation for this condition, let's combine the volatility and correlation terms in Eq. 11.18 to define the *beta of investment i with portfolio P*:

$$\beta_i^P \equiv \frac{SD(R_i) \times Corr(R_i, R_P)}{SD(R_P)} \tag{11.19}$$

β_i^P measures the sensitivity of the investment i to the fluctuations of the portfolio P. That is, for each 1% change in the portfolio's return, investment i's return is expected to change by β_i^P% due to risks that i has in common with P. With this definition, we can restate Eq. 11.18 as follows:

$$E[R_i] > r_f + \beta_i^P \times (E[R_P] - r_f)$$

That is, *increasing the amount invested in i will increase the Sharpe ratio of portfolio P if its expected return* $E[R_i]$ *exceeds its required return given portfolio P, defined as*

$$r_i \equiv r_f + \beta_i^P \times (E[R_P] - r_f) \tag{11.20}$$

The **required return** is the expected return that is necessary to compensate for the risk investment i will contribute to the portfolio. The required return for an investment i is equal to the risk-free interest rate plus the risk premium of the current portfolio, P, scaled by i's sensitivity to P, β_i^P. If i's expected return exceeds this required return, then adding more of it will improve the performance of the portfolio.

[10]We can also write Eq. 11.18 as a comparison of the Sharpe ratio of investment i with the Sharpe ratio of the portfolio scaled by their correlation (the fraction of the risk they have in common):

$$\frac{E[R_i] - r_f}{SD(R_i)} > Corr(R_i, R_p) \times \frac{E[R_p] - r_f}{SD(R_p)}$$

EXAMPLE 11.13 **The Required Return of a New Investment**

Problem

You are currently invested in the Omega Fund, a broad-based fund with an expected return of 15% and a volatility of 20%, as well as in risk-free Treasuries paying 3%. Your broker suggests that you add a real estate fund to your portfolio. The real estate fund has an expected return of 9%, a volatility of 35%, and a correlation of 0.10 with the Omega Fund. Will adding the real estate fund improve your portfolio?

Solution

Let R_{re} be the return of the real estate fund and R_O be the return of the Omega Fund. From Eq. 11.19, the beta of the real estate fund with the Omega Fund is

$$\beta_{re}^{O} = \frac{SD(R_{re})\,Corr(R_{re}, R_O)}{SD(R_O)} = \frac{35\% \times 0.10}{20\%} = 0.175$$

We can then use Eq. 11.20 to determine the required return that makes the real estate fund an attractive addition to our portfolio:

$$r_{re} = r_f + \beta_{re}^{O}(E[R_O] - r_f) = 3\% + 0.175 \times (15\% - 3\%) = 5.1\%$$

Because its expected return of 9% exceeds the required return of 5.1%, investing some amount in the real estate fund will improve our portfolio's Sharpe ratio.

Expected Returns and the Efficient Portfolio

If a security's expected return exceeds its required return, then we can improve the performance of portfolio P by adding more of the security. But how much more should we add? As we buy shares of security i, its correlation (and therefore its beta) with our portfolio will increase, ultimately raising its required return until $E[R_i] = r_i$. At this point, our holdings of security i are optimal. Similarly, if security i's expected return is less than the required return r_i, we should reduce our holdings of i. As we do so the correlation and the required return r_i will fall until $E[R_i] = r_i$.

Thus, if we have no restrictions on our ability to buy or sell securities that are traded in the market, we will continue to trade until the expected return of each security equals its required return—that is, until $E[R_i] = r_i$ holds for all i. At this point, no trade can possibly improve the risk–reward ratio of the portfolio, so our portfolio is the optimal, efficient portfolio. That is, *a portfolio is efficient if and only if the expected return of every available security equals its required return.*

From Eq. 11.20, this result implies the following relationship between the expected return of any security and its beta with the efficient portfolio:

Expected Return of a Security

$$E[R_i] = r_i \equiv r_f + \beta_i^{eff} \times (E[R_{eff}] - r_f) \tag{11.21}$$

where R_{eff} is the return of the efficient portfolio, the portfolio with the highest Sharpe ratio of any portfolio in the economy.

EXAMPLE 11.14 Identifying the Efficient Portfolio

Problem

Consider the Omega Fund and real estate fund of Example 11.13. Suppose you have $100 million invested in the Omega Fund. In addition to this position, how much should you invest in the real estate fund to form an efficient portfolio of these two funds?

Solution

Suppose that for each $1 invested in the Omega Fund, we borrow x_{re} dollars (or sell x_{re} worth of Treasury bills) to invest in the real estate fund. Then our portfolio has a return of $R_P = R_O + x_{re}(R_{re} - r_f)$, where R_O is the return of the Omega Fund and R_{re} is the return of the real estate fund. Table 11.5 shows the change to the expected return and volatility of our portfolio as we increase the investment x_{re} in the real estate fund, using the formulas

$$E[R_P] = E[R_O] + x_{re}(E[R_{re}] - r_f)$$

$$Var(R_P) = Var[R_O + x_{re}(R_{re} - r_f)] = Var(R_O) + x_{re}^2 Var(R_{re}) + 2x_{re} Cov(R_{re}, R_O)$$

Adding the real estate fund initially improves the Sharpe ratio of the portfolio, as defined by Eq. 11.17. As we add more of the real estate fund, however, its correlation with our portfolio rises, computed as

$$Corr(R_{re}, R_P) = \frac{Cov(R_{re}, R_P)}{SD(R_{re})SD(R_P)} = \frac{Cov(R_{re}, R_O + x_{re}(R_{re} - r_f))}{SD(R_{re})SD(R_P)}$$

$$= \frac{x_{re} Var(R_{re}) + Cov(R_{re}, R_O)}{SD(R_{re})SD(R_P)}$$

The beta of the real estate fund—computed from Eq. 11.19—also rises, increasing the required return. The required return equals the 9% expected return of the real estate fund at about $x_{re} = 11\%$, which is the same level of investment that maximizes the Sharpe ratio. Thus, the efficient portfolio of these two funds includes $0.11 in the real estate fund per $1 invested in the Omega Fund.

TABLE 11.5 Sharpe Ratio and Required Return for Different Investments in the Real Estate Fund

x_{re}	$E[R_P]$	$SD(R_P)$	Sharpe Ratio	$Corr(R_{re}, R_P)$	β_{re}^P	Required Return r_{re}
0%	15.00%	20.00%	0.6000	10.0%	0.18	5.10%
4%	15.24%	20.19%	0.6063	16.8%	0.29	6.57%
8%	15.48%	20.47%	0.6097	23.4%	0.40	8.00%
10%	15.60%	20.65%	0.6103	26.6%	0.45	8.69%
11%	15.66%	20.74%	0.6104	28.2%	0.48	9.03%
12%	15.72%	20.84%	0.6103	29.7%	0.50	9.35%
16%	15.96%	21.30%	0.6084	35.7%	0.59	10.60%

Before we move on, note the significance of Eq. 11.21. This equation establishes the relation between an investment's risk and its expected return. It states that *we can determine the appropriate risk premium for an investment from its beta with the efficient portfolio.* The efficient or tangent portfolio, which has the highest possible Sharpe ratio of any portfolio in the market, provides the benchmark that identifies the systematic risk present in the economy.

In Chapter 10, we argued that the *market portfolio* of all risky securities should be well diversified, and therefore could be used as a benchmark to measure systematic risk. To understand the connection between the market portfolio and the efficient portfolio, we must consider the implications of the collective investment decisions of all investors, which we turn to next.

CONCEPT CHECK

1. When will a new investment improve the Sharpe ratio of a portfolio?
2. An investment's cost of capital is determined by its beta with what portfolio?

11.7 The Capital Asset Pricing Model

As shown in Section 11.6, once we can identify the efficient portfolio, we can compute the expected return of any security based on its beta with the efficient portfolio according to Eq. 11.21. But to implement this approach, we face an important practical problem: To identify the efficient portfolio we must know the expected returns, volatilities, and correlations between investments. These quantities are difficult to forecast. Under these circumstances, how do we put the theory into practice?

To answer this question, we revisit the Capital Asset Pricing Model (CAPM), which we introduced in Chapter 10. This model allows us to identify the efficient portfolio of risky assets without having any knowledge of the expected return of each security. Instead, the CAPM uses the optimal choices investors make to identify the efficient portfolio as the market portfolio, the portfolio of all stocks and securities in the market. To obtain this remarkable result, we make three assumptions regarding the behavior of investors.[11]

The CAPM Assumptions

Three main assumptions underlie the CAPM. The first is a familiar one that we have adopted since Chapter 3:

1. *Investors can buy and sell all securities at competitive market prices (without incurring taxes or transactions costs) and can borrow and lend at the risk-free interest rate.*

The second assumption is that *all* investors behave as we have described thus far in this chapter, and choose a portfolio of traded securities that offers the highest possible expected return given the level of volatility they are willing to accept:

2. *Investors hold only efficient portfolios of traded securities—portfolios that yield the maximum expected return for a given level of volatility.*

Of course, there are many investors in the world, and each may have his or her own estimates of the volatilities, correlations, and expected returns of the available securities. But investors don't come up with these estimates arbitrarily; they base them on historical patterns and other information (including market prices) that is widely available to the public. If all investors use publicly available information sources, then their estimates are likely to be similar. Consequently, it is not unreasonable to consider a special case in which all investors have the same estimates concerning future investments and returns, called

[11]The CAPM was proposed as a model of risk and return by William Sharpe in a 1964 paper, as well as in related papers by Jack Treynor (1962), John Lintner (1965), and Jan Mossin (1966).

homogeneous expectations. Although investors' expectations are not completely identical in reality, assuming homogeneous expectations should be a reasonable approximation in many markets, and represents the third simplifying assumption of the CAPM:

3. *Investors have homogeneous expectations regarding the volatilities, correlations, and expected returns of securities.*

Supply, Demand, and the Efficiency of the Market Portfolio

If investors have homogeneous expectations, then each investor will identify the same portfolio as having the highest Sharpe ratio in the economy. Thus, all investors will demand the *same* efficient portfolio of risky securities—the tangent portfolio in Figure 11.10—adjusting only their investment in risk-free securities to suit their particular appetite for risk.

But if every investor is holding the tangent portfolio, then the combined portfolio of risky securities of *all* investors must also equal the tangent portfolio. Furthermore, because every security is owned by someone, the sum of all investors' portfolios must equal the portfolio of all risky securities available in the market, which we defined in Chapter 10 as the market portfolio. Therefore, *the efficient, tangent portfolio of risky securities (the portfolio that all investors hold) must equal the market portfolio.*

The insight that the market portfolio is efficient is really just the statement that *demand must equal supply.* All investors demand the efficient portfolio, and the supply of securities is the market portfolio; hence the two must coincide. If a security were not part of the efficient portfolio, then no investor would want to own it, and demand for this security would not equal its supply. This security's price would fall, causing its expected return to rise until it became an attractive investment. In this way, prices in the market will adjust so that the efficient portfolio and the market portfolio coincide, and demand equals supply.

EXAMPLE 11.15 Portfolio Weights and the Market Portfolio

Problem

Suppose that after much research, you have identified the efficient portfolio. As part of your holdings, you have decided to invest \$10,000 in Microsoft, and \$5000 in Pfizer stock. Suppose your friend, who is a wealthier but more conservative investor, has \$2000 invested in Pfizer. If your friend's portfolio is also efficient, how much has she invested in Microsoft? If all investors are holding efficient portfolios, what can you conclude about Microsoft's market capitalization, compared to Pfizer's?

Solution

Because all efficient portfolios are combination of the risk-free investment and the tangent portfolio, they share the same proportions of risky stocks. Thus, since you have invested twice as much in Microsoft as in Pfizer, the same must be true for your friend; therefore, she has invested \$4000 in Microsoft stock. If all investors hold efficient portfolios, the same must be true of each of their portfolios. Because, collectively, all investors own all shares of Microsoft and Pfizer, Microsoft's market capitalization must therefore be twice that of Pfizer's.

Optimal Investing: The Capital Market Line

When the CAPM assumptions hold, the market portfolio is efficient, so the tangent portfolio in Figure 11.10 is actually the market portfolio. We illustrate this result in Figure 11.11. Recall that the tangent line graphs the highest possible expected return we can achieve for

FIGURE 11.11

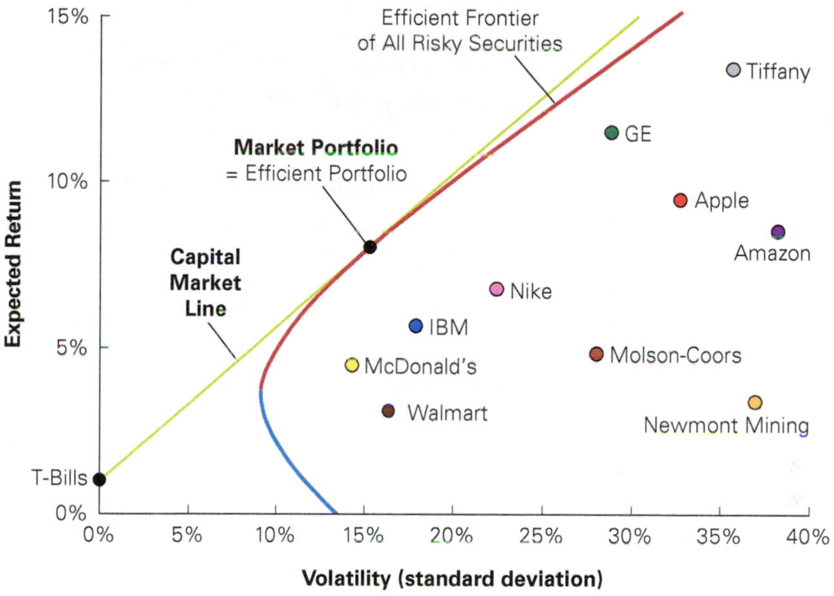

The Capital Market Line

When investors have homogeneous expectations, the market portfolio and the efficient portfolio coincide. Therefore, the capital market line (CML), which is the line from the risk-free investment through the market portfolio, represents the highest-expected return available for any level of volatility. (Data from Figure 11.8.)

any level of volatility. When the tangent line goes through the market portfolio, it is called the **capital market line (CML)**. According to the CAPM, all investors should choose a portfolio on the capital market line, by holding some combination of the risk-free security and the market portfolio.

CONCEPT CHECK

1. Explain why the market portfolio is efficient according to the CAPM.
2. What is the capital market line (CML)?

11.8 Determining the Risk Premium

Under the CAPM assumptions, we can identify the efficient portfolio: It is equal to the market portfolio. Thus, if we don't know the expected return of a security or the cost of capital of an investment, *we can use the CAPM to find it by using the market portfolio as a benchmark*.

Market Risk and Beta

In Eq. 11.21, we showed that the expected return of an investment is given by its beta with the efficient portfolio. But if the market portfolio is efficient, we can rewrite Eq. 11.21 as

The CAPM Equation for the Expected Return

$$E[R_i] = r_i = r_f + \underbrace{\beta_i \times (E[R_{Mkt}] - r_f)}_{\text{Risk premium for security } i} \tag{11.22}$$

where β_i is the beta of the security with respect to the market portfolio, defined as (using Eq. 11.19 and Eq. 11.6)

$$\beta_i = \frac{\overbrace{SD(R_i) \times Corr(R_i, R_{Mkt})}^{\text{Volatility of } i \text{ that is common with the market}}}{SD(R_{Mkt})} = \frac{Cov(R_i, R_{Mkt})}{Var(R_{Mkt})} \tag{11.23}$$

The beta of a security measures its volatility due to market risk relative to the market as a whole, and thus captures the security's sensitivity to market risk.

Equation 11.22 is the same result that we derived intuitively at the conclusion of Chapter 10. It states that to determine the appropriate risk premium for any investment, we must rescale the market risk premium (the amount by which the market's expected return exceeds the risk-free rate) by the amount of market risk present in the security's returns, measured by its beta with the market.

We can interpret the CAPM equation as follows. Following the Law of One Price, in a competitive market, investments with similar risk should have the same expected return. Because investors can eliminate firm-specific risk by diversifying their portfolios, the right measure of risk is the investment's beta with the market portfolio, β_i. As the next example demonstrates, the CAPM Eq. 11.22 states that the investment's expected return should therefore match the expected return of the capital market line portfolio with the same level of market risk.

EXAMPLE 11.16 Computing the Expected Return for a Stock

Problem

Suppose the risk-free return is 4% and the market portfolio has an expected return of 10% and a volatility of 16%. 3M stock has a 22% volatility and a correlation with the market of 0.50. What is 3M's beta with the market? What capital market line portfolio has equivalent market risk, and what is its expected return?

Solution

We can compute beta using Eq. 11.23:

$$\beta_{MMM} = \frac{SD(R_{MMM})\,Corr(R_{MMM}, R_{Mkt})}{SD(R_{Mkt})} = \frac{22\% \times 0.50}{16\%} = 0.69$$

That is, for each 1% move of the market portfolio, 3M stock tends to move 0.69%. We could obtain the same sensitivity to market risk by investing 69% in the market portfolio, and 31% in the risk-free security. Because it has the same market risk, 3M's stock should have the same expected return as this portfolio, which is (using Eq. 11.15 with $x = 0.69$),

$$\begin{aligned} E[R_{MMM}] &= r_f + x(E[R_{Mkt}] - r_f) = 4\% + 0.69(10\% - 4\%) \\ &= 8.1\% \end{aligned}$$

Because $x = \beta_{MMM}$, this calculation is precisely the CAPM Eq. 11.22. Thus, investors will require an expected return of 8.1% to compensate for the risk associated with 3M stock.

EXAMPLE 11.17 A Negative-Beta Stock

Problem

Suppose the stock of Bankruptcy Auction Services, Inc. (BAS), has a negative beta of −0.30. How does its expected return compare to the risk-free rate, according to the CAPM? Does this result make sense?

Solution

Because the expected return of the market is higher than the risk-free rate, Eq. 11.22 implies that the expected return of BAS will be *below* the risk-free rate. For example, if the risk-free rate is 4% and the expected return on the market is 10%,

$$E[R_{BAS}] = 4\% - 0.30(10\% - 4\%) = 2.2\%$$

This result seems odd: Why would investors be willing to accept a 2.2% expected return on this stock when they can invest in a safe investment and earn 4%? A savvy investor will not hold BAS alone; instead, she will hold it in combination with other securities as part of a well-diversified portfolio. Because BAS will tend to rise when the market and most other securities fall, BAS provides "recession insurance" for the portfolio. That is, when times are bad and most stocks are down, BAS will do well and offset some of this negative return. Investors are willing to pay for this insurance by accepting an expected return below the risk-free rate.

NOBEL PRIZE William Sharpe on the CAPM

William Sharpe received the Nobel Prize in 1990 for his development of the Capital Asset Pricing Model. Here are his comments on the CAPM from a 1998 interview with Jonathan Burton:*

Portfolio theory focused on the actions of a single investor with an optimal portfolio. I said, What if everyone was optimizing? They've all got their copies of Markowitz and they're doing what he says. Then some people decide they want to hold more IBM, but there aren't enough shares to satisfy demand. So they put price pressure on IBM and up it goes, at which point they have to change their estimates of risk and return, because now they're paying more for the stock. That process of upward and downward pressure on prices continues until prices reach an equilibrium and everyone collectively wants to hold what's available. At that point, what can you say about the relationship between risk and return? The answer is that expected return is proportionate to beta relative to the market portfolio.

The CAPM was and is a theory of equilibrium. Why should anyone expect to earn more by investing in one security as opposed to another? You need to be compensated for doing badly when times are bad. The security that is going to do badly just when you need money when times are bad is a security you have to hate, and there had better be some redeeming virtue or else who will hold it? That redeeming virtue has to be that in normal times you expect to do better. The key insight of the Capital Asset Pricing Model is that higher expected returns go with the greater risk of doing badly in bad times. Beta is a measure of that. Securities or asset classes with high betas tend to do worse in bad times than those with low betas.

The CAPM was a very simple, very strong set of assumptions that got a nice, clean, pretty result. And then almost immediately, we all said: Let's bring more complexity into it to try to get closer to the real world. People went on—myself and others—to what I call "extended" Capital Asset Pricing Models, in which expected return is a function of beta, taxes, liquidity, dividend yield, and other things people might care about.

Did the CAPM evolve? Of course. But the fundamental idea remains that there's no reason to expect reward just for bearing risk. Otherwise, you'd make a lot of money in Las Vegas. If there's reward for risk, it's got to be special. There's got to be some economics behind it or else the world is a very crazy place. I don't think differently about those basic ideas at all.

*Jonathan Burton, "Revisiting the Capital Asset Pricing Model," *Dow Jones Asset Manager* (May/June 1998): 20–28.

FIGURE 11.12 **The Capital Market Line and the Security Market Line**

(a) The CML depicts portfolios combining the risk-free investment and the efficient portfolio, and shows the highest expected return that we can attain for each level of volatility. According to the CAPM, the market portfolio is on the CML and all other stocks and portfolios contain diversifiable risk and lie to the right of the CML, as illustrated for McDonald's (MCD).

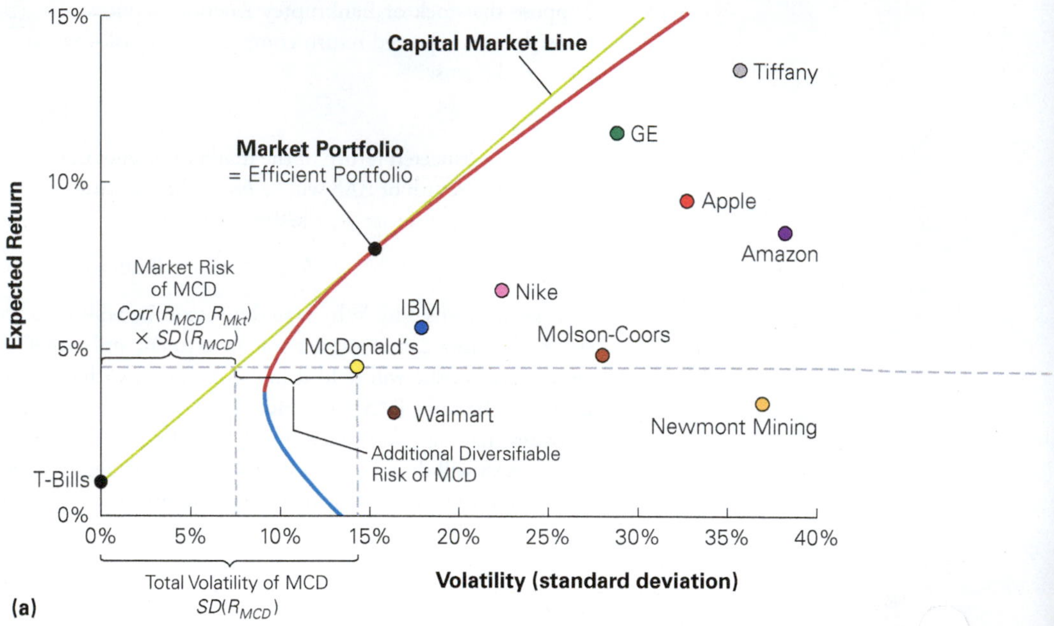

The Security Market Line

Equation 11.22 implies that there is a linear relationship between a stock's beta and its expected return. Panel (b) of Figure 11.12 graphs this line through the risk-free investment (with a beta of 0) and the market (with a beta of 1); it is called the *security market line (SML)*. Under the CAPM assumptions, the **security market line (SML)** is the line along which all individual securities should lie when plotted according to their expected return and beta, as shown in panel (b).

Contrast this result with the capital market line shown in panel (a) of Figure 11.12, where there is no clear relationship between an individual stock's volatility and its expected return. As we illustrate for McDonald's (MCD), a stock's expected return is due only to the fraction of its volatility that is common with the market—$Corr(R_{MCD}, R_{Mkt}) \times SD(R_{MCD})$; the distance of each stock to the right of the capital market line is due to its diversifiable risk. The relationship between risk and return for individual securities becomes evident only when we measure market risk rather than total risk.

Beta of a Portfolio

Because the security market line applies to all tradable investment opportunities, we can apply it to portfolios as well. Consequently, the expected return of a portfolio is given by Eq. 11.22 and therefore depends on the portfolio's beta. Using Eq. 11.23, we calculate the beta of a portfolio $R_p = \sum_i x_i R_i$ as follows:

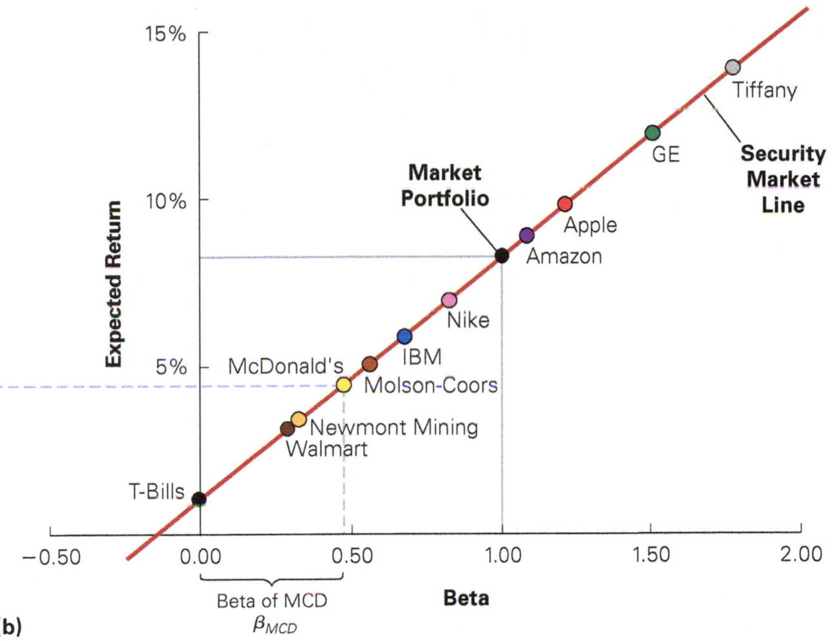

(b)

(b) The SML shows the expected return for each security as a function of its beta with the market. According to the CAPM, the market portfolio is efficient, so all stocks and portfolios should lie on the SML.

$$\beta_P = \frac{Cov(R_P, R_{Mkt})}{Var(R_{Mkt})} = \frac{Cov\left(\sum_i x_i R_i, R_{Mkt}\right)}{Var(R_{Mkt})} = \sum_i x_i \frac{Cov(R_i, R_{Mkt})}{Var(R_{Mkt})}$$

$$= \sum_i x_i \beta_i \tag{11.24}$$

In other words, *the beta of a portfolio is the weighted average beta of the securities in the portfolio.*

EXAMPLE 11.18 The Expected Return of a Portfolio

Problem

Suppose Kraft Foods' stock has a beta of 0.50, whereas Boeing's beta is 1.25. If the risk-free rate is 4%, and the expected return of the market portfolio is 10%, what is the expected return of an equally weighted portfolio of Kraft Foods and Boeing stocks, according to the CAPM?

Solution

We can compute the expected return of the portfolio in two ways. First, we can use the SML to compute the expected return of Kraft Foods (KFT) and Boeing (BA) separately:

$$E[R_{KFT}] = r_f + \beta_{KFT}(E[R_{Mkt}] - r_f) = 4\% + 0.50(10\% - 4\%) = 7.0\%$$

$$E[R_{BA}] = r_f + \beta_{BA}(E[R_{Mkt}] - r_f) = 4\% + 1.25(10\% - 4\%) = 11.5\%$$

Then, the expected return of the equally weighted portfolio P is

$$E[R_P] = \tfrac{1}{2}E[R_{KFT}] + \tfrac{1}{2}E[R_{BA}] = \tfrac{1}{2}(7.0\%) + \tfrac{1}{2}(11.5\%) = 9.25\%$$

Alternatively, we can compute the beta of the portfolio using Eq. 11.24:

$$\beta_P = \tfrac{1}{2}\beta_{KFT} + \tfrac{1}{2}\beta_{BA} = \tfrac{1}{2}(0.50) + \tfrac{1}{2}(1.25) = 0.875$$

We can then find the portfolio's expected return from the SML:

$$E[R_P] = r_f + \beta_P(E[R_{Mkt}] - r_f) = 4\% + 0.875(10\% - 4\%) = 9.25\%$$

Summary of the Capital Asset Pricing Model

In these last two sections, we have explored the consequences of the CAPM assumptions that markets are competitive, investors choose efficient portfolios, and investors have homogeneous expectations. The CAPM leads to two major conclusions:

- The market portfolio is the efficient portfolio. Therefore, the highest expected return for any given level of volatility is obtained by a portfolio on the capital market line, which combines the market portfolio with risk-free saving or borrowing.
- The risk premium for any investment is proportional to its beta with the market. Therefore, the relationship between risk and the required return is given by the security market line described by Eq. 11.22 and Eq. 11.23.

The CAPM model is based on strong assumptions. Because some of these assumptions do not fully describe investors' behavior, some of the model's conclusions are not completely accurate—it is certainly not the case that every investor holds the market portfolio, for instance. We will examine individual investor behavior in more detail in Chapter 13, where we also consider proposed extensions to the CAPM. Nevertheless, financial economists find the qualitative intuition underlying the CAPM compelling, so it is still the most common and important model of risk and return. While not perfect, it is widely regarded as a very useful approximation and is used by firms and practitioners as a practical means to estimate a security's expected return and an investment's cost of capital. In Chapter 12, we will explain in more detail how to implement the model, looking more closely at the construction of the market portfolio and developing a means to estimate the betas of firms' securities as well as their underlying investments.

CONCEPT CHECK

1. What is the security market line (SML)?
2. According to the CAPM, how can we determine a stock's expected return?

MyFinanceLab Here is what you should know after reading this chapter. MyFinanceLab will help you identify what you know and where to go when you need to practice.

11.1 The Expected Return of a Portfolio

- The portfolio weight is the initial fraction x_i of an investor's money invested in each asset. Portfolio weights add up to 1.

$$x_i = \frac{\text{Value of investment } i}{\text{Total value of portfolio}} \tag{11.1}$$

- The expected return of a portfolio is the weighted average of the expected returns of the investments within it, using the portfolio weights.

$$E[R_p] = \sum_i x_i E[R_i] \tag{11.3}$$

11.2 The Volatility of a Two-Stock Portfolio

- To find the risk of a portfolio, we need to know the degree to which stock returns move together. Covariance and correlation measure the co-movement of returns.
  - The covariance between returns R_i and R_j is defined by

$$Cov(R_i, R_j) = E[(R_i - E[R_i])(R_j - E[R_j])] \tag{11.4}$$

  and is estimated from historical data using

$$Cov(R_i, R_j) = \frac{1}{T-1}\sum_t (R_{i,t} - \overline{R}_i)(R_{j,t} - \overline{R}_j) \tag{11.5}$$

  - The correlation is defined as the covariance of the returns divided by the standard deviation of each return. The correlation is always between -1 and $+1$. It represents the fraction of the volatility due to risk that is common to the securities.

$$Corr(R_i, R_j) = \frac{Cov(R_i, R_j)}{SD(R_i)\,SD(R_j)} \tag{11.6}$$

- The variance of a portfolio depends on the covariance of the stocks within it.
  - For a portfolio with two stocks, the portfolio variance is

$$\begin{aligned} Var(R_P) &= x_1^2 Var(R_1) + x_2^2 Var(R_2) + 2x_1x_2 Cov(R_1, R_2) \\ &= x_1^2 SD(R_1)^2 + x_2^2 SD(R_2)^2 + 2x_1x_2 Corr(R_1, R_2) SD(R_1) SD(R_2) \end{aligned} \tag{11.8 and 11.9}$$

  - If the portfolio weights are positive, as we lower the covariance or correlation between the two stocks in a portfolio, we lower the portfolio variance.

11.3 The Volatility of a Large Portfolio

- The variance of an equally weighted portfolio is

$$\begin{aligned} Var(R_P) &= \frac{1}{n}(\text{Average Variance of the Individual Stocks}) \\ &+ \left(1 - \frac{1}{n}\right)(\text{Average Covariance between the Stocks}) \end{aligned} \tag{11.12}$$

- Diversification eliminates independent risks. The volatility of a large portfolio results from the common risk between the stocks in the portfolio.
- Each security contributes to the volatility of the portfolio according to its total risk scaled by its correlation with the portfolio, which adjusts for the fraction of the total risk that is common to the portfolio.

$$SD(R_P) = \sum_i x_i \times SD(R_i) \times Corr(R_i, R_P) \tag{11.13}$$

11.4 Risk Versus Return: Choosing an Efficient Portfolio

- Efficient portfolios offer investors the highest possible expected return for a given level of risk. The set of efficient portfolios is called the efficient frontier. As investors add stocks to a portfolio, the efficient portfolio improves.
  - An investor seeking high expected returns and low volatility should invest only in efficient portfolios.
  - Investors will choose from the set of efficient portfolios based on their risk tolerance.

- Investors may use short sales in their portfolios. A portfolio is short those stocks with negative portfolio weights. Short selling extends the set of possible portfolios.

11.5 Risk-Free Saving and Borrowing

- Portfolios can be formed by combining the risk-free asset with a portfolio of risky assets.
  - The expected return and volatility for this type of portfolio is

$$E[R_{xP}] = r_f + x(E[R_p] - r_f) \tag{11.15}$$

$$SD(R_{xP}) = x\,SD(R_P) \tag{11.16}$$

  - The risk–return combinations of the risk-free investment and a risky portfolio lie on a straight line connecting the two investments.
- The goal of an investor who is seeking to earn the highest possible expected return for any level of volatility is to find the portfolio that generates the steepest possible line when combined with the risk-free investment. The slope of this line is called the Sharpe ratio of the portfolio.

$$\text{Sharpe Ratio} = \frac{\text{Portfolio Excess Return}}{\text{Portfolio Volatility}} = \frac{E[R_P] - r_f}{SD(R_P)} \tag{11.17}$$

- The risky portfolio with the highest Sharpe ratio is called the efficient portfolio. The efficient portfolio is the optimal combination of risky investments independent of the investor's appetite for risk. An investor can select a desired degree of risk by choosing the amount to invest in the efficient portfolio relative to the risk-free investment.

11.6 The Efficient Portfolio and Required Returns

- Beta indicates the sensitivity of the investment's return to fluctuations in the portfolio's return. The beta of an investment with a portfolio is

$$\beta_i^P \equiv \frac{SD(R_i) \times Corr(R_i, R_P)}{SD(R_P)} \tag{11.19}$$

- Buying shares of security i improves the Sharpe ratio of a portfolio if its expected return exceeds the required return:

$$r_i \equiv r_f + \beta_i^P \times (E[R_P] - r_f) \tag{11.20}$$

- A portfolio is efficient when $E[R_i] = r_i$ for all securities. The following relationship therefore holds between beta and expected returns for traded securities:

$$E[R_i] = r_i \equiv r_f + \beta_i^{eff} \times (E[R_{eff}] - r_f) \tag{11.21}$$

11.7 The Capital Asset Pricing Model

- Three main assumptions underlie the Capital Asset Pricing Model (CAPM):
  - Investors trade securities at competitive market prices (without incurring taxes or transaction costs) and can borrow and lend at the risk-free rate.
  - Investors choose efficient portfolios.
  - Investors have homogeneous expectations regarding the volatilities, correlations, and expected returns of securities.
- Because the supply of securities must equal the demand for securities, the CAPM implies that the market portfolio of all risky securities is the efficient portfolio.
- Under the CAPM assumptions, the capital market line (CML), which is the set of portfolios obtained by combining the risk-free security and the market portfolio, is the set of portfolios with the highest possible expected return for any level of volatility.

- The CAPM equation states that the risk premium of any security is equal to the market risk premium multiplied by the beta of the security. This relationship is called the security market line (SML), and it determines the required return for an investment:

$$E[R_i] = r_i = r_f + \underbrace{\beta_i \times (E[R_{Mkt}] - r_f)}_{\text{Risk premium for security } i} \tag{11.22}$$

- The beta of a security measures the amount of the security's risk that is common to the market portfolio or market risk. Beta is defined as follows:

$$\beta_i = \frac{\overbrace{SD(R_i) \times Corr(R_i, R_{Mkt})}^{\text{Volatility of } i \text{ that is common with the market}}}{SD(R_{Mkt})} = \frac{Cov(R_i, R_{Mkt})}{Var(R_{Mkt})} \tag{11.23}$$

- The beta of a portfolio is the weighted-average beta of the securities in the portfolio.

Key Terms

buying stocks on margin *p. 378*
capital market line (CML) *p. 387*
correlation *p. 361*
covariance *p. 360*
efficient frontier *p. 376*
efficient portfolio *p. 380*
equally weighted portfolio *p. 366*
homogeneous expectations *p. 386*
inefficient portfolio *p. 371*
long position *p. 373*
portfolio weights *p. 358*
required return *p. 382*
security market line (SML) *p. 390*
Sharpe ratio *p. 379*
short position *p. 373*
tangent portfolio *p. 380*

Further Reading

The following text presents in more depth optimal portfolio choice: W. Sharpe, G. Alexander, and J. Bailey, *Investments* (Prentice Hall, 1999).

Two seminal papers on optimal portfolio choice are: H. Markowitz, "Portfolio Selection," *Journal of Finance* 7 (March 1952): 77–91; and J. Tobin, "Liquidity Preference as Behavior Toward Risk," *Review of Economic Studies* 25 (February 1958): 65–86. While Markowitz's paper had the greatest influence, the application of mean-variance optimization to portfolio theory was developed concurrently by Andrew Roy ("Safety First and the Holding of Assets," *Econometrica* 20 (1952): 431–449). For an analysis of earlier related work by Bruno de Finetti, see M. Rubinstein, "Bruno de Finetti and Mean-Variance Portfolio Selection," *Journal of Investment Management* 4 (2006): 3–4; the issue also contains a translation of de Finetti's work and comments by Harry Markowitz.

For a historical account of how researchers recognized the impact that short-sales constraints may have in the expected returns of assets, see M. Rubinstein, "Great Moments in Financial Economics: III. Short-Sales and Stock Prices," *Journal of Investment Management* 2(1) (First Quarter 2004): 16–31.

The insight that the expected return of a security is given by its beta with an efficient portfolio was first derived in the following paper: R. Roll, "A Critique of the Asset Pricing Theory's Tests," *Journal of Financial Economics* 4 (1977): 129–176.

The following classic papers developed the CAPM: J. Lintner, "The Valuation of Risk Assets and the Selection of Risky Investments in Stock Portfolios and Capital Budgets," *Review of Economics and Statistics* 47 (February 1965): 13–37; J. Mossin, "Equilibrium in a Capital Asset Market," *Econometrica* 34 (1966): 768–783; W. Sharpe, "Capital Asset Prices: A Theory of Market Equilibrium under Conditions of Risk," *Journal of Finance* 19 (September 1964): 425–442; and J. Treynor, "Toward a Theory of the Market Value of Risky Assets," unpublished manuscript (1961).

Problems

All problems are available in MyFinanceLab. *An asterisk (*) indicates problems with a higher level of difficulty.*

The Expected Return of a Portfolio

1. You are considering how to invest part of your retirement savings. You have decided to put $200,000 into three stocks: 50% of the money in GoldFinger (currently $25/share), 25% of the money in Moosehead (currently $80/share), and the remainder in Venture Associates (currently $2/share). If GoldFinger stock goes up to $30/share, Moosehead stock drops to $60/share, and Venture Associates stock rises to $3 per share,
a. What is the new value of the portfolio?
b. What return did the portfolio earn?
c. If you don't buy or sell shares after the price change, what are your new portfolio weights?

2. You own three stocks: 600 shares of Apple Computer, 10,000 shares of Cisco Systems, and 5000 shares of Colgate-Palmolive. The current share prices and expected returns of Apple, Cisco, and Colgate-Palmolive are, respectively, $500, $20, $100 and 12%, 10%, 8%.
a. What are the portfolio weights of the three stocks in your portfolio?
b. What is the expected return of your portfolio?
c. Suppose the price of Apple stock goes up by $25, Cisco rises by $5, and Colgate-Palmolive falls by $13. What are the new portfolio weights?
d. Assuming the stocks' expected returns remain the same, what is the expected return of the portfolio at the new prices?

3. Consider a world that only consists of the three stocks shown in the following table:

Stock	Total Number of Shares Outstanding	Current Price per Share	Expected Return
First Bank	100 Million	$100	18%
Fast Mover	50 Million	$120	12%
Funny Bone	200 Million	$30	15%

a. Calculate the total value of all shares outstanding currently.
b. What fraction of the total value outstanding does each stock make up?
c. You hold the market portfolio, that is, you have picked portfolio weights equal to the answer to part b (that is, each stock's weight is equal to its contribution to the fraction of the total value of all stocks). What is the expected return of your portfolio?

4. There are two ways to calculate the expected return of a portfolio: either calculate the expected return using the value and dividend stream of the portfolio as a whole, or calculate the weighted average of the expected returns of the individual stocks that make up the portfolio. Which return is higher?

The Volatility of a Two-Stock Portfolio

5. Using the data in the following table, estimate (a) the average return and volatility for each stock, (b) the covariance between the stocks, and (c) the correlation between these two stocks.

Year	2010	2011	2012	2013	2014	2015
Stock A	−10%	20%	5%	−5%	2%	9%
Stock B	21%	7%	30%	−3%	−8%	25%

6. Use the data in Problem 5, consider a portfolio that maintains a 50% weight on stock A and a 50% weight on stock B.
a. What is the return each year of this portfolio?
b. Based on your results from part a, compute the average return and volatility of the portfolio.

c. Show that (i) the average return of the portfolio is equal to the average of the average returns of the two stocks, and (ii) the volatility of the portfolio equals the same result as from the calculation in Eq. 11.9.

d. Explain why the portfolio has a lower volatility than the average volatility of the two stocks.

7. Using your estimates from Problem 5, calculate the volatility (standard deviation) of a portfolio that is 70% invested in stock A and 30% invested in stock B.

8. Using the data from Table 11.3, what is the covariance between the stocks of Alaska Air and Southwest Airlines?

9. Suppose two stocks have a correlation of 1. If the first stock has an above average return this year, what is the probability that the second stock will have an above average return?

10. Arbor Systems and Gencore stocks both have a volatility of 40%. Compute the volatility of a portfolio with 50% invested in each stock if the correlation between the stocks is (a) $+1$, (b) 0.50, (c) 0, (d) -0.50, and (e) -1.0. In which cases is the volatility lower than that of the original stocks?

11. Suppose Wesley Publishing's stock has a volatility of 60%, while Addison Printing's stock has a volatility of 30%. If the correlation between these stocks is 25%, what is the volatility of the following portfolios of Addison and Wesley: (a) 100% Addison, (b) 75% Addison and 25% Wesley, and (c) 50% Addison and 50% Wesley.

12. Suppose Avon and Nova stocks have volatilities of 50% and 25%, respectively, and they are perfectly negatively correlated. What portfolio of these two stocks has zero risk?

13. Suppose Tex stock has a volatility of 40%, and Mex stock has a volatility of 20%. If Tex and Mex are uncorrelated,

a. Construct a portfolio with positive weights in both stocks and that has the same volatility as MEX alone.

b. What portfolio of the two stocks has the smallest possible volatility?

The Volatility of a Large Portfolio

14. Using the data in Table 11.1,

a. Compute the annual returns for a portfolio with 25% invested in North Air, 25% invested in West Air, and 50% invested in Tex Oil.

b. What is the lowest annual return for your portfolio in part a? How does it compare with the lowest annual return of the individual stocks or portfolios in Table 11.1?

15. Using the data from Table 11.3, what is the volatility of an equally weighted portfolio of Microsoft, Alaska Air, and Ford Motor stock?

16. Suppose the average stock has a volatility of 50%, and the correlation between pairs of stocks is 20%. Estimate the volatility of an equally weighted portfolio with (a) 1 stock, (b) 30 stocks, (c) 1000 stocks.

17. What is the volatility (standard deviation) of an equally weighted portfolio of stocks within an industry in which the stocks have a volatility of 50% and a correlation of 40% as the portfolio becomes arbitrarily large?

18. Consider an equally weighted portfolio of stocks in which each stock has a volatility of 40%, and the correlation between each pair of stocks is 20%.

a. What is the volatility of the portfolio as the number of stocks becomes arbitrarily large?

b. What is the average correlation of each stock with this large portfolio?

19. Stock A has a volatility of 65% and a correlation of 10% with your current portfolio. Stock B has a volatility of 30% and a correlation of 25% with your current portfolio. You currently hold both stocks. Which will increase the volatility of your portfolio: (i) selling a small amount of stock B and investing the proceeds in stock A, or (ii) selling a small amount of stock A and investing the proceeds in stock B?

20. You currently hold a portfolio of three stocks, Delta, Gamma, and Omega. Delta has a volatility of 60%, Gamma has a volatility of 30%, and Omega has a volatility of 20%. Suppose you invest 50% of your money in Delta, and 25% each in Gamma and Omega.

a. What is the highest possible volatility of your portfolio?

b. If your portfolio has the volatility in (a), what can you conclude about the correlation between Delta and Omega?

Risk Versus Return: Choosing an Efficient Portfolio

21. Suppose Ford Motor stock has an expected return of 20% and a volatility of 40%, and Molson-Coors Brewing has an expected return of 10% and a volatility of 30%. If the two stocks are uncorrelated,

a. What is the expected return and volatility of an equally weighted portfolio of the two stocks?

b. Given your answer to part a, is investing all of your money in Molson-Coors stock an efficient portfolio of these two stocks?

c. Is investing all of your money in Ford Motor an efficient portfolio of these two stocks?

22. Suppose Intel's stock has an expected return of 26% and a volatility of 50%, while Coca-Cola's has an expected return of 6% and volatility of 25%. If these two stocks were perfectly negatively correlated (i.e., their correlation coefficient is -1),

a. Calculate the portfolio weights that remove all risk.

b. If there are no arbitrage opportunities, what is the risk-free rate of interest in this economy?

For Problems 23–26, suppose Johnson & Johnson and Walgreens Boots Alliance have expected returns and volatilities shown below, with a correlation of 22%.

	Expected Return	Standard Deviation
Johnson & Johnson	7%	16%
Walgreens Boots Alliance	10%	20%

23. Calculate (a) the expected return and (b) the volatility (standard deviation) of a portfolio that is equally invested in Johnson & Johnson's and Walgreens' stock.

24. For the portfolio in Problem 23, if the correlation between Johnson & Johnson's and Walgreens' stock were to increase,

a. Would the expected return of the portfolio rise or fall?

b. Would the volatility of the portfolio rise or fall?

25. Calculate (a) the expected return and (b) the volatility (standard deviation) of a portfolio that consists of a long position of $10,000 in Johnson & Johnson and a short position of $2000 in Walgreens.

***26.** Using the same data as for Problem 23, calculate the expected return and the volatility (standard deviation) of a portfolio consisting of Johnson & Johnson's and Walgreens' stocks using a wide range of portfolio weights. Plot the expected return as a function of the portfolio volatility. Using your graph, identify the range of Johnson & Johnson's portfolio weights that yield efficient combinations of the two stocks, rounded to the nearest percentage point.

27. A hedge fund has created a portfolio using just two stocks. It has shorted $35,000,000 worth of Oracle stock and has purchased $85,000,000 of Intel stock. The correlation between Oracle's and Intel's returns is 0.65. The expected returns and standard deviations of the two stocks are given in the table below:

	Expected Return	Standard Deviation
Oracle	12.00%	45.00%
Intel	14.50%	40.00%

a. What is the expected return of the hedge fund's portfolio?

b. What is the standard deviation of the hedge fund's portfolio?

28. Consider the portfolio in Problem 27. Suppose the correlation between Intel and Oracle's stock increases, but nothing else changes. Would the portfolio be more or less risky with this change?

***29.** Fred holds a portfolio with a 30% volatility. He decides to short sell a small amount of stock with a 40% volatility and use the proceeds to invest more in his portfolio. If this transaction reduces the risk of his portfolio, what is the minimum possible correlation between the stock he shorted and his original portfolio?

30. Suppose Target's stock has an expected return of 20% and a volatility of 40%, Hershey's stock has an expected return of 12% and a volatility of 30%, and these two stocks are uncorrelated.

a. What is the expected return and volatility of an equally weighted portfolio of the two stocks?

Consider a new stock with an expected return of 16% and a volatility of 30%. Suppose this new stock is uncorrelated with Target's and Hershey's stock.

b. Is holding this stock alone attractive compared to holding the portfolio in (a)?

c. Can you improve upon your portfolio in (a) by adding this new stock to your portfolio? Explain.

31. You have $10,000 to invest. You decide to invest $20,000 in Google and short sell $10,000 worth of Yahoo! Google's expected return is 15% with a volatility of 30% and Yahoo!'s expected return is 12% with a volatility of 25%. The stocks have a correlation of 0.9. What is the expected return and volatility of the portfolio?

32. You expect HGH stock to have a 20% return next year and a 30% volatility. You have $25,000 to invest, but plan to invest a total of $50,000 in HGH, raising the additional $25,000 by shorting *either* KBH or LWI stock. Both KBH and LWI have an expected return of 10% and a volatility of 20%. If KBH has a correlation of +0.5 with HGH, and LWI has a correlation of −0.50 with HGH, which stock should you short?

Risk-Free Saving and Borrowing

***33.** Suppose you have $100,000 in cash, and you decide to borrow another $15,000 at a 4% interest rate to invest in the stock market. You invest the entire $115,000 in a portfolio J with a 15% expected return and a 25% volatility.

a. What is the expected return and volatility (standard deviation) of your investment?

b. What is your realized return if J goes up 25% over the year?

c. What return do you realize if J falls by 20% over the year?

34. You have $100,000 to invest. You choose to put $150,000 into the market by borrowing $50,000.

a. If the risk-free interest rate is 5% and the market expected return is 10%, what is the expected return of your investment?

b. If the market volatility is 15%, what is the volatility of your investment?

35. You currently have $100,000 invested in a portfolio that has an expected return of 12% and a volatility of 8%. Suppose the risk-free rate is 5%, and there is another portfolio that has an expected return of 20% and a volatility of 12%.

a. What portfolio has a higher expected return than your portfolio but with the same volatility?

b. What portfolio has a lower volatility than your portfolio but with the same expected return?

36. Assume the risk-free rate is 4%. You are a financial advisor, and must choose *one* of the funds below to recommend to each of your clients. Whichever fund you recommend, your clients will then combine it with risk-free borrowing and lending depending on their desired level of risk.

	Expected Return	Volatility
Fund A	10%	10%
Fund B	15%	22%
Fund C	6%	2%

Which fund would you recommend without knowing your client's risk preference?

37. Assume all investors want to hold a portfolio that, for a given level of volatility, has the maximum possible expected return. Explain why, when a risk-free asset exists, all investors will choose to hold the same portfolio of risky stocks.

The Efficient Portfolio and Required Returns

38. In addition to risk-free securities, you are currently invested in the Tanglewood Fund, a broad-based fund of stocks and other securities with an expected return of 12% and a volatility of 25%. Currently, the risk-free rate of interest is 4%. Your broker suggests that you add a venture capital fund to your current portfolio. The venture capital fund has an expected return of 20%, a volatility of 80%, and a correlation of 0.2 with the Tanglewood Fund. Calculate the required return and use it to decide whether you should add the venture capital fund to your portfolio.

39. You have noticed a market investment opportunity that, given your current portfolio, has an expected return that exceeds your required return. What can you conclude about your current portfolio?

40. The Optima Mutual Fund has an expected return of 20%, and a volatility of 20%. Optima claims that no other portfolio offers a higher Sharpe ratio. Suppose this claim is true, and the risk-free interest rate is 5%.

a. What is Optima's Sharpe Ratio?

b. If eBay's stock has a volatility of 40% and an expected return of 11%, what must be its correlation with the Optima Fund?

c. If the SubOptima Fund has a correlation of 80% with the Optima Fund, what is the Sharpe ratio of the SubOptima Fund?

41. You are currently only invested in the Natasha Fund (aside from risk-free securities). It has an expected return of 14% with a volatility of 20%. Currently, the risk-free rate of interest is 3.8%. Your broker suggests that you add Hannah Corporation to your portfolio. Hannah Corporation has an expected return of 20%, a volatility of 60%, and a correlation of 0 with the Natasha Fund.

a. Is your broker right?

b. You follow your broker's advice and make a substantial investment in Hannah stock so that, considering only your risky investments, 60% is in the Natasha Fund and 40% is in Hannah stock. When you tell your finance professor about your investment, he says that you made a mistake and should reduce your investment in Hannah. Is your finance professor right?

c. You decide to follow your finance professor's advice and reduce your exposure to Hannah. Now Hannah represents 15% of your risky portfolio, with the rest in the Natasha fund. Is this the correct amount of Hannah stock to hold?

42. Calculate the Sharpe ratio of each of the three portfolios in Problem 41. What portfolio weight in Hannah stock maximizes the Sharpe ratio?

43. Returning to Problem 38, assume you follow your broker's advice and put 50% of your money in the venture fund.

a. What is the Sharpe ratio of the Tanglewood Fund?

b. What is the Sharpe ratio of your new portfolio?

c. What is the optimal fraction of your wealth to invest in the venture fund? (*Hint*: Use Excel and round your answer to two decimal places.)

The Capital Asset Pricing Model

44. When the CAPM correctly prices risk, the market portfolio is an efficient portfolio. Explain why.

45. A big pharmaceutical company, DRIg, has just announced a potential cure for cancer. The stock price increased from $5 to $100 in one day. A friend calls to tell you that he owns DRIg.

You proudly reply that you do, too. Since you have been friends for some time, you know that he holds the market, as do you, and so you both are invested in this stock. Both of you care only about expected return and volatility. The risk-free rate is 3%, quoted as an APR based on a 365-day year. DRIg made up 0.2% of the market portfolio before the news announcement.

a. On the announcement your overall wealth went up by 1% (assume all other price changes canceled out so that without DRIg, the market return would have been zero). How is your wealth invested?

b. Your friend's wealth went up by 2%. How is he invested?

46. Your investment portfolio consists of $15,000 invested in only one stock—Microsoft. Suppose the risk-free rate is 5%, Microsoft stock has an expected return of 12% and a volatility of 40%, and the market portfolio has an expected return of 10% and a volatility of 18%. Under the CAPM assumptions,

a. What alternative investment has the lowest possible volatility while having the same expected return as Microsoft? What is the volatility of this investment?

b. What investment has the highest possible expected return while having the same volatility as Microsoft? What is the expected return of this investment?

47. Suppose you group all the stocks in the world into two mutually exclusive portfolios (each stock is in only one portfolio): growth stocks and value stocks. Suppose the two portfolios have equal size (in terms of total value), a correlation of 0.5, and the following characteristics:

	Expected Return	Volatility
Value Stocks	13%	12%
Growth Stocks	17%	25%

The risk-free rate is 2%.

a. What is the expected return and volatility of the market portfolio (which is a 50–50 combination of the two portfolios)?

b. Does the CAPM hold in this economy? (*Hint*: Is the market portfolio efficient?)

Determining the Risk Premium

48. Suppose the risk-free return is 4% and the market portfolio has an expected return of 10% and a volatility of 16%. Merck & Co. (Ticker: MRK) stock has a 20% volatility and a correlation with the market of 0.06.

a. What is Merck's beta with respect to the market?

b. Under the CAPM assumptions, what is its expected return?

49. Consider a portfolio consisting of the following three stocks:

	Portfolio Weight	Volatility	Correlation with the Market Portfolio
HEC Corp	0.25	12%	0.4
Green Midget	0.35	25%	0.6
Alive And Well	0.4	13%	0.5

The volatility of the market portfolio is 10% and it has an expected return of 8%. The risk-free rate is 3%.

a. Compute the beta and expected return of each stock.

b. Using your answer from part a, calculate the expected return of the portfolio.

c. What is the beta of the portfolio?

d. Using your answer from part c, calculate the expected return of the portfolio and verify that it matches your answer to part b.

50. Suppose Autodesk stock has a beta of 2.16, whereas Costco stock has a beta of 0.69. If the risk-free interest rate is 4% and the expected return of the market portfolio is 10%, what is the expected return of a portfolio that consists of 60% Autodesk stock and 40% Costco stock, according to the CAPM?

***51.** What is the risk premium of a zero-beta stock? Does this mean you can lower the volatility of a portfolio without changing the expected return by substituting out any zero-beta stock in a portfolio and replacing it with the risk-free asset?

Data Case

Your manager was so impressed with your work analyzing the return and standard deviations of the 12 stocks from Chapter 10 that he would like you to continue your analysis.

Specifically, he wants you to update the stock portfolio by:

- Rebalancing the portfolio with the optimum weights that will provide the best risk and return combinations for the new 12-stock portfolio.
- Determining the improvement in the return and risk that would result from these optimum weights compared to the current method of equally weighting the stocks in the portfolio.

Use the Solver function in Excel to perform this analysis (the time-consuming alternative is to find the optimum weights by trial-and-error).

1. Begin with the equally weighted portfolio analyzed in Chapter 10. Establish the portfolio returns for the stocks in the portfolio using a formula that depends on the portfolio weights. Initially, these weights will all equal 1/12. You would like to allow the portfolio weights to vary, so you will need to list the weights for each stock in separate cells and establish another cell that sums the weights of the stocks. The portfolio returns for each month *must* reference these weights for Excel Solver to be useful.
2. Compute the values for the monthly mean return and standard deviation of the portfolio. Convert these values to annual numbers (as you did in Chapter 10) for easier interpretation.
3. Compute the efficient frontier when short sales are not allowed. Use the Solver tool in Excel (on the Data tab in the analysis section).* To set the Solver parameters:
   a. Set the target cell as the cell of interest, making it the cell that computes the (annual) portfolio standard deviation. Minimize this value.
   b. Establish the "By Changing Cells" by holding the Control key and clicking in each of the 12 cells containing the weights of each stock.
   c. Add constraints by clicking the Add button next to the "Subject to the Constraints" box. One set of constraints will be the weight of each stock that is greater than or equal to zero. Calculate the constraints individually. A second constraint is that the weights will sum to one.
   d. Compute the portfolio with the lowest standard deviation. If the parameters are set correctly, you should get a solution when you click "Solve." If there is an error, you will need to double-check the parameters, especially the constraints.

---

*If the Solver tool is not available, you must load it into Excel as follows:

1. On the File Tab, click Excel Options.
2. Click Add-Ins, and then, in the Manage box, select Excel Add-ins.
3. Click Go.
4. In the Add-Ins available box, select the Solver Add-in check box, and then click OK.
   Tip: If Solver Add-in is not listed in the Add-Ins available box, click Browse to locate the add-in. If you are prompted that the Solver Add-in is not currently installed on your computer, click Yes to install it.
5. After you load the Solver Add-in, the Solver command is available in the Analysis group on the Data tab.

4. Next, compute portfolios that have the lowest standard deviation for a target level of the expected return.
   a. Start by finding the portfolio with an expected return 2% higher than that of the minimum variance portfolio. To do this, add a constraint that the (annual) portfolio return equals this target level. Click "Solve" and record the standard deviation and mean return of the solution (and be sure the mean return equals target—if not, check your constraint).
   b. Repeat Step (a) raising the target return in 2% increments, recording the result for each step. Continue to increase the target return and record the result until Solver can no longer find a solution.
   c. At what level does Solver fail to find a solution? Why?

5. Plot the efficient frontier with the constraint of no short sales. To do this, create an XY Scatter Plot (similar to what you did in Chapter 10), with portfolio standard deviation on the *x*-axis and the return on the *y*-axis, using the data for the minimum variance portfolio and the portfolios you computed in Step 4. How do these portfolios compare to the mean and standard deviation for the equally weighted portfolio analyzed in Chapter 10?

6. Redo your analysis to allow for short sales by removing the constraint that each portfolio weight is greater than or equal to zero. Use Solver to calculate the (annual) portfolio standard deviation for the minimum variance portfolio, and when the annual portfolio returns are set to 0.05, 0.1, 0.2, 0.3, and 0.4. Plot the unconstrained efficient frontier on an XY Scatter Plot. How does allowing short sales affect the frontier?

7. Redo your analysis adding a new risk-free security that has a return of 0.5% (0.005) each month. Include a weight for this security when calculating the monthly portfolio returns. That is, there will now be 13 weights, one for each of the 12 stocks and one for the risk-free security. Again, these weights must sum to 1. Allow for short sales, and use Solver to calculate the (annual) portfolio standard deviation when the annual portfolio returns are set to 0.05, 0.1, 0.2, 0.3, and 0.4. Plot the results on the same XY Scatter Plot, and in addition keep track of the portfolio weights of the optimal portfolio. What do you notice about the relative weights of the different stocks in the portfolio as you change the target return? Can you identify the tangent portfolio?

Note: Updates to this data case may be found at www.berkdemarzo.com.

CHAPTER 11 APPENDIX

The CAPM with Differing Interest Rates

In this chapter, we assumed that investors faced the same risk-free interest rate whether they were saving or borrowing. In practice, investors receive a lower rate when they save than they must pay when they borrow. For example, short-term margin loans from a broker are often 1–2% higher than the rates paid on short-term Treasury securities. Banks, pension funds, and other investors with large amounts of collateral can borrow at rates that are generally within 1% of the rate on risk-free securities, but there is still a difference. Do these differences in interest rates affect the conclusions of the CAPM?

The Efficient Frontier with Differing Saving and Borrowing Rates

Figure 11A.1 plots the risk and return possibilities when the saving and borrowing rates differ. In this graph, $r_S = 3\%$ is the rate earned on risk-free savings or lending, and $r_B = 6\%$ is the rate paid on borrowing. Each rate is associated with a different tangent portfolio, labeled T_S and T_B, respectively. A conservative investor who desires a low-risk portfolio can combine the portfolio T_S with saving at rate r_S to achieve risk and return combinations along the lower green line. An aggressive investor who desires high expected returns can invest in the portfolio T_B, using some amount of borrowed funds at rate r_B. By adjusting the amount of borrowing, the investor can achieve risk and return combinations on the upper green line. The combinations on the upper line are not as desirable as the combinations that would result if the investor could borrow at rate r_S, but the investor is unable to borrow at the lower rate. Finally, investors with intermediate preferences may choose portfolios on the portion of the red curve between T_S and T_B, which do not involve borrowing or lending.

Thus, if borrowing and lending rates differ, investors with different preferences will choose different portfolios of risky securities. Any portfolio on the curve from T_S to T_B might be chosen. So, the first conclusion of the CAPM—that the market portfolio is the unique efficient portfolio of risky investments—is no longer valid.

The Security Market Line with Differing Interest Rates

The more important conclusion of the CAPM for corporate finance is the security market line, which relates the risk of an investment to its required return. It turns out that the SML is still valid when interest rates differ. To see why, we make use of the following result:

> *A combination of portfolios on the efficient frontier of risky investments is also on the efficient frontier of risky investments.*[12]

Because all investors hold portfolios on the efficient frontier between T_S and T_B, and because all investors collectively hold the market portfolio, the market portfolio must lie

[12] To understand this result intuitively, note that portfolios on the efficient frontier contain no diversifiable risk (otherwise we could reduce risk further without lowering the expected return). But a combination of portfolios that contain no diversifiable risk also contains no diversifiable risk, so it is also efficient.

FIGURE 11A.1

The CAPM with Different Saving and Borrowing Rates

Investors who save at rate r_S will invest in portfolio T_S, and investors who borrow at rate r_B will invest in portfolio T_B. Some investors may neither save nor borrow and invest in a portfolio on the efficient frontier between T_S and T_B. Because all investors choose portfolios on the efficient frontier from T_S to T_B, the market portfolio is on the efficient frontier between them. The dotted tangent line through the market portfolio determines the interest rate r^* that can be used in the SML.

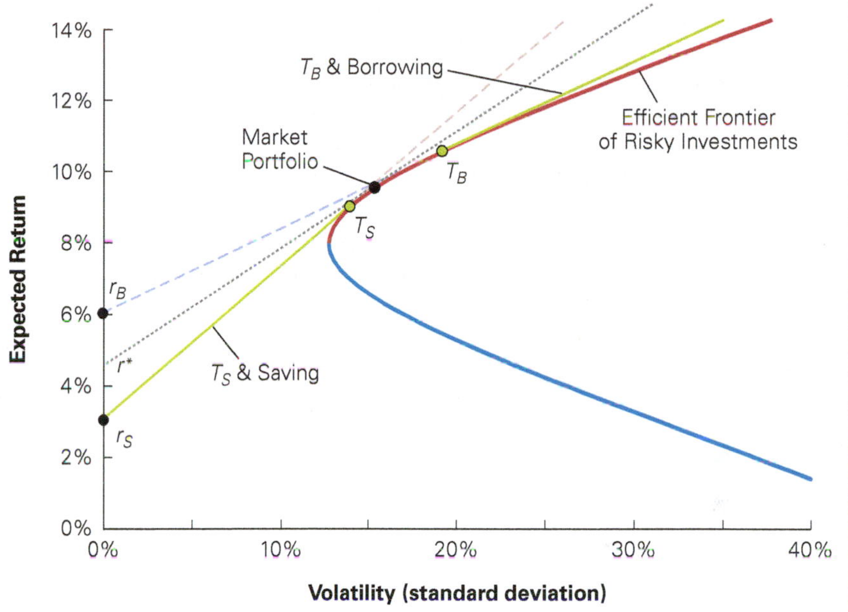

on the frontier between T_S and T_B. As a result, the market portfolio will be tangent for some risk-free interest rate r^* between r_S and r_B, as illustrated by the dotted line in Figure 11A.1. Because our determination of the security market line depends only on the market portfolio being tangent for some interest rate, the SML still holds in the following form:

$$E[R_i] = r^* + \beta_i \times (E[R_{Mkt}] - r^*) \tag{11A.1}$$

That is, the SML holds with some rate r^* between r_S and r_B in place of r_f. The rate r^* depends on the proportion of savers and borrowers in the economy. But even without knowing those proportions, because saving and borrowing rates tend to be close to each other, r^* must be in a narrow range and we can use Eq. 11A.1 to provide reasonable estimates of expected returns.[13]

We can make a similar argument regarding the choice of which risk-free rate to use. As discussed in Chapter 6, the risk-free rate varies with the investment horizon according to the yield curve. When an investor chooses her optimal portfolio, she will do so by finding the tangent line using the risk-free rate that corresponds to her investment horizon. If all investors have the same horizon, then the risk-free rate corresponding to that horizon will determine the SML. If investors have different horizons (but still have homogeneous expectations), then Eq. 11A.1 will hold for some r^* on the current yield curve, with the rate depending on the proportion of investors with each investment horizon.[14]

[13]This result was shown by M. Brennan, "Capital Market Equilibrium with Divergent Borrowing and Lending Rates," *Journal of Financial and Quantitative Analysis* 6 (1971): 1197–1205.

[14]We can generalize the arguments in this section further to settings in which there is no risk-free asset; see Fischer Black, "Capital Market Equilibrium with Restricted Borrowing," *Journal of Business* 45 (1972): 444–455, and Mark Rubinstein, "The Fundamental Theorem of Parameter-Preference Security Valuation," *Journal of Financial and Quantitative Analysis* 1 (1973): 61–69.

CHAPTER

12

Estimating the Cost of Capital

EVALUATING INVESTMENT OPPORTUNITIES REQUIRES FINANCIAL managers to estimate the cost of capital. For example, when executives at Intel Corporation evaluate a capital investment project, they must estimate the appropriate cost of capital for the project in order to determine its NPV. The cost of capital should include a risk premium that compensates Intel's investors for taking on the risk of the new project. How can Intel estimate this risk premium and, therefore, the cost of capital?

In the last two chapters, we have developed a method to answer this question—the Capital Asset Pricing Model. In this chapter, we will apply this knowledge to compute the cost of capital for an investment opportunity. We begin the chapter by focusing on an investment in the firm's stock. We show how to estimate the firm's equity cost of capital, including the practical details of identifying the market portfolio and estimating equity betas. Next, we develop methods to estimate the firm's debt cost of capital, based either on its yield or on its beta. We then consider investing in a new project, and show how to estimate a project's cost of capital based on the unlevered cost of capital of comparable firms. Finally, we introduce the concept of the weighted-average cost of capital as a tool for evaluating levered projects and investments.

NOTATION

r_i	required return for security i
$E[R_i]$	expected return of security i
r_f	risk-free interest rate
r_{wacc}	weighted-average cost of capital
β_i	beta of investment i with respect to the market portfolio
MV_i	total market capitalization of security i
E	Value of Equity
D	Value of Debt
α_i	alpha of security i
τ_C	corporate tax rate
β_U	unlevered or asset beta
β_E	equity beta
β_D	debt beta
r_E	equity cost of capital
r_D	debt cost of capital
r_u	unlevered cost of capital

12.1 The Equity Cost of Capital

Recall that the cost of capital is the best expected return available in the market on investments with *similar* risk. The Capital Asset Pricing Model (CAPM) provides a practical way to identify an investment with similar risk. Under the CAPM, the market portfolio is a well-diversified, efficient portfolio representing the non-diversifiable risk in the economy. Therefore, investments have similar risk if they have the same sensitivity to market risk, as measured by their beta with the market portfolio.

So, the cost of capital of any investment opportunity equals the expected return of available investments with the same beta. This estimate is provided by the Security Market Line equation of the CAPM, which states that, given the beta, β_i, of the investment opportunity, its cost of capital is:

The CAPM Equation for the Cost of Capital (Security Market Line)

$$r_i = r_f + \underbrace{\beta_i \times (E[R_{Mkt}] - r_f)}_{\text{Risk premium for security } i} \tag{12.1}$$

In other words, investors will require a risk premium comparable to what they would earn taking the same market risk through an investment in the market portfolio.

As our first application of the CAPM, consider an investment in the firm's stock. As we demonstrated in Chapter 9, to value a share of stock, we need to calculate the equity cost of capital. We can do so using Eq. 12.1 if we know the beta of the firm's stock.

EXAMPLE 12.1 Computing the Equity Cost of Capital

Problem

Suppose you estimate that Disney's stock (DIS) has a volatility of 20% and a beta of 1.25. A similar process for Chipotle (CMG) yields a volatility of 30% and a beta of 0.55. Which stock carries more total risk? Which has more market risk? If the risk-free interest rate is 3% and you estimate the market's expected return to be 8%, calculate the equity cost of capital for Disney and Chipotle. Which company has a higher cost of equity capital?

Solution

Total risk is measured by volatility; therefore, Chipotle stock has more total risk than Disney. Systematic risk is measured by beta. Disney has a higher beta, so it has more market risk than Chipotle.

Given Disney's estimated beta of 1.25, we expect the price for Disney's stock to move by 1.25% for every 1% move of the market. Therefore, Disney's risk premium will be 1.25 times the risk premium of the market, and Disney's equity cost of capital (from Eq. 12.1) is

$$r_{DIS} = 3\% + 1.25 \times (8\% - 3\%) = 3\% + 6.25\% = 9.25\%$$

Chipotle has a lower beta of 0.55. The equity cost of capital for Chipotle is

$$r_{CMG} = 3\% + 0.55 \times (8\% - 3\%) = 3\% + 2.75\% = 5.75\%$$

Because market risk cannot be diversified, it is market risk that determines the cost of capital; thus Disney has a higher cost of equity capital than Chipotle, even though it is less volatile.

While the calculations in Example 12.1 are straightforward, to implement them we need a number of key inputs. In particular, we must do the following:

- Construct the market portfolio, and determine its expected excess return over the risk-free interest rate
- Estimate the stock's beta, or sensitivity to the market portfolio

We explain how to estimate these inputs in more detail in the next two sections.

CONCEPT CHECK

1. According to the CAPM, we can determine the cost of capital of an investment by comparing it to what portfolio?
2. What inputs do we need to estimate a firm's equity cost of capital using the CAPM?

12.2 The Market Portfolio

To apply the CAPM, we must identify the market portfolio. In this section we examine how the market portfolio is constructed, common proxies that are used to represent the market portfolio, and how we can estimate the market risk premium.

Constructing the Market Portfolio

Because the market portfolio is the total supply of securities, the proportions of each security should correspond to the proportion of the total market that each security represents. Thus, the market portfolio contains more of the largest stocks and less of the smallest stocks. Specifically, the investment in each security *i* is proportional to its market capitalization, which is the total market value of its outstanding shares:

$$MV_i = (\text{Number of Shares of } i \text{ Outstanding}) \times (\text{Price of } i \text{ per Share}) \quad (12.2)$$

We then calculate the portfolio weights of each security as follows:

$$x_i = \frac{\text{Market Value of } i}{\text{Total Market Value of All Securities in the Portfolio}} = \frac{MV_i}{\sum_j MV_j} \quad (12.3)$$

A portfolio like the market portfolio, in which each security is held in proportion to its market capitalization, is called a **value-weighted portfolio**. A value-weighted portfolio is also an **equal-ownership portfolio**: We hold an equal fraction of the total number of shares outstanding of each security in the portfolio. This last observation implies that even when market prices change, to maintain a value-weighted portfolio, we do not need to trade unless the number of shares outstanding of some security changes. Because very little trading is required to maintain it, a value-weighted portfolio is also a **passive portfolio**.

Market Indexes

If we focus our attention on U.S. stocks, then rather than construct the market portfolio ourselves, we can make use of several popular market indexes that try to represent the performance of the U.S. stock market.

Examples of Market Indexes. A **market index** reports the value of a particular portfolio of securities. The S&P 500 is an index that represents a value-weighted portfolio of 500 of the largest U.S. stocks.[1] The S&P 500 was the first widely publicized value-weighted index and is the standard portfolio used to represent "the market portfolio" when using the

[1] Standard and Poor's periodically replaces stocks in the index (on average about 20–25 per year). While size is one criterion, S&P tries to maintain appropriate representation of different sectors of the economy and chooses firms that are leaders in their industries. Also, starting in 2005, the value weights in the index are based on the number of shares actually available for public trading, referred to as its **free float**.

Value-Weighted Portfolios and Rebalancing

Because they are passive, value-weighted portfolios are very efficient from a transaction cost perspective because there is no need to rebalance the portfolio weights in the face of price changes. To see why, consider the following example. Suppose we invest $50,000 in a value-weighted portfolio of General Electric, Home Depot, and Cisco, as shown below:

	Market Data				Our Portfolio	
Stock	**Stock Price**	**Shares Outstanding (billions)**	**Market Cap ($ billion)**	**Percent of Total**	**Initial Investment**	**Shares Purchased**
General Electric	$25.00	10.00	250	50%	$25,000	1000
Home Depot	$100.00	1.50	150	30%	$15,000	150
Cisco	$20.00	5.00	100	20%	$10,000	500
		Total	500	100%	$50,000	

Note that our investment in each stock is proportional to each stock's market capitalization. In addition, the number of shares purchased is proportional to each stock's outstanding shares.

Now suppose that the price of GE's stock increases to $30 per share and Home Depot's stock price drops to $80 per share. Let's compute the new value weights as well as the effect on our portfolio:

Stock	Stock Price	Shares Outstanding (billions)	Market Cap ($ billion)	Percent of Total	Shares Held	New Investment Value
General Electric	$30.00	10.00	300	57.7%	1000	$30,000
Home Depot	$80.00	1.50	120	23.1%	150	$12,000
Cisco	$20.00	5.00	100	19.2%	500	$10,000
		Total	520	100%		$52,000

Note that although the value weights have changed, the value of our investment in each stock has also changed and remains proportional to each stock's market cap. For example, our weight in GE's stock is $30,000/$52,000 = 57.7%, matching its market weight. Thus, there is no need to trade in response to price changes to maintain a value-weighted portfolio. Rebalancing is only required if firms issue or retire shares, or if the set of firms represented by the portfolio changes.

CAPM in practice. Even though the S&P 500 includes only 500 of the roughly 5000 publicly traded stocks in the U.S., because the S&P 500 includes the largest stocks, it represents almost 80% of the U.S. stock market in terms of market capitalization.

More recently created indexes, such as the Wilshire 5000, provide a value-weighted index of *all* U.S. stocks listed on the major stock exchanges.[2] While more complete than the S&P 500, and therefore more representative of the overall market, its returns are very similar; between 1990 and 2015, the correlation between their weekly returns was nearly 99%. Given this similarity, many investors view the S&P 500 as an adequate measure of overall U.S. stock market performance.

The most widely quoted U.S. stock index is the Dow Jones Industrial Average (DJIA), which consists of a portfolio of 30 large industrial stocks. While somewhat representative, the DJIA clearly does not represent the entire market. Also, the DJIA is a *price-weighted*

[2]The Wilshire 5000 began with approximately 5000 stocks when it was first published in 1974 but since then the number of stocks in the index has changed over time with U.S. equity markets. Similar indices are the Dow Jones U.S. Total Market Index and the S&P Total Market Index.

(rather than value-weighted) *portfolio*. A **price-weighted portfolio** holds an equal number of shares of each stock, independent of their size. Despite being nonrepresentative of the entire market, the DJIA remains widely cited because it is one of the oldest stock market indexes (first published in 1884).

Investing in a Market Index. In addition to capturing the performance of the U.S. market, the S&P 500 and the Wilshire 5000 are both easy to invest in. Many mutual fund companies offer funds, called **index funds**, that invest in these portfolios. In addition, *exchange-traded funds* represent these portfolios. An **exchange-traded fund (ETF)** is a security that trades directly on an exchange, like a stock, but represents ownership in a portfolio of stocks. For example, Standard and Poor's Depository Receipts (SPDR, nicknamed "spiders") trade on the American Stock Exchange (symbol SPY) and represent ownership in the S&P 500. Vanguard's Total Stock Market ETF (symbol VTI, nicknamed "viper") is based on the Wilshire 5000 index. By investing in an index or an exchange-traded fund, an individual investor with only a small amount to invest can easily achieve the benefits of broad diversification.

Although practitioners commonly use the S&P 500 as the market portfolio in the CAPM, no one does so because of a belief that this index is *actually* the market portfolio. Instead they view the index as a **market proxy**—a portfolio whose return they believe closely tracks the true market portfolio. Of course, how well the model works will depend on how closely the market proxy actually tracks the true market portfolio. We will return to this issue in Chapter 13.

The Market Risk Premium

Recall that a key ingredient to the CAPM is the market risk premium, which is the expected excess return of the market portfolio: $E[R_{Mkt}] - r_f$. The market risk premium provides the benchmark by which we assess investors' willingness to hold market risk. Before we can estimate it, we must first discuss the choice of the risk-free interest rate to use in the CAPM.

Determining the Risk-Free Rate. The risk-free interest rate in the CAPM model corresponds to the risk-free rate at which investors can both borrow and save. We generally determine the risk-free saving rate using the yields on U.S. Treasury securities. Most investors, however, must pay a substantially higher rate to borrow funds. In mid-2015, for example, even the highest credit quality borrowers had to pay almost 0.35% over U.S. Treasury rates on short-term loans. Even if a loan is essentially risk-free, this premium compensates lenders for the difference in liquidity compared with an investment in Treasuries. As a result, practitioners sometimes use rates from the highest quality corporate bonds in place of Treasury rates in Eq. 12.1.

While U.S. Treasuries are free from default risk, they are subject to interest rate risk unless we select a maturity equal to our investment horizon. Which horizon should we choose when selecting an interest rate from the yield curve? Again, we can extend the CAPM to allow for different investment horizons, and the risk-free rate we choose should correspond to the yield for an "average" horizon.[3] When surveyed, the vast majority of

[3]As explained in the Chapter 11 appendix, the precise rate to use depends on investors' horizons and their propensity to borrow or save. As there is no easy way to know these characteristics, judgment is required. Throughout this chapter, we'll try to make clear these gray areas and highlight common practices.

large firms and financial analysts report using the yields of long-term (10- to 30-year) bonds to determine the risk-free interest rate.[4]

The Historical Risk Premium. One approach to estimating the market risk premium, $E[R_{Mkt}] - r_f$, is to use the historical average excess return of the market over the risk-free interest rate.[5] With this approach, it is important to measure historical stock returns over the same time horizon as that used for the risk-free interest rate.

Because we are interested in the *future* market risk premium, we face a trade-off in selecting the amount of data we use. As we noted in Chapter 10, it takes many years of data to produce even moderately accurate estimates of expected returns. Yet very old data may have little relevance for investors' expectations of the market risk premium today.

Table 12.1 reports excess returns of the S&P 500 versus one-year and ten-year Treasury rates, based on data since 1926, as well as just the last 50 years. For each time period, note the lower risk premium when we compare the S&P 500 to longer-term Treasuries. This difference primarily arises because, historically, the yield curve has tended to be upward sloping, with long-term interest rates higher than short-term rates.

Table 12.1 also suggests that the market risk premium has declined over time, with the S&P 500 showing a significantly lower excess return over the past 50 years than over the full sample. There are several potential explanations for this decline. First, more investors participate in the stock market today, so that the risk can be shared more broadly. Second, financial innovations such as mutual funds and exchange-traded funds have greatly reduced the costs of diversifying. Third, except for the recent increase in the wake of the 2008 financial crisis, the overall volatility of the market has declined over time. All of these reasons may have reduced the risk of holding stocks, and so diminished the premium investors require. Most researchers and analysts believe that future expected returns for the market are likely to be closer to these more recent historical numbers, in a range of about 4–6% over Treasury bills (and 3–5% over longer term bonds).[6]

TABLE 12.1 **Historical Excess Returns of the S&P 500 Compared to One-Year and Ten-Year U.S. Treasury Securities**

	Period	
S&P 500 Excess Return Versus	1926–2015	1965–2015
One-year Treasury	7.7%	5.0%
Ten-year Treasury*	5.9%	3.9%

*Based on a comparison of compounded returns over a ten-year holding period.

[4]See Robert Bruner, et al., "Best Practices in Estimating the Cost of Capital: Survey and Synthesis," *Financial Practice and Education* 8 (1998): 13–28.

[5]Because we are forecasting the expected return, it is appropriate to use the arithmetic average. See Chapter 10.

[6]I. Welch, "Views of Financial Economists on the Equity Premium and on Professional Controversies," *Journal of Business* 73 (2000): 501–537 (with 2009 update), J. Graham and C. Harvey, "The Equity Risk Premium in 2008: Evidence from the Global CFO Outlook Survey," SSRN 2008, and Ivo Welch and Amit Goyal, "A Comprehensive Look at The Empirical Performance of Equity Premium Prediction," *Review of Financial Studies* 21 (2008): 1455–1508.

A Fundamental Approach. Using historical data to estimate the market risk premium suffers from two drawbacks. First, despite using 50 years (or more) of data, the standard errors of the estimates are large (e.g., even using data from 1926, the 95% confidence interval for the excess return is $\pm$ 4.3%). Second, because they are backward looking, we cannot be sure they are representative of current expectations.

As an alternative, we can take a fundamental approach toward estimating the market risk premium. Given an assessment of firms' future cash flows, we can estimate the expected return of the market by solving for the discount rate that is consistent with the current level of the index. For example, if we use the constant expected growth model presented in Chapter 9, the expected market return is equal to

$$r_{Mkt} = \frac{Div_1}{P_0} + g = \text{Dividend Yield} + \text{Expected Dividend Growth Rate} \qquad (12.4)$$

While this model is highly inaccurate for an individual firm, the assumption of constant expected growth is more reasonable when considering the overall market. If, for instance, the S&P 500 has a current dividend yield of 2%, and we assume that both earnings and dividends are expected to grow 6% per year, this model would estimate the expected return of the S&P 500 as 8%. Following such methods, researchers generally report estimates in the 3–5% range for the future equity risk premium.[7]

CONCEPT CHECK

1. How do you determine the weight of a stock in the market portfolio?
2. What is a market proxy?
3. How can you estimate the market risk premium?

12.3 Beta Estimation

Having identified a market proxy, the next step in implementing the CAPM is to determine the security's beta, which measures the sensitivity of the security's returns to those of the market. Because beta captures the market risk of a security, as opposed to its diversifiable risk, it is the appropriate measure of risk for a well-diversified investor.

Using Historical Returns

Ideally, we would like to know a stock's beta *in the future;* that is, how sensitive will its future returns be to market risk. In practice, we estimate beta based on the stock's historical sensitivity. This approach makes sense if a stock's beta remains relatively stable over time, which appears to be the case for most firms.

Many data sources provide estimates of beta based on historical data. Typically, these data sources estimate correlations and volatilities from two to five years of weekly or monthly returns and use the S&P 500 as the market portfolio. Table 10.6 on page 345 shows estimated betas for a number of large firms in different industries.

---

[7]See e.g., E. Fama and K. French, "The Equity Premium," *Journal of Finance* 57 (2002): 637–659; and J. Siegel, "The Long-Run Equity Risk Premium," CFA Institute Conference Proceedings *Points of Inflection: New Directions for Portfolio Management* (2004). Similarly, L. Pástor, M. Sinha, and B. Swaminathan report a 2–4% implied risk premium over 10-year Treasuries ["Estimating the Intertemporal Risk-Return Tradeoff Using the Implied Cost of Capital," *Journal of Finance* 63 (2008): 2859–2897].

As we discussed in Chapter 10, the differences in betas reflect the sensitivity of each firm's profits to the general health of the economy. For example, Apple, Autodesk, and other technology stocks have high betas (well over 1) because demand for their products usually varies with the business cycle: Companies and consumers tend to invest in technology when times are good, but they cut back on these expenditures when the economy slows. In contrast, the demand for personal and household products has very little relation to the state of the economy. Firms producing these goods, such as Procter & Gamble, tend to have very low betas (near 0.5).

Let's look at Cisco Systems stock as an example. Figure 12.1 shows the monthly returns for Cisco and the monthly returns for the S&P 500 from the beginning of 2000 to 2015. Note the overall tendency for Cisco to have a high return when the market is up and a low return when the market is down. Indeed, Cisco tends to move in the same direction as the market, but with greater amplitude. The pattern suggests that Cisco's beta is larger than 1.

Rather than plot the returns over time, we can see Cisco's sensitivity to the market even more clearly by plotting Cisco's excess return as a function of the S&P 500 excess return, as shown in Figure 12.2. Each point in this figure represents the excess return of Cisco and the S&P 500 from one of the months in Figure 12.1. For example, in November 2002, Cisco was up 33.4% and the S&P 500 was up 6.1% (while risk-free Treasuries returned only 0.12%). Once we have plotted each month in this way, we can then plot the best-fitting line drawn through these points.[8]

FIGURE 12.1 **Monthly Returns for Cisco Stock and for the S&P 500, 2000–2015**

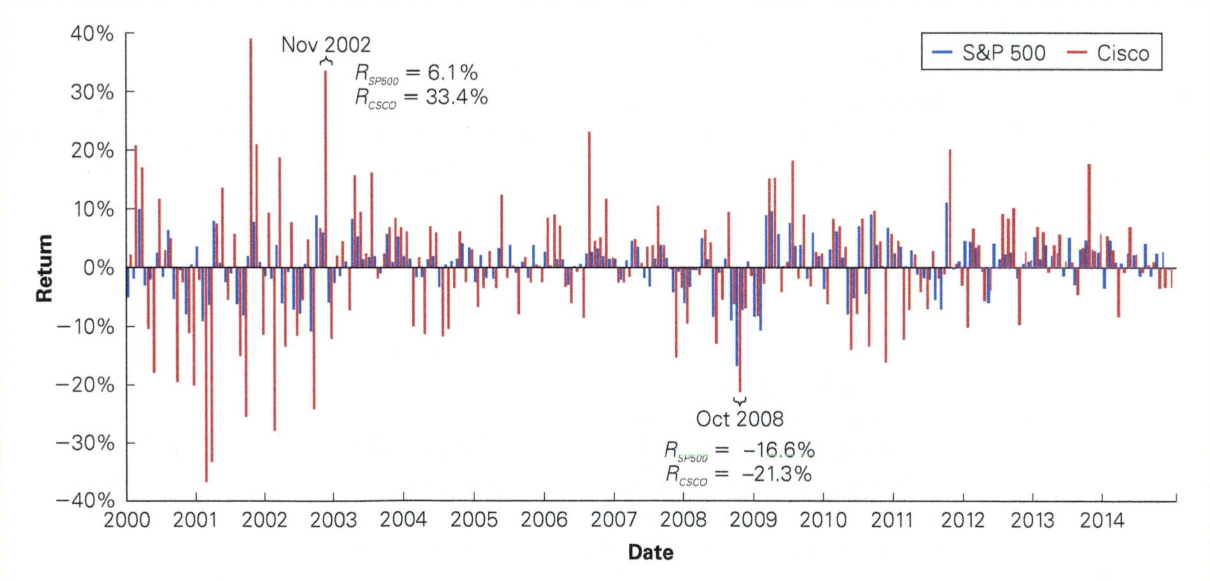

Cisco's returns tend to move in the same direction, but with greater amplitude, than those of the S&P 500.

[8]By "best fitting," we mean the line that minimizes the sum of the squared deviations from the line. In Excel, it can be found by adding a linear trendline to the chart.

Identifying the Best-Fitting Line

As the scatterplot makes clear, Cisco's returns have a positive covariance with the market: Cisco tends to be up when the market is up, and vice versa. Moreover, from the best-fitting line, we can see visually that a 10% change in the market's return corresponds to around a 15% change in Cisco's return. That is, Cisco's return moves near one and a half times that of the overall market, and Cisco's estimated beta is about 1.5. More generally,

Beta corresponds to the slope of the best-fitting line in the plot of the security's excess returns versus the market excess return.[9]

To understand this result fully, recall that beta measures the market risk of a security—the percentage change in the return of a security for a 1% change in the return of the market portfolio. The best-fitting line in Figure 12.2 captures the components of a security's return that we can explain based on market risk, so its slope is the security's beta. Note though, that in any individual month, the security's returns will be higher or lower than the best-fitting line. Such deviations from the best-fitting line result from risk that is not related to the market as a whole. These deviations are zero on average in the graph, as the points above the line balance out the points below the line. They represent firm-specific risk that is diversifiable and that averages out in a large portfolio.

FIGURE 12.2

Scatterplot of Monthly Excess Returns for Cisco Versus the S&P 500, 2000–2015

Beta corresponds to the slope of the best-fitting line. Beta measures the expected change in Cisco's excess return per 1% change in the market's excess return. Deviations from the best-fitting line correspond to diversifiable, non-market-related risk. In this case, Cisco's estimated beta is approximately 1.57.

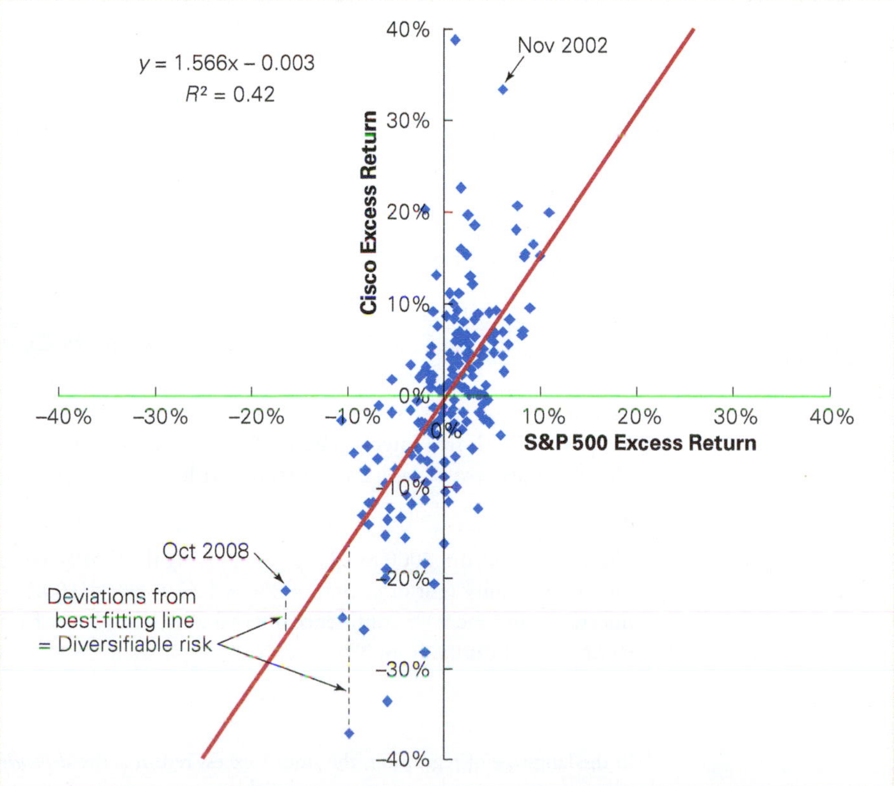

[9]The slope can be calculated using Excel's SLOPE() function, or by displaying the equation for the trendline on the chart (R^2 is the square of the correlation between the returns). See appendix for further details.

Using Linear Regression

The statistical technique that identifies the best-fitting line through a set of points is called **linear regression**. In Figure 12.2, linear regression corresponds to writing the excess return of a security as the sum of three components:[10]

$$(R_i - r_f) = \alpha_i + \beta_i\,(R_{Mkt} - r_f) + \varepsilon_i \tag{12.5}$$

The first term, α_i, is the constant or intercept term of the regression. The second term, $\beta_i(R_{Mkt} - r_f)$, represents the sensitivity of the stock to market risk. For example, if the market's return is 1% higher, there is a β_i% increase in the security's return. We refer to the last term, ε_i, as the **error (or residual) term**: It represents the deviation from the best-fitting line and is zero on average (or else we could improve the fit). This error term corresponds to the diversifiable risk of the stock, which is the risk that is unrelated to the market.

If we take expectations of both sides of Eq. 12.5 and rearrange the result, because the average error is zero (that is, $E[\varepsilon_i] = 0$), we get

$$E[R_i] = \underbrace{r_f + \beta_i(E[R_{Mkt}] - r_f)}_{\text{Expected return for } i \text{ from the SML}} + \underbrace{\alpha_i}_{\text{Distance above/below the SML}} \tag{12.6}$$

The constant α_i, referred to as the stock's **alpha**, measures the historical performance of the security relative to the expected return predicted by the security market line—it is the distance the stock's average return is above or below the SML. Thus, we can interpret α_i as a risk-adjusted measure of the stock's historical performance.[11] According to the CAPM, α_i should not be significantly different from zero.

Using Excel's regression data analysis tool for the monthly returns from 2000–2015, Cisco's estimated beta is 1.57, with a 95% confidence interval from 1.3 to 1.8. Assuming Cisco's sensitivity to market risk will remain stable over time, we would expect Cisco's beta to be in this range in the near future. With this estimate in hand, we are ready to estimate Cisco's equity cost of capital.

EXAMPLE 12.2 Using Regression Estimates to Estimate the Equity Cost of Capital

Problem

Suppose the risk-free interest rate is 3%, and the market risk premium is 5%. What range for Cisco's equity cost of capital is consistent with the 95% confidence interval for its beta?

Solution

Using the data from 2000 to 2015, and applying the CAPM equation, the estimated beta of 1.53 implies an equity cost of capital of 3% + 1.57 × 5% = 10.85% for Cisco. But our estimate is uncertain, and the 95% confidence interval for Cisco's beta of 1.3 to 1.8 gives a range for Cisco's equity cost of capital from 3% + 1.3 × 5% = 9.5% to 3% + 1.8 × 5% = 12%.

---

[10] In the language of regression, the stock's excess return is the *dependent (or y) variable*, and the market's excess return is the *independent (or x) variable.*

[11] When used in this way, α_i is often referred to as Jensen's alpha. It can be calculated using the INTERCEPT() function in Excel (see appendix). Using this regression as a test of the CAPM was introduced by F. Black, M. Jensen, and M. Scholes in "The Capital Asset Pricing Model: Some Empirical Tests." In M. Jensen, ed., *Studies in the Theory of Capital Markets* (Praeger, 1972).

Why Not Estimate Expected Returns Directly?

If the CAPM requires us to use historical data to estimate beta and determine a security's expected return (or an investment's cost of capital), why not just use the security's historical average return as an estimate for its expected return instead? This method would certainly be simpler and more direct.

As we saw in Chapter 10, however, it is extremely difficult to infer the average return of individual stocks from historical data. For example, consider Cisco's stock, which had an average annualized return of 3.3%, and a volatility of 37%, based on monthly data from 2000–2015. Given 15 years of data, the standard error of our estimate of the expected return is $37\%/\sqrt{15} = 9.6\%$, leading to a 95% confidence interval of 3.3% $\pm$ 19%! Even with 100 years of data, the confidence bounds would be $\pm$ 7.4%. Of course, Cisco has not existed for 100 years, and even if it had, the firm today would bear little resemblance today to what it was like 100 years ago.

At the same time, using the methods described in this section, we can infer beta from historical data reasonably accurately even with as little as two years of data. In theory at least, the CAPM can provide much more accurate estimates of expected returns for stocks than we could obtain from their historical average return.

The estimate of Cisco's alpha from the regression is −0.33%. In other words, given its beta, Cisco's average monthly return was 0.33% lower than required by the security market line. The standard error of the alpha estimate is about 0.6%, however, so that statistically the estimate is not significantly different from zero. Alphas, like expected returns, are difficult to estimate with much accuracy without a very long data series. Moreover, the alphas for individual stocks have very little persistence.[12] Thus, although Cisco's return underperformed its required return over this time period, it may not necessarily continue to do so.

In this section we have provided an overview of the main methodology for estimating a security's market risk. In the appendix to this chapter, we discuss some additional practical considerations and common techniques for forecasting beta.

CONCEPT CHECK

1. How can you estimate a stock's beta from historical returns?
2. How do we define a stock's alpha, and what is its interpretation?

12.4 The Debt Cost of Capital

In the preceding sections, we have shown how to use the CAPM to estimate the cost of capital of a firm's equity. What about a firm's debt—what expected return is required by a firm's creditors? In this section, we'll consider some of the main methods for estimating a firm's **debt cost of capital**, the cost of capital that a firm must pay on its debt. In addition to being useful information for the firm and its investors, we will see in the next section that knowing the debt cost of capital will be helpful when estimating the cost of capital of a project.

Debt Yields Versus Returns

Recall from Chapter 6 that the yield to maturity of a bond is the IRR an investor will earn from holding the bond to maturity and receiving its promised payments. Therefore, if there is little risk the firm will default, we can use the bond's yield to maturity as an estimate of investors' expected return. If there is a significant risk that the firm will default on its obligation, however, the yield to maturity of the firm's debt, which is its promised return, will overstate investors' expected return.

[12] Indeed, over the period 1996–2000, Cisco's return had an alpha of 3% per month, significantly outperforming its required return, but as we have seen this positive alpha did not forecast superior future returns.

COMMON MISTAKE Using the Debt Yield as Its Cost of Capital

While firms often use the yield on their debt to estimate their debt cost of capital, this approximation is reasonable only if the debt is very safe. Otherwise, as we explained in Chapter 6, the debt's yield—which is based on its promised payments—will overstate the true expected return from holding the bond once default risk is taken into account.

Consider, for example, that in mid-2009 long-term bonds issued by AMR Corp. (parent company of American Airlines) had a yield to maturity exceeding 20%. Because these bonds were very risky, with a CCC rating, their yield greatly overstated their expected return given AMR's significant default risk. Indeed, with risk-free rates of 3% and a market risk premium of 5%, an expected return of 20% would imply a *debt* beta greater than 3 for AMR, which is unreasonably high, and higher even than the equity betas of many firms in the industry.

Again, the problem is the yield is computed using the promised debt payments, which in this case were quite different from the actual payments investors were expecting: When AMR filed for bankruptcy in 2011, bondholders lost close to 80% of what they were owed. The methods described in this section can provide a much better estimate of a firm's debt cost of capital in cases like AMR's when the likelihood of default is significant.

To understand the relationship between a debt's yield and its expected return, consider a one-year bond with a yield to maturity of y. Thus, for each \$1 invested in the bond today, the bond promises to pay $\$(1 + y)$ in one year. Suppose, however, the bond will default with probability p, in which case bond holders will receive only $\$(1 + y - L)$, where L represents the expected loss per \$1 of debt in the event of default. Then the expected return of the bond is[13]

$$r_d = (1 - p)y + p(y - L) = y - pL$$

$$= \text{Yield to Maturity} - \text{Prob(default)} \times \text{Expected Loss Rate} \tag{12.7}$$

The importance of these adjustments will naturally depend on the riskiness of the bond, with lower-rated (and higher-yielding) bonds having a greater risk of default. Table 12.2 shows average annual default rates by debt rating, as well as the peak default rates experienced during recessionary periods. To get a sense of the impact on the expected return to debt holders, note that the average loss rate for unsecured debt is about 60%. Thus, for a B-rated bond, during average times the expected return to debt holders would be approximately $0.055 \times 0.60 = 3.3\%$ below the bond's quoted yield. On the other hand, outside of recessionary periods, given its negligible default rate the yield on an AA-rated bond provides a reasonable estimate of its expected return.

TABLE 12.2 Annual Default Rates by Debt Rating (1983–2011)*

Rating:	AAA	AA	A	BBB	BB	B	CCC	CC-C
Default Rate:								
Average	0.0%	0.1%	0.2%	0.5%	2.2%	5.5%	12.2%	14.1%
In Recessions	0.0%	1.0%	3.0%	3.0%	8.0%	16.0%	48.0%	79.0%

Source: "Corporate Defaults and Recovery Rates, 1920–2011," *Moody's Global Credit Policy*, February 2012.

*Average rates are annualized based on a 10-year holding period; recession estimates are based on peak annual rates.

[13] While we derived this equation for a one-year bond, the same formula holds for a multi-year bond assuming a constant yield to maturity, default rate, and loss rate. We can also express the loss in default according to the bond's recovery rate R: $(1 + y - L) = (1 + y)R$, or $L = (1 + y)(1 - R)$.

Debt Betas

Alternatively, we can estimate the debt cost of capital using the CAPM. In principle it would be possible to estimate debt betas using their historical returns in the same way that we estimated equity betas. However, because bank loans and many corporate bonds are traded infrequently if at all, as a practical matter we can rarely obtain reliable data for the returns of individual debt securities. Thus, we need another means of estimating debt betas. We will develop a method for estimating debt betas for an individual firm using stock price data in Chapter 21. We can also approximate beta using estimates of betas of bond indices by rating category, as shown in Table 12.3. As the table indicates, debt betas tend to be low, though they can be significantly higher for risky debt with a low credit rating and a long maturity.

TABLE 12.3 Average Debt Betas by Rating and Maturity*

By Rating	*A and above*	*BBB*	*BB*	*B*	*CCC*
Avg. Beta	< 0.05	0.10	0.17	0.26	0.31
By Maturity	(BBB and above)	*1–5 Year*	*5–10 Year*	*10–15 Year*	> 15 *Year*
Avg. Beta		0.01	0.06	0.07	0.14

Source: S. Schaefer and I. Strebulaev, "Risk in Capital Structure Arbitrage," Stanford GSB working paper, 2009.

*Note that these are average debt betas across industries. We would expect debt betas to be lower (higher) for industries that are less (more) exposed to market risk. One simple way to approximate this difference is to scale the debt betas in Table 12.3 by the relative asset beta for the industry (see Figure 12.4 on page 425).

EXAMPLE 12.3 Estimating the Debt Cost of Capital

Problem

In mid-2015, homebuilder KB Home had outstanding 6-year bonds with a yield to maturity of 6% and a B rating. If corresponding risk-free rates were 1%, and the market risk premium is 5%, estimate the expected return of KB Home's debt.

Solution

Given the low rating of debt, we know the yield to maturity of KB Home's debt is likely to significantly overstate its expected return. Using the average estimates in Table 12.2 and an expected loss rate of 60%, from Eq. 12.7 we have

$$r_d = 6\% - 5.5\%(0.60) = 2.7\%$$

Alternatively, we can estimate the bond's expected return using the CAPM and an estimated beta of 0.26 from Table 12.3. In that case,

$$r_d = 1\% + 0.26(5\%) = 2.3\%$$

While both estimates are rough approximations, they both confirm that the expected return of KB Home's debt is well below its promised yield.

Note that both of the methods discussed in this section are approximations; more specific information about the firm and its default risk could obviously improve them. Also, we have focused on the debt cost of capital from the perspective of an outside investor. The effective cost of debt to the firm can be lower once the tax deductibility of interest payments is considered. We will return to this issue in Section 12.6.

CONCEPT CHECK

1. Why does the yield to maturity of a firm's debt generally overestimate its debt cost of capital?
2. Describe two methods that can be used to estimate a firm's debt cost of capital.

12.5 A Project's Cost of Capital

In Chapter 8, we explained how to decide whether or not to undertake a project. Although the project's cost of capital is required to make this decision, we indicated then that we would explain later how to estimate it. We are now ready to fulfill this promise. As we did in Chapter 8, we will assume the project will be evaluated on its own, separate from any financing decisions. Thus, we will assume that the project will be purely equity financed (there will be no debt used to finance it) and consider project financing in Section 12.6.

In the case of a firm's equity or debt, we estimate the cost of capital based on the historical risks of these securities. Because a new project is not itself a publicly traded security, this approach is not possible. Instead, the most common method for estimating a project's beta is to identify comparable firms in the same line of business as the project we are considering undertaking. Indeed, the firm undertaking the project will often be one such comparable firm (and sometimes the only one). Then, if we can estimate the cost of capital of the assets of comparable firms, we can use that estimate as a proxy for the project's cost of capital.

All-Equity Comparables

The simplest setting is one in which we can find an all-equity financed firm (i.e., a firm with no debt) in a single line of business that is comparable to the project. Because the firm is all equity, holding the firm's stock is equivalent to owning the portfolio of its underlying assets. Thus, if the firm's average investment has similar market risk to our project, then we can use the comparable firm's equity beta and cost of capital as estimates for beta and the cost of capital of the project.

EXAMPLE 12.4 **Estimating the Beta of a Project from a Single-Product Firm**

Problem

You have just graduated with an MBA, and decide to pursue your dream of starting a line of women's designer clothes and accessories. You are working on your business plan, and have decided that Michael Kors is the kind of company you would like to build. To develop your financial plan, estimate the cost of capital of this opportunity assuming a risk-free rate of 3% and a market risk premium of 5%.

Solution

Checking Google: Finance, we find that Michael Kors Holdings Limited (KORS) has almost no debt, and an estimated beta of 1.13. Using KORS's beta as the estimate of the project beta, we can apply Eq. 12.1 to estimate the cost of capital of this investment opportunity as

$$r_{project} = r_f + \beta_{KORS}\,(E[R_{Mkt}] - r) = 3\% + 1.13 \times 5\% = 8.65\%$$

Thus, assuming your business has a similar sensitivity to market risk as KORS, you can estimate the appropriate cost of capital as 8.65%. In other words, rather than investing in the new business, you could invest in the fashion industry simply by buying KORS stock. Given this alternative, to be attractive, the new investment must have an expected return at least equal to that of KORS, which from the CAPM is 8.65%.

Levered Firms as Comparables

The situation is a bit more complicated if the comparable firm has debt. In that case, the cash flows generated by the firm's assets are used to pay both debt and equity holders. As a result, the returns of the firm's equity alone are not representative of the underlying assets; in fact, because of the firm's leverage, the equity will often be much riskier. Thus, the beta of a levered firm's equity will not be a good estimate of the beta of its assets and of our project.

How can we estimate the beta of the comparable firm's assets in this case? As shown in Figure 12.3 we can recreate a claim on the firm's assets by holding *both* its debt and equity simultaneously. Because the firm's cash flows will either be used to pay debt or equity holders, by holding both securities we are entitled to all of the cash flows generated by the firm's assets. The return of the firm's assets is therefore the same as the return of a portfolio of the firm's debt and equity combined. For the same reason, the beta of the firm's assets will match the beta of this portfolio.

The Unlevered Cost of Capital

As we saw in Chapter 11, the expected return of a portfolio is equal to the weighted average of the expected returns of the securities in the portfolio, where the weights correspond to the relative market values of the different securities held. Thus, a firm's **asset cost of capital** or **unlevered cost of capital**, which is the expected return required by the firm's investors to hold the firm's underlying assets, is the weighted average of the firm's equity and debt costs of capital:

$$\begin{matrix}\text{Asset or Unlevered}\\ \text{Cost of Capital}\end{matrix} = \begin{pmatrix}\text{Fraction of Firm Value}\\ \text{Financed by Equity}\end{pmatrix}\begin{pmatrix}\text{Equity Cost}\\ \text{of Capital}\end{pmatrix} + \begin{pmatrix}\text{Fraction of Firm Value}\\ \text{Financed by Debt}\end{pmatrix}\begin{pmatrix}\text{Debt Cost}\\ \text{of Capital}\end{pmatrix}$$

FIGURE 12.3 **Using a Levered Firm as a Comparable for a Project's Risk**

If we identify a levered firm whose assets have comparable market risk to our project, then we can estimate the project's cost of capital based on a portfolio of the firm's debt and equity.

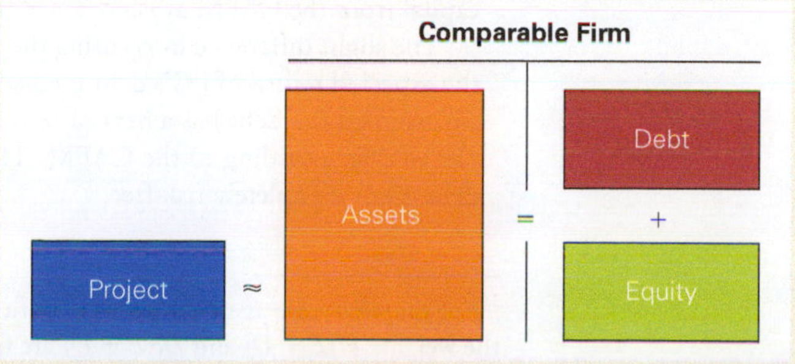

Writing this out, if we let E and D be the total market value of equity and debt of the comparable firm, with equity and debt costs of capital r_E and r_D, then we can estimate a firm's asset or unlevered cost of capital r_U as follows:[14]

Asset or Unlevered Cost of Capital

$$r_U = \frac{E}{E+D} r_E + \frac{D}{E+D} r_D \tag{12.8}$$

Unlevered Beta. Because the beta of a portfolio is the weighted-average of the betas of the securities in the portfolio, we have a similar expression for the firm's **asset or unlevered beta**, which we can use to estimate the beta of our project:

Asset or Unlevered Beta

$$\beta_U = \frac{E}{E+D} \beta_E + \frac{D}{E+D} \beta_D \tag{12.9}$$

Let's apply these formulas in an example.

EXAMPLE 12.5 Unlevering the Cost of Capital

Problem

Your firm is considering expanding its household products division. You identify Procter & Gamble (PG) as a firm with comparable investments. Suppose PG's equity has a market capitalization of \$144 billion and a beta of 0.57. PG also has \$37 billion of AA-rated debt outstanding, with an average yield of 3.1%. Estimate the cost of capital of your firm's investment given a risk-free rate of 3% and a market risk-premium of 5%.

Solution

Because investing in this division is like investing in PG's assets by holding its debt and equity, we can estimate our cost of capital based on PG's unlevered cost of capital. First, we estimate PG's equity cost of capital using the CAPM as $r_E = 3\% + 0.57(5\%) = 5.85\%$. Because PG's debt is highly rated, we approximate its debt cost of capital using the debt yield of 3.1%. Thus, PG's unlevered cost of capital is

$$r_U = \frac{144}{144+37} 5.85\% + \frac{37}{144+37} 3.1\% = 5.29\%$$

Alternatively, we can estimate PG's unlevered beta. Given its high rating, if we assume PG's debt beta is zero we have

$$\beta_U = \frac{144}{144+37} 0.57 + \frac{37}{144+37} 0 = 0.453$$

Taking this result as an estimate of the beta of our project, we can compute our project's cost of capital from the CAPM as $r_U = 3\% + 0.453(5\%) = 5.27\%$.

The slight difference in r_U using the two methods arises because in the first case, we assumed the expected return of PG's debt is equal to its promised yield of 3.1%, while in the second case, we assumed the debt has a beta of zero, which implies an expected return equal to the risk-free rate of 3% according to the CAPM. The truth is somewhere between the two results, as PG's debt is not completely risk-free.

[14] For simplicity, we assume here that the firm in question maintains a constant debt-equity ratio, so that the weights $E/(E+D)$ and $D/(E+D)$ are fixed. As a result, Eq. 12.8 and Eq. 12.9 hold *even in the presence of taxes*. See Chapter 18 for details and an analysis of settings with a changing leverage ratio.

Cash and Net Debt. Sometimes firms maintain large cash balances in excess of their operating needs. This cash represents a risk-free asset on the firm's balance sheet, and reduces the average risk of the firm's assets. Often, we are interested in the risk of the firm's underlying business operations, separate from its cash holdings. That is, we are interested in the risk of the firm's *enterprise value*, which we defined in Chapter 2 as the combined market value of the firm's equity and debt, less any excess cash. In that case, we can measure the leverage of the firm in terms of its **net debt**:

$$\text{Net Debt} = \text{Debt} - \text{Excess Cash and Short-Term Investments} \quad (12.10)$$

The intuition for using net debt is that if the firm holds \$1 in cash and \$1 in risk-free debt, then the interest earned on the cash will equal the interest paid on the debt. The cash flows from each source cancel each other, just as if the firm held no cash and no debt.[15]

Note that if the firm has more cash than debt, its net debt will be negative. In this case, its unlevered beta and cost of capital will exceed its equity beta and cost of capital, as the risk of the firm's equity is mitigated by its cash holdings.

EXAMPLE 12.6 **Cash and Beta**

Problem

In mid-2015, Microsoft Corporation had a market capitalization of \$340 billion, \$35 billion in debt, and \$96 billion in cash. If its estimated equity beta was 0.87, estimate the beta of Microsoft's underlying business enterprise.

Solution

Microsoft has net debt = (35 − 96) = −\$61 billion. Therefore, Microsoft's enterprise value is (340 − 61) = \$279 billion, which is the total value of its underlying business on a debt-free basis and excluding cash. Assuming Microsoft's debt and cash investments are both risk-free, we can estimate the beta of this enterprise value as

$$\beta_U = \frac{E}{E+D}\beta_E + \frac{D}{E+D}\beta_D = \frac{340}{340-61}0.87 + \frac{-61}{340-61}0 = 1.06$$

Note that in this case, Microsoft's equity is *less* risky than its underlying business activities due to its cash holdings.

Industry Asset Betas

Now that we can adjust for the leverage of different firms to determine their asset betas, it is possible to combine estimates of asset betas for multiple firms in the same industry or line of business. Doing so is extremely useful, as it will enable us to reduce our estimation error and improve the accuracy of the estimated beta for our project.

---

[15]We can also think of the firm's enterprise value V in terms of a portfolio of equity and debt less cash: $V = E + D - C$, where C is excess cash. In that case, the natural extension of Eq. 12.9 is

$$\beta_U = \frac{E}{E+D-C}\beta_E + \frac{D}{E+D-C}\beta_D - \frac{C}{E+D-C}\beta_C$$

(and similarly for Eq. 12.8). The shortcut of using net debt is equivalent if the firm's cash investments and debt have similar market risk, or if the debt beta reflects the combined risk of the firm's debt and cash positions.

EXAMPLE 12.7 Estimating an Industry Asset Beta

Problem

Consider the following data for U.S. department stores in mid-2009, showing the equity beta, ratio of net debt to enterprise value (D/V), and debt rating for each firm. Estimate the average and median asset beta for the industry.

Company	Ticker	Equity Beta	D/V	Debt Rating
Dillard's	DDS	2.38	0.59	B
JCPenney	JCP	1.60	0.17	BB
Kohl's	KSS	1.37	0.08	BBB
Macy's	M	2.16	0.62	BB
Nordstrom	JWN	1.94	0.35	BBB
Saks	SKS	1.85	0.50	CCC
Sears Holdings	SHLD	1.36	0.23	BB

Solution

Note that D/V provides the fraction of debt financing, and $(1 - D/V)$ the fraction of equity financing, for each firm. Using the data for debt betas from Table 12.3, we can apply Eq. 12.9 for each firm. For example, for Dillard's:

$$\beta_U = \frac{E}{E+D}\beta_E + \frac{D}{E+D}\beta_D = (1 - 0.59)2.38 + (0.59)0.26 = 1.13$$

Doing this calculation for each firm, we obtain the following estimates:

Ticker	Equity Beta	D/V	Debt Rating	Debt Beta	Asset Beta
DDS	2.38	0.59	B	0.26	1.13
JCP	1.60	0.17	BB	0.17	1.36
KSS	1.37	0.08	BBB	0.10	1.27
M	2.16	0.62	BB	0.17	0.93
JWN	1.94	0.35	BBB	0.10	1.30
SKS	1.85	0.50	CCC	0.31	1.08
SHLD	1.36	0.23	BB	0.17	1.09
				Average	1.16
				Median	1.13

The large differences in the firms' equity betas are mainly due to differences in leverage. The firms' asset betas are much more similar, suggesting that the underlying businesses in this industry have similar market risk. By combining estimates from several closely related firms in this way, we can get a more accurate estimate of the beta for investments in this industry.

Figure 12.4 shows estimates of industry asset betas for U.S. firms. Note that businesses that are less sensitive to market and economic conditions, such as utilities and household product firms, tend to have lower asset betas than more cyclical industries, such as autos and high technology.

CONCEPT CHECK

1. What data can we use to estimate the beta of a project?
2. Why does the equity beta of a levered firm differ from the beta of its assets?

FIGURE 12.4 **Industry Asset Betas (2016)**

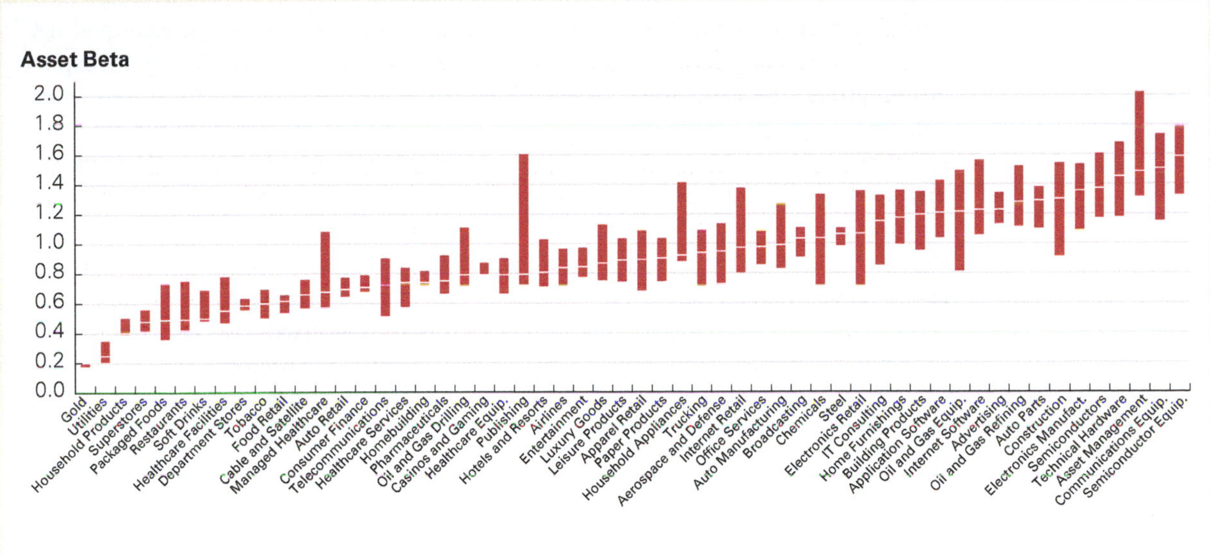

The plot shows the median, as well as upper and lower quartiles, for estimated asset betas of S&P 1500 firms in selected industries. Note the low asset betas for less cyclical industries such as utilities and household products, versus the much higher asset betas of technology firms, asset management, and capital-intensive cyclical industries (like autos and construction).

Source: Author calculations based on data from CapitalIQ.

12.6 Project Risk Characteristics and Financing

Thus far, we have evaluated a project's cost of capital by comparing it with the unlevered assets of firms in the same line of business. We have also assumed the project itself is unlevered—specifically, it is to be financed solely with equity. In this section we consider why and how we may need to adjust our analysis to account for differences between projects, both in terms of their risk and their mode of financing.

Differences in Project Risk

Firm asset betas reflect the market risk of the *average* project in a firm. But individual projects may be more or less sensitive to market risk. A financial manager evaluating a new investment should try to assess how this project might compare with the average project.

As an example, conglomerate 3M has both a health care division and a computer display and graphics division. These divisions are likely to have very different market risks (note the difference in asset betas between healthcare supplies and computer peripherals in Figure 12.4). 3M's own asset beta will represent an average of the risk of these and 3M's other divisions, and would not be an appropriate measure of risk for projects in either division. Instead, financial managers should evaluate projects based on asset betas of firms that concentrate in a similar line of business. Thus, for multi-divisional firms, identifying a set of "pure play" comparables for each division is helpful in estimating appropriate divisional costs of capital.

Even within a firm with a single line of business, some projects obviously have different market risk characteristics from the firm's other activities. For example, if Cisco Systems were considering whether to buy or lease an office building to expand its headquarters, the cash flows associated with this decision have very different market risk from the cash flows associated with its typical project of developing networking software and hardware, and it should use a different cost of capital. (Indeed, we will discuss the risk and appropriate cost of capital associated with leasing in more detail in Chapter 25.)

Another factor that can affect the market risk of a project is its degree of **operating leverage**, which is the relative proportion of fixed versus variable costs. Holding fixed the cyclicality of the project's revenues, a higher proportion of fixed costs will increase the sensitivity of the project's cash flows to market risk and raise the project's beta. To account for this effect, we should assign projects with an above-average proportion of fixed costs, and thus greater-than-average operating leverage, a higher cost of capital.

EXAMPLE 12.8 Operating Leverage and Beta

Problem

Consider a project with expected annual revenues of \$120 and costs of \$50 in perpetuity. The costs are completely variable, so that the profit margin of the project will remain constant. Suppose the project has a beta of 1.0, the risk-free rate is 5%, and the expected return of the market is 10%. What is the value of this project? What would its value and beta be if the revenues continued to vary with a beta of 1.0, but the costs were instead completely fixed at \$50 per year?

Solution

The expected cash flow of the project is $\$120 - \$50 = \$70$ per year. Given a beta of 1.0, the appropriate cost of capital is $r = 5\% + 1.0(10\% - 5\%) = 10\%$. Thus, the value of the project if the costs are completely variable is $\$70/10\% = \$700$.

If instead the costs are fixed, then we can compute the value of the project by discounting the revenues and costs separately. The revenues still have a beta of 1.0, and thus a cost of capital of 10%, for a present value of $\$120/10\% = \$1200$. Because the costs are fixed, we should discount them at the risk-free rate of 5%, so their present value is $\$50/5\% = \$1000$. Thus, with fixed costs the project has a value of only $\$1200 - \$1000 = \$200$.

What is the beta of the project now? We can think of the project as a portfolio that is long the revenues and short the costs. The project's beta is the weighted average of the revenue and cost betas, or

$$\beta_P = \frac{R}{R-C}\beta_R - \frac{C}{R-C}\beta_C = \frac{1200}{1200-1000}1.0 - \frac{1000}{1200-1000}0 = 6.0$$

Given a beta of 6.0, the project's cost of capital with fixed costs is $r = 5\% + 6.0(10\% - 5\%) = 35\%$. To verify this result, note that the present value of the expected profits is then $\$70/35\% = 200$. As this example shows, increasing the proportion of fixed versus variable costs can significantly increase a project's beta (and reduce its value).

COMMON MISTAKE **Adjusting for Execution Risk**

When a company launches a new product or makes some other type of new investment, it is often subject to a greater degree of **execution risk**, which is the risk that—due to missteps in the firm's execution—the project may fail to generate the forecasted cash flows. For example, there may be a greater chance of manufacturing delays or marketing mistakes.

Firms sometimes try to adjust for this risk by assigning a higher cost of capital to new projects. Such adjustments are generally incorrect, as this execution risk is typically firm-specific risk, which is diversifiable. (Intuitively, as a shareholder investing in many firms, you can diversify the risk that some firms may suffer execution failures while others do not.) The cost of capital for the project should only depend on its sensitivity to market-wide risks.

Of course, this does not mean that we should ignore execution risk. We should capture this risk in the expected cash flows generated by the project. For example, if a project is expected to generate a free cash flow of $100 next year, but there is a 20% chance it might fail and generate nothing, then our expected free cash flow is only $80. Thus, while the cost of capital remains the same, the expected free cash flow that we discount will be lower the greater the degree of execution risk.

Financing and the Weighted Average Cost of Capital

In Section 12.5, we presumed the project we are evaluating is all-equity financed; that is, the firm does not plan any additional borrowing as a result of the project. What is the importance of this financing assumption, and how might the project's cost of capital change if the firm does use leverage to finance the project?

The complete answer to this question will be the topic of Part 5, where we consider the many implications of the firm's choice of financing policy. We provide a quick preview here of some key results.

Perfect Capital Markets. Let's begin by recalling our discussion in Chapter 3 where we argued that with perfect capital markets—by which we mean no taxes, transactions costs, or other frictions—the choice of financing does not affect the cost of capital or NPV of a project. Rather, a project's cost of capital and NPV are solely determined by its free cash flows. In this setting then, our assumption regarding the project's financing is innocuous. Its cost of capital would be the same whether, and to what extent, it is financed in part with debt. The intuition for this result, which we gave in Chapter 3, is that in a competitive and perfect market, all financing transactions are zero-NPV transactions that do not affect value.

Taxes—A Big Imperfection. When market frictions do exist, the firm's decision regarding how to finance the project may have consequences that affect the project's value. Perhaps the most important example comes from the corporate tax code, which allows the firm to deduct interest payments on debt from its taxable income. As we saw in Chapter 5, if the firm pays interest rate r on its debt, then once the tax deduction is accounted for, the net cost to the firm is given by

$$\text{Effective after-tax interest rate} = r(1 - \tau_C) \quad (12.11)$$

where τ_C is the firm's corporate tax rate.

The Weighted Average Cost of Capital. As we will see in Chapter 15, when the firm finances its own project using debt, it will benefit from the interest tax deduction. One way

INTERVIEW WITH SHELAGH GLASER

Shelagh M. Glaser is vice president of Finance and Group Controller of the Client Computing Group at Intel Corporation. Her responsibilities include profit and loss forecasting, reporting and controls.

QUESTION: *Does Intel set the discount rate at the corporate or project level?*

ANSWER: We typically set the discount rate at the corporate level. As a company, Intel makes a broad set of products that sell into similar markets so one hurdle rate makes sense for our core business. To justify an investment, every project has to earn or exceed that level of return for our shareholders.

We may use a different discount rate for mergers and acquisitions. For example, recently we've done more software acquisitions. That industry is very different from semi-conductors and has different risk factors, so we take those considerations into account to set the hurdle rate.

QUESTION: *How does Intel compute the cost of capital for new investment opportunities?*

ANSWER: We reexamine our weighted average cost of capital (WACC) each year to see that we have the right inputs and if any have changed: What is the current market risk premium? Are we using the right risk-free rate? How should we weight historical data? We use the CAPM to determine beta but consider whether to continue using the 5-year weekly beta or to change to a daily or monthly beta in the calculation. We also look at the latest studies from academia on what the inputs should be.

Once we have estimated the WACC, we think about the appropriate hurdle rate for our circumstances. We have not changed the hurdle rate in recent years—even though the WACC may have changed—and continue to use a hurdle rate that is above the WACC. This higher hurdle rate reflects our ability to time our investments and helps us choose projects that maximize our expected returns. Intel has more projects with returns above our hurdle than we can invest in, so assessing opportunity cost is a significant aspect of decision making. We may invest in some projects with NPVs below the hurdle rate if they are of strategic importance.

QUESTION: *How do project-specific considerations affect Intel's cost of capital calculation?*

ANSWER: When deciding whether to invest billions in wafer fabrication plants, Intel considers both the physical plant and the product line. We calculate the margin we would need from the product and develop a comprehensive set of metrics to justify the large capital investment. Typically we use our standard hurdle rate and also look at risk factors and the timing of the product launch. Intel's business is driven by the economics of Moore's Law, allowing us to double transistors every 2 years. Each generation of new technology creates cost reductions that enable new fabrication plants to clear the hurdle rate. These plants produce our leading-edge product, which earn our highest margins. To get a premium price, our customers require a product that takes advantage of the performance and power efficiency of the latest technology.

QUESTION: *Has the 2008 financial crisis affected how you evaluate investment opportunities?*

ANSWER: In 2008, the market was very depressed. We continued making R&D investments and reduced spending in other areas, such as marketing and short-term promotion. Cutting R&D would have left us with a gap in our product line in several years, because product development cycles typically run 4 years. In this industry, not keeping the R&D machine flowing, to boost short-term earnings, will harm the company's long-term viability. R&D is critical to our fundamental business model, which may require long-term decisions that negatively impact short-term results.

Intel has a long history of investing to maintain performance leadership during downturns. Intel carries almost no debt. Our capital policy is to maintain sufficient cash for fabrication plants and multiple years of R&D expenses, to avoid depending on capital markets to finance ongoing operations. A painful experience in the 1980s, when Intel's access to capital markets was curtailed, highlighted how this conservative capital policy pays off. Going into this crisis with no debt and an extremely strong cash position has served us well.

COMMON MISTAKE Using a Single Cost of Capital in Multi-Divisional Firms

Many firms combine business units with widely different market risk. Yet some of them use a single cost of capital to evaluate projects throughout the organization. Using the same cost of capital for projects that have different riskiness, is, of course, a mistake, and will result in the firm taking on too many risky projects and too few safer projects. That is, when the same cost of capital is used for all investment opportunities, regardless of their riskiness, riskier projects will be discounted at too low a cost of capital, making negative NPV investments appear to be positive NPV and be accepted. Similarly, less risky projects will be discounted at too high a cost of capital, and so may be erroneously rejected.

Because survey evidence suggests that this mistake is quite common, Professors Philipp Krüger, Augustin Landier and David Thesmar* looked at the behavior of conglomerates and found evidence that they were making this mistake. For each conglomerate, they identified the most important division, what they termed the *core-division*. They then demonstrated that, on average, conglomerates invest relatively less in divisions that are less risky than the core-division, and relatively more in divisions that are more risky than the core-division.

*"The WACC Fallacy: The Real Effects of Using a Unique Discount Rate," *Journal of Finance* 70 (2015): 1253–1285.

of including this benefit when calculating the NPV is by using the firm's effective after-tax cost of capital, which we call the **weighted-average cost of capital** or **WACC**:[16]

Weighted Average Cost of Capital (WACC)

$$r_{wacc} = \frac{E}{E+D} r_E + \frac{D}{E+D} r_D (1 - \tau_C) \tag{12.12}$$

Comparing the weighted average cost of capital, r_{wacc}, with the unlevered cost of capital, r_U, defined in Eq. 12.8, note that the WACC is based on the effective after-tax cost of debt, whereas the unlevered cost of capital is based on the firm's pretax cost of debt. The unlevered cost of capital is therefore also referred to as the **pretax WACC**. Let's review the key distinctions between them:

1. The unlevered cost of capital (or pretax WACC) is the expected return investors will earn holding the firm's assets. In a world with taxes, it can be used to evaluate an *all-equity financed project* with the same risk as the firm.
2. The weighted average cost of capital (or WACC) is the effective after-tax cost of capital to the firm. Because interest expense is tax deductible, the WACC is less than the expected return of the firm's assets. In a world with taxes, the WACC can be used to evaluate a project with the same risk and *the same financing as the firm itself.*

Comparing Eq. 12.8 with Eq. 12.12, given a target leverage ratio we can also calculate the WACC as follows:

$$r_{wacc} = r_U - \frac{D}{E+D} \tau_C r_D \tag{12.13}$$

That is, the WACC is equal to the unlevered cost of capital less the tax savings associated with debt. This version of the WACC formula allows us to take advantage of the

[16]The Chapter 18 appendix contains a formal derivation of this formula. Eq. 12.12 assumes the interest on debt equals its expected return r_D, a reasonable approximation if the debt has low risk and trades near par. If not, we can estimate the after-tax debt cost of capital more precisely as $(r_D - \tau_c \bar{r}_D)$, where $\bar{r}_D$ = (current interest expense)/(market value of debt), the *current yield* of the debt.

industry asset betas we estimated in Section 12.5 when determining the WACC.[17] We'll return to consider the WACC in additional detail, as well other implications of the firm's financing decisions, in Part 5.

EXAMPLE 12.9 **Estimating the WACC**

Problem

Dunlap Corp. has a market capitalization of $100 million, and $25 million in outstanding debt. Dunlap's equity cost of capital is 10%, and its debt cost of capital is 6%. What is Dunlap's unlevered cost of capital? If its corporate tax rate is 40%, what is Dunlap's weighted average cost of capital?

Solution

Dunlap's unlevered cost of capital, or pretax WACC, is given by

$$r_U = \frac{E}{E+D} r_E + \frac{D}{E+D} r_D = \frac{100}{125} 10\% + \frac{25}{125} 6\% = 9.2\%$$

Thus, we would use a cost of capital of 9.2% to evaluate all-equity financed projects with the same risk as Dunlap's assets.

Dunlap's weighted average cost of capital, or WACC, can be calculated using either Eq. 12.12 or 12.13:

$$r_{wacc} = \frac{E}{E+D} r_E + \frac{D}{E+D} r_D (1 - \tau_C) = \frac{100}{125} 10\% + \frac{25}{125} 6\% (1 - 40\%) = 8.72\%$$

$$= r_U - \frac{D}{E+D} \tau_C r_D = 9.2\% - \frac{25}{125} (40\%) 6\% = 8.72\%$$

We can use the WACC of 8.72% to evaluate projects with the same risk and the same mix of debt and equity financing as Dunlap's assets. It is a lower rate than the unlevered cost of capital to reflect the tax deductibility of interest expenses.

CONCEPT CHECK

1. Why might projects within the same firm have different costs of capital?
2. Under what conditions can we evaluate a project using the firm's weighted average cost of capital?

12.7 Final Thoughts on Using the CAPM

In this chapter, we have developed an approach to estimating a firm's or project's cost of capital using the CAPM. Along the way, we have had to make a number of practical choices, approximations, and estimations. And these decisions were on top of the assumptions of the CAPM itself, which are not completely realistic. At this point, you might be wondering: How reliable, and thus worthwhile, are the results that we obtain following this approach?

While there is no definitive answer to this question, we offer several thoughts. First, the types of approximations that we used to estimate the cost of capital are no different from

[17] Eq. 12.13 has an additional advantage: Because we are just using it to estimate the tax shield, we can use the current yield of the debt ($\bar{r}_D$) in place of r_D when debt is risky (see footnote 17).

our other approximations throughout the capital budgeting process. In particular, the revenue and other cash flow projections we must make when valuing a stock or an investment in a new product are likely to be far more speculative than any we have made in estimating the cost of capital. Thus, the imperfections of the CAPM may not be critical in the context of capital budgeting and corporate finance, where errors in estimating project cash flows are likely to have a far greater impact than small discrepancies in the cost of capital.

Second, in addition to being very practical and straightforward to implement, the CAPM-based approach is very robust. While perhaps not perfectly accurate, when the CAPM does generate errors, they tend to be small. Other methods, such as relying on average historical returns, can lead to much larger errors.

Third, the CAPM imposes a disciplined process on managers to identify the cost of capital. There are few parameters available to manipulate in order to achieve a desired result, and the assumptions made are straightforward to document. As a result, the CAPM may make the capital budgeting process less subject to managerial manipulation than if managers could set project costs of capital without clear justification.

Finally, and perhaps most importantly, even if the CAPM model is not perfectly accurate, *it gets managers to think about risk in the correct way*. Managers of widely held corporations should not worry about diversifiable risk, which shareholders can easily eliminate in their own portfolios. They should focus on, and be prepared to compensate investors for, the market risk in the decisions that they make.

Thus, despite its potential flaws, there are very good reasons to use the CAPM as a basis for calculating the cost of capital. In our view, the CAPM is viable, especially when measured relative to the effort required to implement a more sophisticated model (such as the one we will develop in Chapter 13). Consequently, it is no surprise that the CAPM remains the predominant model used in practice to determine the cost of capital.

While the CAPM is likely to be an adequate and practical approach for capital budgeting, you may still wonder how reliable its conclusions are for investors. For example, is holding the market index really the best strategy for investors, or can they do better by trading on news, or hiring a professional fund manager? We consider these questions in Chapter 13.

CONCEPT CHECK

1. Which errors in the capital budgeting process are likely to be more important than discrepancies in the cost of capital estimate?
2. Even if the CAPM is not perfect, why might we continue to use it in corporate finance?

MyFinanceLab Here is what you should know after reading this chapter. MyFinanceLab will help you identify what you know and where to go when you need to practice.

12.1 The Equity Cost of Capital

- Given a security's beta, we can estimate its cost of capital using the CAPM equation for the security market line:

$$r_i = r_f + \underbrace{\beta_i \times (E[R_{Mkt}] - r_f)}_{\text{Risk premium for security } i} \tag{12.1}$$

12.2 The Market Portfolio

- To implement the CAPM, we must (a) construct the market portfolio, and determine its expected excess return over the risk-free interest rate, and (b) estimate the stock's beta, or sensitivity to the market portfolio.
- The market portfolio is a value-weighted portfolio of all securities traded in the market. According to the CAPM, the market portfolio is efficient.
- In a value-weighted portfolio, the amount invested in each security is proportional to its market capitalization.
- A value-weighted portfolio is also an equal-ownership portfolio. Thus, it is a passive portfolio, meaning no rebalancing is necessary due to daily price changes.
- Because the true market portfolio is difficult if not impossible to construct, in practice we use a proxy for the market portfolio, such as the S&P 500 or Wilshire 5000 indices.
- The risk-free rate in the security market line should reflect an average of the risk-free borrowing and lending rates. Practitioners generally choose the risk-free rate from the yield curve based on the investment horizon.
- While the historical return of the S&P 500 has been about 7.7% more than one-year Treasuries since 1926, research suggests that future excess returns are likely to be lower. Since 1965, the average excess return of the S&P 500 has been 5% over one-year Treasuries, and 3.9% over ten-year Treasuries.

12.3 Beta Estimation

- Beta measures a security's sensitivity to market risk. Specifically, beta is the expected change (in %) in the return of a security given a 1% change in the return of the market portfolio.
- To estimate beta, we often use historical returns. Beta corresponds to the slope of the best-fitting line in the plot of a security's excess returns versus the market's excess returns.
- If we regress a stock's excess returns against the market's excess returns, the intercept is the stock's alpha. It measures how the stock has performed historically relative to the security market line.
- Unlike estimating an average return, reliable beta estimates can be obtained with just a few years of data.
- Betas tend to remain stable over time, whereas alphas do not seem to be persistent.

12.4 The Debt Cost of Capital

- Because of default risk, the debt cost of capital, which is its expected return to investors, is less than its yield to maturity, which is its promised return.
- Given annual default and expected loss rates, the debt cost of capital can be estimated as

$$r_d = \text{Yield to Maturity} - \text{Prob(default)} \times \text{Expected Loss Rate} \tag{12.7}$$

- We can also estimate the expected return for debt based on its beta using the CAPM. However, beta estimates for individual debt securities are hard to obtain. In practice, estimates based on the debt's rating may be used.

12.5 A Project's Cost of Capital

- We can estimate a project's cost of capital based on the asset or unlevered cost of capital of comparable firms in the same line of business. Given a target leverage ratio based on the *market* value of the firm's equity and debt, the firm's unlevered cost of capital is:

$$r_U = \frac{E}{E+D} r_E + \frac{D}{E+D} r_D \tag{12.8}$$

- We can also estimate the beta of a project as the unlevered beta of a comparable firm:

$$\beta_U = \frac{E}{E+D} \beta_E + \frac{D}{E+D} \beta_D \tag{12.9}$$

- Because cash holdings will reduce a firm's equity beta, when unlevering betas we can use the firm's net debt, which is debt less excess cash.
- We can reduce estimation error by averaging unlevered betas for several firms in the same industry to determine an industry asset beta.

12.6 Project Risk Characteristics and Financing

- Firm or industry asset betas reflect the market risk of the average project in that firm or industry. Individual projects may be more or less sensitive to the overall market. Operating leverage is one factor that can increase a project's market risk.
- We should not adjust the cost of capital for project-specific risks (such as execution risk). These risks should be reflected in the project's cash flow estimates.
- An unlevered cost of capital can be used to evaluate an equity-financed project. If the project will be financed in part with debt, the firm's effective after-tax cost of debt is less than its expected return to investors. In that case, the weighted average cost of capital can be used:

$$r_{wacc} = \frac{E}{E+D} r_E + \frac{D}{E+D} r_D (1 - \tau_C) \quad (12.12)$$

- The WACC can also be estimated using industry asset betas as follows:

$$r_{wacc} = r_U - \frac{D}{E+D} \tau_C r_D \quad (12.13)$$

12.7 Final Thoughts on Using the CAPM

- While the CAPM is not perfect, it is straightforward to use, relatively robust, hard to manipulate, and correctly emphasizes the importance of market risk. As a result, it is the most popular and best available method to use for capital budgeting.

Key Terms

alpha *p. 416*
asset beta *p. 422*
asset cost of capital *p. 421*
debt cost of capital *p. 417*
equal-ownership portfolio *p. 409*
error (or residual) term *p. 416*
exchange-traded fund (ETF) *p. 411*
execution risk *p. 427*
free float *p. 409*
index funds *p. 411*
linear regression *p. 416*
market index *p. 409*
market proxy *p. 411*
net debt *p. 423*
operating leverage *p. 426*
passive portfolio *p. 409*
pretax WACC *p. 429*
price-weighted portfolio *p. 411*
unlevered beta *p. 422*
unlevered cost of capital *p. 421*
value-weighted portfolio *p. 409*
weighted average cost of capital (WACC) *p. 429*

Further Reading

The following articles provide some additional insights on the CAPM: F. Black, "Beta and Return," *Journal of Portfolio Management* 20 (Fall 1993): 8–18; and B. Rosenberg and J. Guy, "Beta and Investment Fundamentals," *Financial Analysts Journal* (May–June 1976): 60–72.

Although not a focus of this chapter, there is an extensive body of literature on testing the CAPM. Besides the articles mentioned in the text, here are a few others that an interested reader might want to consult: W. Ferson and C. Harvey, "The Variation of Economic Risk Premiums," *Journal of Political Economy* 99 (1991): 385–415; M. Gibbons, S. Ross, and J. Shanken, "A Test of the Efficiency of a Given Portfolio," *Econometrica* 57 (1989): 1121–1152; S. Kothari, J. Shanken, and R. Sloan, "Another Look at the Cross-Section of Expected Stock Returns," *Journal of Finance* 50 (March 1995): 185–224; and R. Levy, "On the Short-Term Stationarity of Beta Coefficients," *Financial Analysts Journal* (November–December 1971): 55–62.

Problems

All problems are available in MyFinanceLab. *An asterisk (*) indicates problems with a higher level of difficulty.*

The Equity Cost of Capital

1. Suppose Pepsico's stock has a beta of 0.57. If the risk-free rate is 3% and the expected return of the market portfolio is 8%, what is Pepsico's equity cost of capital?

2. Suppose the market portfolio has an expected return of 10% and a volatility of 20%, while Microsoft's stock has a volatility of 30%.

a. Given its higher volatility, should we expect Microsoft to have an equity cost of capital that is higher than 10%?

b. What would have to be true for Microsoft's equity cost of capital to be equal to 10%?

3. Aluminum maker Alcoa has a beta of about 2.0, whereas Hormel Foods has a beta of 0.45. If the expected excess return of the marker portfolio is 5%, which of these firms has a higher equity cost of capital, and how much higher is it?

The Market Portfolio

4. Suppose all possible investment opportunities in the world are limited to the five stocks listed in the table below. What does the market portfolio consist of (what are the portfolio weights)?

Stock	Price/Share ($)	Number of Shares Outstanding (millions)
A	10	10
B	20	12
C	8	3
D	50	1
E	45	20

5. Using the data in Problem 4, suppose you are holding a market portfolio, and have invested $12,000 in Stock C.

a. How much have you invested in Stock A?

b. How many shares of Stock B do you hold?

c. If the price of Stock C suddenly drops to $4 per share, what trades would you need to make to maintain a market portfolio?

6. Suppose Best Buy stock is trading for $30 per share for a total market cap of $9 billion, and Walt Disney has 1.65 billion shares outstanding. If you hold the market portfolio, and as part of it hold 100 shares of Best Buy, how many shares of Walt Disney do you hold?

7. Standard and Poor's also publishes the S&P Equal Weight Index, which is an equally weighted version of the S&P 500.

a. To maintain a portfolio that tracks this index, what trades would need to be made in response to daily price changes?

b. Is this index suitable as a market proxy?

8. Suppose that in place of the S&P 500, you wanted to use a broader market portfolio of all U.S. stocks and bonds as the market proxy. Could you use the same estimate for the market risk premium when applying the CAPM? If not, how would you estimate the correct risk premium to use?

9. From the start of 1999 to the start of 2009, the S&P 500 had a negative return. Does this mean the market risk premium we should haved used in the CAPM was negative?

Beta Estimation

10. You need to estimate the equity cost of capital for XYZ Corp. You have the following data available regarding past returns:

Year	Risk-free Return	Market Return	XYZ Return
2007	3%	6%	10%
2008	1%	−37%	−45%

a. What was XYZ's average historical return?
b. Compute the market's and XYZ's excess returns for each year. Estimate XYZ's beta.
c. Estimate XYZ's historical alpha.
d. Suppose the current risk-free rate is 3%, and you expect the market's return to be 8%. Use the CAPM to estimate an expected return for XYZ Corp.'s stock.
e. Would you base your estimate of XYZ's equity cost of capital on your answer in part (a) or in part (d)? How does your answer to part (c) affect your estimate? Explain.

***11.** Go to Chapter Resources on MyFinanceLab and use the data in the spreadsheet provided to estimate the beta of Nike and HPQ stock based on their monthly returns from 2011–2015. (*Hint*: You can use the slope() function in Excel.)

***12.** Using the same data as in Problem 11, estimate the alpha of Nike and HPQ stock, expressed as % per month. (*Hint*: You can use the intercept() function in Excel.)

***13.** Using the same data as in Problem 11, estimate the 95% confidence interval for the alpha and beta of Nike and HPQ stock using Excel's regression tool (from the data analysis menu) or the linest() function.

The Debt Cost of Capital

14. In mid-2012, Ralston Purina had AA-rated, 10-year bonds outstanding with a yield to maturity of 2.05%.
a. What is the highest expected return these bonds could have?
b. At the time, similar maturity Treasuries have a yield of 1.5%. Could these bonds actually have an expected return equal to your answer in part (a)?
c. If you believe Ralston Purina's bonds have 0.5% chance of default per year, and that expected loss rate in the event of default is 60%, what is your estimate of the expected return for these bonds?

15. In mid-2009, Rite Aid had CCC-rated, 6-year bonds outstanding with a yield to maturity of 17.3%. At the time, similar maturity Treasuries had a yield of 3%. Suppose the market risk premium is 5% and you believe Rite Aid's bonds have a beta of 0.31. The expected loss rate of these bonds in the event of default is 60%.
a. What annual probability of default would be consistent with the yield to maturity of these bonds in mid-2009?
b. In mid-2015, Rite-Aid's bonds had a yield of 7.1%, while similar maturity Treasuries had a yield of 1.5%. What probability of default would you estimate now?

16. During the recession in mid-2009, homebuilder KB Home had outstanding 6-year bonds with a yield to maturity of 8.5% and a BB rating. If corresponding risk-free rates were 3%, and the market risk premium was 5%, estimate the expected return of KB Home's debt using two different methods. How do your results compare?

17. The Dunley Corp. plans to issue 5-year bonds. It believes the bonds will have a BBB rating. Suppose AAA bonds with the same maturity have a 4% yield. Assume the market risk premium is 5% and use the data in Table 12.2 and Table 12.3.
a. Estimate the yield Dunley will have to pay, assuming an expected 60% loss rate in the event of default during average economic times. What spread over AAA bonds will it have to pay?
b. Estimate the yield Dunley would have to pay if it were a recession, assuming the expected loss rate is 80% at that time, but the beta of debt and market risk premium are the same as in average economic times. What is Dunley's spread over AAA now?

c. In fact, one might expect risk premia and betas to increase in recessions. Redo part (b) assuming that the market risk premium and the beta of debt both increase by 20%; that is, they equal 1.2 times their value in recessions.

A Project's Cost of Capital

18. Your firm is planning to invest in an automated packaging plant. Harburtin Industries is an all-equity firm that specializes in this business. Suppose Harburtin's equity beta is 0.85, the risk-free rate is 4%, and the market risk premium is 5%. If your firm's project is all equity financed, estimate its cost of capital.

19. Consider the setting of Problem 18. You decided to look for other comparables to reduce estimation error in your cost of capital estimate. You find a second firm, Thurbinar Design, which is also engaged in a similar line of business. Thurbinar has a stock price of $20 per share, with 15 million shares outstanding. It also has $100 million in outstanding debt, with a yield on the debt of 4.5%. Thurbinar's equity beta is 1.00.

a. Assume Thurbinar's debt has a beta of zero. Estimate Thurbinar's unlevered beta. Use the unlevered beta and the CAPM to estimate Thurbinar's unlevered cost of capital.
b. Estimate Thurbinar's equity cost of capital using the CAPM. Then assume its debt cost of capital equals its yield, and using these results, estimate Thurbinar's unlevered cost of capital.
c. Explain the difference between your estimates in part (a) and part (b).
d. You decide to average your results in part (a) and part (b), and then average this result with your estimate from Problem 17. What is your estimate for the cost of capital of your firm's project?

20. IDX Tech is looking to expand its investment in advanced security systems. The project will be financed with equity. You are trying to assess the value of the investment, and must estimate its cost of capital. You find the following data for a publicly traded firm in the same line of business:

Debt Outstanding (book value, AA-rated)	$400 million
Number of shares of common stock	80 million
Stock price per share	$15.00
Book value of equity per share	$6.00
Beta of equity	1.20

What is your estimate of the project's beta? What assumptions do you need to make?

21. In mid-2015, Cisco Systems had a market capitalization of $130 billion. It had A-rated debt of $25 billion as well as cash and short-term investments of $60 billion, and its estimated equity beta at the time was 1.11.

a. What is Cisco's enterprise value?
b. Assuming Cisco's debt has a beta of zero, estimate the beta of Cisco's underlying business enterprise.

22. Consider the following airline industry data from mid-2009:

Company Name	Market Capitalization ($mm)	Total Enterprise Value ($mm)	Equity Beta	Debt Ratings
Delta Air Lines (DAL)	4,938.5	17,026.5	2.04	BB
Southwest Airlines (LUV)	4,896.8	6,372.8	0.966	A/BBB
JetBlue Airways (JBLU)	1,245.5	3,833.5	1.91	B/CCC
Continental Airlines (CAL)	1,124.0	4,414.0	1.99	B

a. Use the estimates in Table 12.3 to estimate the debt beta for each firm (use an average if multiple ratings are listed).
b. Estimate the asset beta for each firm.
c. What is the average asset beta for the industry, based on these firms?

Project Risk Characteristics and Financing

23. Weston Enterprises is an all-equity firm with two divisions. The soft drink division has an asset beta of 0.60, expects to generate free cash flow of $50 million this year, and anticipates a 3% perpetual growth rate. The industrial chemicals division has an asset beta of 1.20, expects to generate free cash flow of $70 million this year, and anticipates a 2% perpetual growth rate. Suppose the risk-free rate is 4% and the market risk premium is 5%.
a. Estimate the value of each division.
b. Estimate Weston's current equity beta and cost of capital. Is this cost of capital useful for valuing Weston's projects? How is Weston's equity beta likely to change over time?

***24.** Harrison Holdings, Inc. (HHI) is publicly traded, with a current share price of $32 per share. HHI has 20 million shares outstanding, as well as $64 million in debt. The founder of HHI, Harry Harrison, made his fortune in the fast food business. He sold off part of his fast food empire, and purchased a professional hockey team. HHI's only assets are the hockey team, together with 50% of the outstanding shares of Harry's Hotdogs restaurant chain. Harry's Hotdogs (HDG) has a market capitalization of $850 million, and an enterprise value of $1.05 billion. After a little research, you find that the average asset beta of other fast food restaurant chains is 0.75. You also find that the debt of HHI and HDG is highly rated, and so you decide to estimate the beta of both firms' debt as zero. Finally, you do a regression analysis on HHI's historical stock returns in comparison to the S&P 500, and estimate an equity beta of 1.33. Given this information, estimate the beta of HHI's investment in the hockey team.

25. Your company operates a steel plant. On average, revenues from the plant are $30 million per year. All of the plants costs are variable costs and are consistently 80% of revenues, including energy costs associated with powering the plant, which represent one quarter of the plant's costs, or an average of $6 million per year. Suppose the plant has an asset beta of 1.25, the risk-free rate is 4%, and the market risk premium is 5%. The tax rate is 40%, and there are no other costs.
a. Estimate the value of the plant today assuming no growth.
b. Suppose you enter a long-term contract which will supply all of the plant's energy needs for a fixed cost of $3 million per year (before tax). What is the value of the plant if you take this contract?
c. How would taking the contract in (b) change the plant's cost of capital? Explain.

26. Unida Systems has 40 million shares outstanding trading for $10 per share. In addition, Unida has $100 million in outstanding debt. Suppose Unida's equity cost of capital is 15%, its debt cost of capital is 8%, and the corporate tax rate is 40%.
a. What is Unida's unlevered cost of capital?
b. What is Unida's after-tax debt cost of capital?
c. What is Unida's weighted average cost of capital?

27. You would like to estimate the weighted average cost of capital for a new airline business. Based on its industry asset beta, you have already estimated an unlevered cost of capital for the firm of 9%. However, the new business will be 25% debt financed, and you anticipate its debt cost of capital will be 6%. If its corporate tax rate is 40%, what is your estimate of its WACC?

Data Case

You work in Walt Disney Company's corporate finance and treasury department and have just been assigned to the team estimating Disney's WACC. You must estimate this WACC in preparation for a team meeting later today. You quickly realize that the information you need is readily available online.

1. Go to finance.yahoo.com. Under the "Investing Tab" and then "Market Overview," you will find the yield to maturity for ten-year Treasury bonds listed as "10 Yr Bond(%)." Collect this number as your risk-free rate.

2. In the box next to the "Get Quotes" button, type Walt Disney's ticker symbol (DIS) and press enter. Once you see the basic information for Disney, find and click "Key Statistics" on the left side of the screen. From the key statistics, collect Disney's market capitalization (its market value of equity), enterprise value (market-value equity + net debt), cash, and beta.

3. To get Disney's cost of debt and the market value of its long-term debt, you will need the price and yield to maturity on the firm's existing long-term bonds. Go to finra-markets.morningstar.com. Under "Market Data," select "Bonds." Under "Search," click "Corporate," and type Disney's ticker symbol. A list of Disney's outstanding bond issues will appear. Assume that Disney's policy is to use the expected return on noncallable ten-year obligations as its cost of debt. Find the noncallable bond issue that is at least 10 years from maturity. (*Hint*: You will see a column titled "Callable"; make sure the issue you choose has "No" in this column. Bonds may appear on multiple pages.) Find the credit rating and yield to maturity for your chosen bond issue (it is in the column titled "Yield"). Hold the mouse over the table of Disney's bonds and right-click. Select "Export to Microsoft Excel." (Note that this option is available in IE, but may not be in other browsers.) An Excel spreadsheet with all of the data in the table will appear.

4. You now have the price for each bond issue, but you need to know the size of the issue. Returning to the Web page, click "Walt Disney Company" in the first row. This brings up a Web page with all of the information about the bond issue. Scroll down until you find "Amount Outstanding" on the right side. Noting that this amount is quoted in thousands of dollars (e.g., $60,000 means $60 million = $60,000,000), record the issue amount in the appropriate row of your spreadsheet. Repeat this step for all of the bond issues.

5. The price for each bond issue in your spreadsheet is reported as a percentage of the bond's par value. For example, 104.50 means that the bond issue is trading at 104.5% of its par value. You can calculate the market value of each bond issue by multiplying the amount outstanding by (Price ÷ 100). Do so for each issue and then calculate the total of all the bond issues. This is the market value of Disney's debt.

6. Compute the weights for Disney's equity and debt based on the market value of equity and Disney's market value of debt, computed in Step 5.

7. Calculate Disney's cost of equity capital using the CAPM, the risk-free rate you collected in step 1, and a market risk premium of 5%.

8. Assuming that Disney has a tax rate of 35%, calculate its after-tax debt cost of capital.

9. Calculate Disney's WACC.

10. Calculate Disney's net debt by subtracting its cash (collected in Step 2) from its debt. Recalculate the weights for the WACC using the market value of equity, net debt, and enterprise value. Recalculate Disney's WACC using the weights based on the net debt. How much does it change?

11. How confident are you of your estimate? Which implicit assumptions did you make during your data collection efforts?

CHAPTER 12 APPENDIX

Practical Considerations When Forecasting Beta

As discussed in Section 12.3, we can estimate stock betas in practice by regressing past stock returns on returns of the market portfolio. Several practical considerations arise when doing so. Important choices in estimating beta include (1) the time horizon used, (2) the index used as the market portfolio, (3) the method used to extrapolate from past betas to future betas, and (4) the treatment of outliers in the data.

Time Horizon

When estimating beta by using past returns, there is a trade-off regarding which time horizon to use to measure returns. If we use too short a time horizon, our estimate of beta will be unreliable. If we use very old data, they may be unrepresentative of the current market risk of the security. For stocks, common practice is to use at least two years of weekly return data or five years of monthly return data.[18]

The Market Proxy

The CAPM predicts that a security's expected return depends on its beta with regard to the market portfolio of *all* risky investments available to investors. As mentioned earlier, in practice the S&P 500 is used as the market proxy. Other proxies, such as the NYSE Composite Index (a value-weighted index of all NYSE stocks), the Wilshire 5000 index of all U.S. stocks, or an even broader market index that includes both equities and fixed-income securities, are sometimes used as well. When evaluating international stocks, it is common practice to use a country or international market index. It is important to remember, however, that the market risk premium used in Eq. 12.1 must reflect the choice of the market proxy. For example, a lower risk premium should be used if the market proxy includes fixed-income securities.

Beta Variation and Extrapolation

The estimated beta for a firm will tend to vary over time. For example, Figure 12A.1 shows variation in an estimate of Cisco's beta from 1999–2015. Much of this variation is likely due to estimation error. Thus, we should be suspicious of estimates that are extreme relative to historical or industry norms; in fact, many practitioners prefer to use average industry asset betas rather than individual stock betas (see Figure 12.4) in order to reduce estimation error. In addition, evidence suggests that betas tend to regress toward the average beta of 1.0 over time.[19] For both of these reasons, many practitioners use **adjusted betas**,

[18]While daily returns would provide even more sample points, we often do not use them due to the concern—especially for smaller, less liquid stocks—that short-term factors might influence daily returns that are not representative of the longer-term risks affecting the security. Ideally, we should use a return interval equal to our investment horizon. The need for sufficient data, however, makes monthly returns the longest practical choice.

[19]See M. Blume, "Betas and Their Regression Tendencies," *Journal of Finance* 30 (1975): 785–795.

FIGURE 12A.1 **Estimated Betas for Cisco Systems, 1999–2015**

Estimated betas will vary over time. The estimate for Cisco's beta, based on three years of monthly data, has fallen from a high of 2.5 in 2002 to below 1 in 2015. While some of this variation is likely estimation error, this trend is typical of many technology stocks that have grown and matured.

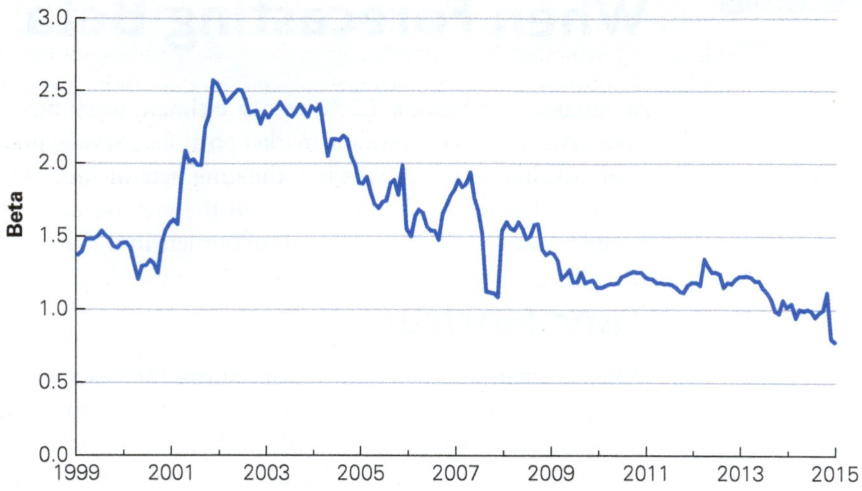

which are calculated by averaging the estimated beta with 1.0. For example, Bloomberg computes adjusted betas using the following formula:

$$\text{Adjusted Beta of Security } i = \tfrac{2}{3}\beta_i + \tfrac{1}{3}(1.0) \tag{12A.1}$$

The estimation methodologies of five data providers appear in Table 12A.1. Each employs a unique methodology, which leads to differences in the reported betas.

Outliers

The beta estimates we obtain from linear regression can be very sensitive to outliers, which are returns of unusually large magnitude.[20] As an example, Figure 12A.2 shows a scatterplot of Genentech's monthly returns versus the S&P 500 for 2002–2004. Based on these returns, we estimate a beta of 1.21 for Genentech. Looking closely at the monthly returns, however, we find two data points with unusually large returns: In April 2002, Genentech's stock price fell by almost 30%, and in May 2003, Genentech's stock price rose by almost 65%. In each case the extreme moves were a reaction to Genentech's announcement of news related to

TABLE 12A.1 **Estimation Methodologies Used by Selected Data Providers**

	Value Line	Google	Bloomberg	Yahoo!	Capital IQ
Returns	Weekly	Monthly	Weekly	Monthly	Weekly, Monthly (5yr)
Horizon	5 years	5 years	2 years	3 years	1, 2, 5 years
Market Index	NYSE Composite	S&P 500	S&P 500	S&P 500	S&P 500 (U.S. Stocks) MSCI (International Stocks)
Adjusted	Adjusted	Unadjusted	Both	Unadjusted	Unadjusted

[20] See, for example, Peter Knez and Mark Ready, "On the Robustness of Size and Book-to-Market in Cross-Sectional Regressions," *Journal of Finance* 52 (1997): 1355–1382.

COMMON MISTAKE **Changing the Index to Improve the Fit**

Because we can use regression analysis to estimate beta, it is often incorrectly assumed that a higher goodness of fit will lead to more accurate results. This goodness of fit is measured by the **R-squared** of the regression, which is equal to the square of the correlation between the stock's and market's excess returns.

For example, our regression of Cisco's returns would show a much higher R-squared if we used the NASDAQ 100 index, which has a much heavier concentration of technology stocks, in place of the S&P 500. But remember, the goal of the regression analysis is to determine Cisco's sensitivity to *market* risk. Because the NASDAQ 100 index itself is not well-diversified, it does not capture market risk. Thus, Cisco's beta with respect to the NASDAQ 100 is not a meaningful assessment of its market risk.

new drug development. In April 2002, Genentech reported a setback in the development of psoriasis drug Raptiva. In May 2003, the company reported the successful clinical trial of its anticancer drug Avastin. These two returns more likely represent firm-specific rather than market-wide risk. But because these large returns happened to occur during months when the market also moved in the same direction, they bias the estimate of beta that results from a standard regression. If we redo the regression replacing Genentech's returns during these two months with the average return of similar biotechnology firms during the same months, we obtain a much lower estimate of 0.60 for Genentech's beta, as shown in Figure 12A.2. This latter estimate is probably a much more accurate assessment of Genentech's true market risk during this period.

There may be other reasons to exclude certain historical data as anomalous when estimating beta. For example, some practitioners advocate ignoring data from 1998–2001 to avoid distortions related to the technology, media, and telecommunications speculative bubble.[21] A similar concern could be raised with regard to the performance of financial

FIGURE 12A.2

Beta Estimation with and without Outliers for Genentech Using Monthly Returns for 2002–2004

Genentech's returns in April 2002 and May 2003 are largely due to firm-specific news. By replacing those returns (blue points) with industry average returns (red points), we obtain a more accurate assessment of Genentech's market risk during this period.

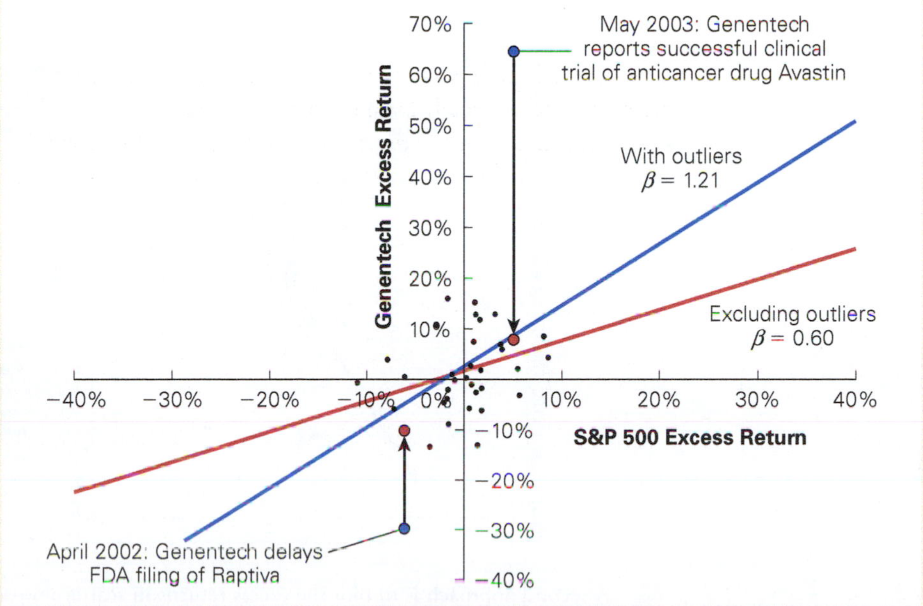

[21]For example, see A. Annema and M. H. Goedhart, "Better Betas," *McKinsey on Finance* (Winter 2003): 10–13.

USING EXCEL

Estimating Beta Using Excel

Given data on past stock returns and interest rates, it is relatively easy to estimate beta using Excel. We begin by computing the excess returns for both the stock and the market for the desired historical period. Here we illustrate the calculation used for Figure 12.2. Columns C and D show monthly adjusted closing prices downloaded from finance.yahoo.com for SPY (ticker symbol for the SPDR S&P500 exchange traded fund, which we use as a proxy for the market portfolio) and CSCO (ticker symbol for Cisco). We also downloaded short-term (13-week) Treasury Bill rates using ticker ^IRX. Because adjusted closing prices are adjusted for both splits and dividends, we can compute total returns directly from them, and then the subtract one month's interest to calculate the excess return (see columns G and H, with the formula for H5 shown).

	A	B	C	D	E	F	G	H	I	J	K	L	M	N
1														
2			Adjusted Close	Adjusted Close	Interest Rate		Monthly Excess Return							
3		Date	SPY	CSCO	^IRX		SPY	CSCO						
4		Dec-99	$155.73	$ 964.13										
5		Jan-00	$147.97	$ 985.50	5.53%		(5.44%)	1.76%	=(D5/D4-1)-$E5/12					
6		Feb-00	$145.72	$ 1,189.69	5.64%		(1.99%)	20.25%						
7		Mar-00	$159.83	$ 1,391.63	5.72%		9.21%	16.50%		Beta	1.57	=SLOPE($H$5:$H$184,$G$5:$G$184)		
8		Apr-00	$154.22	$ 1,247.91	5.65%		(3.98%)	(10.80%)		Alpha	(0.33%)	=INTERCEPT($H$5:$H$184,$G$5:$G$184)		
9		May-00	$151.79	$ 1,024.88	5.49%		(2.03%)	(18.33%)						
10		Jun-00	$154.79	$ 1,144.13	5.70%		1.50%	11.16%				Beta	Alpha	
11		Jul-00	$152.36	$ 1,177.88	6.02%		(2.07%)	2.45%			Value	1.57	(0.33%)	
12		Aug-00	$162.31	$ 1,235.25	6.11%		6.02%	4.36%			Standard Error	0.14	0.61%	
13		Sep-00	$153.02	$ 994.50	6.03%		(6.23%)	(19.99%)				↑		
14		Oct-00	$152.31	$ 969.75	6.15%		(0.98%)	(3.00%)				{=LINEST($H$5:$H$184,$G$5:$G$184,1,1)}		
181		Sep-14	$273.27	$ 496.30	0.01%		(1.37%)	1.48%						
182		Oct-14	$279.70	$ 482.50	0.00%		2.35%	(2.78%)						
183		Nov-14	$287.39	$ 545.00	0.01%		2.75%	12.95%						
184		Dec-14	$286.66	$ 548.55	0.04%		(0.26%)	0.65%						
185														

Once we have calculated the excess returns by month, we can estimate beta using Excel's SLOPE function. The first argument is the "y" or dependent variable, in this case Cisco's excess returns in column H, and the second argument is the "x" or independent variable, where we use the market's excess return in column G. We can similarly estimate the alpha of the regression using the INTERCEPT function with the same arguments. (See K7 and K8.)

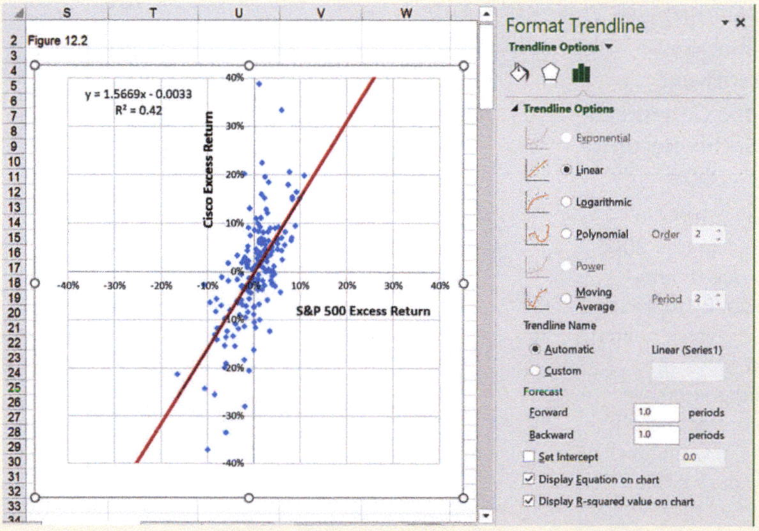

A second approach is to plot the excess returns in scatterplot; see the Charts menu on Excel's insert tab. Once the series has been added (again, using market excess returns for "x" and Cisco's excess returns for "y"), select the plotted data, right click, and choose "Add Trendline." Format the trendline and choose "Linear," leave "Set Intercept" unchecked, and check "Display Equation on Chart" to see the estimated regression equation in the chart.

Finally, to estimate the confidence interval for alpha or beta, we calculate their standard errors using Excel's LINEST function. LINEST is an array formula which returns beta, alpha, and their standard errors as a 2x2 matrix. To input this function, first select all four cells L11:M12 as shown above, and type the LINEST formula as shown (without braces). Finally, type "Ctrl-Shift-Enter" to tell Excel this is an array formula which will have output in all four cells (braces will appear). Once we have the estimates and their standard errors, we can compute the 95% confidence interval using Eq. 10.9. For example, the confidence interval for Cisco's beta during this period is $1.57 \pm (2 \times 0.14) = 1.29$ to 1.85.

stocks during the financial crisis in 2008–2009. On the other hand, including data from recessionary periods may be helpful in evaluating the stock's likely sensitivity to future downturns.

Other Considerations

When using historical returns to forecast future betas, we must be mindful of changes in the environment that might cause the future to differ from the past. For example, if a firm were to change industries, using its historical beta would be inferior to using the beta of other firms in the new industry. Also bear in mind that many practitioners analyze other information in addition to past returns, such as industry characteristics, firm size, and other financial characteristics of a firm, when they forecast betas. In the end, forecasting betas, like most types of forecasting, is as much art as science, and the best estimates require a thorough knowledge of the particulars of a firm and its industry.

Key Terms

adjusted betas *p. 439*
R-squared *p. 441*

Data Case

In the earlier data case for this chapter, you relied on the beta estimate for Walt Disney provided by Yahoo! Finance. You decide to dig deeper and estimate Disney's equity beta on your own.

1. Get the monthly adjusted closing prices for Disney and the S&P 500 from Yahoo! Finance (finance.yahoo.com) using the same time period and procedure as in the Chapter 10 Data Case. (The symbol for the S&P 500 in Yahoo! Finance is ^GSPC.)
2. Get the one-month Eurodollar rate from the Federal Reserve Web site (www.federalreserve.gov/releases/h15/data.htm).[22] Click on Data Download Program ("DDP" on the top right of the screen). Click the Build Package button and make the following selections:
   1. Series Type—Selected Interest Rates
   2. Instrument—ED Eurodollar deposits (London)
   3. Maturity—1-month
   4. Frequency—Monthly

[22]The Eurodollar deposit rate is the average rate paid on dollar deposits in the London interbank market. It is widely regarded as a close proxy for the risk-free rate because it is a measure of the average borrowing/lending rate between financial institutions (see the Chapter 11 appendix).

Click Go to Package and then Format Package. Select Dates—From 2010 May to 2015 April, and select File Type—Excel. Click Go to download and Download file. Then open and save these rates to an Excel file.

3. To convert the Eurodollar rate to a monthly rate, take the yield and divide it by 100 to convert it to a decimal. Then divide the decimal by 12. The resulting rate will be the monthly risk-free return in the CAPM (you may need to re-sort the dates to match the Yahoo! data).
4. Create separate return columns that compute the excess returns for Walt Disney and the S&P 500. Recall that the excess return is the actual monthly return minus the risk-free rate.
5. Compute the beta of Disney stock based on Eq. 12.5 from this chapter, using the SLOPE function in Excel. How does it compare with the beta currently reported by Yahoo! Finance? Why might the results differ?
6. Compute Disney's alpha over this period using the INTERCEPT function in Excel. How might you interpret this alpha?

Note: Updates to this data case may be found at www.berkdemarzo.com.

Investor Behavior and Capital Market Efficiency

CHAPTER

13

NOTATION

x_i portfolio weight of investment in i

R_s return of stock or portfolio s

r_f risk-free rate of interest

α_s alpha of stock s

β_s^i beta of stock s with portfolio i

ε_s residual risk of stock s

AS FUND MANAGER OF LEGG MASON VALUE TRUST, WILLIAM H. MILLER had built a reputation as one of the world's savviest investors. Miller's fund outperformed the overall market every year from 1991–2005, a winning streak no other fund manager came close to matching. But in 2007–2008, Legg Mason Value Trust fell by nearly 65%, almost twice as much as the broader market. While Legg Mason Value Trust outperformed the market in 2009, it lagged again from 2010 until Miller ultimately stepped down as manager and chief investment officer in 2012. As a result of this performance, investors in the fund since 1991 effectively gave back all of the gains they had earned relative to the market in the intervening years and Miller's reputation lay in tatters.[1] Was Miller's performance prior to 2007 merely luck or was his performance in post-2007 the aberration?

According to the CAPM, the market portfolio is efficient, so it should be impossible to consistently do better than the market without taking on additional risk. In this chapter, we will take a close look at this prediction of the CAPM, and assess to what extent the market portfolio is or is not efficient. We will begin by looking at the role of competition in driving the CAPM results, noting that for some investors to beat the market, other investors must be willing to hold portfolios that underperform the market. We then look at the behavior of individual investors, who tend to make a number of mistakes that reduce their returns. But while some professional fund managers are able to exploit these mistakes and profit from them, it does not appear that much, if any, of these profits make it into the hands of the investors who hold their funds.

We will also consider evidence that certain investment "styles," namely holding small stocks, value stocks, and stocks with high recent returns, perform better than predicted by the CAPM, indicating that the market portfolio may not be efficient. We explore this evidence, and then consider how to calculate the cost of capital if indeed the market portfolio is not efficient by deriving an alternative model of risk—the multifactor asset pricing model.

[1] T. Lauricella, "The Stock Picker's Defeat," *Wall Street Journal*, December 10, 2008.

13.1 Competition and Capital Markets

To understand the role of competition in the market, it is useful to consider how the CAPM equilibrium we derived in Chapter 11 might arise based on the behavior of individual investors. In this section, we explain how investors who care only about expected return and variance react to new information and how their actions lead to the CAPM equilibrium.

Identifying a Stock's Alpha

Consider the equilibrium, as we depicted in Figure 11.12 on pages 390–391, where the CAPM holds and the market portfolio is efficient. Now suppose new information arrives such that, *if market prices remain unchanged*, this news would raise the expected return of Walmart and Nike stocks by 2% and lower the expected return of McDonald's and Tiffany stocks by 2%, leaving the expected return of the market unchanged.[2] Figure 13.1 illustrates the effect of this change on the efficient frontier. With the new information, the market portfolio is no longer efficient. Alternative portfolios offer a higher expected return and a lower volatility than we can obtain by holding the market portfolio. Investors who are aware of this fact will alter their investments in order to make their portfolios efficient.

To improve the performance of their portfolios, investors who are holding the market portfolio will compare the expected return of each security s with its required return from the CAPM (Eq. 12.1):

$$r_s = r_f + \beta_s \times (E[R_{Mkt}] - r_f) \tag{13.1}$$

FIGURE 13.1

An Inefficient Market Portfolio

If the market portfolio is not equal to the efficient portfolio, then the market is not in the CAPM equilibrium. The figure illustrates this possibility if news is announced that raises the expected return of Walmart and Nike stocks and lowers the expected return of McDonald's and Tiffany stocks compared to the situation depicted in Figure 11.12.

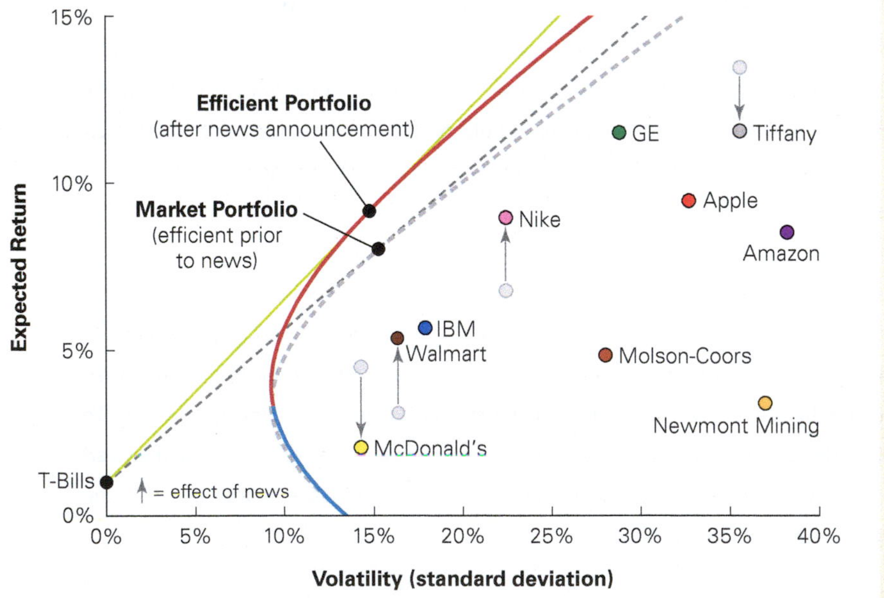

[2]In general, news about individual stocks will affect the market's expected return because these stocks are part of the market portfolio. To keep things simple, we assume the individual stock effects cancel out so that the market's expected return remains unchanged.

FIGURE 13.2

Deviations from the Security Market Line

If the market portfolio is not efficient, then stocks will not all lie on the security market line. The distance of a stock above or below the security market line is the stock's alpha. We can improve upon the market portfolio by buying stocks with positive alphas and selling stocks with negative alphas, but as we do so, prices will change and their alphas will shrink toward zero.

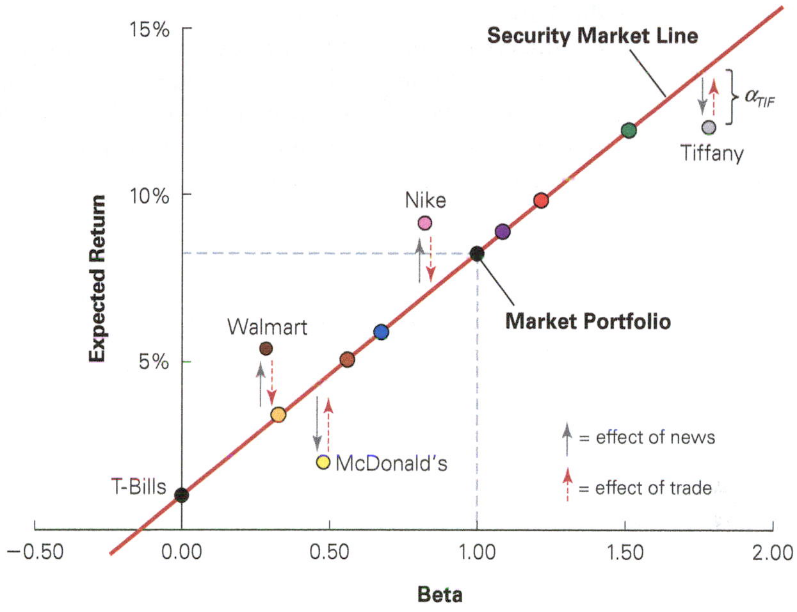

Figure 13.2 shows this comparison. Note that the stocks whose returns have changed are no longer on the security market line. The difference between a stock's expected return and its required return according to the security market line is the stock's alpha:

$$\alpha_s = E[R_s] - r_s \tag{13.2}$$

When the market portfolio is efficient, all stocks are on the security market line and have an alpha of zero. When a stock's alpha is not zero, investors can improve upon the performance of the market portfolio. As we saw in Chapter 11, the Sharpe ratio of a portfolio will increase if we buy stocks whose expected return exceeds their required return—that is, if we buy stocks with positive alphas. Similarly, we can improve the performance of our portfolio by selling stocks with negative alphas.

Profiting from Non-Zero Alpha Stocks

Faced with the situation in Figure 13.2, savvy investors who are holding the market portfolio will want to buy stock in Walmart and Nike, and sell stock in McDonald's and Tiffany. The surge of buy orders for Walmart and Nike will cause their stock prices to rise, and the surge of sell orders for McDonald's and Tiffany will cause their stock prices to fall. As stock prices change, so do expected returns. Recall that a stock's total return is equal to its dividend yield plus the capital gain rate. All else equal, an increase in the current stock price will lower the stock's dividend yield and future capital gain rate, thereby lowering its expected return. Thus, as savvy investors attempt to trade to improve their portfolios, they raise the price and lower the expected return of the positive-alpha stocks, and they depress the price and raise the expected return of the negative-alpha stocks, until the stocks are once again on the security market line and the market portfolio is efficient.

Notice that the actions of investors have two important consequences. First, while the CAPM conclusion that the market is always efficient may not literally be true, competition among savvy investors who try to "beat the market" and earn a positive alpha should keep the market portfolio close to efficient much of the time. In that sense, we can view the CAPM as an approximate description of a competitive market.

Second, there may exist trading strategies that take advantage of non-zero alpha stocks, and by doing so actually can beat the market. In the remainder of this chapter we will explore both of these consequences, looking at evidence of the approximate efficiency of the market, as well as identifying trading strategies that may actually do better than the market.

CONCEPT CHECK

1. If investors attempt to buy a stock with a positive alpha, what is likely to happen to its price and expected return? How will this affect its alpha?
2. What is the consequence of investors exploiting non-zero alpha stocks for the efficiency of the market portfolio?

13.2 Information and Rational Expectations

Under what circumstances could an investor profit from trading a non-zero alpha stock? Consider the situation in Figure 13.2 after the news announcement. Because Exxon Mobil has a positive alpha before prices adjust, investors will anticipate that the price will rise and will likely put in buy orders at the current prices. If the information that altered Exxon Mobil's expected return is publically announced, there are likely to be a large number of investors who receive this news and act on it. Similarly, anybody who hears the news will not want to sell at the old prices. That is, there will be a large order imbalance. The only way to remove this imbalance is for the price to rise so that the alpha is zero. Note that in this case it is quite possible for the new prices to come about *without trade*. That is, the competition between investors may be so intense that prices move before any investor can actually trade at the old prices, so no investor can profit from the news.[3]

Informed Versus Uninformed Investors

As the above discussion makes clear, *in order to profit by buying a positive-alpha stock, there must be someone willing to sell it.* Under the CAPM assumption of homogeneous expectations, which states that all investors have the same information, it would seem that all investors would be aware that the stock had a positive alpha and none would be willing to sell.

Of course, the assumption of homogeneous expectations is not necessarily a good description of the real world. In reality, investors have different information and spend varying amounts of effort researching stocks. Consequently, we might expect that sophisticated investors would learn that Exxon Mobil has a positive alpha, and that they would be able to purchase shares from more naïve investors.

However, even differences in the quality of investors' information will not necessarily be enough to generate trade in this situation. An important conclusion of the CAPM is that investors should hold the market portfolio (combined with risk-free investments), and this investment advice *does not depend on the quality of an investor's information or trading skill.* Even naïve investors with no information can follow this investment advice, and as

[3]The idea that prices will adjust to information without trade is sometimes referred to as the *no-trade theorem*. (P. Milgrom and N. Stokey, "Information, Trade and Common Knowledge," *Journal of Economic Theory* 26 (1982): 17–27.)

the following example shows, by doing so they can avoid being taken advantage of by more sophisticated investors.

EXAMPLE 13.1 **How to Avoid Being Outsmarted in Financial Markets**

Problem

Suppose you are an investor without access to any information regarding stocks. You know that other investors in the market possess a great deal of information and are actively using that information to select an efficient portfolio. You are concerned that because you are less informed than the average investor, your portfolio will underperform the portfolio of the average investor. How can you prevent that outcome and guarantee that your portfolio will do as well as that of the average investor?

Solution

Even though you are not as well informed, you can guarantee yourself the same return as the average investor simply by holding the market portfolio. Because the aggregate of all investors' portfolios must equal the market portfolio (i.e., demand must equal supply), if you hold the market portfolio then you must make the same return as the average investor.

On the other hand, suppose you don't hold the market portfolio, but instead hold less of some stock, such as Google, than its market weight. This must mean that in aggregate all other investors have over-weighted Google relative to the market. But because other investors are more informed than you are, they must realize Google is a good deal, and so are happy to profit at your expense.

Rational Expectations

Example 13.1 is very powerful. It implies that every investor, regardless of how little information he has access to, can guarantee himself the average return and earn an alpha of zero simply by holding the market portfolio. Thus, no investor should choose a portfolio with a negative alpha. However, because the average portfolio of all investors is the market portfolio, the average alpha of all investors is zero. If no investor earns a negative alpha, then no investor can earn a positive alpha, implying that the market portfolio must be efficient. As a result, the CAPM does not depend on the assumption of homogeneous expectations. Rather it requires only that investors have **rational expectations**, which means that all investors correctly interpret and use their own information, as well as information that can be inferred from market prices or the trades of others.[4]

For an investor to earn a positive alpha and beat the market, some investors must hold portfolios with negative alphas. Because these investors could have earned a zero alpha by holding the market portfolio, we reach the following important conclusion:

The market portfolio can be inefficient (so it is possible to beat the market) only if a significant number of investors either

1. *Do not have rational expectations so that they misinterpret information and believe they are earning a positive alpha when they are actually earning a negative alpha, or*
2. *Care about aspects of their portfolios other than expected return and volatility, and so are willing to hold inefficient portfolios of securities.*

[4]See P. DeMarzo and C. Skiadas, "Aggregation, Determinacy, and Informational Efficiency for a Class of Economies with Asymmetric Information," *Journal of Economic Theory* 80 (1998): 123–152.

How do investors actually behave? Do uninformed investors follow the CAPM advice and hold the market portfolio? To shed light on these questions, in the next section we review the evidence on individual investor behavior.

CONCEPT CHECK

1. How can an uninformed or unskilled investor guarantee herself a non-negative alpha?
2. Under what conditions will it be possible to earn a positive alpha and beat the market?

13.3 The Behavior of Individual Investors

In this section, we examine whether small, individual investors heed the advice of the CAPM and hold the market portfolio. As we will see, many investors do not appear to hold an efficient portfolio, but instead fail to diversify and trade too much. We then consider whether these departures from the market create an opportunity for more sophisticated investors to profit at individual investors' expense.

Underdiversification and Portfolio Biases

One of the most important implications of our discussion of risk and return is the benefit of diversification. By appropriately diversifying their portfolios, investors can reduce risk without reducing their expected return. In that sense, diversification is a "free lunch" that all investors should take advantage of.

Despite this benefit, there is much evidence that individual investors fail to diversify their portfolios adequately. Evidence from the U.S. Survey of Consumer Finances shows that, for households that held stocks, the median number of stocks held by investors in 2001 was four, and 90% of investors held fewer than ten different stocks.[5] Moreover, these investments are often concentrated in stocks of companies that are in the same industry or are geographically close, further limiting the degree of diversification attained. A related finding comes from studying how individuals allocate their retirement savings accounts (401K plans). A study of large plans found that employees invested close to a third of their assets in their employer's own stock.[6] These underdiversification results are not unique to U.S. investors: A comprehensive study of Swedish investors documents that approximately one-half of the volatility in investors' portfolios is due to firm-specific risk.[7]

There are a number of potential explanations for this behavior. One is that investors suffer from a **familiarity bias**, so that they favor investments in companies they are familiar with.[8] Another is that investors have **relative wealth concerns** and care most about the performance of their portfolio relative to that of their peers. This desire to "keep up with the Joneses" can lead investors to choose undiversified portfolios that match those of their colleagues or neighbors.[9] In any case, this underdiversification is one important piece of evidence that individual investors may choose sub-optimal portfolios.

---

[5]V. Polkovnichenko, "Household Portfolio Diversification: A Case for Rank Dependent Preferences, *Review of Financial Studies* 18 (2005): 1467–1502.

[6]S. Benartzi, "Excessive Extrapolation and the Allocation of 401(k) Accounts to Company Stock," *Journal of Finance* 56 (2001): 1747–1764.

[7]J. Campbell, "Household Finance," *Journal of Finance* 61 (2006): 1553–1604.

[8]G. Huberman, "Familiarity Breeds Investment," *Review of Financial Studies* 14 (2001): 659–680.

[9]P. DeMarzo, R. Kaniel, and I. Kremer, "Diversification as a Public Good: Community Effects in Portfolio Choice," *Journal of Finance* 59 (2004): 1677–1715.

Excessive Trading and Overconfidence

According to the CAPM, investors should hold risk-free assets in combination with the market portfolio of all risky securities. In Chapter 12, we demonstrated that because the market portfolio is a value-weighted portfolio, it is also a passive portfolio in the sense that an investor does not need to trade in response to daily price changes in order to maintain it. Thus, if all investors held the market, we would see relatively little trading volume in financial markets.

In reality, a tremendous amount of trading occurs each day. At its peak in 2008, for example, annual turnover on the NYSE was nearly 140%, implying that each share of each stock was traded 1.4 times on average. While average turnover has declined dramatically in the wake of the financial crisis, as shown in Figure 13.3, it is still at levels far in excess of that predicted by the CAPM. Moreover, in a study of trading in individual accounts at a discount brokerage, Professors Brad Barber and Terrance Odean found that individual investors tend to trade very actively, with average turnover almost one and a half times the overall rates reported in Figure 13.3 during the time period of their study.[10]

What might explain this trading behavior? Psychologists have known since the 1960s that uninformed individuals tend to overestimate the precision of their knowledge. For example, many sports fans sitting in the stands confidently second guess the coaching decisions on the field, truly believing that they can do a better job. In finance we call this presumptuousness the **overconfidence bias**. Barber and Odean hypothesized that this kind of behavior also characterizes individual investment decision making: Like sports fans, individual investors believe they can pick winners and losers when, in fact, they cannot; this overconfidence leads them to trade too much.

An implication of this overconfidence bias is that, assuming they have no true ability, investors who trade more will not earn higher returns. Instead, their performance will be

FIGURE 13.3

NYSE Annual Share Turnover, 1970–2015

The plot shows the annual share turnover (number of shares traded in the year/total number of shares). Such high turnover is difficult to reconcile with the CAPM, which implies that investors should hold passive market portfolios. Note also the rapid increase in turnover up through 2008, followed by a dramatic decline post-crisis.

Source: www.nyxdata.com

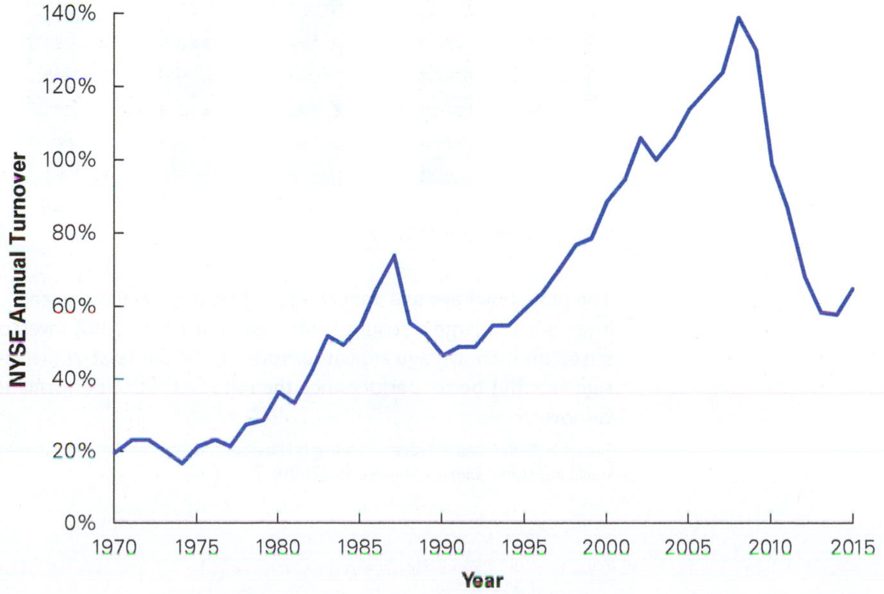

[10]B. Barber and T. Odean, "Trading Is Hazardous to Your Wealth: The Common Stock Investment Performance of Individual Investors," *Journal of Finance* 55 (2000): 773–806.

worse once we take into account the costs of trading (due to both commissions and bid-ask spreads). Figure 13.4 documents precisely this result, showing that much investor trading appears not to be based on rational assessments of performance.

As additional evidence, Barber and Odean contrasted the behavior and performance of men versus women.[11] Psychological studies have shown that, in areas such as finance, men tend to be more overconfident than women. Consistent with the overconfidence hypothesis, they documented that men tend to trade more than women, and that their portfolios have lower returns as a result. These differences are even more pronounced for single men and women.

Researchers have obtained similar results in an international context. Using an extraordinarily detailed database on Finnish investors, Professors Mark Grinblatt and Matti Keloharju find that trading activity increases with psychological measures of overconfidence. Interestingly, they also find that trading activity increases with the number of speeding tickets an individual receives, which they interpret as a measure of **sensation seeking**, or the individual's desire for novel and intense risk-taking experiences. In both cases, the increased trading does not appear to be profitable for investors.[12]

FIGURE 13.4 **Individual Investor Returns Versus Portfolio Turnover**

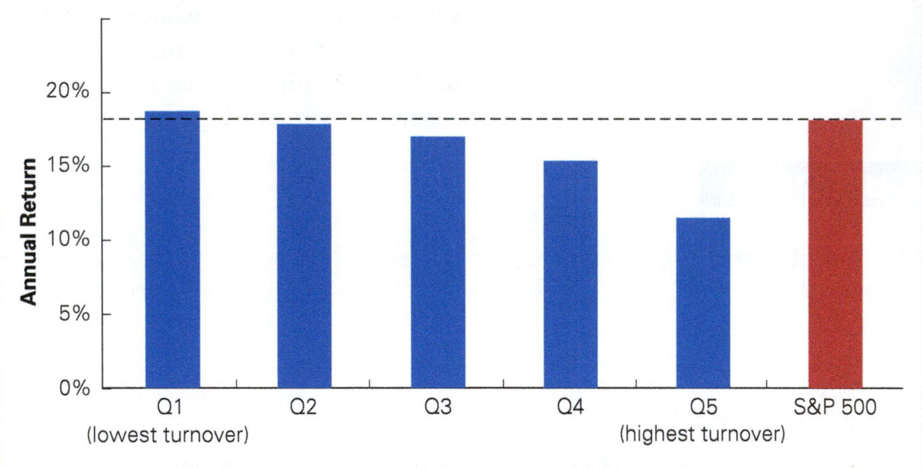

The plot shows average annual return (net of commissions and trading costs) for individual investors at a large discount brokerage from 1991–1997. Investors are grouped into quintiles based on their average annual turnover. While the least-active investors had slightly (but not significantly) better performance than the S&P 500, performance declined with the rate of turnover.

Source: B. Barber and T. Odean, "Trading Is Hazardous to Your Wealth: The Common Stock Investment Performance of Individual Investors," *Journal of Finance* 55 (2000): 773–806.

[11] B. Barber and T. Odean, "Boys Will Be Boys: Gender, Overconfidence, and Common Stock Investment," *Quarterly Journal of Economics* 116 (2001): 261–292.

[12] M. Grinblatt and M. Keloharju, "Sensation Seeking, Overconfidence, and Trading Activity," *Journal of Finance* 64 (2009): 549–578.

Individual Behavior and Market Prices

Thus, in reality, individual investors are underdiversified and trade too much, violating a key prediction of the CAPM. But does this observation imply that the remaining conclusions of the CAPM are invalid?

The answer is not necessarily. If individuals depart from the CAPM in random, idiosyncratic ways, then despite the fact that each individual doesn't hold the market, when we combine their portfolios together these departures will tend to cancel out just like any other idiosyncratic risk. In that case, individuals will hold the market portfolio *in aggregate*, and there will be no effect on market prices or returns. These uninformed investors may simply be trading with themselves—generating trading commissions for their brokers, but without impacting the efficiency of the market.

So, in order for the behavior of uninformed investors to have an impact on the market, there must be patterns to their behavior that lead them to depart from the CAPM in systematic ways, thus imparting systematic uncertainty into prices. For investors' trades to be correlated in this way, they must share a common motivation. Consequently, in Section 13.4, we investigate what might motivate investors to depart from the market portfolio, and show that investors appear to suffer from some common, and predictable, biases.

CONCEPT CHECK

1. Do investors hold well-diversified portfolios?
2. Why is the high trading volume observed in markets inconsistent with the CAPM equilibrium?
3. What must be true about the behavior of small, uninformed investors for them to have an impact on market prices?

13.4 Systematic Trading Biases

For the behavior of individual investors to impact market prices, and thus create a profitable opportunity for more sophisticated investors, there must be predictable, systematic patterns in the types of errors individual investors make. In this section we review some of the evidence researchers have found of such systematic trading biases.

Hanging on to Losers and the Disposition Effect

Investors tend to hold on to stocks that have lost value and sell stocks that have risen in value since the time of purchase. We call this tendency to hang on to losers and sell winners the **disposition effect**. Professors Hersh Shefrin and Meir Statman, building on the work of psychologists Daniel Kahneman and Amos Tversky, posited that this effect arises due to investors' increased willingness to take on risk in the face of possible losses.[13] It may also reflect a reluctance to "admit a mistake" by taking the loss.

Researchers have verified the disposition effect in many studies. For example, in a study of all trades in the Taiwanese stock market from 1995–1999, investors in aggregate were twice as likely to realize gains as they were to realize losses. Also, nearly 85% of individual investors were subject to this bias.[14] On the other hand, mutual funds and foreign investors

[13] H. Shefrin and M. Statman, "The Disposition to Sell Winners Too Early and Ride Losers Too Long: Theory and Evidence," *Journal of Finance* 40 (1985): 777–790; and D. Kahneman and A. Tversky, "Prospect Theory: An Analysis of Decision under Risk," *Econometrica* 47 (1979): 263–291.

[14] B. Barber, Y. T. Lee, Y. J. Liu, and T. Odean, "Is the Aggregate Investor Reluctant to Realize Losses? Evidence from Taiwan," *European Financial Management* 13 (2007): 423–447.

NOBEL PRIZE **Kahneman and Tversky's Prospect Theory**

In 2002, the Nobel Prize for Economics was awarded to Daniel Kahneman for his development of Prospect Theory with fellow psychologist Amos Tversky (who would have surely shared the prize if not for his death in 1996). Prospect Theory provides a descriptive model of the way individuals make decisions under uncertainty, predicting the choices people *do* make rather than the ones they *should* make. It posits that people evaluate outcomes relative to the status quo or similar reference point (the *framing effect*), will take on risk to avoid realizing losses, and put too much weight on unlikely events. The disposition effect follows from Prospect Theory by assuming investors frame their decisions by comparing the sale price with the purchase price for each stock. In a similar way, Prospect Theory provides an important foundation for much research in behavioral economics and finance.

did not exhibit the same tendency, and other studies have shown that more sophisticated investors appear to be less susceptible to the disposition effect.[15]

This behavioral tendency to sell winners and hang on to losers is costly from a tax perspective. Because capital gains are taxed only when the asset is sold, it is optimal for tax purposes to postpone taxable gains by continuing to hold profitable investments, delaying the tax payment and reducing its present value. On the other hand, investors should capture tax losses by selling their losing investments, especially near the year's end, in order to accelerate the tax write-off.

Of course, hanging on to losers and selling winners might make sense if investors forecast that the losing stocks would ultimately "bounce back" and outperform the winners going forward. While investors may in fact have this belief, it does not appear to be justified—if anything, the losing stocks that small investors continue to hold tend to *underperform* the winners that they sell. According to one study, losers underperformed winners by 3.4% over the year after the winners were sold.[16]

Investor Attention, Mood, and Experience

Individual investors generally are not full-time traders. As a result, they have limited time and attention to spend on their investment decisions, and so may be influenced by attention-grabbing news stories or other events. Studies show that individuals are more likely to buy stocks that have recently been in the news, engaged in advertising, experienced exceptionally high trading volume, or have had extreme (positive or negative) returns.[17]

Investment behavior also seems to be affected by investors' moods. For example, sunshine generally has a positive effect on mood, and studies have found that stock returns tend to be higher when it is a sunny day at the location of the stock exchange. In New York City, the annualized market return on perfectly sunny days is approximately 24.8% per year versus 8.7% per year on perfectly cloudy days.[18] Further evidence of the link between investor mood and stock returns comes from the effect of major sports events on returns.

[15] R. Dhar and N. Zhu, "Up Close and Personal: Investor Sophistication and the Disposition Effect," *Management Science* 52 (2006): 726–740.

[16] T. Odean, "Are Investors Reluctant to Realize Their Losses? " *Journal of Finance* 53 (1998): 1775–1798.

[17] See G. Grullon, G. Kanatas, and J. Weston, "Advertising, Breadth of Ownership, and Liquidity," *Review of Financial Studies* 17 (2004): 439–461; M. Seasholes and G. Wu, "Predictable Behavior, Profits, and Attention," *Journal of Empirical Finance* 14 (2007): 590–610; Barber and T. Odean, "All That Glitters: The Effect of Attention and News on the Buying Behavior of Individual and Institutional Investors," *Review of Financial Studies* 21 (2008): 785–818.

[18] Based on data from 1982–1997; see D. Hirshleifer and T. Shumway, "Good Day Sunshine: Stock Returns and the Weather," *Journal of Finance* 58 (2003): 1009–1032.

One study estimates that a loss in the World Cup elimination stage lowers the next day's stock returns in the losing country by about 0.50%, presumably due to investors' poor mood.[19]

Finally, investors appear to put too much weight on their own experience rather than considering all the historical evidence. As a result, people who grew up and lived during a time of high stock returns are more likely to invest in stocks than people who experienced times when stocks performed poorly.[20]

Herd Behavior

Thus far, we have considered common factors that might lead to correlated trading behavior by investors. An alternative reason why investors make similar trading errors is that they are actively *trying* to follow each other's behavior. This phenomenon, in which individuals imitate each other's actions, is referred to as **herd behavior**.

There are several reasons why traders might herd in their portfolio choices. First, they might believe others have superior information that they can take advantage of by copying their trades. This behavior can lead to an **informational cascade effect** in which traders ignore their own information hoping to profit from the information of others.[21] A second possibility is that, due to relative wealth concerns, individuals choose to herd in order to avoid the risk of underperforming their peers.[22] Third, professional fund managers may face reputational risk if they stray too far from the actions of their peers.[23]

Implications of Behavioral Biases

The insight that investors make mistakes is not news. What is surprising, however, is that these mistakes persist even though they may be economically costly and there is a relatively easy way to avoid them—buying and holding the market portfolio.

Regardless of why individual investors choose not to protect themselves by holding the market portfolio, the fact that they don't has potential implications for the CAPM. If individual investors are engaging in strategies that earn negative alphas, it may be possible for more sophisticated investors to take advantage of this behavior and earn positive alphas. Is there evidence that such savvy investors exist? In Section 13.5, we examine evidence regarding this possibility.

CONCEPT CHECK

1. What are several systematic behavioral biases that individual investors fall prey to?
2. What implication might these behavioral biases have for the CAPM?

---

[19] A. Edmans, D. Garcia, and O. Norli, "Sports Sentiment and Stock Returns," *Journal of Finance* 62 (2007): 1967–1998.

[20] U. Malmendier and S. Nagel, "Depression Babies: Do Macroeconomic Experiences Affect Risk-Taking?", *Quarterly Journal of Economics* 126 (2011): 373–416.

[21] For example, see S. Bikhchandani, D. Hirshleifer, and I. Welch, "A Theory of Fads, Fashion, Custom and Cultural Change as Informational Cascades," *Journal of Political Economy* 100 (1992): 992–1026; and C. Avery and P. Zemsky, "Multidimensional Uncertainty and Herd Behavior in Financial Markets," *American Economic Review* 88 (1998): 724–748.

[22] P. DeMarzo, R. Kaniel, and I. Kremer, "Relative Wealth Concerns and Financial Bubbles," *Review of Financial Studies* 21 (2008): 19–50.

[23] D. Scharfstein and J. Stein, "Herd Behavior and Investment," *American Economic Review* 80 (1990): 465–479.

13.5 The Efficiency of the Market Portfolio

When individual investors make mistakes, can sophisticated investors easily profit at their expense? In order for sophisticated investors to profit from investor mistakes, two conditions must hold. First, the mistakes must be sufficiently pervasive and persistent to affect stock prices. That is, investor behavior must push prices so that non-zero alpha trading opportunities become apparent, as in Figure 13.2. Second, there must be limited competition to exploit these non-zero alpha opportunities. If competition is too intense, these opportunities will be quickly eliminated before any trader can take advantage of them in a significant way. In this section, we examine whether there is any evidence that individual or professional investors can outperform the market without taking on additional risk.

Trading on News or Recommendations

A natural place to look for profitable trading opportunities is in reaction to big news announcements or analysts' recommendations. If enough other investors are not paying attention, perhaps one can profit from these public sources of information.

Takeover Offers. One of the biggest news announcements for a firm, in terms of stock price impact, is when it is the target of a takeover offer. Typically, the offer is for a significant premium to the target's current stock price, and while the target's stock price typically jumps on the announcement, it often does not jump completely to the offer price. While it might seem that this difference creates a profitable trading opportunity, in most cases there is usually remaining uncertainty regarding whether the deal will occur at the initially offered price, at a higher price, or fail to occur at all. Figure 13.5 shows the average

FIGURE 13.5 Returns to Holding Target Stocks Subsequent to Takeover Announcements

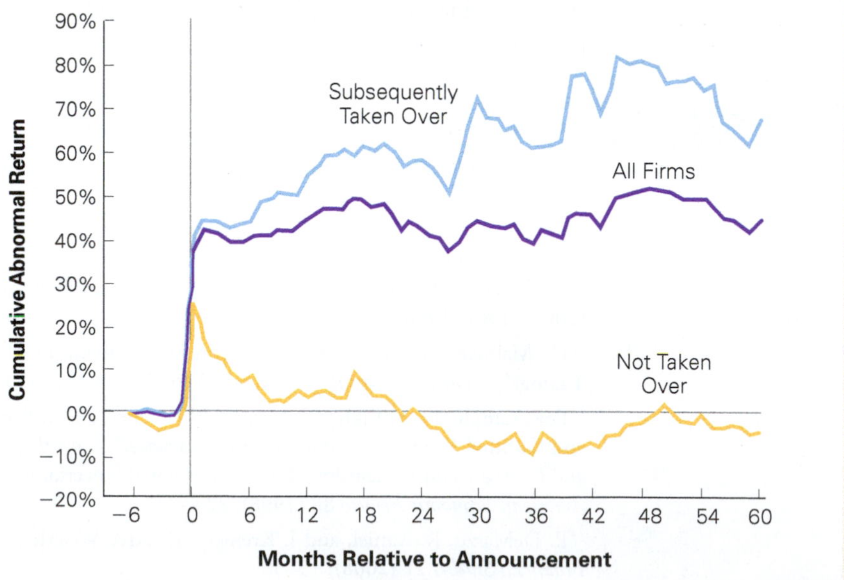

After the initial jump in the stock price at the time of the announcement, target stocks do not appear to earn abnormal subsequent returns on average. However, stocks that are ultimately acquired tend to appreciate and have positive alphas, while those that are not acquired have negative alphas. Thus, an investor could profit from correctly predicting the outcome.

Source: Adapted from M. Bradley, A. Desai, and E. H. Kim, "The Rationale Behind Interfirm Tender Offers: Information or Synergy?" *Journal of Financial Economics* 11 (1983): 183–206.

response to many such takeover announcements, showing the target stock's **cumulative abnormal return**, which measures the stock's return relative to that predicted based on its beta, at the time of the event. Figure 13.5 reveals that the initial jump in the stock price is high enough so that the stock's future returns do not outperform the market, on average. However, if we *could* predict whether the firm would ultimately be acquired, we could earn profits trading on that information.

Stock Recommendations. We could also consider stock recommendations. For example, popular commentator Jim Cramer makes numerous stock recommendations on his evening television show, *Mad Money*. Do investors profit from following these recommendations? Figure 13.6 shows the results of a recent study that analyzed the average stock price reaction to these recommendations, based on whether the recommendation coincided with a news story about the company. In the case where there is news, it appears that the stock price correctly reflects this information the next day, and stays flat (relative to the market) subsequently. On the other hand, for the stocks without news, there appears to be a significant jump in the stock price the next day, but the stock price then tends to fall relative to the market, generating a negative alpha, over the next several weeks. The authors of the study found that the stocks without news tended to be smaller, less liquid stocks; it appears that the individual investors who buy these stocks based on the recommendation push the price too high. They appear to be subject to an overconfidence bias, trusting too much in Cramer's recommendation and not adequately taking into account the behavior of their fellow investors. The more interesting question is why don't smart investors short these stocks and prevent the overreaction? In fact they do (the amount of short interest rises for these stocks), but because these small stocks are difficult to locate and borrow and therefore costly to short, the price does not correct immediately.

FIGURE 13.6 Stock Price Reactions to Recommendations on *Mad Money*

When recommendations coincide with news, the initial stock price reaction appears correct and future alphas are not significantly different from zero. Without news, the stock price appears to overreact. While sophisticated investors gain by shorting these stocks, costs of shorting limit their ability to do so.

Source: Adapted from J. Engelberg, C. Sasseville, J. Williams, "Market Madness? The Case of Mad Money," *Management Science*, 2011.

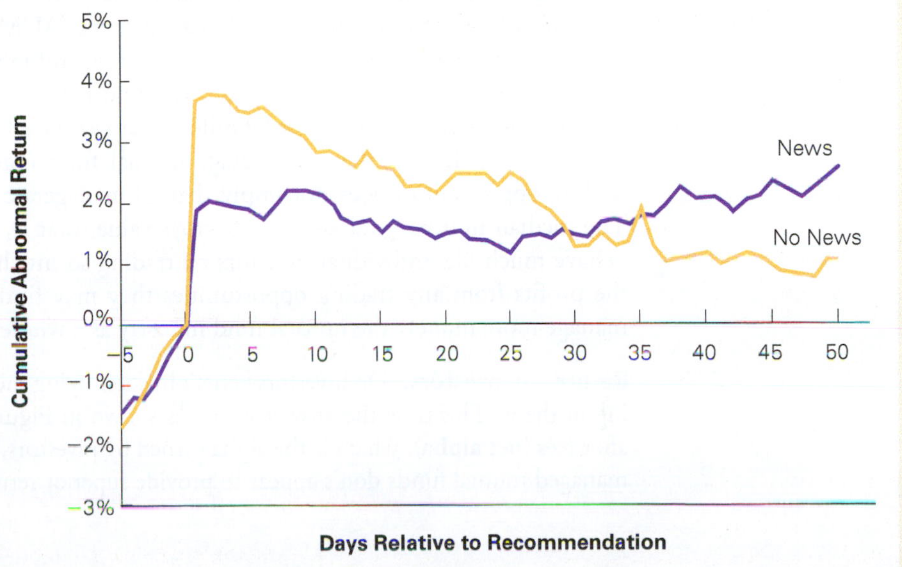

NOBEL PRIZE **The 2013 Prize: An Enigma?**

When the 2013 Nobel Prize in Economics was awarded to three financial economists, most people were surprised. The surprise was not that Eugene Fama, Robert Shiller, and Lars Peter Hansen had won the prize—most economists would agree they certainly deserved the prize for their contributions—rather it was that they won it *together*. After all, Fama is most well-known for what he termed the *efficient market hypothesis*, the assertion that markets are so competitive it is impossible to make money by trying to predict stock price movements. On the other hand, Robert Shiller argued the opposite, that the excess volatility in markets results from irrational behavior that can be exploited. Lars Peter Hansen is credited with developing statistical tools that can help distinguish these opposing views. Here is how the Nobel Prize committee justified its decision:

"Beginning in the 1960s, Eugene Fama and several collaborators demonstrated that stock prices are extremely difficult to predict in the short run, and that new information is very quickly incorporated into prices. . . . If prices are nearly impossible to predict over days or weeks, then shouldn't they be even harder to predict over several years? The answer is no, as Robert Shiller discovered in the early 1980s. He found that stock prices fluctuate much more than corporate dividends, and that the ratio of prices to dividends tends to fall when it is high, and to increase when it is low. This pattern holds not only for stocks, but also for bonds and other assets. Lars Peter Hansen developed a statistical method that is particularly well suited to testing rational theories of asset pricing. Using this method, Hansen and other researchers have found that modifications of these theories go a long way toward explaining asset prices."

Source: "The Prize in Economic Sciences 2013—Press Release." Nobelprize.org.

The Performance of Fund Managers

The previous results suggest that though it may not be easy to profit simply by trading on news, sophisticated investors might be able to do so (for example, by being better able to predict takeover outcomes, or short small stocks). Presumably, professional fund managers, such as those who manage mutual funds, should be in the best position to take advantage of such opportunities. Are they able to find profit-making opportunities in financial markets?

Fund Manager Value-Added. The answer is yes. The value a fund manager adds by engaging in profit-making trades is equal to the fund's alpha before fees (**gross alpha**) multiplied by the fund's assets under management (AUM). The evidence shows that the average mutual fund manager is able to identify profitable trading opportunities worth approximately \$3 million per year, and for fund managers with at least five years experience, the number rises to almost \$9 million per year (see Figure 13.7).[24]

Of course, the fact that the average mutual fund manager is able to find profitable trading opportunities does not imply that all managers can do so. In fact, most cannot. The median mutual fund actually destroys value; that is, most fund managers appear to behave much like individual investors by trading so much that their trading costs exceed the profits from any trading opportunities they may find. But because skilled managers manage more money, the mutual fund industry as a whole has positive value added.

Returns to Investors. Do investors benefit by identifying the profit-making funds and investing in them? This time the answer is no. As shown in Figure 13.7, the average fund's alpha after fees (**net alpha**), which is the alpha earned by investors, is −0.34%. On average actively managed mutual funds don't appear to provide superior returns for their investors compared

[24] J. Berk and J. van Binsbergen, "Measuring Managerial Skill in the Mutual Fund Industry," *Journal of Financial Economics* 118 (2015): 1–20.

FIGURE 13.7

Manager Value Added and Investor Returns for U.S. Mutual Funds (1977–2011)

Value added is alpha before fees (gross alpha) times assets under management with alpha computed relative to available passive index funds. Net alpha is the alpha earned by fund investors (the gross alpha net of fees). Results are averaged across all fund managers with at least 5 years experience for each size quintile. While mutual fund managers do add value on average, they capture this value through their fees, so that investors do not earn positive alphas.

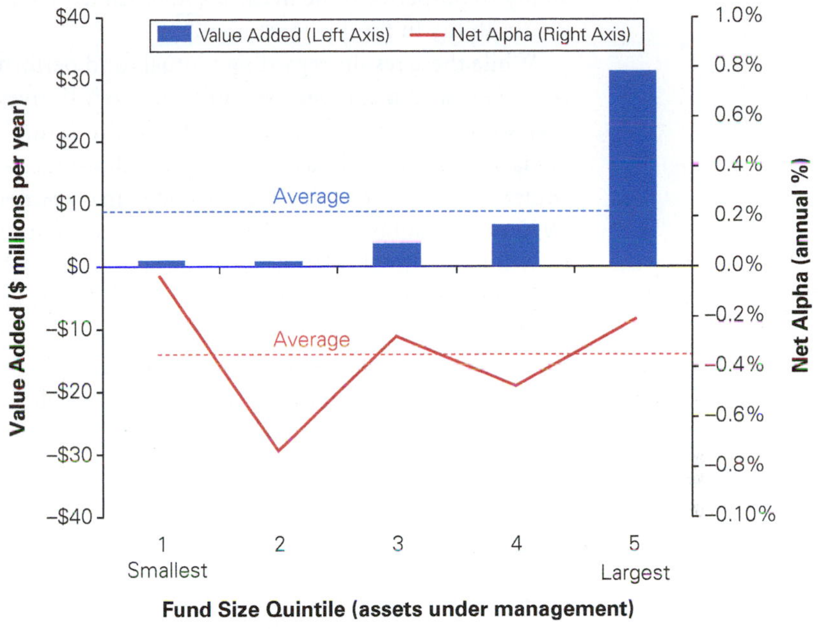

to investing in passive index funds.[25] The reason fund managers can add value but investors do not benefit is that on average the value added is offset by the fees the funds charge.

While the average mutual fund does not provide a positive alpha to its investors, it is possible that some funds might. Can investors identify funds that consistently deliver positive alphas to their investors? Morningstar ranks fund managers each year based on their historical performance. For example, Morningstar named Legg Mason's William Miller, whose performance we highlighted in the introduction to this chapter, as manager of the year in 1998 and manager of the decade the following year. As we have already noted, investors who were motivated to invest based on these awards saw poor performance over the next 10 years. Miller's experience is not exceptional. At the end of each year Forbes publishes an Honor Roll of top mutual funds based on an analysis of the past performance and riskiness of the fund. In a famous 1994 study, Vanguard CEO John Bogle compared the returns from investing in the market index with the returns from investing each year in the newly announced Honor Roll funds. Over a 19-year period, the Honor Roll portfolio had an annual return of 11.2%, whereas the market index fund had an annual return of 13.1%.[26]

---

[25] Many studies report negative average alphas for investments in U.S equity mutual funds; see e.g., R. Kosowski, A. Timmermann, R. Wermers, and H. White, "Can Mutual Fund 'Stars' Really Pick Stocks? New Evidence from a Bootstrap Analysis," *Journal of Finance* 61 (2006): 2551–2596 and E. Fama, and K. French, "Luck versus Skill in the Cross Section of Mutual Fund Alpha Estimates," *Journal of Finance* 65 (2010) 1915–1947. Using an expanded time period, and considering funds that hold international as well as domestic stocks, J. Berk and J. van Binsbergen, find that alphas are not significantly different from zero ("Measuring Managerial Skill in the Mutual Fund Industry," *Journal of Financial Economics* 118 (2015): 1–20).

[26] J. Bogle, *Bogle on Mutual Funds: New Perspectives for the Intelligent Investor*, McGraw-Hill, 1994.

Thus, the superior past performance of these funds was not a good predictor of their future ability to outperform the market. Other studies have confirmed this result, and found little predictability in fund performance.[27]

While these results regarding mutual fund performance might seem surprising, they are consistent with a competitive capital market. If investors could predict that a skilled manager would generate a positive alpha in the future, they would rush to invest with this manager, who would then be flooded with capital. During Legg Mason manager William Miller's meteoric rise, his capital under management grew from about $700 million in 1992 to $28 billion in 2007. But the more capital the manager has to invest, the harder it is to find profitable trading opportunities. Once these opportunities are exhausted, the manager can no longer produce better-than-average performance.[28] Ultimately, as new capital arrives the fund's returns should fall. The inflow of capital will cease when the fund's alpha is no longer positive.[29] Indeed, alphas could be somewhat negative to reflect other benefits these funds provide, or could result from overconfidence. Investors put too much confidence in their ability to select fund managers and thus commit too much capital to them.

The argument above suggests that because skilled managers attract more capital, they will manage the largest funds. Consequently, fund size is a strong predictor of the future value added by fund managers.[30] But while investors appear to be good at picking managers, in the end they derive little benefit, because this superior performance is captured by the manager in the form of fees—mutual funds charge approximately the same percentage fee, so the larger funds collect higher aggregate fees. This result is exactly as we should expect: In a competitive labor market, the fund manager should capture the economic rents associated with his or her unique skill. In summary, while the profits of mutual fund managers imply it is possible to find profitable trading opportunities in markets, being able to do so consistently is a rare talent possessed by only the most skilled fund managers, and these managers earn fees commensurate with their talent.

Researchers have obtained similar results when evaluating institutional fund managers responsible for managing retirement plans, pension funds, and endowment assets. A study investigating the hiring decisions of plan sponsors found that sponsors picked managers that had significantly outperformed their benchmarks historically (see Figure 13.8). Once

---

[27]See M. Carhart, "On Persistence in Mutual Fund Performance," *Journal of Finance* 52 (1997): 57–82. One possible exception is fund fees—ironically, small funds that charge a higher percentage fee seem to generate predictably *lower* returns for their investors.

[28]In Miller's case most investors paid dearly for their confidence in him—although his losses post-2007 equaled his gains from 1992, most investors were not invested in 1992, and so they experienced overall performance that lagged the S&P 500. Not surprisingly, after 2007 he experienced large capital outflows, so by the end of 2008 he had only about $1.2 billion under management.

[29]This mechanism was proposed by J. Berk and R. Green, "Mutual Fund Flows in Rational Markets," *Journal of Political Economy* 112 (2004): 1269–1295. The following studies all find that new capital flows into funds that do well and out of funds that do poorly: M. Gruber, "Another Puzzle: The Growth in Actively Managed Mutual Funds," *Journal of Finance* 51 (1996): 783–810; E. Sirri and P. Tufano, "Costly Search and Mutual Fund Flows," *Journal of Finance* 53 (1998): 1589–1622; J. Chevalier and G. Ellison, "Risk Taking by Mutual Funds as a Response to Incentives," *Journal of Political Economy* 105 (1997): 1167–1200.

[30]J. Berk and J. van Binsbergen, "Measuring Managerial Skill in the Mutual Fund Industry," *Journal of Financial Economics* 118 (2015): 1–20.

FIGURE 13.8 **Before and After Hiring Returns of Investment Managers**

While plan sponsors tend to hire managers that have significantly outperformed their benchmarks historically, after-hiring performance is similar to the excess return of the average fund (0.64% on a value-weighted basis). Data based on 8755 hiring decisions of 3400 plan sponsors from 1994–2003, and returns are gross of management fees (which tend to range from 0.5%–0.7%/year).

Sources: A. Goyal and S. Wahal, "The Selection and Termination of Investment Management Firms by Plan Sponsors," *Journal of Finance* 63 (2008): 1805–1847 and with J. Busse, "Performance and Persistence in Institutional Investment Management," *Journal of Finance* 63 (2008): 1805–1847.

hired, however, the performance of these new managers looked very similar to the average fund, with returns exceeding their benchmarks by an amount roughly equal to their management fees.

The Winners and Losers

The evidence in this section suggests that while it may be possible to improve on the market portfolio, it isn't easy. This result is perhaps not so surprising, for as we noted in Section 13.2, the average investor (on a value-weighted basis) earns an alpha of zero, *before* including trading costs. So beating the market should require special skills, such as better analysis of information, or lower trading costs.

Because individual investors are likely to be at a disadvantage on both counts, as well as subject to behavioral biases, the CAPM wisdom that investors should "hold the market" is probably the best advice for most people. Indeed, a comprehensive study of the Taiwan stock market found that individual investors there lose an average of 3.8% per year by trading, with roughly 1/3 of the losses due to poor trades and the remaining 2/3 due to transactions costs.[31]

[31]Taiwan provides a unique opportunity to study how profits are distributed, because unlike the U.S., the identity of buyers and sellers is tracked for all trades. See B. Barber, Y. Lee, Y. Liu, and T. Odean, "Just How Much Do Individual Investors Lose by Trading?" *Review of Financial Studies* 22 (2009): 609–632.

The same study reported that institutions earn 1.5% per year on average from their trades. But while professional fund managers may profit due to their talent, information, and superior trading infrastructure, the results in this section suggest that little of those profits go to the investors who invest with them.

CONCEPT CHECK

1. Should uninformed investors expect to make money by trading based on news announcements?
2. If fund managers are talented, why do the returns of their funds to investors not have positive alphas?

13.6 Style-Based Techniques and the Market Efficiency Debate

In Section 13.5, we looked for evidence that professional investors could profit at small investors' expense and outperform the market. In this section, we will take a different tack. Rather than looking at managers' profits, we will look at possible *trading strategies.* In particular, many fund managers distinguish their trading strategies based on the types of stocks they tend to hold; specifically, small versus large stocks, and value versus growth stocks. In this section, we will consider these alternative investment styles, and see whether some strategies have generated higher returns historically than the CAPM predicts.

Size Effects

As we reported in Chapter 10, small stocks (those with smaller market capitalizations) have historically earned higher average returns than the market portfolio. Moreover, while small stocks do tend to have high market risk, their returns appear high even accounting for their higher beta, an empirical result we call the **size effect.**

Excess Return and Market Capitalizations. To compare the performance of portfolios formed based on size, Professors Eugene Fama and Kenneth French[32] divided stocks each year into ten portfolios by ranking them based on their market capitalizations, and collecting the smallest 10% of stocks into the first portfolio, the next 10% into the second portfolio, up to the biggest 10% into the tenth portfolio. They then recorded the monthly excess returns of each decile portfolio over the following year. After repeating this process for each year, they calculated the average excess return of each portfolio and the beta of the portfolio; Figure 13.9 shows the result. As you can see, although the portfolios with higher betas yield higher returns, most portfolios plot above the security market line (SML)—all except one portfolio had a positive alpha. The smallest deciles exhibit the most extreme effect.

Of course, this result could be due to estimation error; as the figure shows, the standard errors are large and none of the alpha estimates is significantly different from zero. However, nine of the ten portfolios plot above the SML. If the positive alphas were due purely to statistical error, we would expect as many portfolios to appear above the line as below it. Consequently, a test of whether the alphas of all ten portfolios are jointly all equal to zero can be statistically rejected.

---

[32]See E. Fama and K. French, "The Cross-Section of Stock Returns," *Journal of Finance* 47 (1992): 427–465.

FIGURE 13.9 **Excess Return of Size Portfolios, 1926–2015**

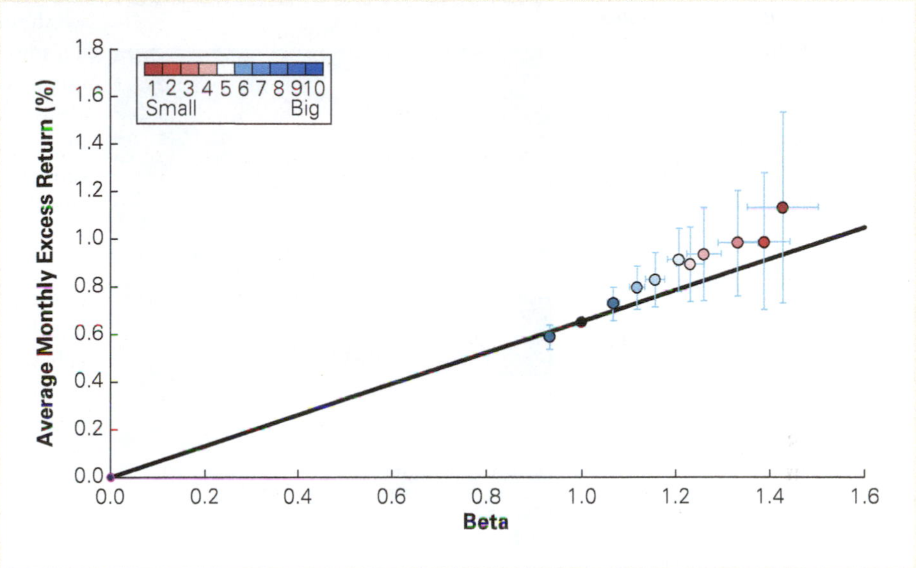

The plot shows the average monthly excess return (the return minus the one-month risk-free rate) for ten portfolios formed in each year based on firms' market capitalizations, plotted as a function of the portfolio's estimated beta. The black line is the security market line. If the market portfolio is efficient and there is no measurement error, all portfolios would plot along this line. The error bars mark the 95% confidence bands of the beta and expected excess return estimates. Note the tendency of small stocks to be above the security market line.

Source: Data courtesy of Kenneth French.

Excess Return and Book-to-Market Ratio. Researchers have found similar results using the **book-to-market ratio**, the ratio of the book value of equity to the market value of equity, to form stocks into portfolios. Recall from Chapter 2 that practitioners refer to stocks with high book-to-market ratios as value stocks, and those with low book-to-market ratios as growth stocks. Figure 13.10 demonstrates that value stocks tend to have positive alphas, and growth stocks tend to have low or negative alphas. Once again, a joint test of whether all 10 portfolios have an alpha of zero is rejected.

Size Effects and Empirical Evidence. The size effect—the observation that small stocks (or stocks with a high book-to-market ratio) have positive alphas—was first discovered in 1981 by Rolf Banz.[33] At the time, researchers did not find the evidence to be convincing because financial economists had been *searching* the data, looking for stocks with positive alphas. Because of estimation error, it is always possible to find stocks with estimated positive alphas; indeed, if we look hard enough, it is also always possible to find

[33]See R. Banz, "The Relationship between Return and Market Values of Common Stock," *Journal of Financial Economics* 9 (1981): 3–18. A similar relation between stock price (rather than size) and future returns was found by M. Blume and F. Husic, "Price, Beta and Exchange Listing," *Journal of Finance* 28 (1973): 283–299.

INTERVIEW WITH

JONATHAN CLEMENTS

Jonathan Clements is the former personal finance columnist for *The Wall Street Journal* and author of *The Little Book of Main Street Money* (Wiley 2009).

QUESTION: *You have written for years on personal finance. How has academic theory influenced investor behavior?*

ANSWER: When I started writing about mutual funds in the 1980s, investors would ask, "What are the best funds?" Today, they are more likely to say, "I'm looking to add a foreign-stock fund to my portfolio. Which funds in that category do you like? Or should I index instead?"

We have gotten away from the blind pursuit of market-beating returns, and there is more focus on portfolio construction and a growing willingness to consider indexing. That reflects the impact of academic research.

What has really influenced investors has been the academic "grunt work" of the past four decades, which has given us a decent grasp of what historical market returns look like. Thanks to that research, many ordinary investors have a better understanding of how stocks have performed relative to bonds. They realize that most actively managed stock mutual funds don't beat the market, and thus, there is a case for indexing. They appreciate that different market sectors perform well at different times, so there is a real value in diversifying.

QUESTION: *Some have critiqued the idea of holding a well-diversified portfolio, arguing that diversification hasn't worked in the 2008–2009 financial crisis. Is diversification still the best strategy?*

ANSWER: Yes, when markets collapse, pretty much every sector gets bludgeoned. But just because investments rise and fall in sync with one another doesn't mean they rise and fall by the same amount. You might have a portfolio where one sector falls 40 percent and another loses 20 percent. Sure, losing 20 percent stings. Still, holding that sector is reducing your portfolio's overall loss, so you are indeed benefiting from diversification.

QUESTION: *Academics talk about efficient frontiers and optimal portfolios. How does that translate into advice for someone looking to build a portfolio?*

ANSWER: While academic research has influenced ordinary investors, we shouldn't overstate the case. To some extent, the research has merely codified what investors already knew intuitively. For instance, investors have always thought about risk as well as return, and they have always been inclined to diversify. The academic research may have made investors a little more rigorous in their thinking, but it didn't radically change their behavior.

Moreover, to the extent that the research doesn't fit with investors' intuition, they have clearly rejected it. Investors still behave in ways that academics would consider sub-optimal. They don't build well-diversified portfolios and then focus on the risk and return of the overall portfolio. Instead, they build moderately diversified portfolios—and then pay a lot of attention to the risk and reward of each investment they own.

QUESTION: *How does risk tolerance affect the type of portfolio a person should build?*

ANSWER: In theory, investors should hold the globally diversified all-asset "market portfolio" and then, depending on their risk tolerance, either add risk-free assets to reduce volatility or use leverage to boost returns. But almost nobody invests that way. In fact, I once tried to find out what the market portfolio looks like—and discovered nobody knows for sure.

Among the vast majority of ordinary investors, the idea of using leverage to buy investments is an anathema. In practice, many are doing just that. They hold a portfolio of assets, including stocks, bonds, and real estate, and they have a heap of debt, including their mortgage, auto loans, and credit card balances. But the implication—that they effectively have a leveraged stock market bet—would horrify most investors.

While nobody seems to know what the market portfolio looks like, investors have become willing to consider a broader array of assets, including foreign stocks, real estate investment trusts, and commodities. I think the trend will continue, as people come to realize that they can lower a portfolio's risk level by adding apparently risky investments.

FIGURE 13.10

Excess Return of Book-to-Market Portfolios, 1926–2015

The plot shows the same data as Figure 13.9, with portfolios formed based on stocks' book-to-market ratios rather than size. Note the tendency of value stocks (high book-to-market) to be above the security market line, and growth stocks (low book-to-market) to be near or below the line.

Source: Data courtesy of Kenneth French.

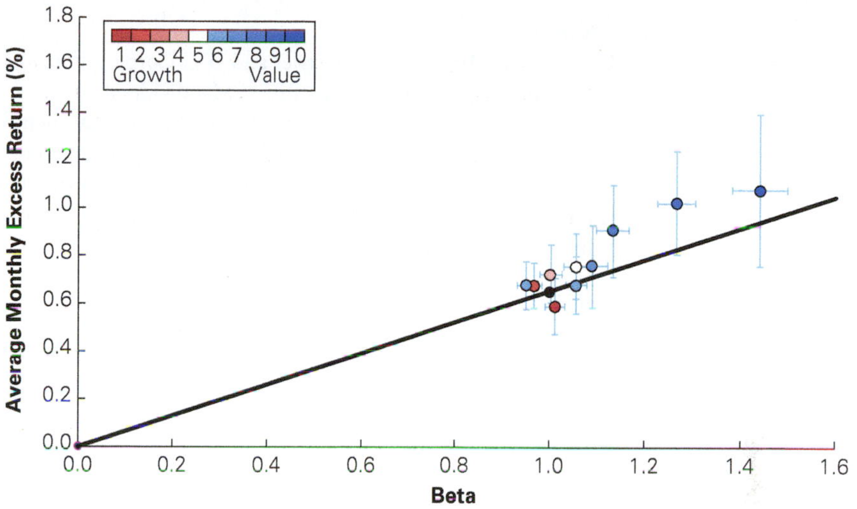

something these stocks have in common. As a consequence, many researchers were inclined to attribute Banz's findings to a **data snooping bias**, which is the idea that given enough characteristics, it will always be possible to find some characteristic that by pure chance happens to be correlated with the estimation error of average returns.[34]

After the publication of Banz's study, however, a theoretical reason emerged that explained the relationship between market capitalization and expected returns. Financial economists realized that as long as beta is not a *perfect* measure of risk—either due to estimation error, or because the market portfolio is not efficient—we should *expect* to observe the size effect.[35] To understand why, consider a stock with a positive alpha. All else equal, a positive alpha implies that the stock also has a relatively high expected return. A higher expected return implies a lower price—the only way to offer a higher expected return is for investors to buy the stock's dividend stream at a lower price. A lower price means a lower market capitalization (and similarly a higher book-to-market ratio—market capitalization is in the *denominator* of the book-to-market ratio). Thus, when a financial economist forms a portfolio of stocks with low market capitalizations (or high book-to-market ratios), that collection contains stocks that will likely have higher expected returns and, if the market portfolio is not efficient, positive alphas. Similarly, a stock that plots below the security market line will have a lower expected return and, all else equal, a higher price, implying that it has a higher market capitalization and lower book-to-market ratio. Hence a portfolio of stocks with high market capitalizations or low book-to-market ratios will have negative alphas if the market portfolio is not efficient. Let's illustrate with a simple example.

[34] David Leinweber, in his book *Nerds on Wall Street* (Wiley Financial, 2008), illustrates this point by searching the data for a patently absurd characteristic that is correlated with returns. He found that over a 13-year period annual butter production in Bangladesh can "explain" annual variation in S&P 500 returns!

[35] See J. Berk, "A Critique of Size-Related Anomalies," *Review of Financial Studies* 8 (1995): 275–286.

EXAMPLE 13.2 Risk and the Market Value of Equity

Problem

Consider two firms, SM Industries and BiG Corporation, which are expected to pay dividends of $1 million per year in perpetuity. SM's dividend stream is riskier than BiG's, so its cost of capital is 14% per year. BiG's cost of capital is 10%. Which firm has the higher market value? Which firm has the higher expected return? Now assume both stocks have the same estimated beta, either because of estimation error, or because the market portfolio is not efficient. Based on this beta, the CAPM would assign an expected return of 12% to both stocks. How do the market values of the firms relate to their alphas?

Solution

The timeline of dividends is the same for both firms:

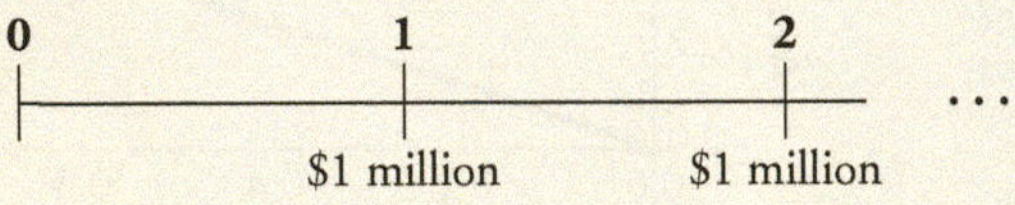

To calculate the market value of SM, we calculate the present value of its future expected dividends using the perpetuity formula and a cost of capital of 14%:

$$\text{Market Value of SM} = \frac{1}{0.14} = \$7.143 \text{ million}$$

Similarly, the market value of BiG is

$$\text{Market Value of BiG} = \frac{1}{0.10} = \$10 \text{ million}$$

SM has the lower market value, and a higher expected return (14% vs. 10%). It also has the higher alpha:

$$\alpha_{SM} = 0.14 - 0.12 = 2\%$$

$$\alpha_{BiG} = 0.10 - 0.12 = -2\%$$

Consequently, the firm with the lower market value has the higher alpha.

When the market portfolio is not efficient, theory predicts that stocks with low market capitalizations or high book-to-market ratios will have positive alphas. In light of this observation, the size effect is, indeed, potential evidence against the efficiency of the market portfolio.

Momentum

Researchers have also used past stock returns to form portfolios with positive alphas. For example, for the years 1965 to 1989, Narishiman Jegadeesh and Sheridan Titman[36] ranked stocks each month by their realized returns over the prior 6–12 months. They found that the best-performing stocks had positive alphas over the next 3–12 months.

[36]See N. Jegadeesh and S. Titman, "Returns to Buying Winners and Selling Losers: Implications for Market Efficiency," *Journal of Finance* 48 (1993): 65–91.

Market Efficiency and the Efficiency of the Market Portfolio

In Chapter 9 we introduced the *efficient markets hypothesis*, which states that competition should eliminate positive-NPV trading opportunities or, equivalently, that securities with equivalent risk should have the same expected return. But because "equivalent risk" is not well defined, we cannot test the efficient markets hypothesis directly. The risk measure is well defined under the CAPM assumptions, however, and thus we can test the idea that no positive-NPV trading opportunities exist in the CAPM by testing whether the market portfolio is efficient and all trading strategies have zero alpha.

Some researchers further categorize such tests as tests of *weak form, semi-strong form*, and *strong form efficiency*. **Weak form efficiency** states that it should not be possible to profit by trading on information in past prices by, for example, selling winners and hanging on to losers or, conversely, by trading on momentum. **Semi-strong form efficiency** states that it should not be possible to consistently profit by trading on any public information, such as news announcements or analysts' recommendations. Finally **strong form efficiency** states that it should not be possible to consistently profit even by trading on private information.

Note that the efficient markets hypothesis does *not* state that market prices are always correct given *future* information. For example, the 2008 financial crisis made clear that the share prices of many banks and other firms were overvalued in 2007. Given this information, selling bank stocks in 2007 would have been a positive-NPV trading opportunity. But this fact on its own does not contradict market efficiency. We would need to demonstrate that the financial crisis was easily predictable in 2007, and that many investors profited by trading on that knowledge. The scarcity of "winners" in the wake of the financial crisis makes clear that this prediction was by no means obvious at the time. Indeed, the trader most famous for anticipating the banking crisis by shorting mortgage-backed securities, John Paulson, has had mediocre performance since then, with his Advantage Plus fund recording a *60% loss* from August 2010 to August 2015, suggesting, perhaps, that his earlier bet might have had to do more with luck, and a healthy appetite for risk, rather than skill.

As the evidence in this chapter makes clear, when we use the CAPM to measure risk, the evidence for market efficiency is mixed: individual investors don't seem to "beat the market" on average, yet at the same time certain trading strategies do appear to be profitable. The key question facing finance researchers is how to correctly measure risk. Do these "profitable" strategies entail systematic risks not identified by the CAPM—making them fairly priced according to some more general model of risk than the CAPM? Or do they represent a true opportunity to earn higher returns without increasing risk?

This evidence goes against the CAPM: When the market portfolio is efficient, past returns should not predict alphas.

Investors can exploit this result by buying stocks that have had past high returns and (short) selling stocks that have had past low returns, which is called a **momentum strategy**. Jegadeesh and Titman showed that over the period 1965–1989, this strategy would have produced an alpha of over 12% per year.

Implications of Positive-Alpha Trading Strategies

Over the years since the discovery of the CAPM, it has become increasingly clear to researchers and practitioners alike that by forming portfolios based on market capitalization, book-to-market ratios, and past returns, investors can construct trading strategies that have a positive alpha. Given these results, we are left to draw one of two conclusions:

1. Investors are systematically ignoring positive-NPV investment opportunities. That is, the CAPM correctly computes required risk premiums, but investors are ignoring opportunities to earn extra returns without bearing any extra risk, either because they are unaware of them or because the costs to implement the strategies are larger than the NPV of undertaking them.
2. The positive-alpha trading strategies contain risk that investors are unwilling to bear but the CAPM does not capture. That is, a stock's beta with the market portfolio

does not adequately measure a stock's systematic risk, and so the CAPM does not correctly compute the risk premium.

The only way a positive-NPV opportunity can persist in a market is if some barrier to entry restricts competition. In this case, it is very difficult to identify what these barriers might be. The existence of these trading strategies has been widely known for more than 15 years. Not only is the information required to form the portfolios readily available, but many mutual funds follow momentum-based and market capitalization/book-to-market–based strategies. Hence, the first conclusion does not seem likely.

That leaves the second possibility: The market portfolio is not efficient, and therefore a stock's beta with the market is not an adequate measure of its systematic risk. Stated another way, the profits (positive alphas) from the trading strategy are really returns for bearing risk that investors are averse to and the CAPM does not capture. There are several reasons why the market portfolio might not be efficient. Let's examine each possibility in turn.

Proxy Error. The true market portfolio may be efficient, but the proxy we have used for it may be inaccurate. The true market portfolio consists of all traded investment wealth in the economy, including bonds, real estate, art, precious metals, and so on. We cannot include most of these investments in the market proxy because competitive price data is not available. Consequently, standard proxies like the S&P 500 may be inefficient compared with the true market, and stocks will have nonzero alphas.[37] In this case, the alphas merely indicate that the wrong proxy is being used; they do not indicate foregone positive-NPV investment opportunities.[38]

Behavioral Biases. As we discussed in Section 13.4, some investors may be subject to systematic behavioral biases. For example, they may be attracted to large growth stocks that receive greater news coverage. Or they may sell winners and hang on to losers, following a contrarian strategy. By falling prey to these biases, these investors are holding inefficient portfolios. More sophisticated investors hold an efficient portfolio, but because supply must equal demand, this efficient portfolio must include more small, value, and momentum stocks to offset the trades of biased investors. While alphas are zero with respect to this efficient portfolio, they are positive when compared with the market portfolio (which is the combined holdings of the biased and sophisticated investors).

Alternative Risk Preferences and Non-Tradable Wealth. Investors may also choose inefficient portfolios because they care about risk characteristics other than the volatility of their traded portfolio. For example, they may be attracted to investments with

---

[37]When the true market portfolio is efficient, even a small difference between the proxy and true market portfolio can lead to an insignificant relation between beta and returns. See R. Roll and S. Ross, "On the Cross-Sectional Relation between Expected Returns and Beta," *Journal of Finance* 49(1) (1994): 101–121.

[38]Because we cannot actually construct the *true* market portfolio of *all* risky investments, the CAPM theory is in some sense untestable (see R. Roll, "A Critique of the Asset Pricing Theory's Tests," *Journal of Financial Economics* 4 (1977): 129–176). Of course, from a corporate manager's perspective, whether the CAPM is testable is irrelevant—as long as an efficient portfolio can be identified, he or she can use it to compute the cost of capital.

skewed distributions that have a small probability of an extremely high payoff. As a result, they might be willing to hold some diversifiable risk in order to obtain such a payoff. In addition, investors are exposed to other significant risks outside their portfolio that are not tradable, the most important of which is due to their human capital.[39] For example, a banker at Goldman Sachs is exposed to financial sector risk, while a software engineer is exposed to risk in the high-tech sector. When choosing a portfolio, investors may deviate from the market portfolio to offset these inherent exposures.[40]

It is important to appreciate that just because the market portfolio is not efficient, this does not rule out the possibility of *another* portfolio being efficient. In fact, as we pointed out in Chapter 11, the CAPM pricing relationship holds with *any* efficient portfolio. Consequently, in light of the evidence against the efficiency of the market portfolio, researchers have developed alternative models of risk and return that do not rely on the efficiency of the market portfolio in particular. We develop such a model in Section 13.7.

CONCEPT CHECK

1. What does the existence of a positive-alpha trading strategy imply?
2. If investors have a significant amount of non-tradable (but risky) wealth, why might the market portfolio not be efficient?

13.7 Multifactor Models of Risk

In Chapter 11, we presented the expected return of any marketable security as a function of the expected return of the efficient portfolio:

$$E[R_s] = r_f + \beta_s^{eff} \times (E[R_{eff}] - r_f) \tag{13.3}$$

When the market portfolio is not efficient, to use Eq.13.3 we need to find an alternative method to identify an efficient portfolio.

As a practical matter, it is extremely difficult to identify portfolios that are efficient because we cannot measure the expected return and the standard deviation of a portfolio with great accuracy. Yet, although we might not be able to identify the efficient portfolio itself, we do know some characteristics of the efficient portfolio. First, any efficient portfolio will be well diversified. Second, we can construct an efficient portfolio from other well-diversified portfolios. This latter observation may seem trivial, but it is actually quite useful: It implies that *it is not actually necessary to identify the efficient portfolio itself.* As long as we can identify a *collection* of well-diversified portfolios from which an efficient portfolio can be constructed, we can use the collection itself to measure risk.

[39] Although rare, there are innovative new markets that allow people to trade their human capital to finance their education; see M. Palacios, *Investing in Human Capital: A Capital Markets Approach to Student Funding*, Cambridge University Press, 2004.

[40] Indeed, human capital risk can explain some of the inefficiency of common market proxies. See R. Jagannathan and Z. Wang, "The Conditional CAPM and the Cross-Sections of Expected Returns," *Journal of Finance* 51 (1996): 3–53; and I. Palacios-Huerta, "The Robustness of the Conditional CAPM with Human Capital," *Journal of Financial Econometrics* 1 (2003): 272–289.

Using Factor Portfolios

Assume that we have identified portfolios that we can combine to form an efficient portfolio; we call these portfolios **factor portfolios**. Then, as we show in the appendix, if we use N factor portfolios with returns $R_{F1}, \ldots, R_{FN}$, the expected return of asset s is given by

Multifactor Model of Risk

$$E[R_s] = r_f + \beta_s^{F1}(E[R_{F1}] - r_f) + \beta_s^{F2}(E[R_{F2}] - r_f) + \cdots + \beta_s^{FN}(E[R_{FN}] - r_f)$$

$$= r_f + \sum_{n=1}^{N} \beta_s^{Fn}(E[R_{Fn}] - r_f) \qquad (13.4)$$

Here $\beta_s^{F1}, \ldots, \beta_s^{FN}$ are the **factor betas**, one for each risk factor, and have the same interpretation as the beta in the CAPM. Each factor beta is the expected % change in the excess return of a security for a 1% change in the excess return of the factor portfolio (holding the other factors constant).

Equation 13.4 says that we can write the risk premium of any marketable security as the sum of the risk premium of each factor multiplied by the sensitivity of the stock with that factor—the *factor betas*. There is nothing inconsistent between Eq.13.4, which gives the expected return in terms of multiple factors, and Eq.13.3, which gives the expected return in terms of just the efficient portfolio. *Both* equations hold; the difference between them is simply the portfolios that we use. When we use an efficient portfolio, it alone will capture all systematic risk. Consequently, we often refer to this model as a **single-factor model**. If we use multiple portfolios as factors, then together these factors will capture all systematic risk, but note that each factor in Eq.13.4 captures different components of the systematic risk. When we use more than one portfolio to capture risk, the model is known as a **multifactor model**. Each portfolio can be interpreted as either a risk factor itself or a portfolio of stocks correlated with an unobservable risk factor.[41] The model is also referred to as the **Arbitrage Pricing Theory (APT)**.

We can simplify Eq.13.4 a bit further. Think of the expected excess return of each factor, $E[R_{Fn}] - r_f$, as the expected return of a portfolio in which we borrow the funds at rate r_f to invest in the factor portfolio. Because this portfolio costs nothing to construct (we are borrowing the funds to invest), it is called a **self-financing portfolio**. We can also construct a self-financing portfolio by going long some stocks, and going short other stocks with equal market value. In general, a self-financing portfolio is any portfolio with portfolio weights that sum to zero rather than one. If we require that all factor portfolios are self-financing (either by borrowing funds or shorting stocks), then we can rewrite Eq.13.4 as

Multifactor Model of Risk with Self-Financing Portfolios

$$E[R_s] = r_f + \beta_s^{F1}E[R_{F1}] + \beta_s^{F2}E[R_{F2}] + \cdots + \beta_s^{FN}E[R_{FN}]$$

$$= r_f + \sum_{n=1}^{N} \beta_s^{Fn}E[R_{Fn}] \qquad (13.5)$$

[41] This form of the multifactor model was originally developed by Stephen Ross, although Robert Merton had developed an alternative multifactor model earlier. See S. Ross, "The Arbitrage Theory of Capital Asset Pricing," *Journal of Economic Theory* 13 (1976): 341–360; and R. Merton, "An Intertemporal Capital Asset Pricing Model," *Econometrica* 41 (1973): 867–887.

To recap, it is possible to calculate the cost of capital without actually identifying the efficient portfolio using a multifactor risk model. Rather than relying on the efficiency of a single portfolio (such as the market), multifactor models rely on the weaker condition that we can construct an efficient portfolio from a collection of well-diversified portfolios or factors. We next explain how to select the factors.

Selecting the Portfolios

The most obvious portfolio to use when identifying a collection of portfolios that contain the efficient portfolio is the market portfolio itself. Historically, the market portfolio has commanded a large premium over short-term risk-free investments, such as Treasury bills. Even if the market portfolio is not efficient, it still captures many components of systematic risk. As Figures 13.9 and 13.10 demonstrate, even when the model fails, portfolios with higher average returns *do* tend to have higher betas. Thus, the first portfolio in the collection is a self-financing portfolio that consists of a long position in the market portfolio that is financed by a short position in the risk-free security.

How do we go about picking the other portfolios? As we pointed out earlier, trading strategies based on market capitalization, book-to-market ratios, and momentum appear to have positive alphas, meaning that the portfolios that implement the trading strategy capture risk that is not captured by the market portfolio. Hence, these portfolios are good candidates for the other portfolios in a multifactor model. We will construct three additional portfolios out of these trading strategies: The first trading strategy selects stocks based on their market capitalization, the second uses the book-to-market ratio, and the third uses past returns.

Market Capitalization Strategy. Each year, we place firms into one of two portfolios based on their market value of equity: Firms with market values below the median of NYSE firms form an equally weighted portfolio, S, and firms above the median market value form an equally weighted portfolio, B. A trading strategy that each year buys portfolio S (small stocks) and finances this position by short selling portfolio B (big stocks) has produced positive risk-adjusted returns historically. This self-financing portfolio is widely known as the **small-minus-big (SMB) portfolio**.

Book-to-Market Ratio Strategy. A second trading strategy that has produced positive risk-adjusted returns historically uses the book-to-market ratio to select stocks. Each year firms with book-to-market ratios less than the 30th percentile of NYSE firms form an equally weighted portfolio called the low portfolio, L. Firms with book-to-market ratios greater than the 70th percentile of NYSE firms form an equally weighted portfolio called the high portfolio, H. A trading strategy that each year takes a long position in portfolio H, which it finances with a short position in portfolio L, has produced positive risk-adjusted returns. We add this self-financing portfolio (high minus low book-to-market stocks) to our collection and call it the **high-minus-low (HML) portfolio** (we can also think of this portfolio as long value stocks, and short growth stocks).

Past Returns Strategy. The third trading strategy is a momentum strategy. Each year we rank stocks by their return over the last one year,[42] and construct a portfolio that goes long the top 30% of stocks and short the bottom 30%. This trading strategy requires holding this portfolio for a year; we then form a new self-financing portfolio and hold it

[42]Because of short-term trading effects, the most recent month's return is often dropped, so we actually use an 11-month return.

for another year. We repeat this process annually. The resulting self-financing portfolio is known as the **prior one-year momentum (PR1YR) portfolio.**

Fama-French-Carhart Factor Specification. The collection of these four portfolios—the excess return of the market ($Mkt - r_f$), SMB, HML, and PR1YR—is currently the most popular choice for the multifactor model. Using this collection, the expected return of security s is given by:

Fama-French-Carhart Factor Specification

$$E[R_s] = r_f + \beta_s^{Mkt}(E[R_{Mkt}] - r_f) + \beta_s^{SMB}E[R_{SMB}] \\ + \beta_s^{HML}E[R_{HML}] + \beta_s^{PR1YR}E[R_{PR1YR}] \tag{13.6}$$

where β_s^{Mkt}, β_s^{SMB}, β_s^{HML}, and β_s^{PR1YR} are the factor betas of stock s and measure the sensitivity of the stock to each portfolio. Because the four portfolios in Eq. 13.6 were identified by Eugene Fama, Kenneth French, and Mark Carhart, we will refer to this collection of portfolios as the **Fama-French-Carhart (FFC) factor specification.**

The Cost of Capital with Fama-French-Carhart Factor Specification

Multifactor models have a distinct advantage over single-factor models in that it is much easier to identify a collection of portfolios that captures systematic risk than just a single portfolio. They also have an important disadvantage, however: We must estimate the expected return of *each* portfolio. Because expected returns are not easy to estimate, each portfolio we add to the collection increases the difficulty of implementing the model. This task is especially complex because it is unclear *which* economic risk the portfolios capture, so we cannot hope to come up with a reasonable estimate of what the return should be (as we did with the CAPM) based on an economic argument. To implement the model, we have little choice other than to use historical average returns on the portfolios.[43]

Because the returns on the FFC portfolios are so volatile, we use over 80 years of data to estimate the expected return. Table 13.1 shows the monthly average return as well as the 95% confidence bands of the FFC portfolios (we use a value-weighted portfolio of all NYSE, AMEX, and NASDAQ stocks as the proxy for the market portfolio). Even with 80 years of data, however, all of the estimates of the expected returns are imprecise.

TABLE 13.1 FFC Portfolio Average Monthly Returns, 1927–2015

Factor Portfolio	Average Monthly Return (%)	95% Confidence Band (%)
$Mkt - r_f$	0.65	±0.33
SMB	0.23	±0.19
HML	0.39	±0.21
PR1YR	0.68	±0.29

Source: Kenneth French mba.tuck.dartmouth.edu/pages/faculty/ken.french/data_library.html

[43]There is a second, more subtle disadvantage to most factor models. Because factor models are designed to price traded securities, there is no guarantee that they will accurately price risks that are not currently traded (e.g., the risk associated with a new technology). In practice, it is assumed that any non-traded risk is idiosyncratic, and therefore does not command a risk premium.

EXAMPLE 13.3 **Using the FFC Factor Specification to Calculate the Cost of Capital**

Problem

You are considering making an investment in a project in the fast food industry. You determine that the project has the same level of non-diversifiable risk as investing in McDonald's stock. Determine the cost of capital by using the FFC factor specification.

Solution

You decide to use data over the past ten years to estimate the factor betas of McDonald's stock (ticker: MCD). Therefore, you regress the monthly excess return (the realized return in each month minus the risk-free rate) of McDonald's stock on the return of each portfolio. The coefficient estimates are the factor betas. Here are the estimates of the four factor betas and their 95% confidence interval based on data from 2005–2015:

Factor	Beta Estimate	Lower 95%	Upper 95%
Mkt	0.62	0.44	0.81
SMB	−0.47	−0.80	−0.15
HML	−0.10	−0.41	0.22
PR1YR	0.12	−0.03	0.28

Using these estimates and a risk-free monthly rate of 1.2%/12 = 0.10%, you can calculate the monthly expected return for investing in McDonald's stock:

$$E[R_{MCD}] = r_f + \beta_{MCD}^{Mkt}(E[R_{Mkt}] - r_f) + \beta_{MCD}^{SMB}\,E[R_{SMB}] + \beta_{MCD}^{HML}E[R_{HML}] + \beta_{MCD}^{PR1YR}E[R_{PR1YR}]$$
$$= 0.10\% + 0.62 \times 0.65\% - 0.47 \times 0.23\% - 0.10 \times 0.39\% + 0.12 \times 0.68\%$$
$$= 0.44\%$$

Expressed as an APR, the expected return is 0.44% × 12 = 5.28%. Thus, the annual cost of capital of the investment opportunity is about 5.3%. (Note, however the substantial uncertainty both in the factor betas and their expected returns.)

As a comparison, a standard CAPM regression over the same time period leads to an estimated market beta of 0.46 for McDonald's—the market beta differs from the estimate of 0.62 above because we are using only a single factor in the CAPM regression. Using the historical excess return on the market implies an expected return of 0.10% + 0.46 × 0.65% = 0.40% per month, or about 4.8% per year.

The FFC factor specification was identified a little more than 20 years ago. Although it is widely used in academic literature to measure risk, much debate persists about whether it really is a significant improvement over the CAPM.[44] The one area where researchers have found that the FFC factor specification does appear to do better than the CAPM is measuring the risk of actively managed mutual funds. Researchers have found that funds with high returns in the past have positive alphas under the CAPM.[45] When Mark Carhart

[44]See M. Cooper, R. Gutierrez, Jr., and B. Marcum, "On the Predictability of Stock Returns in Real Time," *Journal of Business* 78 (2005): 469–500.

[45]See M. Grinblatt and S. Titman, "The Persistence of Mutual Fund Performance," *Journal of Finance* 47 (1992): 1977–1984; and D. Hendricks, J. Patel, and R. Zeckhauser, "Hot Hands in Mutual Funds: Short-Run Persistence of Performance 1974–1988," *Journal of Finance* 4 (1993): 93–130.

repeated the same test using the FFC factor specification to compute alphas, he found no evidence that mutual funds with high past returns had future positive alphas.[46]

CONCEPT CHECK

1. What is the advantage of a multifactor model over a single factor model?
2. How can you use the Fama-French-Carhart factor specification to estimate the cost of capital?

13.8 Methods Used in Practice

Given the evidence for and against the efficiency of the market portfolio, what method do people actually use in practice? There are two reasons why people are interested in computing the expected returns of marketable securities. First, it provides a reliable way for financial managers to estimate the cost of capital for investment decisions. Second, it allows investors to assess the riskiness of investing in these securities. Let's examine which methods people use to make both of these decisions.

Financial Managers

How do financial managers actually calculate the cost of capital? A survey of 392 CFOs conducted by Professors John Graham and Campbell Harvey[47] found that 73.5% of the firms that they questioned use the CAPM to calculate the cost of capital, as indicated in Figure 13.11. They also found that larger firms were more likely to use the CAPM than were smaller firms. What about the other methods? Among the firms Graham and Harvey surveyed, only about one-third reported using a multifactor model to calculate the cost of capital. Two other methods that some firms in the survey reported using are historical average returns (40%) and the dividend discount model (16%). By dividend discount model, practitioners mean Eq. 9.7 in Chapter 9: They estimate the firm's expected future growth rate and add the current dividend yield to determine the stock's expected total return.

FIGURE 13.11 How Firms Calculate the Cost of Capital

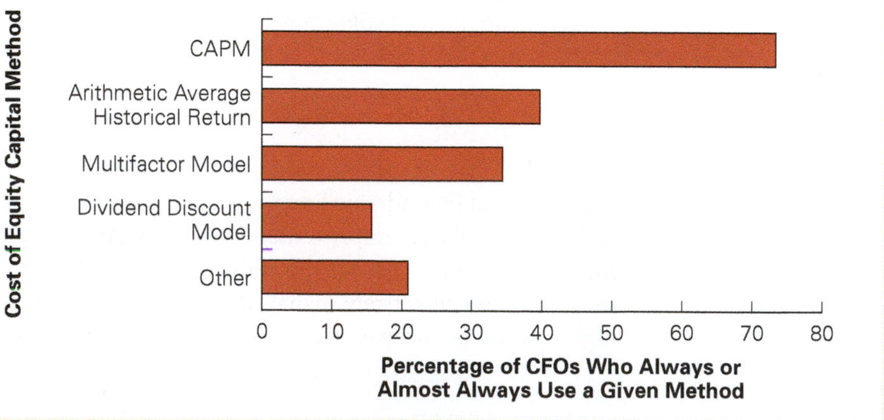

The figure shows the percentage of firms that use the CAPM, multifactor models, the historical average return, and the dividend discount model. The dividend discount model was presented in Chapter 9.

Source: J. R. Graham and C. R. Harvey, "The Theory and Practice of Corporate Finance: Evidence from the Field," *Journal of Financial Economics* 60 (2001): 187–243.

[46]See M. Carhart, "On Persistence in Mutual Fund Performance," *Journal of Finance* 52 (1997): 57–82.

[47]"How Do CFOs Make Capital Budgeting and Capital Structure Decisions?" *Journal of Applied Corporate Finance* 15 (2002): 8–23.

Investors

How do investors measure risk? In this case we can do better than simply asking them. We can look at what investors actually do. Recall, from the discussion in Section 13.1, that when a positive alpha investment opportunity presents itself in a market, investors should rush to invest and thereby eliminate the opportunity. To calculate the alpha of an investment opportunity, investors must first adjust for risk, which requires a risk model. Thus, by observing which investments investors rush into, it is possible to infer the risk model they are using.

In a recent study, Professors Jonathan Berk and Jules van Binsbergen use this insight to infer the risk model investors use when they invest in mutual funds.[48] Figure 13.12 reports their results: Of the different risk models they examined, investor behavior is most consistent with the CAPM. (That said, it also shows that a large percentage of mutual fund investment decisions are not consistent with any model.)

In short, the evidence from both sources is similar. Although most firms, and most investors, appear to use the CAPM, other methods are used as well. The choice of methodology depends on the organization and the sector. It is not difficult to see why different organizations choose to use different techniques. All the techniques we covered are imprecise. Financial economics has not yet reached the point where it can provide a theory of expected returns that gives a precise estimate of the cost of capital. Consider, too, that all techniques are not equally simple to implement. Because the trade-off between simplicity and precision varies across sectors, practitioners apply the techniques that best suit their particular circumstances.

FIGURE 13.12 **Which Risk Model Determines Mutual Fund Inflows**

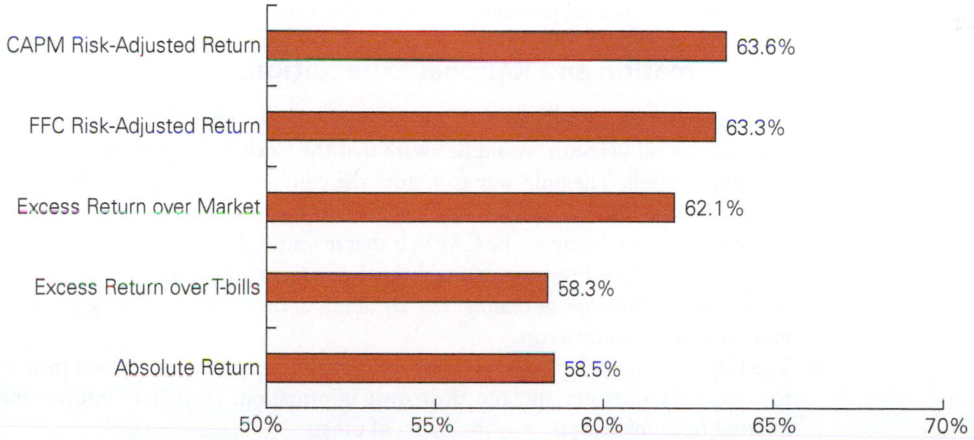

This figure reports the frequency that the sign of fund inflows match the sign of last quarter's risk-adjusted return based on alternative risk models. If fund inflows and outflows were random, the frequency would be 50%. We can see that fund flows are more likely to be positive if the fund has a positive return, even more likely if the fund outperforms the market, and most likely if the fund outperforms the return predicted by the CAPM, implying that investors do not ignore risk when making their investment decisions. The CAPM even outperforms the FFC factor model of Section 13.7, suggesting that the added factors do not help predict investor behavior.

[48]"Assessing Asset Pricing Models Using Revealed Preference," *Journal of Financial Economics* 119 (2016): 1–23.

When making a capital budgeting decision, the cost of capital is just one of several imprecise estimates that go into the NPV calculation. Indeed, in many cases, the imprecision in the cost of capital estimate is less important than the imprecision in the estimate of future cash flows. Often the least complicated models to implement are used. In this regard, the CAPM has the virtues of being simple to implement, theoretically justifiable, and reasonably consistent with investor behavior.

CONCEPT CHECK

1. Which is the most popular method used by corporations to calculate the cost of capital?
2. What other techniques do corporations use to calculate the cost of capital?
3. What risk model is most consistent with investors' choices in their mutual fund investments?

MyFinanceLab Here is what you should know after reading this chapter. MyFinanceLab will help you identify what you know and where to go when you need to practice.

13.1 Competition and Capital Markets

- The difference between a stock's expected return and its required return according to the security market line is the stock's alpha:

$$\alpha_s = E[R_s] - r_s \tag{13.2}$$

- While the CAPM conclusion that the market is always efficient may not literally be true, competition among savvy investors who try to "beat the market" and earn a positive alpha should keep the market portfolio close to efficient much of the time.

13.2 Information and Rational Expectations

- If all investors have homogeneous expectations, which states that all investors have the same information, all investors would be aware that the stock had a positive alpha and none would be willing to sell. The only way to restore the equilibrium in this case is for the price to rise immediately so that the alpha is zero.
- An important conclusion of the CAPM is that investors should hold the market portfolio (combined with risk-free investments), and this investment advice *does not depend on the quality of an investor's information or trading skill.* By doing so they can avoid being taken advantage of by more sophisticated investors.
- The CAPM requires only that investors have rational expectations, which means that all investors correctly interpret and use their own information, as well as information that can be inferred from market prices or the trades of others.
- The market portfolio can be inefficient only if a significant number of investors either do not have rational expectations or care about aspects of their portfolios other than expected return and volatility.

13.3 The Behavior of Individual Investors

- There is evidence that individual investors fail to diversify their portfolios adequately (underdiversification bias) and favor investments in companies they are familiar with (familiarity bias).
- Investors appear to trade too much. This behavior stems, at least in part, from investor overconfidence: the tendency of uninformed individuals to overestimate the precision of their knowledge.

13.4 Systematic Trading Biases

- In order for the behavior of uninformed investors to have an impact on the market, there must be patterns to their behavior that lead them to depart from the CAPM in systematic ways, thus imparting systematic uncertainty into prices.
- Examples of behavior that could be systematic across investors include the disposition effect (the tendency to hang on to losers and sell winners), investor mood swings that result from common events like weather, and putting too much weight on their own experience. Investors could also herd—actively trying to follow each other's behavior. Stock prices appear to have more volatility than one would expect based on the volatility of dividends.

13.5 The Efficiency of the Market Portfolio

- It is not easy to profit simply by trading on news, but professional investors might be able to do so by, for example, being better able to predict takeover outcomes. However, in equilibrium, individual investors should not expect to share any of the benefit of this skill by investing with such professional investors. The empirical evidence supports this—on average, investors earn zero alphas when they invest in managed mutual funds.
- Because beating the market requires enough trading skill to overcome transaction costs as well as behavioral biases, CAPM wisdom that investors should "hold the market" is probably the best advice for most people.

13.6 Style-Based Techniques and the Market Efficiency Debate

- The size effect refers to the observation that historically stocks with low market capitalizations have had positive alphas compared to the predictions of the CAPM. The size effect is evidence that the market portfolio is not efficient, which suggests that the CAPM does not accurately model expected returns. Researchers find similar results using the book-to-market ratio instead of firm size.
- A momentum trading strategy that goes long stocks with high past risk-adjusted returns and short stocks with low past returns also generates positive CAPM alphas, providing further evidence that the market portfolio is not efficient and that the CAPM does not accurately model expected returns.
- Securities may have non-zero alphas if the market portfolio that is used is not a good proxy for the true market portfolio.
- The market portfolio will be inefficient if some investors' portfolio holdings are subject to systematic behavioral biases.
- The market portfolio will be inefficient if either investors care about risk characteristics other than the volatility of their traded portfolio or if investors are exposed to other significant risks outside their portfolio that are not tradable, the most important of which is due to their human capital.

13.7 Multifactor Models of Risk

- When more than one portfolio is used to capture risk, the model is known as a multifactor model. This model is also sometimes called the Arbitrage Pricing Theory (APT). Using a collection of N well-diversified portfolios, the expected return of stock s is

$$E[R_s] = r_f + \beta_s^{F1}(E[R_{F1}] - r_f) + \beta_s^{F2}(E[R_{F2}] - r_f) + \cdots + \beta_s^{FN}(E[R_{FN}] - r_f)$$

$$= r_f + \sum_{n=1}^{N} \beta_s^{Fn}(E[R_{Fn}] - r_f) \qquad (13.4)$$

- A simpler way to write multifactor models is to express risk premiums as the expected return on a self-financing portfolio. A self-financing portfolio is a portfolio that costs nothing to construct. By using the expected returns of self-financing portfolios, the expected return of a stock can be expressed as

$$E[R_s] = r_f + \beta_s^{F1}E[R_{F1}] + \beta_s^{F2}E[R_{F2}] + \cdots + \beta_s^{FN}E[R_{FN}]$$
$$= r_f + \sum_{n=1}^{N}\beta_s^{Fn}E[R_{Fn}] \qquad (13.5)$$

- The portfolios that are most commonly used in a multifactor model are the market portfolio (Mkt), small-minus-big (SMB) portfolio, high-minus-low (HML) portfolio, and prior one-year momentum (PR1YR) portfolio. This model is known as the Fama-French-Carhart factor specification:

$$E[R_s] = r_f + \beta_s^{Mkt}(E[R_{Mkt}] - r_f) + \beta_s^{SMB}E[R_{SMB}]$$
$$+ \beta_s^{HML}E[R_{HML}] + \beta_s^{PR1YR}E[R_{PR1YR}] \qquad (13.6)$$

13.8 Methods Used in Practice

- The CAPM is the most commonly used method in practice to estimate the cost of capital. It has the virtues of being simple to implement, theoretically justifiable, and reasonably consistent with investor behavior.

Key Terms

Arbitrage Pricing Theory (APT) *p. 470*
book-to-market ratio *p. 463*
cumulative abnormal return *p. 457*
data snooping bias *p. 465*
disposition effect *p. 453*
factor betas *p. 470*
factor portfolios *p. 470*
Fama-French-Carhart (FFC) factor specification *p. 472*
familiarity bias *p. 450*
gross alpha *p. 458*
herd behavior *p. 455*
high-minus-low (HML) portfolio *p. 471*
informational cascade effect *p. 455*
momentum strategy *p. 467*
multifactor model *p. 470*
net alpha *p. 458*
overconfidence bias *p. 451*
prior one-year momentum (PR1YR) portfolio *p. 472*
rational expectations *p. 449*
relative wealth concerns *p. 450*
self-financing portfolio *p. 470*
semi-strong form efficiency *p. 467*
sensation seeking *p. 452*
single-factor model *p. 470*
size effect *p. 462*
small-minus-big (SMB) portfolio *p. 471*
strong form efficiency *p. 467*
weak form efficiency *p. 467*

Further Reading

For a simple insightful discussion of why some investors must lose if others win and what this means for mutual fund managers, see W. Sharpe, "The Arithmetic of Active Management," *Financial Analysts Journal*, 47(1) (January–February 1991): 7–9. The ideas on how information affects markets were developed in a series of influential articles: P. Milgrom and N. Stokey, "Information, Trade and Common Knowledge," *Journal of Economic Theory* 26(11) (1982): 17–27; S. Grossman and J. Stiglitz, "On the Impossibility of Informationally Efficient Markets," *The American Economic Review* 70(3) (June 1980): 393–408; M. Hellwig, "On the Aggregation of Information in Competitive Markets," *Journal of Economic Theory* 22 (1980): 477–498; D. Diamond and R. Verrecchia, "Information Aggregation in a Noisy Rational Expectations Economy," *Journal of Financial Economics* 9 (September 1981): 221–235.

For an overview of the Barber and Odean results on individual investor behavior, see B. Barber and T. Odean, "The Courage of Misguided Convictions: The Trading Behavior of Individual Investors," *Financial Analyst Journal* (November/December 1999): 41–55. For a broad introduction to the topic of behavioral finance, see N. Barberis and R. Thaler, "A Survey of Behavioral Finance," in G. Constantinides, M. Harris, and R. Stulz (ed.), *Handbook of the Economics of Finance Vol. 1*, Elsevier, 2003. For a review of the impact of behavioral theories on corporate finance, see M. Baker, R. Ruback, and J. Wurgler, "Behavioral Corporate Finance: A Survey," in E. Eckbo (ed.), *The Handbook of Corporate Finance: Empirical Corporate Finance*, Elsevier/North Holland, 2007. For a review of the evidence on the relative volatility of short and long maturity risk assets, see J. van Binsbergen and R. Koijen, "The Term Structure of Returns: Facts and Theory," NBER working paper 21234.

For a review of rational explanations for herd behavior in financial markets, see S. Sharma and S. Bikhchandani, "Herd Behavior in Financial Markets—A Review," IMF Working Papers 00/48, 2000. For its role in mispricing and crashes, see M. Brunnermeier, *Asset Pricing under Asymmetric Information: Bubbles, Crashes, Technical Analysis, and Herding*, Oxford University Press, 2001.

Readers interested in a more in-depth exposition of the performance of active managers can consult: J. Berk, "Five Myths of Active Portfolio Management," *Journal of Portfolio Management* 31(3): 27; and J. Berk and J. van Binsbergen, "Active Managers Are Skilled," *Journal of Porfolio Management* (January 2016).

More detail on the theoretical relation between firm size and returns can be found in J. Berk, "Does Size Really Matter?" *Financial Analysts Journal* (September/October 1997): 12–18.

A summary of the empirical evidence on the relationship between risk-adjusted return and market value can be found in the following article: E. Fama and K. French, "The Cross-Section of Expected Stock Returns," *Journal of Finance* 47 (June 1992): 427–465.

The evidence that momentum strategies produce positive risk-adjusted returns was first published in the following article: N. Jegadeesh and S. Titman, "Returns to Buying Winners and Selling Losers: Implications for Stock Market Efficiency," *Journal of Finance* 48 (March 1993): 65–91.

The following two articles provide details on the FFC factor specification: E. Fama and K. French, "Common Risk Factors in the Returns on Stocks and Bonds," *Journal of Financial Economics* 33 (1993): 3–56; and M. Carhart, "On Persistence in Mutual Fund Performance," *Journal of Finance* 52 (March 1997): 57–82.

Finally, because the value of a firm also includes the value of future growth options, Z. Da, R. Guo, and R. Jagannathan, "CAPM for Estimating the Cost of Equity Capital: Interpreting the Empirical Evidence," *Journal of Financial Economics* 103 (2012): 204–220 argue that when it comes to evaluating projects (rather than securities), the CAPM may be *more* reliable than multi-factor models.

Problems

All problems are available in MyFinanceLab. *An asterisk (*) indicates problems with a higher level of difficulty.*

Competition and Capital Markets

1. Assume that all investors have the same information and care only about expected return and volatility. If new information arrives about one stock, can this information affect the price and return of other stocks? If so, explain why?

2. Assume that the CAPM is a good description of stock price returns. The market expected return is 7% with 10% volatility and the risk-free rate is 3%. New news arrives that does not change any of these numbers but it does change the expected return of the following stocks:

	Expected Return	Volatility	Beta
Green Leaf	12%	20%	1.5
NatSam	10%	40%	1.8
HanBel	9%	30%	0.75
Rebecca Automobile	6%	35%	1.2

a. At current market prices, which stocks represent buying opportunities?
b. On which stocks should you put a sell order in?

3. Suppose the CAPM equilibrium holds perfectly. Then the risk-free interest rate increases, *and nothing else changes*.
a. Is the market portfolio still efficient?
b. If your answer to part a is yes, explain why. If not, describe which stocks would be buying opportunities and which stocks would be selling opportunities.

Information and Rational Expectations

4. You know that there are informed traders in the stock market, but you are uninformed. Describe an investment strategy that guarantees you will not lose money to the informed traders and explain why it works.

5. What are the only conditions under which the market portfolio might not be an efficient portfolio?

6. Explain what the following sentence means: The market portfolio is a fence that protects the sheep from the wolves, but nothing can protect the sheep from themselves.

7. You are trading in a market in which you know there are a few highly skilled traders who are better informed than you are. There are no transaction costs. Each day you randomly choose five stocks to buy and five stocks to sell (by, perhaps, throwing darts at a dartboard).
a. Over the long run will your strategy outperform, underperform, or have the same return as a buy and hold strategy of investing in the market portfolio?
b. Would your answer to part a change if all traders in the market were equally well informed and were equally skilled?

The Behavior of Individual Investors

8. Why does the CAPM imply that investors should trade very rarely?

9. Your brother Joe is a surgeon who suffers badly from the overconfidence bias. He loves to trade stocks and believes his predictions with 100% confidence. In fact, he is uninformed like most investors. Rumors are that Vital Signs (a startup that makes warning labels in the medical industry) will receive a takeover offer at $20 per share. Absent the takeover offer, the stock will trade at $15 per share. The uncertainty will be resolved in the next few hours. Your brother believes that the takeover will occur with certainty and has instructed his broker to buy the stock at any price less than $20. In fact, the true probability of a takeover is 50%, but a few people are informed and know whether the takeover will actually occur. They also have submitted orders. Nobody else is trading in the stock.
a. Describe what will happen to the market price once these orders are submitted if in fact the takeover will occur in a few hours. What will your brother's profits be: positive, negative, or zero?

b. What range of possible prices could result once these orders are submitted if the takeover does not occur? What will your brother's profits be: positive, negative, or zero?
c. What are your brother's expected profits?

10. To put the turnover of Figure 13.3 into perspective, let's do a back of the envelope calculation of what an investor's average turnover per stock would be were he to follow a policy of investing in the S&P 500 portfolio. Because the portfolio is value weighted, the trading would be required when Standard and Poor's changes the constituent stocks. (Let's ignore additional, but less important reasons like new share issuances and repurchases.) Assuming they change 23 stocks a year (the historical average since 1962) what would you estimate the investor's per stock share turnover to be? Assume that the average total number of shares outstanding for the stocks that are added or deleted from the index is the same as the average number of shares outstanding for S&P 500 stocks.

Systematic Trading Biases

11. How does the disposition effect impact investors' tax obligations?

12. Consider the price paths of the following two stocks over six time periods:

	1	2	3	4	5	6
Stock 1	10	12	14	12	13	16
Stock 2	15	11	8	16	15	18

Neither stock pays dividends. Assume you are an investor with the disposition effect and you bought at time 1 and right now it is time 3. Assume throughout this question that you do no trading (other than what is specified) in these stocks.
a. Which stock(s) would you be inclined to sell? Which would you be inclined to hold on to?
b. How would your answer change if right now is time 6?
c. What if you bought at time 3 instead of 1 and today is time 6?
d. What if you bought at time 3 instead of 1 and today is time 5?

13. Suppose that all investors have the disposition effect. A new stock has just been issued at a price of $50, so all investors in this stock purchased the stock today. A year from now the stock will be taken over, for a price of $60 or $40 depending on the news that comes out over the year. The stock will pay no dividends. Investors will sell the stock whenever the price goes up by more than 10%.
a. Suppose good news comes out in 6 months (implying the takeover offer will be $60). What equilibrium price will the stock trade for after the news comes out, that is, the price that equates supply and demand?
b. Assume that you are the only investor who does not suffer from the disposition effect and your trades are small enough to not affect prices. Without knowing what will actually transpire, what trading strategy would you instruct your broker to follow?

The Efficiency of the Market Portfolio

14. Davita Spencer is a manager at Half Dome Asset Management. She can generate an alpha of 2% a year up to $100 million. After that her skills are spread too thin, so cannot add value and her alpha is zero. Half Dome charges a fee of 1% per year on the total amount of money under management (at the beginning of each year). Assume that there are always investors looking for positive alpha and no investor would invest in a fund with a negative alpha. In equilibrium, that is, when no investor either takes out money or wishes to invest new money,
a. What alpha do investors in Davita's fund expect to receive?
b. How much money will Davita have under management?
c. How much money will Half Dome generate in fee income?

15. Allison and Bill are both mutual fund managers, although Allison is more skilled than Bill. Both have $100 million in assets under management and charge a fee of 1%/year. Allison is able to generate a 2% alpha before fees and Bill is able to generate a 1% alpha before fees.

a. What is the net alpha investors earn in each fund (that is, the alpha after fees are taken out)?
b. Which fund will experience an inflow of funds?
c. Assume that both managers have exhausted the supply of good investment opportunities and so they will choose to invest any new funds received in the market portfolio and so those new funds will earn a zero alpha. How much new capital will flow into each fund?
d. Once the new capital has stopped flowing in, what is the alpha before and after fees of each fund? Which fund will be larger?
e. Calculate each manager's compensation once the capital has stopped flowing. Which manager has higher compensation?

16. Assume the economy consisted of three types of people. 50% are fad followers, 45% are passive investors (they have read this book and so hold the market portfolio), and 5% are informed traders. The portfolio consisting of all the informed traders has a beta of 1.5 and an expected return of 15%. The market expected return is 11%. The risk-free rate is 5%.

a. What alpha do the informed traders make?
b. What is the alpha of the passive investors?
c. What is the expected return of the fad followers?
d. What alpha do the fad followers make?

Style-Based Techniques and the Market Efficiency Debate

17. Explain what the size effect is.

***18.** Assume all firms have the same expected dividends. If they have different expected returns, how will their market values and expected returns be related? What about the relation between their dividend yields and expected returns?

19. Each of the six firms in the table below is expected to pay the listed dividend payment every year in perpetuity.

Firm	Dividend ($ million)	Cost of Capital (%/Year)
S1	10	8
S2	10	12
S3	10	14
B1	100	8
B2	100	12
B3	100	14

a. Using the cost of capital in the table, calculate the market value of each firm.
b. Rank the three S firms by their market values and look at how their cost of capital is ordered. What would be the expected return for a self-financing portfolio that went long on the firm with the largest market value and shorted the firm with the lowest market value? (The expected return of a self-financing portfolio is the weighted average return of the constituent securities.) Repeat using the B firms.
c. Rank all six firms by their market values. How does this ranking order the cost of capital? What would be the expected return for a self-financing portfolio that went long on the firm with the largest market value and shorted the firm with the lowest market value?
d. Repeat part c but rank the firms by the dividend yield instead of the market value. What can you conclude about the dividend yield ranking compared to the market value ranking?

MFL **20.** Consider the following stocks, all of which will pay a liquidating dividend in a year and nothing in the interim:

	Market Capitalization ($ million)	Expected Liquidating Dividend ($ million)	Beta
Stock A	800	1000	0.77
Stock B	750	1000	1.46
Stock C	950	1000	1.25
Stock D	900	1000	1.07

a. Calculate the expected return of each stock.
b. What is the sign of correlation between the expected return and market capitalization of the stocks?

MFL **21.** In Problem 20, assume the risk-free rate is 3% and the market risk premium is 7%.
a. What does the CAPM predict the expected return for each stock should be?
b. Clearly, the CAPM predictions are not equal to the actual expected returns, so the CAPM does not hold. You decide to investigate this further. To see what kind of mistakes the CAPM is making, you decide to regress the actual expected return onto the expected return predicted by the CAPM.[49] What is the intercept and slope coefficient of this regression?
c. What are the residuals of the regression in (b)? That is, for each stock compute the difference between the actual expected return and the best fitting line given by the intercept and slope coefficient in (b).
d. What is the sign of the correlation between the residuals you calculated in (b) and market capitalization?
e. What can you conclude from your answers to part b of the previous problem and part d of this problem about the relation between firm size (market capitalization) and returns? (The results do not depend on the particular numbers in this problem. You are welcome to verify this for yourself by redoing the problems with another value for the market risk premium, and by picking the stock betas and market capitalizations randomly.[50])

22. Explain how to construct a positive-alpha trading strategy if stocks that have had relatively high returns in the past tend to have positive alphas and stocks that have had relatively low returns in the past tend to have negative alphas.

***23.** If you can use past returns to construct a trading strategy that makes money (has a positive alpha), it is evidence that market portfolio is not efficient. Explain why.

24. Explain why you might expect stocks to have nonzero alphas if the market proxy portfolio is not highly correlated with the true market portfolio, even if the true market portfolio is efficient.

25. Explain why if some investors are subject to systematic behavioral biases, while others pick efficient portfolios, the market portfolio will not be efficient.

26. Explain why an employee who cares only about expected return and volatility will likely underweight the amount of money he invests in his own company's stock relative to an investor who does not work for his company.

---

[49]The Excel function SLOPE will produce the desired answers.

[50]The Excel command RAND will produce a random number between 0 and 1.

Multifactor Models of Risk

For Problems 27–29, refer to the following table of estimated factor betas based on data from 2005–2015.

Factor	MSFT	XOM	GE
MKT	1.06	0.78	1.29
HML	−0.45	−0.62	−0.39
SMB	−0.12	0.21	0.82
PR1YR	−0.06	0.32	−0.22

27. Using the factor beta estimates in the table shown here and the monthly expected return estimates in Table 13.1, calculate the risk premium of General Electric stock (ticker: GE) using the FFC factor specification. (Annualize your result by multiplying by 12.) GE's CAPM beta over the same time period was 1.45. How does the risk premium you would estimate from the CAPM compare?

28. You are currently considering an investment in a project in the energy sector. The investment has the same riskiness as Exxon Mobil stock (ticker: XOM). Using the data in Table 13.1 and the table above, calculate the cost of capital using the FFC factor specification if the current risk-free rate is 3% per year.

29. You work for Microsoft Corporation (ticker: MSFT), and you are considering whether to develop a new software product. The risk of the investment is the same as the risk of the company.

a. Using the data in Table 13.1 and in the table above, calculate the cost of capital using the FFC factor specification if the current risk-free rate is 3% per year.

b. Microsoft's CAPM beta over the same time period was 0.96. What cost of capital would you estimate using the CAPM?

CHAPTER 13 APPENDIX

Building a Multifactor Model

In this appendix, we show that if an efficient portfolio can be constructed out of a collection of well-diversified portfolios, the collection of portfolios will correctly price assets. To keep things simple, assume that we have identified two portfolios that we can combine to form an efficient portfolio; we call these portfolios factor portfolios and denote their returns by R_{F1} and R_{F2}. The efficient portfolio consists of some (unknown) combination of these two factor portfolios, represented by portfolio weights x_1 and x_2:

$$R_{eff} = x_1 R_{F1} + x_2 R_{F2} \tag{13A.1}$$

To see that we can use these factor portfolios to measure risk, consider regressing the excess returns of some stock s on the excess returns of *both* factors:

$$R_s - r_f = \alpha_s + \beta_s^{F1}(R_{F1} - r_f) + \beta_s^{F2}(R_{F2} - r_f) + \varepsilon_s \tag{13A.2}$$

This statistical technique is known as a multiple regression—it is exactly the same as the linear regression technique we described in Chapter 12, except now we have two regressors, $R_{F1} - r_f$ and $R_{F2} - r_f$, whereas in Chapter 12 we only had one regressor, the excess return of the market portfolio. Otherwise the interpretation is the same. We write the excess return of stock s as the sum of a constant, α_s, plus the variation in the stock that is related to each factor, and an error term ε_s that has an expectation of zero and is uncorrelated with either factor. The error term represents the risk of the stock that is unrelated to either factor.

If we can use the two factor portfolios to construct the efficient portfolio, as in Eq. 13A.1, then the constant term α_s in Eq. 13A.2 is zero (up to estimation error). To see why, consider a portfolio in which we buy stock s, then sell a fraction β_s^{F1} of the first factor portfolio and β_s^{F2} of the second factor portfolio, and invest the proceeds from these sales in the risk-free investment. This portfolio, which we call P, has return

$$\begin{aligned} R_P &= R_s - \beta_s^{F1} R_{F1} - \beta_s^{F2} R_{F2} + (\beta_s^{F1} + \beta_s^{F2}) r_f \\ &= R_s - \beta_s^{F1}(R_{F1} - r_f) - \beta_s^{F2}(R_{F2} - r_f) \end{aligned} \tag{13A.3}$$

Using Eq. 13A.2 to replace R_s and simplifying, the return of this portfolio is

$$R_P = r_f + \alpha_s + \varepsilon_s \tag{13A.4}$$

That is, portfolio P has a risk premium of α_s and risk given by ε_s. Now, because ε_s is uncorrelated with each factor, it must be uncorrelated with the efficient portfolio; that is,

$$\begin{aligned} Cov(R_{eff}, \varepsilon_s) &= Cov(x_1 R_{F1} + x_2 R_{F2}, \varepsilon_s) \\ &= x_1\, Cov(R_{F1}, \varepsilon_s) + x_2\, Cov(R_{F2}, \varepsilon_s) = 0 \end{aligned} \tag{13A.5}$$

But recall from Chapter 11 that *risk that is uncorrelated with the efficient portfolio is firm-specific risk that does not command a risk premium*. Therefore, the expected return of portfolio P is r_f, which means α_s must be zero.[51]

Setting α_s equal to zero and taking expectations of both sides of Eq. 13A.2, we get the following two-factor model of expected returns:

$$E[R_s] = r_f + \beta_s^{F1}(E[R_{F1}] - r_f) + \beta_s^{F2}(E[R_{F2}] - r_f) \tag{13A.6}$$

[51] That is, Eq. 13A.5 implies $\beta_P^{eff} = \dfrac{Cov(R_{eff}, \varepsilon_s)}{Var(R_{eff})} = 0$. Substituting this result into Eq. 13.3 gives $E[R_p] = r_f$. But from Eq. 13A.4, $E[R_p] = r_f + \alpha_s$, and hence $\alpha_s = 0$.

Capital Structure

PART

5

THE LAW OF ONE PRICE CONNECTION. One of the fundamental questions in corporate finance is how a firm should choose the set of securities it will issue to raise capital from investors. This decision determines the firm's capital structure, which is the total amount of debt, equity, and other securities that a firm has outstanding. Does the choice of capital structure affect the value of the firm? In Chapter 14, we consider this question in a perfect capital market. There we apply the Law of One Price to show that as long as the cash flows generated by the firm's assets are unchanged, then the value of the firm—which is the total value of its outstanding securities—does not depend on its capital structure. Therefore, if capital structure has a role in determining the firm's value, it must come from changes to the firm's cash flows that result from market imperfections. We explore important market imperfections in subsequent chapters. In Chapter 15, we analyze the role of debt in reducing the taxes a firm or its investors will pay, while in Chapter 16, we consider the costs of financial distress and changes to managerial incentives that result from leverage. Finally, in Chapter 17, we consider the firm's choice of payout policy and ask: Which is the best method for the firm to return capital to its investors? The Law of One Price implies that the firm's choice to pay dividends or repurchase its stock will not affect its value in a perfect capital market. We then examine how market imperfections affect this important insight and shape the firm's optimal payout policy.

CHAPTER

14

Capital Structure in a Perfect Market

NOTATION

PV	present value
NPV	net present value
E	market value of levered equity
D	market value of debt
U	market value of unlevered equity
A	market value of firm assets
R_D	return on debt
R_E	return on levered equity
R_U	return on unlevered equity
r_D	expected return (cost of capital) of debt
r_E	expected return (cost of capital) of levered equity
r_U	expected return (cost of capital) of unlevered equity
r_A	expected return (cost of capital) of firm assets
r_{wacc}	weighted average cost of capital
r_f	risk-free rate of interest
β_E	beta of levered equity
β_U	beta of unlevered equity
β_D	beta of debt
EPS	earnings per share

WHEN A FIRM NEEDS TO RAISE NEW FUNDS TO UNDERTAKE ITS investments, it must decide which type of security it will sell to investors. Even absent a need for new funds, firms can issue new securities and use the funds to repay debt or repurchase shares. What considerations should guide these decisions?

Consider the case of Dan Harris, Chief Financial Officer of Electronic Business Services (EBS), who has been reviewing plans for a major expansion of the firm. To pursue the expansion, EBS plans to raise \$50 million from outside investors. One possibility is to raise the funds by selling shares of EBS stock. Due to the firm's risk, Dan estimates that equity investors will require a 10% risk premium over the 5% risk-free interest rate. That is, the company's equity cost of capital is 15%.

Some senior executives at EBS, however, have argued that the firm should consider borrowing the \$50 million instead. EBS has not borrowed previously and, given its strong balance sheet, it should be able to borrow at a 6% interest rate. Does the low interest rate of debt make borrowing a better choice of financing for EBS? If EBS does borrow, will this choice affect the NPV of the expansion, and therefore change the value of the firm and its share price?

We explore these questions in this chapter in a setting of *perfect capital markets*, in which all securities are fairly priced, there are no taxes or transaction costs, and the total cash flows of the firm's projects are not affected by how the firm finances them. Although in reality capital markets are not perfect, this setting provides an important benchmark. Perhaps surprisingly, with perfect capital markets, the Law of One Price implies that the choice of debt or equity financing will *not* affect the total value of a firm, its share price, or its cost of capital. Thus, in a perfect world, EBS will be indifferent regarding the choice of financing for its expansion.

14.1 Equity Versus Debt Financing

The relative proportions of debt, equity, and other securities that a firm has outstanding constitute its **capital structure**. When corporations raise funds from outside investors, they must choose which type of security to issue. The most common choices are financing through equity alone and financing through a combination of debt and equity. We begin our discussion by considering both of these options.

Financing a Firm with Equity

Consider an entrepreneur with the following investment opportunity. For an initial investment of \$800 this year, a project will generate cash flows of either \$1400 or \$900 next year. The cash flows depend on whether the economy is strong or weak, respectively. Both scenarios are equally likely, and are shown in Table 14.1.

TABLE 14.1 The Project Cash Flows

Date 0	Date 1	
	Strong Economy	Weak Economy
−\$800	\$1400	\$900

Because the project cash flows depend on the overall economy, they contain market risk. As a result, investors demand a risk premium. The current risk-free interest rate is 5%, and suppose that given the market risk of the investment the appropriate risk premium is 10%.

What is the NPV of this investment opportunity? Given a risk-free interest rate of 5% and a risk premium of 10%, the cost of capital for this project is 15%. Because the expected cash flow in one year is $\frac{1}{2}(\$1400) + \frac{1}{2}(\$900) = \$1150$, we get

$$NPV = -\$800 + \frac{\$1150}{1.15} = -\$800 + \$1000$$
$$= \$200$$

Thus, the investment has a positive NPV.

If this project is financed using equity alone, how much would investors be willing to pay for the firm's shares? Recall from Chapter 3 that, in the absence of arbitrage, the price of a security equals the present value of its cash flows. Because the firm has no other liabilities, equity holders will receive all of the cash flows generated by the project on date 1. Hence, the market value of the firm's equity today will be

$$PV(\text{equity cash flows}) = \frac{\$1150}{1.15} = \$1000$$

So, the entrepreneur can raise \$1000 by selling the equity in the firm. After paying the investment cost of \$800, the entrepreneur can keep the remaining \$200—the project's NPV—as a profit. In other words, the project's NPV represents the value to the initial owners of the firm (in this case, the entrepreneur) created by the project.

TABLE 14.2 Cash Flows and Returns for Unlevered Equity

	Date 0	Date 1: Cash Flows		Date 1: Returns	
	Initial Value	Strong Economy	Weak Economy	Strong Economy	Weak Economy
Unlevered equity	$1000	$1400	$900	40%	−10%

Equity in a firm with no debt is called **unlevered equity**. Because there is no debt, the date 1 cash flows of the unlevered equity are equal to those of the project. Given equity's initial value of $1000, shareholders' returns are either 40% or −10%, as shown in Table 14.2.

The strong and weak economy outcomes are equally likely, so the expected return on the unlevered equity is $\frac{1}{2}(40\%) + \frac{1}{2}(-10\%) = 15\%$. Because the risk of unlevered equity equals the risk of the project, shareholders are earning an appropriate return for the risk they are taking.

Financing a Firm with Debt and Equity

Financing the firm exclusively with equity is not the entrepreneur's only option. She can also raise part of the initial capital using debt. Suppose she decides to borrow $500 initially, in addition to selling equity. Because the project's cash flow will always be enough to repay the debt, the debt is risk free. Thus, the firm can borrow at the risk-free interest rate of 5%, and it will owe the debt holders $500 \times 1.05 = \$525$ in one year.

Equity in a firm that also has debt outstanding is called **levered equity**. Promised payments to debt holders must be made *before* any payments to equity holders are distributed. Given the firm's $525 debt obligation, the shareholders will receive only $\$1400 - \$525 = \$875$ if the economy is strong and $\$900 - \$525 = \$375$ if the economy is weak. Table 14.3 shows the cash flows of the debt, the levered equity, and the total cash flows of the firm.

What price E should the levered equity sell for, and which is the best capital structure choice for the entrepreneur? In an important paper, Professors Franco Modigliani and Merton Miller proposed an answer to this question that surprised researchers and practitioners at the time.[1] They argued that with perfect capital markets, the total value of a firm should not depend on its capital structure. Their reasoning: The firm's total cash flows

TABLE 14.3 Values and Cash Flows for Debt and Equity of the Levered Firm

	Date 0	Date 1: Cash Flows	
	Initial Value	Strong Economy	Weak Economy
Debt	$500	$525	$525
Levered equity	$E = ?$	$875	$375
Firm	$1000	$1400	$900

[1] F. Modigliani and M. Miller, "The Cost of Capital, Corporation Finance and the Theory of Investment," *American Economic Review* 48(3) (1958): 261–297.

still equal the cash flows of the project, and therefore have the same present value of $1000 calculated earlier (see the last line in Table 14.3). Because the cash flows of the debt and equity sum to the cash flows of the project, by the Law of One Price the combined values of debt and equity must be $1000. Therefore, if the value of the debt is $500, the value of the levered equity must be $E = \$1000 - \$500 = \$500$.

Because the cash flows of levered equity are smaller than those of unlevered equity, levered equity will sell for a lower price ($500 versus $1000). However, the fact that the equity is less valuable with leverage does not mean that the entrepreneur is worse off. She will still raise a total of $1000 by issuing both debt and levered equity, just as she did with unlevered equity alone. As a consequence, she will be indifferent between these two choices for the firm's capital structure.

The Effect of Leverage on Risk and Return

Modigliani and Miller's conclusion went against the common view, which stated that even with perfect capital markets, leverage would affect a firm's value. In particular, it was thought that the value of the levered equity would exceed $500, because the present value of its expected cash flow at 15% is

$$\frac{\frac{1}{2}(\$875) + \frac{1}{2}(\$375)}{1.15} = \$543$$

The reason this logic is *not* correct is that leverage increases the risk of the equity of a firm. Therefore, it is inappropriate to discount the cash flows of levered equity at the same discount rate of 15% that we used for unlevered equity. Investors in levered equity require a higher expected return to compensate for its increased risk.

Table 14.4 compares the equity returns if the entrepreneur chooses unlevered equity financing with the case in which she borrows $500 and raises an additional $500 using levered equity. Note that the returns to equity holders are very different with and without leverage. Unlevered equity has a return of either 40% or −10%, for an expected return of 15%. But levered equity has higher risk, with a return of either 75% or −25%. To compensate for this risk, levered equity holders receive a higher expected return of 25%.

We can evaluate the relationship between risk and return more formally by computing the sensitivity of each security's return to the systematic risk of the economy. (In our simple two-state example, this sensitivity determines the security's beta; see also the discussion of

TABLE 14.4 Returns to Equity with and without Leverage

	Date 0	Date 1: Cash Flows		Date 1: Returns		
	Initial Value	Strong Economy	Weak Economy	Strong Economy	Weak Economy	Expected Return
Debt	$500	$525	$525	5%	5%	5%
Levered equity	$500	$875	$375	75%	−25%	25%
Unlevered equity	$1000	$1400	$900	40%	−10%	15%

TABLE 14.5 **Systematic Risk and Risk Premiums for Debt, Unlevered Equity, and Levered Equity**

	Return Sensitivity (Systematic Risk)	Risk Premium
	$\Delta R = R(\text{strong}) - R(\text{weak})$	$E[R] - r_f$
Debt	$5\% - 5\% = 0\%$	$5\% - 5\% = 0\%$
Unlevered equity	$40\% - (-10\%) = 50\%$	$15\% - 5\% = 10\%$
Levered equity	$75\% - (-25\%) = 100\%$	$25\% - 5\% = 20\%$

risk in the appendix to Chapter 3.) Table 14.5 shows the return sensitivity and the risk premium for each security. Because the debt's return bears no systematic risk, its risk premium is zero. In this particular case, however, levered equity has twice the systematic risk of unlevered equity. As a result, levered equity holders receive twice the risk premium.

To summarize, in the case of perfect capital markets, if the firm is 100% equity financed, the equity holders will require a 15% expected return. If the firm is financed 50% with debt and 50% with equity, the debt holders will receive a lower return of 5%, while the levered equity holders will require a higher expected return of 25% because of their increased risk. As this example shows, *leverage increases the risk of equity even when there is no risk that the firm will default.* Thus, while debt may be cheaper when considered on its own, it raises the cost of capital for equity. Considering both sources of capital together, the firm's average cost of capital with leverage is $\frac{1}{2}(5\%) + \frac{1}{2}(25\%) = 15\%$, the same as for the unlevered firm.

EXAMPLE 14.1 Leverage and the Equity Cost of Capital

Problem

Suppose the entrepreneur borrows only \$200 when financing the project. According to Modigliani and Miller, what should the value of the equity be? What is the expected return?

Solution

Because the value of the firm's total cash flows is still \$1000, if the firm borrows \$200, its equity will be worth \$800. The firm will owe $\$200 \times 1.05 = \$210$ in one year. Thus, if the economy is strong, equity holders will receive $\$1400 - \$210 = \$1190$, for a return of $\$1190/\$800 - 1 = 48.75\%$. If the economy is weak, equity holders will receive $\$900 - \$210 = \$690$, for a return of $\$690/\$800 - 1 = -13.75\%$. The equity has an expected return of

$$\tfrac{1}{2}(48.75\%) + \tfrac{1}{2}(-13.75\%) = 17.5\%.$$

Note that the equity has a return sensitivity of $48.75\% - (-13.75\%) = 62.5\%$, which is $62.5\%/50\% = 125\%$ of the sensitivity of unlevered equity. Its risk premium is $17.5\% - 5\% = 12.5\%$, which is also 125% of the risk premium of the unlevered equity, so it is appropriate compensation for the risk. With 20% debt financing, the firm's weighted average cost of capital remains $80\%(17.5\%) + 20\%(5\%) = 15\%$.

CONCEPT CHECK

1. Why are the value and cash flows of levered equity less than if the firm had issued unlevered equity?
2. How does the risk and cost of capital of levered equity compare to that of unlevered equity? Which is the superior capital structure choice in a perfect capital market?

14.2 Modigliani-Miller I: Leverage, Arbitrage, and Firm Value

In the previous section, we used the Law of One Price to argue that leverage would not affect the total value of the firm (the amount of money the entrepreneur can raise). Instead, it merely changes the allocation of cash flows between debt and equity, without altering the total cash flows of the firm. Modigliani and Miller (or simply MM) showed that this result holds more generally under a set of conditions referred to as **perfect capital markets**:

1. Investors and firms can trade the same set of securities at competitive market prices equal to the present value of their future cash flows.
2. There are no taxes, transaction costs, or issuance costs associated with security trading.
3. A firm's financing decisions do not change the cash flows generated by its investments, nor do they reveal new information about them.

Under these conditions, MM demonstrated the following result regarding the role of capital structure in determining firm value:[2]

MM Proposition I*: In a perfect capital market, the total value of a firm's securities is equal to the market value of the total cash flows generated by its assets and is not affected by its choice of capital structure.*

MM and the Law of One Price

MM established their result with the following simple argument. In the absence of taxes or other transaction costs, the total cash flow paid out to all of a firm's security holders is equal to the total cash flow generated by the firm's assets. Therefore, by the Law of One Price, the firm's securities and its assets must have the same total market value. Thus, as long as the firm's choice of securities does not change the cash flows generated by its assets, this decision will not change the total value of the firm or the amount of capital it can raise.

We can also view MM's result in terms of the Separation Principle introduced in Chapter 3: If securities are fairly priced, then buying or selling securities has an NPV of zero and, therefore, should not change the value of a firm. The future repayments that the firm must make on its debt are equal in value to the amount of the loan it receives upfront. Thus, there is no net gain or loss from using leverage, and the value of the firm is determined by the present value of the cash flows from its current and future investments.

Homemade Leverage

MM showed that the firm's value is not affected by its choice of capital structure. But suppose investors would prefer an alternative capital structure to the one the firm has chosen. MM demonstrated that in this case, investors can borrow or lend on their own and achieve the same result. For example, an investor who would like more leverage than the firm has chosen can borrow and add leverage to his or her own portfolio. When investors use

[2]Although it was not widely appreciated at the time, the idea that a firm's value does not depend on its capital structure was argued even earlier by John Burr Williams in his pathbreaking book, *The Theory of Investment Value* (North Holland Publishing, 1938; reprinted by Fraser Publishing, 1997).

MM and the Real World

Students often question why Modigliani and Miller's results are important if, after all, capital markets are not perfect in the real world. While it is true that capital markets are not perfect, all scientific theories begin with a set of idealized assumptions from which conclusions can be drawn. When we apply the theory, we must then evaluate how closely the assumptions hold, and consider the consequences of any important deviations.

As a useful analogy, consider Galileo's law of falling bodies. Galileo overturned the conventional wisdom by showing that, without friction, free-falling bodies will fall at the same rate independent of their mass. If you test this law, you will likely find it does not hold exactly. The reason, of course, is that unless we are in a vacuum, air friction tends to slow some objects more than others.

MM's results are similar. In practice, we will find that capital structure can have an effect on firm value. But just as Galileo's law of falling bodies reveals that we must look to air friction, rather than any underlying property of gravity, to explain differences in the speeds of falling objects, MM's proposition reveals that any effects of capital structure must similarly be due to frictions that exist in capital markets. After exploring the full meaning of MM's results in this chapter, we look at the important sources of these frictions, and their consequences, in subsequent chapters.

leverage in their own portfolios to adjust the leverage choice made by the firm, we say that they are using **homemade leverage**. As long as investors can borrow or lend at the same interest rate as the firm,[3] homemade leverage is a perfect substitute for the use of leverage by the firm.

To illustrate, suppose the entrepreneur uses no leverage and creates an all-equity firm. An investor who would prefer to hold levered equity can do so by using leverage in his own portfolio—that is, he can buy the stock on margin, as illustrated in Table 14.6.

TABLE 14.6 Replicating Levered Equity Using Homemade Leverage

	Date 0	Date 1: Cash Flows	
	Initial Cost	Strong Economy	Weak Economy
Unlevered equity	\$1000	\$1400	\$900
Margin loan	−\$500	−\$525	−\$525
Levered equity	\$500	\$875	\$375

If the cash flows of the unlevered equity serve as collateral for the margin loan, then the loan is risk-free and the investor should be able to borrow at the 5% rate. Although the firm is unlevered, by using homemade leverage, the investor has replicated the payoffs to the levered equity illustrated in Table 14.3, for a cost of \$500. Again, by the Law of One Price, the value of levered equity must also be \$500.

Now suppose the entrepreneur uses debt, but the investor would prefer to hold unlevered equity. The investor can replicate the payoffs of unlevered equity by buying both the debt *and* the equity of the firm. Combining the cash flows of the two securities produces cash flows identical to unlevered equity, for a total cost of \$1000, as we see in Table 14.7.

In each case, the entrepreneur's choice of capital structure does not affect the opportunities available to investors. Investors can alter the leverage choice of the firm to suit their

[3] This assumption is implied by perfect capital markets because the interest rate on a loan should depend only on its risk.

TABLE 14.7 Replicating Unlevered Equity by Holding Debt and Equity

	Date 0	Date 1: Cash Flows	
	Initial Cost	Strong Economy	Weak Economy
Debt	$500	$525	$525
Levered equity	$500	$875	$375
Unlevered Equity	$1000	$1400	$900

personal tastes either by borrowing and adding more leverage or by holding bonds and reducing leverage. With perfect capital markets, because different choices of capital structure offer no benefit to investors, they do not affect the value of the firm.

EXAMPLE 14.2 Homemade Leverage and Arbitrage

Problem

Suppose there are two firms, each with date 1 cash flows of $1400 or $900 (as shown in Table 14.1). The firms are identical except for their capital structure. One firm is unlevered, and its equity has a market value of $990. The other firm has borrowed $500, and its equity has a market value of $510. Does MM Proposition I hold? What arbitrage opportunity is available using homemade leverage?

Solution

MM Proposition I states that the total value of each firm should equal the value of its assets. Because these firms hold identical assets, their total values should be the same. However, the problem assumes the unlevered firm has a total market value of $990, whereas the levered firm has a total market value of $510 (equity) + $500 (debt) = $1010. Therefore, these prices violate MM Proposition I.

Because these two identical firms are trading for different total prices, the Law of One Price is violated and an arbitrage opportunity exists. To exploit it, we can borrow $500 and buy the equity of the unlevered firm for $990, re-creating the equity of the levered firm by using homemade leverage for a cost of only $990 − 500 = $490. We can then sell the equity of the levered firm for $510 and enjoy an arbitrage profit of $20.

	Date 0	Date 1: Cash Flows	
	Cash Flow	Strong Economy	Weak Economy
Borrow	$500	−$525	−$525
Buy unlevered equity	−$990	$1400	$900
Sell levered equity	$510	−$875	−$375
Total cash flow	$20	$0	$0

Note that the actions of arbitrageurs buying the unlevered firm and selling the levered firm will cause the price of the unlevered firm's stock to rise and the price of the levered firm's stock to fall until the firms' values are equal and MM Proposition I holds.

The Market Value Balance Sheet

In Section 14.1, we considered just two choices for a firm's capital structure. MM Proposition I, however, applies much more broadly to any choice of debt and equity. In fact, it applies even if the firm issues other types of securities, such as convertible debt or warrants, a type of stock option that we discuss later in the text. The logic is the same: Because investors can buy or sell securities on their own, no value is created when the firm buys or sells securities for them.

One application of MM Proposition I is the useful device known as the market value balance sheet of the firm. A **market value balance sheet** is similar to an accounting balance sheet, with two important distinctions. First, *all* assets and liabilities of the firm are included—even intangible assets such as reputation, brand name, or human capital that are missing from a standard accounting balance sheet. Second, all values are current market values rather than historical costs. On the market value balance sheet, shown in Table 14.8, the total value of all securities issued by the firm must equal the total value of the firm's assets.

The market value balance sheet captures the idea that value is created by a firm's choice of assets and investments. By choosing positive-NPV projects that are worth more than their initial investment, the firm can enhance its value. Holding fixed the cash flows generated by the firm's assets, however, the choice of capital structure does not change the value of the firm. Instead, it merely divides the value of the firm into different securities. Using the market value balance sheet, we can compute the value of equity as follows:

$$\text{Market Value of Equity} = \text{Market Value of Assets} - \text{Market Value of Debt and Other Liabilities} \quad (14.1)$$

EXAMPLE 14.3 **Valuing Equity When There Are Multiple Securities**

Problem

Suppose our entrepreneur decides to sell the firm by splitting it into three securities: equity, $500 of debt, and a third security called a warrant that pays $210 when the firm's cash flows are high and nothing when the cash flows are low. Suppose that this third security is fairly priced at $60. What will the value of the equity be in a perfect capital market?

Solution

According to MM Proposition I, the total value of all securities issued should equal the value of the assets of the firm, which is $1000. Because the debt is worth $500 and the new security is worth $60, the value of the equity must be $440. (You can check this result by verifying that at these prices, the firm's equity and warrants both have risk premia commensurate with their risk in comparison with the securities in Table 14.5.)

Application: A Leveraged Recapitalization

So far, we have looked at capital structure from the perspective of an entrepreneur who is considering financing an investment opportunity. In fact, MM Proposition I applies to capital structure decisions made at any time during the life of the firm.

Let's consider an example. Harrison Industries is currently an all-equity firm operating in a perfect capital market, with 50 million shares outstanding that are trading for $4 per share. Harrison plans to increase its leverage by borrowing $80 million and using the funds to repurchase 20 million of its outstanding shares. When a firm repurchases a significant percentage of its outstanding shares in this way, the transaction is called a **leveraged recapitalization**.

We can view this transaction in two stages. First, Harrison sells debt to raise $80 million in cash. Second, Harrison uses the cash to repurchase shares. Table 14.9 shows the market value balance sheet after each of these stages.

TABLE 14.8 The Market Value Balance Sheet of the Firm

Assets	Liabilities
Collection of Assets and Investments Undertaken by the Firm:	Collection of Securities Issued by the Firm:
Tangible Assets	Debt
Cash	Short-term debt
Plant, property, and equipment	Long-term debt
Inventory and other working capital (and so on)	Convertible debt
Intangible Assets	Equity
Intellectual property	Common stock
Reputation	Preferred stock
Human capital (and so on)	Warrants (options)
Total Market Value of Firm Assets	**Total Market Value of Firm Securities**

Initially, Harrison is an all-equity firm. That is, the market value of Harrison's equity, which is 50 million shares × \$4 per share = \$200 million, equals the market value of its existing assets. After borrowing, Harrison's liabilities grow by \$80 million, which is also equal to the amount of cash the firm has raised. Because both assets and liabilities increase by the same amount, the market value of the equity remains unchanged.

To conduct the share repurchase, Harrison spends the \$80 million in borrowed cash to repurchase \$80 million ÷ \$4 per share = 20 million shares. Because the firm's assets decrease by \$80 million and its debt remains unchanged, the market value of the equity must also fall by \$80 million, from \$200 million to \$120 million, for assets and liabilities to remain balanced. The share price, however, is unchanged—with 30 million shares remaining, the shares are worth \$120 million ÷ 30 million shares = \$4 per share, just as before.

The fact that the share price did not change should not come as a surprise. Because the firm has sold \$80 million worth of new debt and purchased \$80 million worth of

TABLE 14.9 Market Value Balance Sheet after Each Stage of Harrison's Leveraged Recapitalization (in \$ million)

Initial		After Borrowing		After Share Repurchase	
Assets	Liabilities	Assets	Liabilities	Assets	Liabilities
		Cash	Debt	Cash	Debt
		80	80	0	80
Existing assets	Equity	Existing assets	Equity	Existing assets	Equity
200	200	200	200	200	120
200	**200**	**280**	**280**	**200**	**200**
Shares outstanding (million)	50	Shares outstanding (million)	50	Shares outstanding (million)	30
Value per share	\$4.00	Value per share	\$4.00	Value per share	\$4.00

existing equity, this zero-NPV transaction (benefits = costs) does not change the value for shareholders.

CONCEPT CHECK

1. Why are investors indifferent to the firm's capital structure choice?
2. What is a market value balance sheet?
3. In a perfect capital market, how will a firm's market capitalization change if it borrows in order to repurchase shares? How will its share price change?

14.3 Modigliani-Miller II: Leverage, Risk, and the Cost of Capital

Modigliani and Miller showed that a firm's financing choice does not affect its value. But how can we reconcile this conclusion with the fact that the cost of capital differs for different securities? Consider again our entrepreneur from Section 14.1. When the project is financed solely through equity, the equity holders require a 15% expected return. As an alternative, the firm can borrow at the risk-free rate of 5%. In this situation, isn't debt a cheaper and better source of capital than equity?

Although debt does have a lower cost of capital than equity, we cannot consider this cost in isolation. As we saw in Section 14.1, while debt itself may be cheap, it increases the risk and therefore the cost of capital of the firm's equity. In this section, we calculate the impact of leverage on the expected return of a firm's stock, or the equity cost of capital. We then consider how to estimate the cost of capital of the firm's assets, and show that it is unaffected by leverage. In the end, the savings from the low expected return on debt, the debt cost of capital, are exactly offset by a higher equity cost of capital, and there are no net savings for the firm.

Leverage and the Equity Cost of Capital

We can use Modigliani and Miller's first proposition to derive an explicit relationship between leverage and the equity cost of capital. Let E and D denote the market value of equity and debt if the firm is levered, respectively; let U be the market value of equity if the firm is unlevered; and let A be the market value of the firm's assets. Then MM Proposition I states that

$$E + D = U = A \tag{14.2}$$

That is, the total market value of the firm's securities is equal to the market value of its assets, whether the firm is unlevered or levered.

We can interpret the first equality in Eq. 14.2 in terms of homemade leverage: By holding a portfolio of the firm's equity and debt, we can replicate the cash flows from holding unlevered equity. Because the return of a portfolio is equal to the weighted average of the returns of the securities in it, this equality implies the following relationship between the returns of levered equity (R_E), debt (R_D), and unlevered equity (R_U):

$$\frac{E}{E+D}R_E + \frac{D}{E+D}R_D = R_U \tag{14.3}$$

If we solve Eq. 14.3 for R_E, we obtain the following expression for the return of levered equity:

$$R_E = \underbrace{R_U}_{\text{Risk without leverage}} + \underbrace{\frac{D}{E}(R_U - R_D)}_{\text{Additional risk due to leverage}} \tag{14.4}$$

This equation reveals the effect of leverage on the return of the levered equity. The levered equity return equals the unlevered return, plus an extra "kick" due to leverage. This extra effect pushes the returns of levered equity even higher when the firm performs well ($R_U > R_D$), but makes them drop even lower when the firm does poorly ($R_U < R_D$). The amount of additional risk depends on the amount of leverage, measured by the firm's market value debt-equity ratio, *D/E*. Because Eq. 14.4 holds for the realized returns, it holds for the *expected* returns as well (denoted by *r* in place of *R*). This observation leads to Modigliani and Miller's second proposition:

MM Proposition II: *The cost of capital of levered equity increases with the firm's market value debt-equity ratio,*

Cost of Capital of Levered Equity

$$r_E = r_U + \frac{D}{E}(r_U - r_D) \tag{14.5}$$

We can illustrate MM Proposition II for the entrepreneur's project in Section 14.1. Recall that if the firm is all-equity financed, the expected return on unlevered equity is 15% (see Table 14.4). If the firm is financed with $500 of debt, the expected return of the debt is the risk-free interest rate of 5%. Therefore, according to MM Proposition II, the expected return on equity for the levered firm is

$$r_E = 15\% + \frac{500}{500}(15\% - 5\%) = 25\%$$

This result matches the expected return calculated in Table 14.4.

EXAMPLE 14.4 **Computing the Equity Cost of Capital**

Problem

Suppose the entrepreneur of Section 14.1 borrows only $200 when financing the project. According to MM Proposition II, what will be the firm's equity cost of capital?

Solution

Because the firm's assets have a market value of $1000, by MM Proposition I the equity will have a market value of $800. Then, using Eq. 14.5,

$$r_E = 15\% + \frac{200}{800}(15\% - 5\%) = 17.5\%$$

This result matches the expected return calculated in Example 14.1.

Capital Budgeting and the Weighted Average Cost of Capital

We can use the insight of Modigliani and Miller to understand the effect of leverage on the firm's cost of capital for new investments. If a firm is financed with both equity and debt, then the risk of its underlying assets will match the risk of a portfolio of its equity and debt. Thus, the appropriate cost of capital for the firm's assets is the cost of capital of this portfolio, which is simply the weighted average of the firm's equity and debt cost of capital:

Unlevered Cost of Capital (Pretax WACC)

$$r_U \equiv \left(\begin{array}{c}\text{Fraction of Firm Value}\\ \text{Financed by Equity}\end{array}\right)\left(\begin{array}{c}\text{Equity}\\ \text{Cost of Capital}\end{array}\right) + \left(\begin{array}{c}\text{Fraction of Firm Value}\\ \text{Financed by Debt}\end{array}\right)\left(\begin{array}{c}\text{Debt}\\ \text{Cost of Capital}\end{array}\right)$$

$$= \frac{E}{E+D} r_E + \frac{D}{E+D} r_D \tag{14.6}$$

In Chapter 12 we called this cost of capital the firm's unlevered cost of capital, or pretax WACC. There we also introduced the firm's effective after-tax weighted average cost of capital, or WACC, which we compute using the firm's after-tax cost of debt. Because we are in a setting of perfect capital markets, there are no taxes, so the firm's WACC and unlevered cost of capital coincide:

$$r_{wacc} = r_U = r_A \tag{14.7}$$

That is, *with perfect capital markets, a firm's WACC is independent of its capital structure and is equal to its equity cost of capital if it is unlevered, which matches the cost of capital of its assets.*

FIGURE 14.1

WACC and Leverage with Perfect Capital Markets

As the fraction of the firm financed with debt increases, both the equity and the debt become riskier and their cost of capital rises. Yet, because more weight is put on the lower-cost debt, the weighted average cost of capital remains constant.
(a) Equity, debt, and weighted average costs of capital for different amounts of leverage. The rate of increase of r_D and r_E and thus the shape of the curves, depends on the characteristics of the firm's cash flows.
(b) This table calculates the WACC for the specific example in Section 14.1 under different capital structures.

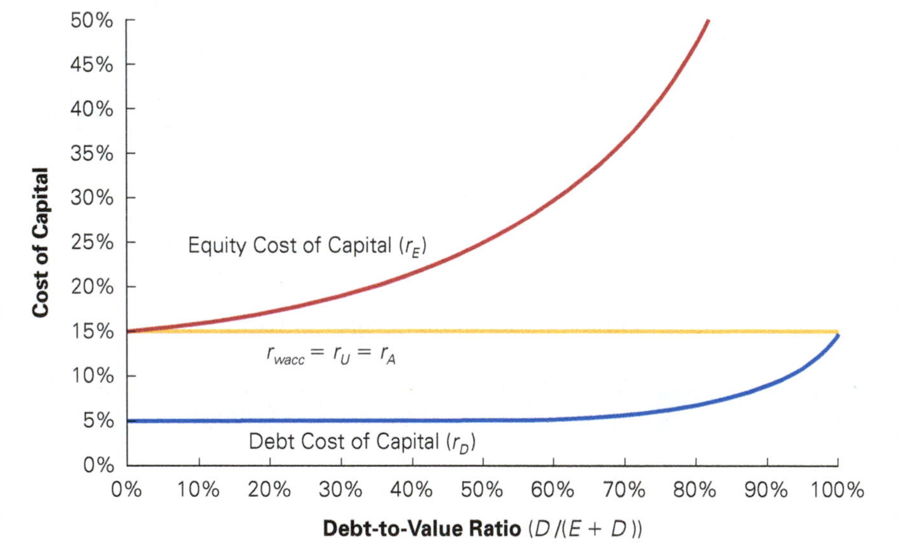

(a)

E	D	r_E	r_D	$\frac{E}{E+D}r_E + \frac{D}{E+D}r_D$	$= r_{wacc}$
1000	0	15.0%	5.0%	1.0 × 15.0% + 0.0 × 5.0%	= 15%
800	200	17.5%	5.0%	0.8 × 17.5% + 0.2 × 5.0%	= 15%
500	500	25.0%	5.0%	0.5 × 25.0% + 0.5 × 5.0%	= 15%
100	900	75.0%	8.3%*	0.1 × 75.0% + 0.9 × 8.3%	= 15%

(b)

*This level of leverage corresponds to a face value of 1050 and thus a promised yield of 16.67%. Because the firm defaults and debt earns a zero return with 50% probability, the expected return of the debt, r_D, is only 8.33%, representing a risk premium of 3.33%. This risk premium is 1/3 that of unlevered equity, which is justified since it has 1/3 the return sensitivity (16.67% versus 50%, see Table 14.5). More generally, we can use No-Arbitrage Pricing to price the securities in this example (see e.g. Problem 14.20 and the Chapter 3 appendix).

Figure 14.1 illustrates the effect of increasing the amount of leverage in a firm's capital structure on its equity cost of capital, its debt cost of capital, and its WACC. In the figure, we measure the firm's leverage in terms of its **debt-to-value ratio**, $D/(E+D)$, which is the fraction of the firm's total value that corresponds to debt. With no debt, the WACC is equal to the unlevered equity cost of capital. As the firm borrows at the low cost of capital for debt, its equity cost of capital rises according to Eq. 14.5. The net effect is that the firm's WACC is unchanged. Of course, as the amount of debt increases, the debt becomes more risky because there is a chance the firm will default; as a result, the debt cost of capital r_D also rises. With 100% debt, the debt would be as risky as the assets themselves (similar to unlevered equity). But even though the debt and equity costs of capital both rise when leverage is high, because more weight is put on the lower-cost debt, the WACC remains constant.

Recall from Chapter 9 that we can calculate the enterprise value of the firm by discounting its future free cash flow using the WACC. Thus, Eq. 14.7 provides the following intuitive interpretation of MM Proposition I: Although debt has a lower cost of capital than equity, leverage does not lower a firm's WACC. As a result, the value of the firm's free cash flow evaluated using the WACC does not change, and so the enterprise value of the firm does not depend on its financing choices. This observation allows us to answer the questions posed for the CFO of EBS at the beginning of this chapter: With perfect capital markets, the firm's weighted average cost of capital, and therefore the NPV of the expansion, is unaffected by how EBS chooses to finance the new investment.

EXAMPLE 14.5 Reducing Leverage and the Cost of Capital

Problem

NRG Energy, Inc. (NRG) is an energy company with a market debt-equity ratio of 3. Suppose its current debt cost of capital is 6%, and its equity cost of capital is 14%. Suppose also that if NRG issues equity and uses the proceeds to repay its debt and reduce its debt-equity ratio to 2, it will lower its debt cost of capital to 5.5%. With perfect capital markets, what effect will this transaction have on NRG's equity cost of capital and WACC? What would happen if NRG issues even more equity and pays off its debt completely? How would these alternative capital structures affect NRG's enterprise value?

Solution

We can calculate NRG's initial WACC and unlevered cost of capital using Eqs. 14.6 and 14.7:

$$r_{wacc} = r_U = \frac{E}{E+D} r_E + \frac{D}{E+D} r_D = \frac{1}{1+3}(14\%) + \frac{3}{1+3}(6\%) = 8\%$$

Given NRG's unlevered cost of capital of 8%, we can use Eq. 14.5 to calculate NRG's equity cost of capital after the reduction in leverage:

$$r_E = r_U + \frac{D}{E}(r_U - r_D) = 8\% + \frac{2}{1}(8\% - 5.5\%) = 13\%$$

The reduction in leverage will cause NRG's equity cost of capital to fall to 13%. Note, though, that with perfect capital markets, NRG's WACC remains unchanged at $8\% = \frac{1}{3}(13\%) + \frac{2}{3}(5.5\%)$, and there is no net gain from this transaction.

If NRG pays off its debt completely, it will be unlevered. Thus, its equity cost of capital will equal its WACC and unlevered cost of capital of 8%.

In either scenario, NRG's WACC and free cash flows remain unchanged. Thus, with perfect capital markets, its enterprise value will not be affected by these different capital structure choices.

COMMON MISTAKE **Is Debt Better Than Equity?**

It is not uncommon to hear people say that because debt has a lower cost of capital than equity, a firm can reduce its overall WACC by increasing the amount of debt financing. If this strategy works, shouldn't a firm take on as much debt as possible, at least as long as the debt is not risky?

This argument ignores the fact that even if the debt is risk free and the firm will not default, adding leverage increases the risk of the equity. Given the increase in risk, equity holders will demand a higher risk premium and, therefore, a higher expected return. The increase in the cost of equity exactly offsets the benefit of a greater reliance on the cheaper debt capital, so that the firm's overall cost of capital remains unchanged.

Computing the WACC with Multiple Securities

We calculated the firm's unlevered cost of capital and WACC in Eqs. 14.6 and 14.7 assuming that the firm has issued only two types of securities (equity and debt). If the firm's capital structure is more complex, however, then r_U and r_{wacc} are calculated by computing the weighted average cost of capital of *all* of the firm's securities.

EXAMPLE 14.6 **WACC with Multiple Securities**

Problem

Compute the WACC for the entrepreneur's project with the capital structure described in Example 14.3.

Solution

Because the firm has three securities in its capital structure (debt, equity, and the warrant), its weighted average cost of capital is the average return it must pay these three groups of investors:

$$r_{wacc} = r_U = \frac{E}{E+D+W} r_E + \frac{D}{E+D+W} r_D + \frac{W}{E+D+W} r_W$$

From Example 14.3, we know $E = 440$, $D = 500$, and $W = 60$. What are the expected returns for each security? Given the cash flows of the firm, the debt is risk free and has an expected return of $r_D = 5\%$. The warrant has an expected payoff of $\frac{1}{2}(\$210) + \frac{1}{2}(\$0) = \$105$, so its expected return is $r_w = \$105/\$60 - 1 = 75\%$. Equity has a payoff of $(\$1400 - \$525 - \$210) = \$665$ when cash flows are high and $(\$900 - \$525) = \$375$ when cash flows are low; thus, its expected payoff is $\frac{1}{2}(\$665) + \frac{1}{2}(\$375) = \$520$. The expected return for equity is then $r_E = \$520/\$440 - 1 = 18.18\%$. We can now compute the WACC:

$$r_{wacc} = \frac{\$440}{\$1000}(18.18\%) + \frac{\$500}{\$1000}(5\%) + \frac{\$60}{\$1000}(75\%) = 15\%$$

Once again, the firm's WACC and unlevered cost of capital is 15%, the same as if it were all-equity financed.

Levered and Unlevered Betas

Note that Eqs. 14.6 and 14.7 for the weighted-average cost of capital match our calculation in Chapter 12 of a firm's unlevered cost of capital. There, we showed that a firm's unlevered or asset beta is the weighted average of its equity and debt beta:

$$\beta_U = \frac{E}{E+D}\beta_E + \frac{D}{E+D}\beta_D \tag{14.8}$$

Recall that the unlevered beta measures the market risk of the firm's underlying assets, and thus can be used to assess the cost of capital for comparable investments. When a firm changes its capital structure without changing its investments, its unlevered beta will remain unaltered. However, its equity beta will change to reflect the effect of the capital structure change on its risk.[4] Let's rearrange Eq. 14.8 to solve for β_E:

$$\beta_E = \beta_U + \frac{D}{E}(\beta_U - \beta_D) \tag{14.9}$$

Eq. 14.9 is analogous to Eq. 14.5, with beta replacing the expected returns. It shows that the firm's equity beta also increases with leverage.

EXAMPLE 14.7 Betas and Leverage

Problem

Suppose drug retailer CVS has an equity beta of 0.8 and a debt-equity ratio of 0.1. Estimate its asset beta assuming its debt beta is zero. Suppose CVS were to increase its leverage so that its debt-equity ratio was 0.5. Assuming its debt beta were still zero, what would you expect its equity beta to be after the increase in leverage?

Solution

We can estimate the unlevered or asset beta for CVS using Eq. 14.8:

$$\beta_U = \frac{E}{E+D}\beta_E + \frac{D}{E+D}\beta_D = \frac{1}{1 + D/E}\beta_E = \frac{1}{1+0.1} \times 0.8 = 0.73$$

With the increase in leverage, CVS's equity beta will increase according to Eq. 14.9:

$$\beta_E = \beta_U + \frac{D}{E}(\beta_U - \beta_D) = 0.73 + 0.5(0.73 - 0) = 1.09$$

Thus, CVS's equity beta (and equity cost of capital) will increase with leverage. Note that if CVS's debt beta also increased, the impact of leverage on its equity beta would be somewhat lower—if debt holders share some of the firm's market risk, the equity holders will need to bear less of it.

The assets on a firm's balance sheet include any holdings of cash or risk-free securities. Because these holdings are risk-free, they reduce the risk—and therefore the required risk premium—of the firm's assets. For this reason, holding excess cash has the opposite effect of leverage on risk and return. From this standpoint, we can view cash as negative debt. Thus, as we stated in Chapter 12, when we are trying to assess a firm's enterprise value—its business assets separate from any cash holdings—it is natural to measure leverage in terms of the firm's net debt, which is its debt less its holdings of excess cash or short-term investments.

[4] The relationship between leverage and equity betas was developed by R. Hamada in "The Effect of the Firm's Capital Structure on the Systematic Risk of Common Stocks," *Journal of Finance* 27(2) (1972): 435–452; and by M. Rubinstein in "A Mean-Variance Synthesis of Corporate Financial Theory," *Journal of Finance* 28(1) (1973): 167–181.

EXAMPLE 14.8 Cash and the Cost of Capital

Problem

In August 2015, Cisco Systems had a market capitalization of \$140 billion. It had debt of \$25.4 billion as well as cash and short-term investments of \$60.4 billion. Its equity beta was 1.09 and its debt beta was approximately zero. What was Cisco's enterprise value at the time? Given a risk-free rate of 2% and a market risk premium of 5%, estimate the unlevered cost of capital of Cisco's business.

Solution

Because Cisco had \$25.4 billion in debt and \$60.4 billion in cash, Cisco's net debt = \$25.4 − \$60.4 billion = −\$35.0 billion. Its enterprise value was therefore \$140 billion − \$35 billion = \$105 billion.

Given a zero beta for its net debt, Cisco's unlevered beta was

$$\beta_U = \frac{E}{E+D}\beta_E + \frac{D}{E+D}\beta_D = \frac{\$140}{\$105}(1.09) + \frac{-\$35}{\$105}(0) = 1.45$$

and we can estimate its unlevered cost of capital as $r_U = 2\% + 1.45 \times 5\% = 9.25\%$. Note that because of its cash holdings, Cisco's equity is less risky than its underlying business.

CONCEPT CHECK

1. How do we compute the weighted average cost of capital of a firm?
2. With perfect capital markets, as a firm increases its leverage, how does its debt cost of capital change? Its equity cost of capital? Its weighted average cost of capital?

NOBEL PRIZE Franco Modigliani and Merton Miller

Franco Modigliani and Merton Miller, the authors of the Modigliani-Miller Propositions, have each won the Nobel Prize in economics for their work in financial economics, including their capital structure propositions. Modigliani won the Nobel Prize in 1985 for his work on personal savings and for his capital structure theorems with Miller. Miller earned his prize in 1990 for his analysis of portfolio theory and capital structure.

Miller once described the MM propositions in an interview this way:

> *People often ask: Can you summarize your theory quickly? Well, I say, you understand the M&M theorem if you know why this is a joke: The pizza delivery man comes to Yogi Berra after the game and says, "Yogi, how do you want this pizza cut, into quarters or eighths?" And Yogi says, "Cut it in eight pieces. I'm feeling hungry tonight."*
>
> *Everyone recognizes that's a joke because obviously the number and shape of the pieces don't affect the size of the pizza. And similarly, the stocks, bonds, warrants, et cetera, issued don't affect the aggregate value of the firm. They just slice up the underlying earnings in different ways.**

Modigliani and Miller each won the Nobel Prize in large part for their observation that the value of a firm should be unaffected by its capital structure in perfect capital markets. While the intuition underlying the MM propositions may be as simple as slicing pizza, their implications for corporate finance are far-reaching. The propositions imply that the true role of a firm's financial policy is to deal with (and potentially exploit) financial market imperfections such as taxes and transactions costs. Modigliani and Miller's work began a long line of research into these market imperfections, which we look at over the next several chapters.

*Peter J. Tanous, *Investment Gurus* (Prentice Hall Press, 1997).

14.4 Capital Structure Fallacies

MM Propositions I and II state that with perfect capital markets, leverage has no effect on firm value or the firm's overall cost of capital. Here we take a critical look at two incorrect arguments that are sometimes cited in favor of leverage.

Leverage and Earnings per Share

Leverage can increase a firm's expected earnings per share. An argument sometimes made is that by doing so, leverage should also increase the firm's stock price.

Consider the following example. Levitron Industries (LVI) is currently an all-equity firm. It expects to generate earnings before interest and taxes (EBIT) of $10 million over the next year. Currently, LVI has 10 million shares outstanding, and its stock is trading for a price of $7.50 per share. LVI is considering changing its capital structure by borrowing $15 million at an interest rate of 8% and using the proceeds to repurchase 2 million shares at $7.50 per share.

Let's consider the consequences of this transaction in a setting of perfect capital markets. Suppose LVI has no debt. Because LVI pays no interest, and because in perfect capital markets there are no taxes, LVI's earnings would equal its EBIT. Therefore, without debt, LVI would expect earnings per share of

$$EPS = \frac{\text{Earnings}}{\text{Number of Shares}} = \frac{\$10 \text{ million}}{10 \text{ million}} = \$1$$

The new debt will obligate LVI to make interest payments each year of

$$\$15 \text{ million} \times 8\% \text{ interest/year} = \$1.2 \text{ million/year}$$

As a result, LVI will have expected earnings after interest of

$$\text{Earnings} = \text{EBIT} - \text{Interest} = \$10 \text{ million} - \$1.2 \text{ million} = \$8.8 \text{ million}$$

The interest payments on the debt will cause LVI's total earnings to fall. But because the number of outstanding shares will also have fallen to 10 million − 2 million = 8 million shares after the share repurchase, LVI's expected earnings per share is

$$EPS = \frac{\$8.8 \text{ million}}{8 \text{ million}} = \$1.10$$

As we can see, LVI's expected earnings per share increases with leverage.[5] This increase might appear to make shareholders better off and could potentially lead to an increase in the stock price. Yet we know from MM Proposition I that as long as the securities are fairly priced, these financial transactions have an NPV of zero and offer no benefit to shareholders. How can we reconcile these seemingly contradictory results?

The answer is that the risk of earnings has changed. Thus far, we have considered only *expected* earnings per share. We have not considered the consequences of this transaction on the risk of the earnings. To do so, we must determine the effect of the increase in leverage on earnings per share in a variety of scenarios.

Suppose earnings before interest payments are only $4 million. Without the increase in leverage, EPS would be $4 million ÷ 10 million shares = $0.40. With the new debt, however, earnings after interest payments would be $4 million − $1.2 million = $2.8 million, leading to earnings per share of $2.8 million ÷ 8 million shares = $0.35. So, when

[5]More generally, leverage will increase expected EPS whenever the firm's after-tax borrowing cost is less than the ratio of expected earnings to the share price (i.e., the reciprocal of its forward P/E multiple, also called the *earnings yield*). For LVI, with no taxes, $8\% < EPS/P = 1/7.50 = 13.33\%$.

FIGURE 14.2

LVI Earnings per Share with and without Leverage

The sensitivity of EPS to EBIT is higher for a levered firm than for an unlevered firm. Thus, given assets with the same risk, the EPS of a levered firm is more volatile.

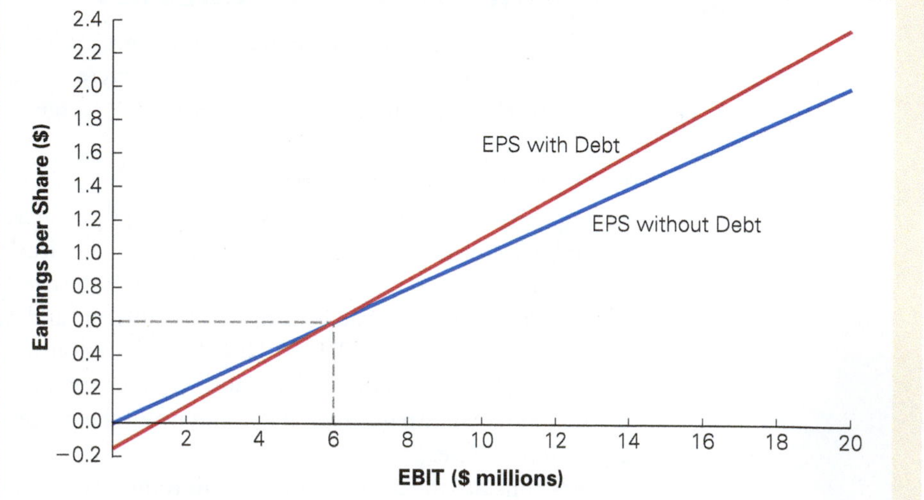

earnings are low, leverage will cause EPS to fall even further than it otherwise would have. Figure 14.2 presents a range of scenarios.

As Figure 14.2 shows, if earnings before interest exceed \$6 million, then EPS is higher with leverage. When earnings fall below \$6 million, however, EPS is lower with leverage than without it. In fact, if earnings before interest fall below \$1.2 million (the level of the interest expense), then after interest LVI will have negative EPS. So, although LVI's expected EPS rises with leverage, the risk of its EPS also increases. The increased risk can be seen because the line showing EPS with leverage in Figure 14.2 is steeper than the line without leverage, implying that the same fluctuation in EBIT will lead to greater fluctuations in EPS once leverage is introduced. Taken together, these observations are consistent with MM Proposition I. While EPS increases on average, this increase is necessary to compensate shareholders for the additional risk they are taking, so LVI's share price does not increase as a result of the transaction. Let's check this result in an example.

EXAMPLE 14.9 **The MM Propositions and Earnings per Share**

Problem

Assume that LVI's EBIT is not expected to grow in the future and that all earnings are paid as dividends. Use MM Propositions I and II to show that the increase in expected EPS for LVI will not lead to an increase in the share price.

Solution

Without leverage, expected earnings per share and therefore dividends are \$1 each year, and the share price is \$7.50. Let r_U be LVI's cost of capital without leverage. Then we can value LVI as a perpetuity:

$$P = 7.50 = \frac{Div}{r_U} = \frac{EPS}{r_U} = \frac{1.00}{r_U}$$

Therefore, LVI's current share price implies $r_U = 1/7.50 = 13.33\%$.

The market value of LVI stock without leverage is \$7.50 per share × 10 million shares = \$75 million. If LVI uses debt to repurchase \$15 million worth of the firm's equity (that is, 2 million shares), then the remaining equity will be worth \$75 million − \$15 million = \$60 million according to MM Proposition I. After the transaction, LVI's debt-equity ratio is $15 million ÷ $60 million = $\frac{1}{4}$. Using MM Proposition II, LVI's equity cost of capital with leverage will be

$$r_E = r_U + \frac{D}{E}(r_U - r_D) = 13.33\% + \frac{1}{4}(13.33\% - 8\%) = 14.66\%$$

Given that expected EPS is now $1.10 per share, the new value of the shares equals

$$P = \frac{\$1.10}{r_E} = \frac{\$1.10}{14.66\%} = \$7.50 \text{ per share}$$

Thus, even though EPS is higher, due to the additional risk, shareholders will demand a higher return. These effects cancel out, so the price per share is unchanged.

Because the firm's earnings per share and price-earnings ratio are affected by leverage, we cannot reliably compare these measures across firms with different capital structures. The same is true for accounting-based performance measures such as return on equity (ROE). Therefore, most analysts prefer to use performance measures and valuation multiples that are based on the firm's earnings before interest has been deducted. For example, the ratio of enterprise value to EBIT (or EBITDA) is more useful when analyzing firms with very different capital structures than is comparing their P/E ratios.

GLOBAL FINANCIAL CRISIS Bank Capital Regulation and the ROE Fallacy

In banking jargon, a "capital requirement" obligates a bank to finance itself with a certain minimum amount of equity to ensure that its debt-to-equity ratio will stay below a set level. The permitted level of leverage is very high—international standards allow common equity to represent as little as 3% of a bank's total funding.* To put this number in perspective, the equity of a typical non-financial firm exceeds 50% of firm value. Such extreme leverage makes bank equity very risky.

These extreme levels of bank leverage were an important contributing factor to the financial meltdown in 2008 and the subsequent recession: With such a small equity cushion, even a minor drop in asset values can lead to insolvency. While stricter international rules post crisis have required banks to reduce leverage, many policymakers believe capital requirements should be increased even further to reduce the risk of the financial sector and the consequent spillovers to the broader economy.

Bankers counter that decreased leverage will lower their return on equity, limiting their ability to compete effectively. According to Josef Ackermann, then CEO of Deutsche Bank, new capital requirements would "depress ROE to levels that make investment into the banking sector unattractive relative to other business sectors."** The return on equity is indeed a function of the firm's leverage. As with EPS, lower leverage will tend to decrease the firm's ROE on average, though it will raise the ROE in bad times. But this decrease in average ROE is compensated for by a reduction in the riskiness of equity and therefore the required risk premium. Thus, from an investor's perspective, the reduction in ROE that results solely from a decrease in leverage does *not* make investing in the firm any less attractive. Franco Modigliani and Merton Miller were awarded the Nobel Prize for pointing out that in a perfect market the bank's capital structure cannot affect its competitiveness.

The only way a change in leverage can affect the "attractiveness" of equity (and the competitiveness of banks) is if there is a market imperfection. In the next two chapters we will discuss these imperfections and explain why they do give banks a strong incentive to maximize their leverage. Unfortunately, the most important imperfections derive from government subsidies, so the banks' gains from leverage come largely at taxpayer expense.

*Prior to the financial crisis, global regulatory standards allowed banks to have as little as 2% equity funding. In 2013 the new Basel III Accord raised this equity requirement to 3% of total assets (and 4.5% of risk-weighted assets). Many countries impose even stricter requirements for systemically important financial institutions (SIFIs); for example the U.S. requires at least 6% for its largest banks.

**J. Ackermann, "The new architecture of financial regulation: Will it prevent another crisis?" Special Paper 194, FMG Deutsche Bank Conference, London School of Economics, October 2010.

Equity Issuances and Dilution

Another often-heard fallacy is that issuing equity will dilute existing shareholders' ownership, so debt financing should be used instead. By **dilution**, the proponents of this fallacy mean that if the firm issues new shares, the cash flows generated by the firm must be divided among a larger number of shares, thereby reducing the value of each individual share. The problem with this line of reasoning is that it ignores the fact that the cash raised by issuing new shares will increase the firm's assets. Let's consider an example.

Suppose Jet Sky Airlines (JSA) is a highly successful discount airline serving the southeastern United States. It currently has no debt and 500 million shares of stock outstanding. These shares are currently trading at \$16. Last month the firm announced that it would expand its operations to the Northeast. The expansion will require the purchase of \$1 billion of new planes, which will be financed by issuing new equity. How will the share price change when the new equity is issued today?

Based on the current share price of the firm (prior to the issue), the equity and therefore the assets of the firm have a market value of 500 million shares $\times$ \$16 per share = \$8 billion. Because the expansion decision has already been made and announced, in perfect capital markets this value incorporates the NPV associated with the expansion.

Suppose JSA sells 62.5 million new shares at the current price of \$16 per share to raise the additional \$1 billion needed to purchase the planes.

Assets (in \$ million)	Before Equity Issue	After Equity Issue
Cash		1000
Existing assets	8000	8000
Total Value	8000	9000
Shares outstanding (million)	500	562.5
Value per share	\$16.00	\$16.00

Two things happen when JSA issues equity. First, the market value of its assets grows because of the additional \$1 billion in cash the firm has raised. Second, the number of shares increases. Although the number of shares has grown to 562.5 million, the value per share is unchanged: \$9 billion $\div$ 562.5 million shares = \$16 per share.

In general, as long as the firm sells the new shares of equity *at a fair price*, there will be no gain or loss to shareholders associated with the equity issue itself. The money taken in by the firm as a result of the share issue exactly offsets the dilution of the shares. *Any gain or loss associated with the transaction will result from the NPV of the investments the firm makes with the funds raised.*[6]

CONCEPT CHECK

1. If a change in leverage raises a firm's earnings per share, should this cause its share price to rise in a perfect market?
2. True or False: When a firm issues equity, it increases the supply of its shares in the market, which should cause its share price to fall.

[6] If JSA had outstanding debt, issuing new equity might reduce its risk, benefiting debt holders at shareholders expense. We will discuss this *debt overhang effect* in Chapter 16.

14.5 MM: Beyond the Propositions

Since the publication of their original paper, Modigliani and Miller's ideas have greatly influenced finance research and practice. Perhaps more important than the specific propositions themselves is the approach that MM took to derive them. Proposition I was one of the first arguments to show that the Law of One Price could have strong implications for security prices and firm values in a competitive market; it marks the beginning of the modern theory of corporate finance.

Modigliani and Miller's work formalized a new way of thinking about financial markets that was first put forth by John Burr Williams in his 1938 book, *The Theory of Investment Value*. In it Williams argues:

> If the investment value of an enterprise as a whole is by definition the present worth of all its future distributions to security holders, whether on interest or dividend account, then this value in no wise depends on what the company's capitalization is. Clearly, if a single individual or a single institutional investor owned all of the bonds, stocks and warrants issued by the corporation, it would not matter to this investor what the company's capitalization was (except for details concerning the income tax). Any earnings collected as interest could not be collected as dividends. To such an individual it would be perfectly obvious that total interest- and dividend-paying power was in no wise dependent on the kind of securities issued to the company's owner. Furthermore no change in the investment value of the enterprise as a whole would result from a change in its capitalization. Bonds could be retired with stock issues, or two classes of junior securities could be combined into one, without changing the investment value of the company as a whole. Such constancy of investment value is analogous to the indestructibility of matter or energy: it leads us to speak of the Law of the Conservation of Investment Value, just as physicists speak of the Law of the Conservation of Matter, or the Law of the Conservation of Energy.

Thus, the results in this chapter can be interpreted more broadly as the **conservation of value principle** for financial markets: *With perfect capital markets, financial transactions neither add nor destroy value, but instead represent a repackaging of risk (and therefore return).*

The conservation of value principle extends far beyond questions of debt versus equity or even capital structure. It implies that any financial transaction that appears to be a good deal in terms of adding value either is too good to be true or is exploiting some type of market imperfection. To make sure the value is not illusory, it is important to identify the market imperfection that is the source of value. In the next several chapters we will examine different types of market imperfections and the potential sources of value that they introduce for the firm's capital structure choice and other financial transactions.

CONCEPT CHECK

1. Consider the questions facing Dan Harris, CFO of EBS, at the beginning of this chapter. What answers would you give based on the Modigliani-Miller Propositions? What considerations should the capital structure decision be based on?
2. State the conservation of value principle for financial markets.

MyFinanceLab Here is what you should know after reading this chapter. MyFinanceLab will help you identify what you know and where to go when you need to practice.

14.1 Equity Versus Debt Financing

- The collection of securities a firm issues to raise capital from investors is called the firm's capital structure. Equity and debt are the securities most commonly used by firms. When equity is used without debt, the firm is said to be unlevered. Otherwise, the amount of debt determines the firm's leverage.
- The owner of a firm should choose the capital structure that maximizes the total value of the securities issued.

14.2 Modigliani-Miller I: Leverage, Arbitrage, and Firm Value

- Capital markets are said to be perfect if they satisfy three conditions:
  - Investors and firms can trade the same set of securities at competitive market prices equal to the present value of their future cash flows.
  - There are no taxes, transaction costs, or issuance costs associated with security trading.
  - A firm's financing decisions do not change the cash flows generated by its investments, nor do they reveal new information about them.
- According to MM Proposition I, with perfect capital markets the value of a firm is independent of its capital structure.
  - With perfect capital markets, homemade leverage is a perfect substitute for firm leverage.
  - If otherwise identical firms with different capital structures have different values, the Law of One Price would be violated and an arbitrage opportunity would exist.
- The market value balance sheet shows that the total market value of a firm's assets equals the total market value of the firm's liabilities, including all securities issued to investors. Changing the capital structure therefore alters how the value of the assets is divided across securities, but not the firm's total value.
- A firm can change its capital structure at any time by issuing new securities and using the funds to pay its existing investors. An example is a leveraged recapitalization in which the firm borrows money (issues debt) and repurchases shares (or pays a dividend). MM Proposition I implies that such transactions will not change the share price.

14.3 Modigliani-Miller II: Leverage, Risk, and the Cost of Capital

- According to MM Proposition II, the cost of capital for levered equity is

$$r_E = r_U + \frac{D}{E}(r_U - r_D) \tag{14.5}$$

- Debt is less risky than equity, so it has a lower cost of capital. Leverage increases the risk of equity, however, raising the equity cost of capital. The benefit of debt's lower cost of capital is offset by the higher equity cost of capital, leaving a firm's weighted average cost of capital (WACC) unchanged with perfect capital markets:

$$r_{wacc} = r_A = r_U = \frac{E}{E+D}r_E + \frac{D}{E+D}r_D \qquad (14.6, 14.7)$$

- The market risk of a firm's assets can be estimated by its unlevered beta:

$$\beta_U = \frac{E}{E+D}\beta_E + \frac{D}{E+D}\beta_D \tag{14.8}$$

- Leverage increases the beta of a firm's equity:

$$\beta_E = \beta_U + \frac{D}{E}(\beta_U - \beta_D) \tag{14.9}$$

- A firm's net debt is equal to its debt less its holdings of cash and other risk-free securities. We can compute the cost of capital and the beta of the firm's business assets, excluding cash, by using its net debt when calculating its WACC or unlevered beta.

14.4 Capital Structure Fallacies

- Leverage can raise a firm's expected earnings per share and its return on equity, but it also increases the volatility of earnings per share and the riskiness of its equity. As a result, in a perfect market shareholders are not better off and the value of equity is unchanged.
- As long as shares are sold to investors at a fair price, there is no cost of dilution associated with issuing equity. While the number of shares increases when equity is issued, the firm's assets also increase because of the cash raised, and the per-share value of equity remains unchanged.

14.5 MM: Beyond the Propositions

- With perfect capital markets, financial transactions are a zero-NPV activity that neither add nor destroy value on their own, but rather repackage the firm's risk and return. Capital structure—and financial transactions more generally—affect a firm's value only because of its impact on some type of market imperfection.

Key Terms

capital structure *p. 489*
conservation of value principle *p. 509*
debt-to-value ratio *p. 501*
dilution *p. 508*
homemade leverage *p. 494*
leveraged recapitalization *p. 496*
levered equity *p. 490*
market value balance sheet *p. 496*
perfect capital markets *p. 493*
unlevered equity *p. 490*

Further Reading

For further details on MM's argument, especially their use of the Law of One Price to derive their results, see MM's original paper: F. Modigliani and M. Miller, "The Cost of Capital, Corporation Finance and the Theory of Investment," *American Economic Review* 48(3) (1958): 261–297.

For a retrospective look at the work of Modigliani and Miller and its importance in corporate finance, see the collection of articles in Volume 2, Issue 4 of the *Journal of Economic Perspectives* (1988), which includes: "The Modigliani-Miller Propositions After Thirty Years," by M. Miller (pp. 99–120); "Comment on the Modigliani-Miller Propositions," by S. Ross (pp. 127–133); "Corporate Finance and the Legacy of Modigliani and Miller," by S. Bhattacharya (pp. 135–147); and "MM—Past, Present, Future," by F. Modigliani (pp. 149–158).

For an interesting interview with Merton Miller about his work, see: P. Tanous, *Investment Gurus* (Prentice Hall Press, 1997).

For a more recent discussion of MM's contribution to the development of capital structure theory, see: R. Cookson, "A Survey of Corporate Finance ('The Party's Over' and 'Debt Is Good for You')," *The Economist* (January 27, 2001): 5–8.

A historical account of Miller-Modigliani's result is provided in these sources: P. Bernstein, *Capital Ideas: The Improbable Origins of Modern Wall Street* (Free Press, 1993); and M. Rubinstein, "Great Moments in Financial Economics: II. Modigliani-Miller Theorem," *Journal of Investment Management* 1(2) (2003).

For more insight into the debate regarding bank capital requirements, and many of the fallacies that have arisen in that debate, see A. Admati, P. DeMarzo, M. Hellwig, and P. Pfleiderer,

"Fallacies, Irrelevant Facts, and Myths in the Discussion of Capital Regulation: Why Bank Equity Is Not Expensive," Rock Center for Corporate Governance Research Paper No. 86, August 2010; and A. Admati and M. Hellwig, *The Bankers' New Clothes: What's Wrong with Banking and What to Do about It* (Princeton University Press, 2013).

Problems

All problems are available in MyFinanceLab. *An asterisk (*) indicates problems with a higher level of difficulty.*

Equity Versus Debt Financing

1. Consider a project with free cash flows in one year of $130,000 or $180,000, with each outcome being equally likely. The initial investment required for the project is $100,000, and the project's cost of capital is 20%. The risk-free interest rate is 10%.
   a. What is the NPV of this project?
   b. Suppose that to raise the funds for the initial investment, the project is sold to investors as an all-equity firm. The equity holders will receive the cash flows of the project in one year. How much money can be raised in this way—that is, what is the initial market value of the unlevered equity?
   c. Suppose the initial $100,000 is instead raised by borrowing at the risk-free interest rate. What are the cash flows of the levered equity, and what is its initial value according to MM?

2. You are an entrepreneur starting a biotechnology firm. If your research is successful, the technology can be sold for $30 million. If your research is unsuccessful, it will be worth nothing. To fund your research, you need to raise $2 million. Investors are willing to provide you with $2 million in initial capital in exchange for 50% of the unlevered equity in the firm.
   a. What is the total market value of the firm without leverage?
   b. Suppose you borrow $1 million. According to MM, what fraction of the firm's equity will you need to sell to raise the additional $1 million you need?
   c. What is the value of your share of the firm's equity in cases (a) and (b)?

3. Acort Industries owns assets that will have an 80% probability of having a market value of $50 million in one year. There is a 20% chance that the assets will be worth only $20 million. The current risk-free rate is 5%, and Acort's assets have a cost of capital of 10%.
   a. If Acort is unlevered, what is the current market value of its equity?
   b. Suppose instead that Acort has debt with a face value of $20 million due in one year. According to MM, what is the value of Acort's equity in this case?
   c. What is the expected return of Acort's equity without leverage? What is the expected return of Acort's equity with leverage?
   d. What is the lowest possible realized return of Acort's equity with and without leverage?

4. Wolfrum Technology (WT) has no debt. Its assets will be worth $450 million in one year if the economy is strong, but only $200 million in one year if the economy is weak. Both events are equally likely. The market value today of its assets is $250 million.
   a. What is the expected return of WT stock without leverage?
   b. Suppose the risk-free interest rate is 5%. If WT borrows $100 million today at this rate and uses the proceeds to pay an immediate cash dividend, what will be the market value of its equity just after the dividend is paid, according to MM?
   c. What is the expected return of WT stock after the dividend is paid in part (b)?

Modigliani-Miller I: Leverage, Arbitrage, and Firm Value

5. Suppose there are no taxes. Firm ABC has no debt, and firm XYZ has debt of $5000 on which it pays interest of 10% each year. Both companies have identical projects that generate free cash flows of $800 or $1000 each year. After paying any interest on debt, both companies use all remaining free cash flows to pay dividends each year.

a. Fill in the table below showing the payments debt and equity holders of each firm will receive given each of the two possible levels of free cash flows.

	ABC		XYZ	
FCF	Debt Payments	Equity Dividends	Debt Payments	Equity Dividends
$ 800				
$1000				

b. Suppose you hold 10% of the equity of ABC. What is another portfolio you could hold that would provide the same cash flows?

c. Suppose you hold 10% of the equity of XYZ. If you can borrow at 10%, what is an alternative strategy that would provide the same cash flows?

6. Suppose Alpha Industries and Omega Technology have identical assets that generate identical cash flows. Alpha Industries is an all-equity firm, with 10 million shares outstanding that trade for a price of $22 per share. Omega Technology has 20 million shares outstanding as well as debt of $60 million.

a. According to MM Proposition I, what is the stock price for Omega Technology?

b. Suppose Omega Technology stock currently trades for $11 per share. What arbitrage opportunity is available? What assumptions are necessary to exploit this opportunity?

7. Cisoft is a highly profitable technology firm that currently has $5 billion in cash. The firm has decided to use this cash to repurchase shares from investors, and it has already announced these plans to investors. Currently, Cisoft is an all-equity firm with 5 billion shares outstanding. These shares currently trade for $12 per share. Cisoft has issued no other securities except for stock options given to its employees. The current market value of these options is $8 billion.

a. What is the market value of Cisoft's non-cash assets?

b. With perfect capital markets, what is the market value of Cisoft's equity after the share repurchase? What is the value per share?

8. Schwartz Industry is an industrial company with 100 million shares outstanding and a market capitalization (equity value) of $4 billion. It has $2 billion of debt outstanding. Management have decided to delever the firm by issuing new equity to repay all outstanding debt.

a. How many new shares must the firm issue?

b. Suppose you are a shareholder holding 100 shares, and you disagree with this decision. Assuming a perfect capital market, describe what you can do to undo the effect of this decision.

9. Zetatron is an all-equity firm with 100 million shares outstanding, which are currently trading for $7.50 per share. A month ago, Zetatron announced it will change its capital structure by borrowing $100 million in short-term debt, borrowing $100 million in long-term debt, and issuing $100 million of preferred stock. The $300 million raised by these issues, plus another $50 million in cash that Zetatron already has, will be used to repurchase existing shares of stock. The transaction is scheduled to occur today. Assume perfect capital markets.

a. What is the market value balance sheet for Zetatron

i. Before this transaction?

ii. After the new securities are issued but before the share repurchase?

iii. After the share repurchase?

b. At the conclusion of this transaction, how many shares outstanding will Zetatron have, and what will the value of those shares be?

Modigliani-Miller II: Leverage, Risk, and the Cost of Capital

10. Explain what is wrong with the following argument: "If a firm issues debt that is risk free, because there is no possibility of default, the risk of the firm's equity does not change. Therefore, risk-free debt allows the firm to get the benefit of a low cost of capital of debt without raising its cost of capital of equity."

11. Consider the entrepreneur described in Section 14.1 (and referenced in Tables 14.1–14.3). Suppose she funds the project by borrowing $750 rather than $500.
   a. According to MM Proposition I, what is the value of the equity? What are its cash flows if the economy is strong? What are its cash flows if the economy is weak?
   b. What is the return of the equity in each case? What is its expected return?
   c. What is the risk premium of equity in each case? What is the sensitivity of the levered equity return to systematic risk? How does its sensitivity compare to that of unlevered equity? How does its risk premium compare to that of unlevered equity?
   d. What is the debt-equity ratio of the firm in this case?
   e. What is the firm's WACC in this case?

12. Hardmon Enterprises is currently an all-equity firm with an expected return of 12%. It is considering a leveraged recapitalization in which it would borrow and repurchase existing shares.
   a. Suppose Hardmon borrows to the point that its debt-equity ratio is 0.50. With this amount of debt, the debt cost of capital is 6%. What will the expected return of equity be after this transaction?
   b. Suppose instead Hardmon borrows to the point that its debt-equity ratio is 1.50. With this amount of debt, Hardmon's debt will be much riskier. As a result, the debt cost of capital will be 8%. What will the expected return of equity be in this case?
   c. A senior manager argues that it is in the best interest of the shareholders to choose the capital structure that leads to the highest expected return for the stock. How would you respond to this argument?

13. Suppose Visa Inc. (V) has no debt and an equity cost of capital of 9.2%. The average debt-to-value ratio for the credit services industry is 13%. What would its cost of equity be if it took on the average amount of debt for its industry at a cost of debt of 6%?

14. Global Pistons (GP) has common stock with a market value of $200 million and debt with a value of $100 million. Investors expect a 15% return on the stock and a 6% return on the debt. Assume perfect capital markets.
   a. Suppose GP issues $100 million of new stock to buy back the debt. What is the expected return of the stock after this transaction?
   b. Suppose instead GP issues $50 million of new debt to repurchase stock.
      i. If the risk of the debt does not change, what is the expected return of the stock after this transaction?
      ii. If the risk of the debt increases, would the expected return of the stock be higher or lower than in part (i)?

15. Hubbard Industries is an all-equity firm whose shares have an expected return of 10%. Hubbard does a leveraged recapitalization, issuing debt and repurchasing stock, until its debt-equity ratio is 0.60. Due to the increased risk, shareholders now expect a return of 13%. Assuming there are no taxes and Hubbard's debt is risk free, what is the interest rate on the debt?

16. Hartford Mining has 50 million shares that are currently trading for $4 per share and $200 million worth of debt. The debt is risk free and has an interest rate of 5%, and the expected return of Hartford stock is 11%. Suppose a mining strike causes the price of Hartford stock to fall 25% to $3 per share. The value of the risk-free debt is unchanged. Assuming there are no taxes and the risk (unlevered beta) of Hartford's assets is unchanged, what happens to Hartford's equity cost of capital?

17. Mercer Corp. has 10 million shares outstanding and $100 million worth of debt outstanding. Its current share price is $75. Mercer's equity cost of capital is 8.5%. Mercer has just announced that it will issue $350 million worth of debt. It will use the proceeds from this debt to pay off its existing debt, and use the remaining $250 million to pay an immediate dividend. Assume perfect capital markets.

a. Estimate Mercer's share price just after the recapitalization is announced, but before the transaction occurs.

b. Estimate Mercer's share price at the conclusion of the transaction. (*Hint*: Use the market value balance sheet.)

c. Suppose Mercer's existing debt was risk-free with a 4.25% expected return, and its new debt is risky with a 5% expected return. Estimate Mercer's equity cost of capital after the transaction.

18. In mid-2015 Qualcomm Inc. had $11 billion in debt, total equity capitalization of $89 billion, and an equity beta of 1.43 (as reported on Yahoo! Finance). Included in Qualcomm's assets was $21 billion in cash and risk-free securities. Assume that the risk-free rate of interest is 3% and the market risk premium is 4%.

a. What is Qualcomm's enterprise value?

b. What is the beta of Qualcomm's business assets?

c. What is Qualcomm's WACC?

***19.** Indell stock has a current market value of $120 million and a beta of 1.50. Indell currently has risk-free debt as well. The firm decides to change its capital structure by issuing $30 million in additional risk-free debt, and then using this $30 million plus another $10 million in cash to repurchase stock. With perfect capital markets, what will be the beta of Indell stock after this transaction?

***20.** Jim Campbell is founder and CEO of OpenStart, an innovative software company. The company is all equity financed, with 100 million shares outstanding. The shares are trading at a price of $1. Campbell currently owns 20 million shares. There are two possible states in one year. Either the new version of their software is a hit, and the company will be worth $160 million, or it will be a disappointment, in which case the value of the company will drop to $75 million. The current risk free rate is 2%. Campbell is considering taking the company private by repurchasing the rest of the outstanding equity by issuing debt due in one year. Assume the debt is zero-coupon and will pay its face value in one year.

a. What is the market value of the new debt that must be issued?

b. Suppose OpenStart issues risk-free debt with a face value of $75 million. How much of its outstanding equity could it repurchase with the proceeds from the debt? What fraction of the remaining equity would Jim still not own?

c. Combine the fraction of the equity Jim does not own with the risk-free debt. What are the payoffs of this combined portfolio? What is the value of this portfolio?

d. What face value of *risky* debt would have the same payoffs as the portfolio in (c)?

e. What is the yield on the risky debt in (d) that will be required to take the company private?

f. If the two outcomes are equally likely, what is OpenStart's current WACC (before the transaction)?

g. What is OpenStart's debt and equity cost of capital after the transaction? Show that the WACC is unchanged by the new leverage.

Capital Structure Fallacies

21. Yerba Industries is an all-equity firm whose stock has a beta of 1.2 and an expected return of 12.5%. Suppose it issues new risk-free debt with a 5% yield and repurchases 40% of its stock. Assume perfect capital markets.

a. What is the beta of Yerba stock after this transaction?

b. What is the expected return of Yerba stock after this transaction?

Suppose that prior to this transaction, Yerba expected earnings per share this coming year of $1.50, with a forward P/E ratio (that is, the share price divided by the expected earnings for the coming year) of 14.

c. What is Yerba's expected earnings per share after this transaction? Does this change benefit shareholders? Explain.

d. What is Yerba's forward P/E ratio after this transaction? Is this change in the P/E ratio reasonable? Explain.

22. You are CEO of a high-growth technology firm. You plan to raise $180 million to fund an expansion by issuing either new shares or new debt. With the expansion, you expect earnings next year of $24 million. The firm currently has 10 million shares outstanding, with a price of $90 per share. Assume perfect capital markets.

a. If you raise the $180 million by selling new shares, what will the forecast for next year's earnings per share be?

b. If you raise the $180 million by issuing new debt with an interest rate of 5%, what will the forecast for next year's earnings per share be?

c. What is the firm's forward P/E ratio (that is, the share price divided by the expected earnings for the coming year) if it issues equity? What is the firm's forward P/E ratio if it issues debt? How can you explain the difference?

23. Zelnor, Inc., is an all-equity firm with 100 million shares outstanding currently trading for $8.50 per share. Suppose Zelnor decides to grant a total of 10 million new shares to employees as part of a new compensation plan. The firm argues that this new compensation plan will motivate employees and is a better strategy than giving salary bonuses because it will not cost the firm anything.

a. If the new compensation plan has no effect on the value of Zelnor's assets, what will be the share price of the stock once this plan is implemented?

b. What is the cost of this plan for Zelnor's investors? Why is issuing equity costly in this case?

***24.** Suppose Levered Bank is funded with 2% equity and 98% debt. Its current market capitalization is $10 billion, and its market to book ratio is 1. Levered Bank earns a 4.22% expected return on its assets (the loans it makes), and pays 4% on its debt.

New capital requirements will necessitate that Levered Bank increase its equity to 4% of its capital structure. It will issue new equity and use the funds to retire existing debt. The interest rate on its debt is expected to remain at 4%.

a. What is Levered Bank's expected ROE with 2% equity?

b. Assuming perfect capital markets, what will Levered Bank's expected ROE be after it increases its equity to 4%?

c. Consider the difference between Levered Bank's ROE and its cost of debt. How does this "premium" compare before and after the Bank's increase in leverage?

d. Suppose the return on Levered Bank's assets has a volatility of 0.25%. What is the volatility of Levered Bank's ROE before and after the increase in equity?

e. Does the reduction in Levered Bank's ROE after the increase equity reduce its attractiveness to shareholders? Explain.

Data Case

You work in the corporate finance division of The Home Depot and your boss has asked you to review the firm's capital structure. Specifically, your boss is considering changing the firm's debt level. Your boss remembers something from his MBA program about capital structure being irrelevant, but isn't quite sure what that means. You know that capital structure is irrelevant under the conditions of perfect markets and will demonstrate this point for your boss by showing that the weighted average cost of capital remains constant under various levels of debt. So, for now, suppose that capital markets are perfect as you prepare responses for your boss.

You would like to analyze relatively modest changes to Home Depot's capital structure. You would like to consider two scenarios: the firm issues $1 billion in new debt to repurchase stock, and the firm issues $1 billion in new stock to repurchase debt. Use Excel to answer the following questions using Eqs. 14.5 and 14.6, and assuming a cost of unlevered equity (r_U) of 12%.

1. Obtain the financial information you need for Home Depot.
   a. Go to www.nasdaq.com, and click "Quotes." Enter Home Depot's stock symbol (HD) and click "Summary Quotes." From the Stock Quote & Summary Data page, get the current stock price. Click "Stock Report" in the left column and find the number of shares outstanding.
   b. Click "Income Statement" and the annual income statement should appear. Put the cursor in the middle of the statement, right-click your mouse, and select "Export to Microsoft Excel." (You will not need the income statement until Chapter 15, but collect all of the background data in one step.) On the Web page, click the Balance Sheet tab. Export the balance sheet to Excel as well and then cut and paste the balance sheet to the same worksheet as the income statement.
   c. To get the cost of debt for Home Depot, go to NASD BondInfo (finra-markets.morningstar.com). Under "Market Data," select "Bonds," then select the "Search" option, enter Home Depot's symbol, select the "Corporate" Bond Type and click "Show Results." The next page will contain information for all of Home Depot's outstanding and recently matured bonds. Select the latest yield on an outstanding bond with the shortest remaining maturity (the maturity date is on the line describing each issue; sometimes the list also contains recently retired bonds, so make sure not to use one of those). For simplicity, since you are just trying to illustrate the main concepts for your boss, you may use the existing yield on the outstanding bond as r_D.
2. Compute the market D/E ratio for Home Depot. Approximate the market value of debt by the book value of net debt; include both Long-Term Debt and Short-Term Debt/Current Portion of Long-Term Debt from the balance sheet and subtract any cash holdings. Use the stock price and number of shares outstanding to calculate the market value of equity.
3. Compute the cost of levered equity (r_E) for Home Depot using their current market debt-to-equity ratio and Eq. 14.5.
4. Compute the current weighted average cost of capital (WACC) for Home Depot using Eq. 14.6 given their current debt-to-equity ratio.
5. Repeat Steps 3 and 4 for the two scenarios you would like to analyze, issuing $1 billion in debt to repurchase stock, and issuing $1 billion in stock to repurchase debt. (Although you realize that the cost of debt capital r_D may change with changes in leverage, for these modestly small changes you decide to assume that r_D remains constant. We will explore the relation between changing leverage and changing r_D more fully in Chapter 24.) What is the market D/E ratio in each of these cases?
6. Prepare a written explanation for your boss explaining the relationship between capital structure and the cost of capital in this exercise.
7. What implicit assumptions in this exercise generate the results found in Question 5? How might your results differ in the "real world"?

Note: Updates to this data case may be found at www.berkdemarzo.com

CHAPTER

15

Debt and Taxes

IN A PERFECT CAPITAL MARKET, THE LAW OF ONE PRICE IMPLIES THAT all financial transactions have an NPV of zero and neither create nor destroy value. Consequently, in Chapter 14, we found that the choice of debt versus equity financing does not affect the value of a firm: The funds raised from issuing debt equal the present value of the future interest and principal payments the firm will make. While leverage increases the risk and cost of capital of the firm's equity, the firm's weighted average cost of capital (WACC), total value, and share price are unaltered by a change in leverage. That is, *in a perfect capital market, a firm's choice of capital structure is unimportant*.

This statement is at odds, however, with the observation that firms invest significant resources, both in terms of managerial time and effort and investment banking fees, in managing their capital structures. In many instances, the choice of leverage is of critical importance to a firm's value and future success. As we will show, there are large and systematic variations in the typical capital structures for different industries. For example, in August 2015, Amgen, a biotechnology and drug company, had debt of $32 billion, cash of $30 billion, and equity worth more than $126 billion, giving the firm a market debt-equity ratio of 0.25, with very little net debt. In contrast, Navistar International, an auto and truck manufacturer, had a debt-equity ratio of 3.7. Truck manufacturers in general have higher debt ratios than biotechnology and drug companies. If capital structure is unimportant, why do we see such consistent differences in capital structures across firms and industries? Why do managers dedicate so much time, effort, and expense to the capital structure choice?

As Modigliani and Miller made clear in their original work, capital structure does not matter in *perfect* capital markets. Recall from Chapter 14 that a perfect capital market exists under the following assumptions:

1. Investors and firms can trade the same set of securities at competitive market prices equal to the present value of their future cash flows.

NOTATION

Int	interest expense
PV	present value
r_f	risk-free interest rate
D	market value of debt
r_E	equity cost of capital
τ_c	marginal corporate tax rate
E	market value of equity
r_{wacc}	weighted average cost of capital
r_D	debt cost of capital
V^U	value of the unlevered firm
V^L	value of the firm with leverage
τ_i	marginal personal tax rate on income from debt
τ_e	marginal personal tax rate on income from equity
τ^*	effective tax advantage of debt
τ^*_{ex}	effective tax advantage on interest in excess of EBIT

2. There are no taxes, transaction costs, or issuance costs associated with security trading.
3. A firm's financing decisions do not change the cash flows generated by its investments, nor do they reveal new information about them.

Thus, if capital structure *does* matter, then it must stem from a market *imperfection*. In this chapter, we focus on one such imperfection—taxes. Corporations and investors must pay taxes on the income they earn from their investments. As we will see, a firm can enhance its value by using leverage to minimize the taxes it, and its investors, pay.

15.1 The Interest Tax Deduction

Corporations must pay taxes on the income that they earn. Because they pay taxes on their profits after interest payments are deducted, interest expenses reduce the amount of corporate tax firms must pay. This feature of the tax code creates an incentive to use debt.

Let's consider the impact of interest expenses on the taxes paid by Macy's, Inc., a retail department store. Macy's had earnings before interest and taxes of approximately \$2.8 billion in 2014, and interest expenses of about \$400 million. Given Macy's marginal corporate tax rate of 35%,[1] the effect of leverage on Macy's earnings is shown in Table 15.1.

TABLE 15.1 **Macy's Income with and without Leverage, Fiscal Year 2014 ($ million)**

	With Leverage	Without Leverage
EBIT	\$2800	\$2800
Interest expense	−400	0
Income before tax	2400	2800
Taxes (35%)	−840	−980
Net income	\$1560	\$1820

As we can see from Table 15.1, Macy's net income in 2014 was lower with leverage than it would have been without leverage. Thus, Macy's debt obligations reduced the income available to equity holders. But more importantly, the *total* amount available to *all* investors was higher with leverage:

	With Leverage	Without Leverage
Interest paid to debt holders	400	0
Income available to equity holders	1560	1820
Total available to all investors	\$1960	\$1820

With leverage, Macy's was able to pay out \$1960 million in total to its investors, versus only \$1820 million without leverage, representing an increase of \$140 million.

[1]Macy's paid an average tax rate of approximately 36.2 % in 2014, after accounting for other credits and deferrals. Because we are interested in the impact of a change in leverage, Macy's marginal tax rate—the tax rate that would apply to additional taxable income—is relevant to our discussion.

It might seem odd that a firm can be better off with leverage even though its earnings are lower. But recall from Chapter 14 that the value of a firm is the total amount it can raise from all investors, not just equity holders. Because leverage allows the firm to pay out more in total to its investors—including interest payments to debt holders—it will be able to raise more total capital initially.

Where does the additional $140 million come from? Looking at Table 15.1, we can see that this gain is equal to the reduction in taxes with leverage: $980 million − $840 million = $140 million. Because Macy's does not owe taxes on the $400 million of earnings it used to make interest payments, this $400 million is *shielded* from the corporate tax, providing the tax savings of 35% × $400 million = $140 million.

In general, the gain to investors from the tax deductibility of interest payments is referred to as the **interest tax shield**. The interest tax shield is the additional amount that a firm would have paid in taxes if it did not have leverage. We can calculate the amount of the interest tax shield each year as follows:

$$\text{Interest Tax Shield} = \text{Corporate Tax Rate} \times \text{Interest Payments} \tag{15.1}$$

EXAMPLE 15.1 Computing the Interest Tax Shield

Problem

Suppose that shown below is the income statement for D.F. Builders (DFB). Given its marginal corporate tax rate of 35%, what is the amount of the interest tax shield for DFB in years 2012 through 2015?

DFB Income Statement ($ million)	2012	2013	2014	2015
Total sales	$3369	$3706	$4077	$4432
Cost of sales	−2359	−2584	−2867	−3116
Selling, general, and administrative expense	−226	−248	−276	−299
Depreciation	−22	−25	−27	−29
Operating income	762	849	907	988
Other income	7	8	10	12
EBIT	769	857	917	1000
Interest expense	−50	−80	−100	−100
Income before tax	719	777	817	900
Taxes (35%)	−252	−272	−286	−315
Net income	$467	$505	$531	$585

Solution

From Eq. 15.1, the interest tax shield is the tax rate of 35% multiplied by the interest payments in each year:

($ million)	2012	2013	2014	2015
Interest expense	−50	−80	−100	−100
Interest tax shield (35% × interest expense)	17.5	28	35	35

Thus, the interest tax shield enabled DFB to pay an additional $115.5 million to its investors over this period.

CONCEPT CHECK

1. With corporate income taxes, explain why a firm's value can be higher with leverage even though its earnings are lower.
2. What is the interest tax shield?

15.2 Valuing the Interest Tax Shield

When a firm uses debt, the interest tax shield provides a corporate tax benefit each year. To determine the benefit of leverage for the value of the firm, we must compute the present value of the stream of future interest tax shields the firm will receive.

The Interest Tax Shield and Firm Value

Each year a firm makes interest payments, the cash flows it pays to investors will be higher than they would be without leverage by the amount of the interest tax shield:

$$\begin{pmatrix}\text{Cash Flows to Investors}\\ \text{with Leverage}\end{pmatrix} = \begin{pmatrix}\text{Cash Flows to Investors}\\ \text{without Leverage}\end{pmatrix} + (\text{Interest Tax Shield})$$

Figure 15.1 illustrates this relationship. Here you can see how each dollar of pretax cash flows is divided. The firm uses some fraction to pay taxes, and it pays the rest to investors. By increasing the amount paid to debt holders through interest payments, the amount of the pretax cash flows that must be paid as taxes decreases. The gain in total cash flows to investors is the interest tax shield.

Because the cash flows of the levered firm are equal to the sum of the cash flows from the unlevered firm plus the interest tax shield, by the Law of One Price the same must be true for the present values of these cash flows. Thus, letting V^L and V^U represent the value of the firm with and without leverage, respectively, we have the following change to MM Proposition I in the presence of taxes:

The total value of the levered firm exceeds the value of the firm without leverage due to the present value of the tax savings from debt:

$$V^L = V^U + PV(\text{Interest Tax Shield}) \tag{15.2}$$

FIGURE 15.1 **The Cash Flows of the Unlevered and Levered Firm**

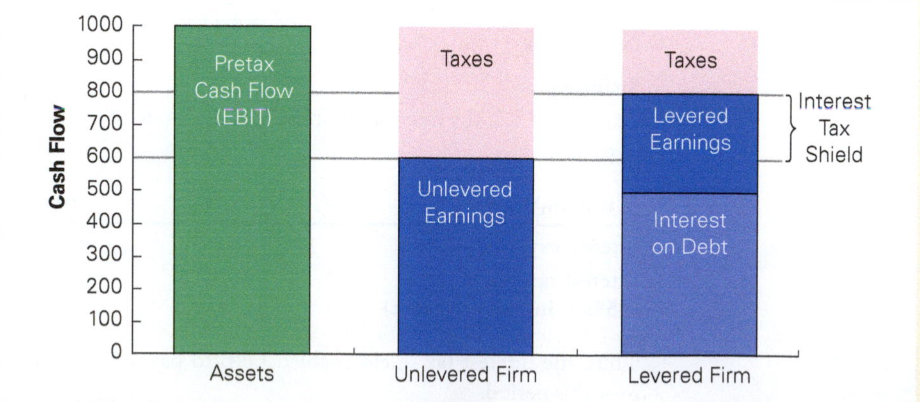

By increasing the cash flows paid to debt holders through interest payments, a firm reduces the amount paid in taxes. Cash flows paid to investors are shown in blue. The increase in total cash flows paid to investors is the interest tax shield. (The figure assumes a 40% marginal corporate tax rate.)

Pizza and Taxes

In Chapter 14, we mentioned the pizza analogy that Merton Miller once used to describe the MM Propositions with perfect capital markets: No matter how you slice it, you still have the same amount of pizza.

We can extend this analogy to the setting with taxes, but the story is a bit different. In this case, every time equity holders get a slice of pizza, Uncle Sam gets a slice as a tax payment. But when debt holders get a slice, there is no tax. Thus, by allocating more slices to debt holders rather than to equity holders, more pizza will be available to investors. While the total amount of pizza does not change, there is more pizza left over for investors to consume because less pizza is consumed by Uncle Sam in taxes.

Clearly, there is an important tax advantage to the use of debt financing. But how large is this tax benefit? To compute the increase in the firm's total value associated with the interest tax shield, we need to forecast how a firm's debt—and therefore its interest payments—will vary over time. Given a forecast of future interest payments, we can determine the interest tax shield and compute its present value by discounting it at a rate that corresponds to its risk.

EXAMPLE 15.2 Valuing the Interest Tax Shield without Risk

Problem

Suppose DFB plans to pay $100 million in interest each year for the next 10 years, and then to repay the principal of $2 billion in year 10. These payments are risk free, and DFB's marginal tax rate will remain 35% throughout this period. If the risk-free interest rate is 5%, by how much does the interest tax shield increase the value of DFB?

Solution

In this case, the interest tax shield is 35% × $100 million = $35 million each year for the next 10 years. Therefore, we can value it as a 10-year annuity. Because the tax savings are known and not risky, we can discount them at the 5% risk-free rate:

$$PV(\text{Interest Tax Shield}) = \$35 \text{ million} \times \frac{1}{0.05}\left(1 - \frac{1}{1.05^{10}}\right)$$
$$= \$270 \text{ million}$$

The final repayment of principal in year 10 is not deductible, so it does not contribute to the tax shield.

The Interest Tax Shield with Permanent Debt

In Example 15.2, we know with certainty the firm's future interest payments and associated tax savings. In practice, this case is rare. Typically, the level of future interest payments varies due to changes the firm makes in the amount of debt outstanding, changes in the interest rate on that debt, and the risk that the firm may default and fail to make an interest payment. In addition, the firm's marginal tax rate may fluctuate due to changes in the tax code and changes in the firm's income bracket.

Rather than attempting to account for all possibilities here, let's consider the special case in which the firm issues debt and plans to keep the dollar amount of debt constant forever.[2]

[2]We discuss how to value the interest tax shield with more complicated leverage policies in Chapter 18.

For example, the firm might issue a perpetual consol bond, making only interest payments but never repaying the principal. More realistically, suppose the firm issues short-term debt, such as a five-year coupon bond. When the principal is due, the firm raises the money needed to pay it by issuing new debt. In this way, the firm never pays off the principal but simply refinances it whenever it comes due. In this situation, the debt is effectively permanent.

Many large firms have a policy of maintaining a certain amount of debt on their balance sheets. As old bonds and loans mature, new borrowing takes place. The key assumption here is that the firm maintains a *fixed* dollar amount of outstanding debt, rather than an amount that changes with the size of the firm.

Suppose a firm borrows debt D and keeps the debt permanently. If the firm's marginal tax rate is τ_c, and if the debt is riskless with a risk-free interest rate r_f, then the interest tax shield each year is $\tau_c \times r_f \times D$, and we can value the tax shield as a perpetuity:

$$PV(\text{Interest Tax Shield}) = \frac{\tau_c \times \text{Interest}}{r_f} = \frac{\tau_c \times (r_f \times D)}{r_f}$$

$$= \tau_c \times D$$

The above calculation assumes the debt is risk free and the risk-free interest rate is constant. These assumptions are not necessary, however. As long as the debt is fairly priced, no arbitrage implies that its market value must equal the present value of the future interest payments:[3]

$$\text{Market Value of Debt} = D = PV(\text{Future Interest Payments}) \tag{15.3}$$

If the firm's marginal tax rate is constant,[4] then we have the following general formula:

Value of the Interest Tax Shield of Permanent Debt

$$\begin{aligned} PV(\text{Interest Tax Shield}) &= PV(\tau_c \times \text{Future Interest Payments}) \\ &= \tau_c \times PV(\text{Future Interest Payments}) \\ &= \tau_c \times D \end{aligned} \tag{15.4}$$

This formula shows the magnitude of the interest tax shield. Given a 35% corporate tax rate, it implies that for every \$1 in new permanent debt that the firm issues, the value of the firm increases by \$0.35.

The Weighted Average Cost of Capital with Taxes

The tax benefit of leverage can also be expressed in terms of the weighted average cost of capital. When a firm uses debt financing, the cost of the interest it must pay is offset to some extent by the tax savings from the interest tax shield. For example, suppose a firm

[3]Equation 15.3 holds even if interest rates fluctuate and the debt is risky. It requires only that the firm never repay the principal on the debt (it either refinances or defaults on the principal). The result follows by the same argument used in Chapter 9 to show that the price of equity should equal the present value of all future dividends.

[4]The tax rate may not be constant if the firm's taxable income fluctuates sufficiently to change the firm's tax bracket (we discuss this possibility further in Section 15.5).

The Repatriation Tax: Why Some Cash-Rich Firms Borrow

In April 2013, Apple Inc. borrowed $17 billion in what was then the largest U.S. corporate bond issuance of all time. But why would a firm with over $100 billion in cash on hand need to borrow money? The answer is that while Apple indeed had plenty of cash, the vast majority of that cash was overseas, and bringing it back to the U.S. would trigger a tax liability in excess of 20%, which Apple wanted to avoid.

Apple's situation is not uncommon. When U.S. firms earn profits overseas, those profits are subject to the foreign corporate tax of the country in which they are earned. But if the profits are then "repatriated" by bringing them back to the U.S. rather than investing them abroad, the firm will owe the difference between the foreign tax paid and the U.S. corporate tax rate. Because foreign corporate tax rates are often very low—for example, 12.5% in Ireland versus 35% in the U.S.—this so-called **repatriation tax** can be a significant cost. Rather than bear this cost, many firms choose to hold the funds abroad in the form of bonds or other marketable securities, and raise the cash they need in the U.S. by issuing bonds domestically. In Apple's case, the $17 billion it borrowed was then used to conduct share repurchases.

So, by holding cash overseas and borrowing at home, firms can avoid or at least delay paying additional taxes on their foreign earnings. Many firms have adopted this strategy in recent years: Shown below are the growth in aggregate cash held overseas by all U.S. corporations, as well as the cash holdings and debt outstanding of several large firms in 2015.

To encourage firms to invest more at home, Congress enacted a one-time "tax holiday" in 2004, allowing firms to repatriate funds at a reduced cost though the policy failed to have much effect. Recent calls by both Democrats and Republicans for a more permanent change to the tax code to reduce or eliminate this repatriation tax have so far been unsuccessful, but in the meantime firms continue to borrow and delay paying the tax in hopes of such change.

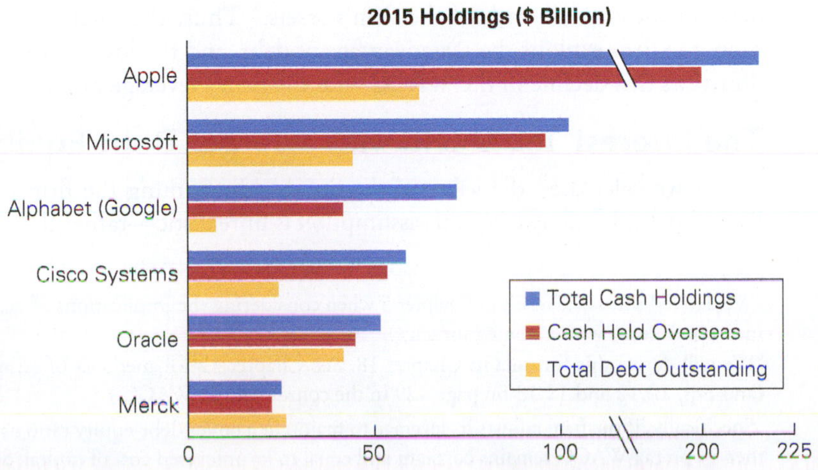

with a 35% tax rate borrows \$100,000 at 10% interest per year. Then its net cost at the end of the year is

		Year-End
Interest expense	$r \times \$100{,}000 =$	\$10,000
Tax savings	$-\tau_c \times r \times \$100{,}000 =$	−3,500
Effective after-tax cost of debt	$r \times (1 - \tau_c) \times \$100{,}000 =$	\$6,500

The effective cost of the debt is only \$6,500/\$100,000 = 6.50% of the loan amount, rather than the full 10% interest. Thus, the tax deductibility of interest lowers the effective cost of debt financing for the firm. More generally,[5]

With tax-deductible interest, the effective after-tax borrowing rate is $r(1 - \tau_c)$.

In Chapter 14, we showed that without taxes, the firm's WACC was equal to its unlevered cost of capital, which is the average return that the firm must pay to its investors (equity holders and debt holders). The tax-deductibility of interest payments, however, lowers the effective after-tax cost of debt *to the firm*. As we discussed in Chapter 12, we can account for the benefit of the interest tax shield by calculating the WACC using the effective after-tax cost of debt:

Weighted Average Cost of Capital (After Tax)[6]

$$r_{wacc} = \frac{E}{E+D} r_E + \frac{D}{E+D} r_D (1 - \tau_c) \tag{15.5}$$

The WACC represents the effective cost of capital to the firm, after including the benefits of the interest tax shield. It is therefore lower than the pretax WACC, which is the average return paid to the firm's investors. From Eq. 15.5, we have the following relationship between the WACC and the firm's pretax WACC:

$$r_{wacc} = \underbrace{\frac{E}{E+D} r_E + \frac{D}{E+D} r_D}_{\text{Pretax WACC}} - \underbrace{\frac{D}{E+D} r_D \tau_c}_{\substack{\text{Reduction Due} \\ \text{to Interest Tax Shield}}} \tag{15.6}$$

As we will show in Chapter 18, even in the presence of taxes, a firm's target leverage ratio does not affect the firm's pretax WACC, which equals its unlevered cost of capital and depends only on the risk of the firm's assets.[7] Thus, the higher the firm's leverage, the more the firm exploits the tax advantage of debt, and the lower its WACC is. Figure 15.2 illustrates this decline in the WACC with the firm's leverage ratio.

The Interest Tax Shield with a Target Debt-Equity Ratio

Earlier we calculated the value of the tax shield assuming the firm maintains a constant level of debt. In many cases this assumption is unrealistic—rather than maintain a constant

[5]We derived this same result in Chapter 5 when considering the implications of tax-deductible interest for individuals (e.g., with a home mortgage).

[6]We will derive this formula in Chapter 18. See Chapter 12 for methods of estimating the cost of debt (and Eqs. 12.12 and 12.13 on page 429 in the context of the WACC.)

[7]Specifically, if the firm adjusts its leverage to maintain a target debt-equity ratio or interest coverage ratio, then its pretax WACC remains constant and equal to its unlevered cost of capital. See Chapter 18 for a full discussion of the relationship between the firm's levered and unlevered costs of capital.

FIGURE 15.2 The WACC with and without Corporate Taxes

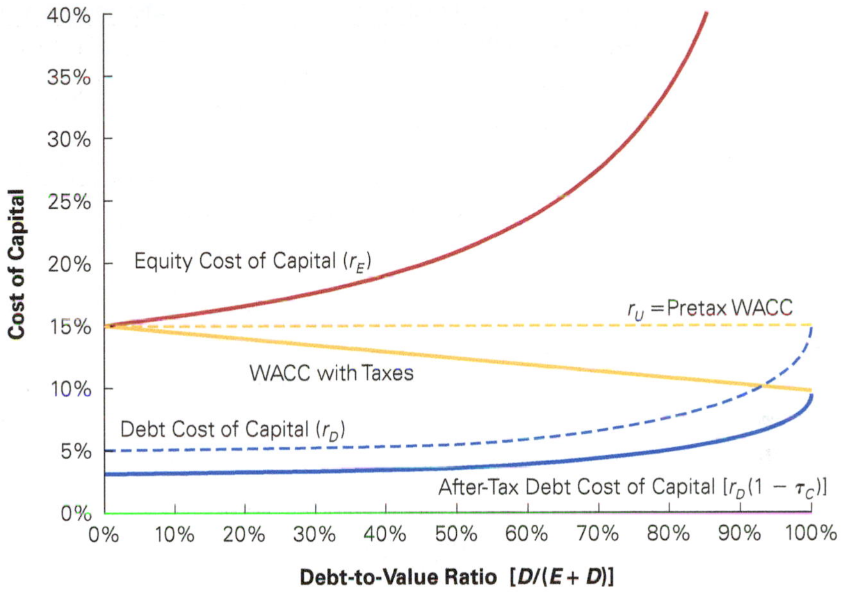

We compute the WACC as a function of the firm's target debt-to-value ratio using Eq. 15.5. As shown in Figure 14.1, the firm's unlevered cost of capital or pretax WACC is constant, reflecting the required return of the firm's investors based on the risk of the firm's assets. However, the (effective after-tax) WACC, which represents the after-tax cost to the firm, declines with leverage as the interest tax shield grows. The figure assumes a marginal corporate income tax rate of $\tau_c = 35\%$.

level of debt, many firms target a specific debt-equity ratio instead. When a firm does so, the level of its debt will grow (or shrink) with the size of the firm.

As we will show formally in Chapter 18, when a firm adjusts its debt over time so that its debt-equity ratio is expected to remain constant, we can compute its value with leverage, V^L, by discounting its free cash flow using the WACC. The value of the interest tax shield can be found by comparing V^L to the unlevered value, V^U, of the free cash flow discounted at the firm's unlevered cost of capital, the pretax WACC.

EXAMPLE 15.3 Valuing the Interest Tax Shield with a Target Debt-Equity Ratio

Problem

Western Lumber Company expects to have free cash flow in the coming year of $4.25 million, and its free cash flow is expected to grow at a rate of 4% per year thereafter. Western Lumber has an equity cost of capital of 10% and a debt cost of capital of 6%, and it pays a corporate tax rate of 35%. If Western Lumber maintains a debt-equity ratio of 0.50, what is the value of its interest tax shield?

Solution

We can estimate the value of Western Lumber's interest tax shield by comparing its value with and without leverage. We compute its unlevered value by discounting its free cash flow at its pretax WACC:

$$\text{Pretax WACC} = \frac{E}{E+D}r_E + \frac{D}{E+D}r_D = \frac{1}{1+0.5}10\% + \frac{0.5}{1+0.5}6\% = 8.67\%$$

Because Western Lumber's free cash flow is expected to grow at a constant rate, we can value it as a constant growth perpetuity:

$$V^U = \frac{4.25}{8.67\% - 4\%} = \$91 \text{ million}$$

To compute Western Lumber's levered value, we calculate its WACC:

$$\text{WACC} = \frac{E}{E+D}r_E + \frac{D}{E+D}r_D(1-\tau_c)$$

$$= \frac{1}{1+0.5}10\% + \frac{0.5}{1+0.5}6\%(1-0.35) = 7.97\%$$

Thus, Western Lumber's value including the interest tax shield is

$$V^L = \frac{4.25}{7.97\% - 4\%} = \$107 \text{ million}$$

The value of the interest tax shield is therefore

$$PV(\text{Interest Tax Shield}) = V^L - V^U = 107 - 91 = \$16 \text{ million}$$

CONCEPT CHECK

1. With corporate taxes as the only market imperfection, how does the value of the firm with leverage differ from its value without leverage?
2. How does leverage affect a firm's weighted average cost of capital?

15.3 Recapitalizing to Capture the Tax Shield

When a firm makes a significant change to its capital structure, the transaction is called a recapitalization (or simply a "recap"). In Chapter 14, we introduced a leveraged recapitalization in which a firm issues a large amount of debt and uses the proceeds to pay a special dividend or to repurchase shares. Leveraged recaps were especially popular in the mid- to late-1980s, when many firms found that these transactions could reduce their tax payments.

Let's see how such a transaction might benefit current shareholders. Midco Industries has 20 million shares outstanding with a market price of $15 per share and no debt. Midco has had consistently stable earnings, and pays a 35% tax rate. Management plans to borrow $100 million on a permanent basis through a leveraged recap in which they would use the borrowed funds to repurchase outstanding shares. Their expectation is that the tax savings from this transaction will boost Midco's stock price and benefit shareholders. Let's see if this expectation is realistic.

The Tax Benefit

First, we examine the tax consequences of Midco's leveraged recap. Without leverage, Midco's total market value is the value of its unlevered equity. Assuming the current stock price is the fair price for the shares without leverage:

$$V^U = (20 \text{ million shares}) \times (\$15/\text{share}) = \$300 \text{ million}$$

With leverage, Midco will reduce its annual tax payments. If Midco borrows $100 million using permanent debt, the present value of the firm's future tax savings is

$$PV(\text{Interest Tax Shield}) = \tau_c D = 35\% \times \$100 \text{ million} = \$35 \text{ million}$$

Thus, the total value of the levered firm will be

$$V^L = V^U + \tau_c D = \$300 \text{ million} + \$35 \text{ million} = \$335 \text{ million}$$

This total value represents the combined value of the debt and the equity after the recapitalization. Because the value of the debt is $100 million, the value of the equity is

$$E = V^L - D = \$335 \text{ million} - \$100 \text{ million} = \$235 \text{ million}$$

While total firm value has increased, the value of equity dropped after the recap. How do shareholders benefit from this transaction?

Even though the value of the shares outstanding drops to $235 million, don't forget that shareholders will also receive the $100 million that Midco will pay out through the share repurchase. In total, they will receive the full $335 million, a gain of $35 million over the value of their shares without leverage. Let's trace the details of the share repurchase and see how it leads to an increase in the stock price.

The Share Repurchase

Suppose Midco repurchases its shares at their current price of $15 per share. The firm will repurchase $100 million ÷ $15 per share = 6.667 million shares, and it will then have 20 − 6.667 = 13.333 million shares outstanding. Because the total value of equity is $235 million, the new share price is

$$\frac{\$235 \text{ million}}{13.333 \text{ million shares}} = \$17.625$$

The shareholders who keep their shares earn a capital gain of $17.625 − $15 = $2.625 per share, for a total gain of

$$\$2.625/\text{share} \times 13.333 \text{ million shares} = \$35 \text{ million}$$

In this case, the shareholders who remain after the recap receive the benefit of the tax shield. However, you may have noticed something odd in the previous calculations. We assumed that Midco was able to repurchase the shares at the initial price of $15 per share, and then demonstrated that the shares would be worth $17.625 after the transaction. Why would a shareholder agree to sell the shares for $15 when they are worth $17.625?

No Arbitrage Pricing

The previous scenario represents an arbitrage opportunity. Investors could *buy* shares for $15 immediately before the repurchase, and they could sell these shares immediately afterward at a higher price. But this activity would raise the share price above $15 even before the repurchase: Once investors know the recap will occur, the share price will rise immediately to a level that reflects the $35 million value of the interest tax shield that the firm will receive. That is, the value of the Midco's equity will rise *immediately* from $300 million to $335 million. With 20 million shares outstanding, the share price will rise to

$$\$335 \text{ million} \div 20 \text{ million shares} = \$16.75 \text{ per share}$$

Midco must offer at least this price to repurchase the shares.

With a repurchase price of \$16.75, the shareholders who tender their shares and the shareholders who hold their shares both gain \$16.75 − \$15 = \$1.75 per share as a result of the transaction. The benefit of the interest tax shield goes to all 20 million of the original shares outstanding for a total benefit of \$1.75/share × 20 million shares = \$35 million. In other words,

When securities are fairly priced, the original shareholders of a firm capture the full benefit of the interest tax shield from an increase in leverage.

EXAMPLE 15.4 **Alternative Repurchase Prices**

Problem

Suppose Midco announces a price at which it will repurchase \$100 million worth of its shares. Show that \$16.75 is the lowest price it could offer and expect shareholders to tender their shares. How will the benefits be divided if Midco offers more than \$16.75 per share?

Solution

For each repurchase price, we can compute the number of shares Midco will repurchase, as well as the number of shares that will remain after the share repurchase. Dividing the \$235 million total value of equity by the number of remaining shares gives Midco's new share price after the transaction. No shareholders will be willing to sell their shares unless the repurchase price is at least as high as the share price after the transaction; otherwise, they would be better off waiting to sell their shares. As the table shows, the repurchase price must be at least \$16.75 for shareholders to be willing to sell rather than waiting to receive a higher price.

Repurchase Price (\$/share)	Shares Repurchased (million)	Shares Remaining (million)	New Share Price (\$/share)
P_R	$R = 100/P_R$	$N = 20 - R$	$P_N = 235/N$
15.00	6.67	13.33	\$17.63
16.25	6.15	13.85	16.97
16.75	5.97	14.03	16.75
17.25	5.80	14.20	16.55
17.50	5.71	14.29	16.45

If Midco offers a price above \$16.75, then all existing shareholders will be eager to sell their shares, because the shares will have a lower value after the transaction is completed. In this case, Midco's offer to repurchase shares will be oversubscribed and Midco will need to use a lottery or some other rationing mechanism to choose from whom it will repurchase shares. In that case, more of the benefits of the recap will go to the shareholders who are lucky enough to be selected for the repurchase.

Analyzing the Recap: The Market Value Balance Sheet

We can analyze the recapitalization using the market value balance sheet, a tool we developed in Chapter 14. It states that the total market value of a firm's securities must equal the total market value of the firm's assets. In the presence of corporate taxes, *we must include the interest tax shield as one of the firm's assets.*

We analyze the leveraged recap by breaking this transaction into steps, as shown in Table 15.2. First, the recap is announced. At this point, investors anticipate the future interest tax shield, raising the value of Midco's assets by \$35 million. Next, Midco issues \$100 million in new debt, increasing both Midco's cash and liabilities by that amount. Finally, Midco uses the cash to repurchase shares at their market price of \$16.75. In this step, Midco's cash declines, as does the number of shares outstanding.

TABLE 15.2 Market Value Balance Sheet for the Steps in Midco's Leveraged Recapitalization

Market Value Balance Sheet ($ million)	Initial	Step 1: Recap Announced	Step 2: Debt Issuance	Step 3: Share Repurchase
Assets				
Cash	0	0	100	0
Original assets (V^U)	300	300	300	300
Interest tax shield	0	35	35	35
Total assets	300	335	435	335
Liabilities				
Debt	0	0	100	100
Equity = Assets − Liabilities	300	335	335	235
Shares outstanding (million)	20	20	20	14.03
Price per share	$15.00	$16.75	$16.75	$16.75

Note that the share price rises at the announcement of the recap. This increase in the share price is due solely to the present value of the (anticipated) interest tax shield. Thus, even though leverage reduces the total market capitalization of the firm's equity, shareholders capture the benefits of the interest tax shield upfront.[8]

CONCEPT CHECK

1. How can shareholders benefit from a leveraged recap when it reduces the total value of equity?
2. How does the interest tax shield enter into the market value balance sheet?

15.4 Personal Taxes

So far, we have looked at the benefits of leverage with regard to the taxes a corporation must pay. By reducing a firm's corporate tax liability, debt allows the firm to pay more of its cash flows to investors.

Unfortunately for investors, after they receive the cash flows, they are generally taxed again. For individuals, interest payments received from debt are taxed as income. Equity investors also must pay taxes on dividends and capital gains. What are the consequences to firm value of these additional taxes?

Including Personal Taxes in the Interest Tax Shield

The value of a firm is equal to the amount of money the firm can raise by issuing securities. The amount of money an investor will pay for a security ultimately depends on the benefits the investor will receive—namely, the cash flows the investor will receive *after all taxes have been paid.* Thus, just like corporate taxes, personal taxes reduce the cash flows to investors and diminish firm value. As a result, the actual interest tax shield depends on the reduction in the total taxes (both corporate and personal) that are paid.[9]

[8] We are ignoring other potential side effects of leverage, such as costs of future financial distress. We discuss such costs in Chapter 16.

[9] This point was made most forcefully in yet another pathbreaking article by Merton Miller, "Debt and Taxes," *Journal of Finance* 32 (1977): 261–275. See also M. Miller and M. Scholes, "Dividends and Taxes," *Journal of Financial Economics* 6 (1978): 333–364.

Personal taxes have the potential to offset some of the corporate tax benefits of leverage that we have described. In particular, in the United States and many other countries, interest income has historically been taxed more heavily than capital gains from equity. Table 15.3 shows recent top federal tax rates in the United States. The average rate on equity income listed in the table is an average of the top capital gains and dividend tax rates.

To determine the true tax benefit of leverage, we need to evaluate the combined effect of both corporate and personal taxes. Consider a firm with \$1 of earnings before interest and taxes. The firm can either pay this \$1 to debt holders as interest, or it can use the \$1 to pay equity holders directly, with a dividend, or indirectly, by retaining earnings so that shareholders receive a capital gain. Figure 15.3 shows the tax consequences of each option.

Using 2015 tax rates, debt offers a clear tax advantage with respect to corporate taxes: For every \$1 in pretax cash flows that debt holders receive, equity holders receive $\tau_c = 35\%$ less under current tax rates. But at the personal level, the highest income tax rate on interest income is $\tau_i = 39.6\%$, whereas the tax rate on equity income is only $\tau_e = 20\%$. Combining corporate and personal rates leads to the following comparison:

	After-Tax Cash Flows	Using Current Tax Rates
To debt holders	$(1 - \tau_i)$	$(1 - 0.396) = 0.604$
To equity holders	$(1 - \tau_c)(1 - \tau_e)$	$(1 - 0.35)(1 - 0.20) = 0.52$

While a tax advantage to debt remains, it is not as large as we calculated based on corporate taxes alone. To express the comparison in relative terms, note that equity holders receive

$$\tau^* = \frac{0.604 - 0.52}{0.604} = 13.9\%$$

less after taxes than debt holders. In this case, personal taxes reduce the tax advantage of debt from 35% to 13.9%.

FIGURE 15.3

After-Tax Investor Cash Flows Resulting from \$1 in EBIT

Interest income is taxed at rate τ_i for the investor. Dividend or capital gain income is taxed at rate τ_c for the corporation, and again at rate τ_e for the investor.

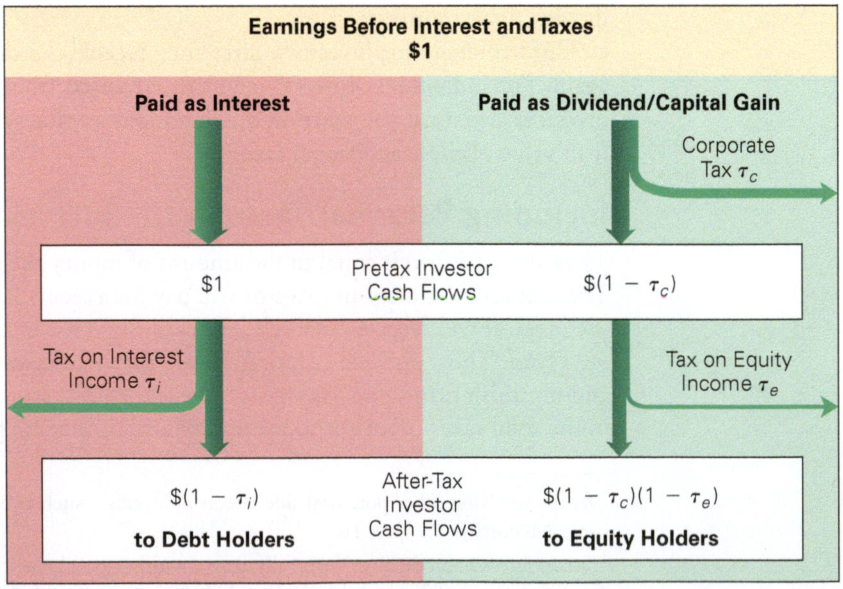

TABLE 15.3 **Top Federal Tax Rates in the United States, 1971–2015**

Year	Corporate Tax Rate†	Personal Tax Rates*			
		Interest Income	Average Rate on Equity Income	Dividends	Capital Gains
1971–1978	48%	70%	53%	70%	35%
1979–1981	46%	70%	49%	70%	28%
1982–1986	46%	50%	35%	50%	20%
1987	40%	39%	33%	39%	28%
1988–1990	34%	28%	28%	28%	28%
1991–1992	34%	31%	30%	31%	28%
1993–1996	35%	40%	34%	40%	28%
1997–2000	35%	40%	30%	40%	20%
2001–2002	35%	39%	30%	39%	20%
2003–2012	35%	35%	15%	15%	15%
2013–2015	35%	39.6%	20%	20%	20%

*Interest income is taxed as ordinary income. Until 2003, dividends were also taxed as ordinary income. The average tax rate on equity income is an average of dividend and capital gain tax rates (consistent with a 50% dividend payout ratio and annual realization of capital gains), where the capital gain tax rate is the long-term rate applicable to assets held more than one year.

†The corporate rate shown is for C corporations with the highest level of income. Marginal rates can be higher for lower brackets. (For example, since 2000, the 35% tax rate applies to income levels above $18.3 million, while the tax rate for income levels between $100,000 and $335,000 is 39%.)

We can interpret τ^* as the effective tax advantage of debt: if the corporation paid $(1 - \tau^*)$ in interest, debt holders would receive the same amount after taxes as equity holders would receive if the firm paid $1 in profits to equity holders. That is,

$$(1 - \tau^*)(1 - \tau_i) = (1 - \tau_c)(1 - \tau_e)$$

Solving this equation for τ^* gives

Effective Tax Advantage of Debt

$$\tau^* = 1 - \frac{(1 - \tau_c)(1 - \tau_e)}{(1 - \tau_i)} \tag{15.7}$$

Said another way, every $1 received after taxes by debt holders from interest payments costs equity holders $\$(1 - \tau^*)$ on an after-tax basis.

When there are no personal taxes, or when the personal tax rates on debt and equity income are the same ($\tau_i = \tau_e$), this formula reduces to $\tau^* = \tau_c$. But when equity income is taxed less heavily ($\tau_i > \tau_e$), then τ^* is less than τ_c.

EXAMPLE 15.5 **Calculating the Effective Tax Advantage of Debt**

Problem

What was the effective tax advantage of debt in 1980? In 1990?

Solution

Using Eq. 15.7 and the tax rates in Table 15.3, we can calculate

$$\tau^*_{1980} = 1 - \frac{(1 - 0.46)(1 - 0.49)}{(1 - 0.70)} = 8.2\% \text{ and } \tau^*_{1990} = 1 - \frac{(1 - 0.34)(1 - 0.28)}{(1 - 0.28)} = 34\%$$

Given the tax rates at the time, the effective tax advantage of debt was much lower in 1980 than in 1990.

FIGURE 15.4

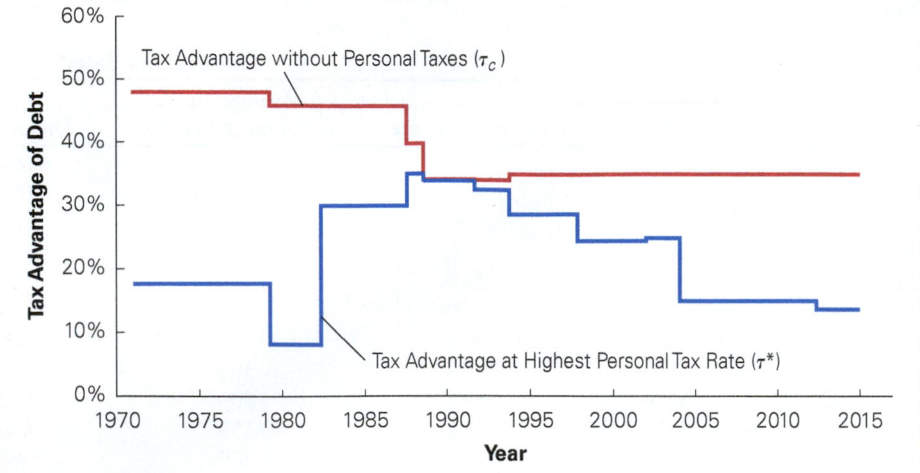

The Effective Tax Advantage of Debt with and without Personal Taxes, 1971–2015

After adjusting for personal taxes, the tax advantage of debt τ^* is generally below τ_c, but still positive. It has also varied widely with changes to the tax code.

Figure 15.4 shows the effective tax advantage of debt since 1971 in the United States. It has varied widely over time with changes in the tax code.

Valuing the Interest Tax Shield with Personal Taxes

How does the foregoing analysis of personal taxes affect our valuation of the debt tax shield? We postpone a detailed answer to this question until Chapter 18, and limit our discussion here to a few important observations. First, as long as $\tau^* > 0$, then despite any tax disadvantage of debt at the personal level, a net tax advantage for leverage remains. In the case of permanent debt, the value of the firm with leverage becomes

$$V^L = V^U + \tau^* D \tag{15.8}$$

Because the personal tax disadvantage of debt generally implies $\tau^* < \tau_c$, comparing Eq. 15.8 with Eq. 15.4 we see that the benefit of leverage is reduced.

Personal taxes have a similar, but indirect, effect on the firm's weighted average cost of capital. While we still compute the WACC using the corporate tax rate τ_c as in Eq. 15.5, with personal taxes the firm's equity and debt costs of capital will adjust to compensate investors for their respective tax burdens. The net result is that a personal tax disadvantage for debt causes the WACC to decline more slowly with leverage than it otherwise would.

EXAMPLE 15.6 **Estimating the Interest Tax Shield with Personal Taxes**

Problem

Estimate the value of Midco after its \$100 million leveraged recap, accounting for personal taxes in 2015.

Solution

Given $\tau^* = 13.9\%$ in 2015, and given Midco's current value $V^U = \$300$ million, we estimate $V^L = V^U + \tau^* D = \$300$ million $+ 13.9\%(\$100$ million$) = \$313.9$ million. With 20 million original shares outstanding, the stock price would increase by \$13.9 million ÷ 20 million shares = \$0.695 share.

Determining the Actual Tax Advantage of Debt

In estimating the effective tax advantage of debt after taking personal taxes into account, we made several assumptions that may need adjustment when determining the actual tax benefit for a particular firm or investor.

First, with regard to the capital gains tax rate, we assumed that investors paid capital gains taxes every year. But unlike taxes on interest income or dividends, which are paid annually, capital gains taxes are paid only at the time the investor sells the stock and realizes the gain. Deferring the payment of capital gains taxes lowers the present value of the taxes, which can be interpreted as a lower *effective* capital gains tax rate. For example, given a capital gains tax rate of 20% and an interest rate of 6%, holding the asset for 10 more years lowers the effective tax rate this year to $(20\%)/1.06^{10} = 11.2\%$. Also, investors with accrued losses that they can use to offset gains face a zero effective capital gains tax rate. As a consequence, investors with longer holding periods or with accrued losses face a lower tax rate on equity income, decreasing the effective tax advantage of debt.

A second key assumption in our analysis is the computation of the tax rate on equity income τ_e. Currently in the United States the dividend and capital gains tax rates are the same. But in other countries they can differ, and so computing the tax rate on equity income requires computing a weighted average of the two rates. In computing the weights, it is important that they reflect a firm's actual payout policy. For example, for firms that do not pay dividends, the capital gains tax rate should be used as the tax rate on equity income.

Finally, we assumed the top marginal federal income tax rates for the investor. In reality, rates vary for individual investors, and many investors face lower rates. (We have also ignored state taxes, which vary widely by state and have an additional impact.) At lower rates, the effects of personal taxes are less substantial. Moreover, *many investors face no personal taxes.* Consider investments held in retirement savings accounts or pension funds that

Cutting the Dividend Tax Rate

In January 2003, President George W. Bush unveiled a proposal to boost the U.S. economy with a $674 billion tax cut plan, half of which would come from eliminating taxes on dividends. From the moment it was announced, this tax cut generated tremendous controversy.

Proponents argued that easing the tax bite on investors' dividend income would boost the stock market and stimulate the sluggish economy. Critics quickly denounced it as a tax cut for the rich. But one of the underlying motives of the plan, authored in large part by economist R. Glenn Hubbard, was to end the current distortion in tax laws that encourage companies to accumulate debt because interest is deductible but dividend payments are not.

Levying taxes both on corporate earnings and on the dividends or capital gains paid to investors is known as *double taxation.* The lower rates on capital gains have provided some relief from double taxation. In 2002, however, dividends were still taxed at the same rate as ordinary income, leading to a combined tax rate in excess of 60% on dividends—one of the highest tax rates on dividends of any industrialized nation. As we have seen, this double taxation results in a tax advantage to debt financing.

Ultimately, policymakers agreed to a compromise that reduced the tax rate for individuals on both dividends (for stocks held for more than 60 days) and capital gains (for assets held for more than one year) to 15%. This compromise still gives a tax advantage to debt, but at a decreased level from prior years (see Figure 15.4).

The "Bush tax cuts" (which also lowered income and capital gains tax rates) were originally set to expire at the end of 2010. Fearing their expiration would slow the nascent economic recovery, in December 2010 Congress extended the tax cuts through 2012. In 2013, the tax cuts were made permanent in a compromise that raised the top tax rates to 39.6% on income and 20% on dividends and capital gains.

are not subject to taxes.[10] For these investors, the effective tax advantage of debt is $\tau^* = \tau_c$, the full corporate tax rate. This full tax advantage would also apply to securities dealers for whom interest, dividends, and capital gains are all taxed equivalently as income.

What is the bottom line? Calculating the effective tax advantage of debt accurately is extremely difficult, and this advantage will vary across firms (and from investor to investor). A firm must consider the tax bracket of its typical debt holders to estimate τ_i, and the tax bracket and holding period of its typical equity holders to determine τ_e. If, for instance, a firm's investors hold shares primarily through their retirement accounts, $\tau^* \approx \tau_c$. While τ^* is likely to be somewhat below τ_c for the typical firm, exactly how much lower is open to debate. Our calculation of τ^* in Figure 15.4 should be interpreted as a very rough guide at best.[11]

CONCEPT CHECK

1. Under current law (in 2015), why is there a personal tax disadvantage of debt?
2. How does this personal tax disadvantage of debt change the value of leverage for the firm?

15.5 Optimal Capital Structure with Taxes

In Modigliani and Miller's setting of perfect capital markets, firms could use any combination of debt and equity to finance their investments without changing the value of the firm. In effect, any capital structure was optimal. In this chapter we have seen that taxes change that conclusion because interest payments create a valuable tax shield. Even after adjusting for personal taxes, the value of a firm with leverage exceeds the value of an unlevered firm, and there is a tax advantage to using debt financing.

Do Firms Prefer Debt?

Do firms show a preference for debt in practice? Figure 15.5 illustrates the net new issues of equity and debt by U.S. corporations. For equity, the figure shows the total

FIGURE 15.5

Net External Financing and Capital Expenditures by U.S. Corporations, 1975–2014

In aggregate, firms have raised external capital primarily by issuing debt. These funds have been used to retire equity and fund investment, but the vast majority of capital expenditures are internally funded. (Amounts adjusted for inflation to reflect 2014 dollars.)

Source: Federal Reserve, *Flow of Funds Accounts of the United States*, 2014.

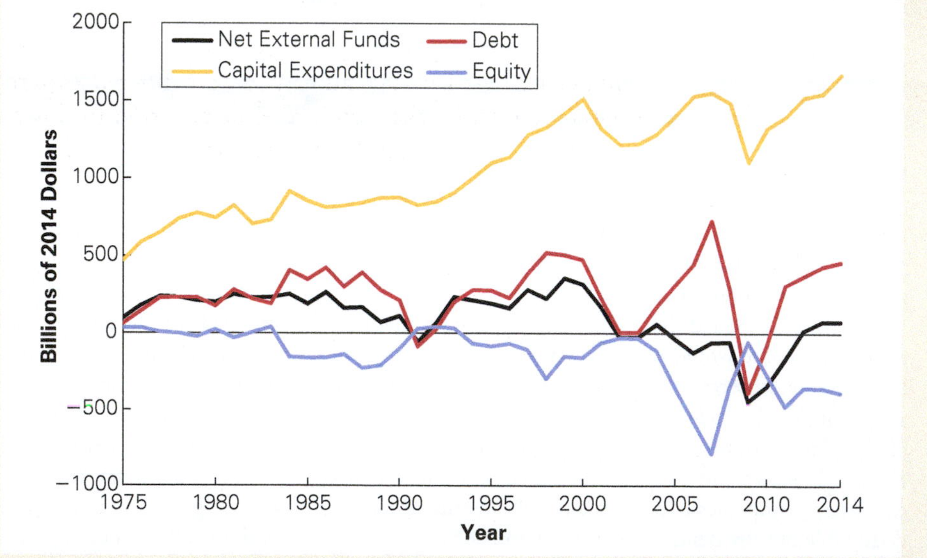

[10]Evidence from the mid-1990s suggests that the growth in pension funds has lowered the average marginal tax rate for investors to about half the rates shown in Table 15.3. See J. Poterba, "The Rate of Return to Corporate Capital and Factor Shares: New Estimates Using Revised National Income Accounts and Capital Stock Data," NBER working paper no. 6263 (1997).

[11]For a discussion of methods of estimating τ^* and the need to include personal taxes, see J. Graham, "Do Personal Taxes Affect Corporate Financing Decisions?" *Journal of Public Economics* 73 (1999): 147–185.

amount of new equity issued, less the amount retired through share repurchases and acquisitions. For debt, it shows the total amount of new borrowing less the amount of loans repaid.

Figure 15.5 makes clear that when firms raise new capital from investors, they do so primarily by issuing debt. In fact, in most years, aggregate equity issues are negative, meaning that firms are reducing the amount of equity outstanding by buying shares. (This observation does not mean that *all* firms raised funds using debt. Many firms may have sold equity to raise funds. However, at the same time, other firms were buying or repurchasing an equal or greater amount.) The data show a clear preference for debt as a source of external financing for the total population of U.S. firms. Indeed, in aggregate, firms appear to be borrowing in excess of the funds they need for internal use in order to repurchase equity.

While firms seem to prefer debt when raising external funds, not all investment is externally funded. As Figure 15.5 also shows, capital expenditures greatly exceed firms' external financing, implying that most investment and growth is supported by internally generated funds, such as retained earnings. Thus, even though firms have not *issued* new equity, the market value of equity has risen over time as firms have grown. In fact, as shown in Figure 15.6, debt as a fraction of firm value has varied in a range from 30–50% for the average firm. The average debt-to-value ratio fell during the 1990s bull market, with the trend reversing post-2000 due to declines in the stock market as well as a dramatic increase in debt issuance in response to falling interest rates.

The aggregate data in Figure 15.6 masks two important tendencies. First, the use of leverage varies greatly by industry. Second, many firms retain large cash balances to reduce their effective leverage. These patterns are revealed in Figure 15.7, which shows both total and *net* debt as a fraction of firm enterprise value for a number of industries and the overall market. Note that net debt is negative if a firm's cash holdings exceed its outstanding debt. Clearly, there are large differences in net leverage across industries. Firms in growth industries like biotechnology or high technology carry very little debt and maintain large cash reserves, whereas wireless telecomms, real estate firms, trucking and automotive firms, and utilities have high leverage ratios. Thus, the differences in the leverage ratios of Amgen and Navistar International noted in the introduction to this chapter are not unique to these firms, but rather are typical of their respective industries.

FIGURE 15.6

Debt-to-Value Ratio [$D/(E + D)$] of U.S. Firms, 1975–2014

Although firms have primarily issued debt rather than equity, the average proportion of debt in their capital structures has not increased due to the growth in value of existing equity.

Source: Compustat and Federal Reserve, *Flow of Funds Accounts of the United States*, 2014.

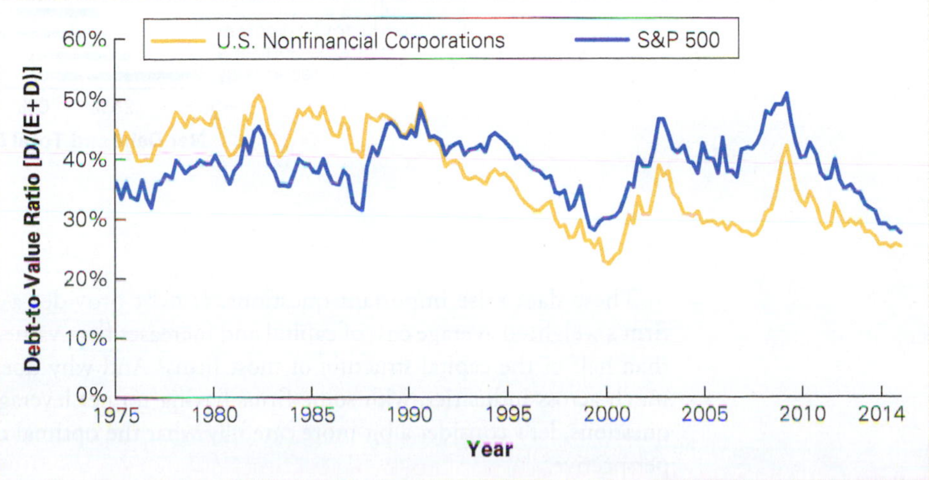

FIGURE 15.7

Debt-to-Enterprise Value Ratio for Select Industries (2015)

Figure shows industry median levels of net debt and total debt as a percentage of firm enterprise value. The spread between them, shown by the blue bars, corresponds to cash holdings. For example, Biotech firms tend to have no debt but hold a great deal of cash, and so have negative net debt. Oil & Gas Drilling firms have much less cash and over 75% total debt. While the median level of debt for all U.S. stocks was about 23% of firm value, note the large differences by industry.

Source: Capital IQ, 2015.

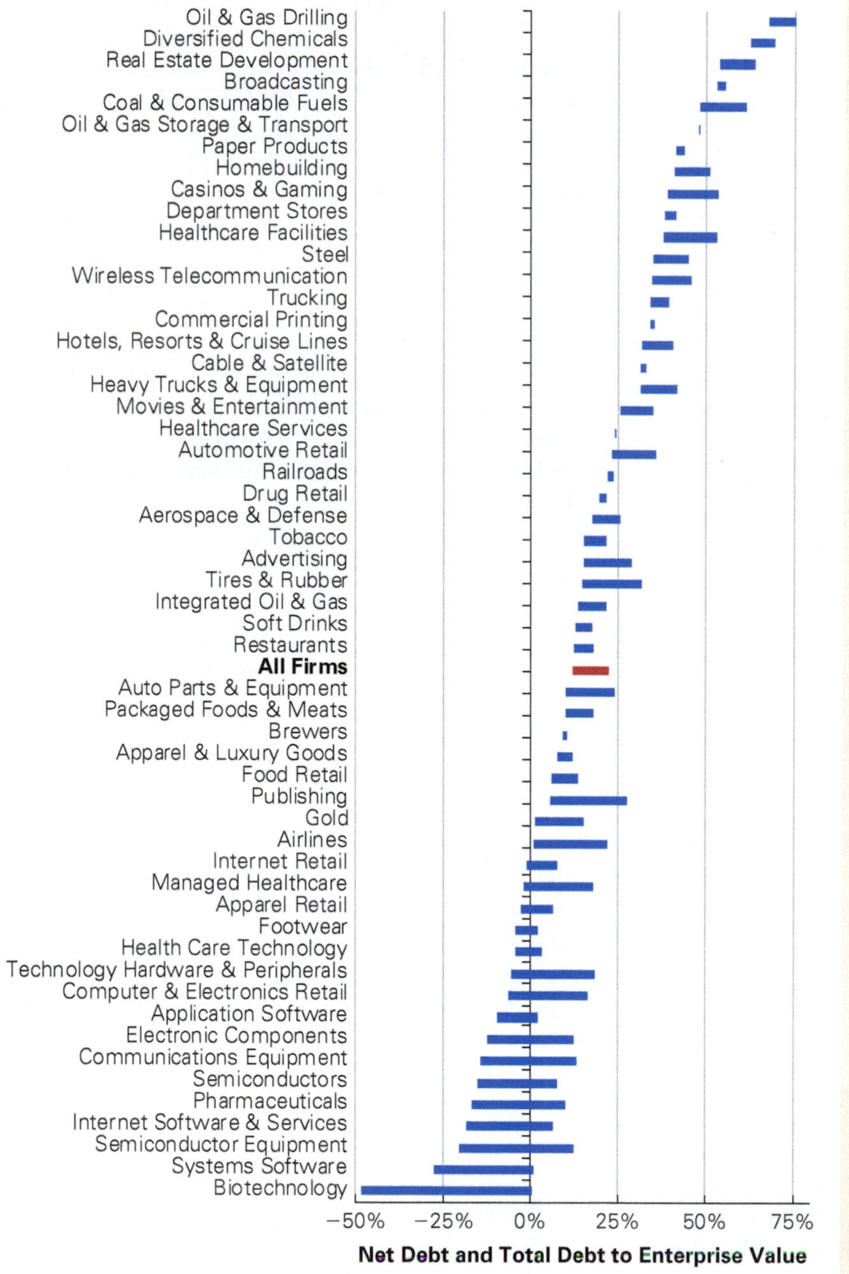

These data raise important questions. If debt provides a tax advantage that lowers a firm's weighted average cost of capital and increases firm value, why does debt make up less than half of the capital structure of most firms? And why does the leverage choice vary so much across industries, with some firms having no net leverage? To begin to answer these questions, let's consider a bit more carefully what the optimal capital structure is from a tax perspective.

Limits to the Tax Benefit of Debt

To receive the full tax benefits of leverage, a firm need not use 100% debt financing. A firm receives a tax benefit only if it is paying taxes in the first place. That is, the firm must have taxable earnings. This constraint may limit the amount of debt needed as a tax shield.

To determine the optimal level of leverage, compare the three leverage choices shown in Table 15.4 for a firm with earnings before interest and taxes (EBIT) equal to $1000 and a corporate tax rate of $\tau_c = 35\%$. With no leverage, the firm owes tax of $350 on the full $1000 of EBIT. If the firm has high leverage with interest payments equal to $1000, then it can shield its earnings from taxes, thereby saving the $350 in taxes. Now consider a third case, in which the firm has excess leverage so that interest payments exceed EBIT. In this case, the firm has a net operating loss, but there is no increase in the tax savings. Because the firm is paying no taxes already, there is no immediate tax shield from the excess leverage.[12]

Thus, no corporate tax benefit arises from incurring interest payments that regularly exceed EBIT. And, because interest payments constitute a tax disadvantage at the investor level as discussed in Section 15.4, investors will pay higher personal taxes with excess leverage, making them worse off.[13] We can quantify the tax disadvantage for excess interest payments by setting $\tau_c = 0$ (assuming there is no reduction in the corporate tax for excess interest payments) in Eq. 15.7 for τ^*:

$$\tau^*_{ex} = 1 - \frac{(1 - \tau_e)}{(1 - \tau_i)} = \frac{\tau_e - \tau_i}{(1 - \tau_i)} < 0 \tag{15.9}$$

Note that τ^*_{ex} is negative because equity is taxed less heavily than interest for investors ($\tau_e > \tau_i$). At 2012 tax rates, this disadvantage is

$$\tau^*_{ex} = \frac{15\% - 35\%}{(1 - 35\%)} = -30.8\%$$

TABLE 15.4 **Tax Savings with Different Amounts of Leverage**

	No Leverage	High Leverage	Excess Leverage
EBIT	$1000	$1000	$1000
Interest expense	0	−1000	−1100
Income before tax	1000	0	0
Taxes (35%)	−350	0	0
Net income	650	0	−100
Tax savings from leverage	$0	$350	$350

[12] If the firm paid taxes during the prior two years, it could "carry back" the current year's net operating loss to apply for a refund of some of those taxes. Alternatively, the firm could "carry forward" the net operating loss up to 20 years to shield future income from taxes (although waiting to receive the credit reduces its present value). Thus, there can be a tax benefit from interest in excess of EBIT if it does not occur on a regular basis. For simplicity, we ignore carrybacks and carryforwards in this discussion.

[13] Of course, another problem can arise from having excess leverage: The firm may not be able to afford the excess interest and could be forced to default on the loan. We discuss financial distress (and its potential costs) in Chapter 16.

INTERVIEW WITH ANDREW BALSON

Andrew Balson was a Managing Director of Bain Capital, a leading private investment firm with nearly $57 billion in assets under management. Bain Capital specializes in private equity (PE) and leveraged buyout (LBO) transactions, in which a firm is purchased and recapitalized with debt-to-value ratios often exceeding 70%. Bain Capital has invested in many well-known companies including Burger King, Domino's Pizza, Dunkin' Brands, HCA, Michael's Stores, Sealy Mattress Company, and Toys 'R Us.

QUESTION: *What is the role of private investment firms such as Bain Capital, and what types of firms make the best LBO candidates?*

ANSWER: Our business serves as an alternate capital market for companies that don't really belong as public companies, either during a transition period or permanently, and don't have a logical fit within another larger corporation. In that context, we've done buyouts for companies across many different industries and types. There really isn't one particular type that is best. We look for companies that are well positioned in their industries, have advantages relative to their competitors, and provide real value to their customers. Some may be underperforming but change can enable them to turn around. Others may be performing well but could do even better. Perhaps the management team has not been given appropriate incentives, or the company has not been optimized or managed aggressively enough. Occasionally, we find a company we can buy at a low price compared to its inherent value. That was a big part of our business 10 years ago but is less so today. We pay relatively full valuations compared to the company's current earnings. This approach works because of our ability to improve current earnings or cash flow.

QUESTION: *How does leverage affect risk and return for investors?*

ANSWER: Based on my experience, if we've found interesting companies where we can change the profit trajectory, leverage will ultimately serve to magnify both the impact of the investments we make and the returns for our investors. Over the past 20 years, the Bain Capital portfolio has far outperformed any equity benchmarks. That performance comes from improved operating profits that are magnified by leverage. Growth is an important driver of our success, so we strive to create efficient capital structures that complement our strategy and enable us to invest in business opportunities. The line between too much and not enough is not distinct, however. We try to use as much debt as we can without changing how our management teams run our businesses.

QUESTION: *How will the 2008 financial crisis affect capital structure and financing policies in the future?*

ANSWER: From 2006 to 2008, debt became more available, and the amount of leverage per $1 of earnings went up dramatically. Companies that typically borrowed four to six times earnings before interest, taxes, depreciation, and amortization (EBITDA) were now borrowing seven to eight times EBITDA. The cost of borrowing went down, spreads tightened, and borrowing terms became more lenient, resulting in "covenant-lite" loans. The market opened its wallet and threw money at PE firms, ultimately driving returns down.

The PE markets began to crack in late spring 2008. Banks had to shore up their balance sheets, leaving no money for buyouts. The PE markets are now reverting to pre-2006 leverage—five times EBITDA—rates, and terms.

QUESTION: *What challenges and opportunities does the financial crisis present for PE firms?*

ANSWER: The fundamental benefits of PE for many companies will persist. PE remains an attractive asset class—at the right leverage and price. The economic uncertainty creates less incentive for sellers of companies, who are more likely to wait out these difficult capital markets. It's a great time to be a PE investor with capital, however. We were able to take substantial minority stakes in companies that interest us, at attractive terms. PE financing is now more expensive, and I think it will remain that way for some time. Companies that need financing now, to grow or make a strategic move, will tap higher-cost capital sources such as PE.

It's also a challenging time for our portfolio companies. Sales in most companies have declined precipitously. We are working with our companies to cut costs and generate liquidity to get them "across the icy river"; and we expect the vast majority to make it.

Therefore, the optimal level of leverage from a tax saving perspective is the level such that interest equals EBIT. The firm shields all of its taxable income, and it does not have any tax-disadvantaged excess interest. Figure 15.8 shows the tax savings at different levels of interest payments when EBIT equals $1000 with certainty. In this case, an interest payment of $1000 maximizes the tax savings.

Of course, it is unlikely that a firm can predict its future EBIT precisely. If there is uncertainty regarding EBIT, then with a higher interest expense there is a greater risk that interest will exceed EBIT. As a result, the tax savings for high levels of interest falls, possibly reducing the optimal level of the interest payment, as shown in Figure 15.8.[14] In general, as a firm's interest expense approaches its expected taxable earnings, the marginal tax advantage of debt declines, limiting the amount of debt the firm should use.

Growth and Debt

In a tax-optimal capital structure, the level of interest payments depends on the level of EBIT. What does this conclusion tell us about the optimal fraction of debt in a firm's capital structure?

If we examine young technology or biotechnology firms, we often find that these firms do not have any taxable income. Their value comes mainly from the prospect that they will produce high future profits. A biotech firm might be developing drugs with tremendous potential, but it has yet to receive any revenue from these drugs. Such a firm will not have taxable earnings. In that case, a tax-optimal capital structure does not include debt. We would expect such a firm to finance its investments with equity alone. Only later, when the firm matures and becomes profitable, will it have taxable cash flows. At that time it should add debt to its capital structure.

Even for a firm with positive earnings, growth will affect the optimal leverage ratio. To avoid excess interest, this type of firm should have debt with interest payments that are below its expected taxable earnings:

$$\text{Interest} = r_D \times \text{Debt} \leq EBIT \quad \text{or} \quad \text{Debt} \leq EBIT / r_D$$

FIGURE 15.8

Tax Savings for Different Levels of Interest

When EBIT is known with certainty, the tax savings is maximized if the interest expense is equal to EBIT. When EBIT is uncertain, the tax savings declines for high levels of interest because of the risk that the interest payment will be in excess of EBIT.

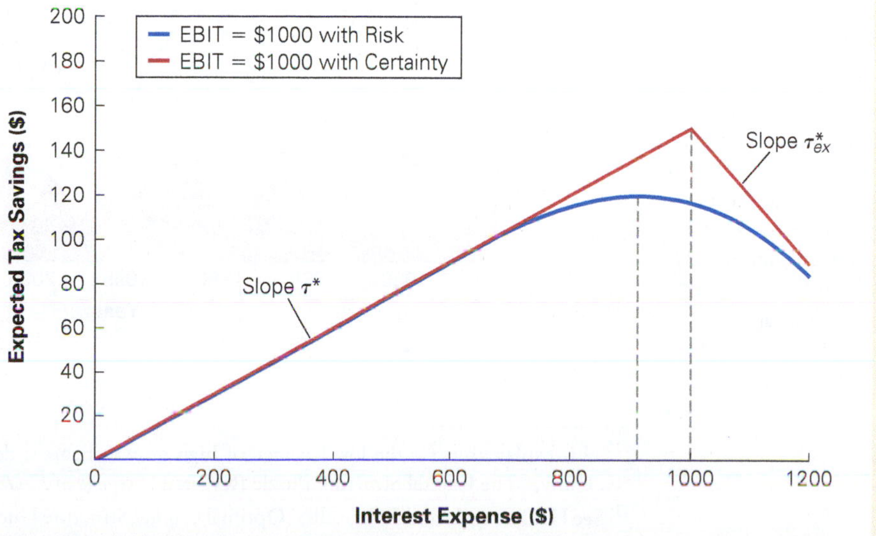

[14]Details of how to compute the optimal level of debt when earnings are risky can be found in a paper by J. Graham, "How Big Are the Tax Benefits of Debt?" *Journal of Finance* 55(5) (2000): 1901–1941.

That is, from a tax perspective, the firm's optimal level of debt is proportional to its current earnings. However, the value of the firm's equity will depend on the growth rate of earnings: The higher the growth rate, the higher the value of equity is (and equivalently, the higher the firm's price-earnings multiple is). As a result, *the optimal proportion of debt in the firm's capital structure* $[D/(E + D)]$ *will be lower, the higher the firm's growth rate.*[15]

Other Tax Shields

Up to this point, we have assumed that interest is the only means by which firms can shield earnings from corporate taxes. But there are numerous other provisions in the tax laws for deductions and tax credits, such as depreciation, investment tax credits, carryforwards of past operating losses, and the like. For example, many high-tech firms pay little or no taxes because of tax deductions related to employee stock options (see box on page 544). To the extent that a firm has other tax shields, its taxable earnings will be reduced and it will rely less heavily on the interest tax shield.[16]

The Low Leverage Puzzle

Do firms choose capital structures that fully exploit the tax advantages of debt? The results of this section imply that to evaluate this question, we should compare the level of firms' interest payments to their taxable income, rather than simply consider the fraction of debt in their capital structures. Figure 15.9 compares interest expenses and EBIT for firms in the S&P 500. It reveals two important patterns. First, firms have used debt to shield less than one third of their income from taxes on average, and only about 50% in downturns

FIGURE 15.9

Interest Payments as a Percentage of EBIT and Percentage of Firms with Negative Pretax Income, S&P 500 1975–2015

On average, firms shield less than one third of their income via interest expenses, and these expenses exceed taxable income only about 10% of the time.

Source: Compustat

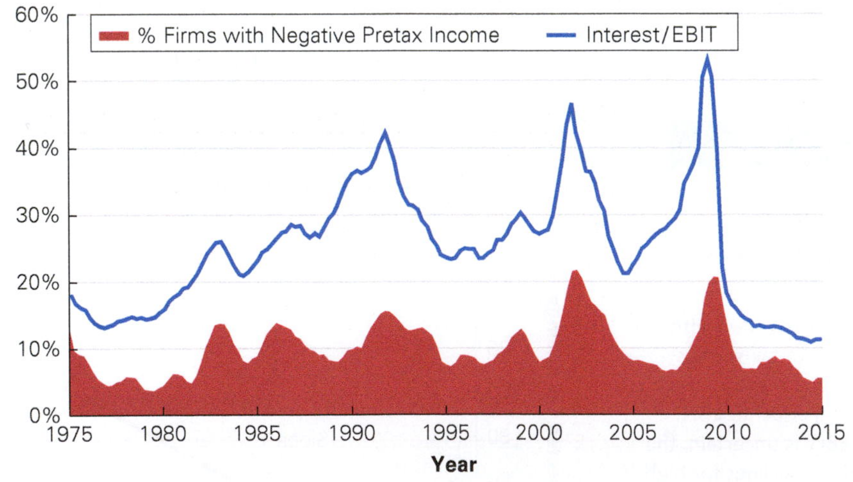

[15]This explanation for the low leverage of high growth firms is developed in a paper by J. Berens and C. Cuny, "The Capital Structure Puzzle Revisited," *Review of Financial Studies* 8 (1995): 1185–1208.

[16]See H. DeAngelo and R. Masulis, "Optimal Capital Structure Under Corporate and Personal Taxation," *Journal of Financial Economics* 8 (1980): 3–27. For a discussion of methods to estimate a firm's marginal tax rate to account for these effects, see J. Graham, "Proxies for the Corporate Marginal Tax Rate," *Journal of Financial Economics* 42 (1996): 187–221.

(when earnings tend to fall). Second, only about 10% of the time do firms have negative taxable income, and thus would not benefit from an increased interest tax shield. Overall, firms have far less leverage than our analysis of the interest tax shield would predict.[17]

This low level of leverage is not unique to U.S. firms. Table 15.5 shows international leverage levels from a 1995 study by Professors Raghuram Rajan and Luigi Zingales using 1990 data. Note that firms worldwide have similar low proportions of debt financing, with firms in the United Kingdom exhibiting especially low leverage. Also, with the exception of Italy and Canada, firms shield less than half of their taxable income using interest payments. The corporate tax codes are similar across all countries in terms of the tax advantage of debt. Personal tax rates vary more significantly, however, leading to greater variation in τ^*.[18]

Why are firms under-leveraged? Either firms are content to pay more taxes than necessary rather than maximize shareholder value, or there is more to the capital structure story than we have uncovered so far. While some firms may deliberately choose a suboptimal capital structure, it is hard to accept that most firms are acting suboptimally. The consensus of so many managers in choosing low levels of leverage suggests that debt financing has other costs that prevent firms from using the interest tax shield fully.

Talk to financial managers and they will quickly point out a key cost of debt missing from our analysis: Increasing the level of debt increases the probability of bankruptcy. Aside from taxes, another important difference between debt and equity financing is that debt payments *must* be made to avoid bankruptcy, whereas firms have no similar obligation to pay dividends or realize capital gains. If bankruptcy is costly, these costs might offset the tax advantages of debt financing. We explore the role of financial bankruptcy costs and other market imperfections in Chapter 16.

TABLE 15.5 International Leverage and Tax Rates (1990)

Country	$D/(E + D)$	Net of Cash $D/(E + D)$	Interest/EBIT	τ_c	τ^*
United States	28%	23%	41%	34.0%	34.0%
Japan	29%	17%	41%	37.5%	31.5%
Germany	23%	15%	31%	50.0%	3.3%
France	41%	28%	38%	37.0%	7.8%
Italy	46%	36%	55%	36.0%	18.6%
United Kingdom	19%	11%	21%	35.0%	24.2%
Canada	35%	32%	65%	38.0%	28.9%

Source: R. Rajan and L. Zingales, "What Do We Know About Capital Structure? Some Evidence from International Data," *Journal of Finance* 50 (1995): 1421–1460. Data is for median firms and top marginal tax rates.

[17] Additional evidence is provided by J. Graham in "How Big Are the Tax Benefits of Debt?" *Journal of Finance* 55 (2000): 1901–1941, where he estimates that the typical firm exploits less than half of the potential tax benefits of debt.

[18] Similar low leverage results continue to hold using more recent data from 2006; see J. Fan, S. Titman, and G. Twite, "An International Comparison of Capital Structure and Debt Maturity Choices," SSRN working paper, 2008.

Employee Stock Options

Employee stock options can serve as an important tax shield for some firms. The typical employee stock option allows employees of a firm to buy the firm's stock at a discounted price (often, the price of the stock when they started employment). When an employee exercises a stock option, the firm is essentially selling shares to the employee at a discount. If the discount is large, the employee can exercise the option and earn a large profit.

The amount of the discount is a cost for the firm's equity holders because selling shares at a price below their market value dilutes the value of the firm's shares. To reflect this cost, the IRS allows firms to deduct the amount of the discount from their earnings for tax purposes. (The IRS taxes employees on the gain, so the tax burden does not go away, but moves from the firm to the employees.) Unlike the interest tax shield, the tax deduction from employee stock options does not add to the value of the firm. If the same amounts were paid to employees through salary rather than options, the firm would be able to deduct the extra salary from its taxable income as well. Until recently, however, employee stock options did not affect EBIT, so that EBIT overstated the taxable income of firms with option expenses.

During the stock market boom of the late 1990s, many technology firms and other firms that issued a large number of employee stock options were able to claim these deductions and lower their taxes relative to what one would naively have imputed from EBIT. In 2000, some of the most profitable companies in the United States (based on net income), such as Microsoft, Cisco Systems, Dell, and Qualcomm, had *no* taxable income—using the stock option deduction, they were able to report a loss for tax purposes.* A study by Professors J. Graham, M. Lang, and D. Shackelford reported that in 2000, stock option deductions for the entire NASDAQ 100 exceeded aggregate pretax earnings.† For these firms, there would have been no tax advantage associated with debt—which may help explain why they used little to no debt financing.

Since 2006, firms have been required to expense employee stock options. However, the rules for expensing the options are not the same as the tax deduction. As a consequence, even after this rule change, stock options may continue to result in a significant difference between firms' accounting income and their income for tax purposes. For example, Mark Zuckerberg's founding options in Facebook led to an accounting expense of under $10 million, yet provided Facebook with a tax deduction exceeding $2 billion.

*See M. Sullivan, "Stock Options Take $50 Billion Bite Out of Corporate Taxes," *Tax Notes* (March 18, 2002): 1396–1401.

†"Employee Stock Options, Corporate Taxes and Debt Policy," *Journal of Finance* 59 (2004): 1585–1618.

CONCEPT CHECK

1. How does the growth rate of a firm affect the optimal fraction of debt in the capital structure?
2. Do firms choose capital structures that fully exploit the tax advantages of debt?

MyFinanceLab Here is what you should know after reading this chapter. MyFinanceLab will help you identify what you know and where to go when you need to practice.

15.1 The Interest Tax Deduction

- Because interest expense is tax deductible, leverage increases the total amount of income available to all investors.
- The gain to investors from the tax deductibility of interest payments is called the interest tax shield.

$$\text{Interest Tax Shield} = \text{Corporate Tax Rate} \times \text{Interest Payments} \tag{15.1}$$

15.2 Valuing the Interest Tax Shield

- When we consider corporate taxes, the total value of a levered firm equals the value of an unlevered firm plus the present value of the interest tax shield.

$$V^L = V^U + PV(\text{Interest Tax Shield}) \tag{15.2}$$

- When a firm's marginal tax rate is constant, and there are no personal taxes, the present value of the interest tax shield from permanent debt equals the tax rate times the value of the debt, $\tau_c D$.
- The firm's pretax WACC measures the required return to the firm's investors. Its effective after-tax WACC, or simply the WACC, measures the cost to the firm after including the benefit of the interest tax shield. The two notions are related as follows:

$$r_{wacc} = \frac{E}{E+D} r_E + \frac{D}{E+D} r_D (1 - \tau_c) \tag{15.5}$$

$$= \underbrace{\frac{E}{E+D} r_E + \frac{D}{E+D} r_D}_{\text{Pretax WACC}} - \underbrace{\frac{D}{E+D} r_D \tau_c}_{\substack{\text{Reduction Due} \\ \text{to Interest Tax Shield}}} \tag{15.6}$$

  Absent other market imperfections, the WACC declines with a firm's leverage.

- When the firm maintains a target leverage ratio, we compute its levered value V^L as the present value of its free cash flows using the WACC, whereas its unlevered value V^U is the present value of its free cash flows using its unlevered cost of capital or pretax WACC.

15.3 Recapitalizing to Capture the Tax Shield

- When securities are fairly priced, the original shareholders of a firm capture the full benefit of the interest tax shield from an increase in leverage.

15.4 Personal Taxes

- Personal taxes offset some of the corporate tax benefits of leverage. Every \$1 received after taxes by debt holders from interest payments costs equity holders $\$(1 - \tau^*)$ on an after-tax basis, where

$$\tau^* = 1 - \frac{(1 - \tau_c)(1 - \tau_e)}{(1 - \tau_i)} \tag{15.7}$$

15.5 Optimal Capital Structure with Taxes

- The optimal level of leverage from a tax-saving perspective is the level such that interest equals EBIT. In this case, the firm takes full advantage of the corporate tax deduction of interest, but avoids the tax disadvantage of excess leverage at the personal level.
- The optimal fraction of debt, as a proportion of a firm's capital structure, declines with the growth rate of the firm.
- The interest expense of the average firm is well below its taxable income, implying that firms do not fully exploit the tax advantages of debt.

Key Terms

interest tax shield *p. 521*

repatriation tax *p. 525*

Further Reading

In their 1963 paper, "Corporate Income Taxes and the Cost of Capital: A Correction," *American Economic Review* 53 (June 1963): 433–443, Modigliani and Miller adjusted their analysis to incorporate the tax benefits of leverage. Other classic works in how taxation affects the cost of capital and optimal capital structure include: M. King, "Taxation and the Cost of Capital," *Review of Economic*

Studies 41 (1974): 21–35; M. Miller, "Debt and Taxes," *Journal of Finance* 32 (1977): 261–275; M. Miller and M. Scholes, "Dividends and Taxes," *Journal of Financial Economics* 6 (1978): 333–364; and J. Stiglitz, "Taxation, Corporate Financial Policy, and the Cost of Capital," *Journal of Public Economics* 2 (1973): 1–34.

For an analysis of how firms respond to tax incentives, see J. MacKie-Mason, "Do Taxes Affect Corporate Financing Decisions?" *Journal of Finance* 45 (1990): 1471–1493. For a recent review of the literature of taxes and corporate finance, see J. Graham, "Taxes and Corporate Finance: A Review," *Review of Financial Studies* 16 (2003): 1075–1129.

These articles analyze in depth several issues regarding taxation and optimal capital structure: M. Bradley, G. Jarrell, and E. Kim, "On the Existence of an Optimal Capital Structure: Theory and Evidence," *The Journal of Finance* 39 (1984): 857–878; M. Brennan and E. Schwartz, "Corporate Income Taxes, Valuation, and the Problem of Optimal Capital Structure," *Journal of Business* 51 (1978): 103–114; H. DeAngelo and R. Masulis, "Optimal Capital Structure Under Corporate and Personal Taxation," *Journal of Financial Economics* 8 (1980): 3–29; and S. Titman and R. Wessels, "The Determinants of Capital Structure Choice," *Journal of Finance* 43 (1988): 1–19.

The following articles contain information on what managers say about their capital structure decisions: J. Graham and C. Harvey, "How Do CFOs Make Capital Budgeting and Capital Structure Decisions?" *Journal of Applied Corporate Finance* 15 (2002): 8–23; R. Kamath, "Long-Term Financing Decisions: Views and Practices of Financial Managers of NYSE Firms," *Financial Review* 32 (1997): 331–356; E. Norton, "Factors Affecting Capital Structure Decisions," *Financial Review* 26 (1991): 431–446; and J. Pinegar and L. Wilbricht, "What Managers Think of Capital Structure Theory: A Survey," *Financial Management* 18 (1989): 82–91.

For additional insight into capital structure decisions internationally, see also F. Bancel and U. Mittoo, "Cross-Country Determinants of Capital Structure Choice: A Survey of European Firms," *Financial Management* 33 (2004): 103–132; R. La Porta, F. Lopez-de-Silanes, A. Shleifer, and R. Vishny, "Legal Determinants of External Finance," *Journal of Finance* 52 (1997): 1131–1152; and L. Booth, V. Aivazian, A. Demirguq-Kunt, and V. Maksimovic, "Capital Structures in Developing Countries," *Journal of Finance* 56 (2001): 87–130.

Problems

All problems are available in MyFinanceLab. *An asterisk (*) indicates problems with a higher level of difficulty.*

The Interest Tax Deduction

1. Pelamed Pharmaceuticals has EBIT of $325 million in 2006. In addition, Pelamed has interest expenses of $125 million and a corporate tax rate of 40%.
   a. What is Pelamed's 2006 net income?
   b. What is the total of Pelamed's 2006 net income and interest payments?
   c. If Pelamed had no interest expenses, what would its 2006 net income be? How does it compare to your answer in part b?
   d. What is the amount of Pelamed's interest tax shield in 2006?

2. Grommit Engineering expects to have net income next year of $20.75 million and free cash flow of $22.15 million. Grommit's marginal corporate tax rate is 35%.
   a. If Grommit increases leverage so that its interest expense rises by $1 million, how will its net income change?
   b. For the same increase in interest expense, how will free cash flow change?

3. Suppose the corporate tax rate is 40%. Consider a firm that earns $1000 before interest and taxes each year with no risk. The firm's capital expenditures equal its depreciation expenses each year, and it will have no changes to its net working capital. The risk-free interest rate is 5%.
   a. Suppose the firm has no debt and pays out its net income as a dividend each year. What is the value of the firm's equity?

b. Suppose instead the firm makes interest payments of $500 per year. What is the value of equity? What is the value of debt?

c. What is the difference between the total value of the firm with leverage and without leverage?

d. The difference in part c is equal to what percentage of the value of the debt?

4. Braxton Enterprises currently has debt outstanding of $35 million and an interest rate of 8%. Braxton plans to reduce its debt by repaying $7 million in principal at the end of each year for the next five years. If Braxton's marginal corporate tax rate is 40%, what is the interest tax shield from Braxton's debt in each of the next five years?

Valuing the Interest Tax Shield

5. Your firm currently has $100 million in debt outstanding with a 10% interest rate. The terms of the loan require the firm to repay $25 million of the balance each year. Suppose that the marginal corporate tax rate is 40%, and that the interest tax shields have the same risk as the loan. What is the present value of the interest tax shields from this debt?

6. Arnell Industries has just issued $10 million in debt (at par). The firm will pay interest only on this debt. Arnell's marginal tax rate is expected to be 35% for the foreseeable future.

a. Suppose Arnell pays interest of 6% per year on its debt. What is its annual interest tax shield?

b. What is the present value of the interest tax shield, assuming its risk is the same as the loan?

c. Suppose instead that the interest rate on the debt is 5%. What is the present value of the interest tax shield in this case?

7. Ten years have passed since Arnell issued $10 million in perpetual interest only debt with a 6% annual coupon, as in Problem 6. Tax rates have remained the same at 35% but interest rates have dropped, so Arnell's current cost of debt capital is 4%.

a. What is Arnell's annual interest tax shield?

b. What is the present value of the interest tax shield today?

8. Bay Transport Systems (BTS) currently has $30 million in debt outstanding. In addition to 6.5% interest, it plans to repay 5% of the remaining balance each year. If BTS has a marginal corporate tax rate of 40%, and if the interest tax shields have the same risk as the loan, what is the present value of the interest tax shield from the debt?

9. Safeco Inc. has no debt, and maintains a policy of holding $10 million in excess cash reserves, invested in risk-free Treasury securities. If Safeco pays a corporate tax rate of 35%, what is the cost of permanently maintaining this $10 million reserve? (*Hint*: What is the present value of the additional taxes that Safeco will pay?)

10. Rogot Instruments makes fine violins and cellos. It has $1 million in debt outstanding, equity valued at $2 million, and pays corporate income tax at rate of 35%. Its cost of equity is 12% and its cost of debt is 7%.

a. What is Rogot's pretax WACC?

b. What is Rogot's (effective after-tax) WACC?

11. Rumolt Motors has 30 million shares outstanding with a price of $15 per share. In addition, Rumolt has issued bonds with a total current market value of $150 million. Suppose Rumolt's equity cost of capital is 10%, and its debt cost of capital is 5%.

a. What is Rumolt's pretax weighted average cost of capital?

b. If Rumolt's corporate tax rate is 35%, what is its after-tax weighted average cost of capital?

12. Summit Builders has a market debt-equity ratio of 0.65 and a corporate tax rate of 40%, and it pays 7% interest on its debt. The interest tax shield from its debt lowers Summit's WACC by what amount?

13. NatNah, a builder of acoustic accessories, has no debt and an equity cost of capital of 15%. Suppose NatNah decides to increase its leverage and maintain a market debt-to-value ratio of 0.5. Suppose its debt cost of capital is 9% and its corporate tax rate is 35%. If NatNah's pre-tax WACC remains constant, what will its (effective after-tax) WACC be with the increase in leverage?

14. Restex maintains a debt-equity ratio of 0.85, and has an equity cost of capital of 12% and a debt cost of capital of 7%. Restex's corporate tax rate is 40%, and its market capitalization is $220 million.

a. If Restex's free cash flow is expected to be $10 million in one year, what constant expected future growth rate is consistent with the firm's current market value?

b. Estimate the value of Restex's interest tax shield.

15. Acme Storage has a market capitalization of $100 million and debt outstanding of $40 million. Acme plans to maintain this same debt-equity ratio in the future. The firm pays an interest rate of 7.5% on its debt and has a corporate tax rate of 35%.

a. If Acme's free cash flow is expected to be $7 million next year and is expected to grow at a rate of 3% per year, what is Acme's WACC?

b. What is the value of Acme's interest tax shield?

16. Milton Industries expects free cash flow of $5 million each year. Milton's corporate tax rate is 35%, and its unlevered cost of capital is 15%. The firm also has outstanding debt of $19.05 million, and it expects to maintain this level of debt permanently.

a. What is the value of Milton Industries without leverage?

b. What is the value of Milton Industries with leverage?

17. Suppose Microsoft has 8.75 billion shares outstanding and pays a marginal corporate tax rate of 35%. If Microsoft announces that it will pay out $50 billion in cash to investors through a combination of a special dividend and a share repurchase, and if investors had previously assumed Microsoft would retain this excess cash permanently, by how much will Microsoft's share price change upon the announcement?

18. Kurz Manufacturing is currently an all-equity firm with 20 million shares outstanding and a stock price of $7.50 per share. Although investors currently expect Kurz to remain an all-equity firm, Kurz plans to announce that it will borrow $50 million and use the funds to repurchase shares. Kurz will pay interest only on this debt, and it has no further plans to increase or decrease the amount of debt. Kurz is subject to a 40% corporate tax rate.

a. What is the market value of Kurz's existing assets before the announcement?

b. What is the market value of Kurz's assets (including any tax shields) just after the debt is issued, but before the shares are repurchased?

c. What is Kurz's share price just before the share repurchase? How many shares will Kurz repurchase?

d. What are Kurz's market value balance sheet and share price after the share repurchase?

19. Rally, Inc., is an all-equity firm with assets worth $25 billion and 10 billion shares outstanding. Rally plans to borrow $10 billion and use these funds to repurchase shares. The firm's corporate tax rate is 35%, and Rally plans to keep its outstanding debt equal to $10 billion permanently.

a. Without the increase in leverage, what would Rally's share price be?

b. Suppose Rally offers $2.75 per share to repurchase its shares. Would shareholders sell for this price?

c. Suppose Rally offers $3.00 per share, and shareholders tender their shares at this price. What will Rally's share price be after the repurchase?

d. What is the lowest price Rally can offer and have shareholders tender their shares? What will its stock price be after the share repurchase in that case?

Personal Taxes

20. Suppose the corporate tax rate is 40%, and investors pay a tax rate of 15% on income from dividends or capital gains and a tax rate of 33.3% on interest income. Your firm decides to add debt so it will pay an additional $15 million in interest each year. It will pay this interest expense by cutting its dividend.

a. How much will debt holders receive after paying taxes on the interest they earn?
b. By how much will the firm need to cut its dividend each year to pay this interest expense?
c. By how much will this cut in the dividend reduce equity holders' annual after-tax income?
d. How much less will the government receive in total tax revenues each year?
e. What is the effective tax advantage of debt τ^*?

21. Facebook, Inc. had no debt on its balance sheet in 2014, but paid $2 billion in taxes. Suppose Facebook were to issue sufficient debt to reduce its taxes by $250 million per year permanently. Assume Facebook's marginal corporate tax rate is 35% and its borrowing cost is 5%.

a. If Facebook's investors do not pay personal taxes (because they hold their Facebook stock in tax-free retirement accounts), how much value would be created (what is the value of the tax shield)?
b. How does your answer change if instead you assume that Facebook's investors pay a 20% tax rate on income from equity and a 39.6% tax rate on interest income?

22. Markum Enterprises is considering permanently adding $100 million of debt to its capital structure. Markum's corporate tax rate is 35%.

a. Absent personal taxes, what is the value of the interest tax shield from the new debt?
b. If investors pay a tax rate of 40% on interest income, and a tax rate of 20% on income from dividends and capital gains, what is the value of the interest tax shield from the new debt?

***23.** Garnet Corporation is considering issuing risk-free debt or risk-free preferred stock. The tax rate on interest income is 35%, and the tax rate on dividends or capital gains from preferred stock is 15%. However, the dividends on preferred stock are not deductible for corporate tax purposes, and the corporate tax rate is 40%.

a. If the risk-free interest rate for debt is 6%, what is the cost of capital for risk-free preferred stock?
b. What is the after-tax debt cost of capital for the firm? Which security is cheaper for the firm?
c. Show that the after-tax debt cost of capital is equal to the preferred stock cost of capital multiplied by $(1 - \tau^*)$.

***24.** Suppose the tax rate on interest income is 35%, and the average tax rate on capital gains and dividend income is 10%. How high must the marginal corporate tax rate be for debt to offer a tax advantage?

Optimal Capital Structure with Taxes

25. With its current leverage, Impi Corporation will have net income next year of $4.5 million. If Impi's corporate tax rate is 35% and it pays 8% interest on its debt, how much additional debt can Impi issue this year and still receive the benefit of the interest tax shield next year?

***26.** Colt Systems will have EBIT this coming year of $15 million. It will also spend $6 million on total capital expenditures and increases in net working capital, and have $3 million in depreciation expenses. Colt is currently an all-equity firm with a corporate tax rate of 35% and a cost of capital of 10%.

a. If Colt's free cash flows are expected to grow by 8.5% per year, what is the market value of its equity today?
b. If the interest rate on its debt is 8%, how much can Colt borrow now and still have non-negative net income this coming year?
c. Is there a tax incentive today for Colt to choose a debt-to-value ratio that exceeds 50%? Explain.

MFL

*27. PMF, Inc., is equally likely to have EBIT this coming year of $10 million, $15 million, or $20 million. Its corporate tax rate is 35%, and investors pay a 15% tax rate on income from equity and a 35% tax rate on interest income.

a. What is the effective tax advantage of debt if PMF has interest expenses of $8 million this coming year?

b. What is the effective tax advantage of debt for interest expenses in excess of $20 million? (Ignore carryforwards.)

c. What is the expected effective tax advantage of debt for interest expenses between $10 million and $15 million? (Ignore carryforwards.)

d. What level of interest expense provides PMF with the greatest tax benefit?

Data Case

Your boss was impressed with your presentation regarding the irrelevance of capital structure from Chapter 14 but, as expected, has realized that market imperfections like taxes must be accounted for. You have now been asked to include taxes in your analysis. Your boss knows that interest is deductible and has decided that the stock price of Home Depot should increase if the firm increases its use of debt. Thus, your boss wants to propose a share repurchase program using the proceeds from a new debt issue and wants to present this plan to the CEO and perhaps to the Board of Directors.

Your boss would like you to examine the impact of two different scenarios, adding a modest level of debt and adding a higher level of debt. In particular, your boss would like to consider issuing $1 billion in new debt or $5 billion in new debt. In either case, Home Depot would use the proceeds to repurchase stock.

1. Using the financial statements for Home Depot that you downloaded in Chapter 14, determine the average corporate tax rate for Home Depot over the last four years by dividing Income Tax by Earnings before Tax for each of the last four years.

2. Begin by analyzing the scenario with $1 billion in new debt. Assuming the firm plans to keep this new debt outstanding forever, determine the present value of the tax shield of the new debt. What additional assumptions did you need to make for this calculation?

3. Determine the new stock price if the $1 billion in debt is used to repurchase stock.
   a. Use the current market value of Home Depot's equity that you calculated in Chapter 14.
   b. Determine the new market value of the equity if the repurchase occurs.
   c. Determine the new number of shares and the stock price after the repurchase is announced.

4. What will Home Depot's D/E ratio based on book values be after it issues new debt and repurchases stock? What will its market value D/E ratio be?

5. Repeat Steps 2–4 for the scenario in which Home Depot issues $5 billion in debt and repurchases stock.

6. Based on the stock price, do the debt increase and stock repurchase appear to be a good idea? Why or why not? What issues might the executives of Home Depot raise that aren't considered in your analysis?

Note: Updates to this data case may be found at www.berkdemarzo.com.

Financial Distress, Managerial Incentives, and Information

CHAPTER

16

MODIGLIANI AND MILLER DEMONSTRATED THAT CAPITAL STRUCTURE does not matter in a perfect capital market. In Chapter 15, we found a tax benefit of leverage, at least up to the point that a firm's EBIT exceeds the interest payments on the debt. Yet we saw that the average U.S. firm shields less than half of its earnings in this way. Why don't firms use more debt?

We can gain some insight by looking at United Airlines (UAL Corporation). For the five-year period 1996 through 2000, UAL paid interest expenses of $1.7 billion, relative to EBIT of more than $6 billion. During this period, it reported a total provision for taxes on its income statement exceeding $2.2 billion. The company appeared to have a level of debt that did not fully exploit its tax shield. Even so, as a result of high fuel and labor costs, a decline in travel following the terrorist attacks of September 11, 2001, and increased competition from discount carriers, UAL filed for bankruptcy court protection in December 2002. United ultimately emerged from bankruptcy in 2006; after a profitable 2007, it suffered losses and renewed creditor concerns in the wake of the financial crisis in 2008. The airline returned to profitability in 2010 when it announced plans to acquire Continental Airlines. A similar fate soon befell American Airlines, whose parent company declared bankruptcy in 2011 with over $29 billion in debt, emerging from bankruptcy 2 years later as part of a merger with US Airways. As these examples illustrate, firms such as airlines whose future cash flows are unstable and highly sensitive to shocks in the economy run the risk of bankruptcy if they use too much leverage.

When a firm has trouble meeting its debt obligations we say the firm is in **financial distress.** In this chapter, we consider how a firm's choice of capital structure can, due to market imperfections, affect its costs of financial distress, alter managers' incentives, and signal information to investors. Each of these consequences of the capital structure decision

NOTATION

E	market value of equity
D	market value of debt
PV	present value
β_E	equity beta
β_D	debt beta
I	investment
NPV	net present value
V^U	value of the unlevered firm
V^L	value of the firm with leverage
τ^*	effective tax advantage of debt

can be significant, and each may offset the tax benefits of leverage when leverage is high. Thus, these imperfections may help to explain the levels of debt that we generally observe. In addition, because their effects are likely to vary widely across different types of firms, they may help to explain the large discrepancies in leverage choices that exist across industries, as documented in Figure 15.7 in the previous chapter.

16.1 Default and Bankruptcy in a Perfect Market

Debt financing puts an obligation on a firm. A firm that fails to make the required interest or principal payments on the debt is in **default**. After the firm defaults, debt holders are given certain rights to the assets of the firm. In the extreme case, the debt holders take legal ownership of the firm's assets through a process called bankruptcy. Recall that equity financing does not carry this risk. While equity holders hope to receive dividends, the firm is not legally obligated to pay them.

Thus, it seems that an important consequence of leverage is the risk of bankruptcy. Does this risk represent a disadvantage to using debt? Not necessarily. As we pointed out in Chapter 14, Modigliani and Miller's results continue to hold in a perfect market even when debt is risky and the firm may default. Let's review that result by considering a hypothetical example.

Armin Industries: Leverage and the Risk of Default

Armin Industries faces an uncertain future in a challenging business environment. Due to increased competition from foreign imports, its revenues have fallen dramatically in the past year. Armin's managers hope that a new product in the company's pipeline will restore its fortunes. While the new product represents a significant advance over Armin's competitors' products, whether that product will be a hit with consumers remains uncertain. If it is a hit, revenues and profits will grow, and Armin will be worth \$150 million at the end of the year. If it fails, Armin will be worth only \$80 million.

Armin Industries may employ one of two alternative capital structures: (1) It can use all-equity financing or (2) it can use debt that matures at the end of the year with a total of \$100 million due. Let's look at the consequences of these capital structure choices when the new product succeeds, and when it fails, in a setting of perfect capital markets.

Scenario 1: New Product Succeeds. If the new product is successful, Armin is worth \$150 million. Without leverage, equity holders own the full amount. With leverage, Armin must make the \$100 million debt payment, and Armin's equity holders will own the remaining \$50 million.

But what if Armin does not have \$100 million in cash available at the end of the year? Although its assets will be worth \$150 million, much of that value may come from anticipated *future* profits from the new product, rather than cash in the bank. In that case, if Armin has debt, will it be forced to default?

With perfect capital markets, the answer is no. As long as the value of the firm's assets exceeds its liabilities, Armin will be able to repay the loan. Even if it does not have the cash immediately available, it can raise the cash by obtaining a new loan or by issuing new shares.

For example, suppose Armin currently has 10 million shares outstanding. Because the value of its equity is \$50 million, these shares are worth \$5 per share. At this price, Armin can raise \$100 million by issuing 20 million new shares and use the proceeds to pay off the debt. After the debt is repaid, the firm's equity is worth \$150 million. Because there is now a total of 30 million shares, the share price remains \$5 per share.

This scenario shows that if a firm has access to capital markets and can issue new securities at a fair price, *then it need not default as long as the market value of its assets exceeds its liabilities.* That is, whether default occurs depends on the relative values of the firm's assets and liabilities, not on its cash flows. Many firms experience years of negative cash flows yet remain solvent.

Scenario 2: New Product Fails. If the new product fails, Armin is worth only $80 million. If the company has all-equity financing, equity holders will be unhappy but there is no immediate legal consequence for the firm. In contrast, if Armin has $100 million in debt due, it will experience financial distress. The firm will be unable to make its $100 million debt payment and will have no choice except to default. In bankruptcy, debt holders will receive legal ownership of the firm's assets, leaving Armin's shareholders with nothing. Because the assets the debt holders receive have a value of $80 million, they will suffer a loss of $20 million relative to the $100 million they were owed. Equity holders in a corporation have limited liability, so the debt holders cannot sue Armin's shareholders for this $20 million—they must accept the loss.

Comparing the Two Scenarios. Table 16.1 compares the outcome of each scenario without leverage and with leverage. Both debt and equity holders are worse off if the product fails rather than succeeds. Without leverage, if the product fails equity holders lose $150 million − $80 million = $70 million. With leverage, equity holders lose $50 million, and debt holders lose $20 million, *but the total loss is the same*—$70 million. Overall, *if the new product fails, Armin's investors are equally unhappy whether the firm is levered and declares bankruptcy or whether it is unlevered and the share price declines.*[1]

TABLE 16.1 **Value of Debt and Equity with and without Leverage (in $ million)**

	Without Leverage		With Leverage	
	Success	Failure	Success	Failure
Debt value	—	—	100	80
Equity value	150	80	50	0
Total to all investors	150	80	150	80

This point is important. When a firm declares bankruptcy, the news often makes headlines. Much attention is paid to the firm's poor results and the loss to investors. But the decline in value is not *caused* by bankruptcy: The decline is the same whether or not the firm has leverage. That is, if the new product fails, Armin will experience **economic distress**, which is a significant decline in the value of a firm's assets, whether or not it experiences financial distress due to leverage.

Bankruptcy and Capital Structure

With perfect capital markets, Modigliani-Miller (MM) Proposition I applies: The total value to all investors does not depend on the firm's capital structure. Investors as a group are *not* worse off because a firm has leverage. While it is true that bankruptcy results from

[1]There is a temptation to look only at shareholders and to say they are worse off when Armin has leverage because their shares are worthless. In fact, shareholders lose $50 million relative to success when the firm is levered, versus $70 million without leverage. What really matters is the total value to all investors, which will determine the total amount of capital the firm can raise initially.

a firm having leverage, bankruptcy alone does not lead to a greater reduction in the total value to investors. Thus, there is no disadvantage to debt financing, and a firm will have the same total value and will be able to raise the same amount initially from investors with either choice of capital structure.

EXAMPLE 16.1 Bankruptcy Risk and Firm Value

Problem

Suppose the risk-free rate is 5%, and Armin's new product is equally likely to succeed or to fail. For simplicity, suppose that Armin's cash flows are unrelated to the state of the economy (i.e., the risk is diversifiable), so that the project has a beta of 0 and the cost of capital is the risk-free rate. Compute the value of Armin's securities at the beginning of the year with and without leverage, and show that MM Proposition I holds.

Solution

Without leverage, the equity is worth either \$150 million or \$80 million at year-end. Because the risk is diversifiable, no risk premium is necessary and we can discount the expected value of the firm at the risk-free rate to determine its value without leverage at the start of the year:[2]

$$\text{Equity (unlevered)} = V^U = \frac{\frac{1}{2}(150) + \frac{1}{2}(80)}{1.05} = \$109.52 \text{ million}$$

With leverage, equity holders receive \$50 million or nothing, and debt holders receive \$100 million or \$80 million. Thus,

$$\text{Equity (levered)} = \frac{\frac{1}{2}(50) + \frac{1}{2}(0)}{1.05} = \$23.81 \text{ million}$$

$$\text{Debt} = \frac{\frac{1}{2}(100) + \frac{1}{2}(80)}{1.05} = \$85.71 \text{ million}$$

Therefore, the value of the levered firm is $V^L = E + D = 23.81 + 85.71 = \$109.52$ million. With or without leverage, the total value of the securities is the same, verifying MM Proposition I. The firm is able to raise the same amount from investors using either capital structure.

CONCEPT CHECK

1. With perfect capital markets, does the possibility of bankruptcy put debt financing at a disadvantage?
2. Does the risk of default reduce the value of the firm?

16.2 The Costs of Bankruptcy and Financial Distress

With perfect capital markets, the *risk* of bankruptcy is not a disadvantage of debt—bankruptcy simply shifts the ownership of the firm from equity holders to debt holders without changing the total value available to all investors.

Is this description of bankruptcy realistic? No. Bankruptcy is rarely simple and straightforward—equity holders don't just "hand the keys" to debt holders the moment the firm defaults on a debt payment. Rather, bankruptcy is a long and complicated process that imposes both direct and indirect costs on the firm and its investors, costs that the assumption of perfect capital markets ignores.

---

[2] If the risk were not diversifiable and a risk premium were needed, the calculations here would become more complicated but the conclusion would not change.

The Bankruptcy Code

When a firm fails to make a required payment to debt holders, it is in default. Debt holders can then take legal action against the firm to collect payment by seizing the firm's assets. Because most firms have multiple creditors, without coordination it is difficult to guarantee that each creditor will be treated fairly. Moreover, because the assets of the firm might be more valuable if kept together, creditors seizing assets in a piecemeal fashion might destroy much of the remaining value of the firm.

The U.S. bankruptcy code was created to organize this process so that creditors are treated fairly and the value of the assets is not needlessly destroyed. According to the provisions of the 1978 Bankruptcy Reform Act, U.S. firms can file for two forms of bankruptcy protection: Chapter 7 or Chapter 11.

In **Chapter 7 liquidation**, a trustee is appointed to oversee the liquidation of the firm's assets through an auction. The proceeds from the liquidation are used to pay the firm's creditors, and the firm ceases to exist.

In the more common form of bankruptcy for large corporations, **Chapter 11 reorganization**, all pending collection attempts are automatically suspended, and the firm's existing management is given the opportunity to propose a reorganization plan. While developing the plan, management continues to operate the business. The reorganization plan specifies the treatment of each creditor of the firm. In addition to cash payment, creditors may receive new debt or equity securities of the firm. The value of cash and securities is generally less than the amount each creditor is owed, but more than the creditors would receive if the firm were shut down immediately and liquidated. The creditors must vote to accept the plan, and it must be approved by the bankruptcy court.[3] If an acceptable plan is not put forth, the court may ultimately force a Chapter 7 liquidation of the firm.

Direct Costs of Bankruptcy

The bankruptcy code is designed to provide an orderly process for settling a firm's debts. However, the process is still complex, time-consuming, and costly. When a corporation becomes financially distressed, outside professionals, such as legal and accounting experts, consultants, appraisers, auctioneers, and others with experience selling distressed assets, are generally hired. Investment bankers may also assist with a potential financial restructuring.

These outside experts are costly. Between 2003 and 2005, United Airlines paid a team of over 30 advisory firms an average of \$8.6 million per month for legal and professional services related to its Chapter 11 reorganization. Enron spent a then-record \$30 million per month on legal and accounting fees in bankruptcy, with the total cost exceeding \$750 million. WorldCom paid its advisors \$620 million as part of its reorganization to become MCI, and the Lehman Brothers bankruptcy, the largest in history, has reportedly entailed fees of \$2.2 billion.[4]

---

[3]Specifically, management holds the exclusive right to propose a reorganization plan for the first 120 days, and this period may be extended indefinitely by the bankruptcy court. Thereafter, any interested party may propose a plan. Creditors who will receive full payment or have their claims fully reinstated under the plan are deemed unimpaired, and do not vote on the reorganization plan. All impaired creditors are grouped according to the nature of their claims. If the plan is approved by creditors holding two-thirds of the claim amount in each group and a majority in the number of the claims in each group, the court will confirm the plan. Even if all groups do not approve the plan, the court may still impose the plan (in a process commonly known as a "cram down") if it deems the plan fair and equitable with respect to each group that objected.

[4]J. O'Toole, "Five years later, Lehman bankruptcy fees hit \$2.2 billion," CNNMoney, September 13, 2013.

In addition to the money spent by the firm, the creditors may incur costs during the bankruptcy process. In the case of Chapter 11 reorganization, creditors must often wait several years for a reorganization plan to be approved and to receive payment. To ensure that their rights and interests are respected, and to assist in valuing their claims in a proposed reorganization, creditors may seek separate legal representation and professional advice.

Whether paid by the firm or its creditors, these direct costs of bankruptcy reduce the value of the assets that the firm's investors will ultimately receive. In some cases, such as Enron, reorganization costs may approach 10% of the value of the assets. Studies typically report that the average direct costs of bankruptcy are approximately 3% to 4% of the pre-bankruptcy market value of total assets.[5] The costs are likely to be higher for firms with more complicated business operations and for firms with larger numbers of creditors, because it may be more difficult to reach agreement among many creditors regarding the final disposition of the firm's assets. Because many aspects of the bankruptcy process are independent of the size of the firm, the costs are typically higher, in percentage terms, for smaller firms. A study of Chapter 7 liquidations of small businesses found that the average direct costs of bankruptcy were 12% of the value of the firm's assets.[6]

Given the substantial legal and other direct costs of bankruptcy, firms in financial distress can avoid filing for bankruptcy by first negotiating directly with creditors. When a financially distressed firm is successful at reorganizing outside of bankruptcy, it is called a **workout**. Consequently, the direct costs of bankruptcy should not substantially exceed the cost of a workout. Another approach is a **prepackaged bankruptcy** (or "prepack"), in which a firm will *first* develop a reorganization plan with the agreement of its main creditors, and *then* file Chapter 11 to implement the plan (and pressure any creditors who attempt to hold out for better terms). With a prepack, the firm emerges from bankruptcy quickly and with minimal direct costs.[7]

Indirect Costs of Financial Distress

Aside from the direct legal and administrative costs of bankruptcy, many other *indirect* costs are associated with financial distress (whether or not the firm has formally filed for bankruptcy). While these costs are difficult to measure accurately, they are often much larger than the direct costs of bankruptcy.

Loss of Customers. Because bankruptcy may enable or encourage firms to walk away from commitments to their customers, customers may be unwilling to purchase

---

[5]See J. Warner, "Bankruptcy Costs: Some Evidence," *Journal of Finance* 32 (1977): 337–347; L. Weiss, "Bankruptcy Resolution: Direct Costs and Violation of Priority of Claims," *Journal of Financial Economics* 27 (1990): 285–314; E. Altman, "A Further Empirical Investigation of the Bankruptcy Cost Question," *Journal of Finance* 39 (1984): 1067–1089; and B. Betker, "The Administrative Costs of Debt Restructurings: Some Recent Evidence," *Financial Management* 26 (1997): 56–68. L. LoPucki and J. Doherty estimate that due to speedier resolution, the direct costs of bankruptcy fell by more than 50% during the 1990s to approximately 1.5% of firm value ("The Determinants of Professional Fees in Large Bankruptcy Reorganization Cases," *Journal of Empirical Legal Studies* 1 (2004): 111–141).

[6]R. Lawless and S. Ferris, "Professional Fees and Other Direct Costs in Chapter 7 Business Liquidations," *Washington University Law Quarterly* (1997): 1207–1236. For comparative international data, see K. Thorburn, "Bankruptcy Auctions: Costs, Debt Recovery and Firm Survival," *Journal of Financial Economics* 58 (2000): 337–368; and A. Raviv and S. Sundgren, "The Comparative Efficiency of Small-firm Bankruptcies: A Study of the U.S. and the Finnish Bankruptcy Codes," *Financial Management* 27 (1998): 28–40.

[7]See E. Tashjian, R. Lease, and J. McConnell, "An Empirical Analysis of Prepackaged Bankruptcies," *Journal of Financial Economics* 40 (1996): 135–162.

products whose value depends on future support or service from the firm. For example, customers will be reluctant to buy plane tickets in advance from a distressed airline that may cease operations, or to purchase autos from a distressed manufacturer that may fail to honor its warranties or provide replacement parts. Similarly, many technology firms' customers may hesitate to commit to a hardware or software platform that may not be supported or upgraded in the future. In contrast, the loss of customers is likely to be small for producers of raw materials (such as sugar or aluminum), as the value of these goods, once delivered, does not depend on the seller's continued success.[8]

Loss of Suppliers. Customers are not the only ones who retreat from a firm in financial distress. Suppliers may also be unwilling to provide a firm with inventory if they fear they will not be paid. For example, Kmart Corporation filed for bankruptcy protection in January 2002 in part because the decline in its stock price scared suppliers, which then refused to ship goods. Similarly, Swiss Air was forced to shut down because its suppliers refused to fuel its planes. This type of disruption is an important financial distress cost for firms that rely heavily on trade credit. In many cases, the bankruptcy filing itself can alleviate these problems through **debtor-in-possession (DIP) financing**. DIP financing is new debt issued by a bankrupt firm. Because this kind of debt is senior to all existing creditors, it allows a firm that has filed for bankruptcy renewed access to financing to keep operating.

Loss of Employees. Because firms in distress cannot offer job security with long-term employment contracts, they may have difficulty hiring new employees, and existing employees may quit or be hired away. Retaining key employees may be costly: Pacific Gas and Electric Corporation implemented a retention program costing over $80 million to retain 17 key employees while in bankruptcy.[9] This type of financial distress cost is likely to be high for firms whose value is derived largely from their human resources.

Loss of Receivables. Firms in financial distress tend to have difficulty collecting money that is owed to them. According to one of Enron's bankruptcy lawyers, "Many customers who owe smaller amounts are trying to hide from us. They must believe that Enron will never bother with them because the amounts are not particularly large in any individual case."[10] Knowing that the firm might go out of business or at least experience significant management turnover reduces the incentive of customers to maintain a reputation for timely payment.

Fire Sales of Assets. In an effort to avoid bankruptcy and its associated costs, companies in distress may attempt to sell assets quickly to raise cash. To do so, the firm may accept a lower price than would be optimal if it were financially healthy. Indeed, a study of airlines by Todd Pulvino shows that companies in bankruptcy or financial distress sell their aircraft at prices that are 15% to 40% below the prices received by healthier rivals.[11]

---

[8]See S. Titman, "The Effect of Capital Structure on a Firm's Liquidation Decision," *Journal of Financial Economics* 13 (1984): 137–151. T. Opler and S. Titman report 17.7% lower sales growth for highly leveraged firms compared to their less leveraged competitors in R&D-intensive industries during downturns ("Financial Distress and Corporate Performance," *Journal of Finance* 49 (1994): 1015–1040).

[9]R. Jurgens, "PG&E to Review Bonus Program," *Contra Costa Times*, December 13, 2003.

[10]K. Hays, "Enron Asks Judge to Get Tough on Deadbeat Customers," *Associated Press*, August 19, 2003.

[11]"Do Asset Fire-Sales Exist? An Empirical Investigation of Commercial Aircraft Transactions," *Journal of Finance* 53 (1998): 939–978; and "Effects of Bankruptcy Court Protection on Asset Sales," *Journal of Financial Economics* 52 (1999): 151–186. For examples from other industries, see T. Kruse, "Asset Liquidity and the Determinants of Asset Sales by Poorly Performing Firms," *Financial Management* 31 (2002): 107–129.

Discounts are also observed when distressed firms attempt to sell subsidiaries. The costs of selling assets below their value are greatest for firms with assets that lack competitive, liquid markets.

Inefficient Liquidation. Bankruptcy protection can be used by management to delay the liquidation of a firm that should be shut down. A study by Lawrence Weiss and Karen Wruck estimates that Eastern Airlines lost more than 50% of its value while in bankruptcy because management was allowed to continue making negative-NPV investments.[12] On the other hand, companies in bankruptcy may be forced to liquidate assets that would be more valuable if held. For example, as a result of its default, Lehman Brothers was forced to terminate 80% of its derivatives contracts with counterparties, in many cases at purportedly unattractive terms.[13]

Costs to Creditors. Aside from the direct legal costs that creditors may incur when a firm defaults, there may be other indirect costs to creditors. If the loan to the firm was a significant asset for the creditor, default of the firm may lead to costly financial distress *for the creditor.*[14] For example, in the 2008 financial crisis, the Lehman Brothers' bankruptcy in turn helped push many of Lehman's creditors into financial distress as well.

Because bankruptcy is a *choice* the firm's investors and creditors make, there is a limit to the direct and indirect costs on them that result from the firm's decision to go through the bankruptcy process. If these costs were too large, they could be largely avoided by negotiating a workout or doing a prepackaged bankruptcy. Thus, these costs should not exceed the cost of renegotiating with the firm's creditors.[15]

On the other hand, there is no such limit on the indirect costs of financial distress that arise from the firm's customers, suppliers, or employees. Many of these costs are incurred even *prior* to bankruptcy, in anticipation of the fact that the firm may use bankruptcy as an opportunity to renegotiate its contracts and commitments. For example, the firm may use bankruptcy as a way to renege on promises of future employment or retirement benefits for employees, to stop honoring warranties on its products, or to back out of unfavorable delivery contracts with its suppliers. Because of this fear that the firm will not honor its long-term commitments in bankruptcy, highly levered firms may need to pay higher wages to their employees, charge less for their products, and pay more to their suppliers than similar firms with less leverage. Because these costs are not limited by the cost of renegotiating to avoid bankruptcy, they may be substantially greater than other kinds of bankruptcy costs.[16]

---

[12]"Information Problems, Conflicts of Interest, and Asset Stripping: Ch. 11's Failure in the Case of Eastern Airlines," *Journal of Financial Economics* 48 (1998): 55–97.

[13]See C. Loomis, "Derivatives: The risk that still won't go away," *Fortune,* June 24, 2009.

[14]While these costs are borne by the creditor and not by the firm, the creditor will consider these potential costs when setting the rate of the loan.

[15]For an insightful discussion of this point, see R. Haugen and L. Senbet, "Bankruptcy and Agency Costs: Their Significance to the Theory of Optimal Capital Structure," *Journal of Financial and Quantitative Analysis* 23 (1988): 27–38.

[16]There is evidence that firms can use bankruptcy to improve efficiency (A. Kalay, R. Singhal, and E. Tashjian, "Is Chapter 11 costly?" *Journal of Financial Economics,* 84 (2007): 772–796) but that these gains may come at the expense of workers (L. Jacobson, R. LaLonde, and D. Sullivan, "Earnings Losses of Displaced Workers," *American Economic Review* 83 (1993): 685–709). J. Berk, R. Stanton, and J. Zechner, "Human Capital, Bankruptcy and Capital Structure," *Journal of Finance* 65 (2009): 891–925, argue that firms may choose not to issue debt in order to increase their ability to commit to long-term labor contracts.

GLOBAL FINANCIAL CRISIS The Chrysler Prepack

In November 2008, Chrysler CEO Robert Nardelli flew by private jet to Washington with a simple message: Without a government bailout, a Chrysler bankruptcy was inevitable. Congress was not convinced—it felt that bankruptcy was inevitable with or without a bailout and that the automaker needed to provide a more convincing plan to justify government funding. A return trip in December (this time by automobile) yielded a similar result. Bypassing Congress, outgoing President Bush decided to bail out Chrysler with funds from the Troubled Asset Relief Program (TARP). In the end the government provided Chrysler with $8 billion in debt financing.

As a durable goods manufacturer, a lengthy bankruptcy would have entailed significant bankruptcy costs. Indeed, sales were already suffering in part due to customer concerns about Chrysler's future. In response, President Obama took the unprecedented step of guaranteeing warranties on all new Chrysler cars in March 2009.

Despite all this assistance, on April 30, 2009, Chrysler declared bankruptcy as part of a government-orchestrated prepack. Just 41 days later, Chrysler emerged from bankruptcy as a Fiat-run, employee-owned,* and government-financed corporation.

Many potential bankruptcy costs were avoided because of the speed with which Chrysler transited the bankruptcy process following the prepack agreement. Yet, getting the debt holders to agree required additional government capital commitments and unprecedented political pressure. In many cases, the senior debt holders were banks that were already receiving TARP aid. Perhaps as a cost of receiving this aid, they accepted a deal that put the claims of unsecured creditors such as the United Auto Workers ahead of their more senior claims.** So, while some creditors may have been harmed, there is no doubt that the unprecedented cooperation among investors, and more importantly, government intervention, avoided a long and costly bankruptcy.

*The Chrysler employee pension plan owned 55% of Chrysler, Fiat 20%, the U.S. Treasury 8%, and the Canadian government 2%. The rest of the equity was split amongst the remaining debt claimants.

**Not all creditors bowed willingly to the government pressure. A group of pension funds opposed the prepack. In the end the Supreme Court sided with the company and refused to hear their appeal. Perhaps not surprisingly, as a result of this intervention, other unionized firms with large pensions saw their borrowing costs increase as creditors anticipated the possibility of similar resolutions. (See B. Blaylock, A. Edwards, and J. Stanfield, "The Role of Government in the Labor-Creditor Relationship: Evidence from the Chrysler Bankruptcy," *Journal of Financial and Quantitative Analysis* 50 (2015): 325–348.

Overall Impact of Indirect Costs. In total, the indirect costs of financial distress can be substantial. When estimating them, however, we must remember two important points. First, we need to identify losses to total firm value (and not solely losses to equity holders or debt holders, or transfers between them). Second, we need to identify the incremental losses that are associated with financial distress, above and beyond any losses that would occur due to the firm's economic distress. A study of highly levered firms by Gregor Andrade and Steven Kaplan estimated a potential loss due to financial distress of 10% to 20% of firm value.[17] Next, we consider the consequences of these potential costs of leverage for firm value.

CONCEPT CHECK

1. If a firm files for bankruptcy under Chapter 11 of the bankruptcy code, which party gets the first opportunity to propose a plan for the firm's reorganization?
2. Why are the losses of debt holders whose claims are not fully repaid not a cost of financial distress, whereas the loss of customers who fear the firm will stop honoring warranties is?

[17]"How Costly Is Financial (Not Economic) Distress? Evidence from Highly Leveraged Transactions That Became Distressed," *Journal of Finance* 53 (1998): 1443–1493.

16.3 Financial Distress Costs and Firm Value

The costs of financial distress described in the previous section represent an important departure from Modigliani and Miller's assumption of perfect capital markets. MM assumed that the cash flows of a firm's assets do not depend on its choice of capital structure. As we have discussed, however, levered firms risk incurring financial distress costs that reduce the cash flows available to investors.

Armin Industries: The Impact of Financial Distress Costs

To illustrate how these financial distress costs affect firm value, consider again the example of Armin Industries. With all-equity financing, Armin's assets will be worth \$150 million if its new product succeeds and \$80 million if the new product fails. In contrast, with debt of \$100 million, Armin will be forced into bankruptcy if the new product fails. In this case, some of the value of Armin's assets will be lost to bankruptcy and financial distress costs. As a result, debt holders will receive less than \$80 million. We show the impact of these costs in Table 16.2, where we assume debt holders receive only \$60 million after accounting for the costs of financial distress.

As Table 16.2 shows, the total value to all investors is now less with leverage than it is without leverage when the new product fails. The difference of \$80 million − \$60 million = \$20 million is due to financial distress costs. These costs will lower the total value of the firm with leverage, and MM's Proposition I will no longer hold, as illustrated in Example 16.2.

EXAMPLE 16.2 **Firm Value When Financial Distress Is Costly**

Problem

Compare the current value of Armin Industries with and without leverage, given the data in Table 16.2. Assume that the risk-free rate is 5%, the new product is equally likely to succeed or fail, and the risk is diversifiable.

Solution

With and without leverage, the payments to equity holders are the same as in Example 16.1. There we computed the value of unlevered equity as \$109.52 million and the value of levered equity as \$23.81 million. But due to bankruptcy costs, the value of the debt is now

$$\text{Debt} = \frac{\frac{1}{2}(100) + \frac{1}{2}(60)}{1.05} = \$76.19 \text{ million}$$

The value of the levered firm is $V^L = E + D = 23.81 + 76.19 = \$100$ million, which is less than the value of the unlevered firm, $V^U = \$109.52$ million. Thus, due to bankruptcy costs, the value of the levered firm is \$9.52 million less than its value without leverage. This loss equals the present value of the \$20 million in financial distress costs the firm will pay if the product fails:

$$PV(\text{Financial Distress Costs}) = \frac{\frac{1}{2}(0) + \frac{1}{2}(20)}{1.05} = \$9.52 \text{ million}$$

Who Pays for Financial Distress Costs?

The financial distress costs in Table 16.2 reduce the payments to the debt holders when the new product has failed. In that case, the equity holders have already lost their investment and have no further interest in the firm. It might seem as though these costs are irrelevant

TABLE 16.2 **Value of Debt and Equity with and without Leverage (in $ million)**

	Without Leverage		With Leverage	
	Success	Failure	Success	Failure
Debt value	—	—	100	60
Equity value	150	80	50	0
Total to all investors	150	80	150	60

from the shareholders' perspective. Why should equity holders care about costs borne by debt holders?

It is true that after a firm is in bankruptcy, equity holders care little about bankruptcy costs. But debt holders are not foolish—they recognize that when the firm defaults, they will not be able to get the full value of the assets. As a result, they will pay less for the debt initially. How much less? Precisely the amount they will ultimately give up—the present value of the bankruptcy costs.

But if the debt holders pay less for the debt, there is less money available for the firm to pay dividends, repurchase shares, and make investments. That is, this difference is money out of the equity holders' pockets. This logic leads to the following general result:

When securities are fairly priced, the original shareholders of a firm pay the present value of the costs associated with bankruptcy and financial distress.

EXAMPLE 16.3 **Financial Distress Costs and the Stock Price**

Problem

Suppose that at the beginning of the year, Armin Industries has 10 million shares outstanding and no debt. Armin then announces plans to issue one-year debt with a face value of $100 million and to use the proceeds to repurchase shares. Given the data in Table 16.2, what will the new share price be? As in the previous examples, assume the risk-free rate is 5%, the new product is equally likely to succeed or fail, and this risk is diversifiable.

Solution

From Example 16.1, the value of the firm without leverage is $109.52 million. With 10 million shares outstanding, this value corresponds to an initial share price of $10.952 per share. In Example 16.2, we saw that with leverage, the total value of the firm is only $100 million. In anticipation of this decline in value, the price of the stock should fall to $100 million ÷ 10 million shares = $10.00 per share on announcement of the recapitalization.

Let's check this result. From Example 16.2, due to bankruptcy costs, the new debt is worth $76.19 million. Thus, at a price of $10 per share, Armin will repurchase 7.619 million shares, leaving 2.381 million shares outstanding. In Example 16.1, we computed the value of levered equity as $23.81 million. Dividing by the number of shares gives a share price after the transaction of

$$\$23.81 \text{ million} \div 2.381 \text{ million shares} = \$10.00 \text{ per share}$$

Thus, the recapitalization will cost shareholders $0.952 per share or $9.52 million in total. This cost matches the present value of financial distress costs computed in Example 16.2. Thus, although debt holders bear these costs in the end, shareholders pay the present value of the costs of financial distress upfront.

CONCEPT CHECK

1. Armin incurred financial distress costs only in the event that the new product failed. Why might Armin incur financial distress costs even before the success or failure of the new product is known?
2. True or False: If bankruptcy costs are only incurred once the firm is in bankruptcy and its equity is worthless, then these costs will not affect the initial value of the firm.

16.4 Optimal Capital Structure: The Trade-Off Theory

We can now combine our knowledge of the benefits of leverage from the interest tax shield (discussed in Chapter 15) with the costs of financial distress to determine the amount of debt that a firm should issue to maximize its value. The analysis presented in this section is called the **trade-off theory** because it weighs the benefits of debt that result from shielding cash flows from taxes against the costs of financial distress associated with leverage.

According to this theory, *the total value of a levered firm equals the value of the firm without leverage plus the present value of the tax savings from debt, less the present value of financial distress costs:*

$$V^L = V^U + PV(\text{Interest Tax Shield}) - PV(\text{Financial Distress Costs}) \qquad (16.1)$$

Equation 16.1 shows that leverage has costs as well as benefits. Firms have an incentive to increase leverage to exploit the tax benefits of debt. But with too much debt, they are more likely to risk default and incur financial distress costs.

The Present Value of Financial Distress Costs

Aside from simple examples, calculating the precise present value of financial distress costs is quite complicated. Three key factors determine the present value of financial distress costs: (1) the probability of financial distress, (2) the magnitude of the costs if the firm is in distress, and (3) the appropriate discount rate for the distress costs. In Example 16.2, when Armin is levered, the present value of its financial distress costs depends on the probability that the new product will fail (50%), the magnitude of the costs if it does fail ($20 million), and the discount rate (5%).

What determines each of these factors? The probability of financial distress depends on the likelihood that a firm will be unable to meet its debt commitments and therefore default. This probability increases with the amount of a firm's liabilities (relative to its assets). It also increases with the volatility of a firm's cash flows and asset values. Thus, firms with steady, reliable cash flows, such as utility companies, are able to use high levels of debt and still have a very low probability of default. Firms whose value and cash flows are very volatile (for example, semiconductor firms) must have much lower levels of debt to avoid a significant risk of default.

The magnitude of the financial distress costs will depend on the relative importance of the costs discussed in Section 16.2, and is also likely to vary by industry. For example, firms, such as technology firms, whose value comes largely from human capital, are likely to incur high costs when they risk financial distress, due to the potential for loss of customers and the need to hire and retain key personnel, as well as a lack of tangible assets that can be easily liquidated. In contrast, firms whose main assets are physical capital, such as real estate firms, are likely to have lower costs of financial distress, because a greater portion of their value derives from assets that can be sold relatively easily.

Finally, the discount rate for the distress costs will depend on the firm's market risk. Note that because distress costs are high when the firm does poorly, the beta of distress costs will have an opposite sign to that of the firm.[18] Also, the higher the firm's beta, the more likely it will be in distress in an economic downturn, and thus the more negative the beta of its distress costs will be. Because a more negative beta leads to a lower cost of capital (below the risk-free rate), other things equal *the present value of distress costs will be higher for high beta firms.*

Optimal Leverage

Figure 16.1 shows how the value of a levered firm, V^L, varies with the level of permanent debt, D, according to Eq. 16.1. With no debt, the value of the firm is V^U. For low levels of debt, the risk of default remains low and the main effect of an increase in leverage is an increase in the interest tax shield, which has present value τ^*D, where τ^* is the effective tax advantage of debt calculated in Chapter 15. If there were no costs of financial distress, the value would continue to increase at this rate until the interest on the debt exceeds the firm's earnings before interest and taxes and the tax shield is exhausted.

The costs of financial distress reduce the value of the levered firm, V^L. The amount of the reduction increases with the probability of default, which in turn increases with the level of the debt D. The trade-off theory states that firms should increase their leverage until it reaches the level D^* for which V^L is maximized. At this point, the tax savings that result from increasing leverage are just offset by the increased probability of incurring the costs of financial distress.

FIGURE 16.1

Optimal Leverage with Taxes and Financial Distress Costs

As the level of debt, D, increases, the tax benefits of debt increase by τ^*D until the interest expense exceeds the firm's EBIT (see Figure 15.8). The probability of default, and hence the present value of financial distress costs, also increase with D. The optimal level of debt, D^*, occurs when these effects balance out and V^L is maximized. D^* will be lower for firms with higher costs of financial distress.

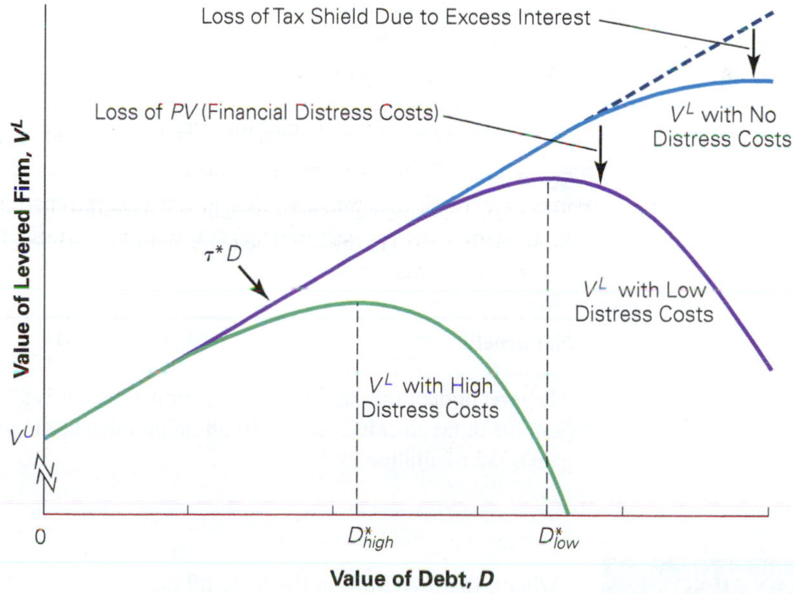

[18] For intuition, consider a law firm specializing in bankruptcy. Because profits will be higher in downturns, the law firm will have negative beta. Formally, the beta of distress costs is similar to the beta of a put option on the firm, which we calculate in Chapter 21 (see Figure 21.8). See also H. Almeida and T. Philippon, "The Risk-Adjusted Cost of Financial Distress," *Journal of Finance* 62 (2007): 2557–2586.

Figure 16.1 also illustrates the optimal debt choices for two types of firms. The optimal debt choice for a firm with low costs of financial distress is indicated by D^*_{low}, and the optimal debt choice for a firm with high costs of financial distress is indicated by D^*_{high}. Not surprisingly, with higher costs of financial distress, it is optimal for the firm to choose lower leverage.

The trade-off theory helps to resolve two puzzles regarding leverage that arose in Chapter 15. First, the presence of financial distress costs can explain why firms choose debt levels that are too low to fully exploit the interest tax shield. Second, differences in the magnitude of financial distress costs and the volatility of cash flows can explain the differences in the use of leverage across industries. That said, bankruptcy costs alone may not be sufficient to explain all of the variation observed. Fortunately, the trade-off theory can be easily extended to include other effects of leverage—which may be even more important than financial distress costs—that we discuss next.

EXAMPLE 16.4 Choosing an Optimal Debt Level

Problem

Greenleaf Industries is considering adding leverage to its capital structure. Greenleaf's managers believe they can add as much as $35 million in debt and exploit the benefits of the tax shield (for which they estimate $\tau^* = 15\%$). However, they also recognize that higher debt increases the risk of financial distress. Based on simulations of the firm's future cash flows, the CFO has made the following estimates (in millions of dollars):[19]

Debt	0	10	20	25	30	35
PV(Interest tax shield)	0.00	1.50	3.00	3.75	4.50	5.25
PV(Financial distress costs)	0.00	0.00	0.38	1.62	4.00	6.38

What is the optimal debt choice for Greenleaf?

Solution

From Eq. 16.1, the net benefit of debt is determined by subtracting *PV*(Financial distress costs) from *PV*(Interest tax shield). The net benefit for each level of debt is

Debt	0	10	20	25	30	35
Net benefit	0.00	1.50	2.62	2.13	0.50	−1.13

The level of debt that leads to the highest net benefit is $20 million. Greenleaf will gain $3 million due to tax shields, and lose $0.38 million due to the present value of distress costs, for a net gain of $2.62 million.

CONCEPT CHECK

1. What is the "trade-off" in the trade-off theory?
2. According to the trade-off theory, all else being equal, which type of firm has a higher optimal level of debt: a firm with very volatile cash flows or a firm with very safe, predictable cash flows?

---

[19]The *PV* of the interest tax shield is computed as $\tau^* D$. The *PV* of financial distress costs is generally difficult to estimate and requires option valuation techniques we introduce in Part 7.

16.5 Exploiting Debt Holders: The Agency Costs of Leverage

In this section, we consider another way that capital structure can affect a firm's cash flows: It can alter managers' incentives and change their investment decisions. If these changes have a negative NPV, they will be costly for the firm.

The type of costs we describe in this section are examples of **agency costs**—costs that arise when there are conflicts of interest between stakeholders. Because top managers often hold shares in the firm and are hired and retained with the approval of the board of directors, which itself is elected by shareholders, managers will generally make decisions that increase the value of the firm's equity. When a firm has leverage, a conflict of interest exists if investment decisions have different consequences for the value of equity and the value of debt. Such a conflict is most likely to occur when the risk of financial distress is high. In some circumstances, managers may take actions that benefit shareholders but harm the firm's creditors and lower the total value of the firm.

We illustrate this possibility by considering Baxter Inc., a firm that is facing financial distress. Baxter has a loan of $1 million due at the end of the year. Without a change in its strategy, the market value of its assets will be only $900,000 at that time, and Baxter will default on its debt. In this situation, let's consider several types of agency costs that might arise.

Excessive Risk-Taking and Asset Substitution

Baxter executives are considering a new strategy that seemed promising initially but appears risky after closer analysis. The new strategy requires no upfront investment, but it has only a 50% chance of success. If it succeeds, it will increase the value of the firm's assets to $1.3 million. If it fails, the value of the firm's assets will fall to $300,000. Therefore, the expected value of the firm's assets under the new strategy is 50% × $1.3 million + 50% × $300,000 = $800,000, a decline of $100,000 from their value of $900,000 under the old strategy. Despite the negative expected payoff, some within the firm have suggested that Baxter should go ahead with the new strategy, in the interest of better serving its shareholders. How can shareholders benefit from this decision?

As Table 16.3 shows, if Baxter does nothing, it will ultimately default and equity holders will get nothing with certainty. Thus, equity holders have nothing to lose if Baxter tries the risky strategy. If the strategy succeeds, equity holders will receive $300,000 after paying off the debt. Given a 50% chance of success, the equity holders' expected payoff is $150,000.

Clearly, equity holders gain from this strategy, even though it has a negative expected payoff. Who loses? The debt holders: If the strategy fails, they bear the loss. As shown in Table 16.3, if the project succeeds, debt holders are fully repaid and receive $1 million. If the project fails, they receive only $300,000. Overall, the debt holders' expected payoff is

TABLE 16.3 Outcomes for Baxter's Debt and Equity under Each Strategy (in $ thousand)

		New Risky Strategy		
	Old Strategy	Success	Failure	Expected
Value of assets	900	1300	300	800
Debt	900	1000	300	650
Equity	0	300	0	150

$650,000, a loss of $250,000 relative to the $900,000 they would have received under the old strategy. This loss corresponds to the $100,000 expected loss of the risky strategy and the $150,000 gain of the equity holders. Effectively, the equity holders are gambling with the debt holders' money.

This example illustrates a general point: *When a firm faces financial distress, shareholders can gain from decisions that increase the risk of the firm sufficiently, even if they have a negative NPV.* Because leverage gives shareholders an incentive to replace low-risk assets with riskier ones, this result is often referred to as the **asset substitution problem.**[20] It can also lead to over-investment, as shareholders may gain if the firm undertakes negative-NPV, but sufficiently risky, projects.

In either case, if the firm increases risk through a negative-NPV decision or investment, the total value of the firm will be reduced. Anticipating this bad behavior, security holders will pay less for the firm initially. This cost is likely to be highest for firms that can easily increase the risk of their investments.

Debt Overhang and Under-Investment

Suppose Baxter does not pursue the risky strategy. Instead, the firm's managers consider an attractive investment opportunity that requires an initial investment of $100,000 and will generate a risk-free return of 50%. That is, it has the following cash flows (in thousands of dollars):

0	1
−100	150

If the current risk-free rate is 5%, this investment clearly has a positive NPV. The only problem is that Baxter does not have the cash on hand to make the investment.

Could Baxter raise the $100,000 by issuing new equity? Unfortunately, it cannot. Suppose equity holders were to contribute the $100,000 in new capital required. Their payoff at the end of the year is shown in Table 16.4.

Thus, if equity holders contribute $100,000 to fund the project, they get back only $50,000. The other $100,000 from the project goes to the debt holders, whose payoff increases from $900,000 to $1 million. Because the debt holders receive most of the benefit, this project is a negative-NPV investment opportunity for equity holders, even though it offers a positive NPV for the firm.

This example illustrates another general point: *When a firm faces financial distress, it may choose not to finance new, positive-NPV projects.* In this case, when shareholders prefer not to

TABLE 16.4 Outcomes for Baxter's Debt and Equity with and without the New Project (in $ thousand)

	Without New Project	With New Project
Existing assets	900	900
New project		150
Total firm value	900	1050
Debt	900	1000
Equity	0	50

[20]See M. Jensen and W. Meckling, "Theory of the Firm: Managerial Behavior, Agency Costs and Ownership Structure," *Journal of Financial Economics* 3 (1976): 305–360.

GLOBAL FINANCIAL CRISIS **Bailouts, Distress Costs, and Debt Overhang**

Firms and financial institutions in or near financial distress in the midst of the 2008 financial crisis experienced many of the costs associated with financial distress that we have described, creating further negative consequences for the real economy.

Of particular concern was the seeming unwillingness of banks to make loans to borrowers at reasonable terms. One possible explanation was that the borrowers were not creditworthy and so lending to them was a negative NPV investment. But many, including the banks themselves, pointed to another culprit: banks were subject to debt overhang that made it extremely difficult to raise the capital needed to make positive-NPV loans. Thus, a primary rationale for governmental bailouts during the crisis was to provide banks with capital directly, alleviating their debt overhang and increasing the availability of credit to the rest of the economy.

invest in a positive-NPV project, we say there is a **debt overhang** or **under-investment problem.**[21] This failure to invest is costly for debt holders and for the overall value of the firm, because it is giving up the NPV of the missed opportunities. The cost is highest for firms that are likely to have profitable future growth opportunities requiring large investments.

Cashing Out. When a firm faces financial distress, shareholders have an incentive to withdraw cash from the firm if possible. As an example, suppose Baxter has equipment it can sell for \$25,000 at the beginning of the year. It will need this equipment to continue normal operations during the year; without it, Baxter will have to shut down some operations and the firm will be worth only \$800,000 at year-end. Although selling the equipment reduces the value of the firm by \$100,000, if it is likely that Baxter will default at year-end, this cost would be borne by the debt holders. So, equity holders gain if Baxter sells the equipment and uses the \$25,000 to pay an immediate cash dividend. This incentive to liquidate assets at prices below their actual value to the firm is an extreme form of under-investment resulting from the debt overhang.

Estimating the Debt Overhang. How much leverage must a firm have for there to be a significant debt overhang problem? While difficult to estimate precisely, we can use a useful approximation. Suppose equity holders invest an amount I in a new investment project with similar risk to the rest of the firm. Let D and E be the market value of the firm's debt and equity, and let β_D and β_E be their respective betas. Then the following approximate rule applies: equity holders will benefit from the new investment only if[22]

$$\frac{NPV}{I} > \frac{\beta_D D}{\beta_E E} \tag{16.2}$$

[21]This agency cost of debt was formalized by S. Myers, "Determinants of Corporate Borrowing," *Journal of Financial Economics* 5 (1977): 147–175.

[22]To understand this result, let dE and dD be the change in the value of equity and debt resulting from an investment with total value $dE + dD = I + NPV$. Equity holders benefit if they gain more than they invest, $I < dE$, which is equivalent to debt holders capturing less than the investment's NPV, $NPV > dD$. Dividing the second inequality by the first, we have $NPV/I > dD/dE$. Eq. 16.2 follows from the approximation $dD/dE \approx \beta_D D/\beta_E E$; that is, the relative sensitivity of debt and equity to changes in asset values are similar whether those changes arise from investment decisions or market conditions. We derive this approximation in Chapter 21.

That is, the project's profitability index (NPV/I) must exceed a cutoff equal to the relative riskiness of the firm's debt (β_D/β_E) times its debt-equity ratio (D/E). Note that if the firm has no debt ($D = 0$) or its debt is risk free ($\beta_D = 0$), then Eq. 16.2 is equivalent to $NPV > 0$. But if the firm's debt is risky, the required cutoff is positive and increases with the firm's leverage. Equity holders will reject positive-NPV projects with profitability indices below the cutoff, leading to under-investment and reduction in firm value.

EXAMPLE 16.5 **Estimating the Debt Overhang**

Problem

In Example 12.7, we estimated that Sears had an equity beta of 1.36, a debt beta of 0.17, and a debt-equity ratio of 0.30, while Saks had an equity beta of 1.85, a debt beta of 0.31, and a debt-equity ratio of 1.0. For both firms, estimate the minimum NPV such that a new $100,000 investment (which does not change the volatility of the firm) will benefit shareholders. Which firm has the more severe debt overhang?

Solution

We can use Eq. 16.2 to estimate the cutoff level of the profitability index for Sears as $(0.17/1.36) \times 0.30 = 0.0375$. Thus, the NPV would need to equal at least $3750 for the investment to benefit shareholders. For Saks, the cutoff is $(0.31/1.85) \times 1.0 = 0.1675$. Thus, the minimum NPV for Saks is $16,750. Saks has the more severe debt overhang, as its shareholders will reject projects with positive NPVs up to this higher cutoff. Similarly, Saks shareholders would benefit if the firm "cashed out" by liquidating up to $116,750 worth of assets to pay out an additional $100,000 in dividends.

Agency Costs and the Value of Leverage

These examples illustrate how leverage can encourage managers and shareholders to act in ways that reduce firm value. In each case, the equity holders benefit at the expense of the debt holders. But, as with financial distress costs, it is the shareholders of the firm who ultimately bear these agency costs. Although equity holders may benefit at debt holders' expense from these negative-NPV decisions in times of distress, debt holders recognize this possibility and pay less for the debt when it is first issued, reducing the amount the firm can distribute to shareholders. The net effect is a reduction in the initial share price of the firm corresponding to the negative NPV of the decisions.

These agency costs of debt can arise only if there is some chance the firm will default and impose losses on its debt holders. The magnitude of the agency costs increases with the risk, and therefore the amount, of the firm's debt. Agency costs, therefore, represent another cost of increasing the firm's leverage that will affect the firm's optimal capital structure choice.

EXAMPLE 16.6 **Agency Costs and the Amount of Leverage**

Problem

Would the agency costs described previously arise if Baxter had less leverage and owed $400,000 rather than $1 million?

Solution

If Baxter makes no new investments or changes to its strategy, the firm will be worth $900,000. Thus, the firm will remain solvent and its equity will be worth $900,000 − $400,000 = $500,000.

Consider first the decision to increase risk. If Baxter takes the risky strategy, its assets will be worth either \$1.3 million or \$300,000, so equity holders will receive \$900,000 or \$0. In this case, the equity holders' expected payoff with the risky project is only $\$900{,}000 \times 0.5 = \$450{,}000$. Thus equity holders will reject the risky strategy.

What about under-investment? If Baxter raises \$100,000 from equity holders to fund a new investment that increases the value of assets by \$150,000, the equity will be worth

$$\$900{,}000 + \$150{,}000 - \$400{,}000 = \$650{,}000$$

This is a gain of \$150,000 over the \$500,000 equity holders would receive without the investment. Because their payoff has gone up by \$150,000 for a \$100,000 investment, they will be willing to invest in the new project.

Similarly, Baxter has no incentive to cash out and sell equipment to pay a dividend. If the firm pays the dividend, equity holders receive \$25,000 today. But their future payoff declines to $\$800{,}000 - \$400{,}000 = \$400{,}000$. Thus, they give up \$100,000 in one year for a \$25,000 gain today. For any reasonable discount rate, this is a bad deal and stockholders will reject the dividend.

The Leverage Ratchet Effect

As we have seen, when an unlevered firm issues new debt, equity holders will bear any anticipated agency or bankruptcy costs via a discount in the price they receive for that new debt. This discount deters the firm from taking on high leverage initially if doing so would reduce the value of the firm.

But once a firm has debt already in place, some of the agency or bankruptcy costs that result from taking on additional leverage will fall on *existing* debt holders. Because that debt has already been sold, the negative consequences for these debt holders will not be borne by shareholders. As a result, shareholders may benefit from taking on higher leverage even though it might reduce the total value of the firm. (This result is another manifestation of the "cashing out" effect of debt overhang—levered firms may have an incentive to borrow further and disburse the proceeds to shareholders.)

In addition, debt overhang will inhibit firms from reducing leverage once it is in place. For if the firm tries to buy back debt, existing debt holders will gain (and debt holders who sell will demand a premium) due to the reduction in risk, agency costs, and bankruptcy costs associated with lower leverage. Thus, debt buybacks benefit the firm's creditors at shareholders' expense.

The **leverage ratchet effect** captures these observations: Once existing debt is in place, (1) shareholders may have an incentive to increase leverage even if it decreases the value of the firm,[23] and (2) shareholders will not have an incentive to decrease leverage by buying back debt, even if it will increase the value of the firm.[24] The leverage ratchet effect is an important additional agency cost of leverage which affects the firm's future financing decisions (rather than its investment decisions). While it will induce firms to borrow less initially in order to avoid these costs, over time it may lead to excessive leverage as shareholders prefer to increase, but not decrease, the firm's debt.

[23]For an analysis of this effect and its consequence on loan markets, see D. Bizer and P. DeMarzo, "Sequential Banking," *Journal of Political Economy* 100 (1992): 41–61.

[24]This result holds quite generally as long as the debt must be repurchased at its ex-post fair value; see A. Admati, P. DeMarzo, M. Hellwig, and P. Pfleiderer, "The Leverage Ratchet Effect," papers.ssrn.com/sol3/papers.cfm?abstract_id=2304969.

EXAMPLE 16.7 Debt Overhang and the Leverage Ratchet Effect

Problem

Show that Baxter's shareholders would not gain by reducing leverage from \$1 million to \$400,000, even though firm value would increase by eliminating the cost of underinvestment.

Solution

Recall that with \$1 million in debt, Baxter would choose to forego an investment in a positive NPV risk-free project (see Table 16.4). Thus, its equity would be worth zero, and its debt would be worth \$900,000. Also, as shown in Example 16.6, if the debt level were \$400,000 instead of \$1 million, the problem would not exist–equity holders would choose to take the positive NPV investment and firm value would increase by the NPV of the project.

Even so, equity holders will not choose to reduce debt. Because the debt will be default-free after the buyback, and given the risk-free rate of 5%, each debt holder must be repaid at least $\$1/1.05 = \$0.952$ per dollar of principal, or would otherwise prefer to hold onto their debt while others sell. Therefore, to reduce its debt to \$400,000, Baxter would need to raise $\$600{,}000/1.05 = \$571{,}429$ from equity holders. Baxter could then raise another \$100,000 from equity holders to invest in the new project. In the end, the value of the firm would be \$1.05 million, and after paying \$400,000 in debt, equity holders would receive \$650,000. But this amount is less than the total of \$671,429 equity holders would need to invest upfront.

The reason equity holders do not gain by reducing debt in Example 16.7 is that in order to buy back the debt, the company must pay its post-transaction market value, which includes the value of the anticipated investment. A similar outcome would apply to the case of excessive risk-taking. By reducing debt, equity holders lose their incentive to take on a risky negative NPV investment. While this effect increases the value of the firm, equity holders would not gain as they would be forced to pay a price for the debt that reflects the value of eliminating the incentives for excessive risk-taking.

Debt Maturity and Covenants

Firms can do several things to mitigate the agency costs of debt. First, note that the magnitude of agency costs likely depends on the maturity of debt. With long-term debt, equity holders have more opportunities to profit at the debt holders' expense before the debt

Why Do Firms Go Bankrupt?

If the costs of excessive leverage are substantial, one might wonder why firms ever default. After all, firms could choose high leverage when they are very profitable and will benefit from the interest tax shield, and then avoid bankruptcy when profits fall by issuing equity to reduce leverage. By doing so firms would avoid the agency, distress and default costs we have described in this chapter—thus preserving the benefits of debt while avoiding its potential costs.

In reality it is rare to see firms behave in this way. Instead, when profits fall, leverage usually increases, often substantially (mainly due to the decrease in the value of equity). Why don't firm's issue new equity to offset this?

The leverage ratchet effect helps to explain this behavior. Lowering leverage by issuing new equity and using the proceeds to retire debt in distressed states would raise the value of the firm because it lowers the probability of incurring bankruptcy costs. But equity holders do not get this value—the bankruptcy cost savings accrue to bondholders, not equity holders. So, if the firm pays off existing debt using cash raised by issuing new equity, or by reducing dividends or share repurchases, its share price will actually decline because equity holders must pay the cost of the leverage reduction while bondholders reap the benefits. Equity holders will therefore not choose such a strategy.

matures. Thus, agency costs are smallest for short-term debt.[25] For example, if Baxter's debt were due today, the firm would be forced to default or renegotiate with debt holders before it could increase risk, fail to invest, or cash out. However, by relying on short-term debt the firm will be obligated to repay or refinance its debt more frequently. Short-term debt may also increase the firm's risk of financial distress and its associated costs.

Second, as a condition of making a loan, creditors often place restrictions on the actions that the firm can take. Such restrictions are referred to as **debt covenants**. Covenants may limit the firm's ability to pay large dividends or restrict the types of investments that the firm can make. They also typically limit the amount of new debt the firm can take on. By preventing management from exploiting debt holders, these covenants may help to reduce agency costs. Conversely, because covenants hinder management flexibility, they have the potential to get in the way of positive NPV opportunities and so can have costs of their own.[26]

CONCEPT CHECK

1. Why do firms have an incentive to both take excessive risk and under-invest when they are in financial distress?
2. Why would debt holders desire covenants that restrict the firm's ability to pay dividends, and why might shareholders also benefit from this restriction?

16.6 Motivating Managers: The Agency Benefits of Leverage

In Section 16.5, we took the view that managers act in the interests of the firm's equity holders, and we considered the potential conflicts of interest between debt holders and equity holders when a firm has leverage. Of course, managers also have their own personal interests, which may differ from those of both equity holders and debt holders. Although managers often do own shares of the firm, in most large corporations they own only a very small fraction of the outstanding shares. And while the shareholders, through the board of directors, have the power to fire managers, they rarely do so unless the firm's performance is exceptionally poor.[27]

This separation of ownership and control creates the possibility of **management entrenchment**: facing little threat of being fired and replaced, managers are free to run the firm in their own best interests. As a result, managers may make decisions that benefit themselves at investors' expense. In this section, we consider how leverage can provide incentives for managers to run the firm more efficiently and effectively. The benefits we describe in this section, in addition to the tax benefits of leverage, give the firm an incentive to use debt rather than equity financing.

---

[25] See S. Johnson, "Debt Maturity and the Effects of Growth Opportunities and Liquidity on Leverage," *Review of Financial Studies* 16 (March 2003): 209–236.

[26] For an analysis of the costs and benefits of bond covenants, see C. Smith and J. Warner, "On Financial Contracting: An Analysis of Bond Covenants," *Journal of Financial Economics* 7 (1979): 117–161.

[27] See, for example, J. Warner, R. Watts, and K. Wruck, "Stock Prices and Top Management Changes," *Journal of Financial Economics* 20 (1988): 461–492, though more recent evidence suggests that management turnover may be more sensitive to poor performance than previously measured (see D. Jenter and K. Lewellen, "Performance-induced CEO Turnover," working paper, 2012).

Concentration of Ownership

One advantage of using leverage is that it allows the original owners of the firm to maintain their equity stake. As major shareholders, they will have a strong interest in doing what is best for the firm. Consider the following simple example:

Ross Jackson is the owner of a successful furniture store. He plans to expand by opening several new stores. Ross can either borrow the funds needed for expansion or raise the money by selling shares in the firm. If he issues equity, he will need to sell 40% of the firm to raise the necessary funds.

If Ross uses debt, he retains ownership of 100% of the firm's equity. As long as the firm does not default, any decision Ross makes that increases the value of the firm by $1 increases the value of his own stake by $1. But if Ross issues equity, he retains only 60% of the equity. Thus, Ross gains only $0.60 for every $1 increase in firm value.

The difference in Ross' ownership stake changes his incentives in running the firm. Suppose the value of the firm depends largely on Ross' personal effort. Ross is then likely to work harder, and the firm will be worth more, if he receives 100% of the gains rather than only 60%.

Another effect of issuing equity is Ross' temptation to enjoy corporate perks, such as a large office with fancy artwork, a corporate limo and driver, a corporate jet, or a large expense account. With leverage, Ross is the sole owner and will bear the full cost of these perks. But with equity, Ross bears only 60% of the cost; the other 40% will be paid for by the new equity holders. Thus, with equity financing, it is more likely that Ross will overspend on these luxuries.

The costs of reduced effort and excessive spending on perks are another form of agency cost. These agency costs arise in this case due to the dilution of ownership that occurs when equity financing is used. Who pays these agency costs? As always, if securities are fairly priced, the original owners of the firm pay the cost. In our example, Ross will find that if he chooses to issue equity, the new investors will discount the price they will pay to reflect Ross' lower effort and increased spending on perks. In this case, using leverage can benefit the firm by preserving ownership concentration and avoiding these agency costs.[28]

Reduction of Wasteful Investment

While ownership is often concentrated for small, young firms, ownership typically becomes diluted over time as a firm grows. First, the original owners of the firm may retire, and the new managers likely will not hold a large ownership stake. Second, firms often need to raise more capital for investment than can be sustained using debt alone (recall the discussion of growth and leverage in Chapter 15). Third, owners will often choose to sell off their stakes and invest in a well-diversified portfolio to reduce risk.[29] As a result, for large U.S. firms, most CEOs own less than 1% of their firms' shares.

With such low ownership stakes, the potential for conflict of interest between managers and equity holders is high. Appropriate monitoring and standards of accountability

---

[28]This potential benefit of leverage is discussed by M. Jensen and W. Meckling, "Theory of the Firm: Managerial Behavior, Agency Costs and Ownership Structure," *Journal of Financial Economics* 3 (1976): 305–360. However, because managers who own a large block of shares are more difficult to replace, increasing ownership concentration at lower levels (e.g., in the 5%–25% range) may increase entrenchment and *reduce* incentives; see R. Morck, A. Shleifer, and R. Vishny, "Management Ownership and Market Valuation," *Journal of Financial Economics* 20 (1988): 293–315.

[29]According to one study, original owners tend to reduce their stake by more than 50% within nine years after the firm becomes a public company (B. Urošević, "Essays in Optimal Dynamic Risk Sharing in Equity and Debt Markets," 2002, University of California, Berkeley).

Excessive Perks and Corporate Scandals

While most CEOs and managers exercise proper restraint when spending shareholders' money, there have been some highly publicized exceptions that have come to light as corporate scandals.

Former Enron CFO Andrew Fastow reportedly used complicated financial transactions to enrich himself with at least $30 million of shareholder money. Tyco Corporation's ex-CEO Dennis Kozlowski will be remembered for his $6000 shower curtain, $6300 sewing basket, and $17 million Fifth Avenue condo, all paid for with Tyco funds. In total, he and former CFO Mark Swartz were convicted of pilfering $600 million from company coffers.* Former WorldCom CEO Bernie Ebbers, who was convicted for his role in the firm's $11 billion accounting scandal, borrowed more than $400 million from the company at favorable terms from late 2000 to early 2002. Among other things, he used the money from these loans to give gifts to friends and family, as well as build a house.† John Rigas and his son Timothy, former CEO and CFO of Adelphia Communications, were convicted of stealing $100 million from the firm as well as hiding $2 billion in corporate debt.

But these are exceptional cases. And they were not, in and of themselves, the cause of the firms' downfalls, but rather a symptom of a broader problem of a lack of oversight and accountability within these firms, together with an opportunistic attitude of the managers involved.

*M. Warner, "Exorcism at Tyco," *Fortune*, April 28, 2003.

†A. Backover, "Report Slams Culture at WorldCom," *USA Today*, November 5, 2002.

are required to prevent abuse. While most successful firms have implemented appropriate mechanisms to protect shareholders, each year scandals are revealed in which managers have acted against shareholders' interests.

While overspending on personal perks may be a problem for large firms, these costs are likely to be small relative to the overall value of the firm. A more serious concern for large corporations is that managers may make large, unprofitable investments: Bad investment decisions have destroyed many otherwise successful firms. But what would motivate managers to make negative-NPV investments?

Some financial economists explain a manager's willingness to engage in negative-NPV investments as *empire building*. According to this view, managers prefer to run large firms rather than small ones, so they will take on investments that increase the size—rather than the profitability—of the firm. One potential reason for this preference is that managers of large firms tend to earn higher salaries, and they may also have more prestige and garner greater publicity than managers of small firms. As a result, managers may expand (or fail to shut down) unprofitable divisions, pay too much for acquisitions, make unnecessary capital expenditures, or hire unnecessary employees.

Another reason that managers may over-invest is that they are overconfident. Even when managers attempt to act in shareholders' interests, they may make mistakes. Managers tend to be bullish on the firm's prospects and so may believe that new opportunities are better than they actually are. They may also become committed to investments the firm has already made and continue to invest in projects that should be canceled.[30]

For managers to engage in wasteful investment, they must have the cash to invest. This observation is the basis of the **free cash flow hypothesis**, the view that wasteful spending is more likely to occur when firms have high levels of cash flow in excess of what is needed

[30]For evidence of the relationship between CEO overconfidence and investment distortions, see U. Malmendier and G. Tate, "CEO Overconfidence and Corporate Investment," *Journal of Finance* 60 (2005): 2661–2700; J. Heaton "Managerial Optimism and Corporate Finance," *Financial Management* 31 (2002): 33–45; and R. Roll, "The Hubris Hypothesis of Corporate Takeovers," *Journal of Business* 59 (1986): 197–216.

GLOBAL FINANCIAL CRISIS Moral Hazard, Government Bailouts, and the Appeal of Leverage

The term **moral hazard** refers to the idea that individuals will change their behavior if they are not fully exposed to its consequences. Discussion of moral hazard's role in the 2008 financial crisis has centered on mortgage brokers, investment bankers, and corporate managers who earned large bonuses when their businesses did well, but did not need to repay these bonuses later when things turned sour. The agency costs described in this chapter represent another form of moral hazard, as equity holders may take excessive risk or pay excessive dividends if the negative consequences will be borne by bondholders.

How are such abuses by equity holders normally held in check? Bondholders will either charge equity holders for the risk of this abuse by increasing the cost of debt, or, more likely, equity holders will credibly commit not to take on excessive risk by, for example, agreeing to very strong bond covenants and other monitoring.

Ironically, despite the potential immediate benefits of the federal bailouts in response to the 2008 financial crisis, by protecting the bondholders of many large corporations, the government may have simultaneously weakened this disciplining mechanism and thereby increased the likelihood of future crises. With this precedent in place, all lenders to corporations deemed "too big to fail" may presume they have an implicit government guarantee, thus lowering their incentives to insist on strong covenants and to monitor whether those covenants are being satisfied.* Without this monitoring the likelihood of future abuses by equity holders and managers has likely been increased, as has the government's liability.

Moral hazard might also help to explain why bankers are opposed to higher capital requirements. As we pointed out in Chapter 14, in a perfect market, capital requirements cannot affect the competitiveness of banks. However, because both deposit insurance and government bailouts subsidize bank debt, banks' borrowing costs do not reflect either their risk or the costs associated with default. Thus, higher leverage *both* reduces banks' tax obligations and increases the benefit they receive in bankruptcy from these subsidies, greatly favoring debt in the trade-off between tax subsidies and bankruptcy costs. Because taxpayers ultimately pay for these subsidies, the benefits of leverage to bank shareholders come largely at taxpayer expense.**

*As an example, a number of large banks continued to pay dividends during the crisis even after receiving bailout funds. Had the funds been raised from outside investors without any government guarantee, it is very likely the new investors would have restricted such payouts.

**See A. Admati, P. DeMarzo, M. Hellwig, and P. Pfleiderer, "Fallacies, Irrelevant Facts, and Myths in the Discussion of Capital Regulation: Why Bank Equity Is Not Socially Expensive," papers.ssrn.com/sol3/papers.cfm?abstract_id=2349739.

to make all positive-NPV investments and payments to debt holders.[31] Only when cash is tight will managers be motivated to run the firm as efficiently as possible. According to this hypothesis, leverage increases firm value because it commits the firm to making future interest payments, thereby reducing excess cash flows and wasteful investment by managers.[32]

A related idea is that leverage can reduce the degree of managerial entrenchment because managers are more likely to be fired when a firm faces financial distress. Managers who are less entrenched may be more concerned about their performance and less likely to engage in wasteful investment. In addition, when the firm is highly levered, creditors themselves will closely monitor the actions of managers, providing an additional layer of management oversight.[33]

---

[31]The hypothesis that excess cash flow induces empire building was put forth by M. Jensen, "Agency Costs of Free Cash Flow, Corporate Finance, and Takeovers," *American Economic Review* 76 (1986): 323–329.

[32]Of course, managers could also raise new capital for wasteful investment. But investors would be reluctant to contribute to such an endeavor and would offer unfavorable terms. In addition, raising external funds would attract greater scrutiny and public criticism regarding the investment.

[33]See, for example, M. Harris and A. Raviv, "Capital Structure and the Informational Role of Debt," *Journal of Finance* 45(2) (1990): 321–349.

Leverage and Commitment

Leverage may also tie managers' hands and commit them to pursue strategies with greater vigor than they would without the threat of financial distress. For example, when American Airlines was in labor negotiations with its unions in April 2003, the firm was able to win wage concessions by explaining that higher costs would push it into bankruptcy. (A similar situation enabled Delta Airlines to persuade its pilots to accept a 33% wage cut in November 2004.) Without the threat of financial distress, American's managers might not have reached agreement with the union as quickly or achieved the same wage concessions.[34]

A firm with greater leverage may also become a fiercer competitor and act more aggressively in protecting its markets because it cannot risk the possibility of bankruptcy. This commitment to aggressive behavior can scare off potential rivals. (This argument could work in reverse: A firm weakened by too much leverage might become so financially fragile that it crumbles in the face of competition, allowing other firms to erode its markets.)[35]

CONCEPT CHECK

1. In what ways might managers benefit by overspending on acquisitions?
2. How might shareholders use the firm's capital structure to prevent this problem?

16.7 Agency Costs and the Trade-Off Theory

We can now adjust Eq. 16.1 for the value of the firm to include the costs and benefits of the incentives that arise when the firm has leverage. This more complete equation follows:

$$V^L = V^U + PV(\text{Interest Tax Shield}) - PV(\text{Financial Distress Costs})$$
$$-PV(\text{Agency Costs of Debt}) + PV(\text{Agency Benefits of Debt}) \qquad (16.3)$$

The net effect of the costs and benefits of leverage on the value of a firm is illustrated in Figure 16.2. With no debt, the value of the firm is V^U. As the debt level increases, the firm benefits from the interest tax shield (which has present value $\tau^* D$). The firm also benefits from improved incentives for management, which reduce wasteful investment and perks. If the debt level is too large, however, firm value is reduced due to the loss of tax benefits (when interest exceeds EBIT), financial distress costs, and the agency costs of leverage. The optimal level of debt, D^*, balances the costs and benefits of leverage.

---

[34]See E. Perotti and K. Spier, "Capital Structure as a Bargaining Tool: The Role of Leverage in Contract Renegotiation," *American Economic Review* 83 (1993): 1131–1141. Debt can also affect a firm's bargaining power with its suppliers; see S. Dasgupta and K. Sengupta, "Sunk Investment, Bargaining and Choice of Capital Structure," *International Economic Review* 34 (1993): 203–220; O. Sarig, "The Effect of Leverage on Bargaining with a Corporation," *Financial Review* 33 (1998): 1–16; and C. Hennessy and D. Livdan, "Debt, Bargaining, and Credibility in Firm-Supplier Relationships," *Journal of Financial Economics* 93 (2009): 382–399. Debt may also enhance a target's bargaining power in a control contest; see M. Harris and A. Raviv, "Corporate Control Contests and Capital Structure," *Journal of Financial Economics* 20 (1988): 55–86; and R. Israel, "Capital Structure and the Market for Corporate Control: The Defensive Role of Debt Financing," *Journal of Finance* 46 (1991): 1391–1409.

[35]See J. Brander and T. Lewis, "Oligopoly and Financial Structure: The Limited Liability Effect," *American Economic Review* 76 (1986): 956–970. In an empirical study, J. Chevalier finds that leverage reduces the competitiveness of supermarket firms ("Capital Structure and Product-Market Competition: Empirical Evidence from the Supermarket Industry," *American Economic Review* 85 (1995): 415–435). P. Bolton and D. Scharfstein discuss the effects of not having deep pockets in "A Theory of Predation Based on Agency Problems in Financial Contracting," *American Economic Review* 80 (1990): 93–106.

FIGURE 16.2

Optimal Leverage with Taxes, Financial Distress, and Agency Costs

As the level of debt, D, increases, the value of the firm increases from the interest tax shield as well as improvements in managerial incentives. If leverage is too high, however, the present value of financial distress costs, as well as the agency costs from debt holder–equity holder conflicts, dominates and reduces firm value. The optimal level of debt, D^*, balances these benefits and costs of leverage.

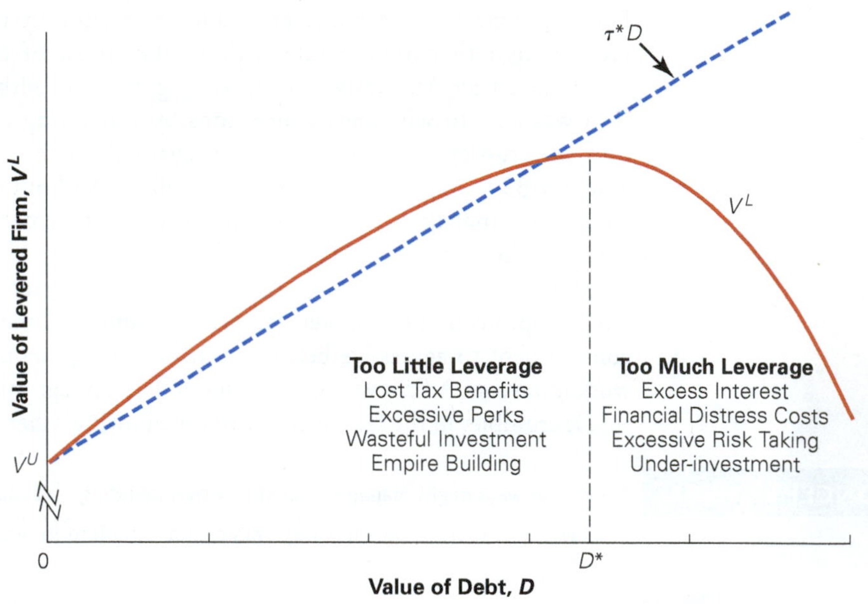

The Optimal Debt Level

It is important to note that the relative magnitudes of the different costs and benefits of debt vary with the characteristics of the firm. Likewise, the optimal level of debt varies. As an example, let's contrast the optimal capital structure choice for two types of firms.[36]

R&D-Intensive Firms. Firms with high R&D costs and future growth opportunities typically maintain low debt levels. These firms tend to have low current free cash flows, so they need little debt to provide a tax shield or to control managerial spending. In addition, they tend to have high human capital, so there will be large costs as a result of financial distress. Also, these firms may find it easy to increase the risk of their business strategy (by pursuing a riskier technology) and often need to raise additional capital to fund new investment opportunities. Thus, their agency costs of debt are also high. Biotechnology and technology firms often maintain less than 10% leverage.

Low-Growth, Mature Firms. Mature, low-growth firms with stable cash flows and tangible assets often fall into the high-debt category. These firms tend to have high free cash flows with few good investment opportunities. Thus, the tax shield and incentive benefits of leverage are likely to be high. With tangible assets, the financial distress costs of leverage are likely to be low, as the assets can be liquidated for close to their full value. Examples of low-growth industries in which firms typically maintain greater than 20% leverage include real estate, utilities, and supermarket chains.

---

[36]For an empirical estimation of the variation in Figure 16.2 across firms and industries, see J. van Binsbergen, J. Graham, and J. Yang, "The Cost of Debt," *Journal of Finance* 65 (2010): 2089–2136; and A. Korteweg, "The Net Benefits to Leverage," *Journal of Finance* 65 (2010): 2137–2170.

Debt Levels in Practice

The trade-off theory explains how firms *should* choose their capital structures to maximize value to current shareholders. Evaluating whether they actually do so is not so straightforward, however, as many of the costs of leverage are hard to measure.

Why might firms *not* choose an optimal capital structure? First, recall from the leverage ratchet effect discussed earlier that if the firm—perhaps due to negative shocks—has debt that exceeds D^*, shareholders will find it costly to reduce leverage because the benefits will accrue to the firm's creditors.

On the other hand, capital structure decisions, like investment decisions, are made by managers who have their own incentives. Proponents of the **management entrenchment theory** of capital structure believe that managers choose a capital structure primarily to avoid the discipline of debt and maintain their own entrenchment. Thus, managers seek to *minimize* leverage to prevent the job loss that would accompany financial distress. Of course, if managers sacrifice too much firm value, disgruntled shareholders may try to replace them or sell the firm to an acquirer. Under this hypothesis, firms will have leverage that is less than the optimal level D^* in Figure 16.2, and increase it toward D^* only in response to a takeover threat or the threat of shareholder activism.[37]

CONCEPT CHECK

1. Coca-Cola Enterprises is almost 50% debt financed, while Intel, a technology firm, has no net debt. Why might these firms choose such different capital structures?
2. Why would a firm with excessive leverage not immediately reduce it?
3. Describe how management entrenchment can affect the value of the firm.

16.8 Asymmetric Information and Capital Structure

Throughout this chapter, we have assumed that managers, stockholders, and creditors have the same information. We have also assumed that securities are fairly priced: The firm's shares and debt are priced according to their true underlying value. These assumptions may not always be accurate in practice. Managers' information about the firm and its future cash flows is likely to be superior to that of outside investors—there is **asymmetric information** between managers and investors. In this section, we consider how asymmetric information may motivate managers to alter a firm's capital structure.

Leverage as a Credible Signal

Consider the plight of Kim Smith, CEO of Beltran International, who believes her company's stock is undervalued. Market analysts and investors are concerned that several of Beltran's key patents will expire soon, and that new competition will force Beltran to cut prices or lose customers. Smith believes that new product innovations and soon-to-be-introduced manufacturing improvements will keep Beltran ahead of its competitors and enable it to sustain its current profitability well into the future. She seeks to convince investors of Beltran's promising future and to increase Beltran's current stock price.

[37] See J. Zwiebel, "Dynamic Capital Structure Under Managerial Entrenchment," *American Economic Review* 86 (1996): 1197–1215; L. Zingales and W. Novaes, "Capital Structure Choice When Managers Are in Control: Entrenchment versus Efficiency," *Journal of Business* 76 (2002): 49–82; and E. Morellec, "Can Managerial Discretion Explain Observed Leverage Ratios?" *Review of Financial Studies* 17 (2004): 257–294.

One potential strategy is to launch an investor relations campaign. Smith can issue press releases, describing the merits of the new innovations and the manufacturing improvements. But Smith knows that investors may be skeptical of these press releases if their claims cannot be verified. After all, managers, much like politicians, have an incentive to sound optimistic and confident about what they can achieve.

Because investors expect her to be biased, to convince the market Smith must take actions that give credible signals of her knowledge of the firm. That is, she must take actions that the market understands she would be unwilling to do unless her statements were true. This idea is more general than manager–investor communication; it is at the heart of much human interaction. We call it the **credibility principle**:

Claims in one's self-interest are credible only if they are supported by actions that would be too costly to take if the claims were untrue.

This principle is the essence behind the adage, "Actions speak louder than words."

One way a firm can credibly convey its strength to investors is by making statements about its future prospects that investors and analysts can ultimately verify. Because the penalties for intentionally deceiving investors are large,[38] investors will generally believe such statements.

For example, suppose Smith announces that pending long-term contracts from the U.S., British, and Japanese governments will increase revenues for Beltran by 30% next year. Because this statement can be verified after the fact, it would be costly to make it if untrue. For deliberate misrepresentation, the U.S. Securities and Exchange Commission (SEC) would likely fine the firm and file charges against Smith. The firm could also be sued by its investors. These large costs would likely outweigh any potential benefits to Smith and Beltran for temporarily misleading investors and boosting the share price. Thus, investors will likely view the announcement as credible.

But what if Beltran cannot yet reveal specific details regarding its future prospects? Perhaps the contracts for the government orders have not yet been signed or cannot be disclosed for other reasons. How can Smith credibly communicate her positive information regarding the firm?

One strategy is to commit the firm to large future debt payments. If Smith is right, then Beltran will have no trouble making the debt payments. But if Smith is making false claims and the firm does not grow, Beltran will have trouble paying its creditors and will experience financial distress. This distress will be costly for the firm and also for Smith, who will likely lose her job. Thus, Smith can use leverage as a way to convince investors that she does have information that the firm will grow, even if she cannot provide verifiable details about the sources of growth. Investors know that Beltran would be at risk of defaulting without growth opportunities, so they will interpret the additional leverage as a credible signal of the CEO's confidence. The use of leverage as a way to signal good information to investors is known as the **signaling theory of debt**.[39]

---

[38]The Sarbanes-Oxley Act of 2002 increased the penalties for securities fraud to include up to 10 years of imprisonment.

[39]See S. Ross, "The Determination of Financial Structure: The Incentive-Signalling Approach," *Bell Journal of Economics* 8 (1977): 23–40.

EXAMPLE 16.8 Debt Signals Strength

Problem

Suppose that Beltran currently uses all-equity financing, and that Beltran's market value in one year's time will be either $100 million or $50 million depending on the success of the new strategy. Currently, investors view the outcomes as equally likely, but Smith has information that success is virtually certain. Will leverage of $25 million make Smith's claims credible? How about leverage of $55 million?

Solution

If leverage is substantially less than $50 million, Beltran will have no risk of financial distress regardless of the outcome. As a result, there is no cost of leverage even if Smith does not have positive information. Thus, leverage of $25 million would not be a credible signal of strength to investors.

However, leverage of $55 million is likely to be a credible signal. If Smith has no positive information, there is a significant chance that Beltran will face bankruptcy under this burden of debt. Thus Smith would be unlikely to agree to this amount of leverage unless she is certain about the firm's prospects.

Issuing Equity and Adverse Selection

Suppose a used-car dealer tells you he is willing to sell you a nice looking sports car for $5000 less than its typical price. Rather than feel lucky, perhaps your first reaction should be one of skepticism: If the dealer is willing to sell it for such a low price, there must be something wrong with the car—it is probably a "lemon."

The idea that buyers will be skeptical of a seller's motivation for selling was formalized by George Akerlof.[40] Akerlof showed that if the seller has private information about the quality of the car, then his *desire to sell* reveals the car is probably of low quality. Buyers are therefore reluctant to buy except at heavily discounted prices. Owners of high-quality cars are reluctant to sell because they know buyers will think they are selling a lemon and offer only a low price. Consequently, the quality and prices of cars sold in the used-car market are both low. This result is referred to as **adverse selection**: The selection of cars sold in the used-car market is worse than average.

Adverse selection extends beyond the used-car market. In fact, it applies in any setting in which the seller has more information than the buyer. Adverse selection leads to the **lemons principle**:

When a seller has private information about the value of a good, buyers will discount the price they are willing to pay due to adverse selection.

We can apply this principle to the market for equity.[41] Suppose the owner of a start-up company tells you that his firm is a wonderful investment opportunity—and then offers to sell you 70% of his stake in the firm. He states that he is selling *only* because he wants to diversify. Although you appreciate this desire, you also suspect the owner may be eager to

---

[40]"The Market for Lemons: Quality, Uncertainty, and the Market Mechanism," *Quarterly Journal of Economics* 84 (1970): 488–500.

[41]See H. Leland and D. Pyle, "Information Asymmetries, Financial Structure and Financial Intermediation," *Journal of Finance* 32 (1977): 371–387.

sell such a large stake because he has negative information about the firm's future prospects. That is, he may be trying to cash out before the bad news becomes known.[42]

As with the used-car dealer, a firm owner's desire to sell equity may lead you to question how good an investment opportunity it really is. Based on the lemons principle, you therefore reduce the price you are willing to pay. This discount of the price due to adverse selection is a potential cost of issuing equity, and it may make owners with good information refrain from issuing equity.

EXAMPLE 16.9 Adverse Selection in Equity Markets

Problem

Zycor stock is worth either $100 per share, $80 per share, or $60 per share. Investors believe each case is equally likely, and the current share price is equal to the average value of $80.

Suppose the CEO of Zycor announces he will sell most of his holdings of the stock to diversify. Diversifying is worth 10% of the share price—that is, the CEO would be willing to receive 10% less than the shares are worth to achieve the benefits of diversification. If investors believe the CEO knows the true value, how will the share price change if he tries to sell? Will the CEO sell at the new share price?

Solution

If the true value of the shares were $100, the CEO would not be willing to sell at the market price of $80 per share, which would be 20% below their true value. So, if the CEO tries to sell, shareholders can conclude the shares are worth either $80 or $60. In that case, share price should fall to the average value of $70. But again, if the true value were $80, the CEO would be willing to sell for $72, but not $70 per share. So, if he still tries to sell, investors will know the true value is $60 per share. Thus, the CEO will sell only if the true value is the lowest possible price, $60 per share, and that is the price he will receive. If the CEO knows the firm's stock is worth $100 or $80 per share, he will not sell even though he would prefer to diversify.

In explaining adverse selection, we considered an owner of a firm selling his or her *own* shares. What if a manager of the firm decides to sell securities on the *firm's* behalf? If the securities are sold at a price below their true value, the buyer's windfall represents a cost for the firm's current shareholders. Acting on behalf of the current shareholders, the manager may be unwilling to sell.[43]

Let's consider a simple example. Gentec is a biotech firm with no debt, and its 20 million shares are currently trading at $10 per share, for a total market value of $200 million. Based on the prospects for one of Gentec's new drugs, management believes the true value of the company is $300 million, or $15 per share. Management believes the share price will reflect this higher value after the clinical trials for the drug are concluded next year.

Gentec has already announced plans to raise $60 million from investors to build a new research lab. It can raise the funds today by issuing 6 million new shares at the current price of $10 per share. In that case, after the good news comes out, the value of the firm's assets will be $300 million (from the existing assets) plus $60 million (new lab), for a total

[42]Again, if the owner of the firm (or the car, in the earlier example) has very specific information that can be verified ex-post, there are potential legal consequences for not revealing that information to a buyer. Generally, however, there is a great deal of subtle information the seller might have that would be impossible to verify.

[43]S. Myers and N. Majluf demonstrated this result, and a number of its implications for capital structure, in an influential paper, "Corporate Financing and Investment Decisions When Firms Have Information that Investors Do Not Have," *Journal of Financial Economics* 13 (1984): 187–221.

NOBEL PRIZE **The 2001 Nobel Prize in Economics**

In 2001, George Akerlof, Michael Spence, and Joseph Stiglitz jointly received the Nobel Prize in economics for their analyses of markets with asymmetric information and adverse selection. In this chapter, we discuss the implications of their theory for firm capital structure. This theory, however, has much broader applications. As described on the Nobel Prize Web site (www.nobelprize.org):

> *Many markets are characterized by asymmetric information: Actors on one side of the market have much better information than those on the other. Borrowers know more than lenders about their repayment prospects, managers and boards know more than shareholders about the firm's profitability, and prospective clients know more than insurance companies about their accident risk. During the 1970s, this year's Laureates laid the foundation for a general theory of markets with asymmetric information. Applications have been abundant, ranging from traditional agricultural markets to modern financial markets. The Laureates' contributions form the core of modern information economics.*

Source: "The Prize in Economic Sciences 2001—Press Release." Nobelprize.org.

value of \$360 million. With 26 million shares outstanding, the new share price will be \$360 million ÷ 26 million shares = \$13.85 per share.

But suppose Gentec waits for the good news to come out and the share price to rise to \$15 *before* issuing the new shares. At that time, the firm will be able to raise the \$60 million by selling 4 million shares. The firm's assets will again be worth a total of \$360 million, but Gentec will have only 24 million shares outstanding, which is consistent with the share price of \$360 million ÷ 24 million shares = \$15 per share.

Thus, issuing new shares when management knows they are underpriced is costly for the original shareholders. Their shares will be worth only \$13.85 rather than \$15. As a result, if Gentec's managers care primarily about the firm's current shareholders, they will be reluctant to sell securities at a price that is below their true value. If they believe the shares are underpriced, managers will prefer to wait until after the share price rises to issue equity.

This preference not to issue equity that is underpriced leads us to the same lemons problem we had before: Managers who know securities have a high value will not sell, and those who know they have a low value will sell. Due to this adverse selection, investors will be willing to pay only a low price for the securities. The lemons problem creates a cost for firms that need to raise capital from investors to fund new investments. If they try to issue equity, investors will discount the price they are willing to pay to reflect the possibility that managers are privy to bad news.

Implications for Equity Issuance

Adverse selection has a number of important implications for equity issuance. First and foremost, the lemons principle directly implies that

1. **The stock price declines on the announcement of an equity issue.** When a firm issues equity, it signals to investors that its equity may be overpriced. As a result, investors are not willing to pay the pre-announcement price for the equity and so the stock price declines. Numerous studies have confirmed this result, finding that the stock price falls about 3% on average on the announcement of an equity issue by a publicly traded U.S. firm.[44]

[44]See, e.g., P. Asquith and D. Mullins, "Equity Issues and Offering Dilution," *Journal of Financial Economics* 15 (1986): 61–89; R. Masulis and A. Korwar, "Seasoned Equity Offerings: An Empirical Investigation," *Journal of Financial Economics* 15 (1986): 91–118; and W. Mikkelson and M. Partch, "Valuation Effects of Security Offerings and the Issuance Process," *Journal of Financial Economics* 15 (1986): 31–60.

As was true for Gentec, managers issuing equity have an incentive to delay the issue until any news that might positively affect the stock price becomes public. In contrast, there is no incentive to delay the issue if managers expect negative news to come out. These incentives lead to the following pattern:

2. **The stock price tends to rise prior to the announcement of an equity issue.** This result is also supported empirically, as illustrated in Figure 16.3 using data from a study by Professors Deborah Lucas and Robert McDonald. They found that stocks with equity issues outperformed the market by almost 50% in the year and a half prior to the announcement of the issue.

Managers may also try to avoid the price decline associated with adverse selection by issuing equity at times when they have the smallest informational advantage over investors. For example, because a great deal of information is released to investors at the time of earnings announcements, equity issues are often timed to occur immediately after these announcements. That is,

3. **Firms tend to issue equity when information asymmetries are minimized, such as immediately after earnings announcements.** Studies have confirmed this timing and reported that the negative stock price reaction is smallest immediately after earnings announcements.[45]

Implications for Capital Structure

Because managers find it costly to issue equity that is underpriced, they may seek alternative forms of financing. While debt issues may also suffer from adverse selection, because the value of low-risk debt is not very sensitive to managers' private information about

FIGURE 16.3

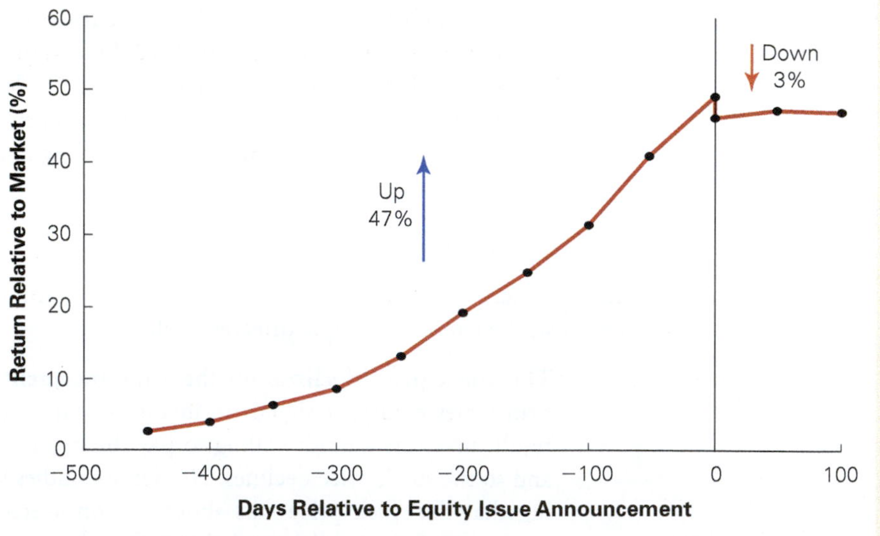

Stock Returns Before and After an Equity Issue
Stocks tend to rise (relative to the market) before an equity issue is announced. Upon announcement, stock prices fall on average. This figure shows the average return relative to the market before and after announcements using data from D. Lucas and R. McDonald, "Equity Issues and Stock Price Dynamics," *Journal of Finance* 45 (1990): 1019–1043.

[45]R. Korajczyk, D. Lucas, and R. McDonald, "The Effect of Information Releases on the Pricing and Timing of Equity Issues," *Review of Financial Studies* 4 (1991): 685–708.

the firm (but is instead determined mainly by interest rates), the degree of underpricing will tend to be smaller for debt than for equity. Of course, a firm can avoid underpricing altogether by financing investment using its cash (retained earnings) when possible. Thus,

Managers who perceive the firm's equity is underpriced will have a preference to fund investment using retained earnings, or debt, rather than equity.

The converse to this statement is also true: Managers who perceive the firm's equity to be overpriced will prefer to issue equity, as opposed to issuing debt or using retained earnings, to fund investment. However, due to the negative stock price reaction when issuing equity, it is less likely that equity will be overpriced. In fact, absent other motives to issue equity, if both managers and investors behave rationally, the price drop upon announcement may be sufficient to deter managers from issuing equity except as a last resort.

The idea that managers will prefer to use retained earnings first, and will issue new equity only as a last resort, is often referred to as the **pecking order hypothesis**, put forth by Stewart Myers.[46] While difficult to test directly, this hypothesis is consistent with the aggregate data on corporate financing in Figure 16.4, which shows that firms tend to be net repurchasers (rather than issuers) of equity, whereas they are issuers of debt. Moreover, the vast majority of investment is funded by retained earnings, with net external financing amounting to less than 25% of capital expenditures in most years, and about 10% on average. These observations can also be consistent with the trade-off theory of capital structure, however, and there is substantial evidence that firms do not follow a *strict* pecking order, as firms often issue equity even when borrowing is possible.[47]

FIGURE 16.4

Aggregate Sources of Funding for Capital Expenditures, U.S. Corporations

The chart shows net equity and debt issues as a percentage of total capital expenditures. In aggregate, firms tend to repurchase equity and issue debt. But more than 75% of capital expenditures are funded from retained earnings.

Source: Federal Reserve Flow of Funds.

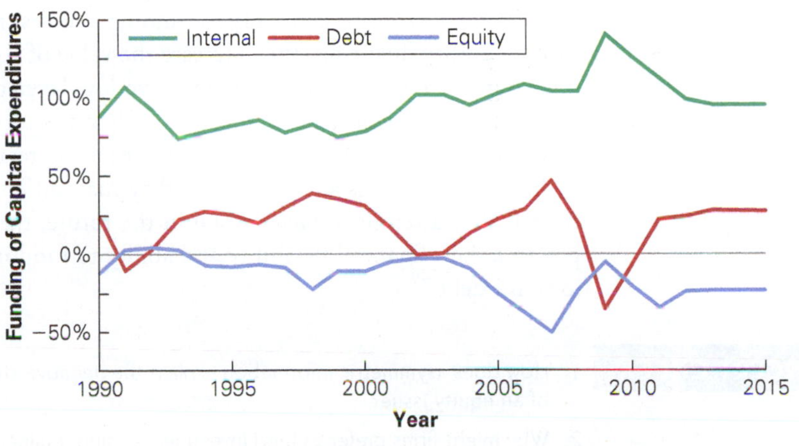

[46]S. Myers, "The Capital Structure Puzzle," *Journal of Finance* 39 (1984): 575–592.

[47]For example, see M. Leary and M. Roberts, "The Pecking Order, Debt Capacity, and Information Asymmetry," *Journal of Financial Economics* 95 (2010): 332–355.

EXAMPLE 16.10 The Pecking Order of Financing Alternatives

Problem

Axon Industries needs to raise \$10 million for a new investment project. If the firm issues one-year debt, it may have to pay an interest rate of 7%, although Axon's managers believe that 6% would be a fair rate given the level of risk. However, if the firm issues equity, they believe the equity may be underpriced by 5%. What is the cost to current shareholders of financing the project out of retained earnings, debt, and equity?

Solution

If the firm spends \$10 million out of retained earnings, rather than paying that money out to shareholders as a dividend, the cost to shareholders is \$10 million. Using debt costs the firm $\$10 \times (1.07) = \$10.7$ million in one year, which has a present value based on management's view of the firm's risk of $\$10.7 \div (1.06) = \$10.094$ million. Finally, if equity is underpriced by 5%, then to raise \$10 million the firm will need to issue \$10.5 million in new equity. Thus, the cost to existing shareholders will be \$10.5 million. Comparing the three, retained earnings are the cheapest source of funds, followed by debt, and finally by equity.

Aside from a general preference for using retained earnings or debt as a source of funding rather than equity, adverse selection costs do not lead to a clear prediction regarding a firm's overall capital structure. Instead, these costs imply that the managers' choice of financing will depend, in addition to the other costs and benefits discussed in this chapter, on whether they believe the firm is currently underpriced or overpriced by investors. This dependence is sometimes referred to as the **market timing** view of capital structure: The firm's overall capital structure depends in part on the market conditions that existed when it sought funding in the past. As a result, similar firms in the same industry might end up with very different, but nonetheless optimal, capital structures.[48]

Indeed, even the pecking order hypothesis does not provide a clear prediction regarding capital structure on its own. While it argues that firms should prefer to use retained earnings, then debt, and then equity as funding sources, retained earnings are merely another form of equity financing (they increase the value of equity while the value of debt remains unchanged). Therefore, firms might have low leverage either because they are unable to issue additional debt and are forced to rely on equity financing or because they are sufficiently profitable to finance all investment using retained earnings.

Moreover, if firms anticipate that they may suffer adverse selection or other financing costs if they attempt to raise capital in the future, they may choose low leverage today to preserve their financial flexibility and ability to fund investment from retained earnings or low-risk debt.[49]

CONCEPT CHECK

1. How does asymmetric information explain the negative stock price reaction to the announcement of an equity issue?
2. Why might firms prefer to fund investments using retained earnings or debt rather than issuing equity?

---

[48] See J. Wurgler and M. Baker, "Market Timing and Capital Structure," *Journal of Finance* 57 (2002): 1–32.

[49] See A. Gamba and A. Triantis, "The Value of Financial Flexibility," *Journal of Finance* 63 (2008): 2263–2296, and H. DeAngelo, L. DeAngelo, and T. Whited, "Capital Structure Dynamics and Transitory Debt," *Journal of Financial Economics* 99 (2011): 235–261.

16.9 Capital Structure: The Bottom Line

Over the past three chapters, we have examined a number of factors that might influence a firm's choice of capital structure. What is the bottom line for a financial manager?

The most important insight regarding capital structure goes back to Modigliani and Miller: With perfect capital markets, a firm's security choice alters the risk of the firm's equity, but it does not change its value or the amount it can raise from outside investors. Thus, the optimal capital structure depends on market imperfections, such as taxes, financial distress costs, agency costs, and asymmetric information.

Of all the different possible imperfections that drive capital structure, the most clear-cut, and possibly the most significant, is taxes. The interest tax shield allows firms to repay investors and avoid the corporate tax. Each dollar of permanent debt financing provides the firm with a tax shield worth τ^* dollars, where τ^* is the effective tax advantage of debt. For firms with consistent taxable income, this benefit of leverage is important to consider.

While firms should use leverage to shield their income from taxes, how much of their income should they shield? If leverage is too high, there is an increased risk that a firm may not be able to meet its debt obligations and will be forced to default. While the risk of default is not itself a problem, financial distress may lead to other consequences that reduce the value of the firm. Firms must, therefore, balance the tax benefits of debt against the costs of financial distress.

Agency costs and benefits of leverage are also important determinants of capital structure. Too much debt can motivate managers and equity holders to take excessive risks or under-invest in a firm. When free cash flows are high, too little leverage may encourage wasteful spending. This effect may be especially important for firms in countries lacking strong protections for investors against self-interested managers.[50] When agency costs are significant, short-term debt may be the most attractive form of external financing.

A firm must also consider the potential signaling and adverse selection consequences of its financing choice. Because bankruptcy is costly for managers, increasing leverage can signal managers' confidence in the firm's ability to meet its debt obligations. When managers have different views regarding the value of securities, managers can benefit current shareholders by issuing the most overpriced securities. However, new investors will respond to this incentive by lowering the price they are willing to pay for securities that the firm issues, leading to negative price reaction when a new issue is announced. This effect is most pronounced for equity issues, because the value of equity is most sensitive to the manager's private information. To avoid this "lemons cost," firms should rely first on retained earnings, then debt, and finally equity. This pecking order of financing alternatives will be most important when managers are likely to have a great deal of private information regarding the value of the firm.

Finally, it is important to recognize that because actively changing a firm's capital structure (for example, by selling or repurchasing shares or bonds) entails transactions costs, firms may be unlikely to change their capital structures unless they depart significantly from the optimal level. As a result, most changes to a firm's debt-equity ratio are likely to occur passively, as the market value of the firm's equity fluctuates with changes in the firm's stock price.[51]

---

[50] See J. Fan, S. Titman, and G. Twite, "An International Comparison of Capital Structure and Debt Maturity Choices," SSRN working paper, 2008.

[51] See I. Strebulaev, "Do Tests of Capital Structure Theory Mean What They Say?," *Journal of Finance* 62 (2007): 1747–1787.

CONCEPT CHECK

1. Consider the differences in leverage across industries shown in Figure 15.7. To what extent can you account for these differences?
2. What are some reasons firms might depart from their optimal capital structure, at least in the short run?

MyFinanceLab Here is what you should know after reading this chapter. MyFinanceLab will help you identify what you know and where to go when you need to practice.

16.1 Default and Bankruptcy in a Perfect Market

- In the Modigliani-Miller setting, leverage may result in bankruptcy, but bankruptcy alone does not reduce the value of the firm. With perfect capital markets, bankruptcy shifts ownership from the equity holders to debt holders without changing the total value available to all investors.

16.2 The Costs of Bankruptcy and Financial Distress

- U.S. firms can file for bankruptcy protection under the provisions of the 1978 Bankruptcy Reform Act.
  - In a Chapter 7 liquidation, a trustee oversees the liquidation of the firm's assets.
  - In a Chapter 11 reorganization, management attempts to develop a reorganization plan that will improve operations and maximize value to investors. If the firm cannot successfully reorganize, it may be liquidated under Chapter 7 bankruptcy.
- Bankruptcy is a costly process that imposes both direct and indirect costs on a firm and its investors.
  - Direct costs include the costs of experts and advisors such as lawyers, accountants, appraisers, and investment bankers hired by the firm or its creditors during the bankruptcy process.
  - Indirect costs include the loss of customers, suppliers, employees, or receivables during bankruptcy. Firms also incur indirect costs when they need to sell assets at distressed prices.

16.3 Financial Distress Costs and Firm Value

- When securities are fairly priced, the original shareholders of a firm pay the present value of the costs associated with bankruptcy and financial distress.

16.4 Optimal Capital Structure: The Trade-Off Theory

- According to the trade-off theory, the total value of a levered firm equals the value of the firm without leverage plus the present value of the tax savings from debt minus the present value of financial distress costs:

$$V^L = V^U + PV(\text{Interest Tax Shield}) - PV(\text{Financial Distress Costs}) \qquad (16.1)$$

  Optimal leverage is the level of debt that maximizes V^L.

16.5 Exploiting Debt Holders: The Agency Costs of Leverage

- Agency costs arise when there are conflicts of interest between stakeholders. A highly levered firm with risky debt faces the following agency costs:
  - Asset substitution: Shareholders can gain by making negative-NPV investments or decisions that sufficiently increase the firm's risk.
  - Debt overhang: Shareholders may be unwilling to finance new, positive-NPV projects.
  - Cashing out: Shareholders have an incentive to liquidate assets at prices below their market values and distribute the proceeds as a dividend.

- With debt overhang, equity holders will benefit from new investment only if

$$\frac{NPV}{I} > \frac{\beta_D D}{\beta_E E} \tag{16.2}$$

- When a firm has existing debt, debt overhang leads to a leverage ratchet effect:
  - Shareholders may have an incentive to increase leverage even if it decreases the value of the firm.
  - Shareholders will not have an incentive to decrease leverage by buying back debt, even if it will increase the value of the firm.

16.6 Motivating Managers: The Agency Benefits of Leverage

- Leverage has agency benefits and can improve incentives for managers to run a firm more efficiently and effectively due to
  - Increased ownership concentration: Managers with higher ownership concentration are more likely to work hard and less likely to consume corporate perks.
  - Reduced free cash flow: Firms with less free cash flow are less likely to pursue wasteful investments.
  - Reduced managerial entrenchment and increased commitment: The threat of financial distress and being fired may commit managers more fully to pursue strategies that improve operations.

16.7 Agency Costs and the Trade-Off Theory

- We can extend the trade-off theory to include agency costs. The value of a firm, including agency costs and benefits, is:

$$V^L = V^U + PV(\text{Interest Tax Shield}) - PV(\text{Financial Distress Costs})$$
$$- PV(\text{Agency Costs of Debt}) + PV(\text{Agency Benefits of Debt}) \tag{16.3}$$

  Optimal leverage is the level of debt that maximizes V^L.

16.8 Asymmetric Information and Capital Structure

- When managers have better information than investors, there is asymmetric information. Given asymmetric information, managers may use leverage as a credible signal to investors of the firm's ability to generate future free cash flow.
- According to the lemons principle, when managers have private information about the value of a firm, investors will discount the price they are willing to pay for a new equity issue due to adverse selection.
- Managers are more likely to sell equity when they know a firm is overvalued. As a result,
  - The stock price declines when a firm announces an equity issue.
  - The stock price tends to rise prior to the announcement of an equity issue because managers tend to delay equity issues until after good news becomes public.
  - Firms tend to issue equity when information asymmetries are minimized.
  - Managers who perceive that the firm's equity is underpriced will have a preference to fund investment using retained earnings, or debt, rather than equity. This result is called the pecking order hypothesis.

16.9 Capital Structure: The Bottom Line

- There are numerous frictions that drive the firm's optimal capital structure. However, if there are substantial transactions costs to changing the firm's capital structure, most changes in the firm's leverage are likely to occur passively, based on fluctuations in the firm's stock price.

Key Terms

adverse selection *p. 579*
agency costs *p. 565*
asset substitution problem *p. 566*
asymmetric information *p. 577*
Chapter 7 liquidation *p. 555*
Chapter 11 reorganization *p. 555*
credibility principle *p. 578*
debt covenants *p. 571*
debtor-in-possession (DIP) financing *p. 557*
debt overhang *p. 567*
default *p. 552*
economic distress *p. 553*
financial distress *p. 551*
free cash flow hypothesis *p. 573*
lemons principle *p. 579*
leverage ratchet effect *p. 569*
management entrenchment *p. 571*
management entrenchment theory *p. 577*
market timing *p. 584*
moral hazard *p. 574*
pecking order hypothesis *p. 583*
prepackaged bankruptcy *p. 556*
signaling theory of debt *p. 578*
trade-off theory *p. 562*
under-investment problem *p. 567*
workout *p. 556*

Further Reading

For a survey of alternative theories of capital structure, see M. Harris and A. Raviv, "The Theory of Capital Structure," *Journal of Finance* 46 (1991): 197–355. For a textbook treatment, see J. Tirole, *The Theory of Corporate Finance*, Princeton University Press, 2005.

In this chapter, we did not discuss how firms dynamically manage their capital structures. Although this topic is beyond the scope of this book, interested readers can consult the following papers: R. Goldstein, N. Ju, and H. Leland, "An EBIT-Based Model of Dynamic Capital Structure," *Journal of Business* 74 (2001): 483–512; O. Hart and J. Moore, "Default and Renegotiation: A Dynamic Model of Debt," *Quarterly Journal of Economics* 113(1) (1998): 1–41; C. Hennessy and T. Whited, "Debt Dynamics," *Journal of Finance* 60(3) (2005): 1129–1165; and H. Leland, "Agency Costs, Risk Management, and Capital Structure," *Journal of Finance* 53(4) (1998): 1213–1243.

For an empirical study of how firms' capital structures evolve in response to changes in their stock price, and how these dynamics relate to existing theories, see I. Welch, "Capital Structure and Stock Returns," *Journal of Political Economy* 112 (2004): 106–131. See also I. Strebulaev, "Do Tests of Capital Structure Theory Mean What They Say?" *Journal of Finance* 62 (2007): 1747–1787, for an analysis of the importance of adjustment costs in interpreting firms' capital structure choices.

Explaining much of the within-industry variation in capital structure remains an important puzzle. Interested readers should consult M. Lemmon, M. Roberts, and J. Zender, "Back to the Beginning: Persistence and the Cross-Section of Corporate Capital Structure," *Journal of Finance* 63 (2008): 1575–1608. For an empirical estimation of Figure 16.2 by industry, see A. Korteweg, "The Net Benefits to Leverage," *Journal of Finance* 65 (2010): 2137–2170.

Results of empirical tests of the pecking order theory can be found in E. Fama and K. French, "Testing Tradeoff and Pecking Order Predictions About Dividends and Debt," *Review of Financial Studies* 15(1): 1–33; M. Frank and V. Goyal, "Testing the Pecking Order Theory of Capital Structure," *Journal of Financial Economics* 67(2) (2003): 217–248; and L. Shyam-Sunder and S. Myers, "Testing Static Tradeoff Against Pecking Order Models of Capital Structure," *Journal of Financial Economics* 51(2) (1999): 219–244.

Problems

All problems in are available in MyFinanceLab. *An asterisk (*) indicates problems with a higher level of difficulty.*

Default and Bankruptcy in a Perfect Market

1. Gladstone Corporation is about to launch a new product. Depending on the success of the new product, Gladstone may have one of four values next year: $150 million, $135 million, $95 million, or $80 million. These outcomes are all equally likely, and this risk is diversifiable.

Gladstone will not make any payouts to investors during the year. Suppose the risk-free interest rate is 5% and assume perfect capital markets.

a. What is the initial value of Gladstone's equity without leverage?

Now suppose Gladstone has zero-coupon debt with a $100 million face value due next year.

b. What is the initial value of Gladstone's debt?
c. What is the yield-to-maturity of the debt? What is its expected return?
d. What is the initial value of Gladstone's equity? What is Gladstone's total value with leverage?

2. Baruk Industries has no cash and a debt obligation of $36 million that is now due. The market value of Baruk's assets is $81 million, and the firm has no other liabilities. Assume perfect capital markets.

a. Suppose Baruk has 10 million shares outstanding. What is Baruk's current share price?
b. How many new shares must Baruk issue to raise the capital needed to pay its debt obligation?
c. After repaying the debt, what will Baruk's share price be?

The Costs of Bankruptcy and Financial Distress

3. When a firm defaults on its debt, debt holders often receive less than 50% of the amount they are owed. Is the difference between the amount debt holders are owed and the amount they receive a *cost* of bankruptcy?

4. Which type of firm is more likely to experience a loss of customers in the event of financial distress:

a. Campbell Soup Company or Intuit, Inc. (a maker of accounting software)?
b. Allstate Corporation (an insurance company) or Adidas AG (maker of athletic footwear, apparel, and sports equipment)?

5. Which type of asset is more likely to be liquidated for close to its full market value in the event of financial distress:

a. An office building or a brand name?
b. Product inventory or raw materials?
c. Patent rights or engineering "know-how"?

6. Suppose Tefco Corp. has a value of $100 million if it continues to operate, but has outstanding debt of $120 million that is now due. If the firm declares bankruptcy, bankruptcy costs will equal $20 million, and the remaining $80 million will go to creditors. Instead of declaring bankruptcy, management proposes to exchange the firm's debt for a fraction of its equity in a workout. What is the minimum fraction of the firm's equity that management would need to offer to creditors for the workout to be successful?

7. You have received two job offers. Firm A offers to pay you $85,000 per year for two years. Firm B offers to pay you $90,000 for two years. Both jobs are equivalent. Suppose that firm A's contract is certain, but that firm B has a 50% chance of going bankrupt at the end of the year. In that event, it will cancel your contract and pay you the lowest amount possible for you to not quit. If you did quit, you expect you could find a new job paying $85,000 per year, but you would be unemployed for 3 months while you search for it.

a. Say you took the job at firm B. What is the least firm B can pay you next year in order to match what you would earn if you quit?
b. Given your answer to part (a), and assuming your cost of capital is 5%, which offer pays you a higher present value of your expected wage?
c. Based on this example, discuss one reason why firms with a higher risk of bankruptcy may need to offer higher wages to attract employees.

Financial Distress Costs and Firm Value

8. As in Problem 1, Gladstone Corporation is about to launch a new product. Depending on the success of the new product, Gladstone may have one of four values next year: $150 million,

$135 million, $95 million, or $80 million. These outcomes are all equally likely, and this risk is diversifiable. Suppose the risk-free interest rate is 5% and that, in the event of default, 25% of the value of Gladstone's assets will be lost to bankruptcy costs. (Ignore all other market imperfections, such as taxes.)

a. What is the initial value of Gladstone's equity without leverage?

Now suppose Gladstone has zero-coupon debt with a $100 million face value due next year.

b. What is the initial value of Gladstone's debt?
c. What is the yield-to-maturity of the debt? What is its expected return?
d. What is the initial value of Gladstone's equity? What is Gladstone's total value with leverage?

Suppose Gladstone has 10 million shares outstanding and no debt at the start of the year.

e. If Gladstone does not issue debt, what is its share price?
f. If Gladstone issues debt of $100 million due next year and uses the proceeds to repurchase shares, what will its share price be? Why does your answer differ from that in part (e)?

9. Kohwe Corporation plans to issue equity to raise $50 million to finance a new investment. After making the investment, Kohwe expects to earn free cash flows of $10 million each year. Kohwe currently has 5 million shares outstanding, and it has no other assets or opportunities. Suppose the appropriate discount rate for Kohwe's future free cash flows is 8%, and the only capital market imperfections are corporate taxes and financial distress costs.

a. What is the NPV of Kohwe's investment?
b. Given these plans, what is Kohwe's value per share today?

Suppose Kohwe borrows the $50 million instead. The firm will pay interest only on this loan each year, and it will maintain an outstanding balance of $50 million on the loan. Suppose that Kohwe's corporate tax rate is 40%, and expected free cash flows are still $10 million each year.

c. What is Kohwe's share price today if the investment is financed with debt?

Now suppose that with leverage, Kohwe's expected free cash flows will decline to $9 million per year due to reduced sales and other financial distress costs. Assume that the appropriate discount rate for Kohwe's future free cash flows is still 8%.

d. What is Kohwe's share price today given the financial distress costs of leverage?

10. You work for a large car manufacturer that is currently financially healthy. Your manager feels that the firm should take on more debt because it can thereby reduce the expense of car warranties. To quote your manager, "If we go bankrupt, we don't have to service the warranties. We therefore have lower bankruptcy costs than most corporations, so we should use more debt." Is he right?

Optimal Capital Structure: The Trade-Off Theory

11. Facebook, Inc. has no debt. As Problem 21 in Chapter 15 makes clear, by issuing debt Facebook can generate a very large tax shield potentially worth nearly $2 billion. Given Facebook's success, one would be hard pressed to argue that Facebook's management are naïve and unaware of this huge potential to create value. A more likely explanation is that issuing debt would entail other costs. What might these costs be?

12. Hawar International is a shipping firm with a current share price of $5.50 and 10 million shares outstanding. Suppose Hawar announces plans to lower its corporate taxes by borrowing $20 million and repurchasing shares.

a. With perfect capital markets, what will the share price be after this announcement?

Suppose that Hawar pays a corporate tax rate of 30%, and that shareholders expect the change in debt to be permanent.

b. If the only imperfection is corporate taxes, what will the share price be after this announcement?
c. Suppose the only imperfections are corporate taxes and financial distress costs. If the share price rises to $5.75 after this announcement, what is the PV of financial distress costs Hawar will incur as the result of this new debt?

13. Your firm is considering issuing one-year debt, and has come up with the following estimates of the value of the interest tax shield and the probability of distress for different levels of debt:

	Debt Level (in $ million)						
	0	40	50	60	70	80	90
PV (interest tax shield, in $ million)	0.00	0.76	0.95	1.14	1.33	1.52	1.71
Probability of Financial Distress	0%	0%	1%	2%	7%	16%	31%

Suppose the firm has a beta of zero, so that the appropriate discount rate for financial distress costs is the risk-free rate of 5%. Which level of debt above is optimal if, in the event of distress, the firm will have distress costs equal to

a. $2 million?

b. $5 million?

c. $25 million?

14. Marpor Industries has no debt and expects to generate free cash flows of $16 million each year. Marpor believes that if it permanently increases its level of debt to $40 million, the risk of financial distress may cause it to lose some customers and receive less favorable terms from its suppliers. As a result, Marpor's expected free cash flows with debt will be only $15 million per year. Suppose Marpor's tax rate is 35%, the risk-free rate is 5%, the expected return of the market is 15%, and the beta of Marpor's free cash flows is 1.10 (with or without leverage).

a. Estimate Marpor's value without leverage.

b. Estimate Marpor's value with the new leverage.

15. Real estate purchases are often financed with at least 80% debt. Most corporations, however, have less than 50% debt financing. Provide an explanation for this difference using the trade-off theory.

Exploiting Debt Holders: The Agency Costs of Leverage

16. On May 14, 2008, General Motors paid a dividend of $0.25 per share. During the same quarter GM lost a staggering $15.5 billion or $27.33 *per share*. Seven months later the company asked for billions of dollars of government aid and ultimately declared bankruptcy just over a year later, on June 1, 2009. At that point a share of GM was worth only a little more than a dollar.

a. If you ignore the possibility of a government bailout, the decision to pay a dividend given how close the company was to financial distress is an example of what kind of cost?

*b. What would your answer be if GM executives anticipated that there was a possibility of a government bailout should the firm be forced to declare bankruptcy?

17. Dynron Corporation's primary business is natural gas transportation using its vast gas pipeline network. Dynron's assets currently have a market value of $150 million. The firm is exploring the possibility of raising $50 million by selling part of its pipeline network and investing the $50 million in a fiber-optic network to generate revenues by selling high-speed network bandwidth. While this new investment is expected to increase profits, it will also substantially increase Dynron's risk. If Dynron is levered, would this investment be more or less attractive to equity holders than if Dynron had no debt?

18. Consider a firm whose only asset is a plot of vacant land, and whose only liability is debt of $15 million due in one year. If left vacant, the land will be worth $10 million in one year. Alternatively, the firm can develop the land at an upfront cost of $20 million. The developed land will be worth $35 million in one year. Suppose the risk-free interest rate is 10%, assume all cash flows are risk-free, and assume there are no taxes.

a. If the firm chooses not to develop the land, what is the value of the firm's equity today? What is the value of the debt today?

b. What is the NPV of developing the land?

c. Suppose the firm raises $20 million from equity holders to develop the land. If the firm develops the land, what is the value of the firm's equity today? What is the value of the firm's debt today?

d. Given your answer to part (c), would equity holders be willing to provide the $20 million needed to develop the land?

19. Sarvon Systems has a debt-equity ratio of 1.2, an equity beta of 2.0, and a debt beta of 0.30. It currently is evaluating the following projects, none of which would change the firm's volatility (amounts in $ million):

Project	A	B	C	D	E
Investment	100	50	85	30	75
NPV	20	6	10	15	18

a. Which project will equity holders agree to fund?

b. What is the cost to the firm of the debt overhang?

20. Zymase is a biotechnology start-up firm. Researchers at Zymase must choose one of three different research strategies. The payoffs (after-tax) and their likelihood for each strategy are shown below. The risk of each project is diversifiable.

Strategy	Probability	Payoff (in $ million)
A	100%	75
B	50%	140
	50%	0
C	10%	300
	90%	40

a. Which project has the highest expected payoff?

b. Suppose Zymase has debt of $40 million due at the time of the project's payoff. Which project has the highest expected payoff for equity holders?

c. Suppose Zymase has debt of $110 million due at the time of the project's payoff. Which project has the highest expected payoff for equity holders?

d. If management chooses the strategy that maximizes the payoff to equity holders, what is the expected agency cost to the firm from having $40 million in debt due? What is the expected agency cost to the firm from having $110 million in debt due?

21. Petron Corporation's management team is meeting to decide on a new corporate strategy. There are four options, each with a different probability of success and total firm value in the event of success, as shown below:

	Strategy			
	A	B	C	D
Probability of Success	100%	80%	60%	40%
Firm Value if Successful (in $ million)	50	60	70	80

Assume that for each strategy, firm value is zero in the event of failure.

a. Which strategy has the highest expected payoff?

b. Suppose Petron's management team will choose the strategy that leads to the highest expected value of Petron's equity. Which strategy will management choose if Petron currently has

i. No debt?
ii. Debt with a face value of $20 million?
iii. Debt with a face value of $40 million?

c. What agency cost of debt is illustrated in your answer to part (b)?

22. Consider the setting of Problem 21, and suppose Petron Corp. has debt with a face value of $40 million outstanding. For simplicity assume all risk is idiosyncratic, the risk-free interest rate is zero, and there are no taxes.

a. What is the expected value of equity, assuming Petron will choose the strategy that maximizes the value of its equity? What is the total expected value of the firm?
b. Suppose Petron issues equity and buys back its debt, reducing the debt's face value to $5 million. If it does so, what strategy will it choose after the transaction? Will the total value of the firm increase?
c. Suppose you are a debt holder, deciding whether to sell your debt back to the firm. If you expect the firm to reduce its debt to $5 million, what price would you demand to sell your debt?
d. Based on your answer to (c), how much will Petron need to raise from equity holders in order to buy back the debt?
e. How much will equity holders gain or lose by recapitalizing to reduce leverage? How much will debt holders gain or lose? Would you expect Petron's management to choose to reduce its leverage?

***23.** Consider the setting of Problems 21 and 22, and suppose Petron Corp. must pay a 25% tax rate on the amount of the final payoff that is paid to equity holders. It pays no tax on payments to, or capital raised from, debt holders.

a. Which strategy will Petron choose with no debt? Which will it choose with a face value of $10 million, $30 million, or $50 million in debt? (Assume management maximizes the value of equity, and in the case of ties, will choose the safer strategy.)
b. Given your answer to (a), show that the total combined value of Petron's equity and debt is maximized with a face value of $30 million in debt.
c. Show that if Petron has $30 million in debt outstanding, shareholders can gain by increasing the face value of debt to $50 million, even though this will reduce the total value of the firm.
d. Show that if Petron has $50 million in debt outstanding, shareholders will lose by buying back debt to reduce the face value of debt to $30 million, even though that will increase the total value of the firm.

Motivating Managers: The Agency Benefits of Leverage

24. You own your own firm, and you want to raise $30 million to fund an expansion. Currently, you own 100% of the firm's equity, and the firm has no debt. To raise the $30 million solely through equity, you will need to sell two-thirds of the firm. However, you would prefer to maintain at least a 50% equity stake in the firm to retain control.

a. If you borrow $20 million, what fraction of the equity will you need to sell to raise the remaining $10 million? (Assume perfect capital markets.)
b. What is the smallest amount you can borrow to raise the $30 million without giving up control? (Assume perfect capital markets.)

25. Empire Industries forecasts net income this coming year as shown below (in thousands of dollars):

EBIT	$1000
Interest expense	0
Income before tax	1000
Taxes	−350
Net income	$650

Approximately $200,000 of Empire's earnings will be needed to make new, positive-NPV investments. Unfortunately, Empire's managers are expected to waste 10% of its net income on needless perks, pet projects, and other expenditures that do not contribute to the firm. All remaining income will be returned to shareholders through dividends and share repurchases.

a. What are the two benefits of debt financing for Empire?
b. By how much would each $1 of interest expense reduce Empire's dividend and share repurchases?
c. What is the increase in the *total* funds Empire will pay to investors for each $1 of interest expense?

26. Ralston Enterprises has assets that will have a market value in one year as follows:

Probability	1%	6%	24%	38%	24%	6%	1%
Value (in $ million)	70	80	90	100	110	120	130

That is, there is a 1% chance the assets will be worth $70 million, a 6% chance the assets will be worth $80 million, and so on. Suppose the CEO is contemplating a decision that will benefit her personally but will reduce the value of the firm's assets by $10 million. The CEO is likely to proceed with this decision unless it substantially increases the firm's risk of bankruptcy.

a. If Ralston has debt due of $75 million in one year, the CEO's decision will increase the probability of bankruptcy by what percentage?
b. What level of debt provides the CEO with the biggest incentive not to proceed with the decision?

Agency Costs and the Trade-Off Theory

27. Although the major benefit of debt financing is easy to observe—the tax shield—many of the indirect costs of debt financing can be quite subtle and difficult to observe. Describe some of these costs.

28. If it is managed efficiently, Remel Inc. will have assets with a market value of $50 million, $100 million, or $150 million next year, with each outcome being equally likely. However, managers may engage in wasteful empire building, which will reduce the firm's market value by $5 million in all cases. Managers may also increase the risk of the firm, changing the probability of each outcome to 50%, 10%, and 40%, respectively.

a. What is the expected value of Remel's assets if it is run efficiently?

Suppose managers will engage in empire building unless that behavior increases the likelihood of bankruptcy. They will choose the risk of the firm to maximize the expected payoff to equity holders.

b. Suppose Remel has debt due in one year as shown below. For each case, indicate whether managers will engage in empire building, and whether they will increase risk. What is the expected value of Remel's assets in each case?
   i. $44 million
   ii. $49 million
   iii. $90 million
   iv. $99 million
c. Suppose the tax savings from the debt, after including investor taxes, is equal to 10% of the expected payoff of the debt. The proceeds from the debt, as well as the value of any tax savings, will be paid out to shareholders immediately as a dividend when the debt is issued. Which debt level in part (b) is optimal for Remel?

29. Which of the following industries have low optimal debt levels according to the trade-off theory? Which have high optimal levels of debt?

a. Tobacco firms
b. Accounting firms
c. Mature restaurant chains
d. Lumber companies
e. Cell phone manufacturers

30. According to the managerial entrenchment theory, managers choose capital structure so as to preserve their control of the firm. On the one hand, debt is costly for managers because they risk losing control in the event of default. On the other hand, if they do not take advantage of the tax shield provided by debt, they risk losing control through a hostile takeover.

Suppose a firm expects to generate free cash flows of $90 million per year, and the discount rate for these cash flows is 10%. The firm pays a tax rate of 40%. A raider is poised to take over the firm and finance it with $750 million in permanent debt. The raider will generate the same free cash flows, and the takeover attempt will be successful if the raider can offer a premium of 20% over the current value of the firm. According to the managerial entrenchment hypothesis, what level of permanent debt will the firm choose?

Asymmetric Information and Capital Structure

31. Info Systems Technology (IST) manufactures microprocessor chips for use in appliances and other applications. IST has no debt and 100 million shares outstanding. The correct price for these shares is either $14.50 or $12.50 per share. Investors view both possibilities as equally likely, so the shares currently trade for $13.50.

IST must raise $500 million to build a new production facility. Because the firm would suffer a large loss of both customers and engineering talent in the event of financial distress, managers believe that if IST borrows the $500 million, the present value of financial distress costs will exceed any tax benefits by $20 million. At the same time, because investors believe that managers know the correct share price, IST faces a lemons problem if it attempts to raise the $500 million by issuing equity.

a. Suppose that if IST issues equity, the share price will remain $13.50. To maximize the long-term share price of the firm once its true value is known, would managers choose to issue equity or borrow the $500 million if
   i. They know the correct value of the shares is $12.50?
   ii. They know the correct value of the shares is $14.50?
b. Given your answer to part (a), what should investors conclude if IST issues equity? What will happen to the share price?
c. Given your answer to part (a), what should investors conclude if IST issues debt? What will happen to the share price in that case?
d. How would your answers change if there were no distress costs, but only tax benefits of leverage?

32. During the Internet boom of the late 1990s, the stock prices of many Internet firms soared to extreme heights. As CEO of such a firm, if you believed your stock was significantly overvalued, would using your stock to acquire non-Internet stocks be a wise idea, even if you had to pay a small premium over their fair market value to make the acquisition?

***33.** "We R Toys" (WRT) is considering expanding into new geographic markets. The expansion will have the same business risk as WRT's existing assets. The expansion will require an initial investment of $50 million and is expected to generate perpetual EBIT of $20 million per year. After the initial investment, future capital expenditures are expected to equal depreciation, and no further additions to net working capital are anticipated.

WRT's existing capital structure is composed of $500 million in equity and $300 million in debt (market values), with 10 million equity shares outstanding. The unlevered cost of capital is 10%, and WRT's debt is risk free with an interest rate of 4%. The corporate tax rate is 35%, and there are no personal taxes.

a. WRT initially proposes to fund the expansion by issuing equity. If investors were not expecting this expansion, and if they share WRT's view of the expansion's profitability, what will the share price be once the firm announces the expansion plan?
b. Suppose investors think that the EBIT from WRT's expansion will be only $4 million. What will the share price be in this case? How many shares will the firm need to issue?
c. Suppose WRT issues equity as in part (b). Shortly after the issue, new information emerges that convinces investors that management was, in fact, correct regarding the cash flows from the expansion. What will the share price be now? Why does it differ from that found in part (a)?
d. Suppose WRT instead finances the expansion with a $50 million issue of permanent risk-free debt. If WRT undertakes the expansion using debt, what is its new share price once the new information comes out? Comparing your answer with that in part (c), what are the two advantages of debt financing in this case?

CHAPTER

17

Payout Policy

NOTATION

PV	present value
P_{cum}	cum-dividend stock price
P_{ex}	ex-dividend stock price
P_{rep}	stock price with share repurchase
τ_d	dividend tax rate
τ_g	capital gains tax rate
τ_d^*	effective dividend tax rate
τ_c	corporate tax rate
P_{retain}	stock price if excess cash is retained
τ_i	tax rate on interest income
τ_{retain}^*	effective tax rate on retained cash
Div	dividend
r_f	risk free rate

FOR MANY YEARS, MICROSOFT CORPORATION CHOSE TO DISTRIBUTE cash to investors primarily by repurchasing its own stock. During the five fiscal years ending June 2004, for example, Microsoft spent an average of $5.4 billion per year on share repurchases. Microsoft began paying dividends to investors in 2003, with what CFO John Connors called "a starter dividend" of $0.08 per share. Then, on July 20, 2004, Microsoft stunned financial markets by announcing plans to pay the largest single cash dividend payment in history, a one-time dividend of $32 billion, or $3 per share, to all shareholders of record on November 17, 2004. Since then Microsoft has repurchased over $120 billion in shares, and raised its quarterly dividend 10 times, so that by late 2015 its dividend was $0.36 per share, representing a 3% annual dividend yield.

When a firm's investments generate free cash flow, the firm must decide how to use that cash. If the firm has new positive-NPV investment opportunities, it can reinvest the cash and increase the value of the firm. Many young, rapidly growing firms reinvest 100% of their cash flows in this way. But mature, profitable firms such as Microsoft often find that they generate more cash than they need to fund all of their attractive investment opportunities. When a firm has excess cash, it can hold those funds as part of its cash reserves or pay the cash out to shareholders. If the firm decides to follow the latter approach, it has two choices: It can pay a dividend or it can repurchase shares from current owners. These decisions represent the firm's payout policy.

In this chapter, we show that, as with capital structure, a firm's payout policy is shaped by market imperfections, such as taxes, agency costs, transaction costs, and asymmetric information between managers and investors. We look at why some firms prefer to pay dividends, whereas others rely exclusively on share repurchases. In addition, we explore why some firms build up large cash reserves, while others pay out their excess cash.

17.1 Distributions to Shareholders

Figure 17.1 illustrates the alternative uses of free cash flow.[1] The way a firm chooses between these alternatives is referred to as its **payout policy**. We begin our discussion of a firm's payout policy by considering the choice between paying dividends and repurchasing shares. In this section, we examine the details of these methods of paying cash to shareholders.

Dividends

A public company's board of directors determines the amount of the firm's dividend. The board sets the amount per share that will be paid and decides when the payment will occur. The date on which the board authorizes the dividend is the **declaration date**. After the board declares the dividend, the firm is legally obligated to make the payment.

The firm will pay the dividend to all shareholders of record on a specific date, set by the board, called the **record date**. Because it takes three business days for shares to be registered, only shareholders who purchase the stock at least three days prior to the record date receive the dividend. As a result, the date two business days prior to the record date is known as the **ex-dividend date**; anyone who purchases the stock on or after the ex-dividend date will not receive the dividend. Finally, on the **payable date** (or **distribution date**), which is generally about a month after the record date, the firm mails dividend checks to the registered shareholders. Figure 17.2 shows these dates for Microsoft's $3.00 dividend.

Most companies that pay dividends pay them at regular, quarterly intervals. Companies typically adjust the amount of their dividends gradually, with little variation in the amount of the dividend from quarter to quarter. Occasionally, a firm may pay a one-time, **special dividend** that is usually much larger than a regular dividend, as was Microsoft's $3.00 dividend in 2004. Figure 17.3 shows the dividends paid by GM from 1983 to 2008. In addition to regular dividends, GM paid special dividends in December 1997 and again in May 1999 (associated with spin-offs of subsidiaries, discussed further in Section 17.7).

FIGURE 17.1

Uses of Free Cash Flow

A firm can retain its free cash flow, either investing or accumulating it, or pay out its free cash flow through a dividend or share repurchase. The choice between holding cash, repurchasing shares, or paying dividends is determined by the firm's payout policy.

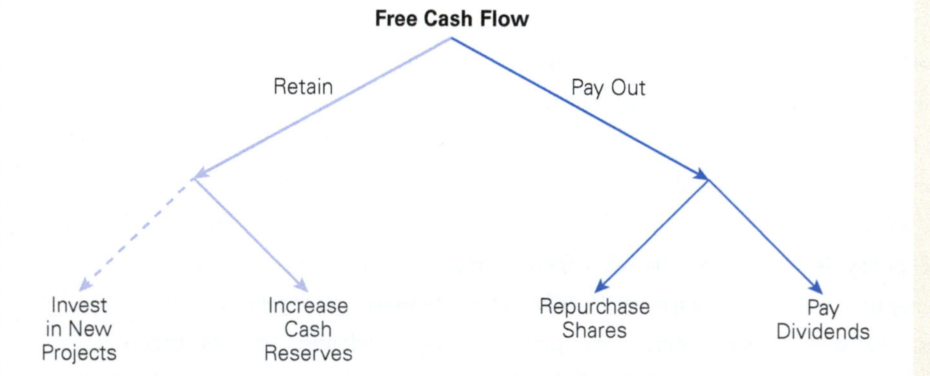

[1] Strictly speaking, Figure 17.1 is for an all-equity firm. For a levered firm, free cash flow would also be used to support interest and principal payments to debt holders.

FIGURE 17.2 Important Dates for Microsoft's Special Dividend

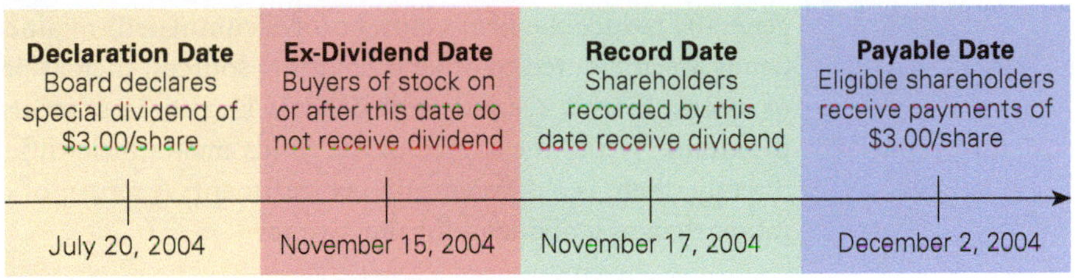

Microsoft declared the dividend on July 20, 2004, payable on December 2 to all shareholders of record on November 17. The ex-dividend date was two business days earlier, or November 15, 2004.

Notice that GM split its stock in March 1989 so that each owner of one share received a second share. This kind of transaction is called a 2-for-1 stock split. More generally, in a **stock split** or **stock dividend**, the company issues additional shares rather than cash to its shareholders. In the case of GM's stock split, the number of shares doubled, but the dividend per share was cut in half (from $1.50 per share to $0.75 per share), so that the total amount GM paid out as a dividend was the same just before and just after the split. (We discuss stock splits and stock dividends further in Section 17.7.) While GM raised its dividends throughout the 1980s, it cut its dividend during the recession in the early 1990s. GM raised its dividends again in the late 1990s, but was forced to cut its dividend again in early 2006 and suspend them altogether in July 2008 in response to financial difficulties. One year later GM filed for Chapter 11 bankruptcy and its existing shareholders were

FIGURE 17.3

Dividend History for GM Stock, 1983–2008

Until suspending its dividends in July 2008, GM had paid a regular dividend each quarter since 1983. GM paid additional special dividends in December 1997 and May 1999, and had a 2-for-1 stock split in March 1989. GM ultimately filed for bankruptcy in June of 2009 wiping out all existing equity holders. GM has since emerged from bankruptcy and issued new stock, reinstating its dividend in 2014.

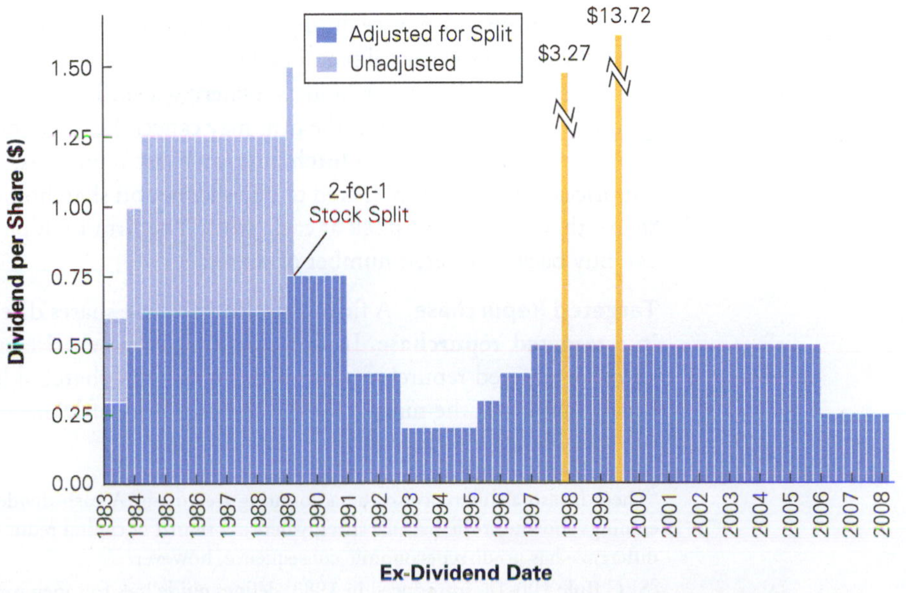

wiped out. GM has since emerged from bankruptcy (in 2009) and issued new shares, but did not reintroduce a dividend payment until 2014.

Dividends are a cash outflow for the firm. From an accounting perspective, dividends generally reduce the firm's current (or accumulated) retained earnings. In some cases, dividends are attributed to other accounting sources, such as paid-in capital or the liquidation of assets. In this case, the dividend is known as a **return of capital** or a **liquidating dividend**. While the source of the funds makes little difference to a firm or to investors directly, there is a difference in tax treatment: A return of capital is taxed as a capital gain rather than as a dividend for the investor.[2]

Share Repurchases

An alternative way to pay cash to investors is through a share repurchase or buyback. In this kind of transaction, the firm uses cash to buy shares of its own outstanding stock. These shares are generally held in the corporate treasury, and they can be resold if the company needs to raise money in the future. We now examine three possible transaction types for a share repurchase.

Open Market Repurchase. An **open market repurchase** is the most common way that firms repurchase shares. A firm announces its intention to buy its own shares in the open market, and then proceeds to do so over time like any other investor. The firm may take a year or more to buy the shares, and it is not obligated to repurchase the full amount it originally stated. Also, the firm must not buy its shares in a way that might appear to manipulate the price. For example, SEC guidelines recommend that the firm not purchase more than 25% of the average daily trading volume in its shares on a single day, nor make purchases at the market open or within 30 minutes of the close of trade.[3]

While open market share repurchases represent about 95% of all repurchase transactions,[4] other methods are available to a firm that wants to buy back its stock. These methods are used when a firm wishes to repurchase a substantial portion of its shares, often as part of a recapitalization.

Tender Offer. A firm can repurchase shares through a **tender offer** in which it offers to buy shares at a prespecified price during a short time period—generally within 20 days. The price is usually set at a substantial premium (10%–20% is typical) to the current market price. The offer often depends on shareholders tendering a sufficient number of shares. If shareholders do not tender enough shares, the firm may cancel the offer and no buyback occurs.

A related method is the **Dutch auction** share repurchase, in which the firm lists different prices at which it is prepared to buy shares, and shareholders in turn indicate how many shares they are willing to sell at each price. The firm then pays the lowest price at which it can buy back its desired number of shares.

Targeted Repurchase. A firm may also purchase shares directly from a major shareholder in a **targeted repurchase**. In this case the purchase price is negotiated directly with the seller. A targeted repurchase may occur if a major shareholder desires to sell a large number of shares but the market for the shares is not sufficiently liquid to sustain such a large

---

[2]There is also a difference in the accounting treatment. A cash dividend reduces the cash and retained earnings shown on the balance sheet, whereas a return of capital reduces paid-in capital. This accounting difference has no direct economic consequence, however.

[3]SEC Rule 10b-18, introduced in 1983, defines guidelines for open market share repurchases.

[4]G. Grullon and D. Ikenberry, "What Do We Know About Stock Repurchases?" *Journal of Applied Corporate Finance* 13(1) (2000): 31–51.

sale without severely affecting the price. Under these circumstances, the shareholder may be willing to sell shares back to the firm at a discount to the current market price. Alternatively, if a major shareholder is threatening to take over the firm and remove its management, the firm may decide to eliminate the threat by buying out the shareholder—often at a large premium over the current market price. This type of transaction is called **greenmail**.

CONCEPT CHECK

1. How is a stock's ex-dividend date determined, and what is its significance?
2. What is a Dutch auction share repurchase?

17.2 Comparison of Dividends and Share Repurchases

If a corporation decides to pay cash to shareholders, it can do so through either dividend payments or share repurchases. How do firms choose between these alternatives? In this section, we show that in the perfect capital markets setting of Modigliani and Miller, the method of payment does not matter.

Consider the case of Genron Corporation, a hypothetical firm. Genron has \$20 million in excess cash and no debt. The firm expects to generate additional free cash flows of \$48 million per year in subsequent years. If Genron's unlevered cost of capital is 12%, then the enterprise value of its ongoing operations is

$$\text{Enterprise Value} = PV(\text{Future FCF}) = \frac{\$48 \text{ million}}{12\%} = \$400 \text{ million}$$

Including the cash, Genron's total market value is \$420 million.

Genron's board is meeting to decide how to pay out its \$20 million in excess cash to shareholders. Some board members have advocated using the \$20 million to pay a \$2 cash dividend for each of Genron's 10 million outstanding shares. Others have suggested repurchasing shares instead of paying a dividend. Still others have proposed that Genron raise additional cash and pay an even larger dividend today, in anticipation of the high future free cash flows it expects to receive. Will the amount of the current dividend affect Genron's share price? Which policy would shareholders prefer?

Let's analyze the consequences of each of these three alternative policies and compare them in a setting of perfect capital markets.

Alternative Policy 1: Pay Dividend with Excess Cash

Suppose the board opts for the first alternative and uses all excess cash to pay a dividend. With 10 million shares outstanding, Genron will be able to pay a \$2 dividend immediately. Because the firm expects to generate future free cash flows of \$48 million per year, it anticipates paying a dividend of \$4.80 per share each year thereafter. The board declares the dividend and sets the record date as December 14, so that the ex-dividend date is December 12. Let's compute Genron's share price just before and after the stock goes ex-dividend.

The fair price for the shares is the present value of the expected dividends given Genron's equity cost of capital. Because Genron has no debt, its equity cost of capital equals its unlevered cost of capital of 12%. Just before the ex-dividend date, the stock is said to trade **cum-dividend** ("with the dividend") because anyone who buys the stock will be entitled to the dividend. In this case,

$$P_{cum} = \text{Current Dividend} + PV(\text{Future Dividends}) = 2 + \frac{4.80}{0.12} = 2 + 40 = \$42$$

After the stock goes ex-dividend, new buyers will not receive the current dividend. At this point the share price will reflect only the dividends in subsequent years:

$$P_{ex} = PV(\text{Future Dividends}) = \frac{4.80}{0.12} = \$40$$

The share price will drop on the ex-dividend date, December 12. The amount of the price drop is equal to the amount of the current dividend, $2. We can also determine this change in the share price using a simple market value balance sheet (values in millions of dollars):

	December 11 (Cum-Dividend)	December 12 (Ex-Dividend)
Cash	20	0
Other assets	400	400
Total market value	420	400
Shares (millions)	10	10
Share price	**$42**	**$40**

As the market value balance sheet shows, the share price falls when a dividend is paid because the reduction in cash decreases the market value of the firm's assets. Although the stock price falls, holders of Genron stock do not incur a loss overall. Before the dividend, their stock was worth $42. After the dividend, their stock is worth $40 and they hold $2 in cash from the dividend, for a total value of $42.[5]

The fact that the stock price falls by the amount of the dividend also follows from the assumption that no opportunity for arbitrage exists. If it fell by less than the dividend, an investor could earn a profit by buying the stock just before it goes ex-dividend and selling it just after, as the dividend would more than cover the capital loss on the stock. Similarly, if the stock price fell by more than the dividend, an investor could profit by selling the stock just before it goes ex-dividend and buying it just after. Therefore, no arbitrage implies

In a perfect capital market, when a dividend is paid, the share price drops by the amount of the dividend when the stock begins to trade ex-dividend.

Alternative Policy 2: Share Repurchase (No Dividend)

Suppose that Genron does not pay a dividend this year, but instead uses the $20 million to repurchase its shares on the open market. How will the repurchase affect the share price?

With an initial share price of $42, Genron will repurchase $20 million ÷ $42 per share $= 0.476$ million shares, leaving only $10 - 0.476 = 9.524$ million shares outstanding. Once again, we can use Genron's market value balance sheet to analyze this transaction:

	December 11 (Before Repurchase)	December 12 (After Repurchase)
Cash	20	0
Other assets	400	400
Total market value of assets	420	400
Shares (millions)	10	9.524
Share price	**$42**	**$42**

[5]For simplicity, we have ignored the short delay between the ex-dividend date and the payable date of the dividend. In reality, the shareholders do not receive the dividend immediately, but rather the *promise* to receive it within several weeks. The stock price adjusts by the present value of this promise, which is effectively equal to the amount of the dividend unless interest rates are extremely high.

In this case, the market value of Genron's assets falls when the company pays out cash, but the number of shares outstanding also falls. The two changes offset each other, so the share price remains the same.

Genron's Future Dividends. We can also see why the share price does not fall after the share repurchase by considering the effect on Genron's future dividends. In future years, Genron expects to have \$48 million in free cash flow, which can be used to pay a dividend of \$48 million ÷ 9.524 million shares = \$5.04 per share each year. Thus, with a share repurchase, Genron's share price today is

$$P_{rep} = \frac{5.04}{0.12} = \$42$$

In other words, by not paying a dividend today and repurchasing shares instead, Genron is able to raise its dividends *per share* in the future. The increase in future dividends compensates shareholders for the dividend they give up today. This example illustrates the following general conclusion about share repurchases:

> *In perfect capital markets, an open market share repurchase has no effect on the stock price, and the stock price is the same as the cum-dividend price if a dividend were paid instead.*

Investor Preferences. Would an investor prefer that Genron issue a dividend or repurchase its stock? Both policies lead to the same *initial* share price of \$42. But is there a difference in shareholder value *after* the transaction? Consider an investor who currently holds 2000 shares of Genron stock. Assuming the investor does not trade the stock, the investor's holdings after a dividend or share repurchase are as follows:

Dividend	Repurchase
\$40 × 2000 = \$80,000 stock	\$42 × 2000 = \$84,000 stock
\$ 2 × 2000 = \$ 4,000 cash	

In either case, the value of the investor's portfolio is \$84,000 immediately after the transaction. The only difference is the distribution between cash and stock holdings. Thus, it might seem the investor would prefer one approach or the other based on whether she needs the cash.

But if Genron repurchases shares and the investor wants cash, she can raise cash by selling shares. For example, she can sell \$4000 ÷ \$42 per share = 95 shares to raise about \$4000 in cash. She will then hold 1905 shares, or 1905 × \$42 ≈ \$80,000 in stock. Thus, in the case of a share repurchase, by selling shares an investor can create a **homemade dividend**.

Similarly, if Genron pays a dividend and the investor does not want the cash, she can use the \$4000 proceeds of the dividend to purchase 100 additional shares at the ex-dividend share price of \$40 per share. As a result she will hold 2100 shares, worth 2100 × \$40 = \$84,000.[6] We summarize these two cases below:

Dividend + Buy 100 shares	Repurchase + Sell 95 shares
\$40 × 2100 = \$84,000 stock	\$42 × 1905 ≈ \$80,000 stock
	\$42 × 95 ≈ \$ 4,000 cash

[6]In fact, many firms allow investors to register for a dividend reinvestment program, or *DRIP*, which automatically reinvests any dividends into new shares of the stock.

COMMON MISTAKE **Repurchases and the Supply of Shares**

There is a misconception that when a firm repurchases its own shares, the price rises due to the decrease in the supply of shares outstanding. This intuition follows naturally from the standard supply and demand analysis taught in microeconomics. Why does that analysis not apply here?

When a firm repurchases its own shares, two things happen. First, the supply of shares is reduced. At the same time, however, the value of the firm's assets declines when it spends its cash to buy the shares. If the firm repurchases its shares at their market price, these two effects offset each other, leaving the share price unchanged.

This result is similar to the dilution fallacy discussed in Chapter 14: When a firm issues shares at their market price, the share price does not fall due to the increase in supply. The increase in supply is offset by the increase in the firm's assets that results from the cash it receives from the issuance.

By selling shares or reinvesting dividends, the investor can create any combination of cash and stock desired. As a result, the investor is indifferent between the various payout methods the firm might employ:

In perfect capital markets, investors are indifferent between the firm distributing funds via dividends or share repurchases. By reinvesting dividends or selling shares, they can replicate either payout method on their own.

Alternative Policy 3: High Dividend (Equity Issue)

Let's look at a third possibility for Genron. Suppose the board wishes to pay an even larger dividend than \$2 per share right now. Is that possible and, if so, will the higher dividend make shareholders better off?

Genron plans to pay \$48 million in dividends starting next year. Suppose the firm wants to start paying that amount today. Because it has only \$20 million in cash today, Genron needs an additional \$28 million to pay the larger dividend now. It could raise cash by scaling back its investments. But if the investments have positive NPV, reducing them would lower firm value. An alternative way to raise more cash is to borrow money or sell new shares. Let's consider an equity issue. Given a current share price of \$42, Genron could raise \$28 million by selling $\$28 \text{ million} \div \$42 \text{ per share} = 0.67$ million shares. Because this equity issue will increase Genron's total number of shares outstanding to 10.67 million, the amount of the dividend per share each year will be

$$\frac{\$48 \text{ million}}{10.67 \text{ million shares}} = \$4.50 \text{ per share}$$

Under this new policy, Genron's cum-dividend share price is

$$P_{cum} = 4.50 + \frac{4.50}{0.12} = 4.50 + 37.50 = \$42$$

As in the previous examples, the initial share value is unchanged by this policy, and increasing the dividend has no benefit to shareholders.

EXAMPLE 17.1 **Homemade Dividends**

Problem

Suppose Genron does not adopt the third alternative policy, and instead pays a \$2 dividend per share today. Show how an investor holding 2000 shares could create a homemade dividend of $\$4.50 \text{ per share} \times 2000 \text{ shares} = \$9000$ per year on her own.

Solution

If Genron pays a $2 dividend, the investor receives $4000 in cash and holds the rest in stock. To receive $9000 in total today, she can raise an additional $5000 by selling 125 shares at $40 per share just after the dividend is paid. In future years, Genron will pay a dividend of $4.80 per share. Because she will own $2000 - 125 = 1875$ shares, the investor will receive dividends of $1875 \times \$4.80 = \$9000$ per year from then on.

Modigliani-Miller and Dividend Policy Irrelevance

In our analysis we considered three possible dividend policies for the firm this year: (1) pay out all cash as a dividend, (2) pay no dividend and use the cash instead to repurchase shares, or (3) issue equity to finance a larger dividend. These policies are illustrated in Table 17.1.

Table 17.1 shows an important trade-off: If Genron pays a higher *current* dividend per share, it will pay lower *future* dividends per share. For example, if the firm raises the current dividend by issuing equity, it will have more shares and therefore smaller free cash flows per share to pay dividends in the future. If the firm lowers the current dividend and repurchases its shares, it will have fewer shares in the future, so it will be able to pay a higher dividend per share. The net effect of this trade-off is to leave the total present value of all future dividends, and hence the current share price, unchanged.

The logic of this section matches that in our discussion of capital structure in Chapter 14. There we explained that in perfect capital markets, buying and selling equity and debt are zero-NPV transactions that do not affect firm value. Moreover, any choice of leverage by a firm could be replicated by investors using homemade leverage. As a result, the firm's choice of capital structure is irrelevant.

Here we have established the same principle for a firm's choice of a dividend. Regardless of the amount of cash the firm has on hand, it can pay a smaller dividend (and use the remaining cash to repurchase shares) or a larger dividend (by selling equity to raise cash). Because buying or selling shares is a zero-NPV transaction, such transactions have no effect on the initial share price. Furthermore, shareholders can create a homemade dividend of any size by buying or selling shares themselves.

Modigliani and Miller developed this idea in another influential paper published in 1961.[7] As with their result on capital structure, it went against the conventional wisdom

TABLE 17.1 **Genron's Dividends per Share Each Year Under the Three Alternative Policies**

	Initial Share Price	Dividend Paid ($ per share)			
		Year 0	Year 1	Year 2	...
Policy 1:	$42.00	2.00	4.80	4.80	...
Policy 2:	$42.00	0	5.04	5.04	...
Policy 3:	$42.00	4.50	4.50	4.50	...

[7]See M. Modigliani and M. Miller, "Dividend Policy, Growth, and the Valuation of Shares," *Journal of Business* 34 (1961): 411–433. See also J. B. Williams, *The Theory of Investment Value* (Harvard University Press, 1938).

COMMON MISTAKE The Bird in the Hand Fallacy

"A bird in the hand is worth two in the bush."

The **bird in the hand hypothesis** states that firms choosing to pay higher current dividends will enjoy higher stock prices because shareholders prefer current dividends to future ones (with the same present value). According to this view, alternative policy 3 would lead to the highest share price for Genron.

Modigliani and Miller's response to this view is that with perfect capital markets, shareholders can generate an equivalent homemade dividend at any time by selling shares. Thus, the dividend choice of the firm should not matter.*

*The bird in the hand hypothesis is proposed in early studies of dividend policy. See M. Gordon, "Optimal Investment and Financing Policy," *Journal of Finance* 18 (1963): 264–272; and J. Lintner, "Dividends, Earnings, Leverage, Stock Prices and the Supply of Capital to Corporations," *Review of Economics and Statistics* 44 (1962): 243–269.

that dividend policy could change a firm's value and make its shareholders better off even absent market imperfections. We state here their important proposition:

MM Dividend Irrelevance: *In perfect capital markets, holding fixed the investment policy of a firm, the firm's choice of dividend policy is irrelevant and does not affect the initial share price.*

Dividend Policy with Perfect Capital Markets

The examples in this section illustrate the idea that by using share repurchases or equity issues a firm can easily alter its dividend payments. Because these transactions do not alter the value of the firm, neither does dividend policy.

This result may at first seem to contradict the idea that the price of a share should equal the present value of its future dividends. As our examples have shown, however, a firm's choice of dividend today affects the dividends it can afford to pay in the future in an offsetting fashion. Thus, while dividends *do* determine share prices, a firm's choice of dividend policy does not.

As Modigliani and Miller make clear, the value of a firm ultimately derives from its underlying free cash flow. A firm's free cash flow determines the level of payouts that it can make to its investors. In a perfect capital market, whether these payouts are made through dividends or share repurchases does not matter. Of course, in reality capital markets are not perfect. As with capital structure, it is the imperfections in capital markets that should determine the firm's dividend and payout policy.

CONCEPT CHECK

1. True or False: When a firm repurchases its own shares, the price rises due to the decrease in the supply of shares outstanding.
2. In a perfect capital market, how important is the firm's decision to pay dividends versus repurchase shares?

17.3 The Tax Disadvantage of Dividends

As with capital structure, taxes are an important market imperfection that influences a firm's decision to pay dividends or repurchase shares.

TABLE 17.2 Long-Term Capital Gains Versus Dividend Tax Rates in the United States, 1971–2012

Year	Capital Gains	Dividends
1971–1978	35%	70%
1979–1981	28%	70%
1982–1986	20%	50%
1987	28%	39%
1988–1990	28%	28%
1991–1992	28%	31%
1993–1996	28%	40%
1997–2000	20%	40%
2001–2002	20%	39%
2003–2012	15%	15%
2013*–	20%	20%

*The tax rates shown are for financial assets held for more than one year. For assets held one year or less, capital gains are taxed at the ordinary income tax rate (currently 39.6% for the highest bracket); the same is true for dividends if the assets are held for less than 61 days. Because the capital gains tax is not paid until the asset is sold, for assets held for longer than one year the *effective* capital gains tax rate is equal to the present value of the rate shown, when discounted by the after-tax risk-free interest rate for the additional number of years the asset is held.

Taxes on Dividends and Capital Gains

Shareholders typically must pay taxes on the dividends they receive. They must also pay capital gains taxes when they sell their shares. Table 17.2 shows the history of U.S. tax rates applied to dividends and long-term capital gains for investors in the highest tax bracket.

Do taxes affect investors' preferences for dividends versus share repurchases? When a firm pays a dividend, shareholders are taxed according to the dividend tax rate. If the firm repurchases shares instead, and shareholders sell shares to create a homemade dividend, the homemade dividend will be taxed according to the capital gains tax rate. If dividends are taxed at a higher rate than capital gains, which was true prior to 2003, shareholders will prefer share repurchases to dividends.[8] And although recent tax code changes equalized the tax rates on dividends and capital gains, because capital gains taxes are deferred until the asset is sold, there is still a tax advantage for share repurchases over dividends for long-term investors.

A higher tax rate on dividends also makes it undesirable for a firm to raise funds to pay a dividend. Absent taxes and issuance costs, if a firm raises money by issuing shares and then gives that money back to shareholders as a dividend, shareholders are no better or worse off—they get back the money they put in. When dividends are taxed at a higher rate than capital gains, however, this transaction hurts shareholders because they will receive less than their initial investment.

[8]Some countries tax dividends at a lower rate than capital gains. The same holds currently in the U.S. for stocks held between 61 days and one year.

EXAMPLE 17.2 **Issuing Equity to Pay a Dividend**

Problem

Suppose a firm raises $10 million from shareholders and uses this cash to pay them $10 million in dividends. If the dividend is taxed at a 40% rate, and if capital gains are taxed at a 15% rate, how much will shareholders receive after taxes?

Solution

Shareholders will owe 40% of $10 million, or $4 million in dividend taxes. Because the value of the firm will fall when the dividend is paid, shareholders' capital gain on the stock will be $10 million less when they sell, lowering their capital gains taxes by 15% of $10 million or $1.5 million. Thus, in total, shareholders will pay $4 million − $1.5 million = $2.5 million in taxes, and they will receive back only $7.5 million of their $10 million investment.

Optimal Dividend Policy with Taxes

When the tax rate on dividends exceeds the tax rate on capital gains, shareholders will pay lower taxes if a firm uses share repurchases for all payouts rather than dividends. This tax savings will increase the value of a firm that uses share repurchases rather than dividends. We can also express the tax savings in terms of a firm's equity cost of capital. Firms that use dividends will have to pay a higher pre-tax return to offer their investors the same after-tax return as firms that use share repurchases.[9] As a result, the optimal dividend policy when the dividend tax rate exceeds the capital gain tax rate is to *pay no dividends at all.*

While firms do still pay dividends, substantial evidence shows that many firms have recognized their tax disadvantage. For example, prior to 1980, a majority of firms used dividends exclusively to distribute cash to shareholders (see Figure 17.4). But the fraction of dividend-paying firms declined dramatically from 1978–2002, falling by more than half.

FIGURE 17.4 **Trends in the Use of Dividends and Repurchases**

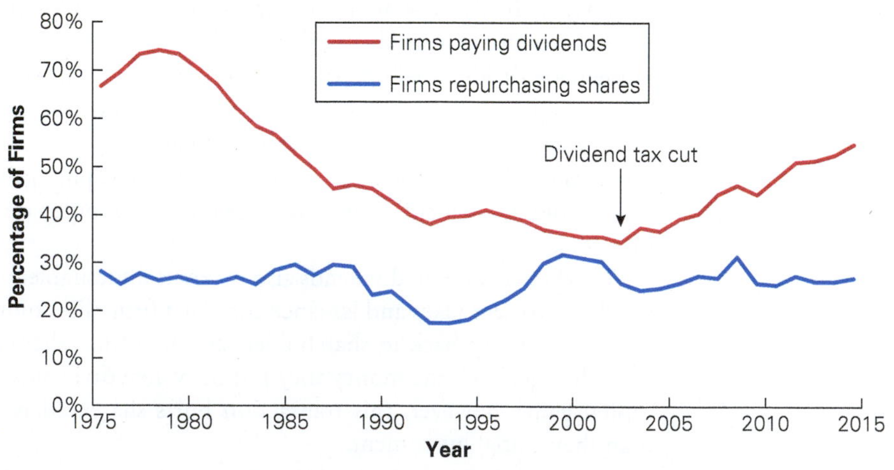

This figure shows the percentage of publicly traded U.S. industrial firms each year that paid dividends or repurchased shares. Note the broad decline in the fraction of firms using dividends from 1975 to 2002, falling from 75% to 35%. This trend has reversed since the 2003 dividend tax cut. The fraction of firms repurchasing shares each year has averaged about 30%.

Source: Compustat

[9]For an extension of the CAPM that includes investor taxes, see M. Brennan, "Taxes, Market Valuation and Corporation Financial Policy," *National Tax Journal* 23 (1970): 417–427.

FIGURE 17.5 **The Changing Composition of Shareholder Payouts**

This figure shows the value of share repurchases as a percentage of total payouts to shareholders (dividends and repurchases). By the late 1990s share repurchases surpassed dividends to become the largest form of corporate payouts for U.S. industrial firms. Note, however, the declines in repurchases during economic downturns.

Source: Compustat data for U.S. firms, excluding financial firms and utilities.

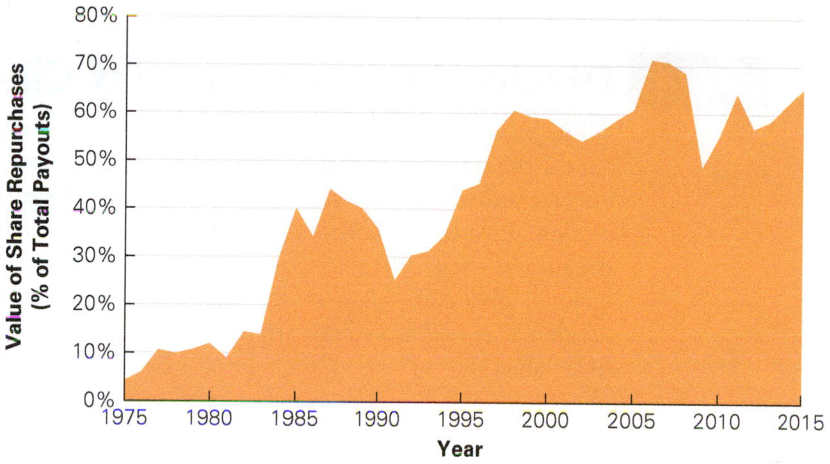

The trend away from dividends has noticeably reversed, however, since the 2003 reduction in the dividend tax rate.[10]

Figure 17.4 does not tell the full story of the shift in corporate payout policy, however. We see a more dramatic trend if we compare the dollar amounts of both forms of corporate payouts. Figure 17.5 shows the relative importance of share repurchases as a proportion of total payouts to shareholders. While dividends accounted for more than 80% of corporate payouts until the early 1980s, the importance of share repurchases grew dramatically in the mid-1980s after the SEC gave guidelines that provided firms a "safe harbor" from accusations of stock-price manipulation.[11] Repurchase activity slowed during the 1990–1991 recession, but by the end of the 1990s repurchases exceeded the value of dividend payments for U.S. industrial firms.[12]

While this evidence is indicative of the growing importance of share repurchases as a part of firms' payout policies, it also shows that dividends still remain a key form of payouts to shareholders. The fact that firms continue to issue dividends despite their tax disadvantage is often referred to as the **dividend puzzle.**[13] In the next section, we consider some factors that may mitigate this tax disadvantage. In Section 17.6, we examine alternative motivations for using dividends based on asymmetric information.

---

[10]See E. Fama and K. French, "Disappearing Dividends: Changing Firm Characteristics or Lower Propensity to Pay?" *Journal of Financial Economics* 60 (2001): 3–43. For an examination of recent trends since 2000, see B. Julio and D. Ikenberry, "Reappearing Dividends," *Journal of Applied Corporate Finance* 16 (2004): 89–100.

[11]SEC Rule 10b-18 (adopted in 1982 and amended in 2003) provides guidelines on the manner of purchase (a single broker on a given day), their timing and price (not at the open nor close of trade, no higher than last transaction or published bid price), and their volume (less than 25% of trading volume).

[12]For further evidence that repurchases are replacing dividends, see G. Grullon and R. Michaely, "Dividends, Share Repurchases, and the Substitution Hypothesis," *Journal of Finance* 57 (2002): 1649–1684; and J. Farre-Mensa, R. Michaely, and M. Schmalz, "Payout Policy," *Annual Review of Financial Economics* 6 (2014): 75–134.

[13]See F. Black, "The Dividend Puzzle," *Journal of Portfolio Management* 2 (1976): 5–8.

CONCEPT CHECK

1. What is the optimal dividend policy when the dividend tax rate exceeds the capital gains tax rate?
2. What is the dividend puzzle?

17.4 Dividend Capture and Tax Clienteles

While many investors have a tax preference for share repurchases rather than dividends, the strength of that preference depends on the difference between the dividend tax rate and the capital gains tax rate that they face. Tax rates vary by income, jurisdiction, investment horizon, and whether the stock is held in a retirement account. Because of these differences, firms may attract different groups of investors depending on their dividend policy. In this section, we look in detail at the tax consequences of dividends as well as investor strategies that may reduce the impact of dividend taxes on firm value.

The Effective Dividend Tax Rate

To compare investor preferences, we must quantify the combined effects of dividend and capital gains taxes to determine an effective dividend tax rate for an investor. For simplicity, consider an investor who buys a stock today just before it goes ex-dividend, and sells the stock just after.[14] By doing so, the investor will qualify for, and capture, the dividend. If the stock pays a dividend of amount *Div*, and the investor's dividend tax rate is τ_d, then her after-tax cash flow from the dividend is $Div(1 - \tau_d)$.

In addition, because the price just before the stock goes ex-dividend, P_{cum}, exceeds the price just after, P_{ex}, the investor will expect to incur a capital loss on her trade. If her tax rate on capital gains is τ_g, her after-tax loss is $(P_{cum} - P_{ex})(1 - \tau_g)$.

Therefore, the investor earns a profit by trading to capture the dividend if the after-tax dividend exceeds the after-tax capital loss. Conversely, if the after-tax capital loss exceeds the after-tax dividend, the investor benefits by selling the stock just before it goes ex-dividend and buying it afterward, thereby avoiding the dividend. In other words, there is an arbitrage opportunity unless the price drop and dividend are equal after taxes:

$$(P_{cum} - P_{ex})(1 - \tau_g) = Div(1 - \tau_d) \qquad (17.1)$$

We can write Eq. 17.1 in terms of the share price drop as

$$P_{cum} - P_{ex} = Div \times \left(\frac{1 - \tau_d}{1 - \tau_g}\right) = Div \times \left(1 - \frac{\tau_d - \tau_g}{1 - \tau_g}\right) = Div \times (1 - \tau_d^*) \qquad (17.2)$$

where we define τ_d^* to be the **effective dividend tax rate:**

$$\tau_d^* = \left(\frac{\tau_d - \tau_g}{1 - \tau_g}\right) \qquad (17.3)$$

[14] We could equally well consider a long-term investor deciding between selling the stock just before or just after the ex-dividend date. The analysis would be identical (although the applicable tax rates will depend on the holding period).

The effective dividend tax rate τ_d^* measures the additional tax paid by the investor per dollar of after-tax capital gains income that is instead received as a dividend.[15]

EXAMPLE 17.3 **Changes in the Effective Dividend Tax Rate**

Problem

Consider an individual investor in the highest U.S. tax bracket who plans to hold a stock for more than one year. What was the effective dividend tax rate for this investor in 2002? How did the effective dividend tax rate change in 2003? (Ignore state taxes.)

Solution

From Table 17.2 , in 2002 we have $\tau_d = 39\%$ and $\tau_g = 20\%$. Thus,

$$\tau_d^* = \frac{0.39 - 0.20}{1 - 0.20} = 23.75\%$$

This indicates a significant tax disadvantage of dividends; each $1 of dividends is worth only $0.7625 in capital gains. However, after the 2003 tax cut, $\tau_d = 15\%$, $\tau_g = 15\%$, and

$$\tau_d^* = \frac{0.15 - 0.15}{1 - 0.15} = 0\%$$

Therefore, the 2003 tax cut eliminated the tax disadvantage of dividends for a one-year investor.

Tax Differences Across Investors

The effective dividend tax rate τ_d^* for an investor depends on the tax rates the investor faces on dividends and capital gains. These rates differ across investors for a variety of reasons.

Income Level. Investors with different levels of income fall into different tax brackets and face different tax rates.

Investment Horizon. Capital gains on stocks held one year or less, and dividends on stocks held for less than 61 days, are taxed at higher ordinary income tax rates. Long-term investors can defer the payment of capital gains taxes (lowering their effective capital gains tax rate even further). Investors who plan to bequeath stocks to their heirs may avoid the capital gains tax altogether.

Tax Jurisdiction. U.S. investors are subject to state taxes that differ by state. For example, New Hampshire imposes a 5% tax on income from interest and dividends, but no tax on capital gains. Foreign investors in U.S. stocks are subject to 30% withholding for dividends they receive (unless that rate is reduced by a tax treaty with their home country). There is no similar withholding for capital gains.

Type of Investor or Investment Account. Stocks held by individual investors in a retirement account are not subject to taxes on dividends or capital gains.[16] Similarly, stocks held through pension funds or nonprofit endowment funds are not subject to

[15] For identification and empirical support for Eq. 17.2 and 17.3, see E. Elton and M. Gruber, "Marginal Stockholder Tax Rates and the Clientele Effect," *Review of Economics and Statistics* 52 (1970): 68–74. For investor reaction to major tax code changes see J. Koski, "A Microstructure Analysis of Ex-Dividend Stock Price Behavior Before and After the 1984 and 1986 Tax Reform Acts," *Journal of Business* 69 (1996): 313–338.

[16] While taxes (or penalties) may be owed when the money is withdrawn from the retirement account, these taxes do not depend on whether the money came from dividends or capital gains.

dividend or capital gains taxes. Corporations that hold stocks are able to exclude 70% of dividends they receive from corporate taxes, but are unable to exclude capital gains.[17]

To illustrate, consider four different investors: (1) a "buy and hold" investor who holds the stock in a taxable account and plans to transfer the stock to her heirs, (2) an investor who holds the stock in a taxable account but plans to sell it after one year, (3) a pension fund, and (4) a corporation. Under the current maximum U.S. federal tax rates, the effective dividend tax rate for each would be as follows:

1. Buy and hold individual investor: $\tau_d = 20\%$, $\tau_g = 0$, and $\tau_d^* = 20\%$
2. One-year individual investor: $\tau_d = 20\%$, $\tau_g = 20\%$, and $\tau_d^* = 0$
3. Pension fund: $\tau_d = 0$, $\tau_g = 0$, and $\tau_d^* = 0$
4. Corporation: Given a corporate tax rate of 35%, $\tau_d = (1 - 70\%) \times 35\% = 10.5\%$, $\tau_g = 35\%$, and $\tau_d^* = -38\%$

As a result of their different tax rates, these investors have varying preferences regarding dividends. Long-term investors are more heavily taxed on dividends, so they would prefer share repurchases to dividend payments. One-year investors, pension funds, and other non-taxed investors have no tax preference for share repurchases over dividends; they would prefer a payout policy that most closely matches their cash needs. For example, a non-taxed investor who desires current income would prefer high dividends so as to avoid the brokerage fees and other transaction costs of selling the stock.

Finally, the negative effective dividend tax rate for corporations implies that corporations enjoy a tax *advantage* associated with dividends. For this reason, a corporation that chooses to invest its cash will prefer to hold stocks with high dividend yields. Table 17.3 summarizes the different preferences of investor groups.

Clientele Effects

Differences in tax preferences across investor groups create **clientele effects**, in which the dividend policy of a firm is optimized for the tax preference of its investor clientele. Individuals in the highest tax brackets have a preference for stocks that pay no or low dividends, whereas tax-free investors and corporations have a preference for stocks with high dividends. In this case, a firm's dividend policy is optimized for the tax preference of its investor clientele.

TABLE 17.3 Differing Dividend Policy Preferences Across Investor Groups

Investor Group	Dividend Policy Preference	Proportion of Investors
Individual investors	Tax disadvantage for dividends Generally prefer share repurchase (except for retirement accounts)	~52%
Institutions, pension funds	No tax preference Prefer dividend policy that matches income needs	~47%
Corporations	Tax advantage for dividends	~1%

Source: Proportions based on *Federal Reserve Flow of Funds Accounts.*

[17] Corporations can exclude 80% if they own more than 20% of the shares of the firm paying the dividend.

INTERVIEW WITH JOHN CONNORS

John Connors was Senior Vice President and Chief Financial Officer of Microsoft. He retired in 2005 and is now a partner at Ignition Partners, a Seattle venture capital firm.

QUESTION: *Microsoft declared a dividend for the first time in 2003. What goes into the decision of a company to initiate a dividend?*

ANSWER: Microsoft was in a unique position. The company had never paid a dividend and was facing shareholder pressure to do something with its $60 billion cash buildup. The company considered five key questions in developing its distribution strategy:

1. Can the company sustain payment of a cash dividend in perpetuity and increase the dividend over time? Microsoft was confident it could meet that commitment and raise the dividend in the future.
2. Is a cash dividend a better return to stockholders than a stock buyback program? These are capital structure decisions: Do we want to reduce our shares outstanding? Is our stock attractively priced for a buyback, or do we want to distribute the cash as a dividend? Microsoft had plenty of capacity to issue a dividend *and* continue a buyback program.
3. What is the tax effect of a cash dividend versus a buyback to the corporation and to shareholders? From a tax perspective to shareholders, it was largely a neutral decision in Microsoft's case.
4. What is the psychological impact on investors, and how does it fit the story of the stock for investors? This is a more qualitative factor. A regular ongoing dividend put Microsoft on a path to becoming an attractive investment for income investors.
5. What are the public relations implications of a dividend program? Investors don't look to Microsoft to hold cash but to be a leader in software development and provide equity growth. So they viewed the dividend program favorably.

QUESTION: *How does a company decide whether to increase its dividend, have a special dividend, or repurchase its stock to return capital to investors?*

ANSWER: The decision to increase the dividend is a function of cash flow projections. Are you confident that you have adequate cash flow to sustain this and future increases? Once you increase the dividend, investors expect future increases as well. Some companies establish explicit criteria for dividend increases. In my experience as a CFO, the analytic framework involves a set of relative comparables. What are the dividend payouts and dividend yields of the market in general and of your peer group, and where are we relative to them? We talk to significant investors and consider what is best for increasing shareholder value long-term.

A special dividend is a very efficient form of cash distribution that generally involves a nonrecurring situation, such as the sale of a business division or a cash award from a legal situation. Also, companies without a comprehensive distribution strategy use special dividends to reduce large cash accumulations. For Microsoft, the 2004 special dividend and announcement of the stock dividend and stock buyback program resolved the issue of what to do with all the cash and clarified our direction going forward.

QUESTION: *What other factors go into dividend decisions?*

ANSWER: Powerful finance and accounting tools help us to make better and broader business decisions. But these decisions involve as much psychology and market thinking as math. You have to consider non-quantifiable factors such as the psychology of investors. Not long ago, everyone wanted growth stocks; no one wanted dividend-paying stocks. Now dividend stocks are in vogue. You must also take into account your industry and what the competition is doing. In many tech companies, employee ownership in the form of options programs represents a fairly significant percentage of fully diluted shares. Dividend distributions reduce the price of the stock and hence the value of options.

At the end of the day, you want to be sure that your cash distribution strategy helps your overall story with investors.

Evidence supports the existence of tax clienteles. For example, Professors Franklin Allen and Roni Michaely[18] report that in 1996 individual investors held 54% of all stocks by market value, yet received only 35% of all dividends paid, indicating that individuals tend to hold stocks with low dividend yields. Of course, the fact that high-tax investors receive any dividends at all implies that the clienteles are not perfect—dividend taxes are not the only determinants of investors' portfolios.

Another clientele strategy is a dynamic clientele effect, also called the **dividend-capture theory.**[19] This theory states that absent transaction costs, investors can trade shares at the time of the dividend so that non-taxed investors receive the dividend. That is, non-taxed investors need not hold the high-dividend-paying stocks all the time; it is necessary only that they hold them when the dividend is actually paid.

An implication of this theory is that we should see large volumes of trade in a stock around the ex-dividend day, as high-tax investors sell and low-tax investors buy the stock in anticipation of the dividend, and then reverse those trades just after the ex-dividend date. Consider Figure 17.6, which illustrates the price and volume for the stock of Value Line, Inc., during 2004. On April 23, Value Line announced it would use its accumulated cash to pay a special dividend of $17.50 per share, with an ex-dividend date of May 20. Note the substantial increase in the volume of trade around the time of the special dividend. The volume of trade in the month following the special dividend announcement was more than 25 times the volume in the month prior to the announcement. In the three months following the announcement of the special dividend, the cumulative volume exceeded 65% of the total shares available for trade.

While this evidence supports the dividend-capture theory, it is also true that many high-tax investors continue to hold stocks even when dividends are paid. For a small ordinary dividend, the transaction costs and risks of trading the stock probably offset the benefits associated with dividend capture.[20] Only large special dividends, such as in the case of Value Line, tend to generate significant increases in volume. Thus, while clientele effects and dividend-capture strategies reduce the relative tax disadvantage of dividends, they do not eliminate it.[21]

---

[18]F. Allen and R. Michaely, "Payout Policy," in G. Constantinides, M. Harris, and R. Stulz, eds., *Handbook of the Economics of Finance: Corporate Finance Volume* 1A (Elsevier, 2003).

[19]This idea is developed by A. Kalay, "The Ex-Dividend Day Behavior of Stock Prices: A Reexamination of the Clientele Effect," *Journal of Finance* 37 (1982): 1059–1070. See also J. Boyd and R. Jagannathan, "Ex-Dividend Price Behavior of Common Stocks," *Review of Financial Studies* 7 (1994): 711–741, who discuss the complications that arise with multiple tax clienteles.

[20]Dividend-capture strategies are risky because the stock price may fluctuate for unrelated reasons before the transaction can be completed. J. Koski and R. Michaely, "Prices, Liquidity, and the Information Content of Trades," *Review of Financial Studies* 13 (2000): 659–696, show that this risk can be eliminated by negotiating a purchase and sale simultaneously, but with settlement dates before and after the ex-dividend date. When such transactions are possible, the amount of dividend-related volume is greatly increased.

[21]Dividend capture strategies are one reason it is difficult to find evidence that dividend yields affect the equity cost of capital. While evidence was found by R. Litzenberger and K. Ramaswamy ["The Effects of Personal Taxes and Dividends on Capital Asset Prices: Theory and Empirical Evidence," *Journal of Financial Economics* 7 (1979): 163–195], this evidence is contradicted by F. Black and M. Scholes ["The Effects of Dividend Yield and Dividend Policy on Common Stock Prices and Returns," *Journal of Financial Economics* 1 (1974): 1–22]. A. Kalay and R. Michaely provide an explanation for these differing results, and do not find a significant impact of dividend yields on expected returns ["Dividends and Taxes: A Reexamination," *Financial Management* 29 (2000): 55–75].

FIGURE 17.6 **Volume and Share Price Effects of Value Line's Special Dividend**

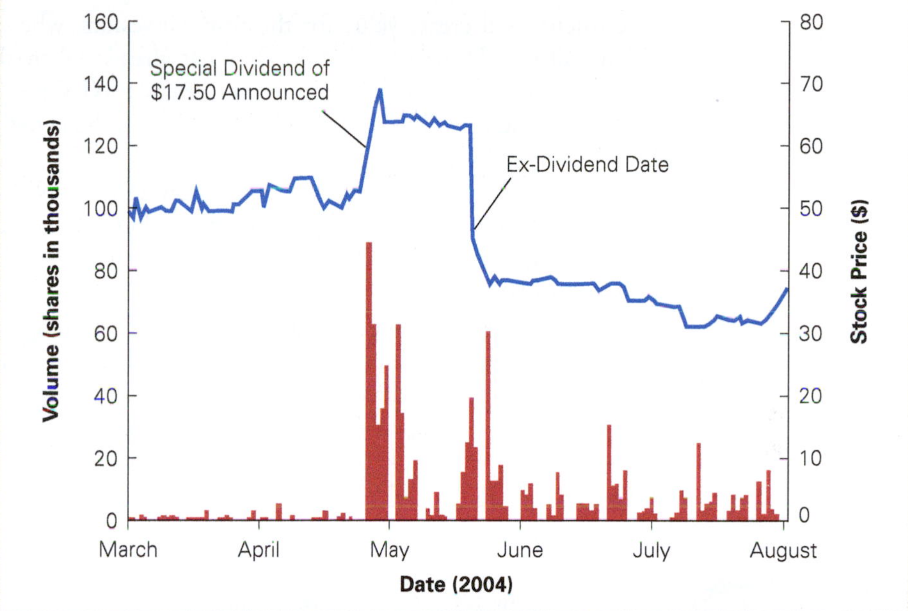

On announcement of the special dividend of $17.50 per share, Value Line's share price rose, as did the volume of trade. The share price dropped by $17.91 on the ex-dividend date, and the volume gradually declined over the following weeks. This pattern of volume is consistent with non-taxed investors buying the stock before the ex-dividend date and selling it afterward. (We consider reasons for the jump in the stock price on the announcement of the dividend in Sections 17.5 and 17.6.)

CONCEPT CHECK

1. Under what conditions will investors have a tax preference for share repurchases rather than dividends?
2. What does the dividend-capture theory imply about the volume of trade in a stock around the ex-dividend day?

17.5 Payout Versus Retention of Cash

Looking back at Figure 17.1, we have thus far considered only one aspect of a firm's payout policy: the choice between paying dividends and repurchasing shares. But how should a firm decide the amount it should pay out to shareholders and the amount it should retain?

To answer this question, first, we must consider what the firm will do with cash that it retains. It can invest the cash in new projects or in financial instruments. We will demonstrate that in the context of perfect capital markets, once a firm has taken all positive-NPV investments, it is indifferent between saving excess cash and paying it out. But once we consider market imperfections, there is a trade-off: Retaining cash can reduce the costs of raising capital in the future, but it can also increase taxes and agency costs.

Retaining Cash with Perfect Capital Markets

If a firm retains cash, it can use those funds to invest in new projects. If new positive-NPV projects are available, this decision is clearly the correct one. Making positive-NPV investments will create value for the firm's investors, whereas saving the cash or paying it out will not. However, once the firm has already taken all positive-NPV projects, any additional projects it takes on are zero or negative-NPV investments. Taking on negative-NPV investments will reduce shareholder value, as the benefits of such investments do not exceed their costs.

Of course, rather than waste excess cash on negative-NPV projects, a firm can hold the cash in the bank or use it to purchase financial assets. The firm can then pay the money to shareholders at a future time or invest it when positive-NPV investment opportunities become available.

What are the advantages and disadvantages of retaining cash and investing in financial securities? In perfect capital markets, buying and selling securities is a zero-NPV transaction, so it should not affect firm value. Shareholders can make any investment a firm makes on their own if the firm pays out the cash. Thus, it should not be surprising that with perfect capital markets, the retention versus payout decision—just like the dividend versus share repurchase decision—is irrelevant to total firm value.

EXAMPLE 17.4 Delaying Dividends with Perfect Markets

Problem

Barston Mining has $100,000 in excess cash. Barston is considering investing the cash in one-year Treasury bills paying 6% interest, and then using the cash to pay a dividend next year. Alternatively, the firm can pay a dividend immediately and shareholders can invest the cash on their own. In a perfect capital market, which option will shareholders prefer?

Solution

If Barston pays an immediate dividend, the shareholders receive $100,000 today. If Barston retains the cash, at the end of one year the company will be able to pay a dividend of

$$\$100{,}000 \times (1.06) = \$106{,}000$$

This payoff is the same as if shareholders had invested the $100,000 in Treasury bills themselves. In other words, the present value of this future dividend is exactly $\$106{,}000 \div (1.06) = \$100{,}000$. Thus, shareholders are indifferent about whether the firm pays the dividend immediately or retains the cash.

As Example 17.4 illustrates, there is no difference for shareholders if the firm pays the cash immediately or retains the cash and pays it out at a future date. This example provides yet another illustration of Modigliani and Miller's fundamental insight regarding financial policy irrelevance in perfect capital markets:

MM Payout Irrelevance: *In perfect capital markets, if a firm invests excess cash flows in financial securities, the firm's choice of payout versus retention is irrelevant and does not affect the initial value of the firm.*

Thus, the decision of whether to retain cash depends on market imperfections, which we turn to next.

Taxes and Cash Retention

Example 17.4 assumed perfect capital markets, and so ignored the effect of taxes. How would our result change with taxes?

EXAMPLE 17.5 Retaining Cash with Corporate Taxes

Problem

Suppose Barston must pay corporate taxes at a 35% rate on the interest it will earn from the one-year Treasury bill paying 6% interest. Would pension fund investors (who do not pay taxes on their investment income) prefer that Barston use its excess cash to pay the $100,000 dividend immediately or retain the cash for one year?

Solution

If Barston pays an immediate dividend, shareholders receive $100,000 today. If Barston retains the cash for one year, it will earn an after-tax return on the Treasury bills of

$$6\% \times (1 - 0.35) = 3.90\%$$

Thus, at the end of the year, Barston will pay a dividend of $100,000 × (1.039) = $103,900.

This amount is less than the $106,000 the investors would have earned if they had invested the $100,000 in Treasury bills themselves. Because Barston must pay corporate taxes on the interest it earns, there is a tax disadvantage to retaining cash. Pension fund investors will therefore prefer that Barston pays the dividend now.

As Example 17.5 shows, corporate taxes make it costly for a firm to retain excess cash. This effect is the very same effect we identified in Chapter 15 with regard to leverage: When a firm pays interest, it receives a tax deduction for that interest, whereas when a firm receives interest, it owes taxes on the interest. As we discussed in Chapter 14, cash is equivalent to *negative* leverage, so the tax advantage of leverage implies a tax disadvantage to holding cash.

EXAMPLE 17.6 Microsoft's Special Dividend

Problem

In the introduction to this chapter, we described Microsoft's special dividend of $3 per share, or $32 billion, during late 2004. If Microsoft had instead retained that cash permanently, what would the present value of the additional taxes be?

Solution

If Microsoft retained the cash, the interest earned on it would be subject to a 35% corporate tax rate. Because the interest payments are risk free, we can discount the tax payments at the risk-free interest rate (assuming Microsoft's marginal corporate tax rate will remain constant or that changes to it have a beta of zero). Thus, the present value of the tax payments on Microsoft's additional interest income would be

$$\frac{\$32 \text{ billion} \times r_f \times 35\%}{r_f} = \$32 \text{ billion} \times 35\% = \$11.2 \text{ billion}$$

Equivalently, on a per share basis, Microsoft's tax savings from paying out the cash rather than retaining it is $3 × 35% = $1.05 per share.

There is one situation when holding cash can lower taxes. Corporations only pay U.S. taxes on their international earnings when they repatriate those earnings. So in some cases corporations can lower their U.S. tax burden by not repatriating earnings and instead holding the cash abroad. If the cash is ultimately spent on future international investments, the corporation can avoid paying U.S. taxes on these earnings. Alternatively, the firm can hold the cash and simultaneously borrow in the U.S. to leave its net debt unchanged. (See "The Repatriation Tax: Why Some Cash-Rich Firms Borrow" in Chapter 15, page 525.)

Adjusting for Investor Taxes

The decision to pay out versus retain cash may also affect the taxes paid by shareholders. While pension and retirement fund investors are tax exempt, most individual investors must pay taxes on interest, dividends, and capital gains. How do investor taxes affect the tax disadvantage of retaining cash?

We illustrate the tax impact with a simple example. Consider a firm whose only asset is \$100 in cash, and suppose all investors face identical tax rates. Let's compare the option of paying out this cash as an immediate dividend of \$100 with the option of retaining the \$100 permanently and using the interest earned to pay dividends.

Suppose the firm pays out its cash immediately as a dividend and shuts down. Because the ex-dividend price of the firm is zero (it has shut down), using Eq. 17.2 we find that before the dividend is paid the firm has a share price of

$$P_{cum} = P_{ex} + Div_0 \times \left(\frac{1 - \tau_d}{1 - \tau_g}\right) = 0 + 100 \times \left(\frac{1 - \tau_d}{1 - \tau_g}\right) \tag{17.4}$$

This price reflects the fact that the investor will pay tax on the dividend at rate τ_d, but will receive a tax credit (at capital gains tax rate τ_g) for the capital loss when the firm shuts down.

Alternatively, the firm can retain the cash and invest it in Treasury bills, earning interest at rate r_f each year. After paying corporate taxes on this interest at rate τ_c, the firm can pay a perpetual dividend of

$$Div = 100 \times r_f \times (1 - \tau_c)$$

each year and retain the \$100 in cash permanently. What price will an investor pay for the firm in this case? The investor's cost of capital is the after-tax return that she could earn by investing in Treasury bills on her own: $r_f \times (1 - \tau_i)$, where τ_i is the investor's tax rate on interest income. Because the investor must pay taxes on the dividends as well, the value of the firm if it retains the \$100 is[22]

$$P_{retain} = \frac{Div \times (1 - \tau_d)}{r_f \times (1 - \tau_i)} = \frac{100 \times r_f \times (1 - \tau_c) \times (1 - \tau_d)}{r_f \times (1 - \tau_i)}$$

$$= 100 \times \frac{(1 - \tau_c)(1 - \tau_d)}{(1 - \tau_i)} \tag{17.5}$$

[22]There is no capital gains tax consequence in this case because the share price will remain the same each year.

Comparing Eq. 17.4 and Eq. 17.5,

$$P_{retain} = P_{cum} \times \frac{(1 - \tau_c)(1 - \tau_g)}{(1 - \tau_i)} = P_{cum} \times (1 - \tau^*_{retain}) \tag{17.6}$$

where τ^*_{retain} measures the effective tax disadvantage of retaining cash:

$$\tau^*_{retain} = \left(1 - \frac{(1 - \tau_c)(1 - \tau_g)}{(1 - \tau_i)}\right) \tag{17.7}$$

Because the dividend tax will be paid whether the firm pays the cash immediately or retains the cash and pays the interest over time, the dividend tax rate does not affect the cost of retaining cash in Eq. 17.7.[23] The intuition for Eq. 17.7 is that when a firm retains cash, it must pay corporate tax on the interest it earns. In addition, the investor will owe capital gains tax on the increased value of the firm. In essence, the interest on retained cash is taxed twice. If the firm paid the cash to its shareholders instead, they could invest it and be taxed only once on the interest that they earn. The cost of retaining cash therefore depends on the combined effect of the corporate and capital gains taxes, compared to the single tax on interest income. Using 2015 tax rates (see Table 15.3), $\tau_c = 35\%$, $\tau_i = 39.6\%$, and $\tau_g = 20\%$, we get an effective tax disadvantage of retained cash of $\tau^*_{retain} = 13.9\%$. Thus, after adjusting for investor taxes, there remains a substantial tax *disadvantage* for the firm to retaining excess cash.

Issuance and Distress Costs

If there is a tax disadvantage to retaining cash, why do some firms accumulate large cash balances? Generally, they retain cash balances to cover potential future cash shortfalls. For example, if there is a reasonable likelihood that future earnings will be insufficient to fund future positive-NPV investment opportunities, a firm may start accumulating cash to make up the difference. This motivation is especially relevant for firms that may need to fund large-scale research and development projects or large acquisitions.

The advantage of holding cash to cover future potential cash needs is that this strategy allows a firm to avoid the transaction costs of raising new capital (through new debt or equity issues). The direct costs of issuance range from 1% to 3% for debt issues and from 3.5% to 7% for equity issues. There can also be substantial indirect costs of raising capital due to the agency and adverse selection (lemons) costs discussed in Chapter 16. Therefore, a firm must balance the tax costs of holding cash with the potential benefits of not having to raise external funds in the future. Firms with very volatile earnings may also build up

[23]Equation 17.7 also holds if the firm uses any (constant) mix of dividends and share repurchases. However, if the firm initially retains cash by cutting back only on share repurchases, and then later uses the cash to pay a mix of dividends and repurchases, then we would replace τ_g in Eq. 17.7 with the average tax rate on dividends and capital gains, $\tau_e = \alpha\tau_d + (1 - \alpha)\tau_g$, where α is the proportion of dividends versus repurchases. In that case, τ^*_{retain} equals the effective tax disadvantage of debt τ^* we derived in Eq. 15.7, where we implicitly assumed that debt was used to fund a share repurchase (or avoid an equity issue), and that the future interest payments displaced a mix of dividends and share repurchases. Using τ_g here is sometimes referred to as the "new view" or "trapped-equity" view of retained earnings; see, for example, A. Auerbach, "Tax Integration and the 'New View' of the Corporate Tax: A 1980s Perspective," *Proceedings of the National Tax Association–Tax Institute of America* (1981): 21–27. Using τ_e corresponds to the "traditional view"; see, for example, J. Poterba and L. Summers, "Dividend Taxes, Corporate Investment, and 'Q'," *Journal of Public Economics* 22 (1983): 135–167.

cash reserves to enable them to weather temporary periods of operating losses. By holding sufficient cash, these firms can avoid financial distress and its associated costs.

Agency Costs of Retaining Cash

There is no benefit to shareholders when a firm holds cash above and beyond its future investment or liquidity needs, however. In fact, in addition to the tax cost, there are likely to be agency costs associated with having too much cash in the firm. As discussed in Chapter 16, when firms have excessive cash, managers may use the funds inefficiently by continuing money-losing pet projects, paying excessive executive perks, or over-paying for acquisitions. In addition, unions, the government, or other entities may take advantage of the firm's "deep pockets."[24] Leverage is one way to reduce a firm's excess cash and avoid these costs; dividends and share repurchases perform a similar role by taking cash out of the firm.

For highly levered firms, equity holders have an additional incentive to pay out cash. Due to the debt overhang problem discussed in Chapter 16, some of the value of the retained cash will benefit debt holders. As a result, equity holders may prefer to "cash out" and increase the firm's payouts. Anticipating this, debt holders will charge a higher cost of debt, or include covenants restricting the firm's payout policy (see the discussion in Section 16.5).

Thus, paying out excess cash through dividends or share repurchases can boost the stock price by reducing waste or the transfer of the firm's resources to other stakeholders. This potential savings, together with tax benefits, likely explains the roughly $10 increase in Value Line's stock price on the announcement of its special dividend, shown in Figure 17.6.

EXAMPLE 17.7 Cutting Negative-NPV Growth

Problem

Rexton Oil is an all-equity firm with 100 million shares outstanding. Rexton has $150 million in cash and expects future free cash flows of $65 million per year. Management plans to use the cash to expand the firm's operations, which will in turn increase future free cash flows by 12%. If the cost of capital of Rexton's investments is 10%, how would a decision to use the cash for a share repurchase rather than the expansion change the share price?

Solution

If Rexton uses the cash to expand, its future free cash flows will increase by 12% to $65 million × 1.12 = $72.8 million per year. Using the perpetuity formula, its market value will be $72.8 million ÷ 10% = $728 million, or $7.28 per share.

If Rexton does not expand, the value of its future free cash flows will be $65 million ÷ 10% = $650 million. Adding the cash, Rexton's market value is $800 million, or $8.00 per share. If Rexton repurchases shares, there will be no change to the share price: It will repurchase $150 million ÷ $8.00/share = 18.75 million shares, so it will have assets worth $650 million with 81.25 million shares outstanding, for a share price of $650 million ÷ 81.25 million shares = $8.00/share.

[24]For example, while Ford's larger cash balances helped it weather the 2008 financial crisis, it also did not receive the same government subsidies or labor concessions as its more troubled competitors.

In this case, cutting investment and growth to fund a share repurchase increases the share price by \$0.72 per share. The reason is the expansion has a negative NPV: It costs \$150 million, but increases future free cash flows by only \$7.8 million, for an NPV of

$$-\$150 \text{ million} + \$7.8 \text{ million}/10\% = -\$72 \text{ million, or } -\$0.72 \text{ per share}$$

Ultimately, firms should choose to retain cash for the same reasons they would use low leverage[25]—to preserve financial slack for future growth opportunities and to avoid financial distress costs. These needs must be balanced against the tax disadvantage of holding cash and the agency cost of wasteful investment. It is not surprising, then, that large global high-tech and biotechnology firms, which typically choose to use little debt, also tend to retain and accumulate large amounts of cash. See Table 17.4 for a list of some U.S. firms with large cash balances.

As with capital structure decisions, however, payout policies are generally set by managers whose incentives may differ from those of shareholders. Managers may prefer to retain and maintain control over the firm's cash rather than pay it out. The retained cash can be used to fund investments that are costly for shareholders but have benefits for managers (for instance, pet projects and excessive salaries), or it can simply be held as a means to reduce leverage and the risk of financial distress that could threaten managers' job security. According to the managerial entrenchment theory of payout policy, managers pay out cash only when pressured to do so by the firm's investors.[26]

CONCEPT CHECK

1. Is there an advantage for a firm to retain its cash instead of paying it out to shareholders in perfect capital markets?
2. How do corporate taxes affect the decision of a firm to retain excess cash?

TABLE 17.4 **Firms with Large Cash Balances (2015)**

Ticker	Company	Cash & Marketable Securities (\$ billion)	Percentage of Market Capitalization
AAPL	Apple Inc.	215.7	37%
GE	General Electric	113.8	39%
MSFT	Microsoft Corporation	102.3	23%
GOOGL	Alphabet (Google)	73.1	14%
CSCO	Cisco Systems	59.1	43%
ORCL	Oracle Corporation	52.3	34%
AMGN	Amgen, Inc.	31.4	26%
GM	General Motors	20.3	38%

[25]As discussed in Chapter 14, we can interpret excess cash as negative debt. As a consequence, the trade-offs from holding excess cash are very similar to those involved in the capital structure decision.

[26]Recall from Section 16.7 that the managerial entrenchment theory of capital structure argued that managers choose low leverage to avoid the discipline of debt and preserve their job security. Applied to payout policy, the same theory implies that managers will reduce leverage further by choosing to hold too much cash.

17.6 Signaling with Payout Policy

One market imperfection that we have not yet considered is asymmetric information. When managers have better information than investors regarding the future prospects of the firm, their payout decisions may signal this information. In this section, we look at managers' motivations when setting a firm's payout policy, and we evaluate what these decisions may communicate to investors.

Dividend Smoothing

Firms can change dividends at any time, but in practice they vary the sizes of their dividends relatively infrequently. For example, General Motors (GM) changed the amount of its regular dividend only eight times over a 20-year period. Yet during that same period, GM's earnings varied widely, as shown in Figure 17.7.

The pattern seen with GM is typical of most firms that pay dividends. Firms adjust dividends relatively infrequently, and dividends are much less volatile than earnings. This practice of maintaining relatively constant dividends is called **dividend smoothing**. Firms also increase dividends much more frequently than they cut them. For example, from 1971 to 2001, only 5.4% of dividend changes by U.S. firms were decreases.[27] In a classic survey of corporate executives, John Lintner[28] suggested that these observations resulted from (1) management's belief that investors prefer stable dividends with sustained growth, and (2) management's desire to maintain a long-term target level of dividends as a fraction of earnings. Thus firms raise their dividends only when they perceive

FIGURE 17.7

GM's Earnings and Dividends per Share, 1985–2008

Compared to GM's earnings, its dividend payments were relatively stable. (Data adjusted for splits, earnings exclude extraordinary items.)

Source: Compustat and CapitalQ

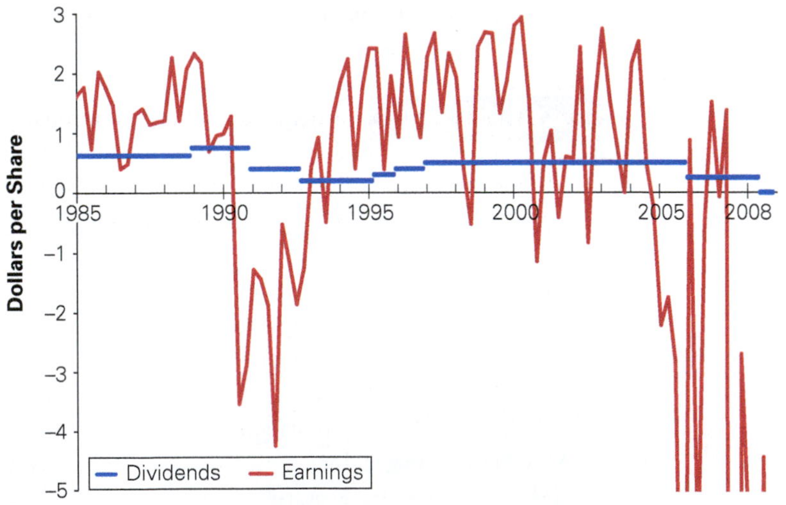

[27]F. Allen and R. Michaely, "Payout Policy," in G. Constantinides, M. Harris, and R. Stulz, eds., *Handbook of the Economics of Finance: Corporate Finance Volume* 1A (Elsevier, 2003).

[28]J. Lintner, "Distribution of Incomes of Corporations Among Dividends, Retained Earnings and Taxes," *American Economic Review* 46 (1956): 97–113.

a long-term sustainable increase in the expected level of future earnings, and cut them only as a last resort.[29]

How can firms keep dividends smooth as earnings vary? As we have already discussed, firms can maintain almost any level of dividend in the short run by adjusting the number of shares they repurchase or issue and the amount of cash they retain. However, due to the tax and transaction costs of funding a dividend with new equity issues, managers do not wish to commit to a dividend that the firm cannot afford to pay out of regular earnings. For this reason, firms generally set dividends at a level they expect to be able to maintain based on the firm's earnings prospects.

Dividend Signaling

If firms smooth dividends, the firm's dividend choice will contain information regarding management's expectations of future earnings. When a firm increases its dividend, it sends a positive signal to investors that management expects to be able to afford the higher dividend for the foreseeable future. Conversely, when managers cut the dividend, it may signal that they have given up hope that earnings will rebound in the near term and so need to reduce the dividend to save cash. The idea that dividend changes reflect managers' views about a firm's future earnings prospects is called the **dividend signaling hypothesis**.

Studies of the market's reaction to dividend changes are consistent with this hypothesis. For example, during the period 1967–1993, firms that raised their dividend by 10% or more saw their stock prices rise by 1.34% after the announcement, while those that cut their dividend by 10% or more experienced a price decline of −3.71%.[30] The average size of the stock price reaction increases with the magnitude of the dividend change, and is larger for dividend cuts.[31]

Dividend signaling is similar to the use of leverage as a signal that we discussed in Chapter 16. Increasing debt signals that management believes the firm can afford the future interest payments, in the same way that raising the dividend signals the firm can afford to maintain the dividends in the future. However, while cutting the dividend is costly for managers in terms of their reputation and the reaction of investors, it is by no means as costly as failing to make debt payments. As a consequence, we would expect dividend changes to be a somewhat weaker signal than leverage changes. Indeed, empirical studies have found average stock price increases of more than 10% when firms replace equity with debt, and decreases of 4% to 10% when firms replace debt with equity.[32]

---

[29]While perhaps a good description of how firms *do* set their dividends, as we have shown in this chapter there is no clear reason why firms *should* smooth their dividends, nor convincing evidence that investors prefer this practice.

[30]See G. Grullon, R. Michaely, and B. Swaminathan, "Are Dividend Changes a Sign of Firm Maturity?" *Journal of Business* 75 (2002): 387–424. The effects are even larger for dividend initiations (+3.4%) and omissions (−7%), according to studies by R. Michaely, R. Thaler, and K. Womack, "Price Reactions to Dividend Initiations and Omissions: Overreaction or Drift?" *Journal of Finance* 50 (1995): 573–608, and similar results by P. Healy and K. Palepu, "Earnings Information Conveyed by Dividend Initiations and Omissions," *Journal of Financial Economics* 21 (1988): 149–176.

[31]Not all of the evidence is consistent with dividend signaling, however. For example, it has been difficult to document a relationship between dividend changes and realized future earnings [S. Benartzi, R. Michaely, and R. Thaler, "Do Changes in Dividends Signal the Future or the Past?" *Journal of Finance* 52 (1997): 1007–1034].

[32]C. Smith, "Raising Capital: Theory and Evidence," in D. Chew, ed., *The New Corporate Finance* (McGraw-Hill, 1993).

Royal & SunAlliance's Dividend Cut

In some quarters, Julian Hance must have seemed like a heretic. On November 8, 2001, the finance director of Royal & SunAlliance, a U.K.-based insurance group with £12.6 billion (€20.2 billion) in annual revenue, did the unthinkable—he announced that he would cut the firm's dividend.

Many observers gasped at the decision. Surely, they argued, cutting the dividend was a sign of weakness. Didn't companies only cut their dividend when profits were falling?

Quite the contrary, countered Hance. With insurance premiums rising around the world, particularly following the World Trade Center tragedy, Royal & SunAlliance believed that its industry offered excellent growth opportunities. "The outlook for business in 2002 and beyond makes a compelling case for reinvesting capital in the business rather than returning it to shareholders," explained Hance.

The stock market agreed with him, sending Royal & SunAlliance's shares up 5% following its dividend news. "Cutting the dividend is a positive move," observes Matthew Wright, an insurance analyst at Credit Lyonnais. "It shows the company expects future profitability to be good."

Source: Justin Wood, CFO Europe.com, December 2001.

While an increase of a firm's dividend may signal management's optimism regarding its future cash flows, it might also signal a lack of investment opportunities. For example, Microsoft's move to initiate dividends in 2003 was largely seen as a result of its declining growth prospects as opposed to a signal about its increased future profitability.[33] Conversely, a firm might cut its dividend to exploit new positive-NPV investment opportunities. In this case, the dividend decrease might lead to a positive—rather than negative—stock price reaction (see the box on Royal and SunAlliance's dividend cut). In general, we must interpret dividends as a signal in the context of the type of new information managers are likely to have.

Signaling and Share Repurchases

Share repurchases, like dividends, may also signal managers' information to the market. However, several important differences distinguish share repurchases and dividends. First, managers are much less committed to share repurchases than to dividend payments. As we noted earlier, when firms announce authorization for an open market share repurchase, they generally announce the maximum amount they plan to spend on repurchases. The actual amount spent, however, may be far less. Also, it may take several years to complete the share repurchase.[34] Second, unlike with dividends, firms do not smooth their repurchase activity from year to year. As a result, announcing a share repurchase today does not necessarily represent a long-term commitment to repurchase shares. In this regard, share repurchases may be less of a signal than dividends about future earnings of a firm.

A third key difference between dividends and share repurchases is that the cost of a share repurchase depends on the market price of the stock. If managers believe the stock is currently overvalued, a share repurchase will be costly to the shareholders who choose to hold on to their shares because buying the stock at its current (overvalued) price is a negative-NPV investment. By contrast, repurchasing shares when managers perceive the stock to

[33]See "An End to Growth?" *The Economist* (July 22, 2004): 61.

[34]C. Stephens and M. Weisbach, "Actual Share Reacquisitions in Open-Market Repurchase Programs," *Journal of Finance* 53 (1998): 313–333, consider how firms' actual repurchases compare to their announced plans. For details on share repurchase programs' implementation, see D. Cook, L. Krigman, and J. Leach, "On the Timing and Execution of Open Market Repurchases," *Review of Financial Studies* 17 (2004): 463–498.

be undervalued is a positive-NPV investment for these shareholders. Thus, if managers are acting in the interest of long-term shareholders and attempting to maximize the firm's future share price, they will be more likely to repurchase shares if they believe the stock to be undervalued. (If, on the other hand, managers act in the interest of all shareholders—including those who sell—then there is no such incentive: Any gain to those who remain is a cost to those who sell at the low price.)

In a 2004 survey, 87% of CFOs agreed that firms should repurchase shares when their stock price is a good value relative to its true value,[35] implicitly indicating that most CFOs believe that they should act in the interests of the long-term shareholders. Share repurchases are therefore a credible signal that management believes its shares are underpriced. Thus, if investors believe that managers have better information regarding the firm's prospects than they do, then investors should react favorably to share repurchase announcements. Indeed they do: The average market price reaction to the announcement of an open market share repurchase program is about 3% (with the size of the reaction increasing in the portion of shares outstanding sought).[36] The reaction is much larger for fixed-price tender offers (12%) and Dutch auction share repurchases (8%).[37] Recall that these methods of repurchase are generally used for very large repurchases conducted in a very short timeframe and are often part of an overall recapitalization. Also, the shares are repurchased at a premium to the current market price. Thus, tender offers and Dutch auction repurchases are even stronger signals than open market repurchases that management views the current share price as undervalued.

EXAMPLE 17.8 Share Repurchases and Market Timing

Problem

Clark Industries has 200 million shares outstanding, a current share price of $30, and no debt. Clark's management believes that the shares are underpriced, and that the true value is $35 per share. Clark plans to pay $600 million in cash to its shareholders by repurchasing shares at the current market price. Suppose that soon after the transaction is completed, new information comes out that causes investors to revise their opinion of the firm and agree with management's assessment of Clark's value. What is Clark's share price after the new information comes out? How would the share price differ if Clark waited until after the new information came out to repurchase the shares?

Solution

Clark's initial market cap is $30/share × 200 million shares = $6 billion, of which $600 million is cash and $5.4 billion corresponds to other assets. At the current share price, Clark will

[35] A. Brav, J. Graham, C. Harvey, and R. Michaely, "Payout Policy in the 21st Century," *Journal of Financial Economics* 77 (2005): 483–527.

[36] See D. Ikenberry, J. Lakonishok, and T. Vermaelen, "Market Underreaction to Open Market Share Repurchases," *Journal of Financial Economics* 39 (1995): 181–208; and G. Grullon and R. Michaely, "Dividends, Share Repurchases, and the Substitution Hypothesis," *Journal of Finance* 57 (2002): 1649–1684. For a signaling explanation of why the stock price will positively react to the announcement even though it is not a commitment to purchase shares, see J. Oded, "Why Do Firms Announce Open-Market Repurchase Programs?" *Review of Financial Studies* 18 (2005): 271–300.

[37] R. Comment and G. Jarrell, "The Relative Signaling Power of Dutch-Auction and Fixed-Price Self-Tender Offers and Open-Market Share Repurchases," *Journal of Finance* 46 (1991): 1243–1271.

repurchase \$600 million ÷ \$30/share = 20 million shares. The market value balance sheet before and after the transaction is shown below (in millions of dollars):

	Before Repurchase	After Repurchase	After New Information
Cash	600	0	0
Other assets	5400	5400	6400
Total market value of assets	6000	5400	6400
Shares (millions)	200	180	180
Share Price	\$30	\$30	\$35.56

According to management, Clark's initial market capitalization should be \$35/share × 200 million shares = \$7 billion, of which \$6.4 billion would correspond to other assets. As the market value balance sheet shows, after the new information comes out, Clark's share price will rise to \$35.556.

If Clark waited for the new information to come out before repurchasing the shares, it would buy shares at a market price of \$35 per share. Thus, it would repurchase only 17.1 million shares. The share price after the repurchase would be \$6.4 billion ÷ 182.9 shares = \$35.

By repurchasing shares while the stock is underpriced, the ultimate share price is \$0.556 higher, representing a gain of \$0.556 × 180 million shares = \$100 million for long-term shareholders. This gain equals the loss to the selling shareholders from selling 20 million shares at a price that is \$5 below their true value.

As this example shows, the gain from buying shares when the stock is underpriced leads to an increase in the firm's long-run share price. Similarly, buying shares when the stock is overpriced will reduce the long-run share price. The firm may therefore try to time its repurchases appropriately. Anticipating this strategy, shareholders may interpret a share repurchase as a signal that the firm is undervalued.

CONCEPT CHECK

1. What possible signals does a firm give when it cuts its dividend?
2. Would managers acting in the interests of long-term shareholders be more likely to repurchase shares if they believe the stock is undervalued or overvalued?

17.7 Stock Dividends, Splits, and Spin-Offs

In this chapter, we have focused on a firm's decision to pay cash to its shareholders. But a firm can pay another type of dividend that does not involve cash: a stock dividend. In this case, each shareholder who owns the stock before it goes ex-dividend receives additional shares of stock of the firm itself (a stock split) or of a subsidiary (a spin-off). Here we briefly review these two types of transactions.

Stock Dividends and Splits

If a company declares a 10% stock dividend, each shareholder will receive one new share of stock for every 10 shares already owned. Stock dividends of 50% or higher are generally referred to as stock splits. For example, with a 50% stock dividend, each shareholder will receive one new share for every two shares owned. Because a holder of two shares will end up holding three new shares, this transaction is also called a 3:2 ("3-for-2") stock split. Similarly, a 100% stock dividend is equivalent to a 2:1 stock split.

With a stock dividend, a firm does not pay out any cash to shareholders. As a result, the total market value of the firm's assets and liabilities, and therefore of its equity, is unchanged. The only thing that is different is the number of shares outstanding. The stock price will therefore fall because the same total equity value is now divided over a larger number of shares.

Let's illustrate a stock dividend for Genron. Suppose Genron paid a 50% stock dividend (a 3:2 stock split) rather than a cash dividend. Table 17.5 shows the market value balance sheet and the resulting share price before and after the stock dividend.

TABLE 17.5 **Cum- and Ex-Dividend Share Price for Genron with a 50% Stock Dividend ($ million)**

	December 11(Cum-Dividend)	December 12(Ex-Dividend)
Cash	20	20
Other assets	400	400
Total market value of assets	420	420
Shares (millions)	10	15
Share price	$42	$28

A shareholder who owns 100 shares before the dividend has a portfolio worth $\$42 \times 100 = \$4200$. After the dividend, the shareholder owns 150 shares worth \$28, giving a portfolio value of $\$28 \times 150 = \$4200$. (Note the important difference between a stock split and a share issuance: When the company issues shares, the number of shares increases, but the firm also raises cash to add to its existing assets. If the shares are sold at a fair price, the stock price should not change.)

Unlike cash dividends, stock dividends are not taxed. Thus, from both the firm's and shareholders' perspectives, there is no real consequence to a stock dividend. The number of shares is proportionally increased and the price per share is proportionally reduced so that there is no change in value.

Why, then, do companies pay stock dividends or split their stock? The typical motivation for a stock split is to keep the share price in a range thought to be attractive to small investors. Stocks generally trade in lots of 100 shares, and in any case do not trade in units less than one share. As a result, if the share price rises significantly, it might be difficult for small investors to afford one share, let alone 100. Making the stock more attractive to small investors can increase the demand for and the liquidity of the stock, which may in turn boost the stock price. On average, announcements of stock splits are associated with a 2% increase in the stock price.[38]

Most firms use splits to keep their share prices from exceeding \$100. From 1990 to 2000, Cisco Systems split its stock nine times, so that one share purchased at the IPO split into 288 shares. Had it not split, Cisco's share price at the time of its last split in March 2000 would have been $288 \times \$72.19$, or \$20,790.72.

---

[38] S. Nayak and N. Prabhala, "Disentangling the Dividend Information in Splits: A Decomposition Using Conditional Event-Study Methods," *Review of Financial Studies* 14 (2001): 1083–1116. For evidence that stock splits attract individual investors, see R. Dhar, W. Goetzmann, and N. Zhu, "The Impact of Clientele Changes: Evidence from Stock Splits," *Yale ICF Working Paper* No. 03-14 (2004). While splits seem to increase the number of shareholders, evidence of their impact on liquidity is mixed; see, for example, T. Copeland, "Liquidity Changes Following Stock Splits," *Journal of Finance* 34 (1979): 115–141; and J. Lakonishok and B. Lev, "Stock Splits and Stock Dividends: Why, Who and When," *Journal of Finance* 42 (1987): 913–932.

Firms also do not want their stock prices to fall too low. First, a stock price that is very low raises transaction costs for investors. For example, the spread between the bid and ask price for a stock has a minimum size of one tick ($0.01 for the NYSE and NASDAQ exchanges) independent of the stock price. In percentage terms, the tick size is larger for stocks with a low price than for stocks with a high price. Also, exchanges require stocks to maintain a minimum price to remain listed on an exchange (for example, the NYSE and NASDAQ require listed firms to maintain a price of at least $1 per share).

If the price of the stock falls too low, a company can engage in a **reverse split** and reduce the number of shares outstanding. For example, in a 1:10 reverse split, every 10 shares of stock are replaced with a single share. As a result, the share price increases tenfold. Reverse splits became necessary for many dot-coms after the Internet bust in 2000, and similarly for some financial firms in the wake of the financial crisis. Citigroup, for instance, split its stock 7 times between 1990 and 2000, for a cumulative increase of 12:1. But in May 2011 it implemented a 1:10 reverse split to increase its stock price from $4.50 to $45 per share.

Through a combination of splits and reverse splits, firms can keep their share prices in any range they desire. As Figure 17.8 shows, almost all firms have share prices below $100 per share, with 90% of firms' share prices between $2.50 and $65 per share.

Spin-Offs

Rather than pay a dividend using cash or shares of its own stock, a firm can also distribute shares of a subsidiary in a transaction referred to as a **spin-off**. Non-cash special dividends are commonly used to spin off assets or a subsidiary as a separate company. For example, after selling 15% of Monsanto Corporation in an IPO in October 2000, Pharmacia Corporation announced in July 2002 that it would spin off its remaining 85% holding of Monsanto Corporation. The spin-off was accomplished through a special dividend in which each Pharmacia shareholder received 0.170593 share of Monsanto per share of Pharmacia owned. After receiving the Monsanto shares, Pharmacia shareholders could trade them separately from the shares of the parent firm.

FIGURE 17.8

Distribution of Share Prices on the NYSE (January 2015)

By using splits and reverse splits, most firms keep their share prices between $10 and $50 to reduce transaction costs for investors. The median share price is $23, though about 6% of firms have share prices above $100.

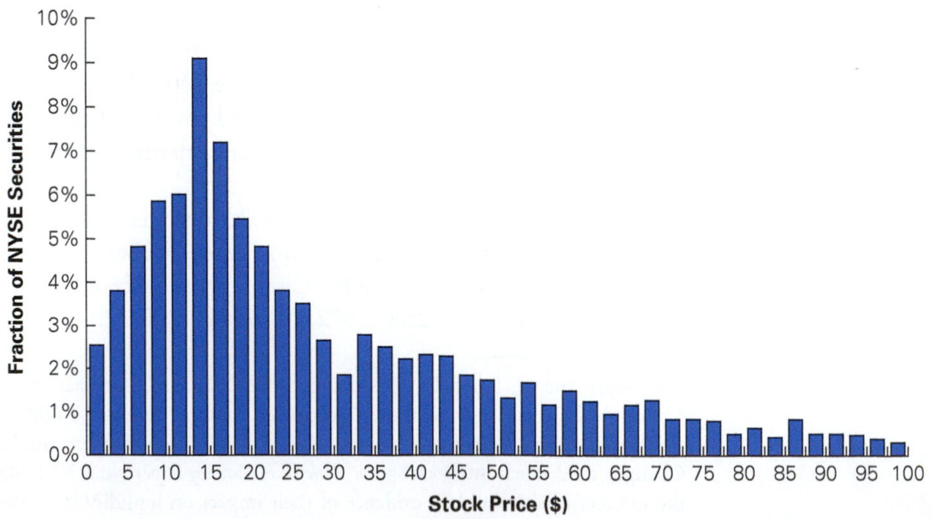

Berkshire Hathaway's A & B Shares

Many managers split their stock to keep the price affordable for small investors, making it easier for them to buy and sell the stock. Warren Buffett, chairman and chief executive of Berkshire Hathaway, disagrees. As he commented in Berkshire's 1983 annual report: "We are often asked why Berkshire does not split its stock . . . we want [shareholders] who think of themselves as business owners with the intention of staying a long time. And, we want those who keep their eyes focused on business results, not market prices." In its 40-year history, Berkshire Hathaway has never split its stock.

As a result of Berkshire Hathaway's strong performance and the lack of stock splits, the stock price climbed. By 1996, it exceeded $30,000 per share. Because this price was much too expensive for some small investors, several financial intermediaries created unit investment trusts whose only investment was Berkshire shares. (Unit investment trusts are similar to mutual funds, but their investment portfolio is fixed.) Investors could buy smaller interests in these trusts, effectively owning Berkshire stock with a much lower initial investment.

In response, in February 1996, Buffett announced the creation of a second class of Berkshire Hathaway stock, the Class B shares. Each owner of the original shares (now called Class A shares) was offered the opportunity to convert each A share into 30 B shares. "We're giving shareholders a do-it-yourself split, if they care to do it," Buffett said. Through the B shares, investors could own Berkshire stock with a smaller investment, and they would not have to pay the extra transaction costs required to buy stock through the unit trusts.

Meanwhile, the value of the A shares has continued to rise. After reaching a peak of almost $230,000 in December 2014, the price of one share has since fallen to $195,000 in early 2016.*

*Buffet's logic for not splitting the stock is a bit puzzling. If an extremely high stock price were advantageous, Buffet could have obtained it much sooner through a reverse split of the stock.

On the distribution date of August 13, 2002, Monsanto shares traded for an average price of $16.21. Thus, the value of the special dividend was

$$0.170593 \text{ Monsanto shares} \times \$16.21 \text{ per share} = \$2.77 \text{ per share}$$

A shareholder who initially owned 100 shares of Pharmacia stock would receive 17 shares of Monsanto stock, plus cash of $0.0593 \times \$16.21 = \$0.96$ in place of the fractional shares.

Alternatively, Pharmacia could have sold the shares of Monsanto and distributed the cash to shareholders as a cash dividend. The transaction Pharmacia chose offers two advantages over a cash distribution: (1) It avoids the transaction costs associated with such a sale, and (2) the special dividend is not taxed as a cash distribution. Instead, Pharmacia shareholders who received Monsanto shares are liable for capital gains tax only at the time they sell the Monsanto shares.[39]

Here we have considered only the methods of distributing the shares of the firm that has been spun off, either by paying a stock dividend or by selling the shares directly and then distributing (or retaining) the cash. The decision of whether to do the spin-off in the first place raises a new question: When is it better for two firms to operate as separate entities, rather than as a single combined firm? The issues that arise in addressing this question are the same as those that arise in the decision to merge two firms, which we discuss further in Chapter 28.

CONCEPT CHECK

1. What is the difference between a stock dividend and a stock split?
2. What is the main purpose of a reverse split?

[39]The capital gain is computed by allocating a fraction of the cost basis of the Pharmacia shares to the Monsanto shares received. Because Pharmacia was trading at an ex-dividend price of $42.54 on the distribution date, the special dividend amounted to $6.1\% = 2.77/(2.77 + 42.54)$ of total value. Thus, the original cost basis of the Pharmacia stock was divided by allocating 6.1% to the Monsanto shares and the remaining 93.9% to the Pharmacia shares.

MyFinanceLab Here is what you should know after reading this chapter. MyFinanceLab will help you identify what you know and where to go when you need to practice.

17.1 Distributions to Shareholders

- When a firm wants to distribute cash to its shareholders, it can pay a cash dividend or it can repurchase shares.
  - Most companies pay regular, quarterly dividends. Sometimes firms announce one-time, special dividends.
  - Firms repurchase shares using an open market repurchase, a tender offer, a Dutch auction repurchase, or a targeted repurchase.
- On the declaration date, firms announce that they will pay dividends to all shareholders of record on the record date. The ex-dividend date is the first day on which the stock trades without the right to an upcoming dividend; it is usually two trading days prior to the record date. Dividend checks are mailed on the payment date.
- In a stock split or a stock dividend, a company distributes additional shares rather than cash to shareholders.

17.2 Comparison of Dividends and Share Repurchases

- In perfect capital markets, the stock price falls by the amount of the dividend when a dividend is paid. An open market share repurchase has no effect on the stock price, and the stock price is the same as the cum-dividend price if a dividend were paid instead.
- The Modigliani-Miller dividend irrelevance proposition states that in perfect capital markets, holding fixed the investment policy of a firm, the firm's choice of dividend policy is irrelevant and does not affect the initial share price.

17.3 The Tax Disadvantage of Dividends

- In reality, capital markets are not perfect, and market imperfections affect firm dividend policy.
- If taxes are the only important market imperfection, when the tax rate on dividends exceeds the tax rate on capital gains, the optimal dividend policy is for firms to pay no dividends. Firms should use share repurchases for all payouts.

17.4 Dividend Capture and Tax Clienteles

- The effective dividend tax rate, τ_d^*, measures the net tax cost to the investor per dollar of dividend income received:

$$\tau_d^* = \left(\frac{\tau_d - \tau_g}{1 - \tau_g}\right) \tag{17.3}$$

- The effective dividend tax rate varies across investors for several reasons, including income level, investment horizon, tax jurisdiction, and type of investment account.
- Different investor taxes create clientele effects, in which the dividend policy of a firm suits the tax preference of its investor clientele.

17.5 Payout Versus Retention of Cash

- Modigliani-Miller payout policy irrelevance says that, in perfect capital markets, if a firm invests excess cash flows in financial securities, the firm's choice of payout versus retention is irrelevant and does not affect the value of the firm.

- Corporate taxes make it costly for a firm to retain excess cash. Even after adjusting for investor taxes, retaining excess cash brings a substantial tax disadvantage for a firm. The effective tax disadvantage of retaining cash is given by

$$\tau^*_{retain} = \left(1 - \frac{(1 - \tau_c)(1 - \tau_g)}{(1 - \tau_i)}\right) \quad (17.7)$$

- Even though there is a tax disadvantage to retaining cash, some firms accumulate cash balances. Cash balances help firms minimize the transaction costs of raising new capital when they have future potential cash needs. However, there is no benefit to shareholders from firms holding cash in excess of future investment needs.
- In addition to the tax disadvantage of holding cash, agency costs may arise, as managers may be tempted to spend excess cash on inefficient investments and perks. Without pressure from shareholders, managers may choose to horde cash to spend in this way or as a means of reducing a firm's leverage and increasing their job security.
- Dividends and share repurchases help minimize the agency problem of wasteful spending when a firm has excess cash. They also reduce the transfer of value to debt holders or other stakeholders.
- Firms typically maintain relatively constant dividends. This practice is called dividend smoothing.

17.6 Signaling with Payout Policy

- The idea that dividend changes reflect managers' views about firms' future earnings prospects is called the dividend signaling hypothesis.
    - Managers usually increase dividends only when they are confident the firm will be able to afford higher dividends for the foreseeable future.
    - When managers cut the dividend, it may signal that they have lost hope that earnings will improve.
- Share repurchases may be used to signal positive information, as repurchases are more attractive if management believes the stock is undervalued at its current price.

17.7 Stock Dividends, Splits, and Spin-Offs

- With a stock dividend, shareholders receive either additional shares of stock of the firm itself (a stock split) or shares of a subsidiary (a spin-off). The stock price generally falls proportionally with the size of the split.
- A reverse split decreases the number of shares outstanding, and therefore results in a higher share price.

Key Terms

bird in the hand hypothesis *p. 606*
clientele effects *p. 612*
cum-dividend *p. 601*
declaration date *p. 598*
dividend-capture theory *p. 614*
dividend puzzle *p. 609*
dividend signaling hypothesis *p. 623*
dividend smoothing *p. 622*
Dutch auction *p. 600*
effective dividend tax rate *p. 610*
ex-dividend date *p. 598*
greenmail *p. 601*
homemade dividend *p. 603*
liquidating dividend *p. 600*
open market repurchase *p. 600*
payable date (distribution date) *p. 598*
payout policy *p. 598*
record date *p. 598*
return of capital *p. 600*
reverse split *p. 628*
special dividend *p. 598*
spin-off *p. 628*
stock dividend *p. 599*
stock split *p. 599*
targeted repurchase *p. 600*
tender offer *p. 600*

Further Reading

For a comprehensive review of the literature on payout policy, see F. Allen and R. Michaely, "Payout Policy," in G. Constantinides, M. Harris, and R. Stulz, eds., *Handbook of the Economics of Finance: Corporate Finance Volume* 1A (Elsevier, 2003), and more recently H. DeAngelo, L. DeAngelo, and D. Skinner, "Corporate Payout Policy," *Foundations and Trends in Finance* 3 (2008): 95–287; and J. Farre-Mensa, Joan, R. Michaely, and M. Schmalz, "Payout Policy," *Annual Review of Financial Economics* 6 (2014): 75–134.

The literature on payout policy is extensive. Readers interested in specific issues might find the following articles interesting:

On the information content of payout policy: K. Dewenter and V. Warther, "Dividends, Asymmetric Information, and Agency Conflicts: Evidence from a Comparison of the Dividend Policies of Japanese and U.S. Firms," *Journal of Finance* 53 (1998): 879–904; E. Dyl and R. Weigand, "The Information Content of Dividend Initiations: Additional Evidence," *Financial Management* 27 (1998): 27–35; and G. Grullon and R. Michaely, "The Information Content of Share Repurchase Programs," *Journal of Finance* 59 (2004): 651–680.

On the decision corporations make between dividends and share repurchases: L. Bagwell and J. Shoven, "Cash Distributions to Shareholders," *Journal of Economic Perspectives* 3 (1989): 129–140; M. Barclay and C. Smith, "Corporate Payout Policy: Cash Dividends Versus Open-Market Repurchases," *Journal of Financial Economics* 22 (1988): 61–82; A. Dittmar, "Why Do Firms Repurchase Stock?" *Journal of Business* 73 (2000): 331–355; G. Fenn and N. Liang, "Corporate Payout Policy and Managerial Stock Incentives," *Journal of Financial Economics* 60 (2001): 45–72; W. Guay and J. Harford, "The Cash-Flow Permanence and Information Content of Dividend Increases Versus Repurchases," *Journal of Financial Economics* 57 (2000): 385–415; M. Jagannathan, C. Stephens, and M. Weisbach, "Financial Flexibility and the Choice Between Dividends and Stock Repurchases," *Journal of Financial Economics* 57 (2000): 355–384; K. Kahle, "When a Buyback Isn't a Buyback: Open Market Repurchases and Employee Options," *Journal of Financial Economics* 63 (2002): 235–261; and M. Rozeff, "How Companies Set Their Dividend Payout Ratios," in Joel M. Stern and Donald H. Chew, eds., *The Revolution in Corporate Finance* (Basil Blackwell, 1986).

On tax clienteles: F. Allen, A. Bernardo, and I. Welch, "A Theory of Dividends Based on Tax Clienteles," *Journal of Finance* 55 (2000): 2499–2536.

On the timing of share repurchases: P. Brockman and D. Chung, "Managerial Timing and Corporate Liquidity: Evidence from Actual Share Repurchases," *Journal of Financial Economics* 61 (2001): 417–448; and D. Cook, L. Krigman, and J. Leach, "On the Timing and Execution of Open Market Repurchases," *Review of Financial Studies* 17 (2004): 463–498.

Problems

All problems are available in MyFinanceLab. *An asterisk (*) indicates problems with a higher level of difficulty.*

Distributions to Shareholders

1. What options does a firm have to spend its free cash flow (after it has satisfied all interest obligations)?

2. ABC Corporation announced that it will pay a dividend to all shareholders of record as of Monday, April 2, 2012. It takes three business days of a purchase for the new owners of a share of stock to be registered.
   a. When is the last day an investor can purchase ABC stock and still get the dividend payment?
   b. When is the ex-dividend day?

3. Describe the different mechanisms available to a firm to use to repurchase shares.

Comparison of Dividends and Share Repurchases

4. RFC Corp. has announced a $1 dividend. If RFC's price last price cum-dividend is $50, what should its first ex-dividend price be (assuming perfect capital markets)?

5. EJH Company has a market capitalization of $1 billion and 20 million shares outstanding. It plans to distribute $100 million through an open market repurchase. Assuming perfect capital markets:
  a. What will the price per share of EJH be right before the repurchase?
  b. How many shares will be repurchased?
  c. What will the price per share of EJH be right after the repurchase?

6. KMS Corporation has assets with a market value of $500 million, $50 million of which are cash. It has debt of $200 million, and 10 million shares outstanding. Assume perfect capital markets.
  a. What is its current stock price?
  b. If KMS distributes $50 million as a dividend, what will its share price be after the dividend is paid?
  c. If instead, KMS distributes $50 million as a share repurchase, what will its share price be once the shares are repurchased?
  d. What will its new market debt-equity ratio be after either transaction?

7. Natsam Corporation has $250 million of excess cash. The firm has no debt and 500 million shares outstanding with a current market price of $15 per share. Natsam's board has decided to pay out this cash as a one-time dividend.
  a. What is the ex-dividend price of a share in a perfect capital market?
  b. If the board instead decided to use the cash to do a one-time share repurchase, in a perfect capital market what is the price of the shares once the repurchase is complete?
  c. In a perfect capital market, which policy, in part a or b, makes investors in the firm better off?

8. Suppose the board of Natsam Corporation decided to do the share repurchase in Problem 7 part b, but you, as an investor, would have preferred to receive a dividend payment. How can you leave yourself in the same position as if the board had elected to make the dividend payment instead?

9. Suppose you work for Oracle Corporation, and part of your compensation takes the form of stock options. The value of the stock option is equal to the difference between Oracle's stock price and an exercise price of $10 per share at the time that you exercise the option. As an option holder, would you prefer that Oracle use dividends or share repurchases to pay out cash to shareholders? Explain.

10. Suppose B&E Press paid dividends at the end of each year according to the schedule below. It also reduced its share count by repurchasing 5 million shares at the end of each year at the ex-dividend stock prices shown. (Assume perfect capital markets.)

	2009	2010	2011	2012	2013
Ex-Dividend Stock Price ($/share)	10.00	12.00	8.00	11.00	15.00
Dividend ($/share)		0.50	0.50	0.50	0.50
Shares Outstanding (millions)	100	95	90	85	80

  a. What is total market value of B&E's equity, and what is the total amount paid out to shareholders, at the end of each year?
  b. If B&E had made the same total payouts using dividends only (and so kept is share count constant), what dividend would it have paid and what would its ex-dividend share price have been each year?
  c. If B&E had made the same total payouts using repurchases only (and so paid no dividends), what share count would it have had and what would its share price have been each year?
  d. Consider a shareholder who owns 10 shares of B&E initially, does not sell any shares, and reinvests all dividends at the ex-dividend share price. Would this shareholder have preferred the payout policy in (b), (c), or the original policy?

The Tax Disadvantage of Dividends

11. The HNH Corporation will pay a constant dividend of $2 per share, per year, in perpetuity. Assume all investors pay a 20% tax on dividends and that there is no capital gains tax. Suppose that other investments with equivalent risk to HNH stock offer an after-tax return of 12%.

a. What is the price of a share of HNH stock?
b. Assume that management makes a surprise announcement that HNH will no longer pay dividends but will use the cash to repurchase stock instead. What is the price of a share of HNH stock now?

12. Using Table 17.2, for each of the following years, state whether dividends were tax disadvantaged or not for individual investors with a one-year investment horizon:
a. 1985 b. 1989 c. 1995 d. 1999 e. 2005

Dividend Capture and Tax Clienteles

13. What was the effective dividend tax rate for a U.S. investor in the highest tax bracket who planned to hold a stock for one year in 1981? How did the effective dividend tax rate change in 1982 when the Reagan tax cuts took effect? (Ignore state taxes.)

14. The dividend tax cut passed in 2003 lowered the effective dividend tax rate for a U.S. investor in the highest tax bracket to a historic low. During which other periods in the last 35 years was the effective dividend tax rate as low?

15. Suppose that all capital gains are taxed at a 25% rate, and that the dividend tax rate is 50%. Arbuckle Corp. is currently trading for $30, and is about to pay a $6 special dividend.
a. Absent any other trading frictions or news, what will its share price be just after the dividend is paid?

Suppose Arbuckle made a surprise announcement that it would do a share repurchase rather than pay a special dividend.
b. What net tax savings per share for an investor would result from this decision?
c. What would happen to Arbuckle's stock price upon the announcement of this change?

16. You purchased CSH stock for $40 one year ago and it is now selling for $50. The company has announced that it plans a $10 special dividend. You are considering whether to sell the stock now, or wait to receive the dividend and then sell.
a. Assuming 2008 tax rates, what ex-dividend price of CSH will make you indifferent between selling now and waiting?
b. Suppose the capital gains tax rate is 20% and the dividend tax rate is 40%, what ex-dividend price would make you indifferent now?

17. On Monday, November 15, 2004, TheStreet.com reported: "An experiment in the efficiency of financial markets will play out Monday following the expiration of a $3.08 dividend privilege for holders of Microsoft." The story went on: "The stock is currently trading ex-dividend both the special $3 payout and Microsoft's regular $0.08 quarterly dividend, meaning a buyer doesn't receive the money if he acquires the shares now." Microsoft stock ultimately opened for trade at $27.34 on the ex-dividend date (November 15), down $2.63 from its previous close.
a. Assuming that this price drop resulted only from the dividend payment (no other information affected the stock price that day), what does this decline in price imply about the effective dividend tax rate for Microsoft?
b. Based on this information, which of the following investors are most likely to be the marginal investors (the ones who determine the price) in Microsoft stock: i. long-term individual investors, ii. one-year individual investors, iii. pension funds, iv. corporations

18. At current tax rates, which of the following investors are most likely to hold a stock that has a high dividend yield:
a. individual investors, b. pension funds, c. mutual funds, d. corporations

19. Que Corporation pays a regular dividend of $1 per share. Typically, the stock price drops by $0.80 per share when the stock goes ex-dividend. Suppose the capital gains tax rate is 20%, but investors pay different tax rates on dividends. Absent transactions costs, what is the highest dividend tax rate of an investor who could gain from trading to capture the dividend?

20. A stock that you know is held by long-term individual investors paid a large one-time dividend. You notice that the price drop on the ex-dividend date is about the size of the dividend payment. You find this relationship puzzling given the tax disadvantage of dividends. Explain how the dividend-capture theory might account for this behavior.

Payout Versus Retention of Cash

21. Clovix Corporation has $50 million in cash, 10 million shares outstanding, and a current share price of $30. Clovix is deciding whether to use the $50 million to pay an immediate special dividend of $5 per share, or to retain and invest it at the risk-free rate of 10% and use the $5 million in interest earned to increase its regular annual dividend of $0.50 per share. Assume perfect capital markets.

a. Suppose Clovix pays the special dividend. How can a shareholder who would prefer an increase in the regular dividend create it on her own?

b. Suppose Clovix increases its regular dividend. How can a shareholder who would prefer the special dividend create it on her own?

22. Assume capital markets are perfect. Kay Industries currently has $100 million invested in short-term Treasury securities paying 7%, and it pays out the interest payments on these securities each year as a dividend. The board is considering selling the Treasury securities and paying out the proceeds as a one-time dividend payment.

a. If the board went ahead with this plan, what would happen to the value of Kay stock upon the announcement of a change in policy?

b. What would happen to the value of Kay stock on the ex-dividend date of the one-time dividend?

c. Given these price reactions, will this decision benefit investors?

23. Redo Problem 22, but assume that Kay must pay a corporate tax rate of 35%, and investors pay no taxes.

24. Harris Corporation has $250 million in cash, and 100 million shares outstanding. Suppose the corporate tax rate is 35%, and investors pay no taxes on dividends, capital gains, or interest income. Investors had expected Harris to pay out the $250 million through a share repurchase. Suppose instead that Harris announces it will permanently retain the cash, and use the interest on the cash to pay a regular dividend. If there are no other benefits of retaining the cash, how will Harris' stock price change upon this announcement?

25. Redo Problem 22, but assume the following:

a. Investors pay a 15% tax on dividends but no capital gains taxes or taxes on interest income, and Kay does not pay corporate taxes.

b. Investors pay a 15% tax on dividends and capital gains, and a 35% tax on interest income, while Kay pays a 35% corporate tax rate.

26. Raviv Industries has $100 million in cash that it can use for a share repurchase. Suppose instead Raviv invests the funds in an account paying 10% interest for one year.

a. If the corporate tax rate is 40%, how much additional cash will Raviv have at the end of the year net of corporate taxes?

b. If investors pay a 20% tax rate on capital gains, by how much will the value of their shares have increased, net of capital gains taxes?

c. If investors pay a 30% tax rate on interest income, how much would they have had if they invested the $100 million on their own?

d. Suppose Raviv retained the cash so that it would not need to raise new funds from outside investors for an expansion it has planned for next year. If it did raise new funds, it would have to pay issuance fees. How much does Raviv need to save in issuance fees to make retaining the cash beneficial for its investors? (Assume fees can be expensed for corporate tax purposes.)

27. Use the data in Table 15.3 to calculate the tax disadvantage of retained cash in the following:
   a. 1998
   b. 1976

Signaling with Payout Policy

28. Explain under which conditions an increase in the dividend payment can be interpreted as a signal of the following:
   a. Good news
   b. Bad news

29. Why is an announcement of a share repurchase considered a positive signal?

***30.** AMC Corporation currently has an enterprise value of $400 million and $100 million in excess cash. The firm has 10 million shares outstanding and no debt. Suppose AMC uses its excess cash to repurchase shares. After the share repurchase, news will come out that will change AMC's enterprise value to either $600 million or $200 million.
   a. What is AMC's share price prior to the share repurchase?
   b. What is AMC's share price after the repurchase if its enterprise value goes up? What is AMC's share price after the repurchase if its enterprise value declines?
   c. Suppose AMC waits until after the news comes out to do the share repurchase. What is AMC's share price after the repurchase if its enterprise value goes up? What is AMC's share price after the repurchase if its enterprise value declines?
   d. Suppose AMC management expects good news to come out. Based on your answers to parts (b) and (c), if management desires to maximize AMC's ultimate share price, will they undertake the repurchase before or after the news comes out? When would management undertake the repurchase if they expect bad news to come out?
   e. Given your answer to part (d), what effect would you expect an announcement of a share repurchase to have on the stock price? Why?

Stock Dividends, Splits, and Spin-Offs

31. Berkshire Hathaway's A shares are trading at $120,000. What split ratio would it need to bring its stock price down to $50?

32. Suppose the stock of Host Hotels & Resorts is currently trading for $20 per share.
   a. If Host issued a 20% stock dividend, what will its new share price be?
   b. If Host does a 3:2 stock split, what will its new share price be?
   c. If Host does a 1:3 reverse split, what will its new share price be?

33. Explain why most companies choose to pay stock dividends (split their stock).

34. When might it be advantageous to undertake a reverse stock split?

35. After the market close on May 11, 2001, Adaptec, Inc., distributed a dividend of shares of the stock of its software division, Roxio, Inc. Each Adaptec shareholder received 0.1646 share of Roxio stock per share of Adaptec stock owned. At the time, Adaptec stock was trading at a price of $10.55 per share (cum-dividend), and Roxio's share price was $14.23 per share. In a perfect market, what would Adaptec's ex-dividend share price be after this transaction?

Data Case

In your role as a consultant at a wealth management firm, you have been assigned a very powerful client who holds one million shares of Cisco Systems, Inc. purchased on February 28, 2003. In researching Cisco, you discovered that they are holding a large amount of cash. Additionally, your client is upset that the Cisco stock price has been somewhat stagnant as of late. The client is considering approaching the Board of Directors with a plan for half of the cash the firm has accumulated, but can't decide whether a share repurchase or a special dividend would be best. You have been asked to determine which initiative would generate the greatest amount of money after taxes, assuming that with a share repurchase your client would keep the same proportion of ownership. Because both dividends and capital gains are taxed at the same rate (20%), your client has assumed that there is no difference between the repurchase and the dividend. To confirm, you need to "run the numbers" for each scenario.

1. Go to finance.yahoo.com, enter the symbol for Cisco (CSCO), and click "Key Statistics."
   a. Record the current price and the number of shares outstanding.
   b. Click on "Balance Sheet" under "Financials." Copy and paste the balance sheet data into Excel.
2. Using one-half of the most recent cash and cash equivalents reported on the balance sheet (in thousands of dollars), compute the following:
   a. The number of shares that would be repurchased given the current market price.
   b. The dividend per share that could be paid given the total number of shares outstanding.
3. Go to finance.yahoo.com to obtain the price at which your client purchased the stock on February 28, 2003.
   a. Enter the symbol for Cisco and click "Get Quotes."
   b. Click "Historical Prices," enter the date your client purchased the stock as the start date and the end date, and hit "Enter." Record the adjusted closing price.
4. Compute the total cash that would be received by your client under the repurchase and the dividend both before taxes and after taxes.
5. The calculation in Step 4 reflects your client's immediate cash flow and tax liability, but it does not consider the final payoff for the client after any shares not sold in a repurchase are liquidated. To incorporate this feature, you first decide to see what happens if the client sells all remaining shares of stock immediately after the dividend or the repurchase. Assume that the stock price will fall by the amount of the dividend if a dividend is paid. What are the client's total after-tax cash flows (considering both the payout and the capital gain) under the repurchase of the dividend in this case?
6. Under which program would your client be better off before taxes? Which program is better after taxes, assuming the remaining shares are sold immediately after the dividend is paid?
7. Because your client is unlikely to sell all 1 million shares today, at the time of dividend/repurchase, you decide to consider two longer holding periods: Assume that under both plans the client sells all remaining shares of stock 5 years later, or the client sells 10 years later. Assume that the stock will return 10% per year going forward. Also assume that Cisco will pay no other dividends over the next 10 years.
   a. What would the stock price be after 5 years or 10 years if a dividend is paid now?
   b. What would the stock price be after 5 years or 10 years if Amazon repurchases shares now?
   c. Calculate the total after-tax cash flows at both points in time (when the dividend payment or the share repurchase takes place, and when the rest of the shares are sold) for your client if the remaining shares are sold in 5 years under both initiatives. Compute the difference between the cash flows under both initiatives at each point in time. Repeat assuming the shares are sold in 10 years.
8. Repeat Question 7 assuming the stock will return 20% per year going forward. What do you notice about the difference in the cash flows under the two initiatives when the return is 20% and 10%?
9. Calculate the NPV of the difference in the cash flows under both holding period assumptions for a range of discount rates. Based on your answer to Question 8, what is the correct discount rate to use?

Note: Updates to this data case may be found at www.berkdemarzo.com.

PART 6

Advanced Valuation

THE LAW OF ONE PRICE CONNECTION. In this part of the text, we return to the topic of valuation and integrate our understanding of risk, return, and the firm's choice of capital structure. Chapter 18 combines the knowledge of the first five parts of the text and develops the three main methods for capital budgeting with leverage and market imperfections: The weighted average cost of capital (WACC) method, the adjusted present value (APV) method, and the flow-to-equity (FTE) method. While the Law of One Price guarantees that all three methods ultimately lead to the same assessment of value, we will identify conditions that can make one method easiest to apply. Chapter 19 applies Chapter 18's methods of valuation to value a corporation in the context of a leveraged acquisition. Chapter 19 thus serves as a capstone case that illustrates how all the concepts developed thus far in the text are used to make complex real-world financial decisions.

CHAPTER

18

Capital Budgeting and Valuation with Leverage

NOTATION

FCF_t	free cash flows at date t
r_{wacc}	weighted average cost of capital
r_E, r_D	equity and debt costs of capital
r_D^*	equity-equivalent debt cost of capital
E	market value of equity
D	market value of debt (net of cash)
τ_c	marginal corporate tax rate
D_t	incremental debt of project on date t
V_t^L	value of a levered investment on date t
d	debt-to-value ratio
r_U	unlevered cost of capital
V^U	unlevered value of investment
T^s	value of predetermined tax shields
k	interest coverage ratio
Int_t	interest expense on date t
D^s	debt net of predetermined tax shields
ϕ	permanence of the debt level
τ_e, τ_i	tax rate on equity and interest income
τ^*	effective tax advantage of debt

IN FALL 2015, GENERAL ELECTRIC COMPANY HAD A MARKET capitalization of approximately $255 billion. With net debt of over $224 billion, GE's total enterprise value was $479 billion, making it the second most valuable business in the world (just behind Apple, and ahead of Alphabet and Exxon Mobil). GE's businesses include power generation and air transportation equipment, health care and medical equipment, consumer appliances, and consumer and commercial financing and insurance. With a debt-to-value ratio exceeding 50%, leverage is clearly part of GE's business strategy. How should a firm that uses leverage, like GE, incorporate the costs and benefits associated with leverage into its capital budgeting decisions? And how should a firm adjust for the differences in risk, and debt capacity, associated with its different business activities?

We introduced capital budgeting in Chapter 7. There, we outlined the following basic procedure: First, we estimate the incremental free cash flow generated by the project; then we discount the free cash flow based on the project's cost of capital to determine the NPV. Thus far, we have focused on all-equity financed projects. In this chapter, we integrate the lessons from Parts 4 and 5 into our capital budgeting framework and consider alternative financing arrangements. In particular, we address how the financing decision of the firm can affect both the cost of capital and the set of cash flows that we ultimately discount.

We begin by introducing the three main methods for capital budgeting with leverage and market imperfections: the weighted average cost of capital (WACC) method, the adjusted present value (APV) method, and the flow-to-equity (FTE) method. While their details differ, when appropriately applied each method produces the same estimate of an investment's (or firm's) value. As we shall see, the choice of method is thus guided by which is the simplest to use in a given setting. Ultimately, we will develop recommendations regarding the best method to use depending on the firm's financing policy.

Throughout this chapter, we focus on the intuition and implementation of the main capital budgeting methods. The appendix to this chapter provides additional details about the justification for and assumptions behind some of the results we use in the chapter. It also introduces advanced computational techniques that can be used in Excel to solve for leverage and value simultaneously.

18.1 Overview of Key Concepts

We introduce the three main methods of capital budgeting in Sections 18.2 through 18.4. Before we turn to the specifics, we will revisit some important ideas we encountered earlier in the text that underpin the valuation methods.

Chapter 15 demonstrated that because interest payments are deductible as an expense for the corporation, debt financing creates a valuable interest tax shield for the firm. We can include the value of this tax shield in the capital budgeting decision in several ways. First, we can use the *WACC method*, explained in Section 18.2, in which we discount the unlevered free cash flows using the weighted-average cost of capital, or WACC. Because we calculate the WACC using the effective *after-tax* interest rate as the cost of debt, this method incorporates the tax benefit of debt implicitly through the cost of capital.

Alternatively, we can first value a project's free cash flows without leverage by discounting them using the unlevered cost of capital. We can then separately estimate and add the present value of the interest tax shields from debt. This method, in which we explicitly add the value of the interest tax shields to the project's unlevered value, is called the *adjusted present value (APV) method*, which we explain in Section 18.3.

Our third method makes use of the observation in Chapter 9 that rather than value the firm based on its free cash flows, we can also value its equity based on the total payouts to shareholders. The *flow-to-equity (FTE) method*, introduced in Section 18.4, applies this idea to value the incremental payouts to equity associated with a project.

To illustrate these methods most clearly, we begin the chapter by applying each method to a single example in which we have made a number of simplifying assumptions:

1. *The project has average risk.* We assume initially that the market risk of the project is equivalent to the average market risk of the firm's investments. In that case, the project's cost of capital can be assessed based on the risk of the firm.
2. *The firm's debt-equity ratio is constant.* Initially, we consider a firm that adjusts its leverage to maintain a constant debt-equity ratio in terms of market values. This policy determines the amount of debt the firm will take on when it accepts a new project. It also implies that the risk of the firm's equity and debt, and therefore its weighted average cost of capital, will not fluctuate due to leverage changes.
3. *Corporate taxes are the only imperfection.* We assume initially that the main effect of leverage on valuation is due to the corporate tax shield. We ignore personal taxes and issuance costs, and we assume that other imperfections (such as financial distress or agency costs) are not significant at the level of debt chosen.

While these assumptions are restrictive, they are also a reasonable approximation for many projects and firms. The first assumption is likely to fit typical projects of firms with investments concentrated in a single industry. The second assumption, while unlikely to hold exactly, reflects the fact that firms tend to increase their levels of debt as they grow larger; some may even have an explicit target for their debt-equity ratio. Finally, for firms without very high levels of debt, the interest tax shield is likely to be the most important market imperfection affecting the capital budgeting decision. Hence, the third assumption is a reasonable starting point to begin our analysis.

Of course, while these three assumptions are reasonable in many situations, there are certainly projects and firms for which they do not apply. The remainder of the chapter therefore relaxes these assumptions and shows how to generalize the methods to more complicated settings. In Section 18.5, we adjust these methods for projects whose risk or debt capacity is substantially different from the rest of the firm. These adjustments are especially important for multidivisional firms, such as GE. In Section 18.6, we consider alternative leverage policies for the firm (rather than maintaining a constant debt-equity ratio) and adapt the APV method to handle such cases. We consider the consequence of other market imperfections, such as issuance, distress, and agency costs, on valuation in Section 18.7. Finally, in Section 18.8, we investigate a number of advanced topics, including periodically adjusted leverage policies and the effect of investor taxes.

CONCEPT CHECK

1. What are the three methods we can use to include the value of the tax shield in the capital budgeting decision?
2. In what situation is the risk of a project likely to match that of the overall firm?

18.2 The Weighted Average Cost of Capital Method

The WACC method takes the interest tax shield into account by using the after-tax cost of capital as the discount rate. When the market risk of the project is similar to the average market risk of the firm's investments, then its cost of capital is equal to the firm's weighted average cost of capital (WACC). As we showed in Chapter 15, the WACC incorporates the benefit of the interest tax shield by using the firm's *after-tax* cost of capital for debt:

$$r_{wacc} = \frac{E}{E+D} r_E + \frac{D}{E+D} r_D(1-\tau_c) \tag{18.1}$$

In this formula,

E = market value of equity　　　r_E = equity cost of capital

D = market value of debt (net of cash)　　　r_D = debt cost of capital

τ_c = marginal corporate tax rate

For now, we assume that the firm maintains a constant debt-equity ratio and that the WACC calculated in Eq. 18.1 remains constant over time. Because the WACC incorporates the tax savings from debt, we can compute the *levered value* of an investment, which is its value including the benefit of interest tax shields given the firm's leverage policy, by discounting its future free cash flow using the WACC. Specifically, if FCF_t is the expected free cash flow of an investment at the end of year t, then the investment's initial levered value, V_0^L, is[1]

$$V_0^L = \frac{FCF_1}{1+r_{wacc}} + \frac{FCF_2}{(1+r_{wacc})^2} + \frac{FCF_3}{(1+r_{wacc})^3} + \dots \tag{18.2}$$

[1] See this chapter's appendix for a formal justification of this result.

INTERVIEW WITH

ZANE ROWE

Zane Rowe is CFO of VMware Corp., a leader in virtualization and cloud infrastructure software solutions, before which he was Executive Vice President and CFO of EMC, an affiliated data storage company. He also spent 19 years in the airline industry, first with Continental Airlines where he became CFO, and then as CFO of United Continental Holdings, Inc.

QUESTION: *When developing a model to analyze a new investment, how do you deal with the uncertainty around future cash flows? Does it differ with new technologies?*

ANSWER: Dealing with uncertainty is an art as well as a science. Companies must take on risk to grow, and that requires a solid investment strategy. The model should support the strategy, not drive it. You can fixate on the model and whether the WACC is 2 points too high or too low, however what's more important is having a team that understands the business proposition and key drivers, such as top-line growth and the expected business environment. By choosing the right inputs for the model, they develop appropriate scenarios to help make the decision.

In the case of an airline's fleet acquisition, you could be fine-tuning a well-defined model with more certain inputs. If you acquire another company—in any industry—you focus on the business rationale for the investment. This involves much greater uncertainty.

QUESTION: *How does the capital budgeting process differ at VMware versus United Continental?*

ANSWER: A mature, capital-intensive, lower margin company such as an airline may emphasize more traditional measures such as NPV, IRR, and WACC. It has more history and lower volatility on the inputs for assumptions—and thus less variability. Airline expenditures can be very large, for example, the decision to purchase or lease new aircraft. The WACC and the timing of cash flows often drive the analysis.

With technology, it's sometimes more difficult to quantify the expected impact of a new product or acquisition. We adapt our model to include more variability and place greater focus on revenue growth and margin assumptions than on certain more detailed factors such as components of WACC. These tend to be more important drivers of the investment's overall value than the precise cost of capital.

QUESTION: *What key financial metrics do you use to make investment decisions? How does it differ between these firms?*

ANSWER: Regardless of the type of company—public or private, technology or capital-intensive—both the fundamentals and metrics are important. Capital budgeting models are only as good as their inputs. The most important element is engaging with all business units affected by the investment to ensure the right variables are in the model.

At the airline we looked at traditional metrics such as NPV and IRR, driven by the right WACC, as well as market multiples. A tech company will use some of those variables, too, but weight them differently. Top-line assumptions such as revenue and margins may carry a larger weight on the ultimate decision. Also, every capital budgeting decision must take into account the competitive and economic environments, the company's growth rate, and geographic risk.

QUESTION: *What is the importance of considering Free Cash Flows as opposed to just the earnings implications of a financial decision?*

ANSWER: Free cash flow (FCF) is important regardless of type of company or industry. Both FCF and earnings affect a financial decision. The airline business can be more sensitive to FCF than earnings, depending on the stage of the business cycle. We went through challenging periods—9/11, oil shocks, financial crisis—where FCF was the decision driver because of our highly levered balance sheet. We may choose a project that is FCF positive but has a minimal or potentially negative short-term impact on earnings.

In technology, FCF carries a fair amount of weight, too. That said, we communicate a number of variables and financial drivers to our analyst and investor base. When earnings and FCF don't perfectly align, we convey the purpose of our decision in greater detail. In an industry or company with a higher growth profile, you have more flexibility to continue to make investments that help drive future growth, placing less emphasis on the details of the capital budgeting model itself.

Using the WACC to Value a Project

Let's apply the WACC method to value a project. Avco, Inc., is a manufacturer of custom packaging products. Avco is considering introducing a new line of packaging, the RFX series, that will include an embedded radio-frequency identification (RFID) tag, which is a miniature radio antenna and transponder that allows a package to be tracked much more efficiently and with fewer errors than standard bar codes.

Avco engineers expect the technology used in these products to become obsolete after four years. During the next four years, however, the marketing group expects annual sales of $60 million per year for this product line. Manufacturing costs and operating expenses are expected to be $25 million and $9 million, respectively, per year. Developing the product will require upfront R&D and marketing expenses of $6.67 million, together with a $24 million investment in equipment. The equipment will be obsolete in four years and will be depreciated via the straight-line method over that period. Avco bills the majority of its customers in advance, and it expects no net working capital requirements for the project. Avco pays a corporate tax rate of 40%. Given this information, the spreadsheet in Table 18.1 forecasts the project's expected free cash flow.[2]

The market risk of the RFX project is expected to be similar to that for the company's other lines of business. Thus, we can use Avco's equity and debt to determine the weighted average cost of capital for the new project. Table 18.2 shows Avco's current market value balance sheet and equity and debt costs of capital. Avco has built up $20 million in cash for investment needs, so that its *net* debt is $D = 320 - 20 = \$300$ million. Avco's enterprise value, which is the market value of its non-cash assets, is $E + D = \$600$ million. Avco intends to maintain a similar (net) debt-equity ratio for the foreseeable future, including any financing related to the RFX project.

TABLE 18.1 SPREADSHEET Expected Free Cash Flow from Avco's RFX Project

	Year	0	1	2	3	4
Incremental Earnings Forecast ($ million)						
1	Sales	—	60.00	60.00	60.00	60.00
2	Cost of Goods Sold	—	(25.00)	(25.00)	(25.00)	(25.00)
3	**Gross Profit**	—	35.00	35.00	35.00	35.00
4	Operating Expenses	(6.67)	(9.00)	(9.00)	(9.00)	(9.00)
5	Depreciation	—	(6.00)	(6.00)	(6.00)	(6.00)
6	**EBIT**	(6.67)	20.00	20.00	20.00	20.00
7	Income Tax at 40%	2.67	(8.00)	(8.00)	(8.00)	(8.00)
8	**Unlevered Net Income**	(4.00)	12.00	12.00	12.00	12.00
Free Cash Flow						
9	Plus: Depreciation	—	6.00	6.00	6.00	6.00
10	Less: Capital Expenditures	(24.00)	—	—	—	—
11	Less: Increases in NWC	—	—	—	—	—
12	**Free Cash Flow**	**(28.00)**	**18.00**	**18.00**	**18.00**	**18.00**

[2]The spreadsheets shown in this chapter are available for download in MyFinanceLab.

TABLE 18.2 Avco's Current Market Value Balance Sheet ($ million) and Cost of Capital without the RFX Project

Assets		Liabilities		Cost of Capital	
Cash	20	Debt	320	Debt	6%
Existing Assets	600	Equity	300	Equity	10%
Total Assets	620	Total Liabilities and Equity	620		

With this capital structure, Avco's weighted average cost of capital is

$$r_{wacc} = \frac{E}{E+D} r_E + \frac{D}{E+D} r_D(1 - \tau_c) = \frac{300}{600}(10.0\%) + \frac{300}{600}(6.0\%)(1 - 0.40)$$
$$= 6.8\%$$

We can determine the value of the project, including the tax shield from debt, by calculating the present value of its future free cash flows, V_0^L, using the WACC:

$$V_0^L = \frac{18}{1.068} + \frac{18}{1.068^2} + \frac{18}{1.068^3} + \frac{18}{1.068^4} = \$61.25 \text{ million}$$

Because the upfront cost of launching the product line is only $28 million, this project is a good idea—taking the project results in an NPV of $61.25 - 28 = \$33.25$ million for the firm.

Summary of the WACC Method

To summarize, the key steps in the WACC valuation method are as follows:

1. Determine the free cash flow of the investment.
2. Compute the weighted average cost of capital using Eq. 18.1.
3. Compute the value of the investment, including the tax benefit of leverage, by discounting the free cash flow of the investment using the WACC.

In many firms, the corporate treasurer performs the second step, calculating the firm's WACC. This rate can then be used throughout the firm as the companywide cost of capital for new investments *that are of comparable risk to the rest of the firm and that will not alter the firm's debt-equity ratio*. Employing the WACC method in this way is very simple and straightforward. As a result, it is the method that is most commonly used in practice for capital budgeting purposes.

EXAMPLE 18.1 Valuing an Acquisition Using the WACC Method

Problem

Suppose Avco is considering the acquisition of another firm in its industry that specializes in custom packaging. The acquisition is expected to increase Avco's free cash flow by $3.8 million the first year, and this contribution is expected to grow at a rate of 3% per year from then on. Avco has negotiated a purchase price of $80 million. After the transaction, Avco will adjust its capital structure to maintain its current debt-equity ratio. If the acquisition has similar risk to the rest of Avco, what is the value of this deal?

Solution

The free cash flows of the acquisition can be valued as a growing perpetuity. Because its risk matches the risk for the rest of Avco, and because Avco will maintain the same debt-equity ratio going forward, we can discount these cash flows using the WACC of 6.8%. Thus, the value of the acquisition is

$$V^L = \frac{3.8}{6.8\% - 3\%} = \$100 \text{ million}$$

Given the purchase price of \$80 million, the acquisition has an NPV of \$20 million.

Implementing a Constant Debt-Equity Ratio

Thus far, we have simply assumed the firm adopted a policy of keeping its debt-equity ratio constant. In fact, an important advantage of the WACC method is that you do not need to know how this leverage policy is implemented in order to make the capital budgeting decision. Nevertheless, keeping the debt-equity ratio constant has implications for how the firm's total debt will change with new investment. For example, Avco currently has a debt-equity ratio of $300/300 = 1$ or, equivalently, a debt-to-value ratio $[D/(E + D)]$ of 50%. To maintain this ratio, the firm's new investments must be financed with debt equal to 50% of their market value.

By undertaking the RFX project, Avco adds new assets to the firm with initial market value $V_0^L = \$61.25$ million. Therefore, to maintain its debt-to-value ratio, Avco must add $50\% \times 61.25 = \$30.625$ million in new net debt.[3] Avco can add this net debt either by reducing cash or by borrowing and increasing debt. Suppose Avco decides to spend its \$20 million in cash and borrow an additional \$10.625 million. Because only \$28 million is required to fund the project, Avco will pay the remaining $30.625 - 28 = \$2.625$ million to shareholders through a dividend (or share repurchase). Table 18.3 shows Avco's market value balance sheet with the RFX project in this case.

TABLE 18.3 **Avco's Current Market Value Balance Sheet ($ million) with the RFX Project**

Assets		Liabilities	
Cash	—	Debt	330.625
Existing Assets	600.00		
RFX Project	61.25	Equity	330.625
Total Assets	661.25	Total Liabilities and Equity	661.25

[3]We can also evaluate the project's debt as follows: Of the \$28 million upfront cost of the project, 50% (\$14 million) will be financed with debt. In addition, the project generates an NPV of \$33.25 million, which will increase the market value of the firm. To maintain a debt-equity ratio of 1, Avco must add debt of $50\% \times 33.25 = \$16.625$ million at the time when the NPV of the project is anticipated (which could occur before the new investment is made). Thus, the total new debt is $14 + 16.625 = \$30.625$ million.

This financing plan maintains Avco's 50% debt-to-value ratio. The market value of Avco's equity increases by 330.625 − 300 = \$30.625 million. Adding the dividend of \$2.625 million, the shareholders' total gain is 30.625 + 2.625 = \$33.25 million, which is exactly the NPV we calculated for the RFX project.

What happens over the life of the project? First, we define an investment's **debt capacity**, D_t, as the amount of debt at date t that is required to maintain the firm's target debt-to-value ratio, d. If V_t^L, is the project's levered continuation value on date t—that is, the levered value of its free cash flow after date t—then

$$D_t = d \times V_t^L \tag{18.3}$$

We compute the debt capacity for the RFX project in the spreadsheet in Table 18.4. Starting with the project's free cash flow, we compute its levered continuation value at each date (line 2) by discounting the future free cash flow at the WACC as in Eq. 18.2. Because the continuation value at each date includes the value of all subsequent cash flows, it is even simpler to compute the value at each date by working backward from period 4, discounting next period's free cash flow and continuation value:

$$V_t^L = \frac{FCF_{t+1} + \overbrace{V_{t+1}^L}^{\substack{\text{Value of FCF in year} \\ t+2 \text{ and beyond}}}}{1 + r_{wacc}} \tag{18.4}$$

Once we have computed the project's value V_t^L at each date, we apply Eq. 18.3 to compute the project's debt capacity at each date (line 3). As the spreadsheet shows, the project's debt capacity declines each year, and falls to zero by the end of year 4.

TABLE 18.4 SPREADSHEET **Continuation Value and Debt Capacity of the RFX Project over Time**

	Year	0	1	2	3	4
Project Debt Capacity (\$ million)						
1	**Free Cash Flow**	(28.00)	18.00	18.00	18.00	18.00
2	Levered Value, V^L (at r_{wacc} = 6.8%)	61.25	47.41	32.63	16.85	—
3	**Debt Capacity, D_t (at d = 50%)**	**30.62**	**23.71**	**16.32**	**8.43**	—

EXAMPLE 18.2 Debt Capacity for an Acquisition

Problem

Suppose Avco proceeds with the acquisition described in Example 18.1. How much debt must Avco use to finance the acquisition and still maintain its debt-to-value ratio? How much of the acquisition cost must be financed with equity?

Solution

From the solution to Example 18.2, the market value of the assets acquired in the acquisition, V^L, is \$100 million. Thus, to maintain a 50% debt-to-value ratio, Avco must increase its debt by \$50 million. The remaining \$30 million of the \$80 million acquisition cost will be financed with new equity. In addition to the \$30 million in new equity, the value of Avco's existing shares will increase by the \$20 million NPV of the acquisition, so in total the market value of Avco's equity will rise by \$50 million.

CONCEPT CHECK

1. Describe the key steps in the WACC valuation method.
2. How does the WACC method take into account the tax shield?

18.3 The Adjusted Present Value Method

The **adjusted present value (APV)** method is an alternative valuation method in which we determine the levered value V^L of an investment by first calculating its *unlevered value* V^U, which is its value without any leverage, and then adding the value of the interest tax shield. That is, as we showed in Chapter 15:[4]

The APV Formula

$$V^L = APV = V^U + PV(\text{Interest Tax Shield}) \tag{18.5}$$

As we did with the WACC method, we focus solely on the corporate tax benefits of debt for now and defer the discussion of other consequences of leverage to Section 18.7. As Eq. 18.5 shows, the APV method incorporates the value of the interest tax shield directly, rather than by adjusting the discount rate as in the WACC method. Let's demonstrate the APV method by returning to Avco's RFX project.

The Unlevered Value of the Project

From the free cash flow estimates in Table 18.1, the RFX project has an upfront cost of \$28 million, and it generates \$18 million per year in free cash flow for the next four years. The first step in the APV method is to calculate the value of these free cash flows using the project's cost of capital if it were financed without leverage.

What is the project's unlevered cost of capital? Because the RFX project has similar risk to Avco's other investments, its unlevered cost of capital is the same as for the firm as a whole. Thus, as we did in Chapter 12, we can calculate the unlevered cost of capital using Avco's pretax WACC, the average return the firm's investors expect to earn:

Unlevered Cost of Capital with a Target Leverage Ratio

$$r_U = \frac{E}{E+D} r_E + \frac{D}{E+D} r_D = \text{Pretax WACC} \tag{18.6}$$

To understand why the firm's unlevered cost of capital equals its pretax WACC, note that the pretax WACC represents investors' required return for holding the entire firm (equity and debt). Thus, it will depend only on the firm's overall risk. So long as the firm's leverage choice does not change the overall risk of the firm, the pretax WACC must be the same whether the firm is levered or unlevered—recall Figure 15.2 on page 527.

Of course, this argument relies on the assumption that the overall risk of the firm is independent of the choice of leverage. As we showed in Chapter 14, this assumption always holds in a perfect market. It will also hold in a world with taxes whenever the risk of the tax shield is the same as the risk of the firm (so the size of the tax shield will not change the overall riskiness of the firm). In this chapter's appendix, we show that the tax shield will have the same risk as the firm if the firm maintains a *target leverage ratio*. A **target leverage ratio**

[4] Stewart Myers developed the application of APV to capital budgeting, see "Interactions of Corporate Financing and Investment Decisions—Implications for Capital Budgeting," *Journal of Finance* 29 (1974): 1–25.

means that the firm adjusts its debt proportionally to the project's value, or its cash flows, so that a constant debt-equity ratio is a special case.

Applying Eq. 18.6 to Avco, we find its unlevered cost of capital to be

$$r_U = 0.50 \times 10.0\% + 0.50 \times 6.0\% = 8.0\%$$

Avco's unlevered cost of capital is less than its equity cost of capital of 10.0% (which includes the financial risk of leverage), but is more than its WACC of 6.8% (which incorporates the tax benefit of leverage).

Given our estimate of the unlevered cost of capital r_U and the project's free cash flows, we calculate the project's value without leverage:

$$V^U = \frac{18}{1.08} + \frac{18}{1.08^2} + \frac{18}{1.08^3} + \frac{18}{1.08^4} = \$59.62 \text{ million}$$

Valuing the Interest Tax Shield

The value of the unlevered project, V^U, calculated above does not include the value of the tax shield provided by the interest payments on debt—it is the value of the project were it purely equity financed. Given the project's debt capacity from Table 18.4, we can estimate the expected interest payments and the tax shield as shown in the spreadsheet in Table 18.5. The interest paid in year t is estimated based on the amount of debt outstanding at the end of the prior year:

$$\text{Interest paid in year } t = r_D \times D_{t-1} \tag{18.7}$$

The interest tax shield is equal to the interest paid multiplied by the corporate tax rate τ_c.

TABLE 18.5 SPREADSHEET **Expected Debt Capacity, Interest Payments, and Tax Shield for Avco's RFX Project**

	Year	0	1	2	3	4
Interest Tax Shield ($ million)						
1	**Debt Capacity, D_t (at d = 50%)**	30.62	23.71	16.32	8.43	—
2	Interest Paid (at r_D = 6%)		1.84	1.42	0.98	0.51
3	**Interest Tax Shield (at τ_c = 40%)**		**0.73**	**0.57**	**0.39**	**0.20**

To compute the present value of the interest tax shield, we need to determine the appropriate cost of capital. The interest tax shields shown in Table 18.5 are expected values, and the true amount of the interest tax shield each year will vary with the cash flows of the project. Because Avco maintains a fixed debt-equity ratio, if the project does well, its value will be higher, it will support more debt, and the interest tax shield will be higher. If the project goes poorly, its value will fall, Avco will reduce its debt level, and the interest tax shield will be lower. Thus, the tax shield will fluctuate with, and therefore share the risk of, the project itself:[5]

When the firm maintains a target leverage ratio, its future interest tax shields have similar risk to the project's cash flows, so they should be discounted at the project's unlevered cost of capital.

[5] In Section 18.6, we consider the case in which the debt levels are fixed in advance, and so do *not* fluctuate with the project cash flows. As we will see, in that case the tax shield has lower risk, and thus a lower cost of capital, than the project.

EXAMPLE 18.3 **Risk of Tax Shields with a Constant Debt-Equity Ratio**

Problem

Suppose ABC Corporation maintains a constant debt-equity ratio of 1, the current total value of the firm is \$100 million, and its existing debt is riskless. Over the next month news will come out that will either raise or lower ABC's value by 20%. How will ABC adjust its debt level in response? What can you conclude about the risk of its interest tax shields?

Solution

Originally ABC has \$50 million in equity and \$50 million in debt. Once the news comes out, ABC's value will rise to \$120 million or fall to \$80 million. Thus, to maintain a debt equity ratio of 1, ABC will either increase its debt level to \$60 million or decrease it to \$40 million. Because the firm's interest payments and tax shield will fall proportionally, they have the same risk as the overall firm.

For Avco's RFX project, we have

$$PV(\text{interest tax shield}) = \frac{0.73}{1.08} + \frac{0.57}{1.08^2} + \frac{0.39}{1.08^3} + \frac{0.20}{1.08^4} = \$1.63 \text{ million}$$

To determine the value of the project with leverage, we add the value of the interest tax shield to the unlevered value of the project:[6]

$$V^L = V^U + PV(\text{interest tax shield}) = 59.62 + 1.63 = \$61.25 \text{ million}$$

Again, given the \$28 million initial investment required, the RFX project has an NPV with leverage of $61.25 - 28 = \$33.25$ million, which matches precisely the value we computed in Section 18.2 using the WACC approach.

Summary of the APV Method

To determine the value of a levered investment using the APV method, we proceed as follows:

1. Determine the investment's value without leverage, V^U, by discounting its free cash flows at the unlevered cost of capital, r_U. With a constant debt-equity ratio, r_U may be estimated using Eq. 18.6.
2. Determine the present value of the interest tax shield.
   a. Determine the expected interest tax shield: Given expected debt D_t on date t, the interest tax shield on date $t+1$ is $\tau_c r_D D_t$.[7]
   b. Discount the interest tax shield. If a constant debt-equity ratio is maintained, using r_U is appropriate.

---

[6]Because we are using the same discount rate for the free cash flow and the tax shield, the cash flows of the project and the tax shield can be combined first and then discounted at the rate r_U. These combined cash flows are also referred to as the capital cash flows (CCF): CCF = FCF + Interest Tax Shield. This method is known as the CCF or "compressed APV" method [see S. Kaplan and R. Ruback, "The Valuation of Cash Flow Forecasts: An Empirical Analysis," *Journal of Finance* 50 (1995): 1059–1093; and R. Ruback, "Capital Cash Flows: A Simple Approach to Valuing Risky Cash Flows," *Financial Management* 31 (2002): 85–103].

[7]The return on the debt need not come solely from interest payments, so this value is an approximation. The same approximation is implicit in the definition of the WACC (for additional precision, see footnote 27 in this chapter's appendix).

3. Add the unlevered value, V^U, to the present value of the interest tax shield to determine the value of the investment with leverage, V^L.

In this case, the APV method is more complicated than the WACC method because we must compute two separate valuations: the unlevered project and the interest tax shield. Furthermore, in this example, to determine the project's debt capacity for the interest tax shield calculation, we relied on the calculation in Table 18.4, *which depended on the value of the project*. Thus, we need to know the debt level to compute the APV, but with a constant debt-equity ratio we need to know the project's value to compute the debt level. As a result, implementing the APV approach with a constant debt-equity ratio requires solving for the project's debt and value *simultaneously*. (See this chapter's appendix for an example of this calculation.)

Despite its complexity, the APV method has some advantages. As we shall see in Section 18.6, it can be easier to apply than the WACC method when the firm does not maintain a constant debt-equity ratio. It also provides managers with an explicit valuation of the tax shield itself. In the case of Avco's RFX project, the benefit of the interest tax shield is relatively small. Even if tax rates were to change, or if Avco decided for other reasons not to increase its debt, the profitability of the project would not be jeopardized. However, this need not always be the case. Consider again the acquisition in Example 18.1, where the APV method makes clear that the gain from the acquisition crucially depends on the interest tax shield.

EXAMPLE 18.4 Using the APV Method to Value an Acquisition

Problem

Consider again Avco's acquisition from Examples 18.1 and 18.2. The acquisition will contribute \$3.8 million in free cash flows the first year, which will grow by 3% per year thereafter. The acquisition cost of \$80 million will be financed with \$50 million in new debt initially. Compute the value of the acquisition using the APV method, assuming Avco will maintain a constant debt-equity ratio for the acquisition.

Solution

First, we compute the value without leverage. Given Avco's unlevered cost of capital of $r_U = 8\%$, we get

$$V^U = 3.8/(8\% - 3\%) = \$76 \text{ million}$$

Avco will add new debt of \$50 million initially to fund the acquisition. At a 6% interest rate, the interest expense the first year is $6\% \times 50 = \$3$ million, which provides an interest tax shield of $40\% \times 3 = \$1.2$ million. Because the value of the acquisition is expected to grow by 3% per year, the amount of debt the acquisition supports—and, therefore, the interest tax shield—is expected to grow at the same rate. The present value of the interest tax shield is

$$PV(\text{interest tax shield}) = 1.2/(8\% - 3\%) = \$24 \text{ million}$$

The value of the acquisition with leverage is given by the APV:

$$V^L = V^U + PV(\text{interest tax shield}) = 76 + 24 = \$100 \text{ million}$$

This value is identical to the value computed in Example 18.1 and implies an NPV of $100 - 80 = \$20$ million for the acquisition. Without the benefit of the interest tax shield, the NPV would be $76 - 80 = -\$4$ million.

We can easily extend the APV approach to include other market imperfections such as financial distress, agency, and issuance costs. We discuss these complexities further in Section 18.7.

CONCEPT CHECK

1. Describe the adjusted present value (APV) method.
2. At what rate should we discount the interest tax shield when a firm maintains a target leverage ratio?

18.4 The Flow-to-Equity Method

In the WACC and APV methods, we value a project based on its free cash flow, which is computed ignoring interest and debt payments. Some students find these methods confusing because, if the goal is to determine the benefit of the project to shareholders, it seems to them that we should focus on the cash flows that *shareholders* will receive.

In the **flow-to-equity (FTE)** valuation method, we explicitly calculate the free cash flow available to equity holders *after taking into account all payments to and from debt holders.* The cash flows to equity holders are then discounted using the *equity* cost of capital.[8] Despite this difference in implementation, the FTE method produces the same assessment of the project's value as the WACC or APV methods.

Calculating the Free Cash Flow to Equity

The first step in the FTE method is to determine the project's **free cash flow to equity (FCFE)**. The FCFE is the free cash flow that remains after adjusting for interest payments, debt issuance, and debt repayment. The spreadsheet shown in Table 18.6 calculates the FCFE for Avco's RFX project.

TABLE 18.6 SPREADSHEET Expected Free Cash Flows to Equity from Avco's RFX Project

	Year	0	1	2	3	4
Incremental Earnings Forecast ($ million)						
1	Sales	—	60.00	60.00	60.00	60.00
2	Cost of Goods Sold	—	(25.00)	(25.00)	(25.00)	(25.00)
3	**Gross Profit**	—	35.00	35.00	35.00	35.00
4	Operating Expenses	(6.67)	(9.00)	(9.00)	(9.00)	(9.00)
5	Depreciation	—	(6.00)	(6.00)	(6.00)	(6.00)
6	**EBIT**	(6.67)	20.00	20.00	20.00	20.00
7	Interest Expense	—	(1.84)	(1.42)	(0.98)	(0.51)
8	**Pretax Income**	(6.67)	18.16	18.58	19.02	19.49
9	Income Tax at 40%	2.67	(7.27)	(7.43)	(7.61)	(7.80)
10	**Net Income**	(4.00)	10.90	11.15	11.41	11.70
Free Cash Flow to Equity						
11	Plus: Depreciation	—	6.00	6.00	6.00	6.00
12	Less: Capital Expenditures	(24.00)	—	—	—	—
13	Less: Increases in NWC	—	—	—	—	—
14	Plus: Net Borrowing	30.62	(6.92)	(7.39)	(7.89)	(8.43)
15	**Free Cash Flow to Equity**	**2.62**	**9.98**	**9.76**	**9.52**	**9.27**

[8]The FTE approach generalizes the total payout method for valuing the firm described in Chapter 9. In that method, we value the total dividends and repurchases that the firm pays to shareholders. It is also equivalent to the residual income valuation method used in accounting (see appendix).

Comparing the FCFE estimates in Table 18.6 with the free cash flow estimates in Table 18.1, we notice two changes. First, we deduct interest expenses (from Table 18.5) on line 7, before taxes. As a consequence, we compute the incremental net income of the project on line 10, rather than its *unlevered* net income as we do when computing free cash flows. The second change is line 14, where we add the proceeds from the firm's net borrowing activity. These proceeds are positive when the firm increases its net debt; they are negative when the firm reduces its net debt by repaying principal (or retaining cash). For the RFX project, Avco issues \$30.62 million in debt initially. At date 1, however, the debt capacity of the project falls to \$23.71 million (see Table 18.4), so that Avco must repay 30.62 − 23.71 = \$6.91 million of the debt.[9] In general, given the project's debt capacity D_t,

$$\text{Net Borrowing at Date } t = D_t - D_{t-1} \tag{18.8}$$

As an alternative to Table 18.6, we can compute a project's FCFE directly from its free cash flow. Because interest payments are deducted before taxes in line 7, we adjust the firm's FCF by their after-tax cost. We then add net borrowing to determine FCFE:

Free Cash Flow to Equity

$$FCFE = FCF - \underbrace{(1 - \tau_c) \times (\text{Interest Payments})}_{\text{After-tax interest expense}} + (\text{Net Borrowing}) \tag{18.9}$$

We illustrate this alternative calculation for Avco's RFX project in Table 18.7. Note that the project's FCFE is lower than its FCF in years 1 through 4 due to the interest and principal payments on the debt. In year 0, however, the proceeds from the loan more than offset the negative free cash flow, so FCFE is positive (and equal to the dividend we calculated in Section 18.2).

Valuing Equity Cash Flows

The project's free cash flow to equity shows the expected amount of additional cash the firm will have available to pay dividends (or conduct share repurchases) each year. Because these cash flows represent payments to equity holders, they should be discounted at the project's equity cost of capital. Given that the risk and leverage of the RFX project are the same as for Avco overall, we can use Avco's equity cost of capital of $r_E = 10.0\%$ to discount the project's FCFE:

$$NPV(FCFE) = 2.62 + \frac{9.98}{1.10} + \frac{9.76}{1.10^2} + \frac{9.52}{1.10^3} + \frac{9.27}{1.10^4} = \$33.25 \text{ million}$$

TABLE 18.7 SPREADSHEET Computing FCFE from FCF for Avco's RFX Project

	Year	0	1	2	3	4
Free Cash Flow to Equity ($ million)						
1	**Free Cash Flow**	(28.00)	18.00	18.00	18.00	18.00
2	After-tax Interest Expense	—	(1.10)	(0.85)	(0.59)	(0.30)
3	Net Borrowing	30.62	(6.92)	(7.39)	(7.89)	(8.43)
4	**Free Cash Flow to Equity**	**2.62**	**9.98**	**9.76**	**9.52**	**9.27**

[9] The \$0.01 million difference in the spreadsheet is due to rounding.

What Counts as "Debt"?

Firms often have many types of debt as well as other liabilities, such as leases. Practitioners use different guidelines to determine which to include as debt when computing the WACC. Some use only long-term debt. Others use both long-term and short-term debt, plus lease obligations. Students are often confused by these different approaches and are left wondering: Which liabilities should be included as debt?

In fact, any choice will work if done correctly. We can view the WACC and FTE methods as special cases of a more general approach in which we *value the after-tax cash flows from a set of the firm's assets and liabilities by discounting them at the after-tax weighted average cost of capital of the firm's remaining assets and liabilities.* In the WACC method, the FCF does not include the interest and principal payments on debt, so debt is included in the calculation of the weighted average cost of capital. In the FTE method, the FCFE incorporates the after-tax cash flows to and from debt holders, so debt is excluded from the weighted average cost of capital (which is simply the equity cost of capital).

Other combinations are also possible. For example, long-term debt can be included in the weighted average cost of capital, and short-term debt can be included as part of the cash flows. Similarly, other assets (such as cash) or liabilities (such as leases) can be included either in the weighted average cost of capital or as part of the cash flow. All such methods, if applied consistently, will lead to an equivalent valuation. Typically, the most convenient choice is the one for which the assumption of a constant debt-to-value ratio is a reasonable approximation.

The value of the project's FCFE represents the gain to shareholders from the project. It is identical to the NPV we computed using the WACC and APV methods.

Why isn't the project's NPV lower now that we have deducted interest and debt payments from the cash flows? Recall that these costs of debt are offset by cash received when the debt is issued. Looking back at Table 18.6, the cash flows from debt in lines 7 and 14 have an NPV of zero assuming the debt is fairly priced.[10] In the end, the only effect on value comes from a reduction in the tax payments, leaving the same result as with the other methods.

Summary of the Flow-to-Equity Method

The key steps in the flow-to-equity method for valuing a levered investment are as follows:

1. Determine the free cash flow to equity of the investment using Eq. 18.9.
2. Determine the equity cost of capital, r_E.
3. Compute the contribution to equity value, E, by discounting the free cash flow to equity using the equity cost of capital.

Applying the FTE method was simplified in our example because the project's risk and leverage matched the firm's, and the firm's equity cost of capital was expected to remain constant. Just as with the WACC, however, this assumption is reasonable only if the firm maintains a constant debt-equity ratio. If the debt-equity ratio changes over time, the risk of equity—and, therefore, its cost of capital—will change as well.

[10] The interest and principal payments for the RFX project are as follows:

		Year 0	1	2	3	4
1	Net Borrowing	30.62	(6.92)	(7.39)	(7.89)	(8.43)
2	Interest Expense	—	(1.84)	(1.42)	(0.98)	(0.51)
3	**Cash Flow from Debt**	**30.62**	**(8.76)**	**(8.81)**	**(8.87)**	**(8.93)**

Because these cash flows have the same risk as the debt, we discount them at the debt cost of capital of 6% to compute their NPV:

$$30.62 + \frac{-8.76}{1.06} + \frac{-8.81}{1.06^2} + \frac{-8.87}{1.06^3} + \frac{-8.93}{1.06^4} = 0.$$

In this setting, the FTE approach has the same disadvantage associated with the APV approach: We need to compute the project's debt capacity to determine interest and net borrowing before we can make the capital budgeting decision. For this reason, in most settings the WACC is easier to apply. The FTE method can offer an advantage when calculating the value of equity for the entire firm, if the firm's capital structure is complex and the market values of other securities in the firm's capital structure are not known. In that case, the FTE method allows us to compute the value of equity directly. In contrast, the WACC and APV methods compute the firm's enterprise value, so that a separate valuation of the other components of the firm's capital structure is needed to determine the value of equity. Finally, by emphasizing a project's implication for equity, the FTE method may be viewed as a more transparent method for discussing a project's benefit to shareholders—a managerial concern.

EXAMPLE 18.5 **Using the FTE Method to Value an Acquisition**

Problem

Consider again Avco's acquisition from Examples 18.1, 18.2, and 18.4. The acquisition will contribute \$3.8 million in free cash flows the first year, growing by 3% per year thereafter. The acquisition cost of \$80 million will be financed with \$50 million in new debt initially. What is the value of this acquisition using the FTE method?

Solution

Because the acquisition is being financed with \$50 million in new debt, the remaining \$30 million of the acquisition cost must come from equity:

$$FCFE_0 = -80 + 50 = -\$30 \text{ million}$$

In one year, the interest on the debt will be $6\% \times 50 = \$3$ million. Because Avco maintains a constant debt-equity ratio, the debt associated with the acquisition is also expected to grow at a 3% rate: $50 \times 1.03 = \$51.5$ million. Therefore, Avco will borrow an additional $51.5 - 50 = \$1.5$ million in one year.

$$FCFE_1 = +3.8 - (1 - 0.40) \times 3 + 1.5 = \$3.5 \text{ million}$$

After year 1, FCFE will also grow at a 3% rate. Using the cost of equity $r_E = 10\%$, we compute the NPV:

$$NPV(FCFE) = -30 + 3.5/(10\% - 3\%) = \$20 \text{ million}$$

This NPV matches the result we obtained with the WACC and APV methods.

CONCEPT CHECK

1. Describe the key steps in the flow to equity method for valuing a levered investment.
2. Why does the assumption that the firm maintains a constant debt-equity ratio simplify the flow-to-equity calculation?

18.5 Project-Based Costs of Capital

Up to this point, we have assumed that both the risk and the leverage of the project under consideration matched those characteristics for the firm as a whole. This assumption allowed us, in turn, to assume that the cost of capital for a project matched the cost of capital of the firm.

In the real world, specific projects often differ from the average investment made by the firm. Consider General Electric Company, discussed in the introduction to this chapter. Projects in its health care division are likely to have different market risk than projects in air transportation equipment or at NBC Universal. Projects may also vary in the amount of leverage they will support—for example, acquisitions of real estate or capital equipment are often highly levered, whereas investments in intellectual property are not. In this section, we show how to calculate the cost of capital for the project's cash flows when a project's risk and leverage differ from those for the firm overall.

Estimating the Unlevered Cost of Capital

We begin by reviewing the method introduced in Chapter 12 to calculate the unlevered cost of capital of a project with market risk that is very different from the rest of the firm. Suppose Avco launches a new plastics manufacturing division that faces different market risks than its main packaging business. What unlevered cost of capital would be appropriate for this division?

We can estimate r_U for the plastics division by looking at other single-division plastics firms that have similar business risks. For example, suppose two firms are comparable to the plastics division and have the following characteristics:

Firm	Equity Cost of Capital	Debt Cost of Capital	Debt-to-Value Ratio, D/(E+ D)
Comparable #1	12.0%	6.0%	40%
Comparable #2	10.7%	5.5%	25%

Assuming that both firms maintain a target leverage ratio, we can estimate the unlevered cost of capital for each competitor by using the pretax WACC from Eq. 18.6:

$$\text{Competitor 1:} \quad r_U = 0.60 \times 12.0\% + 0.40 \times 6.0\% = 9.6\%$$

$$\text{Competitor 2:} \quad r_U = 0.75 \times 10.7\% + 0.25 \times 5.5\% = 9.4\%$$

Based on these comparable firms, we estimate an unlevered cost of capital for the plastics division of about 9.5%.[11] With this rate in hand, we can use the APV approach to calculate the value of Avco's investment in plastic manufacturing. To use either the WACC or FTE method, however, we need to estimate the project's equity cost of capital, which will depend on the incremental debt the firm will take on as a result of the project.

Project Leverage and the Equity Cost of Capital

Suppose the firm will fund the project according to a target leverage ratio. This leverage ratio may differ from the firm's overall leverage ratio, as different divisions or types of investments may have different optimal debt capacities. We can rearrange terms in Eq. 18.6 to get the following expression for the equity cost of capital:[12]

$$r_E = r_U + \frac{D}{E}(r_U - r_D) \tag{18.10}$$

[11] If we are using the CAPM to estimate expected returns, this procedure is equivalent to unlevering the betas of comparable firms using Eq. 12.9:

$$\beta_U = [E/(E+D)]\,\beta_E + [D/(D+E)]\,\beta_D.$$

[12] We derived this same expression with perfect capital markets in Eq. 14.5.

Equation 18.10 shows that the project's equity cost of capital depends on its unlevered cost of capital, r_U, and the debt-equity ratio of the incremental financing that will be put in place to support the project. For example, suppose that Avco plans to maintain an equal mix of debt and equity financing as it expands into plastics manufacturing, and it expects its borrowing cost to remain at 6%. Given its 9.5% unlevered cost of capital, the plastics division's equity cost of capital is

$$r_E = 9.5\% + \frac{0.50}{0.50}(9.5\% - 6\%) = 13.0\%$$

Once we have the equity cost of capital, we can use Eq. 18.1 to determine the division's WACC:

$$r_{wacc} = 0.50 \times 13.0\% + 0.50 \times 6.0\% \times (1 - 0.40) = 8.3\%$$

Based on these estimates, Avco should use a WACC of 8.3% for the plastics division, compared to the WACC of 6.8% for the packaging division that we calculated in Section 18.2.

In fact, we can combine Eq. 18.1 and Eq. 18.10 to obtain a direct formula for the WACC when the firm maintains a target leverage ratio for the project. If d is the project's debt-to-value ratio, $[D/(E + D)]$, then[13]

Project-Based WACC Formula

$$r_{wacc} = r_U - d\tau_c r_D \tag{18.11}$$

For example, in the case of Avco's plastics division:

$$r_{wacc} = 9.5\% - 0.50 \times 0.40 \times 6\% = 8.3\%$$

EXAMPLE 18.6 Computing Divisional Costs of Capital

Problem

Hasco Corporation is a multinational provider of lumber and milling equipment. Currently, Hasco's equity cost of capital is 12.7%, and its borrowing cost is 6%. Hasco has traditionally maintained a 40% debt-to-value ratio. Hasco engineers have developed a GPS-based inventory control tracking system, which the company is considering developing commercially as a separate division. Management views the risk of this investment as similar to that of other technology companies' investments, with comparable firms typically having an unlevered cost of capital of 15%. Suppose Hasco plans to finance the new division using 10% debt financing (a constant debt-to-value ratio of 10%) with a borrowing rate of 6%, and its corporate tax rate is 35%. Estimate the unlevered, equity, and weighted average costs of capital for each division.

Solution

For the lumber and milling division, we can use the firm's current equity cost of capital $r_E = 12.7\%$ and debt-to-value ratio of 40%. Then

$$r_{wacc} = 0.60 \times 12.7\% + 0.40 \times 6\% \times (1 - 0.35) = 9.2\%$$

$$r_U = 0.60 \times 12.7\% + 0.40 \times 6\% = 10.0\%$$

[13] We derive Eq. 18.11 (which is equivalent to Eq. 12.13) by comparing the WACC and pretax WACC in Eq. 18.1 and Eq. 18.6. This formula was proposed by R. Harris and J. Pringle, "Risk Adjusted Discount Rates: Transition from the Average Risk Case," *Journal of Financial Research* 8 (1985): 237–244.

For the technology division, we estimate its unlevered cost of capital using comparable firms: $r_U = 15\%$. Because Hasco's technology division will support 10% debt financing,

$$r_E = 15\% + \frac{0.10}{0.90}(15\% - 6\%) = 16\%$$

$$r_{wacc} = 15\% - 0.10 \times 0.35 \times 6\% = 14.8\%$$

Note that the cost of capital is quite different across the two divisions.

Determining the Incremental Leverage of a Project

To determine the equity or weighted average cost of capital for a project, we need to know the amount of debt to associate with the project. For capital budgeting purposes, the project's financing is the *incremental* financing that results if the firm takes on the project. That is, it is the change in the firm's total debt (net of cash) with the project versus without the project.

The incremental financing of a project need not correspond to the financing that is directly tied to the project. As an example, suppose a project involves buying a new warehouse, and the purchase of the warehouse is financed with a mortgage for 90% of its value. However, if the firm has an overall policy to maintain a 40% debt-to-value ratio, it will reduce debt elsewhere in the firm once the warehouse is purchased in an effort to maintain that ratio. In that case, the appropriate debt-to-value ratio to use when evaluating the warehouse project is 40%, not 90%.

Here are some important concepts to remember when determining the project's incremental financing.

COMMON MISTAKE Re-Levering the WACC

When computing the WACC using its definition in Eq. 18.1, always remember that the equity and debt costs of capital, r_E and r_D, will change for different choices of the firm's leverage ratio. For example, consider a firm with a debt-to-value ratio of 25%, a debt cost of capital of 6.67%, an equity cost of capital of 12%, and a tax rate of 40%. From Eq. 18.1, its current WACC is

$$r_{wacc} = 0.75(12\%) + 0.25(6.67\%)(1 - 0.40)$$
$$= 10\%$$

Suppose the firm increases its debt-to-value ratio to 50%. It is tempting to conclude that its WACC will fall to

$$0.50(12\%) + 0.50(6.67\%)(1 - 0.40) = 8\%$$

In fact, when the firm increases leverage, the risk of its equity and debt will increase, causing its equity and debt cost of capital to rise. To compute the new WACC correctly, we must first determine the firm's unlevered cost of capital from Eq. 18.6:

$$r_U = 0.75(12\%) + 0.25(6.67\%) = 10.67\%$$

If the firm's debt cost of capital rises to 7.34% with the increase in leverage, then from Eq. 18.10 its equity cost of capital will rise as well:

$$r_E = 10.67\% + \frac{0.50}{0.50}(10.67\% - 7.34\%) = 14\%$$

Using Eq. 18.1, with the new equity and debt cost of capital, we can correctly compute the new WACC:

$$r_{wacc} = 0.50(14\%) + 0.50(7.34\%)(1 - 0.40)$$
$$= 9.2\%$$

We can also calculate the new WACC using Eq. 18.11:

$$r_{wacc} = 10.67\% - 0.50(0.40)(7.34\%) = 9.2\%$$

Note that if we fail to incorporate the effect of an increase in leverage on the firm's equity and debt costs of capital, we will overestimate the reduction in its WACC.

Cash Is Negative Debt. A firm's leverage should be evaluated based on its debt net of any cash. Thus, if an investment will reduce the firm's cash holdings, it is equivalent to the firm adding leverage. Similarly, if the positive free cash flow from a project will increase the firm's cash holdings, then this growth in cash is equivalent to a reduction in the firm's leverage.

A Fixed Equity Payout Policy Implies 100% Debt Financing. Consider a firm whose dividend payouts and expenditures on share repurchases are set in advance and will not be affected by a project's free cash flow. In this case, the only source of financing is *debt*—any cash requirement of the project will be funded using the firm's cash or borrowing, and any cash that the project produces will be used to repay debt or increase the firm's cash. As a result, the incremental effect of the project on the firm's financing is to change the level of debt, so this project is 100% debt financed (that is, its debt-to-value ratio $d = 1$). If the firm's payout policy is fixed for the life of a project, the appropriate WACC for the project is $r_U - \tau_c r_D$. This case can be relevant for a highly levered firm that devotes its free cash flow to paying down its debt or for a firm that is hoarding cash.

Optimal Leverage Depends on Project *and* Firm Characteristics. Projects with safer cash flows can support more debt before they increase the risk of financial distress for the firm. But, as we discussed in Part 5, the likelihood of financial distress that a firm can bear depends on the magnitude of the distress, agency, and asymmetric information costs that it may face. These costs are not specific to a project, but rather depend on the characteristics of the entire firm. As a consequence, the optimal leverage for a project will depend on the characteristics of both the project and the firm.

Safe Cash Flows Can Be 100% Debt Financed. When an investment has risk-free cash flows, a firm can offset these cash flows 100% with debt and leave its overall risk unchanged. If it does so, the appropriate discount rate for safe cash flows is $r_D(1 - \tau_c)$.

EXAMPLE 18.7 Debt Financing at Chipotle

Problem

In mid-2015, Chipotle Mexican Grill held nearly 880 million in cash and securities and no debt. Consider a project with an unlevered cost of capital of $r_U = 12\%$. Suppose Chipotle's payout policy is completely fixed during the life of this project, so that the free cash flow from the project will affect only Chipotle's cash balance. If Chipotle earns 4% interest on its cash holdings and pays a 35% corporate tax rate, what cost of capital should Chipotle use to evaluate the project?

Solution

Because the inflows and outflows of the project change Chipotle's cash balance, the project is financed by 100% debt; that is, $d = 1$. The appropriate cost of capital for the project is

$$r_{wacc} = r_U - \tau_c r_D = 12\% - 0.35 \times 4\% = 10.6\%$$

Note that the project is effectively 100% debt financed, because even though Chipotle itself had no debt, if the cash had not been used to finance the project, Chipotle would have had to pay taxes on the interest the cash earned.

CONCEPT CHECK

1. How do we estimate a project's unlevered cost of capital when the project's risk is different from that of a firm?
2. What is the incremental debt associated with a project?

18.6 APV with Other Leverage Policies

To this point, we have assumed that the incremental debt of a project is set to maintain a constant debt-equity (or, equivalently, debt-to-value) ratio. While a constant debt-equity ratio is a convenient assumption that simplifies the analysis, not all firms adopt this leverage policy. In this section, we consider two alternative leverage policies: constant interest coverage and predetermined debt levels.

When we relax the assumption of a constant debt-equity ratio, the equity cost of capital and WACC for a project will change over time as the debt-equity ratio changes. As a result, the WACC and FTE method are difficult to implement (see Section 18.8 for further details). The APV method, however, is relatively straightforward to use and is therefore the preferred method with alternative leverage policies.

Constant Interest Coverage Ratio

As discussed in Chapter 15, if a firm is using leverage to shield income from corporate taxes, then it will adjust its debt level so that its interest expenses grow with its earnings. In this case, it is natural to specify the firm's incremental interest payments as a target fraction, k, of the project's free cash flow:[14]

$$\text{Interest Paid in Year } t = k \times FCF_t \tag{18.12}$$

When the firm keeps its interest payments to a target fraction of its FCF, we say it has a **constant interest coverage ratio.**

To implement the APV approach, we must compute the present value of the tax shield under this policy. Because the tax shield is proportional to the project's free cash flow, it has the same risk as the project's cash flow and so should be discounted at the same rate—that is, the unlevered cost of capital, r_U. But the present value of the project's free cash flow at rate r_U is the unlevered value of the project. Thus,

$$\begin{aligned} PV(\text{Interest Tax Shield}) &= PV(\tau_c k \times FCF) = \tau_c k \times PV(FCF) \\ &= \tau_c k \times V^U \end{aligned} \tag{18.13}$$

That is, with a constant interest coverage policy, the value of the interest tax shield is proportional to the project's unlevered value. Using the APV method, the value of the project with leverage is given by the following formula:

Levered Value with a Constant Interest Coverage Ratio

$$\begin{aligned} V^L &= V^U + PV(\text{Interest Tax Shield}) = V^U + \tau_c k \times V^U \\ &= (1 + \tau_c k) V^U \end{aligned} \tag{18.14}$$

For example, we calculated the unlevered value of Avco's RFX project as $V^U = \$59.62$ million in Section 18.3. If Avco targets interest to be 20% of its free cash flow, the value with leverage is $V^L = [1 + 0.4\,(20\%)]\,59.62 = \$64.39$ million. (This result differs from the value of \$61.25 million for the project that we calculated in Section 18.3, where we assumed a different leverage policy of a 50% debt-to-value ratio.)

---

[14] It might be even better to specify interest as a fraction of taxable earnings. Typically, however, taxable earnings and free cash flows are roughly proportional, so the two specifications are very similar. Also, for Eq. 18.12 to hold exactly, the firm must adjust debt continuously throughout the year. We will relax this assumption in Section 18.8 to a setting in which the firm adjusts debt periodically based on its expected level of future free cash flow (see Example 18.11).

Equation 18.14 provides a simple rule to determine an investment's levered value based on a leverage policy that may be appropriate for many firms.[15] Note also that if the investment's free cash flows are expected to grow at a constant rate, then the assumption of constant interest coverage and a constant debt-equity ratio are equivalent, as in the following example.

EXAMPLE 18.8 Valuing an Acquisition with Target Interest Coverage

Problem

Consider again Avco's acquisition from Examples 18.1 and 18.2. The acquisition will contribute \$3.8 million in free cash flows the first year, growing by 3% per year thereafter. The acquisition cost of \$80 million will be financed with \$50 million in new debt initially. Compute the value of the acquisition using the APV method assuming Avco will maintain a constant interest coverage ratio for the acquisition.

Solution

Given Avco's unlevered cost of capital of $r_U = 8\%$, the acquisition has an unlevered value of

$$V^U = 3.8/(8\% - 3\%) = \$76 \text{ million}$$

With \$50 million in new debt and a 6% interest rate, the interest expense the first year is $6\% \times 50 = \$3$ million, or $k = \text{Interest}/FCF = 3/3.8 = 78.95\%$. Because Avco will maintain this interest coverage, we can use Eq. 18.14 to compute the levered value:

$$V^L = (1 + \tau_c k)V^U = [1 + 0.4\,(78.95\%)]\,76 = \$100 \text{ million}$$

This value is identical to the value computed using the WACC method in Example 18.1, where we assumed a constant debt-equity ratio.

Predetermined Debt Levels

Rather than set debt according to a target debt-equity ratio or interest coverage level, a firm may adjust its debt according to a fixed schedule that is known in advance. Suppose, for example, that Avco plans to borrow \$30.62 million and then will reduce the debt on a fixed schedule to \$20 million after one year, to \$10 million after two years, and to zero after three years. The RFX project will have no other consequences for Avco's leverage, regardless of its success. How can we value an investment like this one when its future *debt levels*, rather than the *debt-equity ratio*, are known in advance?

When the debt levels are known in advance, it is straightforward to compute the interest payments and the corresponding tax shield the firm will obtain. The question is, at what rate should we discount this tax shield to determine the present value? In Section 18.3, we used the project's unlevered cost of capital because the amount of debt—and, therefore, the tax shield—fluctuated with the value of the project itself and so had similar risk. However, with a fixed debt schedule, the amount of the debt will not fluctuate. In this case, the tax shield is less risky than the project, so it should be discounted at a lower rate.

---

[15] J. Graham and C. Harvey report that a majority of firms target a credit rating when issuing debt ["The Theory and Practice of Corporate Finance: Evidence from the Field," *Journal of Financial Economics* 60 (2001)]. The interest coverage ratios are important determinants of credit ratings. Firms and rating agencies also consider the *book* debt-equity ratio, which often fluctuates more closely with a firm's cash flows, rather than with its market value. (For example, book equity increases when the firm invests in physical capital to expand, which generally results in higher cash flows.)

TABLE 18.8 SPREADSHEET Interest Payments and Interest Tax Shield Given a Fixed Debt Schedule for Avco's RFX Project

	Year	0	1	2	3	4
Interest Tax Shield ($ million)						
1	**Debt Capacity, D_t (fixed schedule)**	30.62	20.00	10.00	—	—
2	Interest Paid (at $r_D = 6\%$)		1.84	1.20	0.60	—
3	**Interest Tax Shield (at $\tau_c = 40\%$)**		**0.73**	**0.48**	**0.24**	—

Indeed, the risk of the tax shield is similar to the risk of the debt payments. Therefore, we advise the following general rule:[16]

When debt levels are set according to a fixed schedule, we can discount the predetermined interest tax shields using the debt cost of capital, r_D.

Let's apply this to our Avco example, given the debt schedule and interest tax shield shown in Table 18.8. Using the debt cost of capital, $r_D = 6\%$:

$$PV(\text{Interest Tax Shield}) = \frac{0.73}{1.06} + \frac{0.48}{1.06^2} + \frac{0.24}{1.06^3} = \$1.32 \text{ million}$$

We then combine the value of the tax shield with the unlevered value of the project (which we already computed in Section 18.3) to determine the APV:

$$V^L = V^U + PV(\text{Interest Tax Shield}) = 59.62 + 1.32 = \$60.94 \text{ million}$$

The value of the interest tax shield computed here, $1.32 million, differs from the value of $1.63 million we computed in Section 18.3 based on constant debt-equity ratio. Comparing the firm's debt in the two cases, we see that it is paid off more rapidly in Table 18.8 than in Table 18.4. Also, because the debt-equity ratio for the project changes over time in this example, the project's WACC also changes, making it difficult to apply the WACC method to this case. We show how to do so, and verify that we get the same result, as part of the advanced topics in Section 18.8.

A particularly simple example of a predetermined debt level occurs when the firm has permanent fixed debt, maintaining the same level of debt forever. We discussed this debt policy in Section 15.2 and showed that if the firm maintains a fixed level of debt, D, the value of the tax shield is $\tau_c \times D$.[17] Hence, the value of the levered project in this case is

Levered Value with Permanent Debt

$$V^L = V^U + \tau_c \times D \tag{18.15}$$

A Cautionary Note: When debt levels are predetermined, the firm will not adjust its debt based on fluctuations to its cash flows or value according to a target leverage ratio, and the risk of the interest tax shield differs from the risk of the cash flows. As a result, *the firm's pretax WACC no longer coincides with its unlevered cost of capital, so Eq. 18.6, Eq. 18.10, and Eq. 18.11 do not apply.* (For example, if we compute the WACC using Eq. 18.11 and

[16]The risk of the tax shield is not literally equivalent to that of the debt payments, because it is based on only the interest portion of the payments and is subject to the risk of fluctuations in the firm's marginal tax rate. Nevertheless, this assumption is a reasonable approximation absent much more detailed information.

[17]Because the interest tax shield is $\tau_c r_D D$ in perpetuity, using the discount rate r_D we get $PV(\text{Interest Tax Shield}) = \tau_c r_D D / r_D = \tau_c D$.

apply it in the case of permanent debt, the value we estimate will *not* be consistent with Eq. 18.15.) For the correct relationship between the firm's WACC, unlevered, and equity cost of capital, we need to use more general versions of these equations, which we provide in Eq. 18.20 and Eq. 18.21 in Section 18.8.

A Comparison of Methods

We have introduced three methods for valuing levered investments: WACC, APV, and FTE. How do we decide which method to use in which circumstances?

When used consistently, each method produces the same valuation for the investment. Thus, the choice of method is largely a matter of convenience. As a general rule, the WACC method is the easiest to use when the firm will maintain a fixed debt-to-value ratio over the life of the investment. For alternative leverage policies, the APV method is usually the most straightforward approach. The FTE method is typically used only in complicated settings for which the values of other securities in the firm's capital structure or the interest tax shield are themselves difficult to determine.

CONCEPT CHECK

1. What condition must the firm meet to have a constant interest coverage policy?
2. What is the appropriate discount rate for tax shields when the debt schedule is fixed in advance?

18.7 Other Effects of Financing

The WACC, APV, and FTE methods determine the value of an investment incorporating the tax shields associated with leverage. However, as we discussed in Chapter 16, some other potential imperfections are associated with leverage. In this section, we investigate ways to adjust our valuation to account for imperfections such as issuance costs, security mispricing, and financial distress and agency costs.

Issuance and Other Financing Costs

When a firm takes out a loan or raises capital by issuing securities, the banks that provide the loan or underwrite the sale of the securities charge fees. Table 18.9 lists the typical fees for common transactions. The fees associated with the financing of the project are a cost

TABLE 18.9 Typical Issuance Costs for Different Securities, as a Percentage of Proceeds[18]

Financing Type	Underwriting Fees
Bank loans	< 2%
Corporate bonds	
Investment grade	1–2%
Non-investment grade	2–3%
Equity issues	
Initial public offering	8–9%
Seasoned equity offering	5–6%

[18]Fees vary by transaction size; estimates here are based on typical legal, underwriting, and accounting fees for a $50 million transaction. For example, see I. Lee, S. Lochhead, J. Ritter, and Q. Zhao, "The Cost of Raising Capital," *Journal of Financial Research* 19 (1996): 59–74.

that should be included as part of the project's required investment, reducing the NPV of the project.

For example, suppose a project has a levered value of \$20 million and requires an initial investment of \$15 million. To finance the project, the firm will borrow \$10 million and fund the remaining \$5 million by reducing dividends. If the bank providing the loan charges fees (after any tax deductions) totaling \$200,000, the project NPV is

$$NPV = V^L - (\text{Investment}) - (\text{After Tax Issuance Costs}) = 20 - 15 - 0.2 = \$4.8 \text{ million}$$

This calculation presumes the cash flows generated by the project will be paid out. If instead they will be reinvested in a new project, and thereby save *future* issuance costs, the present value of these savings should also be incorporated and will offset the current issuance costs.

Security Mispricing

With perfect capital markets, all securities are fairly priced and issuing securities is a zero-NPV transaction. However, as discussed in Chapter 16, sometimes management may believe that the securities they are issuing are priced at less than (or more than) their true value. If so, the NPV of the transaction, which is the difference between the actual money raised and the true value of the securities sold, should be included when evaluating the decision. For example, if the financing of the project involves an equity issue, and if management believes that the equity will sell at a price that is less than its true value, this mispricing is a cost of the project for the *existing* shareholders.[19] It can be deducted from the project NPV in addition to other issuance costs.

When a firm borrows funds, a mispricing scenario arises if the interest rate charged differs from the rate that is appropriate given the actual risk of the loan. For example, a firm may pay an interest rate that is too high if news that would improve its credit rating has not yet become public. With the WACC method, the cost of the higher interest rate will result in a higher weighted average cost of capital and a lower value for the investment. With the APV method, we must add to the value of the project the NPV of the loan cash flows when evaluated at the "correct" rate that corresponds to their actual risk.[20]

EXAMPLE 18.9 Valuing a Loan

Problem

Gap, Inc., is considering borrowing \$100 million to fund an expansion of its stores. Given investors' uncertainty regarding its prospects, Gap will pay a 6% interest rate on this loan. The firm's management knows, however, that the actual risk of the loan is extremely low and that the appropriate rate on the loan is 5%. Suppose the loan is for five years, with all principal being repaid in the fifth year. If Gap's marginal corporate tax rate is 40%, what is the net effect of the loan on the value of the expansion?

Solution

The following table shows the cash flows (in \$ million) and interest tax shields of a fair loan, which has a 5% interest rate, and of the above-market rate loan Gap will receive, which has a 6%

[19] New shareholders, of course, benefit from receiving the shares at a low price.

[20] We must also use the correct rate for r_D when levering or unlevering the cost of capital.

interest rate. For each loan, we compute both the NPV of the loan cash flows and the present value of the interest tax shields, using the correct rate $r_D = 5\%$.

		Year	0	1	2	3	4	5
1	Fair Loan		100.00	(5.00)	(5.00)	(5.00)	(5.00)	(105.00)
2	Interest Tax Shield			2.00	2.00	2.00	2.00	2.00
3	At $r_D = 5\%$:							
4	*NPV*(Loan Cash Flows)		0.00					
5	*PV*(Interest Tax Shield)		8.66					
6	Actual Loan		100.00	(6.00)	(6.00)	(6.00)	(6.00)	(106.00)
7	Interest Tax Shield			2.40	2.40	2.40	2.40	2.40
8	At $r_D = 5\%$:							
9	*NPV*(Loan Cash Flows)		(4.33)					
10	*PV*(Interest Tax Shield)		10.39					

For the fair loan, note that the NPV of the loan cash flows is zero. Thus, the benefit of the loan on the project's value is the present value of the interest tax shield of $8.66 million. For the actual loan, the higher interest rate increases the value of the interest tax shield but implies a negative NPV for the loan cash flows. The combined effect of the loan on the project's value is

$$NPV(\text{Loan Cash Flows}) + PV(\text{Interest Tax Shield}) = -4.33 + 10.39 = \$6.06 \text{ million}$$

While leverage is still valuable due to the tax shields, paying the higher interest rate reduces its benefit to the firm by $8.66 - 6.06 = \$2.60$ million.

Financial Distress and Agency Costs

As discussed in Chapter 16, one consequence of debt financing is the possibility of financial distress and agency costs. Because these costs affect the future free cash flows that will be generated by the project, they can be incorporated directly into the estimates of the project's expected free cash flows. When the debt level—and, therefore, the probability of financial distress—is high, the expected free cash flow will be reduced by the expected costs associated with financial distress and agency problems. (Conversely, as we also noted in Chapter 16, in some situations the threat of default can also prompt management to improve efficiency and thereby increase the firm's free cash flow.)

Financial distress and agency costs also have consequences for the cost of capital. For example, financial distress is more likely to occur when economic times are bad. As a result, the costs of distress cause the value of the firm to fall further in a market downturn. Financial distress costs therefore tend to increase the sensitivity of the firm's value to market risk, further raising the cost of capital for highly levered firms.[21]

How do we incorporate financial distress costs into the valuation methods described in this chapter? One approach is to adjust our free cash flow estimates to account for the costs, and increased risk, resulting from financial distress. An alternative method is to first value the project ignoring these costs, and then add the present value of the incremental cash flows associated with financial distress and agency problems separately. Because these costs tend to occur only when a firm is in (or near) default, valuing them is complicated and best done using the option valuation techniques introduced in Part 7. In some special

[21]In other words, distress costs tend to have a negative beta (they are higher in bad times). Because they are a *cost*, including them in the firm's free cash flows will raise the beta of the firm.

GLOBAL FINANCIAL CRISIS **Government Loan Guarantees**

In times of crisis, firms may appeal to the federal government for financial assistance. Often, such aid comes in the form of subsidized loans or loan guarantees. For example, in the wake of the September 11, 2001 tragedy, the U.S. government made available $10 billion in loan guarantees to enable air carriers to obtain credit. U.S. Airways received the largest loan guarantee of $900 million, and America West Airlines received the second largest, for $429 million. Ultimately, these loans were repaid without taxpayer expense.

Loan guarantees were also an important part of the government's response to the 2008 financial crisis. The U.S. government has insured over $1 trillion in debt issued by financial institutions or assets held by the banks. The government also made over $500 billion in direct loans to distressed firms. Moreover, firms and banks viewed as "too big to fail" were thought to have implicit guarantees even if they did not have explicit ones.

These guarantees enabled firms to obtain loans at a lower interest rate than they otherwise would have received without government assistance. If these loans were fairly priced at market rates, then the loans obtained with the help of the federal guarantee had a positive NPV for the borrowers, and were equivalent to a direct cash subsidy. If, on the other hand, market rates for these loans were too high—due perhaps to asymmetric information or a lack of available lenders—then these loans and guarantees may have improved terms for borrowers at a lower cost to taxpayers than a direct cash bailout.

cases, however, we can use the values of the firm's existing securities to estimate the value of distress costs, as in the following example.

EXAMPLE 18.10 **Valuing Distress Costs**

Problem

Your firm has zero coupon debt with a face value of $100 million due in 5 years time, and no other debt outstanding. The current risk-free rate is 5%, but due to default risk the yield to maturity of the debt is 12%. You believe that in the event of default, 10% of the losses are attributable to bankruptcy and distress costs. (For example, if the debt holders lose $60 million and recover $40 million, $6 million of the loss in value would not have occurred if the firm had been unlevered and thus avoided bankruptcy.) Estimate the present value of the distress costs.

Solution

With a 12% yield, the current market value of the firm's debt is $\$100/1.12^5 = \$56.74$ million. If the firm's debt were risk-free, its market value would be $\$100/1.05^5 = \$78.35$ million. The difference in these values, $\$78.35 - \$56.74 = \$21.61$ million, is the present value of the debt holders' expected losses in default. If 10% of these losses is due to bankruptcy and distress costs, then the present value of these costs is $\$21.61 \times 0.10 = \$2.16$ million.

CONCEPT CHECK

1. How do we deal with issuance costs and security mispricing costs in our assessment of a project's value?
2. How would financial distress and agency costs affect a firm's use of leverage?

18.8 Advanced Topics in Capital Budgeting

In the previous sections, we have highlighted the most important methods for capital budgeting with leverage and demonstrated their application in common settings. In this section, we consider several more complicated scenarios and show how our tools can be extended to these cases. First, we consider leverage policies in which firms keep debt fixed in the short run, but adjust to a target leverage ratio in the long run. Second, we look at the relationship between a firm's equity and unlevered cost of capital for alternative leverage policies. Third, we implement the WACC and FTE methods when the firm's debt-equity ratio changes over time. We then conclude the section by incorporating the effects of personal taxes.

Periodically Adjusted Debt

To this point, we have considered leverage policies in which debt is either adjusted continuously to a target leverage ratio[22] or set according to a fixed plan that will never change. More realistically, most firms allow the debt-equity ratio of the firm to stray from the target and periodically adjust leverage to bring it back into line with the target.

Suppose the firm adjusts its leverage every *s* periods, as shown in Figure 18.1. Then the firm's interest tax shields up to date *s* are predetermined, so they should be discounted at rate r_D. In contrast, interest tax shields that occur after date *s* depend on future adjustments the firm will make to its debt, so they are risky. If the firm will adjust the debt according to a target debt-equity ratio or interest coverage level, then the future interest tax shields should be discounted at rate r_D for the periods that they are known, but at rate r_U for all earlier periods when they are still risky.

An important special case is when the debt is adjusted annually. In that case, the expected interest expense on date *t*, Int_t, is known as of date $t-1$. Therefore, we discount the interest tax shield at rate r_D for one period, from date *t* to $t-1$ (because it will be known at that time), and then discount it from date $t-1$ to 0 at rate r_U:

$$PV(\tau_c \times Int_t) = \frac{\tau_c \times Int_t}{(1+r_U)^{t-1}(1+r_D)} = \frac{\tau_c \times Int_t}{(1+r_U)^t} \times \left(\frac{1+r_U}{1+r_D}\right) \tag{18.16}$$

FIGURE 18.1 **Discounting the Tax Shield with Periodic Adjustments**

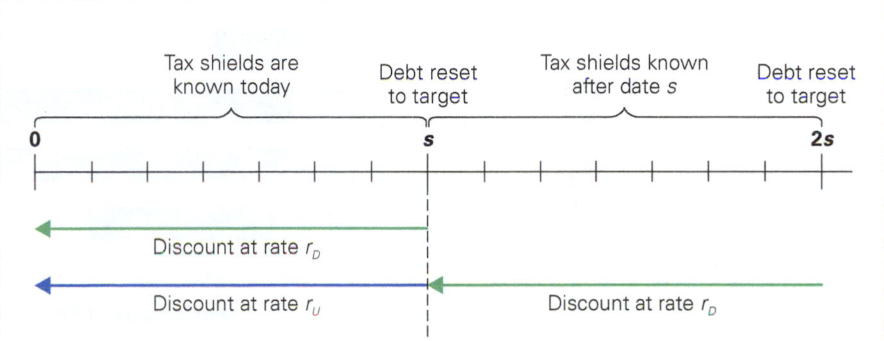

If the debt is reset to a target leverage ratio every *s* periods, then interest tax shields within the first *s* periods are known and should be discounted at rate r_D Interest tax shields that occur after date *s* are not yet known, so they should be discounted at rate r_D for the periods when they will be known and at rate r_U for earlier periods.

[22]While we have simplified our exposition earlier in the chapter by calculating debt and interest payments on an annual basis, the formulas we have used in the case of a target leverage ratio or interest coverage ratio are based on the assumption that the firm maintains the target leverage ratio or interest coverage during the year.

Equation 18.16 implies that we can value the tax shield by discounting it at rate r_U as before, and then multiply the result by the factor $(1 + r_U)/(1 + r_D)$ to account for the fact that the tax shield is known one year in advance.

This same adjustment can be applied to other valuation methods as well. For example, when the debt is adjusted annually rather than continuously to a target debt-to-value ratio d, the project-based WACC formula of Eq. 18.11 becomes[23]

$$r_{wacc} = r_U - d\,\tau_c\, r_D \frac{1 + r_U}{1 + r_D} \tag{18.17}$$

Similarly, when the firm sets debt annually based on its expected future free cash flow, the constant interest coverage model in Eq. 18.14 becomes

$$V^L = \left(1 + \tau_c k \frac{1 + r_U}{1 + r_D}\right) V^U \tag{18.18}$$

How do firm's actually adjust their leverage? As Figure 18.2 shows, approximately 50% of surveyed firms attempt to keep their leverage ratio in tight range. When firm's adjust their debt levels only periodically, the risk of the tax shield declines and its value increases as shown in Eqs. 18.17 and 18.18. Example 18.11 illustrates these methods in a constant growth setting.

FIGURE 18.2 **Firms' Leverage Policies**

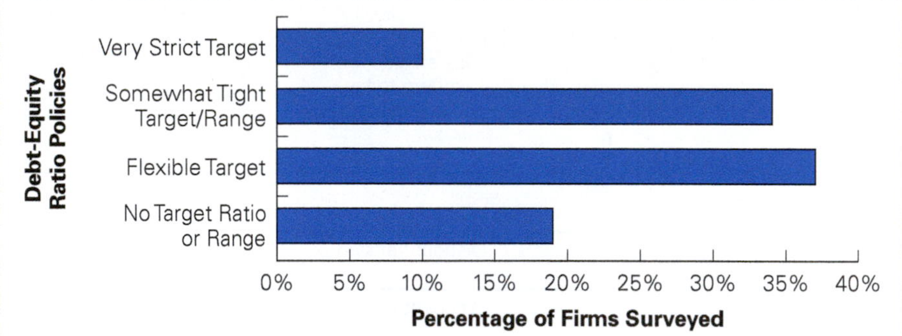

Of 392 CFOs surveyed by Professors J. Graham and C. Harvey, 81% reported having a target debt-equity ratio. However, only 10% of respondents viewed the target as set in stone. Most were willing to let the debt-equity ratio of the firm stray from the target and periodically adjust leverage to bring it back into line.

Source: J. R. Graham and C. Harvey, "The Theory and Practice of Corporate Finance: Evidence from the Field," *Journal of Financial Economics* 60 (2001): 187–243.

[23] An equivalent WACC formula was proposed by J. Miles and J. Ezzell, "The Weighted Average Cost of Capital, Perfect Capital Markets and Project Life: A Clarification," *Journal of Financial and Quantitative Analysis* 15 (1980): 719–730.

EXAMPLE 18.11 **Annual Debt Ratio Targeting**

Problem

Celmax Corporation expects free cash flows this year of \$7.36 million and a future growth rate of 4% per year. The firm currently has \$30 million in debt outstanding. This leverage will remain fixed during the year, but at the end of each year Celmax will increase or decrease its debt to maintain a constant debt-equity ratio. Celmax pays 5% interest on its debt, pays a corporate tax rate of 40%, and has an unlevered cost of capital of 12%. Estimate Celmax's value with this leverage policy.

Solution

Using the APV approach, the unlevered value is $V^U = 7.36/(12\% - 4\%) = \$92.0$ million. In the first year, Celmax will have an interest tax shield of $\tau_c r_D D = 0.40 \times 5\% \times \$30 \text{ million} = \$0.6$ million. Because Celmax will adjust its debt after one year, the tax shields are expected to grow by 4% per year with the firm. The present value of the interest tax shield is therefore

$$PV(\text{Interest Tax Shield}) = \underbrace{\frac{0.6}{(12\% - 4\%)}}_{PV \text{ at rate } r_U} \times \underbrace{\left(\frac{1.12}{1.05}\right)}_{\substack{\text{Debt is set 1 year}\\ \text{in advance}}} = \$8.0 \text{ million}$$

Therefore, $V^L = V^U + PV(\text{Interest Tax Shield}) = 92.0 + 8.0 = \$100.0$ million.

We can also apply the WACC method. From Eq. 18.17, Celmax's WACC is

$$r_{wacc} = r_U - d\,\tau_c\, r_D \frac{1 + r_U}{1 + r_D} = 12\% - \frac{30}{100}(0.40)(5\%)\frac{1.12}{1.05}$$
$$= 11.36\%$$

Therefore, $V^L = 7.36/(11.36\% - 4\%) = \$100$ million.

Finally, the constant interest coverage model can be applied (in this setting with constant growth, a constant debt-equity ratio implies a constant interest coverage ratio). Given interest of $5\% \times \$30$ million $= \$1.50$ million this year, from Eq. 18.18,

$$V^L = \left(1 + \tau_c\, k \frac{1 + r_U}{1 + r_D}\right) V^U$$
$$= \left(1 + 0.40 \times \frac{1.50}{7.36} \times \frac{1.12}{1.05}\right) 92.0 = \$100 \text{ million}$$

Leverage and the Cost of Capital

The relationship between leverage and the project's costs of capital in Eq. 18.6, Eq. 18.10, and Eq.18.11 relies on the assumption that the firm maintains a target leverage ratio. That relationship holds because in that case the interest tax shields have the same risk as the firm's cash flows. But when debt is set according to a fixed schedule for some period of time, the interest tax shields for the scheduled debt are known, relatively safe cash flows. These safe cash flows will reduce the effect of leverage on the risk of the firm's equity. To account for this effect, we should deduct the value of these "safe" tax shields from the debt—in the same way that we deduct cash—when evaluating a firm's leverage. That is, if T^s is the present value of the interest tax shields from predetermined debt, the risk of a firm's equity will depend on its *debt net of the predetermined tax shields:*

$$D^s = D - T^s \qquad (18.19)$$

We show in this chapter's appendix that Eq. 18.6 and Eq. 18.10 continue to apply with D replaced by D^s, so that the more general relationship between the unlevered and equity costs of capital are related as follows:

Leverage and the Cost of Capital with a Fixed Debt Schedule

$$r_U = \frac{E}{E + D^s} r_E + \frac{D^s}{E + D^s} r_D \quad \text{or, equivalently,} \quad r_E = r_U + \frac{D^s}{E}(r_U - r_D) \qquad (18.20)$$

We can also combine Eq. 18.20 with the definition of the WACC in Eq. 18.1 and generalize the project-based WACC formula in Eq. 18.11:

Project WACC with a Fixed Debt Schedule

$$r_{wacc} = r_U - d\tau_c\,[r_D + \phi(r_U - r_D)] \qquad (18.21)$$

where $d = D/(D + E)$ is the debt-to-value ratio, and $\phi = T^s/(\tau_c D)$ is a measure of the permanence of the debt level, D. Here are three cases commonly used in practice, which differ according to the frequency with which the debt is assumed to adjust to the growth of the investment:[24]

1. Continuously adjusted debt: $T^s = 0$, $D^s = D$, and $\phi = 0$
2. Annually adjusted debt: $T^s = \dfrac{\tau_c r_D D}{1 + r_D}$, $D^s = D\left(1 - \tau_c \dfrac{r_D}{1 + r_D}\right)$, and $\phi = \dfrac{r_D}{1 + r_D}$
3. Permanent debt: $T^s = \tau_c D$, $D^s = D(1 - \tau_c)$, and $\phi = 1$

Finally, note that unless d and ϕ remain constant over time, the WACC and equity cost of capital must be computed period by period.

EXAMPLE 18.12 APV and WACC with Permanent Debt

Problem

International Paper Company is considering the acquisition of additional forestland in the southeastern United States. The wood harvested from the land will generate free cash flows of \$4.5 million per year, with an unlevered cost of capital of 7%. As a result of this acquisition, International Paper will permanently increase its debt by \$30 million. If International Paper's tax rate is 35%, what is the value of this acquisition using the APV method? Verify this result using the WACC method.

Solution

Using the APV method, the unlevered value of the land is $V^U = FCF/r_U = 4.5/0.07 = \$64.29$ million. Because the debt is permanent, the value of the tax shield is $\tau_c D = 0.35(30) = 10.50$. Therefore, $V^L = 64.29 + 10.50 = \$74.79$ million.

To use the WACC method, we apply Eq. 18.21 with $\phi = T^s/(\tau_c D) = 1$ and $d = 30/74.79 = 40.1\%$. Therefore, the WACC for the investment is

$$r_{wacc} = r_U - d\tau_c r_U = 7\% - 0.401 \times 0.35 \times 7\% = 6.017\%$$

and $V^L = 4.5/0.06017 = \$74.79$ million.

---

[24]Case 1 reduces to the Harris-Pringle formula (see footnote 14), case 2 is the Miles-Ezzell formula (see footnote 23), and case 3 is equivalent to the Modigliani-Miller-Hamada formula with permanent debt. See F. Modigliani and M. Miller, "Corporate Income Taxes and the Cost of Capital: A Correction," *American Economic Review* 53 (1963): 433–443; and R. Hamada, "The Effect of a Firm's Capital Structure on the Systematic Risks of Common Stocks," *Journal of Finance* 27 (1972): 435–452.

The WACC or FTE Method with Changing Leverage

When a firm does not maintain a constant debt-equity ratio for a project, the APV method is generally the most straightforward method to apply. The WACC and FTE methods become more difficult to use because when the proportion of debt financing changes, the project's equity cost of capital and WACC will not remain constant over time. With a bit of care, however, these methods can still be used (and, of course, will lead to the same result as the APV method).

As an example, let's see how we would apply the WACC or FTE methods to the RFX project when Avco has the fixed debt schedule we analyzed earlier using the APV method. The spreadsheet in Table 18.10 computes the equity cost of capital and WACC for the RFX project each year given the fixed debt schedule shown in line 3. The project's value is computed using the APV method in line 7 as the total of the unlevered and tax shield values. With the project's equity value and net debt D^s in hand, we can use Eq. 18.20 to calculate the project's equity cost of capital each year (line 11). Note that the equity cost of capital declines over time as the project's leverage ratio D^s/E declines. By year 3, the debt is fully repaid and the equity cost of capital equals the unlevered cost of capital of 8%.

Given the project's equity cost of capital, we compute its WACC using Eq. 18.1 in line 12. For example, at the beginning of the project,

$$r_{wacc} = \frac{E}{E+D} r_E + \frac{D}{E+D} r_D(1-\tau_c)$$

$$= \frac{30.32}{60.94} 9.93\% + \frac{30.62}{60.94} 6\%(1-0.40) = 6.75\%$$

Note that as the leverage of the project falls, its WACC rises, until it eventually equals the unlevered cost of capital of 8% when the project debt is fully repaid at year 3.

Once we have computed the WACC or the equity cost of capital, we can value the project using the WACC or FTE method. Because the cost of capital changes over time,

TABLE 18.10 SPREADSHEET **Adjusted Present Value and Cost of Capital for Avco's RFX Project with a Fixed Debt Schedule**

	Year	0	1	2	3	4
Unlevered Value ($ million)						
1	Free Cash Flow	(28.00)	18.00	18.00	18.00	18.00
2	Unlevered Value, V^U (at $r_u = 8.0\%$)	59.62	46.39	32.10	16.67	—
Interest Tax Shield						
3	Debt Schedule, D_t	30.62	20.00	10.00	—	—
4	Interest Paid (at $r_d = 6\%$)	—	1.84	1.20	0.60	—
5	Interest Tax Shield (at $\tau_c = 40\%$)	—	0.73	0.48	0.24	—
6	Tax Shield Value, T^s (at $r_D = 6.0\%$)	1.32	0.67	0.23	—	—
Adjusted Present Value						
7	**Levered Value, $V^L = V^U + T^s$**	**60.94**	**47.05**	**32.33**	**16.67**	—
Effective Leverage and Cost of Capital						
8	Equity, $E = V^L - D$	30.32	27.05	22.33	16.67	—
9	Effective Debt, $D^s = D - T^s$	29.30	19.33	9.77	—	—
10	Effective Debt-Equity Ratio, D^s/E	0.966	0.715	0.438	0.000	
11	**Equity Cost of Capital, r_E**	**9.93%**	**9.43%**	**8.88%**	**8.00%**	
12	**WACC, r_{wacc}**	**6.75%**	**6.95%**	**7.24%**	**8.00%**	

TABLE 18.11 SPREADSHEET **WACC Method for Avco's RFX Project with a Fixed Debt Schedule**

	Year	0	1	2	3	4
WACC Method ($ million)						
1	Free Cash Flow	(28.00)	18.00	18.00	18.00	18.00
2	WACC, r_{wacc}	6.75%	6.95%	7.24%	8.00%	
3	**Levered Value V^L (at r_{wacc})**	**60.94**	**47.05**	**32.33**	**16.67**	**—**

we must use a different discount rate each year when applying these methods. For example, using the WACC method, the levered value each year is computed as

$$V_t^L = \frac{FCF_{t+1} + V_{t+1}^L}{1 + r_{wacc}(t)} \tag{18.22}$$

where $r_{wacc}(t)$ is the project's WACC in year t. This calculation is shown in Table 18.11. Note that the levered value matches the result from the APV method (line 7 in Table 18.10). The same approach can be used when applying the FTE method.[25]

Personal Taxes

As we discussed in Chapter 15, leverage has tax consequences for both investors and corporations. For individuals, interest income from debt is generally taxed more heavily than income from equity (capital gains and dividends). So how do personal taxes affect our valuation methods?

If investors are taxed on the income they receive from holding equity or debt, it will raise the return they require to hold those securities. That is, the equity and debt cost of capital in the market *already* reflects the effects of investor taxes. As a result, *the WACC method does not change in the presence of investor taxes*; we can continue to compute the WACC according to Eq. 18.1 and compute the levered value as in Section 18.2.

The APV approach, however, requires modification in the presence of investor taxes because it requires that we compute the unlevered cost of capital. This computation *is* affected by the presence of investor taxes. Let τ_e be the tax rate investors pay on equity income (dividends) and τ_i be the tax rate investors pay on interest income. Then, given an expected return on debt r_D, define r_D^* as the expected return on equity income that would give investors the same after-tax return: $r_D^*(1 - \tau_e) = r_D(1 - \tau_i)$. So

$$r_D^* \equiv r_D \frac{(1 - \tau_i)}{(1 - \tau_e)} \tag{18.23}$$

Because the unlevered cost of capital is for a hypothetical firm that is all equity, investors' tax rates on income for such a firm are the equity rates, so we must use the rate r_D^* when computing the unlevered cost of capital. Therefore, Eq. 18.20 becomes

Unlevered Cost of Capital with Personal Taxes

$$r_U = \frac{E}{E + D^s} r_E + \frac{D^s}{E + D^s} r_D^* \tag{18.24}$$

[25] You will notice, however, that we used the APV to compute the debt-equity ratio each period, which we needed to calculate r_E and r_{wacc}. If we had not already solved for the APV, we would need to determine the project's value and WACC simultaneously, using the approach described in this chapter's appendix.

Next, we must compute the interest tax shield using the effective tax advantage of debt, τ^*, in place of τ_c. The effective tax rate τ^* incorporates the investors' tax rate on equity income, τ_e, and on interest income, τ_i, and was defined in Chapter 15 as follows:

$$\tau^* = 1 - \frac{(1-\tau_c)(1-\tau_e)}{(1-\tau_i)} \tag{18.25}$$

Then, we calculate the interest tax shield using tax rate τ^* and interest rate r_D^*:

$$\text{Interest Tax Shield in Year } t = \tau^* \times r_D^* \times D_{t-1} \tag{18.26}$$

Finally we discount the interest tax shields at rate r_U if the firm maintains a target leverage ratio or at rate r_D^* if the debt is set according to a predetermined schedule.[26]

EXAMPLE 18.13 Using the APV Method with Personal Taxes

Problem

Apex Corporation has an equity cost of capital of 14.4% and a debt cost of capital of 6%, and the firm maintains a debt-equity ratio of 1. Apex is considering an expansion that will contribute $4 million in free cash flows the first year, growing by 4% per year thereafter. The expansion will cost $60 million and will be financed with $40 million in new debt initially with a constant debt-equity ratio maintained thereafter. Apex's corporate tax rate is 40%; the tax rate on interest income is 40%; and the tax rate on equity income is 20%. Compute the value of the expansion using the APV method.

Solution

First, we compute the value without leverage. From Eq. 18.23, the debt cost of capital of 6% is equivalent to an equity rate of

$$r_D^* = r_D \frac{1-\tau_i}{1-\tau_e} = 6\% \times \frac{1-0.40}{1-0.20} = 4.5\%$$

Because Apex maintains a constant debt-equity ratio, $D^s = D$ and Apex's unlevered cost of capital is, using Eq. 18.24,

$$r_U = \frac{E}{E+D^s} r_E + \frac{D^s}{E+D^s} r_D^* = 0.50 \times 14.4\% + 0.50 \times 4.5\% = 9.45\%$$

Therefore, $V^U = 4/(9.45\% - 4\%) = \$73.39$ million.

From Eq. 18.25, the effective tax advantage of debt is

$$\tau^* = 1 - \frac{(1-\tau_c)(1-\tau_e)}{(1-\tau_i)} = 1 - \frac{(1-0.40)(1-0.20)}{(1-0.40)} = 20\%$$

Apex will add new debt of $40 million initially, so from Eq. 18.26 the interest tax shield is 20% × 4.5% × 40 = $0.36 million the first year (note that we use r_D^* here). With a growth rate of 4%, the present value of the interest tax shield is

$$PV(\text{Interest Tax Shield}) = 0.36/(9.45\% - 4\%) = \$6.61 \text{ million}$$

[26] If the debt is permanent, for example, the value of the tax shield is $\tau^* r_D^* D / r_D^* = \tau^* D$. as shown in Chapter 15.

Therefore, the value of the expansion with leverage is given by the APV:

$$V^L = V^U + PV(\text{Interest Tax Shield}) = 73.39 + 6.61 = \$80 \text{ million}$$

Given the cost of \$60 million, the expansion has an NPV of \$20 million.

Let's check this result using the WACC method. Note that the expansion has the same debt-to-value ratio of 40/80 = 50% as the firm overall. Thus, its WACC is equal to the firm's WACC:

$$r_{wacc} = \frac{E}{E+D} r_E + \frac{D}{E+D} r_D (1 - \tau_c)$$

$$= 0.50 \times 14.4\% + 0.50 \times 6\% \times (1 - 0.40) = 9\%$$

Therefore, $V^L = 4/(9\% - 4\%) = \$80$ million, as before.

As Example 18.13 illustrates, the WACC method is much simpler to apply than the APV method in the case with investor taxes. More significantly, the WACC approach does not require knowledge of investors' tax rates. This fact is important because in practice, estimating the marginal tax rate of the investor can be very difficult.

However, if the investment's leverage or risk does not match the firm's, then investor tax rates are required even with the WACC method, as we must unlever and/or re-lever the firm's cost of capital using Eq. 18.24. When the investor's tax rate on interest income exceeds that on equity income, an increase in leverage will lead to a smaller reduction in the WACC (see Problem 28).

CONCEPT CHECK

1. When a firm has pre-determined tax shields, how do we measure its net debt when calculating its unlevered cost of capital?
2. If the firm's debt-equity ratio changes over time, can the WACC method still be applied?

MyFinanceLab Here is what you should know after reading this chapter. MyFinanceLab will help you identify what you know and where to go when you need to practice.

18.1 Overview of Key Concepts

- The three main methods of capital budgeting are weighted average cost of capital (WACC), adjusted present value (APV), and flow-to-equity (FTE).

18.2 The Weighted Average Cost of Capital

- The key steps in the WACC valuation method are as follows:
  - Determine the unlevered free cash flows of the investment.
  - Compute the weighted average cost of capital:

$$r_{wacc} = \frac{E}{E+D} r_E + \frac{D}{E+D} r_D (1 - \tau_c) \qquad (18.1)$$

  - Compute the value with leverage, V^L, by discounting the free cash flows of the investment using the WACC.

18.3 The Adjusted Present Value Method

- To determine the value of a levered investment using the APV method, proceed as follows:
  - Determine the investment's value without leverage, V^U, by discounting its free cash flows at the unlevered cost of capital, r_U.

- Determine the present value of the interest tax shield.
  a. Given debt D_t on date t, the tax shield on date $t + 1$ is $\tau_c r_D D_t$.
  b. If the debt level varies with the investment's value or free cash flow, use discount rate r_U. (If the debt is predetermined, discount the tax shield at rate r_D. See Section 18.6.)
- Add the unlevered value V^U to the present value of the interest tax shield to determine the value of the investment with leverage, V^L.

18.4 The Flow-to-Equity Method

- The key steps in the flow-to-equity method for valuing a levered investment are as follows:
  - Determine the free cash flow to equity of the investment:

$$FCFE = FCF - (1 - \tau_c) \times (\text{Interest Payments}) + (\text{Net Borrowing}) \quad (18.9)$$

  - Compute the contribution to equity value, E, by discounting the free cash flow to equity using the equity cost of capital.

18.5 Project-Based Costs of Capital

- If a project's risk is different from that of the firm as a whole, we must estimate its cost of capital separately from the firm's cost of capital. We estimate the project's unlevered cost of capital by looking at the unlevered cost of capital for other firms with similar market risk as the project.
- With a target leverage ratio, the unlevered, equity, and weighted average costs of capital are related as follows:

$$r_U = \frac{E}{E+D} r_E + \frac{D}{E+D} r_D = \text{Pretax WACC} \quad (18.6)$$

$$r_E = r_U + \frac{D}{E}(r_U - r_D) \quad (18.10)$$

$$r_{wacc} = r_U - d\,\tau_c\, r_D, \quad (18.11)$$

  where $d = D/(D + E)$ is the project's debt-to-value ratio.
- When assessing the leverage associated with a project, we must consider its incremental impact on the debt, net of cash balances, of the firm overall and not just the specific financing used for that investment.

18.6 APV with Other Leverage Policies

- A firm has a constant interest coverage policy if it sets debt to maintain its interest expenses as a fraction, k, of free cash flow. The levered value of a project with such a leverage policy is $V^L = (1 + \tau_c k)V^U$.
- When debt levels are set according to a fixed schedule:
  - We can discount the predetermined interest tax shields using the debt cost of capital, r_D.
  - The unlevered cost of capital can no longer be computed as the pretax WACC (see Section 18.8).
- If a firm chooses to keep the level of debt at a constant level, D, permanently, then the levered value of a project with such a leverage policy is $V^L = V^U + \tau_c \times D$.
- In general, the WACC method is the easiest to use when a firm has a target debt-equity ratio that it plans to maintain over the life of the investment. For other leverage policies, the APV method is usually the most straightforward method.

18.7 Other Effects of Financing

- Issuance costs and any costs or gains from mispricing of issued securities should be included in the assessment of a project's value.
- Financial distress costs are likely to (1) lower the expected free cash flow of a project and (2) raise the firm's cost of capital. Taking these effects into account, together with other agency and asymmetric information costs, may limit a firm's use of leverage.

18.8 Advanced Topics in Capital Budgeting

- If a firm adjusts its debt annually to a target leverage ratio, the value of the interest tax shield is enhanced by the factor $(1 + r_U)/(1 + r_D)$.
- If the firm does not adjust leverage continuously, so that some of the tax shields are predetermined, the unlevered, equity, and weighted average costs of capital are related as follows:

$$r_U = \frac{E}{E+D^s} r_E + \frac{D^s}{E+D^s} r_D \text{ or, equivalently, } r_E = r_U + \frac{D^s}{E}(r_U - r_D) \quad (18.20)$$

$$r_{wacc} = r_U - d\,\tau_c\,[r_D + \phi(r_U - r_D)] \quad (18.21)$$

where $d = D/(D+E)$ is the debt-to-value ratio of the project, $D^s = D - T^s$, and T^s is the value of predetermined interest tax shields, and $\phi = T^s/(\tau_c D)$ reflects the permanence of the debt level.

- The WACC method does not need to be modified to account for investor taxes. For the APV method, we use the interest rate

$$r_D^* \equiv r_D \frac{(1-\tau_i)}{(1-\tau_e)} \quad (18.23)$$

in place of r_D and we replace τ_c with the effective tax rate:

$$\tau^* = 1 - \frac{(1-\tau_c)(1-\tau_e)}{(1-\tau_i)} \quad (18.25)$$

- If the investment's leverage or risk does not match the firm's, then investor tax rates are required even with the WACC method, as we must unlever and/or re-lever the firm's cost of capital using

$$r_U = \frac{E}{E+D^s} r_E + \frac{D^s}{E+D^s} r_D^* \quad (18.24)$$

Key Terms

adjusted present value (APV) *p. 648*
book enterprise value *p. 690*
constant interest coverage ratio *p. 660*
debt capacity *p. 647*
economic value added *p. 690*
flow-to-equity (FTE) *p. 652*
free cash flow to equity (FCFE) *p. 652*
residual income method *p. 689*
target leverage ratio *p. 648*

Further Reading

For a further treatment of the valuation with leverage, see: T. Copeland, T. Koller, and J. Murrin, *Valuation: Measuring and Managing the Value of Companies* (McGraw-Hill, 2000); and S. Pratt, R. Reilly, and R. Schweihs, *Valuing a Business: The Analysis and Appraisal of Closely Held Companies* (McGraw-Hill, 2000).

For a more detailed treatment of the issues discussed in this chapter, see: E. Arzac and L. Glosten, "A Reconsideration of Tax Shield Valuation," *European Financial Management* 11 (2005): 453–461; R. Harris and J. Pringle, "Risk-Adjusted Discount Rates—Extensions from the Average-Risk Case," *Journal of Financial Research* 8 (1985): 237–244; I. Inselbag and H. Kaufold, "Two DCF Approaches in Valuing Companies Under Alternative Financing Strategies (and How to Choose Between Them)," *Journal of Applied Corporate Finance* 10 (1997): 114–122; T. Luehrman, "Using APV: A Better Tool for Valuing Operations," *Harvard Business Review* 75 (1997): 145–154; J. Miles and J. Ezzell, "The Weighted Average Cost of Capital, Perfect Capital Markets, and Project Life: A Clarification," *Journal of Financial and Quantitative Analysis* 15 (1980): 719–730; J. Miles and J. Ezzell, "Reformulation Tax Shield Valuation: A Note," *Journal of Finance* 40 (1985): 1485–1492; R. Ruback, "Capital Cash Flows: A Simple Approach to Valuing Risky Cash Flows," *Financial Management* 31 (2002): 85–104; and R. Taggart, "Consistent Valuation and Cost of Capital Expressions with Corporate and Personal Taxes," *Financial Management* 20 (1991): 8–20.

Problems

All problems are available in MyFinanceLab. An asterisk (*) indicates problems with a higher level of difficulty.

Overview of Key Concepts

1. Explain whether each of the following projects is likely to have risk similar to the average risk of the firm.
   a. The Clorox Company considers launching a new version of Armor All designed to clean and protect notebook computers.
   b. Google, Inc., plans to purchase real estate to expand its headquarters.
   c. Target Corporation decides to expand the number of stores it has in the southeastern United States.
   d. GE decides to open a new Universal Studios theme park in China.

2. Suppose Caterpillar, Inc., has 665 million shares outstanding with a share price of \$74.77, and \$25 billion in debt. If in three years, Caterpillar has 700 million shares outstanding trading for \$83 per share, how much debt will Caterpillar have if it maintains a constant debt-equity ratio?

3. In 2015, Intel Corporation had a market capitalization of \$134 billion, debt of \$13.2 billion, cash of \$13.8 billion, and EBIT of nearly \$16 billion. If Intel were to increase its debt by \$1 billion and use the cash for a share repurchase, which market imperfections would be most relevant for understanding the consequence for Intel's value? Why?

4. Backcountry Adventures is a Colorado-based outdoor travel agent that operates a series of winter backcountry huts. Currently, the value of the firm (debt + equity) is \$3.5 million. But profits will depend on the amount of snowfall: If it is a good year, the firm will be worth \$5 million, and if it is a bad year it will be worth \$2.5 million. Suppose managers always keep the debt to equity ratio of the firm at 25%, and the debt is riskless.
   a. What is the initial amount of debt?
   b. Calculate the percentage change in the value of the firm, its equity and its debt once the level of snowfall is revealed, but before the firm adjusts the debt level to achieve its target debt to equity ratio.
   c. Calculate the percentage change in the value of outstanding debt once the firm adjusts to its target debt-equity ratio.
   d. What does this imply about the riskiness of the firm's tax shields? Explain.

The Weighted Average Cost of Capital Method

5. Suppose Goodyear Tire and Rubber Company is considering divesting one of its manufacturing plants. The plant is expected to generate free cash flows of \$1.5 million per year, growing at a rate of 2.5% per year. Goodyear has an equity cost of capital of 8.5%, a debt cost of capital of 7%, a marginal corporate tax rate of 35%, and a debt-equity ratio of 2.6. If the plant has average risk and Goodyear plans to maintain a constant debt-equity ratio, what after-tax amount must it receive for the plant for the divestiture to be profitable?

6. Suppose Alcatel-Lucent has an equity cost of capital of 10%, market capitalization of \$10.8 billion, and an enterprise value of \$14.4 billion. Suppose Alcatel-Lucent's debt cost of capital is 6.1% and its marginal tax rate is 35%.
   a. What is Alcatel-Lucent's WACC?
   b. If Alcatel-Lucent maintains a constant debt-equity ratio, what is the value of a project with average risk and the following expected free cash flows?

Year	0	1	2	3
FCF	−100	50	100	70

   c. If Alcatel-Lucent maintains its debt-equity ratio, what is the debt capacity of the project in part b?

7. Acort Industries has 10 million shares outstanding and a current share price of \$40 per share. It also has long-term debt outstanding. This debt is risk free, is four years away from maturity, has annual coupons with a coupon rate of 10%, and has a \$100 million face value. The first of the remaining coupon payments will be due in exactly one year. The riskless interest rates for all maturities are constant at 6%. Acort has EBIT of \$106 million, which is expected to remain constant each year. New capital expenditures are expected to equal depreciation and equal \$13 million per year, while no changes to net working capital are expected in the future. The corporate tax rate is 40%, and Acort is expected to keep its debt-equity ratio constant in the future (by either issuing additional new debt or buying back some debt as time goes on).
a. Based on this information, estimate Acort's WACC.
b. What is Acort's equity cost of capital?

The Adjusted Present Value Method

8. Suppose Goodyear Tire and Rubber Company has an equity cost of capital of 8.5%, a debt cost of capital of 7%, a marginal corporate tax rate of 35%, and a debt-equity ratio of 2.6. Suppose Goodyear maintains a constant debt-equity ratio.
a. What is Goodyear's WACC?
b. What is Goodyear's unlevered cost of capital?
c. Explain, intuitively, why Goodyear's unlevered cost of capital is less than its equity cost of capital and higher than its WACC.

9. You are a consultant who was hired to evaluate a new product line for Markum Enterprises. The upfront investment required to launch the product line is \$10 million. The product will generate free cash flow of \$750,000 the first year, and this free cash flow is expected to grow at a rate of 4% per year. Markum has an equity cost of capital of 11.3%, a debt cost of capital of 5%, and a tax rate of 35%. Markum maintains a debt-equity ratio of 0.40.
a. What is the NPV of the new product line (including any tax shields from leverage)?
b. How much debt will Markum initially take on as a result of launching this product line?
c. How much of the product line's value is attributable to the present value of interest tax shields?

10. Consider Alcatel-Lucent's project in Problem 6.
a. What is Alcatel-Lucent's unlevered cost of capital?
b. What is the unlevered value of the project?
c. What are the interest tax shields from the project? What is their present value?
d. Show that the APV of Alcatel-Lucent's project matches the value computed using the WACC method.

The Flow-to-Equity Method

11. Consider Alcatel-Lucent's project in Problem 6.
a. What is the free cash flow to equity for this project?
b. What is its NPV computed using the FTE method? How does it compare with the NPV based on the WACC method?

12. In year 1, AMC will earn \$2000 before interest and taxes. The market expects these earnings to grow at a rate of 3% per year. The firm will make no net investments (i.e., capital expenditures will equal depreciation) or changes to net working capital. Assume that the corporate tax rate equals 40%. Right now, the firm has \$5000 in risk-free debt. It plans to keep a constant ratio of debt to equity every year, so that on average the debt will also grow by 3% per year. Suppose the risk-free rate equals 5%, and the expected return on the market equals 11%. The asset beta for this industry is 1.11.
a. If AMC were an all-equity (unlevered) firm, what would its market value be?
b. Assuming the debt is fairly priced, what is the amount of interest AMC will pay next year? If AMC's debt is expected to grow by 3% per year, at what rate are its interest payments expected to grow?

c. Even though AMC's debt is *riskless* (the firm will not default), the future growth of AMC's debt is uncertain, so the exact amount of the future interest payments is risky. Assuming the future interest payments have the same beta as AMC's assets, what is the present value of AMC's interest tax shield?
d. Using the APV method, what is AMC's total market value, V^L? What is the market value of AMC's equity?
e. What is AMC's WACC? (*Hint*: Work backward from the FCF and V^L.)
f. Using the WACC method, what is the expected return for AMC equity?
g. Show that the following holds for AMC: $\beta_A = \frac{E}{D+E}\beta_E + \frac{D}{D+E}\beta_D$.
h. Assuming that the proceeds from any increases in debt are paid out to equity holders, what cash flows do the equity holders expect to receive in one year? At what rate are those cash flows expected to grow? Use that information plus your answer to part f to derive the market value of equity using the FTE method. How does that compare to your answer in part d?

Project-Based Costs of Capital

13. Prokter and Gramble (PKGR) has historically maintained a debt-equity ratio of approximately 0.20. Its current stock price is $50 per share, with 2.5 billion shares outstanding. The firm enjoys very stable demand for its products, and consequently it has a low equity beta of 0.50 and can borrow at 4.20%, just 20 basis points over the risk-free rate of 4%. The expected return of the market is 10%, and PKGR's tax rate is 35%.
a. This year, PKGR is expected to have free cash flows of $6.0 billion. What constant expected growth rate of free cash flow is consistent with its current stock price?
b. PKGR believes it can increase debt without any serious risk of distress or other costs. With a higher debt-equity ratio of 0.50, it believes its borrowing costs will rise only slightly to 4.50%. If PKGR announces that it will raise its debt-equity ratio to 0.5 through a leveraged recap, determine the increase in the stock price that would result from the anticipated tax savings.

14. Amarindo, Inc. (AMR), is a newly public firm with 10 million shares outstanding. You are doing a valuation analysis of AMR. You estimate its free cash flow in the coming year to be $15 million, and you expect the firm's free cash flows to grow by 4% per year in subsequent years. Because the firm has only been listed on the stock exchange for a short time, you do not have an accurate assessment of AMR's equity beta. However, you do have beta data for UAL, another firm in the same industry:

	Equity Beta	Debt Beta	Debt-Equity Ratio
UAL	1.5	0.30	1

AMR has a much lower debt-equity ratio of 0.30, which is expected to remain stable, and its debt is risk free. AMR's corporate tax rate is 40%, the risk-free rate is 5%, and the expected return on the market portfolio is 11%.
a. Estimate AMR's equity cost of capital.
b. Estimate AMR's share price.

15. Remex (RMX) currently has no debt in its capital structure. The beta of its equity is 1.50. For each year into the indefinite future, Remex's free cash flow is expected to equal $25 million. Remex is considering changing its capital structure by issuing debt and using the proceeds to buy back stock. It will do so in such a way that it will have a 30% debt-equity ratio after the change, and it will maintain this debt-equity ratio forever. Assume that Remex's debt cost of capital will be 6.5%. Remex faces a corporate tax rate of 35%. Except for the corporate tax rate of 35%, there are no market imperfections. Assume that the CAPM holds, the risk-free rate of interest is 5%, and the expected return on the market is 11%.

a. Using the information provided, complete the following table:

	Debt-Equity Ratio	Debt Cost of Capital	Equity Cost of Capital	Weighted Average Cost of Capital
Before change in capital structure	0	N/A		
After change in capital structure	0.30	6.5%		

b. Using the information provided and your calculations in part a, determine the value of the tax shield acquired by Remex if it changes its capital structure in the way it is considering.

APV with Other Leverage Policies

16. You are evaluating a project that requires an investment of $90 today and provides a single cash flow of $115 for sure one year from now. You decide to use 100% debt financing, that is, you will borrow $90. The risk-free rate is 5% and the tax rate is 40%. Assume that the investment is fully depreciated at the end of the year, so without leverage you would owe taxes on the difference between the project cash flow and the investment, that is, $25.

a. Calculate the NPV of this investment opportunity using the APV method.

b. Using your answer to part a, calculate the WACC of the project.

c. Verify that you get the same answer using the WACC method to calculate NPV.

d. Finally, show that flow-to-equity also correctly gives the NPV of this investment opportunity.

17. Tybo Corporation adjusts its debt so that its interest expenses are 20% of its free cash flow. Tybo is considering an expansion that will generate free cash flows of $2.5 million this year and is expected to grow at a rate of 4% per year from then on. Suppose Tybo's marginal corporate tax rate is 40%.

a. If the unlevered cost of capital for this expansion is 10%, what is its unlevered value?

b. What is the levered value of the expansion?

c. If Tybo pays 5% interest on its debt, what amount of debt will it take on initially for the expansion?

d. What is the debt-to-value ratio for this expansion? What is its WACC?

e. What is the levered value of the expansion using the WACC method?

18. You are on your way to an important budget meeting. In the elevator, you review the project valuation analysis you had your summer associate prepare for one of the projects to be discussed:

	0	1	2	3	4
EBIT		10.0	10.0	10.0	10.0
Interest (5%)		−4.0	−4.0	−3.0	−2.0
Earnings Before Taxes		6.0	6.0	7.0	8.0
Taxes		−2.4	−2.4	−2.8	−3.2
Depreciation		25.0	25.0	25.0	25.0
Cap Ex	−100.0				
Additions to NWC	−20.0				20.0
Net New Debt	80.0	0.0	−20.0	−20.0	−40.0
FCFE	−40.0	28.6	8.6	9.2	9.8
NPV at 11% Equity Cost of Capital	5.9				

Looking over the spreadsheet, you realize that while all of the cash flow estimates are correct, your associate used the flow-to-equity valuation method and discounted the cash flows using the *company's* equity cost of capital of 11%. While the project's risk is similar to the firm's, the project's incremental leverage is very different from the company's historical debt-equity ratio of 0.20: For this project, the company will instead borrow $80 million upfront and repay $20 million in year 2, $20 million in year 3, and $40 million in year 4. Thus, the *project's* equity cost of capital is likely to be higher than the firm's, not constant over time—invalidating your associate's calculation.

Clearly, the FTE approach is not the best way to analyze this project. Fortunately, you have your calculator with you, and with any luck you can use a better method before the meeting starts.

a. What is the present value of the interest tax shield associated with this project?
b. What are the free cash flows of the project?
c. What is the best estimate of the project's value from the information given?

19. Your firm is considering building a $600 million plant to manufacture HDTV circuitry. You expect operating profits (EBITDA) of $145 million per year for the next 10 years. The plant will be depreciated on a straight-line basis over 10 years (assuming no salvage value for tax purposes). After 10 years, the plant will have a salvage value of $300 million (which, since it will be fully depreciated, is then taxable). The project requires $50 million in working capital at the start, which will be recovered in year 10 when the project shuts down. The corporate tax rate is 35%. All cash flows occur at the end of the year.

a. If the risk-free rate is 5%, the expected return of the market is 11%, and the asset beta for the consumer electronics industry is 1.67, what is the NPV of the project?
b. Suppose that you can finance $400 million of the cost of the plant using 10-year, 9% coupon bonds sold at par. This amount is incremental new debt associated specifically with this project and will not alter other aspects of the firm's capital structure. What is the value of the project, including the tax shield of the debt?

Other Effects of Financing

20. Parnassus Corporation plans to invest $150 million in a new generator that will produce free cash flows of $20 million per year in perpetuity. The firm is all equity financed, with an equity cost of capital of 10%.

a. What is the NPV of the project ignoring any costs of raising funds?
b. Suppose the firm will issue new equity to raise the $150 million, and has after-tax issuance costs equal to 8% of the proceeds. What is the NPV of the project including these issuance costs, assuming all future free cash flows generated by it will be paid out?
c. Suppose that instead of paying out the project's future free cash flows, a substantial portion of these free cash flows will be retained and invested in other projects, reducing Parnassus' required fundraising in the future. Specifically, suppose the firm will reinvest all free cash flows for the next 10 years, and then pay out the cash flows after that. If its issuance costs remain constant at 8%, what is the NPV of the project including issuance costs in this case?

MFL **21.** DFS Corporation is currently an all-equity firm, with assets with a market value of $100 million and 4 million shares outstanding. DFS is considering a leveraged recapitalization to boost its share price. The firm plans to raise a fixed amount of permanent debt (i.e., the outstanding principal will remain constant) and use the proceeds to repurchase shares. DFS pays a 35% corporate tax rate, so one motivation for taking on the debt is to reduce the firm's tax liability. However, the upfront investment banking fees associated with the recapitalization will be 5% of the amount of debt raised. Adding leverage will also create the possibility of future financial

Debt amount ($ million):	0	10	20	30	40	50
Present value of expected distress and agency costs ($ million):	0.0	−0.3	−1.8	−4.3	−7.5	−11.3

distress or agency costs; shown below are DFS's estimates for different levels of debt:

a. Based on this information, which level of debt is the best choice for DFS?

b. Estimate the stock price once this transaction is announced.

22. Your firm is considering a $150 million investment to launch a new product line. The project is expected to generate a free cash flow of $20 million per year, and its unlevered cost of capital is 10%. To fund the investment, your firm will take on $100 million in permanent debt.

a. Suppose the marginal corporate tax rate is 35%. Ignoring issuance costs, what is the NPV of the investment?

b. Suppose your firm will pay a 2% underwriting fee when issuing the debt. It will raise the remaining $50 million by issuing equity. In addition to the 5% underwriting fee for the equity issue, you believe that your firm's current share price of $40 is $5 per share less than its true value. What is the NPV of the investment including any tax benefits of leverage? (Assume all fees are on an after-tax basis.)

23. Consider Avco's RFX project from Section 18.3. Suppose that Avco is receiving government loan guarantees that allow it to borrow at the 6% rate. Without these guarantees, Avco would pay 6.5% on its debt.

a. What is Avco's unlevered cost of capital given its true debt cost of capital of 6.5%?

b. What is the unlevered value of the RFX project in this case? What is the present value of the interest tax shield?

c. What is the NPV of the loan guarantees? (*Hint*: Because the actual loan amounts will fluctuate with the value of the project, discount the expected interest savings at the unlevered cost of capital.)

d. What is the levered value of the RFX project, including the interest tax shield and the NPV of the loan guarantees?

Advanced Topics in Capital Budgeting

24. Arden Corporation is considering an investment in a new project with an unlevered cost of capital of 9%. Arden's marginal corporate tax rate is 40%, and its debt cost of capital is 5%.

a. Suppose Arden adjusts its debt continuously to maintain a constant debt-equity ratio of 50%. What is the appropriate WACC for the new project?

b. Suppose Arden adjusts its debt once per year to maintain a constant debt-equity ratio of 50%. What is the appropriate WACC for the new project now?

c. Suppose the project has free cash flows of $10 million per year, which are expected to decline by 2% per year. What is the value of the project in parts a and b now?

25. XL Sports is expected to generate free cash flows of $10.9 million per year. XL has permanent debt of $40 million, a tax rate of 40%, and an unlevered cost of capital of 10%.

a. What is the value of XL's equity using the APV method?

b. What is XL's WACC? What is XL's equity value using the WACC method?

c. If XL's debt cost of capital is 5%, what is XL's equity cost of capital?

d. What is XL's equity value using the FTE method?

***26.** Propel Corporation plans to make a $50 million investment, initially funded completely with debt. The free cash flows of the investment and Propel's incremental debt from the project

Year	0	1	2	3
Free cash flows	−50	40	20	25
Debt	50	30	15	0

follow:

Propel's incremental debt for the project will be paid off according to the predetermined schedule shown. Propel's debt cost of capital is 8%, and its tax rate is 40%. Propel also estimates an unlevered cost of capital for the project of 12%.

a. Use the APV method to determine the levered value of the project at each date and its initial NPV.
b. Calculate the WACC for this project at each date. How does the WACC change over time? Why?
c. Compute the project's NPV using the WACC method.
d. Compute the equity cost of capital for this project at each date. How does the equity cost of capital change over time? Why?
e. Compute the project's equity value using the FTE method. How does the initial equity value compare with the NPV calculated in parts a and c?

***27.** Gartner Systems has no debt and an equity cost of capital of 10%. Gartner's current market capitalization is $100 million, and its free cash flows are expected to grow at 3% per year. Gartner's corporate tax rate is 35%. Investors pay tax rates of 40% on interest income and 20% on equity income.

a. Suppose Gartner adds $50 million in permanent debt and uses the proceeds to repurchase shares. What will Gartner's levered value be in this case?
b. Suppose instead Gartner decides to maintain a 50% debt-to-value ratio going forward. If Gartner's debt cost of capital is 6.67%, what will Gartner's levered value be in this case?

***28.** Revtek, Inc., has an equity cost of capital of 12% and a debt cost of capital of 6%. Revtek maintains a constant debt-equity ratio of 0.5, and its tax rate is 35%.

a. What is Revtek's WACC given its current debt-equity ratio?
b. Assuming no personal taxes, how will Revtek's WACC change if it increases its debt-equity ratio to 2 and its debt cost of capital remains at 6%?
c. Now suppose investors pay tax rates of 40% on interest income and 15% on income from equity. How will Revtek's WACC change if it increases its debt-equity ratio to 2 in this case?
d. Provide an intuitive explanation for the difference in your answers to parts b and c.

Data Case

Toyota Motor Company is expanding the production of their gas-electric hybrid drive systems and plans to shift production in the United States. To enable the expansion, they are contemplating investing $1.5 billion in a new plant with an expected 10-year life. The anticipated free cash flows from the new plant would be $220 million the first year of operation and grow by 10% for each of the next two years and then 5% per year for the remaining seven years. As a newly hired MBA in the capital budgeting division you have been asked to evaluate the new project using the WACC, Adjusted Present Value, and Flow-to-Equity methods. You will compute the appropriate costs of capital and the net present values with each method. Because this is your first major assignment with the firm, they want you to demonstrate that you are capable of handling the different valuation methods. You must seek out the information necessary to value the free cash flows but will be provided some directions to follow. (This is an involved assignment, but at least you don't have to come up with the actual cash flows for the project!)

1. Go to Yahoo! Finance (finance.yahoo.com) and get the quote for Toyota (symbol: TM).

a. Under "Financials," click on the income statement. The income statements for the last three fiscal years will appear. Copy and paste the data into Excel.
b. Go back to the Web page and select "Balance Sheets" from the top of the page. Repeat the download procedure for the balance sheets, then copy and paste them into the same worksheet as the income statements.
c. Click "Historical prices" in the left column, and find Toyota's stock price for the last day of the month at the end of each of the past three fiscal years. Record the stock price on each date in your spreadsheet.

2. Create a timeline in Excel with the free cash flows for the 10 years of the project.
3. Determine the WACC using Eq. 18.1.
   a. For the cost of debt, r_D:
      i. Go to finra-markets.morningstar.com/BondCenter/Default.jsp and click to search. Enter Toyota's symbol, select the Corporate toggle, and press "Enter."
      ii. Look at the average credit rating for Toyota long-term bonds. If you find that they have a rating of A or above, then you can make the approximation that the cost of debt is the risk-free rate. If Toyota's credit rating has slipped, use Table 12.3 to estimate the beta of debt from the credit rating.
   b. For the cost of equity, r_E:
      i. Get the yield on the 10-year U.S. Treasury Bond from Yahoo! Finance (finance.yahoo.com). Click on "Market Data." Scroll down to the Bonds Summary. Enter that yield as the risk-free rate.
      ii. Find the beta for Toyota from Yahoo! Finance. Enter the symbol for Toyota and click "Key Statistics." The beta for Toyota will be listed there.
      iii. Use a market risk premium of 4.50% to compute r_E using the CAPM. If you need to, repeat the exercise to compute r_D.
   c. Determine the values for E and D for Eq. 18.1 for Toyota and the debt-to-value and equity-to-value ratios.
      i. To compute the net debt for Toyota, add the long-term debt and the short-term debt and subtract cash and cash equivalents for each year on the balance sheet.
      ii. Obtain the historical number of shares outstanding from Google Finance (www.google.com/finance). Enter Toyota's ticker in the search box, click "Financials." Look on the income statement for "Diluted Weighted Average Shares." Multiply the historical stock prices by the number of shares outstanding you collected to compute Toyota's market capitalization at the end of each fiscal year.
      iii. Compute Toyota's enterprise value at the end of each fiscal year by combining the values obtained for its equity market capitalization and its net debt.
      iv. Compute Toyota's debt-to-value ratio at the end of each year by dividing its net debt by its enterprise value. Use the average ratio from the last four years as an estimate for Toyota's target debt-to-value ratio.
   d. Determine Toyota's tax rate by dividing the income tax by earnings before tax for each year. Take the average of the four rates as Toyota's marginal corporate tax rate.
   e. Compute the WACC for Toyota using Eq. 18.1.
4. Compute the NPV of the hybrid engine expansion given the free cash flows you calculated using the WACC method of valuation.
5. Determine the NPV using the Adjusted Present Value Method, and also using the Flow-to-Equity method. In both cases, assume Toyota maintains the target leverage ratio you computed in Question 3c.
6. Compare the results under the three methods and explain how the resulting NPVs are achieved under each of the three different methods.

Note: Updates to this data case may be found at www.berkdemarzo.com.

CHAPTER 18 APPENDIX

Foundations and Further Details

In this appendix, we look at the foundations for the WACC method, and for the relationship between a firm's levered and unlevered costs of capital. We also address how we can solve for a firm's leverage policy and value simultaneously.

Deriving the WACC Method

The WACC can be used to value a levered investment, as in Eq. 18.2. Consider an investment that is financed by both debt and equity. Because equity holders require an expected return of r_E on their investment and debt holders require a return of r_D, the firm will have to pay investors a total of

$$E(1 + r_E) + D(1 + r_D) \tag{18.A1}$$

next year. What is the value of the investment next year? The project generates free cash flows of FCF_1 at the end of the year. In addition, the interest tax shield of the debt provides a tax savings of $\tau_c \times$ (interest on debt) $\approx \tau_c\, r_D\, D$.[27] Finally, if the investment will continue beyond next year, it will have a continuation value of V_1^L. Thus, to satisfy investors, the project cash flows must be such that

$$E(1 + r_E) + D(1 + r_D) = FCF_1 + \tau_c r_D D + V_1^L \tag{18A.2}$$

Because $V_0^L = E + D$, we can write the WACC definition in Eq. 18.1 as

$$r_{wacc} = \frac{E}{V_0^L} r_E + \frac{D}{V_0^L} r_D (1 - \tau_c) \tag{18.A3}$$

If we move the interest tax shield to the left side of Eq. 18A.2, we can use the definition of the WACC to rewrite Eq. 18A.2 as follows:

$$\underbrace{E(1 + r_E) + D[1 + r_D(1 - \tau_c)]}_{V_0^L(1 + r_{wacc})} = FCF_1 + V_1^L \tag{18.A4}$$

[27] The return on the debt r_D need not come solely from interest payments. If C_t is the coupon paid and D_t is the market value of the debt in period t, then in period t, r_D is defined as

$$r_D = \frac{E\,[\text{Coupon Payment} + \text{Capital Gain}]}{\text{Current Price}} = \frac{E\,[C_{t+1} + D_{t+1} - D_t]}{D_t}$$

The return that determines the firm's interest expense is

$$\bar{r}_D = \frac{E\,[C_{t+1} + \bar{D}_{t+1} - \bar{D}_t]}{D_t}$$

where $\bar{D}_t$ is the value of the debt on date t according to a fixed schedule set by the tax code based on the difference between the bond's initial price and its face value, which is called the bond's *original issue discount* (OID). (If the bond is issued at par and the firm will not default on the next coupon, then $\bar{D}_t = \bar{D}_{t+1}$ and $\bar{r}_D = C_{t+1}/D_t$, which is the bond's *current yield*.) Thus, the true after-tax cost of debt is $(r_D - \tau_c \bar{r}_D)$. In practice, the distinction between r_D and $\bar{r}_D$ is often ignored, and the after-tax cost of debt is computed as $r_D(1 - \tau_c)$. Also, the debt's yield to maturity is often used in place of r_D. Because the yield ignores default risk, it overstates r_D and thus the WACC. See Chapter 12 for alternative methods.

Dividing by $(1 + r_{wacc})$, we can express the value of the investment today as the present value of next period's free cash flows and continuation value:

$$V_0^L = \frac{FCF_1 + V_1^L}{1 + r_{wacc}} \tag{18.A5}$$

In the same way, we can write the value in one year, V_1^L, as the discounted value of the free cash flows and continuation value of the project in year 2. If the WACC is the same next year, then

$$V_0^L = \frac{FCF_1 + V_1^L}{1 + r_{wacc}} = \frac{FCF_1 + \dfrac{FCF_2 + V_2^L}{1 + r_{wacc}}}{1 + r_{wacc}} = \frac{FCF_1}{1 + r_{wacc}} + \frac{FCF_2 + V_2^L}{(1 + r_{wacc})^2} \tag{18.A6}$$

By repeatedly replacing each continuation value, and *assuming the WACC remains constant*, we can derive Eq. 18.2:[28]

$$V_0^L = \frac{FCF_1}{1 + r_{wacc}} + \frac{FCF_2}{(1 + r_{wacc})^2} + \frac{FCF_3}{(1 + r_{wacc})^3} + \cdots \tag{18.A7}$$

That is, *the value of a levered investment is the present value of its future free cash flows using the weighted average cost of capital.*

The Levered and Unlevered Cost of Capital

In this appendix, we derive the relationship between the levered and unlevered cost of capital for the firm. Suppose an investor holds a portfolio of all of the equity and debt of the firm. Then the investor will receive the free cash flows of the firm plus the tax savings from the interest tax shield. These are the same cash flows an investor would receive from a portfolio of the unlevered firm (which generates the free cash flows) and a separate "tax shield" security that paid the investor the amount of the tax shield each period. Because these two portfolios generate the same cash flows, by the Law of One Price they have the same market values:

$$V^L = E + D = V^U + T \tag{18.A8}$$

where T is the present value of the interest tax shield. Equation 18.A8 is the basis of the APV method. Because these portfolios have equal cash flows, they must also have identical expected returns, which implies

$$E\,r_E + D\,r_D = V^U r_U + T\,r_T \tag{18.A9}$$

where r_T is the expected return associated with the interest tax shields. The relationship between r_E, r_D, and r_U will depend on the expected return r_T, which is determined by the risk of the interest tax shield. Let's consider the two cases discussed in the text.

Target Leverage Ratio

Suppose the firm adjusts its debt continuously to maintain a target debt-to-value ratio, or a target ratio of interest to free cash flow. Because the firm's debt and interest payments will vary with the firm's value and cash flows, it is reasonable to expect the risk of the interest

[28] This expansion is the same approach we took in Chapter 9 to derive the discounted dividend formula for the stock price.

tax shield will equal that of the firm's free cash flow, so $r_T = r_U$. Making this assumption, which we return to below, Eq. 18A.9 becomes

$$E\,r_E + D\,r_D = V^U r_U + T r_U = (V^U + T) r_U$$
$$= (E + D) r_U \qquad (18.A10)$$

Dividing by $(E + D)$ leads to Eq. 18.6.

Predetermined Debt Schedule

Suppose some of the firm's debt is set according to a predetermined schedule that is independent of the growth of the firm. Suppose the value of the tax shield from the scheduled debt is T^s, and the remaining value of the tax shield $T - T^s$ is from debt that will be adjusted according to a target leverage ratio. Because the risk of the interest tax shield from the scheduled debt is similar to the risk of the debt itself, Eq. 18A.9 becomes

$$E\,r_E + D\,r_D = V^U r_U + T r_T = V^U r_U + (T - T^s) r_U + T^s r_D \qquad (18.A11)$$

Subtracting $T^s r_D$ from both sides, and using $D^s = D - T^s$,

$$E\,r_E + D^s r_D = (V^U + T - T^s) r_U = (V^L - T^s) r_U$$
$$= (E + D^s) r_U \qquad (18.A12)$$

Dividing by $(E + D^s)$ leads to Eq. 18.20.

Risk of the Tax Shield with a Target Leverage Ratio

Above, we assumed that with a target leverage ratio, it is reasonable to assume that $r_T = r_U$. Under what circumstances should this be the case?

We define a target leverage ratio as a setting in which the firm adjusts its debt at date t to be a proportion $d(t)$ of the investment's value, or a proportion $k(t)$ of its free cash flow. (The target ratio for either policy need not be constant over time, but can vary according to a predetermined schedule.)

With either policy, the value at date t of the incremental tax shield from the project's free cash flow at date s, FCF_s, is proportional to the value of the cash flow $V_t^L(FCF_s)$, so it should be discounted at the same rate as FCF_s. Therefore, the assumption $r_T = r_U$ follows as long as at each date the cost of capital associated with the value of each future free cash flow is the same (a standard assumption in capital budgeting).[29]

Solving for Leverage and Value Simultaneously

When we use the APV method, we need to know the debt level to compute the interest tax shield and determine the project's value. But if a firm maintains a constant debt-to-value ratio, we need to know the project's value to determine the debt level. How can we apply the APV method in this case?

When a firm maintains a constant leverage ratio, to use the APV method we must solve for the debt level and the project value simultaneously. While complicated to do by hand, it is (fortunately) easy to do in Excel. We begin with the spreadsheet shown in Table 18A.1, which illustrates the standard APV calculation outlined in Section 18.3 of the text. For now, we have just inserted arbitrary values for the project's debt capacity in line 3.

[29]If the risk of the individual cash flows differs, then r_T will be a weighted average of the unlevered costs of capital of the individual cash flows, with the weights depending on the schedule d or k. See P. DeMarzo, "Discounting Tax Shields and the Unlevered Cost of Capital," 2005, ssrn.com/abstract=1488437.

TABLE 18A.1 SPREADSHEET **Adjusted Present Value for Avco's RFX Project with Arbitrary Debt Levels**

	Year	0	1	2	3	4
Unlevered Value ($ million)						
1	Free Cash Flow	(28.00)	18.00	18.00	18.00	18.00
2	Unlevered Value, V^U (at $r_u = 8.0\%$)	59.62	46.39	32.10	16.67	—
Interest Tax Shield						
3	Debt Capacity (arbitrary)	*30.00*	*20.00*	*10.00*	*5.00*	—
4	Interest Paid (at $r_d = 6\%$)	—	1.80	1.20	0.60	0.30
5	Interest Tax Shield (at $\tau_c = 40\%$)	—	0.72	0.48	0.24	0.12
6	Tax Shield Value, T (at $r_u = 8.0\%$)	1.36	0.75	0.33	0.11	—
Adjusted Present Value						
7	**Levered Value, $V^L = V^U + T$**	**60.98**	**47.13**	**32.42**	**16.78**	—

Note that the debt capacity specified in line 3 is not consistent with a 50% debt-to-value ratio for the project. For example, given the value of $60.98 million in year 0, the initial debt capacity should be 50% × $60.98 million = $30.49 million in year 0. But if we change each debt capacity in line 3 to a *numerical* value that is 50% of the value in line 7, the interest tax shield and the project's value will change, and we will still not have a 50% debt-to-value ratio.

The solution is to enter in line 3 a *formula* that sets the debt capacity to be 50% of the project's value in line 7 in the same year. Now line 7 depends on line 3, and line 3 depends on line 7, creating a circular reference in the spreadsheet (and you will most likely receive an error message). By changing the calculation option in Excel to calculate the spreadsheet iteratively (File > Options > Formulas and check the Enable iterative calculation box), Excel will keep calculating until the values in line 3 and line 7 of the spreadsheet are consistent, as shown in Table 18A.2.

TABLE 18A.2 SPREADSHEET **Adjusted Present Value for Avco's RFX Project with Debt Levels Solved Iteratively**

	Year	0	1	2	3	4
Unlevered Value ($ million)						
1	Free Cash Flow	(28.00)	18.00	18.00	18.00	18.00
2	Unlevered Value, V^U (at $r_u = 8.0\%$)	59.62	46.39	32.10	16.67	—
Interest Tax Shield						
3	Debt Capacity (at $d = 50\%$)	30.62	23.71	16.32	8.43	—
4	Interest Paid (at $r_d = 6\%$)	—	1.84	1.42	0.98	0.51
5	Interest Tax Shield (at $\tau_c = 40\%$)	—	0.73	0.57	0.39	0.20
6	Tax Shield Value, T (at $r_u = 8.0\%$)	1.63	1.02	0.54	0.19	—
Adjusted Present Value						
7	**Levered Value, $V^L = V^U + T$**	**61.25**	**47.41**	**32.63**	**16.85**	—

Thus we calculate the same $NPV = V_0^L - FCF_0 = 61.25 - 28 = \$33.25$ million as in Section 18.1.

The same method can be applied when using the WACC method with known debt levels. In that case, we need to know the project's value to determine the debt-to-value ratio and compute the WACC, and we need to know the WACC to compute the project's value. Again, we can use iteration within Excel to determine simultaneously the project's value and debt-to-value ratio.

The Residual Income and Economic Value Added Valuation Methods

An alternative valuation method developed primarily in the accounting literature is the **residual income method**.[30] A company's residual income in year t is defined as its net income less a charge for the required return on stockholders' equity (using the equity cost of capital r_E):

$$\text{Residual Income}_t = \text{Net Income}_t - \underbrace{r_E \times \text{Book Value of Equity}_{t-1}}_{\text{Equity charge}} \qquad (18.A13)$$
$$= (ROE_t - r_E) \times \text{Book Value of Equity}_{t-1}$$

We can think of residual income as the firm's profit in excess of the required return on its equity, and can be thought of as a measure of the equity value added to the firm. The residual income is positive if and only if the firms accounting return on equity, or ROE, exceeds its equity cost of capital.

The residual income valuation method states that the market value of the firm's equity should equal its book value plus the present value of its future residual income. That is, if we write E_0 for the market value and BE_0 for the book value of equity at the *end* of the period, and RI_t for the residual income in year t:

Residual Income Valuation Method

$$E_0 = BE_0 + PV(\text{Residual Income}) = BE_0 + \sum_{t=1}^{\infty} \frac{RI_t}{(1 + r_E)^t} \qquad (18.A14)$$

The residual income method is equivalent to the Flow-to-Equity method described in Section 18.4. Recall that in the FTE method, we value equity as the present value of FCFE, the total cash flows paid out to shareholders. Because the book value of the firm's shares increases each year by net income (NI) less any payouts to shareholders (FCFE), we have

$$BE_t = BE_{t-1} + NI_t - FCFE_t \qquad (18.A15)$$

Then we can rewrite FCFE, using Eq. 18.A15 and Eq. 18.A13, as

$$FCFE_t = NI_t + BE_{t-1} - BE_t = RI_t + (1 + r_E)\, BE_{t-1} - BE_t$$

Taking present values, we see that all of the BE terms with $t \geq 1$ cancel, so that

$$E_0 = PV(FCFE) = PV(RI) + BE_0$$

Note that Eq. 18.A14 presumes the equity cost of capital is constant over time, which only holds if the firm has a target leverage ratio. Otherwise, we must compute r_E period by period as in Table 18.10.

Note that we can also apply the Residual Income method to value a project. In that case, if we assume the initial and ending book value of equity *for the project* is zero, then

$$NPV(\text{Project}) = PV(\text{Incremental Residual Income}) \qquad (18.A16)$$

Table 18A.3 applies this approach to value Avco's RFX project assuming a target leverage ratio of $d = 50\%$. Note that to compute the residual income from the project, we consider only its incremental contribution to the book value of equity from the balance sheet. In this example, because the incremental debt from the project exceeds the book value of the equipment, the incremental equity (and thus the equity charge) is negative.

[30]See e.g. J. A. Ohlson, "Earnings, Book Values, and Dividends in Equity Valuation," *Contemporary Accounting Research* (1995): 661–687.

TABLE 18A.3 SPREADSHEET Evaluating Avco's RFX Project Using the Residual Income Method (assuming a target leverage ratio from Table 18.4)

	Year	0	1	2	3	4
Incremental Earnings Forecast ($ million)						
1	Sales	—	60.00	60.00	60.00	60.00
2	Cost of Goods Sold	—	(25.00)	(25.00)	(25.00)	(25.00)
3	**Gross Profit**	—	35.00	35.00	35.00	35.00
4	Operating Expenses	(6.67)	(9.00)	(9.00)	(9.00)	(9.00)
5	Depreciation	—	(6.00)	(6.00)	(6.00)	(6.00)
6	**EBIT**	(6.67)	20.00	20.00	20.00	20.00
7	Interest Expense	—	(1.84)	(1.42)	(0.98)	(0.51)
8	**Pretax Income**	(6.67)	18.16	18.58	19.02	19.49
9	Income Tax at 40%	2.67	(7.27)	(7.43)	(7.61)	(7.80)
10	**Net Income**	(4.00)	10.90	11.15	11.41	11.70
Project Balance Sheet Data						
11	Property, Plant & Equipment	24.00	18.00	12.00	6.00	—
12	Debt	30.62	23.71	16.32	8.43	—
13	**Incremental Equity**	**(6.62)**	**(5.71)**	**(4.32)**	**(2.43)**	—
Residual Income						
14	Capital Charge (r_e = 10%)	—	0.66	0.57	0.43	0.24
15	Net Income	(4.00)	10.90	11.15	11.41	11.70
16	**Residual Income**	**(4.00)**	**11.56**	**11.72**	**11.84**	**11.94**
17	**PV at r_e = 10%**	**33.25**				

We can use a similar logic to develop an alternative equation for the WACC method. Here we begin with a measure of **economic value added** equal to the firm's *unlevered* net income less a charge for the required return on the firm's *total* invested capital (both equity and debt). We measure total invested capital as the firm's **book enterprise value:**

$$\text{Invested Capital} = \text{Book Value of Equity} + \text{Net Debt} = \text{Book Enterprise Value} \quad (18.A17)$$

Then economic value added in year t is defined as

$$\text{Economic Value Added}_t = \underbrace{\text{EBIT}_t \times (1 - \tau_c)}_{\text{Unlevered Net Income}} - \underbrace{r_{wacc} \times \text{Book Enterprise Value}_{t-1}}_{\text{Capital Charge}}$$
$$= (ROIC_t - r_{wacc}) \times \text{Book Enterprise Value}_{t-1} \quad (18.A18)$$

We can see that economic value added is only positive if the firm's return on invested capital, or ROIC, exceeds its weighted-average cost of capital. Because

$$BEV_t = BEV_{t-1} + \text{EBIT}_t(1 - \tau_c) - FCF_t, \quad (18.A19)$$

we can then show that the WACC method is equivalent to the firm's current (market) enterprise value (V_0) being equal to its book enterprise value (BEV_0) plus the present value of future economic value added (EVA):

Economic Value Added Valuation Method

$$V_0 = BEV_0 + PV(\text{Economic Value Added}) = BEV_0 + \sum_{t=1}^{\infty} \frac{EVA_t}{(1 + r_{wacc})^t} \quad (18.A20)$$

Again, we can apply this method to compute the NPV of a project. Assuming the starting and ending incremental book enterprise value from the project is zero, we have

$$NPV(\text{Project}) = PV(\text{Incremental EVA}) \quad (18.A21)$$

CHAPTER

19

Valuation and Financial Modeling: A Case Study

THE GOAL OF THIS CHAPTER IS TO APPLY THE FINANCIAL TOOLS we have developed thus far to demonstrate how they are used in practice to build a valuation model of a firm. In this chapter, we will value a hypothetical firm, Ideko Corporation. Ideko is a privately held designer and manufacturer of specialty sports eyewear based in Chicago. In mid-2005, its owner and founder, June Wong, has decided to sell the business, after having relinquished management control about four years ago. As a partner in KKP Investments, you are investigating purchasing the company. If a deal can be reached, the acquisition will take place at the end of the current fiscal year. In that event, KKP plans to implement operational and financial improvements at Ideko over the next five years, after which it intends to sell the business.

Ideko has total assets of \$87 million and annual sales of \$75 million. The firm is also quite profitable, with earnings this year of almost \$7 million, for a net profit margin of 9.3%. You believe a deal could be struck to purchase Ideko's equity at the end of this fiscal year for an acquisition price of \$150 million, which is almost double Ideko's current book value of equity. Is this price reasonable?

We begin the chapter by estimating Ideko's value using data for comparable firms. We then review KKP's operating strategies for running the business after the acquisition, to identify potential areas for improvements. We build a financial model to project cash flows that reflect these operating improvements. These cash flow forecasts enable us to value Ideko using the APV model introduced in Chapter 18 and estimate the return on KKP's investment. Finally, we explore the sensitivity of the valuation estimates to our main assumptions.

NOTATION

R_s	return on security s
r_f	risk-free rate
α_s	the alpha of security s
β_s	the beta of security s
R_{mkt}	return of the market portfolio
$E[R_{mkt}]$	expected return of the market portfolio
ε_s	the regression error term
β_U	the beta of an unlevered firm
β_E	the beta of equity
β_D	the beta of debt
r_U	unlevered cost of capital
r_{wacc}	weighted average cost of capital
r_D	debt cost of capital
V_T^L	continuing value of a project at date T
V^U	unlevered value
FCF_t	free cash flow at date t
g	growth rate
T^s	predetermined tax shield value

19.1 Valuation Using Comparables

As a result of preliminary conversations with Ideko's founder, you have estimates of Ideko's income and balance sheet information for the current fiscal year shown in Table 19.1. Ideko currently has debt outstanding of \$4.5 million, but it also has a substantial cash balance. To obtain your first estimate of Ideko's value, you decide to value Ideko by examining comparable firms.

A quick way to gauge the reasonableness of the proposed price for Ideko is to compare it to that of other publicly traded firms using the method of comparable firms introduced in Chapter 9. For example, at a price of \$150 million, Ideko's price-earnings (P/E) ratio is $150,000/6939 = 21.6$, roughly equal to the market average P/E ratio in mid-2005.

It is even more informative to compare Ideko to firms in a similar line of business. Although no firm is exactly comparable to Ideko in terms of its overall product line, three firms with which it has similarities are Oakley, Inc.; Luxottica Group; and Nike, Inc. The closest competitor is Oakley, which also designs and manufactures sports eyewear. Luxottica Group is an Italian eyewear maker, but much of its business is prescription eyewear; it also owns and operates a number of retail eyewear chains. Nike is a manufacturer of specialty sportswear products, but its primary focus is footwear. You also decide to compare Ideko to a portfolio of firms in the sporting goods industry.

A comparison of Ideko's proposed valuation to this peer set, as well as to the average firm in the sporting goods industry, appears in Table 19.2. The table not only lists P/E ratios, but also shows each firm's enterprise value (EV) as a multiple of sales and EBITDA (earnings before interest, taxes, depreciation, and amortization). Recall that enterprise value is the total value of equity plus net debt, where net debt is debt less cash and investments in marketable securities that are not required as part of normal operations. Ideko has \$4.5 million in debt, and you estimate that it holds \$6.5 million of cash in excess of its working capital needs. Thus, Ideko's enterprise value at the proposed acquisition price is $150 + 4.5 - 6.5 = \$148$ million.

At the proposed price, Ideko's P/E ratio is low relative to those of Oakley and Luxottica, although it is somewhat above the P/E ratios of Nike and the industry overall. The same

TABLE 19.1 SPREADSHEET **Estimated 2005 Income Statement and Balance Sheet Data for Ideko Corporation**

	Income Statement ($ 000)	Year 2005
1	**Sales**	75,000
2	Cost of Goods Sold	
3	Raw Materials	(16,000)
4	Direct Labor Costs	(18,000)
5	**Gross Profit**	41,000
6	Sales and Marketing	(11,250)
7	Administrative	(13,500)
8	**EBITDA**	16,250
9	Depreciation	(5,500)
10	**EBIT**	10,750
11	Interest Expense (net)	(75)
12	**Pretax Income**	10,675
13	Income Tax	(3,736)
14	**Net Income**	6,939

	Balance Sheet ($ 000)	Year 2005
	Assets	
1	Cash and Equivalents	12,664
2	Accounts Receivable	18,493
3	Inventories	6,165
4	**Total Current Assets**	37,322
5	Property, Plant, and Equipment	49,500
6	Goodwill	—
7	**Total Assets**	86,822
	Liabilities and Stockholders' Equity	
8	Accounts Payable	4,654
9	Debt	4,500
10	**Total Liabilities**	9,154
11	**Stockholders' Equity**	77,668
12	**Total Liabilities and Equity**	86,822

TABLE 19.2 Ideko Financial Ratios Comparison, Mid-2005

Ratio	Ideko (Proposed)	Oakley, Inc.	Luxottica Group	Nike, Inc.	Sporting Goods Industry
P/E	21.6×	24.8×	28.0×	18.2×	20.3×
EV/Sales	2.0×	2.0×	2.7×	1.5×	1.4×
EV/EBITDA	9.1×	11.6×	14.4×	9.3×	11.4×
EBITDA/Sales	21.7%	17.0%	18.5%	15.9%	12.1%

can be said for Ideko's valuation as a multiple of sales. Thus, based on these two measures, Ideko looks "cheap" relative to Oakley and Luxottica, but is priced at a premium relative to Nike and the average sporting goods firm. The deal stands out, however, when you compare Ideko's enterprise value relative to EBITDA. The acquisition price of just over nine times EBITDA is below that of all of the comparable firms as well as the industry average. Note also Ideko's high profit margins: At 16,250/75,000 = 21.7%, its EBITDA margin exceeds that of all of the comparables.

While Table 19.2 provides some reassurance that the acquisition price is reasonable compared to other firms in the industry, it by no means establishes that the acquisition is a good investment opportunity. As with any such comparison, the multiples in Table 19.2 vary substantially. Furthermore, they ignore important differences such as the operating efficiency and growth prospects of the firms, and they do not reflect KKP's plans to improve Ideko's operations. To assess whether this investment is attractive requires a careful analysis both of the operational aspects of the firm and of the ultimate cash flows the deal is expected to generate and the return that should be required.

EXAMPLE 19.1 Valuation by Comparables

Problem

What range of acquisition prices for Ideko is implied by the range of multiples for P/E, EV/Sales, and EV/EBITDA in Table 19.2?

Solution

For each multiple, we can find the highest and lowest values across all three firms and the industry portfolio. Applying each multiple to the data for Ideko in Table 19.1 yields the following results:

	Range		Price (in $ million)	
Multiple	**Low**	**High**	**Low**	**High**
P/E	18.2×	28.0×	126.3	194.3
EV/Sales	1.4×	2.7×	107.0	204.5
EV/EBITDA	9.3×	14.4×	153.1	236.0

For example, Nike has the lowest P/E multiple of 18.2. Multiplying this P/E by Ideko's earnings of \$6.94 million gives a value of $18.2 \times 6.94 = \$126.3$ million. The highest multiple of enterprise value to sales is 2.7 (Luxottica); at this multiple, Ideko's enterprise value is $2.7 \times 75 = \$202.5$ million. Adding Ideko's excess cash and subtracting its debt implies a purchase price of $202.5 + 6.5 - 4.5 = \$204.5$ million. The table above demonstrates that while comparables provide a useful benchmark, they cannot be relied upon for a precise estimate of value.

CONCEPT CHECK

1. What is the purpose of the valuation using comparables?
2. If the valuation using comparables indicates the acquisition price is reasonable compared to other firms in the industry, does it establish that the acquisition is a good investment opportunity?

19.2 The Business Plan

While comparables provide a useful starting point, whether this acquisition is a successful investment for KKP depends on Ideko's post-acquisition performance. Thus, it is necessary to look in detail at Ideko's operations, investments, and capital structure, and to assess its potential for improvements and future growth.

Operational Improvements

On the operational side, you are quite optimistic regarding the company's prospects. The market is expected to grow by 5% per year, and Ideko produces a superior product. Ideko's market share has not grown in recent years because current management has devoted insufficient resources to product development, sales, and marketing. Conversely, Ideko has overspent on administrative costs. Indeed, Table 19.1 reveals that Ideko's current administrative expenses are 13,500/75,000 = 18% of sales, a rate that exceeds its expenditures on sales and marketing (15% of sales). This is in stark contrast to its rivals, which spend less on administrative overhead than they do on sales and marketing.

KKP plans to cut administrative costs immediately and redirect resources to new product development, sales, and marketing. By doing so, you believe Ideko can increase its market share from 10% to 15% over the next five years. The increased sales demand can be met in the short run using the existing production lines by increasing overtime and running some weekend shifts. However, once the growth in volume exceeds 50%, Ideko will definitely need to undertake a major expansion to increase its manufacturing capacity.

The spreadsheet in Table 19.3 shows sales and operating cost assumptions for the next five years based on this plan. In the spreadsheet, numbers in blue represent data that has been entered, whereas numbers in black are calculated based on the data provided. For example, given the current market size of 10 million units and an expected growth rate of 5% per year, the spreadsheet calculates the expected market size in years 1 through 5. Also shown is the expected growth in Ideko's market share.

TABLE 19.3 SPREADSHEET Ideko Sales and Operating Cost Assumptions

			Year	2005	2006	2007	2008	2009	2010
Sales Data			**Growth/Year**						
1	Market Size	(000 units)	5.0%	10,000	10,500	11,025	11,576	12,155	12,763
2	Market Share		1.0%	10.0%	11.0%	12.0%	13.0%	14.0%	15.0%
3	Average Sales Price	($/unit)	2.0%	75.00	76.50	78.03	79.59	81.18	82.81
Cost of Goods Data									
4	Raw Materials	($/unit)	1.0%	16.00	16.16	16.32	16.48	16.65	16.82
5	Direct Labor Costs	($/unit)	4.0%	18.00	18.72	19.47	20.25	21.06	21.90
Operating Expense and Tax Data									
6	Sales and Marketing	(% sales)		15.0%	16.5%	18.0%	19.5%	20.0%	20.0%
7	Administrative	(% sales)		18.0%	15.0%	15.0%	14.0%	13.0%	13.0%
8	Tax Rate			35.0%	35.0%	35.0%	35.0%	35.0%	35.0%

Note that Ideko's average selling price is expected to increase because of a 2% inflation rate each year. Likewise, manufacturing costs are expected to rise. Raw materials are forecast to increase at a 1% rate and, although you expect some productivity gains, labor costs will rise at a 4% rate due to additional overtime. The table also shows the reallocation of resources from administration to sales and marketing over the five-year period.

EXAMPLE 19.2 **Production Capacity Requirements**

Problem

Based on the data in Table 19.3, what production capacity will Ideko require each year? When will an expansion be necessary?

Solution

Production volume each year can be estimated by multiplying the total market size and Ideko's market share in Table 19.3:

	Year	2005	2006	2007	2008	2009	2010
Production Volume (000 units)							
1	Market Size	10,000	10,500	11,025	11,576	12,155	12,763
2	Market Share	10.0%	11.0%	12.0%	13.0%	14.0%	15.0%
3	Production Volume (1 × 2)	1,000	1,155	1,323	1,505	1,702	1,914

Based on this forecast, production volume will exceed its current level by 50% by 2008, necessitating an expansion then.

Capital Expenditures: A Needed Expansion

The spreadsheet in Table 19.4 shows the forecast for Ideko's capital expenditures over the next five years. Based on the estimates for capital expenditures and depreciation, this spreadsheet tracks the book value of Ideko's plant, property, and equipment starting from its level at the beginning of 2005. Note that investment is expected to remain at its current level over the next two years, which is roughly equal to the level of depreciation. Ideko will expand its production during this period by using its existing plant more efficiently. In 2008, however, a major expansion of the plant will be necessary, leading to a large increase in capital expenditures in 2008 and 2009.

The depreciation entries in Table 19.4 are based on the appropriate depreciation schedule for each type of property. Those calculations are quite specific to the nature of the property and are not detailed here. The depreciation shown will be used for tax purposes.[1]

TABLE 19.4 SPREADSHEET **Ideko Capital Expenditure Assumptions**

	Year	2005	2006	2007	2008	2009	2010
Fixed Assets and Capital Investment ($ 000)							
1	Opening Book Value	50,000	49,500	49,050	48,645	61,781	69,102
2	Capital Investment	5,000	5,000	5,000	20,000	15,000	8,000
3	Depreciation	(5,500)	(5,450)	(5,405)	(6,865)	(7,678)	(7,710)
4	Closing Book Value	49,500	49,050	48,645	61,781	69,102	69,392

[1]Firms often maintain separate books for accounting and tax purposes, and they may use different depreciation assumptions for each. Remember that because depreciation affects cash flows through its tax consequences, tax depreciation is more relevant for valuation.

Working Capital Management

To compensate for its weak sales and marketing efforts, Ideko has sought to retain the loyalty of its retailers in part by maintaining a very lax credit policy. This policy affects Ideko's working capital requirements: For every extra day that customers take to pay, another day's sales revenue is added to accounts receivable (rather than received in cash). From Ideko's current income statement and balance sheet (Table 19.1), we can estimate the number of days of receivables:

$$\text{Accounts Receivable Days} = \frac{\text{Accounts Receivable (\$)}}{\text{Sales Revenue (\$/yr)}} \times 365 \text{ days/yr}$$

$$= \frac{18{,}493}{75{,}000} \times 365 \text{ days} = 90 \text{ days} \qquad (19.1)$$

The standard for the industry is 60 days, and you believe that Ideko can tighten its credit policy to achieve this goal without sacrificing many sales.

You also hope to improve Ideko's inventory management. Ideko's balance sheet in Table 19.1 lists inventory of \$6.165 million. Of this amount, approximately \$2 million corresponds to raw materials, while the rest is finished goods. Given raw material expenditures of \$16 million for the year, Ideko currently holds $(2/16) \times 365 = 45.6$ days' worth of raw material inventory. While maintaining a certain amount of inventory is necessary to avoid production stoppages, you believe that, with tighter controls of the production process, 30 days' worth of inventory will be adequate.

Capital Structure Changes: Levering Up

With little debt, excess cash, and substantial earnings, Ideko appears to be significantly underleveraged. You plan to greatly increase the firm's debt, and have obtained bank commitments for loans of \$100 million should an agreement be reached. These term loans will have an interest rate of 6.8%, and Ideko will pay interest only during the next five years. The firm will seek additional financing in 2008 and 2009 associated with the expansion of its manufacturing plant, as shown in the spreadsheet in Table 19.5. While Ideko's credit quality should improve over time, the steep slope of the yield curve suggests interest rates may increase; therefore, on balance, you expect Ideko's borrowing rate to remain at 6.8%.

Given Ideko's outstanding debt, its interest expense each year is computed as[2]

$$\text{Interest in Year } t = \text{Interest Rate} \times \text{Ending Balance in Year } (t-1) \qquad (19.2)$$

The interest on the debt will provide a valuable tax shield to offset Ideko's taxable income.

TABLE 19.5 SPREADSHEET **Ideko's Planned Debt and Interest Payments**

		Year	2005	2006	2007	2008	2009	2010
Debt and Interest Table ($ 000)								
1	Outstanding Debt		100,000	100,000	100,000	115,000	120,000	120,000
2	Interest on Term Loan	6.80%		(6,800)	(6,800)	(6,800)	(7,820)	(8,160)

[2]Equation 19.2 assumes that changes in debt occur at the end of the year. If debt changes throughout the year, it is more accurate to compute interest expenses based on the average level of debt during the year.

TABLE 19.6 SPREADSHEET Sources and Uses of Funds for the Ideko Acquisition

Acquisition Financing ($ 000)				
	Sources		**Uses**	
1	New Term Loan	100,000	Purchase Ideko Equity	150,000
2	Excess Ideko Cash	6,500	Repay Existing Ideko Debt	4,500
3	KKP Equity Investment	53,000	Advisory and Other Fees	5,000
4	Total Sources of Funds	159,500	Total Uses of Funds	159,500

In addition to the tax benefit, the loan will allow KKP to limit its investment in Ideko and preserve its capital for other investments and acquisitions. The sources and uses of funds for the acquisition are shown in Table 19.6. In addition to the $150 million purchase price for Ideko's equity, $4.5 million will be used to repay Ideko's existing debt. With $5 million in advisory and other fees associated with the transaction, the acquisition will require $159.5 million in total funds. KKP's sources of funds include the new loan of $100 million as well as Ideko's own excess cash (which KKP will have access to). Thus, KKP's required equity contribution to the transaction is 159.5 − 100 − 6.5 = $53 million.

CONCEPT CHECK

1. What are the different operational improvements KKP plans to make?
2. Why is it necessary to consider these improvements to assess whether the acquisition is attractive?

19.3 Building the Financial Model

The value of any investment opportunity arises from the future cash flows it will generate. To estimate the cash flows resulting from the investment in Ideko, we begin by projecting Ideko's future earnings. We then consider Ideko's working capital and investment needs and estimate its free cash flow. With these data in hand, we can forecast Ideko's balance sheet and statement of cash flows.

Forecasting Earnings

We can forecast Ideko's income statement for the five years following the acquisition based on the operational and capital structure changes proposed. This income statement is often referred to as a **pro forma** income statement, because it is not based on actual data but rather depicts the firm's financials under a given set of hypothetical assumptions. The pro forma income statement translates our expectations regarding the operational improvements KKP can achieve at Ideko into consequences for the firm's earnings.

To build the pro forma income statement, we begin with Ideko's sales. Each year, sales can be calculated from the estimates in Table 19.3 as follows:

$$\text{Sales} = \text{Market Size} \times \text{Market Share} \times \text{Average Sales Price} \qquad (19.3)$$

For example, in 2006, Ideko has projected sales of 10.5 million × 11% × 76.5 = $88.358 million. The spreadsheet in Table 19.7 shows Ideko's current (2005) sales as well as projections for five years after the acquisition (2006–2010).

INTERVIEW WITH

JOSEPH L. RICE, III

Joseph L. Rice, III is a founding partner and the former chairman of Clayton, Dubilier & Rice (CD&R). The firm is among the most respected private equity firms in the world. Its investments span a number of industry segments with enterprise values ranging from $1 billion to $15 billion.

QUESTION: *How has private equity business changed since you began in the industry?*

ANSWER: The term "private equity" is very broad and today can cover virtually every kind of investing, short of investing in the stock or bond markets. The buyout business represents a significant component of the private equity market. Since I started in 1966, I've seen many changes as the asset class has matured. In the 1960s and 1970s, the buyout business had relatively little following. Limited capital availability kept transactions small, and we relied on unconventional funding sources. The total purchase price of my first transaction was approximately $3 million, financed through a secured bank line and from individuals contributing amounts ranging from $25,000 to $50,000. In contrast, in 2005, we bought Hertz from Ford for approximately $15 billion.

As the industry has evolved, the attractive returns generated from buyout investments has attracted broader interest from both institutions and high net worth individuals. Buyout firms apply a variety of value creation models, including financial engineering, multiple arbitrage, and industry sector bets, such as technology or healthcare. Today there is more focus on generating returns from improving business performance—which has always been CD&R's underlying investment approach. The character of the businesses that we buy has also changed. Traditionally, this was an asset-heavy business, with much of the financing coming from banks that lent against percentages of inventory and receivables and the liquidation value of hard assets. Now it's become more of a cash flow business.

QUESTION: *What makes a company a good buyout candidate?*

ANSWER: We look to acquire good businesses at fair prices. Acquiring non-core, underperforming divisions of large companies and making them more effective has been a fertile investment area for CD&R. These divestiture buyouts tend to be complex and require experience and patience to execute. For example, we were in discussions with Ford management for three years prior to leading the Hertz division acquisition.

After running a series of projections based on information from management, we develop a capital structure designed to insure the viability of the acquisition candidate. We are relatively unconcerned with EPS but are very return conscious, focusing on cash and creating long-term shareholder value. We must also believe that we can generate a return on equity that meets our standards and justifies our investors' commitments to us.

We also acquire businesses confronting strategic issues where our operating expertise can bring value, such as Kinko's, a great brand franchise that we reorganized and expanded. We prefer service and distribution businesses to large manufacturers because of the wage differential between Asia and the United States and Europe. We also prefer businesses with a diversity of suppliers and customers and where there are multiple levers under our control to improve operating performance.

QUESTION: *Post acquisition, what is the role of the private equity firm?*

ANSWER: CD&R brings both a hands-on ownership style and capital. After closing a transaction, we assess current management's capability to do the job our investment case calls for. If necessary, we build and strengthen the management team. Then we work with them to determine the appropriate strategy to produce outstanding results. Finally, we aggressively pursue productivity, cost reduction, and growth initiatives to enhance operating and financial performance. At Kinko's, we restructured 129 separate S-corporations into one centralized corporation and installed a new management team. Our key strategic decision was transforming Kinko's from a loose confederation of consumer and small business-oriented copy shops into a highly networked company serving major corporations. In the end, that is what made the company an attractive acquisition for FedEx in 2004.

TABLE 19.7 SPREADSHEET **Pro Forma Income Statement for Ideko, 2005–2010**

	Year	2005	2006	2007	2008	2009	2010
Income Statement ($ 000)							
1	**Sales**	75,000	88,358	103,234	119,777	138,149	158,526
2	Cost of Goods Sold						
3	Raw Materials	(16,000)	(18,665)	(21,593)	(24,808)	(28,333)	(32,193)
4	Direct Labor Costs	(18,000)	(21,622)	(25,757)	(30,471)	(35,834)	(41,925)
5	**Gross Profit**	41,000	48,071	55,883	64,498	73,982	84,407
6	Sales and Marketing	(11,250)	(14,579)	(18,582)	(23,356)	(27,630)	(31,705)
7	Administrative	(13,500)	(13,254)	(15,485)	(16,769)	(17,959)	(20,608)
8	**EBITDA**	16,250	20,238	21,816	24,373	28,393	32,094
9	Depreciation	(5,500)	(5,450)	(5,405)	(6,865)	(7,678)	(7,710)
10	**EBIT**	10,750	14,788	16,411	17,508	20,715	24,383
11	Interest Expense (net)	(75)	(6,800)	(6,800)	(6,800)	(7,820)	(8,160)
12	**Pretax Income**	10,675	7,988	9,611	10,708	12,895	16,223
13	Income Tax	(3,736)	(2,796)	(3,364)	(3,748)	(4,513)	(5,678)
14	**Net Income**	**6,939**	**5,193**	**6,247**	**6,960**	**8,382**	**10,545**

The next items in the income statement detail the cost of goods sold. The raw materials cost can be calculated from sales as

$$\text{Raw Materials} = \text{Market Size} \times \text{Market Share} \times \text{Raw Materials per Unit} \quad (19.4)$$

In 2006, the cost of raw materials is 10.5 million $\times$ 11% $\times$ 16.16 $=$ \$18.665 million. The same method can be applied to determine the direct labor costs. Sales, marketing, and administrative costs can be computed directly as a percentage of sales. For example:

$$\text{Sales and Marketing} = \text{Sales} \times (\text{Sales and Marketing \% of Sales}) \quad (19.5)$$

Therefore, sales and marketing costs are forecast to be \$88.358 million $\times$ 16.5% $=$ \$14.579 million in 2006.

Deducting these operating expenses from Ideko's sales, we can project EBITDA over the next five years as shown in line 8 of Table 19.7. Subtracting the depreciation expenses we estimated in Table 19.4, we arrive at Ideko's earnings before interest and taxes. Next, we deduct interest expenses according to the schedule given in Table 19.5.[3] The final expense is the corporate income tax, which we computed using the tax rate in Table 19.3 as

$$\text{Income Tax} = \text{Pretax Income} \times \text{Tax Rate} \quad (19.6)$$

After income taxes, we are left with Ideko's projected pro forma net income as the bottom line in Table 19.7. Based on our projections, net income will rise by 52% from \$6.939 million to \$10.545 million at the end of five years, although it will drop in the near term due to the large increase in interest expense from the new debt.

[3]This interest expense should be offset by any interest earned on investments. As we discuss later in this chapter, we assume that Ideko does not invest its excess cash balances, but instead pays them out to its owner, KKP. Thus, net interest expenses are solely due to Ideko's outstanding debt.

EXAMPLE 19.3 Forecasting Income

Problem

By what percentage is Ideko's EBITDA expected to grow over the five-year period? By how much would it grow if Ideko's market share remained at 10%?

Solution

EBITDA will increase from \$16.25 million to \$32.09 million, or $(32.09/16.25) - 1 = 97\%$, over the five years. With a 10% market share rather than a 15% market share, sales will be only $(10\%/15\%) = 66.7\%$ of the forecast in Table 19.7. Because Ideko's operating expenses are proportional to its unit sales, its expenses and EBITDA will also be 66.7% of the current estimates. Thus, EBITDA will grow to $66.7\% \times 32.09 = \$21.40$ million, which is an increase of only $(21.40/16.25) - 1 = 32\%$.

Working Capital Requirements

The spreadsheet in Table 19.8 lists Ideko's current working capital requirements and forecasts the firm's future working capital needs. (See Chapter 26 for a further discussion of working capital requirements and their determinants.) This forecast includes the plans to tighten Ideko's credit policy, speed up customer payments, and reduce Ideko's inventory of raw materials.

Based on these working capital requirements, the spreadsheet in Table 19.9 forecasts Ideko's net working capital (NWC) over the next five years. Each line item in the spreadsheet is found by computing the appropriate number of days' worth of the corresponding revenue or expense from the income statement (Table 19.7). For example, accounts receivable in 2006 is calculated as[4]

$$\text{Accounts Receivable} = \text{Days Required} \times \frac{\text{Annual Sales}}{365 \text{ days/yr}}$$

$$= 60 \text{ days} \times \frac{\$88.358 \text{ million/yr}}{365 \text{ days/yr}} = \$14.525 \text{ million} \qquad (19.7)$$

TABLE 19.8 SPREADSHEET Ideko's Working Capital Requirements

		Year	2005	>2005
Working Capital Days				
Assets		**Based on:**	**Days**	**Days**
1	Accounts Receivable	Sales Revenue	90	60
2	Raw Materials	Raw Materials Costs	45	30
3	Finished Goods	Raw Materials + Labor Costs	45	45
4	Minimum Cash Balance	Sales Revenue	30	30
Liabilities				
5	Wages Payable	Direct Labor + Admin Costs	15	15
6	Other Accounts Payable	Raw Materials + Sales and Marketing	45	45

[4]If products are highly seasonal, large fluctuations in working capital may occur over the course of the year. When these effects are important, it is best to develop forecasts on a quarterly or monthly basis so that the seasonal effects can be tracked.

TABLE 19.9 SPREADSHEET **Ideko's Net Working Capital Forecast**

	Year	2005	2006	2007	2008	2009	2010
Working Capital ($ 000)							
Assets							
1	Accounts Receivable	18,493	14,525	16,970	19,689	22,709	26,059
2	Raw Materials	1,973	1,534	1,775	2,039	2,329	2,646
3	Finished Goods	4,192	4,967	5,838	6,815	7,911	9,138
4	Minimum Cash Balance	6,164	7,262	8,485	9,845	11,355	13,030
5	Total Current Assets	30,822	28,288	33,067	38,388	44,304	50,872
Liabilities							
6	Wages Payable	1,294	1,433	1,695	1,941	2,211	2,570
7	Other Accounts Payable	3,360	4,099	4,953	5,938	6,900	7,878
8	Total Current Liabilities	4,654	5,532	6,648	7,879	9,110	10,448
Net Working Capital							
9	Net Working Capital (5 − 8)	26,168	22,756	26,419	30,509	35,194	40,425
10	Increase in Net Working Capital		(3,412)	3,663	4,089	4,685	5,231

Similarly, Ideko's inventory of finished goods will be $45 \times (18.665 + 21.622)/365 = \$4.967$ million.

Table 19.9 also lists Ideko's minimum cash balance each year. This balance represents the minimum level of cash needed to keep the business running smoothly, allowing for the daily variations in the timing of income and expenses. Firms generally earn little or no interest on these balances, which are held in cash or in a checking or short-term savings accounts. As a consequence, we account for this opportunity cost by including the minimal cash balance as part of the firm's working capital.

We assume that Ideko will earn no interest on this minimal balance. (If it did, this interest would reduce the firm's net interest expense in the income statement.) We also assume that Ideko will pay out as dividends all cash not needed as part of working capital. Therefore, Ideko will hold no excess cash balances or short-term investments above the minimal level reported in Table 19.9. If Ideko were to retain excess funds, these balances would be considered part of its financing strategy (reducing its net debt), and not as part of its working capital.[5]

Ideko's net working capital for each year is computed in Table 19.9 as the difference between the forecasted current assets and current liabilities. Increases in net working capital represent a cost to the firm. Note that as a result of the improvements in accounts receivable and inventory management, Ideko will reduce its net working capital by more than $3.4 million in 2006. After this initial savings, working capital needs will increase in conjunction with the growth of the firm.

Forecasting Free Cash Flow

We now have the data needed to forecast Ideko's free cash flows over the next five years. Ideko's earnings are available from the income statement (Table 19.7), as are its depreciation and interest expenses. Capital expenditures are available from Table 19.4, and changes in net working capital can be found in Table 19.9. We combine these items to estimate the free cash flows in the spreadsheet in Table 19.10.

[5] Firms often hold excess cash in anticipation of future investment needs or possible cash shortfalls. Because Ideko can rely on KKP to provide needed capital, excess cash reserves are unnecessary.

TABLE 19.10 SPREADSHEET Ideko's Free Cash Flow Forecast

	Year	2005	2006	2007	2008	2009	2010
Free Cash Flow ($ 000)							
1	**Net Income**		5,193	6,247	6,960	8,382	10,545
2	Plus: After-Tax Interest Expense		4,420	4,420	4,420	5,083	5,304
3	**Unlevered Net Income**		9,613	10,667	11,380	13,465	15,849
4	Plus: Depreciation		5,450	5,405	6,865	7,678	7,710
5	Less: Increases in NWC		3,412	(3,663)	(4,089)	(4,685)	(5,231)
6	Less: Capital Expenditures		(5,000)	(5,000)	(20,000)	(15,000)	(8,000)
7	**Free Cash Flow of Firm**		13,475	7,409	(5,845)	1,458	10,328
8	Plus: Net Borrowing		—	—	15,000	5,000	—
9	Less: After-Tax Interest Expense		(4,420)	(4,420)	(4,420)	(5,083)	(5,304)
10	**Free Cash Flow to Equity**		9,055	2,989	4,735	1,375	5,024

To compute Ideko's free cash flow, which excludes cash flows associated with leverage, we first adjust net income by adding back the after-tax interest payments associated with the net debt in its capital structure:[6]

$$\text{After-Tax Interest Expense} = (1 - \text{Tax Rate}) \times (\text{Interest on Debt} - \text{Interest on Excess Cash}) \quad (19.8)$$

Because Ideko has no excess cash, its after-tax interest expense in 2006 is $(1 - 35\%) \times 6.8 = \$4.42$ million, providing unlevered net income of $5.193 + 4.42 = \$9.613$ million. We could also compute the unlevered net income in Table 19.10 by starting with EBIT and deducting taxes. In 2006, for example, EBIT is forecasted as \$14.788 million, which amounts to $14.788 \times (1 - 35\%) = \$9.613$ million after taxes.

To compute Ideko's free cash flow from its unlevered net income, we add back depreciation (which is not a cash expense), and deduct Ideko's increases in net working capital and capital expenditures. The free cash flow on line 7 of Table 19.10 shows the cash the firm will generate for its investors, both debt and equity holders. While Ideko will generate substantial free cash flow over the next five years, the level of free cash flow varies substantially from year to year. It is highest in 2006 (due mostly to the large reduction in working capital) and is forecasted to be negative in 2008 (when the plant expansion will begin).

To determine the free cash flow to equity, we first add Ideko's net borrowing (that is, increases to net debt):

$$\text{Net Borrowing in Year } t = \text{Net Debt in Year } t - \text{Net Debt in Year } (t-1) \quad (19.9)$$

Ideko will borrow in 2008 and 2009 as part of its expansion. We then deduct the after-tax interest payments that were added in line 2.

As shown in the last line of Table 19.10, during the next five years Ideko is expected to generate a positive free cash flow to equity, which will be used to pay dividends to KKP. The free cash flow to equity will be highest in 2006; by 2010, KKP will recoup a significant fraction of its initial investment.

[6] If Ideko had some interest income or expenses from working capital, we would *not* include that interest here. We adjust only for interest that is related to the firm's *financing*—that is, interest associated with debt and *excess* cash (cash not included as part of working capital).

EXAMPLE 19.4 Leverage and Free Cash Flow

Problem

Suppose Ideko does not add leverage in 2008 and 2009, but instead keeps its debt fixed at $100 million until 2010. How would this change in its leverage policy affect its expected free cash flow? How would it affect the free cash flow to equity?

Solution

Because free cash flow is based on unlevered net income, it will not be affected by Ideko's leverage policy. Free cash flow to equity will be affected, however. Net borrowing will be zero each year, and the firm's after-tax interest expense will remain at the 2006 level of $4.42 million:

	Year	2005	2006	2007	2008	2009	2010
Free Cash Flow ($ 000)							
1	**Free Cash Flow of Firm**		13,475	7,409	(5,845)	1,458	10,328
2	Plus: Net Borrowing		—	—	—	—	—
3	Less: After-Tax Interest Expense		(4,420)	(4,420)	(4,420)	(4,420)	(4,420)
4	**Free Cash Flow to Equity**		9,055	2,989	(10,265)	(2,962)	5,908

In this case, Ideko will have a negative free cash flow to equity in 2008 and 2009. That is, without additional borrowing, KKP will have to invest additional capital in the firm to fund the expansion.

USING EXCEL

Summarizing Model Outputs

After completing our earnings and cash flow forecasts, it is helpful to create a summary table with key outputs from the model. The spreadsheet below highlights Ideko's revenue, earnings, and cash flow forecasts. In addition to the raw numbers, we provide further context by calculating annual growth rates, margins, cumulative cash flows, and leverage multiples:

	A B C	D	E	F	G	H	I	J
1								2005-2010
2	**Ideko Key Financials**	**2005**	**2006**	**2007**	**2008**	**2009**	**2010**	**CAGR**
3	Revenue	75,000	88,358	103,234	119,777	138,149	158,526	*16.1%*
4	*% Growth*		*17.8%*	*16.8%*	*16.0%*	*15.3%*	*14.8%*	
5	EBITDA	16,250	20,238	21,816	24,373	28,393	32,094	*14.6%*
6	*% Margin*	*21.7%*	*22.9%*	*21.1%*	*20.3%*	*20.6%*	*20.2%*	
7	EBIT	10,750	14,788	16,411	17,508	20,715	24,383	*17.8%*
8	*% Margin*	*14.3%*	*16.7%*	*15.9%*	*14.6%*	*15.0%*	*15.4%*	
9	Net Income	6,939	5,193	6,247	6,960	8,382	10,545	*8.7%*
10	*% Margin*	*9.3%*	*5.9%*	*6.1%*	*5.8%*	*6.1%*	*6.7%*	
11	*Cash Flows*							*Cumulative*
12	FCF		13,475	7,409	(5,845)	1,458	10,328	26,825
13	Dividends (FCFE)		9,055	2,989	4,735	1,375	5,024	23,178
14	*Leverage*							
15	Debt / EBITDA	6.2x	4.9x	4.6x	4.7x	4.2x	3.7x	
16	EBITDA / Interest		3.0x	3.2x	3.6x	3.6x	3.9x	

The summary above quickly reveals insights not immediately apparent from the raw numbers. First, note that while revenue is growing by 16.1% per year on average (as indicated by the compound annual growth rate), we see that year-over-year growth is declining over the forecast period. Second, EBITDA is growing more slowly than revenue (14.6% versus 16.1%) due to falling margins, indicating that Ideko's operating expenses are growing faster than revenues. EBIT growth is higher, however, at 17.8% per year, because the firm's improved capital efficiency means depreciation grows more slowly than revenues. Finally, net income growth is only 8.7% because of Ideko's increased interest payments, though net profits margins begin to improve after 2008.

Note the higher variability of Ideko's cash flows compared to earnings due to its fluctuating investment needs. The cumulative cash flows show that equity holders hope to recoup over $23 million, or nearly half their investment, from the first five years of dividends alone. Finally, the leverage multiples show that while initial leverage is high, Ideko will quickly reduce leverage and improve its interest coverage ratio.

The Balance Sheet and Statement of Cash Flows (Optional)

The information we have calculated so far can be used to project Ideko's balance sheet and statement of cash flows through 2010. While these statements are not critical for our valuation, they often prove helpful in providing a more complete picture of how a firm will grow during the forecast period. These statements for Ideko are shown in the spreadsheets in Table 19.11 and Table 19.12.

The statement of cash flows in Table 19.11 starts with net income. Cash from operating activities includes depreciation as well as changes to working capital items (other than cash) from Table 19.9. Note that increases in accounts receivable or inventory are a *use* of cash, whereas an increase in accounts payable is a *source* of cash. Cash from investing activities includes the capital expenditures in Table 19.4. Cash from financing activities includes changes in outstanding debt from Table 19.5, and dividends or stock issuance determined by the free cash flow to equity in Table 19.10. (If free cash flow to equity were negative in any year, it would appear as stock issuance in line 13 in Table 19.11.) As a final check on the calculations, note that the change in cash and cash equivalents on line 15 in Table 19.11 equals the change in the minimum cash balance shown in Table 19.9.

For the balance sheet, we must begin by adjusting Ideko's closing 2005 balance sheet from Table 19.1 to account for the transaction. The transaction will affect the firm's goodwill, stockholders' equity, and its cash and debt balances. We show these changes by constructing a new "pro forma" 2005 balance sheet that represents the firm just after the transaction closes (see Table 19.12). Let's consider how each change is determined.

First, we calculate goodwill as the difference between the acquisition price and the value of the net assets acquired:

$$\text{New Goodwill} = \text{Acquisition Price} - \text{Value of Net Assets Acquired} \quad (19.10)$$

In this case, the acquisition price is the $150 million purchase price for Ideko's existing equity. For the net assets acquired, we use Ideko's existing book value of equity, $77.668

TABLE 19.11 SPREADSHEET Pro Forma Statement of Cash Flows for Ideko, 2005–2010

	Year	2005	2006	2007	2008	2009	2010
	Statement of Cash Flows ($ 000)						
1	**Net Income**		5,193	6,247	6,960	8,382	10,545
2	Depreciation		5,450	5,405	6,865	7,678	7,710
3	Changes in Working Capital						
4	Accounts Receivable		3,968	(2,445)	(2,719)	(3,020)	(3,350)
5	Inventory		(336)	(1,112)	(1,242)	(1,385)	(1,544)
6	Accounts Payable		878	1,116	1,231	1,231	1,338
7	**Cash from Operating Activities**		15,153	9,211	11,095	12,885	14,699
8	Capital Expenditures		(5,000)	(5,000)	(20,000)	(15,000)	(8,000)
9	Other Investment		—	—	—	—	—
10	**Cash from Investing Activities**		(5,000)	(5,000)	(20,000)	(15,000)	(8,000)
11	Debt Issuance (or Repayment)		—	—	15,000	5,000	—
12	Dividends		(9,055)	(2,989)	(4,735)	(1,375)	(5,024)
13	Sale (or Purchase) of Stock		—	—	—	—	—
14	**Cash from Financing Activities**		(9,055)	(2,989)	10,265	3,625	(5,024)
15	**Change in Cash** (7 + 10 + 14)		**1,098**	**1,223**	**1,360**	**1,510**	**1,675**

TABLE 19.12 SPREADSHEET **Pro Forma Balance Sheet for Ideko, 2005–2010**

	Year	2005PF	2006	2007	2008	2009	2010
Balance Sheet ($ 000)							
Assets							
1	Cash and Cash Equivalents	6,164	7,262	8,485	9,845	11,355	13,030
2	Accounts Receivable	18,493	14,525	16,970	19,689	22,709	26,059
3	Inventories	6,165	6,501	7,613	8,854	10,240	11,784
4	**Total Current Assets**	30,822	28,288	33,067	38,388	44,304	50,872
5	Property, Plant, and Equipment	49,500	49,050	48,645	61,781	69,102	69,392
6	Goodwill	72,332	72,332	72,332	72,332	72,332	72,332
7	**Total Assets**	152,654	149,670	154,044	172,501	185,738	192,597
Liabilities							
8	Accounts Payable	4,654	5,532	6,648	7,879	9,110	10,448
9	Debt	100,000	100,000	100,000	115,000	120,000	120,000
10	**Total Liabilities**	104,654	105,532	106,648	122,879	129,110	130,448
Stockholders' Equity							
11	Starting Stockholders' Equity		48,000	44,138	47,396	49,621	56,628
12	Net Income	(5,000)	5,193	6,247	6,960	8,382	10,545
13	Dividends		(9,055)	(2,989)	(4,735)	(1,375)	(5,024)
14	Sale (or Purchase) of Stock	53,000	—	—	—	—	—
15	**Stockholders' Equity**	48,000	44,138	47,396	49,621	56,628	62,149
16	**Total Liabilities and Equity**	152,654	149,670	154,044	172,501	185,738	192,597

million, *excluding* any pre-existing goodwill ($0). Thus, new goodwill is 150 − (77.668 − 0) = $72.332 million.[7]

Next, consider stockholders' equity, which we calculate as

$$\text{New Stockholders' Equity} = \text{Equity Contributions} - \text{Expensed Transaction Fees} \quad (19.11)$$

In this case, we deduct the $5 million in advisory fee expenses from KKP's initial equity contribution of $53 million to calculate new shareholders' equity of $48 million.[8]

Finally, we adjust Ideko's cash and debt balances by deducting the excess cash of $6.5 million used to help fund the transaction, eliminating Ideko's existing debt (which will be repaid), and adding the new debt incurred of $100 million. These steps complete the pro forma 2005 balance sheet as of the completion of the transaction and are shown in Table 19.12.

To construct the balance sheet going forward, adjust the cash balance to reflect the change in cash from line 15 of the statement of cash flows in Table 19.11. All other current assets and liabilities come from the net working capital spreadsheet (Table 19.9). The inventory entry on the balance sheet includes both raw materials and finished goods. Property, plant, and equipment information comes from the capital expenditure spreadsheet

[7]We have simplified somewhat the balance sheet adjustments in the goodwill calculation. In particular, the book values of Ideko's assets and liabilities may be "stepped up" to reflect current fair values, and a portion of the excess purchase price may be allocated to intangible assets as opposed to goodwill.

[8]Under SFAS 141R, as of December 2008, acquisition-related advisory and legal fees should be expensed as incurred. To illustrate this method, we have applied it here. Financing fees related to debt issuance, on the other hand, are not deducted from shareholders' equity, but are instead capitalized as a new asset and amortized over the loan's term. For simplicity, we have ignored these fees and any related tax consequences.

USING EXCEL

Auditing Your Financial Model

Building a three-statement financial model is complex, and even experienced financial modelers make mistakes. Audit your model to check for errors using the following best practices.

Do Not Use Stockholders' Equity as a Plug

Because the balance sheet must balance, it is tempting to calculate stockholders' equity in the spreadsheet as the difference between total assets and total liabilities. Doing so, however, nullifies a key benefit of the balance sheet as an audit tool on the rest of the financial model. As a best practice, always calculate stockholders' equity directly as shown here. Then, in a line below the balance sheet, include a "check" line that tests whether total assets equal total liabilities and equity each year—and if the difference is non-zero, display it in a bold red font so the errror is apparent.

If the model does have an error, the amount of the difference will provide a clue to its source: If the difference is a constant each year, it is likely to result from one of the adjustments in the initial pro forma balance sheet; if it varies over time, check each line of the balance sheet to be sure the trends make sense (e.g., that inventories grow with sales), and check the sign of each line item in the statement of cash flows to make sure all sources of cash are positive and all uses of cash are negative (especially working capital).

Check the Cash and Payout Policy

Check that the firm's cash and payouts match its intended policy. In this case, we forecast that Ideko would pay out all excess cash going forward. Thus, its cash balances in the balance sheet should match the minimum balances specified in Table 19.9. If not, be sure to audit the free cash flow to equity calculation in Table 19.10. Note also that in this example, free cash flow to equity (i.e., dividends) was an output of the model. We could have alternatively assumed Ideko would retain its excess cash. In that case, free cash flow to equity would be zero (no dividends would be paid), and changes in cash (and thus the firm's net borrowing) would be outputs.

(Table 19.4), and the debt comes from Table 19.5. From Eq. 2.7, stockholders' equity increases each year through retained earnings (net income less dividends) and new capital contributions (stock issuances net of repurchases). Dividends after 2005 are equal to positive free cash flows to equity from Table 19.10, whereas negative free cash flows to equity represent a stock issuance. As a check on the calculations, note that the balance sheet does, indeed, balance: Total assets equal total liabilities and equity.[9]

Ideko's book value of equity will decline in 2006, as Ideko reduces its working capital and pays out the savings as part of a large dividend. The firm's book value will then rise as it expands. Ideko's book debt-equity ratio will decline from 100,000/48,000 = 2.1 to 120,000/62,149 = 1.9 during the five-year period.

CONCEPT CHECK

1. What is a pro forma income statement?
2. How do we calculate the firm's free cash flow, and the free cash flow to equity?

[9]In Table 19.12, goodwill is assumed to remain constant. If the transaction were structured as an acquisition of assets (as opposed to stock), the goodwill would be amortizable over 15 years for tax reporting as per section 197 of the Internal Revenue Code. For financial accounting purposes, goodwill is not amortized but is subject to an impairment test at least once a year as specified in FASB 142 (though changes in goodwill due to impairment have no tax accounting consequence).

19.4 Estimating the Cost of Capital

To value KKP's investment in Ideko, we need to assess the risk associated with Ideko and estimate an appropriate cost of capital. Because Ideko is a private firm, we cannot use its own past returns to evaluate its risk, but must instead rely on comparable publicly traded firms. In this section, we use data from the comparable firms identified earlier to estimate a cost of capital for Ideko.

Our approach is as follows. First, we use the techniques developed in Part 4 to estimate the equity cost of capital for Oakley, Luxottica Group, and Nike. Then, we estimate the unlevered cost of capital for each firm based on its capital structure. We use the unlevered cost of capital of the comparable firms to estimate Ideko's unlevered cost of capital. Once we have this estimate, we can use Ideko's capital structure to determine its equity cost of capital or WACC, depending on the valuation method employed.

CAPM-Based Estimation

To determine an appropriate cost of capital, we must first determine the appropriate measure of risk. KKP's investment in Ideko will represent a large fraction of its portfolio. As a consequence, KKP itself is not well diversified. But KKP's investors are primarily pension funds and large institutional investors, which are themselves well diversified and which evaluate their performance relative to the market as a benchmark. Thus, you decide that estimating market risk using the CAPM approach is justified.

Using the CAPM, we can estimate the equity cost of capital for each comparable firm based on the beta of its equity. As outlined in Chapter 12, the standard approach to estimating an equity beta is to determine the historical sensitivity of the stock's returns to the market's returns by using linear regression to estimate the slope coefficient in the equation:

$$\underbrace{R_s - r_f}_{\substack{\text{Excess return} \\ \text{of stock } s}} = \alpha_s + \beta_s \underbrace{(R_{mkt} - r_f)}_{\substack{\text{Excess return} \\ \text{of market portfolio}}} + \varepsilon_s \tag{19.12}$$

As a proxy for the market portfolio, we will use a value-weighted portfolio of all NYSE, AMEX, and NASDAQ stocks. With data from 2000 to 2004, we calculate the excess return—the realized return minus the yield on a one-month Treasury security—for each firm and for the market portfolio. We then estimate the equity beta for each firm by regressing its excess return onto the excess return of the market portfolio. We perform the regression for both monthly returns and 10-day returns. The estimated equity betas, together with their 95% confidence intervals, are shown in Table 19.13.

TABLE 19.13 Equity Betas with Confidence Intervals for Comparable Firms

	Monthly Returns		10-Day Returns	
Firm	Beta	95% C.I.	Beta	95% C.I.
Oakley	1.99	1.2 to 2.8	1.37	0.9 to 1.9
Luxottica	0.56	0.0 to 1.1	0.86	0.5 to 1.2
Nike	0.48	−0.1 to 1.0	0.69	0.4 to 1.0

While we would like to assess risk and, therefore, estimate beta based on longer horizon returns (consistent with our investors' investment horizon), the confidence intervals we obtain using monthly data are extremely wide. These confidence intervals narrow somewhat when we use 10-day returns. In any case, the results make clear that a fair amount of uncertainty persists when we estimate the beta for an individual firm.

Unlevering Beta

Given an estimate of each firm's equity beta, we next "unlever" the beta based on the firm's capital structure. Here we use Eq. 12.9 (which is equivalent, in terms of returns, to calculating the pretax WACC as in Eq. 18.6):

$$\beta_U = \left(\frac{\text{Equity Value}}{\text{Enterprise Value}}\right)\beta_E + \left(\frac{\text{Net Debt Value}}{\text{Enterprise Value}}\right)\beta_D \tag{19.13}$$

Recall that we must use the *net* debt of the firm—that is, we must subtract any cash from the level of debt—so we use the enterprise value of the firm as the sum of debt and equity in the formula.[10] Table 19.14 shows the capital structure for each comparable firm. Oakley has no debt, while Luxottica has about 17% debt in its capital structure. Nike holds cash that exceeds its debt, leading to a negative net debt in its capital structure.

Table 19.14 also estimates the unlevered beta of each firm. Here, we have used an equity beta for each firm within the range of the results from Table 19.13. Given the low or negative debt levels for each firm, assuming a beta for debt of zero is a reasonable approximation. Then, we compute an unlevered beta for each firm according to Eq. 19.13.

The range of the unlevered betas for these three firms is large. Both Luxottica and Nike have relatively low betas, presumably reflecting the relative noncyclicality of their core businesses (prescription eyewear for Luxottica and athletic shoes for Nike). Oakley has a much higher unlevered beta, perhaps because the high-end specialty sports eyewear it produces is a discretionary expense for most consumers.

Ideko's Unlevered Cost of Capital

The data from the comparable firms provides guidance to us for estimating Ideko's unlevered cost of capital. Ideko's products are not as high end as Oakley's eyewear, so their sales are unlikely to vary as much with the business cycle as Oakley's sales do. However, Ideko does not have a prescription eyewear division, as Luxottica does. Ideko's products are also fashion items rather than exercise items, so we expect Ideko's cost of capital to be closer to

TABLE 19.14 Capital Structure and Unlevered Beta Estimates for Comparable Firms

Firm	$\frac{E}{E+D}$	$\frac{D}{E+D}$	β_E	β_D	β_U
Oakley	1.00	0.00	1.50	—	1.50
Luxottica	0.83	0.17	0.75	0	0.62
Nike	1.05	−0.05	0.60	0	0.63

[10] Recall from Chapter 18 that Eq. 19.13 assumes that the firm will maintain a target leverage ratio. If the debt is expected to remain fixed for some period, we should also deduct the value of the predetermined tax shields from the firm's net debt.

Oakley's than to Nike's or Luxottica's. Therefore, we use 1.20 as our preliminary estimate for Ideko's unlevered beta, which is somewhat above the average of the comparables in Table 19.14.

We use the security market line of the CAPM to translate this beta into a cost of capital for Ideko. In mid-2005, one-year Treasury rates were approximately 4%; we use this rate for the risk-free interest rate. We also need an estimate of the market risk premium. Since 1960, the average annual return of the value-weighted market portfolio of U.S. stocks has exceeded that of one-year Treasuries by approximately 5%. However, this estimate is a backward-looking number. As we mentioned in Chapter 12, some researchers believe that future stock market excess returns are likely to be lower than this historical average. To be conservative in our valuation of Ideko, we will use 5% as the expected market risk premium.

Based on these choices, our estimate of Ideko's unlevered cost of capital is

$$
\begin{aligned}
r_U &= r_f + \beta_U(E[R_{mkt}] - r_f) = 4\% + 1.20(5\%) \\
&= 10\%
\end{aligned}
$$

Of course, as our discussion has made clear, this estimate contains a large amount of uncertainty. Thus, we will include sensitivity analysis with regard to the unlevered cost of capital in our analysis.

EXAMPLE 19.5 **Estimating the Unlevered Cost of Capital**

Problem

Using the monthly equity beta estimates for each firm in Table 19.13, what range of unlevered cost of capital estimates is possible?

Solution

Oakley has the highest equity beta of 1.99, which is also its unlevered beta (it has no debt). With this beta, the unlevered cost of capital would be $r_U = 4\% + 1.99(5\%) = 13.95\%$. At the other extreme, given its capital structure, Luxottica's equity beta of 0.56 implies an unlevered beta of $(0.56)(0.83) = 0.46$. With this beta, the unlevered cost of capital would be $r_U = 4\% + 0.46(5\%) = 6.3\%$.

As with any analysis based on comparables, experience and judgment are necessary to come up with a reasonable estimate of the unlevered cost of capital. In this case, our choice would be guided by industry norms, an assessment of which comparable is closest in terms of market risk, and possibly knowledge of how cyclical Ideko's revenues have been historically.

CONCEPT CHECK

1. What is a standard approach to estimate an equity beta?
2. How do we estimate a firm's unlevered cost of capital using data from comparable publicly traded firms?

19.5 Valuing the Investment

Thus far, we have forecasted the first five years of cash flows from KKP's investment in Ideko, and we have estimated the investment's unlevered cost of capital. In this section, we combine these inputs to estimate the value of the opportunity. The first step is to develop an estimate of Ideko's value at the end of our five-year forecast horizon. To do so, we consider both a multiples approach and a discounted cash flow (DCF) valuation using the WACC method. Given Ideko's free cash flow and continuation value, we then estimate its total enterprise value in 2005 using the APV method. Deducting the value of debt and KKP's initial investment from our estimate of Ideko's enterprise value gives the NPV of the investment opportunity. In addition to NPV, we look at some other common metrics, including IRR and cash multiples.

The Multiples Approach to Continuation Value

Practitioners generally estimate a firm's continuation value (also called the terminal value) at the end of the forecast horizon using a valuation multiple. While forecasting cash flows explicitly is useful in capturing those specific aspects of a company that distinguish the firm from its competitors in the short run, in the long run firms in the same industry typically have similar expected growth rates, profitability, and risk. As a consequence, multiples are likely to be relatively homogeneous across firms. Thus, applying a multiple is potentially as reliable as estimating the value based on an explicit forecast of distant cash flows.

Of the different valuation multiples available, the EBITDA multiple is most often used in practice. In most settings, the EBITDA multiple is more reliable than sales or earnings multiples because it accounts for the firm's operating efficiency and is not affected by leverage differences between firms. We estimate the continuation value using an EBITDA multiple as follows:

$$\text{Continuation Enterprise Value at Forecast Horizon} = \text{EBITDA at Horizon} \times \text{EBITDA Multiple at Horizon} \tag{19.14}$$

From the income statement in Table 19.7, Ideko's EBITDA in 2010 is forecast to be \$32.09 million. If we assume its EBITDA multiple in 2010 is unchanged from the value of 9.1 that we calculated at the time of the original purchase, then Ideko's continuation value in 2010 is $32.09 \times 9.1 = \$292.05$ million. This calculation is shown in the spreadsheet in Table 19.15. Given Ideko's outstanding debt of \$120 million in 2010, this estimate corresponds to an equity value of \$172.05 million.

Table 19.15 also shows Ideko's sales and P/E multiples based on this continuation value. The continuation value is 1.8 times Ideko's 2010 sales, and the equity value is 16.3 times Ideko's 2010 earnings. Because the P/E multiple is affected by leverage, we also report Ideko's **unlevered P/E ratio**, which is calculated as its continuing enterprise value divided by its unlevered net income in 2010 (listed in Table 19.10). Ideko would have this P/E ratio if it had no debt in 2010, so this information is useful when comparing Ideko to unlevered firms in the industry.

TABLE 19.15 SPREADSHEET Continuation Value Estimate for Ideko

	Continuation Value: Multiples Approach ($ 000)		Common Multiples	
1	EBITDA in 2010	32,094		
2	EBITDA multiple	9.1×	EV/Sales	1.8×
3	**Continuation Enterprise Value**	**292,052**	P/E (levered)	16.3×
4	Debt	(120,000)	P/E (unlevered)	18.4×
5	**Continuation Equity Value**	**172,052**		

We can use the various multiples to assess the reasonableness of our estimated continuation value. While the value-to-sales ratio is high compared to the overall sporting goods industry, these multiples are otherwise low relative to the comparables in Table 19.2. If we expect these industry multiples to remain stable, this estimate of Ideko's continuation value seems reasonable (if not relatively conservative).

The Discounted Cash Flow Approach to Continuation Value

One difficulty with relying solely on comparables when forecasting a continuation value is that we are comparing *future* multiples of the firm with *current* multiples of its competitors. In 2010, the multiples of Ideko and the comparables we have chosen may all be very different, especially if the industry is currently experiencing abnormal growth. To guard against such a bias, it is wise to check our estimate of the continuation value based on fundamentals using a discounted cash flow approach.

To estimate a continuation value in year T using discounted cash flows, we assume a constant expected growth rate, g, and a constant debt-equity ratio. As explained in Chapter 18, when the debt-equity ratio is constant, the WACC valuation method is the simplest to apply:

$$\text{Enterprise Value in Year } T = V_T^L = \frac{FCF_{T+1}}{r_{wacc} - g} \tag{19.15}$$

To estimate free cash flow in year $T + 1$, recall that free cash flow is equal to unlevered net income plus depreciation, less capital expenditures and increases in net working capital (see Table 19.10):

$$\begin{aligned} FCF_{T+1} &= \text{Unlevered Net Income}_{T+1} + \text{Depreciation}_{T+1} \\ &\quad - \text{Increases in NWC}_{T+1} - \text{Capital Expenditures}_{T+1} \end{aligned} \tag{19.16}$$

Suppose the firm's sales are expected to grow at a nominal rate g. If the firm's operating expenses remain a fixed percentage of sales, then its unlevered net income will also grow at rate g. Similarly, the firm's receivables, payables, and other elements of net working capital will grow at rate g.

What about capital expenditures? The firm will need new capital to offset depreciation; it will also need to add capacity as its production volume grows. Given a sales growth rate g, we may expect that the firm will need to expand its investment in fixed assets at about the same rate. In that case,[11]

$$\text{Capital Expenditures}_{T+1} = \text{Depreciation}_{T+1} + g \times \text{Fixed Assets}_T$$

Thus, given a growth rate of g for the firm, we can estimate its free cash flow as

$$\begin{aligned} FCF_{T+1} &= (1 + g) \times \text{Unlevered Net Income}_T \\ &\quad - g \times \text{Net Working Capital}_T - g \times \text{Fixed Assets}_T \end{aligned} \tag{19.17}$$

Together, Eq. 19.15 and Eq. 19.17 allow us to estimate a firm's continuation value based on its long-run growth rate.

---

[11]Here, fixed assets are measured according to their book value net of accumulated depreciation. This level of capital expenditures is required to maintain the firm's ratio of sales to fixed assets (also called its fixed asset turnover ratio). An alternative approach—which is preferable if we anticipate a change in the turnover ratio—is to estimate increases in NWC and net investment (capital expenditures in excess of depreciation) in Eq. 19.16 as a target percentage of the *change* in sales, as we did in Chapter 9 (see Example 9.7), where the target percentage is the expected long-run ratio of NWC and PP&E to sales.

EXAMPLE 19.6 A DCF Estimate of the Continuation Value

Problem

Estimate Ideko's continuation value in 2010 assuming a future expected growth rate of 5%, a future debt-to-value ratio of 40%, and a debt cost of capital of 6.8%.

Solution

In 2010, Ideko's unlevered net income is forecasted to be \$15.849 million (Table 19.10), with working capital of \$40.425 million (Table 19.9). It has fixed assets of \$69.392 million (Table 19.4). From Eq. 19.17, we can estimate Ideko's free cash flow in 2011:

$$FCF_{2011} = (1.05)(15.849) - (5\%)(40.425) - (5\%)(69.392) = \$11.151 \text{ million}$$

This estimate represents nearly an 8% increase over Ideko's 2010 free cash flow of \$10.328 million. It exceeds the 5% growth rate of sales due to the decline in the required additions to Ideko's net working capital as its growth rate slows.

With a debt-to-value ratio of 40%, Ideko's WACC can be calculated from Eq. 18.11 or Eq. 12.13:

$$r_{wacc} = r_U - d\tau_c r_D = 10\% - 0.40(0.35)\,6.8\% = 9.05\%$$

Given the estimate of Ideko's free cash flow and WACC, we can estimate Ideko's continuation value in 2010:

$$V^L_{2010} = \frac{11.151}{9.05\% - 5\%} = \$275.33 \text{ million}$$

This continuation value represents a terminal EBITDA multiple of 275.33/32.09 = 8.6.

Both the multiples approach and the discounted cash flow approach are useful in deriving a realistic continuation value estimate. Our recommendation is to combine both approaches, as we do in Table 19.16. As shown in the spreadsheet, our projected EBITDA multiple of 9.1 can be justified by the discounted cash flow method with a nominal long-term growth rate of about 5.3%.[12] Given an expected future inflation rate of 2.5%, this

TABLE 19.16 SPREADSHEET Discounted Cash Flow Estimate of Continuation Value, with Implied EBITDA Multiple

Continuation Value: DCF and EBITDA Multiple ($ 000)				
1	Long-Term Growth Rate	5.3%		
2	Target *D*/(*E* + *D*)	40.0%		
3	Projected WACC	9.05%		
Free Cash Flow in 2011				
4	Unlevered Net Income	16,695	**Continuation Enterprise Value**	**292,052**
5	Less: Increase in NWC	(2,158)		
6	Less: Net Investment*	(3,705)	**Implied EBITDA Multiple**	**9.1×**
7	Free Cash Flow	10,832		

*Net investment equals the difference between capital expenditures and depreciation, so subtracting this amount is equivalent to adding back depreciation and subtracting capital expenditures (see Eq. 9.20).

[12] The exact nominal growth rate needed to match an EBITDA multiple of 9.1 is 5.33897%, which can be found using Solver in Excel.

COMMON MISTAKE **Continuation Values and Long-Run Growth**

The continuation value is one of the most important estimates when valuing a firm. A common mistake is to use an overly optimistic continuation value, which will lead to an upward bias in the estimated current value of the firm. Be aware of the following pitfalls:

Using multiples based on current high growth rates. Continuation value estimates are often based on current valuation multiples of existing firms. But if these firms are currently experiencing high growth that will eventually slow down, their multiples can be expected to decline over time. In this scenario, if we estimate a continuation value based on today's multiples without accounting for this decline as growth slows, the estimate will be biased upward.

Ignoring investment necessary for growth. When using the discounted cash flow method, we cannot assume that $FCF_{T+1} = FCF_T(1+g)$ if the firm's growth rate has changed between T and $T+1$. Whenever the growth rate changes, expenditures on working and fixed capital will be affected, and we must take this effect into account as we do in Eq. 19.17.

Using unsustainable long-term growth rates. When using the discounted cash flow method, we must choose a long-term growth rate for the firm. By choosing a high rate, we can make the continuation value estimate extremely high. In the long run, however, firms cannot continue to grow faster than the overall economy. Thus, we should be suspicious of long-term growth rates that exceed the expected rate of GDP growth, which has averaged between 2.5% and 3.5% in *real* terms (that is, not including inflation) in the United States over the past several decades.

nominal rate represents a real growth rate of about 2.8%. This implied growth rate is another important reality check for our continuation value estimate. If it is much higher than our expectations of long-run growth for the industry as a whole, we should be more skeptical of the estimate being used.

APV Valuation of Ideko's Equity

Our estimate of Ideko's continuation value summarizes the value of the firm's free cash flow beyond the forecast horizon. We can combine it with our forecast for free cash flow through 2010 (Table 19.10, line 7) to estimate Ideko's value today. Recall from Chapter 18 that because the debt is paid on a fixed schedule during the forecast period, the APV method is the easiest valuation method to apply.

The steps to estimate Ideko's value using the APV method are shown in the spreadsheet in Table 19.17. First, we compute Ideko's unlevered value V^U, which is the firm's value if we were to operate the company without leverage during the forecast period and sell it for its continuation value at the end of the forecast horizon. Thus, the final value in 2010 would be the continuation value we estimated in Table 19.15. The value in earlier periods

TABLE 19.17 SPREADSHEET **APV Estimate of Ideko's Initial Equity Value**

	Year	2005	2006	2007	2008	2009	2010
APV Method ($ 000)							
1	Free Cash Flow		13,475	7,409	(5,845)	1,458	10,328
2	**Unlevered Value** V^U (at 10%)	202,732	209,530	223,075	251,227	274,891	292,052
3	Interest Tax Shield		2,380	2,380	2,380	2,737	2,856
4	**Tax Shield Value** T^S (at 6.8%)	10,428	8,757	6,972	5,067	2,674	—
5	**APV:** $V^L = V^U + T^S$	213,160	218,287	230,047	256,294	277,566	292,052
6	Debt	(100,000)	(100,000)	(100,000)	(115,000)	(120,000)	(120,000)
7	**Equity Value**	**113,160**	**118,287**	**130,047**	**141,294**	**157,566**	**172,052**

includes the free cash flows paid by the firm (from Table 19.10) discounted at the unlevered cost of capital r_U that we estimated in Section 19.4[13]:

$$V_{t-1}^U = \frac{FCF_t + V_t^U}{1 + r_U} \tag{19.18}$$

Next, we incorporate Ideko's interest tax shield during the forecast horizon. The interest tax shield equals the tax rate of 35% (Table 19.3) multiplied by Ideko's scheduled interest payments (see Table 19.5). Because the debt levels are predetermined, we compute the value T^s of the tax shield by discounting the tax savings at the debt interest rate, $r_D = 6.80\%$:

$$T_{t-1}^s = \frac{\text{Interest Tax Shield}_t + T_t^s}{1 + r_D} \tag{19.19}$$

Combining the unlevered value and the tax shield value gives the APV, which is Ideko's enterprise value given the planned leverage policy. By deducting debt, we obtain our estimate for the value of Ideko's equity during the forecast period.

Thus, our estimate for Ideko's initial enterprise value is \$213 million, with an equity value of \$113 million. As KKP's initial cost to acquire Ideko's equity is \$53 million (see Table 19.6), based on these estimates the deal looks attractive, with an NPV of \$113 million − \$53 million = \$60 million.

A Reality Check

At this point, it is wise to step back and assess whether our valuation results make sense. Does an initial enterprise value of \$213 million for Ideko seem reasonable compared to the values of other firms in the industry?

Here again, multiples are helpful. Let's compute the initial valuation multiples that would be implied by our estimated enterprise value of \$213 million and compare them to Ideko's closest competitors as we did in Table 19.2. Table 19.18 provides our results.

Naturally, the valuation multiples based on the estimated enterprise value of \$213 million, which would correspond to a purchase price of \$215 million given Ideko's existing debt and excess cash, are higher than those based on a purchase price of \$150 million. They are now at the top end or somewhat above the range of the values of the other firms

COMMON MISTAKE — Missing Assets or Liabilities

When computing the enterprise value of a firm from its free cash flows, remember that we are valuing only those assets and liabilities whose cash flow consequences are included in our projections. Any "missing" assets or liabilities must be added to the APV estimate to determine the value of equity. In this case, we deduct the firm's debt and add any excess cash or other marketable securities that have not been included (for Ideko, excess cash has already been paid out and will remain at zero, so no adjustment is needed). We also adjust for any other assets or liabilities that have not been explicitly considered. For example, if a firm owns vacant land, or if it has patents or other rights whose potential cash flows were not included in the projections, the value of these assets must be accounted for separately. The same is true for liabilities such as stock option grants, potential legal liabilities, leases (if the lease payments were not included in earnings), or underfunded pension liabilities.

[13]Note that in 2010, we use the continuation value of \$292 million as the final "unlevered" value, even though this value might include future tax shields (as in Example 19.6). This approach is correct as we are using the APV calculation only to value the additional tax shields earned during the forecast horizon. Combining discounting methodologies as we have done here is very useful in situations like this one in which the firm is likely to be recapitalized at the exit horizon.

TABLE 19.18 Ideko Financial Ratios Comparison, Mid-2005, Based on Discounted Cash Flow Estimate Versus Proposed Purchase Price

Ratio	Ideko (Estimated Value)	Ideko (Purchase Price)	Oakley, Inc.	Luxottica Group	Nike, Inc.	Sporting Goods
P/E	31.0×	21.6×	24.8×	28.0×	18.2×	20.3×
EV/Sales	2.8×	2.0×	2.0×	2.7×	1.5×	1.4×
EV/EBITDA	13.1×	9.1×	11.6×	14.4×	9.3×	11.4×

that we used for comparison. While these multiples are not unreasonable given the operational improvements that KKP plans to implement, they indicate that our projections may be somewhat optimistic and depend critically on KKP's ability to achieve the operational improvements it plans.

Our estimated initial EBITDA multiple of 13.1 also exceeds the multiple of 9.1 that we assumed for the continuation value. Thus, our estimate forecasts a decline in the EBITDA multiple, which is appropriate given our expectation that growth will be higher in the short run. If the multiple did not decline, we should question whether our continuation value is too optimistic.

IRR and Cash Multiples

While the NPV method is the most reliable method when evaluating a transaction like KKP's acquisition of Ideko, real-world practitioners often use IRR and the *cash multiple* (or multiple of money) as alternative valuation metrics. We discuss both of these methods in this section.

To compute the IRR, we must compute KKP's cash flows over the life of the transaction. KKP's initial investment in Ideko, from Table 19.6, is $53 million. KKP will then receive cash dividends from Ideko based on the free cash flow to equity reported in Table 19.10. Finally, we assume that KKP will sell its equity share in Ideko at the end of five years, receiving the continuation equity value. We combine these data to determine KKP's cash flows in the spreadsheet in Table 19.19. Given the cash flows, we compute the IRR of the transaction, which is 33.3%.

While an IRR of 33.3% might sound attractive, it is not straightforward to evaluate in this context. To do so, we must compare it to the appropriate cost of capital for KKP's investment. Because KKP holds an equity position in Ideko, we should use Ideko's equity

TABLE 19.19 SPREADSHEET IRR and Cash Multiple for KKP's Investment in Ideko

	Year	2005	2006	2007	2008	2009	2010
IRR and Cash Multiple							
1	Initial Investment	(53,000)					
2	Free Cash Flow to Equity		9,055	2,989	4,735	1,375	5,024
3	Continuation Equity Value						172,052
4	KKP Cash Flows	(53,000)	9,055	2,989	4,735	1,375	177,077
5	**IRR**	**33.3%**					
6	**Cash Multiple**	**3.7×**					

cost of capital. Of course, Ideko's leverage ratio changes over the five-year period, which will change the risk of its equity. Thus, there is no single cost of capital to compare to the IRR.[14]

The spreadsheet in Table 19.19 also computes the cash multiple for the transaction. The **cash multiple** (also called the **multiple of money** or **absolute return**) is the ratio of the total cash received to the total cash invested. The cash multiple for KKP's investment in Ideko is

$$\text{Cash Multiple} = \frac{\text{Total Cash Received}}{\text{Total Cash Invested}}$$
$$= \frac{9055 + 2989 + 4735 + 1375 + 177{,}077}{53{,}000} = 3.7 \qquad (19.20)$$

That is, KKP expects to receive a return that is 3.7 times its investment in Ideko. The cash multiple is a common metric used by investors in transactions such as this one. It has an obvious weakness: The cash multiple does not depend on the amount of time it takes to receive the cash, nor does it account for the risk of the investment. It is therefore useful only for comparing deals with similar time horizons and risk.

CONCEPT CHECK

1. What are the main methods of estimating the continuation value of the firm at the end of the forecast horizon?
2. What are the potential pitfalls of analyzing a transaction like this one based on its IRR or cash multiple?

19.6 Sensitivity Analysis

Any financial valuation is only as accurate as the estimates on which it is based. Before concluding our analysis, it is important to assess the uncertainty of our estimates and to determine their potential impact on the value of the deal.

Once we have developed the spreadsheet model for KKP's investment in Ideko, it is straightforward to perform a sensitivity analysis to determine the impact of changes in different parameters on the deal's value. For example, the spreadsheet in Table 19.20 shows the sensitivity of our estimates of the value of KKP's investment to changes in our assumptions regarding the exit EBITDA multiple that KKP obtains when Ideko is sold, as well as Ideko's unlevered cost of capital.

In our initial analysis, we assumed an exit EBITDA multiple of 9.1. Table 19.20 shows that each 1.0 increase in the multiple represents about $20 million in initial value.[15] KKP will break even on its $53 million investment in Ideko with an exit multiple of slightly more than 6.0. The table also shows, however, that an exit multiple of 6.0 is consistent with a future growth rate for Ideko of less than 2%, which is even less than the expected rate of inflation and perhaps unrealistically low.

Table 19.20 also illustrates the effect of a change to our assumption about Ideko's unlevered cost of capital. A higher unlevered cost of capital reduces the value of KKP's

[14]See the appendix to this chapter for a calculation of Ideko's annual equity cost of capital.

[15]In fact, we can calculate this directly as the present value of Ideko's projected EBITDA in 2010: ($32.094 million)/($1.10^5$) = $19.928 million.

TABLE 19.20 SPREADSHEET Sensitivity Analysis for KKP's Investment in Ideko

Exit EBITDA Multiple		6.0	7.0	8.0	9.1	10.0	11.0
Implied Long-Run Growth Rate		1.60%	3.43%	4.53%	**5.34%**	5.81%	6.21%
Ideko Enterprise Value	(in $ million)	151.4	171.3	191.2	**213.2**	231.1	251.0
KKP Equity Value	(in $ million)	51.4	71.3	91.2	**113.2**	131.1	151.0
KKP IRR		14.8%	22.1%	28.0%	**33.3%**	37.1%	40.8%

Unlevered Cost of Capital		9.0%	10.0%	11.0%	12.0%	13.0%	14.0%
Implied Long-Run Growth Rate		3.86%	**5.34%**	6.81%	8.29%	9.76%	11.24%
Ideko Enterprise Value	(in $ million)	222.1	**213.2**	204.7	196.7	189.1	181.9
KKP Equity Value	(in $ million)	122.1	**113.2**	104.7	96.7	89.1	81.9

investment; yet, even with a rate as high as 14%, the equity value exceeds KKP's initial investment. However, if the unlevered cost of capital exceeds 12%, the implied long-term growth rate that justifies the assumed exit EBITDA multiple of 9.1 is probably unrealistically high. Thus, if we believe the unlevered cost of capital falls within this range, we should lower our forecast for the exit EBITDA multiple, which will further reduce the value of KKP's equity. Conversely, if we are confident in our estimate of the exit multiple, this analysis lends further support to our choice for the unlevered cost of capital.

The exercises at the end of this chapter continue the sensitivity analysis by considering different levels of market share growth and changes to working capital management.

CONCEPT CHECK

1. What is the purpose of the sensitivity analysis?
2. Table 19.20 shows the sensitivity analysis for KKP's investment in Ideko. Given this information, do you recommend the acquisition of Ideko?

MyFinanceLab

Here is what you should know after reading this chapter. MyFinanceLab will help you identify what you know and where to go when you need to practice.

19.1 Valuation Using Comparables

- Valuation using comparables may be used as a preliminary way to estimate the value of a firm. Common multiples include the price-earnings ratio, and the ratio of enterprise value to sales or EBITDA.

19.2 The Business Plan

- When evaluating an acquisition it is necessary to look in detail at the company's operations, investments, and capital structure, and to assess its potential for improvements and future growth.

19.3 Building the Financial Model

- The value of an investment ultimately depends on the firm's future cash flows. To estimate cash flows, one must first develop forecasts for the target firm's operations, investments, and capital structure.
- A financial model may be used to project the future cash flows from an investment.
  - A pro forma income statement projects the firm's earnings under a given set of hypothetical assumptions.
  - The financial model should also consider future working capital needs and capital expenditures to estimate future free cash flows.
  - Based on these estimates, we can forecast the balance sheet and statement of cash flows.

- When forecasting the balance sheet, we must first adjust the firm's initial balance sheet to reflect the transaction, including:

$$\text{New Goodwill} = \text{Acquisition Price} - \text{Value of Net Assets Acquired} \tag{19.10}$$

$$\text{New Stockholders' Equity} = \text{Equity Contributions} - \text{Expensed Transaction Fees} \tag{19.11}$$

- Checking whether the balance sheet balances is an important audit tool for the consistency of the financial model.

19.4 Estimating the Cost of Capital

- To value an investment, we need to assess its risk and estimate an appropriate cost of capital. One method for doing so is to use the CAPM.
  - Use the CAPM to estimate the equity cost of capital for comparable firms, based on their equity betas.
  - Given an estimate of each comparable firm's equity beta, unlever the beta based on the firm's capital structure.
  - Use the CAPM and the estimates of unlevered betas for comparable firms to estimate the unlevered cost of capital for the investment.

19.5 Valuing the Investment

- In addition to forecasting cash flows for a few years, we need to estimate the firm's continuation value at the end of the forecast horizon.
  - One method is to use a valuation multiple based on comparable firms.
  - To estimate a continuation value in year T using discounted cash flows, it is common practice to assume a constant expected growth rate g and a constant debt-equity ratio:

$$\text{Enterprise Value in Year } T = V_T^L = \frac{FCF_{T+1}}{r_{wacc} - g} \tag{19.15}$$

- Given the forecasted cash flows and an estimate of the cost of capital, the final step is to combine these inputs to estimate the value of the opportunity. We may use the valuation methods described in Chapter 18 to calculate firm value.
- While the NPV method is the most reliable approach for evaluating an investment, practitioners often use the IRR and cash multiple as alternative valuation metrics.
  - We use the cash flows over the lifetime of the investment to calculate the IRR.
  - The cash multiple for an investment is the ratio of the total cash received to the total cash invested:

$$\text{Cash Multiple} = \frac{\text{Total Cash Received}}{\text{Total Cash Invested}} \tag{19.20}$$

19.6 Sensitivity Analysis

- Sensitivity analysis is useful for evaluating the uncertainty of estimates used for valuation, and the impact of this uncertainty on the value of the deal.

Key Terms

cash multiple (multiple of money, absolute return) *p. 716*
pro forma *p. 697*
unlevered P/E ratio *p. 710*

Further Reading

For more detail on the issues involved in the valuation and financial modeling of companies and projects, see: T. Koller, M. Goedhart, and D. Wessels, *Valuation: Measuring and Managing the Value of Companies* (John Wiley & Sons, 2010); S. Benninga and O. Sarig, *Corporate Finance: A Valuation Approach* (McGraw-Hill/Irwin, 1996); E. Arzac, *Valuation for Mergers, Buyouts and Restructuring*

(John Wiley & Sons, 2007); S. Pratt, R. Reilly, and R. Schweihs, *Valuing a Business: The Analysis and Appraisal of Closely Held Companies* (McGraw-Hill, 2007); and J. Rosenbaum and J. Pearl, *Investment Banking* (John Wiley & Sons, 2009).

Problems

All problems are available in MyFinanceLab. *An asterisk (*) indicates problems with a higher level of difficulty.*

Valuation Using Comparables

1. You would like to compare Ideko's profitability to its competitors' profitability using the EBITDA/sales multiple. Given Ideko's current sales of $75 million, use the information in Table 19.2 to compute a range of EBITDA for Ideko assuming it is run as profitably as its competitors.

The Business Plan

2. Assume that Ideko's market share will increase by 0.5% per year rather than the 1% used in the chapter. What production capacity will Ideko require each year? When will an expansion become necessary (when production volume will exceed the current level by 50%)?

3. Under the assumption that Ideko market share will increase by 0.5% per year, you determine that the plant will require an expansion in 2010. The cost of this expansion will be $15 million. Assuming the financing of the expansion will be delayed accordingly, calculate the projected interest payments and the amount of the projected interest tax shields (assuming that the interest rates on the term loans remain the same as in the chapter) through 2010.

Building the Financial Model

4. Under the assumption that Ideko's market share will increase by 0.5% per year (and the investment and financing will be adjusted as described in Problem 3), you project the following depreciation:

		Year	2005	2006	2007	2008	2009	2010
Fixed Assets and Capital Investment ($ 000)								
2	New Investment		5,000	5,000	5,000	5,000	5,000	20,000
3	Depreciation		(5,500)	(5,450)	(5,405)	(5,365)	(5,328)	(6,795)

Using this information, project net income through 2010 (that is, reproduce Table 19.7 under the new assumptions).

5. Under the assumptions that Ideko's market share will increase by 0.5% per year (implying that the investment, financing, and depreciation will be adjusted as described in Problems 3 and 4) and that the forecasts in Table 19.8 remain the same, calculate Ideko's working capital requirements though 2010 (that is, reproduce Table 19.9 under the new assumptions).

6. Under the assumptions that Ideko's market share will increase by 0.5% per year (implying that the investment, financing, and depreciation will be adjusted as described in Problems 3 and 4) but that the projected improvements in net working capital do not transpire (so the numbers in Table 19.8 remain at their 2005 levels through 2010), calculate Ideko's working capital requirements though 2010 (that is, reproduce Table 19.9 under these assumptions).

7. Forecast Ideko's free cash flow (reproduce Table 19.10), assuming Ideko's market share will increase by 0.5% per year; investment, financing, and depreciation will be adjusted accordingly; and the projected improvements in working capital occur (that is, under the assumptions in Problem 5).

8. Forecast Ideko's free cash flow (reproduce Table 19.10), assuming Ideko's market share will increase by 0.5% per year; investment, financing, and depreciation will be adjusted accordingly;

and the projected improvements in working capital do *not* occur (that is, under the assumptions in Problem 6).

***9.** Reproduce Ideko's balance sheet and statement of cash flows, assuming Ideko's market share will increase by 0.5% per year; investment, financing, and depreciation will be adjusted accordingly; and the projected improvements in working capital occur (that is, under the assumptions in Problem 5).

***10.** Reproduce Ideko's balance sheet and statement of cash flows, assuming Ideko's market share will increase by 0.5% per year; investment, financing, and depreciation will be adjusted accordingly; and the projected improvements in working capital do *not* occur (that is, under the assumptions in Problem 6).

Estimating the Cost of Capital

11. Calculate Ideko's unlevered cost of capital when Ideko's unlevered beta is 1.1 rather than 1.2, and all other required estimates are the same as in the chapter.

12. Calculate Ideko's unlevered cost of capital when the market risk premium is 6% rather than 5%, the risk-free rate is 5% rather than 4%, and all other required estimates are the same as in the chapter.

Valuing the Investment

13. Using the information produced in the income statement in Problem 4, use EBITDA as a multiple to estimate the continuation value in 2010, assuming the current value remains unchanged (reproduce Table 19.15). Infer the EV/sales and the unlevered and levered P/E ratios implied by the continuation value you calculated.

14. How does the assumption on future improvements in working capital affect your answer to Problem 13?

15. Approximately what expected future long-run growth rate would provide the same EBITDA multiple in 2010 as Ideko has today (i.e., 9.1)? Assume that the future debt-to-value ratio is held constant at 40%; the debt cost of capital is 6.8%; Ideko's market share will increase by 0.5% per year until 2010; investment, financing, and depreciation will be adjusted accordingly; and the projected improvements in working capital occur (i.e., the assumptions in Problem 5).

16. Approximately what expected future long-run growth rate would provide the same EBITDA multiple in 2010 as Ideko has today (i.e., 9.1)? Assume that the future debt-to-value ratio is held constant at 40%; the debt cost of capital is 6.8%; Ideko's market share will increase by 0.5% per year; investment, financing, and depreciation will be adjusted accordingly; and the projected improvements in working capital do *not* occur (i.e., the assumptions in Problem 6).

17. Using the APV method, estimate the value of Ideko and the NPV of the deal using the continuation value you calculated in Problem 13 and the unlevered cost of capital estimate in Section 19.4. Assume that the debt cost of capital is 6.8%; Ideko's market share will increase by 0.5% per year until 2010; investment, financing, and depreciation will be adjusted accordingly; and the projected improvements in working capital occur (i.e., the assumptions in Problem 5).

18. Using the APV method, estimate the value of Ideko and the NPV of the deal using the continuation value you calculated in Problem 13 and the unlevered cost of capital estimate in Section 19.4. Assume that the debt cost of capital is 6.8%; Ideko's market share will increase by 0.5% per year; investment, financing, and depreciation will be adjusted accordingly; and the projected improvements in working capital do *not* occur (i.e., the assumptions in Problem 6).

19. Use your answers from Problems 17 and 18 to infer the value today of the projected improvements in working capital under the assumptions that Ideko's market share will increase by 0.5% per year and that investment, financing, and depreciation will be adjusted accordingly.

CHAPTER 19 APPENDIX

NOTATION

r_E equity cost of capital

Compensating Management

The success of KKP's investment critically depends on its ability to execute the operational improvements laid out in its business plan. KKP has learned from experience that it is much more likely to achieve its goals if the management team responsible for implementing the changes is given a strong incentive to succeed. KKP therefore considers allocating 10% of Ideko's equity to a management incentive plan. This equity stake would be vested over the next five years, and it would provide Ideko's senior executives with a strong financial interest in the success of the venture. What is the cost to KKP of providing this equity stake to the management team? How will this incentive plan affect the NPV of the acquisition?

To determine the value of the acquisition to KKP, we must include the cost of the 10% equity stake granted to management. Because the grant vests after five years, management will not receive any of the dividends paid by Ideko during that time. Instead, management will receive the equity in five years time, at which point we have estimated the value of Ideko's equity to be \$172 million (see Table 19.15). Thus, the cost of management's stake in 2010 is equal to 10% × \$172 million = \$17.2 million according to our estimate. We must determine the present value of this amount today.

Because the payment to the managers is an equity claim, to compute its present value we must use an equity cost of capital. We take an FTE valuation approach to estimate the cost of management's share in Ideko, shown in the spreadsheet in Table 19A.1.

To compute Ideko's equity cost of capital r_E, we use Eq. 18.20, which applies when the debt levels of the firm follow a known schedule:

$$r_E = r_U + \frac{D - T^s}{E}(r_U - r_D)$$

Using the debt, equity, and tax shield values from the spreadsheet in Table 19.17 to compute the effective leverage ratio $(D - T^s)/E$, we compute r_E each year as shown in the spreadsheet. We then compute the cost of management's equity share by discounting at this rate:

$$\text{Cost of Management's Share}_t = \frac{\text{Cost of Management's Share}_{t+1}}{1 + r_E(t)} \qquad (19A.1)$$

Once we have determined the cost of management's equity share, we deduct it from the total value of Ideko's equity (from Table 19.17) to determine the value of KKP's share of Ideko's equity, shown as the last line of the spreadsheet. Given the initial cost of the acquisition to KKP of \$53 million, KKP's NPV from the investment, including the cost of management's compensation, is \$103.58 million − \$53 million = \$50.58 million.

TABLE 19A.1 SPREADSHEET **FTE Estimate of the Cost of Management's Share and KKP's Equity Value**

	Year	2005	2006	2007	2008	2009	2010
Management/KKP Share (\$ 000)							
1	Management Payoff (10% share)						17,205
2	Effective Leverage $(D - T^s)/E$	0.792	0.771	0.715	0.778	0.745	
3	Equity Cost of Capital r_E	12.53%	12.47%	12.29%	12.49%	12.38%	
4	**Cost of Management's Share**	**(9,576)**	**(10,777)**	**(12,120)**	**(13,610)**	**(15,309)**	**(17,205)**
5	Ideko Equity Value	113,160	118,287	130,047	141,294	157,566	172,052
6	**KKP Equity**	**103,583**	**107,511**	**117,927**	**127,684**	**142,256**	**154,847**

PART

7

Options

THE LAW OF ONE PRICE CONNECTION. Having developed the tools to make current investment decisions, we turn to settings in which the firm or an investor has the option to make a future investment decision. Chapter 20 introduces financial options, which give investors the right to buy or sell a security in the future. Financial options are an important tool for corporate financial managers seeking to manage or evaluate risk. Options are an example of a derivative security. In the last 30 years, there has been enormous growth in the derivative securities markets in general and options markets in particular. This growth can be traced directly to the discovery of methods for valuing options, which we derive in Chapter 21 using the Law of One Price. An important corporate application of option theory is in the area of real investment decision making. Future investment decisions within the firm are known as real options and Chapter 22 applies real option theory to corporate decision making.

CHAPTER

20 Financial Options

NOTATION

PV	present value
Div	dividend
C	call option price
P	put option price
S	stock price
K	strike price
dis	discount from face value
NPV	net present value

IN THIS CHAPTER, WE INTRODUCE THE FINANCIAL OPTION, A financial contract between two parties. Since the introduction of publicly traded options on the Chicago Board Options Exchange (CBOE) in 1973, financial options have become one of the most important and actively traded financial assets and important tools for corporate financial managers. Many large corporations have operations in different parts of the world, so they face exposure to exchange rate risk and other types of business risk. To control this risk, they use options as part of their corporate risk management practices. In addition, we can think of the capitalization of the firm itself—that is, its mix of debt and equity—as options on the underlying assets of the firm. As we will see, viewing the firm's capitalization in this way yields important insights into the firm's capital structure as well as the conflicts of interests that arise between equity investors and debt investors.

Before we can discuss the corporate applications of options, we first need to understand what options are and what factors affect their value. In this chapter, we provide an overview of the basic types of financial options, introduce important terminology, and describe the payoffs to various option-based strategies. We next discuss the factors that affect option prices. Finally, we model the equity and debt of the firm as options to gain insight into the conflicts of interest between equity and debt holders, as well as the pricing of risky debt.

20.1 Option Basics

A **financial option** contract gives its owner the right (but not the obligation) to purchase or sell an asset at a fixed price at some future date. Two distinct kinds of option contracts exist: call options and put options. A **call option** gives the owner the right to *buy* the asset; a **put option** gives the owner the right to *sell* the asset. Because an option is a contract between two parties, for every owner of a financial option, there is also an **option writer**, the person who takes the other side of the contract.

The most commonly encountered option contracts are options on shares of stock. A stock option gives the holder the option to buy or sell a share of stock on or before a given date for a given price. For example, a call option on 3M Corporation stock might give the holder the right to purchase a share of 3M for $75 per share at any time up to, for example, January 18, 2019. Similarly, a put option on 3M stock might give the holder the right to sell a share of 3M stock for $50 per share at any time up to, say, January 19, 2018.

Understanding Option Contracts

Practitioners use specific words to describe the details of option contracts. When a holder of an option enforces the agreement and buys or sells a share of stock at the agreed-upon price, he is **exercising** the option. The price at which the holder buys or sells the share of stock when the option is exercised is called the **strike price** or **exercise price**.

There are two kinds of options. **American options**, the most common kind, allow their holders to exercise the option on any date up to and including a final date called the **expiration date**. **European options** allow their holders to exercise the option *only* on the expiration date—holders cannot exercise before the expiration date. The names *American* and *European* have nothing to do with the location where the options are traded: Both types are traded worldwide.

An option contract is a contract between two parties. The option buyer, also called the option holder, holds the right to exercise the option and has a *long* position in the contract. The option seller, also called the option writer, sells (or writes) the option and has a *short* position in the contract. Because the long side has the option to exercise, the short side has an *obligation* to fulfill the contract. For example, suppose you own a call option on Hewlett-Packard stock with an exercise price of $10. Hewlett-Packard stock is currently trading for $25, so you decide to exercise the option. The person holding the short position in the contract is obligated to sell you a share of Hewlett-Packard stock for $10. Your gain, the $15 difference between the price you pay for the share of stock and the price at which you can sell the share in the market, is the short position's loss.

Investors exercise options only when they stand to gain something. Consequently, whenever an option is exercised, the person holding the short position funds the gain. That is, the obligation will be costly. Why, then, do people write options? The answer is that when you sell an option you get paid for it—options always have positive prices. The market price of the option is also called the **option premium**. This upfront payment compensates the seller for the risk of loss in the event that the option holder chooses to exercise the option.

Interpreting Stock Option Quotations

Stock options are traded on organized exchanges. The oldest and largest is the Chicago Board Options Exchange (CBOE). By convention, all traded options expire on the Saturday following the third Friday of the month.

TABLE 20.1 Option Quotes for Amazon.com Stock

AMZN **77.03 +1.40**

Jul 08 2009 @ 15:26 ET **Bid** 77.02 **Ask** 77.03 **Size** 1 x 3 **Vol** 6548487

Calls	Last Sale	Net	Bid	Ask	Vol	Open Int	Puts	Last Sale	Net	Bid	Ask	Vol	Open Int
09 Jul 70.00 (ZQN GN-E)	7.65	1.60	7.20	7.30	221	2637	09 Jul 70.00 (ZQN SN-E)	0.36	−0.18	0.36	0.38	684	11031
09 Jul 75.00 (ZQN GO-E)	3.35	0.86	3.20	3.30	943	6883	09 Jul 75.00 (ZQN SO-E)	1.30	−0.66	1.38	1.40	2394	15545
09 Jul 80.00 (QZN GP-E)	0.94	0.24	0.93	0.96	2456	9877	09 Jul 80.00 (QZN SP-E)	4.15	−1.05	4.00	4.10	700	10718
09 Jul 85.00 (QZN GQ-E)	0.22	0.07	0.19	0.21	497	26679	09 Jul 85.00 (QZN SQ-E)	8.25	−1.25	8.25	8.35	112	7215
09 Aug 70.00 (ZQN HN-E)	9.75	1.04	9.60	9.70	51	326	09 Aug 70.00 (ZQN TN-E)	2.77	−0.39	2.75	2.79	225	1979
09 Aug 75.00 (ZQN HO-E)	6.50	0.70	6.40	6.50	65	1108	09 Aug 75.00 (ZQN TO-E)	4.60	−0.55	4.55	4.60	2322	6832
09 Aug 80.00 (QZN HP-E)	4.00	0.50	3.90	4.00	172	2462	09 Aug 80.00 (QZN TP-E)	6.95	−0.95	7.05	7.15	145	2335
09 Aug 85.00 (QZN HQ-E)	2.15	0.15	2.22	2.26	833	5399	09 Aug 85.00 (QZN TQ-E)	10.15	−1.00	10.30	10.40	43	4599

Source: Chicago Board Options Exchange at www.cboe.com

Table 20.1 shows near-term options on Amazon taken from the CBOE Web site (www.cboe.com) on July 8, 2009. Call options are listed on the left and put options on the right. Each line corresponds to a particular option. The first two digits in the option name refer to the year of expiration. The option name also includes the month of expiration, the strike or exercise price, and the ticker symbol of the individual option (in parentheses). Looking at Table 20.1, the first line of the left column is a call option with an exercise price of $70 that expires on the Saturday following the third Friday of July 2009 (July 18). The columns to the right of the name display market data for the option. The first of these columns shows the last sale price, followed by the net change from the previous day's last reported sales price, the current bid and ask prices, and the daily volume.[1] The final column is the **open interest**, the total number of outstanding contracts of that option.

Above the table, we find information about the stock itself. In this case, Amazon's stock last traded at a price of $77.03 per share. We also see the current bid and ask prices for the stock, the size trade (in hundreds of shares) available at these prices, as well as the volume of trade.

When the exercise price of an option is equal to the current price of the stock, the option is said to be **at-the-money**. Notice that, especially for the near-term options, much of the trading occurs in options that are closest to being at-the-money—that is, calls and puts with exercise prices of either $75 or $80. Note how the July 80 calls have high volume. They last traded for $0.94, midway between the current bid price ($0.93) and the ask price ($0.96), which indicates that the trade likely occurred recently. If it were not recent, the last sale price might be far from the current bid and ask.

Stock option contracts are always written on 100 shares of stock. If, for instance, you decided to purchase one July 75 call contract, you would be purchasing an option to buy 100 shares at $75 per share. Option prices are quoted on a per-share basis, so the ask price of $3.30 implies that you would pay $100 \times 3.30 = \$330$ for the contract. Similarly, if you decide to buy a July 70 put contract, you would pay $100 \times 0.38 = \$38$ for the option to sell 100 shares of Amazon stock for $70 per share.

[1] If no trade has occurred that day, the last sale price is from the previous day, and "pc" appears in the net change column.

Note from Table 20.1 that for each expiration date, call options with lower strike prices have higher market prices—the right to buy the stock at a lower price is more valuable than the right to buy it for a higher price. Conversely, because the put option gives the holder the right to sell the stock at the strike price, for the same expiration date, puts with higher strikes are more valuable. On the other hand, holding fixed the strike price, both calls and puts are more expensive for a longer time to expiration. Because these options are American-style options that can be exercised at any time, having the right to buy or sell for a longer period is more valuable.

If the payoff from exercising an option immediately is positive, the option is said to be **in-the-money**. Call options with strike prices below the current stock price are in-the-money, as are put options with strike prices above the current stock price. Conversely, if the payoff from exercising the option immediately is negative, the option is **out-of-the-money**. Call options with strike prices above the current stock price are out-of-the-money, as are put options with strike prices below the current stock price. Of course, a holder would not exercise an out-of-the-money option. Options where the strike price and the stock price are very far apart are referred to as **deep in-the-money** or **deep out-of-the-money**.

EXAMPLE 20.1 Purchasing Options

Problem

It is the afternoon of July 8, 2009, and you have decided to purchase 10 August call contracts on Amazon stock with an exercise price of $80. Because you are buying, you must pay the ask price. How much money will this purchase cost you? Is this option in-the-money or out-of-the-money?

Solution

From Table 20.1, the ask price of this option is $4.00. You are purchasing 10 contracts and each contract is on 100 shares, so the transaction will cost $4.00 \times 10 \times 100 = \$4,000$ (ignoring any brokerage fees). Because this is a call option and the exercise price is above the current stock price ($77.03), the option is currently out-of-the-money.

Options on Other Financial Securities

Although the most commonly traded options are written on stocks, options on other financial assets do exist. Perhaps the most well-known are options on stock indexes such as the S&P 100 index, the S&P 500 index, the Dow Jones Industrial index, and the NYSE index. These options have become very popular because they allow investors to protect the value of their investments from adverse market changes. As we will see shortly, a stock index put option can be used to offset the losses on an investor's portfolio in a market downturn. Using an option to reduce risk in this way is called **hedging**. Options also allow investors to **speculate**, or place a bet on the direction in which they believe the market is likely to move. Purchasing a call, for example, allows investors to bet on a market rise with a much smaller investment than investing in the market index itself.

Options are also traded on Treasury securities. These options allow investors to bet on or hedge interest rate risk. Similarly, options on currencies and commodities allow investors to hedge or speculate on risks in these markets.

CONCEPT CHECK

1. What is the difference between an American option and a European option?
2. Does the holder of an option have to exercise it?
3. Why does an investor who writes (shorts) an option have an obligation?

20.2 Option Payoffs at Expiration

From the Law of One Price, the value of any security is determined by the future cash flows an investor receives from owning it. Therefore, before we can assess what an option is worth, we must determine an option's payoff at the time of expiration.

Long Position in an Option Contract

Assume you own an option with a strike price of \$20. If, on the expiration date, the stock price is greater than the strike price, say \$30, you can make money by exercising the call (by paying \$20, the strike price, for the stock) and immediately selling the stock in the open market for \$30. The \$10 difference is what the option is worth. Consequently, when the stock price on the expiration date exceeds the strike price, the value of the call is the difference between the stock price and the strike price. When the stock price is less than the strike price at expiration, the holder will not exercise the call, so the option is worth nothing. We plot these payoffs in Figure 20.1.[2]

Thus, if S is the stock price at expiration, K is the exercise price, and C is the value of the call option, the value of the call at expiration is

Call Value at Expiration

$$C = max(S - K, 0) \tag{20.1}$$

FIGURE 20.1

Payoff of a Call Option with a Strike Price of \$20 at Expiration

If the stock price is greater than the strike price (\$20), the call will be exercised, and the holder's payoff is the difference between the stock price and the strike price. If the stock price is less than the strike price, the call will not be exercised, and so has no value.

[2]Payoff diagrams like the ones in this chapter seem to have been introduced by Louis Bachelier in 1900 in his book, *Theorie de la Speculation* (Villars, 1900). Reprinted in English in P. Cootner (ed.), *The Random Character of Stock Market Prices* (M.I.T. Press, 1964).

where *max* is the maximum of the two quantities in the parentheses. The call's value is the maximum of the difference between the stock price and the strike price, $S - K$, and zero.

The holder of a put option will exercise the option if the stock price S is below the strike price K. Because the holder receives K when the stock is worth S, the holder's gain is equal to $K - S$. Thus, the value of a put at expiration is

Put Price at Expiration

$$P = max(K - S, 0) \tag{20.2}$$

EXAMPLE 20.2 **Payoff of a Put Option at Maturity**

Problem

You own a put option on Oracle Corporation stock with an exercise price of $20 that expires today. Plot the value of this option as a function of the stock price.

Solution

Let S be the stock price and P be the value of the put option. The value of the option is

$$P = max(20 - S, 0)$$

Plotting this function gives

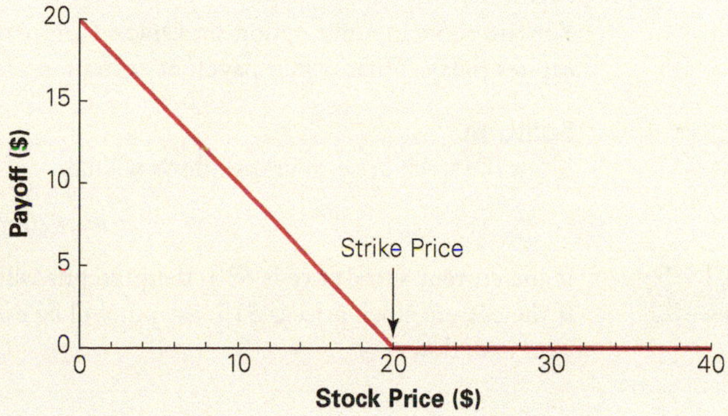

Short Position in an Option Contract

An investor holding a short position in an option has an obligation: This investor takes the opposite side of the contract to the investor who is long. Thus, the short position's cash flows are the negative of the long position's cash flows. Because an investor who is long an option can only receive money at expiration—that is, the investor will not exercise an option that is out-of-the-money—a short investor can only pay money.

To demonstrate, assume you have a short position in a call option with an exercise price of $20. If the stock price is greater than the strike price of a call—for example, $25—the holder will exercise the option. You then have the obligation to sell the stock for the strike price of $20. Because you must purchase the stock at the market price of $25, you lose the difference between the two prices, or $5. However, if the stock price is less than the strike price at the expiration date, the holder will not exercise the option, so in this case you lose nothing; you have no obligation. We plot these payoffs in Figure 20.2.

FIGURE 20.2

Short Position in a Call Option at Expiration

If the stock price is greater than the strike price, the call will be exercised, so a person on the short side of a call will lose the difference between the stock price and the strike price. If the stock price is less than the strike price, the call will not be exercised, and the seller will have no obligation.

EXAMPLE 20.3 Payoff of a Short Position in a Put Option

Problem

You are short in a put option on Oracle Corporation stock with an exercise price of $20 that expires today. What is your payoff at expiration as a function of the stock price?

Solution

If S is the stock price, your cash flows will be

$$-max(20 - S, 0)$$

If the current stock price is $30, then the put will not be exercised and you will owe nothing. If the current stock price is $15, the put will be exercised and you will lose $5. The figure plots your cash flows:

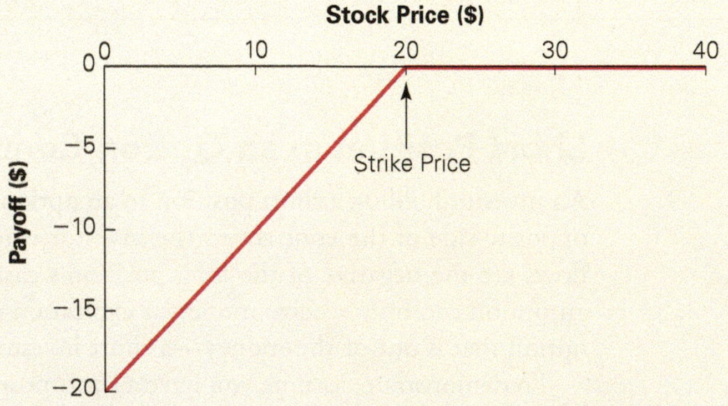

Notice that because the stock price cannot fall below zero, the downside for a short position in a put option is limited to the strike price of the option, as in Example 20.3. A short position in a call, however, has no limit on the downside (see Figure 20.2).

FIGURE 20.3

Profit from Holding a Call Option to Expiration

The curves show the profit per share from purchasing the August call options in Table 20.1 on July 8, 2009, financing this purchase by borrowing at 3%, and holding the position until the expiration date.

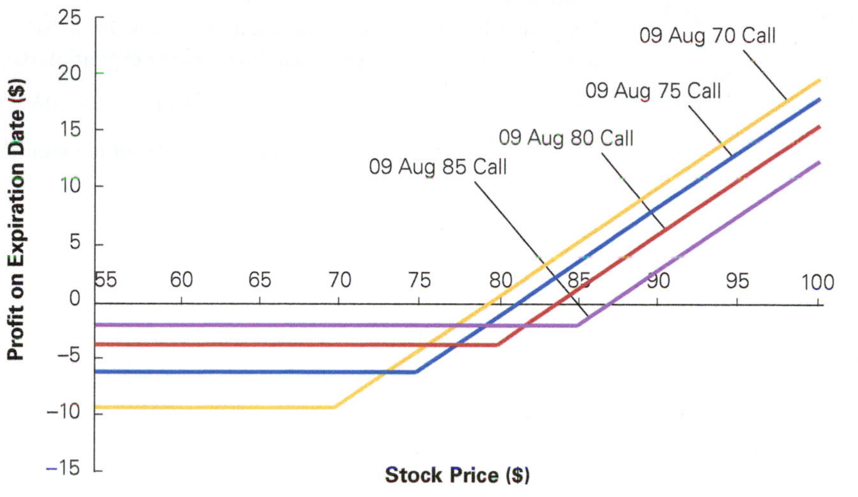

Profits for Holding an Option to Expiration

Although payouts on a long position in an option contract are never negative, the profit from purchasing an option and holding it to expiration could well be negative because the payout at expiration might be less than the initial cost of the option.

To see how this works, let's consider the potential profits from purchasing the 09 August 80 call option on Amazon stock quoted in Table 20.1. The option costs $4.00 and expires in 45 days. Assume you choose to finance the purchase by borrowing $4.00 at an interest rate of 3% per year. If the stock price at expiration is S, then the profit is the call payoff minus the amount owed on the loan: $max(S - 80, 0) - 4.00 \times 1.03^{45/365}$, shown as the red curve in Figure 20.3. Once the cost of the position is taken into account, you make a positive profit only if the stock price exceeds $84.01. As we can see from Table 20.1, the further in-the-money the option is, the higher its initial price and so the larger your potential loss. An out-of-the-money option has a smaller initial cost and hence a smaller potential loss, but the probability of a gain is also smaller because the point where profits become positive is higher.

Because a short position in an option is the other side of a long position, the profits from a short position in an option are just the negative of the profits of a long position. For example, a short position in an out-of-the-money call like the 09 August 85 Amazon call in Figure 20.3 produces a small positive profit if Amazon's stock is below $87.23, but leads to losses if the stock price is above $87.23.

EXAMPLE 20.4 **Profit on Holding a Position in a Put Option until Expiration**

Problem

Assume you decided to purchase each of the August put options quoted in Table 20.1 on July 8, 2009, and you financed each position by shorting a two-month bond with a yield of 3%. Plot the profit of each position as a function of the stock price on expiration.

Solution

Suppose S is the stock price on expiration, K is the strike price, and P is the price of each put option on July 8. Then your cash flows on the expiration date will be

$$\max(K - S, 0) - P \times 1.03^{45/365}$$

The plot is shown below. Note the same trade-off between the maximum loss and the potential for profit as for the call options.

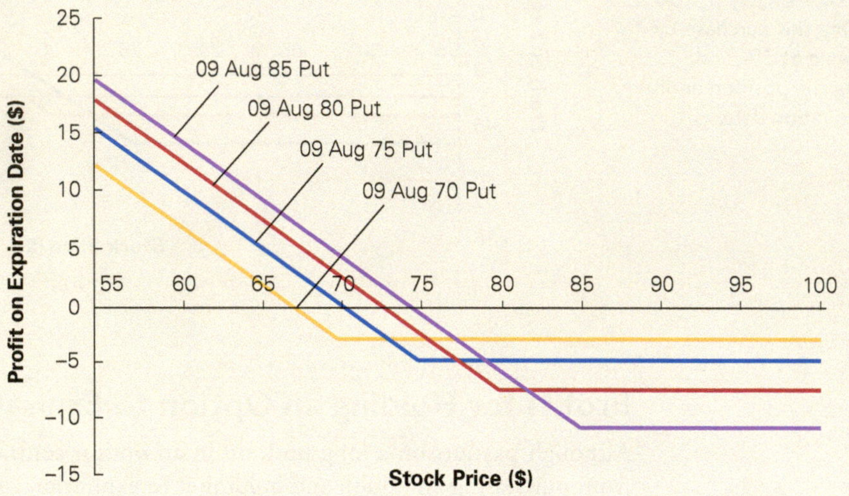

Returns for Holding an Option to Expiration

We can also compare options based on their potential returns. Figure 20.4 shows the return from purchasing one of the August 2009 options in Table 20.1 on July 8, 2009, and holding it until the expiration date. Let's begin by focusing on call options, shown in panel (a). In all cases, the maximum loss is 100%—the option may expire worthless. Notice how the curves change as a function of the strike price—the distribution of returns for out-of-the-money call options are more extreme than those for in-the-money calls. That is, an out-of-the-money call option is more likely to have a −100% return, but if the stock goes up sufficiently it will also have a much higher return than an in-the-money call option. Similarly, all call options have more extreme returns than the stock itself (given Amazon's initial price of $77.03, the range of stock prices shown in the plot represents returns of ±30%). As a consequence, the risk of a call option is amplified relative to the risk of the stock, and the amplification is greater for deeper out-of-the-money calls. Thus, if a stock had a positive beta, call options written on the stock will have even higher betas and expected returns than the stock itself.[3]

Now consider the returns for put options. Look carefully at panel (b) in Figure 20.4. The put position has a higher return with *low* stock prices; that is, if the stock has a positive beta, the put has a negative beta. Hence, put options on positive beta stocks have lower expected returns than the underlying stock. The deeper out-of-the-money the put option is, the more negative its beta, and the lower its expected return. As a result, put options are generally not held as an investment, but rather as insurance to hedge other risk in a portfolio.

[3]In Chapter 21, we explain how to calculate the expected return and risk of an option. In doing so, we will derive these relations rigorously.

FIGURE 20.4 **Option Returns from Purchasing an Option and Holding It to Expiration**

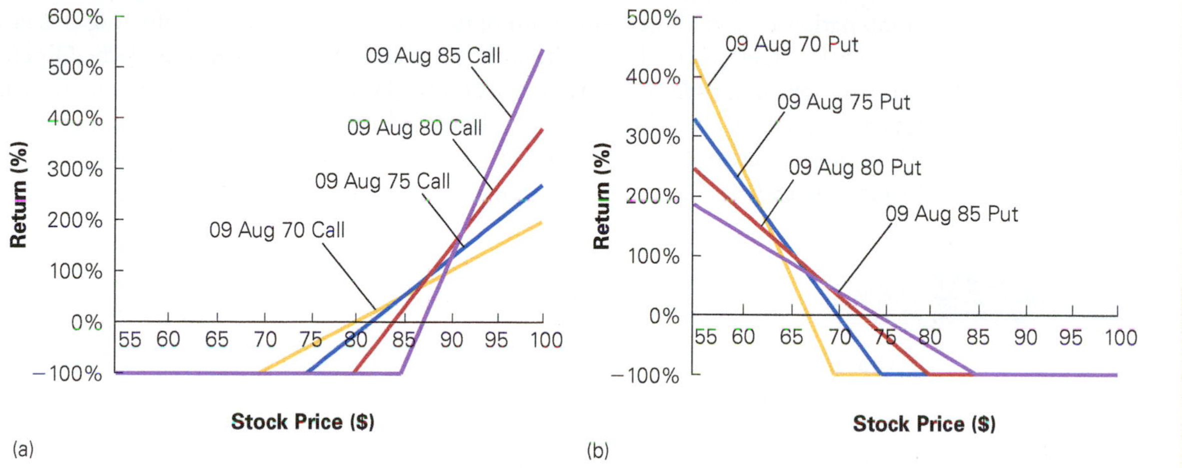

(a) The return on the expiration date from purchasing one of the August call options in Table 20.1 on July 8, 2009, and holding the position until the expiration date; (b) the same return for the August put options in the table.

Combinations of Options

Sometimes investors combine option positions by holding a portfolio of options. In this section, we describe the most common combinations.

Straddle. What would happen at expiration if you were long both a put option and a call option with the same strike price? Figure 20.5 shows the payout on the expiration date of both options.

FIGURE 20.5

Payoff and Profit from a Straddle

A combination of a long position in a put and a call with the same strike price and expiration date provides a positive payoff (solid line) so long as the stock price does not equal the strike price. After deducting the cost of the options, the profit is negative for stock prices close to the strike price and positive elsewhere (dashed line).

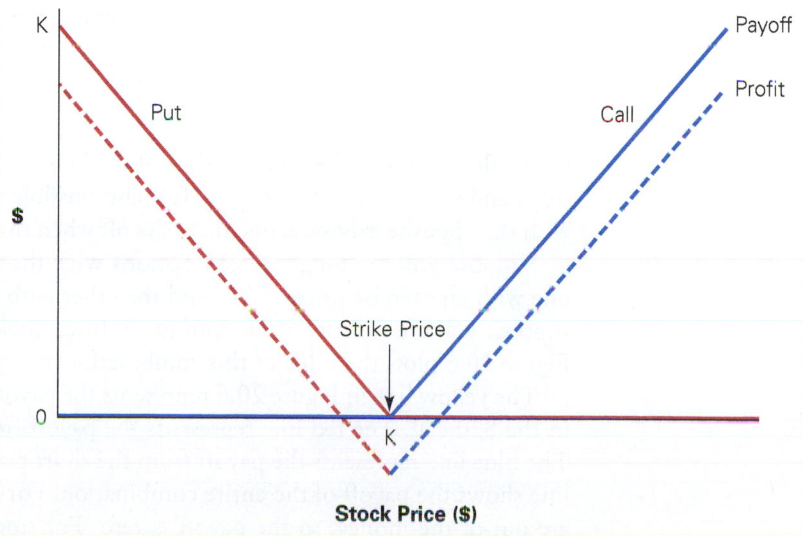

By combining a call option (blue line) with a put option (red line), you will receive cash so long as the options do not expire at-the-money. The farther away from the money the options are, the more money you will make (solid line). However, to construct the combination requires purchasing both options, so the profits after deducting this cost are negative for stock prices close to the strike price and positive elsewhere (dashed line). This combination of options is known as a **straddle**. This strategy is sometimes used by investors who expect the stock to be very volatile and move up or down a large amount, but who do not necessarily have a view on which direction the stock will move. Conversely, investors who expect the stock to end up near the strike price may choose to sell a straddle.

EXAMPLE 20.5 Strangle

Problem

You are long both a call option and a put option on Hewlett-Packard stock with the same expiration date. The exercise price of the call option is $40; the exercise price of the put option is $30. Plot the payoff of the combination at expiration.

Solution

The red line represents the put's payouts and the blue line represents the call's payouts. In this case, you do not receive money if the stock price is between the two strike prices. This option combination is known as a **strangle**.

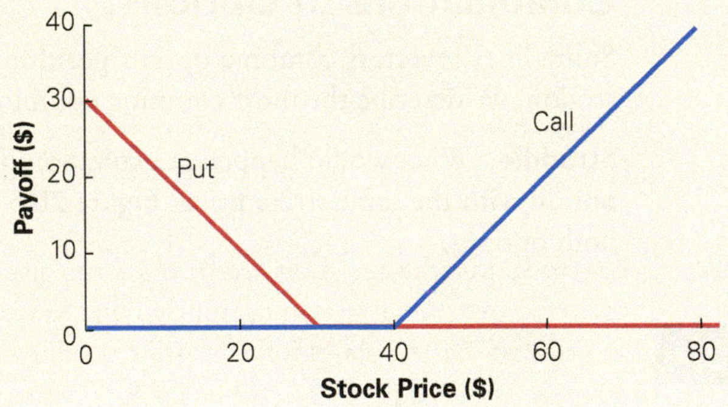

Butterfly Spread. The combination of options in Figure 20.5 makes money when the stock and strike prices are far apart. It is also possible to construct a combination of options with the opposite exposure: one that pays off when the stock price is close to the strike price.

Suppose you are long two call options with the same expiration date on Intel stock: one with an exercise price of $20 and the other with an exercise price of $40. In addition, suppose you are short two call options on Intel stock, both with an exercise price of $30. Figure 20.6 plots the value of this combination at expiration.

The yellow line in Figure 20.6 represents the payoff at expiration from the long position in the $20 call. The red line represents the payoff from the long position in the $40 call. The blue line represents the payoff from the short position in the two $30 calls. The black line shows the payoff of the entire combination. For stock prices less than $20, all options are out-of-the-money, so the payoff is zero. For stock prices greater than $40, the losses from the short position in the $30 calls exactly offset the gain from $20 and $40 options,

FIGURE 20.6

Butterfly Spread

The yellow line represents the payoff from a long position in a \$20 call. The red line represents the payoff from a long position in a \$40 call. The blue line represents the payoff from a short position in two \$30 calls. The black line shows the payoff of the entire combination, called a butterfly spread, at expiration.

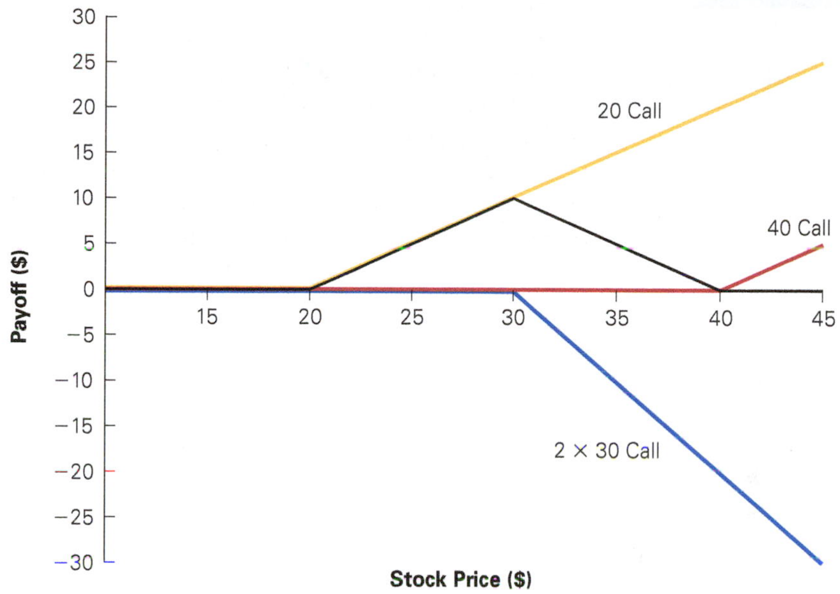

and the value of the entire portfolio of options is zero.[4] Between \$20 and \$40, however, the payoff is positive. It reaches a maximum at \$30. Practitioners call this combination of options a **butterfly spread**.

Because the payoff of the butterfly spread is positive, it must have a positive initial cost. (Otherwise, it would be an arbitrage opportunity.) Therefore, the cost of the \$20 and \$40 call options must exceed the proceeds from selling two \$30 call options.

Portfolio Insurance. Let's see how we can use combinations of options to insure a stock against a loss. Assume you currently own Amazon stock and you would like to insure the stock against the possibility of a price decline. To do so, you could simply sell the stock, but you would also give up the possibility of making money if the stock price increases. How can you insure against a loss without relinquishing the upside? You can purchase a put option, sometimes known as a **protective put**.

For example, suppose you want to insure against the possibility that the price of Amazon stock will drop below \$45. You decide to purchase an August 45 European put option. If Amazon stock is above \$45 in August, you keep the stock, but if it is below \$45 you exercise your put and sell it for \$45. Thus, you get the upside, but are insured against a drop in the price of Amazon's stock. The orange line in Figure 20.7 (a) shows the value of the combined position on the expiration date of the option.

You can use the same strategy to insure against a loss on an entire portfolio of stocks by using put options on the portfolio of stocks as a whole rather than just a single stock. Consequently, holding stocks and put options in this combination is known as **portfolio insurance**.

Purchasing a put option is not the only way to buy portfolio insurance. You can achieve exactly the same effect by purchasing a bond and a call option. Let's return to the insurance we purchased on Amazon stock. Amazon stock does not pay dividends, so there are no cash

[4] To see this, note that $(S - 20) + (S - 40) - 2(S - 30) = 0$.

FIGURE 20.7 **Portfolio Insurance**

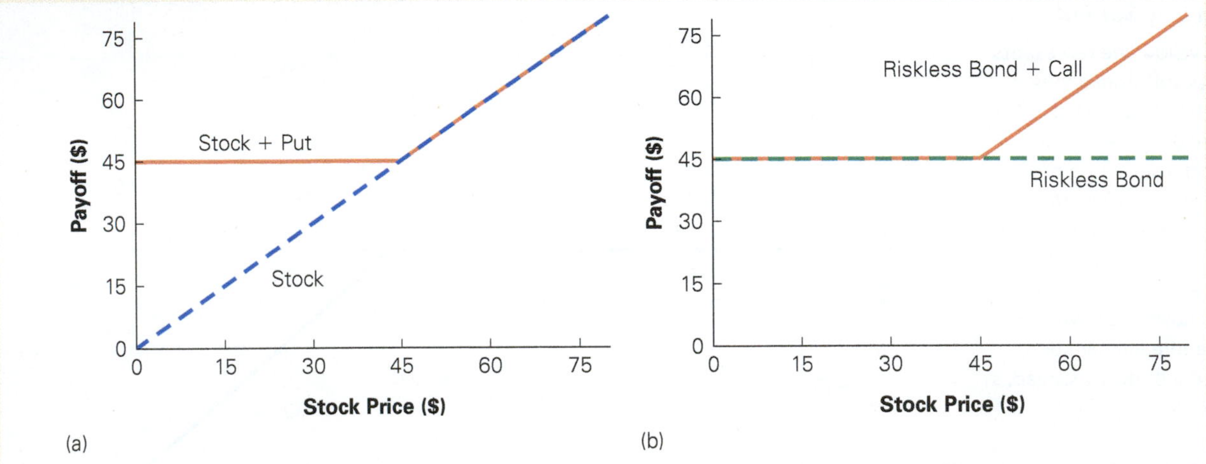

The plots show two different ways to insure against the possibility of the price of Amazon stock falling below \$45. The orange line in (a) indicates the value on the expiration date of a position that is long one share of Amazon stock and one European put option with a strike of \$45 (the blue dashed line is the payoff of the stock itself). The orange line in (b) shows the value on the expiration date of a position that is long a zero-coupon risk-free bond with a face value of \$45 and a European call option on Amazon with a strike price of \$45 (the green dashed line is the bond payoff).

flows before the expiration of the option. Thus, instead of holding a share of Amazon stock and a put, you could get the same payoff by purchasing a risk-free zero-coupon bond with a face value of \$45 and a European call option with a strike price of \$45. In this case, if Amazon is below \$45, you receive the payoff from the bond. If Amazon is above \$45, you can exercise the call and use the payoff from the bond to buy the stock for the strike price of \$45. The orange line in Figure 20.7(b) shows the value of the combined position on the expiration date of the option; it achieves exactly the same payoffs as owning the stock itself along with a put option.

CONCEPT CHECK

1. What is a straddle?
2. Explain how you can use put options to create portfolio insurance. How can you create portfolio insurance using call options?

20.3 Put-Call Parity

Consider the two different ways to construct portfolio insurance illustrated in Figure 20.7: (1) purchase the stock and a put or (2) purchase a bond and a call. Because both positions provide exactly the same payoff, the Law of One Price requires that they must have the same price.

Let's write this concept more formally. Let K be the strike price of the option (the price we want to ensure that the stock will not drop below), C be the call price, P be the put price, and S be the stock price. Then, if both positions have the same price,

$$S + P = PV(K) + C$$

The left side of this equation is the cost of buying the stock and a put (with a strike price of K); the right side is the cost of buying a zero-coupon bond with face value K and a call option (with a strike price of K). Recall that the price of a zero-coupon bond is just the present value of its face value, which we have denoted by $PV(K)$. Rearranging terms gives an expression for the price of a European call option for a non-dividend-paying stock:

$$C = P + S - PV(K) \qquad (20.3)$$

This relationship between the value of the stock, the bond, and call and put options is known as **put-call parity**. It says that the price of a European call equals the price of the stock plus an otherwise identical put minus the price of a bond that matures on the exercise date of the option. In other words, you can think of a call as a combination of a levered position in the stock, $S - PV(K)$, plus insurance against a drop in the stock price, the put P.

EXAMPLE 20.6 Using Put-Call Parity

Problem

You are an options dealer who deals in non-publicly traded options. One of your clients wants to purchase a one-year European call option on HAL Computer Systems stock with a strike price of \$20. Another dealer is willing to write a one-year European put option on HAL stock with a strike price of \$20, and sell you the put option for a price of \$3.50 per share. If HAL pays no dividends and is currently trading for \$18 per share, and if the risk-free interest rate is 6%, what is the lowest price you can charge for the option and guarantee yourself a profit?

Solution

Using put-call parity, we can replicate the payoff of the one-year call option with a strike price of \$20 by holding the following portfolio: Buy the one-year put option with a strike price of \$20 from the dealer, buy the stock, and sell a one-year risk-free zero-coupon bond with a face value of \$20. With this combination, we have the following final payoff depending on the final price of HAL stock in one year, S_1:

	Final HAL Stock Price	
	$S_1 < \$20$	$S_1 > \$20$
Buy Put Option	$20 - S_1$	0
Buy Stock	S_1	S_1
Sell Bond	-20	-20
Portfolio	0	$S_1 - 20$
Sell Call Option	0	$-(S_1 - 20)$
Total Payoff	0	0

Note that the final payoff of the portfolio of the three securities matches the payoff of a call option. Therefore, we can sell the call option to our client and have future payoff of zero no matter what happens. Doing so is worthwhile as long as we can sell the call option for more than the cost of the portfolio, which is

$$P + S - PV(K) = \$3.50 + \$18 - \$20/1.06 = \$2.632$$

What happens if the stock pays a dividend? In that case, the two different ways to construct portfolio insurance do not have the same payout because the stock will pay a dividend while the zero-coupon bond will not. Thus, the two strategies will cost the same to implement only if we add the present value of future dividends to the combination of the bond and the call:

$$S + P = PV(K) + PV(Div) + C$$

The left side of this equation is the value of the stock and a put; the right side is the value of a zero-coupon bond, a call option, and the future dividends paid by the stock during the life of the options, denoted by *Div*. Rearranging terms gives the general put-call parity formula:

Put-Call Parity

$$C = P + S - PV(Div) - PV(K) \tag{20.4}$$

In this case, the call is equivalent to having a levered position in the stock without dividends plus insurance against a fall in the stock price.

EXAMPLE 20.7 Using Options to Value Near-Term Dividends

Problem

It is February 2016 and you have been asked, in your position as a financial analyst, to compare the expected dividends of several popular stock indices over the next several years. Checking the markets, you find the following closing prices for each index, as well as for options expiring December 2018.

	Feb 2016	Dec 2018 Index Options		
Index	**Index Value**	**Strike Price**	**Call Price**	**Put Price**
DJIA	164.85	160	19.78	22.73
S&P 500	1929.80	1900	243.25	278.00
Nasdaq 100	4200.66	4200	636.35	666.85
Russell 2000	1022.08	1000	150.10	166.80

If the current risk-free interest rate is 0.90% for a December 2018 maturity, estimate the relative contribution of the near-term dividends to the value of each index.

Solution

Rearranging the Put-Call Parity relation gives:

$$PV(Div) = P - C + S - PV(K)$$

Applying this to the DJIA, we find that the expected present value of its dividends over the next 34 months is

$$PV(Div) = 22.73 - 19.78 + 164.85 - \frac{160}{1.009^{34/12}} = 11.81$$

Therefore, expected dividends through December 2018 represent 11.81/164.85 = 7.2% of the current value of DJIA index. Doing a similar calculation for the other indices, we find that near-term dividends account for 5.8% of the value of the S&P 500, 3.2% of the NASDAQ 100, and 6.2% of the Russell 2000.

CONCEPT CHECK

1. Explain put-call parity.
2. If a put option trades at a higher price from the value indicated by the put-call parity equation, what action should you take?

20.4 Factors Affecting Option Prices

Put-call parity gives the price of a European call option in terms of the price of a European put, the underlying stock, and a zero-coupon bond. Therefore, to compute the price of a call using put-call parity, you have to know the price of the put. In Chapter 21, we explain how to calculate the price of a call without knowing the price of the put. Before we get there, let's first investigate the factors that affect option prices.

Strike Price and Stock Price

As we noted earlier for the Amazon option quotes in Table 20.1, the value of an otherwise identical call option is higher if the strike price the holder must pay to buy the stock is lower. Because a put is the right to sell the stock, puts with a lower strike price are less valuable.

For a given strike price, the value of a call option is higher if the current price of the stock is higher, as there is a greater likelihood the option will end up in-the-money. Conversely, put options increase in value as the stock price falls.

Arbitrage Bounds on Option Prices

We have already seen that an option's price cannot be negative. Furthermore, because an American option carries all the same rights and privileges as an otherwise equivalent European option, it cannot be worth less than a European option. If it were, you could make arbitrage profits by selling a European call and using part of the proceeds to buy an otherwise equivalent American call option. Thus, *an American option cannot be worth less than its European counterpart.*

The maximum payoff for a put option occurs if the stock becomes worthless (if, say, the company files for bankruptcy). In that case, the put's payoff is equal to the strike price. Because this payoff is the highest possible, *a put option cannot be worth more than its strike price.*

For a call option, the lower the strike price, the more valuable the call option. If the call option had a strike price of zero, the holder would always exercise the option and receive the stock at no cost. This observation gives us an upper bound on the call price: *A call option cannot be worth more than the stock itself.*

The **intrinsic value** of an option is the value it would have if it expired immediately. Therefore, the intrinsic value is the amount by which the option is currently in-the-money, or zero if the option is out-of-the-money. If an American option is worth less than its intrinsic value, you could make arbitrage profits by purchasing the option and immediately exercising it. Thus, *an American option cannot be worth less than its intrinsic value.*

The **time value** of an option is the difference between the current option price and its intrinsic value. Because an American option cannot be worth less than its intrinsic value, it cannot have a negative time value.

Option Prices and the Exercise Date

For American options, the longer the time to the exercise date, the more valuable the option. To see why, let's consider two options: an option with one year until the exercise date and an option with six months until the exercise date. The holder of the one-year option can turn her option into a six-month option by simply exercising it early. That is, the one-year option has all the same rights and privileges as the six-month option, so by the Law of One Price, it cannot be worth less than the six-month option: *An American option with a later exercise date cannot be worth less than an otherwise identical American option with an earlier exercise date.* Usually the right to delay exercising the option is worth something, so the option with the later exercise date will be more valuable.

What about European options? The same argument will not work for European options, because a one-year European option cannot be exercised early at six months. As a consequence, a European option with a later exercise date may potentially trade for less than an otherwise identical option with an earlier exercise date. For example, think about a European call on a stock that pays a liquidating dividend in eight months (a liquidating dividend is paid when a corporation chooses to go out of business, sells off all of its assets, and pays out the proceeds as a dividend). A one-year European call option on this stock would be worthless, but a six-month call would be worth something.

Option Prices and Volatility

An important criterion that determines the price of an option is the volatility of the underlying stock. Consider the following simple example.

EXAMPLE 20.8 **Option Value and Volatility**

Problem

Two European call options with a strike price of \$50 are written on two different stocks. Suppose that tomorrow, the *low-volatility* stock will have a price of \$50 for certain. The *high-volatility* stock will be worth either \$60 or \$40, with each price having equal probability. If the exercise date of both options is tomorrow, which option will be worth more today?

Solution

The expected value of *both* stocks tomorrow is \$50—the low-volatility stock will be worth this amount for sure, and the high-volatility stock has an expected value of $\frac{1}{2}(\$40) + \frac{1}{2}(\$60) = \$50$. However, the options have very different values. The option on the low-volatility stock is worth nothing because there is no chance it will expire in-the-money (the low-volatility stock will be worth \$50 and the strike price is \$50). The option on the high-volatility stock is worth a positive amount because there is a 50% chance that it will be worth $\$60 - \$50 = \$10$, and a 50% chance that it will be worthless. The value today of a 50% chance of a positive payoff (with no chance of a loss) is positive.

Example 20.8 illustrates an important principle: *The value of an option generally increases with the volatility of the stock.* The intuition for this result is that an increase in volatility increases the likelihood of very high and very low returns for the stock. The holder of a call option benefits from a higher payoff when the stock goes up and the option is in-the-money, but earns the same (zero) payoff no matter how far the stock drops once the option is out-of-the-money. Because of this asymmetry of the option's payoff, an option holder gains from an increase in volatility.[5]

Recall that adding a put option to a portfolio is akin to buying insurance against a decline in value. Insurance is more valuable when there is higher volatility—hence put options on more volatile stocks are also worth more.

---

[5]This relation between the stock's volatility and the value of an option holds for realistic distributions of stock prices assumed by practitioners (described in detail in Chapter 21), in which an increase in volatility implies a more "spread out" distribution for the entire range of future stock prices. That said, it need not hold, for example, if the volatility of the stock increases in some ranges but falls in others.

CONCEPT CHECK

1. What is the intrinsic value of an option?
2. Can a European option with a later exercise date be worth less than an identical European option with an earlier exercise date?
3. How does the volatility of a stock affect the value of puts and calls written on the stock?

20.5 Exercising Options Early

One might guess that the ability to exercise the American option early would make an American option more valuable than an equivalent European option. Surprisingly, this is not always the case—sometimes, they have equal value. Let's see why.

Non-Dividend-Paying Stocks

Let's consider first options on a stock that will not pay any dividends prior to the expiration date of the options. In that case, the put-call parity formula for the value of the call option is (see Eq. 20.3):

$$C = P + S - PV(K)$$

We can write the price of the zero-coupon bond as $PV(K) = K - dis(K)$, where $dis(K)$ is the amount of the discount from face value to account for interest. Substituting this expression into put-call parity gives

$$C = \underbrace{S - K}_{\text{Intrinsic value}} + \underbrace{dis(K) + P}_{\text{Time value}} \tag{20.5}$$

In this case, both terms that make up the time value of the call option are positive before the expiration date: As long as interest rates remain positive, the discount on a zero-coupon bond before the maturity date is positive, and the put price is also positive, so a European call always has a positive time value. Because an American option is worth at least as much as a European option, it must also have a positive time value before expiration. Hence, *the price of any call option on a non-dividend-paying stock always exceeds its intrinsic value.*[6]

This result implies that it is *never* optimal to exercise a call option on a non-dividend-paying stock early—you are always better off just selling the option. It is straightforward to see why. When you exercise an option, you get its intrinsic value. But as we have just seen, the price of a call option on a non-dividend-paying stock always exceeds its intrinsic value. Thus, if you want to liquidate your position in a call on a non-dividend-paying stock, you will get a higher price if you sell it rather than exercise it. Because it is never optimal to exercise an American call on a non-dividend-paying stock early, the right to exercise the call early is worthless. For this reason, *an American call on a non-dividend-paying stock has the same price as its European counterpart.*

To understand the economics underlying this result, note that there are two benefits to delaying the exercise of a call option. First, the holder delays paying the strike price, and second, by retaining the right not to exercise, the holder's downside is limited. (These benefits are represented by the discount and put values in Eq. 20.5.)

[6]This conclusion would not hold if the interest rate faced by traders is *negative*; in that case the results for calls and puts in this section would be reversed.

What about an American put option on a non-dividend-paying stock? Does it ever make sense to exercise it early? The answer is yes, under certain circumstances. To see why, note that we can rearrange the put-call parity relationship as expressed in Eq. 20.5 to get the price of a European put option:

$$P = \underbrace{K - S}_{\text{Intrinsic value}} + \underbrace{C - dis(K)}_{\text{Time value}} \tag{20.6}$$

In this case, the time value of the option includes a negative term, the discount on a bond with face value *K*; this term represents the opportunity cost of waiting to receive the strike price *K*. When the strike price is high and the put option is sufficiently deep in-the-money, this discount will be large relative to the value of the call, and the time value of a European put option will be negative. In that case, the European put will sell for less than its intrinsic value. However, its American counterpart cannot sell for less than its intrinsic value (because otherwise arbitrage profits would be possible by immediately exercising it), which implies that the American option can be worth more than an otherwise identical European option. Because the only difference between the two options is the right to exercise the option early, this right must be valuable—there must be states in which it is optimal to exercise the American put early.

Let's examine an extreme case to illustrate when it is optimal to exercise an American put early: Suppose the firm goes bankrupt and the stock is worth nothing. In such a case, the value of the put equals its upper bound—the strike price—so its price cannot go any higher. Thus, no future appreciation is possible. However, if you exercise the put early, you can get the strike price today and earn interest on the proceeds in the interim. Hence it makes sense to exercise this option early. Although this example is extreme, it illustrates that it can be optimal to exercise deep in-the-money put options early.

EXAMPLE 20.9 Early Exercise of a Put Option on a Non-Dividend-Paying Stock

Problem

Table 20.2 lists the quotes from the CBOE on October 5, 2015, for options on Alphabet stock (Google's holding company) expiring in November 2015. Alphabet will not pay a dividend during this period. Identify any option for which exercising the option early is better than selling it.

Solution

Because Alphabet pays no dividends during the life of these options (October 2015 to November 2015), it should not be optimal to exercise the call options early. In fact, we can check that the bid price for each call option exceeds that option's intrinsic value, so it would be better to sell the call than to exercise it. For example, the payoff from exercising a call with a strike of 620 early is $667.50 - 620 = \$47.50$, while the option can be sold for \$59.10.

On the other hand, an Alphabet shareholder holding a put option with a strike price of \$795 or higher would be better off exercising—rather than selling—the option. For example, by exercising the 805 put the shareholder would receive \$805 for her stock, whereas by selling the stock and the option she would only receive $\$667.15 + 127.50 = \$794.65$. The same is not true of the puts with strikes below \$795, however. For example, the holder of the 750 put option who exercises it early would receive \$750 for her stock, but would net $\$667.15 + 86.50 = \$753.65$ by selling the stock and the put instead. Thus, early exercise is only optimal for the deep in-the-money put options.[7]

[7]Selling versus exercising may have different tax consequences or transaction costs for some investors, which could also affect this decision.

TABLE 20.2 Alphabet Option Quotes

GOOGL (ALPHABET INC (A)) **667.35** 10.36

Oct 05 2015 @ 13:40 ET **Bid** 667.15 **Ask** 667.5 **Size** 1 × 1 **Vol** 1111445

Calls	Bid	Ask	Open Int	Puts	Bid	Ask	Open Int
15 Nov 620.00 (GOOGL1520K620)	59.10	62.00	237	15 Nov 620.00 (GOOGL1520W620)	13.20	14.10	167
15 Nov 630.00 (GOOGL1520K630)	51.80	54.00	91	15 Nov 630.00 (GOOGL1520W630)	15.80	16.60	238
15 Nov 640.00 (GOOGL1520K640)	45.10	47.10	103	15 Nov 640.00 (GOOGL1520W640)	18.70	20.00	182
15 Nov 650.00 (GOOGL1520K650)	38.90	40.60	478	15 Nov 650.00 (GOOGL1520W650)	22.30	23.50	326
15 Nov 660.00 (GOOGL1520K660)	33.10	34.70	358	15 Nov 660.00 (GOOGL1520W660)	26.40	27.50	106
15 Nov 670.00 (GOOGL1520K670)	27.60	29.20	281	15 Nov 670.00 (GOOGL1520W670)	30.80	32.10	85
15 Nov 680.00 (GOOGL1520K680)	23.20	24.30	164	15 Nov 680.00 (GOOGL1520W680)	35.60	37.30	66
15 Nov 750.00 (GOOGL1520K750)	4.50	5.10	1897	15 Nov 750.00 (GOOGL1520W750)	86.50	89.10	10
15 Nov 795.00 (GOOGL1520K795)	0.90	1.70	0	15 Nov 795.00 (GOOGL1520W795)	127.50	130.80	0
15 Nov 805.00 (GOOGL1520K805)	0.60	1.35	0	15 Nov 805.00 (GOOGL1520W805)	136.90	140.50	0

Source: Chicago Board Options Exchange at www.cboe.com

Dividend-Paying Stocks

When stocks pay dividends, the right to exercise an option on them early is generally valuable for both calls and puts. To see why, let's write out the put-call parity relationship for a dividend-paying stock:

$$C = \underbrace{S - K}_{\text{Intrinsic value}} + \underbrace{dis(K) + P - PV(Div)}_{\text{Time value}} \tag{20.7}$$

If $PV(Div)$ is large enough, the time value of a European call option can be negative, implying that its price could be less than its intrinsic value. Because an American option can never be worth less than its intrinsic value, the price of the American option can exceed the price of a European option.

To understand when it is optimal to exercise the American call option early, note that when a company pays a dividend, investors expect the price of the stock to drop to reflect the cash paid out. This price drop hurts the owner of a call option because the stock price falls, but unlike the owner of the stock, the option holder does not get the dividend as compensation. However, by exercising early, the owner of the call option can capture the value of the dividend. Thus, the decision to exercise early trades off the benefits of waiting to exercise the call option versus the loss of the dividend. Because a call should only be exercised early to capture the dividend, it will only be optimal to do so just before the stock's ex-dividend date.

Dividends have the opposite effect on the time value of a put option. Again, from the put-call parity relation, we can write the put value as:

$$P = \underbrace{K - S}_{\text{Intrinsic value}} + \underbrace{C - dis(K) + PV(Div)}_{\text{Time value}} \tag{20.8}$$

Intuitively, when a stock pays dividends, the holder of a put option will benefit by waiting for the stock price to drop after it goes ex-dividend before exercising. Thus, it is less likely that a put option on a dividend-paying stock will be exercised early.

EXAMPLE 20.10 Early Exercise of Options on a Dividend-Paying Stock

Problem

General Electric (GE) stock went ex-dividend on December 22, 2005 (only equity holders on the previous day are entitled to the dividend). The dividend amount was \$0.25. Table 20.3 lists the quotes for GE options on December 21, 2005. From the quotes, identify the options that should be exercised early rather than sold.

Solution

The holder of a call option on GE stock with a strike price of \$32.50 or less is better off exercising—rather than selling—the option. For example, exercising the 06 January 10 call and immediately selling the stock would net $35.52 - 10 = \$25.52$. The option itself can be sold for \$25.40, so the holder is better off by \$0.12 by exercising the call rather than selling it. To understand why early exercise can be optimal in this case, note that interest rates were about 0.33% per month, so the value of delaying payment of the \$10 strike price until January was worth only \$0.033, and the put option was worth less than \$0.05. Thus, from Eq. 20.7, the benefit of delay was much less than the \$0.25 value of the dividend.[8]

On the other hand, all of the put options listed have a positive time value and thus should not be exercised early. In this case, waiting for the stock to go ex-dividend is more valuable than the cost of delaying the receipt of the strike price.

Although most traded options are American, options on stock indices, such as the S&P 500, are typically European. Table 20.4 shows quotes for European calls and puts on the S&P 500 index, together with their intrinsic values. At the time of these quotes, the aggregate dividend yield was approximately 2.8% while interest rates were 1.6% for the maturity of the options. Because these are European-style options, it is possible for the option's

TABLE 20.3 Option Quotes for GE on December 21, 2005 (GE paid \$0.25 dividend with ex-dividend date of December 22, 2005)

GE **35.52 −0.02**
Dec 21, 2005 @ 11:50 ET **Vol** 8103000

Calls	Bid	Ask	Open Interest	Puts	Bid	Ask	Open Interest
06 Jan 10.00 (GE AB-E)	25.40	25.60	738	06 Jan 10.00 (GE MB-E)	0	0.05	12525
06 Jan 20.00 (GE AD-E)	15.40	15.60	1090	06 Jan 20.00 (GE MD-E)	0	0.05	8501
06 Jan 25.00 (GE AE-E)	10.40	10.60	29592	06 Jan 25.00 (GE ME-E)	0	0.05	36948
06 Jan 30.00 (GE AF-E)	5.40	5.60	37746	06 Jan 30.00 (GE MF-E)	0	0.05	139548
06 Jan 32.50 (GE AZ-E)	2.95	3.10	13630	06 Jan 32.50 (GE MZ-E)	0	0.05	69047
06 Jan 35.00 (GE AG-E)	0.70	0.75	146682	06 Jan 35.00 (GE MG-E)	0.30	0.35	140014
06 Jan 40.00 (GE AH-E)	0	0.05	84366	06 Jan 40.00 (GE MH-E)	4.70	4.80	4316
06 Jan 45.00 (GE AI-E)	0	0.05	7554	06 Jan 45.00 (GE MI-E)	9.70	9.80	767
06 Jan 50.00 (GE AJ-E)	0	0.05	17836	06 Jan 50.00 (GE MJ-E)	14.70	14.80	383
06 Jan 60.00 (GE AL-E)	0	0.05	7166	06 Jan 60.00 (GE ML-E)	24.70	24.80	413

Source: Chicago Board Options Exchange at www.cboe.com

[8]Again, we have analyzed the early exercise decision ignoring taxes. Some investors may face higher taxes if they exercise the option early rather than sell or hold it.

TABLE 20.4 Two-Year Call and Put Options on the S&P 500 Index

SPX **879.56 −1.47**
JUL 08 2009 @16:25ET

Calls	Bid	Ask	Intrinsic Value	Puts	Bid	Ask	Intrinsic Value
11 Dec 200.00 (SZD-LH-E)	632.5	638.2	679.56	11 Dec 200.00 (SZD-XH-E)	2.20	3.40	0.00
11 Dec 400.00 (SZD-LP-E)	454.9	461.3	479.56	11 Dec 400.00 (SZD-XP-E)	14.7	19.0	0.00
11 Dec 600.00 (SZJ-LR-E)	299.3	306.0	279.56	11 Dec 600.00 (SZJ-XR-E)	53.5	59.3	0.00
11 Dec 800.00 (SZJ-LL-E)	172.2	179.2	79.56	11 Dec 800.00 (SZJ-XL-E)	118.7	125.4	0.00
11 Dec 1000.00 (SZT-LR-E)	82.0	88.7	0.00	11 Dec 1000.00 (SZT-XR-E)	220.1	227.5	120.44
11 Dec 1200.00 (SZT-LU-E)	30.5	36.5	0.00	11 Dec 1200.00 (SZT-XU-E)	360.4	367.9	320.44
11 Dec 1400.00 (SZT-LA-E)	8.60	11.8	0.00	11 Dec 1400.00 (SZT-XA-E)	530.5	537.7	520.44
11 Dec 1600.00 (SZV-LO-E)	2.20	3.40	0.00	11 Dec 1600.00 (SZV-XO-E)	716.5	721.8	720.44
11 Dec 1800.00 (SZV-LD-E)	0.00	1.15	0.00	11 Dec 1800.00 (SZV-XD-E)	907.6	912.0	920.44
11 Dec 2000.00 (SZV-LE-E)	0.00	0.65	0.00	11 Dec 2000.00 (SZV-XE-E)	1099.9	1103.9	1120.44

Source: Chicago Board Options Exchange at www.cboe.com

price to be below its intrinsic value, so that its time value is negative. As the table shows, this occurs for calls with strikes of 400 or below and for puts with strikes of 1600 or above. For the deep in-the-money calls, the present value of the dividends is larger than the interest earned on the low strike prices, making it costly to wait to exercise the option. For the deep in-the-money puts, the interest on the high strike prices exceeds the dividends earned, again making it costly to wait.

CONCEPT CHECK

1. Is it ever optimal to exercise an American call on a non-dividend paying stock early?
2. When might it be optimal to exercise an American put option early?
3. When might it be optimal to exercise an American call early?

20.6 Options and Corporate Finance

Although we will delay much of the discussion of how corporations use options until after we have explained how to value an option, one very important corporate application does not require understanding how to price options: interpreting the capital structure of the firm as options on the firm's assets. We begin by explaining why we can think of equity as an option.

Equity as a Call Option

Think of a share of stock as a call option on the assets of the firm with a strike price equal to the value of debt outstanding.[9] To illustrate, consider a single-period world in which at the end of the period the firm is liquidated. If the firm's value does not exceed the value of debt outstanding at the end of the period, the firm must declare bankruptcy and the equity

[9] Fischer Black and Myron Scholes discussed this insight in their path-breaking option valuation paper, "The Pricing of Options and Corporate Liabilities," *Journal of Political Economy* 81 (1973): 637–654.

FIGURE 20.8

Equity as a Call Option

If the value of the firm's assets exceeds the required debt payment, the equity holders receive the value that remains after the debt is repaid; otherwise, the firm is bankrupt and its equity is worthless. Thus, the payoff to equity is equivalent to a call option on the firm's assets with a strike price equal to the required debt payment.

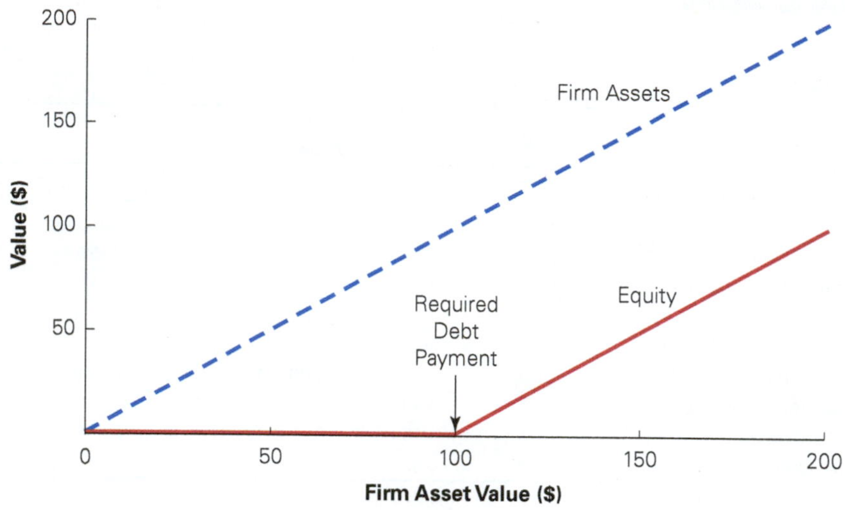

holders receive nothing. Conversely, if the value exceeds the value of debt outstanding, the equity holders get whatever is left once the debt has been repaid. Figure 20.8 illustrates this payoff. Note how the payoff to equity looks exactly the same as the payoff of a call option.

Debt as an Option Portfolio

We can also represent debt using options. In this case, you can think of the debt holders as owning the firm *and* having sold a call option with a strike price equal to the required debt payment. If the value of the firm exceeds the required debt payment, the call will be exercised; the debt holders will therefore receive the strike price (the required debt payment) and "give up" the firm. If the value of the firm does not exceed the required debt payment, the call will be worthless, the firm will declare bankruptcy, and the debt holders will be entitled to the firm's assets. Figure 20.9 illustrates this payoff.

There is also another way to view corporate debt: as a portfolio of risk-free debt and a short position in a put option on the firm's assets with a strike price equal to the required debt payment:

$$\text{Risky debt} = \text{Risk-free debt} - \text{Put option on firm assets} \tag{20.9}$$

When the firm's assets are worth less than the required debt payment, the put is in-the-money; the owner of the put option will therefore exercise the option and receive the difference between the required debt payment and the firm's asset value (see Figure 20.9). This leaves the portfolio holder (debt holder) with just the assets of the firm. If the firm's value is greater than the required debt payment, the put is worthless, leaving the portfolio holder with the required debt payment.

Credit Default Swaps

By rearranging Equation 20.9, notice that we can eliminate a bond's credit risk by buying the very same put option to protect or insure it:

$$\text{Risk-free debt} = \text{Risky debt} + \text{Put option on firm assets}$$

FIGURE 20.9

Debt as an Option Portfolio

If the value of the firm's assets exceeds the required debt payment, debt holders are fully repaid. Otherwise, the firm is bankrupt and the debt holders receive the value of the assets. Note that the payoff to debt (orange line) can be viewed either as (1) the firm's assets, less the equity call option, or (2) a risk-free bond, less a put option on the assets with a strike price equal to the required debt payment.

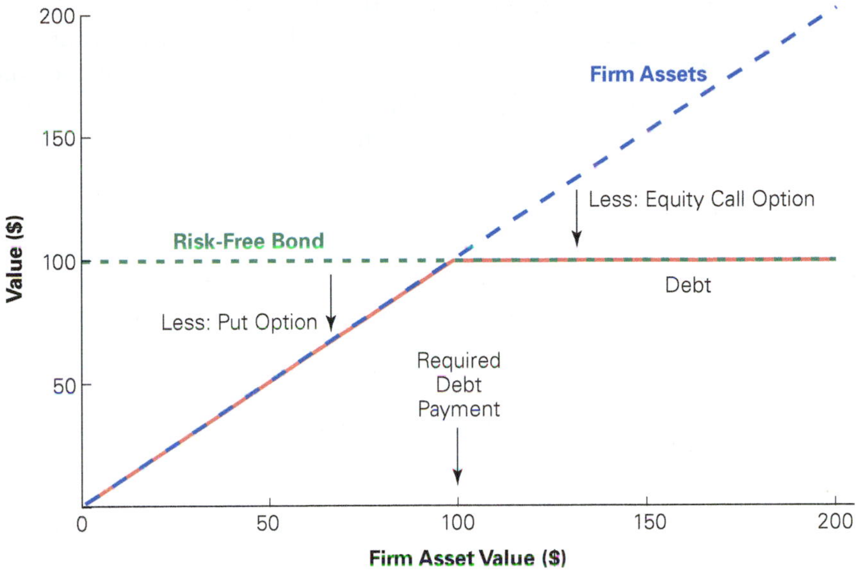

We refer to this put option, which can insure a firm's credit risk, as a credit default swap (or CDS). In a **credit default swap**, the buyer pays a premium to the seller (often in the form of periodic payments) and receives a payment from the seller to make up for the loss if the underlying bond defaults.

Investment banks developed and began trading CDSs in the late 1990s as a means to allow bond investors to insure the credit risk of the bonds in their portfolios. Many hedge funds and other investors soon began using these contracts as a means to speculate on the prospects of a firm and its likelihood of default even if they did not hold its bonds. By late 2007, credit default swaps on over $45 trillion worth of bonds were outstanding—an amount far larger than the total size of the corporate bond market (about $6 trillion).

While this market's large size is impressive, it is also misleading: Because CDSs are contracts written between counterparties, a buyer of a contract who wants to unwind the position cannot simply sell the contract on an exchange like a standard stock option.

GLOBAL FINANCIAL CRISIS **Credit Default Swaps**

Ironically, in the wake of the 2008 financial crisis the CDS market itself became a critical *source* of credit risk of concern to regulators. American International Group (AIG) required a federal bailout in excess of $100 billion due to (1) losses on CDS protection it had sold, and (2) concern that if it defaulted on paying this insurance, banks and other firms who had purchased this insurance to hedge their own exposures would default as well. To reduce these systemic risks in the future, regulators have moved to standardize CDS contracts, as well as provided for trading through a central clearing house that acts as a counterparty to all trades. To protect itself against counterparty default, the clearing house would impose strict margin requirements. In addition to improving transparency, this process allows contracts that offset each other to be cancelled rather than simply offset, which should help reduce the creation of new credit risk by the very market designed to help control it!

Instead, the buyer must enter a new offsetting CDS contract with a possibly new counterparty (e.g., a buyer of insurance on GE could then sell insurance on GE to someone else, leaving no net exposure to GE). In this way, a new contract is created with each trade, even if investors' net exposure is not increased. For example, when Lehman Brothers defaulted in September 2009, buyers of CDS protection against such a default were owed close to $400 billion. However, after netting all offsetting positions, only about $7 billion actually changed hands.

Pricing Risky Debt

Viewing debt as an option portfolio is useful, as it provides insight into how credit spreads for risky debt are determined. Let's illustrate with an example.

EXAMPLE 20.11 Calculating the Yield on New Corporate Debt

Problem

As of September 2012, Google (GOOG) had no debt. Suppose the firm's managers consider recapitalizing the firm by issuing zero-coupon debt with a face value of $163.5 billion due in January of 2014, and using the proceeds to pay a special dividend. Suppose too that Google had 327 million shares outstanding, trading at $700.77 per share, implying a market value of $229.2 billion. The risk-free rate over this horizon is 0.25%. Using the call option quotes in Figure 20.10, estimate the credit spread Google would have to pay on the debt assuming perfect capital markets.

Solution

Assuming perfect capital markets, the total value of Google's equity and debt should remain unchanged after the recapitalization. The $163.5 billion face value of the debt is equivalent to a claim of $163.5 billion/(327 million shares) = $500 per share on Google's current assets. Because Google's shareholders will only receive the value in excess of this debt claim, the value of Google's equity after the recap is equivalent to the current value of a call option with a strike price of $500. From the quotes in Figure 20.10, such a call option has a value of approximately $222.05 per share (using the average of the bid and ask quotes). Multiplying by Google's total number of shares, we can estimate the total value of Google's equity after the recap as $222.05 × 327 million shares = $72.6 billion.

To estimate the value of the new debt, we can subtract the estimated equity value from Google's total value of $229.2 billion; thus, the estimated debt value is 229.2 − 72.6 = $156.6 billion. Because the debt matures 16 months from the date of the quotes, this value corresponds to a yield to maturity of

$$\left(\frac{163.5}{156.6}\right)^{12/16} - 1 = 3.29\%$$

Thus, Google's credit spread for the new debt issue would be about 3.29% − 0.25% = 3.04%.

Using the methodology in Example 20.11, Figure 20.10 plots this yield on Google debt as a function of the amount borrowed and illustrates the relation between the amount borrowed and the yield. The analysis in this example demonstrates the use of option valuation methods to assess credit risk and value risky debt. While here we used data from option quotes, in the next chapter we will develop methods to value options as well as risky debt and other distress costs based on firm fundamentals.

FIGURE 20.10 Google Call Option Quotes and Implied Debt Yields

GOOG (GOOGLE INC) 700.77 − 5.38
Sep 10 2012 @ 21:39 ET Vol 2560067

Calls	Bid	Ask	Open Int
14 Jan 300.00 (GOOG1418A300-E)	402.90	405.90	4
14 Jan 350.00 (GOOG1418A350-E)	355.30	358.00	34
14 Jan 400.00 (GOOG1418A400-E)	308.20	311.60	471
14 Jan 450.00 (GOOG1418A450-E)	263.00	266.50	25
14 Jan 500.00 (GOOG1418A500-E)	220.20	223.90	229
14 Jan 550.00 (GOOG1418A550-E)	181.00	184.70	122
14 Jan 600.00 (GOOG1418A600-E)	145.20	148.60	303
14 Jan 650.00 (GOOG1418A650-E)	114.30	117.30	292
14 Jan 660.00 (GOOG1418A660-E)	108.50	111.60	63
14 Jan 680.00 (GOOG1418A680-E)	97.80	101.70	91
14 Jan 700.00 (GOOG1418A700-E)	87.60	91.00	508
14 Jan 750.00 (GOOG1418A750-E)	66.20	68.10	534

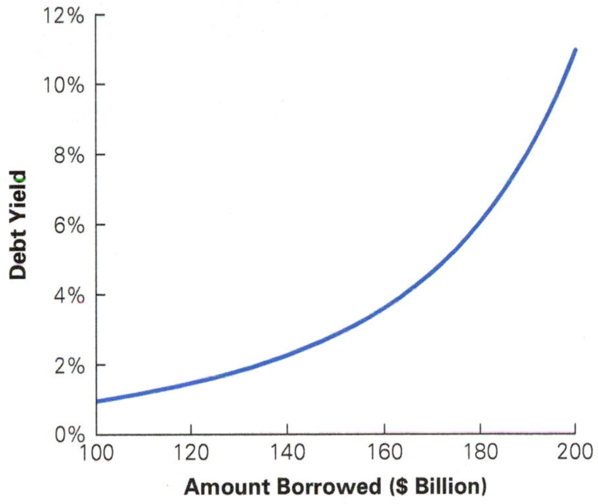

Given the CBOE call option quotes for Google stock, we can calculate the implied debt yield given perfect markets if Google were to borrow by issuing 16-month, zero-coupon bonds. Note the increase in the debt yield with the amount borrowed.

Agency Conflicts

In addition to pricing, the option characterization of equity and debt securities provides a new interpretation of the agency conflicts between debt and equity holders that we discussed in Chapter 16. Recall that the price of an option generally increases with the volatility level of the underlying security. Because equity is like a call option on the firm's assets, equity holders will benefit from investments that increase the risk of the firm. On the other hand, debt holders are short a put option on the firm's assets. Thus, they will be hurt by an increase in the firm's risk. This conflict of interest regarding risk-taking is the asset substitution problem (see Section 16.5), and we can quantify it in terms of the sensitivity of the option values to the firm's volatility.

Similarly, when the firm makes new investments that increase the value of the firm's assets, the value of a put option on the firm will decline. Because debt holders are short a put option, the value of the firm's debt will increase. Thus, some fraction of each dollar increase in the value of the firm's assets will go to debt holders, rather than equity holders, reducing equity holders' incentive to invest. This problem is the debt overhang problem we discussed in Section 16.5, and we can quantify it in terms of the sensitivity of the call and put values to the value of the firm's underlying assets.

The usefulness of options to corporate managers is by no means limited to the applications we discuss in this section. However, to understand the other applications, and to quantify the results we have discussed here, we need deeper knowledge of what determines the option price. In Chapter 21, we develop these tools and explore how to calculate the price of an option.

CONCEPT CHECK

1. Explain how equity can be viewed as a call option on the firm.
2. Explain how debt can be viewed as an option portfolio.

MyFinanceLab Here is what you should know after reading this chapter. MyFinanceLab will help you identify what you know and where to go when you need to practice.

20.1 Option Basics

- A call option gives the holder the right (but not the obligation) to purchase an asset at some future date. A put option gives the holder the right to sell an asset at some future date.
- When a holder of an option enforces the agreement and buys or sells the share of stock at the agreed-upon price, the holder is exercising the option.
- The price at which the holder agrees to buy or sell the share of stock when the option is exercised is called the strike price or exercise price.
- The last date on which the holder has the right to exercise the option is known as the expiration date.
- An American option can be exercised on any date up to, and including, the exercise date. A European option can be exercised only on the expiration date.
- If the payoff from exercising the option immediately is positive, the option is in-the-money. If the stock price equals the strike price, the option is at-the-money. Finally, if you would lose money by exercising an option immediately, the option is out-of-the-money.

20.2 Option Payoffs at Expiration

- Given stock price S and strike price K, the value of a call option at expiration is

$$C = max(S - K, 0) \tag{20.1}$$

- The value of a put option at expiration is

$$P = max(K - S, 0) \tag{20.2}$$

- An investor holding a short position in an option has an obligation; he or she takes the opposite side of the contract to the investor who is long.
- The value an option would have if it expired today is its intrinsic value. The time value of an option is the difference between its current value and its intrinsic value.

20.3 Put-Call Parity

- Put-call parity relates the value of the European call to the value of the European put and the stock.

$$C = P + S - PV(K) - PV(Div) \tag{20.4}$$

20.4 Factors Affecting Option Prices

- Call options with lower strike prices are more valuable than otherwise identical calls with higher strike prices. Conversely, put options are more valuable with higher strike prices.
- Call options increase in value, and put options decrease in value, when the stock price rises.
- Arbitrage bounds for option prices:
  - An American option cannot be worth less than its European counterpart.
  - A put option cannot be worth more than its exercise price.
  - A call option cannot be worth more than the stock itself.
  - An American option cannot be worth less than its intrinsic value.
  - An American option with a later exercise date cannot be worth less than an otherwise identical American option with an earlier exercise date.
- The value of an option generally increases with the volatility of the stock.

20.5 Exercising Options Early

- It is never optimal to exercise an American call option on a non-dividend-paying stock early. Thus, an American call option on a non-dividend-paying stock has the same price as its European counterpart.
- It can be optimal to exercise a deep in-the-money American put option. It can be optimal to exercise an American call option just before the stock goes ex-dividend.

20.6 Options and Corporate Finance

- Equity can be viewed as a call option on the firm's assets.
- The debt holders can be viewed as owning the firm's assets *and* having sold a call option with a strike price equal to the required debt payment.
- Alternatively, corporate debt is a portfolio of riskless debt and a short position in a put option on the firm's cash flow with a strike price equal to the required debt payment. This put option is also referred to as a credit default swap.
- Option valuations can be used to estimate the appropriate yield for risky debt, as well as to estimate the magnitude of agency cost problems within the firm.

Key Terms

American options *p. 725*
at-the-money *p. 726*
butterfly spread *p. 735*
call option *p. 725*
credit default swap (CDS) *p. 747*
deep in-the-money *p. 727*
deep out-of-the-money *p. 727*
European options *p. 725*
exercising (an option) *p. 725*
expiration date *p. 725*
financial option *p. 725*
hedging *p. 727*
in-the-money *p. 727*
intrinsic value *p. 739*
open interest *p. 726*
option premium *p. 725*
option writer *p. 725*
out-of-the-money *p. 727*
portfolio insurance *p. 735*
protective put *p. 735*
put option *p. 725*
put-call parity *p. 737*
speculate *p. 727*
straddle *p. 734*
strangle *p. 734*
strike (exercise) price *p. 725*
time value *p. 739*

Further Reading

For a deeper discussion of options and other derivative securities, see the following books: R. McDonald, *Derivative Markets* (Prentice Hall, 2009); and J. Hull, *Options, Futures, and Other Derivatives* (Prentice Hall, 2011).

Problems

All problems are available in MyFinanceLab. *An asterisk (*) indicates problems with a higher level of difficulty.*

Option Basics

1. Explain the meanings of the following financial terms:
   a. Option
   b. Expiration date
   c. Strike price
   d. Call
   e. Put
2. What is the difference between a European option and an American option? Are European options available exclusively in Europe and American options available exclusively in the United States?

3. Below is an option quote on IBM from the CBOE Web site showing options expiring in October and November 2015.

a. Which option contract had the most trades on that day?
b. Which option contract is being held the most overall?
c. Suppose you purchase one option with symbol IBM1516J150. How much will you need to pay your broker for the option (ignoring commissions)?
d. Explain why the last sale price is not always between the bid and ask prices.
e. Suppose you sell one option with symbol IBM1516V150. How much will you receive for the option (ignoring commissions)?
f. The calls with which strike prices are currently in-the-money? Which puts are in-the-money?
g. What is the difference between the option with symbol IBM1516J140 and the option with symbol IBM1506K140?
h. On what date does the option with symbol IBM1516V140 expire? In what range must IBM's stock price be at expiration for this option to be valuable?

IBM (INTL BUSINESS MACHINES) **149.04** 4.46

Oct 05 2015 @ 16:39 ET **Bid** 148.72 **Ask** 149.04 **Size** 3 × 3 **Vol** 4997840

Calls	Last Sale	Net	Bid	Ask	Vol	Open Int	Puts	Last Sale	Net	Bid	Ask	Vol	Open Int
15 Oct 140.00 (IBM1516J140)	9.55	4.10	9.15	9.50	35	390	15 Oct 140.00 (IBM1516V140)	0.36	−0.62	0.35	0.36	834	3762
15 Oct 145.00 (IBM1516J145)	4.95	2.86	4.80	5.20	234	1689	15 Oct 145.00 (IBM1516V145)	0.89	−1.30	0.86	0.87	855	2395
15 Oct 150.00 (IBM1516J150)	1.50	1.13	1.53	1.54	786	3380	15 Oct 150.00 (IBM1516V150)	2.44	−3.62	2.24	2.47	180	2774
15 Oct 155.00 (IBM1516J155)	0.23	0.19	0.18	0.19	662	4569	15 Oct 155.00 (IBM1516V155)	6.01	−5.99	5.60	6.30	81	2985
15 Nov 140.00 (IBM1506K140)	6.77	0	10.45	11.05	0	73	15 Nov 140.00 (IBM1506W140)	1.76	−1.64	1.93	2.00	34	54
15 Nov 145.00 (IBM1506K145)	5.83	1.58	6.70	6.90	94	191	15 Nov 145.00 (IBM1506W145)	3.00	−2.69	3.20	3.35	33	78
15 Nov 150.00 (IBM1506K150)	3.86	1.84	3.65	3.85	314	43	15 Nov 150.00 (IBM1506W150)	8.66	0	5.40	5.55	0	11
15 Nov 155.00 (IBM1506K155)	1.72	0.90	1.67	1.74	135	123	15 Nov 155.00 (IBM1506W155)	8.30	0	7.85	8.80	2	0

Source: Chicago Board Options Exchange at www.cboe.com

Option Payoffs at Expiration

4. Explain the difference between a long position in a put and a short position in a call.

5. Which of the following positions benefit if the stock price increases?

a. Long position in a call
b. Short position in a call
c. Long position in a put
d. Short position in a put

MFL **6.** You own a call option on Intuit stock with a strike price of $40. The option will expire in exactly three months' time.

a. If the stock is trading at $55 in three months, what will be the payoff of the call?
b. If the stock is trading at $35 in three months, what will be the payoff of the call?
c. Draw a payoff diagram showing the value of the call at expiration as a function of the stock price at expiration.

MFL **7.** Assume that you have shorted the call option in Problem 6.

a. If the stock is trading at $55 in three months, what will you owe?
b. If the stock is trading at $35 in three months, what will you owe?
c. Draw a payoff diagram showing the amount you owe at expiration as a function of the stock price at expiration.

MFL **8.** You own a put option on Ford stock with a strike price of $10. The option will expire in exactly six months' time.

a. If the stock is trading at $8 in six months, what will be the payoff of the put?
b. If the stock is trading at $23 in six months, what will be the payoff of the put?
c. Draw a payoff diagram showing the value of the put at expiration as a function of the stock price at expiration.

MFL

9. Assume that you have shorted the put option in Problem 8.
   a. If the stock is trading at $8 in three months, what will you owe?
   b. If the stock is trading at $23 in three months, what will you owe?
   c. Draw a payoff diagram showing the amount you owe at expiration as a function of the stock price at expiration.

10. What position has more downside exposure: a short position in a call or a short position in a put? That is, in the worst case, in which of these two positions would your losses be greater?

11. Consider the October 2015 IBM call and put options in Problem 3. Ignoring any interest you might earn over the remaining few days' life of the options:
   a. Compute the break-even IBM stock price for each option (i.e., the stock price at which your total profit from buying and then exercising the option would be zero).
   b. Which call option is most likely to have a return of −100%?
   c. If IBM's stock price is $156 on the expiration day, which option will have the highest return?

12. You are long both a call and a put on the same share of stock with the same exercise date. The exercise price of the call is $40 and the exercise price of the put is $45. Plot the value of this combination as a function of the stock price on the exercise date.

13. You are long two calls on the same share of stock with the same exercise date. The exercise price of the first call is $40 and the exercise price of the second call is $60. In addition, you are short two otherwise identical calls, both with an exercise price of $50. Plot the value of this combination as a function of the stock price on the exercise date. What is the name of this combination of options?

*14. A forward contract is a contract to purchase an asset at a fixed price on a particular date in the future. Both parties are obligated to fulfill the contract. Explain how to construct a forward contract on a share of stock from a position in options.

15. You own a share of Costco stock. You are worried that its price will fall and would like to insure yourself against this possibility. How can you purchase insurance against this possibility?

16. It is October 5, 2015, and you own IBM stock. You would like to insure that the value of your holdings will not fall significantly. Using the data in Problem 3, and expressing your answer in terms of a percentage of the current value of your portfolio:
   a. What will it cost to insure that the value of your holdings will not fall below $140 per share between now and the third Friday in October?
   b. What will it cost to insure that the value of your holdings will not fall below $140 per share between now and the third Friday in November?
   c. What will it cost to insure that the value of your holdings will not fall below $145 per share between now and the third Friday in November?

Put-Call Parity

17. Dynamic Energy Systems stock is currently trading for $33 per share. The stock pays no dividends. A one-year European put option on Dynamic with a strike price of $35 is currently trading for $2.10. If the risk-free interest rate is 10% per year, what is the price of a one-year European call option on Dynamic with a strike price of $35?

18. You happen to be checking the newspaper and notice an arbitrage opportunity. The current stock price of Intrawest is $20 per share and the one-year risk-free interest rate is 8%. A one-year put on Intrawest with a strike price of $18 sells for $3.33, while the identical call sells for $7. Explain what you must do to exploit this arbitrage opportunity.

19. Consider the October 2015 IBM call and put options in Problem 3. Ignoring the negligible interest you might earn on T-bills over the remaining few days' life of the options, show that there is no arbitrage opportunity using put-call parity for the options with a $140 strike price. Specifically:
   a. What is your profit/loss if you buy a call and T-bills, and sell IBM stock and a put option?
   b. What is your profit/loss if you buy IBM stock and a put option, and sell a call and T-bills?
   c. Explain why your answers to (a) and (b) are not both zero.

d. Do the same calculation for the October options with a strike price of $150. What do you find? How can you explain this?

20. In mid-February 2016, European-style options on the S&P 100 index (OEX) expiring in December 2017 were priced as follows:

Dec 2017 OEX Index Options

Strike Price	Call Price	Put Price
840	88.00	
860	76.30	102.21
880		111.56

Given an interest rate of 0.40% for a December 2017 maturity (22 months in the future), use put-call parity (with dividends) to determine:

a. The price of a December 2017 OEX put option with a strike price of 840.

b. The price of a December 2017 OEX call option with a strike price of 880.

Factors Affecting Option Prices

21. Suppose Amazon stock is trading for $500 per share, and Amazon pays no dividends.

a. What is the maximum possible price of a call option on Amazon?

b. What is the maximum possible price of a put option on Amazon with a strike price of $550?

c. What is the minimum possible value of a call option on Amazon stock with a strike price of $475?

d. What is the minimum possible value of an American put option on Amazon stock with a strike price of $550?

22. Consider the data for IBM options in Problem 3. Suppose a new American-style put option on IBM is issued with a strike price of $155 and an expiration date of November 1st.

a. What is the maximum possible price for this option?

b. What is the minimum possible price for this option?

23. You are watching the option quotes for your favorite stock, when suddenly there is a news announcement. Explain what type of news would lead to the following effects:

a. Call prices increase, and put prices fall.

b. Call prices fall, and put prices increase.

c. Both call and put prices increase.

Exercising Options Early

***24.** Explain why an American call option on a non-dividend-paying stock always has the same price as its European counterpart.

25. Consider an American put option on XAL stock with a strike price of $55 and one year to expiration. Assume XAL pays no dividends, XAL is currently trading for $10 per share, and the one-year interest rate is 10%. If it is optimal to exercise this option early:

a. What is the price of a one-year American put option on XAL stock with a strike price of $60 per share?

b. What is the maximum price of a one-year American call option on XAL stock with a strike price of $55 per share?

26. The stock of Harford Inc. is about to pay a $0.30 dividend. It will pay no more dividends for the next month. Consider call options that expire in one month. If the interest rate is 6% APR (monthly compounding), what is the maximum strike price where it could be possible that early exercise of the call option is optimal? (Round to the nearest dollar.)

27. Suppose the S&P 500 is at 900, and a one-year European call option with a strike price of $400 has a negative time value. If the interest rate is 5%, what can you conclude about the dividend yield of the S&P 500? (Assume all dividends are paid at the end of the year.)

28. Suppose the S&P 500 is at 900, and it will pay a dividend of $30 at the end of the year. Suppose also that the interest rate is 2%. If a one-year European put option has a negative time value, what is the lowest possible strike price it could have?

Options and Corporate Finance

29. Wesley Corp. stock is trading for $25/share. Wesley has 20 million shares outstanding and a market debt-equity ratio of 0.5. Wesley's debt is zero-coupon debt with a 5-year maturity and a yield to maturity of 10%.

a. Describe Wesley's equity as a call option. What is the maturity of the call option? What is the market value of the asset underlying this call option? What is the strike price of this call option?

b. Describe Wesley's debt using a call option.

c. Describe Wesley's debt using a put option.

***30.** Express the position of an equity holder in terms of put options.

31. Use the option data from July 13, 2009 in the following table to determine the rate Google would have paid if it had issued $128 billion in zero-coupon debt due in January 2011. Suppose Google currently had 320 million shares outstanding, implying a market value of $135.1 billion. (Assume perfect capital markets.)

GOOG — **422.27 +7.87**

Jul 13 2009 @ 13:10 ET — **Vol** 2177516

Calls	Bid	Ask	Open Int
11 Jan 150.0 (OZF AJ)	273.60	276.90	100
11 Jan 160.0 (OZF AL)	264.50	267.20	82
11 Jan 200.0 (OZF AA)	228.90	231.20	172
11 Jan 250.0 (OZF AU)	186.50	188.80	103
11 Jan 280.0 (OZF AX)	162.80	165.00	98
11 Jan 300.0 (OZF AT)	148.20	150.10	408
11 Jan 320.0 (OZF AD)	133.90	135.90	63
11 Jan 340.0 (OZF AI)	120.50	122.60	99
11 Jan 350.0 (OZF AK)	114.10	116.10	269
11 Jan 360.0 (OZF AM)	107.90	110.00	66
11 Jan 380.0 (OZF AZ)	95.80	98.00	88
11 Jan 400.0 (OZF AU)	85.10	87.00	2577
11 Jan 420.0 (OUP AG)	74.60	76.90	66
11 Jan 450.0 (OUP AV)	61.80	63.30	379

***32.** Suppose that in July 2009, Google were to issue $96 billion in zero-coupon senior debt, and another $32 billion in zero-coupon junior debt, both due in January 2011. Use the option data in the preceding table to determine the rate Google would pay on the junior debt issue. (Assume perfect capital markets.)

Data Case

Your uncle owns 10,000 shares of Walmart stock. He is concerned about the short-term outlook for Walmart's stock due to an impending "major announcement." This announcement has received much attention in the press so he expects the stock price will change significantly in the next month, but is unsure whether it will be a profit or a loss. He hopes the price will increase, but he also doesn't want to suffer if the price were to fall in the short term.

His broker recommended he buy a "protective put" on the stock, but your uncle has never traded options before and is not much of a risk taker. He wants you to devise a plan for him to capitalize if the announcement is positive but to still be protected if the news causes the price to drop. You realize that a protective put will protect him from the downside risk, but you think a straddle may offer similar downside protection, while increasing the upside potential. You decide to show him both strategies and the resulting profits and returns he could face from each.

1. Download option quotes on options that expire in approximately one month on Walmart from the Chicago Board Options Exchange (www.cboe.com) into an Excel spreadsheet (click the Quotes & Data tab at the top left portion of the screen and then select "Delayed Quotes"). If you choose to download "near term at-the-money" options you will get a range of options expiring in about a month. *Note*: You can only get active quotes while the exchange is open; bid or ask prices are not available when it is closed.
2. Determine your uncle's profit and return using the protective put.
   a. Identify the expiring put with an exercise price closest to, but not below, the current stock price. Determine the investment required to protect all 10,000 shares.
   b. Determine the put price at expiration for each stock price at $5 increments within a range of $40 of Walmart's current price using Eq. 20.2.
   c. Compute the profit (or loss) on the put for each stock price used in part (b).
   d. Compute the profit on the stock from the current price for each stock price used in part (b).
   e. Compute his overall profit (or loss) of the protective put, that is, combining the put and his stock for each price used in parts (c) and (d).
   f. Compute the overall return of the protective put.
3. Determine your uncle's profit and return using the straddle.
   a. Compute the investment your uncle would have to make to purchase the call and put with the same exercise price and expiration as the put option in Question 2, to cover all 10,000 of his shares.
   b. Determine the value at expiration of the call and the put options at each $5 increment of stock prices within a range of $40 of Walmart's current price using Eqs. 20.1 and 20.2.
   c. Determine the profit (or loss) on the options at each stock price used in part (b).
   d. Determine the profit (or loss) on the stock from the current price for each stock price used in part (b).
   e. Compute his overall profit (or loss) of the stock plus straddle, that is, combining the position in both options and his stock for each price used in parts (c) and (d).
   f. Compute the overall return of this position.
4. Was the broker correct that the protective put would prevent your uncle from losing if the announcement caused a large decrease in the stock value? What is your uncle's maximum possible loss using the protective put?
5. What is the maximum possible loss your uncle could experience using the straddle?
6. Which strategy, the protective put or the straddle, provides the maximum upside potential for your uncle? Why does this occur?

Note: Updates to this data case may be found at www.berkdemarzo.com.

CHAPTER

21

Option Valuation

ROBERT MERTON AND MYRON SCHOLES WERE AWARDED THE 1997 Nobel Prize in economics for their 1973 discovery, together with Fischer Black,[1] of a formula to calculate the price of an option: the *Black-Scholes Option Pricing Model*. Although the formula itself represented an enormous contribution to economics, even more important were the techniques that Black, Scholes, and Merton developed to value options. These techniques changed the course of financial economics and gave birth to a new profession: financial engineering. Routinely, financial engineers use formulas to price financial securities in much the same way as civil engineers use Newton's laws to build bridges. The most important factor contributing to the huge growth in the types of financial securities available in the market are the techniques used to price them, which can all be traced to the Black-Scholes formula. Today, most large corporations rely on these financial securities to manage risk. Without the Black-Scholes formula, the job of corporate managers would be very different: Many corporations would be forced to bear much more risk than they presently do.

These formulas rely primarily on the Law of One Price. That is, they do not depend on knowing unobservable parameters such as investor tastes and beliefs. The great insight that Black, Scholes, and Merton brought to economics is that in the case of options it is not necessary to model preferences. As we will explain in this chapter, their work demonstrated how to apply the Law of One Price to value a vast new range of financial securities based on the current market prices of stocks and bonds.

Our objective in this chapter is to explain the most commonly used techniques (all of which derive from Black and Scholes' insights) for calculating the price of an option: the *Binomial Option Pricing Model*, the *Black-Scholes formula*, and *risk-neutral probabilities*. We apply these techniques to show how to value stock options and quantify their risk and return. We then show how to use the Black-Scholes formula to estimate the beta of

[1] The Black-Scholes formula was derived by Fischer Black and Myron Scholes ("The Pricing of Options and Corporate Liabilities," *Journal of Political Economy* 81, 1973), building on earlier work by Robert Merton. Unfortunately, Black died two years before the prize was awarded.

NOTATION

Δ	shares of stock in the replicating portfolio; sensitivity of option price to stock price
B	risk-free investment in the replicating portfolio
S	stock price
r_f	risk-free rate of interest
C	call option price
T	years until the exercise date of an option
K	strike price
σ	volatility of stock's return
$N(d)$	cumulative normal distribution
ln	natural logarithm
PV	present value
P	put option price
S^x	value of stock excluding dividends
q	dividend yield
ρ	risk-neutral probability
β_S, β_B	beta of the stock, bond
β_E, β_D	beta of the levered equity, debt
β_U	beta of the firm's assets; beta of unlevered equity
A, E, D	market value of assets, equity, debt

risky debt. With this foundation in place, in subsequent chapters we will be able to cover important applications of option pricing for corporate managers.

21.1 The Binomial Option Pricing Model

We begin our study of option pricing with the **Binomial Option Pricing Model**.[2] The model prices options by making the simplifying assumption that at the end of the next period, the stock price has only two possible values. Under this assumption, we demonstrate the key insight of Black and Scholes—that option payoffs can be replicated exactly by constructing a portfolio out of a risk-free bond and the underlying stock. Furthermore, we will see that the model can be quite realistic if we consider stock price movements over very short time intervals.

A Two-State Single-Period Model

Let's start by calculating the price of a single-period option in a very simple world. We will value the option by first constructing a **replicating portfolio**, a portfolio of other securities that has exactly the same value in one period as the option. Then, because they have the same payoffs, the Law of One Price implies that the current value of the call and the replicating portfolio must be equal.

Consider a European call option that expires in one period and has an exercise price of \$50. Assume that the stock price today is equal to \$50. Assume here and throughout the chapter that the stock pays no dividends (unless explicitly indicated). In one period, the stock price will either rise by \$10 or fall by \$10. The one-period risk-free rate is 6%. We can summarize this information on a **binomial tree**—a timeline with two branches at every date representing the possible events that could happen at those times:

0	1		
	Stock	*Bond*	*Call*
	60	1.06	*max* (60 − 50, 0) = 10
Stock 50 **Bond** 1			
	40	1.06	*max* (40 − 50, 0) = 0

The binomial tree contains all the information we currently know: the value of the stock, bond, and call options in each state in one period, as well as the price of the stock and bond today (for simplicity, we assume the bond price today is \$1, so in one period it will be worth \$1.06). We define the state in which the stock price goes up (to \$60) as the *up* state and the state in which the stock price goes down (to \$40) as the *down* state.

In order to determine the value of the option using the Law of One Price, we must show that we can replicate its payoffs using a portfolio of the stock and the bond. Let Δ be the number of shares of stock we purchase, and let B be our initial investment in bonds. To create a call option using the stock and the bond, the value of the portfolio consisting of the

[2]This technique was originally derived by J. Cox, S. Ross, and M. Rubinstein, "Option Pricing, a Simplified Approach," *Journal of Financial Economics* 7 (1979): 229–263; and J. Rendleman and B. Bartter, "Two-State Option Pricing," *Journal of Finance* 34 (December 1979): 1093–1110.

stock and bond must match the value of the option in every possible state. Thus, in the up state, the value of the portfolio must be \$10 (the value of the call in that state):

$$60\Delta + 1.06B = 10 \tag{21.1}$$

In the down state, the value of the portfolio must be zero (the value of the call in that state):

$$40\Delta + 1.06B = 0 \tag{21.2}$$

Equations 21.1 and 21.2 are two simultaneous equations with two unknowns, Δ and B. We'll write down the general formula to solve these equations shortly, but in this case, we can check that the solution is

$$\Delta = 0.5$$
$$B = -18.8679$$

A portfolio that is long 0.5 share of stock and short approximately \$18.87 worth of bonds (i.e., we have borrowed \$18.87 at a 6% interest rate) will have a value in one period that matches the value of the call exactly. Let's verify this explicitly:

$$60 \times 0.5 - 1.06 \times 18.87 = 10$$
$$40 \times 0.5 - 1.06 \times 18.87 = 0$$

Therefore, by the Law of One Price, the price of the call option today must equal the current market value of the replicating portfolio. The value of the portfolio today is the value of 0.5 shares at the current share price of \$50, less the amount borrowed:

$$50\Delta + B = 50(0.5) - 18.87 = 6.13 \tag{21.3}$$

Thus, the price of the call today is \$6.13.[3]

Figure 21.1 illustrates how we can use the stock and the bond to replicate the payoff of the call option in this case. As a function of the future stock price, the payoff of the replicating portfolio is a line with a slope of $\Delta = 0.5$, and an intercept of $FV(B) = 1.06(-18.87) = -20$. This line is very different from the line showing the payoff

FIGURE 21.1

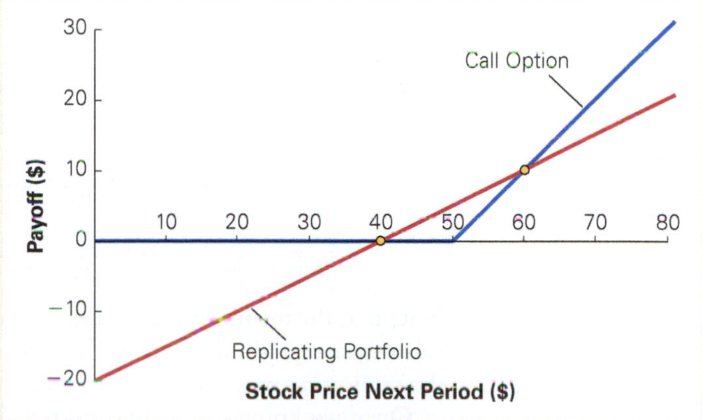

Replicating an Option in the Binomial Model

The red line shows the payoff of the replicating portfolio and the blue line shows the payoff of the call option, as a function of next period's stock price. While they do not match everywhere, they do match for the two possible outcomes of the stock price next period, \$40 and \$60.

[3]If the call's price were different, say \$6.50, there would be an arbitrage opportunity: we could earn a profit by buying the replicating portfolio for \$6.13 and selling the call for \$6.50. Because they have the same payoff, we have taken no risk, and earn an immediate profit of 6.50 − 6.13 = \$0.37 per option.

of the call option, which is zero below the strike price of \$50 and increases 1:1 with the stock price above \$50. The secret of the binomial model is that while the option and the replicating portfolio do not have the same payoffs in general, they have the same payoffs given the only two outcomes we have assumed possible for the stock price: \$40 and \$60.

Note that by using the Law of One Price, we are able to solve for the price of the option *without knowing the probabilities of the states in the binomial tree.* That is, we did not need to specify the likelihood that the stock would go up versus down. This remarkable result was a very important discovery because the probabilities of future states are part of investor beliefs, so they are very difficult to estimate. The preceding argument shows that we do not need to know these probabilities to value options. It also means that we do not need to know the expected return of the stock, which will depend on these probabilities.

The Binomial Pricing Formula

Now that we have seen the basic idea, let's consider a more general example. Suppose the current stock price is S, and the stock price will either go up to S_u or down to S_d next period. The risk-free interest rate is r_f. Let's determine the price of an option that has a value of C_u if the stock goes up, and C_d if the stock goes down:

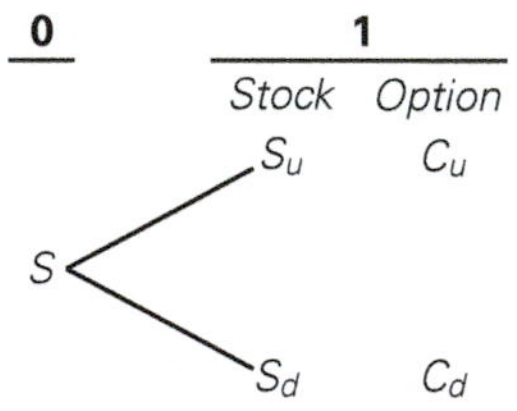

Note that in the depiction of the binomial tree above, for simplicity, we did not write down the bond payoff since it earns a return of r_f in either case.

What is the value of the option today? Again, we must determine the number of shares of stock, Δ, and the position in the bond, B, such that the payoff of the replicating portfolio matches the payoff of the option if the stock goes up or down:

$$S_u \Delta + (1 + r_f)B = C_u \quad \text{and} \quad S_d \Delta + (1 + r_f)B = C_d \tag{21.4}$$

Solving these two equations for the two unknowns Δ and B, we get the general formula for the replicating formula in the binomial model:

Replicating Portfolio in the Binomial Model

$$\Delta = \frac{C_u - C_d}{S_u - S_d} \quad \text{and} \quad B = \frac{C_d - S_d \Delta}{1 + r_f} \tag{21.5}$$

Note that the formula for Δ in Eq. 21.5 can be interpreted as the sensitivity of the option's value to changes in the stock price. It is equal to the slope of the line showing the payoff of the replicating portfolio in Figure 21.1.

Once we know the replicating portfolio, we can calculate the value C of the option today as the cost of this portfolio:

Option Price in the Binomial Model

$$C = S\Delta + B \tag{21.6}$$

Equations 21.5 and 21.6 summarize the binomial option pricing model. Although they are relatively simple, by applying them in different ways we will see that they are quite powerful. For one thing, they do not require that the option we are valuing is a call option—we can use them to value *any* security whose payoff depends on the stock price. For example, we can use them to price a put, as presented in Example 21.1.

EXAMPLE 21.1 **Valuing a Put Option**

Problem

Suppose a stock is currently trading for \$60, and in one period will either go up by 20% or fall by 10%. If the one-period risk-free rate is 3%, what is the price of a European put option that expires in one period and has an exercise price of \$60?

Solution

We begin by constructing a binomial tree:

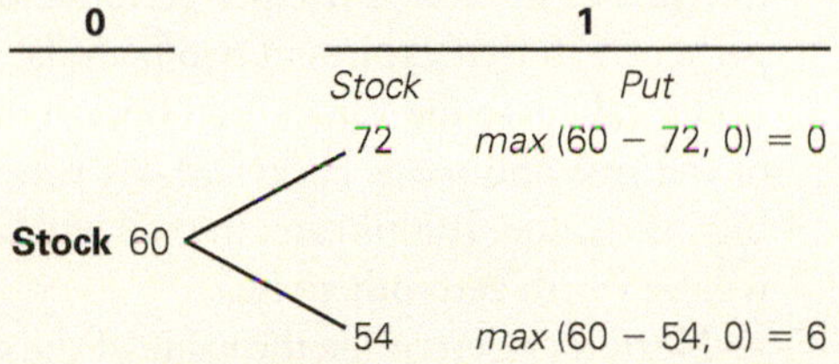

Thus, we can solve for the value of the put by using Eq. 21.5 and Eq. 21.6 with $C_u = 0$ (the value of the put when the stock goes up) and $C_d = 6$ (the value of the put when the stock goes down). Therefore,

$$\Delta = \frac{C_u - C_d}{S_u - S_d} = \frac{0-6}{72-54} = -0.3333 \text{ and } B = \frac{C_d - S_d\,\Delta}{1+r_f} = \frac{6 - 54(-0.3333)}{1.03} = 23.30$$

This portfolio is short 0.3333 shares of the stock, and has \$23.30 invested in the risk-free bond. Let's check that it replicates the put if the stock goes up or down:

$$72(-0.3333) + 1.03(23.30) = 0 \text{ and } 54(-0.3333) + 1.03(23.30) = 6$$

Thus, the value of the put is the initial cost of this portfolio. Using Eq. 21.6:

$$\begin{aligned}\text{Put value} &= C = S\Delta + B \\ &= 60(-0.3333) + 23.30 = \$3.30\end{aligned}$$

You might be skeptical at this point. Showing that we can value call and put options in a simple two-state one-period example is one thing; pricing real-world options is another matter altogether. Yet, as we show in the next section, this simple two-state model is easily generalized.

A Multiperiod Model

The problem with the simple two-state example is that there are many more than two possible outcomes for the stock price in the real world. To make the model more realistic, we must allow for the possibility of many states and periods.

Let's consider a two-period binomial tree for the stock price:[4]

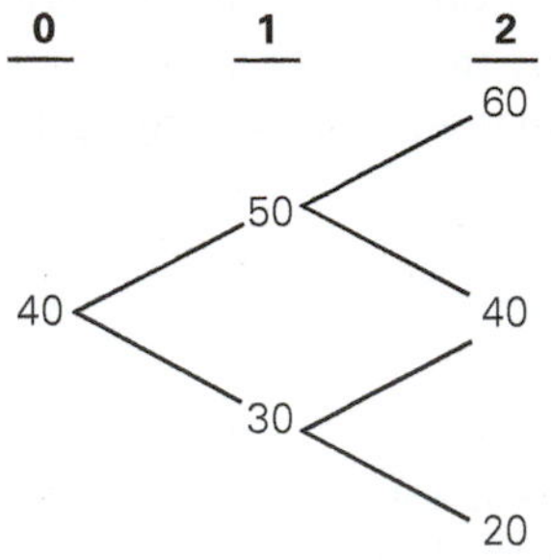

The key property of the binomial model is that in each period, there are only two possible outcomes—the stock either goes up or down. But by adding an additional period, the number of possible stock prices at the end has increased. Let's assume again that the risk-free rate of interest is 6% per period and consider how to price a call option with a strike price of \$50 that expires in two periods.

To calculate the value of an option in a multiperiod binomial tree, we start at the end of the tree and work backward. At time 2, the option expires, so its value is equal to its intrinsic value. In this case, the call will be worth \$10 if the stock price goes up to \$60, and will be worth zero otherwise.

Next, let's determine the value of the option in each possible state at time 1. What is the value of the option if the stock price has gone up to \$50 at time 1? In this case, because the option expires next period, the remaining part of the binomial tree is as follows:

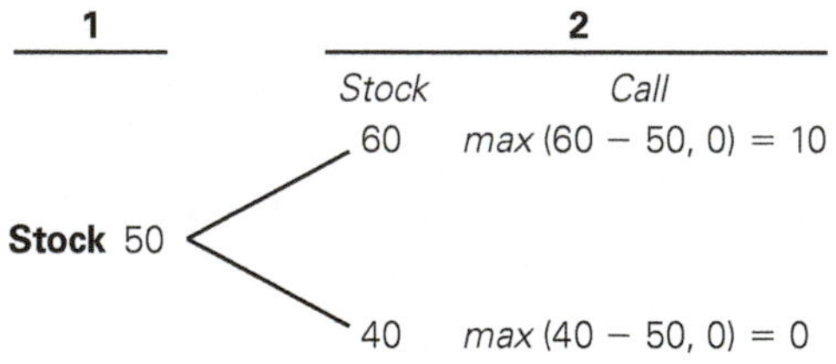

This binomial tree is exactly the same tree that we considered in the one-period model at the start of this section. There, we computed the replicating portfolio as having $\Delta = 0.5$ shares of stock and a bond position of $B = -\$18.87$, for an initial call value of \$6.13 (see Eq. 21.3).

What if the stock price has dropped to \$30 at time 1? In that case, the binomial tree for the next period is

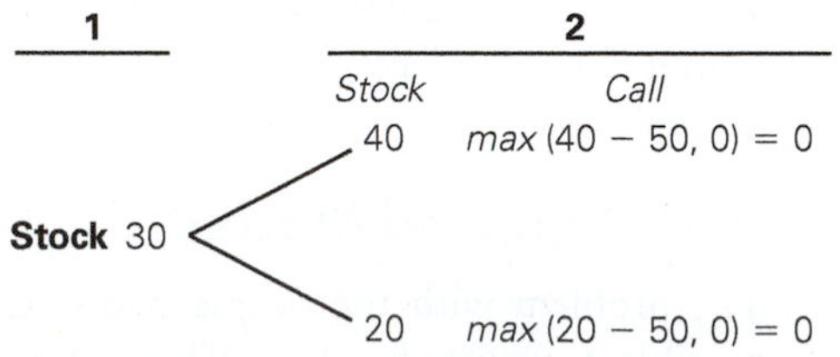

---

[4]The multiperiod tree is sometimes referred to as a *binomial lattice*.

The option is worthless in both states at time 2, so the value of the option in the down state at time 1 must also be zero (and the replicating portfolio is simply $\Delta = 0$ and $B = 0$).

Given the value of the call option in either state at time 1, we can now work backward and determine the value of the call at time 0. In that case, we can write the binomial tree over the next period as follows:

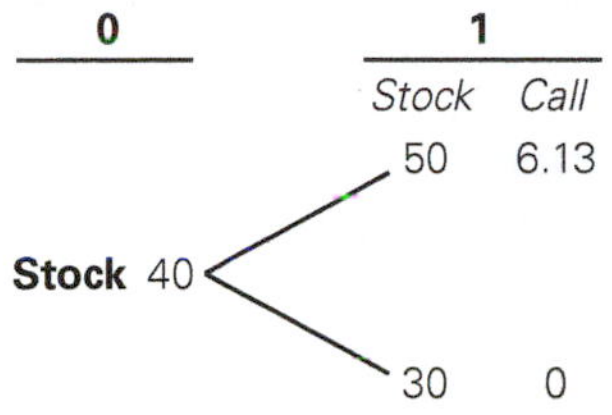

In this case, the call values at the end of the tree (time 1) are not the final payoffs of the option, but are the values of the option one period prior to expiration. Nonetheless, we can use the same binomial formulas to calculate the replicating portfolio at time 0, which is a portfolio whose value will match the value of the option at time 1. From Eq. 21.5:

$$\Delta = \frac{C_u - C_d}{S_u - S_d} = \frac{6.13 - 0}{50 - 30} = 0.3065 \quad \text{and}$$

$$B = \frac{C_d - S_d\,\Delta}{1 + r_f} = \frac{0 - 30(0.3065)}{1.06} = -8.67$$

From Eq. 21.6, the initial value of the call option is equal to the initial cost of this portfolio:

$$C = S\Delta + B = 40(0.3065) - 8.67 = \$3.59$$

Therefore, the initial value of the call option at time 0 is \$3.59.

For this two-period call option, while we can still construct the option out of the stock and the bond, we now need to adjust our replicating portfolio at the end of each period. That is, we start off long 0.3065 shares of stock and borrow \$8.67 (for an initial cost of \$3.59). If the stock price drops to \$30, our shares are worth $\$30 \times 0.3065 = \$9.20$, and our debt has grown to $\$8.67 \times 1.06 = \$9.20$. Thus, the net value of the portfolio is worthless (matching the option value), and we can liquidate the portfolio (at no cost). If the stock price rises to \$50, the net value of the portfolio rises to \$6.13. In that case, the new Δ of the replicating portfolio is 0.5. Therefore, to match the new Δ, we buy $0.50 - 0.3065 = 0.1935$ more shares of stock and pay for it by borrowing $0.1935 \times \$50 = \$9.67$. This re-trading requires no new money; at the end our total debt will be $\$8.67 \times 1.06 + \$9.67 = \$18.87$, which matches the value for B we calculated earlier. Finally, on the expiration date at time 2, the value of the portfolio is \$10 if the stock goes up to \$60, and is zero otherwise.

The idea that you can replicate the option payoff by dynamically trading in a portfolio of the underlying stock and a risk-free bond was one of the most important contributions of the original Black-Scholes paper. Today, this kind of replication strategy is called a **dynamic trading strategy**.

EXAMPLE 21.2 Using the Binomial Option Pricing Model to Value a Put Option

Problem

Suppose the current price of Narver Network Systems stock is \$50 per share. In each of the next two years, the stock price will either increase by 20% or decrease by 10%. The 3% one-year risk-free rate of interest will remain constant. Calculate the price of a two-year European put option on Narver Network Systems stock with a strike price \$60.

Solution

Here is the binomial tree for the stock price, together with the final payoffs of the put option:

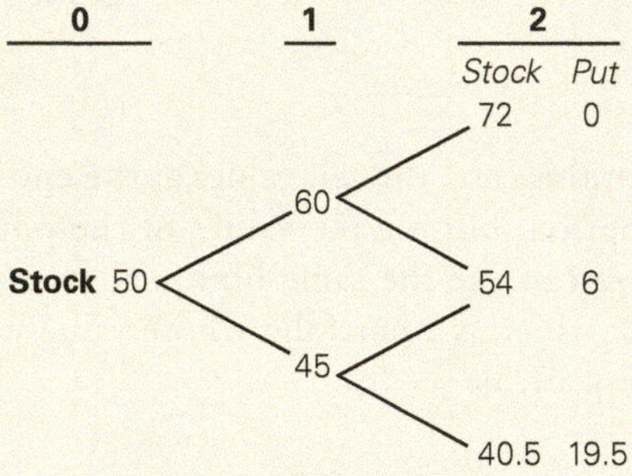

If the stock goes up to \$60 at time 1, we are in exactly the same situation as in Example 21.1. Using our result there, we see that if the stock is worth \$60 at time 1, the value of the put option is \$3.30.

If the stock goes down to \$45 at time 1, then at time 2 the put option will be worth either \$6 if the stock goes up or \$19.50 if the stock goes down. Using Eq. 21.5:

$$\Delta = \frac{C_u - C_d}{S_u - S_d} = \frac{6 - 19.5}{54 - 40.5} = -1 \text{ and } B = \frac{C_d - S_d \Delta}{1 + r_f} = \frac{19.5 - 40.5(-1)}{1.03} = 58.25$$

This portfolio is short one share of the stock, and has \$58.25 invested in the risk-free bond. Because the value of the bond will grow to \$58.25 × 1.03 = \$60 at time 2, the value of the replicating portfolio will be \$60 less the final price of the stock, matching the payoff of the put option. Thus, the value of the put is the cost of this portfolio. Using Eq. 21.6:

$$\text{Put value} = C = S\Delta + B = 45(-1) + 58.25 = \$13.25$$

Now consider the value of the put option at time 0. In period 1, we have calculated that the put will be worth \$3.30 if the stock goes up to \$60 and \$13.25 if the stock falls to \$45. The binomial tree at time 0 is

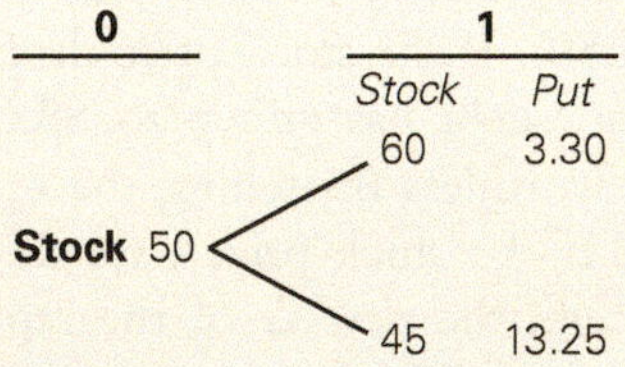

Using Eq. 21.5 and Eq. 21.6, the replicating portfolio and put value at time 0 are

$$\Delta = \frac{C_u - C_d}{S_u - S_d} = \frac{3.30 - 13.25}{60 - 45} = -0.6633,$$

$$B = \frac{C_d - S_d \Delta}{1 + r_f} = \frac{13.25 - 45(-0.6633)}{1.03} = 41.84, \text{ and}$$

$$\text{Put value} = C = S\Delta + B = 50(-0.6633) + 41.84 = \$8.68$$

Thus, the value of a European put option at time 0 is \$8.68.

Making the Model Realistic

Using the methods of the previous section, we can value options given any number of periods in the binomial stock price tree. But of course, to price an option for an actual stock, the binomial tree must be a realistic model of the way the stock is likely to evolve in the future.

While binary up or down movements are not the way stock prices behave on an annual or even daily basis, they are a much more reasonable description of stock prices over very short time periods, such as the time between trades. By decreasing the length of each period, and increasing the number of periods in the stock price tree, we can construct a realistic model for the stock price. Figure 21.2 shows an example of a stock price path in which the stock price moves up or down by 1% in each of 900 periods over the year. With many short periods, these stock price paths look very similar to the price charts for real stocks. Practitioners routinely use this method to calculate the prices of options and other types of derivative securities. With a fast computer, prices can be computed very quickly even with thousands of periods.[5]

As mentioned earlier, the techniques of the binomial option pricing model are not specific to European call and put options. We can use it to price any security whose payoff depends on the stock price. But for the special case of European call and put options, there is an alternative approach. If we let the length of each period shrink to zero, and the number of periods per year grows to infinity, the results of the binomial option pricing model can be calculated using a single, simple formula: the Black-Scholes formula. We consider it next.

FIGURE 21.2

A Binomial Stock Price Path

The figure depicts a stock price path with 900 periods during the year, and a random stock return of +1% or −1% each period. With a large number of periods, and small movements in the stock price each period, the binomial model is a realistic model of stock price behavior.

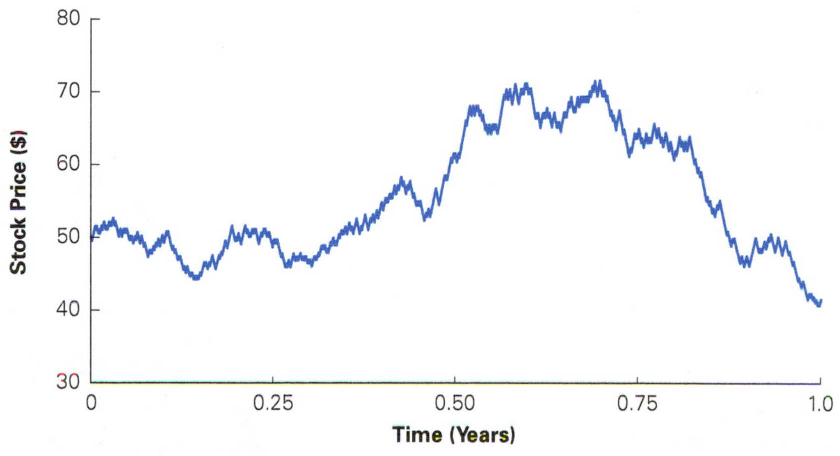

CONCEPT CHECK

1. What is the key assumption of the binomial option pricing model?
2. Why don't we need to know the probabilities of the states in the binominal tree in order to solve for the price of the option?
3. What is a replicating portfolio?

---

[5]There is a question of how to calibrate the up or down movements each period. A standard approach is to assume the stock's return each period is $\pm\sigma/\sqrt{n}$, where σ is the stock's volatility and n is the number of periods per year.

21.2 The Black-Scholes Option Pricing Model

Although Fischer Black and Myron Scholes did not originally derive it that way, the **Black-Scholes Option Pricing Model** can be derived from the Binomial Option Pricing Model by making the length of each period, and the movement of the stock price per period, shrink to zero and letting the number of periods grow infinitely large. Rather than derive the formula here, we will state it and focus on its applications.

The Black-Scholes Formula

Before stating the Black-Scholes formula for the price of an option, it is necessary to introduce some terminology. Let S be the current price of the stock, T be the number of years left to expiration, K be the exercise price, and σ be the annual volatility (standard deviation) of the stock's return. Then, the value, at time t, of a call option on a stock that does not pay dividends prior to the option's expiration date is given by

Black-Scholes Price of a Call Option on a Non-Dividend-Paying Stock

$$C = S \times N(d_1) - PV(K) \times N(d_2) \tag{21.7}$$

where $PV(K)$ is the present value (price) of a risk-free zero-coupon bond that pays K on the expiration date of the option, $N(d)$ is the **cumulative normal distribution**—that is, the probability, as shown in Figure 21.3, that a normally distributed variable is less than d—and

$$d_1 = \frac{\ln[S/PV(K)]}{\sigma\sqrt{T}} + \frac{\sigma\sqrt{T}}{2} \quad \text{and} \quad d_2 = d_1 - \sigma\sqrt{T} \tag{21.8}$$

FIGURE 21.3

Normal Distribution

$N(d)$, the cumulative normal distribution, is the probability that a normally distributed random variable will take on a value less than d. This probability is equal to the area under the normal distribution (bell curve) to the left of the point d—the shaded area in the figure. Because it is a probability, $N(d)$ has a minimum value of 0 and a maximum value of 1. It can be calculated in Excel by using the function NORMSDIST(d).

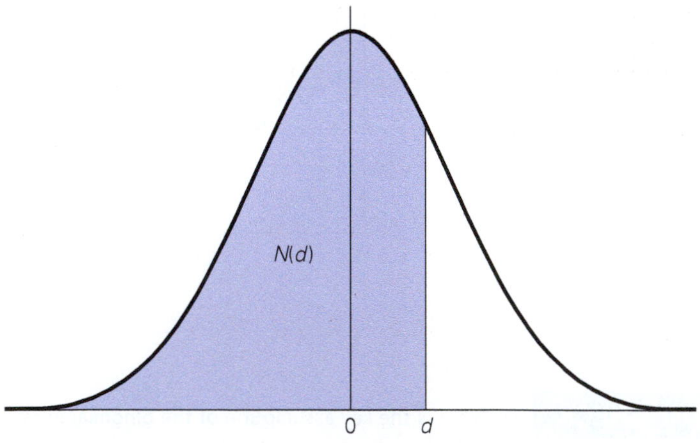

INTERVIEW WITH MYRON S. SCHOLES

Professor Myron S. Scholes is co-inventor of the Black-Scholes options pricing model, for which he won the Nobel Prize for Economic Sciences in 1997. He is the Frank E. Buck Professor of Finance, Emeritus, at Stanford Graduate School of Business.

QUESTION: *At the time you derived the Black-Scholes formula, did you anticipate its influence in the financial world?*

ANSWER: Fischer Black and I believed that the option-pricing technology would be used to value existing contracts such as options on stock, warrants, corporate debt, and mortgage contracts. We did not anticipate that in the future our technology would be used to develop and price new instruments, although we were not alone. For example, several journals rejected our paper. Only after Merton Miller explained to the editors of the *Journal of Political Economy* that our findings were not arcane but had general importance did it accept our paper. Fischer and I rewrote the paper to include a description of the importance of options in the economy, such as how to value the stock of a corporation with risky debt in its capital structure.

QUESTION: *What is the most important contribution of the Black-Scholes formula?*

ANSWER: The Black-Scholes option paper has two parts: a technology to value options and an illustration of that technology to the pricing of options under a stylized set of assumptions that was later called the Black-Scholes options pricing model. The Nobel Prize was awarded, in part, for developing the technology to value derivatives. We showed that if investors could hedge the systematic components of asset returns, then the remaining risks were unsystematic and the expected return of a portfolio of unsystematic risks will equal the risk-free rate. Moreover, as trading-time became continuous, the unsystematic risk would disappear.

When we developed the model we did not believe that the risk-free rate or the volatility of an asset remained constant. We assumed that to be the case, however, to illustrate the application of the model. This illustration became the Black-Scholes model. The underlying technology does not assume the constancy of either parameter. What impressed and particularly pleased me was the realization that investors could price an option without knowing the expected rate of return on the underlying asset or the expected terminal value of the option at its maturity. I believe that the technology to value options and the underlying economics to support its development were the most important part of our paper.

QUESTION: *How did you arrive at the insight that you could create a risk-free portfolio trading the stock and option?*

ANSWER: We first needed to determine how much stock to short against a long position in the underlying option, such that small movements in the price of the underlying stock would be offset by opposite movements in the price of the option—a hedged position. As explained above, if the returns on this combined stock and option investment were uncorrelated with the market portfolio (assuming that CAPM held over short time periods—i.e., the returns were normally distributed) or riskless in continuous time (if investors could trade continuously to adjust their stock position), to prevent arbitrage profits the return on the hedged position had to be equal to the risk-free rate.

QUESTION: *What words of wisdom might you offer future practitioners on using the Black-Scholes formula in light of the 2007–2009 financial crisis?*

ANSWER: Some blamed models such as ours for the financial crisis. In part, the model can't be correct other than for relatively short-dated options; it would not make economic sense to use the same calibration of the pricing technology over long periods of time. Most of the difficulties in using models arise from the incorrect use of technology and assumptions of how to calibrate the models. The crisis highlighted once again that assumptions are important in building and calibrating models.

We need only five input parameters to price the call: the stock price, the strike price, the exercise date, the risk-free interest rate (to compute the present value of the strike price), and the volatility of the stock. What is equally notable is what we do *not* need. Just as we do not need to know the probabilities in the Binomial Option Pricing Model, we do not need to know the expected return on the stock to calculate the option price in the Black-Scholes Option Pricing Model. The expected return of the stock is difficult to measure with great accuracy as we learned in Part 4; if it were a required input, we could not expect the formula to deliver the option price with much accuracy. Indeed, the only parameter in the Black-Scholes formula that we need to forecast is the stock's volatility. Because a stock's volatility is much easier to measure (and forecast) than its expected return, the Black-Scholes formula can be very precise.

You might wonder how it is possible to compute the value of a security like an option that appears to depend critically on the future stock price without knowing the expected return of the stock. In fact, the expected return of the stock is already reflected in the stock's current price (which is the discounted value of its future payoffs). The Black-Scholes formula depends on the stock's current price, and so, in a sense, uses this information implicitly.

The Black-Scholes formula is derived assuming that the call is a European option. Recall from Chapter 20 that an American call option on a non-dividend-paying stock always has the same price as its European counterpart. Thus, the Black-Scholes formula can be used to price American or European call options on non-dividend-paying stocks.

EXAMPLE 21.3 Valuing a Call Option with the Black-Scholes Formula

Problem

JetBlue Airways does not pay dividends. Using the data in Table 21.1, compare the price on July 24, 2009, for the December 2009 American call option on JetBlue with a strike price of \$6 to the price predicted by the Black-Scholes formula. Assume that the volatility of JetBlue is 65% per year and that the risk-free rate of interest is 1% per year.

Solution

We use \$5.03 (the closing price) for the per-share price of JetBlue stock. Because the December contract expires on the Saturday following the third Friday of December (December 19), there are 148 days left until expiration. The present value of the strike price is $PV(K) = 6.00/(1.01)^{148/365} = \$5.976$. Calculating d_1 and d_2 from Eq. 21.8 gives

$$d_1 = \frac{\ln[S/PV(K)]}{\sigma\sqrt{T}} + \frac{\sigma\sqrt{T}}{2}$$

$$= \frac{\ln(5.03/5.976)}{0.65\sqrt{\frac{148}{365}}} + \frac{0.65\sqrt{\frac{148}{365}}}{2} = -0.209$$

$$d_2 = d_1 - \sigma\sqrt{T} = -0.209 - 0.65\sqrt{\tfrac{148}{365}} = -0.623$$

Substituting d_1 and d_2 into the Black-Scholes formula given by Eq. 21.7 results in

$$\begin{aligned} C &= S \times N(d_1) - PV(K) \times N(d_2) \\ &= 5.03 \times 0.417 - 5.976 \times 0.267 \\ &= \$0.50 \end{aligned}$$

In Table 21.1, the bid and ask prices for this option are \$0.45 and \$0.55.

TABLE 21.1 JetBlue Option Quotes

JBLU 5.03 +0.11

Jul 24 2009 @ 17:17 ET **Bid** 5.03 **Ask** 5.04 **Size** 168 × 96 **Vol** 7335887

Calls	Bid	Ask	Vol	Open Int	Puts	Bid	Ask	Vol	Open Int
09 Dec 5.00 (JGQ LA)	0.80	0.90	47	5865	09 Dec 5.00 (JGQ XA)	0.80	0.90	6	1000
09 Dec 6.00 (JGQ LF)	0.45	0.55	2	259	09 Dec 6.00 (JGQ XF)	1.40	1.50	0	84
10 Jan 5.00 (JGQ AA)	0.85	1.00	125	6433	10 Jan 5.00 (JGQ MA)	0.85	0.95	10	14737
10 Jan 6.00 (JGQ AF)	0.50	0.60	28	0	10 Jan 6.00 (JGQ MF)	1.45	1.55	0	22
10 Jan 9.00 (JGQ AI)	0.05	0.15	0	818	10 Jan 9.00 (JGQ MI)	4.00	4.10	0	0
10 Mar 5.00 (JGQ CA)	1.05	1.15	0	50	10 Mar 5.00 (JGQ OA)	1.00	1.10	0	40
10 Mar 6.00 (JGQ CF)	0.65	0.75	0	146	10 Mar 6.00 (JGQ OF)	1.60	1.70	10	41
10 Mar 7.00 (JGQ CG)	0.40	0.50	5	3	10 Mar 7.00 (JGQ OG)	2.30	2.45	10	0

Source: Chicago Board Options Exchange at www.cboe.com

Figure 21.4 plots the value of the call option in Example 21.3 as a function of JetBlue's current stock price. Notice how the value of the option always lies above its intrinsic value.

European Put Options. We can use the Black-Scholes formula to compute the price of a European put option on a non-dividend-paying stock by using the put-call parity formula we derived in Chapter 20 (see Eq. 20.3). The price of a European put from put-call parity is

$$P = C - S + PV(K)$$

Substituting for C using the Black-Scholes formula gives

Black-Scholes Price of a European Put Option on a Non-Dividend-Paying Stock

$$P = PV(K)[1 - N(d_2)] - S[1 - N(d_1)] \tag{21.9}$$

FIGURE 21.4

Black-Scholes Value on July 24, 2009, of the December 2009 $6 Call on JetBlue Stock

The red curve shows the Black-Scholes value of the call option as a function of JetBlue's stock price. The circle shows the value at JetBlue's current price of $5.03. The black line is the intrinsic value of the call.

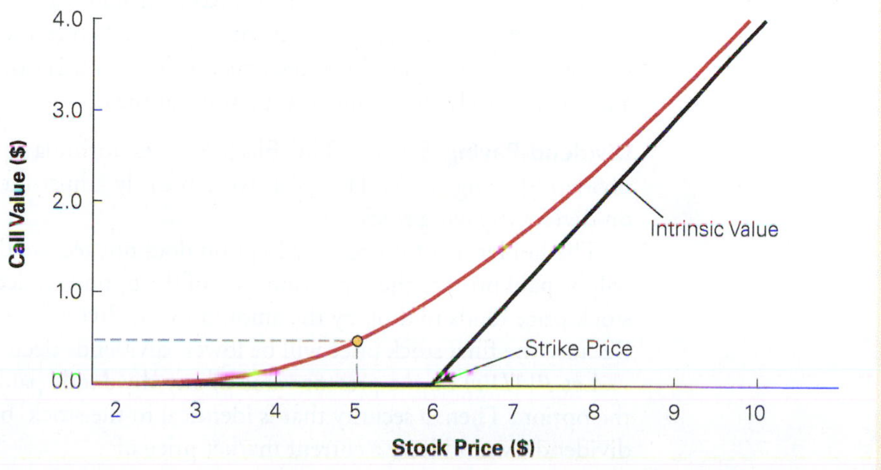

EXAMPLE 21.4 Valuing a Put Option with the Black-Scholes Formula

Problem

Using the Black-Scholes formula and the data in Table 21.1, compute the price of a January 2010 $5 put option and compare it to the price in the market. Is the Black-Scholes formula the correct way to price these options? (As before, assume that the volatility of JetBlue is 65% per year and that the risk-free rate of interest is 1% per year.)

Solution

The contract expires on January 16, 2010, or 176 days from the quote date. The present value of the strike price is $PV(K) = 5.00/(1.01)^{176/365} = \$4.976$. Calculating d_1 and d_2 from Eq. 21.8 gives

$$d_1 = \frac{\ln[S/PV(K)]}{\sigma\sqrt{T}} + \frac{\sigma\sqrt{T}}{2}$$

$$= \frac{\ln(5.03/4.976)}{0.65\sqrt{\frac{176}{365}}} + \frac{0.65\sqrt{\frac{176}{365}}}{2} = 0.250$$

$$d_2 = d_1 - \sigma\sqrt{T} = 0.250 - 0.65\sqrt{\tfrac{176}{365}} = -0.201$$

Substituting d_1 and d_2 into the Black-Scholes formula for a put option, using Eq. 21.9, gives

$$P = PV(K)[1 - N(d_2)] - S[1 - N(d_1)]$$

$$= 4.976 \times (1 - 0.420) - 5.03 \times (1 - 0.599)$$

$$= \$0.87$$

Given the bid and ask prices of $0.85 and $0.95, respectively, for the option, this estimate is within the bid-ask spread. But the Black-Scholes formula for puts is valid for European options, and the quotes are for American options. Hence, in this case, the Black-Scholes option price is a lower bound on the actual value of the put, as an American put might be exercised early to benefit from interest on the strike price. However, given that interest on the $5 strike price is less than $0.03, in this case the approximation is a close one.

Figure 21.5 plots the Black-Scholes value of the European put option in Example 21.4 as a function of JetBlue's stock price. Recall from Chapter 20 that the time value of deep-in-the-money European puts can be negative. While the put value does falls below its intrinsic value in Figure 21.5, the effect is slight in this case given low current interest rates and the relatively short time to expiration of the option.

Dividend-Paying Stocks. The Black-Scholes formula applies to call options on non-dividend-paying stocks. However, we can easily adjust the formula for European options on dividend-paying stocks.

The holder of a European call option does not receive the benefit of any dividends that will be paid prior to the expiration date of the option. Indeed, as we saw in Chapter 17, the stock price tends to drop by the amount of the dividend when the stock goes ex-dividend. Because the final stock price will be lower, dividends decrease the value of a call option.

Let $PV(Div)$ be the present value of any dividends paid prior to the expiration date of the option. Then, a security that is identical to the stock, but that did not pay any of these dividends, would have a current market price of

$$S^x = S - PV(Div) \tag{21.10}$$

FIGURE 21.5

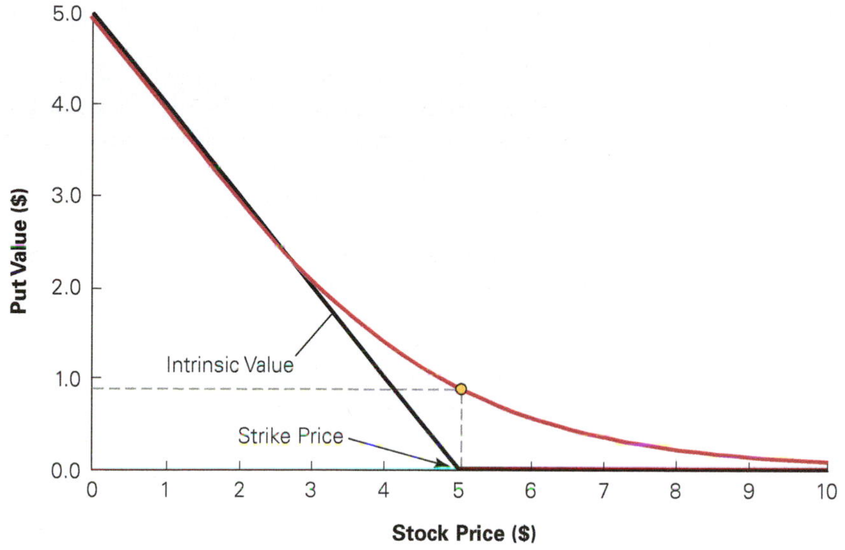

Black-Scholes Value on July 24, 2009, of the January 2010 $5 Put on JetBlue Stock

The red curve shows the Black-Scholes value of the put option as a function of JetBlue's stock price. The circle shows the value at JetBlue's current price of $5.03. The black line is the intrinsic value of the put. For stock prices below $2.25, the European put's value is slightly less than its intrinsic value.

The value S^x is the current price of the stock excluding any dividends prior to expiration. *Because a European call option is the right to buy the stock without these dividends, we can evaluate it using the Black-Scholes formula with S^x in place of S.*

A useful special case is when the stock will pay a dividend that is proportional to its stock price at the time the dividend is paid. If q is the stock's (compounded) dividend yield until the expiration date, then[6]

$$S^x = S/(1 + q) \tag{21.11}$$

EXAMPLE 21.5

Valuing a Dividend-Paying European Call Option with the Black-Scholes Formula

Problem

World Wide Plants will pay an annual dividend yield of 5% on its stock. Plot the value of a one-year European call option with a strike price of $20 on World Wide Plants stock as a function of the stock price. Assume that the volatility of World Wide Plants stock is 20% per year and that the one-year risk-free rate of interest is 4%.

Solution

The price of the call is given by the standard Black-Scholes formula, Eq. 21.7, but with the stock price replaced throughout with $S^x = S/(1.05)$. For example, with a stock price of $30, $S^x = 30/(1.05) = 28.57$, $PV(K) = 20/1.04 = 19.23$, and

[6] To see why, suppose that whenever the dividend is paid, we reinvest it. Then, if we buy $1/(1 + q)$ shares today, at expiration we will own $[1/(1 + q)] \times (1 + q) = 1$ share. Thus, by the Law of One Price, the value today of receiving 1 share at expiration is $S/(1 + q)$.

$$d_1 = \frac{\ln[S^x/PV(K)]}{\sigma\sqrt{T}} + \frac{\sigma\sqrt{T}}{2}$$

$$= \frac{\ln(28.57/19.23)}{0.2} + 0.1 = 2.08$$

$$d_2 = d_1 - \sigma\sqrt{T} = 2.08 - 0.2 = 1.88$$

so

$$C(S) = S^x N(d_1) - PV(K)N(d_2) = 28.57(0.981) - 19.23(0.970) = 9.37$$

The plot below shows the value of the call (in red) for different levels of the stock price. When the stock price is sufficiently high, the call is worth less than its intrinsic value.

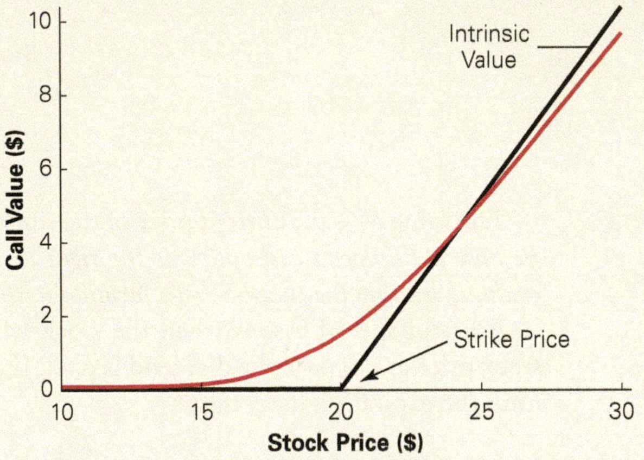

Implied Volatility

Of the five required inputs in the Black-Scholes formula, four are directly observable: S, K, T, and the risk-free interest rate. Only one parameter, σ, the volatility of the stock price, is not directly observable. Practitioners use two strategies to estimate the value of this variable. The first, most straightforward approach is to use historical data on daily stock returns to estimate the volatility of the stock over the past several months. Because volatility tends to be persistent, such estimates can provide a reasonable forecast for the stock's volatility in the near future.

The second approach is to use the current market prices of traded options to "back out" the volatility that is consistent with these prices based on the Black-Scholes formula. An estimate of a stock's volatility that is implied by an option's price is known as an **implied volatility**. The implied volatility from one option can be used to estimate the value of other options on the stock with the same expiration date (as well as those with different expiration dates if the stock's volatility is not expected to change over time).

EXAMPLE 21.6 Computing the Implied Volatility from an Option Price

Problem

Use the price of the March 2010 call on JetBlue with a strike price of \$5 in Table 21.1 to calculate the implied volatility for JetBlue from July 2009 to March 2010. Assume the risk-free rate of interest is 1% per year.

Solution

The call expires on March 20, 2010, or 239 days after the quote date. The stock price is \$5.03, and $PV(K) = 5.00/(1.01)^{239/365} = \$4.968$. Substituting these values into the Black-Scholes formula, Eq. 21.7, gives

$$C = 5.03N(d_1) - 4.968N(d_2)$$

where

$$d_1 = \frac{\ln(5.03/4.968)}{\sigma\sqrt{\frac{239}{365}}} + \frac{\sigma\sqrt{\frac{239}{365}}}{2} \quad \text{and} \quad d_2 = d_1 - \sigma\sqrt{\frac{239}{365}}$$

We can compute the Black-Scholes option value C for different volatilities using this equation. The option value C increases with σ, and equals \$1.10 (average bid and ask price for the call) when $\sigma \approx 67\%$. (You can find this value by trial and error or by using Excel's Solver tool.) If we look at the bid price of \$1.05, the implied volatility is about 64%, and at the ask price of \$1.15, the implied volatility is about 70%. Thus, the 65% volatility we used in Example 21.3 and Example 21.4 is within the bid-ask spread for the option.

GLOBAL FINANCIAL CRISIS The VIX Index

The use of the Black-Scholes option pricing formula to compute implied volatility has become so ubiquitous that in January 1990 the Chicago Board Options Exchange introduced the **VIX Index**, which tracks the one-month implied volatility of options written on the S&P 500 index. Quoted in percent per annum, this index has since become one of the most-cited measures of market volatility. Because it characterizes the level of investor uncertainty, it is often referred to as the "fear index."

As the figure below shows, while the average level of the VIX is about 20%, the index does indeed rise during times of crisis and heightened uncertainty. This effect is illustrated most dramatically during the U.S. financial crisis, with the VIX nearly quadrupling between September and October 2008, to a level almost twice its previous all-time high. The index remained at these historically high levels for several months, reflecting the unprecedented uncertainty that accompanied the financial crisis. As this uncertainty dissipated in mid-2009, the index began to drop, reflecting renewed investor confidence. Since then, however, uncertainty in Europe and Asia has led to time periods when the VIX again topped 40%.

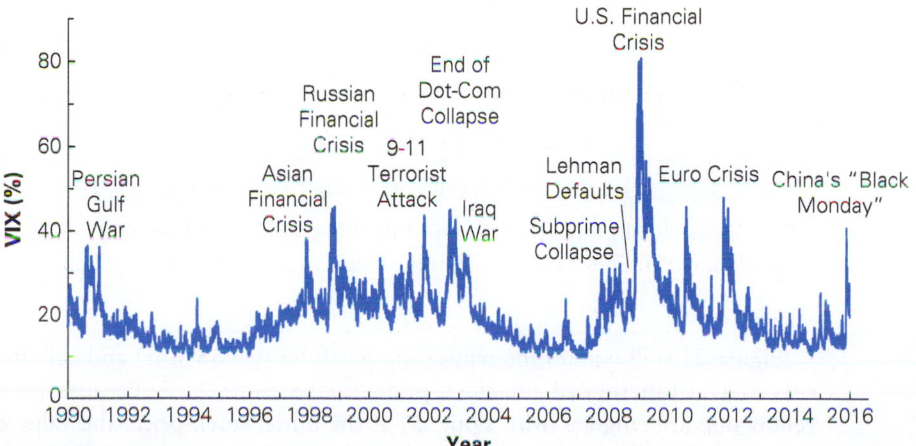

Source: Yahoo! Finance

The Replicating Portfolio

Although we introduced the concept of the replicating portfolio in the discussion of the Binomial Option Pricing Model, it was actually Fischer Black and Myron Scholes who discovered this important insight while deriving their model. To see how the replicating portfolio is constructed in the Black-Scholes Model, recall from the Binomial Option Pricing Model that the price of a call option is given by the price of the replicating portfolio, as shown in Eq. 21.6:

$$C = S\Delta + B$$

Comparing this expression to the Black-Scholes formula from Eq. 21.7 gives the shares of stock and amount in bonds in the Black-Scholes replicating portfolio:

Black-Scholes Replicating Portfolio of a Call Option

$$\begin{aligned} \Delta &= N(d_1) \\ B &= -PV(K)N(d_2) \end{aligned} \tag{21.12}$$

Recall that $N(d)$ is the cumulative normal distribution function; that is, it has a minimum value of 0 and a maximum value of 1. So, Δ is between 0 and 1, and B is between $-K$ and 0. The **option delta**, Δ, has a natural interpretation: It is the change in the price of the option given a $1 change in the price of the stock. Because Δ is always less than 1, the change in the call price is always less than the change in the stock price.

EXAMPLE 21.7 Computing the Replicating Portfolio

Problem

PNA Systems pays no dividends and has a current stock price of $10 per share. If its returns have a volatility of 40% and the risk-free rate is 5%, what portfolio would you hold today to replicate a one-year at-the-money call option on the stock?

Solution

We can apply the Black-Scholes formula with $S = 10$, $PV(K) = 10/1.05 = 9.524$, and

$$d_1 = \frac{\ln[S/PV(K)]}{\sigma\sqrt{T}} + \frac{\sigma\sqrt{T}}{2} = \frac{\ln(10/9.524)}{40\%} + \frac{40\%}{2} = 0.322$$

$$d_2 = d_1 - \sigma\sqrt{T} = 0.322 - 0.40 = -0.078$$

From Eq. 21.12, the replicating portfolio for the option is

$$\Delta = N(d_1) = N(0.322) = 0.626$$

$$B = -PV(K)N(d_2) = -9.524 \times N(-0.078) = -4.47$$

That is, we should buy 0.626 shares of the PNA stock, and borrow $4.47, for a total cost of $10(0.626) − 4.47 = $1.79, which is the Black-Scholes value of the call option.

Figure 21.6 illustrates the replicating portfolio (yellow line) and call option value (red curve), as a function of the stock price, for Example 21.7. Because the red curve and yellow line are tangent (with slope Δ) at the initial stock price, the value of the replicating portfolio will approximate the value of the call option for small changes to the stock price. But as the stock price changes, the replicating portfolio will need to be updated to

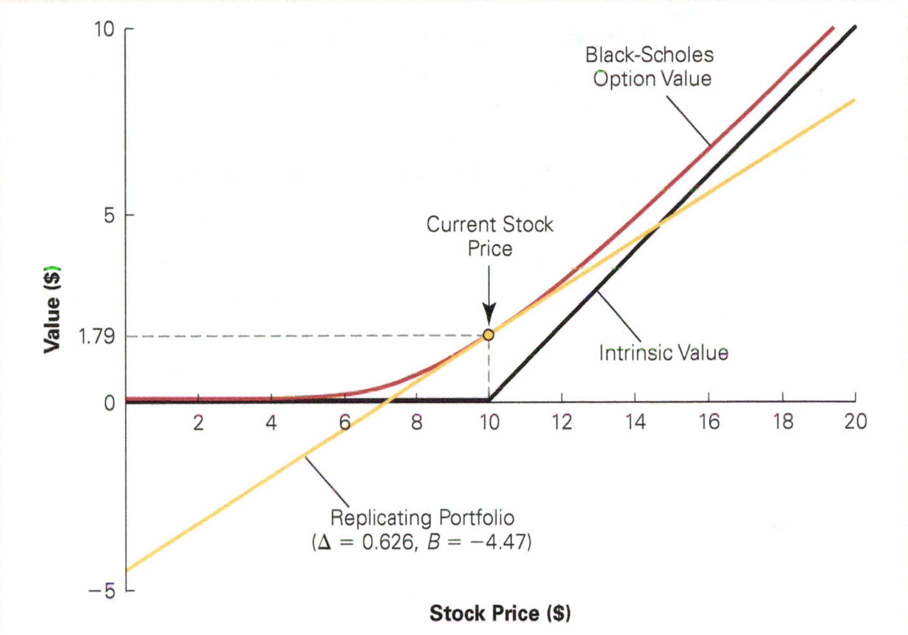

FIGURE 21.6

Replicating Portfolio for the Call Option in Example 21.7

The replicating portfolio has the same initial value as the call option, and the same initial sensitivity to the stock price (given by Δ). Because the red curve and the yellow line are tangent, the value of the replicating portfolio will approximate the value of the call option for small changes to the stock price. But to maintain accuracy, the replicating portfolio must be updated as the stock price changes.

maintain accuracy. For example, if the stock price increases, the replicating portfolio will correspond to a new, steeper tangent line higher on the red curve. Because a steeper line corresponds to a higher Δ, to replicate the option it is necessary to buy shares as the stock price increases.

This dynamic trading strategy is analogous to the ones we derived earlier for the Binomial Option Pricing Model. In the binomial model, we were able to replicate the payoff of an option because we only needed to match two of its payoffs at any time. The great insight of Black, Scholes, and Merton was that if we can update our portfolio continuously, we can replicate an option on the stock by constantly adjusting our portfolio to remain on a line that is tangent to the value of the option.

Notice that the replicating portfolio of a call option always consists of a long position in the stock and a short position in the bond; in other words, the replicating portfolio is a leveraged position in the stock. Because a leveraged position in a stock is riskier than the stock itself, this implies that call options on a positive beta stock are *more* risky than the underlying stock and therefore have higher returns and higher betas.

We can also derive the replicating portfolio for a put option. Comparing the Black-Scholes price of a put from Eq. 21.9 with Eq. 21.6 gives

Black-Scholes Replicating Portfolio of a Put Option

$$\Delta = -[1 - N(d_1)]$$
$$B = PV(K)[1 - N(d_2)] \tag{21.13}$$

In this case, Δ is between -1 and 0, and B is between 0 and K. Thus, the replicating portfolio of a put option always consists of a long position in the bond and a short position in the stock, implying that put options on a positive beta stock will have a negative beta.

CONCEPT CHECK

1. What are the inputs of the Black-Scholes option pricing formula?
2. What is the implied volatility of a stock?
3. How does the delta of a call option change as the stock price increases?

21.3 Risk-Neutral Probabilities

In both the Binomial and Black-Scholes Pricing Models, we do not need to know the probability of each possible future stock price to calculate the option price. But what if we did know these probabilities? In that case, we could calculate the price of the option as we have done for other financial assets: We could calculate the expected payoff of the option and discount it at the appropriate cost of capital. The drawback of this approach is that even if we know the probabilities, it is very difficult to estimate the cost of capital for a particular asset, and options are no exception. There is, however, one case in which the cost of capital can be precisely estimated. If all market participants were risk neutral, then *all* financial assets (including options) would have the same cost of capital—the risk-free rate of interest. Let's consider that scenario and see its implications for option prices.

A Risk-Neutral Two-State Model

Imagine a world consisting of only risk-neutral investors, and consider the two-state example in Section 21.1 in the risk-neutral world. Recall that the stock price today is equal to \$50. In one period it will either go up by \$10 or go down by \$10, and the one-period risk-free rate of interest is 6%. Let ρ be the probability that the stock price will increase, which means $(1 - \rho)$ is the probability that it will go down. The value of the stock today must equal the present value of the expected price next period discounted at the risk-free rate:

$$50 = \frac{60\rho + 40(1 - \rho)}{1.06} \tag{21.14}$$

This equation is solved with $\rho = 65\%$. Because we now know the probability of each state, we can price the call by calculating the present value of its expected payoff next period. Recall that the call option had an exercise price of \$50, so it will be worth either \$10 or nothing at expiration. The present value of the expected payouts is

$$\frac{10(0.65) + 0(1 - 0.65)}{1.06} = 6.13 \tag{21.15}$$

This is precisely the value we calculated in Section 21.1 using the Binomial Option Pricing Model where we did *not* assume that investors were risk neutral. It is not a coincidence. Because no assumption on the risk preferences of investors is necessary to calculate the option price using either the Binomial Model or the Black-Scholes formula, the models must work for any set of preferences, *including* risk-neutral investors.

Implications of the Risk-Neutral World

Let's take a step back and consider the importance of the conclusion that if we use the Binomial Model or Black-Scholes Model to price options, we do not need to make any assumption regarding investor risk preferences, the probability of each state, or the stock's expected return. These models *give the same option price no matter what the actual risk preferences and expected stock returns are.* To understand how these two settings can be consistent with the same prices for securities, consider the following:

- In the real world, investors are risk averse. Thus, the expected return of a typical stock includes a positive risk premium to compensate investors for risk.
- In the hypothetical risk-neutral world, investors do not require compensation for risk. So for the stock price to be the same as in real world, investors must be more pessimistic. Thus, stocks that in reality have expected returns above the risk-free rate, when evaluated using these more pessimistic probabilities, have expected returns that equal the risk-free rate.

In other words, the ρ in Eq. 21.14 and Eq. 21.15 is *not* the *actual* probability of the stock price increasing. Rather, it represents how the actual probability would have to be adjusted to keep the stock price the same in a risk-neutral world. For this reason, we refer to ρ and $(1 - \rho)$ as **risk-neutral probabilities**. These risk-neutral probabilities are known by other names as well: **state-contingent prices**, **state prices**, or **martingale prices**.

To illustrate, suppose the stock considered above, with a current price of \$50, will increase to \$60 with a true probability of 75%, or fall to \$40 with a true probability of 25%:

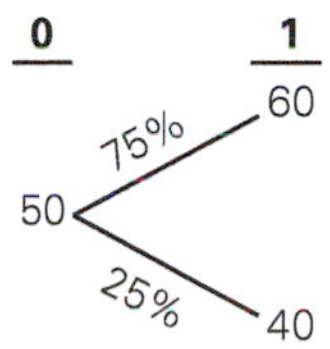

This stock's true expected return is therefore

$$\frac{60 \times 0.75 + 40 \times 0.25}{50} - 1 = 10\%$$

Given the risk-free interest rate of 6%, this stock has a 4% risk premium. But as we calculated earlier in Eq. 21.14, the risk-neutral probability that the stock will increase is $\rho = 65\%$, which is less than the true probability. Thus, the expected return of the stock in the risk-neutral world is $(60 \times 0.65 + 40 \times 0.35)/50 - 1 = 6\%$ (equal to the risk-free rate). To ensure that all assets in the risk-neutral world have an expected return equal to the risk-free rate, relative to the true probabilities, the risk-neutral probabilities overweight the bad states and underweight the good states.

Risk-Neutral Probabilities and Option Pricing

We can exploit the insight that if the stock price dynamics are the same in the risk-neutral and risk-averse worlds, the option prices must be the same, to develop another technique for pricing options. Consider again the general binomial stock price tree:

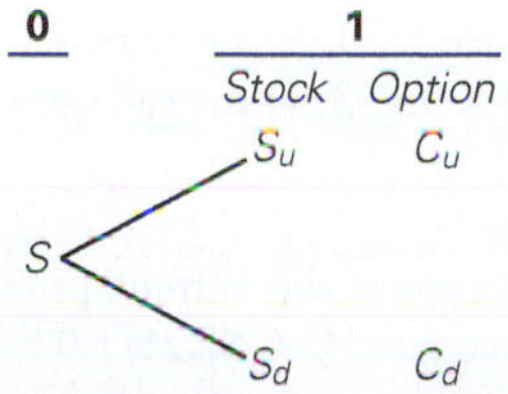

First, we can compute the risk-neutral probability that makes the stock's expected return equal to the risk-free interest rate:

$$\frac{\rho S_u + (1-\rho)S_d}{S} - 1 = r_f$$

Solving this equation for the risk-neutral probability ρ we get

$$\rho = \frac{(1+r_f)S - S_d}{S_u - S_d} \tag{21.16}$$

We can then compute the value of the option by computing its expected payoff using the risk-neutral probabilities, and discount the expected payoff at the risk-free interest rate.

EXAMPLE 21.8 Option Pricing with Risk-Neutral Probabilities

Problem

Using Narver Network Systems stock from Example 21.2, imagine all investors are risk neutral and calculate the probability of every state in the next two years. Use these probabilities to calculate the price of a two-year call option on Narver Network Systems stock with a strike price $60. Then, price a two-year European put option with the same strike price.

Solution

The binomial tree in the three-state example is

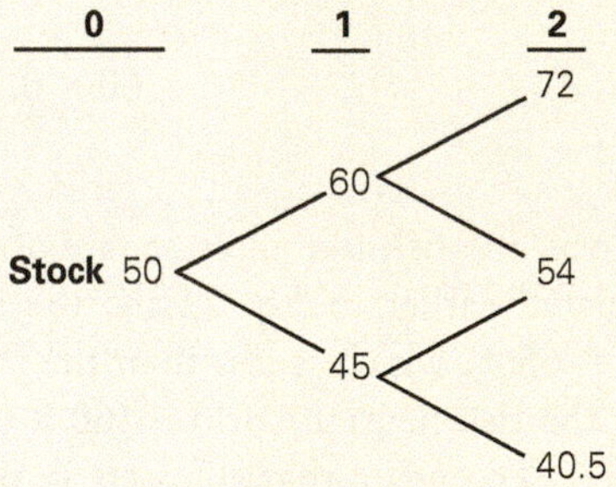

First, we use Eq. 21.16 to compute the risk-neutral probability that the stock price will increase. At time 0, we have

$$\rho = \frac{(1+r_f)S - S_d}{S_u - S_d} = \frac{(1.03)50 - 45}{60 - 45} = 0.433$$

Because the stock has the same returns (up 20% or down 10%) at each date, we can check that the risk-neutral probability is the same at each date as well.

Consider the call option with a strike price of $60. This call pays $12 if the stock goes up twice, and zero otherwise. The risk-neutral probability that the stock will go up twice is 0.433×0.433, so the call option has an expected payoff of

$$0.433 \times 0.433 \times \$12 = \$2.25$$

We compute the current price of the call option by discounting this expected payoff at the risk-free rate: $C = \$2.25/1.03^2 = \$2.12$.

Next, consider the European put option with a strike price of \$60. The put ends up in the money if the stock goes down twice, if it goes up and then down, or if it goes down and then up. Because the risk-neutral probability of a drop in the stock price is $1 - 0.433 = 0.567$, the expected payoff of the put option is

$$0.567 \times 0.567 \times \$19.5 + 0.433 \times 0.567 \times \$6 + 0.567 \times 0.433 \times \$6 = \$9.21$$

The value of the put today is therefore $P = \$9.21/1.03^2 = \$8.68$, which is the price we calculated in Example 21.2.

As the calculation of the put price in Example 21.8 makes clear, by using the probabilities in the risk-neutral world we can price any **derivative security**—that is, any security whose payoff depends solely on the prices of other marketed assets. After we have constructed the tree and calculated the probabilities in the risk-neutral world, we can use them to price the derivative by simply discounting its expected payoff (using the risk-neutral probabilities) at the risk-free rate.

The risk-neutral pricing method is the basis for a common technique for pricing derivative securities called **Monte Carlo simulation**. In this approach, the expected payoff of the derivative security is estimated by calculating its average payoff after simulating many random paths for the underlying stock price. In the randomization, the risk-neutral probabilities are used, and so the average payoff can be discounted at the risk-free rate to estimate the derivative security's value.

CONCEPT CHECK

1. What are risk-neutral probabilities? How can they be used to value options?
2. Does the binominal model or Black-Scholes model assume that investors are risk neutral?

21.4 Risk and Return of an Option

To measure the risk of an option, we must compute the option beta. The simplest way to do so is to compute the beta of the replicating portfolio. Recall that the beta of a portfolio is just the weighted average beta of the constituent securities that make up the portfolio. In this case, the portfolio consists of $S \times \Delta$ dollars invested in the stock and B dollars invested in the bond, so the beta of an option is

$$\beta_{option} = \frac{S\Delta}{S\Delta + B}\beta_S + \frac{B}{S\Delta + B}\beta_B$$

where β_S is the stock's beta and β_B is the bond's beta. In this case the bond is riskless, so $\beta_B = 0$. Thus, the option beta is

Option Beta

$$\beta_{option} = \frac{S\Delta}{S\Delta + B}\beta_S \tag{21.17}$$

Recall that for a call option, Δ is greater than zero and B is less than zero. Thus, for a call written on a stock with positive beta, the beta of the call always exceeds the beta of the stock. For a put option, Δ is less than zero and B is greater than zero; thus the beta of a put option written on a positive beta stock is always negative. This result should not be surprising. A put option is a hedge, so its price goes up when the stock price goes down.

EXAMPLE 21.9 Option Beta

Problem

Calculate the betas of the JetBlue call and put options in Examples 21.3 and 21.4, assuming JetBlue's stock has a beta of 0.85.

Solution

From Example 21.3, the December 2009 \$6 call option has a value of C = \$0.50 and a delta of $N(d_1) = 0.417$. Thus, its beta is given by

$$\beta_{Call} = \frac{S\Delta}{S\Delta + B}\beta_{Stock} = \frac{S \times N(d_1)}{C}\beta_{Stock}$$

$$= \frac{5.03 \times 0.417}{0.50} \times 0.85 = 3.57$$

Similarly, the beta of the January 2010 \$5 put option is given by

$$\beta_{Put} = \frac{S\Delta}{S\Delta + B}\beta_{Stock} = \frac{-S[1 - N(d_1)]}{P}\beta_{Stock}$$

$$= \frac{-5.03[1 - 0.599]}{0.87} \times 0.85 = -1.97$$

The expression $S\Delta/(S\Delta + B)$ is the ratio of the amount of money in the stock position in the replicating portfolio to the value of the replicating portfolio (or the option price); it is known as the option's **leverage ratio**. Figure 21.7 shows how the leverage ratio changes for puts and calls. As the figure shows, the magnitude of the leverage ratio for options can

FIGURE 21.7

Leverage Ratios of Options

The leverage ratio for a call option is always greater than 1, but out-of-the-money calls have higher leverage ratios than in-the-money calls. Put leverage ratios are always negative, and out-of-the-money puts have more negative leverage ratios than in-the-money puts. Data shown is for one-year options on a stock with a 30% volatility, given a risk-free interest rate of 5%.

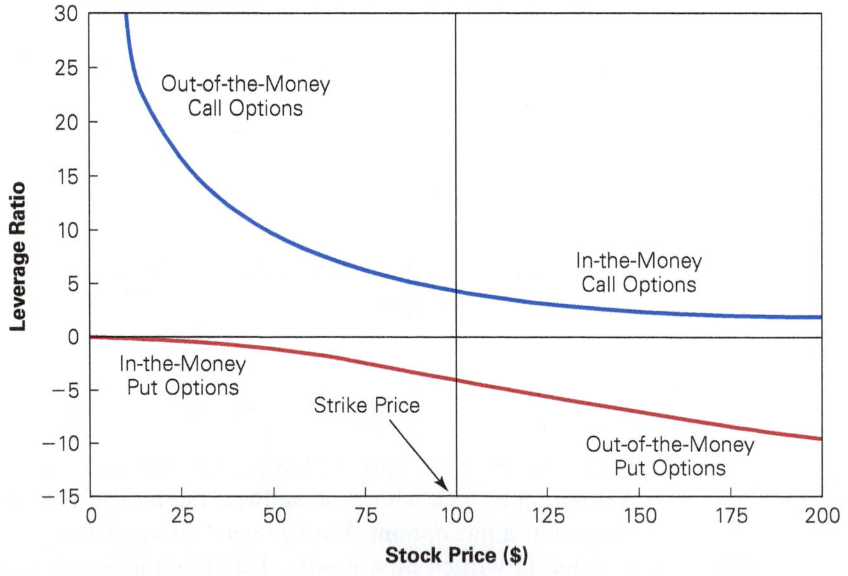

FIGURE 21.8

Security Market Line and Options

The figure shows how the expected return of different options are related.

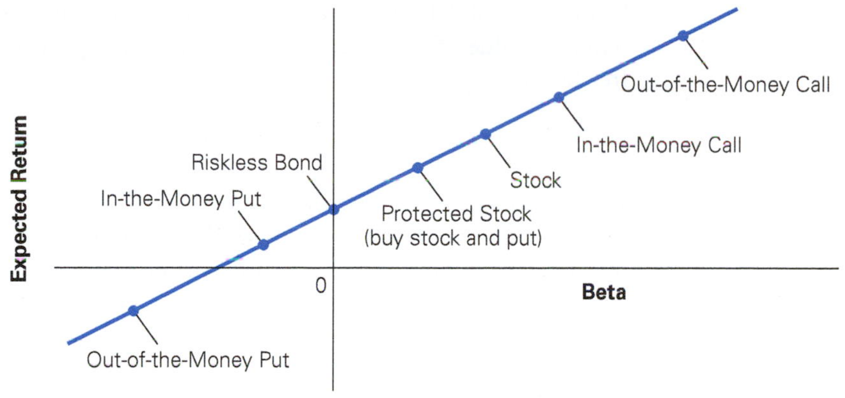

be very large, especially for inexpensive out-of-the-money options. Thus, calls and puts on a positive beta stock have very large positive and negative betas, respectively. Note also that as the stock price changes, the beta of an option will change, with its magnitude falling as the option goes in-the-money.

Recall that expected returns and beta are linearly related. Hence, out-of-the-money calls have the highest expected returns and out-of-the-money puts have the lowest expected returns. The expected returns of different options are plotted on the security market line in Figure 21.8.

CONCEPT CHECK

1. Is the beta of a call greater or smaller than the beta of the underlying stock?
2. What is the leverage ratio of a call?

21.5 Corporate Applications of Option Pricing

We close this chapter by developing two corporate applications of option pricing: (1) unlevering the beta of equity and calculating the beta of risky debt and (2) deriving the approximation formula to value debt overhang that we introduced in Chapter 16.

Beta of Risky Debt

In Chapter 14, we explained how to calculate the beta of equity from the unlevered beta of equity. If we make the common approximation that the beta of debt is zero, then

$$\beta_E = \beta_U + \frac{D}{E}(\beta_U - \beta_D) \approx \left(1 + \frac{D}{E}\right)\beta_U \tag{21.18}$$

where β_E is the beta of equity and β_U is the beta of unlevered equity (or the beta of the firm's assets). However, for companies with high debt-to-equity ratios, the approximation that the beta of debt is zero is unrealistic; such corporations have a positive probability of bankruptcy, and this uncertainty usually has systematic components.

To derive an expression for the beta of equity when the beta of debt is not zero, recall from the discussion in Chapter 20 that equity can be viewed as a call option on the firm's assets.[7] If we let A be the value of the firm's assets, E be the value of equity, and D be the value of debt, then because equity is a call option on the assets of the firm, we can write the value of equity in terms of a replicating portfolio of the firm's assets and a risk-free bond,

$$E = A\Delta + B$$

where the value of the firm's assets $A = E + D$ is used in place of the stock price S to represent the underlying asset on which the option is written. Substituting these expressions into Eq. 21.17 gives an expression for the beta of equity that does not assume the beta of the firm's debt is zero:

$$\beta_E = \frac{A\Delta}{A\Delta + B}\beta_U = \frac{(E + D)\Delta}{E}\beta_U = \Delta\left(1 + \frac{D}{E}\right)\beta_U \tag{21.19}$$

Note that when the debt is risk free, the firm's equity is always in-the-money; thus $\Delta = 1$ and Eq. 21.19 reduces to Eq. 21.18.

We can derive the beta of debt in a similar fashion. Debt, D, is equal to a portfolio consisting of a long position in the assets of the firm and a short position in its equity; i.e., $D = A - E$. The beta of debt is therefore the weighted-average beta of this portfolio:

$$\beta_D = \frac{A}{D}\beta_U - \frac{E}{D}\beta_E$$

Using Eq. 21.19 and simplifying gives an expression for the beta of debt in terms of the beta of assets:

$$\beta_D = (1 - \Delta)\frac{A}{D}\beta_U = (1 - \Delta)\left(1 + \frac{E}{D}\right)\beta_U \tag{21.20}$$

Again, when the debt is riskless, $\Delta = 1$ and $\beta_D = 0$, the assumption we made in Eq. 21.18.

Figure 21.9 plots an example of the beta of debt and equity as a function of the firm's leverage using Eq. 21.12. For low levels of debt, the approximation that the beta of debt is zero works reasonably well. As the debt-to-equity ratio becomes larger, however, the beta of debt begins to rise above zero and the beta of equity no longer increases proportionally with the debt-equity ratio.

In most applications, the beta of equity can be estimated. Using the beta of equity, we can calculate the beta of debt and the unlevered beta. For example, to unlever the beta, we can solve Eq. 21.19 for β_U:

$$\beta_U = \frac{\beta_E}{\Delta\left(1 + \frac{D}{E}\right)} \tag{21.21}$$

[7]The idea to view debt and equity as options was first developed by R. Merton in "On the Pricing of Corporate Debt: The Risk Structure of Interest Rates," *Journal of Finance* 29 (1974): 449–470.

FIGURE 21.9

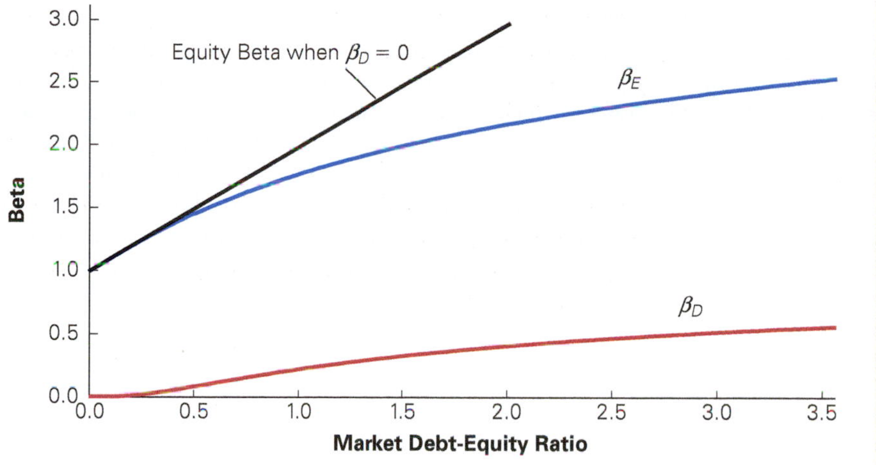

Beta of Debt and Equity

The blue curve is the beta of equity and the red curve is the beta of debt as a function of the firm's debt-to-equity ratio. The black line shows the beta of equity when the beta of debt is assumed to be zero. The firm is assumed to hold five-year zero-coupon debt and reinvest all its earnings. The firm's beta of assets is one, the risk-free interest rate is 3% per year, and the volatility of assets is 30% per year.

EXAMPLE 21.10 Computing the Beta of Debt

Problem

You would like to know the beta of debt for BB Industries. The value of BB's outstanding equity is \$40 million, and you have estimated its beta to be 1.2. However, you cannot find enough market data to estimate the beta of its debt, so you decide to use the Black-Scholes formula to find an approximate value for the debt beta. BB has four-year zero-coupon debt outstanding with a face value of \$100 million that currently trades for \$75 million. BB pays no dividends and reinvests all of its earnings. The four-year risk-free rate of interest is currently 5.13%. What is the beta of BB's debt?

Solution

We can interpret BB's equity as a four-year call option on the firm's assets with a strike price of \$100 million. The present value of the strike price is \$100 million/$(1.0513)^4$ = \$81.86 million. The current market value of BB's assets is \$40 + 75 = \$115 million. Therefore, the implied volatility of BB's assets is equal to the implied volatility of a call option whose price is 40 when the stock price is 115 and the present value of the strike price is 81.86. Using trial and error, we find an implied volatility of about 25%. With this volatility, the delta of the call option is

$$\Delta = N(d_1) = N\left(\frac{\ln(115/81.86)}{0.25(2)} + 0.25\right) = 0.824$$

First, we use Eq. 21.21 to solve for BB's unlevered beta:

$$\beta_U = \frac{\beta_E}{\Delta\left(1 + \dfrac{D}{E}\right)} = \frac{1.2}{0.824\left(1 + \dfrac{75}{40}\right)} = 0.51$$

We can then use Eq. 21.20 to estimate the beta of BB's debt:

$$\beta_D = (1 - \Delta)\left(1 + \frac{E}{D}\right)\beta_U = (1 - 0.824)\left(1 + \frac{40}{75}\right)0.51 = 0.14$$

COMMON MISTAKE Valuing Employee Stock Options

In the last 20 years, it has become common practice to compensate executives by granting them **executive stock options (ESOs)**—call options on their company's stock. Until 2005, U.S. accounting standards did not require firms to include stock option grants as part of their compensation expense. Now, however, firms are required to expense these options when calculating their earnings. Regardless of the accounting requirement, both firms and employees would like to know the value of this compensation. While it is tempting to use the Black-Scholes formula to value an ESO, there are several important pitfalls to be aware of when doing so.

To understand the difficulties of using the Black-Scholes formula to value ESOs, it is important to appreciate how they are usually granted. ESOs are typically American-style options with exercise dates up to 10 years in the future. However, there is usually a vesting period (often as long as four years) during which the employee does not actually own the option. Instead, he or she owns a right to the option at the end of the vesting period. If the employee leaves the firm during this period, the individual forfeits this right and so does not get the option. Once the vesting period has passed, the employee owns the option but *it is not tradable*—the only way the employee can liquidate the option is by exercising it. Furthermore, most executives face restrictions in trading their own company stock, so they effectively cannot construct a replicating portfolio. Because of these restrictions, ESOs are not worth the same amount to the employee and the firm.

One obvious difficulty with applying the Black-Scholes formula to such options is that the formula requires an estimate of the volatility of the stock over the life of the option. Forecasting volatility up to 10 years in the future is extremely difficult. But even if the stock's volatility were known, the Black-Scholes formula does not account for the following important differences between ESOs and ordinary stock options:

1. *ESOs are dilutive.* When exercised, they increase the number of shares outstanding of the firm.
2. *ESOs may be forfeited.* If the employee leaves the firm, options that are not vested are immediately forfeited. Options already vested are forfeited if not exercised within three months of the employee's departure.
3. *ESOs may be exercised early.* Once vested, the employee can exercise the options at any time.

Unless the number of options is large relative to the total number of shares outstanding, the first difference is not that important. The second difference is important for employees and firms with high employee turnover.

The third difference is very important for employees and all firms. Employees are risk-averse, but are not permitted to hedge the risk of the option by trading the replicating portfolio. As a consequence, the employee's preferences and beliefs matter in computing the ESO's value: A more risk-averse or pessimistic employee will attach a lower value to the option than a less risk-averse or optimistic employee. Furthermore, the only way an employee can eliminate his or her risk from the option is to exercise it and sell the stock. *Hence, most employees choose to exercise early.** In this case, employees are forfeiting the (often substantial) remaining time value of their options in exchange for a reduction in their risk.

Thus, the Black-Scholes formula (which assumes no early exercise) overestimates the cost of the option to the firm and its benefit to the employee. Because the firm can hedge its option liabilities, risk is not an issue when evaluating the cost of the option to the firm. Thus, the Black-Scholes formula overstates the cost by not accounting for forfeitures and early exercise. Because the employee cannot sell or hedge the risk of the option, the Black-Scholes formula overstates the value of the option to the employee even further by not accounting for the personal cost of bearing risk.

How important are these differences? The answer appears to be *very* important. In a recent paper, Ashish Jain and Ajay Subramanian adjust for these differences and find that for reasonable parameter values, the Black-Scholes formula can overestimate the *cost to the firm* of a vested five-year option by as much as 40%.[†] And once one considers the personal cost of being under-diversified while holding the option, its value to the employee can be as low as one third of the cost of the option to the firm. To account for these discrepancies, researchers have developed methods based on the binomial model in Section 21.1, that incorporate the probability and effect of forfeiture and early exercise directly into the binomial tree (see Further Readings).

*See S. Huddart and M. Lang, "Employee Stock Option Exercises: An Empirical Analysis," *Journal of Accounting and Economics* 21 (1996): 5–43.

[†] "The Intertemporal Exercise and Valuation of Employee Options," *Accounting Review* 79 (2004): 705–743.

NOBEL PRIZE **The 1997 Nobel Prize in Economics**

In a modern market economy, it is essential that firms and households are able to select an appropriate level of risk in their transactions. Markets for options and other so-called derivatives are important in the sense that agents who anticipate future revenues or payments can ensure a profit above a certain level or insure themselves against a loss above a certain level. A prerequisite for efficient management of risk, however, is that such instruments are correctly valued, or priced. A new method to determine the value of derivatives stands out among the foremost contributions to economic sciences over the last 25 years.

This year's laureates, Robert Merton and Myron Scholes, developed this method in close collaboration with Fischer Black, who died in his mid-fifties in 1995. Black, Merton, and Scholes thus laid the foundation for the rapid growth of markets for derivatives in the last ten years. Their method has more general applicability, however, and has created new areas of research—inside as well as outside of financial economics. A similar method may be used to value insurance contracts and guarantees, or the flexibility of physical investment projects.

Source: "The Prize in Economic Sciences 1997—Press Release." Nobelprize.org.

Agency Costs of Debt

In Chapter 16 we noted that leverage can distort equity holders' incentives to invest. These distortions can be readily understood when we view equity as a call option on the firm's assets. First, leverage creates an asset substitution problem because the value of the equity call option increases with the firm's volatility. Thus, equity holders may have an incentive to take excessive risk. Second, because $\Delta < 1$ for a call option, equity holders gain less than \$1 for each \$1 increase in the value of the firm's assets, reducing their incentive to invest and leading to a debt overhang or underinvestment problem. Example 21.11 illustrates how we can use the methods of this chapter to quantify both of these effects.

EXAMPLE 21.11 **Evaluating Potential Agency Costs**

Problem

Consider BB Industries from Example 21.10. Suppose BB can embark on a risky strategy that would increase the volatility of BB's assets from 25% to 35%. Show that shareholders benefit from this risky strategy even if it has an NPV of −\$5 million. Alternatively, suppose BB tries to raise \$100,000 from shareholders to invest in a new positive NPV project that does not change the firm's risk. What minimum NPV is required for this investment to benefit shareholders?

Solution

Recall that we can interpret BB's equity as a four-year call option on the firm's assets with a strike price of \$100 million. Given the current risk-free rate of 5.13%, asset value of \$115 million, and asset volatility of 25%, the current value of the equity call option is \$40 million, with $\Delta = 0.824$.

If BB follows the risky strategy, the value of its assets will fall to $\$115 - 5 = \$110$ million, and the volatility of the assets will increase to 35%. Applying the Black-Scholes formula with these new parameters, we find the value of the equity call option would *increase* to \$42.5 million, or a \$2.5 million gain for equity holders. Thus, leverage may cause equity holders to support risky negative NPV decisions.

Second, suppose BB raises and invests $I = \$100{,}000$ in a new project with NPV $= V$. Then the value of the firm's assets will increase by $\$100{,}000 + V$. Because Δ represents the sensitivity of a call option to the underlying asset value, the value of equity will increase by approximately Δ times this amount, and so equity holders gain more than they invest if

$$\Delta(100{,}000 + V) > 100{,}000$$

Using Eq. 21.19 and Eq. 21.20, we can rewrite this condition as

$$\frac{NPV}{I} = \frac{V}{100{,}000} > \frac{1-\Delta}{\Delta} = \frac{\beta_D D}{\beta_E E}$$

which matches precisely Eq. 16.2. Using the betas from Example 21.10, we see that the investment benefits shareholders only if its profitability index exceeds $(0.14 \times 75)/(1.2 \times 40) = 0.21875$, so that the project's NPV must exceed \$21,875. Because equity holders may reject projects with a positive NPV below this amount, the debt overhang induced by leverage may cause the firm to underinvest.

Thus, option pricing methods can be used to assess potential investment distortions that might arise due to debt overhang, or the incentive for asset substitution and risk-taking. We can also use these methods to evaluate state-contingent costs, such as financial distress costs.

In the above cases, management's and equity holders' option to default imposes costs on the firm. But in many situations, having "options" when investing can be a good thing, and enhance the value of the firm. We explore these situations in the next chapter.

CONCEPT CHECK

1. How can we estimate the beta of debt?
2. The fact that equity is a call option on the firm's assets leads to what agency costs?

MyFinanceLab Here is what you should know after reading this chapter. MyFinanceLab will help you identify what you know and where to go when you need to practice.

21.1 The Binomial Option Pricing Model

- An option can be valued using a portfolio that replicates the payoffs of the option in different states. The Binomial Option Pricing Model assumes two possible states for the next time period, given today's state.
- The value of an option is the value of the portfolio that replicates its payoffs. The replicating portfolio will hold the underlying asset and risk-free debt, and will need to be rebalanced over time.
- The replicating portfolio for the Binomial Option Pricing Model is

$$\Delta = \frac{C_u - C_d}{S_u - S_d} \quad \text{and} \quad B = \frac{C_d - S_d \Delta}{1 + r_f} \tag{21.5}$$

- Given the replicating portfolio, the value of the option is

$$C = S\Delta + B \tag{21.6}$$

21.2 The Black-Scholes Option Pricing Model

- The Black-Scholes option pricing formula for the price of a call option on a non-dividend-paying stock is

$$C = S \times N(d_1) - PV(K) \times N(d_2) \tag{21.7}$$

where $N(d)$ is the cumulative normal distribution and

$$d_1 = \frac{\ln[S/PV(K)]}{\sigma\sqrt{T}} + \frac{\sigma\sqrt{T}}{2}$$

$$d_2 = d_1 - \sigma\sqrt{T} \tag{21.8}$$

- Only five input parameters are required to price a call: the stock price, the strike price, the exercise date, the risk-free rate, and the volatility of the stock. We do not need to know the expected return on the stock to calculate the option price.
- The Black-Scholes option pricing formula for the price of a European put option on a non-dividend-paying stock is

$$P = PV(K)[1 - N(d_2)] - S[1 - N(d_1)] \tag{21.9}$$

- We can evaluate a European option on a stock that pays dividends using the Black-Scholes formula with S^x in place of S where

$$S^x = S - PV(Div) \tag{21.10}$$

  If the stock pays a (compounded) dividend yield of q prior to the expiration date, then

$$S^x = S/(1 + q) \tag{21.11}$$

- The Black-Scholes replicating portfolio is
  - For a call option on a non-dividend-paying stock

$$\Delta = N(d_1) \quad \text{and} \quad B = -PV(K)N(d_2) \tag{21.12}$$

  - For a European put option on a non-dividend-paying stock

$$\Delta = -[1 - N(d_1)] \quad \text{and} \quad B = PV(K)[1 - N(d_2)] \tag{21.13}$$

  - The replicating portfolio must be continuously updated to remain tangent to the option value

21.3 Risk-Neutral Probabilities

- Risk-neutral probabilities are the probabilities under which the expected return of all securities equals the risk-free rate. These probabilities can be used to price any other asset for which the payoffs in each state are known.
- In a binomial tree, the risk-neutral probability ρ that the stock price will increase is given by

$$\rho = \frac{(1 + r_f)S - S_d}{S_u - S_d} \tag{21.16}$$

- The price of any derivative security can be obtained by discounting the expected cash flows computed using the risk-neutral probabilities at the risk-free rate.

21.4 Risk and Return of an Option

- The beta of an option can also be calculated by computing the beta of its replicating portfolio. For stocks with positive betas, calls will have larger betas than the underlying stock, while puts will have negative betas. The magnitude of the option beta is higher for options that are further out of the money.
- The beta of an option is the beta of the underlying stock times the option's leverage ratio:

$$\beta_{option} = \frac{S\Delta}{S\Delta + B}\beta_S \tag{21.17}$$

21.5 Corporate Applications of Option Pricing

- When debt is risky, the betas of equity and debt increase with leverage according to

$$\beta_E = \Delta\left(1 + \frac{D}{E}\right)\beta_U, \quad \beta_D = (1 - \Delta)\left(1 + \frac{E}{D}\right)\beta_U \qquad (21.19), (21.20)$$

We can also use Eq. 21.19 to solve for the firm's unlevered beta and debt beta, given an estimate of the beta and delta of the firm's equity.

- Option valuation methods can be used to assess the magnitude of agency costs:
  - As a result of debt overhang, equity holders benefit from new investment only if

$$\frac{NPV}{I} > \frac{1-\Delta}{\Delta} = \frac{\beta_D D}{\beta_E E}$$

  verifying Eq. 16.2.
  - Equity holders' incentive to increase volatility can be estimated as the sensitivity of the value of the equity call option to an increase in volatility.

Key Terms

Further Reading

The seminal article on options was written by Fischer Black and Myron Scholes: "The Pricing of Options and Corporate Liabilities," *Journal of Political Economy* 81 (1973): 637–654. It followed an earlier article by Robert Merton, "Theory of Rational Option Pricing," *Bell Journal of Economics and Management Science* 4 (1973): 141–183.

For a deeper discussion of options and other derivative securities, see: R. McDonald, *Derivative Markets* (Prentice Hall, 2006); J. Hull, *Options, Futures, and Other Derivatives* (Prentice Hall, 2008); R. Jarrow and S. Turnbull, *Derivative Securities* (South-Western, 1999); and P. Wilmott, *Paul Wilmott on Quantitative Finance* (John Wiley & Sons, 2006).

The following articles by Fischer Black contain an interesting account of the development of the Black-Scholes formula as well as some of its limitations: "How We Came Up with the Option Formula," *Journal of Portfolio Management* 15 (1989): 4–8; "The Holes in Black-Scholes," *RISK Magazine* 1 (1988): 30–33; and "How to Use the Holes in Black-Scholes," *Journal of Applied Corporate Finance* 1 (Winter 1989): 67–73.

For alternative methods of valuing employee stock options, see, for example, M. Rubinstein, "On the Accounting Valuation of Employee Stock Options," *Journal of Derivatives* (Fall 1995); J. Hull and A. White, "How to Value Employee Stock Options," *Financial Analysts Journal* 60 (2004): 114–119; and N. Brisley and C. Anderson, "Employee Stock Option Valuation with an Early Exercise Boundary," *Financial Analysts Journal* 64 (2008): 88–100.

The use of option pricing methods to gain a deeper understanding of the role of agency costs in the determination of optimal capital structure is developed in H. Leland, "Agency Costs, Risk Management, and Capital Structure," *Journal of Finance* (1998): 1213–1243.

Problems

All problems are available in MyFinanceLab. *An asterisk (*) indicates problems with a higher level of difficulty.*

The Binomial Option Pricing Model

1. The current price of Estelle Corporation stock is $25. In each of the next two years, this stock price will either go up by 20% or go down by 20%. The stock pays no dividends. The one-year

risk-free interest rate is 6% and will remain constant. Using the Binomial Model, calculate the price of a one-year call option on Estelle stock with a strike price of $25.

2. Using the information in Problem 1, use the Binomial Model to calculate the price of a one-year put option on Estelle stock with a strike price of $25.

3. The current price of Natasha Corporation stock is $6. In each of the next two years, this stock price can either go up by $2.50 or go down by $2. The stock pays no dividends. The one-year risk-free interest rate is 3% and will remain constant. Using the Binomial Model, calculate the price of a two-year call option on Natasha stock with a strike price of $7.

4. Using the information in Problem 3, use the Binomial Model to calculate the price of a two-year European put option on Natasha stock with a strike price of $7.

5. Suppose the option in Example 21.1 actually sold in the market for $8. Describe a trading strategy that yields arbitrage profits.

***6.** Suppose the option in Example 21.2 actually sold today for $5. You do not know what the option will trade for next period. Describe a trading strategy that will yield arbitrage profits.

7. Eagletron's current stock price is $10. Suppose that over the current year, the stock price will either increase by 100% or decrease by 50%. Also, the risk-free rate is 25% (EAR).

a. What is the value today of a one-year at-the-money European put option on Eagletron stock?

b. What is the value today of a one-year European put option on Eagletron stock with a strike price of $20?

c. Suppose the put options in parts a and b could either be exercised immediately, or in one year. What would their values be in this case?

8. What is the highest possible value for the delta of a call option? What is the lowest possible value? (*Hint*: See Figure 21.1.)

***9.** Hema Corp. is an all equity firm with a current market value of $1000 million (i.e., $1 billion), and will be worth $900 million or $1400 million in one year. The risk-free interest rate is 5%. Suppose Hema Corp. issues zero-coupon, one-year debt with a face value of $1050 million, and uses the proceeds to pay a special dividend to shareholders. Assuming perfect capital markets, use the binomial model to answer the following:

a. What are the payoffs of the firm's debt in one year?

b. What is the value today of the debt today?

c. What is the yield on the debt?

d. Using Modigliani-Miller, what is the value of Hema's equity before the dividend is paid? What is the value of equity just after the dividend is paid?

e. Show that the ex-dividend value of Hema's equity is consistent with the binomial model. What is the Δ of the equity, when viewed as a call option on the firm's assets?

***10.** Consider the setting of Problem 9. Suppose that in the event Hema Corp. defaults, $90 million of its value will be lost to bankruptcy costs. Assume there are no other market imperfections.

a. What is the present value of these bankruptcy costs, and what is their delta with respect to the firm's assets?

b. In this case, what is the value and yield of Hema's debt?

c. In this case, what is the value of Hema's equity before the dividend is paid? What is the value of equity just after the dividend is paid?

The Black-Scholes Option Pricing Model

11. Roslin Robotics stock has a volatility of 30% and a current stock price of $60 per share. Roslin pays no dividends. The risk-free interest is 5%. Determine the Black-Scholes value of a one-year, at-the-money call option on Roslin stock.

12. Rebecca is interested in purchasing a European call on a hot new stock, Up, Inc. The call has a strike price of $100 and expires in 90 days. The current price of Up stock is $120, and the stock has a standard deviation of 40% per year. The risk-free interest rate is 6.18% per year.

a. Using the Black-Scholes formula, compute the price of the call.
b. Use put-call parity to compute the price of the put with the same strike and expiration date.

13. Using the data in Table 21.1, compare the price on July 24, 2009, of the following options on JetBlue stock to the price predicted by the Black-Scholes formula. Assume that the standard deviation of JetBlue stock is 65% per year and that the short-term risk-free rate of interest is 1% per year.
a. December 2009 call option with a $5 strike price
b. December 2009 put option with a $6 strike price
c. March 2010 put option with a $7 strike price

14. Using the market data in Figure 20.10 and a risk-free rate of 0.25% per annum, calculate the implied volatility of Google stock in September 2012, using the bid price of the 700 January 2014 call option.

15. Using the implied volatility you calculated in Problem 14, and the information in that problem, use the Black-Scholes option pricing formula to calculate the value of the 800 January 2014 call option.

16. Plot the value of a two-year European put option with a strike price of $20 on World Wide Plants as a function of the stock price. Recall that World Wide Plants has a constant dividend yield of 5% per year and that its volatility is 20% per year. The two-year risk-free rate of interest is 4%. Explain why there is a region where the option trades for less than its intrinsic value.

17. Consider the at-the-money call option on Roslin Robotics evaluated in Problem 11. Suppose the call option is not available for trade in the market. You would like to replicate a long position in 1000 call options.
a. What portfolio should you hold today?
b. Suppose you purchase the portfolio in part a. If Roslin stock goes up in value to $62 per share today, what is the value of this portfolio now? If the call option were available for trade, what would be the difference in value between the call option and the portfolio (expressed as percent of the value of the call)?
c. After the stock price change in part b, how should you adjust your portfolio to continue to replicate the options?

18. Consider again the at-the-money call option on Roslin Robotics evaluated in Problem 11. What is the impact on the value of this call option of each of the following changes (evaluated separately)?
a. The stock price increases by $1 to $61.
b. The volatility of the stock goes up by 1% to 31%.
c. Interest rates go up by 1% to 6%.
d. One month elapses, with no other change.
e. The firm announces a $1 dividend, paid immediately.

Risk-Neutral Probabilities

19. Harbin Manufacturing has 10 million shares outstanding with a current share price of $20 per share. In one year, the share price is equally likely to be $30 or $18. The risk-free interest rate is 5%.
a. What is the expected return on Harbin stock?
b. What is the risk-neutral probability that Harbin's stock price will increase?

20. Using the information on Harbin Manufacturing in Problem 19, answer the following:
a. Using the risk-neutral probabilities, what is the value of a one-year call option on Harbin stock with a strike price of $25?
b. What is the expected return of the call option?
c. Using the risk-neutral probabilities, what is the value of a one-year put option on Harbin stock with a strike price of $25?
d. What is the expected return of the put option?

21. Using the information in Problem 1, calculate the risk-neutral probabilities. Then use them to price the option.

22. Using the information in Problem 3, calculate the risk-neutral probabilities. Then use them to price the option.

23. Explain the difference between the risk-neutral and actual probabilities. In which states is one higher than the other? Why?

24. Explain why risk-neutral probabilities can be used to price derivative securities in a world where investors are risk averse.

Risk and Return of an Option

25. Calculate the beta of the January 2010 $9 call option on JetBlue listed in Table 21.1. Assume that the volatility of JetBlue is 65% per year and its beta is 0.85. The short-term risk-free rate of interest is 1% per year. What is the option's leverage ratio?

26. Consider the March 2010 $5 put option on JetBlue listed in Table 21.1. Assume that the volatility of JetBlue is 65% per year and its beta is 0.85. The short-term risk-free rate of interest is 1% per year.

a. What is the put option's leverage ratio?

b. What is the beta of the put option?

c. If the expected risk premium of the market is 6%, what is the expected return of the put option based on the CAPM?

d. Given its expected return, why would an investor buy a put option?

Corporate Applications of Option Pricing

27. Return to Example 20.11 (on page 748), in which Google was contemplating issuing zero-coupon debt due in 16 months with a face value of $163.5 billion, and using the proceeds to pay a special dividend. Google currently has a market value of $229.2 billion and the risk-free rate is 0.25%. Using the market data in Figure 20.10, answer the following:

a. If Google's current equity beta is 1.2, estimate Google's equity beta after the debt is issued.

b. Estimate the beta of the new debt.

***28.** You would like to know the unlevered beta of Schwartz Industries (SI). SI's value of outstanding equity is $400 million, and you have estimated its beta to be 1.2. SI has four-year zero-coupon debt outstanding with a face value of $100 million that currently trades for $75 million. SI pays no dividends and reinvests all of its earnings. The four-year risk-free rate of interest is currently 5.13%. Use the Black-Scholes formula to estimate the unlevered beta of the firm.

***29.** The J. Miles Corp. has 25 million shares outstanding with a share price of $20 per share. Miles also has outstanding zero-coupon debt with a 5-year maturity, a face value of $900 million, and a yield to maturity of 9%. The risk-free interest rate is 5%.

a. What is the implied volatility of Miles' assets?

b. What is the minimum profitability index required for equity holders to gain by funding a new investment that does not change the volatility of the Miles' assets?

c. Suppose Miles is considering investing cash on hand in a new investment that will increase the volatility of its assets by 10%. What is the minimum NPV such that this investment will increase the value of Miles' shares?

CHAPTER 22

Real Options

THE MOST IMPORTANT APPLICATION OF OPTIONS IN CORPORATE finance is in the capital budgeting decision. Let's use Amgen, a global biotechnology company, as an example. Amgen had 2014 revenues of $20 billion, and it spent over 20% of its revenues on research and development. Even though only a very small number of early-stage drug development projects ultimately reach the market, the ones that do can be highly successful. How does Amgen manage its research and development expenses to maximize value?

For Amgen, investing in R&D is like purchasing a call option. When research results on early-stage drug development projects are favorable, Amgen commits additional resources to the next stage of product development. If research results are not promising, Amgen stops funding the project. Amgen, by selectively investing in those technologies that prove to be the most promising, exercises its option to develop a product: The additional investment is equivalent to paying the strike price and acquiring the underlying asset—in this case, the benefits of further product development. By choosing not to make further investments (thereby mothballing or abandoning the research and development project) Amgen chooses not to exercise its option.

While real investment options like Amgen's can be very important in capital budgeting, the effect of such real options on the capital budgeting decision is generally application specific, and no single methodology exists that applies across all settings. In light of this fact, in this chapter we show how the general principles we have already developed that govern capital budgeting and option pricing can be applied to evaluate real options in the capital budgeting decision. We apply these principles to examine the three most common options that occur in capital budgeting: the option to wait for the optimal time to invest, the option to grow in the future, and the option to abandon a poorly performing project. We then consider two important applications: deciding the order in which to complete a staged investment opportunity and deciding which of two mutually exclusive projects of different lengths is the wiser investment. Finally, we explain rules of thumb that managers often use to account for real options in the capital budgeting decision.

NOTATION

NPV	net present value
S^x	value of stock excluding dividends
S	stock price
PV	present value
Div	dividend
K	strike price
ln	natural logarithm
T	years until the exercise date of an option
σ	volatility of the return of the underlying asset
C	call option price
$N(d)$	cumulative normal distribution
ρ	risk-neutral probability
r_f	risk-free rate of interest

22.1 Real Versus Financial Options

The financial options we have studied in the previous two chapters give their holders the right to buy, or sell, a traded asset such as a stock. Amgen's option to invest in research and development for new products is an example of a different type of option, called a *real option*. A **real option** is the right to make a particular business decision, such as a capital investment, after new information may be learned. A key distinction between a real option and a financial option is that real options, and the underlying assets on which they are based, are often not traded in competitive markets; for example, there is no market for Amgen's R&D in a particular drug.

Despite this distinction, many of the principles that we developed in the last two chapters for financial options also apply to real options. In particular, because real options allow a decision maker to choose the most attractive alternative after new information becomes available, the presence of real options adds value to an investment opportunity. This value can be substantial, especially in environments with a great deal of uncertainty. Thus, to make the most accurate investment decisions, the value of these options must be included in the decision-making process.

Our approach to capital budgeting thus far has focused on the initial investment decision without explicitly considering future decisions that may be required over the life of a project. Rather, we assumed that our forecast of the project's expected future cash flows already incorporated the effect of any future decisions made. In this chapter, we take a closer look at how these cash flows, and therefore the NPV of a project, are determined when a firm must react to changing business conditions over the life of a project. To do so, we begin by introducing a new analytical tool called a *decision tree*.

CONCEPT CHECK

1. What is the difference between a real option and a financial option?
2. Why does a real option add value to an investment decision?

22.2 Decision Tree Analysis

Most investment projects allow for the possibility of reevaluating the decision to invest at a later point in time. Let's illustrate this possibility with a natural example.

United Studios holds the movie rights for a national best-seller, and as part of these rights also has the option to produce a sequel based on the same book. The studio is now in the process of developing the production schedule. It believes that shooting both movies simultaneously would allow significant cost savings, and both movies could be produced for a total budget of $525 million. If instead the movies are produced sequentially, the total expected cost will rise to $575 million. On the other hand, by waiting to produce the second movie until after the first movie is released, the studio will have much better information regarding the likely prospects for the sequel. Let's see how we can use a decision tree to analyze this situation.

First consider the case in which the movies are produced simultaneously. Once produced, the studio forecasts it will earn a total of $650 million from both movies, for a net profit of $125 million.[1] We illustrate this simple scenario in Figure 22.1 using a **decision tree**, a graphical representation that shows current and future decisions and their corresponding risks and outcomes over time.

[1] For simplicity, we ignore discounting in this example by assuming a zero interest rate and only idiosyncratic risk. (Alternatively, we can interpret all amounts as their equivalent present values.) In later examples we will incorporate discounting and systematic risk.

FIGURE 22.1

United's Investment without Real Options

This decision tree shows United's options if it produces both movies at once. The optimal decision is shown in blue.

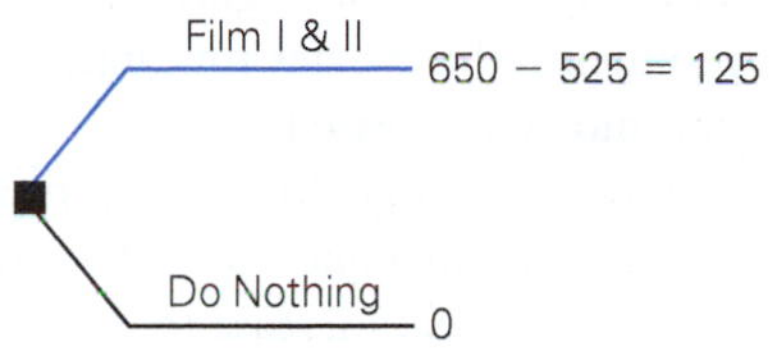

A decision tree differs from the binomial trees used in Chapter 21. In a binomial tree, the branches of the tree represent uncertainty that cannot be controlled. In a decision tree, we also include branches to represent different choices available to the decision maker.

The decision tree in Figure 22.1 is the decision tree for a standard investment problem without real options. We can either invest, and earn the project's NPV, or not invest and earn 0. The square node indicates a decision point, where the decision maker must choose which branch to follow. We highlight the optimal decision in blue; in this case United Studios would choose to invest and produce the movies since the expected payoff exceeds the upfront cost: \$650 million − \$525 million = \$125 million.

Representing Uncertainty

While United's expected earnings imply that the movies are worth producing, there is significant uncertainty regarding the actual outcome. In fact, the expected total revenue of \$650 million for both movies reflects two alternative outcomes. Based on the popularity of the book, United believes there is a 50% chance the first movie will be a blockbuster success, in which case the studio expects it will earn \$500 million from it alone, and another \$400 million for the sequel. If instead the first film is just a moderate hit, it will only bring in \$300 million, and the sequel will only be expected to earn \$100 million. We illustrate this uncertainty in Figure 22.2.

Notice that the decision tree now contains two kinds of nodes: square **decision nodes** (invest versus do nothing), and circular **information nodes** in which uncertainty is resolved that is out of the control of the decision maker (e.g., whether the film is a blockbuster or not). Figure 22.2 also indicates the point at which each cash flow is committed or realized. Because the production cost is paid in advance, that cash flow is incurred before United learns how successful the movies will be.

FIGURE 22.2

Representing Uncertainty

Circular nodes indicate the resolution of uncertainty. Cash flows are shown at the point they are committed or resolved.

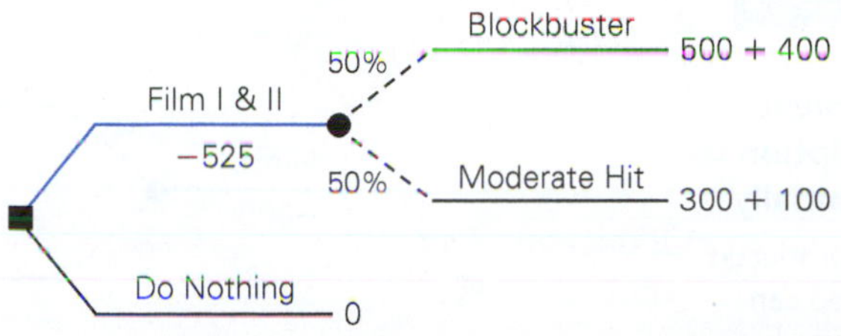

Real Options

The decision tree in Figure 22.2 is not a full description of United's alternatives. Instead of producing the movies simultaneously, United can delay filming the sequel until after the first movie is released.

United's budget for the first film is $300 million. If it is only a moderate hit, they expect to produce the sequel for $250 million. But if the first film is a blockbuster, the cost of the second film will increase to $300 million (it will be worth investing more, and the actors may demand higher wages). Overall, the expected total cost of producing the films sequentially is $575 million, an increase of $50 million over the cost of filming them together.

We illustrate the decision tree for sequential production in Figure 22.3. The key difference between this figure and Figure 22.2 is that we now illustrate the fact that United can wait until it learns how successful the first movie is before deciding whether to produce the sequel. A decision node that occurs *after* an information node in a decision tree is a real option. The option to decide later is valuable because of the new information United will learn.

As Figure 22.3 reveals, it is not optimal for United to produce the sequel unless the first film is a blockbuster. Producing the sequel after a moderate success would cost $250 million and earn only $100 million. Producing the sequel at that point has a negative NPV of –$150 million. Given United's optimal strategy (shown in blue), its expected payoff is as follows:

$$-300 + 50\% \times \overbrace{(500 - 300 + 400)}^{\substack{\text{Blockbuster,} \\ \text{produce sequel}}} + 50\% \times \overbrace{(300)}^{\substack{\text{Moderate hit,} \\ \text{no sequel}}} = \$150 \text{ million}$$

Comparing this payoff to the expected payoff of $125 million if the movies are produced simultaneously, the option to wait and decide later whether to produce the sequel is worth $25 million to United. The option is valuable because United will learn enough information to affect its decision: it will cancel the sequel if the first film is not a blockbuster. The option value is equal to the benefit of avoiding a 50% chance of a loss of $150 million, or $75 million, which exceeds the $50 million increase in expected production costs.

Solving Decision Trees

Many corporate investment decisions contain real options like the one facing United Studios. While the exact nature of these options is investment specific, they can be analyzed by creating a decision tree that identifies

- Decision nodes showing the choices available at each stage
- Information nodes showing the payoff relevant information to be learned
- Investments made and payoffs earned over time

FIGURE 22.3

United's Investment with the Real Option to Produce Sequentially

If the movies are produced sequentially, United can make a more informed decision whether to produce the sequel.

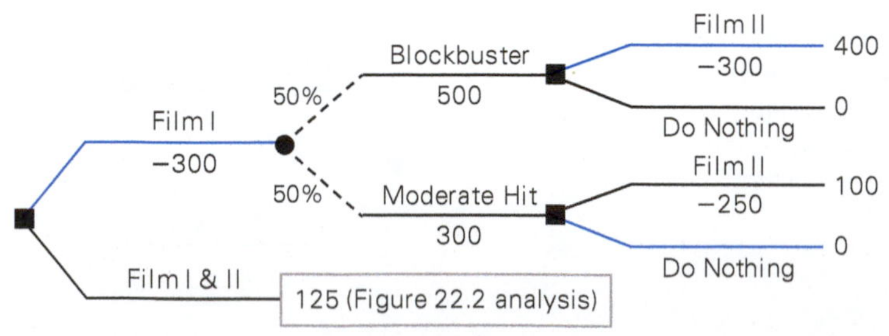

Once the decision tree is created, we can value the investment opportunity by working backward from the end of the tree. At each

(i) **Decision node:** determine the optimal choice by comparing the present value of the remaining payoffs along each branch; and at each

(ii) **Information node:** compute the expected present value of the payoffs from the subsequent branches.

As always, in both Steps (i) and (ii), we compute present values according to the Law of One Price (using the methodologies developed in earlier chapters).

While our example here was highly simplified, with only two states and two choices, the decision tree methodology is quite general and is used in practice to analyze highly complex real world examples. We'll consider a variety of real options in the remainder of this chapter.

CONCEPT CHECK

1. How can you identify a real option in a decision tree?
2. In what circumstances does the real option add value?
3. How do you use a decision tree to make the best investment decision?

22.3 The Option to Delay: Investment as a Call Option

United Studios' option to produce a movie sequel illustrates how choosing the optimal time to make an investment can add value. This option to delay is common in practice. Typically, there are costs from delaying the investment decision: interim profits from the project are lost, costs might rise, competitors may enter, etc. On the other hand, by delaying you will gain additional information regarding the value of the investment. In general, one must trade off the costs from delay with the benefit from gaining information before making a decision. In this section we see how the quantitative methods developed to price financial options can be used to analyze the optimal timing decision.

An Investment Option

Consider the following investment opportunity. You have negotiated a deal with a major electric car manufacturer to open a dealership in your hometown. The terms of the contract specify that you must open the dealership either immediately or in exactly one year. If you do neither, you lose the right to open the dealership at all. Figure 22.4 shows these choices on a decision tree.

FIGURE 22.4

Electric Car Dealership Investment Opportunity

The electric car dealership must be opened either immediately or in exactly one year. If we wait to open the dealership, our decision can be based on new information about the dealership's value, which can take on many values.

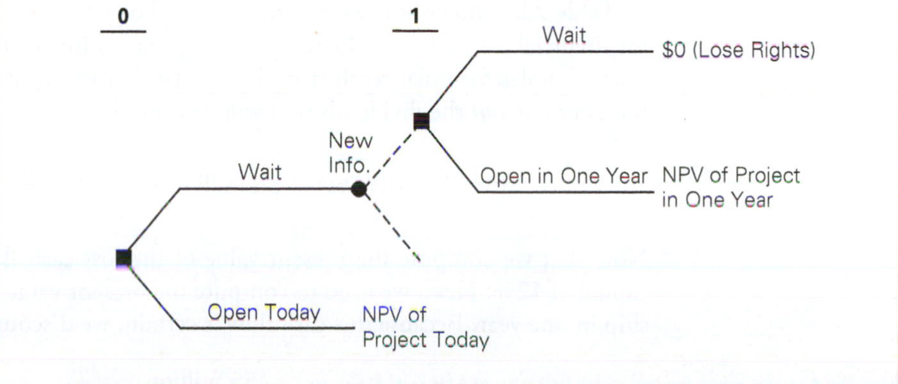

You are wondering how much you should pay for this opportunity. It will cost you \$5 million to open the dealership, whether you open it now or in one year. If you open the dealership immediately, you expect it to generate \$600,000 in free cash flow the first year. While future cash flows will vary with consumer tastes and the state of the economy, on average these cash flows are expected to grow at a rate of 2% per year. The appropriate cost of capital for this investment is 12%, so you estimate that the value of the dealership, if it were open today, would be

$$V = \frac{\$600{,}000}{12\% - 2\%} = \$6 \text{ million} \tag{22.1}$$

You also double-check this value using comparables. A publicly traded firm operating dealerships elsewhere in the state exists, and this firm provides an essentially perfect comparable for your investment. This firm has an enterprise value equal to 10 times its free cash flow, leading to an equivalent valuation.

Thus, the NPV of opening the dealership immediately is \$1 million, implying that the contract is worth at least \$1 million. But given the flexibility you have to delay opening for one year, should you be willing to pay more? And when should you open the dealership?

To answer these questions, we start at the end of the tree and evaluate the NPV of opening the dealership in one year. If we wait, then one year from now we will have the choice to invest \$5 million to open the dealership, or lose our right to open it and receive nothing. Thus, at that time, the decision is easy—we will open the dealership if its value at that time, based on any new information about the economy and consumer tastes and trends, is above \$5 million. But because trends in this industry can change quickly, there is a great deal of uncertainty as to what the expected cash flows and the value of the dealership will be at that time.

Next, to compute the present value at the information node, we can use the Law of One Price. Our payoff if we delay is equivalent to the payoff of a one-year European call option on the dealership with a strike price of \$5 million. Because the final payoff in one year is equivalent to a call option, we can use the techniques from Chapter 21 to value it. Suppose that the risk-free interest rate is 5%. We can estimate the volatility of the value of the dealership by looking at the return volatility of the publicly traded comparable firm; suppose this volatility is 40%. Finally, if we wait to open the dealership we will lose out on the \$600,000 in free cash flow we would have earned in the first year. In terms of a financial option, this free cash flow is equivalent to a dividend paid by a stock—the holder of a call option does not receive the dividend until the option is exercised. Let's assume for now this cost is the only cost of delay—there are no additional costs in terms of lost growth of the dealership's cash flows, for example.

Table 22.1 shows how we can reinterpret the parameters for the Black-Scholes formula for financial options to evaluate this real option to invest in the dealership. To apply the Black-Scholes formula, recall from Eq. 21.10 that we must compute the current value of the asset *without* the dividends that will be missed:

$$S^x = S - PV(Div) = \$6 \text{ million} - \frac{\$0.6 \text{ million}}{1.12} = \$5.46 \text{ million}$$

Note that we compute the present value of the lost cash flow using the project's cost of capital of 12%. Next, we need to compute the present value of the cost to open the dealership in one year. Because this cash flow is certain, we discount it at the risk-free rate:

$$PV(K) = \frac{\$5 \text{ million}}{1.05} = \$4.76 \text{ million}$$

TABLE 22.1 Black-Scholes Option Value Parameters for Evaluating a Real Option to Invest

Financial Option		Real Option	Example
Stock Price	S	Current Market Value of Asset	\$6 million
Strike Price	K	Upfront Investment Required	\$5 million
Expiration Date	T	Final Decision Date	1 year
Risk-Free Rate	r_f	Risk-Free Rate	5%
Volatility of Stock	σ	Volatility of Asset Value	40%
Dividend	Div	FCF Lost from Delay	\$0.6 million

Now we can compute the value of the call option to open the dealership using Eq. 21.7 and Eq. 21.8:

$$d_1 = \frac{\ln[S^x/PV(K)]}{\sigma\sqrt{T}} + \frac{\sigma\sqrt{T}}{2} = \frac{\ln(5.46/4.76)}{0.40} + 0.20 = 0.543$$

$$d_2 = d_1 - \sigma\sqrt{T} = 0.543 - 0.40 = 0.143$$

and therefore,

$$\begin{aligned} C &= S^x N(d_1) - PV(K)N(d_2) \\ &= (\$5.46 \text{ million}) \times (0.706) - (\$4.76 \text{ million}) \times (0.557) \\ &= \$1.20 \text{ million} \end{aligned} \tag{22.2}$$

The result in Eq. 22.2 states that the value today from waiting to invest in the dealership next year, and only opening it if it is profitable to do so, is \$1.20 million. This value exceeds the NPV of \$1 million from opening the dealership today. Thus, we are better off waiting to invest, and the value of the contract is \$1.20 million.

What is the advantage of waiting in this case? If we wait, we will learn more about the likely success of the business by observing the performance of the comparable firm. Because our investment in the dealership is not yet committed, we can cancel our plans if the popularity of electric cars should decline. By opening the dealership today, we give up this option to "walk away."[2]

Of course, there is a trade-off—if we wait to invest we give up the profits the dealership will generate the first year. Whether it is optimal to invest today will depend on the magnitude of these lost profits, compared to the benefit of preserving our right to change our decision. To see this trade-off, suppose instead that the first-year free cash flow of the dealership is projected to be \$700,000, so that the current value of the dealership is \$7 million (using the 10x multiple of the comparable, or a similar calculation to Eq. 22.1). In this case, the same analysis shows that the value of the call option would be \$1.91 million. Because the value of opening the dealership today is \$7 million − 5 million = \$2 million, in this case it would not be optimal to wait, and we would open the dealership immediately.

[2]A second benefit from waiting is that the cost of opening the dealership is assumed to stay the same (\$5 million), so the present value of this cost declines if we wait. This benefit is specific to the example. Depending on the scenario, the cost of investing may rise or fall over time.

Why Are There Empty Lots in Built-Up Areas of Big Cities?

Have you ever wondered why there are empty lots (for example, a parking lot) right next to multi-story buildings in a city? After all, if it was optimal for the next-door neighbor to build a multi-story building, why would someone choose to leave the lot empty? In many cases, the property taxes exceed the revenue generated by the empty lot, so by putting a revenue-producing building on the lot, the owner could turn a negative cash flow into a positive cash flow. However, by building on the lot, the owner gives up the option to construct a different building in the future. If there is a large amount of uncertainty about the kind of building to put on the lot, and if this uncertainty might be resolved in the future, it might make sense to wait for additional information before breaking ground on a building. The value of waiting might exceed the net present value of building today.*

Notice a similar effect in the price of agricultural land that is close to big cities. Even though the land might produce the same agricultural revenue as similar land 100 miles away, the price of the land closer to the city is higher because the price reflects the possibility that the city might grow to the point that it becomes economical to put the land to non-agricultural use—that is, subdivide it and build single-family housing. The option to one day use the land in this way is reflected in the current price of the land.

*S. Titman, "Urban Land Prices Under Uncertainty," *American Economic Review* 75 (1985): 505–514, develops this idea.

Figure 22.5 plots the NPV of investing today and the value of waiting as we vary the expected first-year free cash flow of the dealership, and thus its current operating value. As the figure makes clear, you should invest today (and give up the option to wait) only if the current value of the dealership exceeds \$6.66 million. Thus, your optimal investment strategy is to invest today only if the NPV of the investment opportunity exceeds \$6.66 million − 5 million = \$1.66 million.

FIGURE 22.5

The Decision to Invest in the Dealership

The red line denotes the NPV of investing today. The yellow curve shows the value today of waiting one year to make the decision (i.e., the value of the call option). The black curve indicates the value of the contract, which gives us the option to invest today, in one year, or not at all. The optimal investment strategy is to invest today only if the value of an operating dealership exceeds \$6.66 million.

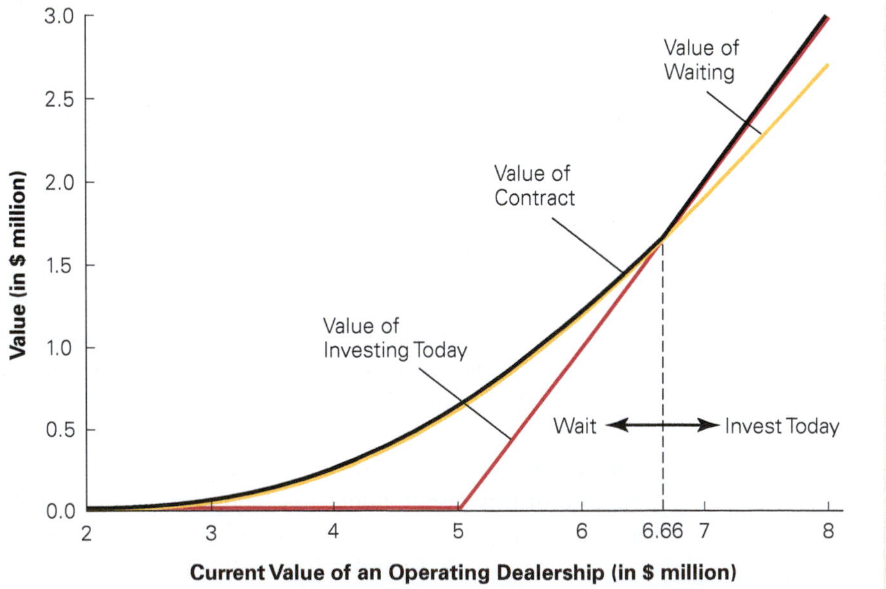

Factors Affecting the Timing of Investment

This example illustrates how the real option to wait affects the capital budgeting decision. Without the option of when to invest, it is optimal to invest as long as NPV > 0. *But when you have the option of deciding when to invest, it is usually optimal to invest only when the NPV is substantially greater than zero.*

To understand this result, think of the timing decision as a choice between two mutually exclusive projects: (1) invest today or (2) wait. Faced with mutually exclusive choices, we should choose the project with the higher NPV. That is, we should invest today only if the NPV of investing today exceeds the value of the option of waiting. If we can always walk away from the project, the option of waiting will be positive, so the NPV of investing today must be even higher for us to choose not to wait.

An interesting aspect of the dealership investment opportunity is the value of the deal when the ongoing value of a dealership is less than $5 million. In this case, the NPV of opening a dealership is negative, so without the option to wait the investment opportunity is worthless. But from Figure 22.5 we see that, with the option to wait, the investment opportunity is clearly not worthless. Even if the current value of an electric car dealership is $4 million (which means the NPV of investing today is −$1 million), the value of the opportunity is still worth about $248,000. That is, you would still be willing to pay up to $248,000 to sign the deal. Thus, *given the option to wait, an investment that currently has a negative NPV can have a positive value.*

Aside from the current NPV of the investment, what other factors affect the value of an investment and the decision to wait? From Figure 22.5 we can see that factors that increase the value of the call option will increase the benefit of waiting. Recall from our study of financial options in Chapters 20 and 21 that both the volatility and the dividends of the stock affect the value of a call option and the optimal time to exercise the call. These factors have their counterparts for real options:

- *Volatility*: By delaying an investment, we can base our decision on additional information. The option to wait is most valuable when there is a great deal of uncertainty regarding what the value of the investment will be in the future. If there is little uncertainty, the benefit of waiting is diminished.
- *Dividends*: Recall that absent dividends, it is not optimal to exercise a call option early. In the real option context, the dividends correspond to any value from the investment that we give up by waiting. It is always better to wait unless there is a cost to doing so. The greater the cost, the less attractive the option to delay becomes.

EXAMPLE 22.1 **Evaluating the Decision to Wait**

Problem

Suppose your current estimate of the electric car dealership's value is $6 million. What would be the value of the dealership contract if the volatility of the dealership's value were 25% rather than 40%? Alternatively, suppose the volatility is 40%, but waiting would lead competitors to expand and reduce the future free cash flows of the dealership by 10%. What is the value of the contract in this case?

Solution

With a lower volatility of 25%, we have

$$d_1 = \frac{\ln[S^x/PV(K)]}{\sigma\sqrt{T}} + \frac{\sigma\sqrt{T}}{2} = \frac{\ln(5.46/4.76)}{0.25} + 0.125 = 0.674$$

$$d_2 = d_1 - \sigma\sqrt{T} = 0.674 - 0.25 = 0.424$$

The value of the call option is

$$\begin{aligned} C &= S^x N(d_1) - PV(K)N(d_2) \\ &= (\$5.46 \text{ million}) \times (0.750) - (\$4.76 \text{ million}) \times (0.664) \\ &= \$0.93 \text{ million} \end{aligned}$$

Therefore, it is better to invest immediately and get an NPV of \$1 million, rather than wait. With the lower volatility, not enough information will be learned over the next year to justify the cost of waiting.

Now let's suppose the volatility is 40%, but waiting leads to increased competition. In this case, we should deduct the loss from increased competition as an additional "dividend" that we forego by waiting. Thus,

$$\begin{aligned} S^x &= S - PV(\text{First-Year FCF}) - PV(\text{Lost FCF from Competition}) \\ &= \left(\$6 \text{ million} - \frac{\$0.6 \text{ million}}{1.12}\right) \times (1 - 0.10) = \$4.92 \text{ million} \end{aligned}$$

Now,

$$d_1 = \frac{\ln[S^x/PV(K)]}{\sigma\sqrt{T}} + \frac{\sigma\sqrt{T}}{2} = \frac{\ln(4.92/4.76)}{0.40} + 0.20 = 0.283$$

$$d_2 = d_1 - \sigma\sqrt{T} = 0.283 - 0.40 = 0.117$$

The value of the call option in this case is

$$\begin{aligned} C &= S^x N(d_1) - PV(K)N(d_2) \\ &= (\$4.92 \text{ million}) \times (0.611) - (\$4.76 \text{ million}) \times (0.453) \\ &= \$0.85 \text{ million} \end{aligned}$$

Again, it would not be optimal to wait. In this case, despite the information to be gained, the costs associated with waiting are too high.

Investment Options and Firm Risk

Imagine that you formed a corporation and, acting on behalf of this corporation, you signed the electric car dealership contract. If the corporation has no other assets, what is the value of the corporation and how risky is it?

We have already calculated the value of the contract as a real option. Indeed, when the value of an operating dealership is \$6 million, the contract—and thus your firm—is worth \$1.2 million. To assess risk, you note that electric car dealerships are very sensitive to the economy and have a beta of about 2. Your firm, however, will not begin operating the

GLOBAL FINANCIAL CRISIS Uncertainty, Investment, and the Option to Delay

In mid-September 2008, with the markets for investment capital frozen, the Treasury announced an unprecedented program to help unfreeze credit markets and stave off a deep recession. The well-founded worry was that the dysfunctional financial markets would effectively cut off business activity and thus precipitate a crash in the real economy. Despite the passage of a $750 billion relief program (the Troubled Asset Relief Program—TARP), the economy plunged into the deepest recession since the Great Depression. What went wrong?

One likely factor was lawmakers' insensitivity to the effect of uncertainty on the real option to delay investment. The original idea behind TARP was to reduce uncertainty by making a huge capital commitment to buy troubled assets and effectively signal the government's intention to stabilize markets. By stabilizing markets and reducing uncertainty, it was hoped that TARP would help stimulate investment.

Unfortunately, however, TARP failed in its primary mission to decrease uncertainty. Indeed, concerns about whether the program would be implemented and how it would be implemented contributed significantly to overall uncertainty in the economy, making the option to delay investment until the uncertainty was resolved more valuable. In the end, the combination of this increased uncertainty together with a gloomy economic forecast led to a 19.1% decline in business investment in the fourth quarter of 2008, the largest decline since 1975.

dealership immediately; instead, it will wait until next year to decide whether to invest. The beta of your firm will therefore equal the beta of the option on a dealership, which we can calculate using the Black-Scholes formula and Equation 21.17 from the last chapter. Given the $6 million value of the operating dealership, and using the values from Eq. 22.2, the beta of the option to open the dealership—and therefore the beta of the corporation—is

$$\beta_{\text{corp}} = \frac{S^x \times N(d_1)}{C}\beta_{\text{dealer}} = \frac{(\$5.46 \text{ million}) \times (0.706)}{\$1.2 \text{ million}}\beta_{\text{dealer}} = 3.2 \times \beta_{\text{dealer}} = 6.4$$

Notice that the beta of a corporation with the option to open a dealership (that is, 6.4) is considerably larger than the beta of a dealership itself (2.0). Moreover, the beta of the corporation will fluctuate with the value of the option, and it will only be equal to the beta of a dealership if it is optimal to open the dealership immediately.

As this example shows, when comparing firms in the same industry, betas may vary depending upon the firms' growth opportunities. All else equal, firms for which a higher fraction of their value depends on future growth will tend to have higher betas.[3]

The fact that the beta of the firm includes the beta of the firm's growth options has implications for capital budgeting. Because the beta of growth options tend to be higher than the beta of the firm's investments in place, the beta of the firm typically overstates the beta of its existing assets. Hence, when financial analysts estimate an individual project beta by using the beta of a firm with substantial growth options, they may be overestimating the project beta.[4]

CONCEPT CHECK

1. What is the economic trade-off between investing immediately or waiting?
2. How does the option to wait affect the capital budgeting decision?
3. Does an option to invest have the same beta as the investment itself?

[3]The apparent failure of the CAPM to explain the cross-section of stock returns has been at least partially attributed to ignoring the effect of future investment options on the beta of the firm—see Z. Da, R. J. Guo, and R. Jagannathan, "CAPM for estimating the cost of equity capital: Interpreting the empirical evidence," *Journal of Financial Economics* 103 (2012): 204–220.

[4]For an analysis of this potential bias and an approach to correct it, see A. Bernardo, B. Chowdhry, and A. Goyal, "Assessing Project Risk," *Journal of Applied Corporate Finance* 24 (2012): 94–100.

22.4 Growth and Abandonment Options

When a firm has a real option to invest in the future, as in the dealership example, it is known as a **growth option**. In other situations, the firm may have the option to reduce the scale of its investment in the future; the option to disinvest is known as an **abandonment option**. Because these options have value, they contribute to the value of any firm with future possible investment opportunities.

Valuing Growth Potential

Future growth opportunities can be thought of as a collection of real call options on potential projects. Out-of-the-money calls are riskier than in-the-money calls, and because most growth options are likely to be out-of-the-money, the growth component of firm value is likely to be riskier than the ongoing assets of the firm. This observation might explain why young firms (and small firms) have higher returns than older, established firms. It also explains why R&D-intensive firms often have higher expected returns even when much of the R&D risk is idiosyncratic.[5]

In the dealership example, the main source of uncertainty was the investment's expected cash flows. Let's consider a second example of a growth option in which the uncertainty is instead about the investment's cost of capital. In this case, we will also illustrate how to value the option using the technique of risk-neutral probabilities introduced in Chapter 21.[6]

StartUp Incorporated is a new company whose only asset is a patent on a new drug. If produced, the drug will generate certain profits of $1 million per year for the life of the patent, which is 17 years (after that, competition will drive profits to zero). It will cost $10 million today to produce the drug. Assume that the yield on a 17-year risk-free annuity is currently 8% per year. What is the value of the patent?

Using the formula for the present value of an annuity, the NPV of investing today in the drug is

$$NPV = \frac{1}{0.08}\left(1 - \frac{1}{1.08^{17}}\right) - 10 = -\$878{,}362$$

Based on this calculation, it does not make sense to invest in the drug today. But what if interest rates change? Let's assume that interest rates will change in exactly one year. At that time, all risk-free interest rates will be either 10% per year or 5% per year, and then will remain at that level forever. Clearly, an increase in interest rates will make matters worse. Because interest rates will remain at the new higher level forever, it will never be optimal to invest. Thus, the value of this growth option is zero in that state. However, if rates drop, the NPV of undertaking the investment, given that the patent will have a remaining life of 16 years, is

$$NPV = \frac{1}{0.05}\left(1 - \frac{1}{1.05^{16}}\right) - 10 = \$837{,}770$$

In this case, it is optimal to invest. We can put this information on a decision tree, as shown in Figure 22.6.

---

[5]Readers interested in a more in-depth discussion of the relation between R&D risk and returns can consult J. Berk, R. Green, and V. Naik, "The Valuation and Return Dynamics of New Ventures," *Review of Financial Studies* 17 (2004): 1–35.

[6]Using risk-neutral probabilities in a decision tree is more general than Black-Scholes, which assumes a log-normal distribution for the asset's value and that the option can only be exercised at a fixed point in time.

FIGURE 22.6

StartUp's Decision to Invest in the Drug

If interest rates rise, it does not make sense to invest. If rates fall, it is optimal to develop the drug.

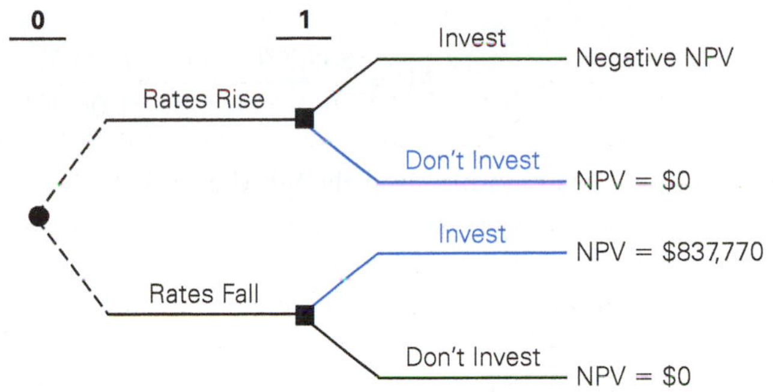

Working back to the information node at time zero, we face two outcomes, \$0 if rates rise and \$837,770 if rates fall. While we don't know the true probability of each outcome, we can compute the present value using risk-neutral probabilities as we showed in Chapter 21. To find the risk-neutral probabilities, we solve for the probabilities so that the expected return of all financial assets is equal to the current risk-free rate. In Chapter 21, we used a stock as the financial asset; in this case, we use the 17-year risk-free annuity that pays \$1000 per year as the financial asset. The value today of this annuity is

$$S = \frac{1000}{0.08}\left(1 - \frac{1}{1.08^{17}}\right) = \$9122$$

A year from now, the annuity will pay \$1000, and it will have 16 years left to maturity. Therefore, including the payment, it will be worth either

$$S_u = 1000 + \frac{1000}{0.1}\left(1 - \frac{1}{1.1^{16}}\right) = \$8824$$

if interest rates go up, or, if interest rates fall,

$$S_d = 1000 + \frac{1000}{0.05}\left(1 - \frac{1}{1.05^{16}}\right) = \$11{,}838$$

Suppose the current one-year risk-free interest rate is equal to 6%. (Note that this rate is below the current 17-year annuity rate of 8%; thus, the current yield curve is upward-sloping.) We can calculate the risk-neutral probability of interest rates increasing, which we denote by ρ using Eq. 21.16:

$$\rho = \frac{(1 + r_f)S - S_d}{S_u - S_d} = \frac{1.06 \times 9122 - 11{,}838}{8824 - 11{,}838} = 71.95\%$$

That is, a risk-neutral probability of 71.95% that interest rates will rise is required for the annuity to have an expected return equal to the risk-free rate of 6% over the next year.

Now that we have calculated the risk-neutral probabilities for the interest rate movements, we can use them to value StartUp's patent. The value today of the investment opportunity is the present value of the expected cash flows (using risk-neutral probabilities) discounted at the risk-free rate:

$$PV = \frac{837{,}770 \times (1 - 0.7195) + 0 \times 0.7195}{1.06} = \$221{,}693$$

In this example, even though the cash flows of the project are known with certainty, the uncertainty regarding future interest rates creates substantial option value for the firm. The firm's ability to use the patent and grow should interest rates fall is worth close to a quarter of a million dollars.

The Option to Expand

Future growth options are not only important to firm value, but can also be important in the value of an individual project. By undertaking a project, a firm often gets the opportunity to invest in new projects that firms outside the industry cannot easily access. For example, a fashion designer might introduce a new line of clothes knowing that if the line proves popular, he has the option to launch a new line of accessories based on those clothes.

Consider an investment opportunity with an option to grow that requires a $10 million investment today. In one year, we will find out whether the project, which entails introducing a new product into the business machines market, is successful. The risk-neutral probability that the project will generate $1 million per year in perpetuity is 50%; otherwise, the project will generate nothing. At any time, we can double the size of the project on the original terms. Figure 22.7 represents these decisions on a decision tree.

Assume that the risk-free rate is constant at 6% per year. If we ignore the option to double the size of the project and we invest today, then the expected cash flows are $1 million × 0.5 = $500,000 per year. Computing the NPV gives

$$NPV_{\text{without growth option}} = \frac{500{,}000}{0.06} - 10{,}000{,}000 = -\$1.667 \text{ million}$$

Based on this analysis, it appears that it is not optimal to undertake the project today. Of course, that also means we will never find out whether the project is successful.

FIGURE 22.7

Staged Investment Opportunity

At any time, the size of the project can be doubled on the original terms. It is optimal to make this decision after we find out whether the project is a success. This growth option can make the initial investment worthwhile.

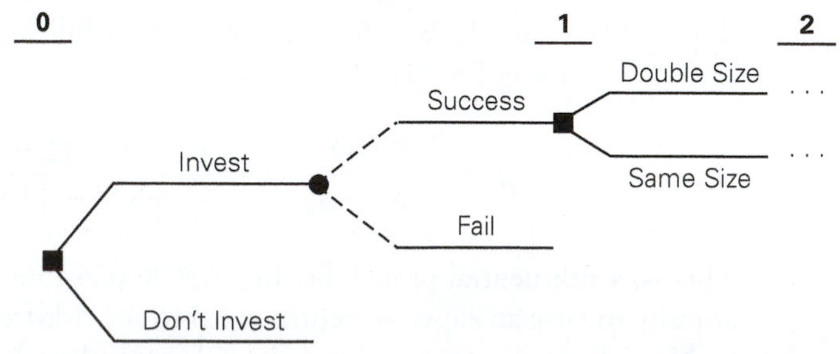

INTERVIEW WITH

SCOTT MATHEWS

Scott Mathews, formerly a Technical Fellow with the Computational Finance and Stochastic Modeling team within Boeing's advanced research and development division. He has expertise in "Business Engineering," a technology that features complex financial and investment risk models applying real asset option pricing for new products and strategically significant projects. Mr. Mathews has a number of patents in the field of real options.

QUESTION: *How can real options be used to manage projects?*

ANSWER: High-potential projects typically have substantial uncertain cash flows owing to technology and market uncertainties, and therefore your corporate finance team has to be more active in managing these projects. Essentially they act as internal venture capitalists, seeking high payoffs from risky projects. We use real options to evaluate these types of investment opportunities. With real options, we can answer the questions: Given the technical and market risks of the project, how much should we spend at the early stages? Does each incremental investment increase my return opportunities or decrease risk, and how? What amount of technology and market "learning" must be accomplished to merit a follow-on investment?

Real options are call options on an opportunity, giving you the right to stop, start, or modify a project at some future date. They are contingent, so you can make a strategic, rather than tactical, investment. By investing a small amount at each stage, you can gather enough information to decide what to do next. This limits your losses but still lets you capitalize on opportunities that arise. You don't reject (or approve) the project outright, but make incremental investments in the technology or market to gather sufficient information to determine whether this investment optimizes the company's strategy and produces positive returns over the long term.

QUESTION: *Explain the concepts of "pilot" and "commercial" stages?*

ANSWER: The "pilot" stage refers to the incremental staged investments we make to move projects through "decision gates," investing a small and appropriate amount to gather information about the technology and the market, while driving down the project risks. At the end of each decision gate, the project is re-evaluated. If there is a reasonable weighted probability of a successful outcome, we invest again and continue to the next decision gate. Projects go through several gates, and at each one we focus on reducing uncertainty, until arriving at a decision point of whether to make a large, discretionary, one-time investment (the "strike price") that launches the "piloted" concepts into production—the "commercial" stage—or terminate the project.

QUESTION: *How does staging development create a real option with value?*

ANSWER: Staging development is how we use real options to manage projects. By staging development we are buying knowledge, especially about the project risks and opportunities. As a project moves through gates, projects compete for funding, and we use this knowledge to decide which projects should proceed and which ones should be deferred. The approach brings together the engineering, marketing, and finance disciplines to give a uniform look at risks and investment opportunities. This is one of the huge powers of the technique.

Boeing's ability to solve aviation challenges with a high degree of efficiency is our competitive advantage and allows us to "buy" these options at below their market value through investments (the "premium") in our engineering processes. Buying an option for less provides direct value to shareholders. We can leverage our internal knowledge with a relatively small amount of money and hedge the risks. It's a tricky process, and is not completely financial. It often requires judgment as well.

Consider undertaking the project and exercising the growth option to double the size in a year if the product takes off. The NPV of doubling the size of the project in a year in this state is

$$NPV_{\text{doubling if successful}} = \frac{1{,}000{,}000}{0.06} - 10{,}000{,}000 = \$6.667 \text{ million}$$

The risk-neutral probability that this state will occur is 50%, so the expected value of this growth option is $6.667 \times 0.5 = \$3.333$ million. The present value of this amount today is

$$PV_{\text{growth option}} = \frac{3.333}{1.06} = \$3.145 \text{ million}$$

We have this option only if we choose to invest today (otherwise, we never find out how the product performs), so the NPV of undertaking this investment is the NPV we calculated above plus the value of the growth option we obtain by undertaking the project:

$$\begin{aligned} NPV &= NPV_{\text{without growth option}} + PV_{\text{growth option}} \\ &= -1.667 + 3.145 = \$1.478 \text{ million} \end{aligned}$$

Our analysis shows that the NPV of the investment opportunity is positive and the firm should undertake it.

Notice that it is optimal to undertake the investment today only because of the existence of the future expansion option. If we could find out how well the product would sell without actually producing it, then it would not make sense to invest until we found out this information. Because the only way to find out if the product is successful is to make and market it, it is optimal to proceed. In this case, the project is viable because we can experiment at a low scale and preserve the option to grow later.

This project is an example of a strategy that many firms use when they undertake big projects. Rather than commit to the entire project initially, a firm experiments by undertaking the project in stages. It implements the project on a smaller scale first; if the small-scale project proves successful, the firm then exercises the option to grow the project.

The Option to Abandon

The previous two examples consider cases in which the firm has the option to grow or expand if the project proves successful. Alternatively, when a project is unsuccessful, the firm may be able to mitigate its loss by abandoning the project. An abandonment option is the option to walk away. Abandonment options can add value to a project because a firm can drop a project if it turns out to be unsuccessful.

To illustrate, assume you are the CFO of a publicly traded nationwide chain of gourmet food stores. Your company is considering opening a new store in the renovated Ferry Building in Boston. If you do not sign the lease on the store today, someone else will, so you will not have the opportunity to open a store later. There is a clause in the lease that allows you to break the lease at no cost in two years.

Including the lease payments, the new store will cost \$10,000 per month to operate. Because the building has just recently reopened, you do not know what the pedestrian traffic will be. If your customers are mainly limited to morning and evening commuters, you expect to generate \$8000 per month in revenue in perpetuity. If, however, the building follows the lead of the Ferry Building in San Francisco and becomes a tourist attraction, you believe that your revenue will be double that amount. You estimate there is a 50% probability that the Ferry Building will become a tourist attraction. The costs to set up the store will be \$400,000. Assume that the cost of capital for the business is 7% per year.

Whether the Boston Ferry Building becomes a tourist attraction represents idiosyncratic uncertainty that investors in your company can costlessly diversify, and hence we do not need to adjust its probability for risk (i.e., the risk-neutral probability equals the true probability of 50%). If you were forced to operate the store under all circumstances, then the expected revenue will be $\$8000 \times 0.5 + \$16{,}000 \times 0.5 = \$12{,}000$. Given the monthly discount rate of $1.07^{1/12} - 1 = 0.565\%$, the NPV of the investment is

$$NPV = \frac{12{,}000 - 10{,}000}{0.00565} - 400{,}000 = -\$46{,}018$$

It would not make sense to open the store.

Of course, you do not have to keep operating the store. You have an option to get out of the lease after two years at no cost, and after the store is open it will be immediately obvious whether the Ferry Building is a tourist attraction. In this case, the decision tree looks like Figure 22.8.

If the Ferry Building is a tourist attraction, the NPV of the investment opportunity is

$$NPV = \frac{16{,}000 - 10{,}000}{0.00565} - 400{,}000 = \$661{,}947$$

If the Ferry Building does not become a tourist attraction, you will close the store after two years. The NPV of the investment opportunity in this state is just the NPV of operating for two years:

$$NPV = \frac{8000 - 10{,}000}{0.00565}\left(1 - \frac{1}{1.00565^{24}}\right) - 400{,}000$$
$$= -\$444{,}770$$

There is an equal probability of each state and again, because the risk is idiosyncratic, the actual and risk-neutral probabilities are the same. Thus, the NPV of opening the store is just the expected value using the actual probabilities:

$$\$661{,}947 \times 0.5 - \$444{,}770 \times 0.5 = \$108{,}589$$

By exercising the option to abandon the venture, you limit your losses and so the NPV of undertaking the investment is positive. The value of the option to abandon is the difference between the NPV with and without the option: $108{,}589 - (-46{,}018) = \$154{,}607$.[7]

FIGURE 22.8

Decision to Open a Store in the Boston Ferry Building

You must decide now whether to sign the lease and open the store, but you have an option to abandon the lease in 24 months (2 years). The profitability of the store depends on whether the Ferry Building becomes a tourist attraction.

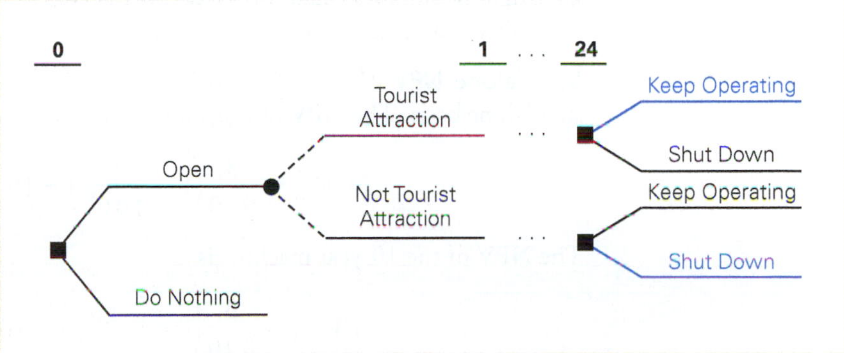

[7]We can also calculate the option value directly; with a 50% probability, we avoid the losses of \$2000 per month starting in two years:

$$50\% \times \frac{1}{1.00565^{24}} \times \frac{2000}{0.00565} = \$154{,}607$$

It is easy to ignore or understate the importance of the option to abandon. In many applications, killing an economically unsuccessful venture can add more value than starting a new venture. Often, however, managers focus on the value created by starting new ventures and de-emphasize the value created by abandoning old ventures. Some of this behavior undoubtedly results from the same behavioral biases that we discussed in Chapter 13 that cause individual investors to hold onto losers. It is also closely tied to the sunk cost fallacy, the idea that once a manager makes a large investment, he should not abandon a project. As we pointed out in Chapter 8, sunk costs should have no bearing on an investment decision. If continuing a project is a negative-NPV undertaking, you can create value by abandoning, regardless of how much investment has already been sunk into the project.

CONCEPT CHECK

1. Why can a firm with no ongoing projects, and investment opportunities that currently have negative NPVs, still be worth a positive amount?
2. Why is it sometimes optimal to invest in stages?
3. How can an abandonment option add value to a project?

22.5 Investments with Different Lives

As we have seen, real options can add substantial value to an investment decision. Therefore, when we are in a position of choosing between alternative investments, it is necessary to assess any differences in the real options each provides. One example that can be particularly important is the case where one is comparing investments with different lives. While longer-term investments may have cost or return advantages, shorter-term investments include reinvestment options that should not be ignored. Let's illustrate this trade-off with an example.

Consider the following problem faced by a financial analyst at Canadian Motors. Last year, an engineering firm named Advanced Mechanics was asked to design a new machine that will attach car chassis to bodies. The firm has produced two designs. The cheaper design will cost \$10 million to implement and last five years. The more expensive design will cost \$16 million and last 10 years. In both cases, the machines are expected to save Canadian Motors \$3 million per year. If the cost of capital is 10%, which design should Canadian Motors approve?

Standalone NPV of Each Design. Let's first calculate the NPV of each decision on a standalone basis. The NPV of adopting the five-year machine is

$$NPV_{5\text{ yr}} = \frac{3}{0.10}\left(1 - \frac{1}{1.10^5}\right) - 10 = \$1.37 \text{ million}$$

The NPV of the 10-year machine is

$$NPV_{10\text{ yr}} = \frac{3}{0.10}\left(1 - \frac{1}{1.10^{10}}\right) - 16 = \$2.43 \text{ million}$$

If the analyst simply picked the design with the higher standalone NPV, he would choose the longer-lived design. However, the preceding NPV calculation ignores the difference in these projects' life spans. The longer-lived design embodies a 10-year production plan. The shorter-lived design only captures what will happen over the next five years. To truly compare the two options, we must consider what will happen once the shorter-lived equipment wears out. Let's consider three possibilities: (1) the technology is not replaced;

(2) it is replaced at the same terms; or (3) technological advances allow us to replace it at improved terms.

No Replacement. If the shorter-lived technology is not replaced (and the firm reverts to its old production process), there will be no additional benefits once its five-year life ends. In that case, the original comparison is correct, and the 10-year machine will increase firm value by 2.43 − 1.37 = $1.06 million more than the shorter-lived design.

One reason we might not replace the technology is if we expect its cost to increase. For example, suppose its cost in five years' time will be $11.37 million or higher (an increase of 2.6% per year). In that case, because the cost of the machine has gone up by more than its current NPV of $1.37 million, replacement will not be optimal.

Replacement at the Same Terms. Suppose that we expect the costs and benefits of the shorter-lived design to be the same in five years. In that case, it will be optimal to replace the machine with a new equivalent machine, as we will again earn its NPV of $1.37 million. We should include this benefit when we evaluate the NPV of the five-year design, leading to a total NPV over the 10-year horizon of

$$NPV_{5\text{ yr, with replacement}} = 1.37 + \frac{1.37}{1.10^5} = \$2.22 \text{ million}$$

Allowing for replacement at the same terms substantially increases the NPV we calculated for the five-year design. However, it is still inferior to the $2.43 million NPV from the 10-year design.

Replacement at Improved Terms. In reality, the future cost of a machine is uncertain. Because of technological advances, machines may become less expensive rather than more expensive (think about the steadily declining prices of computers). Suppose we expect the cost of the new technology to fall to $7 million at the end of five years. Because the cost

Equivalent Annual Benefit Method

Traditionally, managers have accounted for the difference in project lengths by calculating the **equivalent annual benefit (EAB)** of each project, which is the constant annuity payment over the life of the project that is equivalent to receiving its NPV today. The **equivalent annual benefit method** then selects the project with the highest equivalent annual benefit. (When all cash flows are costs, this approach is sometimes referred to as the **equivalent annual cost** method.)

For example, in the case of Canadian Motors, the equivalent annual benefit of each machine is

$$EAB_{5\text{ yr}} = \frac{1.37}{\frac{1}{0.10}\left(1 - \frac{1}{1.10^5}\right)} = \$0.361 \text{ million,}$$

$$EAB_{10\text{ yr}} = \frac{2.43}{\frac{1}{0.10}\left(1 - \frac{1}{1.10^{10}}\right)} = \$0.395 \text{ million}$$

Thus, the 10-year machine has the higher equivalent annual benefit and would be chosen under this method.

The equivalent annual benefit method assumes that we earn the project's EAB over the entire forecast horizon. For the five-year machine, this assumption means that we would earn an NPV over 10 years of

$$NPV_{5\text{ yr }EAB} = \frac{0.361}{0.10}\left(1 - \frac{1}{1.10^{10}}\right) = \$2.22 \text{ million}$$

Comparing this result with our earlier analysis, we see that using the EAB method is equivalent to assuming that we can replace the project at identical terms over the entire horizon. While this assumption may be correct, in most instances there is significant uncertainty regarding the project terms in the future. In that case, real option methods must be used to determine the correct choice.

has declined by \$3 million, its NPV will rise to $3 + 1.37 = \$4.37$ million. In that case, the NPV of the five-year design over a 10-year horizon is

$$NPV_{5\text{ yr, with improved replacement}} = 1.37 + \frac{4.37}{1.10^5} = \$4.08 \text{ million}$$

Thus, if terms are expected to improve in this way, the five-year design is optimal for the firm, increasing firm value by $4.08 - 2.43 = \$1.65$ million compared to the 10-year machine.

Valuing the Replacement Option. As the above analysis reveals, adopting the five-year machine provides the firm with a replacement option in five years' time. In order to compare the two designs correctly, we must determine the value of this replacement option, which will depend on the likelihood that the cost of the machine will decrease or increase.

EXAMPLE 22.2 **Valuing the Replacement Option**

Problem

Suppose the cost of the shorter-lived machine is equally likely to rise to \$13 million, stay equal to \$10 million, or fall to \$7 million, and suppose this risk is idiosyncratic and does not change the project's cost of capital. Which machine should the firm choose?

Solution

If the cost rises to \$13 million, the firm will choose not to replace the machine and get an NPV of 0. If the cost stays the same or falls, the firm will replace the machine and get an NPV of \$1.37 million or \$4.37 million, respectively. Given the probabilities, the NPV of the five-year machine over the 10-year horizon is

$$NPV_{5\text{ yr, with uncertain replacement}} = 1.37 + \frac{\frac{1}{3}(0) + \frac{1}{3}(1.37) + \frac{1}{3}(4.37)}{1.10^5} = \$2.56 \text{ million}$$

Thus, given this uncertainty, the shorter-lived machine offers a higher NPV over 10 years than the \$2.43 million NPV of the longer-lived machine. By committing to the longer-lived project, the firm would give up its real option to react to technological and market changes.

CONCEPT CHECK

1. Why is it inappropriate to simply pick the higher NPV project when comparing mutually exclusive investment opportunities with different lives?
2. What is a major shortcoming of the equivalent annual benefit method?

22.6 Optimally Staging Investments

In analyzing the value of the option to grow, we considered the real option value of a staged investment opportunity. The advantage of staging is that it allows us to postpone investment until after we learn important new information. We can avoid making the investment unless the new information suggests it is worthwhile.

In many applications, the stages have a natural order, for example, investing in a prototype before developing on a large scale. But in some situations, we can choose the order of the development stages. If so, how can we maximize the value of the real options that we create?

An Example: Eclectic Motors. Eclectic Motors is considering developing an electric car that would compete directly with gasoline-powered cars. They must overcome three technological hurdles to produce a successful car:

1. Develop materials to significantly reduce the car's body weight.
2. Develop a method to rapidly recharge the batteries.
3. Advance battery technology to reduce weight and increase storage capacity.

As shown in Table 22.2, although Eclectic's engineers have already made significant breakthroughs, further research and substantial risk remain for each task:

Suppose all three risks are idiosyncratic, and the risk-free interest rate is 6%. Given Eclectic's resources, the company can only work on one technology at a time. Eclectic's managers know that by appropriately staging these investments, they can enhance the firm's value. The question is, assuming that it makes sense to proceed, which technology should they tackle first?

Mutually Dependent Investments. Eclectic's electric car project represents a situation with **mutually dependent investments**, in which the value of one project depends upon the outcome of the others. In this case, we assume that all three challenges must be overcome, or there will be no benefit. Thus, we need to determine the optimal order of investment that will minimize the expected cost of development.

Investment Scale. Consider first the materials and recharger technologies. These two are identical except for the upfront investment costs. Let's compare the expected cost of completing them in different orders. If we begin with the materials technology, the expected cost to complete both is

$$\underbrace{100}_{\substack{\text{Investment}\\\text{in materials}}} + \underbrace{0.50}_{\substack{\text{Probability}\\\text{materials}\\\text{technology}\\\text{succeeds}}} \times \underbrace{\frac{1}{1.06}}_{\substack{\text{PV of}\\\text{delay}}} \times \underbrace{400}_{\substack{\text{Investment}\\\text{in recharger}}} = \$288.7 \text{ million}$$

If we begin with the recharger technology, the expected cost is

$$\underbrace{400}_{\substack{\text{Investment}\\\text{in recharger}}} + \underbrace{0.50}_{\substack{\text{Probability}\\\text{recharger}\\\text{technology}\\\text{succeeds}}} \times \underbrace{\frac{1}{1.06}}_{\substack{\text{PV of}\\\text{delay}}} \times \underbrace{100}_{\substack{\text{Investment}\\\text{in materials}}} = \$447.2 \text{ million}$$

TABLE 22.2 **Required Time, Cost, and Likelihood of Success for Eclectic's Project**

Technology	Cost	Time	Probability of Success
Materials	\$100 million	1 year	50%
Recharger	\$400 million	1 year	50%
Battery	\$100 million	4 years	25%

Thus, it is clear that Eclectic should invest in the materials technology before working on the recharger. Because the cost of the recharger is greater, we don't want to waste our investment in it if the materials technology fails. As this example shows, other things being equal, it is beneficial to make the least costly investments first, delaying more expensive investments until it is clear they are warranted.

Investment Time and Risk. Next, let's compare the materials and battery technologies. These projects have the same cost, but the battery technology will take longer and has a greater chance of failure. Considering only these two projects, if we begin with the materials technology, the expected cost of completing both is

$$\underbrace{100}_{\substack{\text{Investment}\\\text{in materials}}} + \underbrace{0.50}_{\substack{\text{Probability}\\\text{materials}\\\text{technology}\\\text{succeeds}}} \times \underbrace{\frac{1}{1.06}}_{\substack{\text{PV of}\\\text{delay}}} \times \underbrace{100}_{\substack{\text{Investment}\\\text{in battery}}} = \$147.2 \text{ million}$$

If we begin with the battery technology, the expected cost is

$$\underbrace{100}_{\substack{\text{Investment}\\\text{in battery}}} + \underbrace{0.25}_{\substack{\text{Probability}\\\text{battery}\\\text{technology}\\\text{succeeds}}} \times \underbrace{\frac{1}{1.06^4}}_{\substack{\text{PV of}\\\text{delay}}} \times \underbrace{100}_{\substack{\text{Investment}\\\text{in materials}}} = \$119.80 \text{ million}$$

Thus, Eclectic should work on the battery technology before working on the materials. Given its greater risk, we will learn more if the battery project succeeds regarding the viability of the overall project. Due to its longer time requirement, we also benefit from the time value of postponing the following investments further. In general, other things being equal, it is beneficial to invest in riskier and lengthier projects first, delaying future investments until the greatest amount of information can be learned.

A General Rule. As we have seen, the cost, time, and risk of each project will determine the optimal order in which to invest. Intuitively, by making smaller, riskier investments first, we gain the most additional information at the lowest cost. (Thus, the battery project should definitely come before the recharger project.) In general, we can find the optimal order to stage mutually dependent projects by ranking each, from highest to lowest, according to its **failure cost index**:

$$\text{Failure Cost Index} = \frac{1 - PV(\text{success})}{PV(\text{investment})} \tag{22.3}$$

where PV(success) is the value at the start of the project of receiving \$1 if the project succeeds (i.e., the present value of the risk-neutral probability of success) and PV(investment) is the project's required investment, again expressed as a present value at the project's start. The failure cost index orders investments so that we gain the most information at the lowest cost upfront.

EXAMPLE 22.3 **Deciding the Order of Investment with Multiple Stages**

Problem

Use the failure cost index to determine the optimal investment order for Eclectic's electric car project.

Solution

Evaluating the failure cost index for each stage, we have

Materials:	$[1 - (0.50/1.06)]/100 = 0.00528$
Recharger:	$[1 - (0.50/1.06)]/400 = 0.00132$
Battery:	$[1 - (0.25/1.06^4)]/100 = 0.00802$

So, Eclectic should develop the batteries first, then the body materials, and finally the charger, matching our earlier analysis.

Until now, we have ignored the decision about whether it is optimal to develop at all. In evaluating the overall investment decision, the first step is to decide the optimal order of investment in each stage. Once that order has been determined, we can calculate the overall NPV of the opportunity and reach a decision on whether to proceed.

EXAMPLE 22.4 **Deciding Whether to Invest in a Project with Multiple Stages**

Problem

Eclectic's managers estimate that with these technological breakthroughs, they can develop the electric car, and the present value of all future profits will be $4 billion. Does the decision to develop the car make sense?

Solution

Using the optimal order from Example 22.3, the NPV is

$$NPV = -100 - 0.25\frac{100}{1.06^4} - 0.25 \times 0.5\frac{400}{1.06^5} + 0.25 \times 0.5 \times 0.5\frac{4000}{1.06^6} = \$19.1 \text{ million}$$

Thus, it is profitable to develop the electric car. However, this result crucially depends on the optimal staging—the NPV would be negative if Eclectic chose any other order!

CONCEPT CHECK

1. Why can staging investment decisions add value?
2. How can you decide the order of investment in a staged investment decision?

22.7 Rules of Thumb

One of the major drawbacks of using the concepts introduced in this chapter is that they are difficult to implement. In practice, correctly modeling the sources of uncertainty and appropriate dynamic decisions usually requires an extensive amount of time and financial expertise. Furthermore, in most cases, the solutions are problem-specific, so the time and expertise spent on one problem are not transferable to other problems. Consequently, many firms resort to following rules of thumb.[8] Here, we examine two commonly used rules of thumb: the profitability index and hurdle rates.

The Profitability Index Rule

As we explained in Section 22.1, when an investment opportunity can be delayed, it is optimal to invest only when the NPV of the investment project is sufficiently high. In most applications, it is quite difficult to calculate precisely how high the NPV must be to trigger investment. As a result, some firms use the following rule of thumb: *Invest whenever the profitability index exceeds a specified level.*

Recall from Chapter 7 that in the simple case of a project where the only resource is the upfront investment, the profitability index is

$$\text{Profitability Index} = \frac{NPV}{\text{Initial Investment}}$$

The **profitability index rule** directs you to invest whenever the profitability index exceeds some predetermined number. When the investment cannot be delayed, the optimal rule is to invest whenever the profitability index is greater than zero. When there is an option to delay, a common rule of thumb is to invest only when the index exceeds a higher threshold, such as one. Often, firms set high thresholds because the cost of investing at the wrong time is usually asymmetric. It is often better to wait too long (use a profitability index criterion that is too high) than to invest too soon (use a profitability index criterion that is too low).

The Hurdle Rate Rule

The profitability index rule raises the bar on the NPV to take into account the option to wait. Rather than invest when the NPV is zero, you wait until the NPV is a multiple of the initial investment. Instead of raising the bar on the NPV, the **hurdle rate rule** raises the discount rate. The hurdle rate rule uses a higher discount rate than the cost of capital to compute the NPV, but then applies the regular NPV rule: *Invest whenever the NPV calculated using this higher discount rate is positive.* This higher discount rate is known as the **hurdle rate** because if the project can jump this hurdle—that is, have a positive NPV at this higher discount rate—then it should be undertaken.

When the source of uncertainty that creates a motive to wait is interest rate uncertainty, there is a natural way to approximate the optimal hurdle rate. In this case, the rule of thumb is to multiply the cost of capital by the ratio of the **callable annuity rate**, which is the rate on a risk-free annuity that can be repaid (or *called*) at any time, to the risk-free rate:

$$\text{Hurdle Rate} = \text{Cost of Capital} \times \frac{\text{Callable Annuity Rate}}{\text{Risk-Free Rate}} \tag{22.4}$$

We should then invest whenever the NPV of the project is positive using this hurdle rate as the discount rate.

---

[8]See Robert McDonald, "Real Options and Rules of Thumb in Capital Budgeting," in M. Brennan and L. Trigeorgis (eds.), *Project Flexibility, Agency, and Competition* (Oxford University Press, 2000), for a detailed analysis of the performance of different rules of thumb.

What is the intuition for this rule? Let's assume you have a risk-free project that you can delay. It currently has a positive NPV. You intend to borrow the initial investment but you are unsure whether you should wait in the hope that interest rates will fall. If you take out a regular loan and interest rates decrease, you will be stuck paying a higher rate. However, if you take out a callable loan and interest rates fall, then you can refinance the loan and take advantage of the lower rates. So, if the project has a positive NPV using the callable annuity rate as the discount rate, you can have your cake and eat it too: You can immediately get the benefits of the investment by undertaking it and still take advantage of a lower rate if rates fall. Thus, it makes sense to invest immediately. The rule of thumb approximately implements this decision rule.

How large is the difference between the hurdle rate and the cost of capital? Because government-guaranteed mortgages are insured against default and repayable by the borrower at any time, they are an example of a callable annuity (as the box on the next page explains). Based on the difference between mortgage and risk-free rates, using a hurdle rate 20% higher than the firm's cost of capital might be a reasonable adjustment to account for the firm's ability to wait until interest rates are sufficiently favorable to invest.

EXAMPLE 22.5 Using the Hurdle Rate Rule for the Option to Delay

Problem

You can invest in a risk-free technology that requires an upfront payment of $1 million and will provide a perpetual annual cash flow of $90,000. Suppose all interest rates will be either 10% or 5% in one year and remain there forever. The risk-neutral probability that interest rates will drop to 5% is 90%. The one-year risk-free interest rate is 8%, and today's rate on a risk-free perpetual bond is 5.4%. The rate on an equivalent perpetual bond that is repayable at any time (the callable annuity rate) is 9%.[9] Should you invest in the technology today, or wait and see if rates drop and then invest?

Solution

Because the investment is risk free, the cost of capital is the risk-free rate. Thus, Eq. 22.4 suggests using a hurdle rate equal to the callable annuity rate of 9%. With that rate,

$$NPV = \frac{90{,}000}{0.09} - 1{,}000{,}000 = 0$$

The hurdle rate rule implies that you are indifferent. Let's see if this is correct. The actual cost of capital is 5.4% (the rate offered on a risk-free perpetuity), so the investment opportunity clearly has a positive NPV:

$$NPV = \frac{90{,}000}{.054} - 1{,}000{,}000 = \$666{,}667$$

---

[9]To check that these rates make sense, note that a $1000 perpetual bond paying $54 per year would be worth $\$54 + 54/.05 = \$1134$ if interest rates fall and $\$54 + 54/.10 = \$594$ if rates rise, for a (risk-neutral) expected payoff of $0.9 \times 1134 + 0.1 \times 594 = \$1080$, and an expected return equal to the one-year risk-free rate of 8%. Similarly, a $1000 callable bond with a coupon of $90 would be worth $\$90 + 1000 = \$1090$ if rates fall and the bond is prepaid, and $\$90 + 90/.10 = \$990$ if rates rise, again for a risk-neutral expected payoff of $0.9 \times 1090 + 0.1 \times 990 = \$1080$.

Let's see what the NPV of waiting is. If we delay the investment, it makes sense to invest only if rates drop to 5%, in which case

$$NPV_{\text{rates go down}} = \frac{90{,}000}{0.05} - 1{,}000{,}000 = \$800{,}000$$

The present value today of the expected NPV using risk-neutral probabilities is therefore

$$\frac{800{,}000 \times 0.90}{1.08} = \$666{,}667$$

The hurdle rate rule is correct: You really are indifferent between investing today and waiting.

In situations like Example 22.5, when the cash flows are constant and perpetual, and the reason to wait derives solely from interest rate uncertainty, the rule of thumb is exact.[10] However, when these conditions are not satisfied, the rule of thumb merely approximates the correct decision.

While using a hurdle rate rule for deciding when to invest might be a cost-effective way to make investment decisions, it is important to remember that this rule does not provide an accurate measure of *value*. The value of making an investment is the NPV calculated using the cost of capital as the discount rate, not the hurdle rate. Thus, while the rule of thumb provides the correct time to invest in Example 22.5, the actual value of undertaking the investment is $666,667—the NPV when the correct cost of capital is used as the discount rate.

Potentially, there could be an advantage to using the hurdle rate and profitability index rules of thumb simultaneously. That is, the decision when to invest can be made by first computing the NPV using the hurdle rate in Eq. 22.4 to account for interest rate uncertainty. The profitability index can then be calculated using this NPV, with the firm accepting the project only if the profitability index exceeds a threshold that accounts for cash flow uncertainty.

The Option to Repay a Mortgage

As most homeowners know, mortgage interest rates are higher than comparable risk-free rates like the yield on the 30-year U.S. Treasury bond. One reason mortgage rates are higher than Treasury rates is the risk that the homeowner will default. But, for high-quality borrowers, this risk has remained relatively small, even through the financial crisis. Furthermore, in many cases, mortgage lenders are insured against default by government agencies. Yet, mortgage rates for the best borrowers still exceed even the rates on some corporate debt.

Mortgage interest rates are higher than Treasury rates because mortgages have a repayment option that Treasuries do not have: You can repay your mortgage at any time, while the U.S. government cannot. Consequently, if interest rates drop, a mortgage holder can **refinance**—that is, repay the existing mortgage and take out a new mortgage at a lower rate. This option to refinance is valuable to the borrower but costly to the lender: If rates fall, the mortgage holder will repay the mortgage and replace it with a new mortgage at a lower rate, whereas if rates rise, the bank is stuck with a loan that is now below the market rate. Of course, banks understand they have written this option, and so demand a higher rate on the loan than the rate they would if the mortgage did not have the repayment option. As a result, mortgage rates have tended to be at least 20% higher than long-term risk-free interest rates.

[10] See J. Berk, "A Simple Approach for Deciding When to Invest," *American Economic Review* 89 (1999): 1319–1326.

CONCEPT CHECK

1. Explain the profitability index rule of thumb.
2. What is the hurdle rate rule, and what uncertainty does it reflect?

22.8 Key Insights from Real Options

Although a general rule for how to account for all real options does not exist, there are a few simple principles that we have covered in this chapter. In closing, it is worth restating these principles:

Out-of-the-Money Real Options Have Value. Even if an investment opportunity currently has a negative NPV, it does not imply that the opportunity is worthless. So long as there is a chance that the investment opportunity could have a positive NPV in the future, the opportunity is worth something today.

In-the-Money Real Options Need Not Be Exercised Immediately. You should not necessarily take on an investment opportunity that has a positive NPV today. If you can delay the investment opportunity, the option to delay might be worth more than the NPV of undertaking the investment immediately. In this case, you should not undertake the investment and instead delay it.

Waiting Is Valuable. Value can be created by waiting for uncertainty to resolve because once uncertainty is resolved, you can make better decisions with better information. Thus, if there is no cost to waiting, investing early never makes sense. If there is a cost, always weigh the benefits of waiting for resolution of uncertainty against the costs of waiting.

Delay Investment Expenses as Much as Possible. Because waiting is valuable, you should only incur investment expenses at the last possible moment. Committing capital before it is absolutely necessary reduces value because it gives up the option to make a better decision once uncertainty has been resolved.

Create Value by Exploiting Real Options. In an uncertain environment, real options create value for the firm. To realize this value, the firm must continually re-evaluate its investment opportunities and optimize its decision-making dynamically. It is important to keep in mind that often as much value can be created by optimally delaying or abandoning projects as by creating or growing them.

Combining these insights, we find that by staging investments, and using clear valuation-based methods to determine at each stage if the firm should abandon, defer, continue, or grow an investment opportunity, managers can substantially increase firm value.

MyFinanceLab

Here is what you should know after reading this chapter. MyFinanceLab will help you identify what you know and where to go when you need to practice.

22.1 Real Versus Financial Options

- A real option is an option where the underlying asset is physical rather than financial.

22.2 Decision Tree Analysis

- A decision tree is a graphical way to represent alternative decisions and potential outcomes in an uncertain economy. It contains decision nodes and information nodes.

22.3 The Option to Delay: Investment as a Call Option

- By waiting before committing to an investment, a firm can obtain more information about the investment's returns. By correctly choosing the time to invest, it can add value.
- When you have the option of deciding when to invest, it is usually optimal to invest only when the NPV is substantially greater than zero.
- Given the option to wait, an investment that currently has a negative NPV can have a positive value.
- The option to wait is most valuable when there is a great deal of uncertainty regarding what the value of the investment will be in the future.
- In the real option context, the dividends correspond to any value from the investment that we give up by waiting. Absent dividends, a call option should not be exercised early.
- The beta of the option to invest is a multiple of the beta of the underlying investment opportunity, and varies with its value.

22.4 Growth and Abandonment Options

- By undertaking a project, a firm often gets the opportunity to make investments that it would not have otherwise. The opportunity to invest in projects in the future—that is, the firm's growth options—is worth something today.
- When firms find themselves involved in a project that is losing money, with little prospect of turning things around in the future, they can exercise their abandonment option and walk away.

22.5 Investments with Different Lives

- In choosing between investments with different lives, a firm must take into account its option to replace or extend the shorter-lived project at the end of its original life.
- Managers sometimes use the equivalent annual benefit method to compare projects of different lengths. It implicitly assumes that the projects can be replaced at their original terms. Using the equivalent annual benefit method might produce different recommendations when future uncertainty is taken into account.

22.6 Optimally Staging Investments

- When deciding the order of investment for a multi-stage investment decision, there is a benefit to making smaller and riskier investments first in order to gain additional information at low cost. If the projects are mutually dependent so that all projects must succeed for the firm to realize any benefit, the optimal order can be determined by ranking the projects according to the failure cost index in Eq. 22.3.

22.7 Rules of Thumb

- The profitability index rule of thumb calls for investing whenever the profitability index exceeds some predetermined number. It is a way of accounting for the option to wait when there is cash flow uncertainty.
- The hurdle rate rule of thumb computes the NPV using the hurdle rate, a discount rate higher than the cost of capital, and specifies that the investment should be undertaken only when the NPV computed this way is positive. It is a way of accounting for the option to wait when there is interest rate uncertainty.

22.8 Key Insights from Real Options

- Out-of-the-money real options have value.
- In-the-money real options need not be exercised immediately.
- Waiting is valuable.
- Delay investment expenses as much as possible.
- Create value by exploiting real options.

Key Terms

Further Reading

Many people believe that by not explicitly accounting for the real options described in this chapter, managers make costly mistakes. For an in-depth discussion of this issue, see T. Copeland, V. Antikarov, and T. Texere, *Real Options: A Practitioner's Guide* (W. W. Norton & Company, 2003). For a discussion of how to adjust firm betas for capital budgeting purposes see A. Bernardo, B. Chowdhry, and A. Goyal, "Assessing Project Risk," *Journal of Applied Corporate Finance* 24 (2012): 94–100.

These books cover the topics of this chapter in more detail and depth: M. Amran and N. Kulatilaka, *Real Options: Managing Strategic Investments in an Uncertain World* (Harvard Business School Press, 1999); M. Brennan and L. Trigeorgis, eds., *Flexibility, Natural Resources, and Strategic Options* (Oxford University Press, 1998); A. Dixit and R. Pindyck, *Investment Under Uncertainty* (Princeton University Press, 1994); H. Smit and L. Trigeorgis, *Strategic Investment, Real Options and Games* (Princeton University Press, 2004); and L. Trigeorgis, *Real Options* (MIT Press, 1996).

For a discussion of how well the rules of thumb covered in this chapter perform in practice, see R. McDonald, "Real Options and Rules of Thumb in Capital Budgeting," in M. Brennan and L. Trigeorgis (eds.), *Project Flexibility, Agency, and Competition* (Oxford University Press, 2000).

For more information on how real options affect the view academics and practitioners have of corporate finance, see T. Luehrman, "Strategy as a Portfolio of Real Options," *Harvard Business Review* (September–October 1998): 89–99; S. Mason and R. Merton, "The Role of Contingent Claims Analysis in Corporate Finance," in E. Altman and M. Subrahmanyan (eds.), *Recent Advances in Corporate Finance* (Richard D. Irwin, 1985); and A. Triantris and A. Borison, "Real Options: State of the Practice," *Journal of Applied Corporate Finance* 14(2) (2001): 8–24.

Problems

All problems are available in MyFinanceLab. *An asterisk (*) indicates problems with a higher level of difficulty.*

Decision Tree Analysis

1. Your company is planning on opening an office in Japan. Profits depend on how fast the economy in Japan recovers from its current recession. There is a 50% chance of recovery this year. You are trying to decide whether to open the office now or in a year. Construct the decision tree that shows the choices you have to open the office either today or one year from now.

2. You are trying to decide whether to make an investment of $500 million in a new technology to produce Everlasting Gobstoppers. There is a 60% chance that the market for these candies will produce profits of $100 million annually, a 20% chance the market will produce profits of $50 million, and a 20% chance that there will be no profits. The size of the market will become clear one year from now. Currently, the cost of capital of the project is 11% per year. There is a 20% chance that the cost of capital will drop to 9% in a year and stay at that level forever, and an 80% chance that it will stay at 11% forever. Movements in the cost of capital are unrelated to the size of the candy market. Construct the decision tree that shows the choices you have to make the investment either today or one year from now.

3. Consider the United Studios example in Section 22.2. Suppose United has the rights to produce the first film, but has not yet purchased the sequel rights.
   a. How much are the sequel rights worth to United?
   b. Suppose United can purchase the sequel rights now for $30 million. Alternatively, United can pay $10 million now for the option to buy the sequel rights for $30 million in the future. Which should it choose?
4. Using the information in Problem 2, rework the problem assuming you find out the size of the Everlasting Gobstopper market one year *after* you make the investment. That is, if you do not make the investment, you do not find out the size of the market. Construct the decision tree that shows the choices you have under these circumstances.

The Option to Delay: Investment as a Call Option

5. Describe the benefits and costs of delaying an investment opportunity.
6. You are a financial analyst at Global Conglomerate and are considering entering the shoe business. You believe that you have a very narrow window for entering this market. Because of Christmas demand, the time is right today and you believe that exactly a year from now would also be a good opportunity. Other than these two windows, you do not think another opportunity will exist to break into this business. It will cost you $35 million to enter the market. Because other shoe manufacturers exist and are public companies, you can construct a perfectly comparable company. Hence, you have decided to use the Black-Scholes formula to decide when and if you should enter the shoe business. Your analysis implies that the current value of an operating shoe company is $40 million and it has a beta of 1. However, the flow of customers is uncertain, so the value of the company is volatile—your analysis indicates that the volatility is 25% per year. Fifteen percent of the value of the company is attributable to the value of the free cash flows (cash available to you to spend how you wish) expected in the first year. If the one-year risk-free rate of interest is 4%:
   a. Should Global enter this business and, if so, when?
   b. How will the decision change if the current value of a shoe company is $36 million instead of $40 million?
   c. Plot the value of your investment opportunity as a function of the current value of a shoe company.
   d. Plot the beta of the investment opportunity as a function of the current value of a shoe company.
7. It is the beginning of September and you have been offered the following deal to go heli-skiing. If you pick the first week in January and pay for your vacation now, you can get a week of heli-skiing for $2500. However, if you cannot ski because the helicopters cannot fly due to bad weather, there is no snow, or you get sick, you do not get a refund. There is a 40% probability that you will not be able to ski. If you wait until the last minute and go only if you know that the conditions are perfect and you are healthy, the vacation will cost $4000. You estimate that the pleasure you get from heli-skiing is worth $6000 per week to you (if you had to pay any more than that, you would choose not to go). If your cost of capital is 8% per year, should you book ahead or wait?
8. A professor in the Computer Science department at United States Institute of Technology has just patented a new search engine technology and would like to sell it to you, an interested venture capitalist. The patent has a 17-year life. The technology will take a year to implement (there are no cash flows in the first year) and has an upfront cost of $100 million. You believe this technology will be able to capture 1% of the Internet search market, and currently this market generates profits of $1 billion per year. Over the next five years, the risk-neutral probability that profits will grow at 10% per year is 20% and the risk-neutral probability that profits will grow at 5% per year is 80%. This growth rate will become clear one year from now (after the first year of growth). After five years, profits are expected to decline 2% annually. No profits are expected after the patent runs out. Assume that all risk-free interest rates are constant (regardless of the term) at 10% per year.

a. Calculate the NPV of undertaking the investment today.
b. Calculate the NPV of waiting a year to make the investment decision.
c. What is your optimal investment strategy?

9. Consider again the electric car dealership in Section 22.3. Suppose the current value of a dealership is $5 million because the first-year free cash flow is expected to be $500,000 rather than $600,000. What is the beta of a corporation whose only asset is a one-year option to open a dealership? What is the beta if the first year's cash flows are expected to be $700,000, so a working dealership is worth $7 million?

10. Under the same assumptions as in Section 22.3, suppose your corporation owns an operating electric car dealership, together with one-year options to open five more.
a. What is the value and beta of your firm if the expected first-year free cash flow for all dealerships is $600,000?
b. What is the value and beta of your firm if the expected first-year free cash flow for all dealerships is $300,000?
c. In which case do your options have higher beta? In which case does your firm have higher beta? Why?

***11.** The management of Southern Express Corporation is considering investing 10% of all future earnings in growth. The company has a single growth opportunity that it can take either now or in one period. Although the managers do not know the return on investment with certainty, they know it is equally likely to be either 10% or 14% per year. In one period, they will find out which state will occur. Currently the firm pays out all earnings as a dividend of $10 million; if it does not make the investment, dividends are expected to remain at this level forever. If Southern Express undertakes the investment, the new dividend will reflect the realized return on investment and will grow at the realized rate forever. Assuming the opportunity cost of capital is 10.1%, what is the value of the company just before the current dividend is paid (the cum-dividend value)?

***12.** What decision should you make in Problem 2 if the one-year cost of capital is 15.44% and the profits last forever?

Growth and Abandonment Options

13. Your R&D division has just synthesized a material that will superconduct electricity at room temperature; you have given the go-ahead to try to produce this material commercially. It will take five years to find out whether the material is commercially viable, and you estimate that the probability of success is 25%. Development will cost $10 million per year, paid at the beginning of each year. If development is successful and you decide to produce the material, the factory will be built immediately. It will cost $1 billion to put in place, and will generate profits of $100 million at the end of every year in perpetuity. Assume that the current five-year risk-free interest rate is 10% per year, and the yield on a perpetual risk-free bond will be 12%, 10%, 8%, or 5% in five years. Assume that the risk-neutral probability of each possible rate is the same. What is the value today of this project?

***14.** You are an analyst working for Goldman Sachs, and you are trying to value the growth potential of a large, established company, Big Industries. Big Industries has a thriving R&D division that has consistently turned out successful products. You estimate that, on average, the R&D division generates two new product proposals every three years, so that there is a two-thirds chance that a project will be proposed every year. Typically, the investment opportunities the R&D division produces require an initial investment of $10 million and yield profits of $1 million per year that grow at one of three possible growth rates in perpetuity: 3%, 0%, and −3%. All three growth rates are equally likely for any given project. These opportunities are always "take it or leave it" opportunities: If they are not undertaken immediately, they disappear forever. Assume that the cost of capital will always remain at 12% per year. What is the present value of all future growth opportunities Big Industries will produce?

***15.** Repeat Problem 14, but this time assume that all the probabilities are risk-neutral probabilities, which means the cost of capital is always the risk-free rate and risk-free rates are as follows: The current interest rate for a risk-free perpetuity is 8%; in one year, there is a 64.375% chance that all risk-free interest rates will be 10% and stay there forever, and a 35.625% chance that they will be 6% and stay there forever. The current one-year risk-free rate is 7%.

16. You own a small networking startup. You have just received an offer to buy your firm from a large, publicly traded firm, JCH Systems. Under the terms of the offer, you will receive 1 million shares of JCH. JCH stock currently trades for $25 per share. You can sell the shares of JCH that you will receive in the market at any time. But as part of the offer, JCH also agrees that at the end of the next year, it will buy the shares back from you for $25 per share if you desire. Suppose the current one-year risk-free rate is 6.18%, the volatility of JCH stock is 30%, and JCH does not pay dividends.

a. Is this offer worth more than $25 million? Explain.

b. What is the value of the offer?

17. You own a wholesale plumbing supply store. The store currently generates revenues of $1 million per year. Next year, revenues will either decrease by 10% or increase by 5%, with equal probability, and then stay at that level as long as you operate the store. You own the store outright. Other costs run $900,000 per year. There are no costs for shutting down; in that case, you can always sell the store for $500,000. What is the business worth today if the cost of capital is fixed at 10%?

***18.** You own a copper mine. The price of copper is currently $1.50 per pound. The mine produces 1 million pounds of copper per year and costs $2 million per year to operate. It has enough copper to operate for 100 years. Shutting the mine down would entail bringing the land up to EPA standards and is expected to cost $5 million. Reopening the mine once it is shut down would be an impossibility given current environmental standards. The price of copper has an equal (and independent) probability of going up or down by 25% each year for the next two years and then will stay at that level forever. Calculate the NPV of continuing to operate the mine if the cost of capital is fixed at 15%. Is it optimal to abandon the mine or keep it operating?

19. An original silver dollar from the late eighteenth century consists of approximately 24 grams of silver. At a price of $0.19 per gram ($6 per troy ounce), the silver content of the coin is worth about $4.50. Assume that these coins are in plentiful supply and are not collector's items, so they have no numismatic value. If the current price of silver is $0.19 per gram, will the price of the coin be greater than, less than, or equal to $4.50? Justify your answer.

***20.** You own a piece of raw land in an up-and-coming area in Gotham City. The costs to construct a building increase disproportionately with the size of the building. A building of q square feet costs $0.1 \times q^2$ to build. After you construct a building on the lot, it will last forever but you are committed to it: You cannot put another building on the lot. Buildings currently rent at $100 per square foot per month. Rents in this area are expected to increase in five years. There is a 50% chance that they will rise to $200 per square foot per month and stay there forever, and a 50% chance that they will stay at $100 per square foot per month forever. The cost of capital is fixed at 12% per year.

a. Should you construct a building on the lot right away? If so, how large should the building be?

b. If you choose to delay the decision, how large a building will you construct in each possible state in five years?

Investments with Different Lives

21. What implicit assumption is made when managers use the equivalent annual benefit method to decide between two projects with different lives that use the same resource?

22. You own a cab company and are evaluating two options to replace your fleet. Either you can take out a five-year lease on the replacement cabs for $500 per month per cab, or you can purchase the cabs outright for $30,000, in which case the cabs will last eight years. You must return the cabs to the leasing company at the end of the lease. The leasing company is responsible for all maintenance costs, but if you purchase the cabs, you will buy a maintenance contract that will cost $100 per month for the life of each cab. Each cab will generate revenues of $1000 per month. Assume the cost of capital is fixed at 12%.

a. Calculate the NPV per cab of both possibilities: purchasing the cabs or leasing them.
b. Calculate the equivalent monthly annual benefit of both opportunities.
c. If you are leasing a cab, you have the opportunity to buy the used cab after five years. Assume that in five years a five-year-old cab will cost either $10,000 or $16,000 with equal likelihood, will have maintenance costs of $500 per month, and will last three more years. Which option should you take?

Optimally Staging Investments

23. Genenco is developing a new drug that will slow the aging process. In order to succeed, two breakthroughs are needed: one to increase the potency of the drug, and the second to eliminate toxic side effects. Research to improve the drug's potency is expected to require an upfront investment of $10 million and take 2 years; the drug has a 5% chance of success. Reducing the drug's toxicity will require a $30 million upfront investment, take 4 years, and has a 20% chance of success. If both efforts are successful, Genenco can sell the patent for the drug to a major drug company for $2 billion. All risk is idiosyncratic, and the risk-free rate is 6%.

a. What is the NPV of launching both research efforts simultaneously?
b. What is the optimal order to stage the investments?
c. What is the NPV with the optimal staging?

24. Your engineers are developing a new product to launch next year that will require both software and hardware innovations. The software team requests a budget of $5 million and forecasts an 80% chance of success. The hardware team requests a $10 million budget and forecasts a 50% chance of success. Both teams will need 6 months to work on the product, and the risk-free interest rate is 4% APR with semiannual compounding.

a. Which team should work on the project first?
b. Suppose that before anyone has worked on the project, the hardware team comes back and revises their proposal, changing the estimated chance of success to 75% based on new information. Will this affect your decision in (a)?

Rules of Thumb

25. Your firm is thinking of expanding. If you invest today, the expansion will generate $10 million in FCF at the end of the year, and will have a continuation value of either $150 million (if the economy improves) or $50 million (if the economy does not improve). If you wait until next year to invest, you will lose the opportunity to make $10 million in FCF, but you will know the continuation value of the investment in the following year (that is, in a year from now, you will know what the investment continuation value will be in the following year). Suppose the risk-free rate is 5%, and the risk-neutral probability that the economy improves is 45%. Assume the cost of expanding is the same this year or next year.

a. If the cost of expanding is $80 million, should you do so today or wait until next year to decide?
b. At what cost of expanding would there be no difference between expanding now and waiting? To what profitability index does this correspond?

26. Assume that the project in Example 22.5 pays an annual cash flow of $100,000 (instead of $90,000).

a. What is the NPV of investing today?
b. What is the NPV of waiting and investing tomorrow?
c. Verify that the hurdle rate rule of thumb gives the correct time to invest in this case.

27. Assume that the project in Example 22.5 pays an annual cash flow of $80,000 (instead of $90,000).

a. What is the NPV of investing today?
b. What is the NPV of waiting and investing tomorrow?
c. Verify that the hurdle rate rule of thumb gives the correct time to invest in this case.

Long-Term Financing

PART

8

THE LAW OF ONE PRICE CONNECTION. How should a firm raise the funds it needs to undertake its investments? In the capital structure part of the text, we discussed the financial manager's choice between the major categories of financing, debt, and equity. In this part of the book, we explain the mechanics of implementing these decisions. Chapter 23 describes the process a company goes through when it raises equity capital. In Chapter 24, we review firms' use of debt markets to raise capital. Chapter 25 introduces an alternative to long-term debt financing—leasing. By presenting leasing as a financing alternative, we apply the Law of One Price to determine that the benefits of leasing must derive from tax differences, incentive effects, or other market imperfections.

CHAPTER 23

Raising Equity Capital

AS WE POINTED OUT IN CHAPTER 1, MOST BUSINESSES IN THE United States are small sole proprietorships and partnerships. Yet, these firms generate only 10% of total U.S. sales. One limitation of a sole proprietorship is that it does not allow access to outside equity capital, so the business has relatively little capacity for growth. Another limitation is that the sole proprietor is forced to hold a large fraction of his or her wealth in a single asset—the company—and therefore is likely to be undiversified. By incorporating, businesses can gain access to capital and founders can reduce the risk of their portfolios by selling some of their equity and diversifying. Consequently, even though corporations make up less than 20% of U.S. businesses, they account for nearly 85% of sales in the U.S. economy.

In this chapter, we discuss how companies raise equity capital. We begin by looking at sources of equity financing for private firms. These sources include angel investors, venture capital firms, and private equity firms. We then review the initial public offering (IPO) process in which firms list their shares to be traded by all investors on a recognized stock exchange. Finally, we look how public companies may raise additional equity capital through a seasoned offering. To illustrate these concepts, we follow the case of a real company, RealNetworks, Inc. (RNWK). RealNetworks is a leading creator of digital media services and software. Customers use RealNetworks' products to find, play, purchase, and manage digital music, videos, and games. RealNetworks was founded in 1993 and incorporated in 1994. Using the example of RealNetworks, we first discuss the alternative ways new companies can raise capital and then examine the impact of these funding alternatives on current and new investors.

23.1 Equity Financing for Private Companies

The initial capital that is required to start a business is usually provided by the entrepreneur herself and her immediate family. However, few families have the resources to finance a growing business, so growth almost always requires outside capital. A private company must seek sources that can provide this capital, but it must also understand how the infusion of outside capital will affect the control of the company, particularly when outside investors decide to cash out their investments in the company.

Sources of Funding

When a private company decides to raise outside equity capital, it can seek funding from several potential sources: angel investors, venture capital firms, institutional investors, and corporate investors. The source of capital is closely tied to the lifecycle of the firm. Start-up firms in their earliest stages rely on angels. As the firm grows, it is able to tap into the other sources of equity financing.

Angel Investors. Traditionally, when entrepreneurs had an idea and started a firm, they relied on friends and family as the initial source of funding. But today, the market for very early stage financing has become more efficient. Increasingly, early stage entrepreneurs are able to find individual investors, called **angel investors**, who will provide the initial capital to start their business. Angel investors are often rich, successful entrepreneurs themselves who are willing to help new companies get started in exchange for a share of the business.

In recent years the role of angel investors has changed, allowing start-ups to rely on angel financing for much longer into their life cycle. There are two reasons for this change. First, the number of angel investors has grown enormously, and within the angel community, angel groups have formed. An **angel group** is a group of angel investors who pool their money and decide as a group which investments to fund. The Angel Capital Association lists over 400 angel groups on its Web site and estimates that the typical angel group had 42 members and invested an average of $2.42 million in 9.8 deals per year in 2013.[1] In addition it estimates that there are over 100,000 individuals making angel investments in any given year.

The second, and perhaps more important, reason for the growth in importance of angel financing is that the cost of setting up a business has dropped dramatically. Twenty years ago a new company would have to make relatively large capital investments in servers, databases, and other back office technologies. Today, almost all of these functions can be outsourced, allowing individuals to start and grow their businesses with much less capital.

Angel financing often occurs at such an early stage in the business that it is difficult to assess a value for the firm. Angel investors often circumvent this problem by holding a **convertible note** rather than equity. In a typical deal, in exchange for their investment, angels receive a note that is convertible into equity when the company finances with equity for the first time. The note holders convert the value of their initial investment plus accrued interest into equity at a discount (often 20%) to the price paid by new investors. Structuring the deal in this way allows angels and entrepreneurs to agree on terms without agreeing on a value for the firm, instead postponing the valuation until the firm is more mature and becomes attractive to venture capitalists.

[1] "What are angel groups?" on www.angelcapitalassociation.org/faqs/

Crowdfunding: The Wave of the Future?

The last 10 years has seen growth in an entirely new kind of funding for start-ups, known as **crowdfunding**, in which the firm raises very small amounts of money from a large number of people. Investment levels can be minute, in some cases less than $100.

Historically in the U.S., the SEC has enforced strict rules that only allowed "qualified investors" (investors with a high net worth) to invest in private equity issues. These rules effectively barred U.S. crowdfunding sites from offering equity to investors. As a result, companies like Kickstarter and Indiegogo offered investors other payoffs such as the products the company would ultimately produce. In many cases these "financing" contracts looked more like advanced purchase orders.

However, in 2012 the landscape changed dramatically when Congress passed the JOBS Act that exempted crowdfunding from the historical restrictions on private equity investments. The act allowed equity investment by non-qualified individuals so long as the crowdfunding sites did not charge a commission for the transaction. In the wake of this act, a number of equity-based platforms such as AngelList emerged that charged fees based on the performance of the investment. Recently the SEC announced specific restrictions on the size of an equity investment via crowdfunding. For example, in any year, companies may raise no more than $1 million through crowdfunding, and individuals whose annual income or net worth is less than $100,000 can invest no more than $2000, or up to 5% of their annual income or net worth (whichever is less) in crowdfunding-based equity.

The typical size of an angel investment ranges from several hundred thousand dollars for individual investors to a few million dollars for angel groups. Although the pool of capital available from angel financing continues to grow, most firms' financing needs eventually reach the point that they need to tap into larger funding sources, such as venture capital.

Venture Capital Firms. A **venture capital firm** is a limited partnership that specializes in raising money to invest in the private equity of young firms. Table 23.1 lists the 12 most active U.S. venture capital firms in 2015, based on the number of deals completed.

Typically, institutional investors, such as pension funds, are the limited partners. The general partners run the venture capital firm; they are called **venture capitalists.** Venture capital firms offer limited partners a number of advantages over investing directly in start-ups themselves. Venture firms invest in many start-ups, so limited partners get the benefit

TABLE 23.1 Most Active U.S. Venture Capital Firms in 2015 (by number of deals completed)

Venture Capital Firm	Number of Deals	Average Invested per Deal (in $ million)
Sequoia Capital	265	36.3
500 Startups	164	2.1
New Enterprise Associates	163	25.7
Accel Partners	158	31.1
Matrix Partners	143	19.8
Y Combinator	113	3.5
Intel Capital	111	16.1
Tiger Global Management	96	73.4
Kleiner Perkins Caufield & Byers	96	53.4
Silicon Valley Bank	94	29.0
Andreessen Horowitz	93	39.3
Bessemer Venture Partners	92	42.0

Source: Preqin

INTERVIEW WITH KEVIN LAWS

Kevin Laws is an active angel investor, partner at Maiden Lane Ventures, and Chief Operating Officer of AngelList, an online platform where start-up companies can meet investors and recruit talent.

QUESTION: *How has angel investing changed over the last decade?*

ANSWER: Historically, angel investors typically grouped together in regions and markets not well covered by venture capital (VC) or would dispense cash along with advice at the earliest stages of a few technology companies. Often investors viewed funding start-ups as a sideline rather than a full-time business.

The cost of starting a technology company today has dropped significantly. Cloud services, social marketing, Search Engine Optimization, and other platforms and tools allow entrepreneurs to launch for $500,000 rather than $5 million. Because venture investors prefer to invest several million dollars, angels are now the dominant form of fundraising for the earliest (seed stage) cash needs of the company.

QUESTION: *How has angel investing affected the venture capital industry?*

ANSWER: The lines between angel investing and venture capital are blurring. Today's angels ask for terms they didn't when angel investing was more of a hobby—for example, pro rata investment rights (to maintain their level of percentage ownership during later financing rounds) and information rights. The venture industry is adjusting to a host of new players and is responding primarily by ceding the earliest stage markets to angel investors and engaging at Series A (the first round of financing after seed capital) and beyond.

QUESTION: *How do the returns from angel investing compare with other investment classes?*

ANSWER: Historically, angel investing encompassed a wide range of investments (from investing in your nephew's doomed dry cleaner to early Google investors), making it hard to define the returns. An Angel Capital Association's study found that returns of more "professional" angel investors outstripped venture capital investor returns. It is too early to say whether that will continue as angel investing in technology jumps dramatically, because most investments take 7 to 10 years to come to fruition. Early indicators are that it will likely converge with early stage venture returns.

QUESTION: *Is angel investing only for wealthy investors with domain expertise? Or is it accessible/attractive even for smaller investors?*

ANSWER: Currently, active angel investing with large checks is still for wealthy investors with domain expertise. Although a typical angel check is $25,000, the risk profile of each individual investment is such that you want 30 to 50 investments in a good portfolio. You also need domain expertise to recognize good deals and be familiar enough with the management team and markets to move quickly.

While angel investing is still an asset class for sophisticated investors, it no longer requires as much wealth or start-up experience to participate. Services like AngelList allow investors to invest as little as $1,000 per company across hundreds of companies behind the wealthy, experienced investors. This means that the standard for wealth has dropped (because your friends can combine their money with yours to make the appropriate check size), plus by investing behind experienced investors you can get access without having the same expertise. That has broadened the investor base significantly.

QUESTION: *On what basis do angel investors make the decision to invest?*

ANSWER: Team, traction, and social proof, in that order, based on a recent study I co-authored with several economists. The characteristics of the founding team were the most important factor, followed by how much progress the company had made (which varies by industry—downloads, paying customers, pre-orders, etc.). The third factor, social proof, is who else is involved as investor or advisor to the company. When you are writing small checks for companies whose most likely failure reason is "running out of cash too soon," you want to be sure you're investing with many other investors. A successful investor is a lot more likely to be followed by other investors than an unknown one, much as investors buy a stock after Warren Buffett does. Investing in a company that only manages to raise your $25,000 will lose you money for certain, no matter how "right" you were about its product or market.

FIGURE 23.1 **Venture Capital Funding in the United States**

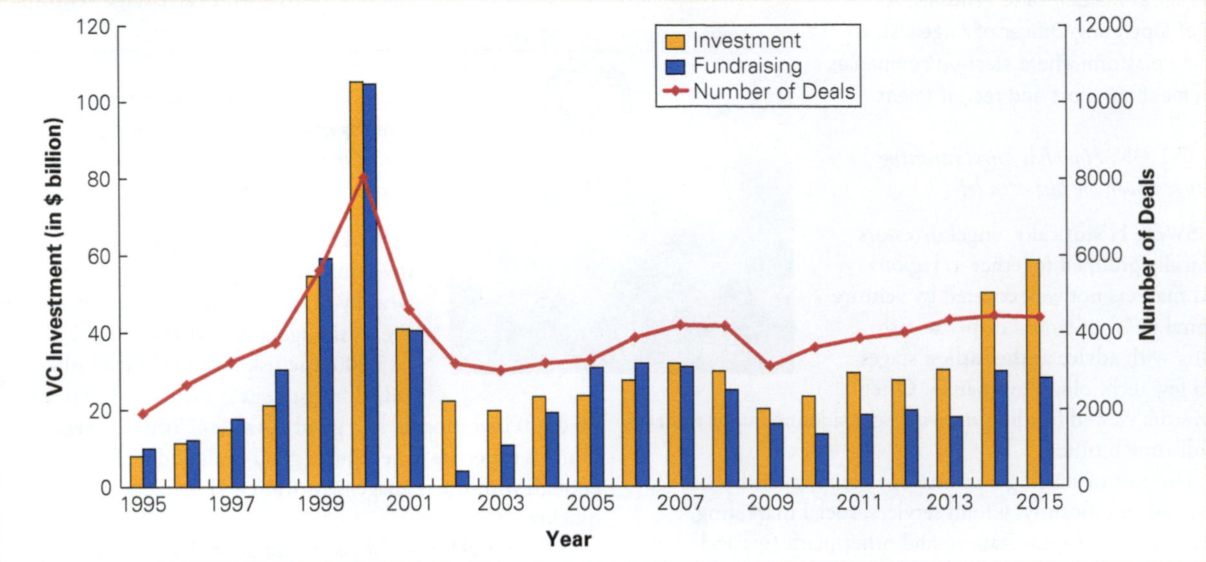

Columns show the aggregate funds raised from investors, and the amount invested in start-up firms, each year by U.S. venture capital firms. The line chart shows the number of separate investment deals. Note the peak in activity in 2000, followed by a sharp decline after the Internet bust. While activity dipped again in the financial crisis, it has since recovered with 2015 showing the highest level of investment since 2000.

Source: National Venture Capital Association

of this diversification. More importantly, limited partners also benefit from the expertise of the general partners. However, these advantages come at a cost—general partners charge substantial fees to run the firm. In addition to an annual management fee of about 1.5%–2.5% of the fund's committed capital, general partners also take a share of any positive return generated by the fund in a fee referred to as **carried interest**. Most firms charge 20%, but some take up to 30%, of any profits as carried interest.

The importance of the venture capital sector has grown enormously in the last 50 years. As Figure 23.1 shows, growth in the sector increased in the 1990s and peaked at the height of the Internet boom. Although the size of the industry decreased substantially in the 2000s, it has since recovered to the level it was in the late 1990s.

Venture capital firms can provide substantial capital for young companies. For example, in 2015, venture capital firms invested $58.8 billion in 4380 separate deals, for an average investment of about $13.4 million per deal. In return, venture capitalists often demand a great deal of control. Professors Paul Gompers and Josh Lerner[2] report that venture capitalists typically control about one-third of the seats on a start-up's board of directors, and often represent the single largest voting block on the board. Although entrepreneurs generally view this control as a necessary cost of obtaining venture capital, it can actually be an important benefit of accepting venture financing. Venture capitalists use their control to

[2]P. Gompers and J. Lerner, *The Venture Capital Cycle* (MIT Press, 1999).

FIGURE 23.2

Global LBO Volume and Number of Deals

Global leveraged buyout volume as measured by dollar volume and number of deals. Private equity activity surged during the 2003–2007 period, reflected in record volume, deal size, and number of deals. Activity declined dramatically, however, with the 2008 financial crisis.

Source: Dealogic

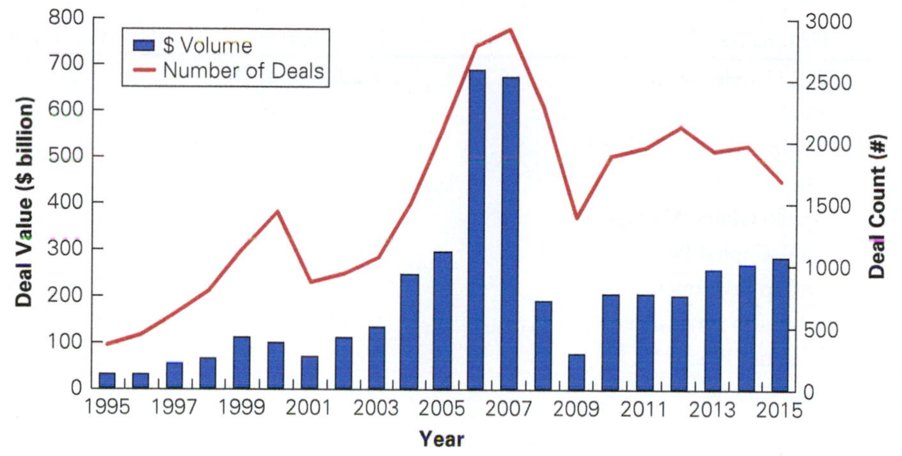

protect their investments; therefore, they may perform a key nurturing and monitoring role for the firm. Professors Shai Bernstein, Xavier Giroud, and Richard Townsend found that when a direct flight between the location of the key venture capitalist and the firm is introduced, making it easier to do this nurturing, the firm does better.[3]

Private Equity Firms. A **private equity firm** is organized very much like a venture capital firm, but it invests in the equity of existing privately held firms rather than start-up companies. Often, private equity firms initiate their investment by finding a publicly traded firm and purchasing the outstanding equity, thereby taking the company private in a transaction called a **leveraged buyout (LBO)**. In most cases, the private equity firms use debt as well as equity to finance the purchase.

Private equity firms share the advantages of venture capital firms, and also charge similar fees. One key difference between private equity and venture capital is the magnitude invested. For example, Figure 23.2 shows that the total LBO transaction volume in 2006–2007 (the peak of the private equity market) was nearly $700 billion, with an average deal size of $250 million. Table 23.2 lists the top 10 private equity funds in 2015 based on the total amount of investment capital each firm raised over the last five years.

Institutional Investors. Institutional investors such as pension funds, insurance companies, endowments, and foundations manage large quantities of money. They are major investors in many different types of assets, so, not surprisingly, they are also active investors in private companies. Institutional investors may invest directly in private firms, or they may invest indirectly by becoming limited partners in venture capital or private equity firms. Institutional interest in private equity has grown dramatically in recent years. For example, in 2015, the California Public Employees' Retirement System (CalPERS) reported that it had $29 billion of its $302 billion portfolio invested in private equity, with another $12 billion in capital committed to the sector.

[3] "The Impact of Venture Capital Monitoring," *Journal of Finance* (2016).

TABLE 23.2 Top 10 Private Equity Funds in 2015

Rank	Firm name	Headquarters	Five-Year Fundraising Total (in $ billion)
1	The Carlyle Group	Washington, DC	31.9
2	TPG	Fort Worth	30.3
3	Kohlberg Kravis Roberts	New York	29.1
4	The Blackstone Group	New York	25.6
5	Apollo Global Management	New York	22.2
6	CVC Capital Partners	London	21.2
7	EnCap Investments	Houston	21.2
8	Advent International	Boston	15.7
9	Warburg Pincus	New York	15.2
10	Bain Capital	Boston	14.6

Source: Private Equity International, www.peimedia.com/pei300

Corporate Investors. Many established corporations purchase equity in younger, private companies. A corporation that invests in private companies is called many different names, including **corporate investor**, **corporate partner**, **strategic partner**, and **strategic investor**. Most of the other types of investors in private firms that we have considered so far are primarily interested in the financial return that they will earn on their investments. Corporate investors, by contrast, might invest for corporate strategic objectives in addition to the desire for investment returns. For example, in May 2009, automaker Daimler invested $50 million for a 10% equity stake in electric car maker Tesla as part of a strategic collaboration on the development of lithium-ion battery systems, electric drive systems, and individual vehicle projects.

Venture Capital Investing

When a company founder decides to sell equity to outside investors for the first time, it is common practice for private companies to issue preferred stock rather than common stock to raise capital. **Preferred stock** issued by mature companies usually has preferential dividend, liquidation, or voting rights relative to common shareholders. While the preferred stock issued by young companies typically does not pay regular cash dividends, it usually gives the owner the option to convert it into common stock, and so is called **convertible preferred stock**. If the company runs into financial difficulties, the preferred stockholders have a senior claim on the assets of the firm relative to any common stockholders (who are often the employees of the firm). If things go well, then these investors will convert their preferred stock and receive all the rights and benefits of common stockholders.

Each time the firm raises money is referred to as a **funding round**, and each round will have its own set of securities with special terms and provisions. After a potential initial "seed round," it is common to name the securities alphabetically, starting with Series A, Series B, etc.

For example, RealNetworks, which was founded by Robert Glaser in 1993, was initially funded with an investment of approximately $1 million by Glaser. As of April 1995, Glaser's $1 million initial investment in RealNetworks represented 13,713,439 shares of Series A preferred stock, implying an initial purchase price of about $0.07 per share. RealNetworks needed more capital, and management decided to raise this money by selling equity in the form of convertible preferred stock.

The company's first round of outside equity funding was Series B preferred stock. RealNetworks sold 2,686,567 shares of Series B preferred stock at $0.67 per share in April 1995.[4] After this funding round, the distribution of ownership was as follows:

	Number of Shares	Price per Share ($)	Total Value (in $ million)	Percentage Ownership
Series A	13,713,439	0.67	9.2	83.6%
Series B	2,686,567	0.67	1.8	16.4%
	16,400,006		11.0	100.0%

The Series B preferred shares were new shares of stock being sold by RealNetworks. At the price the new shares were sold for, Glaser's shares were worth $9.2 million and represented 83.6% of the outstanding shares. The value of the prior shares outstanding at the price in the funding round ($9.2 million in this example) is called the **pre-money valuation.** The value of the whole firm (old plus new shares) at the funding round price ($11.0 million) is known as the **post-money valuation.** The difference between the pre- and post-money valuation is the amount invested. In other words,

$$\text{Post-money Valuation} = \text{Pre-money Valuation} + \text{Amount Invested} \tag{23.1}$$

In addition, the fractional ownership held by the new investors is equal to

$$\text{Percentage Ownership} = \text{Amount Invested/Post-money Valuation} \tag{23.2}$$

EXAMPLE 23.1 **Funding and Ownership**

Problem

You founded your own firm two years ago. Initially, you contributed $100,000 of your money and, in return, received 1,500,000 shares of stock. Since then, you have sold an additional 500,000 shares to angel investors. You are now considering raising even more capital from a venture capitalist. The venture capitalist has agreed to invest $6 million with a post-money valuation of $10 million for the firm. Assuming that this is the venture capitalist's first investment in your company, what percentage of the firm will she end up owning? What percentage will you own? What is the value of your shares?

Solution

Because the VC will invest $6 million out of the $10 million post-money valuation, her ownership percentage is $6/10 = 60\%$. From Eq. 23.1, the pre-money valuation is $10 - 6 = \$4$ million. As there are 2 million pre-money shares outstanding, this implies a share price of $4 million/2 million shares = $2 per share. Thus, the VC will receive 3 million shares for her investment, and after this funding round, there will be a total of 5,000,000 shares outstanding. You will own $1{,}500{,}000/5{,}000{,}000 = 30\%$ of the firm, and the post-transaction valuation of your shares is $3 million.

[4] The number of shares of RealNetworks' preferred stock given here for this and subsequent funding comes from the IPO prospectus (available on EDGAR at www.sec.gov/edgar/searchedgar/webusers.htm). For simplicity, we have ignored warrants to purchase additional shares that were also issued and a small amount of employee common stock that existed.

Over the next few years, RealNetworks raised three more rounds of outside equity in addition to the Series B funding round. Note the increase in the amount of capital raised as the company matured:

Series	Date	Number of Shares	Share Price ($)	Capital Raised (in $ million)
B	April 1995	2,686,567	0.67	1.8
C	Oct. 1995	2,904,305	1.96	5.7
D	Nov. 1996	2,381,010	7.53	17.9
E	July 1997	3,338,374	8.99	30.0

In each case, investors bought preferred stock in the private company. These investors were very similar to the profile of typical investors in private firms that we described earlier. Angel investors purchased the Series B stock. The investors in Series C and D stock were primarily venture capital funds. Microsoft purchased the Series E stock as a corporate investor.

Venture Capital Financing Terms

As we have already pointed out, outside investors generally receive convertible preferred stock. When things go well these securities will ultimately convert to common stock and so all investors are treated equally. But when they don't, these securities generally give preference to outside investors. Here are some typical features these securities have:

Liquidation Preference. The liquidation preference specifies a minimum amount that must be paid to these security holders—before any payments to common stockholders—in the event of a liquidation, sale, or merger of the company. It is typically set to between 1 and 3 times the value of the initial investment.

Seniority. It is not uncommon for investors in later rounds to demand seniority over investors in earlier rounds, to ensure that they are repaid first. When later round investors accept securities with equal priority, they are said to be ***pari passu***.

Participation Rights. Holders of convertible shares without participation rights must choose between demanding their liquidation preference or converting their shares to

COMMON MISTAKE Misinterpreting Start-Up Valuations

When a new valuation round occurs, it is common in the popular press to quote the post-money valuation as the "current value" of the company. Recall that the post-money valuation is calculated as the share price in the round times the total number of shares outstanding assuming all preferred shareholders convert their shares. But although the post-money valuation for a private firm is a similar calculation to the market capitalization of a public company, there is an important difference: While most shareholders of a public company hold the same securities, that is typically not the case for start-ups, where the terms in each funding round can differ substantially. As a result, the post-money value can be misleading.

Consider, for example, a start-up whose prior funding round closed at $3 per share with a post-money value of $300 million (and so has 100 million shares outstanding). They are now looking to raise $100 million to expand their operations. Suppose investors are willing to pay $8.50 per share if the series has a 1x liquidation preference and equal priority, but will pay $10 per share if the series has a 3x liquidation preference and is senior. Thus, depending on the terms, the post-money value will be either $950 million or $1.1 billion; some firms might choose the latter in order to enjoy the publicity of achieving so-called **unicorn** status (start-ups with valuations over $1 billion). Obviously, the actual value of the company does not depend on the liquidation rights of its investors.

In reality, the higher post-money valuation achieved by providing better terms to the new investors is artificial: While the new shares are worth $10 per share, the old shares are not. This scenario can also create a serious conflict of interest—if in the future the firm were to receive an acquisition offer for $400 million, the new investors would receive a 300% return (having priority for their liquidation preference of $300 million), while earlier investors would split the remaining $100 million, and founders and employees would likely receive little or nothing.

common stock and forfeiting their liquidation preference and other rights. Participation rights allow the investors to "double dip" and receive both their liquidation preference *and* any payments to common shareholders as though they had converted their shares. Often, these participation rights are capped once the investor receives 2–3 times their initial investment (when there is no cap, the securities are referred to as *fully participating*).

Anti-Dilution Protection. If things are not going well and the firm raises new funding at a lower price than in a prior round, it is referred to as a "**down round**." **Anti-dilution protection** lowers the price at which investors in earlier rounds can convert their shares to common, effectively increasing their ownership percentage in a down round at the expense of founders and employees.[5]

Board Membership. New investors may also negotiate the right to appoint one or more members to the board of directors of the firm as a way of securing control rights.

All of these provisions are negotiable, and so the actual terms in each funding round will depend on the relative bargaining power between the firm and the new investors at the time. For example, in a selection of Silicon Valley start-ups in 2014–2015, new investors obtained seniority about 30% of the time in up rounds, but more than 50% of the time in down rounds. Similarly, while only about 25% of funding rounds gave investors participation rights, almost 50% received them in down rounds. Over 80% of deals include anti-dilution protection, though the exact form of protection varies.[6] Because of these protections, prior to conversion, preferred shares are generally worth more than the firm's common stock and the true value of each series may differ.

EXAMPLE 23.2

Problem

Suppose that in addition to common shares, your firm raised $6 million in Series A financing with a 1x liquidation preference, no participation rights, and a $20 million post-money valuation, and $10 million in Series B financing with a 3x liquidation preference, no participation rights, and a $40 million post-money valuation, with Series B senior to Series A. If you sell the firm after the Series B financing, what is the minimum sale price such that common shareholders will receive anything? What is the minimum sale price such that all investors will convert their shares?

Solution

Series B has a liquidation preference of $3 \times 10 = \$30$ million, and Series A has a liquidation preference of $1 \times 6 = \$6$ million. Therefore, for a sale price of $30 million or less, only Series B will be paid, and any additional amount up to $36 million will be paid to Series A. Common shareholders will receive nothing unless the share price exceeds $36 million.

Because the Series B investors will receive up to 3x their investment from their liquidation preference, they will not be willing to convert their shares to common (and forfeit their liquidation preference) unless the value of the firm has at least tripled from the time of their investment, or a sale price of $3 \times 40 = \$120$ million. At that price, because Series B investors own $10/40 = 25\%$ of the firm, they will receive $25\% \times 120 = \$30$ million as common shareholders and so are just willing to convert. Series A investors own $6/20 = 30\%$ of the remaining shares, and so receive $30\% \times 75\% \times 120 = \$27$ million (and so will also convert), and the remaining $120 - 30 - 27 = \$63$ million goes to common shareholders.

[5]The simplest form is *full ratchet protection*, which adjusts old investors' conversion price to match that of new investors. The most common form is *broad-based weighted average protection*, which resets the conversion price to a weighted average of the old and new price.

[6]See "Private Company Financing Trends," Wilson Sonsini Goodrich & Rosati, 2015.

From Launch to Liquidity

This chart illustrates the life cycle of a typical successful start-up firm from first launch to its exit as a public firm via an initial public offering. The chart shows changes in the firm valuation as well changes in the distribution of ownership through each funding round. Our representative firm begins with an idea and two cofounders, who raise $500,000 from an angel investor in exchange for 20% of the company. Six months later they have a first prototype and receive $2 million in VC seed funding with a pre-money valuation of $6 million. As part of this round they create an employee option pool with 15% of the shares, which they can use to attract new employees and fill out their executive team.

Within a year they have their first customer, and raise $6 million in a Series A round for a post-money value of $18 million. At this point the founders each hold 16% of the firm's shares, and are sharing control with their VC backers. As the product continues to gain traction and the company grows, they raise $15 million, then $25 million, and finally $50 million in three funding rounds over the next 4 years, watching their valuation grow from $18 million to $200 million. With each round, they top up their employee option pool to 10% so they can retain and recruit top talent.

After 9 years, the company has established itself as a market leader, is consistently profitable, and undertakes

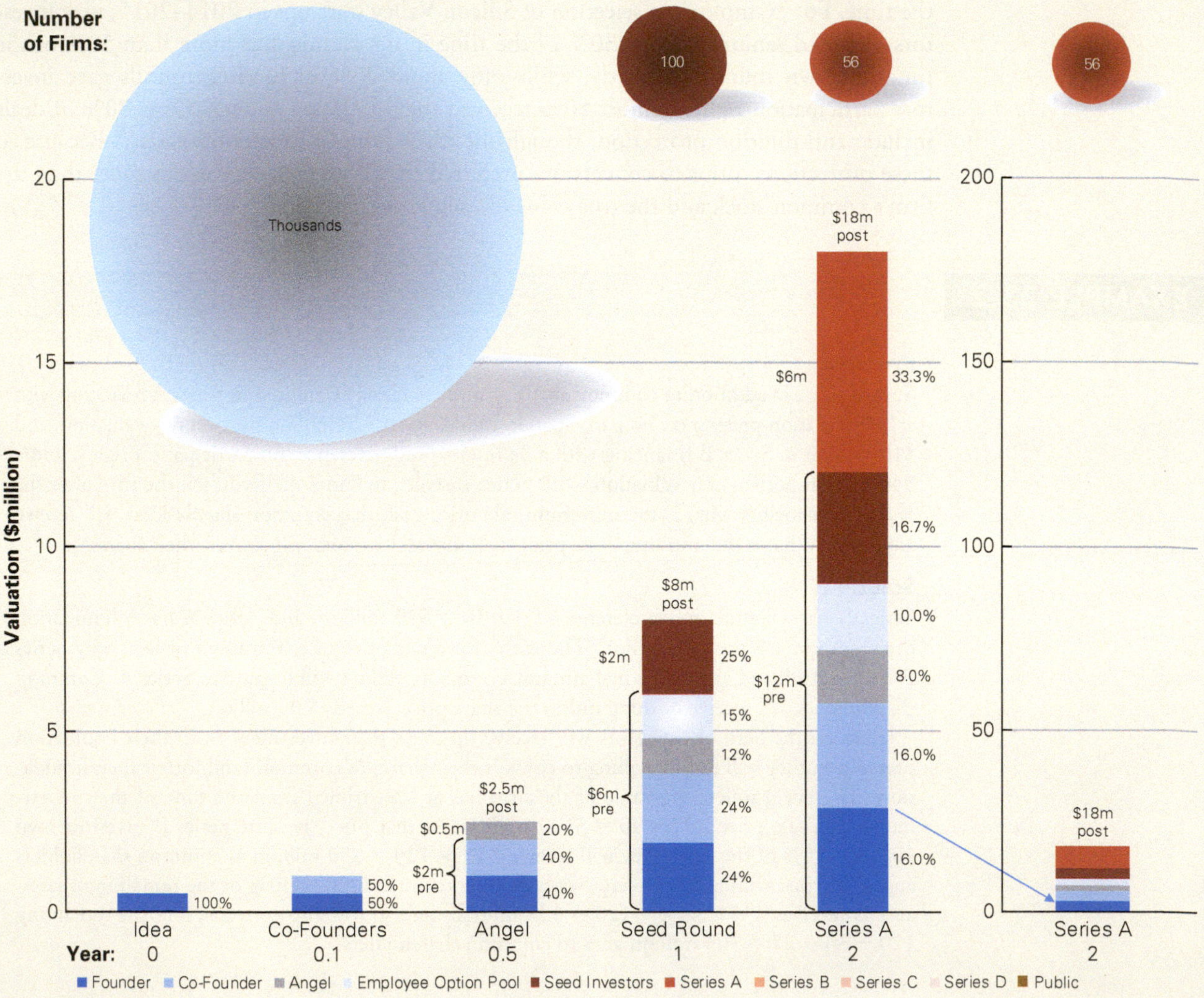

an IPO in which it raises $200 million with an opening market cap of $2.2 billion. At this point the founders hold 5.5% of the company and their shares are each valued at $121 million.

While the figure illustrates a "typical" path of a *successful* firm, it is important to remember that not all start-ups succeed. The top of the chart shows an estimate of the proportion of firms at each stage: VCs will hear thousands of pitches before selecting 100 for seed funding. Of those, only 56 survive to raise a follow-up Series A round, and the pool continues to shrink leaving only 4 of the original 100 to go public. So, while in this example the Series A investors earned $11.4\% \times \$2.2$ billion $= \$250$ million or 42 times their initial investment, their expected multiple of money must take into account that only a small proportion of their investments ever have a successful exit. In this case, if we assume they do not recover anything on their unsuccessful investments, their expected money multiple would only be $4/56 \times 42 = 3x$, corresponding to a $3^{1/7} - 1 = 17\%$ expected annual return over their 7-year investment.

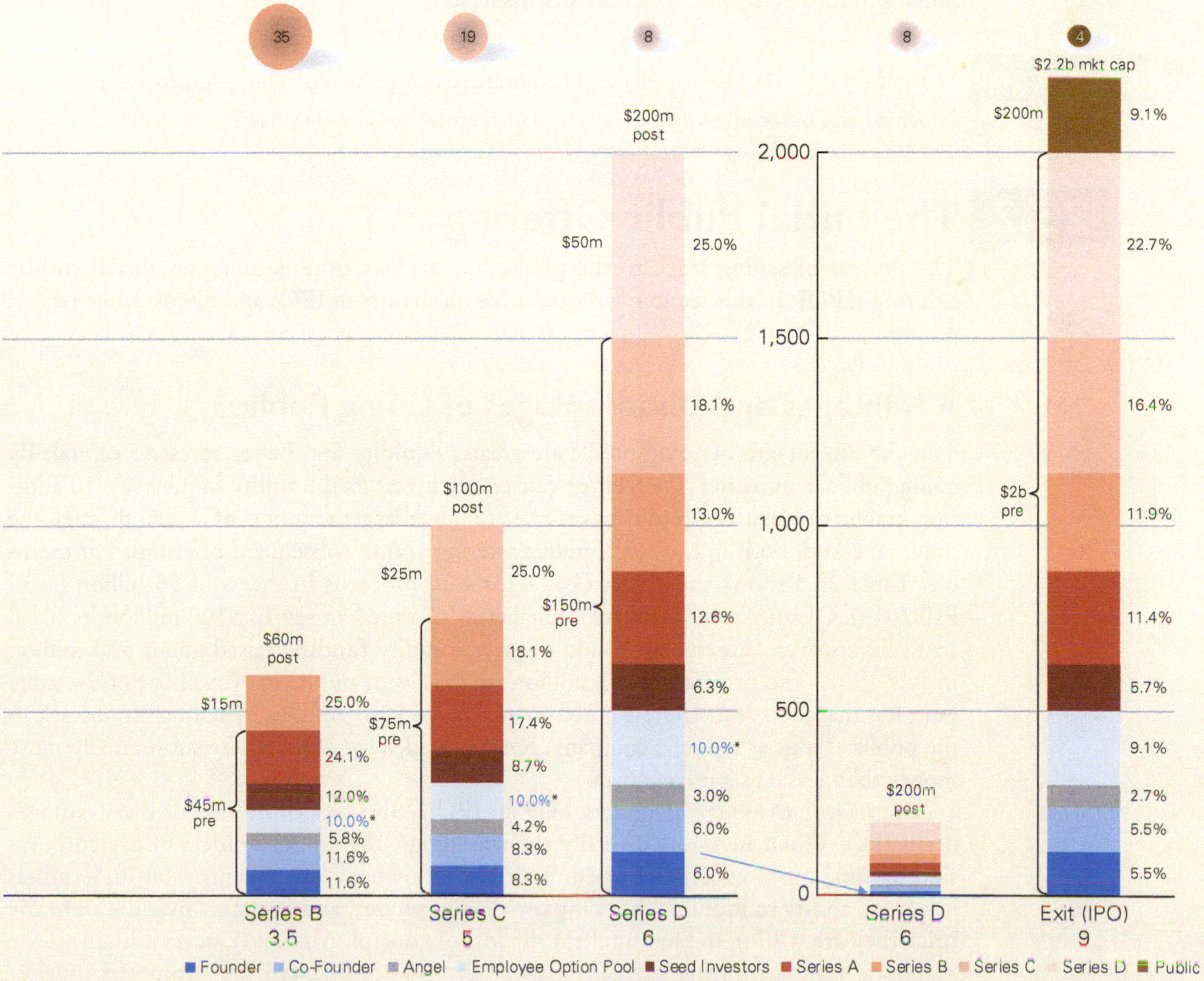

*Includes additional 2.78% increment to Employee Option Pool.

Exiting an Investment in a Private Company

Over time, the value of a share of RealNetworks' stock and the size of its funding rounds increased. Because investors in Series E were willing to pay $8.99 for a share of preferred stock with essentially equivalent rights in July 1997, the valuation of existing preferred stock had increased significantly, representing a substantial capital gain for early investors. Because RealNetworks was still a private company, however, investors could not liquidate their investment by selling their stock in the public stock markets.

An important consideration for investors in private companies is their **exit strategy**—how they will eventually realize the return from their investment. Investors exit in two main ways: through an acquisition or through a public offering. Often, large corporations purchase successful start-up companies. In such a case, the acquiring company purchases the outstanding stock of the private company, allowing all investors to cash out. Roughly 88% of venture capital exits from 2002–2012 occurred through mergers or acquisitions with typical deal sizes in the range of $100 million to $150 million.[6]

The alternative way to provide liquidity to its investors is for the company to become a publicly traded company, which we discuss next.

CONCEPT CHECK

1. What are the main sources of funding for private companies to raise outside equity capital?
2. What types of securities do VCs hold, and what protections do they have?

23.2 The Initial Public Offering

The process of selling stock to the public for the first time is called an **initial public offering (IPO)**. In this section, we look at the mechanics of IPOs and discuss some related puzzles.

Advantages and Disadvantages of Going Public

The two advantages of going public are greater liquidity and better access to capital. By going public, companies give their private equity investors the ability to diversify. In addition, public companies typically have access to much larger amounts of capital through the public markets, both in the initial public offering and in subsequent offerings. For example, Table 23.3 shows the largest U.S. IPOs with proceeds in excess of $5 billion (as of Fall 2015). Of course, most IPOs are smaller, with a median size of $100 million in 2014. In RealNetworks' case, its last round of private equity funding raised about $30 million in July 1997. The firm raised $43 million when it went public in November of the same year; less than two years later, it raised an additional $267 million by selling more stock to the public. Thus, as a public company, RealNetworks was able to raise substantially more money than it did as a private firm.

The major advantage of undertaking an IPO is also one of the major disadvantages of an IPO: When investors diversify their holdings, the equity holders of the corporation become more widely dispersed. This lack of ownership concentration undermines investors' ability to monitor the company's management, and investors may discount the price they are willing to pay to reflect the loss of control. Moreover, several high-profile corporate scandals during the early part of the twenty-first century prompted tougher

[6]The National Venture Capital Association.

regulations designed to address corporate abuses. Organizations such as the Securities and Exchange Commission (SEC), the securities exchanges (including the New York Stock Exchange and the NASDAQ), and Congress (through the Sarbanes-Oxley Act of 2002 and other legislation) adopted new standards that focused on more thorough financial disclosure, greater accountability, and more stringent requirements for the board of directors. These standards, in general, were designed to provide better protection for investors. However, compliance with the new standards is costly and time-consuming for public companies.

Types of Offerings

After deciding to go public, managers of the company work with an **underwriter**, an investment banking firm that manages the offering and designs its structure. Choices include the type of shares to be sold and the mechanism the financial advisor will use to sell the stock.

Primary and Secondary Offerings. At an IPO, a firm offers a large block of shares for sale to the public for the first time. The shares that are sold in the IPO may either be new shares that raise new capital, known as a **primary offering**, or existing shares that are sold by current shareholders (as part of their exit strategy), known as a **secondary offering**.

Best-Efforts, Firm Commitment, and Auction IPOs. For smaller IPOs, the underwriter commonly accepts the deal on a **best-efforts IPO** basis. In this case, the underwriter does not guarantee that the stock will be sold, but instead tries to sell the stock for the best possible price. Often, such deals have an all-or-none clause: either all of the shares are sold in the IPO, or the deal is called off.

More commonly, an underwriter and an issuing firm agree to a **firm commitment IPO**, in which the underwriter guarantees that it will sell all of the stock at the offer price. The underwriter purchases the entire issue (at a slightly lower price than the offer price) and then resells it at the offer price. If the entire issue does not sell out, the underwriter is on the hook: The remaining shares must be sold at a lower price and the underwriter must

TABLE 23.3 Largest U.S. IPOs

Company Name	Offer Date	Exchange	Industry	Underwriter	Deal Size (in $ million)
Alibaba Group Holding	09/18/2014	NYSE	Technology	Credit Suisse	$21,767
Visa	03/18/2008	NYSE	Financial	J.P. Morgan	$17,864
ENEL SpA	11/01/1999	NYSE	Utilities	Merrill Lynch	$16,452
Facebook	05/17/2012	NASDAQ	Technology	Morgan Stanley	$16,007
General Motors	11/17/2010	NYSE	Capital Goods & Services	Morgan Stanley	$15,774
Deutsche Telekom	11/17/1996	NYSE	Communications	Goldman Sachs	$13,034
AT&T Wireless Group	04/26/2000	NYSE	Communications	Goldman Sachs	$10,620
Kraft Foods	06/12/2001	NYSE	Consumer	Credit Suisse	$8,680
France Telecom	10/17/1997	NYSE	Communications	Merrill Lynch	$7,289
Telstra Corporation	11/17/1997	NYSE	Communications	Credit Suisse	$5,646
Swisscom	10/04/1998	NYSE	Communications	Warburg Dillon Read	$5,582
United Parcel Service	11/09/1999	NYSE	Transportation	Morgan Stanley	$5,470

Source: Renaissance Capital IPO Home

take the loss. The most notorious loss in the industry happened when the British government privatized British Petroleum. In a highly unusual deal, the company was taken public gradually. The British government sold its final stake in British Petroleum at the time of the October 1987 stock market crash. The offer price was set just before the crash, but the offering occurred after the crash.[7] At the end of the first day's trading, the underwriters were facing a loss of $1.29 billion. The price then fell even further, until the Kuwaiti Investment Office stepped in and purchased a large stake in the company.

In the late 1990s, the investment banking firm of WR Hambrecht and Company attempted to change the IPO process by selling new issues directly to the public using an online **auction IPO** mechanism called OpenIPO. Rather than setting the price itself in the traditional way, Hambrecht lets the market determine the price of the stock by auctioning off the company. Investors place bids over a set period of time. An auction IPO then sets the highest price such that the number of bids at or above that price equals the number of offered shares. All winning bidders pay this price, even if their bid was higher. The first OpenIPO was the $11.55 million IPO for Ravenswood Winery, completed in 1999.

EXAMPLE 23.3 Auction IPO Pricing

Problem

Fleming Educational Software, Inc., is selling 500,000 shares of stock in an auction IPO. At the end of the bidding period, Fleming's investment bank has received the following bids:

Price ($)	Number of Shares Bid
8.00	25,000
7.75	100,000
7.50	75,000
7.25	150,000
7.00	150,000
6.75	275,000
6.50	125,000

What will the offer price of the shares be?

Solution

First, we compute the total number of shares demanded at or above any given price:

Price ($)	Cumulative Demand
8.00	25,000
7.75	125,000
7.50	200,000
7.25	350,000
7.00	500,000
6.75	775,000
6.50	900,000

For example, the company has received bids for a total of 125,000 shares at $7.75 per share or higher (25,000 + 100,000 = 125,000).

[7]This deal was exceptional in that the offer price was determined more than a week before the issue date. In the United States, the underwriter usually sets the final offer price within a day of the IPO date.

Fleming is offering a total of 500,000 shares. The winning auction price would be $7 per share, because investors have placed orders for a total of 500,000 shares at a price of $7 or higher. All investors who placed bids of at least this price will be able to buy the stock for $7 per share, even if their initial bid was higher.

In this example, the cumulative demand at the winning price exactly equals the supply. If total demand at this price were greater than the supply, all auction participants who bid prices higher than the winning price would receive their full bid (at the winning price). Shares would be awarded on a pro rata basis to bidders who bid exactly the winning price.

In 2004, Google went public using the auction mechanism, generating substantial interest in this alternative. In May 2005, Morningstar raised $140 million in its IPO using a Hambrecht OpenIPO auction.[8] But although the auction IPO mechanism seems to represent a viable alternative to traditional IPO procedures, it has not been widely adopted either in the United States or abroad. After completing fewer than 30 transactions between 1999 and 2008, Hambrecht has completed only one other auction IPO since.

The Mechanics of an IPO

The traditional IPO process follows a standardized form. In this section, we explore the steps that underwriters go through during an IPO.

Underwriters and the Syndicate. Many IPOs, especially the larger offerings, are managed by a group of underwriters. The **lead underwriter** is the primary banking firm responsible for managing the deal. The lead underwriter provides most of the advice and

Google's IPO

On April 29, 2004, Google, Inc., announced plans to go public. Breaking with tradition, Google startled Wall Street by declaring its intention to rely heavily on the auction IPO mechanism for distributing its shares. Google had been profitable since 2001, so, according to Google executives, access to capital was not the only motive to go public. The company also wanted to provide employees and private equity investors with liquidity.

One of the major attractions of the auction mechanism was the possibility of allocating shares to more individual investors. Google also hoped to discourage short-term speculation by letting market bidders set the IPO price. After the Internet stock market boom, there were many lawsuits related to the way underwriters allocated shares. Google hoped to avoid the allocation scandals by letting the auction allocate shares.

Investors who wanted to bid opened a brokerage account with one of the deal's underwriters and then placed their bids with the brokerage house. Google and its underwriters identified the highest bid that allowed the company to sell all of the shares being offered. They also had the flexibility to choose to offer shares at a lower price.

On August 18, 2004, Google sold 19.6 million shares at $85 per share. At the time, the $1.67 billion raised was easily the largest auction IPO ever in the United States. Google stock (ticker: GOOG) opened trading on the NASDAQ market the next day at $100 per share. Although the Google IPO sometimes stumbled along the way, it represented the most significant example of the use of the auction mechanism as an alternative to the traditional IPO mechanism.

Sources: K. Delaney and R. Sidel, "Google IPO Aims to Change the Rules," *The Wall Street Journal*, April 30, 2004, p. C1; R. Simon and E. Weinstein, "Investors Eagerly Anticipate Google's IPO," *The Wall Street Journal*, April 30, 2004, p. C1; and G. Zuckerman, "Google Shares Prove Big Winners—for a Day," *The Wall Street Journal*, August 20, 2004, p. C1.

---

[8] For a comparison of auction and traditional IPOs see A. Sherman, "Global Trends in IPO Methods: Book Building versus Auctions with Endogenous Entry," *Journal of Financial Economics* 78(3) (2005): 615–649.

TABLE 23.4 Top Global IPO Underwriters, Ranked by 2014 Proceeds

	2014				2013		
Manager	Proceeds ($ billion)	Market Share	No. of Issues	Manager	Proceeds ($ billion)	Market Share	No. of Issues
Morgan Stanley	22.19	8.9%	130	Goldman Sachs	15.80	9.6%	113
Goldman Sachs	21.32	8.6%	114	JPMorgan	12.59	7.6%	106
JPMorgan	17.67	7.1%	126	Morgan Stanley	11.93	7.2%	100
Deutsche Bank	17.35	7.0%	95	Bank of America Merrill Lynch	11.45	6.9%	106
Credit Suisse	16.19	6.5%	113	Deutsche Bank	10.57	6.4%	93
Citi	14.68	5.8%	96	Credit Suisse	9.91	6.0%	102
UBS	11.02	4.4%	86	Citi	9.40	5.7%	87
Bank of America Merrill Lynch	10.23	4.1%	88	UBS	7.35	4.5%	68
Barclays Capital	7.41	3.0%	76	Barclays Capital	6.77	4.1%	69
HSBC Holdings	6.12	2.5%	23	Nomura	5.39	3.3%	42
Top 10 Totals	144.18	57.9%	947	**Top 10 Totals**	101.16	61.3%	886
Industry Totals	249.02	100.0%	1205	**Industry Totals**	164.91	100.0%	843*

Source: dmi.thomsonreuters.com/Content/Files/4Q2014_Global_Equity_Capital_Markets_Review.pdf, 2014

*Total issues is less than the sum of individual totals as there are often multiple managers for the same issue.

arranges for a group of other underwriters, called the **syndicate**, to help market and sell the issue. Table 23.4 shows the underwriters who were responsible for the largest number of IPOs in the United States during 2014. As you can see, the major investment and commercial banks dominate the underwriting business, with the top 10 firms capturing about one-half of the total market. The data for 2013–2014 also reveal a strong turnaround from 2008, when the aggregate number of issues was a paltry 29, with only $26 billion raised.

Underwriters market the IPO, and they help the company with all the necessary filings. More importantly, they actively participate in determining the offer price. In many cases, the underwriter will also commit to making a market in the stock after the issue, thereby guaranteeing that the stock will be liquid.

SEC Filings. The SEC requires that companies prepare a **registration statement**, a legal document that provides financial and other information about the company to investors, prior to an IPO. Company managers work closely with the underwriters to prepare this registration statement and submit it to the SEC. Part of the registration statement, called the **preliminary prospectus** or **red herring**, circulates to investors before the stock is offered.

The SEC reviews the registration statement to make sure that the company has disclosed all of the information necessary for investors to decide whether to purchase the stock. Once the company has satisfied the SEC's disclosure requirements, the SEC approves the stock for sale to the general public. The company prepares the final registration statement and **final prospectus** containing all the details of the IPO, including the number of shares offered and the offer price.[9]

To illustrate this process, let's return to RealNetworks. Figure 23.3 shows the cover page for the final prospectus for RealNetworks' IPO. This cover page includes the name of the

[9]Registration statements may be found at EDGAR, the SEC Web site providing registration information to investors: www.sec.gov/edgar/searchedgar/webusers.htm.

FIGURE 23.3

The Cover Page of RealNetworks' IPO Prospectus

The cover page includes the name of the company, a list of underwriters, and summary information about the pricing of the deal.

Source: www.sec.gov/edgar.shtml

3,000,000 Shares

RealNetworks

RealNetworks, Inc.

(formerly "Progressive Networks, Inc.")

Common Stock

(par value $.001 per share)

All of the 3,000,000 shares of Common Stock offered hereby are being sold by RealNetworks, Inc. Prior to the offering, there has been no public market for the Common Stock. For factors considered in determining the initial public offering price, see "Underwriting".

The Common Stock offered hereby involves a high degree of risk. See "Risk Factors" beginning on page 6.

The Common Stock has been approved for quotation on the Nasdaq National Market under the symbol "RNWK," subject to notice of issuance.

THESE SECURITIES HAVE NOT BEEN APPROVED OR DISAPPROVED BY THE SECURITIES AND EXCHANGE COMMISSION OR ANY STATE SECURITIES COMMISSION NOR HAS THE SECURITIES AND EXCHANGE COMMISSION OR ANY STATE SECURITIES COMMISSION PASSED UPON THE ACCURACY OR ADEQUACY OF THIS PROSPECTUS. ANY REPRESENTATION TO THE CONTRARY IS A CRIMINAL OFFENSE.

	Initial Public Offering Price(1)	Underwriting Discount(2)	Proceeds to Company(3)
Per Share	$12.50	$0.875	$11.625
Total(4)	$37,500,000	$2,625,000	$34,875,000

(1) In connection with the offering, the Underwriters have reserved up to 300,000 shares of Common Stock for sale at the initial public offering price to employees and friends of the Company.

(2) The Company has agreed to indemnify the Underwriters against certain liabilities, including liabilities under the Securities Act of 1933, as amended. See "Underwriting".

(3) Before deducting estimated expenses of $950,000 payable by the Company.

(4) The Company has granted the Underwriters an option for 30 days to purchase up to an additional 450,000 shares at the initial public offering price per share, less the underwriting discount, solely to cover over-allotments. If such option is exercised in full, the total initial public offering price, underwriting discount and proceeds to Company will be $43,125,000, $3,018,750 and $40,106,250, respectively. See "Underwriting".

The shares offered hereby are offered severally by the Underwriters, as specified herein, subject to receipt and acceptance by them and subject to their right to reject any order in whole or in part. It is expected that certificates for the shares will be ready for delivery in New York, New York on or about November 26, 1997, against payment therefor in immediately available funds.

Goldman, Sachs & Co.

BancAmerica Robertson Stephens

NationsBanc Montgomery Securities, Inc.

The date of this Prospectus is November 21, 1997.

company, the list of underwriters (with the lead underwriter shown first) and summary information about the pricing of the deal. The offering was a primary offering of 3 million shares.

Valuation. Before the offer price is set, the underwriters work closely with the company to come up with a price range that they believe provides a reasonable valuation for the firm using the techniques described in Chapter 9. As we pointed out in that chapter, there are two ways to value a company: estimate the future cash flows and compute the present value, or estimate the value by examining comparable companies. Most underwriters use both techniques. However, when these techniques give substantially different answers, they often rely on comparables based on recent IPOs.

Once an initial price range is established, the underwriters try to determine what the market thinks of the valuation. They begin by arranging a **road show**, in which senior management and the lead underwriters travel around the country (and sometimes around the world) promoting the company and explaining their rationale for the offer price to the underwriters' largest customers—mainly institutional investors such as mutual funds and pension funds.

EXAMPLE 23.4 Valuing an IPO Using Comparables

Problem

Wagner, Inc. is a private company that designs, manufactures, and distributes branded consumer products. During the most recent fiscal year, Wagner had revenues of $325 million and earnings of $15 million. Wagner has filed a registration statement with the SEC for its IPO. Before the stock is offered, Wagner's investment bankers would like to estimate the value of the company using comparable companies. The investment bankers have assembled the following information based on data for other companies in the same industry that have recently gone public. In each case, the ratios are based on the IPO price.

Company	Price/Earnings	Price/Revenues
Ray Products Corp.	18.8×	1.2×
Byce-Frasier, Inc.	19.5×	0.9×
Fashion Industries Group	24.1×	0.8×
Recreation International	22.4×	0.7×
Mean	21.2×	0.9×

After the IPO, Wagner will have 20 million shares outstanding. Estimate the IPO price for Wagner using the price/earnings ratio and the price/revenues ratio.

Solution

If the IPO price of Wagner is based on a price/earnings ratio that is similar to those for recent IPOs, then this ratio will equal the mean of recent deals, or 21.2. Given earnings of $15 million, the total market value of Wagner's stock will be ($15 million)(21.2) = $318 million. With 20 million shares outstanding, the price per share should be $15.90.

Similarly, if Wagner's IPO price implies a price/revenues ratio equal to the recent average of 0.9, then using its revenues of $325 million, the total market value of Wagner will be ($325 million)(0.9) = $292.5 million, or ($292.5 million/20) = $14.63 per share.

Based on these estimates, the underwriters will probably establish an initial price range for Wagner stock of $13 to $17 per share to take on the road show.

At the end of the road show, customers inform the underwriters of their interest by telling the underwriters how many shares they may want to purchase. Although these commitments are nonbinding, the underwriters' customers value their long-term relationships with the underwriters, so they rarely go back on their word. The underwriters then add up the total demand and adjust the price until it is unlikely that the issue will fail. This process for coming up with the offer price based on customers' expressions of interest is called **book building**.

Because no offer price is set in an auction IPO, book building is not as important in that venue as it is in traditional IPOs. Professors Ravi Jagannathan and Ann Sherman examined why auctions have failed to become a popular IPO method and have been plagued by inaccurate pricing and poor aftermarket performance. They suggest that, since auctions do not use the book-building process which aids in price discovery, investors are discouraged from participating in auctions.[10]

Pricing the Deal and Managing Risk. In the RealNetworks' IPO, the final offer price was \$12.50 per share.[11] Also, the company agreed to pay the underwriters a fee, called an **underwriting spread**, of \$0.875 per share—exactly 7% of the issue price. Because this was a firm commitment deal, the underwriters bought the stock from RealNetworks for \$12.50 − \$0.875 = \$11.625 per share and then resold it to their customers for \$12.50 per share.

Recall that when an underwriter provides a firm commitment, it is potentially exposing itself to the risk that the banking firm might have to sell the shares at less than the offer price and take a loss. However, according to Tim Loughran and Jay Ritter, between 1990 and 1998, just 9% of U.S. IPOs experienced a fall in share price on the first day.[12] For another 16% of firms, the price at the end of the first day was the same as the offer price. Therefore, the vast majority of IPOs experienced a price increase on the first day of trading, indicating that the initial offer price was generally lower than the price that stock market investors were willing to pay.

Underwriters appear to use the information they acquire during the book-building stage to intentionally underprice the IPO, thereby reducing their exposure to losses. Furthermore, once the issue price (or offer price) is set, underwriters may invoke another mechanism to protect themselves against a loss—the **over-allotment allocation**, or **greenshoe provision**.[13] This option allows the underwriter to issue more stock, amounting to 15% of the original offer size, at the IPO offer price. Look at footnote 4 on the front page of the RealNetworks' prospectus in Figure 23.3. This footnote is a greenshoe provision.

Let's illustrate how underwriters use the greenshoe provision to protect themselves against a loss and thereby manage risk. The RealNetworks' prospectus specified that 3 million shares would be offered at \$12.50 per share. In addition, the greenshoe provision allowed for the issue of an additional 450,000 shares at \$12.50 per share. Underwriters initially market both the initial and the greenshoe allotment—in RealNetworks' case, the \$12.50 per share price is set so that all 3.45 million shares are expected to sell—and thereby "short sell" the greenshoe allotment. Then, if the issue is a success, the underwriter exercises the greenshoe option, covering its short position. If the issue is not a success and its price falls, the underwriter covers the short position by repurchasing the greenshoe allotment (450,000 shares in the RealNetworks' IPO) in the aftermarket, thereby supporting the price.[14]

Once the IPO process is complete, the company's shares trade publicly on an exchange. The lead underwriter usually makes a market in the stock and assigns an analyst to cover it. By doing so, the underwriter increases the liquidity of the stock in the secondary market.

[10]"Why Do IPO Auctions Fail?," NBER working paper 12151, March 2006.

[11]Stock prices for RealNetworks throughout this chapter have not been adjusted for stock splits. (RealNetworks split 2:1 in 1999 and again in 2000, followed by a 1:4 reverse split in 2011.)

[12]"Why Don't Issuers Get Upset About Leaving Money on the Table in IPOs?" *Review of Financial Studies* 15(2) (2002): 413–443.

[13]The name derives from the Green Shoe Company, the first issuer to have an over-allotment option in its IPO.

[14]R. Aggarwal, "Stabilization Activities by Underwriters After IPOs," *Journal of Finance* 55(3) (2000): 1075–1103, finds that underwriters initially oversell by an average of 10.75% and then cover themselves if necessary using the greenshoe option.

This service is of value to both the issuing company and the underwriter's customers. A liquid market ensures that investors who purchased shares via the IPO are able to easily trade those shares. If the stock is actively traded, the issuer will have continued access to the equity markets in the event that the company decides to issue more shares in a new offering. In most cases, the preexisting shareholders are subject to a 180-day **lockup**; they cannot sell their shares for 180 days after the IPO. Once the lockup period expires, they are free to sell their shares.

CONCEPT CHECK

1. What are some advantages and disadvantages of going public?
2. Explain the mechanics of an auction IPO.

23.3 IPO Puzzles

Four characteristics of IPOs puzzle financial economists and are relevant for the financial manager:

1. On average, IPOs appear to be underpriced: The price at the end of trading on the first day is often substantially higher than the IPO price.
2. The number of issues is highly cyclical: When times are good, the market is flooded with new issues; when times are bad, the number of issues dries up.
3. The costs of an IPO are very high, and it is unclear why firms willingly incur them.
4. The long-run performance of a newly public company (three to five years from the date of issue) is poor. That is, on average, a three- to five-year buy and hold strategy appears to be a bad investment.

We will now examine each of these puzzles that financial economists seek to understand.

Underpricing

Generally, underwriters set the issue price so that the average first-day return is positive. For RealNetworks, the underwriters offered the stock at an IPO price of $12.50 per share on November 21, 1997. RealNetworks' stock opened trading on the NASDAQ market at a price of $19.375 per share, and it closed at the end of its first trading day at $17.875. Such performance is not atypical. On average, between 1960 and 2015, the price in the U.S. aftermarket was 17% higher at the end of the first day of trading. As is evident in Figure 23.4, the one-day average return for IPOs has historically been very large around the world.

Who benefits from the underpricing? We have already explained how the underwriters benefit by controlling their risk. Of course, investors who are able to buy stock from underwriters at the IPO price also gain from the first-day underpricing. Who bears the cost? The pre-IPO shareholders of the issuing firms. In effect, these owners are selling stock in their firm for less than they could get in the aftermarket.

So why do shareholders of issuing firms put up with this underpricing? A naive view is that they have no choice because a relatively small number of underwriters controls the market. In fact, this is unlikely to be the explanation. The industry, at least anecdotally, appears to be highly competitive. In addition, entrants offering cheaper alternatives to the traditional underwriting process, like WR Hambrecht, have not been very successful at gaining significant market share.

FIGURE 23.4 **International Comparison of First-Day IPO Returns**

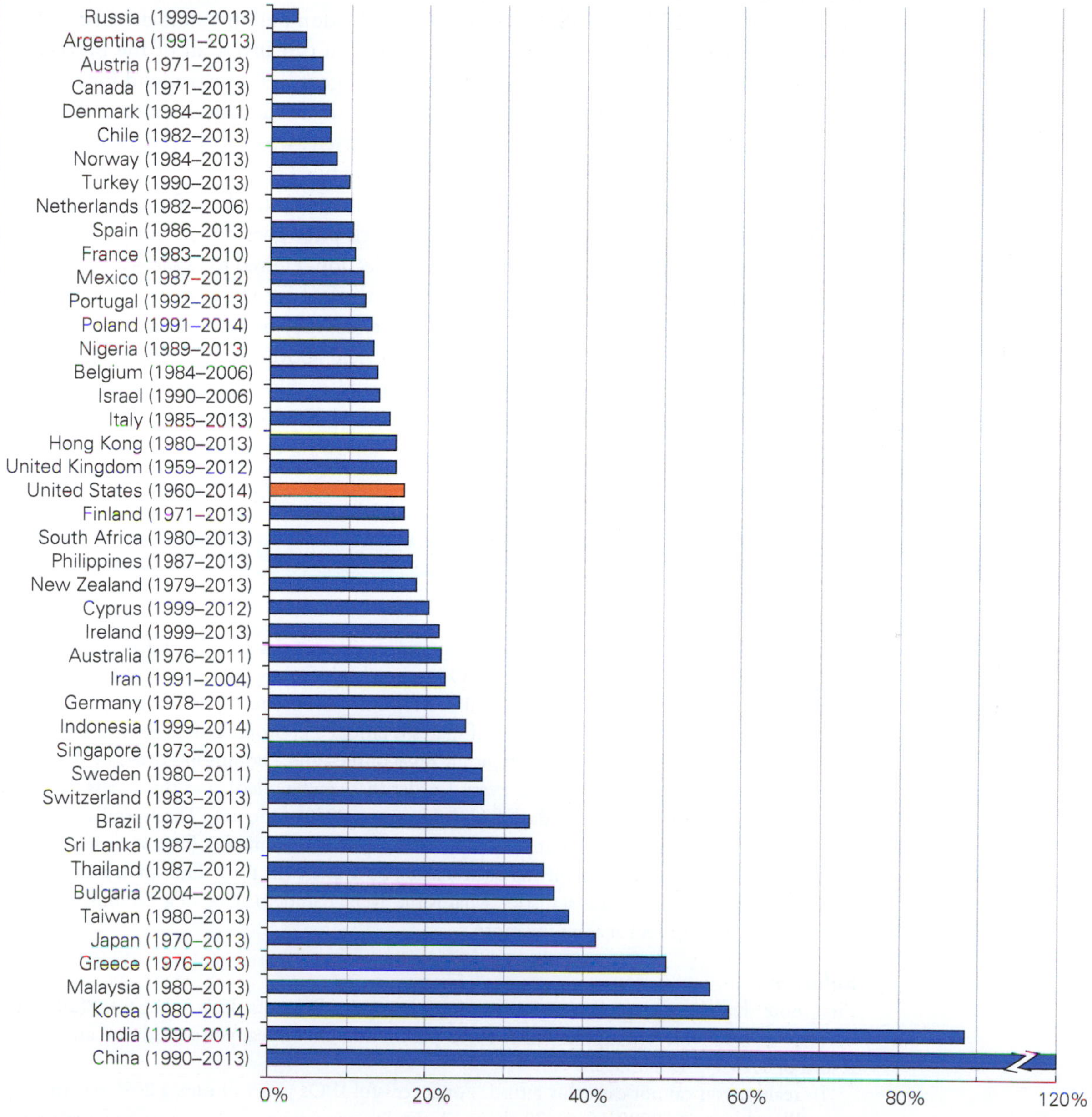

The bars show the average initial returns from the offer price to the first closing market price. For China, the bar shows the average initial return on A share IPOs, available only to residents of China. The dates indicate the sample period for each country.

Source: Adapted courtesy of Jay Ritter (bear.warrington.ufl.edu/ritter/)

Given the existence of underpricing, it might appear that investing in new IPOs would be a very lucrative deal. If the average one-day return is 17%, and you could invest in a new IPO at the beginning of every working day and sell your shares at the end of the day for 250 business days per year, your cumulative annual return would be $(1.17)^{250} - 1 = 11{,}129{,}238{,}168{,}937{,}200{,}000\%$. Why don't all investors do this?

The preceding calculation assumes that each day you can invest all of the proceeds of the previous day's investment. However, when an IPO goes well, the demand for the stock exceeds the supply. (This is another way of saying that the stock is underpriced.) Thus, the allocation of shares for each investor is rationed. Conversely, when an IPO does not go well, demand at the issue price is weak, so all initial orders are filled completely. In this scenario, if you followed the strategy of reinvesting whatever you made on the last IPO in the next one, your orders would be completely filled when the stock price goes down, but you would be rationed when it goes up. This is a form of adverse selection referred to as the **winner's curse**: You "win" (get all the shares you requested) when demand for the shares by others is low, and the IPO is more likely to perform poorly. This effect may be substantial enough so that the strategy of investing in every IPO does not even yield above-market returns, never mind the stratospheric number calculated above.[15] Furthermore, this effect implies that it may be necessary for the underwriter to underprice its issues on average in order for less informed investors to be willing to participate in IPOs, as the following example demonstrates.

EXAMPLE 23.5 IPO Investors and the Winner's Curse

Problem

Thompson Brothers, a large underwriter, is offering its customers the following opportunity: Thompson will guarantee a piece of every IPO it is involved in. Suppose you are a customer. On each deal you must commit to buying 2000 shares. If the shares are available, you get them. If the deal is oversubscribed, your allocation of shares is rationed in proportion to the oversubscription. Your market research shows that typically 80% of the time Thompson's deals are oversubscribed 16 to 1 (there are 16 orders for every 1 order that can be filled), and this excess demand leads to a price increase on the first day of 20%. However, 20% of the time Thompson's deals are not oversubscribed, and while Thompson supports the price in the market (by not exercising the greenshoe provision and instead buying back shares), on average the price tends to decline by 5% on the first day. Based on these statistics, what is the average underpricing of a Thompson IPO? What is your average return as an investor?

Solution

First, note that the average first-day return for Thompson Brothers deals is large: $0.8(20\%) + 0.2(-5\%) = 15\%$. If Thompson had one IPO per month, after a year you would earn an annual return of $1.15^{12} - 1 = 435\%$!

In reality, you cannot earn this return. For successful IPOs you will earn a 20% return, but you will only receive $2000/16 = 125$ shares. Assuming an average IPO price of $15 per share, your profit is

$$\$15/\text{share} \times (125 \text{ shares}) \times (20\% \text{ return}) = \$375$$

[15] This explanation was first proposed by K. Rock: "Why New Issues Are Underpriced," *Journal of Financial Economics* 15(2) (1986): 197–212. See also M. Levis, "The Winner's Curse Problem, Interest Costs and the Underpricing of Initial Public Offerings," *Economic Journal* 100 (1990): 76–89.

For unsuccessful IPOs you will receive your full allocation of 2000 shares. Because these stocks tend to fall by 5%, your profit is

$$\$15/\text{share} \times (2000 \text{ shares}) \times (-5\% \text{ return}) = -\$1500$$

Because 80% of Thompson's IPOs are successful, your average profit is therefore

$$0.80(\$375) + 0.20(-\$1500) = \$0$$

That is, on average you are just breaking even! As this example shows, even though the average IPO may be profitable, because you receive a higher allocation of the less successful IPOs, your average return may be much lower. Also, if Thompson's average underpricing were less than 15%, uninformed investors would lose money and be unwilling to participate in its IPOs.

Cyclicality

Figure 23.5 shows the number and dollar volume of IPOs by year from 1975 to 2014. As the figure makes clear, the dollar volume of IPOs reached a peak in 1999–2000. An even more important feature of the data is the clear cycle pattern in the volume and number of issues. Sometimes, such as in 2000, the volume of IPOs is unprecedented by historical standards; yet, within a year or two, the volume of IPOs may decrease significantly. This cyclicality by itself is not particularly surprising. We would expect there to be a greater need for capital in times with more growth opportunities than in times with fewer growth

FIGURE 23.5 **Cyclicality of Initial Public Offerings in the United States**

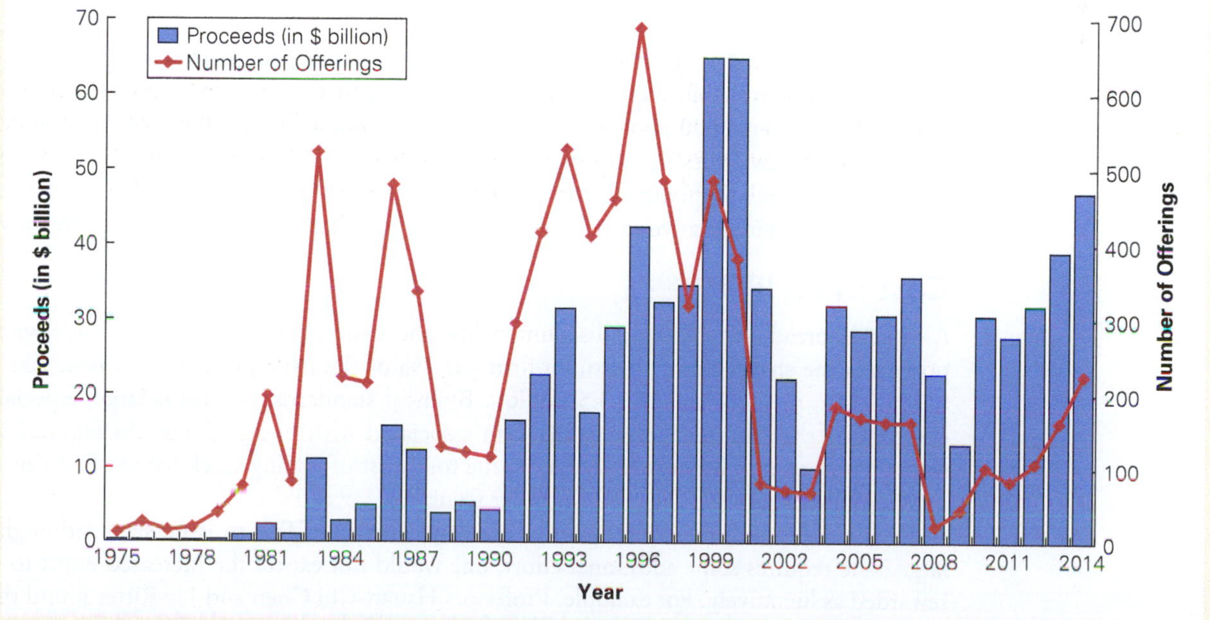

The graph shows the number of IPOs and the annual cumulative dollar volume of shares offered. The number and volume of IPOs reached a peak in the late 1990s and is highly cyclical.

Source: Adapted courtesy of Jay R. Ritter from "Initial Public Offerings: Tables Updated through 2014" (bear.warrington.ufl.edu/ritter/).

GLOBAL FINANCIAL CRISIS Worldwide IPO Deals in 2008–2009

The drop in IPO issues during the 2008 financial crisis was both global and dramatic. The figure below shows the total worldwide dollar volume of IPO proceeds in billions of dollars (blue bars) and number of deals (red line) by quarter, from the last quarter of 2006 to the first quarter of 2009. Comparing the fourth quarter of 2007 (a record quarter for IPO issues) to the fourth quarter of 2008, dollar volume dropped a stunning 97% from $102 billion to just $3 billion. Things got even worse in the first quarter of 2009 with just $1.4 billion raised. The market for IPOs essentially dried up altogether.

During the 2008 financial crisis, IPO markets were not the only equity issue markets that saw a collapse in volume. Markets for seasoned equity offerings and leveraged buyouts also collapsed. The extreme market uncertainty at the time created a "flight to quality." Investors, wary of taking risk, sought to move their capital into risk-free investments like U.S. Treasury securities. The result was a crash in existing equity prices and a greatly reduced supply of new capital to risky asset classes.

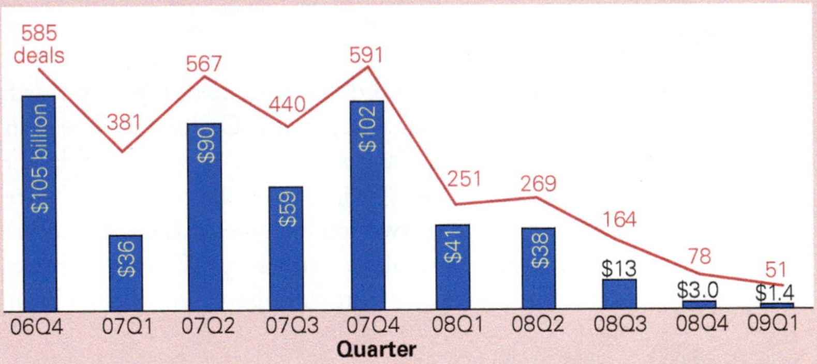

Source: Shifting Landscape—Are You Ready? Global IPO Trends report 2009, Ernst & Young

opportunities. What is surprising is the magnitude of the swings. It is very difficult to believe that the availability of growth opportunities and the need for capital changed so drastically between 2000 and 2003 as to cause a decline of more than 75% in the dollar volume of new issues. It appears that the number of IPOs is not solely driven by the demand for capital. Sometimes firms and investors seem to favor IPOs; at other times firms appear to rely on alternative sources of capital and financial economists are not sure why.

Cost of an IPO

A typical spread—that is, the discount below the issue price at which the underwriter purchases the shares from the issuing firm—is 7% of the issue price. For an issue size of $50 million, this amounts to $3.5 million. By most standards, this fee is large, especially considering the additional cost to the firm associated with underpricing. As Figure 23.6 shows, compared to other security issues, the total cost of issuing stock for the first time is substantially larger than the costs for other securities.

Even more puzzling is the seeming lack of sensitivity of fees to issue size. Although a large issue requires some additional effort, one would not expect the increased effort to be rewarded as lucratively. For example, Professors Hsuan-Chi Chen and Jay Ritter found that almost all issues ranging in size from $20 million to $80 million paid fees of about 7%.[16]

[16] "The Seven Percent Solution," *Journal of Finance* 55(3) (2000): 1105–1131.

FIGURE 23.6

Relative Costs of Issuing Securities

This figure shows the total direct costs (all underwriting, legal, and auditing costs) of issuing securities as a percentage of the amount of money raised. The figure reports results for IPOs, seasoned equity offerings, convertible bonds, and straight bonds, for issues of different sizes from 1990–1994.

Source: Adapted from I. Lee, S. Lochhead, J. Ritter, and Q. Zhao, "The Costs of Raising Capital," *Journal of Financial Research* 19(1) (1996): 59–74.

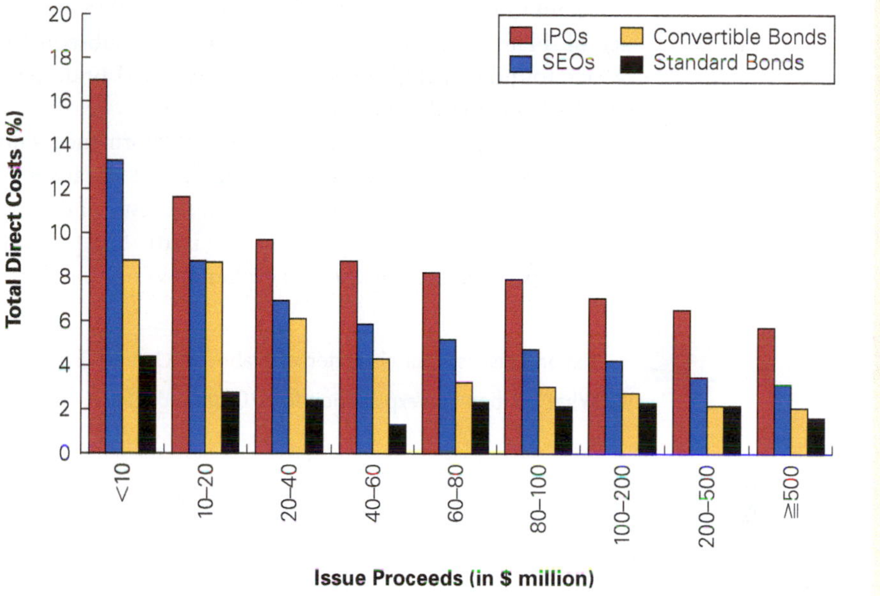

It is difficult to understand how a $20 million issue can be profitably done for "only" $1.4 million, while an $80 million issue requires paying fees of $5.6 million.

No researcher has provided a satisfactory answer to this puzzle. Chen and Ritter argue for implicit collusion by the underwriters, but in response to their paper Robert Hansen finds no evidence of any such collusion.[17] He shows that there is low underwriting industry concentration, that there have been significant new entrants in the IPO-underwriting market, and that a 7% spread is less profitable than normal investment banking activities.

One possible explanation is that by attempting to undercut its rivals, an underwriter may risk signaling that it is not the same quality as its higher-priced competitors, making firms less likely to select that underwriter. Professor Craig Dunbar examined this hypothesis.[18] He found that underwriters charging slightly lower fees appear to enjoy a greater market share, but those charging significantly lower fees have smaller market shares. Indeed, in support of the idea that the quality of the underwriter is important, underwriters that charge very high fees gain market share.

Long-Run Underperformance

We know that the shares of IPOs generally perform very well immediately following the public offering. It is perhaps surprising, then, that Professor Jay Ritter found that newly listed firms subsequently appear to perform relatively poorly over the following three to

---

[17]"Do Investment Banks Compete in IPOs?: The Advent of the '7% Plus Contract,'" *Journal of Financial Economics* 59(3) (2001): 313–346.

[18]"Factors Affecting Investment Banks Initial Public Offering Market Share," *Journal of Financial Economics* 55(1) (2000): 3–41.

five years after their IPOs.[19] In follow-up studies, Professors Alon Brav, Christopher Geczy, and Paul Gompers found that IPOs between 1975 and 1992 underperformed by an average of 44% relative to the S&P 500 over the subsequent five years.[20] Jay Ritter and Ivo Welch found that IPOs between 1980 and 2001 underperformed the market by an average of 23.4% during the subsequent three years.[21]

As we will see in the next section, underperformance is not unique to an initial public issuance of equity: It is associated with subsequent issuances as well, raising the possibility that underperformance might not result from the issue of equity itself, but rather from the conditions that motivated the equity issuance in the first place. We will explain this idea in more detail in the next section after we explain how a public company issues additional equity.

CONCEPT CHECK

1. List and discuss four characteristics about IPOs that financial economists find puzzling.
2. What is a possible explanation for IPO underpricing?

23.4 The Seasoned Equity Offering

A firm's need for outside capital rarely ends at the IPO. Usually, profitable growth opportunities occur throughout the life of the firm, and in some cases it is not feasible to finance these opportunities out of retained earnings. Thus, more often than not, firms return to the equity markets and offer new shares for sale, a type of offering called a **seasoned equity offering (SEO)**.

The Mechanics of an SEO

When a firm issues stock using an SEO, it follows many of the same steps as for an IPO. The main difference is that a market price for the stock already exists, so the price-setting process is not necessary.

RealNetworks has conducted several SEOs since its IPO in 1997. On June 17, 1999, the firm offered 4 million shares in an SEO at a price of $58 per share. Of these shares, 3,525,000 were **primary shares**—new shares issued by the company. The remaining 475,000 shares were **secondary shares**—shares sold by existing shareholders, including the company's founder, Robert Glaser, who sold 310,000 of his shares. Most of the rest of RealNetworks' SEOs occurred between 1999 and 2004 and included secondary shares sold by existing shareholders rather than directly by RealNetworks.

Historically, intermediaries would advertise the sale of stock (both IPOs and SEOs) by taking out advertisements in newspapers called **tombstones**. Through these ads, investors would know who to call to buy stock. Today, investors become informed about the impending sale of stock by the news media, from the Internet, via a road show, or through the book-building process, so these tombstones are purely ceremonial.

Two kinds of seasoned equity offerings exist: a cash offer and a rights offer. In a **cash offer**, the firm offers the new shares to investors at large. In a **rights offer**, the firm offers the new shares only to existing shareholders. In the United States, most offers are cash

[19] "The Long-Run Performance of Initial Public Offerings," *Journal of Finance* 46(1) (1991): 3–27.

[20] "Is the Abnormal Return Following Equity Issuances Anomalous?" *Journal of Financial Economics* 56 (2000): 209–249.

[21] "A Review of IPO Activity, Pricing, and Allocations," *Journal of Finance* 57(4) (2002): 1795–1828.

offers, but the same is not true internationally. For example, in the United Kingdom, most seasoned offerings of new shares are rights offers.

Rights offers protect existing shareholders from underpricing. To see how, suppose a company holds $100 in cash and has 50 shares outstanding. Each share is worth $2. The company announces a cash offer for 50 shares at $1 per share. Once this offer is complete, the company will have $150 in cash and 100 shares outstanding. The price per share is now $1.50 to reflect the fact that the new shares were sold at a discount. The new shareholders therefore receive a $0.50 windfall at the expense of the old shareholders.

The old shareholders would be protected if, instead of a cash offer, the company did a rights offer. In this case, rather than offer the new shares for general sale, every shareholder would have the right to purchase an additional share for $1 per share. If all shareholders chose to exercise their rights, then after the sale, the value of the company would be the same as with a cash offer: It would be worth $150 with 100 shares outstanding and a price of $1.50 per share. In this case, however, the $0.50 windfall accrues to existing shareholders, which exactly offsets the drop in the stock price. Thus, if a firm's management is concerned that its equity may be underpriced in the market, by using a rights offering the firm can continue to issue equity without imposing a loss on its current shareholders.

EXAMPLE 23.6 Raising Money with Rights Offers

Problem

You are the CFO of a company that is currently worth $1 billion. The firm has 100 million shares outstanding, so the shares are trading at $10 per share. You need to raise $200 million and have announced a rights issue. Each existing shareholder is sent one right for every share he or she owns. You have not decided how many rights you will require to purchase a share of new stock. You will require either four rights to purchase one share at a price of $8 per share, or five rights to purchase two new shares at a price of $5 per share. Which approach will raise more money?

Solution

If all shareholders exercise their rights, then in the first case, 25 million new shares will be purchased at a price of $8 per share, raising $200 million. In the second case, 40 million new shares will be purchased at a price of $5 per share, also raising $200 million. If all shareholders exercise their rights, both approaches will raise the same amount of money.

In both cases, the value of the firm after the issue is $1.2 billion. In the first case, there are 125 million shares outstanding, so the price per share after the issue is $9.60. This price exceeds the issue price of $8, so the shareholders will exercise their rights. In the second case, the number of shares outstanding will grow to 140 million, resulting in a post-issue stock price of $1.2 billion for 140 million shares = $8.57 per share (also higher than the issue price). Again, the shareholders will exercise their rights. In both cases, the same amount of money is raised.

The arguments in favor of rights offers presume, however, that all shareholders participate. Surprisingly, even though participation is profitable (because the new shares are priced at a discount), Professors Clifford Holderness and Jeffrey Pontiff report that on average less than 70% of shareholders participate in U.S. rights offerings.[22] Rights offers therefore lead to a wealth transfer from non-participating shareholders, who tend to be small individual investors, to those who do participate.

[22] "Shareholder Nonparticipation in Valuable Rights Offerings: New Findings for an Old Puzzle," *Journal of Financial Economics* (2016).

FIGURE 23.7

Post-SEO Performance

The figure plots the cumulative abnormal returns (realized alpha using the Fama-French-Carhart factor specification) for portfolios made up of seasoned equity offerings between 1976 and 1996. The long-run underperformance appears much more pronounced among smaller firms.

Source: Adapted from A. Brav, C. Geczy, and P. Gompers, "Is the Abnormal Return Following Equity Issuances Anomalous?" *Journal of Financial Economics* 56 (2000): 209–249, Figure 3.

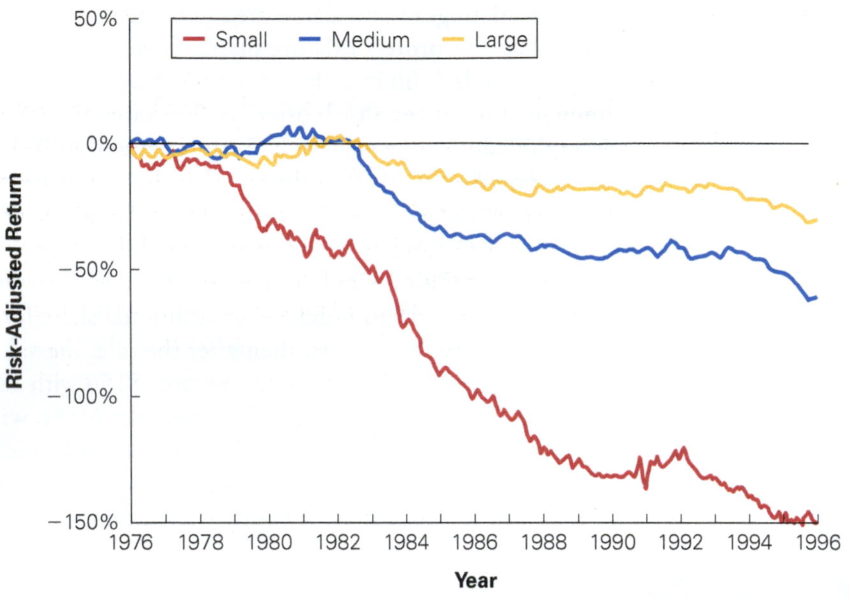

Price Reaction

Researchers have found that, on average, the market greets the news of an SEO with a price decline. Often the value destroyed by the price decline can be a significant fraction of the new money raised. This price decline is consistent with the adverse selection we discussed in Chapter 16. Because a company concerned about protecting its existing shareholders will tend to sell only at a price that correctly values or overvalues the firm, investors infer from the decision to sell that the company is likely to be overvalued; hence, the price drops with the announcement of the SEO.

Although adverse selection is a plausible explanation for SEO price reaction, some puzzles remain unexplained. First, by offering a rights issue, a company can mitigate the adverse selection. It is not clear, then, at least in the United States, why companies do not initiate more rights issues. Second, as with IPOs, evidence suggests that companies underperform following a seasoned offering (see Figure 23.7). At first glance, this underperformance appears to suggest that the stock price decrease is not large enough, because underperformance implies that the price following the issue was too high.

A possible explanation for SEO subsequent underperformance, put forward by Professors Murray Carlson, Adlai Fisher, and Ron Giammarino, is that this outcome might not have to do with the SEO announcement itself, but rather with the conditions that led the firm to choose an SEO.[23] The decision to raise financing externally usually implies that a firm plans to pursue an investment opportunity. As explained in Chapter 22, when a firm invests, it is exercising its growth options. Growth options are riskier than projects

[23]M. Carlson, A. Fisher, and R. Giammarino, "Corporate Investment and Asset Price Dynamics: Implications for the Cross-section of Returns," *Journal of Finance* 59(6) (2004): 2577–2603.

themselves, so upon exercise, the firm's beta decreases, which explains the post-SEO lower returns. Researchers have found empirical support for this hypothesis.[24]

Issuance Costs

Although not as costly as IPOs, as Figure 23.6 shows, seasoned offerings are still expensive. Underwriting fees amount to 5% of the proceeds of the issue and, as with IPOs, the variation across issues of different sizes is relatively small. Furthermore, rights offers have lower costs than cash offers.[25] Given the other advantages of a rights offer, it is a puzzle why the majority of offers in the United States are cash offers. The one advantage of a cash offer is that the underwriter takes on a larger role and, therefore, can credibly certify the issue's quality. If there is a large amount of asymmetric information and a large proportion of existing shareholders are buying the offering anyway, the benefits of certification might overcome the cost difference. Professors Espen Eckbo and Ronald Masulis have found empirical support for this hypothesis.[26]

CONCEPT CHECK

1. What is the difference between a cash offer and a rights offer for a seasoned equity offering?
2. What is the average stock price reaction to an SEO?

MyFinanceLab

Here is what you should know after reading this chapter. MyFinanceLab will help you identify what you know and where to go when you need to practice.

23.1 Equity Financing for Private Companies

- Private companies can raise outside equity capital from angel investors, venture capital firms, private equity firms, institutional investors, or corporate investors.
- Increasingly, early stage entrepreneurs are able to find angel investors who provide the initial capital to start their business.
- When a company founder sells stock to an outsider to raise capital, the founder's ownership share and control over the company are reduced.
- Venture capital investors in private firms are often negotiated in terms of the pre-money valuation of the firm, which is the number of prior shares outstanding times the share price used in the funding round.
- Given the pre-money valuation and the amount invested:

$$\text{Post-money Valuation} = \text{Pre-money Valuation} + \text{Amount Invested} \tag{23.1}$$

  In addition, the fractional ownership held by the new investors is equal to

$$\text{Percentage Ownership} = \text{Amount Invested/Post-money Valuation.} \tag{23.2}$$

- Venture capital investors hold convertible preferred stock. Convertible preferred differs from common shares due to provisions such as liquidation preference, seniority, anti-dilution protection, participation rights, and board membership rights.

---

[24]A. Brav, C. Geczy, and P. Gompers (see footnote 20); B. E. Eckbo, R. Masulis, and O. Norli, "Seasoned Public Offerings: Resolution of the New Issues Puzzle," *Journal of Financial Economics* 56(2) (2000): 251–291; E. Lyandres, L. Sun, and L. Zhang, "The New Issues Puzzle: Testing the Investment-Based Explanation" *Review of Financial Studies* 21 (6) (2008): 2825–2855; and M. Carlson, A. Fisher, and R. Giammarino, "SEO Risk Dynamics," University of British Columbia working paper (2009).

[25]In the United Kingdom, M. Slovin, M. Sushka, and K. Lai [*Journal of Financial Economics* 57(2) (2000)] found that the average fee for a cash offer is 6.1% versus 4.6% for an underwritten rights offer.

[26]"Adverse Selection and the Rights Offer Paradox," *Journal of Financial Economics* 32 (1992): 293–332.

- Equity investors in private companies plan to sell their stock eventually through one of two main exit strategies: an acquisition or a public offering.

23.2 The Initial Public Offering

- An initial public offering (IPO) is the first time a company sells its stock to the public.
- The main advantages of going public are greater liquidity and better access to capital. Disadvantages include regulatory and financial reporting requirements and the undermining of the investors' ability to monitor the company's management.
- During an IPO, the shares sold may represent either a primary offering (if the shares are being sold to raise new capital) or a secondary offering (if the shares are sold by earlier investors).
- Stock may be sold during an IPO on a best-efforts basis, as a firm commitment IPO, or using an auction IPO. The firm commitment process is the most common practice in the United States.
- An underwriter is an investment bank that manages the IPO process and helps the company sell its stock.
  - The lead underwriter is responsible for managing the IPO.
  - The lead underwriter forms a group of underwriters, called the syndicate, to help sell the stock.
- The SEC requires that a company file a registration statement prior to an IPO. The preliminary prospectus is part of the registration statement that circulates to investors before the stock is offered. After the deal is completed, the company files a final prospectus.
- Underwriters value a company before an IPO using valuation techniques and by book building.
- Underwriters face risk during an IPO. A greenshoe provision is one way underwriters manage the risk associated with IPOs.

23.3 IPO Puzzles

- Several puzzles are associated with IPOs.
  - IPOs are underpriced on average.
  - New issues are highly cyclical.
  - The transaction costs of an IPO are high.
  - Long-run performance after an IPO is poor on average.

23.4 The Seasoned Equity Offering

- A seasoned equity offering (SEO) is the sale of stock by a company that is already publicly traded.
- Two kinds of SEOs exist: a cash offer (when new shares are sold to investors at large) and a rights offer (when new shares are offered only to existing shareholders).
- The stock price reaction to an SEO is negative on average.

Key Terms

angel group *p. 829*
angel investors *p. 829*
anti-dilution protection *p. 837*
auction IPO *p. 842*
best-efforts IPO *p. 841*
board membership *p. 837*
book building *p. 846*
carried interest *p. 831*
cash offer *p. 854*
convertible note *p. 829*
convertible preferred stock *p. 834*
corporate investor *p. 834*
corporate partner *p. 834*
crowdfunding *p. 830*
down round *p. 837*
exit strategy *p. 840*
final prospectus *p. 844*
firm commitment IPO *p. 841*
funding round *p. 834*
initial public offering (IPO) *p. 840*
lead underwriter *p. 843*
leveraged buyout (LBO) *p. 833*
liquidation preference *p. 836*
lockup *p. 848*
over-allotment allocation (greenshoe provision) *p. 847*
pari passu *p. 836*
participation rights *p. 836*
post-money valuation *p. 835*
pre-money valuation *p. 835*

preferred stock *p. 834*
preliminary prospectus (red herring) *p. 844*
primary offering *p. 841*
primary shares *p. 854*
private equity firm *p. 833*
registration statement *p. 844*
rights offer *p. 854*
road show *p. 846*
seasoned equity offering (SEO) *p. 854*
secondary offering *p. 841*
secondary shares *p. 854*
seniority *p. 836*
strategic investor *p. 834*
strategic partner *p. 834*
syndicate *p. 844*
tombstones *p. 854*
underwriter *p. 841*
underwriting spread *p. 847*
unicorn *p. 836*
venture capital firm *p. 830*
venture capitalists *p. 830*
winner's curse *p. 850*

Further Reading

For more detailed coverage of the topics in this chapter, read one of the following survey articles on security issuance: B. E. Eckbo, R. Masulis, and O. Norli, "Security Offerings: A Survey," in B. E. Eckbo (ed.), *Handbook of Corporate Finance, Vol. 1: Empirical Corporate Finance* (Elsevier/North Holland, 2007); and J. Ritter, "Investment Banking and Securities Issuance," in G. Constantinides, M. Harris, and R. Stulz (eds.), *Handbook of the Economics of Finance* (North-Holland, 2012).

For more detailed coverage of specific topics, consult the following resources:

Angel Financing. The Angel Capital Association (www.angelcapitalassociation.org) and the Angel Resource Institute (www.angelresourceinstitute.org) provides up-to-date information on angel financing. W. Kerr, J. Lerner and A. Schoar, "The Consequences of Entrepreneurial Finance: Evidence from Angel Financings," *Review of Financial Studies* 27 (2014), study the success of angel investments; and S Bernstein, A. Korteweg, and K. Laws, "Attracting Early Stage Investors: Evidence from a Randomized Field Experiment," *Journal of Finance* (2016) uses a randomized field experiment on AngelList to identify which start-up characteristics are most important to investors in early stage firms.

Venture Capital. P. Gompers, "Venture Capital," in B. E. Eckbo (ed.), *Handbook of Corporate Finance, Vol. 1: Empirical Corporate Finance* (Elsevier/North Holland, 2007); P. Gompers and L. Lerner, "The Venture Capital Revolution," *Journal of Economic Perspectives* 15(2) (2001): 145–168; and S. Kaplan and P. Stromberg, "Contract, Characteristics and Actions: Evidence from Venture Capitalist Analysis," *Journal of Finance* 59(5) (2004): 2177–2210.

IPOs. Jay Ritter's Web site (bear.warrington.ufl.edu/ritter/) contains a wealth of information and links to cutting-edge research on the subject of IPOs. Other references of interest include L. Benveniste and W. Wilhelm, "Initial Public Offerings: Going by the Book," *Journal of Applied Corporate Finance* 10(1) (1997): 98–108; F. Cornelli and D. Goldreich, "Bookbuilding and Strategic Allocation," *Journal of Finance* 56(6) (2001): 2337–2369; A. Ljungqvist, "IPO Underpricing," in B. E. Eckbo (ed.), *Handbook of Corporate Finance, Vol. 1: Empirical Corporate Finance* (Elsevier/North Holland, 2007); T. Jenkinson and A. Ljungqvist, *Going Public: The Theory and Evidence on How Companies Raise Equity Finance* (Oxford University Press, 2001); M. Lowry and G. W. Schwert, "IPO Market Cycles: Bubbles or Sequential Learning?" *Journal of Finance* 57(3) (2002): 1171–1200; M. Pagano, F. Panetta, and L. Zingales, "Why Do Companies Go Public? An Empirical Analysis," *Journal of Finance* 53(1) (1998): 27–64; L. Pástor and P. Veronesi, "Rational IPO Waves," *Journal of Finance* 60(4) (2005): 1713–1757; and I. Welch, "Seasoned Offerings, Imitation Costs and the Underpricing of Initial Public Offerings," *Journal of Finance* 44(2) (1989): 421–449.

SEOs. A. Brav, C. Geczy, and P. Gompers, "Is the Abnormal Return Following Equity Issuances Anomalous?" *Journal of Financial Economics* 56(2) (2000): 209–249; J. Clarke, C. Dunbar, and K. Kahle, "Long-Run Performance and Insider Trading in Completed and Canceled Seasoned Equity Offerings," *Journal of Financial and Quantitative Analysis* 36(2) (2001): 415–430; and B. E. Eckbo and R. Masulis, "Seasoned Equity Offerings: A Survey." In R. Jarrow et al. (eds.), *Handbooks in Operations Research and Management Science*, 9th ed. (1995): 1017–1059; C. Holderness and J. Pontiff, "Shareholder Nonparticipation in Valuable Rights Offerings: New findings for an Old Puzzle," *Journal of Financial Economics* (2016).

Costs of Raising Equity. O. Altinkilic and R. Hansen, "Are There Economies of Scale in Underwriting Fees? Evidence of Rising External Financing Costs," *Review of Financial Studies* 13(1) (2000): 191–218.

Problems

All problems are available in MyFinanceLab.

Equity Financing for Private Companies

1. What are some of the alternative sources from which private companies can raise equity capital?
2. What are the advantages and the disadvantages to a private company of raising money from a corporate investor?
3. Starware Software was founded last year to develop software for gaming applications. Initially, the founder invested $800,000 and received 8 million shares of stock. Starware now needs to raise a second round of capital, and it has identified an interested venture capitalist. This venture capitalist will invest $1 million and wants to own 20% of the company after the investment is completed.
   a. How many shares must the venture capitalist receive to end up with 20% of the company? What is the implied price per share of this funding round?
   b. What will the value of the whole firm be after this investment (the post-money valuation)?
4. Suppose venture capital firm GSB partners raised $100 million of committed capital. Each year over the 10-year life of the fund, 2% of this committed capital will be used to pay GSB's management fee. As is typical in the venture capital industry, GSB will only invest $80 million (committed capital less lifetime management fees). At the end of 10 years, the investments made by the fund are worth $400 million. GSB also charges 20% carried interest on the profits of the fund (net of management fees).
   a. Assuming the $80 million in invested capital is invested immediately and all proceeds were received at the end of 10 years, what is the IRR of the investments GSB partners made? That is, compute IRR ignoring all management fees.
   b. Of course, as an investor, or limited partner, you are more interested in your own IRR—that is, the IRR including all fees paid. Assuming that investors gave GSB partners the full $100 million up front, what is the IRR for GSB's limited partners (that is, the IRR net of *all* fees paid).
5. Three years ago, you founded your own company. You invested $100,000 of your money and received 5 million shares of Series A preferred stock. Since then, your company has been through three additional rounds of financing.

Round	Price ($)	Number of Shares
Series B	0.50	1,000,000
Series C	2.00	500,000
Series D	4.00	500,000

   a. What is the pre-money valuation for the Series D funding round?
   b. What is the post-money valuation for the Series D funding round?
   c. Assuming that you own only the Series A preferred stock (and that each share of all series of preferred stock is convertible into one share of common stock), what percentage of the firm do you own after the last funding round?

6. Your robotic automation start-up, Kela Controls, has raised capital as follows:

Funding Round	Pre-Money	Post-Money
Series A	$8 million	$12 million
Series B	$25 million	$40 million
Series C	$100 million	$150 million

a. How much did Kela raise in each round?
b. Assuming no other securities were issued, what fraction of the firm's shares were held by common shareholders (founders and employees) after each round?
c. What is the distribution of ownership across each security after the Series C financing?
d. If the firm is ultimately sold for $500 million, what multiple of money did each series earn? What will founders and employees receive? (Assume all preferred shares convert to common.)

7. Beru.com recently raised $5 million with a pre-money value of $9 million. They are seeking to raise another $6 million. What is the largest fraction of the firm they can offer and avoid a down round?

***8.** BitBox has raised $10 million in a Series A round with $40 million post-money value and a 1.5x liquidation preference, and $25 million in a Series B round with a $75 million post-money value and a 3x liquidation preference plus seniority over Series A. What will Series A, Series B, and common shareholders receive if BitBox is sold for
a. $85 million?
b. $100 million?
c. $200 million?
d. $300 million?

The Initial Public Offering

9. What are the main advantages and disadvantages of going public?

10. Do underwriters face the most risk from a best-efforts IPO, a firm commitment IPO, or an auction IPO? Why?

11. Roundtree Software is going public using an auction IPO. The firm has received the following bids:

Price ($)	Number of Shares
14.00	100,000
13.80	200,000
13.60	500,000
13.40	1,000,000
13.20	1,200,000
13.00	800,000
12.80	400,000

Assuming Roundtree would like to sell 1.8 million shares in its IPO, what will the winning auction offer price be?

12. Three years ago, you founded Outdoor Recreation, Inc., a retailer specializing in the sale of equipment and clothing for recreational activities such as camping, skiing, and hiking. So far, your company has gone through three funding rounds:

Round	Date	Investor	Shares	Share Price ($)
Series A	Feb. 2009	You	500,000	1.00
Series B	Aug. 2010	Angels	1,000,000	2.00
Series C	Sept. 2011	Venture capital	2,000,000	3.50

Currently, it is 2012 and you need to raise additional capital to expand your business. You have decided to take your firm public through an IPO. You would like to issue an additional 6.5 million new shares through this IPO. Assuming that your firm successfully completes its IPO, you forecast that 2012 net income will be $7.5 million.

a. Your investment banker advises you that the prices of other recent IPOs have been set such that the P/E ratios based on 2012 forecasted earnings average 20.0. Assuming that your IPO is set at a price that implies a similar multiple, what will your IPO price per share be?
b. What percentage of the firm will you own after the IPO?

IPO Puzzles

13. What is IPO underpricing? If you decide to try to buy shares in every IPO, will you necessarily make money from the underpricing?

14. Margoles Publishing recently completed its IPO. The stock was offered at a price of $14 per share. On the first day of trading, the stock closed at $19 per share. What was the initial return on Margoles? Who benefited from this underpricing? Who lost, and why?

15. Chen Brothers, Inc., sold 4 million shares in its IPO, at a price of $18.50 per share. Management negotiated a fee (the underwriting spread) of 7% on this transaction. What was the dollar cost of this fee?

16. Your firm has 10 million shares outstanding, and you are about to issue 5 million new shares in an IPO. The IPO price has been set at $20 per share, and the underwriting spread is 7%. The IPO is a big success with investors, and the share price rises to $50 the first day of trading.

a. How much did your firm raise from the IPO?
b. What is the market value of the firm after the IPO?
c. Assume that the post-IPO value of your firm is its fair market value. Suppose your firm could have issued shares directly to investors at their fair market value, in a perfect market with no underwriting spread and no underpricing. What would the share price have been in this case, if you raise the same amount as in part (a)?
d. Comparing part (b) and part (c), what is the total cost to the firm's original investors due to market imperfections from the IPO?

17. You have an arrangement with your broker to request 1000 shares of all available IPOs. Suppose that 10% of the time, the IPO is "very successful" and appreciates by 100% on the first day, 80% of the time it is "successful" and appreciates by 10%, and 10% of the time it "fails" and falls by 15%.

a. By what amount does the average IPO appreciate the first day; that is, what is the average IPO underpricing?
b. Suppose you expect to receive 50 shares when the IPO is very successful, 200 shares when it is successful, and 1000 shares when it fails. Assume the average IPO price is $15. What is your expected one-day return on your IPO investments?

The Seasoned Equity Offering

18. On January 20, Metropolitan, Inc., sold 8 million shares of stock in an SEO. The current market price of Metropolitan at the time was $42.50 per share. Of the 8 million shares sold, 5 million shares were primary shares being sold by the company, and the remaining 3 million shares were being sold by the venture capital investors. Assume the underwriter charges 5% of the gross proceeds as an underwriting fee (which is shared proportionately between primary and secondary shares).

a. How much money did Metropolitan raise?

b. How much money did the venture capitalists receive?

19. What are the advantages to a company of selling stock in an SEO using a cash offer? What are the advantages of a rights offer?

20. MacKenzie Corporation currently has 10 million shares of stock outstanding at a price of $40 per share. The company would like to raise money and has announced a rights issue. Every existing shareholder will be sent one right per share of stock that he or she owns. The company plans to require five rights to purchase one share at a price of $40 per share.

a. Assuming the rights issue is successful, how much money will it raise?

b. What will the share price be after the rights issue? (Assume perfect capital markets.)

Suppose instead that the firm changes the plan so that *each* right gives the holder the right to purchase one share at $8 per share.

c. How much money will the new plan raise?

d. What will the share price be after the rights issue?

e. Which plan is better for the firm's shareholders? Which is more likely to raise the full amount of capital?

Data Case

Few IPOs have garnered as much attention as social media giant Facebook's public offering on May 18, 2012. It was the biggest IPO in Internet history, easily topping Google's initial public offering eight years earlier. Let's take a closer look at the IPO itself, as well as the payoffs to some of Facebook's early investors.

1. Begin by navigating to the SEC EDGAR Web site, which provides access to company filings: www.sec.gov/edgar.shtml. Choose "Search for Company Filings" and pick search by company name. Enter "Facebook" and then search for its IPO prospectus, which was filed on the date of the IPO and is listed as filing "424B4" (this acronym derives from the rule number requiring the firm to file a prospectus, Rule 424(b)(4)). From the prospectus, calculate the following information:

a. The underwriting spread in percentage terms. How does this spread compare to a typical IPO?

b. The fraction of the offering that comprised primary shares and the fraction that comprised secondary shares.

c. The size, in number of shares, of the greenshoe provision. What percent of the deal did the greenshoe provision represent?

2. Next, navigate to Google Finance and search for "Facebook." Determine the closing price of the stock on the day of the IPO (use the "Historical prices" link). What was the first day return? How does this return compare to the typical IPO?

3. Using the data provided by Google Finance, calculate the performance of Facebook in the three-month post-IPO period. That is, calculate the annualized return an investor would have received if he had invested in Facebook at the closing price on the IPO day and sold the stock three months later. What was the return for a one-year holding period?

4. Prior to the public offering, Facebook was able to raise capital from all the sources mentioned in the chapter. Let's concentrate on one particular source, Microsoft Corporation.

a. Microsoft made one investment in Facebook, during October 2007. Go to Facebook's corporate news Web site (newsroom.fb.com) and locate the press release announcing this investment. Using the information in that press release and the number of shares owned by Microsoft listed in the IPO prospectus, calculate the per share price Microsoft paid.

b. Calculate the return (expressed on an annual basis) Microsoft earned on its investment up to the IPO (using the IPO price).

c. How much money did Microsoft receive from the IPO (assuming it sold all its shares at the IPO price)?

5. Facebook had only one angel investor, Peter Thiel (one of the founders of PayPal). Mr. Thiel invested more than once in Facebook, both as an angel and, in later rounds, on behalf of investors in his venture capital firm, Founders Fund. As an angel, Mr. Thiel invested $500,000 in September 2004. Assuming that all the shares he received in the angel round were registered under the name Rivendell One LLC,[27] use the information in the prospectus to calculate:

a. The per share price he paid as an angel.

b. The annualized return (using the IPO price) he made on his investment.

c. The amount of angel money Mr. Thiel received from the proceeds of the IPO assuming he sold his entire stake at the IPO price, (that is, from his Rivendell investments alone).

Note: Updates to this data case may be found at www.berkdemarzo.com.

[27]How Mr. Thiel holds his investments in Facebook is private information, so there is no substantive basis on which to make this assumption. That said, Mr. Thiel is reported to be a fan of *The Lord of the Rings.*

CHAPTER

24

Debt Financing

NOTATION

YTC	yield to call on a callable bond
YTM	yield to maturity on a bond
PV	present value

IN THE MIDDLE OF 2005, FORD MOTOR COMPANY DECIDED TO put one of its subsidiaries, Hertz Corporation, up for competitive bid. On September 13, 2005, *The Wall Street Journal* reported that a group of private investors led by Clayton, Dubilier & Rice (CDR), a private equity firm, had reached a deal with Ford to purchase Hertz's outstanding equity for $5.6 billion. In addition, Hertz had $9.1 billion in existing debt that needed to be refinanced as part of the deal. CDR planned to finance the transaction in part by raising over $11 billion in new debt. Using this Hertz deal as an illustrative example, in this chapter, we examine how corporations use the debt markets to raise capital.

When companies raise capital by issuing debt, they have several potential sources from which to seek funds. To complete the Hertz purchase, the group led by CDR ended up relying on at least four different kinds of debt: domestic- and foreign-denominated high-yield bonds, bank loans, and asset-backed securities. In addition, each debt issue has its own specific terms, determined at the time of issue. We therefore begin our exploration of debt financing by explaining the process of issuing debt.

Corporations are not the only entities that use debt financing. Governments, municipalities, and other local entities as well as quasi-government entities (such as state-owned corporations) also use the debt markets to raise capital. Hence, the scope of this chapter is necessarily broader than that of Chapter 23. Here, we introduce all of the important types of debt that exist—not just corporate debt. Finally, we discuss some of the more advanced features of bonds such as call provisions and conversion options.

24.1 Corporate Debt

Recall from Chapter 23 our discussion of how private companies become public companies. The deal in which CDR bought Hertz is an example of the opposite transition—a public company becoming private, in this case through a leveraged buyout. Recall that in a leveraged buyout (LBO), a group of private investors purchases all the equity of a public corporation.[1] With a total value of $15.2 billion,[2] the leveraged buyout of Hertz was the second largest transaction of its kind at the time of its announcement (the largest LBO at the time was the $31.3 billion takeover of RJR-Nabisco in 1989). Taking a public corporation private in this way requires issuing large amounts of corporate debt. Table 24.1 shows the debt that was issued to finance the Hertz LBO. Using these debt issues as an example, let's begin by explaining how corporations issue debt.

TABLE 24.1 New Debt Issued as Part of the Hertz LBO

Type of Debt	Amount (in $ million)
Public debt	
Junk bond issues	2,668.9
Private debt	
Term loan	1,707.0
Asset-backed revolving line of credit	400.0
Asset-backed "fleet" debt	6,348.0
Total	**$11,123.9**

Public Debt

Corporate bonds are securities issued by corporations. They account for a significant amount of invested capital. As of mid-2015, the value of outstanding U.S. corporate bonds was about $8.1 trillion.

The Prospectus. A public bond issue is similar to a stock issue. A prospectus or offering memorandum must be produced that describes the details of the offering (see Figure 24.1). In addition, for public offerings, the prospectus must include an **indenture**, a formal contract between the bond issuer and a trust company. The trust company represents the bondholders and makes sure that the terms of the indenture are enforced. In the case of default, the trust company represents the bondholders' interests.

While corporate bonds almost always pay coupons semiannually, a few corporations (e.g., Coca-Cola) have issued zero-coupon bonds. Historically, corporate bonds have been issued with a wide range of maturities. Most corporate bonds have maturities of 30 years or less, although in the past there have been original maturities of up to 999 years.

[1]At the time of the deal, Hertz was a wholly owned subsidiary of Ford Motor Company, which itself is a public company. Prior to Ford's acquisition of Hertz's outstanding shares in 2001, Hertz was publicly traded.

[2]The total value includes $5.6 billion in equity, $9.1 billion in debt, and $0.5 billion in fees and expenses. In addition to $11.1 billion in new debt, the transaction was financed using $1.8 billion of Hertz's own cash and securities (including a $1.2 billion obligation from Ford, which was forgiven as part of the payment to Ford). The remaining $2.3 billion in private equity was contributed by Clayton, Dubilier & Rice; The Carlyle Group; and Merrill Lynch Global Private Equity.

FIGURE 24.1

Front Cover of the Offering Memorandum of the Hertz Junk Bond Issue

Source: Courtesy Hertz Corporation

OFFERING MEMORANDUM CONFIDENTIAL

Hertz®

CCMG Acquisition Corporation
to be merged with and into The Hertz Corporation
$1,800,000,000 8.875% Senior Notes due 2014
$600,000,000 10.5% Senior Subordinated Notes due 2016
€225,000,000 7.875% Senior Notes due 2014

The Company is offering $1,800,000,000 aggregate principal amount of its 8.875% Senior Notes due 2014 (the "Senior Dollar Notes"), $600,000,000 aggregate principal amount of its 10.5% Senior Subordinated Notes due 2016 (the "Senior Subordinated Notes" and, together with the Senior Dollar Notes, the "Dollar Notes"), and €225,000,000 aggregate principal amount of its 7.875% Senior Notes due 2014 (the "Senior Euro Notes"). The Senior Dollar Notes and the Senior Euro Notes are collectively referred to as the "Senior Notes," and the Dollar Notes and the Senior Euro Notes are collectively referred to as the "Notes."

The Senior Notes will mature on January 1, 2014 and the Senior Subordinated Notes will mature on January 1, 2016. Interest on the Notes will accrue from December 21, 2005. We will pay interest on the Notes on January 1 and July 1 of each year, commencing July 1, 2006.

We have the option to redeem all or a portion of the Senior Notes and the Senior Subordinated Notes at any time (1) before January 1, 2010 and January 1, 2011, respectively, at a redemption price equal to 100% of their principal amount plus the applicable make-whole premium set forth in this offering memorandum and (2) on or after January 1, 2010 and January 1, 2011, respectively, at the redemption prices set forth in this offering memorandum. In addition, on or before January 1, 2009, we may, on one or more occasions, apply funds equal to the proceeds from one or more equity offerings to redeem up to 35% of each series of Notes at the redemption prices set forth in this offering memorandum. If we undergo a change of control or sell certain of our assets, we may be required to offer to purchase Notes from holders.

The Senior Notes will be senior unsecured obligations and will rank equally with all of our senior unsecured indebtedness. The Senior Subordinated Notes will be unsecured obligations and subordinated in right of payment to all of our existing and future senior indebtedness. Each of our domestic subsidiaries that guarantees specified bank indebtedness will guarantee the Senior Notes with guarantees that will rank equally with all of the senior unsecured indebtedness of such subsidiaries and the Senior Subordinated Notes with guarantees that will be unsecured and subordinated in right of payment to all existing and future senior indebtedness of such subsidiaries.

We have agreed to make an offer to exchange the Notes for registered, publicly tradable notes that have substantially identical terms as the Notes. The Dollar Notes are expected to be eligible for trading in the Private Offering, Resale and Trading Automated Linkages (PORTAL℠) market. This offering memorandum includes additional information on the terms of the Notes, including redemption and repurchase prices, covenants and transfer restrictions.

Investing in the Notes involves a high degree of risk. See "Risk Factors" beginning on page 23.

We have not registered the Notes under the federal securities laws of the United States or the securities laws of any other jurisdiction. The Initial Purchasers named below are offering the Notes only to qualified institutional buyers under Rule 144A and to persons outside the United States under Regulation S. See "Notice to Investors" for additional information about eligible offerees and transfer restrictions.

Price for each series of Notes: 100%

We expect that (i) delivery of the Dollar Notes will be made to investors in book-entry form through the facilities of The Depository Trust Company on or about December 21, 2005 and (ii) delivery of the Senior Euro Notes will be made to investors in book-entry form through the facilities of the Euroclear System and Clearstream Banking, S.A. on or about December 21, 2005.

Joint Book-Running Managers

Deutsche Bank Securities **Lehman Brothers**

Merrill Lynch & Co. **Goldman, Sachs & Co.** **JPMorgan**

Co-Lead Managers

BNP PARIBAS **RBS Greenwich Capital** **Calyon**

The date of this offering memorandum is December 15, 2005.

In July 1993, for example, Walt Disney Company issued $150 million in bonds with a maturity of 100 years; these bonds soon became known as the "Sleeping Beauty" bonds.

The face value or principal amount of the bond is denominated in standard increments, most often $1000. The face value does not always correspond to the actual money raised because of underwriting fees and the possibility that the bond might not actually sell for its face value when it is offered for sale initially. If a coupon bond is issued at a discount, it is called an **original issue discount (OID)** bond.

Bearer Bonds and Registered Bonds. In a public offering, the indenture lays out the terms of the bond issue. Most corporate bonds are coupon bonds, and coupons are paid in one of two ways. Historically, most bonds were bearer bonds. **Bearer bonds** are like currency: Whoever physically holds the bond certificate owns the bond. To receive a coupon payment, the holder of a bearer bond must provide explicit proof of ownership. The holder does so by literally clipping a coupon off the bond certificate and remitting it to the paying agent. Anyone producing such a coupon is entitled to the payment—hence, the name "coupon" payment. Besides the obvious hassles associated with clipping coupons and mailing them in, there are serious security concerns with bearer bonds. Losing such a bond certificate is like losing currency.

Consequently, almost all bonds that are issued today are **registered bonds**. The issuer maintains a list of all holders of its bonds. Brokers keep issuers informed of any changes in ownership. On each coupon payment date, the bond issuer consults its list of registered owners and mails each owner a check (or directly deposits the coupon payment into the owner's brokerage account). This system also facilitates tax collection because the government can easily keep track of all interest payments made.

Types of Corporate Debt. Four types of corporate debt are typically issued: **notes**, **debentures**, **mortgage bonds**, and **asset-backed bonds** (see Table 24.2). Debentures and notes are **unsecured debt**, which means that in the event of a bankruptcy bondholders have a claim to only the assets of the firm that are not already pledged as collateral on other debt. Typically, notes have shorter maturities (less than 10 years) than debentures. Asset-backed bonds and mortgage bonds are **secured debt**: Specific assets are pledged as collateral that bondholders have a direct claim to in the event of bankruptcy. Mortgage bonds are secured by real property, whereas asset-backed bonds can be secured by any kind of asset. Although the word "bond" is commonly used to mean any kind of debt security, technically a corporate bond must be secured.

Let's illustrate these concepts by returning to the Hertz LBO. Recall that CDR intended to refinance approximately \$9 billion of existing Hertz corporate debt. So, subsequent to the agreement, Hertz made a tender offer—a public announcement of an offer to all existing bondholders to buy back its existing debt. This debt repurchase was financed by issuing several kinds of new debt (both secured and unsecured), all of which were claims on Hertz's corporate assets.

As part of the financing, CDR planned to issue \$2.7 billion worth of unsecured debt[3]—in this case, high-yield notes known as junk bonds (bonds rated below investment grade).[4] The high-yield issue was divided into three kinds of debt or **tranches** (see Table 24.3), all of

TABLE 24.2 Types of Corporate Debt

Secured	Unsecured
Mortgage bonds (secured with property)	Notes (original maturity less than 10 years)
Asset-backed bonds (secured with any asset)	Debentures

[3]In the end, the firm issued only \$2 billion in debt because fewer existing bondholders tendered their bonds than expected (\$1.6 billion of existing debt remained on the balance sheet after the LBO was completed).

[4]A description of corporate credit ratings can be found in Chapter 6 (see Table 6.4).

TABLE 24.3 Hertz's December 2005 Junk Bond Issues

	Senior Dollar-Denominated Note	Senior Euro-Denominated Note	Subordinated Dollar-Denominated Note
Face value	$1.8 billion	€225 million	$600 million
Maturity	December 1, 2014	December 1, 2014	December 1, 2016
Coupon	8.875%	7.875%	10.5%
Issue price	Par	Par	Par
Yield	8.875%	7.875%	10.5%
Call features	Up to 35% of the outstanding principal callable at 108.875% in the first three years.	Up to 35% of the outstanding principal callable at 107.875% in the first three years.	Up to 35% of the outstanding principal callable at 110.5% in the first three years.
	After four years, fully callable at:	After four years, fully callable at:	After five years, fully callable at:
	• 104.438% in 2010	• 103.938% in 2010	• 105.25% in 2011
	• 102.219% in 2011	• 101.969% in 2011	• 103.50% in 2012
	• Par thereafter	• Par thereafter	• 101.75% in 2013
			• Par thereafter
Settlement	December 21, 2005	December 21, 2005	December 21, 2005
Rating			
Standard & Poor's	B	B	B
Moody's	B1	B1	B3
Fitch	BB−	BB−	B+

which made semiannual coupon payments and were issued at par. The largest tranche was a $1.8 billion face-value note maturing in nine years. It paid a coupon of 8.875%, which at the time represented a 4.45% spread over Treasuries. A second tranche was denominated in euros, and the third tranche was junior to the other two and paid a coupon of 10.5%. The rest of the debt financing was made up of asset-backed debt that was sold privately, and bank loans.

Seniority. Recall that debentures and notes are unsecured. Because more than one debenture might be outstanding, the bondholder's priority in claiming assets in the event of default, known as the bond's **seniority**, is important. As a result, most debenture issues contain clauses restricting the company from issuing new debt with equal or higher priority than existing debt.

When a firm conducts a subsequent debenture issue that has lower priority than its outstanding debt, the new debt is known as a **subordinated debenture**. In the event of default, the assets not pledged as collateral for outstanding bonds cannot be used to pay off the holders of subordinated debentures until all more senior debt has been paid off. In Hertz's case, one tranche of the junk bond issue is a note that is subordinated to the other two tranches. In the event of bankruptcy, this note has a lower-priority claim on the firm's assets. Because holders of this tranche are likely to receive less in the event of a Hertz default, the yield on this debt is higher than that of the other tranches—10.5% compared to 8.875% for the first tranche.

Bond Markets. The remaining tranche of Hertz's junk bond issue is a note that is denominated in euros rather than U.S. dollars—it is an international bond. International bonds are classified into four broadly defined categories. **Domestic bonds** are bonds issued by a local entity and traded in a local market, but purchased by foreigners. They are denominated in the local currency. **Foreign bonds** are bonds issued by a foreign company in a local market and are intended for local investors. They are also denominated in the local currency. Foreign bonds in the United States are known as **Yankee bonds**. In other countries, foreign bonds also have special names. For example, in Japan they are called **Samurai bonds**; in the United Kingdom, they are known as **Bulldogs**.

Eurobonds are international bonds that are not denominated in the local currency of the country in which they are issued. Consequently, there is no connection between the physical location of the market on which they trade and the location of the issuing entity. They can be denominated in any number of currencies that might or might not be connected to the location of the issuer. The trading of these bonds is not subject to any particular nation's regulations. **Global bonds** combine the features of domestic, foreign, and Eurobonds, and are offered for sale in several different markets simultaneously. The Hertz junk bond issue is an example of a global bond issue: It was simultaneously offered for sale in the United States and Europe.

A bond that makes its payments in a foreign currency contains the risk of holding that currency and, therefore, is priced off the yields of similar bonds in that currency. Hence, the euro-denominated note of the Hertz junk bond issue has a different yield from the dollar-denominated note, even though both bonds have the same seniority and maturity. While they have the same default risk, they differ in their exchange rate risk—the risk that the foreign currency will depreciate in value relative to the local currency.

Private Debt

In addition to the junk bond issue, Hertz took out more than $2 billion in bank loans. Bank loans are an example of **private debt**, debt that is not publicly traded. The private debt market is larger than the public debt market. Private debt has the advantage that it avoids the cost of registration but has the disadvantage of being illiquid.

There are two segments of the private debt market: term loans and private placements.

Term Loans. Hertz negotiated a $1.7 billion **term loan**, a bank loan that lasts for a specific term. The term of the Hertz loan was seven years. This particular loan is an example of a **syndicated bank loan**: a single loan that is funded by a group of banks rather than just a single bank. Usually, one member of the syndicate (the lead bank) negotiates the terms of the bank loan. In the Hertz case, Deutsche Bank AG negotiated the loan with CDR and then sold portions of it off to other banks—mostly smaller regional banks that had excess cash but lacked the resources to negotiate a loan of this magnitude by themselves.

Most syndicated loans are rated as investment grade. However, Hertz's term loan is an exception. Term loans such as Hertz's that are associated with LBOs are known as leveraged syndicated loans and are rated as speculative grade; in Hertz's case, Standard and Poor's rated the term loan as BB and Moody's rated it as Ba2.

In addition to the term loan, Dow Jones reported that Hertz negotiated an asset-backed revolving line of credit. A **revolving line of credit** is a credit commitment for a specific time period up to some limit (five years and $1.6 billion in Hertz's case), which a company can use as needed. Hertz's initial draw on the line of credit was $400 million. Because the line of credit is backed by specific assets, it is more secure than the term loan, so Standard and Poor's gave it a BB+ rating.

Private Placements. A **private placement** is a bond issue that does not trade on a public market but rather is sold to a small group of investors. Because a private placement does not need to be registered, it is less costly to issue. Instead of an indenture, often a simple promissory note is sufficient. Privately placed debt also need not conform to the same standards as public debt; as a consequence, it can be tailored to the particular situation.

Returning to the Hertz deal, CDR privately placed an additional $4.2 billion of U.S. asset-backed securities and $2.1 billion of international asset-backed securities. In this case, the assets backing the debt were the fleet of rental cars Hertz owned; hence, this debt was termed "Fleet Debt" in the offering memorandum.

In 1990, the U.S. Securities and Exchange Commission (SEC) issued Rule 144A, which significantly increased the liquidity of certain privately placed debt. Private debt issued under this rule can be traded by large financial institutions among themselves. The rule was motivated by a desire to increase the access of foreign corporations to U.S. debt markets. Bonds that are issued under this rule are nominally private debt, but because they are tradable between financial institutions they are only slightly less liquid than public debt. In fact, the $2.8 billion Hertz junk bond issue in Table 24.3 is actually debt issued under Rule 144A (which explains why the offering document in Figure 24.1 is called an "offering memorandum" rather than a "prospectus," because the latter term is reserved for public offerings). As part of the offering, however, the issuers agreed to publicly register the bonds within 390 days.[5] Because the debt was marketed and sold with the understanding that it would become public debt, we classified that issue as public debt.

CONCEPT CHECK

1. List four types of corporate debt that are typically issued.
2. What are the four categories of international bonds?

24.2 Other Types of Debt

Corporations are not the only entities that use debt. We begin with the largest debt sector—loans to government entities.

Sovereign Debt

Recall from Chapter 6 that **sovereign debt** is debt issued by national governments. Recall too that bonds issued by the U.S. government are called Treasury securities. Treasury securities represent the single largest sector of the U.S. bond market. On June 30, 2015, the market value of outstanding Treasury securities was $12.70 trillion. These bonds enable the U.S. government to borrow money so that it can engage in deficit spending (that is, spending more than what is received in tax revenues).

The U.S. Treasury issues four kinds of securities (see Table 24.4). Treasury bills are pure discount bonds with maturities ranging from a few days to one year. Currently,

TABLE 24.4 Existing U.S. Treasury Securities

Treasury Security	Type	Original Maturity
Bills	Discount	4, 13, 26, and 52 weeks
Notes	Coupon	2, 3, 5, 7, and 10 years
Bonds	Coupon	30 years
Inflation indexed	Coupon	5, 10, and 30 years

[5] If Hertz failed to fulfill this commitment, the interest rate on all the outstanding bonds would increase by 0.5%.

the Treasury issues bills with original maturities of 4, 13, 26, and 52 weeks. Treasury notes are semiannual coupon bonds with original maturities of between 1 and 10 years. The Treasury issues notes with maturities of 2, 3, 5, 7, and 10 years at the present time. Treasury bonds are semiannual coupon bonds with maturities longer than 10 years. The Treasury currently issues bonds with maturities of 30 years (often called **long bonds**). All of these Treasury securities trade in the bond market.

The last type of security that the U.S. Treasury is currently issuing is inflation-indexed bonds called **TIPS** (Treasury Inflation-Protected Securities) with maturities of 5, 10, and 30 years. These bonds are standard coupon bonds with one difference: The outstanding principal is adjusted for inflation. Thus, although the coupon *rate* is fixed, the dollar coupon varies because the semiannual coupon payments are a fixed rate of the inflation-adjusted principal. In addition, the final repayment of principal at maturity (but not the interest payments) is protected against deflation. That is, if the final inflation-adjusted principal amount is less than the original principal amount, the original principal amount is repaid.

EXAMPLE 24.1 Coupon Payments on Inflation-Indexed Bonds

Problem

On January 15, 2008, the U.S. Treasury issued a 10-year inflation-indexed note with a coupon of 1⅝%. On the date of issue, the consumer price index (CPI) was 209.49645. On January 15, 2015, the CPI had increased to 236.85403. What coupon payment was made on January 15, 2015?

Solution

Between the issue date and January 15, 2015, the CPI appreciated by 226.33474/184.77419 = 1.13059. Consequently, the principal amount of the bond increased by this amount; that is, the original face value of \$1000 increased to \$1130.59. Because the bond pays semiannual coupons, the coupon payment was $\$1130.59 \times 0.01625/2 = \$9.19$

Treasury securities are initially sold to the public by auction. Two kinds of bids are allowed: competitive bids and noncompetitive bids. Noncompetitive bidders (usually individuals) just submit the amount of bonds they wish to purchase and are guaranteed to have their orders filled at the auction. All competitive bidders submit sealed bids in terms of yields and the amount of bonds they are willing to purchase. The Treasury then accepts the lowest-yield (highest-price) competitive bids up to the amount required to fund the deal. The highest yield accepted is termed the **stop-out yield**. All successful bidders (including the noncompetitive bidders) are awarded this yield. In the case of a Treasury bill offering, the stop-out yield is used to set the price of the bill and all bidders then pay this price. In the case of a Treasury note or Treasury bond offering, this yield determines the coupon of the bond and then all bidders pay the par value for the bond or note.[6] All income from Treasury securities is taxable at the federal level. This income, however, is not taxable at the state or local level.[7]

Zero-coupon Treasury securities with maturities longer than one year also trade in the bond market. They are called **STRIPS** (Separate Trading of Registered Interest and Principal Securities). The Treasury itself does not issue STRIPS. Instead, investors (or, more

[6]Because coupons are specified in eighths, if the winning yield is not divisible by eight, the coupon is set at the rate that produces a price closest to, but not over, par.

[7]For more details, see the U.S. Treasury Web site: www.treasurydirect.gov/.

commonly, investment banks) purchase Treasury notes and bonds and then resell each coupon and principal payment separately as a zero-coupon bond.

Municipal Bonds

Municipal bonds ("munis") are issued by state and local governments. Their distinguishing characteristic is that the income on municipal bonds is not taxable at the federal level. Consequently, municipal bonds are sometimes also referred to as tax-exempt bonds. Some issues are also exempt from state and local taxes.

Most municipal bonds pay semiannual coupons. A single issue will often contain a number of different maturity dates. Such issues are often called **serial bonds** because the bonds are scheduled to mature serially over a number of years. The coupons on municipal bonds can be either *fixed* or *floating*. A fixed-coupon bond has the same coupon over the life of the bond. In a floating-rate issue, the coupon of the bond is adjusted periodically. The reset formula is a spread over a reference rate like the rate on Treasury bills that is established when the bond is first issued. There are also a few zero-coupon municipal bond issues.

Municipal bonds can differ in terms of the source of funds that guarantee them. **Revenue bonds** pledge specific revenues generated by projects that were initially financed by the bond issue. For example, the State of Nevada issued revenue bonds to finance the Las Vegas Monorail, to be repaid from fare revenues. Bonds backed by the full faith and credit of a local government are known as **general obligation bonds**. Sometimes local governments strengthen the commitment further by tying the promise to a particular revenue source, such as a special fee. Because a local government can always use its general revenue to repay such bonds, this commitment is over and above the usual commitment, so these bonds are called **double-barreled**. Despite these protections, municipal bonds are not nearly as secure as bonds backed by the federal government. Since 1970, about 4% of municipal bonds have defaulted, with the frequency and magnitude of default increasing in the aftermath of the 2008 financial crisis (including the aforementioned Las Vegas Monorail bonds).[8] The largest municipal bond defaults in U.S. history were Detroit's default in 2013 on over $7 billion in debt, soon surpassed by Puerto Rico's 2016 default on as much as $72 billion in debt.

Detroit's Art Museum at Risk

In July 2013, the city of Detroit filed for Chapter 9 bankruptcy protection, making history as the largest-ever municipal default. The city emerged from bankruptcy 15 months later, defaulting on $7 billion of its debt and cutting pension payments by 4.5%. But the cuts might have been worse, had not the city effectively "sold" its art museum.

The trouble for the city's art museum began prior to the bankruptcy filing when Kevyn Orr was appointed as an emergency manager of the city and demanded that the art museum sell $500 million of its art to help pay off city debts. The museum responded by raising $800 million from donors and using the money to buy its independence from the city. Following the bankruptcy, the ownership of the art museum transferred from the city to an independent trust.

Compared to a corporate bankruptcy, which allows the debtors to claim all the assets of the corporation, the ability of the debtors to claim assets in a municipal bankruptcy is very limited. Although the museum did ultimately contribute to the bankruptcy settlement, the amount of the contribution was far less than the $4.6 billion appraised value of its art. Similarly, although the pensioners did take cuts, the assets that backed their pensions were left intact in the pension plans and were not used to pay off debt holders. In the end, the debt holders took losses even when city assets existed, that if liquidated, could have covered some, if not all, of those losses.

Source: Slate 11/7/2014 "Detroit Exits Bankruptcy, Thanks to Its Art Museum" and *New York Times*, 11/7/2014, "'Grand Bargain' Saves the Detroit Institute of Arts."

[8]M. Walsh, "Muni Bonds Not as Safe as Thought," *The New York Times*, August 15, 2012.

Asset-Backed Securities

An **asset-backed security (ABS)** is a security that is made up of other financial securities; that is, the security's cash flows come from the cash flows of the underlying financial securities that "back" it. We refer to the process of creating an asset-backed security—packaging a portfolio of financial securities and issuing an asset-backed security backed by this portfolio—as **asset securitization.**

By far, the largest sector of the asset-backed security market is the *mortgage-backed security* market. A **mortgage-backed security (MBS)** is an asset-backed security backed by home mortgages. U.S. government agencies and sponsored enterprises, such as The Government National Mortgage Association (GNMA, or "Ginnie Mae") are the largest issuers

GLOBAL FINANCIAL CRISIS — CDOs, Subprime Mortgages, and the Financial Crisis

GNMA and the other government agencies that issue mortgage-backed securities restrict the type of mortgages that they are prepared to securitize. For example, they will only securitize mortgages below a certain face value and, more importantly, that meet certain credit criteria. Mortgages that do not satisfy these criteria and have a high default probability are known as **subprime mortgages**. Part of the housing boom in the mid-2000s can be attributed to the increased availability of subprime mortgages. As the number of subprime mortgages exploded so, too, did the incentives to securitize them. Private institutions, such as banks, issued large amounts of mortgage-backed securities backed by subprime mortgages.

To understand the origins of the crisis, it is helpful to understand how subprime loans were securitized. Banks originating these loans first combined them into large **asset pools.** The cash flows from these mortgage-backed security pools were then used to back promises to different tranches of securities, distinguished by their seniority, known as **collateralized mortgage obligations (CMOs)**. By first pooling and diversifying the mortgages, and then tranching them into senior and subordinated securities, it is possible to create senior securities that have much lower risk than the underlying mortgages themselves. For example, consider a security with a senior claim to any principal repayments, for up to one half of the total principal outstanding. This security would be impaired only if more than 50% of the mortgages in the pool defaulted.

The figure below illustrates this idea, showing the flow of mortgage cash flows, first into MBS pools, and then into buckets representing the CMO security tranches. The buckets that are first in line are very likely to be filled. These senior tranches received AAA ratings and were attractive to investors because of their high yields given their perceived safety. Of course, as we move further down, the later buckets face a much higher

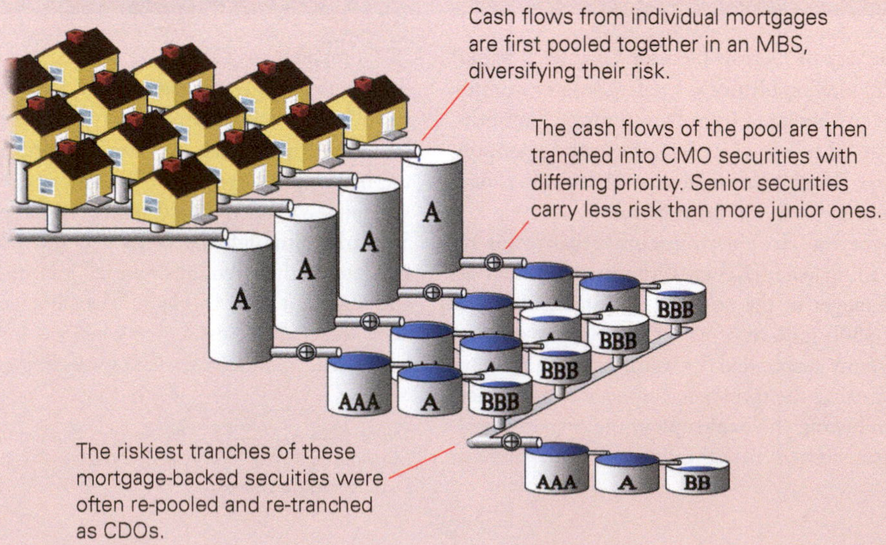

in this sector. When homeowners in the underlying mortgages make their mortgage payments, this cash is passed through (minus servicing fees) to the holders of the mortgage-backed security. The cash flows of mortgage-backed securities therefore mirror the cash flows of home mortgages.

In the case of GNMA-issued mortgage-backed securities, the U.S. government provides an explicit guarantee to investors against default risk. This guarantee does not mean that these securities are risk-free, however. As discussed in Chapter 22, a mortgage borrower always has an option to repay some or all of the mortgage loan early (often because the borrower moves or refinances), and this early repayment of principal is passed through to owners of mortgage-backed securities. Thus, holders of mortgage-backed securities face **prepayment risk**—the risk that the bond will be partially (or wholly) repaid earlier than expected.

risk of not filling completely. The most junior tranches had low ratings (or were even unrated), and were much riskier than the original pools (if even one mortgage in the entire pool defaulted, these securities would be affected). As a result, these junior tranches appealed only to very sophisticated investors with an appetite for, and an ability to assess, their risk.

As the subprime market grew, finding investors willing to hold the junior tranches became more problematic. To resolve this problem, investment banks created pools of these junior securities, which they then tranched into a new series of senior and junior securities (CDOs). By the same reasoning as before, the senior tranches of these new CDOs were perceived to be very low risk and received AAA ratings, making them easy to sell to a wide range of investors. (Note also that, due to diversification, the CDO securities can have a higher average rating than the individual assets backing them.)

What went wrong? From 2002 through 2005, default rates on subprime mortgages were quite low, dropping to below 6%. As a result, ratings agencies relaxed their requirements and increased the size of the tranches that received AAA ratings. However, these low default rates occurred because house prices were rising, making it easy for subprime borrowers to refinance their loans and avoid default. Once the housing market slowed and began to decline in 2006–2007, refinancing was no longer possible (as banks would not lend more than the house was worth), and the default rate skyrocketed to over 40%.

The increased default rate had two important consequences. First, the original mortgage-backed securities turned out to be riskier than anticipated: Securities that were protected against default rates in excess of 20%, which seemed extremely safe in 2005, began to experience losses. But the damage was even more dramatic in the CDO securities that were created from the junior mortgage-backed securities. The safety of the senior tranches of these CDOs relied on diversification—if no more than 20% of the junior mortgage-backed securities defaulted, these securities would be fully repaid. But the unexpectedly pervasive nature of the housing crisis meant that almost *all* of the securities that were backing these CDOs were running dry. As a result, many of the most senior, AAA-rated, CDO tranches were virtually wiped out, with their values declining to pennies on the dollar. This outcome was an extreme shock for the many investors who held them believing they were safe investments.

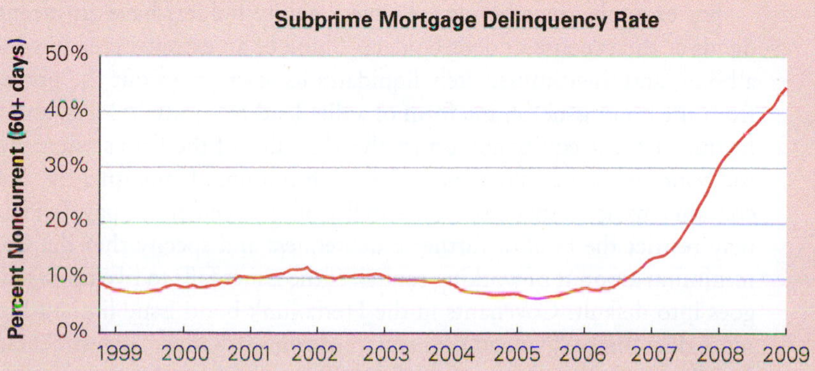

Other government-sponsored enterprises issuing mortgage-backed securities are the Federal National Mortgage Association (FNMA or "Fannie Mae") and the Federal Home Loan Mortgage Corporation (FHLMC or "Freddie Mac"). The Student Loan Marketing Association ("Sallie Mae") issues asset-backed securities backed by student loans. While, unlike Ginnie Mae, these enterprises are not explicitly backed by the full faith and credit of the U.S. government, most investors doubt that the government would allow any of its agencies to default and so believe these issues contain an implicit guarantee. In September 2008, this confidence was borne out when both Fannie Mae and Freddie Mac, which were both on the brink of failure, were placed into conservatorship of the Federal Housing Finance Agency, effectively bailing them out. On June 16, 2010, Fannie Mae's and Freddie Mac's stocks were delisted from the NYSE.

Private organizations, such as banks, also issue asset-backed securities. These securities can be backed by home mortgages (typically loans that do not meet the criteria to be included in the asset-backed securities issued by the government agencies) or other kinds of consumer loans such as automobile loans and credit card receivables. In addition, private asset-backed securities can be backed by other asset-backed securities. When banks re-securitize asset-backed and other fixed income securities, the new asset-backed security is known as a **collateralized debt obligation (CDO)**. CDO cash flows are usually divided into different tranches that are assigned different priorities. For example, investors in the junior tranche of an asset-backed security do not receive any cash flows until investors in the senior tranche have received their promised cash flows. Because of this prioritization, different CDO securities can have very different risk characteristics from each other, and from the underlying assets themselves (see the box on pages 874 and 875).

CONCEPT CHECK

1. List four different kinds of securities issued by the U.S. Treasury.
2. What is the distinguishing characteristic of municipal bonds?
3. What is an asset-backed security?

24.3 Bond Covenants

Covenants are restrictive clauses in a bond contract that limit the issuer from taking actions that may undercut its ability to repay the bonds. One might guess that such covenants would not be necessary—after all, why would managers voluntarily take actions that increase the firm's default risk? However, recall from Chapter 16 that when a firm is levered, managers may have an incentive to take actions that benefit equity holders at the expense of debt holders.

For example, once bonds are issued, equity holders have an incentive to increase dividends at the expense of debt holders. Think of an extreme case in which a company issues a bond, and then immediately liquidates its assets, pays out the proceeds (including those from the bond issue) in the form of a dividend to equity holders, and declares bankruptcy. In this case, the equity holders receive the value of the firm's assets plus the proceeds from the bond, while bondholders are left with nothing. Consequently, bond agreements often contain covenants that restrict the ability of management to pay dividends. Other covenants may restrict the level of further indebtedness and specify that the issuer must maintain a minimum amount of working capital. If the issuer fails to live up to any covenant, the bond goes into default. Covenants in the Hertz junk bond issue limited Hertz's ability to incur more debt, make dividend payments, redeem stock, make investments, create liens, transfer or sell assets, and merge or consolidate. They also included a requirement to offer to repurchase the bonds at 101% of face value if the corporation experiences a change in control.

Recall that CDR made a tender offer to repurchase all of Hertz's outstanding debt. CDR made this offer because the outstanding debt had a restrictive covenant that made it difficult to complete a merger or takeover of Hertz. Once the group led by CDR owned more that 50% of this debt, the terms of the prospectus gave CDR the ability to unilaterally change any covenant, thus allowing them to proceed with the LBO.

You might expect that equity holders would try to include as few covenants as possible in a bond agreement. In fact, this is not necessarily the case. The stronger the covenants in the bond contract, the less likely the issuer will default on the bond, and so the lower the interest rate required by investors who buy the bond. That is, by including more covenants, issuers can reduce their costs of borrowing. As discussed in Chapter 16, if the covenants are designed to reduce agency costs by restricting management's ability to take negative NPV actions that exploit debt holders, then the reduction in the firm's borrowing cost can more than outweigh the cost of the loss of flexibility associated with covenants.

CONCEPT CHECK

1. What happens if an issuer fails to live up to a bond covenant?
2. Why can bond covenants reduce a firm's borrowing cost?

24.4 Repayment Provisions

A bond issuer repays its bonds by making coupon and principal payments as specified in the bond contract. However, this is not the only way an issuer can repay bonds. For example, the issuer can repurchase a fraction of the outstanding bonds in the market, or it can make a tender offer for the entire issue, as Hertz did on its existing bonds. Another way issuers repay bonds is to exercise a *call* provision that allows the issuer to repurchase the bonds at a predetermined price. Bonds that contain such a provision are known as **callable bonds**.

Call Provisions

Hertz's junk bonds are examples of callable bonds. Table 24.3 lists the call features in each tranche. A call feature allows the issuer of the bond the right (but not the obligation) to retire all outstanding bonds on (or after) a specific date (the **call date**), for the **call price**. The call price is generally set at or above, and expressed as a percentage of, the bond's face value. In Hertz's case, the call dates of the two senior tranches are at the end of the fourth year. For the duration of 2010, the $1.8 billion issue could be called at price of 104.438% of the face value of the bond. In the following years, the call price declined until in 2012 the bond could be called at par. The euro-denominated bond has similar terms at slightly different call prices. The subordinated tranche's call date is a year later and has a different call price structure.

The Hertz bonds could also be partially called in the first three years. Hertz had the option to retire up to 35% of the outstanding principal at the call prices listed in Table 24.3, as long as the funds needed to repurchase the bonds were derived from the proceeds of an equity issuance.

To understand how call provisions affect the price of a bond, we first need to consider when an issuer will exercise its right to call the bond. An issuer can always retire one of its bonds early by repurchasing the bond in the open market. If the call provision offers a cheaper way to retire the bonds, however, the issuer will forgo the option of purchasing the bonds in the open market and call the bonds instead.

Let's examine a more concrete example. Consider a case in which an issuer has issued two bonds that are identical in every respect except that one is callable at par (redeemable at face value) and the other is not callable. This issuer wants to retire one of the two bonds. How does it decide which bond to retire? If bond yields have dropped since the issue date, the non-callable bond will be trading at a premium. Thus, if the issuer wished to retire this bond (by repurchasing it in the open market), it would have to repay more than the outstanding principal. If it chose to call the callable bond instead, the issuer would simply pay the outstanding principal. Hence, if yields have dropped, it is cheaper to retire the callable bond. In other words, by exercising the call on the callable bond and then immediately refinancing, the issuer can lower its borrowing costs. Conversely, if yields have increased after the issue date, there is no reason to refinance. Both bonds would be trading at a discount. Even if the issuer wished to retire some bonds, it would be better off by repurchasing either bond at less than par in the market than by calling the callable bond for par. Thus, when yields have risen, the issuer will not choose to exercise the call on the callable bond.

Let's consider this scenario from the perspective of a bondholder. As we have seen, the issuer will exercise the call option only when the coupon rate of the bond exceeds the prevailing market rate. Therefore, the only time the call is exercised, the bondholder finds herself in the position of looking for an alternative investment when market rates are lower than the bond's coupon rate. That is, the holder of a callable bond faces reinvestment risk precisely when it hurts: when market rates are lower than the coupon rate she is currently receiving. This makes the callable bond relatively less attractive to the bondholder than the identical non-callable bond. Consequently, a callable bond will trade at a lower price (and therefore a higher yield) than an otherwise equivalent non-callable bond.

Let's take a concrete example—a bond that is callable at par on only one specific date. Figure 24.2 plots the price of a callable bond and an otherwise identical non-callable bond on the call date as a function of the yield on the non-callable bond. When the yield of the non-callable bond is less than the coupon, the callable bond will be called, so its price is \$100. If this yield is greater than the coupon, then the callable bond will not be called, so it has the same price as the non-callable bond. Note that the callable bond price is capped at

FIGURE 24.2

Prices of Callable and Non-Callable Bonds on the Call Date

This figure shows the prices of a callable bond (gold line) and an otherwise identical non-callable bond (blue line) on the call date as a function of the yield on the non-callable bond. Both bonds have a 5% coupon rate. (The callable bond is assumed to be callable at par on one date only.)

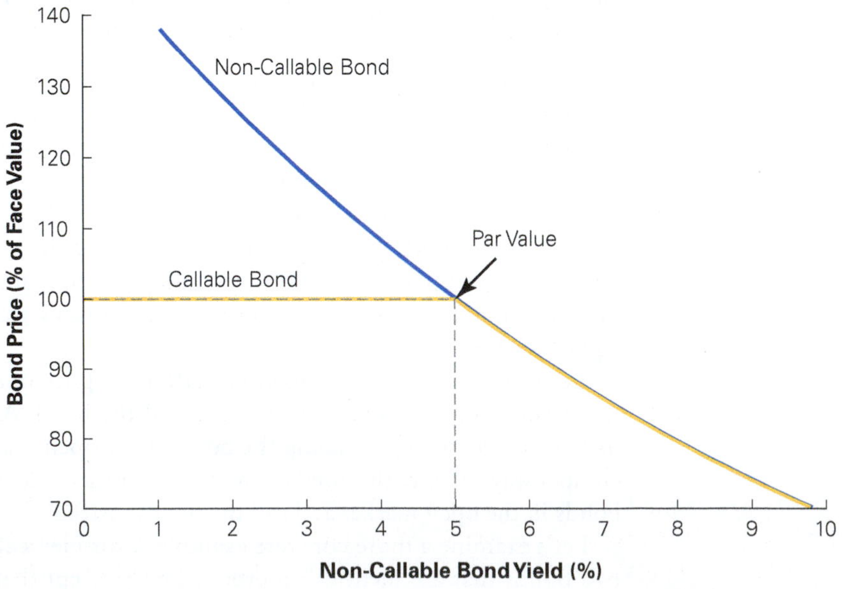

FIGURE 24.3

Prices of Callable and Non-Callable Bonds Prior to the Call Date

When non-callable bond yields are high relative to the callable bond coupon, investors anticipate that the likelihood of exercising the call is low and the callable bond price is similar to that of an otherwise identical non-callable bond. When market yields are low relative to the bond coupon, investors anticipate that the bond will likely be called, so its price is close to the price of a non-callable bond that matures on the call date.

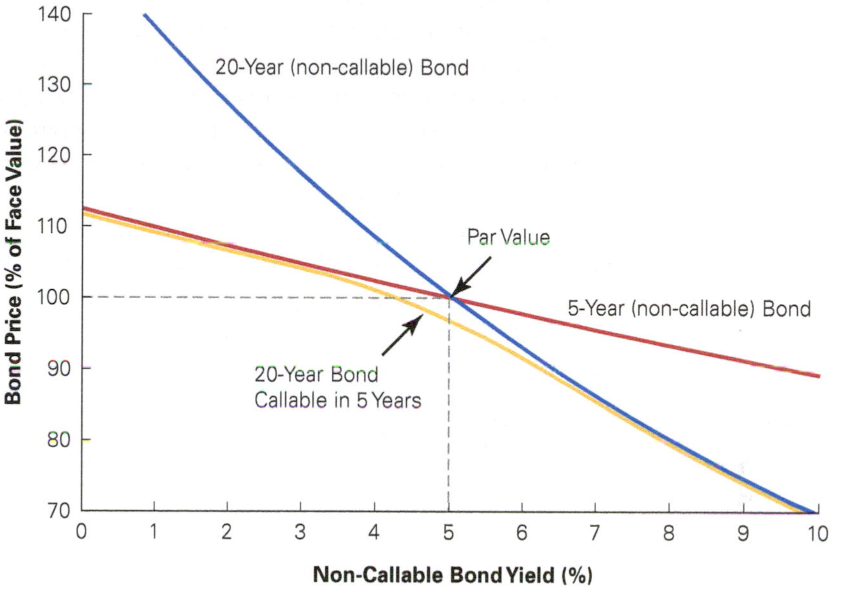

par: The price can be low when yields are high, but does not rise above the par value when the yield is low.

Before the call date, investors anticipate the optimal strategy that the issuer will follow, and the bond price reflects this strategy, as Figure 24.3 illustrates. When market yields are high relative to the bond coupon, investors anticipate that the likelihood of exercising the call is low and the bond price is similar to an otherwise identical non-callable bond. On the other hand, when market yields are low relative to the bond coupon, investors anticipate that the bond will likely be called, so its price is close to the price of a non-callable bond that matures on the call date. Because the issuer holds the option of whether to call the bond, the callable bond's price is always below that of the non-callable bonds.

New York City Calls Its Municipal Bonds

In November 2004, New York City announced plans to call \$430 million of its municipal bonds. New York City was an AAA-rated borrower, and these bonds paid relatively high interest rates of 6% to 8%. The city would be refinancing the bonds with new bonds that paid interest rates between 3% and 5%. In total, New York City called 63 individual bond issues with original maturities between 2012 and 2019.

Investors were attracted to the older municipal bonds because of their higher yields. Despite these yields, they did not expect New York City to call these bonds, so the market price for these bonds earlier in the year was 10% to 20% higher than their face value. When New York City announced its plans to call the bonds at prices slightly higher than the face value investors were caught off guard and the market value of the bonds fell accordingly. Investors suffered losses of 15% or more on their AAA-rated investment.

Investors did not expect New York City to call these bonds because it had already refinanced the debt in the early 1990s. According to Internal Revenue Service rules, the city could not refinance again with another tax-exempt issue. However, New York City surprised the market when it decided to refinance the bonds by issuing taxable bonds instead. Although it happens rarely, this example illustrates that investors are sometimes surprised by issuer call strategies.

The yield to maturity of a callable bond is calculated as if the bond were not callable. That is, the yield is still defined as the discount rate that sets the present value of the promised payments equal to the current price, *ignoring* the call feature. We can think of the yield of a callable bond as the interest rate the bondholder receives if the bond is not called and repaid in full. Because the price of a callable bond is lower than the price of an otherwise identical non-callable bond, the yield to maturity of a callable bond will be higher than the yield to maturity for its non-callable counterpart.

The assumption that underlies the yield calculation of a callable bond—that it will not be called—is not always realistic, so bond traders often quote the *yield to call.* The **yield to call (YTC)** is the annual yield of a callable bond assuming that the bond is called at the earliest opportunity. Again, because the issuer has the option not to call the bond on its call date, its yield to call will be higher than an identical non-callable bond that matures on the call date.

EXAMPLE 24.2 Calculating the Yield to Call

Problem

IBM has just issued a callable (at par) five-year, 8% coupon bond with annual coupon payments. The bond can be called at par in one year or anytime thereafter on a coupon payment date. It has a price of $103 per $100 face value. What is the bond's yield to maturity and yield to call?

Solution

The timeline of the promised payments for this bond (if it is not called) is

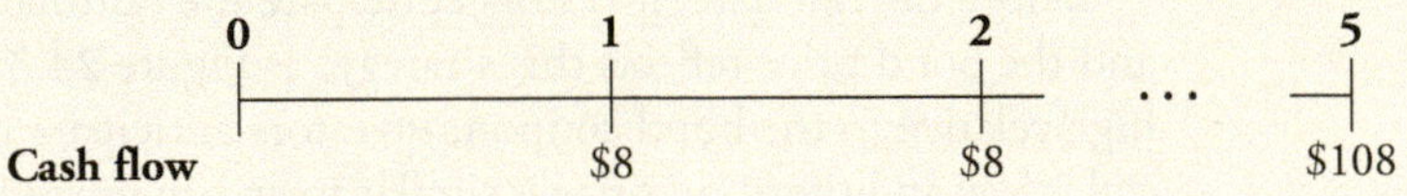

Setting the present value of the payments equal to the current price gives

$$103 = \frac{8}{(YTM)}\left(1 - \frac{1}{(1 + YTM)^5}\right) + \frac{100}{(1 + YTM)^5}$$

Solving for YTM (using the annuity spreadsheet) gives the bond's yield to maturity:

	NPER	RATE	PV	PMT	FV	Excel Formula
Given	5		−103	8	100	
Solve for Rate		7.26%				=RATE(5,8,−103,100)

The bond has a yield to maturity of 7.26%.

The timeline of the payments if the bond is called at the first available opportunity is

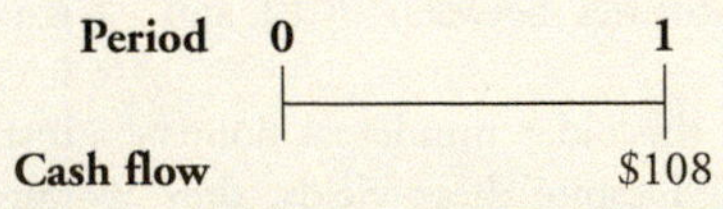

Setting the present value of these payments equal to the current price gives

$$103 = \frac{108}{(1 + YTC)}$$

Solving for YTC gives the yield to call:

$$YTC = \frac{108}{103} - 1 = 4.85\%$$

The annuity spreadsheet can be used to derive the same result:

	NPER	RATE	PV	PMT	FV	Excel Formula
Given	1		−103	8	100	
Solve for Rate		**4.85%**				=RATE(1,8,−103,100)

Sinking Funds

Another way bonds are repaid is through a **sinking fund**. Instead of repaying the entire principal balance on the maturity date, the company makes regular payments into a sinking fund administered by a trustee over the life of the bond. These payments are then used to repurchase bonds. In this way, the company can reduce the amount of outstanding debt without affecting the cash flows of the remaining bonds.

How does the trustee decide which bonds to repurchase? If the bonds are trading below their face value, the company simply repurchases the bonds in the market. But if a bond is trading above its face value, because the bonds are repurchased at par the decision is made by lottery.

Sinking fund provisions usually specify a minimum rate at which the issuer must contribute to the fund. In some cases, the issuer has the option to accelerate these payments. Because the sinking fund allows the issuer to repurchase the bonds at par, the option to accelerate the payments is another form of call provision.

The manner in which an outstanding balance is paid off using a sinking fund depends on the issue. Some issues specify equal payments over the life of the bond, ultimately retiring the issue on the maturity date of the bond. In other cases, the sinking fund payments are not sufficient to retire the entire issue and the company must make a large payment on the maturity date, known as a **balloon payment**. Often, sinking fund payments start only a few years after the bond issue. Bonds can be issued with both a sinking fund and call provision.

Convertible Provisions

Another way bonds are retired is by converting them into equity. Some corporate bonds have a provision that gives the bondholder an option to convert each bond owned into a fixed number of shares of common stock at a ratio called the **conversion ratio**. Such bonds are called **convertible bonds**. The provision usually gives bondholders the right to convert the bond into stock at any time up to the maturity date for the bond.[9]

To understand how a conversion feature changes the value of a bond, note that this provision gives a call option to the holder of a bond. Thus, a convertible bond can be thought of as a regular bond plus a special type of call option called a **warrant**. A warrant is a call option written by the company itself on *new* stock (whereas a regular call option is written on existing stock). That is, when a holder of a warrant exercises it and thereby

[9]Some convertible bonds do not allow conversion for a specified amount of time after the issue date.

purchases stock, the company delivers this stock by issuing new stock. In all other respects, a warrant is identical to a call option.[10]

On the maturity date of the bond, the strike price of the embedded warrant in a convertible bond is equal to the face value of the bond divided by the conversion ratio—that is, the **conversion price**. So, on the maturity date of a convertible bond with a $1000 face value and a conversion ratio of 15, if you converted the bond into stock, you would receive 15 shares. If you did not convert, you would receive $1000. Hence, by converting, you essentially "paid" $1000 for 15 shares, implying a price per share of 1000/15 = $66.67. If the price of the stock exceeds $66.67, you would choose to convert; otherwise, you would take the cash. At maturity, you will choose to convert whenever the stock price exceeds the conversion price. As shown in Figure 24.4, the value of the bond is the maximum of its face value ($1000) and the value of 15 shares of stock.

What about prior to the maturity date? If the stock does not pay a dividend, then we know from our discussion of call options in Chapter 20 that it is never optimal to exercise a call early. Hence, the holder of a convertible bond should wait until the maturity date of the bond before deciding whether to convert. The value of the bond prior to maturity is plotted in Figure 24.4. If the stock price is low so that the embedded warrant is deep out-of-the-money, the conversion provision is not worth much and the bond's value is close to the value of a straight bond—an otherwise identical bond without the conversion provision. When the stock price is high and the embedded warrant is deep in-the-money, then the convertible bond trades close to—but higher than (to reflect the time value of the option)—the value of the bond if converted.

FIGURE 24.4

Convertible Bond Value

At maturity, the value of a convertible bond is the maximum of the value of a $1000 straight bond and 15 shares of stock, and will be converted if the stock is above the conversion price. Prior to maturity, the value of the convertible bond will depend upon the likelihood of conversion, and will be above that of a straight bond or 15 shares of stock.

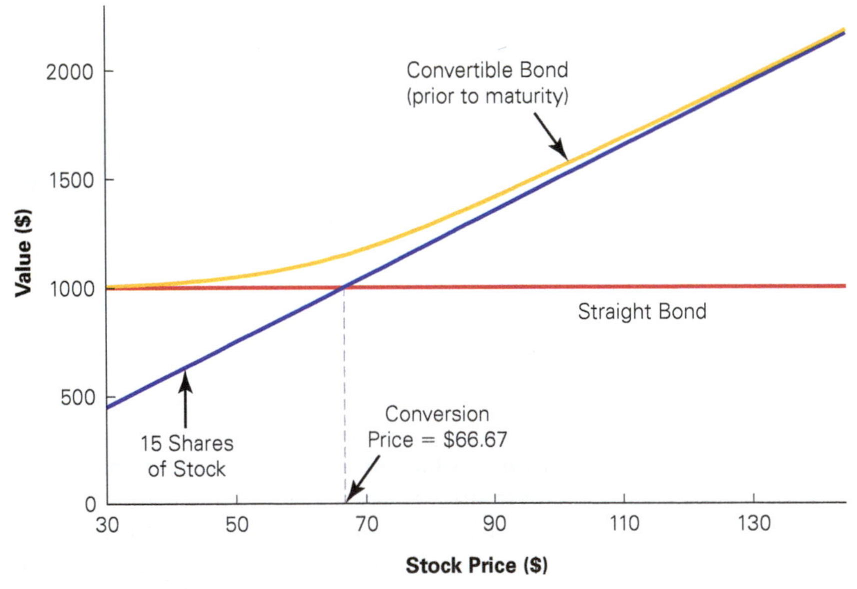

[10]When a regular call is exercised, the loss incurred by the writer of the call accrues to an unknown third party. However, when a warrant is exercised, the loss accrues to the equity holders of the firm (because they are forced to sell new equity at below-market value), which *includes* the holder of the warrant (upon exercise, the warrant holder becomes an equity holder). This dilution effect implies that the gain from exercising a warrant is less than that from a call, so warrants are worth less than calls.

Often, companies issue convertible bonds that are callable. With these bonds, if the issuer calls them, the holder can choose to convert rather than let the bonds be called. When the bonds are called, the holder faces exactly the same decision as he would on the maturity date of the bonds: He will choose to convert if the stock price exceeds the conversion price and let the bonds be called otherwise. Thus, by calling the bonds, a company can force bondholders to make their decision to exercise the conversion option earlier than they would otherwise like to. Therefore, calling a convertible bond transfers the remaining time value of the conversion option from bondholders to shareholders.

When a corporation issues convertible debt, it is giving the holder an option—a warrant, in this case. As we learned in Chapter 20, options always have a positive value; hence, a convertible bond is worth more than an otherwise identical straight bond. Consequently, if both bonds are issued at par, the non-convertible bond must offer a higher interest rate. Many people point to the lower interest rates of convertible bonds and argue that therefore convertible debt is cheaper than straight debt.

As we learned in Chapter 14, in a perfect market, the choice of financing cannot affect the value of a firm. Hence, the argument that convertible debt is cheaper because it has a lower interest rate is fallacious. Convertible debt carries a lower interest rate because it has an embedded warrant. If the price of a firm were subsequently to rise so that the bondholders choose to convert, the current shareholders will have to sell an equity stake in their firm for below-market value. The lower interest rate is compensation for the possibility that this event will occur.

CONCEPT CHECK

1. What is a sinking fund?
2. Do callable bonds have a higher or lower yield than otherwise identical bonds without a call feature? Why?
3. Why does a convertible bond have a lower yield than an otherwise identical bond without the option to convert?

MyFinanceLab

Here is what you should know after reading this chapter. MyFinanceLab will help you identify what you know and where to go when you need to practice.

24.1 Corporate Debt

- Companies can raise debt using different sources. Typical types of debt are public debt, which trades in a public market, and private debt, which is negotiated directly with a bank or a small group of investors. The securities that companies issue when raising debt are called corporate bonds.
- For public offerings, the bond agreement takes the form of an indenture, a formal contract between the bond issuer and a trust company. The indenture lays out the terms of the bond issue.
- Four types of corporate bonds are typically issued: notes, debentures, mortgage bonds, and asset-backed bonds. Notes and debentures are unsecured; mortgage bonds and asset-backed bonds are secured.
- Corporate bonds differ in their level of seniority. In case of bankruptcy, senior debt is paid in full first before subordinated debt is paid.
- International bonds are classified into four broadly defined categories: domestic bonds, which trade in foreign markets; foreign bonds, which are issued in a local market by a foreign entity; Eurobonds, which are not denominated in the local currency of the country in which they are issued; and global bonds, which trade in several markets simultaneously.

- Private debt can be in the form of term loans or private placements. A term loan is a bank loan that lasts for a specific term. A private placement is a bond issue that is sold to a small group of investors.

24.2 Other Types of Debt

- Governments, states, and other state-sponsored enterprises issue bonds as well.
- The U.S. Treasury has issued four different kinds of securities: Treasury bills, Treasury notes, Treasury bonds, and TIPS.
- Municipal bonds ("munis") are issued by state and local governments. Their distinguishing characteristic is that the income on municipal bonds is not taxable at the federal level.
- An asset-backed security (ABS) is a security that is made up of other financial securities, that is, the security's cash flows come from the cash flows of the underlying financial securities that "back" it.
- A mortgage-backed security (MBS) is an asset-backed security backed by home mortgages. U.S. government agencies, such as the Government National Mortgage Association (GNMA, or "Ginnie Mae"), are the largest issuers in this sector.
- Holders of agency-issued mortgage-backed securities face prepayment risk, which is the risk that they will find that the bond will be partially (or wholly) repaid earlier than expected. Holders of privately issued mortgage-backed securities also face default risk.
- A collateralized debt obligation is an asset-backed security that is backed by other asset-backed securities.

24.3 Bond Covenants

- Covenants are restrictive clauses in the bond contract that help investors by limiting the issuer's ability to take actions that will increase the default risk and reduce the value of the bonds.

24.4 Repayment Provisions

- A call provision gives the issuer of the bond the right (but not the obligation) to retire the bond after a specific date (but before maturity).
- A callable bond will generally trade at a lower price than an otherwise equivalent non-callable bond.
- The yield to call is the yield of a callable bond assuming that the bond is called at the earliest opportunity.
- Another way in which a bond is repaid before maturity is by periodically repurchasing part of the debt through a sinking fund.
- Some corporate bonds, known as convertible bonds, have a provision that allows the holder to convert them into equity.
- Convertible debt carries a lower interest rate than other comparable non-convertible debt.

Key Terms

asset-backed bonds *p. 868*
asset-backed security (ABS) *p. 874*
asset pools *p. 874*
asset securitization *p. 874*
balloon payment *p. 881*
bearer bonds *p. 868*
Bulldogs *p. 870*
call date *p. 877*
call price *p. 877*
callable bonds *p. 877*
collateralized debt obligation (CDO) *p. 876*
collateralized mortgage obligation (CMO) *p. 874*
conversion price *p. 882*
conversion ratio *p. 881*
convertible bonds *p. 881*
covenants *p. 876*
debentures *p. 868*
domestic bonds *p. 869*
double-barreled *p. 873*
Eurobonds *p. 870*
foreign bonds *p. 870*
general obligation bonds *p. 873*
global bonds *p. 870*
indenture *p. 866*

long bonds *p. 872*
mortgage-backed security (MBS) *p. 874*
mortgage bonds *p. 868*
municipal bonds *p. 873*
notes *p. 868*
original issue discount (OID) *p. 867*
prepayment risk *p. 875*
private debt *p. 870*
private placement *p. 870*
registered bonds *p. 868*
revenue bonds *p. 873*
revolving line of credit *p. 870*
Samurai bonds *p. 870*
secured debt *p. 868*
seniority *p. 869*
serial bonds *p. 873*
sinking fund *p. 881*
sovereign debt *p. 871*
stop-out yield *p. 872*
STRIPS *p. 872*
subordinated debenture *p. 869*
subprime mortgages *p. 874*
syndicated bank loan *p. 870*
term loan *p. 870*
TIPS *p. 872*
tranches *p. 868*
unsecured debt *p. 868*
warrant *p. 881*
Yankee bonds *p. 870*
yield to call (YTC) *p. 880*

Further Reading

For a comprehensive summary of the bond market, consult either of the following texts: F. Fabozzi (ed.), *Handbook of Fixed Income Securities* (McGraw-Hill, 2011); M. Stigum and A. Crescenzi, *The Money Market* (McGraw-Hill, 2007).

Readers interested in more depth on subjects covered in this chapter can consult the following sources:

Convertible Debt. R. Billingsley and D. Smith, "Why Do Firms Issue Convertible Debt?" *Financial Management* 25(2) (1996): 93–99; M. Brennan and E. Schwartz, "The Case for Convertibles," *Journal of Applied Corporate Finance* 1(1) (1988): 55–64; W. Bühler and C. Koziol, "Valuation of Convertible Bonds with Sequential Conversion," *Schmalenback Business Review* 54 (October 2002): 302–334; R. Green, "Investment Incentives, Debt and Warrants," *Journal of Financial Economics* 13 (1984), 115–136; C. Hennessy and Y. Tserlukevich, "Taxation, Agency Conflicts and the Choice between Callable and Convertible Debt," *Journal of Economic Theory* 143 (2008): 374–404; and J. Stein, "Convertible Bonds as Backdoor Equity Financing," *Journal of Financial Economics* 32(1) (1992): 3–21.

Callable Debt. P. Asquith, "Convertible Bonds Are Not Called Late," *Journal of Finance* 50(4) (1995): 1275–1289; and M. Brennan and E. Schwartz, "Savings Bonds, Retractable Bonds, and Callable Bonds," *Journal of Financial Economics* 5(1) (1997): 67–88.

For an analysis of how callable convertible debt may reduce the lemons problem, see B. Yilmaz and A. Chakraborty, "Adverse Selection and Convertible Bonds," *Review of Economic Studies* (2011) 78: 148–175.

Bond Covenants. C. Smith and J. Warner, "On Financial Contracting: An Analysis of Bond Covenants," *Journal of Financial Economics* 7 (1979): 117–161; and M. Bradley and M. Roberts, "The Structure and Pricing of Corporate Debt Covenants," SSRN working paper (2004).

Problems

All problems are available in MyFinanceLab.

Corporate Debt

1. Explain some of the differences between a public debt offering and a private debt offering.
2. Why do bonds with lower seniority have higher yields than equivalent bonds with higher seniority?

3. Explain the difference between a secured corporate bond and an unsecured corporate bond.
4. What is the difference between a foreign bond and a Eurobond?

Other Types of Debt

5. Describe the kinds of securities the U.S. government uses to finance the federal debt.
6. Suppose on January 15, 2013, the U.S. Treasury issued a five-year inflation-indexed note with a coupon of 3%. On the date of issue, the consumer price index (CPI) was 250. By January 15, 2018, the CPI had increased to 300. What principal and coupon payment was made on January 15, 2018?
7. On January 15, 2020, the U.S. Treasury issued a 10-year inflation-indexed note with a coupon of 6%. On the date of issue, the CPI was 400. By January 15, 2030, the CPI had decreased to 300. What principal and coupon payment was made on January 15, 2030?
8. Describe what prepayment risk in a GNMA is.
9. What is the distinguishing feature of how municipal bonds are taxed?

Bond Covenants

10. Explain why bond issuers might voluntarily choose to put restrictive covenants into a new bond issue.

Repayment Provisions

11. General Electric has just issued a callable 10-year, 6% coupon bond with annual coupon payments. The bond can be called at par in one year or anytime thereafter on a coupon payment date. It has a price of $102. What is the bond's yield to maturity and yield to call?
12. Boeing Corporation has just issued a callable (at par) three-year, 5% coupon bond with semiannual coupon payments. The bond can be called at par in two years or anytime thereafter on a coupon payment date. It has a price of $99. What is the bond's yield to maturity and yield to call?
13. Explain why the yield on a convertible bond is lower than the yield on an otherwise identical bond without a conversion feature.
14. You own a bond with a face value of $10,000 and a conversion ratio of 450. What is the conversion price?

Data Case

You are still employed at The Home Depot. Recall the presentation of Chapter 15's plan to increase leverage to the Board of Directors. The idea of changing Home Depot's capital structure stirred some conversations among top executives. The CFO and other top managers in the finance division are all aware that increasing the debt load will have ramifications in the credit markets. Specifically, they realize that the firm's debt rating could change, which will raise the cost of borrowing as well as possibly lower the value of the existing debt. No one is exactly sure what the impact will be, but they all agree that it deserves investigation.

Because you prepared the spreadsheet data, you have been summoned to an executive-level meeting and asked to estimate the impact of increasing the debt of the firm. Use the spreadsheet from Chapter 15's Data Case as a starting point. You are to consider four different scenarios: issuing $1 billion, $10 billion, $20 billion, and $30 billion in new debt. In each case, proceeds from the debt will be used to repurchase stock. The CFO believes that the $1 billion level will not affect the firm's credit rating. However, each larger increase in debt will cause the debt to be downgraded one letter grade (e.g., from Baa to Ba). For example, the $10 billion scenario will lower the current debt rating one level, the $20 billion scenario would lower the rating still another level, and so on. Your job is to determine the impact of additional debt on borrowing costs at each debt level. Assume the new debt will be raised by issuing 10-year bonds.

1. Determine the current debt rating for The Home Depot.
   - Research the current bond rating at FINRA (finra-markets.morningstar.com/BondCenter/). Select the "Corporate" toggle, enter the symbol for Home Depot (HD), and click "Show Results."
   - What is the Moody's bond rating on the Home Depot bond with the maturity closest to 10 years from today? What is the yield on this bond?
2. Because lower bond ratings will lead to higher interest costs, you will need to determine those costs. Go to Bonds Online (www.bondsonline.com) and click "Today's Market." Next, click "US Corporate Bond Spreads." You will see a table of bond spreads prepared by Reuters and the date the table was prepared right below it. These spreads represent the increased yield a bond must pay over the U.S. Treasury of the same maturity. Choose the 10-year spread for Home Depot's current rating and the three ratings below it. The spreads are in basis points; a basis point is 1/100th of a percentage point (thus, 50 basis points is 0.5%). We will adjust these old spreads to estimate the current spread.
   - Because these spreads are dated, you will need to create new yield spreads for the various ratings. Use the current difference between the Home Depot bond's yield and the 10-year Treasury as the true spread for the rating. Using Excel, compute the spreads for the other ratings, by adding the *difference* in spreads from the table to the new true spread for Home Depot's rating. Finally, determine the yield for each rating by adding the new spread to the yield on the 10-year Treasury bond.
   - Compute the required yields on 10-year bonds at each of the new debt levels requested.
3. What factors cause the bond rating to fall, and the bond yields to increase, as Home Depot increases its debt levels?

Note: Updates to this data case may be found at www.berkdemarzo.com.

CHAPTER

25

Leasing

NOTATION

L	lease payments
PV	present value
r_D	debt cost of capital
τ_c	marginal corporate income tax rate
r_U	unlevered cost of capital
r_{wacc}	weighted average cost of capital

TO IMPLEMENT AN INVESTMENT PROJECT, A FIRM MUST ACQUIRE the necessary property, plant, and equipment. As an alternative to purchasing these assets outright, the firm can lease them. You are probably familiar with leases if you have leased a car or rented an apartment. These consumer rentals are similar to the leases used by businesses: The owner retains title to the asset, and the firm pays for its use of the asset through regular lease payments. When firms lease property, plant, or equipment, the leases generally exceed one year. This chapter focuses on such long-term leases.

If you can purchase an asset, you can probably lease it. Commercial real estate, computers, trucks, copy machines, airplanes, and even power plants are examples of assets that firms can lease rather than buy. Equipment leasing is a rapidly growing industry, with more than one-half of the world's leasing now being done by companies in Europe and Japan. In 2012 more than 33% of the productive assets acquired by U.S. companies were procured through leasing contracts, for a total leasing volume exceeding $264 billion. Eighty-five percent of U.S. companies lease all or some of their equipment.[1] For example, it may come as a surprise that airlines do not own many of their own airplanes. The top aircraft leasing company by fleet size at the start of 2015 was GE Commercial Aviation Services. GE owns and manages over 2200 aircraft, the world's largest commercial airplane fleet.[2] GE leases these commercial aircraft to some 270 airline customers in 75 countries.

As you will learn, leases are not merely an alternative to purchasing; they also function as an important financing method for tangible assets. In fact, long-term leasing is the most common method of equipment financing. How do companies such as

[1]Beacon Funding (www.beaconfunding.com/vendor_programs/statistics.aspx).

[2]GE Capital Aviation Services Global Fact Sheet www.gecas.com/en/common/docs/GECAS_FactSheet.pdf.

GE Commercial Aviation Services set the terms for their leases? How do their customers—the commercial airlines—evaluate and negotiate these leases? In this chapter, we first discuss the basic types of leases and provide an overview of the accounting and tax treatment of leases. We next show how to evaluate the lease-versus-buy decision. Firms often cite various benefits to leasing as compared to purchasing property and equipment, and we conclude the chapter with an evaluation of their reasoning.

25.1 The Basics of Leasing

A lease is a contract between two parties: the *lessee* and the *lessor*. The **lessee** is liable for periodic payments in exchange for the right to use the asset. The **lessor** is the owner of the asset, who is entitled to the lease payments in exchange for lending the asset.

Most leases involve little or no upfront payment. Instead, the lessee commits to make regular lease (or rental) payments for the term of the contract. At the end of the contract term, the lease specifies who will retain ownership of the asset and at what terms. The lease also specifies any cancellation provisions, the options for renewal and purchase, and the obligations for maintenance and related servicing costs.

Examples of Lease Transactions

Many types of lease transactions are possible based on the relationship between the lessee and the lessor. In a **sales-type lease**, the lessor is the manufacturer (or a primary dealer) of the asset. For example, IBM both manufactures and leases computers. Similarly, Xerox leases its copy machines. Manufacturers generally set the terms of these leases as part of a broader sales and pricing strategy, and they may bundle other services or goods (such as software, maintenance, or product upgrades) as part of the lease.

In a **direct lease**, the lessor is not the manufacturer, but is often an independent company that specializes in purchasing assets and leasing them to customers. For example, Ryder Systems, Inc., owns more than 135,000 commercial trucks, tractors, and trailers, which it leases to small businesses and large enterprises throughout the United States, Canada, and the United Kingdom. In many instances of direct leases, the lessee identifies the equipment it needs first and then finds a leasing company to purchase the asset.

If a firm already owns an asset it would prefer to lease, it can arrange a **sale and leaseback** transaction. In this type of lease, the lessee receives cash from the sale of the asset and then makes lease payments to retain the use of the asset. In 2002, San Francisco Municipal Railway (Muni) used the $35 million in proceeds from the sale and leaseback of 118 of its light-rail vehicles to offset a large operating budget deficit. The purchaser, CIBC World Markets of Canada, received a tax benefit from depreciating the rail cars, something Muni could not do as a public transit agency.

With many leases, the lessor provides the initial capital necessary to purchase the asset, and then receives and retains the lease payments. In a **leveraged lease**, however, the lessor borrows from a bank or other lender to obtain the initial capital for the purchase, using the lease payments to pay interest and principal on the loan. Also, in some circumstances, the lessor is not an independent company but rather a separate business partnership, called a **special-purpose entity (SPE)**, which is created by the lessee for the sole purpose of obtaining the lease. SPEs are commonly used in **synthetic leases**, which are designed to obtain specific accounting and tax treatment (discussed further in Section 25.2).

Lease Payments and Residual Values

Suppose your business needs a new \$20,000 electric forklift for its warehouse operations, and you are considering leasing the forklift for four years. In this case, the lessor will purchase the forklift and allow you to use it for four years. At that point, you will return the forklift to the lessor. How much should you expect to pay for the right to use the forklift for the first four years of its life?

The cost of the lease will depend on the asset's **residual value**, which is its market value at the end of the lease. Suppose the residual value of the forklift in four years will be \$6000. If lease payments of amount L are made monthly, then the lessor's cash flows from the transaction are as follows (note that lease payments are typically made at the beginning of each payment period):

	0	1	2	. . .	47	48
Purchase price	$-\$20{,}000$					
Lease payment	$+L$	L	L	. . .	L	
Residual value						\$6000

In a perfect capital market (where lessors compete with one another in initiating leases), the lease payment should be set so that the NPV of the transaction is zero and the lessor breaks even:

$$PV(\text{Lease Payments}) = \text{Purchase Price} - PV(\text{Residual Value}) \tag{25.1}$$

In other words, *in a perfect market, the cost of leasing is equivalent to the cost of purchasing and reselling the asset.*

Thus, the amount of the lease payment will depend on the purchase price, the residual value, and the appropriate discount rate for the cash flows.

EXAMPLE 25.1 Lease Terms in a Perfect Market

Problem

Suppose the purchase price of the forklift is \$20,000, its residual value in four years is certain to be \$6000, and there is no risk that the lessee will default on the lease. If the risk-free interest rate is a 6% APR with monthly compounding, what would be the monthly lease payment for a four-year lease in a perfect capital market?

Solution

Because all cash flows are risk free, we can discount them using the risk-free interest rate of 6%/12 = 0.5% per month. From Eq. 25.1,

$$PV(\text{Lease Payments}) = \$20{,}000 - \$6000/1.005^{48} = \$15{,}277.41$$

What monthly lease payment L has this present value? We can interpret the lease payments as an annuity. Because the first lease payment starts today, we can view the lease as an initial payment of L plus a 47-month annuity of L. Thus, using the annuity formula, we need to find L so that

$$15{,}277.41 = L + L \times \frac{1}{0.005}\left(1 - \frac{1}{1.005^{47}}\right) = L \times \left[1 + \frac{1}{0.005}\left(1 - \frac{1}{1.005^{47}}\right)\right]$$

Solving for L, we get

$$L = \frac{15{,}277.41}{1 + \frac{1}{0.005}\left(1 - \frac{1}{1.005^{47}}\right)} = \$357.01 \text{ per month}$$

Leases Versus Loans

Alternatively, you could obtain a four-year loan for the purchase price and buy the forklift outright. If M is the monthly payment for a fully amortizing loan, the lender's cash flows will be as follows:

	0	1	2	...	47	48
Purchase price	−\$20,000					
Loan payments		M	M	...	M	M

Assuming the loan is fairly priced, the loan payments would be such that

$$PV(\text{Loan Payments}) = \text{Purchase Price} \qquad (25.2)$$

Comparing Eq. 25.2 with Eq. 25.1, we see that while with a standard loan we are financing the entire cost of the asset, with a lease we are financing only the cost of the economic depreciation of the asset during the term of the lease. Because we are getting the entire asset when we purchase it with the loan, the loan payments are higher than the lease payments.

EXAMPLE 25.2 **Loan Payments in a Perfect Market**

Problem

Suppose that you purchase the forklift for \$20,000 by borrowing the purchase price using a four-year annuity loan. What would the monthly loan payment be in a perfect capital market where the risk-free interest rate is a 6% APR with monthly compounding, assuming no risk of default? How does this compare with the lease payment of Example 25.1?

Solution

Because all cash flows are risk free, we can discount them using the risk-free interest rate of 6%/12 = 0.5% per month. Because loan payments are made at the end of each month, using the annuity formula to value the loan payments, Eq. 25.2 becomes

$$M \times \frac{1}{0.005}\left(1 - \frac{1}{1.005^{48}}\right) = 20{,}000$$

Solving for M gives the loan payments:

$$M = \frac{20{,}000}{\frac{1}{0.005}\left(1 - \frac{1}{1.005^{48}}\right)} = \$469.70 \text{ per month}$$

Of course, while the lease payments are lower, with the lease, we have the use of the forklift for four years only. With the loan, we own the forklift for its entire life.

Calculating Auto Lease Payments

Rather than use the annuity formula to calculate the lease payments, as we did in Example 25.1, in many cases, practitioners use the following approximation to calculate the lease payments:

$$L = \underbrace{\frac{\text{Purchase Price} - \text{Residual Value}}{\text{Term}}}_{\text{Avg. Depreciation}} + \underbrace{\left(\frac{\text{Purchase Price} + \text{Residual Value}}{2}\right) \times \text{Interest Rate}}_{\text{Financing Cost}}$$

where the purchase price includes any fees charged on the lease (and is net of any down payment), the term is the number of payment periods, and the interest rate is for a payment period. The idea behind this approximation is that the first term is the average depreciation over a payment period and the second term is the interest cost associated with the average value of the asset. The sum is what you have to pay to use the asset over one payment period.

Despite its simplicity, this formula is very accurate for lease terms up to five years and interest rates up to 10%. Using it to calculate the lease payments in Example 25.1 gives

$$\frac{20{,}000 - 6000}{48} + \left(\frac{20{,}000 + 6000}{2}\right) \times 0.005 = \$356.67$$

which is within $1 of the amount calculated in Example 25.1.

This approximation for the lease payment is used to calculate the payment on automobile leases. In that case, the formula is often stated as

$$L = \frac{\text{Purchase Price} - \text{Residual Value}}{\text{Term}} + (\text{Purchase Price} + \text{Residual Value}) \times \text{Money Factor}$$

leaving many first-time car lessees wondering why they have to pay interest on both the purchase price and the residual value. In reality, all that has happened is that the factor of 2 is subsumed into the money factor; that is, the money factor is half the interest rate.

The monthly loan payments in Example 25.2 exceed the lease payments in Example 25.1. This difference does not mean the lease is superior to the loan. While the lease payments are lower, with the lease, we have use of the forklift for four years only. If we purchase the forklift using the loan, we own it after four years and can sell it for its residual value of $6000. Alternatively, if we lease the forklift and want to keep it after the lease terminates, we can purchase it for its fair market value of $6000. Once we consider the benefit of this residual value, by the Law of One Price, the total cost of purchasing with either the loan or the lease is the same. That is, combining Eq. 25.2 and Eq. 25.1, we have

$$PV(\text{Lease Payments}) + PV(\text{Residual Value}) = PV(\text{Loan Payments}) \tag{25.3}$$

In other words, *in a perfect market, the cost of leasing and then purchasing the asset is equivalent to the cost of borrowing to purchase the asset.*[3]

End-of-Term Lease Options

In Example 25.1, we assumed that at the end of the lease the forklift would be returned to the lessor, who would then obtain its residual market value of $6000. In reality, other lease terms are possible. In many cases, the lease allows the lessee to obtain ownership of the asset for some price.

- A **fair market value (FMV) lease** gives the lessee the option to purchase the asset at its fair market value at the termination of the lease. (Depending on the asset, determining

[3]For a theoretical analysis of competitive lease pricing, see M. Miller and C. Upton, "Leasing, Buying, and the Cost of Capital Services," *Journal of Finance* 31(3) (1976): 761–786; and W. Lewellen, M. Long, and J. McConnell, "Asset Leasing in Competitive Capital Markets," *Journal of Finance* 31(3) (1976): 787–798.

its fair market value may be complicated. The lease will typically stipulate a procedure for doing so, and it often will require estimates of the fair market value to be provided by an independent third party.) With perfect capital markets, there is no difference between an FMV lease and a lease in which the assets are retained by the lessor, because acquiring the asset at its fair market value is a zero-NPV transaction.

- In a **\$1.00 out lease** (also known as a finance lease), ownership of the asset transfers to the lessee at the end of the lease for a nominal cost of \$1.00. Thus, the lessee will continue to have use of the asset for its entire economic life. The lessee has effectively purchased the asset by making the lease payments. As a result, this type of lease is in many ways equivalent to financing the asset with a standard loan.
- In a **fixed price lease**, the lessee has the option to purchase the asset at the end of the lease for a fixed price that is set upfront in the lease contract. This type of lease is very common for consumer leases (such as for autos). Notice that this kind of lease gives the lessee an option: At the end of the lease, if the market value of the asset exceeds the fixed price, the lessee can buy the asset at below its market value; if the market value of the asset does not exceed the fixed price, however, the lessee can walk away from the lease and purchase the asset for less money elsewhere. Consequently, the lessor will set a higher lease rate to compensate for the value of this option to the lessee.
- In a **fair market value cap lease**, the lessee can purchase the asset at the minimum of its fair market value and a fixed price (the "cap"). The lessee has the same option as in a fixed price lease, although the option in this case is easier to exercise because the lessee does not have to find a similar asset elsewhere to buy when the fixed price exceeds the market value.

EXAMPLE 25.3 Lease Payments and End-of-Lease Options

Problem

Compute the lease payments for the forklift lease of Example 25.1 if the lease is (a) a fair market value lease, (b) a \$1.00 out lease, or (c) a fixed price lease that allows the lessee to buy the asset at the end of the lease for \$4000.

Solution

With the FMV lease, the lessee can buy the forklift for its fair market value of \$6000 at the end of the lease. The lessor obtains a residual value of \$6000, either from the forklift itself or from the payment from the lessee. Thus, the lease payments will be unchanged from Example 25.1, or \$357 per month.

With the \$1.00 out lease, the lessor receives essentially no residual value. Thus, the lease payments themselves will have to compensate the lessor for the full \$20,000 purchase price. The lease payments are therefore

$$L = \frac{20{,}000}{1 + \frac{1}{0.005}\left(1 - \frac{1}{1.005^{47}}\right)} = \$467.36 \text{ per month}$$

These payments are slightly less than the loan payments of \$470 per month calculated in Example 25.2 because the lease payments occur at the beginning—rather than the end—of the month.

With the fixed price lease, because the forklift will be worth \$6000 for certain, the lessee will exercise the option to purchase it for \$4000. As a result, the lessor will receive only \$4000 at the end of the lease. For the lease to have an NPV of zero, the present value of the lease payments must be $\$20{,}000 - \$4000/1.005^{48} = \$16{,}851.61$. Therefore, the lease payment will be

$$L = \frac{16{,}851.61}{1 + \frac{1}{0.005}\left(1 - \frac{1}{1.005^{47}}\right)} = \$393.79 \text{ per month}$$

This payment exceeds that of the FMV lease due to the lessee's ability to buy the asset at a discount at the end of the lease.

Other Lease Provisions

Leases are privately negotiated contracts and can contain many more provisions than are described here. For example, they may include early cancellation options that allow the lessee to end the lease early (perhaps for a fee). They may contain buyout options that allow the lessee to purchase the asset before the end of the lease term. Clauses may allow the lessee to trade in and upgrade the equipment to a newer model at certain points in the lease. Each lease agreement can be tailored to fit the precise nature of the asset and the needs of the parties at hand.

These features of leases will be priced as part of the lease payment. Terms that give valuable options to the lessee raise the amount of the lease payments, whereas terms that restrict these options will lower them. Absent market imperfections, leases represent another form of zero-NPV financing available to a firm, and the Modigliani-Miller propositions apply: Leases neither increase nor decrease firm value, but serve only to divide the firm's cash flows and risks in different ways.[4]

CONCEPT CHECK

1. In a perfect capital market, how is the amount of a lease payment determined?
2. What types of lease options would raise the amount of the lease payment?

25.2 Accounting, Tax, and Legal Consequences of Leasing

We have seen that with perfect capital markets, leasing represents yet another zero-NPV financing alternative for a firm. Thus, the decision to lease is often driven by real-world market imperfections related to leasing's accounting, tax, and legal treatment.[5] In particular, when a firm leases an asset, a number of important questions arise: Should the firm list the asset on its balance sheet and deduct depreciation expenses? Should the firm list the lease as a liability? Can the lease payments be deducted for tax purposes? In the event of bankruptcy, is the leased asset protected from creditors? As we will see in this section, the answers to these questions depend on how the lease is structured.

---

[4]For an analysis of options embedded in lease contracts, see J. McConnell and J. Schallheim, "Valuation of Asset Leasing Contracts," *Journal of Financial Economics* 12(2) (1983): 237–261; and S. Grenadier, "Valuing Lease Contracts: A Real-Options Approach," *Journal of Financial Economics* 38(3) (1995): 297–331.

[5]Anyone who has ever considered leasing a car will be familiar with one such imperfection. In most states, lessees do not pay sales tax on the purchase price of the car, only on the lease payments, which usually means lessees can avoid paying a substantial part of the sales tax purchasers must pay.

Lease Accounting

When publicly traded firms disclose leasing transactions in their financial statements, they must follow the recommendations of the Financial Accounting Standards Board (FASB). For lessees, the FASB has historically distinguished two types of leases based on the lease terms, and this classification determines the lease's accounting treatment:

- An **operating lease** is viewed as a rental for accounting purposes. In this case, the lessee reports the entire lease payment as an operating expense. The lessee does not deduct a depreciation expense for the asset and does not report the asset, or the lease payment liability, on its balance sheet. Operating leases are disclosed in the footnotes of the lessee's financial statements.
- A **capital lease** (also called a **finance lease**) is viewed as an acquisition for accounting purposes. The asset acquired is listed on the lessee's balance sheet, and the lessee incurs depreciation expenses for the asset. In addition, the present value of the future lease payments is listed as a liability, and the interest portion of the lease payment is deducted as an interest expense.[6]

The different accounting treatment for each type of lease will affect the firm's balance sheet as well as its debt-equity ratio, as shown in Example 25.4.

EXAMPLE 25.4 Leasing and the Balance Sheet

Problem

Harbord Cruise Lines currently has the following balance sheet (in millions of dollars):

Assets		**Liabilities**	
Cash	100	Debt	900
Property, Plant, and Equipment	1500	Equity	700
Total Assets	1600	**Total Debt plus Equity**	1600

Harbord is about to add a new fleet of cruise ships. The price of the fleet is \$400 million. What will Harbord's balance sheet look like if (a) it purchases the fleet by borrowing the \$400 million, (b) it acquires the fleet through a \$400 million capital lease, or (c) it acquires the fleet through an operating lease?

Solution

For parts (a) and (b), the balance sheet consequences are the same: The fleet becomes a new asset of the firm, and the \$400 million becomes an additional liability.

Assets		**Liabilities**	
Cash	100	Debt	1300
Property, Plant, and Equipment	1900	Equity	700
Total Assets	2000	**Total Debt plus Equity**	2000

Note that the firm's debt-equity ratio increases in this case (from $900/700 = 1.29$ to $1300/700 = 1.86$).

[6]The accounting treatment of a capital lease for the lessor will depend on whether it is a sales-type lease, a direct lease, or a leveraged lease (a direct lease in which the lessor obtains more than 60% debt financing to purchase the asset, and the debt is non-recourse in that it is backed solely by the income from the asset).

If the fleet is acquired through an operating lease, as described in part (c), there is no change in the original balance sheet: The fleet is not listed as an asset, and the lease is not viewed as a liability. Thus, the apparent leverage ratio is unchanged.

Because capital leases increase the apparent leverage on the firm's balance sheet, firms sometimes prefer to have a lease categorized as an operating lease to keep it off the balance sheet. In its Statement of Financial Accounting Standards No. 13 (FAS13), the FASB provides specific criteria that distinguish an operating lease from a capital lease. The lease is treated as a capital lease for the lessee and must be listed on the firm's balance sheet if it satisfies any of the following conditions:

1. Title to the property transfers to the lessee at the end of the lease term.
2. The lease contains an option to purchase the asset at a bargain price that is substantially less than its fair market value.
3. The lease term is 75% or more of the estimated economic life of the asset.
4. The present value of the minimum lease payments at the start of the lease is 90% or more of the asset's fair market value.

These conditions are designed to identify situations in which the lease provides the lessee with use of the asset for a large fraction of its useful life. For example, a $1.00 out lease satisfies the second condition and so would be ruled a capital lease for accounting purposes. Firms that prefer to keep a lease off-balance-sheet will often structure lease contracts to avoid these conditions.

Despite FASB's strict rules about which leases could be characterized as operating leases, many investors as well as the SEC believed that these rules were being abused. In response, in 2006 the FASB and the International Accounting Standards Board (IASB) embarked on a joint project to reform the rules. The result is a new standard, announced in 2016 and slated to take full effect in 2019. While the reporting of lease expenses will continue to depend on the lease characterization, under the new rules firms will now have to recognize *all* leases with terms longer than one year on their balance sheets.

Operating Leases at Alaska Air Group

Alaska Air Group, Inc., was incorporated in 1985 as a holding company with two main subsidiaries: Alaska Airlines, Inc., and Horizon Air Industries. Alaska Airlines is a major airline with flights throughout the United States. Horizon Air is a regional airline concentrated in the Pacific Northwest. Typical for airlines, Alaska Air Group leases many of its aircraft, as is summarized in the following table:

	Owned	Leased	Total
Alaska Airlines	111	34	145
Horizon Air	36	15	51

Source: Alaska Air Group, Inc., December 2014 10-K

Alaska Airlines leases more than a quarter of its aircraft, and Horizon leases almost one third. These leases are almost exclusively operating leases. (In many cases, the lessors are trusts established by a third party specifically to purchase, finance, and lease aircraft to Alaska.) In addition, Alaska leases the majority of its airport and terminal facilities.

Because these leases are operating leases, Alaska Air Group reports the entire lease payment as an operating expense. During 2014, Alaska Air reported aircraft rent expenses of $110 million relative to operating revenues of $5.4 billion. The firm did not deduct a depreciation expense for its leased aircraft, and these aircraft did not show up as an asset on its balance sheet (although Alaska Air does report the value of the aircraft that it owns as assets on its balance sheet). And though the lease obligations are not listed as a liability, if they were they would more than double Alaska Air's reported debt.

EXAMPLE 25.5 Operating Versus Capital Leases

Problem

Consider a seven-year fair market value lease for a $12.5 million Gulfstream Jet with a remaining useful life of 10 years. Suppose the monthly lease payments are $175,000 and the appropriate discount rate is a 6% APR with monthly compounding. Would this lease be classified as an operating lease or a capital lease for the lessee? What if the lease contract gave the lessee the option to cancel the contract after five years?

Solution

We compute the present value of the monthly lease payments at the beginning of the lease using the annuity formula with a monthly interest rate of $6\%/12 = 0.5\%$ and $7 \times 12 - 1 = 83$ monthly payments after the initial payment. Thus,

$$PV(\text{Lease Payments}) = 175{,}000 \times \left[1 + \frac{1}{0.005}\left(1 - \frac{1}{1.005^{83}}\right)\right] = \$12.04 \text{ million}$$

Because the present value of the lease payments is $12.04/12.50 = 96.3\%$ of the value of the jet, the lease satisfies condition 4 and so it is a capital lease.

If the lessee can cancel the contract after five years, then the minimum number of lease payments is 60 under the contract. In this case,

$$PV(\text{Lease Payments}) = 175{,}000 \times \left[1 + \frac{1}{0.005}\left(1 - \frac{1}{1.005^{59}}\right)\right] = \$9.10 \text{ million}$$

This is only $9.10/12.5 = 73\%$ of the value of the jet. As no other conditions for a capital lease are satisfied, the lease would be classified as an operating lease.

The Tax Treatment of Leases

The categories used to report leases on the financial statements affect the values of assets on the balance sheet, but they have no direct effect on the cash flows that result from a leasing transaction. The IRS has its own classification rules that determine the tax treatment of a lease. Because the tax treatment does affect the cash flows, these rules are more significant from a financial valuation perspective.

The IRS separates leases into two broad categories: true tax leases and non-tax leases. These categories are roughly equivalent to operating and capital leases, although the defining criteria are not identical.

In a **true tax lease**, the lessor receives the depreciation deductions associated with the ownership of the asset. The lessee can deduct the full amount of the lease payments as an operating expense, and these lease payments are treated as revenue for the lessor.

Although the legal ownership of the asset resides with the lessor, in a **non-tax lease**, the lessee receives the depreciation deductions. The lessee can also deduct the interest portion of the lease payments as an interest expense. The interest portion of the lease payment is interest income for the lessor.

IRS Revenue Ruling 55–540 provides the conditions that determine the tax classification of a lease. If the lease satisfies any of these conditions, it is treated as a non-tax lease:

1. The lessee obtains equity in the leased asset.
2. The lessee receives ownership of the asset on completion of all lease payments.
3. The total amount that the lessee is required to pay for a relatively short period of use constitutes an inordinately large proportion of the total value of the asset.

4. The lease payments greatly exceed the current fair rental value of the asset.
5. The property may be acquired at a bargain price in relation to the fair market value of the asset at the time when the option may be exercised.
6. Some portion of the lease payments is specifically designated as interest or its equivalent.[7]

As with the accounting criteria, these rules attempt to identify cases in which a lease is likely to provide the lessee with use of the asset for a large fraction of its useful life. These rules are somewhat vague and are designed to provide the IRS with sufficient latitude to prevent the use of leases solely for tax avoidance.

For example, suppose a $200,000 asset was required to be depreciated by $20,000 per year for 10 years for tax purposes. By acquiring the asset through a four-year $1.00 out lease with payments of $50,000 per year, a firm could receive the same $200,000 total deduction at a faster rate if the lease were categorized as a true tax lease.[8] The IRS rules prevent this type of transaction by categorizing such a lease as a non-tax lease (via conditions 3 and 5).

Leases and Bankruptcy

Recall from Chapter 16 that when a firm files for bankruptcy under Chapter 11 of the U.S. bankruptcy code, its assets are protected from seizure by the firm's creditors while existing management is given the opportunity to propose a reorganization plan. Even secured lenders are prevented from taking the assets that serve as collateral for their loans during this period, which can last from a few months to several years. Instead, bankruptcy law permits the firm to continue to use the assets in an effort to remain a going concern.

The treatment of leased property in bankruptcy will depend on whether the lease is classified as a security interest or a true lease by the bankruptcy judge. If the lease is deemed to be a **security interest**, the firm is assumed to have effective ownership of the asset and the asset is protected against seizure. The lessor is then treated as any other secured creditor and must await the firm's reorganization or ultimate liquidation.

If the lease is classified as a **true lease** in bankruptcy, then the lessor retains ownership rights over the asset. Within 120 days of filing Chapter 11, the bankrupt firm must choose whether to assume or reject the lease. If it assumes the lease, it must settle all pending claims and continue to make all promised lease payments. If it rejects the lease, the asset must be returned to the lessor (with any pending claims of the lessor becoming unsecured claims against the bankrupt firm).

Thus, if a lease contract is characterized as a true lease in bankruptcy, the lessor is in a superior position than a lender if the firm defaults. By retaining ownership of the asset, the lessor has the right to repossess it if the lease payments are not made, even if the firm seeks bankruptcy protection. A lease therefore allows the lessee to commit to give the lessor superior treatment in default compared to ordinary creditors. Such commitment is efficient if the asset would be more valuable in the hands of the lessor than if retained by the defaulted firm. In this case, the firm might choose to lease assets it would otherwise choose not to finance.[9]

---

[7]IRS Revenue Ruling 55–540, 1955. Additional considerations exist for the tax treatment for the lessor if the lease is a leveraged lease.

[8]This transaction would have the opposite tax consequence for the lessor: The lease payments would be taxed as revenues, but the cost of the asset would be depreciated at the slower rate. However, there can be an advantage if the lessor is in a lower tax bracket than the lessee.

[9]For an analysis of the consequences of this treatment of leases for a firm's borrowing capacity, see A. Eisfeldt and A. Rampini, "Leasing, Ability to Repossess, and Debt Capacity," *Review of Financial Studies* 22(4) (2008): 1621–1657.

Synthetic Leases

Synthetic leases are designed to be treated as an operating lease for accounting purposes and as a non-tax lease for tax purposes. With a synthetic lease, the lessee is able to deduct depreciation and interest expenses for tax purposes, just as if it had borrowed to purchase the asset, but does not need to report the asset or the debt on its balance sheet.

To obtain this accounting and tax treatment, synthetic leases have typically been structured by creating a special-purpose entity that will act as the lessor and obtain financing, acquire the asset, and lease it to the firm. To ensure that the lease qualifies as an operating lease, the lease is structured so that it (1) provides a fixed purchase price at the end of the lease term based on an initial appraised value (and so is not a bargain price), (2) has a term less than 75% of the economic life of the asset (which is renewable under certain conditions), and (3) has minimum lease payments with a present value less than 90% of the fair value of the property. In addition, to avoid balance sheet consolidation, the owner of record of the SPE must make an initial minimum equity investment of 3% that remains at risk during the entire lease term. The lease can qualify as a non-tax lease by designating some portion of the lease payments as interest.

A major motivation for such leases appears to be that they allow firms to use debt while avoiding the accounting consequences of debt. In particular, by keeping the debt off the balance sheet, the firm's debt-equity ratio is improved, its return on assets is generally raised, and, if the lease payments are less than the interest and depreciation expenses, its reported earnings per share will be higher.

These types of transactions were used and abused by Enron Corporation to boost its earnings and hide its liabilities prior to its downfall. In the wake of the Enron scandal, the FASB significantly tightened the requirements for SPEs, raising the at-risk equity investment of the SPE to 10% and requiring that ownership truly be independent from the lessor. Investors have also reacted skeptically to such deals, forcing many firms to avoid synthetic leases or unwind structures that were already in place. For example, in 2002, Krispy Kreme Doughnuts Corporation reversed its decision to use a synthetic lease to fund a new $35 million plant after an article critical of the transaction was published in *Forbes* magazine. Because of abuses like these, starting in 2019, the FASB will require all leases to be on-balance sheet items.

Whether a transaction is classified as a true lease or a security interest will depend on the facts of each case, but the distinction is very similar to the accounting and tax distinctions made earlier. Operating and true tax leases are generally viewed as true leases by the courts, whereas capital and non-tax leases are more likely to be viewed as a security interest. In particular, leases for which the lessee obtains possession of the asset for its remaining economic life (either within the contract or through an option to renew or purchase at a nominal charge) are generally deemed security interests.[10]

CONCEPT CHECK

1. What is the difference between the accounting treatment of operating and capital leases? What aspect of this accounting treatment will change in 2019?
2. Is it possible for a lease to be treated as an operating lease for accounting purposes and as a non-tax lease for tax purposes?

25.3 The Leasing Decision

How should a firm decide whether to buy or lease an asset? Recall that in a perfect market the decision is irrelevant, so the real-world decision depends on market frictions. In this section, we consider one important market friction—taxes—and evaluate the financial consequences of the leasing decision from the perspective of the lessee. We show how to determine whether it is more attractive to lease an asset or to buy it and (potentially)

[10]See Article 1 of the Uniform Commercial Code, Section 1-203 at www.law.upenn.edu/bll/ulc/ulc.htm#ucc1.

finance the purchase with debt. First, we consider a true tax lease; then, we turn to non-tax leases at the end of the section.

Cash Flows for a True Tax Lease

If a firm purchases a piece of equipment, the expense is a capital expenditure. Therefore, the purchase price can be depreciated over time, generating a depreciation tax shield. If the equipment is leased and the lease is a true tax lease, there is no capital expenditure, but the lease payments are an operating expense.

Let's compare the cash flows arising from a true tax lease with those arising from a purchase using an example. Emory Printing needs a new high-speed printing press. It can purchase one for $50,000 in cash. The machine will last five years, and it will be depreciated for tax purposes using straight-line depreciation over that period.[11] This means that Emory can deduct $10,000 per year for depreciation. Given its tax rate of 35%, Emory will therefore save $3500 per year in taxes from the depreciation deduction.

Alternatively, Emory can lease the machine instead of purchasing it. A five-year lease contract will cost $12,500 per year. Emory must make these payments at the beginning of each year. Because the lease is a true tax lease, Emory deducts the lease payments as an operating expense when they are paid. Thus, the after-tax cost of each lease payment is $(1 - 35\%) \times 12{,}500 = \$8125$. The lease contract does not provide for maintenance or servicing of the machine, so these costs are identical whether the machine is leased or purchased.

Table 25.1 shows the free cash flow consequences of buying and leasing. Here, we consider only the cash flows that differ as a result of leasing versus buying. We do not need to consider cash flows that would be the same in both situations, such as the sales revenues generated by having the machine and maintenance expenses. We have also assumed the machine has no residual value after five years if it is purchased. If any of these differences existed, we would include them in the cash flows. Recall from Eq. 8.6 of Chapter 8 that free cash flow can be calculated as EBITDA less taxes, capital expenditures and increases in net working capital, plus the depreciation tax shield (i.e., tax rate × depreciation expense). Thus, if Emory buys, the only change to FCF is from capital expenditures and the depreciation tax shield, and if Emory leases, the only change is a reduction in EBITDA, and therefore taxes, from the lease payment.

TABLE 25.1 SPREADSHEET **Cash Flow ($) Consequences from Leasing Versus Buying**

		Year 0	1	2	3	4	5
Buy							
1	Capital Expenditures	(50,000)	—	—	—	—	—
2	Depreciation Tax Shield at 35%	—	3,500	3,500	3,500	3,500	3,500
3	**Free Cash Flow (Buy)**	(50,000)	3,500	3,500	3,500	3,500	3,500
Lease							
4	Lease Payments	(12,500)	(12,500)	(12,500)	(12,500)	(12,500)	—
5	Income Tax Savings at 35%	4,375	4,375	4,375	4,375	4,375	—
6	**Free Cash Flow (Lease)**	(8,125)	(8,125)	(8,125)	(8,125)	(8,125)	—

[11] In practice, a more accelerated depreciation schedule would be used for tax purposes. We use straight-line depreciation here for simplicity.

Note that the cash flows of leasing differ from buying. A purchase requires a large initial outlay followed by a series of depreciation tax credits. In contrast, the cost of a leased machine is more evenly spread over time.

Lease Versus Buy (An Unfair Comparison)

Is it better for Emory to lease or buy the printing press? To begin to answer this question, let's compare the present value of the cash flows in each transaction (or, equivalently, we can compute the NPV of the difference between the cash flows). To compute the present value, we need to determine the cost of capital.

The appropriate cost of capital depends, of course, on the risk of the cash flows. Lease payments are a fixed obligation of the firm. If Emory fails to make the lease payments, it will default on the lease. The lessor will seek the remaining lease payments and, in addition, will take back the printing press. In that sense, a lease is similar to a loan secured with the leased asset as collateral. Moreover, as discussed in Section 25.2, in a true lease the lessor is in an even better position than a secured creditor if the firm files for bankruptcy. Thus, *the risk of the lease payments is no greater than the risk of secured debt*, so it is reasonable to discount the lease payments at the firm's secured borrowing rate.

The tax savings from the lease payments and from depreciation expenses are also low-risk cash flows, as they are predetermined and will be realized as long as the firm generates positive income.[12] Therefore, a common assumption in practice is to use the firm's borrowing rate for these cash flows as well.

If Emory's borrowing rate is 8%, the cost of buying the machine has present value

$$PV(\text{Buy}) = -50{,}000 + \frac{3500}{1.08} + \frac{3500}{1.08^2} + \frac{3500}{1.08^3} + \frac{3500}{1.08^4} + \frac{3500}{1.08^5}$$

$$= -\$36{,}026$$

The cost of leasing the machine has present value

$$PV(\text{Lease}) = -8125 - \frac{8125}{1.08} - \frac{8125}{1.08^2} - \frac{8125}{1.08^3} - \frac{8125}{1.08^4}$$

$$= -\$35{,}036$$

Thus, leasing is cheaper than buying, with a net savings of $36,026 − $35,036 = $990.

The preceding analysis ignores an important point, however. When a firm enters into a lease, it is committing to lease payments that are a fixed future obligation of the firm. If the firm is in financial distress and cannot make the lease payments, the lessor can seize the machine. Moreover, the lease obligations themselves could trigger financial distress. Therefore, when a firm leases an asset, it is effectively adding leverage to its capital structure (whether or not the lease appears on the balance sheet for accounting purposes).

Because leasing is a form of financing, we should compare it to other financing options that Emory may have. Rather than buy the asset outright, Emory could borrow funds (or reduce its planned cash balances, and thereby increase its net debt) to finance the purchase of the machine, thus matching the leverage of the lease. If Emory does borrow, it

[12] Even if income is negative, these tax benefits may still be obtained through carryback or carryforward provisions that allow the firm to apply these credits against income that was generated in past or future years.

will also benefit from the interest tax shield provided by leverage. This tax advantage may make borrowing to buy the machine more attractive than leasing. Thus, to evaluate a lease correctly, we should compare it to purchasing the asset using an equivalent amount of leverage. In other words, the appropriate comparison is not lease versus buy, but rather lease versus borrow.

Lease Versus Borrow (The Right Comparison)

To compare leasing to borrowing, we must determine the amount of the loan that leads to the same level of fixed obligations that Emory would have with the lease. We call this loan the **lease-equivalent loan**. That is, the lease-equivalent loan is the loan that is required on the purchase of the asset that leaves the purchaser with the same obligations as the lessee would have.[13]

The Lease-Equivalent Loan. To compute the lease-equivalent loan in Emory's case, we first compute the difference between the cash flows from leasing versus buying, which we refer to as the incremental free cash flow of leasing. As Table 25.2 shows, relative to buying, leasing saves cash upfront but results in lower future cash flows. The incremental free cash flow in years 1 through 5 represents the effective leverage the firm takes on by leasing. Alternatively, Emory could take on this same leverage by purchasing the printing press and taking on a loan with these same after-tax debt payments. How much could Emory borrow by taking on such a loan? Because the future incremental cash flows are the after-tax payments Emory will make on the loan, the initial balance on the lease-equivalent loan is the present value of these cash flows using Emory's after-tax cost of debt:

$$\text{Loan Balance} = PV[\text{Future FCF of Lease Versus Buy at } r_D(1 - \tau_c)] \tag{25.4}$$

Using Emory's after-tax borrowing cost of 8% (1 − 35%) = 5.2%, the initial loan balance is

$$\text{Loan Balance} = \frac{11{,}625}{1.052} + \frac{11{,}625}{1.052^2} + \frac{11{,}625}{1.052^3} + \frac{11{,}625}{1.052^4} + \frac{3500}{1.052^5} = \$43{,}747 \tag{25.5}$$

Eq. 25.5 implies that if Emory is willing to take on the future obligations implied by leasing, it could instead buy the printing press and borrow $43,747. This exceeds the savings of $41,875 in year 0 from leasing shown in Table 25.2. Thus, by buying and borrowing using the lease-equivalent loan, Emory saves an additional $43,747 − 41,875 = $1872 initially, and so leasing the machine is unattractive relative to this alternative.

TABLE 25.2 SPREADSHEET **Incremental Free Cash Flows of Leasing Versus Buying**

	Year	0	1	2	3	4	5
	Lease vs. Buy ($)						
1	FCF Lease (Line 6, Table 25.1)	(8,125)	(8,125)	(8,125)	(8,125)	(8,125)	—
2	Less: FCF Buy (Line 3, Table 25.1)	50,000	(3,500)	(3,500)	(3,500)	(3,500)	(3,500)
3	**Lease–Buy**	**41,875**	**(11,625)**	**(11,625)**	**(11,625)**	**(11,625)**	**(3,500)**

[13]See S. Myers, D. Dill, and A. Bautista, "Valuation of Financial Lease Contracts," *Journal of Finance* 31(3) (1976): 799–819, for a development of this method.

TABLE 25.3 SPREADSHEET **Cash Flows from Buying and Borrowing Using the Lease-Equivalent Loan**

	Year	0	1	2	3	4	5
Lease–Equivalent Loan ($)							
1	Loan Balance (PV at 5.2%)	43,747	34,397	24,561	14,213	3,327	—
Buy with Lease Equivalent Loan ($)							
2	Net Borrowing (Repayment)	43,747	(9,350)	(9,836)	(10,348)	(10,886)	(3,327)
3	Interest (at 8%)		(3,500)	(2,752)	(1,965)	(1,137)	(266)
4	Interest Tax Shield at 35%		1,225	963	688	398	93
5	Cash Flows of Loan (After-Tax)	43,747	(11,625)	(11,625)	(11,625)	(11,625)	(3,500)
6	FCF Buy	(50,000)	3,500	3,500	3,500	3,500	3,500
7	Cash Flows of Borrow + Buy	(6,253)	(8,125)	(8,125)	(8,125)	(8,125)	—

We verify this result explicitly in the spreadsheet in Table 25.3. There, we compute the cash flows that result from buying the machine and borrowing using the lease-equivalent loan. Line 1 shows the lease-equivalent loan balance, which we compute at each date by applying Eq. 25.4. Line 2 shows the initial borrowing and principal payments of the loan (computed as the change in the loan balance from the prior year). Line 3 shows the interest due each year (8% of the prior loan balance), and line 4 computes the interest tax shield (35% of the interest amount). Line 5 then totals the after-tax cash flows of the loan, which we combine with the free cash flow from buying the printing press, to compute the total cash flow from buying and borrowing on line 7.

Comparing the cash flows from buying the printing press and financing it with the lease-equivalent loan (line 7 of Table 25.3) with the cash flows of the lease (e.g., line 1 of Table 25.2), we see that in both cases Emory has a net future obligation of $8125 per year for four years. But while the leverage is the same for the two strategies, the initial cash flow is not. With the lease, Emory will pay $8125 initially; with the loan, Emory will pay the purchase price of the printing press minus the amount borrowed, or $50,000 − $43,747 = $6253. Again, we see that borrowing to buy the machine is cheaper than the lease, with a savings of $8125 − $6253 = $1872. For Emory, the lease is not attractive. If Emory is willing to take on that much leverage, it would be better off doing so by borrowing to purchase the printing press, rather than leasing it.

A Direct Method. Now that we have seen the role of the lease-equivalent loan, we can use the tools of Chapter 18 to directly compare leasing with an equivalent debt-financed purchase. Recall from Chapter 18 that when the cash flows of an investment will be offset completely with leverage, the appropriate weighted average cost of capital is given by $r_U - \tau_c r_D$, where r_U is the unlevered cost of capital for the investment (see Eq. 18.11 and the discussion on pages 656–658). Because the incremental cash flows from leasing versus borrowing are relatively safe, $r_U = r_D$ and so $r_{wacc} = r_D(1 - \tau_c)$. Thus, *we can compare leasing to buying the asset using equivalent leverage by discounting the incremental cash flows of leasing versus buying using the after-tax borrowing rate.*

In Emory's case, discounting the incremental free cash flow in Table 25.2 at Emory's after-tax borrowing cost of 8% × (1 − 35%) = 5.2%, we get

$$PV(\text{Lease Versus Borrow}) = 41{,}875 - \frac{11{,}625}{1.052} - \frac{11{,}625}{1.052^2} - \frac{11{,}625}{1.052^3} - \frac{11{,}625}{1.052^4} - \frac{3500}{1.052^5}$$
$$= -\$1872$$

Note that this is precisely the difference we calculated earlier.

The Effective After-Tax Lease Borrowing Rate. We can also compare leasing and buying in terms of an effective after-tax borrowing rate associated with the lease. This is given by the IRR of the incremental lease cash flows in Table 25.2, which we can calculate as 7%:

$$41{,}875 - \frac{11{,}625}{1.07} - \frac{11{,}625}{1.07^2} - \frac{11{,}625}{1.07^3} - \frac{11{,}625}{1.07^4} - \frac{3500}{1.07^5} = 0$$

Thus, the lease is equivalent to borrowing at an after-tax rate of 7%. This option is not attractive compared to the after-tax rate of only $8\% \times (1 - 35\%) = 5.2\%$ that Emory pays on its debt. Because we are borrowing (positive followed by negative cash flows), a lower IRR is better. But be careful with this approach—as discussed in Chapter 7, if the cash flows alternate signs more than once, the IRR method cannot be relied upon.

Evaluating a True Tax Lease

In summary, when evaluating a true-tax lease, we should compare leasing to a purchase that is financed with equivalent leverage. We suggest the following approach:

1. Compute the *incremental cash flows* for leasing versus buying, as we did in Table 25.2. Include the depreciation tax shield (if buying) and the tax deductibility of the lease payments if leasing.
2. Compute the NPV of leasing versus buying using equivalent leverage by discounting the incremental cash flows at the *after-tax borrowing rate.*

If the NPV computed in Step 2 is negative, then leasing is unattractive compared to traditional debt financing. In this case, the firm should not lease, but rather should acquire the asset using an optimal amount of leverage (based on the trade-offs and techniques discussed in Parts 5 and 6).

If the NPV computed in Step 2 is positive, then leasing does provide an advantage over traditional debt financing and should be considered. Management should recognize, however, that while it may not be listed on the balance sheet, the lease increases the firm's effective leverage by the amount of the lease-equivalent loan.[14]

EXAMPLE 25.6 Evaluating New Lease Terms

Problem

Suppose Emory rejects the lease we analyzed, and the lessor agrees to lower the lease rate to $11,800 per year. Does this change make the lease attractive?

Solution

The incremental cash flows are shown in the following table:

Year	0	1	2	3	4	5
Buy						
1 Capital Expenditures	(50,000)	—	—	—	—	—
2 Depreciation Tax Shield at 35%	—	3,500	3,500	3,500	3,500	3,500
3 **Free Cash Flow (Buy)**	(50,000)	3,500	3,500	3,500	3,500	3,500
Lease						
4 Lease Payments	(11,800)	(11,800)	(11,800)	(11,800)	(11,800)	—
5 Income Tax Savings at 35%	4,130	4,130	4,130	4,130	4,130	—
6 **Free Cash Flow (Lease)**	(7,670)	(7,670)	(7,670)	(7,670)	(7,670)	—
Lease vs. Buy						
7 **Lease–Buy**	**42,330**	**(11,170)**	**(11,170)**	**(11,170)**	**(11,170)**	**(3,500)**

[14]If financial distress or other costs of leverage are large, the firm may wish to offset some of this increase in leverage by reducing other debt of the firm.

Using Emory's after-tax borrowing cost of 5.2%, the gain from leasing versus an equivalently leveraged purchase is

$$\begin{aligned} NPV(\text{Lease Versus Borrow}) &= 42{,}330 - \frac{11{,}170}{1.052} - \frac{11{,}170}{1.052^2} - \frac{11{,}170}{1.052^3} - \frac{11{,}170}{1.052^4} - \frac{3500}{1.052^5} \\ &= 42{,}330 - 42{,}141 \\ &= \$189 \end{aligned}$$

Therefore, the lease is attractive at the new terms.

Evaluating a Non-Tax Lease

Evaluating a non-tax lease is much more straightforward than evaluating a true tax lease. For a non-tax lease, the lessee still receives the depreciation deductions (as though the asset were purchased). Only the interest portion of the lease payment is deductible, however. Thus, in terms of cash flows, a non-tax lease is directly comparable to a traditional loan. Therefore, it is attractive if it offers a better interest rate than would be available with a loan. To determine whether it does offer a better rate, we can discount the lease payments at the firm's *pretax* borrowing rate and compare it to the purchase price of the asset.

EXAMPLE 25.7 Comparing a Non-Tax Lease with a Standard Loan

Problem

Suppose the lease in Example 25.6 is a non-tax lease. Would it be attractive for Emory in this case?

Solution

Instead of purchasing the machine for \$50,000, Emory will pay lease payments of \$11,800 per year. That is, Emory is effectively borrowing \$50,000 by making payments of \$11,800 per year. Given Emory's 8% borrowing rate, payments of \$11,800 per year on a standard loan would allow Emory to borrow

$$PV(\text{Lease Payments}) = 11{,}800 + \frac{11{,}800}{1.08} + \frac{11{,}800}{1.08^2} + \frac{11{,}800}{1.08^3} + \frac{11{,}800}{1.08^4} = \$50{,}883$$

That is, by making the same payments on a loan, Emory could raise more than \$50,000. Thus, the lease is not attractive at these terms if it is a non-tax lease.

For both the true tax lease and the non-tax lease, we have ignored the residual value of the asset, any differences in the maintenance and service arrangements with a lease versus a purchase, and any cancellation or other lease options. If these features are present, they should also be included when comparing leasing versus a debt-financed purchase.

CONCEPT CHECK

1. Why is it inappropriate to compare leasing to buying?
2. What discount rate should be used for the incremental lease cash flows to compare a true tax lease to borrowing?
3. How can we compare a non-tax lease to borrowing?

25.4 Reasons for Leasing

In Section 25.3, we saw how to determine whether a lease is attractive for the potential lessee. A similar, but reverse argument can be used from the standpoint of the lessor. The lessor could compare leasing the equipment to lending the money to the firm so that it can purchase the equipment. Under what circumstances would leasing be profitable for both the lessor and the lessee? If a lease is a good deal for one of the parties, is it a bad deal for the other? Or are there underlying economic sources of value in a lease contract?

Valid Arguments for Leasing

For a lease to be attractive to both the lessee and the lessor, the gains must come from some underlying economic benefits that the leasing arrangement provides. Here, we consider some valid reasons for leasing.

Tax Differences. With a true tax lease, the lessee replaces depreciation and interest tax deductions with a deduction for the lease payments. Depending on the timing of the payments, one set of deductions will have a larger present value. A tax gain occurs if the lease shifts the more valuable deductions to the party with the higher tax rate. Generally speaking, if the asset's tax depreciation deductions are more rapid than its lease payments, a true tax lease is advantageous if the lessor is in a higher tax bracket than the lessee.[15] In contrast, if the asset's tax depreciation deductions are slower than its lease payments, there are tax gains from a true tax lease if the lessor is in a lower tax bracket than the lessee.

EXAMPLE 25.8 Exploiting Tax Differences Through Leasing

Problem

Suppose Emory is offered a true tax lease for the printing press at a lease rate of $11,800 per year. Show that this lease is profitable for Emory as well as for a lessor with a 15% tax rate and an 8% borrowing cost.

Solution

We already evaluated the lease with these terms in Example 25.6. There, we found that the NPV of leasing versus borrowing was $189 for Emory. Now let's consider the lease from the standpoint of the lessor. The lessor will buy the printing press and then lease it to Emory. The incremental cash flows for the lessor from buying and leasing are as follows:

	Year	0	1	2	3	4	5
Buy							
1	Capital Expenditures	(50,000)	—	—	—	—	—
2	Depreciation Tax Shield at 15%	—	1,500	1,500	1,500	1,500	1,500
3	**Free Cash Flow (Buy)**	(50,000)	1,500	1,500	1,500	1,500	1,500
Lease							
4	Lease Payments	11,800	11,800	11,800	11,800	11,800	—
5	Income Tax at 15%	(1,770)	(1,770)	(1,770)	(1,770)	(1,770)	—
6	**Free Cash Flow (Lease)**	10,030	10,030	10,030	10,030	10,030	—
Lessor Free Cash Flow							
7	**Buy and Lease**	**(39,970)**	**11,530**	**11,530**	**11,530**	**11,530**	**1,500**

Evaluating the cash flows at the after-tax rate of $8\% \times (1 - 15\%) = 6.8\%$, we find the NPV $= \$341 > 0$ for the lessor. (Using the after-tax rate for the lessor implies that the lessor will borrow against the future free cash flows of the transaction.) Thus, both sides gain from the transaction due to the difference in tax rates. The gain comes from the fact that for Emory, the lease provides more accelerated tax deductions than the company would receive from depreciating the printing press. Because Emory is in a higher tax bracket than the leasing company, shifting the faster tax deductions to Emory is advantageous.

[15] See J. Graham, M. Lemmon, and J. Schallheim, "Debt, Leases, Taxes, and the Endogeneity of Corporate Tax Status," *Journal of Finance* 53(1) (1998): 131–162, for evidence that low tax rate firms tend to lease more than high tax rate firms.

Reduced Resale Costs. Many assets are time consuming and costly to sell. If a firm only needs to use the asset for a short time, it is probably less costly to lease it than to buy and resell the asset. In this case, the lessor is responsible for finding a new user for the asset, but lessors are often specialized to do so and so face much lower costs. For example, car dealerships are in a better position to sell a used car at the end of a lease than a consumer is. Some of this advantage can be passed along through a lower lease rate. In addition, while owners of assets are likely to resell them only if the assets are "lemons," a short-term lease can commit the user of an asset to return it regardless of its quality. In this way, leases can help mitigate the adverse selection problem in the used goods market.[16]

Efficiency Gains from Specialization. Lessors often have efficiency advantages over lessees in maintaining or operating certain types of assets. For example, a lessor of office copy machines can employ expert technicians and maintain an inventory of spare parts required for maintenance. Some types of leases may even come with an operator, such as a truck with a driver (in fact, the term "operating lease" originated from such leases). By offering assets together with these complementary services, lessors can achieve efficiency gains and offer attractive lease rates. In addition, if the value of the asset depends upon these additional services, then a firm that purchases the asset would be dependent on the service provider, who could then raise the price for services and exploit the firm.[17] By leasing the asset and the services as a bundle, the firm maintains its bargaining power by retaining its flexibility to switch to competing equipment.

Reduced Distress Costs and Increased Debt Capacity. As noted in Section 25.2, assets leased under a true lease are not afforded bankruptcy protection and can be seized in the event of default. As a result, lease obligations effectively have higher priority and lower risk than even secured debt. In addition, the lessor may be better able to recover the full economic value of the asset (by releasing it) than a lender would. Because of the reduced risk and higher recovery value in the event of default, a lessor may be able to offer more attractive financing through the lease than an ordinary lender could. Studies suggest that this effect is important for small firms and firms that are capital constrained.[18]

Mitigating Debt Overhang. Leasing may have an additional benefit to firms that suffer from debt overhang. Recall that with debt overhang, a firm may fail to make positive NPV investments because the existing debt holders will capture much of the value of any new assets. Because of its effective seniority, a lease may allow the firm to finance its expansion while effectively segregating the claim on the new assets, and thus overcome the debt overhang problem.[19]

For example, suppose clothing designer Andreano Ltd. has an opportunity that requires use of a new \$1.1 million robotic sewing machine. The machine does not depreciate and so can be sold for \$1.1 million at the end of the year, and the project will generate an

[16]For evidence of this effect, see T. Gilligan, "Lemons and Leases in the Used Business Aircraft Market," *Journal of Political Economy* 112(5) (2004): 1157–1180.

[17]This concern is often referred to as the hold-up problem. The importance of the hold-up problem in determining the optimal ownership of assets was identified by B. Klein, R. Crawford, and A. Alchian, "Vertical Integration, Appropriable Rents, and the Competitive Contracting Process," *Journal of Law and Economics* 21 (1978): 297–326.

[18]See S. Sharpe and H. Nguyen, "Capital Market Imperfections and the Incentive to Lease," *Journal of Financial Economics* 39(2–3) (1995): 271–294; and A. Eisfeldt and A. Rampini (referenced in footnote 9).

[19]See R. Stulz and H. Johnson, "An Analysis of Secured Debt," *Journal of Financial Economics*, 14 (1985): 501–521.

INTERVIEW WITH

MARK LONG

Mark Long, XOJET's Executive Vice President and Chief Financial Officer since 2009, has more than 25 years' aviation finance experience. He is responsible for maximizing XOJET's operating performance, achieving financial goals, and managing financial risks, as well as aircraft fleet planning and asset management at the company.

QUESTION: *How is XOJET financed?*

ANSWER: XOJET, one of the largest private aviation companies in North America, owns and operates the largest chartered fleet of super midsize jets and also leases jets to supplement its fleet. XOJET is financed by equity, secured and unsecured debt, and operating leases. As a private company in a capital-intensive business, XOJET maximizes use of debt financing secured by aircraft primarily funded through an established credit facility. Using aircraft as security reduces lender risk and therefore expands our access to debt capital markets and minimizes our cost of financing.

QUESTION: *How do you make the decision whether to expand your fleet? How do you compare buying versus leasing airplanes?*

ANSWER: XOJET's fleet expansion criteria include such factors as:

- Positive contribution to maintain a 15% or higher ROIC (return on invested capital).
- Sufficient and sustainable customer demand generated through our retail channel.
- Availability of suitable lease or debt financing.
- Evaluation of the business environment: economic cycle stage, competitive environment, and growth outlook.
- Availability of suitably priced used aircraft for sale or lease that comport to our business model at the right capital cost.

Because paying all cash ("buying") an aircraft is typically not an optimal use of our cash resources, the decision focuses on the type of financing available and the terms, as well as lease accounting treatment. Operating leases are off-balance sheet, whereas capital leases (essentially full-payout loans like a mortgage) are carried on the balance sheet. Thus it's also important to consider XOJET's ability to add more balance-sheet debt.

We first assess the market availability for lease financing and any potential asset utilization penalties for excess use. Then we consider current and future residual values for a particular aircraft, secondary market conditions, the cash deposits required for the lease, and the potential extra cost of acceptable return condition obligations (beyond normal wear). In addition, some individuals and small businesses have tax incentives to purchase an aircraft and then lease it to an operator like XOJET. These special situations may offer preferred lease terms to XOJET that may not otherwise be available in traditional debt markets, making leasing an attractive option.

QUESTION: *What are some of the advantages/disadvantages associated with leasing?*

ANSWER: The leasing arena offers a broader marketplace of investors, expanding our financing avenues. Another benefit is the transfer of the residual value risk to the lessor. An operating (off-balance sheet) lease reported in a financial footnote helps us manage compliance with leverage and coverage ratio covenants. Leases also allow us to structure both the lease term to best match the cash flow production over an asset's planned life of the asset and the most tax efficient use of the asset.

A major disadvantage of an operating lease, which is expensed, is its negative impact on EBITDA, a common profitability measure. (The interest expense associated with loans does not impact EBITDA.) Leases are also non-cancellable and incur large early-termination penalties, which means less flexibility for XOJET to respond to changing market conditions.

QUESTION: *Do you view leasing as another form of financing that is similar to debt, and why?*

ANSWER: XOJET views each form of financing type as similar, although each has its advantages and disadvantages as mentioned previously. In some cases lease financing may be the best option, depending on the situational facts and seller motivation. Leasing is typically—but not always—a more expensive source of financing because the lessor wants to earn a premium over its cost of funds, mitigate potential credit risk through significant cash deposits, and be compensated for potential future residual value risk.

additional \$550,000 with certainty, for a total payoff of \$1.65 million. If the risk-free rate is 10%, then this opportunity has NPV of \$1.65 million/1.10 − 1.1 million = \$400,000.

But suppose there is a 40% probability that Andreano will be in bankruptcy next year and its equity will be wiped out. In that case, the present value of the project's payoff to equity holders is only 60% × \$1.65 million/1.10 = \$900,000, and it will not be willing to invest the \$1.1 million needed to purchase the machine upfront.[20]

On the other hand, suppose Andreano can lease the machine for the year. From Eq. 25.1, the competitive one-year lease rate is \$1.1 million − 1.1 million/1.10 = \$100,000. Equity holders would be willing to contribute this amount, as the present value of the equity holders' payoff from the new project is 60% × \$550,000/1.10 = \$300,000. Leasing solves the debt overhang by allowing Andreano to use the machine without giving existing debt holders a claim to it in the event of default.[21]

Transferring Risk. At the beginning of a lease, there may be significant uncertainty about the residual value of the leased asset, and whoever owns the asset bears this risk. Leasing allows the party best able to bear the risk to hold it. For example, small firms with a low tolerance for risk may prefer to lease rather than purchase assets.

Improved Incentives. When the lessor is the manufacturer, a lease in which the lessor bears the risk of the residual value can improve incentives and lower agency costs. Such a lease provides the manufacturer with an incentive to produce a high-quality, durable product that will retain its value over time. In addition, if the manufacturer is a monopolist, leasing the product gives the manufacturer an incentive not to overproduce and lower the product's residual value, as well as an ability to restrict competition from sales of used goods.

Despite these potential benefits, significant agency costs may also be associated with leasing. For leases in which the lessor retains a substantial interest in the asset's residual value, the lessee has less of an incentive to take proper care of an asset that is leased rather than purchased.[22]

Suspect Arguments for Leasing

Some reasons that lessees and lessors cite for preferring leasing to purchasing are difficult to justify economically. While they may be important in some circumstances, they deserve careful scrutiny.

Avoiding Capital Expenditure Controls. One reason some managers will choose to lease equipment rather than purchase it is to avoid the scrutiny from superiors that often accompanies large capital expenditures. For example, some companies may place limits on the dollar amounts a manager can invest over a certain period; lease payments may fall below these limits, whereas the cost of the purchase would not. By leasing, the manager

[20]For simplicity, we have assumed in this example that all risk is idiosyncratic so that we can discount at the risk-free rate. More generally, the same results hold even if the risk is not idiosyncratic as long as we interpret the probabilities as risk-neutral probabilities, as discussed in Chapter 21.

[21]While secured debt might also be beneficial in this example, there is some risk that secured debt holders might not be able to repossess the assets in a timely fashion in the event of bankruptcy, and thus would not receive its full liquidation value.

[22]As an example, auto manufacturers require individuals who lease their cars to provide proper maintenance. Without such requirements, individuals would be tempted to avoid paying for oil changes and other maintenance near the end of the lease term. Of course, there are other ways lessees may abuse their cars (driving at excessive speeds, for example) that cannot be easily controlled.

avoids having to make a special request for funds. This reason for leasing is also apparent in the public sector, where large assets are often leased to avoid asking the government or the public to approve the funds necessary to purchase the assets. However, the lease may cost more than the purchase, wasting stockholder or taxpayer dollars in the long run.

Preserving Capital. A common argument made in favor of leasing is that it provides "100% financing" because no down payment is required, so the lessee can save cash to use for other needs. Of course, in a perfect market financing is irrelevant, so for leases to have a financing advantage, some friction must exist. Possible imperfections include the distress costs, debt overhang, and tax differentials discussed above. But it is important to appreciate that the advantage of a lease derives from its differential treatment for tax purposes and in bankruptcy, not because leases provide 100% financing. For firms that are not subject to these frictions, the amount of leverage the firm can obtain through a lease is unlikely to exceed the amount of leverage the firm can obtain through a loan.

Reducing Leverage Through Off-Balance-Sheet Financing. By carefully avoiding the four criteria that define a capital lease for accounting purposes, a firm can avoid listing the long-term lease as a liability. Because a lease is equivalent to a loan, the firm can increase its actual leverage without increasing the debt-to-equity ratio on its balance sheet. But whether they appear on the balance sheet or not, lease commitments are liabilities for the firm. As a result, they will have the same effect on the risk and return characteristics of the firm as other forms of leverage do. Most financial analysts and sophisticated investors understand this fact and consider operating leases (which must be listed in the footnotes of the financial statements) to be additional sources of leverage.

CONCEPT CHECK

1. What are some of the potential gains from leasing if the lessee plans to hold the asset for only a small fraction of its useful life?
2. If a lease is not listed as a liability on the firm's balance sheet, does it mean that a firm that leases rather than borrows is less risky?

MyFinanceLab Here is what you should know after reading this chapter. MyFinanceLab will help you identify what you know and where to go when you need to practice.

25.1 The Basics of Leasing

- A lease is a contract between two parties: the lessee and the lessor. The lessee is liable for periodic payments in exchange for the right to use the asset. The lessor, who is the owner of the asset, is entitled to the lease payments in exchange for lending the asset.
- Many types of lease transactions are possible depending on the relationship between the lessee and the lessor.
  - In a sales-type lease, the lessor is the manufacturer or primary dealer of the asset.
  - In a direct lease, the lessor is an independent company that specializes in purchasing assets and leasing them to customers.
  - If a firm already owns an asset it would prefer to lease, it can arrange a sale and leaseback transaction.
- In a perfect market, the cost of leasing is equivalent to the cost of purchasing and reselling the asset. Also, the cost of leasing and then purchasing the asset is equivalent to the cost of borrowing to purchase the asset.

- In many cases, the lease provides options for the lessee to obtain ownership of the asset at the end of the lease. Some examples include fair market value leases, $1.00 out leases, and fixed price or fair market value cap leases.

25.2 Accounting, Tax, and Legal Consequences of Leasing

- The FASB recognizes two types of leases based on the lease terms: operating leases and capital leases. Operating leases do not appear on the balance sheet, and lease payments are deducted as a rental expense. Capital leases are treated as a purchase and a loan, with interest and depreciation expenses. Beginning in 2019, firms will also list operating lease obligations on the balance sheet.
- The IRS separates leases into two broad categories: true tax leases and non-tax leases. With a true tax lease, the lessee deducts lease payments as an operating expense. A non-tax lease is treated as a loan for tax purposes, so the lessee must depreciate the asset and can expense only the interest portion of the lease payments.
- In a true lease, the asset is not protected in the event that the lessee declares bankruptcy, and the lessor can seize the asset if lease payments are not made. If the lease is deemed a security interest by the bankruptcy court, then the asset is protected and the lessor becomes a secured creditor.

25.3 The Leasing Decision

- To evaluate the leasing decision for a true tax lease, managers should compare the cost of leasing with the cost of financing using an equivalent amount of leverage.
  - Compute the incremental cash flows for leasing versus buying.
  - Compute the NPV by discounting the incremental cash flows at the after-tax borrowing rate.
- The cash flows of a non-tax lease are directly comparable to the cash flows of a traditional loan, so a non-tax lease is attractive only if it offers a better interest rate than a loan.

25.4 Reasons for Leasing

- Good reasons for leasing include tax differences, reduced resale costs, efficiency gains from specialization, reduced bankruptcy costs, mitigating debt overhang, risk transfer, and improved incentives.
- Suspect reasons for leasing include avoiding capital expenditure controls, preserving capital, and reducing leverage through off-balance-sheet financing.

Key Terms

$1.00 out lease *p. 894*
capital (finance) lease *p. 896*
direct lease *p. 890*
fair market value cap lease *p. 894*
fair market value (FMV) lease *p. 893*
fixed price lease *p. 894*
lease-equivalent loan *p. 903*
lessee *p. 890*
lessor *p. 890*
leveraged lease *p. 890*
non-tax lease *p. 898*
operating lease *p. 896*
residual value *p. 891*
sale and leaseback *p. 890*
sales-type lease *p. 890*
security interest *p. 899*
special-purpose entity (SPE) *p. 890*
synthetic lease *p. 890*
true lease *p. 899*
true tax lease *p. 898*

Further Reading

The following books analyze leasing in greater depth: P. Nevitt and F. Fabozzi, *Equipment Leasing* (Frank Fabozzi Associates, 2000); and J. Schallheim, *Lease or Buy? Principles for Sound Decision Making* (Harvard Business School Press, 1994).

To keep abreast of the changes to how leases are accounted for, consult the lease section of FASB Web site: www.fasb.org/jsp/FASB/Page/BridgePage&cid=1351027207574#section_1.

The academic literature on leasing has been active since the 1970s. Empirical studies on the use and effects of leasing include: J. Ang and P. Peterson, "The Leasing Puzzle," *Journal of Finance* 39(4) (1984): 1055–1065; R. Bowman, "The Debt Equivalence of Leases: An Empirical Investigation," *Accounting Review* 55(2) (1980): 237–253; T. Mukherjee, "A Survey of Corporate Leasing Analysis," *Financial Management* 20(3) (1991): 96–107; C. Smith and L. Wakeman, "Determinations of Corporate Leasing Policy," *Journal of Finance* 40(3) (1985): 895–908; J. Schallheim, K. Wells, R. Whitby, "Do Leases Expand Debt Capacity?," *Journal of Corporate Finance* 23 (2013): 368–381; and A. Rampini and A. Eisfeldt, "Leasing, Ability to Repossess, and Debt Capacity," *Review of Financial Studies* 22 (2009): 1621–1657.

Readers interested in exploring the effects of other market frictions on the leasing decision can consult the following sources: C. Lewis and J. Schallheim, "Are Debt and Leases Substitutes?," *Journal of Financial and Quantitative Analysis* 27(4) (1992): 497–511; I. Hendel and A. Lizzeri, "The Role of Leasing Under Adverse Selection," *Journal of Political Economy* 110(1) (2002): 113–143; and K. Sivarama and R. Moyer, "Bankruptcy Costs and Financial Leasing Decisions," *Financial Management* 23(2) (1994): 31–42.

An in-depth analysis of lease valuation is beyond the scope of this book. Readers interested in some of the issues that complicate the analysis can consult these sources: S. Grenadier, "An Equilibrium Analysis of Real Estate Leases," *Journal of Business* 78(4) (2005): 1173–1214; J. McConnell and J. Schallheim, "Valuation of Asset Leasing Contracts," *Journal of Financial Economics* 12(2) (1983): 237–261; J. Schallheim, R. Johnson, R. Lease, and J. McConnell, "The Determinants of Yields on Financial Leasing Contracts," *Journal of Financial Economics* 19(1) (1987): 45–67; and R. Stanton and N. Wallace, "An Empirical Test of a Contingent Claims Lease Valuation Model," *Journal of Real Estate Research* 31 (2008): 1–26.

Problems

All problems are available in MyFinanceLab. *An asterisk (*) indicates problems with a higher level of difficulty.*

The Basics of Leasing

1. Suppose an H1200 supercomputer has a cost of $200,000 and will have a residual market value of $60,000 in five years. The risk-free interest rate is 5% APR with monthly compounding.
   a. What is the risk-free monthly lease rate for a five-year lease in a perfect market?
   b. What would be the monthly payment for a five-year $200,000 risk-free loan to purchase the H1200?

2. Suppose the risk-free interest rate is 5% APR with monthly compounding. If a $2 million MRI machine can be leased for seven years for $22,000 per month, what residual value must the lessor recover to break even in a perfect market with no risk?

3. Consider a five-year lease for a $400,000 bottling machine, with a residual market value of $150,000 at the end of the five years. If the risk-free interest rate is 6% APR with monthly compounding, compute the monthly lease payment in a perfect market for the following leases:
   a. A fair market value lease
   b. A $1.00 out lease
   c. A fixed price lease with an $80,000 final price

Accounting, Tax, and Legal Consequences of Leasing

MFL **4.** Acme Distribution currently has the following items on its balance sheet:

Assets		Liabilities	
Cash	20	Debt	70
Property, Plant, and Equipment	175	Equity	125

Under current FASB accounting standards (that is, prior to 2019), how will Acme's balance sheet change if it enters into an $80 million capital lease for new warehouses? What will its book debt-equity ratio be? How will Acme's balance sheet and debt-equity ratio change if the lease is an operating lease?

5. Your firm is considering leasing a $50,000 copier. The copier has an estimated economic life of eight years. Suppose the appropriate discount rate is 9% APR with monthly compounding. Classify each lease below as a capital lease or operating lease, and explain why:
   a. A four-year fair market value lease with payments of $1150 per month
   b. A six-year fair market value lease with payments of $790 per month
   c. A five-year fair market value lease with payments of $925 per month
   d. A five-year fair market value lease with payments of $1000 per month and an option to cancel after three years with a $9000 cancellation penalty

The Leasing Decision

6. Craxton Engineering will either purchase or lease a new $756,000 fabricator. If purchased, the fabricator will be depreciated on a straight-line basis over seven years. Craxton can lease the fabricator for $130,000 per year for seven years. Craxton's tax rate is 35%. (Assume the fabricator has no residual value at the end of the seven years.)
   a. What are the free cash flow consequences of buying the fabricator if the lease is a true tax lease?
   b. What are the free cash flow consequences of leasing the fabricator if the lease is a true tax lease?
   c. What are the incremental free cash flows of leasing versus buying?

7. Riverton Mining plans to purchase or lease $220,000 worth of excavation equipment. If purchased, the equipment will be depreciated on a straight-line basis over five years, after which it will be worthless. If leased, the annual lease payments will be $55,000 per year for five years. Assume Riverton's borrowing cost is 8%, its tax rate is 35%, and the lease qualifies as a true tax lease.
   a. If Riverton purchases the equipment, what is the amount of the lease-equivalent loan?
   b. Is Riverton better off leasing the equipment or financing the purchase using the lease-equivalent loan?
   c. What is the effective after-tax lease borrowing rate? How does this compare to Riverton's actual after-tax borrowing rate?

8. Suppose Clorox can lease a new computer data processing system for $975,000 per year for five years. Alternatively, it can purchase the system for $4.25 million. Assume Clorox has a borrowing cost of 7% and a tax rate of 35%, and the system will be obsolete at the end of five years.
   a. If Clorox will depreciate the computer equipment on a straight-line basis over the next five years, and if the lease qualifies as a true tax lease, is it better to lease or finance the purchase of the equipment?
   b. Suppose that if Clorox buys the equipment, it will use accelerated depreciation for tax purposes. Specifically, suppose it can expense 20% of the purchase price immediately and can take depreciation deductions equal to 32%, 19.2%, 11.52%, 11.52%, and 5.76% of the purchase price over the next five years. Compare leasing with purchase in this case.

***9.** Suppose Procter and Gamble (P&G) is considering purchasing $15 million in new manufacturing equipment. If it purchases the equipment, it will depreciate it on a straight-line basis over the five years, after which the equipment will be worthless. It will also be responsible for maintenance expenses of $1 million per year. Alternatively, it can lease the equipment for $4.2 million per year for the five years, in which case the lessor will provide necessary maintenance. Assume P&G's tax rate is 35% and its borrowing cost is 7%.

a. What is the NPV associated with leasing the equipment versus financing it with the lease-equivalent loan?
b. What is the break-even lease rate—that is, what lease amount could P&G pay each year and be indifferent between leasing and financing a purchase?

Reasons for Leasing

*10. Suppose Amazon is considering the purchase of computer servers and network infrastructure to expand its very successful business offering cloud-based computing. In total, it will purchase $48 million in new equipment. This equipment will qualify for accelerated depreciation: 20% can be expensed immediately, followed by 32%, 19.2%, 11.52%, 11.52%, and 5.76% over the next five years. However, because of the firm's substantial loss carryforwards and other credits, Amazon estimates its marginal tax rate to be 10% over the next five years, so it will get very little tax benefit from the depreciation expenses. Thus, Amazon considers leasing the equipment instead. Suppose Amazon and the lessor face the same 8% borrowing rate, but the lessor has a 35% tax rate. For the purpose of this question, assume the equipment is worthless after five years, the lease term is five years, and the lease qualifies as a true tax lease.
a. What is the lease rate for which the lessor will break even?
b. What is the gain to Amazon with this lease rate?
c. What is the source of the gain in this transaction?

11. Western Airlines is considering a new route that will require adding an additional Boeing 777 to its fleet. Western can purchase the airplane for $225 million or lease it for $25 million per year. If it purchases the airplane, its seating can be optimized, and the new route is expected to generate profits of $50 million per year. If leased, the route will only generate profits of $35 million per year. Suppose the appropriate cost of capital is 12.5% and that, if purchased, the plane can be sold at any time for an expected resale price of $225 million. Ignore taxes.
a. As a one-year decision, does purchasing or leasing the plane have higher NPV?
b. Suppose the funds to purchase or lease the plane will come from equity holders (for example, by reducing the amount of Western's current dividend). Western also has one-year debt outstanding, and there is a 10% (risk-neutral[23]) probability that over the next year Western will declare bankruptcy and its equity holders will be wiped out. Otherwise, the debt will be rolled over at the end of the year. Is purchasing or leasing the plane more attractive to equity holders?
c. At what (risk-neutral) probability of default would equity holders' preference for leasing versus purchasing the plane change?

[23]Chapter 21 explains risk-neutral probabilities. If you have not read that chapter, you can work the problem and get the same answers by assuming that the specified probabilities are the actual probabilities of default but the risk of default is purely idiosyncratic risk.

PART

9

Short-Term Financing

THE LAW OF ONE PRICE CONNECTION. Most of the financial decisions we have studied so far have been long term, that is, decisions involving cash flows that occur over a period of time longer than one year. In Part 9, we turn to the details of running the financial side of a corporation and focus on short-term financial management. In a perfect capital market, the Law of One Price and the Modigliani-Miller propositions imply that the way a firm chooses to manage its short-term financial needs does not affect the value of the firm. In reality, short-term financial policy does matter because of the existence of market frictions. In this part of the book, we identify these frictions and explain how firms set their short-term financial policies. In Chapter 26, we discuss how firms manage their working capital requirements, including accounts receivable, accounts payable, and inventory. In Chapter 27, we explain how firms finance their short-term cash needs.

CHAPTER

26 Working Capital Management

NOTATION

CCC	cash conversion cycle
NPV	net present value
EAR	effective annual rate

IN CHAPTER 2, WE DEFINED A FIRM'S NET WORKING CAPITAL as its current assets minus its current liabilities. Net working capital is the capital required in the short term to run the business. Thus, working capital management involves short-term asset accounts such as cash, inventory, and accounts receivable, as well as short-term liability accounts such as accounts payable.

The level of investment in each of these accounts differs from firm to firm and from industry to industry. It also depends on factors such as the type of business and industry standards. Some firms, for example, require heavy inventory investments because of the nature of their business. Consider The Kroger Company, a retail grocery chain, and Carnival Corporation, a cruise ship operator. Inventory amounted to nearly 20% of Kroger's total assets at the start of 2015, whereas Carnival's investment in inventory was less than 1%. A grocery store requires a large investment in inventory, while a cruise line's profitability is generated primarily from its investment in plant, property, and equipment—that is, its 100 cruise ships.

There are opportunity costs associated with investing in inventories and accounts receivable, and from holding cash. Excess funds invested in these accounts could instead be used to pay down debt or returned to shareholders in the form of a dividend or share repurchase. This chapter focuses on the tools firms use to manage their working capital efficiently and thereby minimize these opportunity costs. We begin by discussing why firms have working capital and how it affects firm value. In a perfectly competitive market, many of the working capital accounts would be irrelevant. Not surprisingly, the existence of these accounts for real firms can be traced to market frictions. We discuss the costs and benefits of trade credit and evaluate the trade-offs firms make in managing various working capital accounts. Finally, we discuss the cash balance of a firm and provide an overview of the short-term investments in which a firm may choose to invest its cash.

26.1 Overview of Working Capital

Most projects require the firm to invest in net working capital. The main components of net working capital are cash, inventory, receivables, and payables. Working capital includes the cash that is needed to run the firm on a day-to-day basis. It does not include excess cash, which is cash that is not required to run the business and can be invested at a market rate. As we discussed in Chapter 14, excess cash may be viewed as part of the firm's capital structure, offsetting firm debt. In Chapter 8, we discussed how any increases in net working capital represent an investment that reduces the cash that is available to the firm. Therefore, working capital alters a firm's value by affecting its free cash flow. In this section, we examine the components of net working capital and their effects on the firm's value.

The Cash Cycle

The level of working capital reflects the length of time between when cash goes out of a firm at the beginning of the production process and when it comes back in. A company first buys inventory from its suppliers, in the form of either raw materials or finished goods. A firm typically buys its inventory on credit, which means that the firm does not have to pay cash immediately at the time of purchase. After receiving the inventory, even if the inventory is in the form of finished goods, it may sit on the shelf for some time. Finally, when the inventory is ultimately sold, the firm may extend credit to its customers, delaying when it will receive the cash. A firm's **cash cycle** is the length of time between when the firm pays cash to purchase its initial inventory and when it receives cash from the sale of the output produced from that inventory. Figure 26.1 illustrates the cash cycle.

Some practitioners measure the cash cycle by calculating the cash conversion cycle. The **cash conversion cycle (CCC)** is defined as

$$\text{CCC} = \text{Accounts Receivable Days} + \text{Inventory Days} - \text{Accounts Payable Days} \quad (26.1)$$

where

$$\text{Accounts Receivable Days} = \frac{\text{Accounts Receivable}}{\text{Average Daily Sales}}$$

$$\text{Inventory Days} = \frac{\text{Inventory}}{\text{Average Daily Cost of Goods Sold}}$$

$$\text{Accounts Payable Days} = \frac{\text{Accounts Payable}}{\text{Average Daily Cost of Goods Sold}}$$

FIGURE 26.1

The Cash and Operating Cycles for a Firm

The cash cycle is the average time between when a firm pays for its inventory and when it receives cash from the sale of its product.

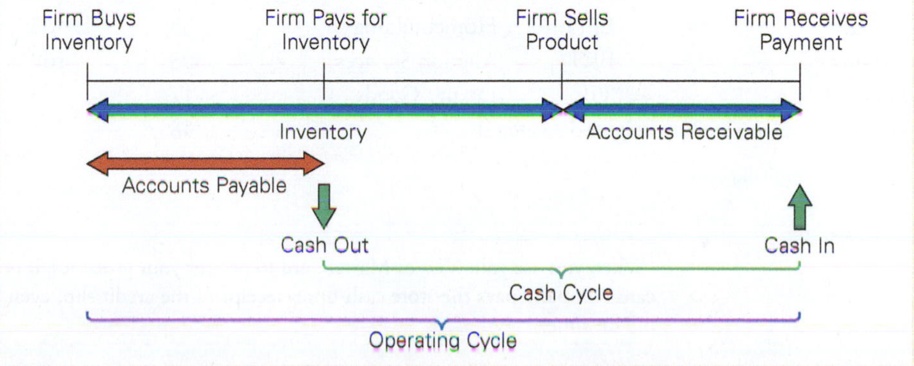

The firm's **operating cycle** is the average length of time between when a firm originally purchases its inventory and when it receives the cash back from selling its product. If the firm pays cash for its inventory, this period is identical to the firm's cash cycle. However, most firms buy their inventory on credit, which reduces the amount of time between the cash investment and the receipt of cash from that investment.

The longer a firm's cash cycle, the more working capital it has, and the more cash it needs to carry to conduct its daily operations. Table 26.1 provides data on the working capital needs for selected firms in a variety of industries.

Because of the characteristics of different industries, working capital levels vary significantly. For example, grocery stores (Kroger) and fast-food restaurants (Chipotle Mexican Grill) typically sell on a cash-only basis, and thus have very short accounts receivable days.[1] Similar results hold for Southwest Airlines, because many of its customers pay in advance for airline tickets with cash or credit cards. Inventory represents the largest percentage of

TABLE 26.1 Working Capital in Various Industries (2015)

Company	Ticker	Industry	Accounts Receivable Days	Inventory Days	Accounts Payable Days	CCC
Molson Coors Brewing	TAP	Brewing	48	37	184	−99
Pepsico	PEP	Beverages	40	40	164	−84
Verizon Communications	VZ	Telecommunications	37	8	117	−72
Apple	AAPL	Computer Hardware	20	7	76	−49
Bristol-Myers Squibb	BMY	Pharmaceuticals	72	126	223	−25
Southwest Airlines	LUV	Airlines	9	9	32	−14
Amazon.com	AMZN	Internet Retail	19	45	73	−9
The New York Times	NYT	Publishing	41	0	49	−8
Chipotle Mexican Grill	CMG	Restaurants	2	2	10	−6
The Kroger Co.	KR	Grocery Stores	4	24	23	5
Wal-Mart Stores	WMT	Superstores	4	47	39	12
Microsoft	MSFT	Software	62	33	77	18
Macy's	SHLD	Department Stores	4	147	133	18
FedEx	FDX	Air Freight	43	5	22	26
Starbucks	SBUX	Restaurants	12	30	16	26
Nordstrom	JWN	Department Stores	29	79	62	46
Nike	NKE	Footwear	36	91	41	86
Brown-Forman	BF.B	Distillers and Vintners	72	440	90	422
Lennar	LEN	Homebuilding	3	463	23	443
Sotheby's	BID	Auction Services	393	169	117	445
Tiffany & Co.	TIF	Luxury Goods	17	546	66	497
Major U.S. Firms (value-weighted Average)			48	71	76	43

Source: www.capitaliq.com

[1]When you use your Visa or MasterCard to pay for your groceries, it is a cash sale for the store. The credit card company pays the store cash upon receipt of the credit slip, even if you do not pay your credit card bill on time.

sales for firms such as Tiffany, Brown-Forman, and Lennar, whose products have long production and sales cycles, whereas Chipotle and The New York Times hold minimal inventory. Note also the wide variation in the firms' cash conversion cycles; Amazon.com and Southwest's cash conversion cycle is negative, reflecting the fact that they receive cash from their customers before having to pay suppliers, whereas firms such as Tiffany must spend cash to produce their products more than one year before they receive revenues from them.

Firm Value and Working Capital

Any reduction in working capital requirements generates a positive free cash flow that the firm can distribute immediately to shareholders. For example, if a firm is able to reduce its required net working capital by \$50,000 permanently, it will be able to distribute this \$50,000 as a dividend to its shareholders immediately and thus increase firm value by the same amount. Similarly, when evaluating a project, reducing the project's net working capital needs over the project's life reduces the opportunity cost associated with this use of capital.

EXAMPLE 26.1 Costly Working Capital for a Project

Problem

Emerald City Paints would like to construct a new facility that will manufacture paint. In addition to the capital expenditure on the plant, management estimates that the project will require an investment today of \$450,000 for net working capital. The firm will recover the investment in net working capital eight years from today, when management anticipates closing the plant. The discount rate for this type of cash flow is 6% per year. What is the present value of the cost of working capital for the paint facility? What is the value of an inventory policy that would halve the plant's net working capital requirements?

Solution

The cash flows for the investment in net working capital are −\$450,000 today and +\$450,000 eight years from today. Putting this on a timeline:

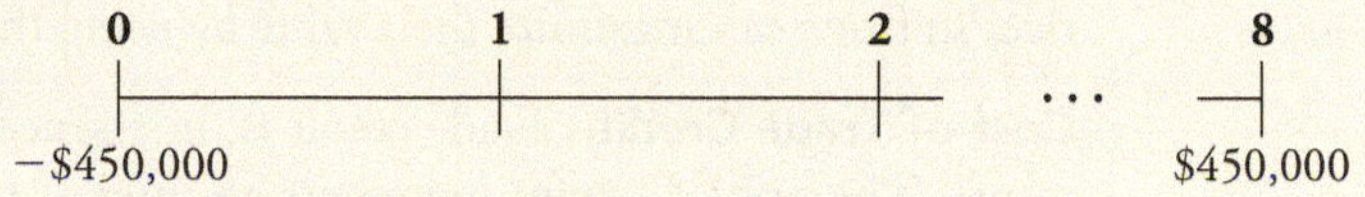

Given a discount rate of 6% per year, the NPV of these cash flows is

$$NPV = -\$450{,}000 + \frac{\$450{,}000}{(1 + 0.06)^8} = -\$167{,}664$$

Although Emerald City Paints receives back all of its investment in working capital, it loses the time value of money on this cash. If a new inventory policy could halve this requirement, it would be worth \$167,664/2 = \$83,832 to the firm.

Managing working capital efficiently will maximize firm value. We now turn our attention to some specific working capital accounts.

CONCEPT CHECK

1. What is the firm's cash cycle? How does it differ from the operating cycle?
2. How does working capital impact a firm's value?

26.2 Trade Credit

When a firm allows a customer to pay for goods at some date later than the date of purchase, it creates an account receivable for the firm and an account payable for the customer. Accounts receivable represent the credit sales for which a firm has yet to receive payment. The accounts payable balance represents the amount that a firm owes its suppliers for goods that it has received but for which it has not yet paid. The credit that the firm is extending to its customer is known as **trade credit**. A firm would, of course, prefer to be paid in cash at the time of purchase, but a "cash-only" policy may cause it to lose its customers to competition. In this section, we demonstrate how managers can compare the costs and benefits of trade credit to determine optimal credit policies.

Trade Credit Terms

To see how the terms of trade credit are quoted, let's consider some examples. If a supplier offers its customers terms of "Net 30," payment is not due until 30 days from the date of the invoice. Essentially, the supplier is letting the customer use its money for an extra 30 days. (Note that "30" is not a magic number; the invoice could specify "Net 40," "Net 15," or any other number of days as the payment due date.)

Sometimes the selling firm will offer the buying firm a discount if payment is made early. The terms "2/10, Net 30" mean that the buying firm will receive a 2% discount if it pays for the goods within 10 days; otherwise, the full amount is due in 30 days. Firms offer discounts to encourage customers to pay early so that the selling firm gets cash from the sale sooner. However, the amount of the discount also represents a cost to the selling firm because it does not receive the full selling price for the product.

Trade Credit and Market Frictions

In a perfectly competitive market, trade credit is just another form of financing. Under the Modigliani-Miller assumptions of perfect capital markets, the amounts of payables and receivables are therefore irrelevant. In reality, product markets are rarely perfectly competitive, so firms can maximize their value by using their trade credit options effectively.

Cost of Trade Credit. Trade credit is, in essence, a loan from the selling firm to its customer. The price discount represents an interest rate. Often, firms offer favorable interest rates on trade credit as a price discount to their customers. Therefore, financial managers should evaluate the terms of trade credit to decide whether to use it.

How do we compute the interest rate on trade credit? Suppose a firm sells a product for \$100 but offers its customer terms of 2/10, Net 30. The customer doesn't have to pay anything for the first 10 days, so it effectively has a zero-interest loan for this period. If the customer takes advantage of the discount and pays within the 10-day discount period, the customer pays only \$98 for the product. The cost of the discount to the selling firm is equal to the discount percentage times the selling price. In this case, it is $0.02 \times \$100$, or \$2.

Rather than pay within 10 days, the customer has the option to use the \$98 for an additional 20 days $(30 - 10 = 20)$. The interest rate for the 20-day term of the loan is $\$2/\$98 = 2.04\%$. With a 365-day year, this rate over 20 days corresponds to an effective annual rate of[2]

$$EAR = (1.0204)^{365/20} - 1 = 44.6\%$$

[2]See Eq. 5.1 in Chapter 5.

Thus, by not taking the discount, the firm is effectively paying 2.04% to borrow the money for 20 days, which translates to an effective annual rate of 44.6%! If the firm can obtain a bank loan at a lower interest rate, it would be better off borrowing at the lower rate and using the cash proceeds of the loan to take advantage of the discount offered by the supplier.

EXAMPLE 26.2 **Estimating the Effective Cost of Trade Credit**

Problem

Your firm purchases goods from its supplier on terms of 1/15, Net 40. What is the effective annual cost to your firm if it chooses not to take advantage of the trade discount offered?

Solution

Because the discount is 1%, for a $100 purchase your firm must pay either $99 in 15 days or $100 in 40 days. Given the difference of 25 days (40 − 15), these terms correspond to an effective annual rate of $(100/99)^{365/25} - 1 = 15.8\%$.

Benefits of Trade Credit. For a number of reasons, trade credit can be an attractive source of funds. First, trade credit is simple and convenient to use, and it therefore has lower transaction costs than alternative sources of funds. For example, no paperwork must be completed, as would be the case for a loan from a bank. Second, it is a flexible source of funds, and can be used as needed. Finally, it is sometimes the only source of funding available to a firm.

Trade Credit Versus Standard Loans. You might wonder why companies would ever provide trade credit. After all, most companies are not banks, so why are they in the business of making loans? Several reasons explain their willingness to offer trade credit.[3] First, providing financing at below-market rates is an indirect way to lower prices for only certain customers. Consider, for example, an automobile manufacturer. Rather than lower prices on all cars, the financing division may offer specific credit terms that are attractive to customers with bad credit, but unattractive to customers with good credit. In this way, the car manufacturer is able to discount the price only for those customers with bad credit who otherwise might not be able to afford the car.

Second, because a supplier may have an ongoing business relationship with its customer, it may have more information about the credit quality of the customer than a traditional outside lender such as a bank. The supplier may also be able to increase the likelihood of payment by threatening to cut off future supplies if payment is not made. Finally, if the buyer defaults, the supplier may be able to seize the inventory as collateral. This inventory is likely to be more valuable to a company within the industry such as the supplier (which presumably has other customers) than to an outsider.

Managing Float

One factor that contributes to the length of a firm's receivables and payables is the delay between the time a bill is paid and the cash is actually received. This delay, or processing float, will impact a firm's working capital requirements.

[3]For a detailed discussion of these issues, see B. Biais and C. Gollier, "Trade Credit and Credit Rationing," *Review of Financial Studies* 10 (1997): 903–937; and M. Petersen and R. Rajan, "Trade Credit: Theories and Evidence," *Review of Financial Studies* 10 (1997): 661–691.

Collection Float. Collection float is the amount of time it takes for a firm to be able to use funds after a customer has paid for its goods. Firms can reduce their working capital needs by reducing their collection float. Collection float is determined by three factors:

- **Mail float**: How long it takes the firm to receive the check after the customer has mailed it
- **Processing float**: How long it takes the firm to process the check and deposit it in the bank
- **Availability float**: How long it takes before the bank gives the firm credit for the funds

Disbursement Float. Disbursement float is the amount of time it takes before payments to suppliers actually result in a cash outflow for the firm. Like collection float, it is a function of mail time, processing time, and check-clearing time. Although a firm may try to extend its disbursement float in order to lengthen its payables and reduce its working capital needs, it risks making late payments to suppliers. In such a case, the firm may be charged an additional fee for paying late or may be required to pay cash before delivery (CBD) or on delivery (COD) for future purchases. In some cases, the supplier may refuse to do business in the future with the delinquent firm.

Electronic Check Processing. Firms can employ several methods to reduce their collection and disbursement floats. The **Check Clearing for the 21st Century Act (Check 21)**, which became effective on October 28, 2004, eliminated the disbursement float due to the check-clearing process. Under the Act, banks can process check information electronically, and the funds are deducted from a firm's checking account on the same day that the firm's supplier deposits the check in its bank in most cases. Unfortunately, even though under Check 21 the funds are taken out of the check writer's account almost immediately, the check recipient's account is not credited as quickly. As a result, the act does not serve to reduce collection float.

There are, however, several ways that a firm *can* reduce its collection float. For example, the firm may streamline its in-house check-processing procedures. In addition, with electronic collection, funds are automatically transferred from the customer's bank account to the firm's bank account on the payment date, reducing the collection float to zero. The methods a firm employs to reduce its collection float are not without costs, of course. Therefore, to decide which, if any, to employ, the firm must compare the costs and benefits of systems that allow it to use its cash for a longer period.

CONCEPT CHECK

1. What does the term "2/10, Net 30" mean?
2. Why do companies provide trade credit?

26.3 Receivables Management

So far, we have discussed the costs and benefits of trade credit in general. Next, we look at some issues that arise specifically from the management of a firm's accounts receivable. In particular, we focus on how a firm adopts a policy for offering credit to its customers and how it monitors its accounts receivable on an ongoing basis.

Determining the Credit Policy

Establishing a credit policy involves three steps that we will discuss in turn:

1. Establishing credit standards
2. Establishing credit terms
3. Establishing a collection policy

Establishing Credit Standards. Management must first decide on its credit standards. Will it extend credit to anyone who applies for it? Or will it be selective and extend credit only to those customers who have very low credit risk? Unless the firm adopts the former policy, it will need to assess the credit risk of each customer before deciding whether to grant credit. Large firms often perform this analysis in-house with their own credit departments. Many small firms purchase credit reports from credit rating agencies such as Dun & Bradstreet.

The decision of how much credit risk to assume plays a large role in determining how much money a firm ties up in its receivables. While a restrictive policy can result in a lower sales volume, the firm will have a smaller investment in receivables. Conversely, a less selective policy will produce higher sales, but the level of receivables will also rise.

Establishing Credit Terms. After a firm decides on its credit standards, it must next establish its credit terms. The firm decides on the length of the period before payment must be made (the "net" period) and chooses whether to offer a discount to encourage early payments. If it offers a discount, it must also determine the discount percentage and the discount period. If the firm is relatively small, it will probably follow the lead of other firms in the industry in establishing these terms.

Establishing a Collection Policy. The last step in the development of a credit policy is to decide on a collection policy. The content of this policy can range from doing nothing if a customer is paying late (generally not a good choice), to sending a polite letter of inquiry, to charging interest on payments extending beyond a specified period, to threatening legal action at the first late payment.

Monitoring Accounts Receivable

After establishing a credit policy, a firm must monitor its accounts receivable to analyze whether its credit policy is working effectively. Two tools that firms use to monitor the accounts receivable are the accounts receivable days (or average collection period) and the aging schedule.

Accounts Receivable Days. The accounts receivable days is the average number of days that it takes a firm to collect on its sales. A firm can compare this number to the payment policy specified in its credit terms to judge the effectiveness of its credit policy. If the credit terms specify "Net 30" and the accounts receivable days outstanding is 50 days, the firm can conclude that its customers are paying 20 days late, on average.

The firm should also look at the trend in the accounts receivable days over time. If the accounts receivable days ratio of a firm has been approximately 35 days for the past few years and it is 43 days this year, the firm may want to reexamine its credit policy. Of course, if the economy is sluggish, the entire industry may be affected. Under these circumstances, the increase might have little to do with the firm itself.

Because accounts receivable days can be calculated from the firm's financial statements, outside investors commonly use this measure to evaluate a firm's credit management policy. A major weakness of the accounts receivable days is that it is merely one number and conceals much useful information. Seasonal sales patterns may cause the number calculated for the accounts receivable days to change, depending on when the calculation takes place. The number can also look reasonable even when a substantial percentage of the firm's customers are paying late.

Aging Schedule. An **aging schedule** categorizes accounts by the number of days they have been on the firm's books. It can be prepared using either the number of accounts or the dollar amount of the accounts receivable outstanding. For example, assume that a firm selling on terms of 2/15, Net 30, has \$530,000 in accounts receivable that has been on the books for 15 or fewer days in 220 accounts. Another \$450,000 has been on the books for 16 to 30 days and is made up of 190 accounts, and \$350,000 has been on the books for 31 to 45 days and represents 80 accounts. The firm has \$200,000 that has been on the books for 46 to 60 days in 60 accounts. Yet another \$70,000 has been on the books for more than 60 days and is made up of 20 accounts. Table 26.2 includes aging schedules based on the number of accounts and dollar amounts outstanding.

In this case, if the firm's average daily sales is \$65,000, its accounts receivable days is \$1,600,000/\$65,000 = 25 days. But on closer examination, using the aging schedules in Table 26.2, we can see that 28% of the firm's credit customers (and 39% by dollar amounts) are paying late.

TABLE 26.2 Aging Schedules

Days Outstanding	Number of Accounts	Percentage of Accounts (%)	Amount Outstanding (\$)	Percentage Outstanding (%)
1–15	220	38.6	530,000	33.1
16–30	190	33.3	450,000	28.1
31–45	80	14.0	350,000	21.9
46–60	60	10.5	200,000	12.5
60+	20	3.5	70,000	4.4
	570	100.0	1,600,000	100.0

EXAMPLE 26.3 Aging Schedules

Problem

Financial Training Systems (FTS) bills its accounts on terms of 3/10, Net 30. The firm's accounts receivable include \$100,000 that has been outstanding for 10 or fewer days, \$300,000 outstanding for 11 to 30 days, \$100,000 outstanding for 31 to 40 days, \$20,000 outstanding for 41 to 50 days, \$10,000 outstanding for 51 to 60 days, and \$2000 outstanding for more than 60 days. Prepare an aging schedule for FTS.

Solution

With the available information, we can calculate the aging schedule based on dollar amounts outstanding.

Days Outstanding	Amount Outstanding (\$)	Percentage Outstanding (%)
1–10	100,000	18.8
11–30	300,000	56.4
31–40	100,000	18.8
41–50	20,000	3.8
51–60	10,000	1.9
60+	2,000	0.3
	532,000	100.0

If the aging schedule gets "bottom-heavy"—that is, if the percentages in the lower half of the schedule begin to increase—the firm will likely need to revisit its credit policy. The aging schedule is also sometimes augmented by analysis of the **payments pattern**, which provides information on the percentage of monthly sales that the firm collects in each month after the sale. By examining past data, a firm may observe that 10% of its sales are usually collected in the month of the sale, 40% in the month following the sale, 25% two months after the sale, 20% three months after the sale, and 5% four months after the sale. Management can compare this normal payments pattern to the current payments pattern. Knowledge of the payments pattern is also useful for forecasting the firm's working capital requirements.

CONCEPT CHECK

1. Describe three steps in establishing a credit policy.
2. What is the difference between accounts receivable days and an aging schedule?

26.4 Payables Management

A firm should choose to borrow using accounts payable only if trade credit is the cheapest source of funding. The cost of the trade credit depends on the credit terms. The higher the discount percentage offered, the greater the cost of forgoing the discount. The cost of forgoing the discount is also higher with a shorter loan period. When a company has a choice between trade credit from two different suppliers, it should take the less expensive alternative.

In addition, a firm should always pay on the latest day allowed. For example, if the discount period is 10 days and the firm is taking the discount, payment should be made on day 10, not on day 2. If the discount is not taken and the terms are 2/10, Net 30, the full payment should be made on day 30, not on day 16. A firm should strive to keep its money working for it as long as possible without developing a bad relationship with its suppliers or engaging in unethical practices. In this section, we examine two techniques that firms use to monitor their accounts payable.

Determining Accounts Payable Days Outstanding

Similar to the situation with its accounts receivable, a firm should monitor its accounts payable to ensure that it is making its payments at an optimal time. One method is to calculate the accounts payable days outstanding and compare it to the credit terms. The accounts payable days outstanding is the accounts payable balance expressed in terms of the number of days of cost of goods sold. If the accounts payable outstanding is 40 days and the terms are 2/10, Net 30, the firm can conclude that it generally pays late and may be risking supplier difficulties. Conversely, if the accounts payable days outstanding is 25 days and the firm has not been taking the discount, the firm is paying too early. It could be earning another five days' interest on its money.

EXAMPLE 26.4 **Accounts Payable Management**

Problem

The Rowd Company has an average accounts payable balance of $250,000. Its average daily cost of goods sold is $14,000, and it receives terms of 2/15, Net 40, from its suppliers. Rowd chooses to forgo the discount. Is the firm managing its accounts payable well?

Solution

The firm is not managing its accounts payable well. Rowd's accounts payable days outstanding is $250,000/$14,000 = 17.9 days. If Rowd made payment three days earlier, it could take advantage of the 2% discount. If for some reason it chooses to forgo the discount, it should not be paying the full amount until the fortieth day.

Stretching Accounts Payable

Some firms ignore the payment due period and pay later, in a practice referred to as **stretching the accounts payable**. Given terms of 2/10, Net 30, for example, a firm may choose to not pay until 45 days have passed. Doing so reduces the direct cost of trade credit because it lengthens the time that a firm has use of the funds. While the interest rate per period remains the same—$2/$98 = 2.04%—the firm is now using the $98 for 35 days beyond the discount period, rather than 20 days as provided by the trade credit terms.

EXAMPLE 26.5 **Cost of Trade Credit with Stretched Accounts Payable**

Problem

What is the effective annual cost of credit terms of 1/15, Net 40, if the firm stretches the accounts payable to 60 days?

Solution

The interest rate per period is $1/$99 = 1.01%. If the firm delays payment until the sixtieth day, it has use of the funds for 45 days beyond the discount period. There are 365/45 = 8.11 45-day periods in one year. Thus, the effective annual cost is $(1.0101)^{8.11} - 1 = 8.49\%$.

Firms may also make a payment on the thirtieth day but pay only the discounted price. Some may pay only the discounted price and pay even later than the thirtieth day. While all of these actions will reduce the effective annual rate associated with the trade credit, the firm may incur costs as a result of these actions. Suppliers may react to a firm whose payments are always late by imposing terms of cash on delivery (COD) or cash before delivery (CBD). The delinquent firm then bears the additional costs associated with these terms and may have to negotiate a bank loan to have the cash available to pay. The supplier may also discontinue business with the delinquent customer, leaving the customer to find another source, which may be more expensive or of lower quality. A poor credit rating might also result, making it difficult for the firm to obtain good terms with any other supplier. Moreover, when a firm explicitly agrees to the terms of the sale, violating these terms constitutes unethical business behavior in most people's minds.

CONCEPT CHECK

1. What is accounts payable days outstanding?
2. What are the costs of stretching accounts payable?

26.5 Inventory Management

As we discussed earlier, in a perfect markets setting, firms would not need payables or receivables. Interest rates on trade credit would be competitive, and firms could use alternative sources of financing. However, unlike trade credit, inventory represents one of the required factors of production. Therefore, even in a perfect markets setting in which the Modigliani-Miller propositions hold, firms still need inventory.

Inventory management receives extensive coverage in courses on operations management. Nevertheless, it is the firm's financial manager who must arrange for the financing necessary to support the firm's inventory policy and who is responsible for ensuring the firm's overall profitability. Therefore, the role of the inventory manager is to balance the costs and benefits associated with inventory. Because excessive inventory uses cash, efficient management of inventory increases firm value.

Benefits of Holding Inventory

A firm needs its inventory to operate for several reasons. First, inventory helps minimize the risk that the firm will not be able to obtain an input it needs for production. If a firm holds too little inventory, **stock-outs**, the situation when a firm runs out of goods, may occur, leading to lost sales. Disappointed customers may switch to one of the firm's competitors.

Second, firms may hold inventory because factors such as seasonality in demand mean that customer purchases do not perfectly match the most efficient production cycle. Consider the case of the Sandpoint Toy Company. As is typical for many toy manufacturers, 80% of Sandpoint's annual sales occur between September and December, during the holiday gift season. It is more efficient for Sandpoint to manufacture toys at relatively constant levels throughout the year. If Sandpoint produces its toys at a constant rate, its inventory levels will increase to very high levels by August, in anticipation of the increase in sales beginning in September. In contrast, Sandpoint may consider a seasonal manufacturing strategy, producing more toys between September and December when sales are high. Under this strategy, inventory would not accumulate, freeing up cash flow from working capital and reducing the costs of inventory. However, seasonal manufacturing incurs additional costs, such as increased wear and tear on the manufacturing equipment during peak demand and the need to hire and train seasonal workers. Sandpoint must weigh the costs of the inventory buildup under constant production against the benefits of more efficient production. The optimal choice is likely to involve a compromise between the two extremes, so that Sandpoint will carry some inventory throughout the year.

Costs of Holding Inventory

As suggested by the Sandpoint Toy example, tying up capital in inventory is costly for a firm. We can classify the direct costs associated with inventory into three categories:

- *Acquisition costs* are the costs of the inventory itself over the period being analyzed (usually one year).
- *Order costs* are the total costs of placing an order over the period being analyzed.
- *Carrying costs* include storage costs, insurance, taxes, spoilage, obsolescence, and the opportunity cost of the funds tied up in the inventory.

Minimizing these total costs involves some trade-offs. For example, if we assume no quantity discounts are available, the lower the level of inventory a firm carries, the lower its carrying cost, but the higher its annual order costs, because it needs to place more orders during the year.

That said, the benefits from reducing inventory requirements can be substantial. In 2003, the apparel chain GAP reduced its investment in inventory significantly by reducing its inventory days outstanding by 24%. This change freed up $344 million for other purposes. GAP invested some of this cash in short-term securities—primarily in U.S.

government and agency securities and in bank certificates of deposits with maturities between three months and one year. The firm reported an increase of $1.2 million in interest income in fiscal year 2003 compared with fiscal year 2002. It attributed the increase to increases in the average cash balances available for investment.[4]

Some firms seek to reduce their carrying costs as much as possible. With **"just-in-time" (JIT) inventory management**, a firm acquires inventory precisely when needed so that its inventory balance is always zero, or very close to it. This technique requires exceptional coordination with suppliers as well as a predictable demand for the firm's products. In addition, there may be a trickle-down effect when one firm in an industry adopts JIT. For example, in 1999, Toys 'R Us instituted JIT, which caused one of its suppliers, toy manufacturer Hasbro, to make changes in its production schedule.[5]

CONCEPT CHECK

1. What are the benefits and costs of holding inventory?
2. Describe "just-in-time" inventory management.

26.6 Cash Management

In the Modigliani-Miller setting, the level of cash is irrelevant. With perfect capital markets, a firm is able to raise new money instantly at a fair rate, so it can never be short of cash. Similarly, the firm can invest excess cash at a fair rate to earn an NPV of zero.

In the real world, of course, markets are not perfect. Liquidity has a cost; for example, holding liquid assets may earn a below-market return, and a firm may face transaction costs if it needs to raise cash quickly. Similarly, recall from Chapters 15 and 17 that due to the double taxation of corporate interest income, holding excess cash has a tax disadvantage. In these cases, the optimal strategy for a firm is to hold cash in anticipation of seasonalities in its operating or investment cash flows, as well as to buffer random shocks that affect the business. Risky firms and firms with high-growth opportunities tend to hold a relatively high percentage of assets as cash. Firms with easy access to capital markets (for which the transaction costs of raising cash are lower) tend to hold less cash.[6] In this section, we examine the firm's motivation for holding cash, tools for managing cash, and the short-term securities in which firms invest.

Motivation for Holding Cash

There are three reasons why a firm holds cash:

- To meet its day-to-day needs
- To compensate for the uncertainty associated with its cash flows
- To satisfy bank requirements

Let's discuss each of these motivations in more detail.

Transactions Balance. Just like you, a firm must hold enough cash to pay its bills. The amount of cash a firm needs to be able to pay its bills is sometimes referred to as a **transactions balance**. The amount of cash a firm needs to satisfy the transactions balance

---

[4]GAP 2003 annual report.

[5]Hasbro 1999 annual report.

[6]See T. Opler, L. Pinkowitz, R. Stulz, and R. Williamson, "The Determinants and Implications of Corporate Cash Holdings," *Journal of Financial Economics* 52(1) (1999): 3–46.

requirement depends on both the average size of the transactions made by the firm and the firm's cash cycle, discussed earlier in the chapter. Firms set the transactions balance so that the firm's cash and other liquid securities are adequate to pay its near-term liabilities. One common measure used to assess whether the firm has adequate liquidity to meet short-term needs is its quick ratio, which is the ratio of current assets other than inventory to current liabilities. By increasing its cash balance, the firm can raise its quick ratio to its desired level.

Precautionary Balance. The amount of cash a firm holds to counter the uncertainty surrounding its future cash needs is known as a **precautionary balance**. The size of this balance depends on the degree of uncertainty surrounding a firm's cash flows. The more uncertain future cash flows are, the harder it is for a firm to predict its transactions need, so the larger the precautionary balance must be. A useful measure to assess the firm's desired precautionary balance is the volatility of its operating cash flows over different horizons. Firms will typically choose to maintain liquid assets equal to some multiple of this volatility, in order to avoid the risk of experiencing a cash shortfall.

Compensating Balance. A firm's bank may require it to hold a **compensating balance** in an account at the bank as compensation for services that the bank performs. Compensating balances are typically deposited in accounts that either earn no interest or pay a very low interest rate. This arrangement is similar to a bank offering individuals free checking so long as their balances do not fall below a certain level—say, $1000. Essentially, the customer has $1000 cash that he cannot use unless he is willing to pay a service charge. Similarly, the cash that a firm has tied up to meet a compensating balance requirement is unavailable for other uses.

Alternative Investments

In our discussion of collection and disbursement floats, we assumed that the firm will invest any cash in short-term securities. In fact, the firm may choose from a variety of short-term securities that differ somewhat with regard to their default risk and liquidity risk. The greater

Hoarding Cash

Corporate liquidity is measured as corporate investments in short-term, marketable securities. According to IRS statistics, the cash holdings of U.S. corporations more than tripled between 1999 and 2009, rising from $1.6 trillion to more than $4.8 trillion. Indeed, in 2015 more than 39% of U.S. publicly traded firms were net investors, having more cash and short-term investments than debt outstanding.

Why have companies been accumulating more cash? Factors include (i) a shift away from industries such as manufacturing that spend heavily on plant and equipment, (ii) growth in service sectors that have low capital expenditures and high cash flows, (iii) avoidance of repatriation taxes by multi-national firms (see box on page 525), and (iv) a desire by companies to preserve liquidity and financial flexibility. As a result, corporate savings has reached an all-time high.

How are companies investing their cash? A 2007 survey by Treasury Strategies indicated that 20% is invested in money market funds (which in turn invest in a diversified portfolio of the short-term securities described in Table 26.3), 18% is invested in bonds and notes, and the remainder is invested directly in commercial paper, CDs, repurchase agreements, and other investments.

During the 2008 financial crisis, short-term credit markets froze and many businesses that relied on short-term credit found themselves unable to conduct business. Even firms with sufficient cash balances had to worry about how secure their cash was: many banks were in or on the verge of default, and even traditionally safe money market funds risked losses. As a result, the breakdown in credit markets in the early days of the financial crisis was potentially as disruptive for firms that relied on cash balances to conduct business as it was for firms that relied on credit.

the risk, the higher the expected return on the investment. The financial manager must decide how much risk she is willing to accept in return for a higher yield. If her firm expects to need the funds within the next 30 days, the manager will probably avoid the less liquid options. Table 26.3 briefly describes the most frequently used short-term investments; these short-term debt securities are collectively referred to as **money market** securities. Firms may invest in these securities directly, or through money market mutual funds.

TABLE 26.3 Money Market Investment Options

Investment	Description	Maturity	Risk	Liquidity
Treasury Bills	Short-term debt of the U.S. government.	Four weeks, three months (91 days), six months (182 days), or one year when newly issued	Default risk free.	Very liquid and marketable.
Certificates of Deposit (CDs)	Short-term debt issued by banks, minimum denomination of $100,000.	Varying maturities up to one year	If the issuing bank is insured by the FDIC, any amount up to $250,000 is free of default risk because it is covered by the insurance. Any amount in excess of $250,000 is not insured and is subject to default risk.	Unlike CDs purchased by individuals, these CDs sell on the secondary market, but are less liquid than Treasury bills.
Repurchase Agreements	Essentially a loan arrangement wherein a securities dealer is the "borrower" and the investor is the "lender"; the investor buys securities, such as U.S. Treasury bills, from the securities dealer, with an agreement to sell the securities back to the dealer at a later date for a specified higher price.	Very short term, ranging from overnight to approximately three months in duration	The security serves as collateral for the loan, and therefore the investor is exposed to very little risk. However, the investor needs to consider the creditworthiness of the securities dealer when assessing the risk.	No secondary market for repurchase agreements.
Banker's Acceptances	Drafts written by the borrower and guaranteed by the bank on which the draft is drawn, typically used in international trade transactions; the borrower is an importer who writes the draft in payment for goods.	Typically one to six months	Because both the borrower and a bank have guaranteed the draft, there is usually very little risk.	When the exporter receives the draft, he may hold it until maturity and receive its full value or he may sell the draft at a discount prior to maturity.
Commercial Paper	Short-term, unsecured debt issued by large corporations. The minimum denomination is $25,000, but most commercial paper has a face value of $100,000 or more.	Typically one to six months	Default risk depends on the creditworthiness of the issuing corporation.	No active secondary market, but issuer may repurchase commercial paper.
Short-Term Tax Exempts	Short-term debt of state and local governments; these instruments pay interest that is exempt from federal taxation, so their pre-tax yield is lower than that of a similar-risk, fully taxable investment.	Typically one to six months	Default risk depends on the creditworthiness of the issuing government.	Moderate secondary market.

Thus, a financial manager who wants to invest the firm's funds in the least risky security will choose to invest in Treasury bills. However, if the financial manager wishes to earn a higher return on the firm's short-term investments, she may opt to invest some or all of the firm's excess cash in a riskier alternative, such as commercial paper.

CONCEPT CHECK

1. List three reasons why a firm holds cash.
2. What trade-off does a firm face when choosing how to invest its cash?

MyFinanceLab

Here is what you should know after reading this chapter. MyFinanceLab will help you identify what you know and where to go when you need to practice.

26.1 Overview of Working Capital

- Working capital management involves managing the firm's short-term assets and short-term liabilities.
- A firm's cash cycle is the length of time between when the firm pays cash to purchase its initial inventory and when it receives cash from the sale of the output produced from that inventory. The operating cycle is the average length of time between when a firm originally purchases its inventory and when it receives the cash back from selling its product.

26.2 Trade Credit

- Trade credit is effectively a loan from the selling firm to its customer. The cost of trade credit depends on the credit terms. The cost of not taking a discount that is offered by a supplier implies an interest rate for the loan.
- Companies provide trade credit to their customers for two reasons: (1) as an indirect way to lower prices, and (2) because they may have advantages in making loans to their customers relative to other potential sources of credit.
- A firm should compare the cost of trade credit with the cost of alternative sources of financing in deciding whether to use the trade credit offered.
- Establishing a credit policy involves three steps: establishing credit standards, establishing credit terms, and establishing a collection policy.

26.3 Receivables Management

- Accounts receivable days and the aging schedule are two methods used to monitor the effectiveness of a firm's credit policy.

26.4 Payables Management

- Firms should monitor accounts payable to ensure that they are making payments at an optimal time.

26.5 Inventory Management

- Firms hold inventory to avoid lost sales due to stock-outs and because of factors such as seasonal demand.
  - Because excessive inventory uses cash, efficient inventory management increases the firm's free cash flow and thus increases firm value.
  - The costs of inventory include acquisition costs, order costs, and carrying costs.

26.6 Cash Management

- If a firm's need to hold cash is reduced, the funds can be invested in a number of different short-term securities, including Treasury bills, certificates of deposit, commercial paper, repurchase agreements, banker's acceptances, and short-term tax exempts.

Key Terms

aging schedule *p. 926*
availability float *p. 924*
cash conversion cycle (CCC) *p. 919*
cash cycle *p. 919*
Check Clearing for the 21st Century Act (Check 21) *p. 924*
collection float *p. 924*
compensating balance *p. 931*
disbursement float *p. 924*
"just-in-time" (JIT) inventory management *p. 930*
mail float *p. 924*
money market *p. 932*
operating cycle *p. 920*
payments pattern *p. 927*
precautionary balance *p. 931*
processing float *p. 924*
stock-outs *p. 929*
stretching the accounts payable *p. 928*
trade credit *p. 922*
transactions balance *p. 930*

Further Reading

For more advanced analysis of working capital management, consult the following textbooks: R. Cole and L. Mishler, *Consumer and Business Credit Management* (McGraw-Hill, 1998); F. Fabozzi, S. Mann, and M. Choudhry, *The Global Money Markets* (John Wiley, 2002); and T. Maness and J. Zietlow, *Short-Term Financial Management* (South-Western, 2004).

The following articles address some of the research questions in working capital management.

Cash Management Issues. H. Almeida, M. Campello, and M. Weisbach, "The Cash Flow Sensitivity of Cash," *Journal of Finance* 59(4), (2004): 1777–1804; W. Baumol, "The Transactions Demand for Cash: An Inventory Theoretic Approach," *Quarterly Journal of Economics* 66(4) (1952): 545–556; J. Gentry, "State of the Art of Short-Run Financial Management," *Financial Management* 17(2) (1988): 41–57; M. Miller and D. Orr, "A Model of the Demand for Money by Firms," *Quarterly Journal of Economics* 80(3) (1966): 413–435; T. Opler, L. Pinkowitz, R. Stulz, and R. Williamson, "The Determinants and Implications of Corporate Cash Holdings," *Journal of Financial Economics* 52(1) (1999): 3–46; C. Payne, "The ABCs of Cash Management," *Journal of Corporate Accounting and Finance* 16(1) (2004): 3–8; L. Pinkowitz and R. Williamson, "What Is the Market Value of a Dollar of Corporate Cash?" *Journal of Applied Corporate Finance* 19 (2007): 74–81; and L. Pinkowitz, R. Stulz, and R. Williamson, "Does the Contribution of Corporate Cash Holdings and Dividends to Firm Value Depend on Governance? A Cross-Country Analysis," *Journal of Finance* 61 (2006): 2725–2751.

Trade Credit. Y. Lee and J. Stowe, "Product Risk, Asymmetric Information and Trade Credit," *Journal of Financial and Quantitative Analysis* 28(2) (1993): 285–300; M. Long, I. Malitz, and S. A. Ravid, "Trade Credit, Quality Guarantees, and Product Marketability," *Financial Management* 22(4) (1993): 117–127; S. Mian and C. Smith, "Extending Trade Credit and Financing Receivables," *Journal of Applied Corporate Finance* 7(1) (1994): 75–84; S. Mian and C. Smith, "Accounts Receivable Management Policy: Theory and Evidence," *Journal of Finance* 47(1) (1992): 169–200; O. Ng, J. Smith, and R. Smith, "Evidence on the Determinants of Credit Terms Used in Interfirm Trade," *Journal of Finance* 54(3) (1999): 1109–1129; F. Scherr, "Optimal Trade Credit Limits," *Financial Management* 25(1) (Spring 1996): 71–85; and J. Smith, "Trade Credit and Information Asymmetry," *Journal of Finance* 42(4) (1987): 863–872.

Problems

All problems are available in MyFinanceLab. An asterisk (*) indicates problems with a higher level of difficulty.

Overview of Working Capital

1. Answer the following questions:
   a. What is the difference between a firm's cash cycle and its operating cycle?
   b. How will a firm's cash cycle be affected if a firm increases its inventory, all else being equal?
   c. How will a firm's cash cycle be affected if a firm begins to take the discounts offered by its suppliers, all else being equal?
2. Does an increase in a firm's cash cycle necessarily mean that a firm is managing its cash poorly?
3. Aberdeen Outboard Motors is contemplating building a new plant. The company anticipates that the plant will require an initial investment of $2 million in net working capital today. The plant will last 10 years, at which point the full investment in net working capital will be recovered. Given an annual discount rate of 6%, what is the net present value of this working capital investment?
4. The Greek Connection had sales of $32 million in 2015, and a cost of goods sold of $20 million. A simplified balance sheet for the firm appears below:

THE GREEK CONNECTION
Balance Sheet
As of December 31, 2015
(in $ thousand)

Assets		Liabilities and Equity	
Cash	$ 2,000	Accounts payable	$ 1,500
Accounts receivable	3,950	Notes payable	1,000
Inventory	1,300	Accruals	1,220
Total current assets	$ 7,250	Total current liabilities	$ 3,720
		Long-term debt	
		Total liabilities	$ 6,720
Net plant, property, and equipment	$ 8,500	Common equity	$ 9,030
Total assets	$ 15,750	Total liabilities and equity	$ 15,750

   a. Calculate The Greek Connection's net working capital in 2015.
   b. Calculate the cash conversion cycle of The Greek Connection in 2015.
   c. The industry average accounts receivable days is 30 days. What would the cash conversion cycle for The Greek Connection have been in 2015 had it matched the industry average for accounts receivable days?

Trade Credit

5. Assume the credit terms offered to your firm by your suppliers are 3/5, Net 30. Calculate the cost of the trade credit if your firm does not take the discount and pays on day 30.
6. Your supplier offers terms of 1/10, Net 45. What is the effective annual cost of trade credit if you choose to forgo the discount and pay on day 45?
7. The Fast Reader Company supplies bulletin board services to numerous hotel chains nationwide. The owner of the firm is investigating the benefit of employing a billing firm to do her billing and collections. Because the billing firm specializes in these services, collection float will be reduced by 20 days. Average daily collections are $1200, and the owner can earn 8% annually (expressed as an APR with monthly compounding) on her investments. If the billing firm charges $250 per month, should the owner employ the billing firm?

8. The Saban Corporation is trying to decide whether to switch to a bank that will accommodate electronic funds transfers from Saban's customers. Saban's financial manager believes the new system would decrease its collection float by as much as five days. The new bank would require a compensating balance of $30,000, whereas its present bank has no compensating balance requirement. Saban's average daily collections are $10,000, and it can earn 8% on its short-term investments. Should Saban make the switch? (Assume the compensating balance at the new bank will be deposited in a non-interest-earning account.)

Receivables Management

9. What are the three steps involved in establishing a credit policy?

10. The Manana Corporation had sales of $60 million this year. Its accounts receivable balance averaged $2 million. How long, on average, does it take the firm to collect on its sales?

11. The Mighty Power Tool Company has the following accounts on its books:

Customer	Amount Owed ($)	Age (days)
ABC	50,000	35
DEF	35,000	5
GHI	15,000	10
KLM	75,000	22
NOP	42,000	40
QRS	18,000	12
TUV	82,000	53
WXY	36,000	90

The firm extends credit on terms of 1/15, Net 30. Develop an aging schedule using 15-day increments through 60 days, and then indicate any accounts that have been outstanding for more than 60 days.

Payables Management

12. What is meant by "stretching the accounts payable"?

13. Simple Simon's Bakery purchases supplies on terms of 1/10, Net 25. If Simple Simon's chooses to take the discount offered, it must obtain a bank loan to meet its short-term financing needs. A local bank has quoted Simple Simon's owner an interest rate of 12% on borrowed funds. Should Simple Simon's enter the loan agreement with the bank and begin taking the discount?

14. Your firm purchases goods from its supplier on terms of 3/15, Net 40.
- a. What is the effective annual cost to your firm if it chooses not to take the discount and makes its payment on day 40?
- b. What is the effective annual cost to your firm if it chooses not to take the discount and makes its payment on day 50?

***15.** Use the financial statements supplied on the next page for International Motor Corporation (IMC) to answer the following questions.
- a. Calculate the cash conversion cycle for IMC for both 2015 and 2016. What change has occurred, if any? All else being equal, how does this change affect IMC's need for cash?
- b. IMC's suppliers offer terms of Net 30. Does it appear that IMC is doing a good job of managing its accounts payable?

INTERNATIONAL MOTOR CORPORATION

Income Statement (in $ million)
for the Years Ending December 31

	2015	2016
Sales	$ 60,000	$ 75,000
Cost of goods sold	52,000	61,000
Gross profit	$ 8,000	$ 14,000
Selling and general and administrative expenses	6,000	8,000
Operating profit	$ 2,000	$ 6,000
Interest expense	1,400	1,300
Earnings before tax	$ 600	$ 4,700
Taxes	300	2,350
Earnings after tax	$ 300	$ 2,350

INTERNATIONAL MOTOR CORPORATION

Balance Sheet (in $ million)
as of December 31

	2015	2016		2015	2016
Assets			**Liabilities**		
Cash	$ 3,080	$ 6,100	Accounts payable	$ 3,600	$ 4,600
Accounts receivable	2,800	6,900	Notes payable	1,180	1,250
Inventory	6,200	6,600	Accruals	5,600	6,211
Total current assets	$ 12,080	$ 19,600	Total current liabilities	$ 10,380	$ 12,061
Net plant, property, and equipment	$ 23,087	$ 20,098	Long-term debt	$ 6,500	$ 7,000
Total assets	$ 35,167	$ 39,698	Total liabilities	$ 16,880	$ 19,061
			Equity		
			Common stock	$ 2,735	$ 2,735
			Retained earnings	$ 15,552	$ 17,902
			Total equity	$ 18,287	$ 20,637
			Total liabilities and equity	$ 35,167	$ 39,698

Inventory Management

16. Ohio Valley Homecare Suppliers, Inc. (OVHS) had $20 million in sales in 2015. Its cost of goods sold was $8 million, and its average inventory balance was $2,000,000.
  a. Calculate the average number of inventory days outstanding for OVHS.
  b. The average days of inventory in the industry is 73 days. By how much would OVHS reduce its investment in inventory if it could improve its inventory days to meet the industry average?

Cash Management

17. Which of the following short-term securities would you expect to offer the highest before-tax return: Treasury bills, certificates of deposit, short-term tax exempts, or commercial paper? Why?

Data Case

You are the Chief Financial Officer (CFO) of BP. This afternoon you played golf with a member of the company's board of directors. Somewhere during the back nine, the board member enthusiastically described a recent article she had read in a leading management journal. This article noted several companies that had improved their stock price performance through effective working capital management, and the board member was intrigued. She wondered whether BP was managing its working capital effectively and, if not, whether BP could accomplish something similar. How was BP managing its working capital, and how does it compare to its competitors?

Upon returning home, you decide to do a quick preliminary investigation using information freely available on the Internet.

1. Obtain BP's financial statements for the past three years from Yahoo! Finance (finance.yahoo.com).
   a. Enter the stock symbol (BP) in the box and click "Get Quotes."
   b. Under "Financials," click "Income Statement." Copy and paste the statement into Excel (if using Internet Explorer, place the cursor in the statement and right-click the mouse, then choose "Export to Microsoft Excel" from the menu).
   c. Go back to the Web page and under "Financials," click "Balance Sheet"; repeat the download procedure for the balance sheet.
   d. Copy and paste the balance sheet so that it is on the same worksheet as the income statement.
2. Obtain the competitors' ratios for comparison from Yahoo! Finance (finance.yahoo.com).
   a. Enter ExxonMobil Corporation's stock symbol (XOM) in the box at the top and click "Get Quotes."
   b. Follow the steps in Part 1 to obtain "net receivables" and "inventory" from the most recent annual balance sheet, and "total revenue" and "cost of revenue" from the most recent annual income statement.
   c. Repeat the two steps above for Chevron Corporation (CVX).
3. Compute the cash conversion cycle for BP for each of the last three years.
   a. Compute the inventory days using "cost of revenue" as cost of goods sold and a 365-day year.
   b. Compute accounts receivable days using a 365-day year.
   c. Compute accounts payable days.
   d. Compute the cash conversion cycle for each year.
4. How has BP's CCC changed over the last few years?
5. Compare BP's inventory and receivables turnover ratios for the most recent year to those of its competitors.
   a. Compute BP's inventory turnover ratio as cost of revenue/inventory.
   b. Compute BP's receivable turnover ratio as total revenue/net receivables.
   c. Compute the average inventory turnover ratio and average receivable turnover ratio of Chevron and ExxonMobil. How do BP's numbers compare to the average ratios of its competitors? Do they confirm or refute your answer to Question 4?
6. Determine how BP's free cash flow would change if BP's inventory and accounts receivable balances were adjusted to meet the industry averages.
7. Determine the amount of additional free cash flow that would be available if BP adjusted its accounts payable days to 75 days.
8. Determine the net amount of additional free cash flow and BP's cash conversion cycle if its inventory and receivables turnover ratios were at the industry average and its payable days were 75 days.

9. What are your impressions regarding BP's working capital management based on this preliminary analysis? Discuss any advantages and disadvantages of bringing the cash conversion cycle more in line with the industry averages.

10. You are somewhat concerned about the reliability of financial data from the Internet, and decide to check the data versus BP's SEC filings. To obtain these filings, go to the SEC Web site and use the EDGAR system to search for BP's financial statements: www.sec.gov/edgar/searchedgar/companysearch.html. Enter BP in the ticker symbol field and then click "Search." Enter 20-F in the "Filing Type" field, and then click "Search." Click on the latest 20-F, "Annual and transition report of foreign private issuers," and then click on the 20-F document link. Once you are in the document, scroll down to the table of contents and select "Financial Statements," and then find either the balance sheet or income statement to find the numbers you need. Is there any discrepancy between these numbers and the data you downloaded originally?

Note: Updates to this data case may be found at www.berkdemarzo.com.

CHAPTER

27

Short-Term Financial Planning

NOTATION

EAR	effective annual rate
APR	annual percentage rate

MATTEL, INC. IS A COMPANY IN THE STANDARD AND POOR'S 500 INDEX, with year-end 2014 assets of over $6.7 billion. Mattel designs and manufactures toys throughout the world; its major product lines include the Barbie, Fisher-Price, and American Girl brands. The demand for toys is typically highly seasonal, peaking during the fall in anticipation of December's holiday retailing season. As a result, Mattel's revenues vary dramatically throughout the calendar year. For example, revenues during the fourth quarter of the calendar year are typically more than twice as high as revenues in the first quarter.

Mattel's varying business revenues cause its cash flows to be highly cyclical. The firm generates surplus cash during some months; it has a great demand for capital during other months. These seasonal financing requirements are quite different from its ongoing, long-term demand for permanent capital. How does a company such as Mattel manage its short-term cash needs within each calendar year?

In this chapter, we analyze short-term financial planning. We begin by showing how companies forecast their cash flows to determine their short-term financing needs, and we explore reasons why firms use short-term financing. We next discuss financing policies that guide these financing decisions. Finally, we compare alternative ways a company can finance a shortfall during periods when it is not generating enough cash, including short-term financing with bank loans, commercial paper, and secured financing.

27.1 Forecasting Short-Term Financing Needs

The first step in short-term financial planning is to forecast the company's future cash flows. This exercise has two distinct objectives. First, a company forecasts its cash flows to determine whether it will have surplus cash or a cash deficit for each period. Second, management needs to decide whether that surplus or deficit is temporary or permanent. If it is permanent, it may affect the firm's long-term financial decisions. For example, if a company anticipates an ongoing surplus of cash, it may choose to increase its dividend payout. Deficits resulting from investments in long-term projects are often financed using long-term sources of capital, such as equity or long-term bonds.

In this chapter, we focus specifically on short-term financial planning. With this perspective, we are interested in analyzing the types of cash surpluses or deficits that are temporary and, therefore, short term in nature. When a company analyzes its short-term financing needs, it typically examines cash flows at quarterly intervals. To illustrate, let's assume that it is currently December 2018 and consider the case of Springfield Snowboards, Inc. Springfield manufactures snowboarding equipment, which it sells primarily to sports retailers. Springfield anticipates that in 2019 its sales will grow by 10% to \$20 million and its total net income will be \$1,950,000. Assuming that both sales and production will occur uniformly throughout the year, management's forecast of its quarterly net income and statement of cash flows for 2019 is presented in the spreadsheet in Table 27.1 (also shown, in gray, is the income statement for the fourth quarter of 2018).[1]

From this forecast, we see that Springfield is a profitable company. Its quarterly net income is almost \$500,000. Springfield's capital expenditures are equal to depreciation, and while Springfield's working capital requirements increase in the first quarter due to the increase in sales, they remain constant thereafter and so have no further cash flow consequence. Based on these projections, Springfield will be able to fund projected sales growth from its operating profit and, in fact, will accumulate excess cash on an ongoing basis. Given similar growth forecasts for next year and beyond, this surplus is likely to be long term. Springfield could reduce the surplus by paying some of it out as a dividend or by repurchasing shares.

Let's now turn to Springfield's potential short-term financing needs. Firms typically require short-term financing for three reasons: seasonalities, negative cash flow shocks, and positive cash flow shocks.

Seasonalities

In many industries, sales are seasonal. Figure 27.1 shows the seasonal pattern of sales for department stores, sporting goods, and building materials. Department store and sporting good sales are concentrated during the Christmas holiday season, while for building materials, sales peak in the spring ahead of the summer building season. When sales are concentrated during a few months, sources and uses of cash are also likely to be seasonal. Firms in this position may find themselves with a surplus of cash during some months that is sufficient to compensate for a shortfall during other months. However, because of timing differences, such firms often have short-term financing needs.

---

[1] Given the extensive coverage we have provided in Chapters 2 and 19 on how to construct pro forma financial statements, we do not rehash those details here. The full Excel model for all spreadsheets in this chapter is available from MyFinanceLab or www.pearsonhighered.com/berk_demarzo. Note that, for simplicity, we have assumed Springfield has no debt, and earns no interest on retained cash.

TABLE 27.1 SPREADSHEET **Projected Financial Statements for Springfield Snowboards, 2019, Assuming Level Sales**

	Quarter	2018Q4	2019Q1	2019Q2	2019Q3	2019Q4
	Income Statement ($000)					
1	Sales	4,545	5,000	5,000	5,000	5,000
2	Cost of Goods Sold	(2,955)	(3,250)	(3,250)	(3,250)	(3,250)
3	Selling, General and Administrative	(455)	(500)	(500)	(500)	(500)
4	EBITDA	1,136	1,250	1,250	1,250	1,250
5	Depreciation	(455)	(500)	(500)	(500)	(500)
6	EBIT	682	750	750	750	750
7	Taxes	(239)	(263)	(263)	(263)	(263)
8	**Net Income**	443	488	488	488	488
	Statement of Cash Flows					
9	Net Income		488	488	488	488
10	Depreciation		500	500	500	500
11	Changes in Working Capital					
12	Accounts Receivable		(136)	—	—	—
13	Inventory		—	—	—	—
14	Accounts Payable		48	—	—	—
15	**Cash from Operating Activities**		899	988	988	988
16	Capital Expenditures		(500)	(500)	(500)	(500)
17	Other Investment		—	—	—	—
18	**Cash from Investing Activities**		(500)	(500)	(500)	(500)
19	Net Borrowing		—	—	—	—
20	Dividends		—	—	—	—
21	Capital Contributions		—	—	—	—
22	**Cash from Financing Activities**		—	—	—	—
23	**Change in Cash and Equivalents** (15 + 18 + 22)		399	488	488	488

To illustrate, let's return to the example of Springfield Snowboards. In Table 27.1, management assumed that Springfield's sales occur uniformly throughout the year. In reality, for a snowboard manufacturer, sales are likely to be highly seasonal. Assume that 20% of sales occur during the first quarter, 10% during each of the second and third quarters (largely Southern Hemisphere sales), and 60% occur in the fourth quarter, in anticipation

FIGURE 27.1

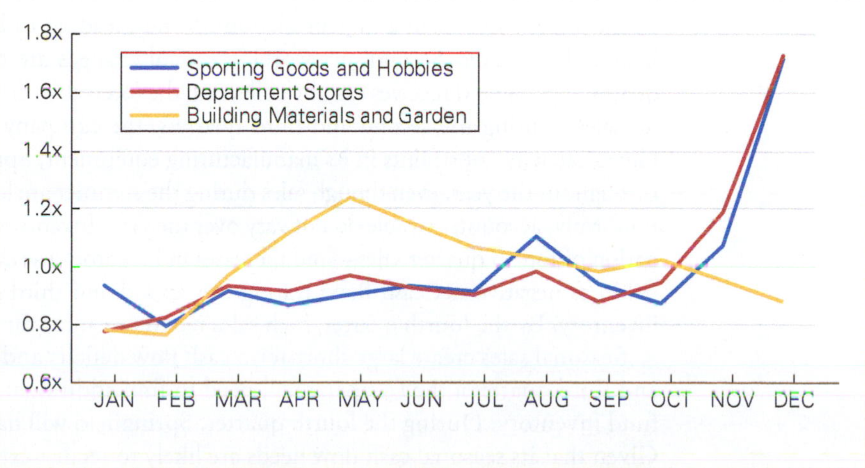

Sales Seasonality (2010–2015)

Monthly sales specified as a multiple of average monthly sales for each industry.

TABLE 27.2 SPREADSHEET Projected Financial Statements for Springfield Snowboards, 2019, Assuming Seasonal Sales

	Quarter	2018Q4	2019Q1	2019Q2	2019Q3	2019Q4
Income Statement ($000)						
1	Sales	10,909	4,000	2,000	2,000	12,000
2	Cost of Goods Sold	(7,091)	(2,600)	(1,300)	(1,300)	(7,800)
3	Selling, General and Administrative	(773)	(450)	(350)	(350)	(850)
4	EBITDA	3,045	950	350	350	3,350
5	Depreciation	(455)	(500)	(500)	(500)	(500)
6	EBIT	2,591	450	(150)	(150)	2,850
7	Taxes	(907)	(158)	53	53	(998)
8	**Net Income**	1,684	293	(98)	(98)	1,853
Statement of Cash Flows						
9	Net Income		293	(98)	(98)	1,853
10	Depreciation		500	500	500	500
11	Changes in Working Capital					
12	Accounts Receivable		2,073	600	—	(3,000)
13	Inventory		(650)	(1,950)	(1,950)	4,550
14	Accounts Payable		48	—	—	—
15	**Cash from Operating Activities**		2,263	(948)	(1,548)	3,903
16	Capital Expenditures		(500)	(500)	(500)	(500)
17	Other Investment		—	—	—	—
18	**Cash from Investing Activities**		(500)	(500)	(500)	(500)
19	Net Borrowing		—	—	—	—
20	Dividends		—	—	—	—
21	Capital Contributions		—	—	—	—
22	**Cash from Financing Activities**		—	—	—	—
23	**Change in Cash and Equivalents** (15 + 18 + 22)		1,763	(1,448)	(2,048)	3,403

of the (Northern Hemisphere) winter snowboarding season. The spreadsheet in Table 27.2 presents the resulting statement of cash flows. These forecasts continue to assume production occurs uniformly throughout the year.

From Table 27.2, we see that Springfield is still a profitable company, and its annual net income still totals $1,950,000. However, the introduction of seasonal sales creates some dramatic swings in Springfield's short-term cash flows. There are two effects of seasonality on cash flows. First, while cost of goods sold fluctuates proportionally with sales, other costs (such as administrative overhead and depreciation) do not, leading to large changes in the firm's net income by quarter. Second, net working capital changes are more pronounced. In the first quarter, Springfield receives cash by collecting the receivables from last year's high fourth quarter sales. During the second and third quarters, the company's inventory balance increases. Given capacity constraints in its manufacturing equipment, Springfield produces snowboards throughout the year, even though sales during the summer are low. Because production occurs uniformly, accounts payable do not vary over the year. Inventory, however, builds up in anticipation of fourth quarter sales—and increases in inventory use cash. As a consequence, Springfield has negative net cash flows during the second and third quarters, primarily to fund its inventory. By the fourth quarter, high sales recover cash for the company.

Seasonal sales create large short-term cash flow deficits and surpluses. During the second and third quarters, the company will need to find additional short-term sources of cash to fund inventory. During the fourth quarter, Springfield will have a large short-term surplus. Given that its seasonal cash flow needs are likely to recur next year, Springfield may choose to invest this cash in one of the short-term investment options discussed in Chapter 26.

TABLE 27.3 SPREADSHEET **Projected Financial Statements for Springfield Snowboards, 2019, Assuming Level Sales and a Negative Cash Flow Shock**

	Quarter	2018Q4	2019Q1	2019Q2	2019Q3	2019Q4
Income Statement ($000)						
1	Sales	4,545	5,000	5,000	5,000	5,000
2	Cost of Goods Sold	(2,955)	(3,250)	(3,250)	(3,250)	(3,250)
3	Selling, General and Administrative	(455)	(500)	(500)	(500)	(500)
4	EBITDA	1,136	1,250	1,250	1,250	1,250
5	Depreciation	(455)	(500)	(500)	(525)	(525)
6	EBIT	682	750	750	725	725
7	Taxes	(239)	(263)	(263)	(254)	(254)
8	**Net Income**	443	488	488	471	471
Statement of Cash Flows						
9	Net Income		488	488	471	471
10	Depreciation		500	500	525	525
11	Changes in Working Capital					
12	Accounts Receivable		(136)	—	—	—
13	Inventory		—	—	—	—
14	Accounts Payable		48	—	—	—
15	**Cash from Operating Activities**		899	988	996	996
16	Capital Expenditures		(500)	(1,500)	(525)	(525)
17	Other Investment		—	—	—	—
18	**Cash from Investing Activities**		(500)	(1,500)	(525)	(525)
19	Net Borrowing		—	—	—	—
20	Dividends		—	—	—	—
21	Capital Contributions		—	—	—	—
22	**Cash from Financing Activities**		—	—	—	—
23	**Change in Cash and Equivalents** (15 + 18 + 22)		399	(513)	471	471

Management can then use this cash to fund some of its short-term working capital needs during the following year.

Negative Cash Flow Shocks

Occasionally, a company will encounter circumstances in which cash flows are temporarily negative for an unexpected reason. We refer to such a situation as a negative cash flow shock. Like seasonalities, negative cash flow shocks can create short-term financing needs.

Returning to the Springfield Snowboards example, assume that during April 2019, management learns that some manufacturing equipment has broken unexpectedly. It will cost an additional $1,000,000 to replace the equipment.[2] To illustrate the effect of this negative cash flow shock, we return to the base case in which Springfield's sales are level rather than seasonal. (The marginal impact of this negative shock given seasonal sales would be similar.) The spreadsheet in Table 27.3 presents cash flows with level sales and the broken equipment.

In this case, the one-time expenditure of $1 million to replace equipment results in a negative net cash flow of $513,000 during the second quarter of 2019. If its cash reserves

[2]For simplicity, assume the book value of the replaced equipment is zero, so the equipment change does not have any immediate tax implications. Also, assume that Springfield obtains the replacement equipment quickly, so that any interruption in production is negligible. Finally, assume that Springfield increases investment by an amount equal to any increase in depreciation. The general results discussed here still hold absent these assumptions, although the calculations become more complicated.

are insufficient, Springfield will have to borrow (or arrange for another financing source) to cover the \$513,000 shortfall. However, the company continues to generate positive cash flow in subsequent quarters, and by the fourth quarter it will have generated enough in cumulative cash flow to repay any loan. Therefore, this negative cash flow shock has created the need for short-term financing.

Positive Cash Flow Shocks

We next analyze a case in which a positive cash flow shock affects short-term financing needs. Although this surprise is good news, it still creates demand for short-term financing.

During the first quarter of 2019, the director of marketing at Springfield Snowboards announces a deal with a chain of outdoor sporting goods stores located in the Midwest. Springfield will be the exclusive supplier to this customer, leading to an overall sales increase of 20% for the firm, with other operating expenses expected to increase accordingly. The increased sales will begin in the second quarter. As part of the deal, Springfield has agreed to a one-time expense of \$500,000 for marketing in areas where the stores are located. An extra \$1 million in capital expenditures is also required during the first quarter to increase production capacity. Likewise, sales growth will affect required working capital.

Managers at Springfield prepared the projected financial statement in Table 27.4 to reflect this new business. Notice that net income is lower during the first quarter, reflecting the \$500,000 increase in marketing expenses. By contrast, net income in subsequent quarters is higher, reflecting the higher sales. Sales increases in each of the first two quarters result in increases in accounts receivable and accounts payable.

TABLE 27.4 SPREADSHEET **Projected Financial Statements for Springfield Snowboards, 2019, Assuming Level Sales and a Growth Opportunity**

Quarter	2018Q4	2019Q1	2019Q2	2019Q3	2019Q4
Income Statement ($000)					
1 Sales	4,545	5,000	6,000	6,000	6,000
2 Cost of Goods Sold	(2,955)	(3,250)	(3,900)	(3,900)	(3,900)
3 Selling, General and Administrative	(455)	(1,000)	(600)	(600)	(600)
4 EBITDA	1,136	750	1,500	1,500	1,500
5 Depreciation	(455)	(500)	(525)	(525)	(525)
6 EBIT	682	250	975	975	975
7 Taxes	(239)	(88)	(341)	(341)	(341)
8 **Net Income**	443	163	634	634	634
Statement of Cash Flows					
9 Net Income		163	634	634	634
10 Depreciation		500	525	525	525
11 Changes in Working Capital					
12 Accounts Receivable		(136)	(300)	—	—
13 Inventory		—	—	—	—
14 Accounts Payable		48	105	—	—
15 **Cash from Operating Activities**		574	964	1,159	1,159
16 Capital Expenditures		(1,500)	(525)	(525)	(525)
17 Other Investment		—	—	—	—
18 **Cash from Investing Activities**		(1,500)	(525)	(525)	(525)
19 Net Borrowing		—	—	—	—
20 Dividends		—	—	—	—
21 Capital Contributions		—	—	—	—
22 **Cash from Financing Activities**		—	—	—	—
23 **Change in Cash and Equivalents** (15 + 18 + 22)		(926)	439	634	634

Even though the unexpected event in this case—the opportunity to grow more rapidly—is positive, it results in a negative net cash flow during the first quarter, due primarily to the new marketing expenses and capital expenditures. However, because the company will be even more profitable in subsequent quarters, this financing need is temporary.

Now that we have explained how a company determines its short-term needs, let's explore how these needs are financed.

CONCEPT CHECK

1. How do we forecast the firm's future cash requirements?
2. What is the effect of seasonalities on short-term cash flows?

27.2 The Matching Principle

In a perfect capital market, the choice of financing is irrelevant; thus, how the firm chooses to finance its short-term cash needs cannot affect value. In reality, important market frictions exist, including transaction costs. For example, one transaction cost is the opportunity cost of holding cash in accounts that pay little or no interest. Firms also face high transaction costs if they need to negotiate a loan on short notice to cover a cash shortfall. Firms can increase their value by adopting a policy that minimizes these kinds of costs. One such policy is known as the matching principle. The **matching principle** states that short-term needs should be financed with short-term debt and long-term needs should be financed with long-term sources of funds.[3]

Permanent Working Capital

Permanent working capital is the amount that a firm must keep invested in its short-term assets to support its continuing operations. Because this investment in working capital is required so long as the firm remains in business, it constitutes a long-term investment. The matching principle indicates that the firm should finance this permanent investment in working capital with long-term sources of funds. Such sources have lower transaction costs than short-term sources of funds, which would have to be replaced more often.

Temporary Working Capital

Another portion of a firm's investment in its accounts receivable and inventory is temporary and results from seasonal fluctuations in the firm's business or unanticipated shocks. This **temporary working capital** is the difference between the actual level of investment in short-term assets and the permanent working capital investment. Because temporary working capital represents a short-term need, the firm should finance this portion of its investment with short-term financing.

To illustrate the distinction between permanent and temporary working capital, we return to the Springfield Snowboards example. Table 27.2 presented cash flow forecasts assuming seasonal sales. In the spreadsheet in Table 27.5, we report the underlying levels of working capital that correspond to these forecasts.

[3]Some evidence indicates that most firms appear to follow the matching principle. See W. Beranek, C. Cornwell, and S. Choi, "External Financing, Liquidity, and Capital Expenditures," *Journal of Financial Research* (Summer 1995): 207–222; and M. Stohs and D. Mauer, "The Determinants of Corporate Debt Maturity Structure," *Journal of Business* 69(3) (1996): 279–312.

TABLE 27.5 SPREADSHEET Projected Levels of Working Capital for Springfield Snowboards, 2019, Assuming Seasonal Sales

	Quarter	2018Q4	2019Q1	2019Q2	2019Q3	2019Q4
Net Working Capital Requirements ($000)						
1	Minimum Cash Balance	500	500	500	500	500
2	Accounts Receivable	3,273	1,200	600	600	3,600
3	Inventory	300	950	2,900	4,850	300
4	Accounts Payable	(477)	(525)	(525)	(525)	(525)
5	**Net Working Capital**	3,595	2,125	3,475	5,425	3,875

In Table 27.5, we see that working capital for Springfield varies from a minimum of \$2,125,000 in the first quarter of 2019 to \$5,425,000 in the third quarter. The minimum level of working capital, or \$2,125,000, can be thought of as the firm's permanent working capital. The difference between this minimum level and the higher levels in subsequent quarters (for example, $\$5{,}425{,}000 - \$2{,}125{,}000 = \$3{,}300{,}000$ in the third quarter) reflects Springfield's temporary working capital requirements.

Financing Policy Choices

Following the matching principle should, in the long run, help minimize a firm's transaction costs. But what if, instead of using the matching principle, a firm financed its permanent working capital needs with short-term debt? When the short-term debt comes due, the firm will have to negotiate a new loan. This new loan will involve additional transaction costs, and it will carry whatever market interest rate exists at the time. As a result, the firm is also exposed to interest rate risk. Financing part or all of the permanent working capital with short-term debt is known as an **aggressive financing policy**. An ultra-aggressive policy would involve financing even some of the plant, property, and equipment with short-term sources of funds.

When the yield curve is upward sloping, the interest rate on short-term debt is lower than the rate on long-term debt. In that case, short-term debt may appear cheaper than long-term debt. However, we know that with perfect capital markets, Modigliani and Miller's results from Chapter 14 apply: The benefit of the lower rate from short-term debt is offset by the risk that the firm will have to refinance the debt in the future at a higher rate. This risk is borne by the equity holders, and so the firm's equity cost of capital will rise to offset any benefit from the lower borrowing rate.

Why, then, might a firm choose an aggressive financing policy? Such a policy might be beneficial if the market imperfections mentioned in Chapter 16, such as agency costs and asymmetric information, are important. The value of short-term debt is less sensitive to the firm's credit quality than long-term debt; therefore, its value will be less affected by management's actions or information. As a result, short-term debt can have lower agency and "lemons" costs than long-term debt, and an aggressive financing policy can benefit shareholders. On the other hand, by relying on short-term debt, the firm exposes itself to **funding risk**, which is the risk of incurring financial distress costs, should the firm not be able to refinance its debt in a timely manner or at a reasonable rate.

Alternatively, a firm could finance its short-term needs with long-term debt, a practice known as a **conservative financing policy**. For example, when following such a policy, a firm would use long-term sources of funds to finance its fixed assets, permanent working capital, and some of its seasonal needs. The firm would use short-term debt very sparingly to meet its peak seasonal needs. To implement such a policy effectively, there will necessarily be periods when excess cash is available—those periods when the firm requires little or no investment in temporary working capital. While a conservative financing policy reduces funding risk, it entails other costs: First, excess cash may earn a below-market interest rate, thereby reducing the firm's value. Second, even if the cash is invested at a competitive rate, interest income on the cash will be subject to double taxation, an additional cost. Finally, holding excess cash within the firm also increases the possibility that managers of the firm will use it nonproductively—for example, on perquisites for themselves.

Once a firm determines its short-term financing needs, it must choose which instruments it will use for this purpose. In the rest of this chapter, we survey the specific financing options available: bank loans, commercial paper, and secured financing.

CONCEPT CHECK

1. What is the matching principle?
2. What is the difference between temporary and permanent working capital?

27.3 Short-Term Financing with Bank Loans

One of the primary sources of short-term financing, especially for small businesses, is the commercial bank. Bank loans are typically initiated with a **promissory note**, which is a written statement that indicates the amount of the loan, the date payment is due, and the interest rate. In this section, we examine three types of bank loans: single, end-of-period payment loans; lines of credit; and bridge loans. In addition, we compare the interest rates, common stipulations, and fees associated with these bank loans.

Single, End-of-Period Payment Loan

The most straightforward type of bank loan is a single, end-of-period-payment loan. Such a loan agreement requires that the firm pay interest on the loan and pay back the principal in one lump sum at the end of the loan. The interest rate may be fixed or variable. With a fixed interest rate, the specific rate that the commercial bank will charge is stipulated at the time the loan is made. With a variable interest rate, the terms of the loan may indicate that the rate will vary with some spread relative to a benchmark rate, such as the yield on one-year Treasury securities or the prime rate. The **prime rate** is the rate banks charge their most creditworthy customers. However, large corporations can sometimes negotiate bank loans at an interest rate that is *below* the prime rate. For example, in its 2007 annual report, Mattel indicated that the weighted average interest rate it paid on average short-term borrowings from domestic institutions was 5.5% in 2007. By comparison, the average prime rate in 2007 was 8.05%.[4] Another common benchmark rate is the **London Inter-Bank Offered Rate**, or **LIBOR**, which is the rate of interest at which banks borrow funds from each other in the London interbank market. It is quoted for maturities of one day to one year for 10 major currencies. As it is a rate paid by banks with the highest credit quality, most firms will borrow at a rate that exceeds LIBOR.

Line of Credit

Another common type of bank loan arrangement is a **line of credit**, in which a bank agrees to lend a firm any amount up to a stated maximum. This flexible agreement allows the firm to draw upon the line of credit whenever it chooses.

Firms frequently use lines of credit to finance seasonal needs.[5] The line of credit may be an **uncommitted line of credit**, meaning it is an informal agreement that does not legally bind

[4]Mattel 2007 annual report and *Federal Reserve Statistical Release* Web site. On the other hand, in 2015 Mattel was paying over 10% while the prime rate was only 3.25%.

[5]Lines of credit may be used for other purposes as well. For example, Gartner, Inc., which provides research and analysis on information technology, announced that it would use both cash on hand and an existing bank line of credit to finance its 2005 acquisition of competitor Meta Group (Craig Schneider, "Dealwatch," ww2.CFO.com, January 5, 2005).

the bank to provide the funds. As long as the borrower's financial condition remains good, the bank is happy to advance additional funds. A **committed line of credit** consists of a written, legally binding agreement that obligates the bank to provide the funds regardless of the financial condition of the firm (unless the firm is bankrupt), as long as the firm satisfies any restrictions in the agreement. These arrangements are typically accompanied by a compensating balance requirement (that is, a requirement that the firm maintain a minimum level of deposits with the bank) and restrictions regarding the level of the firm's working capital. The firm pays a commitment fee based on a percentage of the unused portion of the line of credit plus interest on the amount that the firm borrowed. The line of credit agreement may also stipulate that at some point in time the outstanding balance must be zero. This policy ensures that the firm does not use the short-term financing to finance its long-term obligations.

Banks usually renegotiate the terms of a line of credit on an annual basis. A **revolving line of credit** is a committed line of credit that involves a solid commitment from the bank for a longer period of time, typically two to three years. A revolving line of credit with no fixed maturity is called **evergreen credit**. In its 2014 annual report, Mattel reported that it relied on a $1.6 billion revolving credit facility as a source of financing for its seasonal working capital requirements.

Bridge Loan

A **bridge loan** is another type of short-term bank loan that is often used to "bridge the gap" until a firm can arrange for long-term financing. For example, a real estate developer may use a bridge loan to finance the construction of a shopping mall. After the mall is completed, the developer will obtain long-term financing. Other firms use bridge loans to finance their plant and equipment costs until they receive the proceeds from the sale of a long-term debt or an equity issue. After a natural disaster, lenders may provide businesses with short-term loans to serve as bridges until they receive insurance payments or long-term disaster relief.

Bridge loans are often quoted as discount loans with fixed interest rates. With a **discount loan**, the borrower is required to pay the interest at the *beginning* of the loan period. The lender deducts interest from the loan proceeds when the loan is made.

Common Loan Stipulations and Fees

We now turn to common loan stipulations and fees that affect the effective interest rate on a loan. Specifically, we look at loan commitment fees, loan origination fees, and compensating balance requirements.

Commitment Fees. Various loan fees charged by banks affect the effective interest rate that the borrower pays. For example, the commitment fee associated with a committed line of credit increases the effective cost of the loan to the firm. The "fee" can really be considered an interest charge under another name. Suppose that a firm has negotiated a committed line of credit with a stated maximum of $1 million and an interest rate of 10% (EAR) with a bank. The commitment fee is 0.5% (EAR). At the beginning of the year, the firm borrows $800,000. It then repays this loan at the end of the year, leaving $200,000 unused for the rest of the year. The total cost of the loan is

Interest on borrowed funds = 0.10($800,000)	=	$80,000
Commitment fee paid on unused portion = 0.005($200,000)	=	$ 1,000
Total cost		$81,000

Loan Origination Fee. Another common type of fee is a **loan origination fee**, which a bank charges to cover credit checks and legal fees. The firm pays the fee when the loan is initiated; like a discount loan, it reduces the amount of usable proceeds that the firm receives. And like the commitment fee, it is effectively an additional interest charge.

To illustrate, assume that Timmons Towel and Diaper Service is offered a \$500,000 loan for three months at an APR of 12%. This loan has a loan origination fee of 1%. The loan origination fee is charged on the principal of the loan. In this case, the fee amounts to $0.01 \times \$500{,}000 = \$5000$, so the actual amount borrowed is \$495,000. The interest payment for three months is $\$500{,}000(0.12/4) = \$15{,}000$. Putting these cash flows on a timeline:

Thus, the actual three-month interest rate paid is

$$\frac{515{,}000}{495{,}000} - 1 = 4.04\%$$

Expressing this rate as an EAR gives $1.0404^4 - 1 = 17.17\%$.

Compensating Balance Requirements. Regardless of the loan structure, the bank may include a compensating balance requirement in the loan agreement that reduces the usable loan proceeds. Recall from Chapter 26 that a compensating balance requirement means that the firm must hold a certain percentage of the principal of the loan in an account at the bank. Assume that, rather than charging a loan origination fee, Timmons Towel and Diaper Service's bank requires that the firm keep an amount equal to 10% of the loan principal in a non-interest-bearing account with the bank as long as the loan remains outstanding. The loan was for \$500,000, so this requirement means that Timmons must hold $0.10 \times 500{,}000 = \$50{,}000$ in an account at the bank. Thus, the firm has only \$450,000 of the loan proceeds actually available for use, although it must pay interest on the full loan amount. At the end of the loan period, the firm owes $\$500{,}000 \times (1 + 0.12/4) = \$515{,}000$, and so must pay $\$515{,}000 - 50{,}000 = \$465{,}000$ after using its compensating balance. Putting these cash flows on a timeline:

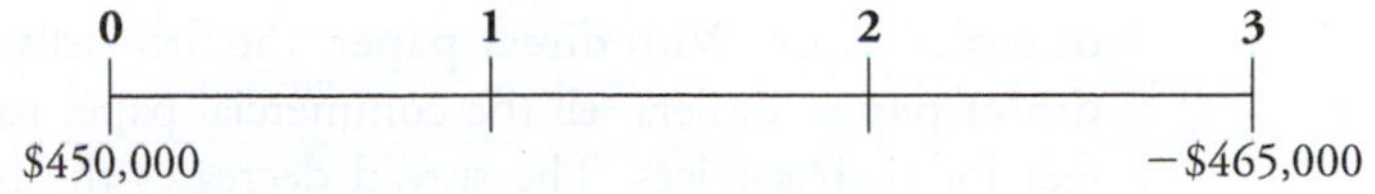

The actual three-month interest rate paid is

$$\frac{465{,}000}{450{,}000} - 1 = 3.33\%$$

Expressing this as an EAR gives $1.0333^4 - 1 = 14.01\%$.

We assumed that Timmons' compensating balance is held in a non-interest-earning account. Sometimes a bank will allow the compensating balance to be held in an account that pays a small amount of interest to offset part of the interest expense of the loan.

EXAMPLE 27.1 Compensating Balance Requirements and the Effective Annual Rate

Problem

Assume that Timmons Towel and Diaper Service's bank pays 1% (APR with quarterly compounding) on its compensating balance accounts. What is the EAR of Timmons' three-month loan?

Solution

The balance held in the compensating balance account will grow to $50{,}000(1 + 0.01/4) = \$50{,}125$. Thus, the final loan payment will be $500{,}000 + 15{,}000 - 50{,}125 = \$464{,}875$. Notice that the interest on the compensating balance accounts offsets some of the interest that Timmons pays on the loan. Putting the new cash flows on a timeline:

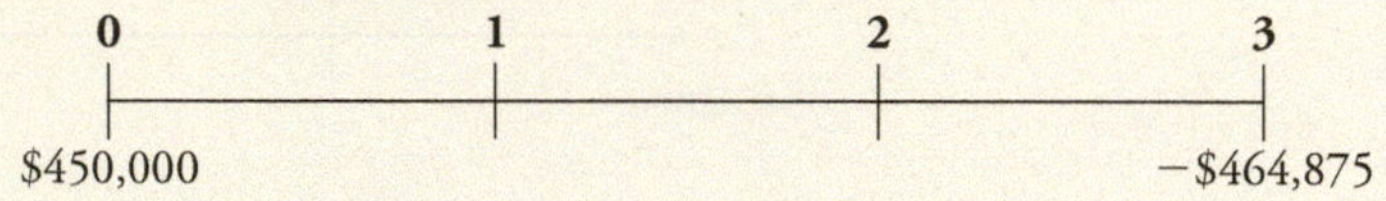

The actual three-month interest rate paid is

$$\frac{464{,}875}{450{,}000} - 1 = 3.31\%$$

Expressing this as an EAR gives $1.0331^4 - 1 = 13.89\%$.

CONCEPT CHECK

1. What is the difference between an uncommitted line of credit and a committed line of credit?
2. Describe common loan stipulations and fees.

27.4 Short-Term Financing with Commercial Paper

Commercial paper is short-term, unsecured debt used by large corporations that is usually a cheaper source of funds than a short-term bank loan. The minimum face value is $25,000, and most commercial paper has a face value of at least $100,000. The interest on commercial paper is typically paid by selling it at an initial discount.

The average maturity of commercial paper is 30 days and the maximum maturity is 270 days. Extending the maturity beyond 270 days triggers a registration requirement with the Securities and Exchange Commission (SEC), which increases issue costs and creates a time delay in the sale of the issue. Commercial paper is referred to as either direct paper or dealer paper. With **direct paper**, the firm sells the security directly to investors. With **dealer paper**, dealers sell the commercial paper to investors in exchange for a spread (or fee) for their services. The spread decreases the proceeds that the issuing firm receives, thereby increasing the effective cost of the paper. Like long-term debt, commercial paper is rated by credit rating agencies.

EXAMPLE 27.2 The Effective Annual Rate of Commercial Paper

Problem

A firm issues three-month commercial paper with a $100,000 face value and receives $98,000. What effective annual rate is the firm paying for its funds?

Solution

Let's put the firm's cash flows on a timeline:

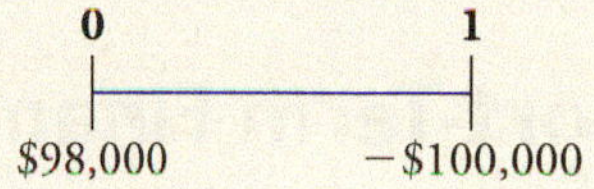

The actual three-month interest rate paid is

$$\frac{100{,}000}{98{,}000} - 1 = 2.04\%$$

Expressing this as an EAR gives $1.0204^4 - 1 = 8.42\%$.

GLOBAL FINANCIAL CRISIS Short-Term Financing in Fall 2008

One of the biggest problems firms faced during the financial crisis was short-term financing. In the weeks following the bankruptcy of Lehman Brothers, the short-term credit markets froze. Many investors lost confidence in money market mutual funds and withdrew their capital. In response, fund managers liquidated their short-term investments, causing the availability of short-term credit to contract dramatically and short-term yields to skyrocket. Nowhere was this more evident than in the commercial paper market. The figure below shows the spread (difference) between the yields on the highest-rated commercial paper (P1) and the second-highest-rated commercial paper (P2) for two maturities: overnight (red) and 30 day (blue).

Before the collapse of housing prices and the subprime crisis in 2007, spreads were tiny—less than 0.2%. Then, in the latter half of 2007, spreads increased dramatically, at times exceeding 1% and consistently remaining above 0.5%. The onset of the financial crisis in the fall of 2008 precipitated an explosion in the spread. By October, spreads were over 4%. Government intervention helped reduce the overnight spread, but the more risky 30-day spread remained elevated and actually topped 6% on the last day of the year. The new year brought more calm to the short-term debt markets and by late 2009 spreads were back to their fall 2007 levels. Since that time, spreads have remained low (although have trended mildly upward through 2015).

Credit spreads at the level witnessed during the financial crisis effectively shut firms like Mattel out of the commercial paper market and severely hampered their ability to conduct business. In addition, the increased uncertainty in financial markets made firms less likely to invest. Both effects were significant contributors to the global recession that accompanied the financial crisis.

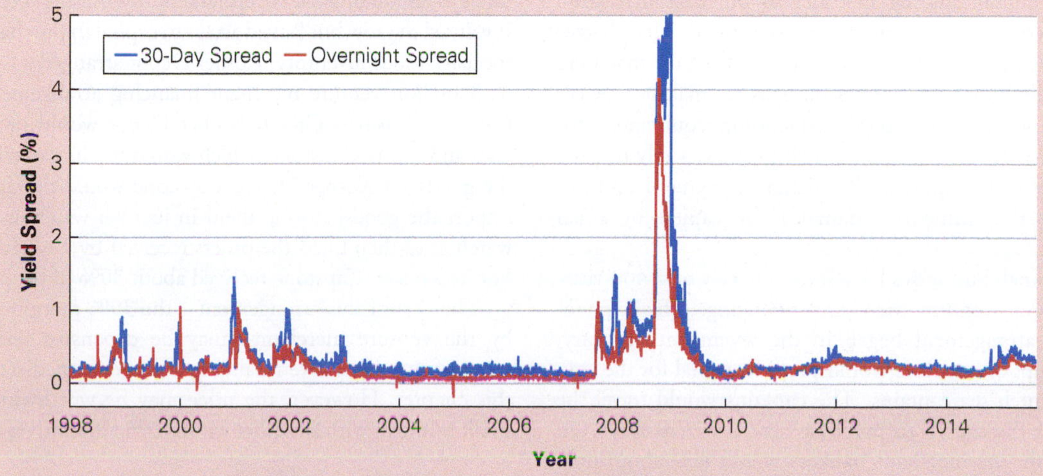

Source: Federal Reserve Board (www.federalreserve.gov/DataDownload/Choose.aspx?rel=CP)

CONCEPT CHECK

1. What is commercial paper?
2. How is interest paid on commercial paper?

27.5 Short-Term Financing with Secured Financing

Businesses can also obtain short-term financing by using **secured loans**, which are loans collateralized with short-term assets—most typically the firm's accounts receivables or inventory. Commercial banks, finance companies, and **factors**, which are firms that purchase the receivables of other companies, are the most common sources for secured short-term loans.

Accounts Receivable as Collateral

Firms can use accounts receivable as security for a loan by pledging or factoring.

Pledging of Accounts Receivable. In a **pledging of accounts receivable** agreement, the lender reviews the invoices that represent the credit sales of the borrowing firm and decides which credit accounts it will accept as collateral for the loan, based on its own credit standards. The lender then typically lends the borrower some percentage of the value of the accepted invoices—say, 75%. If the borrowing firm's customers default on their bills, the firm is still responsible to the lender for the money.

Factoring of Accounts Receivable. In a **factoring of accounts receivable** arrangement, the firm sells receivables to the lender (i.e., the factor), and the lender agrees to pay the firm the amount due from its customers at the end of the firm's payment period. For example, if a firm sells its goods on terms of Net 30, then the factor will pay the firm the face value of its receivables, less a factor's fee, at the end of 30 days. The firm's customers are usually instructed to make payments directly to the lender. In many cases, the firm

A Seventeenth-Century Financing Solution

In recent years, it has become more difficult for small businesses to obtain funding in order to purchase inventory. Several factors have contributed to this trend. First, bigger banks have acquired many small, regional banks that were traditionally important sources of loans to small businesses. Second, large banks have tightened lending requirements for small borrowers. Third, many small businesses rely increasingly on foreign suppliers that demand payment upfront, increasing the immediate demand for capital by small businesses.

Some small businesses have started to rely on a 400-year-old solution: venture merchant financing. This type of financing arrangement began in the seventeenth century, when groups of investors would provide capital for the voyages of Dutch sea captains. The captains would travel the seas, using the capital to purchase exotic merchandise. On their return, the merchant bankers would take about one-third of the captain's profits when the goods were sold as compensation for the financing.

Now consider the Kosher Depot, which sells exotic kosher foods to restaurants and supermarkets in Westbury, New York. It wanted to grow but lacked access to capital to purchase more specialty-foods inventory. Kosher Depot arranged a two-year, $3.3 million venture merchant financing arrangement with Capstone Business Credit. Kosher Depot would prearrange sales and notify Capstone, which would use its capital to buy the goods for Kosher Depot. Capstone would purchase and import the goods, storing them in its own warehouses. The warehouses then filled the orders received by Kosher Depot. For its services, Capstone received about 30% of the profits.

The cost of this arrangement—the 30% margin charged by the venture merchant—may be expensive relative to some of the alternative financing arrangements discussed in this chapter. However, the price may be worthwhile for a small business with no other short-term alternatives.

Source: Marie Leone, "Capital Ideas: A Little Cash'll Do Ya," ww2.CFO.com, March 3, 2005

can borrow as much as 80% of the face value of its receivables from the factor, thereby receiving its funds in advance. In such a case, the lender will charge interest on the loan in addition to the factor's fee. The lender charges the factor's fee, which may range from 1% to 2% of the face value of the accounts receivable, whether or not the firm borrows any of the available funds. Both the interest rate and the factor's fee vary depending on such issues as the size of the borrowing firm, the dollar volume of its receivables, and the creditworthiness of its customers. The dollar amounts involved in factoring agreements may be substantial. In 2014, for example, Mattel had sold nearly $23 million of its accounts receivable under factoring arrangements.

A factoring arrangement may be **with recourse**, meaning that the lender can seek payment from the borrower should the borrower's customers default on their bills. Alternatively, the financing arrangement may be **without recourse**, in which case the lender bears the risk of bad-debt losses. In this latter case, the factor will pay the firm the amount due regardless of whether the factor receives payment from the firm's customers. If the arrangement is with recourse, the lender may not require that it approve the customers' accounts before sales are made. If the factoring agreement is without recourse, the borrowing firm must receive credit approval for a customer from the factor prior to shipping the goods. If the factor gives its approval, the firm ships the goods and the customer is directed to make payment directly to the lender.

Inventory as Collateral

Inventory can be used as collateral for a loan in one of three ways: as a floating lien, as a trust receipt, or in a warehouse arrangement.

Floating Lien. In a **floating lien**, **general lien**, or **blanket lien** arrangement, all of the inventory is used to secure the loan. This arrangement is the riskiest setup from the standpoint of the lender because the value of the collateral used to secure the loan dwindles as inventory is sold. When a firm becomes financially distressed, management may be tempted to sell the inventory without making payments on the loan. In such a case, the firm may not have enough funds to replenish its inventory. As a result, the loan may become under-collateralized. To counter this risk, this type of loan bears a higher interest rate than the next two arrangements that we discuss. In addition, lenders will loan a low percentage of the value of the inventory.

Trust Receipt. With a **trust receipts loan** or **floor planning**, distinguishable inventory items are held in a trust as security for the loan. As these items are sold, the firm remits the proceeds from their sale to the lender in repayment of the loan. The lender will periodically send someone to ensure that the borrower has not sold some of the specified inventory and failed to make a repayment on the loan. Car dealerships often use this type of secured financing arrangement to obtain the funds needed to purchase vehicles from the manufacturer.

Warehouse Arrangement. In a **warehouse arrangement**, the inventory that serves as collateral for the loan is stored in a warehouse. A warehouse arrangement is the least risky collateral arrangement from the standpoint of the lender. This type of arrangement can be set up in one of two ways.

The first method is to use a **public warehouse**, which is a business that exists for the sole purpose of storing and tracking the inflow and outflow of the inventory. The lender extends a loan to the borrowing firm, based on the value of the inventory stored. When the

Loan Guarantees: The Ex-Im Bank Controversy

Exporters looking to finance working capital needs often face difficulty obtaining loans from domestic lenders. Lenders may feel unable to evaluate adequately the credit risk of foreign customers, for example, making them unwilling to lend against the exporter's accounts receivables, or to finance its purchases of inventory.

The Export-Import Bank of the United States, or Ex-Im Bank, was established in 1934 by President Franklin D. Roosevelt as an independent export credit agency that serves to "assist in financing the export of U.S. goods and services to international markets." It does so by providing loan guarantees which insure exporters' receivables against the risk of default by foreign customers, as well as risks of non-payment due to war or inconvertibility of the foreign currency. After obtaining such a loan guarantee, it is then usually possible for the exporter to arrange for short-term financing of its working capital needs from traditional lenders.

Critics of the Ex-Im Bank argue that because the bank is government sponsored, these loan guarantees implicitly pass the risk of the loans to U.S. taxpayers. If defaults were to exceed the bank's reserves, the federal government would need to bail out the bank. Supporters of the bank emphasize that the bank creates U.S. jobs by supporting the growth of U.S. exporters, and that without these guarantees the firms it serves would be unable to obtain competitive financing terms.

After facing controversial reauthorization votes in 2012 and 2014, the U.S. Congress let the Ex-Im Bank's authorization expire on June 30, 2015, closing the bank. After months of strong lobbying by U.S. businesses, Congress voted in a rare bipartisan effort to reauthorize and reopen the bank in December 2015.

borrowing firm needs the inventory to sell, it returns to the warehouse and retrieves it upon receiving permission from the lender. This arrangement provides the lender with the tightest control over the inventory. Public warehouses work well for some types of inventory, such as wine and tobacco products, which must age before they are ready to be sold. It is not practical for items that are subject to spoilage or are bulky and, therefore, difficult to transport to and from the warehouse.

The second option, a **field warehouse**, is operated by a third party, but is set up on the borrower's premises in a separate area so that the inventory collateralizing the loan is kept apart from the borrower's main plant. This type of arrangement is convenient for the borrower but gives the lender the added security of having the inventory that serves as collateral controlled by a third party.

Warehouse arrangements are expensive. The business operating the warehouse charges a fee on top of the interest that the borrower must pay the lender for the loan. However, the borrower may also save on the costs of storing the inventory herself. Because the warehouser is a professional at inventory control, there is likely to be little loss due to damaged goods or theft, which in turn lowers insurance costs. Because the control of the inventory remains in the hands of a third party, lenders may be willing to lend a greater percentage of the market value of the inventory than they would under other inventory arrangements.

EXAMPLE 27.3 Calculating the Effective Annual Cost of Warehouse Financing

Problem

The Row Cannery wants to borrow \$2 million for one month. Using its inventory as collateral, it can obtain a 12% (APR) loan. The lender requires that a warehouse arrangement be used. The warehouse fee is \$10,000, payable at the end of the month. Calculate the effective annual rate of this loan for Row Cannery.

Solution

The monthly interest rate is 12%/12 = 1%. At the end of the month, Row will owe $\$2{,}000{,}000 \times 1.01 = \$2{,}020{,}000$ plus the warehouse fee of $10,000. Putting the cash flows on a timeline gives:

0	1
$2,000,000	−$2,030,000

The actual one-month interest rate paid is

$$\frac{2{,}030{,}000}{2{,}000{,}000} - 1 = 1.5\%$$

Expressing this as an EAR gives $1.015^{12} - 1 = 19.6\%$.

The method that a firm adopts when using its inventory to collateralize a loan will affect the ultimate cost of the loan. The blanket lien agreement exposes the lender to the most risk, and will therefore carry the highest interest rate of the three types of arrangements discussed. While a warehousing arrangement provides the greatest amount of control over the inventory to the lender, resulting in a lower interest rate on the loan itself, the borrowing firm must pay the additional fees charged by the warehouser and accept the inconvenience associated with the loss of control. Although a trust receipts arrangement may offer a lower interest rate than a blanket lien, and it allows the firm to avoid the high fees associated with a warehouse arrangement, it can be used only with certain types of inventory.

CONCEPT CHECK

1. What is factoring of accounts receivable?
2. What is the difference between a floating lien and a trust receipt?

MyFinanceLab

Here is what you should know after reading this chapter. MyFinanceLab will help you identify what you know and where to go when you need to practice.

27.1 Forecasting Short-Term Financing Needs

- The first step in short-term financial planning is to forecast future cash flows. The cash flow forecasts allow a company to determine whether it has a cash flow surplus or deficit, and whether the surplus or deficit is short term or long term.
- Firms need short-term financing to deal with seasonal working capital requirements, negative cash flow shocks, or positive cash flow shocks.

27.2 The Matching Principle

- The matching principle specifies that short-term needs for funds should be financed with short-term sources of funds, and long-term needs with long-term sources of funds.

27.3 Short-Term Financing with Bank Loans

- Bank loans are a primary source of short-term financing, especially for small firms.
  - The most straightforward type of bank loan is a single, end-of-period payment loan.
  - Bank lines of credit allow a firm to borrow any amount up to a stated maximum. The line of credit may be uncommitted, which is a nonbinding informal agreement, or may more typically be committed.

- A bridge loan is a short-term bank loan that is used to bridge the gap until the firm can arrange for long-term financing.
- The number of compounding periods and other loan stipulations, such as commitment fees, loan origination fees, and compensating balance requirements, affect the effective annual rate of a bank loan.

27.4 Short-Term Financing with Commercial Paper

- Commercial paper is a method of short-term financing that is usually available only to large, well-known firms. It is a low-cost alternative to a short-term bank loan for those firms with access to the commercial paper market.

27.5 Short-Term Financing with Secured Financing

- Short-term loans may also be structured as secured loans. The accounts receivable and inventory of a firm typically serve as collateral in short-term secured financing arrangements.
- Accounts receivable may be either pledged as security for a loan or factored. In a factoring arrangement, the accounts receivable are sold to the lender (or factor), and the firm's customers are usually instructed to make payments directly to the factor.
- Inventory can be used as collateral for a loan in several ways: a floating lien (also called a general or blanket lien), a trust receipts loan (or floor planning), or a warehouse arrangement. These arrangements vary in the extent to which specific items of inventory are identified as collateral; consequently, they vary in the amount of risk the lender faces.

Key Terms

aggressive financing policy *p. 948*
blanket lien *p. 955*
bridge loan *p. 950*
commercial paper *p. 952*
committed line of credit *p. 950*
conservative financing policy *p. 948*
dealer paper *p. 952*
direct paper *p. 952*
discount loan *p. 950*
evergreen credit *p. 950*
factors *p. 954*
factoring of accounts receivable *p. 954*
field warehouse *p. 956*
floating lien *p. 955*
floor planning *p. 955*
funding risk *p. 948*
general lien *p. 955*
line of credit *p. 949*
loan origination fee *p. 951*
London Inter-Bank Offered Rate (LIBOR) *p. 949*
matching principle *p. 947*
permanent working capital *p. 947*
pledging of accounts receivable *p. 954*
prime rate *p. 949*
promissory note *p. 949*
public warehouse *p. 955*
revolving line of credit *p. 950*
secured loans *p. 954*
temporary working capital *p. 947*
trust receipts loan *p. 955*
uncommitted line of credit *p. 949*
warehouse arrangement *p. 955*
with recourse *p. 955*
without recourse *p. 955*

Further Reading

For an in-depth discussion of short-term financing, see: G. Gallinger and B. Healey, *Liquidity Analysis and Management* (Addison-Wesley, 1991); N. Hill and W. Sartoris, *Short-Term Financial Management: Text and Cases* (Prentice-Hall, 1994); J. Kallberg and K. Parkinson, *Corporate Liquidity: Management and Measurement* (Irwin/McGraw Hill, 1996); F. Scherr, *Modern Working Capital Management: Text and Cases* (Prentice-Hall, 1989); and K. Smith and G. Gallinger, *Readings on Short-Term Financial Management* (West, 1988).

Problems

All problems are available in MyFinanceLab.

Forecasting Short-Term Financing Needs

1. Which of the following companies are likely to have high short-term financing needs? Why?
   a. A clothing retailer
   b. A professional sports team
   c. An electric utility
   d. A company that operates toll roads
   e. A restaurant chain

2. Sailboats Etc. is a retail company specializing in sailboats and other sailing-related equipment. The following table contains financial forecasts as well as current (month 0) working capital levels. During which months are the firm's seasonal working capital needs the greatest? When does it have surplus cash?

	Month						
($000)	**0**	**1**	**2**	**3**	**4**	**5**	**6**
Net Income		$10	$12	$15	$25	$30	$18
Depreciation		2	3	3	4	5	4
Capital Expenditures		1	0	0	1	0	0
Levels of Working Capital							
Accounts Receivable	$2	3	4	5	7	10	6
Inventory	3	2	4	5	5	4	2
Accounts Payable	2	2	2	2	2	2	2

The Matching Principle

3. What is the difference between permanent working capital and temporary working capital?

4. Quarterly working capital levels for your firm for the next year are included in the following table. What are the permanent working capital needs of your company? What are the temporary needs?

	Quarter			
($000)	**1**	**2**	**3**	**4**
Cash	$100	$100	$100	$100
Accounts Receivable	200	100	100	600
Inventory	200	500	900	50
Accounts Payable	100	100	100	100

5. Why might a company choose to finance permanent working capital with short-term debt?

Short-Term Financing with Bank Loans

6. Hand-to-Mouth (H2M) is currently cash-constrained, and must make a decision about whether to delay paying one of its suppliers, or take out a loan. They owe the supplier $10,000 with terms of 2/10 Net 40, so the supplier will give them a 2% discount if they pay today (when the discount period expires). Alternatively, they can pay the full $10,000 in one month when the invoice is due. H2M is considering three options:

Alternative A: Forgo the discount on its trade credit agreement, wait and pay the full $10,000 in one month.

Alternative B: Borrow the money needed to pay its supplier today from Bank A, which has offered a one-month loan at an APR of 12%. The bank will require a (no-interest) compensating balance of 5% of the face value of the loan and will charge a $100 loan origination fee. Because H2M has no cash, it will need to borrow the funds to cover these additional amounts as well.

Alternative C: Borrow the money needed to pay its supplier today from Bank B, which has offered a one-month loan at an APR of 15%. The loan has a 1% loan origination fee, which again H2M will need to borrow to cover.

Which alternative is the cheapest source of financing for Hand-to-Mouth?

7. Consider two loans with a 1-year maturity and identical face values: an 8% loan with a 1% loan origination fee and an 8% loan with a 5% (no-interest) compensating balance requirement. Which loan would have the higher effective annual rate? Why?

8. What is the difference between evergreen credit and a revolving line of credit?

9. Which of the following one-year $1000 bank loans offers the lowest effective annual rate?
  a. A loan with an APR of 6%, compounded monthly
  b. A loan with an APR of 6%, compounded annually, that also has a compensating balance requirement of 10% (on which no interest is paid)
  c. A loan with an APR of 6%, compounded annually, that has a 1% loan origination fee

10. The Needy Corporation borrowed $10,000 from Bank Ease. According to the terms of the loan, Needy must pay the bank $400 in interest every three months for the three-year life of the loan, with the principal to be repaid at the maturity of the loan. What effective annual rate is Needy paying?

Short-Term Financing with Commercial Paper

11. The Treadwater Bank wants to raise $1 million using three-month commercial paper. The net proceeds to the bank will be $985,000. What is the effective annual rate of this financing for Treadwater?

12. Magna Corporation has an issue of commercial paper with a face value of $1,000,000 and a maturity of six months. Magna received net proceeds of $973,710 when it sold the paper. What is the effective annual rate of the paper to Magna?

13. What is the difference between direct paper and dealer paper?

14. The Signet Corporation has issued four-month commercial paper with a $6 million face value. The firm netted $5,870,850 on the sale. What effective annual rate is Signet paying for these funds?

Short-Term Financing with Secured Financing

15. What is the difference between pledging accounts receivable to secure a loan and factoring accounts receivable?

16. The Ohio Valley Steel Corporation has borrowed $5 million for one month at a stated annual rate of 9%, using inventory stored in a field warehouse as collateral. The warehouser charges a $5000 fee, payable at the end of the month. What is the effective annual rate of this loan?

17. Discuss the three different arrangements under which a firm may use inventory to secure a loan.

18. The Rasputin Brewery is considering using a public warehouse loan as part of its short-term financing. The firm will require a loan of $500,000. Interest on the loan will be 10% (APR, annual compounding) to be paid at the end of the year. The warehouse charges 1% of the face value of the loan, payable at the beginning of the year. What is the effective annual rate of this warehousing arrangement?

Special Topics

PART

10

THE LAW OF ONE PRICE CONNECTION. In Part 10, the final section of the text, we address special topics in corporate financial management. The Law of One Price continues to provide a unifying framework as we consider these topics. Chapter 28 discusses mergers and acquisitions and Chapter 29 provides an overview of corporate governance. In Chapter 30, we focus on corporations' use of derivatives to manage risk. We use the Law of One Price to evaluate the costs and benefits of risk management. Chapter 31 introduces the issues a firm faces when making a foreign investment and addresses the valuation of foreign projects. We value foreign currency cash flows in the context of internationally integrated capital markets, a condition that we demonstrate with the Law of One Price.

CHAPTER

28

Mergers and Acquisitions

NOTATION

EPS	earnings per share
P/E	price-earnings ratio
A	premerger total value of acquirer
T	premerger total value of target
S	value of all synergies
N_A	premerger number of shares of acquirer outstanding
x	number of new shares issued by acquirer to pay for target
P_T	premerger share price of target
P_A	premerger share price of acquirer
N_T	premerger number of shares of target outstanding

ON JULY 14, 2008, ST. LOUIS-BASED ANHEUSER-BUSCH AGREED to an acquisition by Belgian-based beer giant InBev for $70 per share in cash. The agreement ended 150 years of independence for the brewer of iconic Budweiser beer. In fact, Anheuser-Busch's board flatly rejected InBev's initial $65 per share offer, preferring to remain independent. However, the sweetened offer, valuing the company at $60 billion, was too compelling a deal for Anheuser's board to pass up. Next, InBev's managers faced the daunting task of integrating Anheuser's organization and brands into their global company and generating enough value from the transaction to justify the price they paid. Given the complexity and potential sums of money at stake, it is clear that some of the most important decisions financial managers make concern mergers and acquisitions.

In this chapter, we first provide some historical background about the market for mergers and acquisitions (M&A). Next, we discuss some of the reasons why a corporate financial manager may decide to pursue an acquisition. We then review the takeover process. Finally, we address the question of who benefits from the value that is added when a takeover occurs.

28.1 Background and Historical Trends

Mergers and acquisitions are part of what is often referred to as "the market for corporate control." When one firm acquires another, there is typically a buyer, the **acquirer** or **bidder**, and a seller, the **target** firm. There are two primary mechanisms by which ownership and control of a public corporation can change: Either another corporation or group of individuals can acquire the target firm, or the target firm can merge with another firm. In both cases, the acquiring entity must purchase the stock or existing assets of the target either for cash or for something of equivalent value (such as shares in the acquiring or newly merged corporation). For simplicity, we refer to either mechanism as a **takeover**.

The global takeover market is highly active, averaging more than $1 trillion per year in transaction value. Table 28.1 lists the twenty largest mergers of publicly traded firms completed from 1998 through fall 2015. As the table indicates, takeovers happen between well-known companies, and individual transactions can involve huge sums of money.

Merger Waves

The takeover market is also characterized by **merger waves**—peaks of heavy activity followed by quiet troughs of few transactions. Figure 28.1 displays the time series of takeover activity from 1926 to 2015. Merger activity is greater during economic expansions than during contractions and correlates with bull markets. Many of the same technological and

TABLE 28.1 Twenty Largest Merger Transactions, 1998–2015

Date Announced	Date Completed	Target Name	Acquirer Name	Equity Value (in $ billion)
Nov. 1999	June 2000	Mannesmann AG	Vodafone AirTouch PLC	203
Oct. 2004	Aug. 2005	Shell Transport & Trading Co.	Royal Dutch Petroleum Co.	185
Jan. 2000	Jan. 2001	Time Warner	America Online Inc.	182
Apr. 2007	Nov. 2007	ABN-AMRO Holding NV	RFS Holdings BV	98
Mar. 2006	Dec. 2006	BellSouth Corp.	AT&T Inc.	89
Nov. 1999	June 2000	Warner-Lambert Co.	Pfizer Inc.	89
Dec. 1998	Nov. 1999	Mobil Corp.	Exxon Corp.	85
Jan. 2000	Dec. 2000	SmithKline Beecham PLC	Glaxo Wellcome PLC	79
Feb. 2006	July 2008	Suez SA	Gaz de France SA	75
Apr. 1998	Oct. 1998	Citicorp	Travelers Group Inc.	73
July 1998	June 2000	GTE Corp.	Bell Atlantic Corp.	71
May 1998	Oct. 1999	Ameritech Corp.	SBC Communications Inc.	70
June 1998	Mar. 1999	Tele-Communications Inc. (TCI)	AT&T Corp.	70
Nov. 2014	Mar. 2015	Allergan Inc.	Actavis PLC	68
Jan. 2009	Oct. 2009	Wyeth	Pfizer Inc.	67
Jan. 1999	June 1999	AirTouch Communications Inc.	Vodafone Group PLC	66
Jan. 2004	Aug. 2004	Aventis SA	Sanofi-Synthelabo SA	66
Apr. 1998	Sep. 1998	BankAmerica Corp.	NationsBank Corp.	62
July 2002	Apr. 2003	Pharmacia Corp.	Pfizer Inc.	61
June 2008	Nov. 2008	Anheuser-Busch Cos. Inc.	InBev NV	60

Source: Thomson Reuters' SDC M&A Database

FIGURE 28.1

Fraction of U.S. Public Companies Acquired Each Year, 1926–2015

Shown is the fraction, by number and by value, of U.S. public firms acquired each year. Mergers appear to occur in distinct waves, with the most recent waves occurring in the 1980s, 1990s, and 2000s.

Source: Authors' calculations based on Center for Research in Securities Prices data

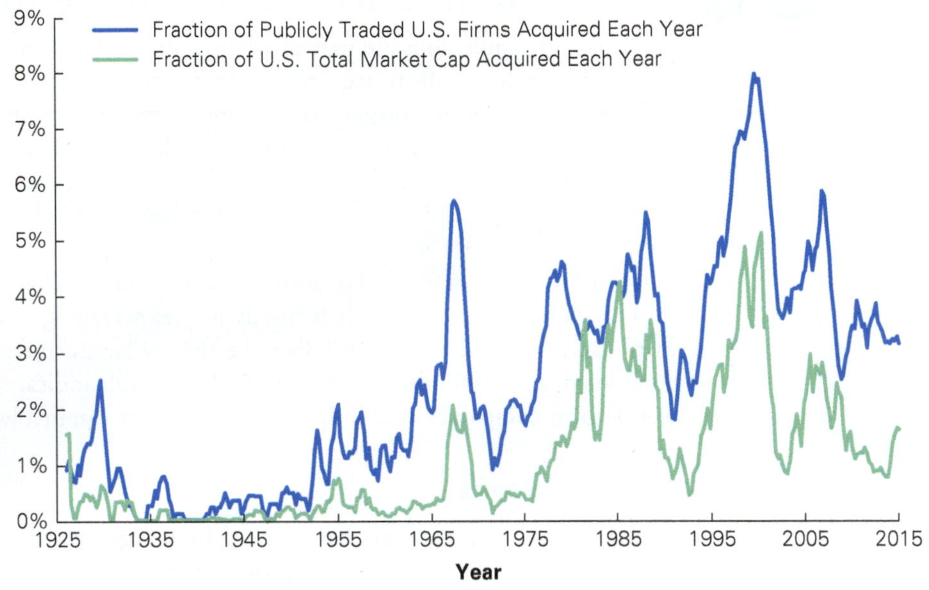

economic conditions that lead to bull markets also motivate managers to reshuffle assets through mergers and acquisitions. Thus, the same economic activities that drive expansions most likely also drive peaks in merger activity.[1]

Figure 28.1 shows that the periods of the greatest takeover activity occurred in the 1960s, 1980s, 1990s, and 2000s. Each merger wave was characterized by a typical type of deal. The increase in activity in the 1960s is known as the "conglomerate wave" because firms typically acquired firms in unrelated businesses. At the time, it was thought that managerial expertise was portable across business lines and that the conglomerate business form offered great financial advantages. This conglomerate fad eventually fell out of favor, and the 1980s were known for hostile, "bust-up" takeovers, in which the acquirer purchased a poorly performing conglomerate and sold off its individual business units for more than the purchase price. The 1990s, in contrast, were known for "strategic" or "global" deals that were more likely to be friendly and to involve companies in related businesses; these mergers often were designed to create strong firms on a scale that would allow them to compete globally. At the end of 2004, takeover activity began to pick up again, starting the next big merger wave, marked by consolidation in many industries such as telecommunications and software. This wave also saw private equity playing a larger role than it had in the past, with some private equity groups such as KKR, TPG, Blackrock, and Cerberus taking ever-larger firms such as Hertz (see Chapter 24), Chrysler, and Harrah's private. The financial crisis and severe contraction of credit in 2008 brought an abrupt end to the last merger wave, though activity, in terms of dollar value, has again picked up in 2014–2015. In fact, according to data from Thomson Reuters, nearly $5 trillion in global M&A deals were announced in 2015, setting a new record.

[1] See J. Harford, "What Drives Merger Waves," *Journal of Financial Economics* 77 (2005): 529–560, for an analysis of why these waves occur.

Types of Mergers

While we tend to talk about merger waves and mergers in general, the term "merger," as commonly used, encompasses several types of transactions that vary by the relation between the target and the acquirer and by the method of payment used in the transaction. If the target and acquirer are in the same industry, the merger is typically called a **horizontal merger**, whereas if the target's industry buys or sells to the acquirer's industry, it is called a **vertical merger**. Finally, if the target and acquirer operate in unrelated industries, the deal is a **conglomerate merger**. Conglomerate mergers, while popular in the 1960s, have generally fallen out of favor with shareholders because of the difficulty in creating value when combining two unrelated businesses.

Deals also vary based on whether the target shareholders receive stock or cash as payment for target shares. When they receive stock, the deal is often called a **stock swap**, because target shareholders are swapping their old stock for new stock in either the acquirer or the newly created merged firm. The consideration paid to target shareholders can be very complex, including debt instruments, options, and mixes of any of these with cash and/or stock. Commonly, however, target shareholders receive stock, cash, or a mix of the two.

While news reports understandably focus on the price and method of payment, the structure of a merger transaction, summarized in a **term sheet**, can be simple or incredibly complex. The items to negotiate include, among other things, who will run the new company, the size and composition of the new board, the location of the headquarters, and even the name of the new company.

CONCEPT CHECK

1. What are merger waves?
2. What is the difference between a horizontal and vertical merger?

28.2 Market Reaction to a Takeover

In most U.S. states, the law requires that when existing shareholders of a target firm are forced to sell their shares, they receive a fair value for their shares. Typically this concept is interpreted as the value exclusive of any value that arises because of the merger itself. For practical purposes, this principle translates into the share price prior to the merger. As a consequence, a bidder is unlikely to acquire a target company for less than its current market value. Instead, most acquirers pay a substantial **acquisition premium**, which is the percentage difference between the acquisition price and the premerger price of the target firm.

Table 28.2 lists the average historical premium and market reaction to a takeover.[2] As the table shows, acquirers pay an average premium of 43% over the premerger price of the

[2]The original research done in the 1970s and 1980s documented that shareholders experience significant gains (between 20% and 30%) upon a successful takeover of their firms. See G. Mandelker, "Risk and Return: The Case of the Merging Firm," *Journal of Financial Economics* 1(4) (1974): 303–335; M. Jensen and R. Ruback, "The Market for Corporate Control: The Scientific Evidence," *Journal of Financial Economics* 11(1) (1983): 5–50; and M. Bradley, A. Desai, and E. Kim, "The Rationale Behind Interfirm Tender Offers: Information or Synergy?" *Journal of Financial Economics* 11(1) (1983): 183–206. More recent papers have found combined losses on the order of $240 billion in capitalization at the announcement of takeover bids. This finding appears to be driven by spectacular losses from some large takeovers of public targets, especially in the late 1990s. See T. Loughran and A. Vijh, "Do Long-Term Shareholders Benefit from Corporate Acquisitions?" *Journal of Finance* 52(5) (1997): 1765–1790; and S. Moeller, R. Stulz, and F. Schlingemann, "Wealth Destruction on a Massive Scale: A Study of Acquiring Firm Returns in the Recent Merger Wave," *Journal of Finance* 60(2) (2005): 757–782.

TABLE 28.2 Average Acquisition Premium and Stock Price Reactions to Mergers

Premium Paid over Premerger Price	Announcement Price Reaction	
	Target	Acquirer
43%	15%	1%

Source: Data based on all U.S. deals from 1980 to 2005, as reported in *Handbook of Corporate Finance: Empirical Corporate Finance,* Vol. 2, Chapter 15, pp. 291–430, B. E. Eckbo, ed., Elsevier/North-Holland Handbook of Finance Series, 2008.

target. When a bid is announced, the target shareholders enjoy a gain of 15% on average in their stock price. Although acquirer shareholders see an *average* gain of 1%, in half of the transactions, the bidder price *decreases.* These facts raise three important questions that we answer in this chapter:

1. Why do acquirers pay a premium over the market value for a target company?
2. Although the price of the target company rises on average upon the announcement of the takeover, why does it rise less than the premium offered by the acquirer?
3. If the transaction is a good idea, why does the acquirer not consistently experience a large price increase?

Let's start with the first question—why do acquirers pay a premium over market value? In fact, this question has two parts: (1) Why is the target worth a premium over the current market value? and (2) Even if the target is worth more than its premerger value, why do acquirers pay more than the premerger market price? In the next section, we answer the first part of this question. We delay the discussion of the second part until the end of the chapter, when we fully understand the mechanics of the takeover process.

CONCEPT CHECK

1. On average, what happens to the target share price on the announcement of a takeover?
2. On average, what happens to the acquirer share price on the announcement of a takeover?

28.3 Reasons to Acquire

For most investors, an investment in the stock market is a zero-NPV investment. How, then, can an acquirer pay a premium for a target and still satisfy the requirement that the investment is a positive-NPV investment opportunity? The answer is that an acquirer might be able to add economic value, as a result of the acquisition, that an individual investor cannot add.

Large synergies are by far the most common justification that bidders give for the premium they pay for a target. An extreme example is SBC's acquisition of AT&T in 2005 for more than $15 billion. In interviews immediately after the announcement, SBC's Chairman Ed Whitacre was quick to point out that the projected synergies of $15 billion alone could justify the price SBC agreed to pay for AT&T, let alone AT&T's assets.

Such synergies usually fall into two categories: cost reductions and revenue enhancements. Cost-reduction synergies are more common and easier to achieve because they generally translate into layoffs of overlapping employees and elimination of redundant resources. This was the case in the SBC/AT&T acquisition, which forecasted 13,000 layoffs in the first year. If the merger will create possibilities to expand into new markets or gain more customers, then the merger partners will predict synergies that enhance their revenue. For example, when Dell and EMC announced their merger agreement in October 2015, they forecasted $1 billion in revenue-enhancement synergies, partially through providing new opportunities for VMWare, partially held by EMC, to sell its virtualization software.

Let's examine in detail the synergies most often cited by acquirers to justify takeovers.

Economies of Scale and Scope

A large company can enjoy **economies of scale**, or savings from producing goods in high volume, that are not available to a small company. For example, in Stride Rite's acquisition of sports shoemaker Saucony in 2005, one motivation was to reduce Saucony's manufacturing costs because, due to its larger size, Stride Rite could negotiate superior manufacturing contracts in China. Larger firms can also benefit from **economies of scope**, which are savings that come from combining the marketing and distribution of different types of related products (e.g., soft drinks and snack foods). Many analysts believed that Kraft's decision in 2009 to purchase the British chocolate maker Cadbury was motivated by a desire to expand Kraft's snack foods into emerging markets where Cadbury already had a large presence.

There may also be costs associated with size. Chief among these is that larger firms are more difficult to manage. In a small firm, the CEO is often close to the firm's operations. He or she can keep in touch with the firm's largest customers and most important personnel, thereby keeping abreast of changing market conditions and potential problems. Because they receive information quickly, small firms are often able to react in a timely way to changes in the economic environment.

Vertical Integration

Vertical integration refers to the merger of two companies in the same industry that make products required at different stages of the production cycle. A company might conclude that it can enhance its product if it has direct control of the inputs required to make the product. Similarly, another company might not be happy with how its products are being distributed, so it might decide to take control of its distribution channels.

The principal benefit of vertical integration is coordination. By putting two companies under central control, management can ensure that both companies work toward a common goal. For example, oil companies are often vertically integrated. They generally own all stages of the production process, from the oil fields to the refineries and so on, even down to the gas stations that distribute their primary product—gasoline. Many also have divisions that prospect for new oil.

Vertically integrated companies are large, and as we have already pointed out, large corporations are more difficult to run. Consequently, not all successful corporations are vertically integrated. A good example is Microsoft Corporation. Microsoft has chosen to make the operating system that the vast majority of computers use, but not the computers themselves. Many experts have argued that a key factor in Microsoft's early success over rivals IBM and Apple was its decision not to integrate vertically.

Expertise

Firms often need expertise in particular areas to compete more effectively. Faced with this situation, a firm can enter the labor market and attempt to hire personnel with the required skills. However, hiring experienced workers with the appropriate talent might be difficult with an unfamiliar, new technology. A more efficient solution may be to purchase the talent as an already functioning unit by acquiring an existing firm. For example, in

2000 Paris-based AXA bought Sanford C. Bernstein, a Wall Street private partnership, to gain expertise and a preexisting client base in the huge U.S. asset management market. Similarly, U.K. builder Amec bought a large stake in Spie Batignolles, a French contractor, to gain local contacts and expertise in the French building industry. Such mergers are common in high-tech industries. Networking firm Cisco Systems is known for its strategy of buying young startup firms that have developed promising new networking technologies.

Monopoly Gains

It is often argued that merging with or acquiring a major rival enables a firm to substantially reduce competition within the industry and thereby increase profits. Society as a whole bears the cost of monopoly strategies, so most countries have antitrust laws that limit such activity.

The extent to which these laws are enforced tends to vary across countries and over time depending on the policy of current leaders. When General Electric (GE) agreed to buy Honeywell in October 2000, the U.S. Justice Department approved the deal with limited conditions. However, the European Commission (EC) determined that putting GE's aircraft leasing division and Honeywell's extensive avionics product line under the same management would lead to unacceptable anticompetitive effects in the avionics market. Despite substantial concessions by GE and top-level political lobbying by U.S. officials, the EC refused to approve the deal, and it was eventually called off. The GE/Honeywell deal was the first time a merger of two U.S. companies that had been approved by U.S. authorities was blocked by European officials. The EC had no direct jurisdiction over the merger of the companies, but it was in the position to impose crippling restrictions on sales inside the European Union.[3]

Monopoly power could be very valuable, and we would expect that in the absence of strong antitrust laws, many companies would merge. However, while all companies in an industry benefit when competition is reduced, only the merging company pays the associated costs (from, for instance, integrating the target and managing a larger corporation). Perhaps this reason, along with existing antitrust regulation, accounts for the lack of convincing evidence that monopoly gains result from the reduction of competition following takeovers. For example, financial researchers have found that the share prices of other firms in the same industry did not significantly increase following the announcement of a merger within the industry.[4]

Efficiency Gains

Another justification acquirers cite for paying a premium for a target is efficiency gains, which are often achieved through an elimination of duplication—for example, as in the SBC/AT&T merger mentioned earlier. Acquirers also often argue that they can run the target organization more efficiently than existing management could.

While in theory a chief executive of an inefficiently run corporation can be ousted by current shareholders voting to replace the board of directors, very few managers are replaced in this way. Instead, unhappy investors typically sell their stock, so the stock of a corporation with an inept chief executive trades at a discount relative to the price at which it would trade if it had more capable leadership. In such a situation, an acquirer could purchase shares at the discounted price to take control of the corporation and replace the

---

[3]The European Commissioner for Competition at the time was Mario Monti, who later was the prime minister of Italy from 2011–2013 and helped resolve the Italian debt crisis.

[4]See B. E. Eckbo, "Horizontal Mergers, Collusion and Stockholder Wealth," *Journal of Financial Economics* 11(1) (1983): 241–273; and R. Stillman, "Examining Antitrust Policy Toward Horizontal Mergers," *Journal of Financial Economics* 11(1) (1983): 225–240.

chief executive with a more effective one. Once the benefits of the new management team become obvious to investors, the discount for the old management will likely disappear and the acquirer can resell its shares for a profit.[5]

Although identifying poorly performing corporations is relatively easy, fixing them is another matter entirely. Takeovers relying on the improvement of target management are difficult to complete, and post-takeover resistance to change can be great. Thus, not all inefficiently run organizations necessarily become more efficient following a takeover.

Tax Savings from Operating Losses

When a firm makes a profit, it must pay taxes on the profit. However, when it incurs a loss, the government does not rebate taxes. Thus, it might appear that a conglomerate has a tax advantage over a single-product firm simply because losses in one division can be offset by profits in another division. Let's illustrate this scenario with an example.

EXAMPLE 28.1 Taxes for a Merged Corporation

Problem

Consider two firms, Ying Corporation and Yang Corporation. Both corporations will either make $50 million or lose $20 million every year with equal probability. The only difference is that the firms' profits are perfectly negatively correlated. That is, any year Yang Corporation earns $50 million, Ying Corporation loses $20 million, and vice versa. Assume that the corporate tax rate is 34%. What are the total expected after-tax profits of both firms when they are two separate firms? What are the expected after-tax profits if the two firms are combined into one corporation called Ying-Yang Corporation, but are run as two independent divisions? (Assume it is not possible to carry back or carry forward any losses.)

Solution

Let's start with Ying Corporation. In the profitable state, the firm must pay corporate taxes, so after-tax profits are $\$50 \times (1 - 0.34) = \$33$ million. No taxes are owed when the firm reports losses, so the expected after-tax profits of Ying Corporation are $33(0.5) - 20(0.5) = \$6.5$ million. Because Yang Corporation has identical expected profits, its expected profits are also $6.5 million. Thus, the expected profit of both companies operated separately is $13 million.

The merged corporation, Ying-Yang Corporation, always makes a pretax profit equal to $50 - 20 = \$30$ million. After taxes, expected profits are therefore $\$30 \times (1 - 0.34) = \$19.8$ million. So Ying-Yang Corporation has significantly higher after-tax profits than the total stand-alone after-tax profits of Ying Corporation and Yang Corporation.

Although Example 28.1 is an extreme case, it illustrates a benefit of conglomeration. In the United States, however, these benefits are mitigated because the IRS typically allows companies to carry back losses up to 2 years, or forward up to 20 years, to offset earnings. While that rule would reduce the tax benefit in Example 28.1, it also creates a motive for profitable firms to acquire targets with large tax loss carryforwards in order to reap the tax savings from them. However, the IRS will disallow a tax break if it can show that the principal reason for a takeover is tax avoidance, so it is unlikely that such a tax benefit could, by itself, be a valid reason to acquire another firm.

[5] There are a number of papers that document operational improvements in the context of private equity buyouts; see for example, S. Kaplan, "The Effects of Management Buyouts on Operating Performance and Value," *Journal of Financial Economics* 24 (1989): 217–254; and S. Bernstein and A. Sheen "The Operational Consequences of Private Equity Buyouts: Evidence from the Restaurant Industry," *Review of Financial Studies* (2016), forthcoming.

Diversification

The benefits of diversification are frequently cited as a reason for a conglomerate merger. The justification for these benefits comes in three forms: direct risk reduction, lower cost of debt or increased debt capacity, and liquidity enhancement. We discuss each in turn.

Risk Reduction. Like a large portfolio, large firms bear less idiosyncratic risk, so often mergers are justified on the basis that the combined firm is less risky. The problem with this argument is that it ignores the fact that investors can achieve the benefits of diversification themselves by purchasing shares in the two separate firms. Because most stockholders will already be holding a well-diversified portfolio, they get no further benefit from the firm diversifying through acquisition. Moreover, as we have already pointed out, there are costs associated with merging and with running a large diversified firm. Because it may be harder to measure performance accurately in a conglomerate, agency costs may increase and resources may be inefficiently allocated across divisions.[6] As a result, it is cheaper for investors to diversify their own portfolios than to have the corporation do it through acquisition.

Debt Capacity and Borrowing Costs. All else being equal, larger, more diversified firms have a lower probability of bankruptcy given the same degree of leverage. Consequently, such firms can increase leverage further and enjoy greater tax savings without incurring significant costs of financial distress. Thus, increased tax benefits and reduction in bankruptcy costs from leverage are potential benefits of diversifying mergers. Of course, to justify a merger, these gains must be large enough to offset any disadvantages of running a larger, less-focused firm.

Liquidity. Shareholders of private companies are often under-diversified: They have a disproportionate share of their wealth invested in the private company. Consequently, when an acquirer buys a private target, it provides the target's owners with a way to reduce their risk exposure by cashing out their investment in the private target and reinvesting in a diversified portfolio. This liquidity that the bidder provides to the owners of a private firm can be valuable and often is an important incentive for the target shareholders to agree to the takeover.

Earnings Growth

It is possible to combine two companies with the result that the earnings per share of the merged company exceed the premerger earnings per share of either company, *even when the merger itself creates no economic value*. Let's look at how this can happen.

EXAMPLE 28.2 Mergers and Earnings per Share

Problem

Consider two corporations that both have earnings of $5 per share. The first firm, OldWorld Enterprises, is a mature company with few growth opportunities. It has 1 million shares that are currently outstanding, priced at $60 per share. The second company, NewWorld Corporation, is a young company with much more lucrative growth opportunities. Consequently, it has a higher value: Although it has the same number of shares outstanding, its stock price is $100 per share. Assume NewWorld acquires OldWorld using its own stock, and the takeover adds no value. In a perfect market, what is the value of NewWorld after the acquisition? At current market prices, how many shares must NewWorld offer to OldWorld's shareholders in exchange for their shares? Finally, what are NewWorld's earnings per share after the acquisition?

---

[6]See, for example, A. Goel, V. Nanda, and M. P. Narayanan, "Career Concerns and Resource Allocation in Conglomerates," *Review of Financial Studies* 17(1) (2004): 99–128.

Solution

Because the takeover adds no value, the post-takeover value of NewWorld is just the sum of the values of the two separate companies: 100×1 million $+ 60 \times 1$ million $= \$160$ million. To acquire OldWorld, NewWorld must pay \$60 million. At its pre-takeover stock price of \$100 per share, the deal requires issuing 600,000 shares. As a group, OldWorld's shareholders will then exchange 1 million shares in OldWorld for 600,000 shares in NewWorld, or each shareholder will get 0.6 share in NewWorld for each 1 share in OldWorld. Notice that the price per share of NewWorld stock is the same after the takeover: The new value of NewWorld is \$160 million and there are 1.6 million shares outstanding, giving it a stock price of \$100 per share.

However, NewWorld's earnings per share have changed. Prior to the takeover, both companies earned \$5/share $\times$ 1 million shares $= \$5$ million. The combined corporation thus earns \$10 million. There are 1.6 million shares outstanding after the takeover, so NewWorld's post-takeover earnings per share are

$$EPS = \frac{\$10 \text{ million}}{1.6 \text{ million shares}} = \$6.25/\text{share}$$

By taking over OldWorld, NewWorld has raised its earnings per share by \$1.25.

As Example 28.2 demonstrates, by acquiring a company with low growth potential (and thus a low P/E multiple), a company with high growth potential (and high P/E multiple) can raise its earnings per share. In the past, people have cited this increase as a reason to merge. Of course, a savvy investor will see that the merger *adds no economic value*. All that has happened is that the high-growth company, by combining with a low-growth company, has lowered its overall growth rate. As a result, its P/E multiple should fall, which results from its earnings per share rising. Thus, we can draw no conclusion regarding whether a merger was beneficial solely by looking at its impact on the acquirer's earnings.

EXAMPLE 28.3 Mergers and the Price-Earnings Ratio

Problem

Calculate NewWorld's price-earnings ratio before and after the takeover described in Example 28.2.

Solution

Before the takeover, NewWorld's price-earnings ratio is

$$\text{P/E} = \frac{\$100/\text{share}}{\$5/\text{share}} = 20$$

After the takeover, NewWorld's price-earnings ratio is

$$\text{P/E} = \frac{\$100/\text{share}}{\$6.25/\text{share}} = 16$$

The price-earnings ratio has dropped to reflect the fact that after taking over OldWorld, more of the value of NewWorld comes from earnings from current projects than from its future growth potential.

Managerial Motives to Merge

Most of the reasons given so far are economically motivated, shareholder-driven incentives to merge. However, managers sometimes have their own reasons to merge. Studies have consistently found that the stock price of large bidders drops on average when a bid is announced, especially when the target is publicly traded. Two possible explanations might be conflicts of interest with their shareholders and overconfidence.

Conflicts of Interest. Managers may prefer to run a larger company due to the additional pay and prestige it brings. Because most CEOs hold only a small fraction of their firm's stock, they may not bear enough of the cost of an otherwise bad merger that increases their personal benefits.[7] For example, a CEO who owns 1% of her firm's stock bears 1% of every dollar lost on a bad acquisition, but enjoys 100% of the gains in compensation and prestige that come with being the CEO of a larger company. If the acquisition destroys $100 million in shareholder value, but increases the present value of her compensation by more than $1 million, she will prefer to execute the merger anyway. Why would the board of directors create these incentives? Either due to poor monitoring of the manager, or belief that the strategy is correct even if the stock market disagrees, boards typically increase the pay of CEOs along with the size of the firm, even if the size comes at the expense of poorly performing acquisitions.[8] We will discuss corporate governance further in the next chapter.

Overconfidence. As explained in Chapter 13, people in general tend to be overconfident in their abilities. Psychological research has shown that it takes repeated failures for a person to change his belief that he is above-average at some activity. Most CEOs perform at most one large acquisition during their tenure as CEO. In a well-known 1986 paper,[9] Richard Roll proposed the "hubris hypothesis" to explain takeovers, which maintains that overconfident CEOs pursue mergers that have low chance of creating value because they truly believe that their ability to manage is great enough to succeed. The critical distinction between this hypothesis and the incentive conflict discussed above is that overconfident managers believe they are doing the right thing for their shareholders, but irrationally overestimate their own abilities. Under the incentive conflict explanation, managers know they are destroying shareholder value, but personally gain from doing so.

CONCEPT CHECK

1. What are the reasons most often cited for a takeover?
2. Explain why risk diversification benefits and earnings growth are not good justifications for a takeover intended to increase shareholder wealth.

28.4 Valuation and the Takeover Process

In this section, we explore how the takeover process works. We begin by establishing how a bidder determines the initial offer. We then review the tax and accounting issues specific to a takeover and explain the regulatory approval process. We end by discussing board approval, including defensive strategies that boards implement to discourage takeovers.

---

[7] M. Jensen highlighted the agency conflict in acquisition decisions in his 1986 paper, "Agency Costs of Free Cash Flow, Corporate Finance and Takeovers," *American Economic Review* 76 (1986): 323–329.

[8] J. Harford and K. Li, "Decoupling CEO Wealth and Firm Performance: The Case of Acquiring CEOs," *Journal of Finance* 62 (2007): 917–949, shows that in 75% of mergers where the acquiring shareholders lose money, acquiring CEOs are financially better off.

[9] R. Roll, "The Hubris Hypothesis of Corporate Takeovers," *Journal of Business* 59(2) (1986): 197–216.

Valuation

In Chapter 19, we demonstrated how a bidder values a target company. Recall that we explained, in the context of a case study, how an acquirer values a target by using two different approaches. The first—and simpler—approach compares the target to other comparable companies. Although this approach is easy to implement, it gives at best a rough estimate of value. Valuing the target using a multiple based on comparable firms does not directly incorporate the operational improvements and other synergistic efficiencies that the acquirer intends to implement. Purchasing a corporation usually constitutes a very large capital investment decision, so it requires a more accurate estimate of value including careful analysis of both operational aspects of the firm and the ultimate cash flows the deal will generate. Thus, the second approach to valuation requires making a projection of the expected cash flows that will result from the deal, and valuing those cash flows.

A key issue for takeovers is quantifying and discounting the value added as a result of the merger. In Chapter 19, the acquirer was expected to implement operational improvements, as well as changes to the target's capital structure (potentially increasing its tax efficiency). As demonstrated in Section 28.3, a takeover can generate other sources of value. For simplicity, in this section we refer to any additional value created as the **takeover synergies**.

Conceptually, we can separate the price paid for a target into its pre-bid market value plus a premium:

$$\text{Amount Paid} = \text{Target's Pre-Bid Market Capitalization} + \text{Acquisition Premium} \quad (28.1)$$

From the bidder's standpoint, the benefit from the acquisition includes both the stand-alone value of the target (what it is worth on its own) and any synergies created:

$$\text{Value Acquired} = \text{Target Stand-Alone Value} + \text{PV(Synergies)} \quad (28.2)$$

Comparing Eqs. 28.1 and 28.2, if we equate the pre-bid market capitalization with the stand-alone value of the target,[10] then from the bidder's perspective, the takeover is a positive-NPV project only if the premium it pays does not exceed the synergies created. Although the premium that is offered is a concrete number, the synergies are not—investors might well be skeptical of the acquirer's estimate of their magnitude. The bidder's stock price reaction to the announcement of the merger is one way to gauge investors' assessments of whether the bidder overpaid or underpaid for the target. As Table 28.2 shows, the average stock price reaction is 1%, but the median is closer to zero. Thus, the market, on average, believes that the premium is approximately equal to the synergies. Nonetheless, there is large variation in the premium across deals. One large-scale study of the value effects of mergers found that positive reactions to bids are concentrated in smaller bidders. In fact, during the 1990s, 87 large public acquirers announced bids that resulted in $1 billion or more in value reduction at announcement.[11] This finding is likely explained by some of the managerial motives discussed in the previous section.

[10] Rumors about a potential bid for the target will often push its share price up in anticipation of the premium offer. Practitioners refer to the "unaffected" target price, meaning the target's share price before it was affected by rumors of a takeover. This price would be used to compute the stand-alone value of the target.

[11] S. Moeller, R. Stulz, and F. Schlingemann, "Wealth Destruction on a Massive Scale: A Study of Acquiring Firm Returns in the Recent Merger Wave," *Journal of Finance* 60(2) (2005): 757–782.

The Offer

Once the acquirer has completed the valuation process, it is in the position to make a **tender offer**—that is, a public announcement of its intention to purchase a large block of shares for a specified price. A bidder can use either of two methods to pay for a target: cash or stock. In a cash transaction, the bidder simply pays for the target, including any premium, in cash. In a stock-swap transaction, the bidder pays for the target by issuing new stock and giving it to the target shareholders. The "price" offered is determined by the **exchange ratio**—the number of bidder shares received in exchange for each target share—multiplied by the market price of the acquirer's stock.

A stock-swap merger is a positive-NPV investment for the acquiring shareholders if the share price of the merged firm (the acquirer's share price after the takeover) exceeds the premerger price of the acquiring firm. We can write this condition as follows. Let A be the premerger, or stand-alone, value of the acquirer, and T be the premerger (stand-alone) value of the target. Let S be the value of the synergies created by the merger. If the acquirer has N_A shares outstanding before the merger, at share price P_A, and issues x new shares to pay for the target, then the acquirer's share price should increase post-acquisition if

$$\frac{A+T+S}{N_A+x} > \frac{A}{N_A} = P_A \tag{28.3}$$

The left side of Eq. 28.3 is the share price of the merged firm. The numerator indicates the total value of the merged firm: the stand-alone value of the acquirer and target plus the value of the synergies created by the merger. The denominator represents the total number of shares outstanding once the merger is complete. The ratio is the post-merger share price. The right side of Eq. 28.3 is the premerger share price of the acquirer: the total premerger value of the acquirer divided by the premerger number of shares outstanding.

We can rearrange Eq. 28.3 to find the following condition for the acquirer to earn a positive NPV:

$$x\,P_A < T + S \tag{28.4}$$

Eq. 28.4 simply states that the value of the shares offered, xP_A, must be less than the value of the target plus the synergies created. If we let $P_T = T/N_T$ be the premerger value of the target, then we can rewrite this condition to find the maximum exchange ratio the acquirer should offer:

$$\text{Exchange ratio} = \frac{x}{N_T} < \frac{P_T}{P_A}\left(1 + \frac{S}{T}\right) \tag{28.5}$$

For example, if the value of synergies equals 20% of the value of the target, you would be willing to pay an exchange ratio 20% higher than the current price ratio.

EXAMPLE 28.4 Maximum Exchange Ratio in a Stock Takeover

Problem

At the time Sprint announced plans to acquire Nextel in December 2004, Sprint stock was trading for $25 per share and Nextel stock was trading for $30 per share. If the projected synergies were $12 billion, and Nextel had 1.033 billion shares outstanding, what is the maximum exchange ratio Sprint could offer in a stock swap and still generate a positive NPV? What is the maximum cash offer Sprint could make?

Solution

Nextel's premerger market cap was $T = 1.033 \times 30 = \$31$ billion. Thus using Eq. 28.5,

$$\text{Exchange ratio} < \frac{P_T}{P_A}\left(1 + \frac{S}{T}\right) = \frac{30}{25}\left(1 + \frac{12}{31}\right) = 1.665$$

That is, Sprint could offer up to 1.665 shares of Sprint stock for each share of Nextel stock and generate a positive NPV. For a cash offer, given synergies of \$12 billion/1.033 billion shares = \$11.62 per share, Sprint could offer up to \$30 + 11.62 = \$41.62. Note that this cash amount equals the cash value of the exchange offer: \$25 × 1.665 = \$41.62.

Merger "Arbitrage"

Once a tender offer is announced, there is no guarantee that, in fact, the takeover will take place at this price. Often acquirers have to raise the price to consummate the deal. Alternatively, the offer may fail. When an acquirer bids for a target, the target firm's board may not accept the bid and recommend that existing shareholders not tender their shares, even when the acquirer offers a significant premium over the pre-offer share price. Even if the target board supports the deal, there is also the possibility that regulators might not approve the takeover. Because of this uncertainty about whether a takeover will succeed, the market price generally does not rise by the amount of the premium when the takeover is announced.

This uncertainty creates an opportunity for investors to speculate on the outcome of the deal. Traders known as **risk arbitrageurs**, who believe that they can predict the outcome of a deal, take positions based on their beliefs. While the strategies these traders use are sometimes referred to as arbitrage, they are actually quite risky, so they do not represent a true arbitrage opportunity in the sense we have defined in this book. Let's illustrate the strategy using the 2002 stock-swap merger of Hewlett-Packard (HP) and Compaq.

In September 2001, HP announced that it would purchase Compaq by swapping 0.6325 shares of HP stock for each share of Compaq stock. After the announcement, HP traded for \$18.87 per share, so the implied value of HP's offer was \$18.87 × 0.6325 = \$11.9353. Yet, the price of Compaq was only \$11.08 per share after the announcement, \$0.8553 below the value of HP's offer. Thus, a risk arbitrageur who simultaneously purchased 10,000 Compaq shares and short sold 6325 HP shares, would net 6325 × \$18.87 − 10,000 × \$11.08 = \$8553 immediately. Then, if the takeover was successfully completed on the original terms, the 10,000 Compaq shares would convert into 6325 HP shares, allowing the risk arbitrageur to cover the short position in HP and be left with no net exposure. Thus, the arbitrageur would pocket the original \$8553 as a profit.[12]

The potential profit described above arises from the difference between the target's stock price and the implied offer price, and is referred to as the **merger-arbitrage spread**. However, it is not a true arbitrage opportunity because there is a risk that the deal will not go through. If the takeover did not ultimately succeed, the risk arbitrageur would eventually have to unwind his position at whatever market prices prevailed. In most cases, these prices would have moved against him (in particular, the price of Compaq would be likely to decline if the takeover did not occur), so he would face losses on the position.

[12] For simplicity, we are ignoring dividend payments made during the period. HP paid \$0.24 and Compaq paid \$0.075 in dividends prior to the completion of the merger, reducing slightly the profit from the trade by 10,000 × \$0.075 − 6325 × \$0.24 = −\$768.

FIGURE 28.2

Merger-Arbitrage Spread for the Merger of HP and Compaq

The plot shows the potential profit, given that the merger was ultimately successfully completed, from purchasing 10,000 Compaq shares and short-selling 6325 HP shares on the indicated date. A risk arbitrageur who expects the deal to go through can profit by opening the position when the spread is large, and closing the position after it declines.

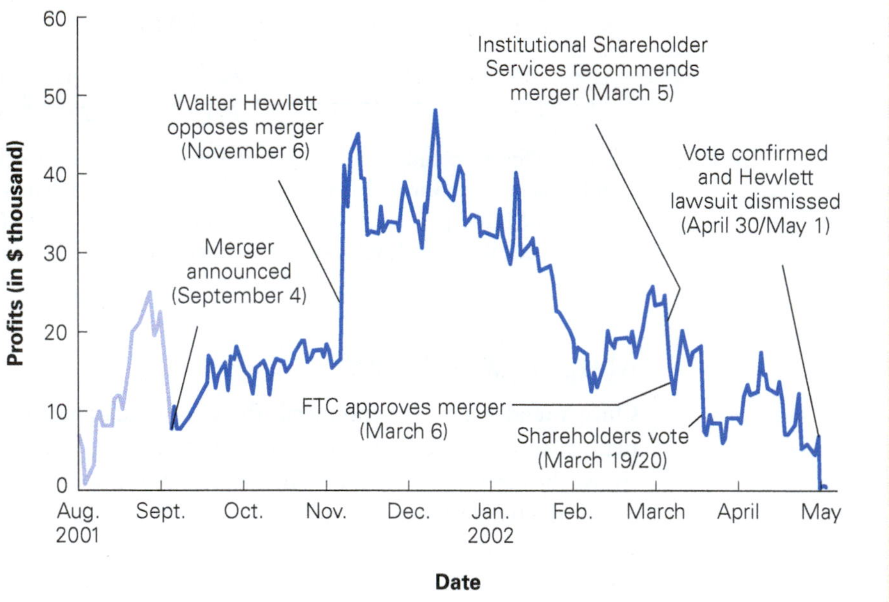

The HP-Compaq takeover was distinctive in that the uncertainty about the success of the deal stemmed largely from acquirer discomfort with the deal rather than from target shareholder discomfort. Although initially supportive of the merger, the Hewlett family got cold feet. About two months after the deal was announced, Walter Hewlett disclosed his family's opposition to it. On the day of Walter Hewlett's announcement, the price of HP stock rose to \$19.81, while Compaq's stock price fell to \$8.50, causing the merger-arbitrage spread to widen to $\$19.81 \times 6325 - \$8.5 \times 10{,}000 = \$40{,}298$. We plot the merger-arbitrage spread for the HP-Compaq merger in Figure 28.2. The risk-arbitrage strategy outlined above is effectively a short position on this spread, which pays off if the spread declines. Thus, an arbitrageur who opened the strategy when the deal was announced and closed it after Walter Hewlett announced his opposition would face a loss of $\$40{,}298 - \$8553 = \$31{,}745$.

Although the Hewlett family members were large shareholders of HP, they were not controlling shareholders; they did not have enough shares to block the deal single-handedly. Hence, a battle for control of HP ensued between the Hewlett family and CEO Carly Fiorina, the driving force behind the acquisition of Compaq. This conflict was only resolved months later when HP shareholders, by a slim margin, voted in favor of issuing new shares, thereby effectively approving the merger and netting a profit for any risk arbitrageur who stayed the course. As is clear from Figure 28.2, arbitrageurs who did not have the stomach to hold on would have faced large losses at several points during the roller-coaster ride. And while HP CEO Carly Fiorina survived this early challenge to her authority, the performance of HP following the merger vindicated Hewlett's position. HP's board ultimately fired Fiorina in 2005.

Tax and Accounting Issues

Once the terms of trade have been decided, the tax and accounting implications of a merger can be determined. How the acquirer pays for the target affects the taxes of both the target shareholders and the combined firm. Any cash received in full or partial exchange for shares triggers an immediate tax liability for target shareholders. They will have to pay a capital gains tax on the difference between the price paid for their shares in the takeover and the price they paid when they first bought the shares. If the acquirer pays for the takeover entirely by exchanging bidder stock for target stock, then the tax liability is deferred until the target shareholders actually sell their new shares of bidder stock.

If the acquirer purchases the target assets directly (rather than the target stock), then it can **step up** the book value of the target's assets to the purchase price. This higher depreciable basis reduces future taxes through larger depreciation charges. Further, any goodwill created could also be amortized for tax purposes over 15 years. The same treatment applies to a forward cash-out merger, where the target is merged into the acquirer and target shareholders receive cash in exchange for their shares.

Many transactions are carried out as acquisitive reorganizations under the tax code. These structures allow the target shareholders to defer their tax liability on the part of the payment made in acquirer stock but they do not allow the acquirer to step up the book value of the target assets. However, they provide a mechanism for isolating the target's assets and liabilities in a subsidiary of the acquirer. This can be very attractive for an acquirer that does not want to be exposed to the known (or unknown) liabilities of the target.

While the method of payment (cash or stock) affects how the value of the target's assets is recorded for tax purposes, it does not affect the combined firm's financial statements for financial reporting. The combined firm must mark up the value assigned to the target's assets on the financial statements by allocating the purchase price to target assets according to their fair market value. If the purchase price exceeds the fair market value of the target's identifiable assets, then the remainder is recorded as goodwill and is examined annually by the firm's accountants to determine whether its value has decreased. For example, in HP's takeover of Compaq, HP recorded more than $10 billion in goodwill. The footnotes to the statements attributed the goodwill to the value of the Compaq brand name, which is assumed to have an indefinite life.

Even when a merger has a positive NPV, bidding managers are typically very concerned with the effect of the merger on earnings. This is the other side of the earnings-growth argument as a reason to merge. Just as merging two companies can increase earnings without affecting economic value, it can also decrease earnings without affecting economic value. Nevertheless, acquirers are hesitant to commit to a deal that would be dilutive to earnings per share, even if only in the short run.

Board and Shareholder Approval

For a merger to proceed, both the target and the acquiring board of directors must approve the deal and put the question to a vote of the shareholders of the target (and, in some cases, the shareholders of the acquiring firm as well).

In a **friendly takeover**, the target board of directors supports the merger, negotiates with potential acquirers, and agrees on a price that is ultimately put to a shareholder vote. Although it is rare for acquiring boards to oppose a merger, target boards sometimes do not support the deal even when the acquirer offers a large premium. In a **hostile takeover**, the board of directors (together with upper-level management) fights the takeover attempt. To succeed, the acquirer must garner enough shares to take control of the target and replace the board of directors. When a takeover is hostile, the acquirer is often called a **raider**.

If the shareholders of a target company receive a premium over the current market value of their shares, why would a board of directors ever oppose a takeover? There are a number of reasons. The board might legitimately believe that the offer price is too low. In this case, a suitor that is willing to pay more might be found or the original bidder might be convinced to raise its offer. Alternatively, if the offer is a stock-swap, target management may oppose the offer because they feel the acquirer's shares are over-valued, and therefore that the value of the offer is actually less than the stand-alone value of the target. Finally, managers (and the board) might oppose a takeover because of their own self-interests, especially if the primary motivation for the takeover is efficiency gains. In this case, the acquirer most likely plans to undertake a complete change of leadership of the corporation. Upper-level managers could view opposing the merger as a way of protecting their jobs (and the jobs of their employees). In fact, this concern is perhaps the single biggest reason for the negative associations that hostile takeovers generate. Bear in mind that if substantial efficiency gains are indeed possible, current management is not doing an effective job. A takeover, or threat thereof, might be the only recourse investors have to fix the problem.

In theory, the duty of the target board of directors is to choose the course of action that is in the best interests of the target shareholders. In practice, the courts have given target directors wide latitude under what is called the "business judgment rule" to determine the best course for their companies, including spurning a premium offer if the directors can reasonably argue that more value will eventually be realized for their shareholders by remaining independent. The premise of this rule is that absent evidence of misconduct or self-dealing, the court will not substitute its judgment for that of the elected, informed directors.

In merger transactions, however, there is heightened judicial scrutiny under what is commonly referred to as the "Revlon duties" and "Unocal," named after the cases in which they were established. The Revlon duties state that if a change of control is going to occur, then directors must seek the highest value (they cannot favor one controlling entity over another based on anything other than value to shareholders). The Unocal case established that when the board takes actions deemed as defensive (we discuss these in detail in the next section), its actions are subject to extra scrutiny to ensure that they are not coercive or designed simply to preclude a deal. The board must believe that there is a threat to its corporate strategy and its defenses must be proportional to the magnitude of the threat.

CONCEPT CHECK

1. What are the steps in the takeover process?
2. What do risk arbitrageurs do?

28.5 Takeover Defenses

For a hostile takeover to succeed, the acquirer must go around the target board and appeal directly to the target shareholders. The acquirer can do this by making an unsolicited offer to buy target stock directly from the shareholders (a tender offer). The acquirer will usually couple this with a **proxy fight**: The acquirer attempts to convince target shareholders to unseat the target board by using their proxy votes to support the acquirers' candidates for election to the target board. Target companies have a number of strategies available to them to stop this process. These strategies can force a bidder to raise its bid or entrench management more securely, depending on the independence of the target board. We begin with the most effective defensive strategy, the poison pill.

Poison Pills

A **poison pill** is a rights offering that gives existing target shareholders the right to buy shares in the target at a deeply discounted price once certain conditions are met. The acquirer is specifically excluded from this right. Because target shareholders can purchase shares at less than the market price, the rights offering dilutes the value of any shares held by the acquirer. This dilution makes the takeover so expensive for the acquiring shareholders that they choose to pass on the deal.

The poison pill was invented in 1982 by a takeover lawyer, Martin Lipton, who successfully warded off a takeover attempt of El Paso Electric by General American Oil.[13] Because the original poison pill goes into effect only in the event of a complete takeover (that is, a purchase of 100% of the outstanding shares), one way to circumvent it is to not do a complete takeover. The first time this work-around was used was by Sir James Goldsmith, who took control of Crown Zellerbach by purchasing slightly more than 50% of the outstanding stock. Because he did not purchase the rest, Crown Zellerbach's poison pill was ineffective.

In response to the takeover of Crown Zellerbach, corporate lawyers have perfected the original poison pill. Most poison pills now specify that if a raider acquires more than a trigger amount (typically 20%) of the target shares (but chooses not to execute a complete takeover by purchasing all outstanding shares), existing shareholders—with the exception of the acquirer—have the right to buy more shares in the target at a discounted price.

The name *poison pill* comes from the world of espionage. Once caught, a spy is supposed to take his own life by swallowing a poison pill rather than give up important secrets. Poison pills are very effective in stopping takeovers, but where is the suicide analogy? The answer is that by adopting a poison pill, a company effectively entrenches its management by making it much more difficult for shareholders to replace bad managers, thereby potentially destroying value. Financial research has verified this effect. A firm's stock price typically drops when it adopts a poison pill. Furthermore, once adopted, firms with poison pills have below-average financial performance.[14]

Not surprisingly, companies adopting poison pills are harder to take over, and when a takeover occurs, the premium that existing shareholders receive for their stock is higher. Therefore, because a poison pill increases the cost of a takeover, all else being equal, a target company must be in worse shape (there must be a greater opportunity for profit) to justify the expense of waging a takeover battle.

Poison pills also increase the bargaining power of the target firm when negotiating with the acquirer because they make it difficult to complete the takeover without the cooperation of the target board. If used effectively, this bargaining power can allow target shareholders to capture more of the takeover gains by negotiating a higher premium than they would get if no pill existed. Numerous studies on the impact of anti-takeover provisions on takeovers have found that such provisions result in higher premiums accruing to existing shareholders of the target company.[15]

Staggered Boards

A determined bidder in the face of a poison pill has another available option: Get its own slate of directors elected to the target board, which it can submit at the next annual shareholders meeting. If the target shareholders elect those candidates, then the new directors

---

[13]For a brief history, see Len Costa, "The Perfect Pill," *Legal Affairs* (March 2005), www.legalaffairs.org.

[14]P. Malatesta and R. Walkling, "Poison Pill Securities: Stockholder Wealth, Profitability and Ownership Structure," *Journal of Financial Economics* 20(1) (1988): 347–376; and M. Ryngaert, "The Effects of Poison Pills Securities on Stockholder Wealth," *Journal of Financial Economics* 20(1) (1988): 377–417.

[15]Georgeson and Company (1988) study; R. Comment and G. W. Schwert, "Poison or Placebo: Evidence on the Deterrence and Wealth Effects of Modern Antitakeover Measures," *Journal of Financial Economics* 39(1) (1995): 3–43; N. Varaiya, "Determinants of Premiums in Acquisition Transactions," *Managerial and Decision Economics* 8(3) (1987): 175–184; and R. Heron and E. Lie, "On the Use of Poison Pills and Defensive Payouts by Takeover Targets," *Journal of Business* 79(4) (2006): 1783–1807.

can cancel the poison pill and accept the bidder's offer. To prevent such a coup from happening, about two-thirds of public companies have a **staggered** (or **classified**) **board**. In a typical staggered board, every director serves a three-year term and the terms are staggered so that only one-third of the directors are up for election each year. Thus, even if the bidder's candidates win board seats, it will control only a minority of the target board. A bidder's candidate would have to win a proxy fight two years in a row before the bidder had a majority presence on the target board. The length of time required to execute this maneuver can deter a bidder from making a takeover attempt when the target board is staggered. Most experts consider a poison pill combined with a staggered board to be the most effective defense available to a target company.

While staggered boards and poison pills are an effective defense against hostile takeovers, preventing such takeovers may not be in shareholders' best interest. Indeed, many investors have come to view these mechanisms as fostering management entrenchment, allowing subpar managers to escape market discipline. Increased shareholder activism in the 2000s has led to dramatic decline in the use of these devices, as shown in Figure 28.3.

White Knights

When a hostile takeover appears to be inevitable, a target company will sometimes look for another, friendlier company to acquire it. This company that comes charging to the target's rescue is known as a **white knight**. The white knight will make a more lucrative offer for the target than the hostile bidder. Incumbent managers of the target maintain control by reaching an agreement with the white knight to retain their positions.

One variant on the white knight defense is the **white squire** defense. In this case, a large investor or firm agrees to purchase a substantial block of shares in the target with special voting rights. This action prevents a hostile raider from acquiring control of the target. The idea is that the white squire itself will not choose to exercise its control rights.

FIGURE 28.3

Disappearing Defenses

The fraction of U.S. firms with poison pill and staggerred board defenses against hostile takeovers has declined dramatically since 2002 in response to shareholder activism.

Source: Factset

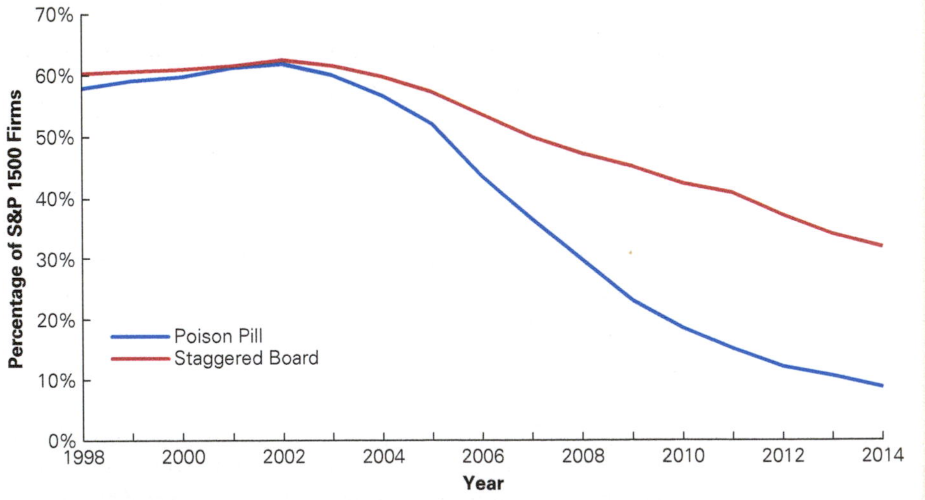

Golden Parachutes

A **golden parachute** is an extremely lucrative severance package that is guaranteed to a firm's senior managers in the event that the firm is taken over and the managers are let go. For example, when Procter & Gamble acquired The Gillette Company in 2005, Gillette CEO James Kilts was reported to have received a severence package worth $165 million.

Golden parachutes have been criticized because they are seen both as excessive and a misuse of shareholder wealth. In fact, the empirical evidence does not support this view.[16] If anything, it supports the view that an adoption of a golden parachute actually creates value. If a golden parachute exists, management will be more likely to be receptive to a takeover. Gillette CEO James Kilts is a case in point. He reportedly solicited the offer from Procter & Gamble, which long coveted Gillette. This means the existence of golden parachutes lessens the likelihood of managerial entrenchment. Researchers have found that stock prices rise on average when companies announce that they plan to implement a golden parachute policy, and that the number of firms bidding against one another for the target and the size of the takeover premium are higher if a golden parachute agreement exists.

Recapitalization

Another defense against a takeover is a recapitalization, in which a company changes its capital structure to make itself less attractive as a target. For example, a company with a lot of cash might choose to pay out a large dividend. Companies without a lot of cash might instead choose to issue debt and then use the proceeds to pay a dividend or repurchase stock.

Why does increasing leverage make a firm less attractive as a target? In many cases, a substantial portion of the synergy gains that an acquirer anticipates from a takeover are from tax savings from an increase in leverage as well as other cost reductions. By increasing leverage on its own, the target firm can reap the benefit of the interest tax shields. In addition, the need to generate cash to meet the debt service obligations provides a powerful motivation to managers to run a corporation efficiently. In effect, the restructuring itself can produce efficiency gains, often removing the principal motivation for the takeover in the first place.

Other Defensive Strategies

Corporate managers and defense advisors have devised other mechanisms to forestall a takeover. A corporation's charter can require a supermajority (sometimes as much as 80%) of votes to approve a merger. It can also restrict the voting rights of very large shareholders. Finally, a firm can require that a "fair" price be paid for the company, where the determination of what is "fair" is up to the board of directors or senior management. Beauty is always in the eye of the beholder, so "fair" in this case usually implies an optimistic determination of value.

We might expect the presence of defensive strategies to reduce firm value. However, Professors Gregg Jarrell and Annette Poulsen[17] found that, on average, the public announcement of anti-takeover amendments by 600 firms in the period 1979–1985 had an insignificant effect on the value of announcing firms' shares.

---

[16]M. Narayanan and A. Sundaram, "A Safe Landing? Golden Parachutes and Corporate Behavior," University of Michigan Business School Working Paper No. 98015 (1998).

[17]G. Jarrell and A. Poulsen, "Shark Repellents and Stock Prices: The Effects of Antitakeover Amendments Since 1980," *Journal of Financial Economics* 19 (1988): 127–168.

Regulatory Approval

All mergers must be approved by regulators. In Section 28.2, we discussed monopoly gains from takeovers and the use of antitrust regulations to limit them. In the United States, antitrust enforcement is governed by three main statutes: the Sherman Act, the Clayton Act, and the Hart-Scott-Rodino Act. The Sherman Act of 1890, which was passed in response to the formation of huge oil trusts such as Standard Oil, prohibits mergers that would create a monopoly or undue market control. The Clayton Act, enacted in 1914, strengthened the government's hand by prohibiting companies from acquiring the stock (or, as later amended, the assets) of another company if it would adversely affect competition. Under both the Sherman and Clayton acts, the government had to sue to block a merger. Often by the time a decision was rendered, the merger had taken place and it was difficult to undo it. The Hart-Scott-Rodino (HSR) Act of 1976 put the burden of proof on the merging parties. Under HSR, all mergers above a certain size (the formula for determining whether a transaction qualifies is complicated, but it comes out to approximately $60 million) must be approved by the government before the proposed takeovers occur. The government cannot delay the deal indefinitely, however, because it must respond with approval or a request for additional information within 20 days of receiving notification of the proposed merger.

The European Commission has established a process similar to the HSR process, which requires merging parties to notify the EC, provide additional information if requested about the proposed merger, and wait for approval before proceeding. As discussed in the Honeywell/GE example, even though the EC technically lacks legal authority to block a merger of U.S. companies, it can stop a takeover by imposing restrictions on the combined firm's operations and sales in Europe. Although globally a proposed takeover might have to satisfy antitrust rules in more than 80 jurisdictions, practically the most important jurisdictions besides the home jurisdiction of the firm are Europe and the United States.

Weyerhaeuser's Hostile Bid for Willamette Industries

In November 2000, Weyerhaeuser, a forest products company based in Federal Way, Washington, announced a hostile bid of $48 per share for its smaller neighbor, Willamette Industries, based in Portland, Oregon. Weyerhaeuser had been pursuing Willamette in private since 1998, when Steve Rogel unexpectedly resigned as CEO of Willamette to become CEO of Weyerhaeuser. Each time Rogel approached his old employer in private, he was rebuffed. The response to the hostile tender offer was no different. Despite the fact that the bid represented a substantial premium to the firm's pre-bid stock price, the Willamette board rejected the offer and urged its shareholders not to tender their shares to Weyerhaeuser.

Willamette's defenses included a staggered board and a poison pill, so Weyerhaeuser made its tender offer conditional on Willamette's board canceling the poison pill. Consequently, Weyerhaeuser initiated a proxy fight at the next annual shareholders' meeting in June 2001. One of the directors up for reelection at that time was Duane McDougall, Willamette's CEO. One month before the meeting, Weyerhaeuser increased its offer to $50 per share, but Willamette's board still believed that the offer was too low and worried that too many of its long-time employees would face layoffs after the merger. Nonetheless, at the annual meeting, Weyerhaeuser's slate received 1.4% more votes than Willamette's, thereby removing Willamette's CEO from its board.

The loss of the board seats did not change Willamette's position. Willamette unsuccessfully searched for a white knight to generate a bidding contest that would force Weyerhaeuser to up its bid. It also entered into talks to buy Georgia-Pacific's building products division. Such a deal would have increased its size and added enough debt to its balance sheet to render the firm unattractive to Weyerhaeuser.

In the end, Weyerhaeuser increased its offer to $55.50 per share in January 2002, and Willamette finally agreed to a deal and called off its negotiations with Georgia-Pacific. Even without the presence of other bidders, Willamette's board was able to get what it considered to be a fair price from Weyerhaeuser.

CONCEPT CHECK

1. What defensive strategies are available to help target companies resist an unwanted takeover?
2. How can a hostile acquirer get around a poison pill?

28.6 Who Gets the Value Added from a Takeover?

Now that we have explained the takeover process, we can return to the remaining questions posed at the beginning of this chapter: why the price of the acquiring company does not rise at the announcement of the takeover and why the bidder is forced to pay a premium for the target.

You might imagine that the people who do the work of acquiring the corporation and replacing its management will capture the value created by the merger. Based on the average stock price reaction, it does not appear that the acquiring corporation generally captures this value. Instead, the premium the acquirer pays is approximately equal to the value it adds, which means the *target* shareholders ultimately capture the value added by the acquirer. To see why, we need to understand how market forces react to a takeover announcement.

The Free Rider Problem

Assume you are one of the 1 million shareholders of HighLife Corporation, all of whom own 1 share of stock. HighLife has no debt. Its chief executive is not doing a good job, preferring to spend his time using the company's jets to fly to the corporate condo in Aspen, Colorado, rather than running the company in Chicago. As such, the shares are trading at a substantial discount. They currently have a price of \$45 per share, giving HighLife a market value of \$45 million. Under a competent manager, the company would be worth \$75 million. HighLife's corporate charter specifies that a simple majority is required to make all decisions, so to take control of HighLife a shareholder must purchase half the outstanding shares.

T. Boone Icon decides to fix the situation (and make a profit at the same time) by making a tender offer to buy half the outstanding shares for \$60 per share in cash. If fewer than 50% of the shareholders tender their shares, the deal is off.

In principle, this idea could land T. Boone a handsome profit. If 50% of shareholders tender their shares, those shares will cost him $\$60 \times 500{,}000 = \$30$ million. Once he has control of the firm, he can replace the managers. When the executive jets and the Aspen condo are sold and the market realizes that the new managers are serious about improving performance, the market value of the firm will rise to \$75 million. Hence T. Boone's shares will be worth \$75 per share, netting him a profit of $\$15 \times 500{,}000 = \$7.5$ million. But will 50% of the shareholders tender their shares?

The offer price of \$60 per share exceeds the value of the firm if the takeover does not go through (\$45 per share). Hence, the offer is a good deal for shareholders overall. But if all shareholders tender their shares, as an individual shareholder, you could do better by not tendering your share. Then if T. Boone takes control, each of your shares will be worth \$75 rather than the \$60 you would get by tendering. In this case it is wiser to not tender. Of course, if all shareholders think this way no one will tender their shares, and T. Boone's deal will not get off the ground. The only way to persuade shareholders to tender their shares is to offer them at least \$75 per share, which removes any profit opportunity for T. Boone. The problem here is that existing shareholders do not have to invest time and effort, but they still participate in all the gains from the takeover that T. Boone Icon generates—hence the term "free rider problem." By sharing the gains in this way, T. Boone Icon is forced to give up substantial profits and thus will likely choose not to bother at all.[18]

Toeholds

One way for T. Boone to get around the problem of shareholders' reluctance to tender their shares is to buy the shares in the market anonymously. However, SEC rules make it difficult for investors to buy much more than about 10% of a firm in secret.[19] After T. Boone acquires such an initial stake in the target, called a **toehold**, he would have to make his intentions public by informing investors of his large stake. To successfully gain control of HighLife, he would have to announce a tender offer to buy an additional 40% of the shares for $75 per share. Once in control, he would be able to sell his stake for $75 per share. Assuming he accumulated the first 10% for $50 per share, his profits in this case will be $\$25 \times 100{,}000 = \$2.5$ million. Not bad, but substantially less than the value he is adding.

Why should investors care whether T. Boone's profits are substantially lower than the value he is adding? The answer is that people like T. Boone perform an important service. Because of the threat that such a person might attempt to take over their company and fire them, chief executives are less likely to shirk their duties. Thus, the more profitable we make this activity, the less likely we will have to resort to it. If $2.5 million is not enough to justify T. Boone's time and effort, he will not try to acquire HighLife. Current management will remain entrenched and T. Boone will think about acquiring the company only if further erosion in the stock price makes the deal lucrative enough for him.

A number of legal mechanisms exist that allow acquirers to avoid the free rider problem and capture more of the gains from the acquisition. We describe the two most common, the leveraged buyout and the freezeout merger, next.

The Leveraged Buyout

The good news for shareholders is that another significantly lower-cost mechanism allows people like T. Boone Icon to take over companies and fire underperforming managers. Recall from Chapter 24 that this mechanism is called the leveraged buyout (LBO). Let's illustrate how it works by returning to HighLife Corporation.[20]

Assume that T. Boone chooses not to buy any shares in the market secretly, but instead announces a tender offer for half the outstanding shares at a price of $50 per share. However, instead of using his own cash to pay for these shares, he borrows the money through a shell corporation by *pledging the shares themselves as collateral on the loan*. The only time he will need the money is if the tender offer succeeds, so the banks lending the money can be certain that he will have control of the collateral. Even more important, if the tender offer succeeds, with control of the company, T. Boone can merge the target with the shell corporation, effectively attaching the loans directly to the target—that is, it is as if the

---

[18]A rigorous analysis of the free rider problem in mergers can be found in S. Grossman and O. Hart, "Takeover Bids, the Free-Rider Problem, and the Theory of the Corporation," *Bell Journal of Economics* 11(1) (1980): 42–64.

[19]The rules actually require that any shareholder who owns more than 5% of a firm publicly disclose this fact, but the time delays in the disclosure process allow investors to accumulate more than 5% of the firm before this information is made public.

[20]For a further discussion of this mechanism, see H. Mueller and F. Panunzi, "Tender Offers and Leverage," *The Quarterly Journal of Economics* 119 (2004): 1217–1248.

The Leveraged Buyout of RJR-Nabisco by KKR

By the summer of 1988, Ross Johnson, CEO of RJR Nabisco (RJR), was becoming increasingly worried about the poor stock price performance of the conglomerate. Despite a strong earnings record, management had not been able to shake loose its image as a tobacco company, and the stock price was languishing at $55 per share. In October 1988, Johnson and a small team of RJR's executives, backed by the Wall Street firms of Shearson Lehman Hutton and Salomon Brothers, announced a bid of $75 per share for the company. At this price, the deal would have been valued at $17.6 billion, more than twice as large as the largest LBO completed up to that point. Because this deal involved the current management of the company, it falls into a special category of LBO deals called **management buyouts (MBOs)**.

The announcement focused Wall Street's attention on RJR. Even at this substantial premium, the MBO appeared to be a good deal for Johnson and his team, because soon after the offer went public, it became hotly contested. Foremost among the contenders was the firm of Kohlberg, Kravis, and Roberts (KKR). KKR launched its own bid with a cash offer of $90 per share. A bidding war ensued that saw the offer price ultimately rise to $109 per share, valuing the deal at more than $25 billion. In the end, both Johnson and KKR offered very similar deals, although management's final bid was slightly higher than KKR's. Eventually, RJR's board accepted KKR's bid of $109 per RJR share. The offer price comprised $81 per share in cash, $18 per share in preferred stock, and $10 per share in debenture securities.

From an economic point of view, this outcome is surprising. One would think that given their inside knowledge of the company, management would be in the best position not only to value it, but also to run it. Why, then, would an outsider choose to outbid an insider for a company? The answer in RJR's case appeared to point to the managers themselves. As the deal proceeded, it became increasingly obvious to investors that executives (and members of the board of directors) enjoyed perks that were unprecedented. For example, Johnson had the personal use of numerous corporate apartments in different cities and literally a fleet of corporate jets that he, the top executives, and members of the corporate board used for personal travel. In their leveraged buyout proposal, they had obtained a 4% equity stake for top executives that was worth almost $1 billion, $52.5 million in golden parachutes, and assurances that the RJR air force (the fleet of corporate jets) and the flamboyant Atlanta headquarters would not be subject to budget cutting.

EXAMPLE 28.5 Leveraged Buyout

Problem

FAT Corporation stock is currently trading at $40 per share. There are 20 million shares outstanding, and the company has no debt. You are a partner in a firm that specializes in leveraged buyouts. Your analysis indicates that the management of this corporation could be improved considerably. If the managers were replaced with more capable ones, you estimate that the value of the company would increase by 50%. You decide to initiate a leveraged buyout and issue a tender offer for at least a controlling interest—50% of the outstanding shares. What is the maximum amount of value you can extract and still complete the deal?

Solution

Currently, the value of the company is $\$40 \times 20$ million = $800 million, and you estimate you can add an additional 50%, or $400 million. If you borrow $400 million and the tender offer succeeds, you will take control of the company and install new management. The total value of the company will increase by 50% to $1.2 billion. You will also attach the debt to the company, so the company will now have $400 million in debt. The value of the equity once the deal is done is the total value minus the debt outstanding:

$$\text{Total Equity} = 1200 - 400 = \$800 \text{ million}$$

The value of the equity is the same as the premerger value. You own half the shares, which are worth $400 million, and paid nothing for them, so you have captured the value you anticipated adding to FAT.

What if you borrowed more than $400 million? Assume you were able to borrow $450 million. The value of equity after the merger would be

$$\text{Total Equity} = 1200 - 450 = \$750 \text{ million}$$

This is lower than the premerger value. Recall, however, that in the United States, existing shareholders must be offered at least the premerger price for their shares. Because existing shareholders anticipate that the share price will be lower once the deal is complete, all shareholders will tender their shares. This implies that you will have to pay $800 million for these shares, and so to complete the deal, you will have to pay 800 − 450 = $350 million out of your own pocket. In the end, you will own all the equity, which is worth $750 million. You paid $350 million for it, so your profit is again $400 million. Thus, you cannot extract more value than the value you add to the company by taking it over.

target corporation, and not T. Boone, has borrowed the money. At the end of this process, T. Boone still owns half the shares, but the *corporation* is responsible for repaying the loan. T. Boone has effectively acquired half the shares without paying for them!

You might imagine that no shareholder would be willing to tender her shares under these circumstances. Surprisingly, this conclusion is wrong. If you tender your shares, you will receive $50 for each of them. If you do not tender your shares, but enough other shareholders do, then T. Boone will take control of the company. After he replaces the managers, the enterprise value of the company will be $75 million. What will your shares be worth if you did not tender them?

For simplicity, assume that there are no frictions or taxes. To gain control of the firm, T. Boone borrowed $25 million to purchase half the outstanding shares ($50 × 500,000). Because this debt is now attached to HighLife, the total value of HighLife's equity is just the total value of the company, minus the value of debt:

$$\text{Total Value of HighLife's Equity} = \$75 \text{ million} - \$25 \text{ million} = \$50 \text{ million}$$

The total number of outstanding shares is the same (remember that T. Boone purchased existing shares), so the price per share is $50 million ÷ 1 million = $50/share. If the tender offer succeeds, you will be indifferent. Whether you tender your shares or keep them, each is always worth $50. If you keep your shares and the tender offer fails, the price per share stays at $45. Clearly, it is always in your best interests to tender your shares, so T. Boone's tender offer will succeed. T. Boone also makes substantially more profits than he would if he used a toehold strategy—his profits are the value of his shares upon completion of the takeover: $50 × 500,000 = $25 million.

The examples we have illustrated are extreme in that the acquirer takes over the target without paying any premium and with no initial investment. In practice, premiums in LBO transactions are often quite substantial—while they can avoid the free rider problem, acquirers must still get board approval to overcome other defenses such as poison pills, as well as outbid other potential acquirers. And while in earlier times it was possible to fund deals with over 90% leverage, lenders today typically require that the acquirer have a significant equity stake as protection for the debt holders, in case the claimed post-acquisition benefits do not materialize. In the $15.2 billion Hertz LBO (at the time in 2006, the second largest in history), which we described in Chapter 24, the acquirers contributed $2.3 billion in equity out of $12.9 billion of total capital raised. As shown in Figure 28.4, recent LBOs tend to have equity stakes closer to 40%.

From 2003 to 2007, there was a surge in leveraged buyout activity, fueled by a combination of huge flows of capital to buy out (private equity) firms, and increased appetite for risk by

FIGURE 28.4

Average Equity Stake in LBO Transactions, 1987–2015

While early LBOs were often financed with over 90% leverage, average equity stakes for U.S. LBOs have averaged about 40% over the past decade. They exceeded 50% during the 2008–2009 financial crisis, when debt markets were extremely tight.

Source: Standard & Poor's Leveraged Commentary & Data (LCD), 2015

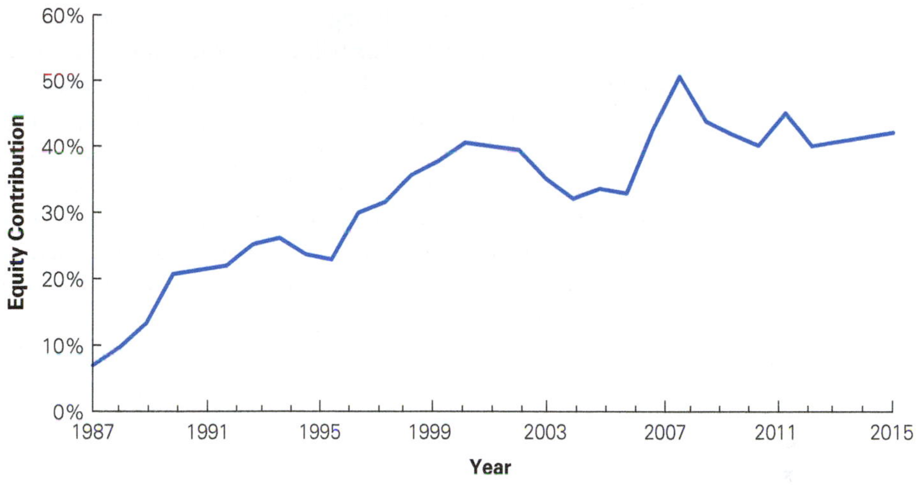

lenders willing to allow buyout groups to leverage their equity investment at attractive terms (see Figure 23.2 on page 833). Buyout firms took many companies private with the stated goal of increasing their performance without concern for perceived pressure from public investors to meet short-term earnings targets. They also employed so-called "roll-up" strategies whereby they would buy many smaller, already private firms in a particular industry and consolidate them into a larger player. The typical LBO has a planned exit in five years, either by taking the firm public again, or selling it to an operating firm or another private equity group. In 2008, the financial crisis and contraction of credit put an almost complete halt to private equity activity. Some highly levered private equity transactions from the peak faltered under their debt load during the recession. For example, Chrysler, which had been purchased and taken private from Daimler Chrysler AG by private equity firm Cerberus Group, declared bankruptcy in 2009, wiping out Cerberus' stake in the firm.The LBO market has gradually recovered in the years since the financial crisis, and by 2015 the annual dollar volume of deals is back at 2005 levels (see Figure 23.2 on page 833).

The Freezeout Merger

Although a leveraged buyout is an effective tool for a group of investors to use to purchase a company, it is less well suited to the case of one company acquiring another. An alternative is the **freezeout merger**: The laws on tender offers allow the acquiring company to freeze existing shareholders out of the gains from merging by forcing non-tendering shareholders to sell their shares for the tender offer price. Let's see how this is accomplished.

An acquiring company makes a tender offer at an amount slightly higher than the current target stock price. If the tender offer succeeds, the acquirer gains control of the target and merges its assets into a new corporation, which is fully owned by the acquirer. In effect, the non-tendering shareholders lose their shares because the target corporation no longer exists. In compensation, non-tendering shareholders get the right to receive the tender offer price for their shares. The bidder, in essence, gets complete ownership of the target for the tender offer price.[21]

[21] Y. Amihud, M. Kahan, and R. K. Sundaram, "The Foundations of Freezeout Laws in Takeovers," *Journal of Finance* 59 (2004): 1325–1344, contains a detailed discussion of the mechanics of freezeout mergers.

Because the value the non-tendering shareholders receive for their shares is equal to the tender price (which is more than the premerger stock price), the law generally recognizes it as fair value and non-tendering shareholders have no legal recourse. Under these circumstances, existing shareholders will tender their stock, reasoning that there is no benefit to holding out: If the tender offer succeeds, they get the tender price anyway; if they hold out, they risk jeopardizing the deal and forgoing the small gain. Hence the acquirer is able to capture almost all the value added from the merger and, as in a leveraged buyout, is able to effectively eliminate the free rider problem.

The freezeout tender offer has a significant advantage over a leveraged buyout because an acquiring corporation need not make an all-cash offer. Instead of paying the target's shareholders in cash, it can use shares of its own stock to pay for the acquisition. In this case, the bidder offers to exchange each shareholder's stock in the target for stock in the acquiring company. As long as the exchange rate is set so that the value in the acquirer's stock exceeds the premerger market value of the target stock, the non-tendering shareholders will receive fair value for their shares and will have no legal recourse.

Competition

The empirical evidence in Table 28.2 suggests that, despite the availability of both the freezeout merger and the leveraged buyout as acquisition strategies, most of the value added still appears to accrue to the target shareholders. That is, on average, acquirers do not have a positive price reaction on the announcement of a takeover. Why do acquirers choose to pay so large a premium that they effectively hand the value they create to the target company's shareholders?

In addition to the presence of the takeover defenses we have previously discussed, the most likely explanation is the competition that exists in the takeover market. Once an acquirer starts bidding on a target company and it becomes clear that a significant gain exists, other potential acquirers may submit their own bids. The result is effectively an auction in which the target is sold to the highest bidder. Even when a bidding war does not result, most likely it is because, rather than participate in a bidding war, an acquirer offered a large enough initial premium to forestall the process. In essence, it must give up most of the value added to the target shareholders.

CONCEPT CHECK

1. What mechanisms allow corporate raiders to get around the free rider problem in takeovers?
2. Based on the empirical evidence, who gets the value added from a takeover? What is the most likely explanation of this fact?

MyFinanceLab Here is what you should know after reading this chapter. MyFinanceLab will help you identify what you know and where to go when you need to practice.

28.1 Background and Historical Trends

- Mergers can be horizontal, vertical, or conglomerate. The global takeover market is active, averaging more than $1 trillion per year in transaction value. The periods of greatest activity have been the 1960s, 1980s, 1990s, and 2000s. During the 1960s, deals were aimed at building conglomerates. In the 1980s, the trend reversed and conglomerates were split into individual businesses. The 1990s saw a rise in "strategic" or "global" deals designed to create firms that could compete globally. From 2004–2008, further consolidation and global-scale deals contributed to the most recent merger wave.

28.2 Market Reaction to a Takeover

- While on average the shareholders of the acquiring firm obtain small or no gains, shareholders from the acquired firm typically enjoy gains of 15% on the announcement of a takeover bid.

28.3 Reasons to Acquire

- The most common justifications given for acquiring a firm are the synergies that can be gained through an acquisition. The most commonly cited sources of synergies are economies of scale and scope, the control provided by vertical integration, gaining monopolistic power, the expertise gained from the acquired company, improvements in operating efficiency, and benefits related to diversification such as increased borrowing capacity and tax savings. Shareholders of a private company that is acquired gain by switching to a more liquid investment. Some mergers are motivated by incentive conflicts or overconfidence of the acquirer's management.
- From the bidder's perspective, a takeover is a positive-NPV project only if the premium paid does not exceed the synergies created. The bidder's stock price reaction to the announcement of the merger is one way to gauge investors' assessments of whether the bidder overpaid or underpaid for the target.

28.4 Valuation and the Takeover Process

- The acquisition is positive-NPV for the acquirer only if the total amount paid does not exceed the standalone value of the target plus the value of the synergies from the transaction.
- If we equate the standalone value with the pre-bid value of the target, the transaction is positive-NPV for the acquirer if the value of the synergies exceeds the premium paid. For an all stock transaction, this requires

$$\text{Exchange ratio} = \frac{x}{N_T} < \frac{P_T}{P_A}\left(1 + \frac{S}{T}\right) \tag{28.5}$$

- A tender offer is a public announcement of an intention to purchase a large block of shares for a specified price. Making a tender offer does not guarantee that a deal will take place.
- Bidders use either of two methods to pay for a target: cash or stock. In a cash transaction, the bidder simply pays for the target in cash. In a stock-swap transaction, the bidder pays for the target by issuing new stock and giving it to the target shareholders. The method used by the bidder to pay for the acquired firm has tax and accounting implications.
- For a merger to proceed, both the target and the acquiring board of directors must approve the merger and put the question to a vote of the shareholders of the target (and, in some cases, the shareholders of the acquiring firm as well). In a friendly takeover, the target board of directors supports the merger and negotiates with the potential acquirers. If the target board opposes the merger, then the acquirer must go around the target board and appeal directly to the target shareholders, asking them to elect a new board that will support the merger.

28.5 Takeover Defenses

- The most effective takeover defense strategy is the poison pill, which gives target shareholders the right to buy shares in either the target or the acquirer at a deeply discounted price. The purchase is effectively subsidized by the existing shareholders of the acquirer, making the takeover very expensive.
- Another effective defense strategy is having a staggered board, which prevents a bidder from acquiring control over the board in a short period of time.
- Other defenses include looking for a friendly bidder (a white knight), making it expensive to replace management, and changing the capital structure of the firm.

28.6 Who Gets the Value Added from a Takeover?

- When a bidder makes an offer for a firm, the target shareholders can benefit by keeping their shares and letting other shareholders sell at a low price. However, because all shareholders have the incentive to keep their shares, no one will sell. This scenario is known as the free rider problem. To overcome this problem, bidders can acquire a toehold in the target, attempt a leveraged buyout, or, in the case when the acquirer is a corporation, offer a freezeout merger.

Key Terms

Further Reading

The literature on mergers and acquisitions is extensive. It is impossible to cover it all in a single chapter, but the following books address the topics of this chapter in more detail: J. Weston, M. Mitchell, and J. Mulherin, *Takeovers, Restructuring and Corporate Finance* (Prentice-Hall, 2004); L. Herzel and R. Shepro, *Bidders and Targets: Mergers and Acquisitions in the U.S.* (Basil Blackwell, 1990); and S. Kaplan (ed.), *Mergers and Productivity* (University of Chicago Press, 2000).

Problems

All problems are available in MyFinanceLab.

Background and Historical Trends

1. What are the two primary mechanisms under which ownership and control of a public corporation can change?
2. Why do you think mergers cluster in time, causing merger waves?
3. What are some reasons why a horizontal merger might create value for shareholders?

Market Reaction to a Takeover

4. Why do you think shareholders from target companies enjoy an average gain when acquired, while acquiring shareholders on average often do not gain anything?

Reasons to Acquire

5. If you are planning an acquisition that is motivated by trying to acquire expertise, you are basically seeking to gain intellectual capital. What concerns would you have in structuring the deal and the post-merger integration that would be different from the concerns you would have when buying physical capital?

6. Do you agree that the European Union should be able to block mergers between two U.S.-based firms? Why or why not?

7. How do the carryforward and carryback provisions of the U.S. tax code affect the benefits of merging to capture operating losses?

8. Diversification is good for shareholders. So why shouldn't managers acquire firms in different industries to diversify a company?

9. Your company has earnings per share of $4. It has 1 million shares outstanding, each of which has a price of $40. You are thinking of buying TargetCo, which has earnings per share of $2, 1 million shares outstanding, and a price per share of $25. You will pay for TargetCo by issuing new shares. There are no expected synergies from the transaction.
   a. If you pay no premium to buy TargetCo, what will your earnings per share be after the merger?
   b. Suppose you offer an exchange ratio such that, at current pre-announcement share prices for both firms, the offer represents a 20% premium to buy TargetCo. What will your earnings per share be after the merger?
   c. What explains the change in earnings per share in part (a)? Are your shareholders any better or worse off?
   d. What will your price-earnings ratio be after the merger (if you pay no premium)? How does this compare to your P/E ratio before the merger? How does this compare to TargetCo's premerger P/E ratio?

10. If companies in the same industry as TargetCo (from Problem 9) are trading at multiples of 14 times earnings, what would be one estimate of an appropriate premium for TargetCo?

11. You are invested in GreenFrame, Inc. The CEO owns 3% of GreenFrame and is considering an acquisition. If the acquisition destroys $50 million of GreenFrame's value, but the present value of the CEO's compensation increases by $5 million, will he be better or worse off?

Valuation and the Takeover Process

12. Loki, Inc., and Thor, Inc., have entered into a stock swap merger agreement whereby Loki will pay a 40% premium over Thor's premerger price. If Thor's premerger price per share was $40 and Loki's was $50, what exchange ratio will Loki need to offer?

13. The NFF Corporation has announced plans to acquire LE Corporation. NFF is trading for $35 per share and LE is trading for $25 per share, implying a premerger value of LE of approximately $4 billion. If the projected synergies are $1 billion, what is the maximum exchange ratio NFF could offer in a stock swap and still generate a positive NPV?

14. Let's reconsider part (b) of Problem 9. The actual premium that your company will pay for TargetCo will not be 20%, because on the announcement the target price will go up and your price will go down to reflect the fact that you are willing to pay a premium for TargetCo. Assume that the takeover will occur with certainty and all market participants know this on the announcement of the takeover.
   a. What is the price per share of the combined corporation immediately after the merger is completed?
   b. What is the price of your company immediately after the announcement?

c. What is the price of TargetCo immediately after the announcement?
d. What is the actual premium your company will pay?

15. ABC has 1 million shares outstanding, each of which has a price of $20. It has made a takeover offer of XYZ Corporation, which has 1 million shares outstanding and a price per share of $2.50. Assume that the takeover will occur with certainty and all market participants know this. Furthermore, there are no synergies to merging the two firms.
a. Assume ABC made a cash offer to purchase XYZ for $3 million. What happens to the price of ABC and XYZ on the announcement? What premium over the current market price does this offer represent?
b. Assume ABC makes a stock offer with an exchange ratio of 0.15. What happens to the price of ABC and XYZ this time? What premium over the current market price does this offer represent?
c. At current market prices, both offers are offers to purchase XYZ for $3 million. Does that mean that your answers to parts (a) and (b) must be identical? Explain.

Takeover Defenses

16. BAD Company's stock price is $20, and the firm has 2 million shares outstanding. You believe you can increase the company's value if you buy it and replace the management. Assume that BAD has a poison pill with a 20% trigger. If it is triggered, all BAD's shareholders—other than the acquirer—will be able to buy one new share in BAD for each share they own at a 50% discount. Assume that the price remains at $20 while you are acquiring your shares. If BAD's management decides to resist your buyout attempt, and you cross the 20% threshold of ownership:
a. How many new shares will be issued and at what price?
b. What will happen to your percentage ownership of BAD?
c. What will happen to the price of your shares of BAD?
d. Do you lose or gain from triggering the poison pill? If you lose, where does the loss go (who benefits)? If you gain, from where does the gain come (who loses)?

Who Gets the Value Added from a Takeover?

17. How does a toehold help overcome the free rider problem?

18. You work for a leveraged buyout firm and are evaluating a potential buyout of UnderWater Company. UnderWater's stock price is $20, and it has 2 million shares outstanding. You believe that if you buy the company and replace its management, its value will increase by 40%. You are planning on doing a leveraged buyout of UnderWater, and will offer $25 per share for control of the company.
a. Assuming you get 50% control, what will happen to the price of non-tendered shares?
b. Given the answer in part (a), will shareholders tender their shares, not tender their shares, or be indifferent?
c. What will your gain from the transaction be?

CHAPTER

29

Corporate Governance

THE TURN OF THE TWENTY-FIRST CENTURY WITNESSED SCANDALS and corporate fraud in the United States. The names of once well-respected companies like Enron, WorldCom, Tyco, and Adelphia filled the news. Enron, with stock worth $68 billion at its peak, became almost worthless in a matter of months, wiping out the retirement savings of thousands of employees and other stockholders. The story at WorldCom was similar. The once high-flying stock peaked at a market value of $115 billion after a string of acquisitions that included well-known phone company MCI. In 2002, WorldCom filed what was at the time the largest bankruptcy ever. After building one of the nation's largest cable companies from scratch, the Rigas family of Adelphia was forced to endure the indignity of watching their own cable system convey the image of Adelphia's demise into millions of homes.

The common theme among these companies is the accusation of fraud, perpetrated by the manipulation of accounting statements. Shareholders, analysts, and regulators were kept in the dark as the companies' financial situations became ever more precarious, resulting, in the end, in total collapse. How did this happen? Aren't managers supposed to act in the interests of shareholders? Why did auditors go along with the fraud? Where were the boards of directors when all of this was happening?

There is an opportunity cost to bad governance; thus, by replacing bad governance with good governance, it is possible to increase firm *value*—in other words, good governance is a positive-NPV project. Hence, we begin by discussing various governance mechanisms that are designed to mitigate the agency conflicts between managers and owners. These agency conflicts cannot be removed completely by a firm's governance mechanisms, so we next discuss regulations that are designed to prohibit managers from taking certain acts that are not in the interests of shareholders. We conclude the chapter with a discussion of corporate governance around the world.

29.1 Corporate Governance and Agency Costs

Any discussion of **corporate governance**—the system of controls, regulations, and incentives designed to prevent fraud—is a story of conflicts of interest and attempts to minimize them. As we saw in Chapter 16, the different stakeholders in a firm all have their own interests. When those interests diverge, we may have agency conflicts. That chapter emphasized the sources of conflicts between bondholders and shareholders. In this chapter, we focus on the conflicts between managers and investors.

The conflict of interest between managers and investors derives from the separation of ownership and control in a corporation. As we pointed out in Chapter 1, the separation of ownership and control is perhaps the most important reason for the success of the corporate organizational form. Because any investor can hold an ownership stake in a corporation, investors are able to diversify and thus reduce their risk exposures without cost. This is especially true for the managers of a corporation: Because they are not also required to own the firm, their risk exposures are much lower than they would be if ownership and control were not separate.

Once control and ownership are separated, however, a conflict of interest arises between the owners and the people in control of a corporation. For example, in Chapter 28, we talked about mergers that are motivated by managers' desire to manage a larger firm, gaining them more prestige and greater pay, even if that might not be in the best interests of shareholders. Other examples of agency problems are excessive perquisites, such as using corporate jets for family vacations, or managers not working as diligently as they would if it were their own business. Agency conflicts are likely to arise any time the manager does not internalize the full cost of his or her actions—just think about how you order at a restaurant when you are paying compared to when the company is paying!

The seriousness of this conflict of interest depends on how closely aligned the interests of the managers and shareholders are. Aligning their interests comes at a cost—it increases the risk exposure of the managers. For example, tying managerial compensation to performance aligns managers' incentives with investors' interests, but then managers are exposed to the firm's risk (because the firm might do poorly for reasons unrelated to the manager's performance).

The role of the corporate governance system is to mitigate the conflict of interest that results from the separation of ownership and control without unduly burdening managers with the risk of the firm. The system attempts to align these interests by providing incentives for taking the right action and punishments for taking the wrong action. The incentives come from owning stock in the company and from compensation that is sensitive to performance. Punishment comes when a board fires a manager for poor performance or fraud, or when, upon failure of the board to act, shareholders or raiders launch control contests to replace the board and management. As we will see, these actions interact in complicated ways. For example, as a manager owns more stock in the firm, his incentives become better aligned, but, in addition to the increase in risk the manager must bear, the manager also becomes harder to fire because the block of stock gives him significant voting rights.

Let's now take a closer look at the components of the corporate governance system.

CONCEPT CHECK

1. What is corporate governance?
2. What agency conflict do corporate governance structures address?

29.2 Monitoring by the Board of Directors and Others

At first glance, one might think that there is a simple solution to the conflict of interest problem: monitor the firm's managers closely. The problem with this reasoning is that it ignores the cost of monitoring. When the ownership of a corporation is widely held, no one shareholder has an incentive to bear this cost (because she bears the full cost of monitoring but the benefit is divided among all shareholders). Instead, the shareholders as a group elect a board of directors to monitor managers. The directors themselves, however, have the same conflict of interest—monitoring is costly and in many cases directors do not get significantly greater benefits than other shareholders from monitoring the managers closely. Consequently, in most cases, shareholders understand that there are reasonable limits on how much monitoring they can expect from the board of directors.

In principle, the board of directors hires the executive team, sets its compensation, approves major investments and acquisitions, and dismisses executives if necessary. In the United States, the board of directors has a clear fiduciary duty to protect the interests of the owners of the firm—the shareholders. Most other countries give some weight to the interests of other stakeholders in the firm, such as the employees. In Germany, this concept is formalized through a two-tier board structure that gives half of the seats on the upper board—called the supervisory board—to employees.

Types of Directors

Generally, researchers have categorized directors into three groups: inside, gray, and outside (or independent). **Inside directors** are employees, former employees, or family members of employees. **Gray directors** are people who are not as directly connected to the firm as insiders are, but who have existing or potential business relationships with the firm. For example, bankers, lawyers, and consultants who are already retained by the firm or who would be interested in being retained may sit on a board. Thus, their judgment could be compromised by their desire to keep the CEO happy. Finally, all other directors are considered **outside** (or **independent**) **directors** and are the most likely to make decisions solely in the interests of the shareholders.

Board Independence

Researchers have hypothesized that boards with a majority of outside directors are better monitors of managerial effort and actions. One early study showed that a board was more likely to fire the firm's CEO for poor performance if the board had a majority of outside directors.[1] Other studies have found that firms with independent boards make fewer value-destroying acquisitions and are more likely to act in shareholders' interests if targeted in an acquisition.[2]

---

[1] M. Weisbach, "Outside Directors and CEO Turnover," *Journal of Financial Economics* 20(1–2) (1988): 431–460.

[2] J. Byrd and K. Hickman, "Do Outside Directors Monitor Managers? Evidence from Tender Offer Bids," *Journal of Financial Economics* 32(2) (1992): 195–207; and J. Cotter, A. Shivdasani, and M. Zenner, "Do Independent Directors Enhance Target Shareholder Wealth During Tender Offers?" *Journal of Financial Economics* 43(2) (1997): 195–218. H. Ryan and R. Wiggins show that firms with more outsiders on their boards award directors more equity-based compensation, increasing incentives for the board to monitor. ("Who Is in Whose Pocket? Director Compensation, Board Independence, and Barriers to Effective Monitoring," *Journal of Financial Economics* 73 (2204): 497–525.

Despite evidence that board independence matters for major activities such as firing CEOs and making corporate acquisitions, researchers have struggled to find a connection between board structure and firm performance. Although the firm's stock price increases on the announcement of its addition of an independent board member, the increased firm value appears to come from the potential for the board to make better decisions on acquisitions and CEO turnover rather than from improvements in the firm's operating performance. Researchers have argued, however, that so many other factors affect firm performance that the effect of a more or less independent board is very difficult to detect.

Another reason why it may be difficult to explicate a relationship between board independence and firm performance is the nature of the role of the independent director. On a board composed of insider, gray, and independent directors, the role of the independent director is really that of a watchdog. But because independent directors' personal wealth is likely to be less sensitive to performance than that of insider and gray directors, they have less incentive to closely monitor the firm. However, there has been a trend toward more equity-based pay for outside directors. As recently as the early 1990s, it was very common for directors to be paid a fixed annual cash fee plus perhaps an extra nominal fee per meeting attended. It is now standard for outside directors to be granted shares of stock and/or options to more closely align their interests with those of the shareholders they serve.

Incentives notwithstanding, even the most active independent directors spend only one or two days per month on firm business, and many independent directors sit on multiple boards, further dividing their attention. In fact, some studies have found value decreases when too many of a board's directors are "busy," meaning that they sit on three or more boards.[3]

A board is said to be **captured** when its monitoring duties have been compromised by connections or perceived loyalties to management. Theoretical and empirical research support the notion that the longer a CEO has served, especially when that person is also chairman of the board, the more likely the board is to become captured. Over time, most of the independent directors will have been nominated by the CEO. Even though they have no business ties to the firm, they are still likely to be friends or at least acquaintances of the CEO. The CEO can be expected to stack the board with directors who are less likely to challenge her. When the CEO is also chairman of the board, the nominating letter offering a seat to a new director comes from her. This process merely serves to reinforce the sense that the outside directors owe their positions to the CEO and work for the CEO rather than for the shareholders.

The Sarbanes-Oxley Act of 2002 (SOX), which we discuss in more depth in Section 29.5, required that the audit committee of the board, charged with overseeing the audit of the firm's financial statements, be composed entirely of independent directors. Following the implementation of SOX, major U.S. exchanges (NYSE and NASDAQ) changed their listing requirements such that firms listed on those exchanges must have a majority of independent directors on their board. Most recently, the Dodd-Frank Act of 2010 further requires that *all* members of a firm's compensation committee be independent board members. Ideally, these changes will reduce entrenchment and improve governance. However, all such changes come at a cost, because the other major role of the board is to advise managers on strategic issues. Independent directors, while unbiased, are also the least likely to be experts in the firm's business, thus reducing their ability to advise.

---

[3]E. Fich and A. Shivdasani, "Are Busy Boards Effective Monitors?," *Journal of Finance* 61(2) (2006): 689–724.

Board Size and Performance

Researchers have found the surprisingly robust result that smaller boards are associated with greater firm value and performance.[4] The likely explanation for this phenomenon comes from the psychology and sociology research, which finds that smaller groups make better decisions than larger groups. Most firms that have just gone public either as young companies or as older firms returning to public status after a leveraged buyout (LBO) choose to start with smaller boards. Boards tend to grow over time as members are added for various reasons. For example, boards are often expanded by one or two seats after an acquisition to accommodate the target CEO and perhaps one other target director.

Other Monitors

The board is complemented by other monitors, both inside and outside the firm. We discuss direct shareholder monitoring and action in Section 29.4, but other monitors include security analysts, lenders, the SEC, and employees within the firm itself.

Securities analysts produce independent valuations of the firms they cover so that they can make buy and sell recommendations to clients. They collect as much information as they can, becoming an expert on the firm and its competitors by poring over a company's financial statements and filings. As a result, they are in a position to uncover irregularities first. Analysts often ask difficult and probing questions of CEOs and CFOs during quarterly earnings releases. Anyone can listen to these conference calls, which are typically simulcast on the company's investor relations Web site.

Lenders also carefully monitor firms to which they are exposed as creditors. Loans and lines of credit also contain financial covenants designed to provide early warning signs of trouble. These covenants, such as requiring maintenance of a certain quick ratio or profitability level, are primarily designed to capture the firm's ability to repay the loan. Nonetheless, they complement other signals of potential governance problems. A stockholder must keep in mind, however, that her interests are not perfectly aligned with the creditors' interests. The creditor, lacking upside participation, is particularly interested in minimizing risk, even at the expense of some positive-NPV projects.

Employees of the firm are most likely to detect outright fraud because of their inside knowledge. However, they do not always have strong incentives to report the fraud. They may personally benefit from the fraud, or they may fear retribution from "blowing the whistle." Some states have whistle-blower statutes to protect employees who report fraud to the authorities; there are federal statutes to protect employees who expose fraud against the U.S. government.

The SEC is charged with the task of protecting the investing public against fraud and stock price manipulation. But while the SEC's enforcement powers are extensive and carry with them the weight of criminal prosecution, its detection resources are limited. Out of necessity, the SEC must rely on the array of other monitors, each with vested interests in detecting governance problems, to alert it to potential wrongdoing.

CONCEPT CHECK

1. What is the difference between gray directors and outside directors?
2. What does it mean for a board to be captured?

[4] D. Yermack, "Higher Market Valuation of Companies with Small Boards of Directors," *Journal of Financial Economics* 40(2) (1996): 185–211.

29.3 Compensation Policies

In the absence of monitoring, the other way the conflict of interest between managers and owners can be mitigated is by closely aligning their interests through the managers' compensation policy. That is, by tying compensation to performance, the shareholders effectively give the manager an ownership stake in the firm.

Stock and Options

Managers' pay can be linked to the performance of a firm in many ways. The most basic approach is through bonuses based on, for example, earnings growth. During the 1990s, most companies adopted compensation policies that more directly gave managers an ownership stake by including grants of stock or stock options to executives. These grants give managers a direct incentive to increase the stock price to make their stock or options as valuable as possible. Consequently, stock and option grants naturally tie managerial wealth to the wealth of shareholders.

Many studies have examined firms' compensation policies. One of the earlier studies examined the sensitivity of managers' compensation to the performance of their firms.[5] The authors found that for every $1000 increase in firm value, CEO pay changed, on average, by $3.25. Most of this increase came from changes in the value of their stock ownership ($2). The rest was driven by options, bonuses, and other compensation changes. The authors of the study argued that this seemed too small a sensitivity to provide managers with the proper incentives to exert extra effort on the behalf of shareholders. Recall, however, that increasing the pay-for-performance sensitivity comes at the cost of burdening managers with risk. As a consequence, the optimal level of sensitivity depends on the managers' level of risk aversion, which is hard to measure.

Pay and Performance Sensitivity

Figure 29.1 shows the dramatic rise in CEO pay during the economic expansion of the 1990s. As the figure shows, median cash pay, consisting of salary and bonuses, has

FIGURE 29.1

CEO Compensation

This figure shows the median cash pay, stock and option grants, and deferred compensation and other pay (for example, long-term incentive payouts and retirement packages) for CEOs of the 1600 largest public companies over the period 1993 through 2014.

Source: Execucomp

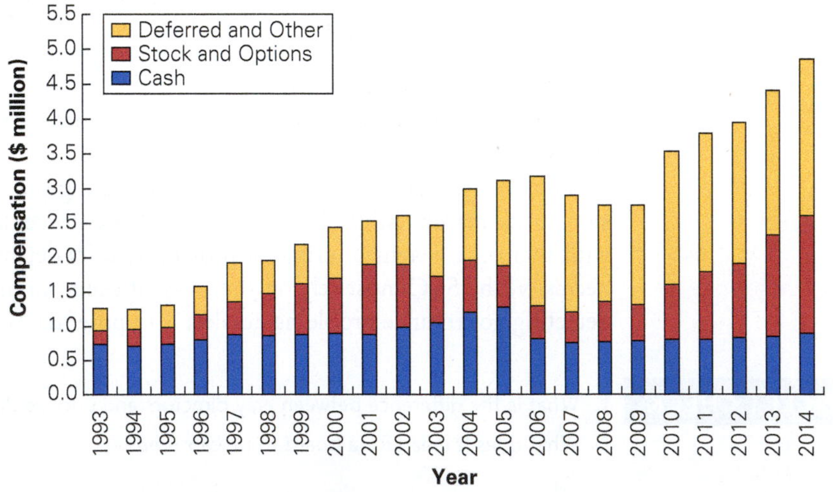

[5]M. Jensen and K. Murphy, "Performance Pay and Top-Management Incentives," *Journal of Political Economy* 98(2) (1990): 225–264.

fluctuated only moderately. The climb in CEO total compensation has been driven instead by the sharp increase in the value of stock, options, and deferred compensation granted each year. The median value of options granted rose from less than $200,000 in 1993 to more than $1 million by 2001. Not surprisingly, the substantial use of stock and option grants in the 1990s greatly increased managers' pay-for-performance sensitivity. Consequently, subsequent estimates put this sensitivity at $25 per $1000 change in wealth.[6] While the value of stock and option grants have fluctuated in the 2000s with the performance of the overall stock market, there appears to have been some substitution toward deferred compensation and retirement packages, with median amounts exceeding $2 million in 2014.

Besides increasing managers' risk exposure, increasing the sensitivity of managerial pay and wealth to firm performance has some other negative effects. For example, often options are granted "at the money," meaning that the exercise price is equal to the current stock price. Therefore, managers have an incentive to manipulate the release of financial forecasts so that bad news comes out before options are granted (to drive the exercise price down) and good news comes out after options are granted. Studies have found evidence that the practice of timing the release of information to maximize the value of CEO stock options is widespread.[7]

More recently, Professor Erik Lie has found evidence suggesting that many executives have engaged in a more direct form of manipulating their stock option compensation: backdating their option grants.[8] **Backdating** refers to the practice of choosing the grant date of a stock option retroactively, so that the date of the grant would coincide with a date when the stock price was at its low for the quarter or for the year. By backdating the option in this way, the executive receives a stock option that is already in-the-money, with a strike price equal to the lower price on the supposed grant date.

The use of backdating suggests that some executive stock option compensation may not truly have been earned as the result of good *future* performance of the firm. Furthermore, unless it is reported in a timely manner to the IRS and to shareholders, and reflected in the firm's financial statements, backdating is illegal. In mid-2006, SEC and U.S. Justice Department investigations into alleged backdating were ongoing for more than 70 firms. New SEC rules require firms to report option grants within two days of the grant date, which may help prevent further abuses.

CONCEPT CHECK

1. What is the main reason for tying managers' compensation to firm performance?
2. What is the negative effect of increasing the sensitivity of managerial pay to firm performance?

---

[6] B. Hall and J. Liebman, "Are CEOs Really Paid Like Bureaucrats?," *Quarterly Journal of Economics* 103(3) (1998): 653–691.

[7] D. Yermack, "Good Timing: CEO Stock Option Awards and Company News Announcements," *Journal of Finance* 52(2) (1997): 449–476. For evidence the option compensation may induce misreporting, see N. Burns and S. Kedia, "The Impact of Performance-Based Compensation on Misreporting," *Journal of Financial Economics* 79 (2006): 35–67.

[8] See E. Lie, "On the Timing of CEO Stock Option Awards," *Management Science* 51 (2005): 802–812. Also, R. Heron and E. Lie show that new rules enacted as part of the Sarbanes-Oxley legislation in 2002 that require grants to be reported within two business days have curbed the practice of backdating ("Does Backdating Explain the Stock Price Pattern Around Executive Stock Option Grants?" *Journal of Financial Economics* 83(2) (2007): 271–295).

29.4 Managing Agency Conflict

Even with the risk benefits of separating ownership and control, there are still examples of corporations in which the top managers have substantial ownership interests (for example, Microsoft Corporation). One might conjecture that such corporations have suffered less from the conflict of interest between managers and shareholders.

Academic studies have supported the notion that greater managerial ownership is associated with fewer value-reducing actions by managers.[9] But while increasing managerial ownership may reduce perquisite consumption, it also makes managers harder to fire—thus reducing the incentive effect of the threat of dismissal. Therefore, the relationship between managerial ownership and firm value is unlikely to be the same for every firm, or even for different executives of the same firm. Shareholders will use all of the tools at their disposal to manage the agency conflict. Thus, if managers have small ownership stakes, shareholders may use compensation policies or a stronger board to create the desired incentives. Harold Demsetz and Kenneth Lehn argue that if you look at a group of firms at any time, you should not necessarily see any relationship between ownership and value, unless you are able to control for all of the other, sometimes unobservable, parts of the governance system, including the risk aversion of the manager.[10] More recent studies have supported their position.[11]

Direct Action by Shareholders

If all else fails, the shareholders' last line of defense against expropriation by self-interested managers is direct action. Recall that shareholders elect the board of directors. Typically, these elections look like those in the former Soviet Union—there is only one slate of candidates and you vote "yes" or "no" for the slate as a whole. When shareholders are angry about the management of the company and frustrated by a board unwilling to take action, however, they have at their disposal a variety of options for expressing that displeasure.

Shareholder Voice. First, any shareholder can submit a resolution that is put to a vote at the annual meeting. A resolution could direct the board to take a specific action, such as discontinue investing in a particular line of business or country, or remove a poison pill. Such resolutions rarely receive majority support, but if large shareholders back them, they can be embarrassing for the board. Studies show that the market responds positively when such resolutions are adopted, presumably indicating that they positively impact the governance of firms.[12] Some large public pension funds, such as the California Public Employees Retirement System (CalPERS), take an activist role in corporate governance. Typically, these funds target firms that are taking actions without considering the concerns of the stockholders; for example, they may privately approach the board of the firm and ask it to reverse its course.

---

[9]See, for example, R. Walkling and M. Long, "Agency Theory, Managerial Welfare, and Takeover Bid Resistance," *Rand Journal of Economics* 15(1) (1984): 54–68.

[10]H. Demsetz and K. Lehn, "The Structure of Corporate Ownership: Causes and Consequences," *Journal of Political Economy* 93(6) (1985): 1155–1177.

[11]C. Himmelberg, R. G. Hubbard, and D. Palia, "Understanding the Determinants of Managerial Ownership and the Link Between Ownership and Performance," *Journal of Financial Economics* 53(3) (1999): 353–384; and J. Coles, M. Lemmon, and J. Meschke, "Structural Models and Endogeneity in Corporate Finance: the Link Between Managerial Ownership and Corporate Performance," *Journal of Financial Economics* 103(1) (2012): 149–168.

[12]See D. Levit and N. Malenko, "Non-Binding Voting for Shareholder Proposals," *Journal of Finance* 66(5) (2011): 1579–1614, for a theoretical analysis of the informativeness and effectiveness of such votes and V. Cuñat, M. Guadalupe, and M. Gine, "The Vote Is Cast: The Effect of Corporate Governance on Shareholder Value. *The Journal of Finance* 67 (2012): 1943–1977.

The explicit threat at that stage is that if the board fails to comply, the pension fund will put the issue to a shareholder vote. Studies have reported that such activist investors are usually successful in achieving their goals without having to take matters public.[13] Such activism has been very effective, for example, in removing poison pills and other defenses designed to entrench management (see Figure 28.3 on page 980).

Recently, shareholders have started organizing "no" votes. That is, when they are dissatisfied with a board, they simply refuse to vote to approve the slate of nominees for the board. The most high-profile example of this type of action occurred in 2004 with the Walt Disney Company. Major shareholders were dissatisfied with the recent performance of Disney under long-time CEO and Chairman Michael Eisner. They began an organized campaign to convince the majority of Disney shareholders to withhold their approval of the reelection of Eisner as director and chairman of the board. When the votes were counted, 45% of Disney's shareholders had voted to withhold approval of Eisner. While Eisner technically had won reelection, a 45% "no" vote is practically unprecedented in large public companies. The signal was clear, and an embarrassed Eisner and the Disney board decided that Eisner would remain CEO, but relinquish the chairman title. Shortly thereafter, Eisner announced plans to retire completely in 2006.

Shareholder Approval. In addition to electing the directors of the company, shareholders must approve many major actions taken by the board. For example, target shareholders must approve merger agreements and, in some cases, so must bidder shareholders. Even in cases where bidder shareholders are not required to approve a merger directly, listing requirements on the NYSE, for example, demand that shareholders approve any large issue of new shares, such as might be necessary in a stock-swap merger. Normally, approval is perfunctory, but it cannot be taken for granted. As we saw in Chapter 28, after Hewlett-Packard CEO Carly Fiorina negotiated the merger of HP and Compaq, the Hewlett family used their board seats and voting block to oppose the deal.

A recent movement, which gained momentum and regulators' interest during the 2008 financial crisis, is to let shareholders have a "say on pay," vote. Typically, this is a nonbinding vote to approve or disapprove of the compensation plan for senior executives each year. Even though the votes are nonbinding, firms that narrowly passed shareholder resolutions

Shareholder Activism at *The New York Times*

New York Times Co., publisher of *The New York Times*, is closely controlled by the Ochs-Sulzberger family, which owns most of the Class B voting shares, allowing it to elect 70% of the board members. However, in December 2007 and January 2008, two hedge funds working together started acquiring a large stake in the publicly traded Class A shares. The two funds, Harbinger Capital Partners and Firebrand Partners, initially acquired 5% of the shares, subsequently raising the stake to 19%. The funds also filed to nominate four dissident directors to the NYT Co. board, arguing that the *Times* was moving too slowly to develop digital content and should shed non-core assets. After initially resisting, the Company agreed to accept two of the funds' nominees and the funds withdrew their competing proxy statement. Over the two-month period starting when the funds began their activism, the stock price of the Company increased by close to 30%. This episode is indicative of two emerging trends in investor activism: hedge funds taking a more activist role and working in concert to effect change at a company, and an increased willingness of targeted companies to negotiate a settlement with activists (see Figure 29.2).

Source: "New York Times Co. Relents on Board Seats—Dissident Group Secures 2 on Expanded Panel; Dual-Stock Handcuffs," Merissa Marr, 18 March 2008, *The Wall Street Journal*, B3.

[13] W. Carleton, J. Nelson, and M. Weisbach, "The Influence of Institutions on Corporate Governance Through Private Negotiations: Evidence from TIAA-CREF," *Journal of Finance* 53(4) (1998): 1335–1362.

FIGURE 29.2

Proxy Contest Outcomes

Outcomes of proxy fights involving dissident proposals, showing the fraction of cases management lost or compromised. While dissidents do not often win these fights outright, they are becoming more successful in getting management to settle.

Source: FactSet SharkWatch

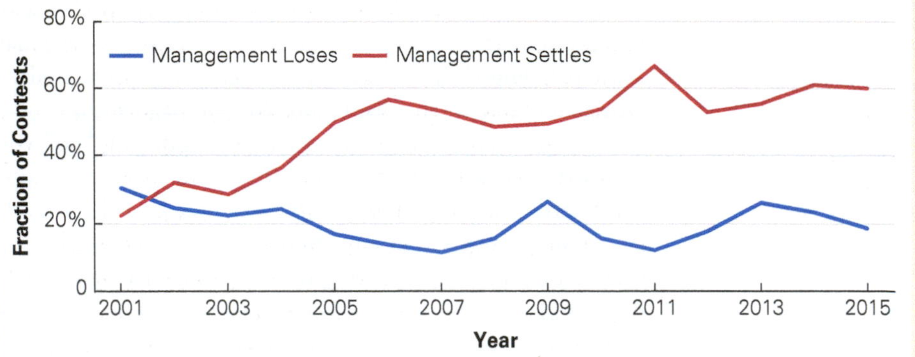

requiring say on pay votes subsequently saw their stock prices increase in response (relative to firms that narrowly rejected such resolutions).[14]

In 2010 the Dodd-Frank Act required advisory votes of shareholders on executive pay for *all* large U.S. corporations. While shareholders do tend to support executive pay packages—voting them down a mere 8% of the time in 2011—firms with poor performance or unusually high executive pay are more likely to see their compensation proposals rejected by shareholders.[15]

Proxy Contests. Perhaps the most extreme form of direct action that disgruntled shareholders can take is to hold a proxy contest and introduce a rival slate of directors for election to the board (see Figure 29.2). This action gives shareholders an actual choice between the nominees put forth by management and the current board and a completely different slate of nominees put forth by dissident shareholders.

For example, in February 2008 Microsoft made an unsolicited offer to buy Yahoo! for $31 per share. While many shareholders supported the offer, which represented a 60% premium to its stock price, Yahoo!'s management and board of directors resisted and Microsoft eventually withdrew its offer that May. Immediately thereafter, dissident Carl Icahn launched an effort aimed at replacing Yahoo!'s board via a proxy contest. Yahoo! settled the contest in July by agreeing to give board seats to Icahn and two of his supporters.

Perhaps because proxy fights can push management to take needed action, one early study of proxy contests found that the announcement of a contest increased firm stock price by 8% on average, even if the challenge was eventually unsuccessful and the incumbents won reelection.[16]

Management Entrenchment

Given the importance of shareholder action in corporate governance, researchers and large investors alike have become increasingly interested in measuring the balance of power between shareholders and managers in a firm. Over time, the tools that managers can use to

[14]V. Cuñat, M. Guadalupe, and M. Gine, "Say Pays!: Shareholder Voice and Firm Performance," Financial Markets Group Working Paper, The London School of Economics (2012).

[15]ISS White Paper: 2011 U.S. Postseason Report; and J. Cotter, A. Palmiter, and R. Thomas "The First Year of 'Say on Pay' Under Dodd-Frank: An Empirical Analysis and Look Forward" (February 17, 2013). Vanderbilt Law and Economics Research Paper No. 12–32.

[16]P. Dodd and J. Warner, "On Corporate Governance: A Study of Proxy Contests," *Journal of Financial Economics* 11(1) (1983): 401–438.

entrench themselves have evolved, including antitakeover protections such as those discussed in Chapter 28. The Investor Responsibility Research Center (IRRC) has collected information on 24 different characteristics that can entrench, or give more power, to managers vis-à-vis shareholders. These provisions include state antitakeover statutes, poison pills, staggered boards, and restrictions on the ability of shareholders to call special meetings themselves.

Researchers have begun using data from the IRRC as a way of measuring how entrenched managers are. One study found that firms with more restrictions on shareholder power performed worse than firms with fewer restrictions during the 1990s.[17] Other studies have found connections between the degree of entrenchment and the compensation offered to managers, and even to the value of acquisitions made.[18] While the index offered by the IRRC does not capture every aspect of corporate governance, many practitioners are finding it to be a useful summary measure of the degree to which managers are entrenched and less likely to have their actions checked by shareholders.

The Threat of Takeover

Many of the provisions listed in the IRRC index concern protection from takeovers. As we discussed in Chapter 28, one motivation for a takeover can be to replace poorly performing management. When internal governance systems such as ownership, compensation, board oversight, and shareholder activism fail, the one remaining way to remove poorly performing managers is by mounting a hostile takeover. Thus, the effectiveness of the corporate governance structure of a firm depends on how well protected its managers are from removal in a hostile takeover.

An active takeover market is part of the system through which the threat of dismissal is maintained. In fact, some research has suggested that an active takeover market complements a board's own vigilance in dismissing incompetent managers. That research found that boards are actually more likely to fire managers for poor performance during active takeover markets than they are during lulls in takeover activity.[19] This finding also has implications internationally because some countries have much more active takeover markets than others. In particular, hostile takeovers are far more common in the United States than in other countries.

CONCEPT CHECK

1. Describe and explain a proxy contest.
2. What is the role of takeovers in corporate governance?

29.5 Regulation

So far, we've focused on those parts of the corporate governance system that have evolved over time as economic responses to the need for shareholders to mitigate the conflict of interest between themselves and managers. For example, boards of directors came into being long before there was any regulation of the governance of a company, and CEOs

[17]P. Gompers, J. Ishii, and A. Metrick, "Corporate Governance and Equity Prices," *Quarterly Journal of Economics* 118(1) (2003): 107–155. The cause of this effect, however, is not clear; see J. Core, W. Guay, and T. Rusticus, "Does Weak Governance Cause Weak Stock Returns? An Examination of Firm Operating Performance and Investors' Expectations," *Journal of Finance* 61(2) (2006): 655–687.

[18]G. Garvey and T. Milbourn, "Asymmetric Benchmarking in Compensation: Executives Are Paid for Good Luck but Not Punished for Bad," *Journal of Financial Economics* (2006) 82: 197–225; and R. Masulis, C. Wang, and F. Xie, "Corporate Governance and Acquirer Returns," *Journal of Finance* 62(4) (2007): 1851–1889.

[19]W. Mikkelson and M. Partch, "The Decline of Takeovers and Disciplinary Managerial Turnover," *Journal of Financial Economics* 44(2) (1997): 205–228.

have long appointed independent directors to their boards without being required to do so. Nonetheless, from time to time, government has added to existing requirements by passing laws that force minimum standards of governance. Recent examples include the Sarbanes-Oxley Act of 2002 (SOX) and the Dodd-Frank Act of 2010.

In the wake of the massive failures of large public companies and corporate fraud scandals in the early 2000s mentioned in the introduction to this chapter, Congress rushed to enact legislation to fix what it saw as inadequate safeguards against malfeasance by managers of public corporations. The result was the Sarbanes-Oxley Act. Prior to SOX, the largest overhaul of securities markets and introduction of regulation came in response to the stock market crash of 1929 and the Great Depression that followed. The Exchange Acts of 1933 and 1934, among other things, established the Securities and Exchange Commission (SEC) and prohibited trading on private information gained as an insider of a firm.

The Sarbanes-Oxley Act

One of the most critical inputs to the monitoring process is accurate information. If a board of directors has inaccurate information, it cannot do its job. While SOX contains many provisions, the overall intent of the legislation was to improve the accuracy of information given to both boards and to shareholders. SOX attempted to achieve this goal in three ways: (1) by overhauling incentives and independence in the auditing process, (2) by stiffening penalties for providing false information, and (3) by forcing companies to validate their internal financial control processes.

Many of the problems at Enron, WorldCom, and elsewhere were kept hidden from boards and shareholders until it was too late. In the wake of these scandals, many people felt that the accounting statements of these companies, while often remaining true to the letter of GAAP, did not present an accurate picture of the financial health of the company.

Auditing firms are supposed to ensure that a company's financial statements accurately reflect the financial state of the firm. In reality, most auditors have a long–standing relationship with their audit clients; this extended relationship and the auditors' desire to keep the lucrative auditing fees makes auditors less willing to challenge management. More important perhaps, most accounting firms have developed large and extremely profitable consulting divisions. Obviously, if an audit team refuses to accommodate a request by a client's management, that client will be less likely to choose the accounting firm's consulting division for its next consulting contract. SOX addressed this concern by putting strict limits on the amount of non-audit fees (consulting or otherwise) that an accounting firm can earn from the same firm that it audits. It also required that audit partners rotate every five years to limit the likelihood that auditing relationships become too cozy over long periods of time. Finally, SOX called on the SEC to force companies to have audit committees that are dominated by outside directors and required that at least one outside director have a financial background.

SOX also stiffened the criminal penalties for providing false information to shareholders. It required both the CEO and the CFO to personally attest to the accuracy of the financial statements presented to shareholders and to sign a statement to that effect. Penalties for providing false or misleading financial statements were increased under SOX—fines of as much as $5 million and imprisonment of a maximum of 20 years are permitted. Furthermore, CEOs and CFOs must return bonuses or profits from the sale of stock or the exercise of options during any period covered by statements that are later restated.

Finally, Section 404 of SOX requires senior management and the boards of public companies to be comfortable enough with the process through which funds are allocated and controlled, and outcomes monitored throughout the firm, to be willing to attest to their effectiveness and validity. Section 404 has arguably garnered more attention than any other

INTERVIEW WITH

LAWRENCE E. HARRIS

As Chief Economist of the U.S. Securities and Exchange Commission from 2002 to 2004, Dr. Lawrence E. Harris was the primary advisor to the SEC on all economic issues. He participated extensively in the development of Sarbanes-Oxley (SOX) regulations. Currently Dr. Harris holds the Fred V. Keenan Chair in Finance at the University of Southern California's Marshall School of Business.

QUESTION: *Why is legislation such as Sarbanes-Oxley necessary to protect shareholders?*

ANSWER: Public investors will supply capital to entrepreneurs seeking to fund new business ventures only if they believe it will be used wisely. Regrettably, history has shown that management too often has violated that trust.

The interests of managers and shareholders often conflict. To solve this agency problem, shareholders rely upon information produced by corporate accounting systems. Sarbanes-Oxley mandated accounting and audit standards to improve the quality of corporate financial disclosure.

Opponents of governance regulation believe that shareholders can—and should—take care of themselves. Unfortunately, shareholders often cannot exercise the control necessary to solve agency problems that they could not have anticipated when the firm was first founded. The firm's governance structure, which may have been sensible when the firm was a small company funded primarily by its founders, may no longer be appropriate for a large, widely held corporation operating in the modern economy. Management with little ownership stake may be entrenched, and the directors may be conflicted. When shareholders cannot solve their agency problems, the government must intervene with the lightest possible hand.

QUESTION: *What are the costs and benefits of Sarbanes-Oxley?*

ANSWER: Good corporate disclosure is essential to public finance. SOX improved the quality of disclosure by strengthening accounting and auditing standards. By requiring the CEO and CFO to sign accounts and attest to their accuracy, SOX also put teeth into enforcement if fraud is discovered.

What many people perceive as costs of SOX are really expenditures that weak firms avoided. All well-managed firms must ensure the integrity of their accounting. SOX merely requires that people adopt *existing* best practice. Many companies were already fully compliant with SOX in most essential respects.

Critics claim that SOX made going public more difficult for small firms by increasing the cost of being a public firm. But a public firm *must* have secure control mechanisms to protect shareholders. SOX may decrease the number of firms that go public, but it will also decrease the losses suffered by public investors.

SOX established the Public Corporation Auditing Oversight Board (PCAOB) to regulate auditors. Previous efforts at self-regulation failed because accountants would not discipline their peers. Following numerous notable failures, Congress stepped in and created the PCAOB.

QUESTION: *Is SOX a good law?*

ANSWER: Regulators are blamed for failing to regulate when crises occur, but they do not bear the costs of their regulations. This asymmetry often causes them to underestimate the costs of their regulations and thus adopt unnecessary regulations. The problem is greatest when political considerations force Congress to write regulations that would be better written by well-informed specialists in regulatory agencies such as the SEC. Congress wrote SOX in response to the financial accounting crises that greatly offended the public. Although SOX permits the SEC to essentially rewrite any provision that it determines not to be in the public interest, under the circumstances, it could not do so.

SOX is generally good regulation, but it has some notable unintended consequences. The power it gives audit firms over their corporate clients allows them to interpret SOX to their advantage and thereby increase the work necessary to comply with SOX. SOX also imposes unnecessary costs upon mutual funds. Investment companies are subject to SOX because they are public corporations, but they do not face the same accounting problems that operating companies face. In its haste to appease the public, Congress failed to be as discriminating as it could have been.

section in SOX because of the potentially enormous burden it places on every firm to validate its entire financial control system. When the SEC estimated the cost of implementing Section 404, its staff economists put the total cost at $1.24 billion. Recent estimates based on surveys by Financial Executives International and the American Electronics Association predict that the actual cost will be between $20 billion and $35 billion.[20] The burden of complying with this provision is greater, as a fraction of revenue, for smaller companies. The surveys cited earlier found that multibillion-dollar companies will pay less than 0.05% of their revenues to comply, whereas small companies with less than $20 million in revenues will pay more than 3% of their revenues to comply.

The Cadbury Commission

It is difficult to determine definitively whether the costs of SOX outweigh its benefits: Even if we could measure the total direct and indirect costs of a law, we could never accurately estimate how much fraud is deterred by that law. One place to turn to for guidance is the experiences of other countries. The following quote from *The Independent*[21] sounds like it was written to describe the motivation behind the Sarbanes-Oxley legislation:

> *Prompted by public concern over a string of unexpected collapses of recently audited firms and over big rises in executive pay, exchanges and public officials rode a wave of public outrage to institute corporate governance reforms to strengthen the independence of the board and address the conflicts of interest in the auditing process.*

In actuality, this passage was written in 1992, and it described what happened in the United Kingdom in 1991. Following the collapse of some large public companies, the U.K. government commissioned Sir Adrian Cadbury to form a committee to develop a code of best practices in corporate governance. Sir Cadbury, in introducing his recommendations, reportedly said the following:

> *The fundamental issue is one of pressure. There is pressure on the company to show the results that the market expects. There is pressure on the auditors who don't want to lose their jobs. The question is whether a structure can emerge out of the dialogue which is robust enough to give the shareholders what they ought to get and what they can rely upon. Internal controls are a part of the legitimate expectations of those who receive accounts.*[22]

The problems that the Cadbury Commission identified are the same as those that SOX attempted to address in the United States 10 years later. Perhaps not surprisingly, the resulting recommendations were quite similar as well. According to the commission's findings, audit and compensation committees should be made up entirely of independent directors or, at least, have a majority of them. The CEO should not be chairman of the board, and at the very least there should be a lead independent director with similar agenda-setting powers. Auditors should be rotated, and there should be fuller disclosure of non-audit work. Unlike SOX, these recommendations were not backed up by the force of law. Rather, companies could adopt them or instead explain why they chose not to adopt them in their annual reports. Some researchers have studied firms that adopted the Cadbury recommendations versus those that

[20]American Electronics Association, "Sarbanes-Oxley Section 404: The 'Section' of Unintended Consequences and Its Impact on Small Business" (2005).

[21]S. Pincombe, "Accountancy and Management: Auditors Look to Pass the Buck as Pressure for Reform Increases," *The Independent* (London), November 12, 1991, p. 21.

[22]Ibid.

did not. The results are mixed. While one study found that those firms that separated the position of CEO and chairman performed better, another found no relation between the independence of key board committees and firm performance in the post-Cadbury era.[23]

Dodd-Frank Act

As the previous cases illustrate, regulatory change is often prompted by crisis. As we explained in Chapter 1, the Dodd-Frank Act of 2010 was spurred by the 2008 financial crisis. Many people believed that poor corporate governance was an important factor that contributed to the crisis and so the act has numerous clauses designed to strengthen governance, including:

- **Independent Compensation Committee:** All U.S. exchanges must require that the listed firms' compensation committees be composed of only independent board members, and have the authority to hire outside compensation consultants.
- **Nominating Directors:** Large shareholders owning at least 3% of a company's stock for at least three years may nominate candidates for the board of directors, with the candidates listed on the firm's proxy statement alongside the nominees of management.
- **Vote on Executive Pay and Golden Parachutes:** At least once every three years, firms must provide shareholders with a nonbinding vote on the compensation of the firm's CEO, CFO, and the three other most highly paid executives. While the vote is nonbinding, companies must formally respond regarding how they have taken into account the results of the vote.
- **Clawback Provisions:** Public companies must establish policies that allow firms to take back up to three years of any executive incentive compensation erroneously awarded in the event of an accounting restatement.
- **Pay Disclosure:** Companies must disclose the ratio of CEO annual total compensation to that of the median employee. Companies are also required to disclose the relationship between executive compensation and the firm's financial performance. Finally, firms are required to disclose whether they permit employees and directors to hedge against decreases in the market value of the company's stock.

Insider Trading

One aspect of the conflict of interest between managers and outside shareholders that we have not yet addressed is **insider trading**. Insider trading occurs when a person makes a trade based on privileged information. Managers have access to information that outside investors do not have. By using this information, managers can exploit profitable trading opportunities that are not available to outside investors. If they were allowed to trade on their information, their profits would come at the expense of outside investors and, as a result, outside investors would be less willing to invest in corporations. Insider trading regulation was passed to address this problem.

In the United States, regulation against insider trading traces back to the Great Depression—specifically, to the Exchange Act of 1934. Insiders of a company are defined broadly to include managers, directors, and anyone else who has access to material nonpublic information, including temporary insiders—for example, lawyers working on a

[23] J. Dahya, A. Lonie, and D. Power, "The Case for Separating the Roles of Chairman and CEO: An Analysis of Stock Market and Accounting Data," *Corporate Governance* 4(2) (1996): 71–77; and N. Vafeas and E. Theodorou, "The Association Between Board Structure and Firm Performance in the UK," *British Accounting Review* 30(4) (1998): 383–407.

Martha Stewart and ImClone

One of the most famous insider trading cases involved Martha Stewart, self-made celebrity, billionaire, and CEO of a media empire built around her name. Stewart sold 3928 shares of ImClone Systems in December 2001, just before the Food and Drug Administration announced that it was rejecting ImClone's application to review a new cancer drug. The SEC investigated, alleging that Stewart sold the shares after receiving a tip from her broker that the ImClone founder and his family had been selling shares. Even though Stewart was not an employee of ImClone, insider trading laws prohibited her from trading on information gained through a tip, as the origin of the information violated the duty of trust. Nonetheless, in the end, Stewart was charged only with lying to a federal officer and conspiracy to obstruct justice (the investigation of her trades). She was convicted and served five months in prison and an additional five months of home confinement. In addition, she was fined $30,000.

While Stewart's case made the headlines, it was relatively minor by SEC standards. From 2009–2015, the SEC has charged over 600 individuals for insider trading, with some of those convicted facing penalties exceeding $100 million and jail terms of up to 11 years. The largest penalty ever imposed was $1.8 billion against hedge fund SAC Capital in 2013, with at least 8 individuals at the firm convicted or pleading guilty to a series of violations.

merger deal or commercial printers contracted to print the merger agreement documents. Whether information is material has been defined in the courts as referring to whether the information would have been a significant factor in an investor's decision about the value of the security. Some examples include knowledge of an upcoming merger announcement, earnings release, or change in payout policy. The law is especially strict with regard to takeover announcements, prohibiting anyone (whether an insider or not) with nonpublic information about a pending or ongoing tender offer from trading on that information or revealing it to someone who is likely to trade on it.

The penalties for violating insider trading laws include jail time, fines, and civil penalties. Only the U.S. Justice Department—on its own or at the request of the SEC—can bring charges that carry the possibility of a prison sentence. However, the SEC can bring civil actions if it chooses. In 1984, Congress stiffened the civil penalties for insider trading by passing the Insider Trading Sanctions Act, which allowed for civil penalties of up to three times the gain from insider trading.

CONCEPT CHECK

1. Describe the main requirements of the Sarbanes-Oxley Act of 2002.
2. What new requirements for corporate governance were added in the Dodd-Frank Act of 2010?
3. What is insider trading, and how can it harm investors?

29.6 Corporate Governance Around the World

Most of our discussion in this chapter has focused on corporate governance in the United States. Yet, both the protection of shareholder rights and the basic ownership and control structure of corporations vary across countries. We explore some of those differences here.

Protection of Shareholder Rights

Recent events notwithstanding, investor protection in the United States is generally seen as being among the best in the world. The degree to which investors are protected against expropriation of company funds by managers and even the degree to which their rights are enforced vary widely across countries and legal regimes. In an important study, researchers collected data on aspects of shareholder rights across more than 30 countries.[24] They claimed that the degree of investor protection was largely determined by the legal origin of the country—specifically, whether its legal system was based on British common law (more protection) or French, German, and Scandinavian civil law (less protection). This purported link between legal origin and investor protection has been challenged by other researchers, however, who demonstrate that formal legal protection for investors is a relatively recent development in Great Britain.[25] In the late nineteenth and early twentieth centuries, there was essentially no formal legal protection of minority investors.

Controlling Owners and Pyramids

Much of the focus in the United States is on the agency conflict between shareholders, who own the majority of a firm but are a dispersed group, and managers, who own little of the firm and must be monitored. In many other countries, the central conflict is between what are called "controlling shareholders" and "minority shareholders." In Europe, many corporations are run by families that own controlling blocks of shares. For most practical purposes, blocks of shares in excess of 20% are considered to be controlling, as long as no one else has any large concentration of shares. The idea is that if you own 20% and the other 80% is dispersed among many different shareholders, you will have considerable say in the operation of the firm; other shareholders would have to coordinate their activities to try to outvote you—a formidable challenge.

In these firms, there is usually little conflict between the controlling family and the management (it is often made up of family members). Instead, the conflict arises between the minority shareholders (those without the controlling block) and the controlling shareholders. Controlling shareholders can make decisions that benefit them disproportionately relative to the minority shareholders, such as employing family members rather than the most talented managers or establishing contracts favorable to other family-controlled firms.

Dual Class Shares and the Value of Control. One way for families to gain control over firms even when they do not own more than half the shares is to issue **dual class shares**—a scenario in which companies have more than one class of shares and one class has superior voting rights over the other class. For example, Mark Zuckerberg controls more than 50% of the voting power of Facebook because he controls the majority of Facebook's class B shares, and these shares have ten votes for every one vote of a class A share. Controlling shareholders—often families—will hold all or most of the shares with superior voting rights and issue the inferior voting class to the public. This approach allows the controlling shareholders to raise capital without diluting their control. Dual class shares are common in Brazil, Canada, Denmark, Finland, Germany, Italy, Korea, Mexico, Norway, Sweden, and Switzerland. In the United States, they are far less common. Some countries, such as Belgium, China, Japan, Singapore, and Spain, outlaw differential voting rights altogether.

Pyramid Structures. Another way families can control a corporation without owning 50% of the equity is to create a pyramid structure. In a **pyramid structure**, a family first creates a company in which it owns more than 50% of the shares and therefore has a controlling interest. This company then owns a controlling interest—that is, at least 50% of

[24] R. La Porta, F. Lopez-de-Silanes, A. Shleifer, and R. Vishny, "Law and Finance," *Journal of Political Economy* 106 (1998): 1113–1155.

[25] J. Franks, C. Mayer, and S. Rossi, "Ownership: Evolution and Regulation," *Review of Financial Studies* 22 (2009): 4009–4056.

the shares—in another company. Notice that the family controls *both* companies, but *owns* only 25% of the second company. Indeed, if the second company purchased 50% of the shares of a third company, then the family would control all three companies, even though it would own only 12.5% of the third company. The farther you move down the pyramid the less ownership the family has, but it still remains in complete control of all the companies. Although this example is stylized, a variety of pyramid structures based on this idea are quite common outside the United States.

Figure 29.3 details the actual pyramid controlled by the Pesenti family in Italy as of 1995.[26] The Pesenti family effectively controls five companies primarily concentrated in the construction industry—Italmobiliare, Italcementi, Franco Tosi, Cementerie Siciliane, and Cementerie de Sardegna—even though it does not have more than 50% ownership of any one of them. In this case, the family uses a pyramid structure plus shares with special voting rights to control companies even when its ownership share is as little as 7%.

A controlling family has many opportunities to expropriate minority shareholders in a pyramid structure. The source of the problem is that as you move down the pyramid, the difference between the family's control and its cash flow rights increases. Cash flow rights refer simply to the family's direct ownership stake and, therefore, the portion of the cash flows generated by the firm that the family has a right to. Notice that Italcementi gets 74% of the dividends of Cementerie Siciliane; Italmobiliare gets 32% of the dividends of Italcementi. Finally, the Pesenti family has rights to 29% of the dividends of Italmobiliare.

FIGURE 29.3 **Pesenti Family Pyramid, 1995**

Each box contains both ownership and voting rights (which can differ when preferred stock with superior voting rights is used). The first set of numbers (in blue) indicates the rights of the preceding company one step up the pyramid. The second set of numbers (in red) shows the effective rights of the Pesenti family in that company. For example, Italmobiliare controls Italcementi through its 54% voting block, but it owns only 32% of the company. The Pesenti family's investment in Italmobiliare gives it a 10% ownership of Italcementi but, because it is controlled by Italmobiliare, 45% of the effective voting rights in Italcementi.

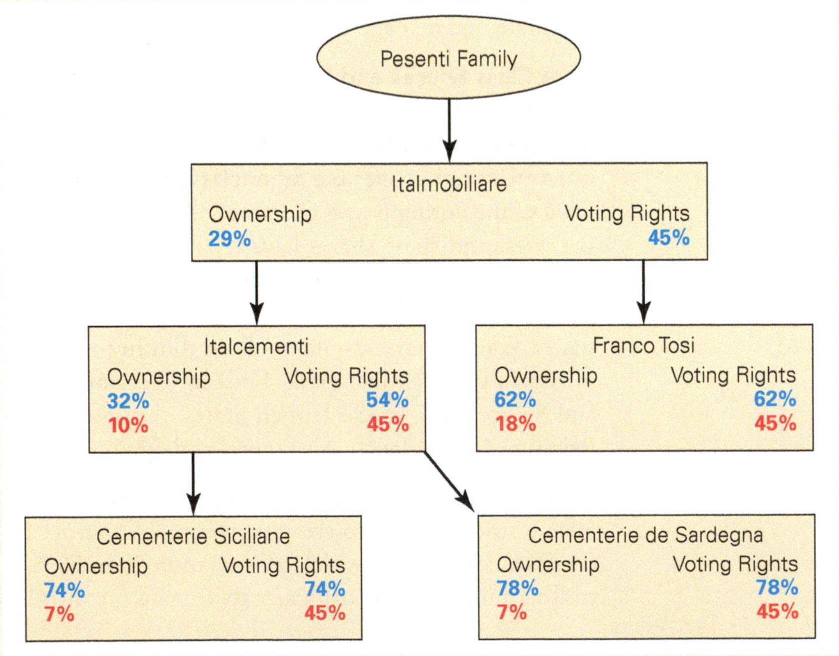

[26] P. Volpin, "Governance with Poor Investor Protection: Evidence from Top Executive Turnover in Italy," *Journal of Financial Economics* 64(1) (2002): 61–90.

Thus, the family receives only 29% × 32% × 74% = 7% of the dividends of Cementerie Siciliane but still controls it.

A conflict of interest arises because the family has an incentive to try to move profits (and hence dividends) up the pyramid—that is, away from companies in which it has few cash flow rights and toward firms in which it has more cash flow rights. This process is called **tunneling**. An example of how this might occur is if the Pesenti family would have Cementerie Siciliane enter into an agreement to be supplied by Italmobiliare at prices that are extremely favorable to Italmobiliare. Such a move would reduce Cementerie Siciliane's profits and increase Italmobiliare's profits.

Of course, if you are a minority shareholder in one of these subsidiaries, you would rationally anticipate this expropriation and so you would pay less for the shares of firms in which a family has control, especially if it is low in the pyramid. In effect, you would factor in your expected loss from being a minority shareholder rather than a controlling shareholder. Many studies have confirmed this intuition, finding sharp differences between the value of controlling blocks and minority shares.[27] Thus, controlling shareholders pay for their control rights because the firm effectively faces a higher cost of equity for outside capital.

The Stakeholder Model

The agency costs and the ways to control them that we have discussed are general to all companies anywhere in the world. However, the United States is somewhat of an exception, in that it focuses solely on maximizing shareholder welfare. Most countries follow what is called the **stakeholder model**, giving explicit consideration to other stakeholders—in particular, rank-and-file employees. As noted earlier, countries such as Germany give employees board representation. Others have mandated works councils, local versions of labor unions that are to be informed and consulted on major corporate decisions. Finally, some countries mandate employee participation in decision making in their constitutions. Table 29.1 summarizes employee standing in the governance of firms in OECD (Organization for Economic Cooperation and Development) countries.

It is important to keep in mind that in countries like the U.S. where other stakeholders are not explicitly considered in the firm's objective, the interests of these stakeholders are not necessarily ignored. Most firms are constrained because they operate in competitive markets. If they mistreat other stakeholders such as employees or customers, these

[27]For estimates based on research on mergers and acquisitions, see P. Hanouna, A. Sarin, and A. Shapiro, "Value of Corporate Control: Some International Evidence," SSRN working paper (2004). Estimates of the value of control have also been done comparing the value of shares with different voting rights. In the United States, see C. Doidge, "U.S. Cross-listings and the Private Benefits of Control: Evidence from Dual Class Shares," *Journal of Financial Economics* 72(3) (2004): 519–553. Italy is a country where the value of control is much larger. Zingales reports a premium of 82% on voting shares, presumably because of lower protection to minority investors. See L. Zingales, "The Value of the Voting Right: A Study of the Milan Stock Exchange Experience," *Review of Financial Studies* 7(1) (1994): 125–148. Other work includes H. Almeida and D. Wolfenzon, "A Theory of Pyramidal Ownership and Family Business Groups," *Journal of Finance* 61(6) (2006): 2637–2680; L. Bebchuk, R. Kraakman, and G. Triantis, "Stock Pyramids, Cross-Ownership, and Dual Class Equity," in R. Morck (ed.), *Concentrated Corporate Ownership* (Chicago: University of Chicago Press, 2000): 295–318; M. Bertrand, P. Mehta, and S. Mullainathan, "Ferreting Out Tunneling: An Application to Indian Business Groups," *Quarterly Journal of Economics* 117(1) (2002): 121–148; S. Johnson, R. La Porta, F. Lopez-de-Silanes, and A. Shleifer, "Tunneling," *American Economic Review* 90(2) (2000): 22–27.

TABLE 29.1 Employee Participation in Corporate Governance in OECD Countries

Mandated Works Councils	Employee Appointed Board Members	Constitutional Employee Protections	No Explicit Requirements
Austria	Austria	France	Australia
Belgium	Czech Republic	Italy	Canada
Denmark	Denmark	Norway	Ireland
Finland	Germany		Japan
France	Netherlands		Mexico
Germany	Norway		New Zealand
Greece	Sweden		Poland
Hungary			Slovak Republic
Korea			Switzerland
Netherlands			Turkey
Portugal			United Kingdom
Spain			United States

Source: Based on Organization for Economic Cooperation and Development, *Survey of Corporate Governance Developments in OECD Countries* (2004).

stakeholders will be tempted to sever their relationship with the firm. Thus an objective that maximizes shareholder value must also implicitly consider stakeholder preferences.

Cross-Holdings

While in the United States it is rare for one company's largest shareholder to be another company, in many countries, such as Germany, Japan, and Korea, it is the norm. In Japan, groups of firms connected through cross-holdings and a common relation to a bank are known as *keiretsu*. Monitoring of each company comes from others in the group holding blocks of its stock and primarily from the main bank of the group, which as a creditor monitors the financial well-being of the group companies closely. In Korea, huge conglomerate groups such as Hyundai, Samsung, LG, and SK comprise companies in widely diversified lines of business and are known as *chaebol*. For example, SK Corporation has subsidiary and group companies in energy, chemicals, pharmaceuticals, and telecommunications. An important difference between the Korean chaebol and the Japanese keiretsu is that in Korea the firms do not share a common relationship with a single bank.

CONCEPT CHECK

1. How does shareholder protection vary across countries?
2. How can a minority owner in a business gain a controlling interest?

29.7 The Trade-Off of Corporate Governance

Corporate governance is a system of checks and balances that trades off costs and benefits. As this chapter makes clear, this trade-off is very complicated. No one structure works for all firms. For example, it would be hard to argue that having Bill Gates as a controlling shareholder of Microsoft was bad for minority investors. For Microsoft, the alignment of incentives assured by Gates' large stake in Microsoft appeared to outweigh the costs of having such an entrenched CEO. In other cases, however, this is unlikely to be true.

The costs and benefits of a corporate governance system also depend on cultural norms. Acceptable business practice in one culture is unacceptable in another culture, and thus it is not surprising that there is such wide variation in governance structures across countries.[28]

It is important to keep in mind that good governance is value enhancing and so, in principle, is something investors in the firm should strive for. Because there are many ways to implement good governance, one should expect firms to display—and firms do display—wide variation in their governance structures.

MyFinanceLab

Here is what you should know after reading this chapter. MyFinanceLab will help you identify what you know and where to go when you need to practice.

29.1 Corporate Governance and Agency Costs

- Corporate governance refers to the system of controls, regulations, and incentives designed to prevent fraud from happening.
- The conflicts between those who control the operations of a firm and those who supply capital to the firm are as old as the corporate organizational structure. Shareholders use a combination of incentives and threats of dismissal to mitigate this conflict.

29.2 Monitoring by the Board of Directors and Others

- The board of directors hires managers, sets their compensation, and fires them if necessary. Some boards become captured, meaning that they act in the interests of managers rather than shareholders. Boards with strong, outside directors who were nominated before the current CEO took the helm of the firm are the least likely to be captured.

29.3 Compensation Policies

- Ownership of a company's stock by management can reduce managers' perquisite consumption. However, moderate holdings of shares can have a negative effect by making the managers harder to fire (reducing the threat of dismissal), without fully aligning their interests with those of shareholders.
- By tying managers' compensation to firm performance, boards can better align managers' interests with shareholders' interests. Care must be taken to make sure managers do not have incentives to try to manipulate the firm's stock price to garner a big compensation payout.

29.4 Managing Agency Conflict

- If a board fails to act, shareholders are not without recourse. They can propose an alternate slate of directors or vote not to ratify certain actions of the board.
- A board and management can adopt provisions, such as staggered boards and limitations on special shareholder meetings that serve to entrench them. These provisions also have the effect of limiting the efficacy of a hostile takeover bid.

[28]Resources that detail how governance differs across the world include J. Charkham, *Keeping Good Company: A Study of Corporate Governance in Five Countries* (Oxford: Clarendon Press, 1994); J. Franks and C. Mayer, "Corporate Ownership and Control in the U.K., Germany and France," *Journal of Applied Corporate Finance* 9(4) (1997): 30–45; R. La Porta, F. Lopez-de-Silanes, and A. Shleifer, "Corporate Ownership Around the World," *Journal of Finance* 54(4) (1999): 471–517; and D. Denis and J. McConnell, "International Corporate Governance," *Journal of Financial and Quantitative Analysis* 38(1) (2003): 1–38.

- Despite the defenses that a determined management can erect, one source of the threat of dismissal comes from a hostile acquirer, which can take over a firm and fire the management, even if the board fails to do so.

29.5 Regulation

- Regulation is an important piece of the total corporate governance environment. Regulation can be beneficial by reducing asymmetric information between managers and capital providers and thus reducing the overall cost of capital. Regulation also carries with it costs of compliance and enforcement. Good regulation balances these forces to produce a net benefit for society.
- The Sarbanes-Oxley Act was intended to improve shareholder monitoring of managers by increasing the accuracy of their information.
  - It overhauls incentives and independence in the auditing process.
  - It stiffens the penalties for providing false information.
  - It forces companies to validate their internal financial control process.
- The most recent overhaul of U.S. governance regulation is the Dodd-Frank Act of 2010. The act requires that firms
  - Choose independent compensation committees and allow long-term large shareholders to nominate directors.
  - Allow shareholders to vote on executive pay and to clawback incentive pay that was erroneously awarded.
  - Disclose how executive pay compares with that of the median employee, as well as how it is related to the firm's financial performance.
- The Exchange Acts of 1933 and 1934 are the basis of insider trading regulation. Over time, the SEC and the courts have developed interpretations of the law that
  - Prohibit insiders with a fiduciary duty to their shareholders from trading on material nonpublic information in that stock.
  - Prohibit anyone with nonpublic information about a pending or ongoing tender offer from trading on that information or revealing it to someone who is likely to trade on it.

29.6 Corporate Governance Around the World

- Corporate governance, regulations, and practices vary widely across countries.
  - Some studies suggest that countries with common-law roots generally provide better shareholder protection than countries with civil-law origin.
  - Ownership structures in Europe and Asia often involve pyramidal control of a group of companies by a single family. In these situations, the controlling family has many opportunities for expropriation of minority shareholders through tunneling.
  - Dual class shares with differential voting rights allow a controlling shareholder or family to maintain control of a company or group even if their cash flow rights are relatively small. Dual class shares are common outside the United States.
  - Most countries give employees some role in governing a firm. Employee involvement usually takes the form of board seats or works councils that are consulted before major decisions.
  - It is common outside the United States for a company's largest shareholder to be another company. These cross-holdings create incentives for firms to monitor each other.

29.7 The Trade-Off of Corporate Governance

- Corporate governance is a system of checks and balances that trades off costs and benefits.
- Good governance is value enhancing and so, in principle, is something investors in the firm should strive for. Because there are many ways to implement good governance, one should expect firms to display—and firms do display—wide variation in their governance structures.

Key Terms

backdating *p. 999*
captured *p. 996*
corporate governance *p. 994*
dual class shares *p. 1009*
gray directors *p. 995*
inside directors *p. 995*
insider trading *p. 1007*
outside (independent) directors *p. 995*
pyramid structure *p. 1009*
stakeholder model *p. 1011*
tunneling *p. 1011*

Further Reading

The literature on corporate governance is extensive; we cannot hope to do it justice in this single chapter. Readers interested in delving into this subject more thoroughly can begin by consulting the following surveys: M. Becht, P. Bolton, and A. Roell, "Corporate Governance and Control," in G. Constantinides, M. Harris, and R. Stulz (eds.), *Handbook of the Economics of Finance* (North-Holland, 2003: 1–109); and A. Shleifer and R. W. Vishny, "A Survey of Corporate Governance," *Journal of Finance* 52(2) (1997): 737–783.

Problems

All problems are available in MyFinanceLab.

Corporate Governance and Agency Costs

1. What inherent characteristic of corporations creates the need for a system of checks on manager behavior?
2. What are some examples of agency problems?
3. What are the advantages and disadvantages of the corporate organizational structure?

Monitoring by the Board of Directors and Others

4. What is the role of the board of directors in corporate governance?
5. How does a board become captured by a CEO?
6. What role do security analysts play in monitoring?
7. How are lenders part of corporate governance?
8. What is a whistle-blower?

Compensation Policies

9. What are the advantages and disadvantages of increasing the options granted to CEOs?

Managing Agency Conflict

10. Is it necessarily true that increasing managerial ownership stakes will improve firm performance?
11. How can proxy contests be used to overcome a captured board?
12. What is a say-on-pay vote?
13. What are a board's options when confronted with dissident shareholders?

Regulation

14. What is the essential trade-off faced by government in designing regulation of public firms?

15. Many of the provisions of the Sarbanes-Oxley Act of 2002 were aimed at auditors. How does this affect corporate governance?

16. The Dodd-Frank Act requires that firms disclose whether employees and directors are permitted to hedge against declines in the firm's stock price. Why might this matter for corporate governance?

17. What are the costs and benefits of prohibiting insider trading?

18. How do the laws on insider trading differ for merger- versus non-merger-related trading?

Corporate Governance Around the World

19. Are the rights of shareholders better protected in the United States or in France?

20. How can a controlling family use a pyramidal control structure to benefit itself at the expense of other shareholders?

CHAPTER

30

Risk Management

ALL FIRMS ARE SUBJECT TO RISK FROM A VARIETY OF SOURCES: CHANGES in consumer tastes and demand for their products, fluctuations in the cost of raw materials, employee turnover, the entry of new competitors, and countless other uncertainties. Entrepreneurs and corporate managers willingly take on these risks in the pursuit of high returns and accept them as part of the cost of doing business. But as with any other cost, firms should manage risk to minimize the effect on the value of the firm.

The primary method of risk management is prevention. For example, firms can avoid or at least reduce many potential risks by increasing safety standards in the workplace, by making prudent investment decisions, and by conducting appropriate due diligence when entering into new relationships. But some risks are too costly to prevent and are inevitable consequences of running a business. As discussed in Part 5, the firm shares these business risks with its investors through its capital structure. Some of the risk is passed on to debt holders, who bear the risk that the firm will default. Most of the risk is held by equity holders, who are exposed to the volatility of the stock's realized return. Both types of investors can reduce their risk by holding the firm's securities in a well-diversified portfolio.

Not all risks need to be passed on to the firm's debt and equity holders. Insurance and financial markets allow firms to trade risk and shield their debt and equity holders from some types of risk. For example, after a fire shut down its processing plant in January 2005, Suncor Energy received more than $200 million in settlements from insurance contracts covering both the damage to the plant and the lost business while the plant was being repaired. Much of the loss from the fire was thus borne by Suncor's insurers rather than by its investors. In 2008, Southwest Airlines received $1.3 billion from financial contracts that compensated it for the rise in the cost of jet fuel. In July 2015, Cisco held contracts to protect nearly $3.5 billion worth of projected foreign revenues from fluctuations in exchange rates, and General Electric held contracts, with a total market value exceeding $5 billion, designed to reduce its exposure to interest rate fluctuations.

NOTATION

r_f	risk-free interest rate
r	current interest rate
r_L	cost of capital for an insured loss
β_L	beta of an insured loss
$r_\$$, $r_€$	dollar and euro interest rate
S	spot exchange rate
F, F_T	one-year and T-year forward exchange rate
K	option strike price
σ	exchange rate volatility
T	option (or forward) expiration date
$N(\ )$	normal distribution function
C_t	cash flow on date t
P	price of a security
ε	change in interest rate
k	compounding periods per year
A, L, E	market value of assets, liabilities, equity
D_P	duration of security or portfolio P
$\tilde{r}_t$	floating interest rate on date t
δ_t	credit spread on date t
N	notational principal of a swap contract
NPV	net present value

In this chapter, we consider the strategies that firms use to manage and reduce the risk borne by their investors. We begin with the most common form of risk management, insurance. After carefully considering the costs and benefits of insurance, we look at the ways firms can use financial markets to offload the risks associated with changes in commodity prices, exchange rate fluctuations, and interest rate movements.

30.1 Insurance

Insurance is the most common method firms use to reduce risk. Many firms purchase **property insurance** to insure their assets against hazards such as fire, storm damage, vandalism, earthquakes, and other natural and environmental risks. Other common types of insurance include:

- **Business liability insurance**, which covers the costs that result if some aspect of the business causes harm to a third party or someone else's property
- **Business interruption insurance**, which protects the firm against the loss of earnings if the business is interrupted due to fire, accident, or some other insured peril
- **Key personnel insurance**, which compensates for the loss or unavoidable absence of crucial employees in the firm

In this section, we illustrate the role of insurance in reducing risk and examine its pricing and potential benefits and costs for a firm.

The Role of Insurance: An Example

To understand the role of insurance in reducing risk, consider an oil refinery with a 1-in-5000, or 0.02%, chance of being destroyed by a fire in the next year. If it is destroyed, the firm estimates that it will lose \$150 million in rebuilding costs and lost business. We can summarize the risk from fire with a probability distribution:

Event	Probability	Loss (in \$ million)
No fire	99.98%	0
Fire	0.02%	150

Given this probability distribution, the firm's expected loss from fire each year is

$$99.98\% \times (\$0) + 0.02\% \times (\$150 \text{ million}) = \$30{,}000$$

While the expected loss is relatively small, the firm faces a large downside risk if a fire does occur. If the firm could completely eliminate the chance of fire for less than the present value of \$30,000 per year, it would do so; such an investment would have a positive NPV. But avoiding *any* chance of a fire is probably not feasible with current technology (or at least would cost far more than \$30,000 per year). Consequently, the firm can manage the risk by instead purchasing insurance to compensate its loss of \$150 million. In exchange, the firm will pay an annual fee, called an **insurance premium**, to the insurance company. In this way, insurance allows the firm to exchange a random future loss for a certain upfront expense.

Insurance Pricing in a Perfect Market

When a firm buys insurance, it transfers the risk of the loss to an insurance company. The insurance company charges an upfront premium to take on that risk. At what price will the insurance company be willing to bear the risk in a perfect market?

In a perfect market without other frictions, insurance companies should compete until they are just earning a fair return and the NPV from selling insurance is zero. The NPV is zero if the price of insurance equals the present value of the expected payment; in that case, we say the price is **actuarially fair**. If r_L is the appropriate cost of capital given the risk of the loss, we can calculate the actuarially fair premium as follows:[1]

Actuarially Fair Insurance Premium

$$\text{Insurance Premium} = \frac{\Pr(\text{Loss}) \times E[\text{Payment in the Event of Loss}]}{1 + r_L} \tag{30.1}$$

where Pr(Loss) is the probability that the loss will occur, $E[\cdot]$ is the expected payment if the loss occurs, and r_L is the appropriate cost of capital.

The cost of capital r_L used in Eq. 30.1 depends on the risk being insured. Consider again the oil refinery. The risk of fire is surely unrelated to the performance of the stock market or the economy. Instead, this risk is specific to this firm and, therefore, diversifiable in a large portfolio. As we discussed in Chapter 10, by pooling together the risks from many policies, insurance companies can create very-low-risk portfolios whose annual claims are relatively predictable. In other words, the risk of fire has a beta of zero, so it will not command a risk premium. In this case, $r_L = r_f$, the risk-free interest rate.

Not all insurable risks have a beta of zero. Some risks, such as hurricanes and earthquakes, create losses of tens of billions of dollars and may be difficult to diversify completely.[2] Other types of losses may be correlated across firms. Increases in the cost of health care or more stringent environmental regulations raise the potential claims from health insurance and liability insurance for all firms. Finally, some risks can have a causal effect on the stock market: The September 11, 2001, terrorist attacks cost insurers $34 billion[3] and also led to a 12% decline in the S&P 500 in the first week of trading following the attacks.

For risks that cannot be fully diversified, the cost of capital r_L will include a risk premium.[4] By its very nature, insurance for nondiversifiable hazards is generally a negative-beta asset (it pays off in bad times); the insurance payment to the firm tends to be *larger* when total losses are high and the market portfolio is low. Thus, the risk-adjusted rate r_L for losses is *less than* the risk-free rate r_f, leading to a *higher* insurance premium in Eq. 30.1. While firms that purchase insurance earn a return $r_L < r_f$ on their investment, because of the negative beta of the insurance payoff, it is still a zero-NPV transaction.[5]

---

[1] Equation 30.1 assumes insurance premiums are paid at the start of the year, and payments in the event of loss are made at the end of the year. It is straightforward to extend it to alternative timing assumptions.

[2] For example, insured losses from hurricanes Katrina, Rita, and Wilma, which pummeled the southeastern United States in 2005, exceeded $40 billion, with total economic losses topping $100 billion. When insuring large risks like these, many insurance companies buy insurance on their own portfolios from reinsurance companies. Reinsurance firms pool risks globally from different insurance companies worldwide. For natural disasters, typically, one-fourth to one-third of the insured losses is passed on to reinsurers.

[3] This number includes property, life, and liability insurance, as estimated by the Insurance Information Institute, www.iii.org.

[4] Alternatively, we can use *risk-neutral* probabilities, as defined in Chapter 21, to calculate the expected loss in the numerator of Eq. 30.1, in which case we would continue to discount using the risk-free interest rate.

[5] Not all insurance must have a zero or negative beta; a positive beta is possible if the amount of the insured loss is higher when market returns are also high.

EXAMPLE 30.1 **Insurance Pricing and the CAPM**

Problem

As the owner of a landmark Chicago skyscraper, you decide to purchase insurance that will pay \$1 billion in the event the building is destroyed by terrorists. Suppose the likelihood of such a loss is 0.1%, the risk-free interest rate is 4%, and the expected return of the market is 10%. If the risk has a beta of zero, what is the actuarially fair insurance premium? What is the premium if the beta of terrorism insurance is −2.5?[6]

Solution

The expected loss is 0.1% × \$1 billion = \$1 million. If the risk has a beta of zero, we compute the insurance premium using the risk-free interest rate: (\$1 million)/1.04 = \$961,538.

If the beta of the risk is not zero, we can use the CAPM to estimate the appropriate cost of capital. Given a beta for the loss, β_L, of −2.5, and an expected market return, r_{mkt}, of 10%:

$$r_L = r_f + \beta_L(r_{mkt} - r_f) = 4\% - 2.5(10\% - 4\%) = -11\%$$

In this case, the actuarially fair premium is (\$1 million)/(1 − 0.11) = \$1.124 million. Although this premium exceeds the expected loss, it is a fair price given the negative beta of the risk.

The Value of Insurance

In a perfect capital market, insurance will be priced so that it has an NPV of zero for both the insurer and the insured. But if purchasing insurance has an NPV of zero, what benefit does it have for the firm?

Modigliani and Miller have already provided us with the answer to this question: In a perfect capital market, there is no benefit to the firm from any financial transaction, *including insurance.* Insurance is a zero-NPV transaction that has no effect on value. Although insurance allows the firm to divide its risk in a new way (e.g., the risk of fire is held by insurers, rather than by debt and equity holders), the firm's total risk—and, therefore, its value—remains unchanged.

Thus, just like a firm's capital structure, the value of insurance must come from reducing the cost of market imperfections on the firm. Let's consider the potential benefits of insurance with respect to the market imperfections that we considered in Part 5.

Bankruptcy and Financial Distress Costs. When a firm borrows, it increases its chances of experiencing financial distress. In Chapter 16, we saw that financial distress may impose significant direct and indirect costs on the firm, including agency costs such as excessive risk taking and underinvestment. By insuring risks that could lead to distress, the firm can reduce the likelihood that it will incur these costs.

For example, for an airline with a large amount of leverage, the losses associated with an accident involving one of its planes may lead to financial distress. While the actual losses from the incident might be \$150 million, the costs from distress might be an additional \$40 million. The airline can avoid these distress costs by purchasing insurance that will cover the \$150 million loss. In this case, the \$150 million paid by the insurer is worth \$190 million to the firm.

Issuance Costs. When a firm experiences losses, it may need to raise cash from outside investors by issuing securities. Issuing securities is an expensive endeavor. In addition to underwriting fees and transaction costs, there are costs from underpricing due to adverse

[6]Given a market volatility of 18%, a beta of −2.5 is consistent with a market decline of roughly 9% in the event of an attack.

selection as well as potential agency costs due to reduced ownership concentration. Because insurance provides cash to the firm to offset losses, it can reduce the firm's need for external capital and thus reduce issuance costs.

EXAMPLE 30.2 Avoiding Distress and Issuance Costs

Problem

Suppose the risk of an airline accident for a major airline is 1% per year, with a beta of zero. If the risk-free rate is 4%, what is the actuarially fair premium for a policy that pays $150 million in the event of a loss? What is the NPV of purchasing insurance for an airline that would experience $40 million in financial distress costs and $10 million in issuance costs in the event of a loss if it were uninsured?

Solution

The expected loss is 1% × $150 million = $1.50 million, so the actuarially fair premium is $1.50 million/1.04 = $1.44 million.

The total benefit of the insurance to the airline is $150 million plus an additional $50 million in distress and issuance costs that it can avoid if it has insurance. Thus, the NPV from purchasing the insurance is

$$NPV = -1.44 + 1\% \times (150 + 50)/1.04 = \$0.48 \text{ million}$$

Tax Rate Fluctuations. When a firm is subject to graduated income tax rates, insurance can produce a tax savings if the firm is in a higher tax bracket when it pays the premium than the tax bracket it is in when it receives the insurance payment in the event of a loss.

Consider an almond grower with a 10% chance of a weather-related crop failure. If the risk of crop failure has a beta of zero and the risk-free rate is 4%, the actuarially fair premium per $100,000 of insurance is

$$\frac{1}{1.04} \times 10\% \times \$100{,}000 = \$9615$$

Suppose the grower's current tax rate is 35%. In the event of a crop failure, however, the grower expects to earn much less income and face a lower 15% tax rate. Then, the grower's NPV from purchasing insurance is positive:

$$\begin{aligned} NPV &= -\$9615 \times (1 - 0.35) + \underbrace{\frac{1}{1.04} \times 10\% \times \$100{,}000}_{=\,\$9615} \times (1 - 0.15) \\ &= \$1923 \end{aligned}$$

The benefit arises because the grower is able to shift income from a period in which it has a high tax rate to a period in which it has a low rate. This tax benefit of insurance can be large if the potential losses are significant enough to have a substantial impact on the firm's marginal tax rate.

Debt Capacity. Firms limit their leverage to avoid financial distress costs. Because insurance reduces the risk of financial distress, it can relax this trade-off and allow the firm to increase its use of debt financing.[7] In Chapter 16, we found that debt financing provides

[7] Indeed, it is not unusual for creditors to require the firm to carry insurance as part of a covenant.

several important advantages for the firm, including lower corporate tax payments due to the interest tax shield, lower issuance costs, and lower agency costs (through an increase in equity ownership concentration and a reduction in excess cash flow).

Managerial Incentives. By eliminating the volatility that results from perils outside management's control, insurance turns the firm's earnings and share price into informative indicators of management's performance. Therefore, the firm can increase its reliance on these measures as part of performance-based compensation schemes, without exposing managers to unnecessary risk. In addition, by lowering the volatility of the stock, insurance can encourage concentrated ownership by an outside director or investor who will monitor the firm and its management.

Risk Assessment. Insurance companies specialize in assessing risk. In many instances, they may be better informed about the extent of certain risks faced by the firm than the firm's own managers. This knowledge can benefit the firm by improving its investment decisions. Requiring the firm to purchase fire insurance, for example, implies that the firm will consider differences in fire safety, through their effects on the insurance premium, when choosing a warehouse. Otherwise, the managers might overlook such differences. Insurance firms also routinely monitor the firms they insure and can make value-enhancing safety recommendations.

The Costs of Insurance

When insurance premiums are actuarially fair, using insurance to manage the firm's risk can reduce costs and improve investment decisions. But in reality, market imperfections exist that can raise the cost of insurance above the actuarially fair price and offset some of these benefits.

Insurance Market Imperfections. Three main frictions may arise between the firm and its insurer. First, transferring the risk to an insurance company entails administrative and overhead costs. The insurance company must employ sales personnel who seek out clients, underwriters who assess the risks of a given property, appraisers and adjusters who assess the damages in the event of a loss, and lawyers who can resolve potential disputes that arise over the claims. Insurance companies will include these expenses when setting their premiums. In 2014, expenses for the property and casualty insurance industry amounted to over 28% of premiums charged.[8]

A second factor that raises the cost of insurance is adverse selection. Just as a manager's desire to sell equity may signal that the manager knows the firm is likely to perform poorly, so a firm's desire to buy insurance may signal that it has above-average risk. If firms have private information about how risky they are, insurance companies must be compensated for this adverse selection with higher premiums.

Agency costs are a third factor that contributes to the price of insurance. Insurance reduces the firm's incentive to avoid risk. For example, after purchasing fire insurance, a firm may decide to cut costs by reducing expenditures on fire prevention. This change in behavior that results from the presence of insurance is referred to as **moral hazard**. The extreme case of moral hazard is insurance fraud, in which insured parties falsify or deliberately cause losses to collect insurance money. Property and casualty insurance companies estimate that moral hazard costs account for more than 11% of premiums.[9]

[8] "2014 Year End Results," Insurance Information Institute.

[9] Insurance Research Council estimate (2002).

Addressing Market Imperfections. Insurance companies try to mitigate adverse selection and moral hazard costs in a number of ways. To prevent adverse selection, they screen applicants to assess their risk as accurately as possible. Just as medical examinations are often required for individuals seeking life insurance, plant inspections and reviews of safety procedures are required to obtain large commercial insurance policies. To deter moral hazard, insurance companies routinely investigate losses to look for evidence of fraud or deliberate intent.

Insurance companies also structure their policies in such a way as to reduce these costs. For example, most policies include both a **deductible**, which is the initial amount of the loss that is not covered by insurance, and **policy limits**, which limit the amount of the loss that is covered regardless of the extent of the damage. These provisions mean that the firm continues to bear some of the risk of the loss even after it is insured. In this way, the firm retains an incentive to avoid the loss, reducing moral hazard. Also, because risky firms will prefer lower deductibles and higher limits (because they are more likely to experience a loss), insurers can use the firm's policy choice to help identify its risk and reduce adverse selection.[10]

EXAMPLE 30.3 Adverse Selection and Policy Limits

Problem

Your firm faces a potential $100 million loss that it would like to insure. Because of tax benefits and the avoidance of financial distress and issuance costs, each $1 received in the event of a loss is worth $1.50 to the firm. Two policies are available: One pays $55 million and the other pays $100 million if a loss occurs. The insurance company charges 20% more than the actuarially fair premium to cover administrative expenses. To account for adverse selection, the insurance company estimates a 5% probability of loss for the $55 million policy and a 6% probability of loss for $100 million policy.

Suppose the beta of the risk is zero and the risk-free rate is 5%. Which policy should the firm choose if its risk of loss is 5%? Which should it choose if its risk of loss is 6%?

Solution

The premium charged for each policy is

$$\text{Premium (\$55 million policy)} = \frac{5\% \times \$55 \text{ million}}{1.05} \times 1.20 = \$3.14 \text{ million}$$

$$\text{Premium (\$100 million policy)} = \frac{6\% \times \$100 \text{ million}}{1.05} \times 1.20 = \$6.86 \text{ million}$$

If the risk of a loss is 5%, the NPV of each policy is

$$NPV(\$55 \text{ million policy})$$

$$= -\$3.14 \text{ million} + \frac{5\% \times \$55 \text{ million}}{1.05} \times 1.50 = \$0.79 \text{ million}$$

[10] Articles that investigate optimal insurance policy design include A. Raviv, "The Design of an Optimal Insurance Policy," *American Economic Review* 69 (1979): 84–96; G. Huberman, D. Mayers, and C. Smith, "Optimal Insurance Policy Indemnity Schedules," *Bell Journal of Economics* 14 (1983): 415–426; and M. Rothschild and J. Stiglitz, "Equilibrium in Competitive Insurance Markets: An Essay on the Economics of Imperfect Information," *Quarterly Journal of Economics* 90 (1976): 629–649.

NPV($100 million policy)

$$= -\$6.86 \text{ million} + \frac{5\% \times \$100 \text{ million}}{1.05} \times 1.50 = \$0.28 \text{ million}$$

Thus, with a 5% risk, the firm should choose the policy with lower coverage. If the risk of a loss is 6%, the policy with higher coverage is superior:

NPV($55 million policy)

$$= -\$3.14 \text{ million} + \frac{6\% \times \$55 \text{ million}}{1.05} \times 1.50 = \$1.57 \text{ million}$$

NPV($100 million policy)

$$= -\$6.86 \text{ million} + \frac{6\% \times \$100 \text{ million}}{1.05} \times 1.50 = \$1.71 \text{ million}$$

Note that the insurance company's concerns regarding adverse selection are justified: Firms that are riskier will choose the higher-coverage policy.

The Insurance Decision

In a perfect capital market, purchasing insurance does not add value to the firm. It can add value in the presence of market imperfections, but market imperfections are also likely to raise the premiums charged by insurers. For insurance to be attractive, the benefit to the firm must exceed the additional premium charged by the insurer.

For these reasons, insurance is most likely to be attractive to firms that are currently financially healthy, do not need external capital, and are paying high current tax rates. They will benefit most from insuring risks that can lead to cash shortfalls or financial distress, and that insurers can accurately assess and monitor to prevent moral hazard.

Full insurance is unlikely to be attractive for risks about which firms have a great deal of private information or that are subject to severe moral hazard. Also, firms that are already in financial distress have a strong incentive not to purchase insurance—they need cash today and have an incentive to take risk because future losses are likely to be borne by their debt holders.

CONCEPT CHECK

1. How can insurance add value to a firm?
2. Identify the costs of insurance that arise due to market imperfections.

30.2 Commodity Price Risk

Firms use insurance to protect against the unlikely event that their real assets are damaged or destroyed by hazards such as fires, hurricanes, accidents, and other catastrophes that are outside their normal course of business. At the same time, many risks that firms face arise naturally as part of their business operations. For many firms, changes in the market prices of the raw materials they use and the goods they produce may be the most important source of risk to their profitability. For example, in the airline industry, the second-largest expense after labor is jet fuel. With oil prices increasing from a low of $17 a barrel in 2001, to nearly $150 a barrel in mid-2008, most major carriers struggled to achieve profitability. Industry analysts estimate that each $1 per barrel increase in the price of oil equates to a $425 million increase in the industry's annual jet fuel expenses. United Airlines alone spent more than $11 billion on fuel in 2014, nearly 30% of its annual revenue. For an airline, oil price fluctuations are clearly an important source of risk.

In this section, we discuss ways firms can reduce, or *hedge*, their exposure to commodity price movements. Like insurance, hedging involves contracts or transactions that provide the firm with cash flows that offset its losses from price changes.

Hedging with Vertical Integration and Storage

Firms can hedge risk by making real investments in assets with offsetting risk. The most common strategies are vertical integration and storage.

Vertical integration entails the merger of a firm and its supplier (or a firm and its customer). Because an increase in the price of the commodity raises the firm's costs and the supplier's revenues, these firms can offset their risks by merging. For example, in 2005 Japanese tire maker Bridgestone purchased a large Indonesian rubber plantation to control its costs. As the price of rubber increases, so will the profits of the rubber plantation, offsetting the higher costs of making tires. Similarly, airlines could offset their oil price risk by merging with an oil company.

While vertical integration can reduce risk, it does not always increase value. Recall the key lesson of Modigliani and Miller: Firms add no value by doing something investors can do for themselves. Investors concerned about commodity price risk can diversify by "vertically integrating" their portfolios and buying shares of the firm and its supplier. Because the acquiring firm often pays a substantial premium over the current share price of the firm being acquired, the shareholders of the acquiring firm would generally find it cheaper to diversify on their own.

Vertical integration can add value if combining the firms results in important synergies. For example, Boeing ultimately decided to purchase a number of its suppliers involved in its 787 "Dreamliner" to improve quality control and coordination, and reduce production delays. In many instances, however, diseconomies would be the more likely outcome of vertical integration, as the combined firm would lack a strategic focus (e.g., airlines and oil producers). Finally, vertical integration is not a perfect hedge: A firm's supplier is exposed to many other risks besides commodity prices. By integrating vertically, the firm eliminates one risk but acquires others.

A related strategy is the long-term storage of inventory. An airline concerned about rising fuel costs could purchase a large quantity of fuel today and store the fuel until it is needed. By doing so, the firm locks in its cost for fuel at today's price plus storage costs. But for many commodities, storage costs are much too high for this strategy to be attractive. Such a strategy also requires a substantial cash outlay upfront. If the firm does not have the required cash, it would need to raise external capital—and consequently would suffer issuance and adverse selection costs. Finally, maintaining large amounts of inventory would dramatically increase working capital requirements, a cost for the firm.

Hedging with Long-Term Contracts

An alternative to vertical integration or storage is a long-term supply contract. Firms routinely enter into long-term lease contracts for real estate, fixing the price at which they will obtain office space many years in advance. Similarly, utility companies sign long-term supply contracts with power generators, and steelmakers sign long-term contracts with mining firms for iron ore. Through these contracts, both parties can achieve price stability for their product or input.

A good example is provided by Southwest Airlines. In early 2000, when oil prices were close to $20 per barrel, Chief Financial Officer Gary Kelly developed a strategy to protect the airline from a surge in oil prices. By the time oil prices soared above $30 per barrel later that year and put the airline industry into a financial crisis, Southwest had signed contracts guaranteeing a price for its fuel equivalent to $23 per barrel. The savings from its fuel hedge

FIGURE 30.1

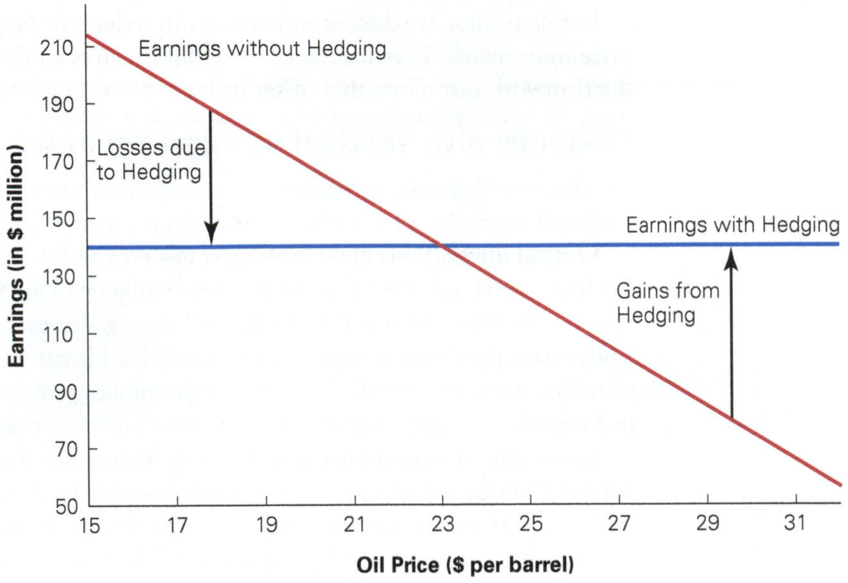

Commodity Hedging Smoothes Earnings

By locking in its fuel costs through long-term supply contracts, Southwest Airlines has kept its earnings stable in the face of fluctuating fuel prices. With a long-term contract at a price of $23 per barrel, Southwest would gain by buying at this price if oil prices go above $23 per barrel. If oil prices fall below $23 per barrel, Southwest would lose from its commitment to buy at a higher price.

amounted to almost 50% of Southwest's earnings that year, as shown in Figure 30.1. Kelly went on to become Southwest's CEO, and Southwest has continued this strategy to hedge fuel costs. Between 1998 and 2008, Southwest saved $3.5 billion over what it would have spent if it had paid the industry's average price for jet fuel, accounting for 83% of the company's profits during that period.

Of course, like insurance, commodity hedging does not always boost a firm's profits. Had oil prices fallen below $23 per barrel in the fall of 2000, Southwest's hedging policy would have *reduced* the firm's earnings by obligating it to pay $23 per barrel for its oil (and perhaps Kelly might not have gone on to be CEO). Presumably, Southwest felt that it could afford to pay $23 per barrel for oil even if the price fell. In fact, in recent years oil prices have fallen dramatically leaving Southwest with a loss of $1.8 billion for outstanding hedges through 2018. In response, the airline significantly reduced its hedging program in 2016, from about 70% of its fuel consumption, to 30%. But although these hedges have turned out to be a bad bet recently, the losses from them were offset by Southwest's higher profit margins resulting from low fuel costs. Thus, in either case, as Figure 30.1 illustrates, hedging stabilizes earnings.

EXAMPLE 30.4 Hedging with Long-Term Contracts

Problem

Consider a chocolate maker that will need 10,000 tons of cocoa beans next year. Suppose the current market price of cocoa beans is $1400 per ton. At this price, the firm expects earnings before interest and taxes of $22 million next year. What will the firm's EBIT be if the price of cocoa beans rises to $1950 per ton? What will EBIT be if the price of cocoa beans falls to $1200 per ton? What will EBIT be in each scenario if the firm enters into a supply contract for cocoa beans for a fixed price of $1450 per ton?

Solution

If the price of cocoa beans increases to \$1950 per ton, the firm's costs will increase by $(1950 - 1400) \times 10{,}000 = \$5.5$ million. Other things equal, EBIT will decline to \$22 million − \$5.5 million = \$16.5 million. If the price of cocoa beans falls to \$1200 per ton, EBIT will rise to \$22 million $- (1200 - 1400) \times 10{,}000 = \$24$ million. Alternatively, the firm can avoid this risk by entering into the supply contract that fixes the price in either scenario at \$1450 per ton, for an EBIT of \$22 million $- (1450 - 1400) \times 10{,}000 = \$21.5$ million.

Often, long-term supply contracts are bilateral contracts negotiated by a buyer and a seller. Such contracts have several potential disadvantages. First, they expose each party to the risk that the other party may default and fail to live up to the terms of the contract. Thus, while they insulate the firms from commodity price risk, they expose them to credit risk. Second, such contracts cannot be entered into anonymously; the buyer and seller know each other's identity. This lack of anonymity may have strategic disadvantages. Finally, the market value of the contract at any point in time may not be easy to determine, making it difficult to track gains and losses, and it may be difficult or even impossible to cancel the contract if necessary.

An alternative strategy that avoids these disadvantages is to hedge with futures contracts. We investigate this strategy in the next section.

Hedging with Futures Contracts

A commodity futures contract is a type of long-term contract designed to avoid the disadvantages cited above. A **futures contract** is an agreement to trade an asset on some future date, at a price that is locked in today. Futures contracts are traded anonymously on an exchange at a publicly observed market price and are generally very liquid. Both the buyer and the seller can get out of the contract at any time by selling it to a third party at the current market price. Finally, through a mechanism we will describe shortly, futures contracts are designed to eliminate credit risk.

Figure 30.2 shows the prices in September 2015 of futures contracts for light, sweet crude oil traded on the New York Mercantile Exchange (NYMEX). Each contract represents a

FIGURE 30.2

Futures Prices for Light, Sweet Crude Oil, September 2015

Each point represents the futures price per barrel that was available in September 2015 for the delivery of oil in the month indicated. While the spot price of oil at the time was \$45 per barrel, the futures contract price for delivery in March 2019 was \$57.

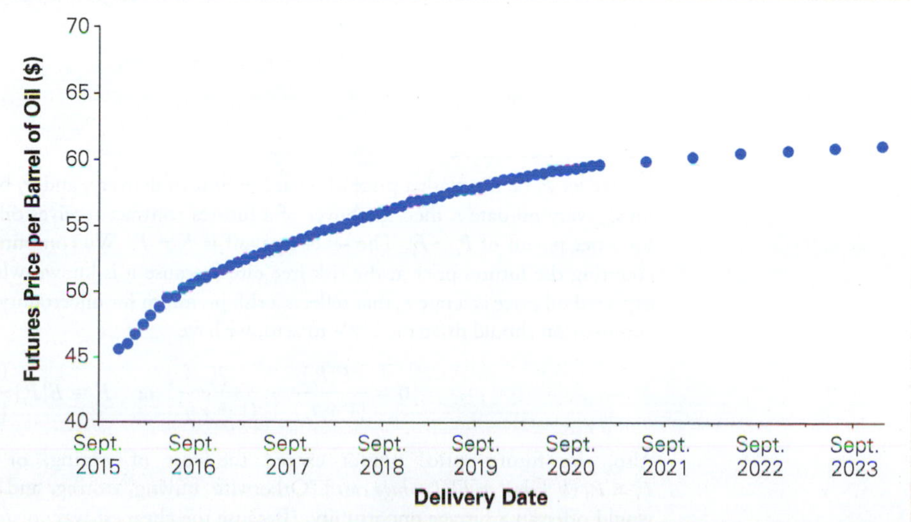

commitment to trade 1000 barrels of oil at the futures price on its delivery date. For example, by trading the March 2019 contract, buyers and sellers in September 2015 agreed to exchange 1000 barrels of oil in March 2019 at a price of \$57 per barrel. By doing so, they were able to lock in the price they will pay or receive for oil more than three years in advance.

The futures prices shown in Figure 30.2 are not prices that are paid today. Rather, they are prices *agreed to* today, to be paid in the future. The futures prices are determined in the market based on supply and demand for each delivery date. They depend on expectations of future oil prices, adjusted by an appropriate risk premium.[11]

Eliminating Credit Risk. If a buyer commits to purchase crude oil in March 2019 for \$57 per barrel, how can the seller be assured that the buyer will honor that commitment? If the actual price of oil in March 2019 is only \$35 per barrel, the buyer will have a strong incentive to renege and default on the contract. Similarly, the seller will have an incentive to default if the actual price of oil is more than \$57 in March 2019.

Futures exchanges use two mechanisms to prevent buyers or sellers from defaulting. First, traders are required to post collateral, called **margin**, when buying or selling commodities using futures contracts. This collateral serves as a guarantee that traders will meet their obligations. In addition, rather than waiting until the end of the contract, there is **daily settlement** of all profits and losses through a procedure called **marking to market.** That is, gains and losses are computed and exchanged each day based on the change in the price of the futures contract.

Marking to Market: An Example. Suppose that the price of the March 2019 futures contract varies as shown in Table 30.1 over the 900 remaining trading days between September 2015 and the delivery date in March 2019. A buyer who enters into the

TABLE 30.1 **Example of Marking to Market and Daily Settlement for the December 2018 Light, Sweet Crude Oil Futures Contract (\$/bbl)**

	September 2015								March 2019
Trading Day	0	1	2	3	4	...	898	899	900
Futures price	57	55	56	54	53	...	32	34	35
Daily marked to market profit/loss		−2	1	−2	−1	...	...	2	1
Cumulative profit/loss		−2	−1	−3	−4	...	−25	−23	−22

[11]If we let P_t be the market price of oil at the time of delivery, and F_t be the futures price agreed to today for delivery on date t, then the buyer of a futures contract receives oil worth P_t and pays F_t at delivery, for a net payoff of $P_t - F_t$. The seller's payoff is $F_t - P_t$. We compute the NPV of the contract by discounting the futures price at the risk-free rate (because it is known when we enter the contract) and the expected oil price at a rate r_p that reflects a risk premium for uncertainty regarding the price of oil. Because competition should drive the NPV to zero, we have

$$0 = \frac{E[P_t]}{(1+r_p)^t} - \frac{F_t}{(1+r_f)^t} \quad \text{or} \quad F_t = E[P_t]\frac{(1+r_f)^t}{(1+r_p)^t}$$

Also, the futures price cannot exceed the cost of storing, or "carrying," oil for the future: $F_t \le P_0\,(1+r_f)^t + FV(\textit{storage costs})$. Otherwise, buying, storing, and selling oil using futures contracts would offer an arbitrage opportunity. (Because the cheapest way to store oil is to leave it in the ground, the futures price is often well below this "cost-of-carry" price. Thus, the relationship between the current price, P_0, and the futures price, F_t, will depend on oil producers' ability to shift production across time.)

COMMON MISTAKE Hedging Risk

There are several common mistakes to be avoided when hedging risk:

Account for Natural Hedges. Even though purchases of a commodity may be a firm's largest expense, they may not be a source of risk if the firm can pass along those costs to its customers. For example, gas stations do not need to hedge their cost of oil, because the price of gasoline—and thus their revenues—fluctuate with it. When a firm can pass on cost increases to its customers or revenue decreases to its suppliers, it has a **natural hedge** for these risks. A firm should hedge risks to its profits only after such natural hedges are accounted for, lest it over-hedge and increase risk.

Liquidity Risk. When hedging with futures contracts, the firm stabilizes its earnings by offsetting business losses with gains on the futures contracts and by offsetting business gains with losses on the futures contracts. In the latter scenario, the firm runs the risk of receiving margin calls on its futures positions before it realizes the cash flows from the business gains. To effectively hedge, the firm must have, or be able to raise, the cash required to meet these margin calls or it may be forced to default on its positions. Hence, when hedging with future contracts, the firm is exposed to **liquidity risk**. Such was the case for Metallgesellschaft Refining and Marketing (MGRM), which shut down in 1993 with more than $1 billion in losses in the oil futures market. MGRM had written long-term contracts to supply oil to its customers and hedged its risk that oil prices might rise by buying oil futures. When oil prices subsequently dropped, MGRM faced a cash flow crisis and could not meet the margin calls on its futures positions.

Basis Risk. Futures contracts are available only for a set of standardized commodities, with specific delivery dates and locations. Thus, while a futures contract that promises to deliver crude oil in Oklahoma in June 2018 is a reasonable hedge for the cost of jet fuel in Dallas in July 2018, it will not be a perfect match. **Basis risk** is the risk that arises because the value of the futures contract will not be perfectly correlated with the firm's exposure.

contract on date 0 has committed to pay the futures price of $57 per barrel for oil. If the next day the futures price is only $55 per barrel, the buyer has a loss of $2 per barrel on her position. This loss is settled immediately by deducting $2 from the buyer's margin account. If the price rises to $56 per barrel on day 2, the gain of $1 is added to the buyer's margin account. This process continues until the contract delivery date, with the daily gains and losses shown. The buyer's cumulative loss is the sum of these daily amounts and always equals the difference between the original contract price of $57 per barrel and the current contract price.

In December 2018, delivery takes place at the final futures price, which is equal to the actual price of oil at that time.[12] In the example in Table 30.1, the buyer ultimately pays $35 per barrel for oil and has lost $22 per barrel in her margin account. Thus, her total cost is $\$35 + \$22 = \$57$ per barrel, the price for oil she originally committed to. Through this daily marking to market, buyers and sellers pay for any losses as they occur, rather than waiting until the final delivery date. Thus, as long as the margin balance is sufficient to cover the daily variation in price, this mechanism avoids the risk of default.[13]

In essence, the March 2019 futures contract is the same as a long-term supply contract with a set price of $57 per barrel of oil.[14] But unlike a bilateral contract, the buyer and the seller can close their positions at any time (and accept the cumulative losses or gains in

---

[12] At its delivery date, a futures contract is a contract for immediate delivery. Thus, by the Law of One Price, its price must be the actual price of oil in the market.

[13] The futures exchange sets a minimum balance for the margin account to be sure it is sufficient to cover one day's loss. If a buyer's remaining margin in the account is too low, the exchange will require the buyer to replenish the account in a margin call. If the buyer fails to do so, the account will be closed and the buyer's contract will be assigned to a new buyer.

[14] Because the daily marked-to-market gains and losses occur over the life of the contract rather than at the end, after we account for interest, the future value of the loss is somewhat higher with a futures contract than with a supply contract. To account for this effect, which can be sizable for a multiyear contract, practitioners generally reduce the magnitude of their initial futures position to reflect the interest earned over the life of the contract. This adjustment is called *tailing the hedge*.

Differing Hedging Strategies

In mid-2005, oil prices rose to more than $60 per barrel. As a result of its aggressive hedging policy, Southwest Airlines was paying slightly more than $26 per barrel for 85% of its oil at the time. But many other U.S. airlines lacked, at that time, the cash or creditworthiness necessary to enter into long-term contracts. In 2004, Delta was forced to sell its supply contracts to raise cash so as to avoid defaulting on its debt. United Airlines, which filed for bankruptcy protection in December 2002, had only 30% of its fuel hedged in 2005 at a price of $45 per barrel. Researchers have documented these patterns more generally: Risk management drops substantially as airlines approach distress and recovers only slowly afterward.*

These differences in strategy are somewhat understandable given the airlines' differing financial positions. Southwest was profitable and desired to reduce its risk of becoming financially distressed by hedging its fuel costs. Moreover, it had the collateral necessary to do so. Delta and United were already financially constrained and in financial distress. Hedging would therefore tie up scarce collateral without avoiding distress costs. And for Delta and United's equity holders, taking a risk by not hedging may be the best strategy—a sudden drop in oil prices would lead to a windfall for equity holders, while losses from further increases would likely be borne by debt holders in default.

As the financial health of United and Delta improved, they too became active hedgers, resulting in large losses when oil prices fell dramatically in 2014–15. United and Delta combined reported over $3 billion in hedging losses in 2015, and along with Southwest Airlines, have decided to scale back their hedging programs.

*A. Rampini, A. Sufi, and S. Viswanathan, "Dynamic Risk Management," *Journal of Financial Economics* 111 (2014): 271–296.

their margin accounts), and the contract will then be reassigned to a new buyer or seller at its current price. Because of this liquidity and the lack of credit risk, commodity futures contracts are the predominant method by which many firms hedge oil price risk. Similar futures contracts exist for many other commodities, including natural gas, coal, electricity, silver, gold, aluminum, soybeans, corn, wheat, rice, cattle, pork bellies, cocoa, sugar, carbon dioxide emissions, and even frozen orange juice.

Deciding to Hedge Commodity Price Risk

In a perfect market, commodity supply contracts and futures contracts are zero-NPV investments that do not change the value of the firm. But hedging commodity price risk can benefit the firm by reducing the costs of other frictions. Just as with insurance, the potential benefits include reduced financial distress and issuance costs, tax savings, increased debt capacity, and improved managerial incentives and risk assessment. Commodity futures markets, in particular, provide valuable information to commodity producers and users. For example, an oil firm can lock in the future price of oil before it spends millions of dollars on drilling a new well. A farmer unsure of future crop prices can lock in the futures price of wheat when deciding the quantity to plant.

But while hedging commodity price risk has similar potential benefits as buying insurance, it does not have the same costs. In comparison to the market for hazard insurance, the commodity markets are less vulnerable to the problems of adverse selection and moral hazard. Firms generally do not possess better information than outside investors regarding the risk of future commodity price changes, nor can they influence that risk through their actions. Also, futures contracts are very liquid and do not entail large administrative costs.

Trading in these contracts carries other costs, however. First, as Figure 30.1 illustrates, when a firm hedges, sometimes it will lose money. These losses will be offset by other gains or savings, but the firm must be sure it can weather the losses until it realizes the offsetting gains. Therefore, the firm must have access to capital it can post as collateral until the ultimate delivery date. Second, the firm may speculate by entering into contracts that do not offset its actual risks. Speculating increases the firm's risk rather than reducing it. When a firm authorizes managers to trade contracts to hedge, it opens the door to the possibility of speculation. The firm must guard against the potential to speculate and add risk to the firm through appropriate governance procedures.

CONCEPT CHECK

1. Discuss risk management strategies that firms use to hedge commodity price risk.
2. What are the potential risks associated with hedging using futures contracts?

30.3 Exchange Rate Risk

Multinational firms face the risk of exchange rate fluctuations. In this section, we consider two strategies that firms use to hedge this risk: currency forward contracts and currency options.

Exchange Rate Fluctuations

Recall from Chapter 3 that an exchange rate is the market rate at which one currency can be exchanged for another currency. Consider the relationship between the U.S. dollar and the euro. In April 2008, the value of the euro (€) relative to the dollar peaked at an exchange rate of 0.625 euros per dollar or, equivalently,

$$\frac{1}{€0.625/\$} = \$1.60 \text{ per euro}$$

Like most foreign exchange rates, the dollar/euro rate is a **floating rate**, which means it changes constantly depending on the quantity supplied and demanded for each currency in the market. The supply and demand for each currency is driven by three factors:

- *Firms trading goods*: A U.S. dealer exchanges dollars for euros to buy cars from a German automaker.
- *Investors trading securities*: A Japanese investor exchanges yen for dollars to purchase U.S. bonds.
- *The actions of central banks in each country*: The British central bank may exchange pounds for euros to attempt to keep down the value of the pound.

Because the supply and demand for currencies varies with global economic conditions, exchange rates are volatile. Figure 30.3 shows the dollar price of euros from January 1999

FIGURE 30.3

Dollars per Euro ($/€), 1999–2015

Note the dramatic changes in the exchange rate over short periods.

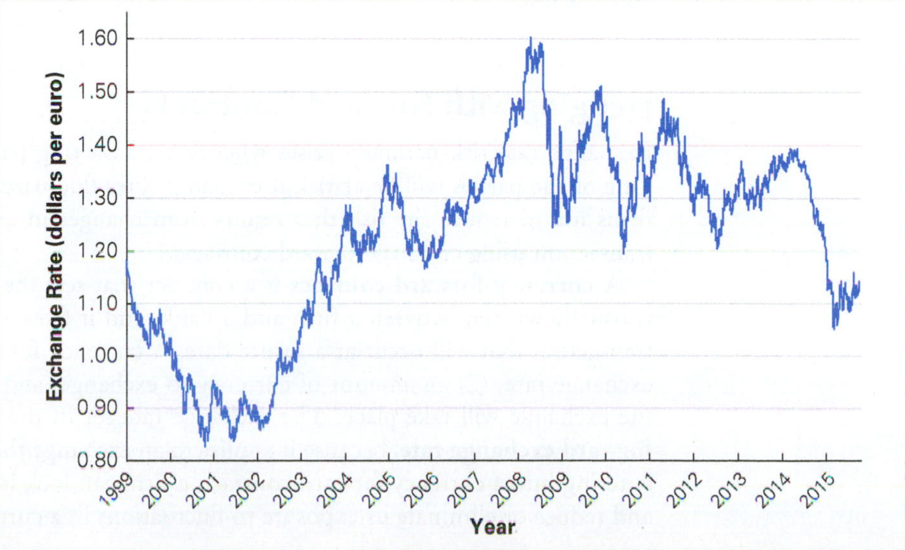

through October 2015. Notice that the price of the euro often varies by as much as 20% over periods as short as a few months. From its low in 2000 to the summer of 2008, the value of the euro nearly doubled relative to the dollar, only to fall by close to 20% between August and October 2008 in the wake of the financial crisis, and again in 2014 in response to continued instability in the eurozone.

Fluctuating exchange rates cause a problem, known as the *importer–exporter dilemma*, for firms doing business in international markets. To illustrate, consider the problem faced by Manzini Cyclery, a small U.S. maker of custom bicycles. Manzini needs to import parts from an Italian supplier, Campagnolo. If Campagnolo sets the price of its parts in euros, then Manzini faces the risk that the dollar may fall, making euros, and therefore the parts, more expensive. If Campagnolo sets its prices in dollars, then Campagnolo faces the risk that the dollar may fall and it will receive fewer euros for the parts it sells to the U.S. manufacturer.

The problem of exchange rate risk is a general problem in any import–export relationship. If neither company will accept the exchange rate risk, the transaction may be difficult or impossible to negotiate. Example 30.5 demonstrates the potential magnitude of the problem.

EXAMPLE 30.5 **The Effect of Exchange Rate Risk**

Problem

In December 2002, when the exchange rate was \$1 per euro, Manzini ordered parts for next year's production from Campagnolo. They agreed to a price of 500,000 euros, to be paid when the parts were delivered in one year's time. One year later, the exchange rate was \$1.22 per euro. What was the actual cost in dollars for Manzini when the payment was due? If the price had instead been set at \$500,000 (which had equivalent value at the time of the agreement), how many euros would Campagnolo have received?

Solution

With the price set at 500,000 euros, Manzini had to pay (\$1.22/euro) × (500,000 euros) = \$610,000. This cost is \$110,000, or 22% higher than it would have been if the price had been set in dollars.

If the price had been set in dollars, Manzini would have paid \$500,000, which would have been worth only \$500,000 ÷ (\$1.22/euro) = 409,836 euros to Campagnolo, or more than 18% less. Whether the price was set in euros or dollars, one of the parties would have suffered a substantial loss.

Hedging with Forward Contracts

Exchange rate risk naturally arises whenever transacting parties use different currencies: One of the parties will be at risk if exchange rates fluctuate. The most common method firms use to reduce the risk that results from changes in exchange rates is to hedge the transaction using currency forward contracts.

A **currency forward contract** is a contract that sets the exchange rate in advance. It is usually written between a firm and a bank, and it fixes a currency exchange rate for a transaction that will occur at a future date. A currency forward contract specifies (1) an exchange rate, (2) an amount of currency to exchange, and (3) a delivery date on which the exchange will take place. The exchange rate set in the contract is referred to as the **forward exchange rate**, because it applies to an exchange that will occur in the future. By entering into a currency forward contract, a firm can lock in an exchange rate in advance and reduce or eliminate its exposure to fluctuations in a currency's value.

EXAMPLE 30.6 Using a Forward Contract to Lock In an Exchange Rate

Problem

In December 2002, banks were offering one-year currency forward contracts with a forward exchange rate of \$0.987/€. Suppose that at that time, Manzini placed the order with Campagnolo with a price of 500,000 euros and simultaneously entered into a forward contract to purchase 500,000 euros at a forward exchange rate of \$0.987/€ in December 2003. What payment would Manzini be required to make in December 2003?

Solution

Even though the exchange rate rose to \$1.22/€ in December 2003, making the euro more expensive, Manzini would obtain the 500,000 euros using the forward contract at the forward exchange rate of \$0.987/€. Thus, Manzini must pay

$$500{,}000 \text{ euros} \times \$0.987/€ = \$493{,}500 \text{ in December 2003}$$

Manzini would pay this amount to the bank in exchange for 500,000 euros, which are then paid to Campagnolo.

This forward contract would have been a good deal for Manzini because without the hedge, it would have had to exchange dollars for euros at the prevailing rate of \$1.22/€, raising its cost to \$610,000. However, the exchange rate could have moved the other way. If the exchange rate had fallen to \$0.85/€, the forward contract still commits Manzini to pay \$0.987/€. In other words, the forward contract locks in the exchange rate and eliminates the risk—whether the movement of the exchange rate is favorable or unfavorable.

If the forward contract allows the importer to eliminate the risk of a stronger euro, where does the risk go? At least initially, the risk passes to the bank that has written the forward contract. Because the bank agrees to exchange dollars for euros at a fixed rate, it will experience a loss if the euro increases in value. In Example 30.6, the bank receives only \$493,500 in the forward contract, but gives up euros that are worth \$610,000.

Why is the bank willing to bear this risk? First, generally the bank is much larger and has more capital than a small importer, so it can bear the risk without being in jeopardy of financial distress. More importantly, in most settings the bank will not even hold the risk. Instead, the bank will find another party willing to trade euros for dollars. By entering into a second forward contract with offsetting risk, the bank can eliminate its risk altogether.

This situation is illustrated in Figure 30.4. A U.S. importer, who must pay for goods with euros, purchases euros from the bank through a forward contract with a forward exchange rate of \$0.987 per euro. This transaction locks in the importer's cost at \$493,500. Similarly, a U.S. exporter, who will receive payment in euros, uses a forward contract to sell the euros to the bank, locking in the exporter's revenue at \$493,500. The bank holds both forward contracts—the first to exchange dollars for euros and the second to exchange euros for dollars. The bank bears no exchange rate risk and earns fees from both the exporter and the importer.

Cash-and-Carry and the Pricing of Currency Forwards

An alternative method, the cash-and-carry strategy, also enables a firm or bank to eliminate exchange rate risk. Because this strategy provides the same cash flows as the forward contract, we can use it to determine the forward exchange rate using the Law of One Price. Let's begin by considering the different ways investors can exchange foreign currency in the future for dollars in the future.

FIGURE 30.4

The Use of Currency Forwards to Eliminate Exchange Rate Risk

In this example, the U.S. importer and the U.S. exporter both hedge their exchange rate risk by using currency-forward contracts (shown in blue). By writing offsetting contracts, the bank bears no exchange rate risk and earns a fee from each transaction.

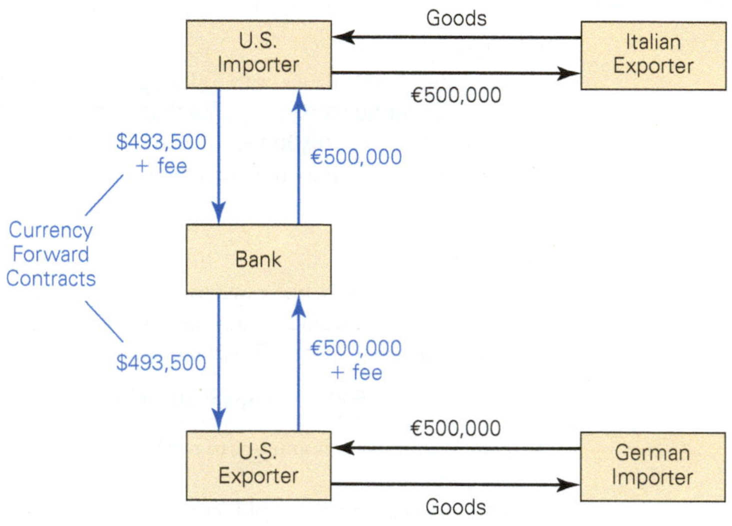

The Law of One Price and the Forward Exchange Rate. Currency forward contracts allow investors to exchange a foreign currency in the future for dollars in the future at the forward exchange rate. We illustrate such an exchange in the **currency timeline** in Figure 30.5, which indicates time horizontally by dates (as in a standard timeline) and currencies vertically (dollars and euros). Thus, "dollars in one year" corresponds to the upper-right point in the timeline and "euros in one year" corresponds to the lower-right point in the timeline. To convert cash flows between points, we must convert them at an appropriate rate. The forward exchange rate, indicated by $F\$/€$, tells us the rate at which we can exchange euros for dollars in one year using a forward contract.

Figure 30.5 also illustrates other transactions that we can use to move between dates or currencies in the timeline. We can convert euros to dollars today at the current exchange rate, also referred to as the **spot exchange rate**, $S\$/€$. By borrowing or lending at the dollar interest rate $r_\$$, we can exchange dollars today for dollars in one year. Finally, we can convert euros today for euros in one year at the euro interest rate $r_€$, which is the rate at which banks will borrow or lend on euro-denominated accounts.

FIGURE 30.5

Currency Timeline Showing Forward Contract and Cash-and-Carry Strategy

The cash-and-carry strategy (three transactions in red) replicates the forward contract (in blue) by borrowing in one currency, converting to the other currency at the spot exchange rate, and investing in the new currency.

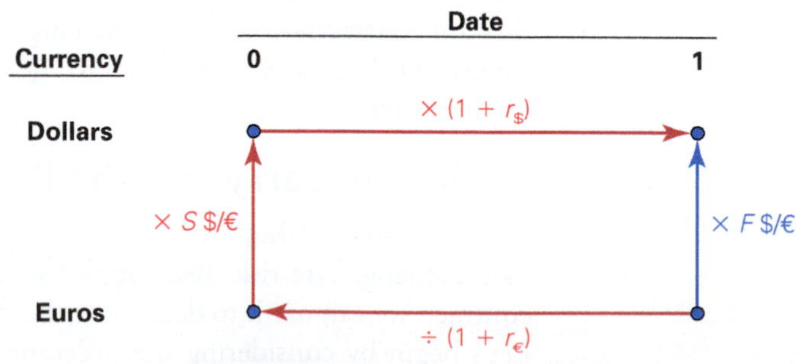

As Figure 30.5 shows, combining these other transactions provides an alternative way to convert euros to dollars in one year. The **cash-and-carry strategy** consists of the following three simultaneous trades:

1. Borrow euros today using a one-year loan with the interest rate $r_€$.
2. Exchange the euros for dollars today at the spot exchange rate S \$/€.
3. Invest the dollars today for one year at the interest rate $r_\$$.

In one year's time, we will owe euros (from the loan in transaction 1) and receive dollars (from the investment in transaction 3). That is, we have converted euros in one year to dollars in one year, just as with the forward contract. This method is called a cash-and-carry strategy because we borrow cash that we then carry (invest) in the future.

GLOBAL FINANCIAL CRISIS Arbitrage in Currency Markets?

Currency markets are amongst the largest and most liquid markets in the world. Consequently, they are one of the last places we would expect to find arbitrage opportunities. Yet, for a short time during the 2008 financial crisis there were arbitrage opportunities in these markets when the cash-and-carry strategy and the forward exchange rate did not provide the same rate of exchange in the forward market. The figure below shows the profits per dollar from borrowing for one month in dollars, converting the proceeds into euros at the spot exchange rate, investing for one month in euros, and simultaneously entering into a forward contract to convert euros back to dollars in a month. Prior to the 2008 crisis, the strategy did not make economically meaningful profits, but during the crisis the strategy appears to have been quite profitable—at the peak generating about \$0.25 for each borrowed dollar.

What explains these apparent profits? One possibility is the risk of default. The arbitrage requires borrowing and lending, and during the crisis the risk of default was perceived to be very high. In addition, there is also counter-party risk—the entity on the other side of the forward contract might default on their obligation. Because of the heightened uncertainty during the crisis, investors might very well have viewed this one-month commitment as risky. Hence, the strategy was not really risk free—these "profits" were at least in part compensation for this risk. Finally, Professors Loriano Mancini, Angelo Ranaldo, and Jan Wrampelmeyer* provide evidence that liquidity might also have been a contributing factor. U.S. short-term credit markets (including even overnight markets) froze during the crisis, so banks and other traders might have had difficulty taking advantage of the apparent arbitrage opportunity because borrowing dollars was very difficult. In other words, during the financial crisis the natural arbitrageurs in these markets were themselves capital constrained!

*"Liquidity in the Foreign Exchange Market: Measurement, Commonality, and Risk Premiums," *Journal of Finance* 68 (2012): 1805–1841.

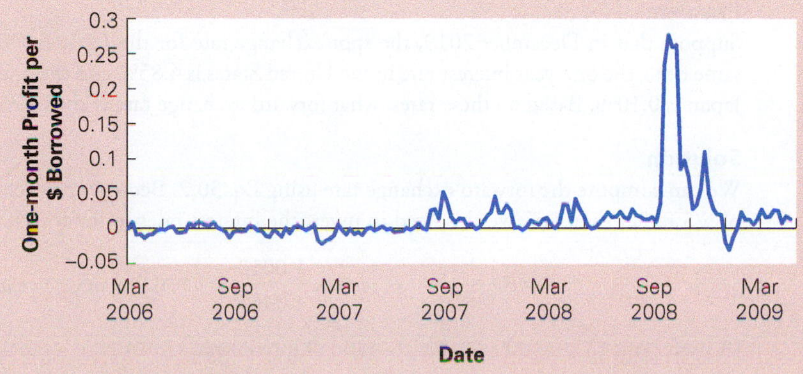

Source: Adapted from T. Griffoli and A. Ranaldo, "Deviations from covered interest parity during the crisis; a story of funding liquidity constraints," Swiss National Bank, 2009.

Because the forward contract and the cash-and-carry strategy accomplish the same conversion, by the Law of One Price they must do so at the same rate. Combining the rates used in the cash-and-carry strategy leads to the following no-arbitrage formula for the forward exchange rate:

Covered Interest Parity

$$\underbrace{F}_{\frac{\$\text{ in one year}}{€\text{ in one year}}} = \underbrace{S}_{\frac{\$\text{ today}}{€\text{ today}}} \times \underbrace{\frac{1 + r_\$}{1 + r_€}}_{\frac{\$\text{ in one year}/\$\text{ today}}{€\text{ in one year}/€\text{ today}}} \tag{30.2}$$

Equation 30.2 expresses the forward exchange rate in terms of the spot exchange rate and the interest rates in each currency. Note that on both sides of the equation, the ultimate units are \$/€ in one year.

Let's evaluate Eq. 30.2 in an example. In December 2002, the spot exchange rate was \$1/€, while one-year interest rates were 1.66% for dollars and 3% for euros. From Eq. 30.2, the no-arbitrage forward exchange rate in December 2002 for an exchange to take place one year later was

$$F = S \times \frac{1 + r_\$}{1 + r_€} = (\$1/€) \times \frac{1.0166}{1.0300} = \$0.987/€$$

which is the rate offered by the bank in Example 30.6.

Equation 30.2 is referred to as the **covered interest parity equation**; it states that the difference between the forward and spot exchange rates is related to the interest rate differential between the currencies. When the interest rate differs across countries, investors have an incentive to borrow in the low-interest rate currency and invest in the high-interest rate currency. Of course, there is always the risk that the high-interest rate currency could depreciate while the investment is held. If you try to avoid this risk by locking in the future exchange rate using a forward contract, Eq. 30.2 implies that the forward exchange rate will exactly offset any benefit from the higher interest rate, eliminating any arbitrage opportunity.

EXAMPLE 30.7 Computing the No-Arbitrage Forward Exchange Rate

Problem

Suppose that in December 2019, the spot exchange rate for the Japanese yen is ¥116/\$. At the same time, the one-year interest rate in the United States is 4.85% and the one-year interest rate in Japan is 0.10%. Based on these rates, what forward exchange rate is consistent with no arbitrage?

Solution

We can compute the forward exchange rate using Eq. 30.2. Because the exchange rate is in terms of ¥/\$ rather than \$/¥, we also need to invert the interest rates in the formula:

$$F = S\frac{1 + r_¥}{1 + r_\$} = ¥116/\$ \times \frac{1.0010}{1.0485} = ¥110.7/\$ \text{ in one year}$$

(A useful rule to remember is that the ratio of interest rates must match the units of the exchange rate. Because the exchange rate is ¥/\$, we multiply by the yen interest rate and divide by the dollar interest rate. Of course, we could also solve the problem by converting all the rates to \$/¥.) The forward exchange rate is lower than the spot exchange rate, offsetting the higher interest rate on dollar investments.

Advantages of Forward Contracts. Why do firms use forward contracts rather than the cash-and-carry strategy? First, the forward contract is simpler, requiring one transaction rather than three, so it may have lower transaction fees. Second, many firms are not able to borrow easily in different currencies and may pay a higher interest rate if their credit quality is poor. Generally speaking, cash-and-carry strategies are used primarily by large banks, which can borrow most easily and face the lowest transaction costs. Banks use such a strategy to hedge their currency exposures that result from commitments to forward contracts.

EXAMPLE 30.8 **Using the Cash-and-Carry Strategy**

Problem

In December 2019, a Japanese bank enters into a forward contract with Japanese exporter Shimano, in which Shimano agrees to exchange \$100 million for yen in December 2020 at the forward exchange rate of ¥110.7/\$. If the current exchange rate is ¥116/\$, and one-year interest rates are 4.85% in the United States and 0.10% in Japan, how can the bank hedge its risk if it has no other clients interested in currency forward contracts?

Solution

The forward contract specifies that Shimano will pay \$100 million to the bank in exchange for \$100 million × ¥110.7/\$ = 11.07 billion yen. To hedge its risk, the bank may find another client or clients who would like to exchange yen for dollars. When no such clients can be found, the bank can still hedge its risk using a cash-and-carry strategy:

1. Borrow dollars today at the dollar interest rate of 4.85%. The bank can borrow \$100 million/1.0485 = \$95.37 million today and repay the loan using the cash received from Shimano.
2. Convert dollars to yen at the spot exchange rate of ¥116/\$. The bank can convert the dollars borrowed to \$95.37 million × ¥116/\$ = ¥11.06 billion.
3. Invest the yen today at the yen interest rate of 0.10%. By depositing the yen for one year, the bank will have 11.06 billion × 1.001 = ¥11.07 billion in one year.

Through this combination of transactions, the bank can lock in its ability to convert dollars to yen at the rate agreed upon in the forward contract with Shimano.

Equation 30.2 easily generalizes to a forward contract longer than one year. Using the same logic, but investing or borrowing for T years rather than one year, the no-arbitrage forward rate for an exchange that will occur T years in the future is

$$F_T = S \times \frac{(1 + r_{\$})^T}{(1 + r_{€})^T} \tag{30.3}$$

where the spot and forward rates are in units of \$/€ and the interest rates are the current risk-free T-year rates from the yield curve for each currency.

Hedging with Options

Currency options are another method that firms commonly use to manage exchange rate risk. Currency options, like the stock options introduced in Chapter 20, give the holder the right—but not the obligation—to exchange currency at a given exchange rate. Currency forward contracts allow firms to lock in a future exchange rate; currency options allow firms to insure themselves against the exchange rate moving beyond a certain level.

TABLE 30.2 **Cost of Euros ($/€) When Hedging with a Currency Option with a Strike Price of $1.20/€ and an Initial Premium of $0.05/€**

Dec. 2006 Spot Exchange Rate	Exercise Option?	Exchange Rate Taken	+	Cost of Option	=	Total Cost
1.00	No	1.00		0.05		1.05
1.15	No	1.15		0.05		1.20
1.30	Yes	1.20		0.05		1.25
1.45	Yes	1.20		0.05		1.25

To demonstrate the difference between hedging with forward contracts and hedging with options, let's examine a specific situation. In December 2005, the one-year forward exchange rate was $1.20 per euro. Instead of locking in this exchange rate using a forward contract, a firm that will need euros in one year can buy a call option on the euro, giving it the right to buy euros at a maximum price.[15] Suppose a one-year European call option on the euro with a strike price of $1.20 per euro trades for $0.05 per euro. That is, for a cost of $0.05 per euro, the firm can buy the right—but not the obligation—to purchase euros for $1.20 per euro in one year's time. By doing so, the firm protects itself against a large increase in the value of the euro, but still benefits if the euro declines.

Table 30.2 shows the outcome from hedging with a call option if the actual exchange rate in one year is one of the values listed in the first column. If the spot exchange rate is less than the $1.20 per euro strike price of the option, the firm will not exercise the option and will convert dollars to euros at the spot exchange rate. If the spot exchange rate is more than $1.20 per euro, the firm will exercise the option and convert dollars to euros at the rate of $1.20 per euro (see the second and third columns). We then add the initial cost of the option (fourth column) to determine the total dollar cost per euro paid by the firm (fifth column).[16]

FIGURE 30.6

Comparison of Hedging the Exchange Rate Using a Forward Contract, an Option, or No Hedge

The forward hedge locks in an exchange rate and thus eliminates all risk. Not hedging leaves the firm fully exposed. Hedging with an option allows the firm to benefit if the exchange rate falls and protects the firm from a very large increase.

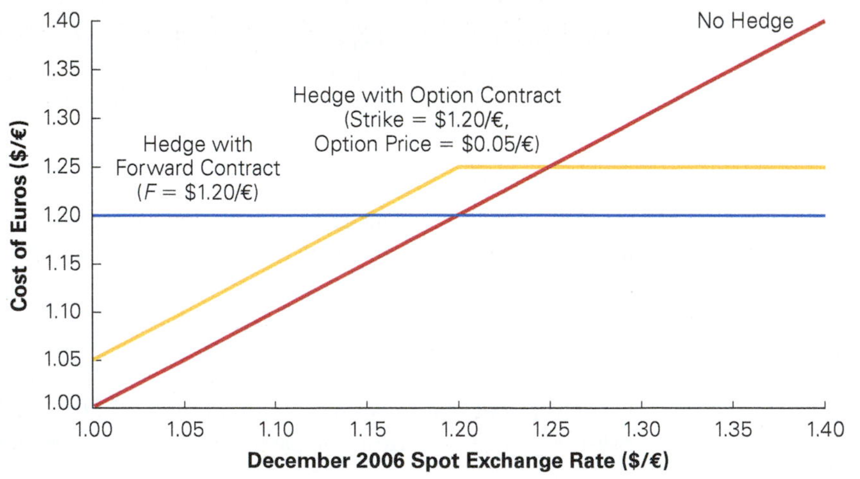

---

[15]Currency options can be purchased over the counter from a bank or on an exchange. The Philadelphia Stock Exchange (PHLX, now part of NASDAQ OMX) is one exchange offering currency options.

[16]In computing the total cost, we have ignored the small amount of interest that could be earned on the option premium.

We plot the data from Table 30.2 in Figure 30.6, where we compare hedging with options to the alternative of hedging with a forward contract or not hedging at all. If the firm does not hedge at all, its cost for euros is simply the spot exchange rate. If the firm hedges with a forward contract, it locks in the cost of euros at the forward exchange rate and the firm's cost is fixed. As Figure 30.6 shows, hedging with options represents a middle ground: The firm puts a *cap* on its potential cost, but will benefit if the euro depreciates in value. (In this case, the actual exchange rate turned out to be $1.30/€ in December 2006, for a total cost of $1.25.)

Options Versus Forward Contracts. Why might a firm choose to hedge with options rather than forward contracts? Many managers want the firm to benefit if the exchange rate moves in their favor, rather than being stuck paying an above-market rate. Firms also prefer options to forward contracts if the transaction they are hedging might not take place. In this case, a forward contract could commit them to making an exchange at an unfavorable rate for currency they do not need, whereas an option allows them to walk away from the exchange.

EXAMPLE 30.9 Using Options to Hedge a Conditional Exposure

Problem

ICTV is a U.S. company that develops software for cable television networks. Executives at ICTV have just negotiated a £20 million deal with British cable operator Telewest. ICTV will receive the payment in six months' time, after ICTV demonstrates a prototype proving the viability of its technology. If Telewest is not satisfied with the technology, it can cancel the contract at that time and pay nothing. ICTV executives have two major concerns: (1) their engineers may not be able to meet Telewest's technology requirements and (2) even if the deal succeeds, the British pound may fall, reducing the dollar value of the £20 million payment.

Suppose the current exchange rate is $1.752/£, the six-month forward exchange rate is $1.75/£, and a six-month put option on the British pound with a strike price of $1.75/£ is trading for $0.05/£. Compare ICTV's outcomes if it does not hedge, hedges using a forward contract, or hedges using the put option.

Solution

First, let's plot ICTV's revenue if it chooses not to hedge (the red lines in the plot):

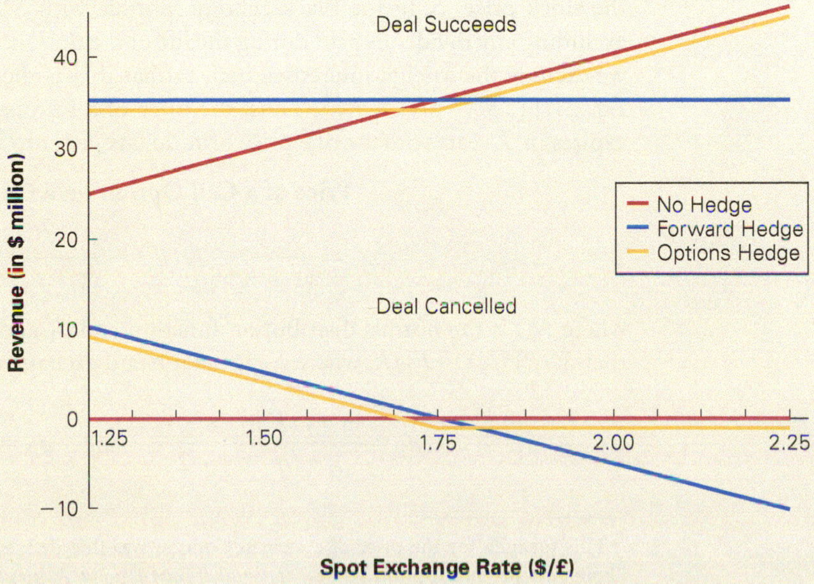

Suppose ICTV does not hedge, and the British pound falls to \$1.50/£. Then, ICTV's dollar revenue from the deal will be only £20 million × \$1.50/£ = \$30 million. However, if ICTV hedges the £20 million payment using a forward contract, it will be guaranteed revenue of £20 million × \$1.75/£ = \$35 million if the deal succeeds (the upper blue line). But if Telewest cancels the deal, ICTV will still be obligated by the forward contract to pay the bank £20 million in exchange for \$35 million. If the spot exchange rate rises to \$2.00/£, then the £20 million will be worth £20 million × \$2.00/£ = \$40 million, and ICTV will have a loss of 40 − 35 = \$5 million on its forward contract (see the lower blue line).

Thus, if ICTV does not hedge or hedges with a forward contract, there are scenarios that lead to large losses. Now consider hedging with the put option. The upfront cost of the put option is £20 million × \$0.05/£ = \$1 million, and the results of this hedge are plotted as the yellow curves. For example, if the deal succeeds and the pound falls below \$1.75/£, ICTV can exercise the put and receive, net of the cost of the put,

£20 million × \$1.75/£ − \$1 million = \$35 million − \$1 million = \$34 million

(We have ignored the small amount of interest on the cost of the put over six months.) If Telewest cancels the deal and the spot exchange rate rises, ICTV will lose the \$1 million cost of the put. In either case, Telewest has limited its potential losses.

Currency Option Pricing. In the preceding example, we assumed that ICTV could purchase a currency option at a price of \$0.05/£. But how do we determine the price of a currency option? Just as we determined the forward exchange rate by assessing banks' ability to replicate a forward contract using a cash-and-carry strategy, the prices of currency options are determined by identifying banks' ability to replicate them using dynamic trading strategies of the type introduced in Chapter 21 for stock options. In fact, we can apply the same pricing methodologies discussed in Chapter 21, such as the Black-Scholes formula or the binomial model, to currency options. In this case, the underlying asset is the currency, so we use the spot exchange rate in place of the stock price. The foreign interest rate you earn while holding the currency is analogous to the dividend yield for a stock.

Recall that to price a European option on a dividend-paying stock, you simply replace the stock price, S, in the Black-Scholes formula with S^x, the current value of the stock excluding any dividends paid during the life of the option. In the case of a currency option, we exclude the foreign interest earned, so that if $r_€$ is the foreign interest rate, then from Eq. 21.11, $S^x = S/(1 + r_€)^T$. Thus, the price of a European call option on the euro that expires in T years with a strike price of K dollars per euro is[17]

Price of a Call Option on a Currency

$$C = \frac{S}{(1 + r_€)^T} N(d_1) - \frac{K}{(1 + r_\$)^T} N(d_2) \tag{30.4}$$

where $N()$ is the normal distribution function and d_1 and d_2 are calculated using the fact that $S^x/PV(K) = F_T/K$, where F_T is the forward exchange rate from Eq. 30.3:

$$d_1 = \frac{\ln(F_T/K)}{\sigma\sqrt{T}} + \frac{\sigma\sqrt{T}}{2} \quad \text{and} \quad d_2 = d_1 - \sigma\sqrt{T} \tag{30.5}$$

[17]This formula for the price of a currency option was first derived by M. Garman and S. Kohlhagen, "Foreign-Currency Option Values," *Journal of International Money and Finance* 2 (1983): 231–237.

We can also use option pricing techniques to estimate the implied volatility of the exchange rate.

EXAMPLE 30.10 **Implied Volatility of Exchange Rates**

Problem

Suppose the current exchange rate is \$1.752/£, the interest rate in the United States is 4.25%, the interest rate in the United Kingdom is 4.5%, and a six-month European call option on the British pound with a strike price of \$1.75/£ trades for a price of \$0.05/£. Use the Black-Scholes formula to determine the implied volatility of the \$/£ exchange rate.

Solution

We can use Eq. 30.4 and Eq. 30.5 to compute the Black-Scholes price of a call option on the British pound. The inputs are S = spot exchange rate = 1.752, $K = 1.75$, $T = 0.5$, $r_\$ = 4.25\%$, and the U.K. interest rate $r_£ = 4.5\%$. The forward exchange rate is $F_{0.5} = 1.752 \times (1.0425)^{1/2}/(1.045)^{1/2} = 1.75$. With a volatility of 10%, we have $d_1 = 0.035$ and $d_2 = -0.035$, with $N(d_1) = 0.514$ and $N(d_2) = 0.486$, so the Black-Scholes value of the call is \$.048/£. With a volatility of 11%, the Black-Scholes value is \$.055/£. Thus, the implied volatility of the \$/£ exchange rate is between 10% and 11% per year.

CONCEPT CHECK

1. How can firms hedge exchange rate risk?
2. Why may a firm prefer to hedge exchange rate risk with options rather than forward contracts?

30.4 Interest Rate Risk

Firms that borrow must pay interest on their debt. An increase in interest rates raises firms' borrowing costs and can reduce their profitability. In addition, many firms have fixed long-term future liabilities, such as capital leases or pension fund liabilities. A decrease in interest rates raises the present value of these liabilities and can lower the value of the firm. Thus, when interest rates are volatile, interest rate risk is a concern for many firms.

In this chapter, we have considered several methods that firms use to manage interest rate risk. Before firms can manage it, however, they must be able to measure it. Thus, we begin by discussing the primary tool used to measure interest rate risk, duration. We will then see how firms can use *duration-hedging* to minimize their interest rate risk.

Interest Rate Risk Measurement: Duration

In Chapter 6, we informally introduced the notion of a bond's duration as a measure of its sensitivity to interest rate changes. There, we saw that the sensitivity of zero-coupon bonds to interest rates increases with their maturity. For example, for a 10-year, zero-coupon bond, an increase of one percentage point in the yield to maturity from 5% to 6% causes the bond price per \$100 face value to fall from

$$\frac{100}{1.05^{10}} = \$61.39 \quad \text{to} \quad \frac{100}{1.06^{10}} = \$55.84$$

or a price change of (55.84 − 61.39)/61.39 = −9%. The price of a five-year bond drops only 4.6% for the same yield change. The interest rate sensitivity of a *single* cash flow is roughly proportional to its maturity. The farther away the cash flow is, the larger the effect of interest rate changes on its present value.

Now consider a bond or portfolio with *multiple* cash flows. How will its value change if interest rates rise? As we saw in Chapter 11, the return of a portfolio is the value-weighted average of the returns of the elements of the portfolio. Because the interest rate sensitivity of a cash flow depends on its maturity, the interest rate sensitivity of a security with multiple cash flows depends on their value-weighted maturity. Thus, we formally define a security's duration as follows:[18]

Duration of a Security

$$\text{Duration} = \sum_t \frac{PV(C_t)}{P} \times t \tag{30.6}$$

where C_t is the cash flow on date t, $PV(C_t)$ is its present value (evaluated at the bond's yield), and $P = \sum_t PV(C_t)$ is the total present value of the cash flows, which is equal to the bond's current price. Therefore, the duration weights each maturity t by the percentage contribution of its cash flow to the total present value, $PV(C_t)/P$.

EXAMPLE 30.11 The Duration of a Coupon Bond

Problem

What is the duration of a 10-year, zero-coupon bond? What is the duration of a 10-year bond with 10% annual coupons trading at par?

Solution

For a zero-coupon bond, there is only a single cash flow. Thus, in Eq. 30.6, $PV(C_{10}) = P$ and the duration is equal to the bond's maturity of 10 years.

For the coupon bond, because the bond trades at par, its yield to maturity equals its 10% coupon rate. Table 30.3 shows the calculation of the duration of the bond using Eq. 30.6.

Note that, because the bond pays coupons prior to maturity, its duration is shorter than its 10-year maturity. Moreover, the higher the coupon rate, the more weight is put on these earlier cash flows, shortening the duration of the bond.

TABLE 30.3 Computing the Duration of a Coupon Bond

t(years)	C_t	$PV(C_t)$	$PV(C_t)/P$	$[PV(C_t)/P] \times t$
1	10	9.09	9.09%	0.09
2	10	8.26	8.26%	0.17
3	10	7.51	7.51%	0.23
4	10	6.83	6.83%	0.27
5	10	6.21	6.21%	0.31
6	10	5.64	5.64%	0.34
7	10	5.13	5.13%	0.36
8	10	4.67	4.67%	0.37
9	10	4.24	4.24%	0.38
10	110	42.41	42.41%	4.24
		Bond price = 100.00	100.00%	Duration = 6.76 yrs

[18]This measure is also called the Macaulay duration.

Just as the interest rate sensitivity of a single cash flow increases with its maturity, the interest rate sensitivity of a stream of cash flows increases with its duration, as shown by the following result:

Duration and Interest Rate Sensitivity: *If r, the APR used to discount a stream of cash flows, increases to $r + \varepsilon$, where ε is a small change, then the present value of the cash flows changes by approximately*[19]

$$\text{Percent Change in Value} \approx -\text{Duration} \times \frac{\varepsilon}{1 + r/k} \tag{30.7}$$

where k is the number of compounding periods per year of the APR.

EXAMPLE 30.12 **Estimating Interest Rate Sensitivity Using Duration**

Problem

Suppose the yield of a 10-year bond with 10% annual coupons increases from 10% to 10.25%. Use duration to estimate the percentage price change. How does it compare to the actual price change?

Solution

In Example 30.11, we found that the duration of the bond is 6.76 years. We can use Eq. 30.7 to estimate the percentage price change:

$$\%\text{Price Change} \approx -6.76 \times \frac{0.25\%}{1.10} = -1.54\%$$

Indeed, calculating the bond's price with a 10.25% yield to maturity, we get

$$10 \times \frac{1}{0.1025}\left(1 - \frac{1}{(1.1025)^{10}}\right) + \frac{100}{(1.1025)^{10}} = \$98.48$$

which represents a 1.52% price drop.

As we see, we can use duration to measure the interest rate sensitivity of a security or a portfolio. We now consider ways firms can hedge this risk.

Duration-Based Hedging

A firm's market capitalization is determined by the difference in the market value of its assets and its liabilities. If changes in interest rates affect these values, they will affect the firm's equity value. We can measure a firm's sensitivity to interest rates by computing the duration of its balance sheet. Moreover, by restructuring the balance sheet to reduce its duration, we can hedge the firm's interest rate risk.

---

[19] The term Duration/$(1 + r/k)$ is called the *modified duration.* Thus, Eq. 30.7 can also be written as

$$\%\text{ change in value} \approx -(\text{Modified Duration}) \times \varepsilon$$

To see how Eq. 30.7 is derived, note that the approximate price change for a small change in r is equal to the derivative of the price with respect to r:

$$\partial P / \partial r = \sum_t \frac{\partial}{\partial r}\left(\frac{C_t}{(1 + r/k)^{kt}}\right) = \sum_t -\left(\frac{C_t}{(1 + r/k)^{kt+1}}\right)t = -\frac{1}{1 + r/k}\sum_t - PV(C_t)^t$$

Equation 30.7 follows by dividing by P to express the price change in percentage terms.

Savings and Loans: An Example. Consider a typical savings and loan (S&L). These institutions hold short-term deposits, in the form of checking and savings accounts, as well as certificates of deposit. They also make long-term loans such as car loans and home mortgages. Most S&Ls face a problem because the duration of the loans they make is generally longer than the duration of their deposits. When the durations of a firm's assets and liabilities are significantly different, the firm has a **duration mismatch**. This mismatch puts the S&L at risk if interest rates change significantly.

As an example, Table 30.4 provides the market-value balance sheet for Acorn Savings and Loan, listing the market value and duration of each asset and liability. What is the combined duration of Acorn's assets and liabilities? The duration of a portfolio of investments is the value-weighted average of the durations of each investment in the portfolio. That is, a portfolio of securities with market values A and B and durations D_A and D_B, respectively, has the following duration:

Duration of a Portfolio

$$D_{A+B} = \frac{A}{A+B} D_A + \frac{B}{A+B} D_B \tag{30.8}$$

Therefore, the duration of Acorn's assets is

$$D_A = \frac{10}{300} \times 0 + \frac{120}{300} \times 2 + \frac{170}{300} \times 8 = 5.33 \text{ years}$$

Similarly, the duration of Acorn's liabilities is

$$D_L = \frac{120}{285} \times 0 + \frac{90}{285} \times 1 + \frac{75}{285} \times 12 = 3.47 \text{ years}$$

Note the mismatch between Acorn's assets and liabilities. Given their long duration, if interest rates rise, Acorn's assets will fall in value much faster than its liabilities. As a result, the value of equity, which is the difference between assets and liabilities, may drop significantly with a rise in interest rates.

In fact, we can calculate the duration of Acorn's equity by expressing it as a portfolio that is long the assets and short the liabilities:

$$\text{Equity} = \text{Assets} - \text{Liabilities}$$

TABLE 30.4 **Market-Value Balance Sheet for Acorn Savings and Loan**

	Market Value (in $ million)	Duration (years)
Assets		
Cash Reserves	10	0
Auto Loans	120	2
Mortgages	170	8
Total Assets	300	
Liabilities		
Checking and Savings	120	0
Certificates of Deposit	90	1
Long-Term Financing	75	12
Total Liabilities	285	
Owner's Equity	15	
Total Liabilities and Equity	300	

We can then apply Eq. 30.8 to compute the duration of equity:

Equity Duration

$$D_E = D_{A-L} = \frac{A}{A-L}D_A - \frac{L}{A-L}D_L$$
$$= \frac{300}{15} \times 5.33 - \frac{285}{15} \times 3.47 = 40.67 \text{ years} \tag{30.9}$$

Therefore, if interest rates rise by 1%, the value of Acorn's equity will fall by about 40%. This decline in the value of equity will occur as a result of the value of Acorn's assets decreasing by approximately 5.33% × 300 = \$16 million, while the value of its liabilities decrease by only 3.47% × 285 = \$9.9 million. Acorn's market value of equity therefore declines by about 16 − 9.9 = \$6.1 million or (6.1/15) = 40.67%.

How can Acorn reduce its sensitivity to interest rates? To fully protect its equity from an overall increase or decrease in the level of interest rates, Acorn needs an equity duration of zero. A portfolio with a zero duration is called a **duration-neutral portfolio** or an **immunized portfolio**, which means that for small interest rate fluctuations, the value of equity should remain unchanged.

To make its equity duration neutral, Acorn must reduce the duration of its assets or increase the duration of its liabilities. The firm can lower the duration of its assets by selling some of its mortgages in exchange for cash. We compute the amount to sell from the following formula:[20]

$$\text{Amount to Exchange} = \frac{\text{Change in Portfolio Duration} \times \text{Portfolio Value}}{\text{Change in Asset Duration}} \tag{30.10}$$

To reduce its risk from interest rate fluctuations, Acorn would like to reduce the duration of its equity from 40.7 to 0. Because the duration of the mortgages will change from 8 to 0 if the S&L sells the mortgages for cash, Eq. 30.10 implies that Acorn must sell (40.7 − 0) × 15/(8 − 0) = \$76.3 million worth of mortgages. If it does so, the duration of its assets will decline to

$$\overbrace{\frac{10 + 76.3}{300}}^{\text{Increased cash balance}} \times 0 + \frac{120}{300} \times 2 + \overbrace{\frac{170 - 76.3}{300}}^{\text{Decreased mortgage holdings}} \times 8 = 3.30 \text{ years}$$

Thus, its equity duration will fall to $\frac{300}{15} \times 3.30 - \frac{285}{15} \times 3.47 = 0$, as desired.

Adjusting a portfolio to make its duration neutral is sometimes referred to as **immunizing** the portfolio, a term that indicates it is being protected against interest rate changes. Table 30.5 shows Acorn's market-value balance sheet after immunization. Note that the duration of equity is now zero.

A Cautionary Note. While duration matching is a useful method of interest rate risk management, it has some important limitations. First, the duration of a portfolio depends on the current interest rate. As interest rates change, the market values of the

[20] To derive Eq. 30.10, let P be the value of the original portfolio and S be the amount of assets sold, and let D_P and D_S be their respective durations. Let D_B be the duration of the new assets bought. Then, new portfolio duration D_P^* is

$$D_P^* = \frac{P}{P}D_P + \frac{S}{P}D_B - \frac{S}{P}D_S$$

Solving for S leads to $S = (D_P - D_P^*)P/(D_S - D_B)$.

TABLE 30.5 **Market-Value Balance Sheet for Acorn Savings and Loan After Immunization**

	Market Value (in $ million)	Duration (years)
Assets		
Cash Reserves	86.3	0
Auto Loans	120	2
Mortgages	93.7	8
Total Assets	300	3.30
Liabilities		
Checking and Savings	120	0
Certificates of Deposit	90	1
Long-Term Financing	75	12
Total Liabilities	285	3.47
Owner's Equity	15	0
Total Liabilities and Equity	300	3.30

securities and cash flows in the portfolio change as well, which in turn alters the weights used when computing the duration as the value-weighted average maturity. Hence, maintaining a duration-neutral portfolio will require constant adjustment as interest rates change.[21]

The second important limitation is that a duration-neutral portfolio is only protected against interest rate changes that affect *all yields identically*. In other words, it offers protection in the case of parallel up or down movements in the yield curve. If short-term interest rates were to rise while long-term rates remained stable, then short-term securities would fall in value relative to long-term securities, despite their shorter duration. Additional methods (beyond the scope of this text) are required to hedge the risk of such changes in the slope of the yield curve.

Finally, even if assets have similar maturities, if the assets have different credit risks, duration-based hedging will not protect against fluctuations in the relative credit spreads of the assets. For example, during the financial crisis in the fall of 2008, Treasury interest rates fell dramatically, while at the same time the yields of similar maturity corporate bonds increased (e.g., see the Global Financial Crisis box on page 193 in Chapter 6.)

Swap-Based Hedging

Acorn Savings and Loan was able to reduce its interest rate sensitivity by selling assets. For most firms, selling assets is not an attractive prospect, as those assets are typically necessary to conduct the firms' normal business operations. Interest rate swaps are an alternative means of modifying the firm's interest rate risk exposure without buying or selling assets. An **interest rate swap** is a contract entered into with a bank, much like a forward contract, in which the firm and the bank agree to exchange the coupons from two different types

[21]Another measure of interest rate sensitivity, convexity, provides a measure of the change in duration of a portfolio as interest rates change. For example, see F. Fabozzi, *Duration, Convexity, and Other Bond Risk Measures* (John Wiley & Sons, 1999).

of loans. In this section, we describe interest rate swaps and explore how they are used to manage interest rate risk.[22]

In a standard interest rate swap, one party agrees to pay coupons based on a fixed interest rate in exchange for receiving coupons based on the prevailing market interest rate during each coupon period. An interest rate that adjusts to current market conditions is called a *floating rate*. Thus, the parties exchange a fixed-rate coupon for a floating-rate coupon, which explains why this swap is also called a "fixed-for-floating interest rate swap."

To demonstrate how an interest swap works, consider a five-year, \$100 million interest rate swap with a 7.8% fixed rate. Standard swaps have semiannual coupons, so the fixed coupon amounts would be $\frac{1}{2}(7.8\% \times \$100 \text{ million}) = \$3.9$ million every six months. The floating-rate coupons are typically based on a six-month market interest rate, such as the six-month Treasury bill rate or the six-month London Interbank Offered Rate (LIBOR).[23] This rate varies over the life of the contract. Each coupon is calculated based on the six-month interest rate that prevailed in the market six months prior to the coupon payment date. Table 30.6 calculates the cash flows of the swap under a hypothetical scenario for LIBOR rates over the life of the swap. For example, at the first coupon date in six months, the fixed coupon is \$3.9 million and the floating-rate coupon is $\frac{1}{2}(6.8\% \times \$10 \text{ million}) = \$3.4$ million, for a net payment of \$0.5 million from the fixed- to the floating-rate payer.

Each payment of the swap is equal to the difference between the fixed- and floating-rate coupons. Unlike with an ordinary loan, there is no payment of principal. Because the \$100 million swap amount is used only to calculate the coupons but is never actually paid, it is referred to as the **notional principal** of the swap. Finally, there is no initial cash flow associated with the swap. That is, the swap contract—like forward and futures contracts—is typically structured as a "zero-cost" security. The fixed rate of the swap contract is set based on current market conditions so that the swap is a fair deal (i.e., has an NPV of zero) for both sides.

TABLE 30.6 Cash Flows (in \$ million) for a \$100 Million Fixed-for-Floating Interest Rate Swap

Year	Six-Month LIBOR	Fixed Coupon	Floating-Rate Coupon	Swap Cash Flow: Fixed–Floating
0.0	6.8%			0.0
0.5	7.2%	3.9	3.4	0.5
1.0	8.0%	3.9	3.6	0.3
1.5	7.4%	3.9	4.0	−0.1
2.0	7.8%	3.9	3.7	0.2
2.5	8.6%	3.9	3.9	0.0
3.0	9.0%	3.9	4.3	−0.4
3.5	9.2%	3.9	4.5	−0.6
4.0	8.4%	3.9	4.6	−0.7
4.5	7.6%	3.9	4.2	−0.3
5.0		3.9	3.8	0.1

[22]Interest rate forward contracts, futures contracts, and options contracts also exist and can be used to manage interest rate risk. Swaps, however, are by far the most common strategy used by corporations.

[23]LIBOR is the rate at which major international banks with offices in London estimate they would be able to borrow in the interbank market. It is a common benchmark interest rate for swaps and other financial agreements. However, charges emerged in 2012 that some banks were skewing their estimates to manipulate LIBOR, prompting calls for its redefinition.

The Savings and Loan Crisis

In the late 1970s, many U.S. savings and loans were in exactly the same position as Acorn. The rates offered on deposits by S&Ls were highly regulated by the government, which encouraged these institutions to use their deposits to make long-term home loans at fixed rates to borrowers. As in our Acorn example, these S&Ls were especially vulnerable to a rise in interest rates.

That increase in rates occurred in the early 1980s, with rates rising from less than 9% to more than 15% in less than one year. As a result, many S&Ls quickly became insolvent, with the value of their liabilities being close to or exceeding the value of their assets.

Most firms in this situation would be unable to raise new funds and would quickly default. However, because their deposits were protected by federal deposit insurance, these insolvent S&Ls were able to attract new depositors to pay off old ones and keep their doors open. Many of them embarked on a strategy of making very risky investments in junk bonds and other securities in hopes of a high return that would reestablish their solvency. (Recall the discussion in Chapter 16 regarding the incentives of equity holders to take excessive risk when the firm is near default.) Most of these risky investments also failed, compounding the S&Ls' problems. By the late 1980s, the U.S. government had to shut down more than 50% of the nation's S&Ls and fulfill its deposit insurance obligations by bailing out S&L depositors at a cost of more than $100 billion to taxpayers.

Combining Swaps with Standard Loans. Corporations use interest rate swaps routinely to alter their exposure to interest rate fluctuations. The interest rate a firm pays on its loans can fluctuate for two reasons. First, the risk-free interest rate in the market may change. Second, the firm's credit quality, which determines the spread the firm must pay over the risk-free interest rate, can vary over time. By combining swaps with loans, firms can choose which of these sources of interest rate risk they will tolerate and which they will eliminate. Let's consider a typical example.

Alloy Cutting Corporation (ACC), a manufacturer of machine tools, is in the process of expanding its operations. It needs to borrow $10 million to fund this expansion. Currently, the six-month interest rate (LIBOR) is 4% and the 10-year interest rate is 6%—but these rates are for AA-rated firms. Given ACC's low current credit rating, the bank will charge the firm a spread of 1% above these rates.

ACC's managers are considering whether they should borrow on a short-term basis and then refinance the loan every six months or whether they should borrow using a long-term, 10-year loan. If they borrow for the short term, they worry that if interest rates rise substantially, the higher interest rates they will have to pay when they refinance the debt could lead to financial distress for ACC. They can avoid this risk if they borrow for the long term and lock in the interest rate for 10 years. But long-term borrowing also has a downside. ACC's managers believe that their firm's credit rating will improve over the next few years as the expansion generates additional revenue. If they borrow using a 10-year loan, ACC will be stuck paying a spread based on its current credit quality.

Table 30.7 highlights these trade-offs. Borrowing long term has the advantage of locking in interest rates, but the disadvantage of not allowing ACC to get the benefit of its improving credit quality. Borrowing short term enables ACC to benefit as its credit quality improves, but it risks an increase in interest rates.

In this situation, ACC can use an interest rate swap to combine the best of both strategies. First, ACC can borrow the $10 million it needs for expansion using a short-term loan that is rolled over every six months. The interest rate on each loan will be $\tilde{r}_t + \delta_t$, where $\tilde{r}_t$ is the new (LIBOR) market rate and δ_t is the spread ACC must pay based on its credit rating at the time. Given ACC's belief that its credit quality will improve over time, δ_t should decline from its current 1% level.

TABLE 30.7 Trade-Offs of Long-Term Versus Short-Term Borrowing for ACC

Strategy	Pro	Con
Borrow long term at 6% + 1% = 7% fixed rate	Lock in current low interest rates at 6%	Lock in current high spread of 1% given low initial credit rating
Borrow short-term at $\tilde{r}_t + \delta_t$	Get benefit of spread δ_t falling below 1% as credit rating improves	Risk of an increase in interest rates $\tilde{r}_t$ above 6%

Note: $\tilde{r}_t$ is the six-month interest rate (LIBOR) on date t. δ_t is the spread ACC must pay based on its credit rating on date t.

Next, to eliminate the risk of an increase in the interest rate it will pay in the future, $\tilde{r}_t$, ACC can enter into a 10-year interest rate swap in which it agrees to pay a fixed rate of 6% per year in exchange for receiving the floating rate $\tilde{r}_t$.[24] Combining the cash flows from the swap with ACC's short-term borrowing, we can compute ACC's net borrowing cost as follows:

Short-Term Loan Rate		Fixed Rate Due on Swap		Floating Rate Received from Swap		Net Borrowing Cost
$\tilde{r}_t + \delta_t$	+	6%	−	$\tilde{r}_t$	=	$6\% + \delta_t$

That is, ACC will have an initial net borrowing cost of 7% (given its current credit spread of 1%), but this cost will decline in the future as its credit rating improves and the spread δ_t declines. At the same time, this strategy protects ACC from an increase in interest rates.

EXAMPLE 30.13 Using Interest Rate Swaps

Problem

Bolt Industries is facing increased competition and wants to borrow $10 million in cash to protect against future revenue shortfalls. Currently, long-term AA rates are 10%. Bolt can borrow at 10.5% given its credit rating. The company is expecting interest rates to fall over the next few years, so it would prefer to borrow at short-term rates and refinance after rates drop. However, Bolt's management is afraid that its credit rating may deteriorate as competition intensifies, which may greatly increase the spread the firm must pay on a new loan. How can Bolt benefit from declining interest rates without worrying about changes in its credit rating?

Solution

Bolt can borrow at the long-term rate of 10.5% and then enter into a swap in which it *receives* a fixed rate of 10% and *pays* the short-term rate $\tilde{r}_t$. Its net borrowing cost will then be

Long-Term Loan Rate		Floating Rate Due on Swap		Floating Rate Received from Swap		Net Borrowing Cost
10.5%	+	$\tilde{r}_t$	−	10%	=	$\tilde{r}_t + 0.5\%$

In this way, Bolt locks in its current credit spread of 0.5% but gets the benefit of lower rates as rates decline.

[24]The fixed rate on the swap corresponds to the 10-year market rate for a AA-rated borrower. ACC would be able to get this rate on a swap, even though it is not AA-rated, because there is very little credit risk in a swap (because there is no exchange of the $10 million principal associated with a swap contract). As a result, swap rates are relatively independent of the user's credit quality.

Using a Swap to Change Duration. Firms can also use interest rate swaps with duration-hedging strategies. The value of a swap, while initially zero, will fluctuate over time as interest rates change. When interest rates rise, the swap's value will fall for the party receiving the fixed rate; conversely, it will rise for the party paying the fixed rate.

For the party receiving the fixed rate, we can calculate the interest rate sensitivity of a swap by thinking of it as a portfolio that is long a long-term bond and short a short-term bond, each with a face value equal to the notional principal. Thus, a 10-year, $10 million interest swap with a 6% fixed rate is equivalent to a portfolio that is long a 10-year, $10 million bond with a 6% coupon rate, and short a six-month, $10 million bond at the current short-term rate. Likewise, the party paying the fixed rate is short a 10-year bond and long a six-month bond.

A swap contract will therefore alter the duration of a portfolio according to the difference in the duration of the corresponding long-term and short-term bonds. We can apply Eq. 30.10 to compute the notional principal required to achieve a particular change in duration. Used in this way, swaps are a convenient way to alter the duration of a portfolio without buying or selling assets.

EXAMPLE 30.14 Using a Swap to Immunize a Portfolio

Problem

How can Acorn Savings and Loan use a swap to hedge its interest rate exposure rather than sell its mortgages?

Solution

Acorn needs to reduce the duration of its $15 million in equity from 40.7 to 0. To compute the correct notional amount of the swap, we must first compute the duration of a current 10-year bond. Suppose the duration is 6.76. The duration of a six-month bond is 0.5. Then, from Eq. 30.10,

$$N = \frac{40.7 \times 15}{(6.76 - 0.5)} = \$97.5 \text{ million}$$

Acorn should enter into a swap with the notional amount of $97.5 million. Because Acorn would like to reduce the duration of its equity, it should enter into a swap of this size in which it *pays* fixed and *receives* floating interest rates, as this swap will increase in value if interest rates rise, immunizing its balance sheet.

CONCEPT CHECK

1. How do we calculate the duration of a portfolio?
2. How do firms manage interest rate risk?

MyFinanceLab

Here is what you should know after reading this chapter. MyFinanceLab will help you identify what you know and where to go when you need to practice.

30.1 Insurance

- Insurance is a common method firms use to reduce risk. In a perfect market, the price of insurance is actuarially fair. An actuarially fair insurance premium is equal to the present value of the expected loss:

$$\frac{\Pr(\text{Loss}) \times E[\text{Payment in the Event of Loss}]}{1 + r_L} \tag{30.1}$$

- Insurance for large risks that cannot be well diversified has a negative beta, which raises its cost.
- The value of insurance comes from its ability to reduce the cost of market imperfections for the firm. Insurance may be beneficial to a firm because of its effects on bankruptcy and financial distress costs, issuance costs, taxes, debt capacity, and risk assessment.
- The costs of insurance include administrative and overhead costs, adverse selection, and moral hazard.

30.2 Commodity Price Risk

- Firms use several risk management strategies to hedge their exposure to commodity price movements.
  - Firms can make real investments in assets with offsetting risk using techniques such as vertical integration and storage.
  - Firms can enter into long-term contracts with suppliers or customers to achieve price stability.
  - Firms can hedge risk by trading commodity futures contracts in financial markets.
  - Futures contracts eliminate credit risk of long-term contracts via margin requirements, marking to market, and daily settlement.
  - While futures contracts are liquid and therefore easy to enter into or cancel, they expose the firm to liquidity risk from possible margin calls, as well as basis risk if the hedge is imperfect.

30.3 Exchange Rate Risk

- Firms can manage exchange rate risk in financial markets using currency forward contracts to lock in an exchange rate in advance and currency option contracts to protect against an exchange rate moving beyond a certain level.
- The cash-and-carry strategy is an alternative strategy that provides the same cash flows as the currency forward contract. By the Law of One Price, we determine the forward exchange rate by the cost-of-carry formula, called the covered interest parity equation. For an exchange that will take place in T years, the corresponding forward exchange rate (in \$/€) is:

$$F_T = S \times \frac{(1 + r_\$)^T}{(1 + r_€)^T} \tag{30.3}$$

- Currency options allow firms to insure themselves against the exchange rate moving beyond a certain level. A firm may choose to use options rather than forward contracts if
  - It would like to benefit from favorable exchange rate movements but not be obligated to make an exchange at unfavorable rates.
  - There is some chance that the transaction it is hedging will not take place.
- Currency options can be priced (in \$/€) using the Black-Scholes formula, with the foreign interest rate as a dividend yield:

$$C = \frac{S}{(1 + r_€)^T} N(d_1) - \frac{K}{(1 + r_\$)^T} N(d_2) \tag{30.4}$$

where

$$d_1 = \frac{\ln(F_T / K)}{\sigma\sqrt{T}} + \frac{\sigma\sqrt{T}}{2} \text{ and } d_2 = d_1 - \sigma\sqrt{T} \tag{30.5}$$

- Firms face interest rate risk when exchange rates are volatile. The primary tool they use to measure interest rate risk is duration. Duration measures the value-weighted maturity of an asset.

$$\text{Duration} = \sum_t \frac{PV(C_t)}{P} \times t \tag{30.6}$$

30.4 Interest Rate Risk

- The interest rate sensitivity of a stream of cash flows increases with its duration. For a small change, ε, in the interest rate, the change in the present value of a stream of cash flows is given by

$$\text{Percent Change in Value} \approx -\text{Duration} \times \frac{\varepsilon}{1 + r/k} \tag{30.7}$$

  where r is the current interest rate, expressed as an APR with k compounding periods per year.
- The duration of a portfolio is equal to the value-weighted average duration of each security in the portfolio. The duration of a firm's equity is determined from the duration of its assets and liabilities:

$$D_E = D_{A-L} = \frac{A}{A-L}D_A - \frac{L}{A-L}D_L \tag{30.9}$$

- Firms manage interest rate risk by buying or selling assets to make their equity duration neutral.
- Interest rate swaps allow firms to separate the risk of interest rate changes from the risk of fluctuations in the firm's credit quality.
  - By borrowing long term and entering into an interest rate swap in which the firm receives a fixed coupon and pays a floating-rate coupon, the firm will pay a floating interest rate plus a spread that is fixed based on its initial credit quality.
  - By borrowing short term and entering into an interest rate swap in which the firm receives a floating-rate coupon and pays a fixed coupon, the firm will pay a fixed interest rate plus a spread that will float with its credit quality.
- Firms use interest rate swaps to modify their interest rate risk exposure without buying or selling assets.

Key Terms

actuarially fair *p. 1019*
basis risk *p. 1029*
business interruption insurance *p. 1018*
business liability insurance *p. 1018*
cash-and-carry strategy *p. 1035*
covered interest parity equation *p. 1036*
currency forward contract *p. 1032*
currency timeline *p. 1034*
daily settlement *p. 1028*
deductible *p. 1023*
duration mismatch *p. 1044*
duration-neutral portfolio *p. 1045*
floating rate *p. 1031*
forward exchange rate *p. 1032*
futures contract *p. 1027*
immunized portfolio *p. 1045*
immunizing *p. 1045*
insurance premium *p. 1018*
interest rate swap *p. 1046*
key personnel insurance *p. 1018*
liquidity risk *p. 1029*
margin *p. 1028*
marking to market *p. 1028*
moral hazard *p. 1022*
natural hedge *p. 1029*
notional principal *p. 1047*
policy limits *p. 1023*
property insurance *p. 1018*
spot exchange rate *p. 1034*
vertical integration *p. 1025*

Further Reading

For a discussion of the benefits of insurance and risk management for the corporation, see the following article: D. Mayers and C. Smith, "On the Corporate Demand for Insurance," *Journal of Business* 55(2) (1982): 281–296.

Several textbooks specialize in risk management topics: D. Chance and R. Brooks, *An Introduction to Derivatives and Risk Management* (South-Western College Publishing, 2009); M. Crouhy, D. Galai, and R. Mark, *Risk Management* (McGraw-Hill Professional, 2000); C. Smith, C. Smithson, and D. Wilford, *Managing Financial Risk* (McGraw-Hill, 1998); and S. Sundaresan, *Fixed Income Markets and Their Derivatives* (Academic Press, 2009).

Other textbooks have an emphasis on international risk management: D. Eiteman, A. Stonehill, and M. Moffett, *Multinational Business Finance* (Prentice Hall, 2012); P. Sercu and R. Uppal, *International Financial Markets and the Firm* (South-Western College Publishing, 1995); and A. Shapiro, *Multinational Financial Management* (John Wiley & Sons, 2009).

For an in-depth treatment of the use of forwards, futures, and options for risk management, see the following text: R. McDonald, *Derivatives Markets* (Pearson, 2012).

These two articles integrate risk management and the overall strategy of the firm: K. Froot, D. Scharfstein, and J. Stein, "A Framework for Risk Management," *Harvard Business Review* 72 (November–December 1994): 59–71; and P. Tufano, "How Financial Engineering Can Advance Corporate Strategy," *Harvard Business Review* (January–February 1996).

Interested readers can look deeper into why firms may want to hedge and how to implement a hedging strategy: K. Brown and D. Smith, "Default Risk and Innovations in the Design of Interest Rate Swaps," *Financial Management* 22(2) (1993): 94–105; P. DeMarzo and D. Duffie, "Corporate Incentives for Hedging and Hedge Accounting," *Review of Financial Studies* 8(3) (1995): 743–771; W. Dolde, "The Trajectory of Corporate Financial Risk Management," *Journal of Applied Corporate Finance* 6(3) (1993): 33–41; K. Froot, D. Scharfstein, and J. Stein, "Risk Management: Coordinating Corporate Investment and Financing Policies," *Journal of Finance* 48(5) (1993): 1629–1658; J. Graham and C. Smith, "Tax Incentives to Hedge," *Journal of Finance* 54(6) (1999): 2241–2262; M. Levi and P. Sercu, "Erroneous and Valid Reasons for Hedging Foreign Exchange Exposure," *Journal of Multinational Financial Management* 1(2) (1991): 25–37; and R. Stulz, "Rethinking Risk Management," *Journal of Applied Corporate Finance* 9(3) (1996): 8–24.

Many articles have been written on what firms actually do to manage their risks and on the impact of risk management on stock returns: G. Allayannis and E. Ofek, "Exchange Rate Exposure, Hedging, and the Use of Foreign Currency Derivatives," *Journal of International Money and Finance* 20 (2001): 273–296; H. Berkman and M. Bradbury, "Empirical Evidence on the Corporate Use of Derivatives," *Financial Management* 25(2) (1996): 5–13; D. Carter, D. Rogers, and B. Simkins, "Hedging and Value in the US Airline Industry," *Journal of Applied Corporate Finance* 18 (2006): 21–33. C. Geczy, B. Minton, and C. Schrand, "Why Firms Use Currency Derivatives," *Journal of Finance* 52(4) (1997): 1323–1354; R. Graham and D. Rogers, "Do Firms Hedge in Response to Tax Incentives?" *Journal of Finance* 58(2) (2002): 815–839; W. Guay and S. Kothari, "How Much Do Firms Hedge with Derivatives?" *Journal of Financial Economics* 70(3) (2003): 423–461; S. Howton and S. Perfect, "Currency and Interest-Rate Derivatives Use in U.S. Firms," *Financial Management* 27(4) (1998): 111–121; J. Koski and J. Pontiff, "How Are Derivatives Used? Evidence from the Mutual Fund Industry," *Journal of Finance* 54(2) (1999): 791–816; S. Mian, "Evidence on Corporate Hedging Policy," *Journal of Financial and Quantitative Analysis* 31(3) (1996): 419–439; D. Nance, C. Smith, and C. Smithson, "On the Determinants of Corporate Hedging," *Journal of Finance* 48(1) (1993): 267–284; A. Rampini, A. Sufi, and S. Viswanathan, "Dynamic Risk Management," *Journal of Financial Economics* 111 (2014): 271–296; and P. Tufano, "The Determinants of Stock Price Exposure: Financial Engineering and the Gold Mining Industry," *Journal of Finance* 53(3) (1998): 1014–1052.

Problems

All problems are available in MyFinanceLab.

Insurance

1. The William Companies (WMB) owns and operates natural gas pipelines that deliver 12% of the natural gas consumed in the United States. WMB is concerned that a major hurricane could disrupt its Gulfstream pipeline, which runs 691 miles through the Gulf of Mexico. In the

event of a disruption, the firm anticipates a loss of profits of $65 million. Suppose the likelihood of a disruption is 3% per year, and the beta associated with such a loss is −0.25. If the risk-free interest rate is 5% and the expected return of the market is 10%, what is the actuarially fair insurance premium?

2. Genentech's main facility is located in South San Francisco. Suppose that Genentech would experience a direct loss of $450 million in the event of a major earthquake that disrupted its operations. The chance of such an earthquake is 2% per year, with a beta of −0.5.
   a. If the risk-free interest rate is 5% and the expected return of the market is 10%, what is the actuarially fair insurance premium required to cover Genentech's loss?
   b. Suppose the insurance company raises the premium by an additional 15% over the amount calculated in part (a) to cover its administrative and overhead costs. What amount of financial distress or issuance costs would Genentech have to suffer if it were not insured to justify purchasing the insurance?

3. Your firm imports manufactured goods from China. You are worried that U.S.–China trade negotiations could break down next year, leading to a moratorium on imports. In the event of a moratorium, your firm expects its operating profits to decline substantially and its marginal tax rate to fall from its current level of 40% to 10%.

   An insurance firm has agreed to write a trade insurance policy that will pay $500,000 in the event of an import moratorium. The chance of a moratorium is estimated to be 10%, with a beta of −1.5. Suppose the risk-free interest rate is 5% and the expected return of the market is 10%.
   a. What is the actuarially fair premium for this insurance?
   b. What is the NPV of purchasing this insurance for your firm? What is the source of this gain?

4. Your firm faces a 9% chance of a potential loss of $10 million next year. If your firm implements new policies, it can reduce the chance of this loss to 4%, but these new policies have an upfront cost of $100,000. Suppose the beta of the loss is 0, and the risk-free interest rate is 5%.
   a. If the firm is uninsured, what is the NPV of implementing the new policies?
   b. If the firm is fully insured, what is the NPV of implementing the new policies?
   c. Given your answer to part (b), what is the actuarially fair cost of full insurance?
   d. What is the minimum-size deductible that would leave your firm with an incentive to implement the new policies?
   e. What is the actuarially fair price of an insurance policy with the deductible in part (d)?

Commodity Price Risk

5. BHP Billiton is the world's largest mining firm. BHP expects to produce 2 billion pounds of copper next year, with a production cost of $0.90 per pound.
   a. What will be BHP's operating profit from copper next year if the price of copper is $1.25, $1.50, or $1.75 per pound, and the firm plans to sell all of its copper next year at the going price?
   b. What will be BHP's operating profit from copper next year if the firm enters into a contract to supply copper to end users at an average price of $1.45 per pound?
   c. What will be BHP's operating profit from copper next year if copper prices are described as in part (a), and the firm enters into supply contracts as in part (b) for only 50% of its total output?
   d. Describe situations for which each of the strategies in parts (a), (b), and (c) might be optimal.

MFL **6.** Your utility company will need to buy 100,000 barrels of oil in 10 days' time, and it is worried about fuel costs. Suppose you go long 100 oil futures contracts, each for 1000 barrels of oil, at the current futures price of $60 per barrel. Suppose futures prices change each day as follows:

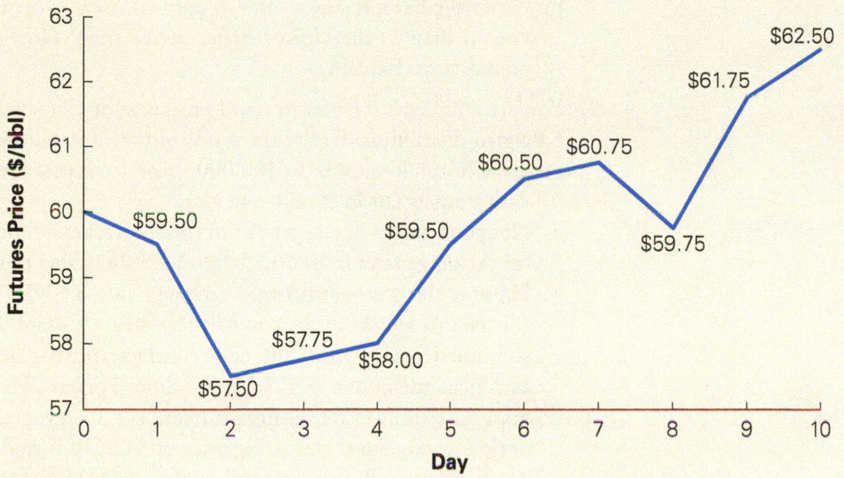

a. What is the mark-to-market profit or loss (in dollars) that you will have on each date?
b. What is your total profit or loss after 10 days? Have you been protected against a rise in oil prices?
c. What is the largest cumulative loss you will experience over the 10-day period? In what case might this be a problem?

7. Suppose Starbucks consumes 100 million pounds of coffee beans per year. As the price of coffee rises, Starbucks expects to pass along 60% of the cost to its customers through higher prices per cup of coffee. To hedge its profits from fluctuations in coffee prices, Starbucks should lock in the price of how many pounds of coffee beans using supply contracts?

Exchange Rate Risk

MFL

8. Your start-up company has negotiated a contract to provide a database installation for a manufacturing company in Poland. That firm has agreed to pay you $100,000 in three months' time when the installation will occur. However, it insists on paying in Polish zloty (PLN). You don't want to lose the deal (the company is your first client!), but are worried about the exchange rate risk. In particular, you are worried the zloty could depreciate relative to the dollar. You contact Fortis Bank in Poland to see if you can lock in an exchange rate for the zloty in advance.
a. You find the following table posted on the bank's Web site, showing zloty per dollar, per euro, and per British pound:

	1 week	2 weeks	1 month	2 months	3 months
			USD		
purchase	3.1433	3.1429	3.1419	3.1390	3.1361
sale	3.1764	3.1761	3.1755	3.1735	3.1712
			EUR		
purchase	3.7804	3.7814	3.7836	3.7871	3.7906
sale	3.8214	3.8226	3.8254	3.8298	3.8342
			GBP		
purchase	5.5131	5.5131	5.5112	5.5078	5.5048
sale	5.5750	5.5750	5.5735	5.5705	5.5681

What exchange rate could you lock in for the zloty in three months? How many zloty should you demand in the contract to receive $100,000?

b. Given the bank forward rates in part (a), were short-term interest rates higher or lower in Poland than in the United States at the time? How did Polish rates compare to euro or pound rates? Explain.

9. You are a broker for frozen seafood products for Choyce Products. You just signed a deal with a Belgian distributor. Under the terms of the contract, in one year you will deliver 4000 kilograms of frozen king crab for 100,000 euros. Your cost for obtaining the king crab is $110,000. All cash flows occur in exactly one year.

a. Plot your profits in one year from the contract as a function of the exchange rate in one year, for exchange rates from $0.75/€ to $1.50/€. Label this line "Unhedged Profits."

b. Suppose the one-year forward exchange rate is $1.25/€, and that you enter into a forward contract to sell the euros you will receive at this rate. In the figure from part (a), plot your combined profits from the crab contract and the forward contract as a function of the exchange rate in one year. Label this line "Forward Hedge."

c. Suppose that instead of using a forward contract, you consider using options. A one-year call option to buy euros at a strike price of $1.25/€ is trading for $0.10/€. Similarly a one-year put option to sell euros at a strike price of $1.25/€ is trading for $0.10/€. To hedge the risk of your profits, should you buy or sell the call or the put?

d. In the figure from parts (a) and (b), plot your "all in" profits using the option hedge (combined profits of crab contract, option contract, and option price) as a function of the exchange rate in one year. Label this line "Option Hedge." (*Note*: You can ignore the effect of interest on the option price.)

e. Suppose that by the end of the year, a trade war erupts, leading to a European embargo on U.S. food products. As a result, your deal is cancelled, and you don't receive the euros or incur the costs of procuring the crab. However, you still have the profits (or losses) associated with your forward or options contract. In a new figure, plot the profits associated with the forward hedge and the options hedge (labeling each line). When there is a risk of cancellation, which type of hedge has the least downside risk? Explain briefly.

10. Suppose the current exchange rate is $1.80/£, the interest rate in the United States is 5.25%, the interest rate in the United Kingdom is 4%, and the volatility of the $/£ exchange rate is 10%. Use the Black-Scholes formula to determine the price of a six-month European call option on the British pound with a strike price of $1.80/£.

Interest Rate Risk

11. Assume each of the following securities has the same yield-to-maturity: a five-year, zero-coupon bond; a nine-year, zero-coupon bond; a five-year annuity; and a nine-year annuity. Rank these securities from lowest to highest duration.

12. You have been hired as a risk manager for Acorn Savings and Loan. Currently, Acorn's balance sheet is as follows (in millions of dollars):

Assets		**Liabilities**	
Cash Reserves	50	Checking and Savings	80
Auto Loans	100	Certificates of Deposit	100
Mortgages	150	Long-Term Financing	100
Total Assets	300	Total Liabilities	280
		Owner's Equity	20
		Total Liabilities and Equity	300

When you analyze the duration of loans, you find that the duration of the auto loans is two years, while the mortgages have a duration of seven years. Both the cash reserves and the checking and savings accounts have a zero duration. The CDs have a duration of two years and the long-term financing has a 10-year duration.

a. What is the duration of Acorn's equity?

b. Suppose Acorn experiences a rash of mortgage prepayments, reducing the size of the mortgage portfolio from \$150 million to \$100 million, and increasing cash reserves to \$100 million. What is the duration of Acorn's equity now? If interest rates are currently 4% but fall to 3%, estimate the approximate change in the value of Acorn's equity.

c. Suppose that after the prepayments in part (b), but before a change in interest rates, Acorn considers managing its risk by selling mortgages and/or buying 10-year Treasury STRIPS (zero-coupon bonds). How many should the firm buy or sell to eliminate its current interest rate risk?

13. The Citrix Fund has invested in a portfolio of government bonds that has a current market value of \$44.8 million. The duration of this portfolio of bonds is 13.5 years. The fund has borrowed to purchase these bonds, and the current value of its liabilities (i.e., the current value of the bonds it has issued) is \$39.2 million. The duration of these liabilities is four years. The equity in the Citrix Fund (or its net worth) is obviously \$5.6 million. The market-value balance sheet below summarizes this information:

Assets		**Liabilities (Debt) and Equity**	
Portfolio of Government Bonds (duration = 13.5)	\$44,800,000	Short- and Long-Term Debt (duration = 4.0)	\$39,200,000
		Equity	\$5,600,000
Total	\$44,800,000	Total	\$44,800,000

Assume that the current yield curve is flat at 5.5%. You have been hired by the board of directors to evaluate the risk of this fund.

a. Consider the effect of a surprise increase in interest rates, such that the yields rise by 50 basis points (i.e., the yield curve is now flat at 6%). What would happen to the value of the assets in the Citrix Fund? What would happen to the value of the liabilities? What can you conclude about the change in the value of the equity under these conditions?

b. What is the initial duration of the Citrix Fund (i.e., the duration of the equity)?

c. As a result of your analysis, the board of directors fires the current manager of the fund. You are hired and given the objective of minimizing the fund's exposure to interest rate fluctuations. You are instructed to do so by liquidating a portion of the fund's assets and reinvesting the proceeds in short-term Treasury bills and notes with an average duration of two years. How many dollars do you need to liquidate and reinvest to minimize the fund's interest rate sensitivity?

d. Rather than immunizing the fund using the strategy in part (c), you consider using a swap contract. If the duration of a 10-year, fixed-coupon bond is seven years, what is the notational amount of the swap you should enter into? Should you receive or pay the fixed-rate portion of the swap?

14. Your firm needs to raise \$100 million in funds. You can borrow short term at a spread of 1% over LIBOR. Alternatively, you can issue 10-year, fixed-rate bonds at a spread of 2.50% over 10-year Treasuries, which currently yield 7.60%. Current 10-year interest rate swaps are quoted at the LIBOR rate versus the 8% fixed rate.

Management believes that the firm is currently "underrated" and that its credit rating is likely to improve in the next year or two. Nevertheless, the managers are not comfortable with the interest rate risk associated with using short-term debt.

a. Suggest a strategy for borrowing the \$100 million. What is your effective borrowing rate?

b. Suppose the firm's credit rating does improve three years later. It can now borrow at a spread of 0.50% over Treasuries, which now yield 9.10% for a seven-year maturity. Also, seven-year interest rate swaps are quoted at LIBOR versus 9.50%. How would you lock in your new credit quality for the next seven years? What is your effective borrowing rate now?

International Corporate Finance

CHAPTER

31

IN THE 1990s, STARBUCKS COFFEE COMPANY IDENTIFIED JAPAN AS A potentially lucrative new market for its coffee products and decided to invest as much as $10 million in fiscal year 1996 to begin operations there. Because Starbucks realized it needed specialized knowledge of the Japanese market, it established a joint venture with Sazaby, Inc., a Japanese retailer and restaurateur. This venture, called Starbucks Coffee Japan Ltd., intended to open as many as 12 stores in this initial phase. Although stores opened more slowly than expected, the venture had more than 200 stores and sales of ¥29 billion ($252 million) by 2001, and it opened its 500th store in November 2003. To finance this growth, Starbucks Coffee Japan Ltd. used the Japanese capital markets. It held an initial public offering of shares on the Osaka Stock Exchange in October 2001 with a market capitalization of ¥90.88 billion ($756 million), raising ¥18.8 billion ($156 million) in additional capital for expansion. As of 2015, Starbucks had over 1000 stores in Japan. How did Starbucks' managers decide to undertake this investment opportunity? Why did they decide to use the Japanese domestic market to finance it rather than U.S. markets?

This chapter focuses on some of the factors a firm faces when making a foreign investment that it does not encounter when making a domestic investment. There are three key issues that arise when considering an investment in a foreign project like Starbucks Coffee Japan Ltd.:

- The project will most likely generate foreign currency cash flows, although the firm cares about the home currency value of the project.
- Interest rates and costs of capital will likely be different in the foreign country as a result of the macroeconomic environment.
- The firm will probably face a different tax rate in the foreign country and will be subject to both foreign and domestic tax codes.

NOTATION

C_{FC}	foreign currency cash flow
S	spot exchange rate
F	forward exchange rate
$r_{\$}^{*}$	dollar cost of capital
$r_{\$}$	dollar risk-free interest rate
r_{FC}^{*}	foreign currency cost of capital
r_{FC}	foreign currency risk-free interest rate
r_{wacc}	weighted average cost of capital
D	market value of debt
E	market value of equity
r_E	required return on equity
r_D	required return on debt
τ_C	corporate tax rate

As a first step toward evaluating foreign projects, this chapter discusses international capital markets. We begin by examining internationally integrated capital markets, which provide a useful benchmark for comparing different methods of valuing a foreign project. We next explain how to value a foreign project and address the three key issues mentioned above. We then value foreign currency cash flows using two valuation methodologies and consider the implications of foreign and domestic tax codes. Finally, we explore the implications of internationally segmented capital markets.

31.1 Internationally Integrated Capital Markets

We begin our examination of valuing foreign projects by developing a conceptual benchmark based on the integration of capital markets across currencies and borders. In this framework, capital markets are internationally integrated when the value of a foreign investment does not depend on the currency (home or foreign) we use in the analysis.

Consider a risky foreign asset that is expected to pay the cash flow, C_{FC}, in one period. In a normal market, the price of this asset in a foreign market is the present value of this cash flow using the cost of capital of a local investor:

$$C_{FC}/(1 + r^*_{FC}) \tag{31.1}$$

A U.S. investor who wants to purchase this asset in dollars will have to pay

$$S \times \frac{C_{FC}}{(1 + r^*_{FC})} \tag{31.2}$$

where S is the current spot exchange rate in dollars per foreign currency. Now any U.S. investor who actually purchased this security would have to convert the future cash flow into dollars, so the payoff to such an investor is the dollar cash flow it produces. To value this cash flow, assume that the U.S. investor contracts today to convert the *expected* cash flow in one period at the forward rate, F, quoted as dollars per foreign currency. If we assume that spot exchange rates and the foreign currency cash flows of the security are uncorrelated, then this U.S. investor's expected dollar cash flow is $F \times C_{FC}$.[1] If $r^*_{\$}$ is the appropriate cost of capital from the standpoint of a U.S. investor, the present value of this expected cash flow is

$$\frac{F \times C_{FC}}{(1 + r^*_{\$})} \tag{31.3}$$

By the Law of One Price, this value must be equal to what the U.S. investor paid for the security:

$$S \times \frac{C_{FC}}{(1 + r^*_{FC})} = \frac{F \times C_{FC}}{(1 + r^*_{\$})}$$

[1] The actual cash flow in foreign currency will be $C_{FC} + \varepsilon$ where ε is the uncertainty in the cash flow and has an expected value of zero. In U.S. dollars, this cash flow is $F \times C_{FC} + S_1 \times \varepsilon$ because the forward contract is only for the amount C_{FC}; the rest must be converted at the prevailing spot rate in one period, S_1. Then, because spot rates are uncorrelated with the project cash flows, $E[S_1 \times \varepsilon] = E[S_1] \times E[\varepsilon] = E[S_1] \times 0 = 0$.

Rearranging terms gives

$$F = \frac{(1 + r^*_{\$})}{(1 + r^*_{FC})} S \tag{31.4}$$

This condition ought to look familiar from Chapter 30, because Eq. 31.4 is simply covered interest parity, here derived for risky rather than riskless discount rates.

At this point, it is worth taking a step back and considering the assumptions specific to the international context that we needed to derive Eq. 31.4. Recall from Chapter 3 that in a normal market, prices are competitive. In this context, this concept means, among other things, that any investor can exchange either currency in any amount at the spot rate or forward rates, and is free to purchase or sell any security in any amount in either country at their current market prices. Under these conditions, which we term **internationally integrated capital markets**, the value of an investment does not depend on the currency we use in the analysis.

EXAMPLE 31.1 **Present Values and Internationally Integrated Capital Markets**

Problem

You are an American who is trying to calculate the present value of a ¥10 million cash flow that will occur one year in the future. You know that the spot exchange rate is $S =$ ¥110/\$ and the one-year forward rate is $F =$ ¥105.8095/\$. You also know that the appropriate dollar cost of capital for this cash flow is $r^*_{\$} = 5\%$ and that the appropriate yen cost of capital for this cash flow is $r^* = 1\%$. What is the present value of the ¥10 million cash flow from the standpoint of a Japanese investor, and what is the dollar equivalent of this amount? What is the present value of the ¥10 million cash flow from the standpoint of a U.S. investor who first converts the ¥10 million into dollars, and then applies the dollar discount rate?

Solution

The present value of the yen cash flow is ¥10,000,000/(1.01) = ¥9,900,990, and the dollar equivalent is ¥9,900,990/(110 ¥/\$) = \$90,009. (Note that we adjusted the formula in Eq. 31.2 because the exchange rate is expressed as yen per dollar rather than dollars per yen.) The present value from the standpoint of a U.S. investor who first converts the ¥10 million into dollars using the forward rate and then applies the dollar cost of capital is (¥10,000,000 ÷ 105.8095 ¥/\$)/1.05 = \$90,009. (Again, we have adjusted the formula in Eq. 31.3 because the exchange rate is expressed as yen per dollar.) Because the U.S. and Japanese capital markets are internationally integrated, both methods produce the same result.

CONCEPT CHECK

1. What assumptions are necessary for internationally integrated capital markets?
2. What implication do internationally integrated capital markets have for the value of the same asset in different countries?

31.2 Valuation of Foreign Currency Cash Flows

The most obvious difference between a domestic project and a foreign project is that the foreign project will most likely generate cash flows in a foreign currency. If the foreign project is owned by a domestic corporation, managers and shareholders need to determine the home currency value of the foreign currency cash flows.

In an internationally integrated capital market, two equivalent methods are available for calculating the NPV of a foreign project: Either we can calculate the NPV in the foreign country and convert it to the local currency at the spot rate, or we can convert the cash flows of the foreign project into the local currency and then calculate the NPV of these cash flows. The first method is essentially what we have done throughout this book (calculating the NPV of a project in a single currency) with the added step at the end of converting the NPV into the local currency using spot rates. Because this method should be familiar to you at this stage, we will concentrate on the second method.

WACC Valuation Method in Domestic Currency

The second valuation method requires converting the expected dollar value of the foreign currency cash flows and then proceeding to value the project as if it were a domestic project.

Application: Ityesi, Inc. Ityesi, Inc., a manufacturer of custom packaging products headquartered in the United States, wants to apply the weighted average cost of capital (WACC) technique to value a project in the United Kingdom. Ityesi is considering introducing a new line of packaging in the United Kingdom that will be its first foreign project. The project will be completely self-contained within the United Kingdom, such that all revenues are generated and all costs are incurred there.

Engineers expect the technology used in the new products to be obsolete after four years. The marketing group expects annual sales of £37.5 million per year for this product line. Manufacturing costs and operating expenses are expected to total £15.625 million and £5.625 million per year, respectively. Developing the product will require an upfront investment of £15 million in capital equipment that will be obsolete in four years, and an initial marketing expense of £4.167 million. Ityesi pays a corporate tax rate of 40% regardless of where it manufactures its products. The expected pound free cash flows of the proposed project are projected in the spreadsheet in Table 31.1.

Ityesi's managers have determined that there is no correlation between the uncertainty in these cash flows and the uncertainty in the spot dollar-pound exchange rate. As we explained in the last section, under this condition, the expected value of the future cash flows in dollars is the expected value in pounds multiplied by the forward exchange rate. Obtaining forward rate quotes for as long as four years in the future is difficult, so

TABLE 31.1 SPREADSHEET **Expected Foreign Free Cash Flows from Ityesi's U.K. Project**

	Year	0	1	2	3	4
	Incremental Earnings Forecast (£ millions)					
1	Sales	—	37.500	37.500	37.500	37.500
2	Cost of Goods Sold	—	(15.625)	(15.625)	(15.625)	(15.625)
3	**Gross Profit**	—	21.875	21.875	21.875	21.875
4	Operating Expenses	(4.167)	(5.625)	(5.625)	(5.625)	(5.625)
5	Depreciation	—	(3.750)	(3.750)	(3.750)	(3.750)
6	**EBIT**	(4.167)	12.500	12.500	12.500	12.500
7	Income tax at 40%	1.667	(5.000)	(5.000)	(5.000)	(5.000)
8	**Unlevered Net Income**	(2.500)	7.500	7.500	7.500	7.500
	Free Cash Flow					
9	Plus: Depreciation	—	3.750	3.750	3.750	3.750
10	Less: Capital Expenditures	(15.000)	—	—	—	—
11	Less: Increases in NWC	—	—	—	—	—
12	**Pound Free Cash Flow**	**(17.500)**	**11.250**	**11.250**	**11.250**	**11.250**

Ityesi's managers have decided to use the covered interest rate parity formula (Eq. 30.3 in Chapter 30) to compute the forward rates.

Forward Exchange Rates. The current spot exchange rate, S, is \$1.60/£. Suppose that the yield curve in both countries is flat: The risk-free rate on dollars, $r_{\$}$, is 4%, and the risk-free interest rate on pounds, $r_{£}$, is 7%. Using the covered interest parity condition for a multi-year forward exchange rate (Eq. 30.3):

$$F_1 = S \times \frac{(1 + r_{\$})}{(1 + r_{£})} = (\$1.60/£)\frac{(1.04)}{(1.07)} = \$1.5551/£$$

$$F_2 = S \times \frac{(1 + r_{\$})^2}{(1 + r_{£})^2} = (\$1.60/£)\frac{(1.04)^2}{(1.07)^2} = \$1.5115/£$$

$$F_3 = S \times \frac{(1 + r_{\$})^3}{(1 + r_{£})^3} = (\$1.60/£)\frac{(1.04)^3}{(1.07)^3} = \$1.4692/£$$

$$F_4 = S \times \frac{(1 + r_{\$})^4}{(1 + r_{£})^4} = (\$1.60/£)\frac{(1.04)^4}{(1.07)^4} = \$1.4280/£$$

Free Cash Flow Conversion. Using these forward exchange rates, we can now calculate the expected free cash flows in dollars by multiplying the expected cash flows in pounds by the forward exchange rate, as shown in the spreadsheet in Table 31.2.

The Value of Ityesi's Foreign Project with WACC. With the cash flows of the U.K. project now expressed in dollars, we can value the foreign project as if it were a domestic U.S. project. We proceed, as we did in Chapter 18, under the assumption that the market risk of the U.K. project is similar to that of the company as a whole. As a consequence, we can use Ityesi's costs of equity and debt in the United States to calculate the WACC.[2]

Ityesi has built up \$20 million in cash for investment needs and has debt of \$320 million, so its net debt is $D = 320 - 20 = \$300$ million. This amount is equal to the market value of its equity, implying a (net) debt-equity ratio of 1. Ityesi intends to maintain a similar (net) debt-equity ratio for the foreseeable future. The WACC thus assigns equal weights to equity and debt (Table 31.3).

TABLE 31.2 SPREADSHEET Expected Dollar Free Cash Flows from Ityesi's U.K. Project

		0	1	2	3	4
	Dollar Free Cash Flow (\$ millions)					
1	Pound FCF (£ millions)	(17.500)	11.250	11.250	11.250	11.250
2	Forward Exchange Rate (\$/£)	1.600	1.555	1.512	1.469	1.428
3	**Dollar Value of Pound FCF** (1 × 2)	(28.000)	17.495	17.004	16.528	16.065

[2]The risk of the foreign project is unlikely to be *exactly* the same as the risk of domestic projects (or the firm as a whole), because it may be exposed to foreign economic and exchange rate risk factors. Ityesi's managers have assessed these additional risks to be small, and so for practical purposes have chosen to ignore it. Alternatively, one could estimate a domestic cost of capital for the project based on return data for a foreign firm in the same industry with stock that is traded on the U.S. market.

TABLE 31.3 **Ityesi's Current Market Value Balance Sheet ($ million) and Cost of Capital without the U.K. Project**

Assets		Liabilities		Cost of Capital	
Cash	20	Debt	320	Debt	6%
Existing Assets	600	Equity	300	Equity	10%
	620		620		

With Ityesi's cost of equity at 10% and its cost of debt at 6%, we calculate Ityesi's WACC as follows:

$$r_{wacc} = \frac{E}{E+D} r_E + \frac{D}{E+D} r_D (1 - \tau_C)$$

$$= (0.5)(10.0\%) + (0.5)(6.0\%)(1 - 40\%) = 6.8\%$$

We can now determine the value of the foreign project, including the tax shield from debt, by calculating the present value of the future free cash flows using the WACC:

$$\frac{17.495}{1.068} + \frac{17.004}{1.068^2} + \frac{16.528}{1.068^3} + \frac{16.065}{1.068^4} = \$57.20 \text{ million}$$

Because the upfront cost of launching the product line in dollars is only $28 million, the net present value is 57.20 − 28 = $29.20 million. Thus, Ityesi should undertake the U.K. project.

Using the Law of One Price as a Robustness Check

To arrive at the NPV of Ityesi's project requires making a number of assumptions—for example, that international markets are integrated, and that the exchange rate and the cash flows of the project are uncorrelated. The managers of Ityesi will naturally worry about whether these assumptions are justified. Luckily, there is a way to check the analysis.

Recall that there are two ways to compute the NPV of the foreign project. Ityesi could just have easily computed the foreign NPV by discounting the foreign cash flows at the foreign cost of capital and converting this result to a domestic NPV using the spot rate. Except for the last step, this method requires doing the same calculation we have performed throughout this book—that is, calculate the NPV of a (domestic) project. Determining the NPV requires knowing the cost of capital—in this case, the cost of capital for an investment in the United Kingdom. Recall that to estimate this cost of capital we use return data for publicly traded single-product companies—in this case, U.K. firms. For this method to provide the same answer as the alternative method, the estimate for the foreign cost of capital, $r_{£}^{*}$, must satisfy the Law of One Price, which from Eq. 31.4 implies:

$$(1 + r_{£}^{*}) = \frac{S}{F}(1 + r_{\$}^{*}) \tag{31.5}$$

If it does not, then Ityesi's managers should be concerned that the simplifying assumptions in their analysis are not valid: Either there are market frictions that prevent integration, or there is a significant correlation between the project's cash flows and the exchange rate.

We can further interpret Eq. 31.5 by using the covered interest rate parity relation derived in Chapter 30 (Eq. 30.3):

$$\frac{S}{F} = \frac{1 + r_{£}}{1 + r_{\$}} \tag{31.6}$$

where $r_{£}$ and $r_{\$}$ are the foreign and domestic risk-free interest rates, respectively. Combining Eq. 31.5 and Eq. 31.6 and rearranging terms gives the foreign cost of capital in terms of the domestic cost of capital and interest rates:

The Foreign-Denominated Cost of Capital

$$r^*_{£} = \frac{1 + r_{£}}{1 + r_{\$}}(1 + r^*_{\$}) - 1$$
$$\approx r_{£} + (r^*_{\$} - r_{\$}) \tag{31.7}$$

In other words, the foreign risk premium is approximately equal to the domestic risk premium, so the foreign cost of capital is roughly equal to the foreign risk-free rate plus the domestic risk premium. If the simplifying assumptions Ityesi made in calculating the NPV of its U.K. project are valid, then the cost of capital estimate calculated using Eq. 31.7 will be close to the cost of capital estimate calculated directly using comparable single-product companies in the United Kingdom.

EXAMPLE 31.2 Internationalizing the Cost of Capital

Problem

Use the Law of One Price to infer the pound WACC from Ityesi's dollar WACC. Verify that the NPV of Ityesi's project is the same when its pound free cash flows are discounted at this WACC and converted at the spot rate.

Solution

Using Eq. 31.7 to compute the pound WACC gives

$$r^*_{£} = \frac{1 + r_{£}}{1 + r_{\$}}(1 - r^*_{\$}) - 1\left(\frac{1.07}{1.04}\right)(1.068) - 1 = 0.0988$$

The pound WACC is 9.88%.

We can now use Ityesi's pound WACC to calculate the present value of the pound free cash flows in Table 31.3:

$$\frac{11.25}{1.0988} + \frac{11.25}{1.0988^2} + \frac{11.25}{1.0988^3} + \frac{11.25}{1.0988^4} = £35.75 \text{ million}$$

The NPV in pounds of the investment opportunity is 35.75 − 17.5 = £18.25 million. Converting this amount to dollars at the spot rate gives £18.25 million × 1.6\$/£ = \$29.20 million, which is exactly the NPV we calculated before.

CONCEPT CHECK

1. Explain two methods we use to calculate the NPV of a foreign project.
2. When do these two methods give the same NPV of the foreign project?

31.3 Valuation and International Taxation

In this chapter, we assume that Ityesi pays a corporate tax rate of 40% no matter where its earnings are generated. In practice, determining the corporate tax rate on foreign income is complicated because corporate income taxes must be paid to two national governments:

the host government (the United Kingdom in this example) and the home government (the United States). If the foreign project is a separately incorporated subsidiary of the parent, the amount of taxes a firm pays generally depends on the amount of profits **repatriated** (brought back to the home country).

Single Foreign Project with Immediate Repatriation of Earnings

We begin by assuming that the firm has a single foreign project and that all foreign profits are repatriated immediately. The general international arrangement prevailing with respect to taxation of corporate profits is that the host country gets the first opportunity to tax income produced within its borders. The home government then gets an opportunity to tax the income from a foreign project to the domestic firm. In particular, the home government must establish a tax policy specifying its treatment of foreign income and foreign taxes paid on that income. In addition, it needs to establish the timing of taxation.

U.S. tax policy requires U.S. corporations to pay taxes on their foreign income at the same rate as profits earned in the United States. However, a full tax credit is given for foreign taxes paid *up to* the amount of the U.S. tax liability. In other words, if the foreign tax rate is less than the U.S. tax rate, the company pays total taxes equal to the U.S. tax rate on its foreign earnings. In this case, all of the company's earnings are taxed at the same rate no matter where they are earned—the working assumption we used for Ityesi.

If the foreign tax rate exceeds the U.S. tax rate, companies must pay this higher rate on foreign earnings. Because the U.S. tax credit exceeds the amount of U.S. taxes owed, no tax is owed in the United States. Note that U.S. tax policy does not allow companies to apply the part of the tax credit that is not used to offset domestic taxes owed, so this extra tax credit is wasted. In this scenario, companies pay a higher tax rate on foreign income and a lower (U.S.) tax rate on income generated in the United States.

Multiple Foreign Projects and Deferral of Earnings Repatriation

Thus far, we have assumed that the firm has only one foreign project and that it repatriates earnings immediately. Neither assumption is realistic. Firms can lower their taxes by pooling multiple foreign projects and deferring the repatriation of earnings. Let's begin by considering the benefits of pooling the income on all foreign projects.

Pooling Multiple Foreign Projects. Under U.S. tax law, multinational corporations may use any excess tax credits generated in high-tax foreign countries to offset their net U.S. tax liabilities on earnings in low-tax foreign countries. Thus, if the U.S. tax rate exceeds the combined tax rate on all foreign income, it is valid to assume that the firm pays the same tax rate on all income no matter where it is earned. Otherwise, the firm must pay a higher tax rate on its foreign income.

Deferring Repatriation of Earnings. Now consider an opportunity to defer repatriation of foreign profits. This consideration is important because U.S. tax liability is not incurred until the profits are brought back home, if the foreign operation is set up as a separately incorporated subsidiary (rather than as a foreign branch). If a company chooses not to repatriate £12.5 million in pre-tax earnings, for example, it effectively reinvests those earnings abroad and defers its U.S. tax liability. When the foreign tax rates exceed the U.S. tax rates, there are no benefits to deferral because in such a case there is no additional U.S. tax liability.

When the foreign tax rate is less than the U.S. tax rate, deferral can provide significant benefits. Deferring repatriation of earnings lowers the overall tax burden in much the same way as deferring capital gains lowers the tax burden imposed by the capital gains tax. Other benefits from deferral arise because the firm effectively gains a real option to repatriate income at times when repatriation might be cheaper. For example, we have already noted that by pooling foreign income, the firm effectively pays the combined tax rate on all foreign income. Because the income generated across countries changes, this combined tax rate will vary from year to year. In years in which it exceeds the U.S. tax rate, the repatriation of additional income does not incur an additional U.S. tax liability, so the earnings can be repatriated tax-free. In addition, there have been occasions in the past when the U.S. Congress has granted a "tax holiday," allowing firms to repatriate funds at a temporarily reduced tax rate. For example, the American Jobs Creation Act passed in 2004 allowed firms to repatriate funds at a 5.25% tax rate rather than the standard 35% corporate tax rate.[3]

This tax treatment leads many U.S. firms with significant profits abroad to opt to defer repatriation and accumulate cash overseas. For instance, in July 2015, Cisco reported total cash and short-term investments on its balance sheet of over $60 billion. However, nearly 90% of this cash was held overseas, with only $7 billion held in the United States.

CONCEPT CHECK

1. What tax rate should we use to value a foreign project?
2. How can a U.S. firm lower its taxes on foreign projects?

31.4 Internationally Segmented Capital Markets

To this point, we have worked under the assumption that international capital markets are integrated. Often, however, this assumption is not appropriate. In some countries, especially in the developing world, all investors do not have equal access to financial securities. In this section, we consider why countries' capital markets might not be integrated—a case called **segmented capital markets**.

Many of the interesting questions in international corporate finance address the issues that result when capital markets are internationally segmented. In this section, we briefly consider the main reasons for segmentation of the capital markets and the implications for international corporate finance.

Differential Access to Markets

In some cases, a country's risk-free securities are internationally integrated but markets for a specific firm's securities are not. Firms may face differential access to markets if there is any kind of asymmetry with respect to information about them. For example, Ityesi may be well known in the United States and enjoy easy access to dollar equity and debt markets there because it regularly provides information to an established community of analysts tracking the firm. It may not be equally well known in the United Kingdom and, therefore, may have difficulty tapping into the pound capital markets because it has no track record there. For this reason, investors in the United Kingdom may require a higher rate of return to persuade them to hold pound stocks and bonds issued by the U.S. firm.

With differential access to national markets, Ityesi would face a higher pound WACC than the pound WACC implied by Eq. 31.7. Ityesi would then view the foreign project as less valuable if it raises capital in the United Kingdom rather than in the United States. In fact, to maximize shareholder value, the firm should raise capital at home; the method of valuing the foreign project as if it were a domestic project would then provide the correct NPV. Differential access to national capital markets is common enough that it provides the best explanation for the existence of **currency swaps**, which are like the interest rate swap

[3]For further discussion see the "Repatriation Tax" box on page 525 in Chapter 15.

contracts we discussed in Chapter 30, but with the holder receiving coupons in one currency and paying coupons denominated in a different currency. Currency swaps generally also have final face value payments, also in different currencies. Using a currency swap, a firm can borrow in the market where it has the best access to capital, and then "swap" the coupon and principal payments to the currency in which it would prefer to make payments. Thus, swaps allow firms to mitigate their exchange rate risk exposure between assets and liabilities, while still making investments in the most profitable locales and raising funds where their cost of capital is lowest.

Macro-Level Distortions

Markets for risk-free instruments may also be segmented. Important macroeconomic reasons for segmented capital markets include capital controls and foreign exchange controls that create barriers to international capital flows, and thus segment national markets. Many countries regulate or limit capital inflows or outflows, and many do not allow their currencies to be freely converted into dollars, thereby creating capital market segmentation. Similarly, some countries restrict who can hold financial securities.

Political, legal, social, and cultural characteristics that differ across countries may require compensation in the form of a country risk premium. For example, the rate of interest paid on government bonds or other securities in a country with a tradition of weak enforcement of property rights is likely not really a risk-free rate. Instead, interest rates in the country will reflect a risk premium for the possibility of default, so relations such as covered interest rate parity will not hold exactly.

EXAMPLE 31.3 Risky Government Bonds

Problem

On July 27, 2009, the spot ruble-dollar exchange rate was R30.9845/\$ and the one-year forward exchange rate was R33.7382/\$. At the time, the yield on short-term Russian government bonds was about 11%, while the comparable one-year yield on U.S. Treasury securities was 0.5%. Using the covered interest parity relationship, calculate the implied one-year forward rate. Compare this rate to the actual forward rate, and explain why the two rates differ.

Solution

Using the covered interest parity formula, the implied forward rate is

$$F = S \times \frac{(1 + r_R)}{(1 + r_\$)} = (\text{R}30.9845/\$)\frac{1.110}{1.005} = \text{R}34.2217/\$$$

The implied forward rate is higher than the current spot rate because Russian government bonds have higher yields than U.S. government bonds. The difference between the implied forward rate and the actual forward rate likely reflects the default risk in Russian government bonds (the Russian government defaulted on its debt as recently as 1998). A holder of 100,000 rubles seeking a true risk-free investment could convert the rubles to dollars, invest in U.S. Treasuries, and convert the proceeds back to rubles at a rate locked in with a forward contract. By doing so, the investor would earn

$$\frac{\text{R}100{,}000}{\text{R}30.9845/\$ \text{ today}} \times \frac{\$1.005 \text{ in 1 year}}{\$ \text{ today}} \times (\text{R}33.7382/\$ \text{ in 1 year}) = \text{R}109{,}432 \text{ in 1 year}$$

for an effective ruble risk-free rate of 9.432%. The higher rate of 11% on Russian bonds reflects a credit spread of 11% − 9.432% = 1.568% to compensate bondholders for default risk.

Implications

A segmented financial market has an important implication for international corporate finance: One country or currency has a higher rate of return than another country or currency, when the two rates are compared in the same currency. If the return difference results from a market friction such as capital controls, corporations can exploit this friction by setting up projects in the high-return country/currency and raising capital in the low-return country/currency. Of course, the extent to which corporations can capitalize on this strategy is naturally limited: If such a strategy were easy to implement, the return difference would quickly disappear as corporations competed to use the strategy. Nevertheless, certain corporations might realize a competitive advantage by implementing such a strategy. For example, as an incentive to invest, a foreign government might strike a deal with a particular corporation that relaxes capital controls for that corporation alone.

EXAMPLE 31.4 Valuing a Foreign Acquisition in a Segmented Market

Problem

Camacho Enterprises is a U.S. company that is considering expanding by acquiring Xtapa, Inc., a firm in Mexico. The acquisition is expected to increase Camacho's free cash flows by 21 million pesos the first year; this amount is then expected to grow at a rate of 8% per year. The price of the investment is 525 million pesos, which is $52.5 million at the current exchange rate of 10 pesos/$. Based on an analysis in the Mexican market, Camacho has determined that the appropriate after-tax peso WACC is 12%. If Camacho has also determined that its after-tax dollar WACC for this expansion is 7.5%, what is the value of the Mexican acquisition? Assume that the Mexican and U.S. markets for risk-free securities are integrated and that the yield curve in both countries is flat. U.S. risk-free interest rates are 6%, and Mexican risk-free interest rates are 9%.

Solution

Let's begin by calculating the NPV of the expansion in pesos and converting the result into dollars at the spot rate. Putting the free cash flows on a timeline:

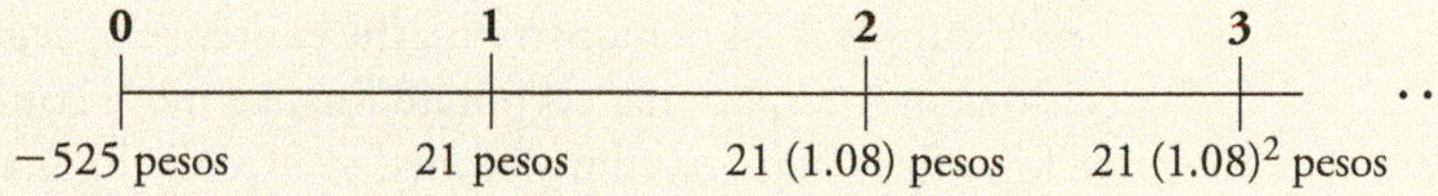

The net present value of these cash flows at the peso WACC is

$$NPV = \frac{21}{0.12 - 0.08} - 525 = 0$$

so the purchase is a zero-NPV transaction. Presumably, Camacho is competing with other Mexican companies for the purchase, and they have bid up the price to the point that NPV = 0.

We can also compute the NPV in dollars by converting the expected cash flows into dollars using forward rates. The N-year forward rate (Eq. 30.3 in Chapter 30) expressed in pesos/$ is

$$F_N = S \times \frac{(1 + r_p)^N}{(1 + r_\$)^N} = 10 \times \left(\frac{1.09}{1.06}\right)^N = 10 \times 1.0283^N = 10.283 \times 1.0283^{N-1}$$

Thus, the dollar expected cash flows are the peso cash flows (from the earlier timeline) converted at the appropriate forward rate (we divide by the forward rate because it is in pesos/$):

$$C_p^N / F_N = \frac{21(1.08)^{N-1}}{10.283 \times 1.0283^{N-1}} = 2.0422 \times 1.0503^{N-1}$$

The dollar expected cash flows are therefore

0	1	2	3	...
$-\$52.5$	$\$2.0422$	$\$2.0422\ (1.0503)$	$\$2.0422\ (1.0503)^2$	

so the dollar cash flows grow at about 5% per year. The NPV of these cash flows is

$$NPV = \frac{2.0422}{0.075 - 0.0503} - 52.5 = \$30.18 \text{ million}$$

Which NPV more accurately represents the benefits of the expansion? The answer depends on the source of the difference. To compute the dollar expected cash flows by converting the peso expected cash flows at the forward rate, we must accept the assumption that spot rates and the project cash flows are uncorrelated. The difference might simply reflect that this assumption failed to hold. Another possibility is that the difference reflects estimation error in the respective WACC estimates.

If Camacho is relatively confident in its assumptions about spot rates and its WACC estimates, a third possibility is that Mexican and U.S. capital markets are not integrated. In this case, Camacho, because of its access to U.S. capital markets, might have a competitive advantage. Perhaps other companies with which it is competing for the purchase of Xtapa are all Mexican firms that do not have access to capital markets outside of Mexico. Hence Camacho can raise capital at a cheaper rate. Of course, this argument also requires that other U.S. companies are not competing for the purchase of Xtapa. Camacho, however, might have special knowledge of Xtapa's markets that other U.S.-based companies lack. This knowledge would give Camacho a competitive advantage in the product market over other U.S. companies and puts it on an equal footing in the product market with other Mexican companies. Because it has a competitive advantage in capital markets over other Mexican companies, the NPV of the purchase is positive for Camacho, but zero for the other bidders for Xtapa.

As Example 31.4 demonstrates, the existence of segmented capital markets makes many decisions in international corporate finance more complicated but potentially more lucrative for a firm that is well positioned to exploit the market segmentation.

CONCEPT CHECK

1. What is the main implication for international corporate finance of a segmented financial market?
2. What are the reasons for segmentation of the capital markets?

31.5 Capital Budgeting with Exchange Risk

The final issue that arises when a firm is considering a foreign project is that the cash flows of the project may be affected by exchange rate risk. The risk is that the cash flows generated by the project will depend upon the future level of the exchange rate. A large part of international corporate finance addresses this foreign exchange risk. This section offers an overview with respect to valuation of foreign currency cash flows.

The working assumptions made thus far in this chapter are that the project's free cash flows are uncorrelated with the spot exchange rates. Such an assumption often makes sense if the firm operates as a local firm in the foreign market—it purchases its inputs and sells its outputs in that market, and price changes of the inputs and outputs are uncorrelated with exchange rates. However, many firms use imported inputs in their production processes or export some of their output to foreign countries. These scenarios alter the nature of a project's foreign exchange risk and, in turn, change the valuation of the foreign currency cash flows.

As an example, let's reconsider what happens if the Ityesi project in the United Kingdom imports some materials from the United States. In this case, the project's pound free cash flows will be correlated with exchange rates. Assuming the cost of the material in the United States remains stable, if the value of a dollar appreciates against the pound, the pound cost of these materials will increase, thereby reducing the pound free cash flows. The reverse is also true: If the dollar depreciates, then the pound free cash flows will increase. Hence, our working assumption that changes in the free cash flows are uncorrelated with changes in the exchange rate is violated, and it is no longer appropriate to calculate the expected dollar free cash flows by converting the expected pound free cash flows at the forward rate.

INTERVIEW WITH

Bill Barrett

William (Bill) Barrett is Co-Chair of Barrett Corporation and CEO of Barrett Explorer. Barrett Corporation is a Canadian family business headquartered in Woodstock, New Brunswick, that distributes recreation and outdoor goods, consumer electronics, wireless broadband services, and other products.

QUESTION: *What are the benefits to being international?*

ANSWER: When a business seeks growth, sooner or later it must look at the international market. In today's world, you are usually involved in international business because so much production and manufacturing occurs in China. We have had longstanding relationships with Chinese companies and have been importing from China and Japan for 30 years. We have also invested and become partners in other businesses: one in India, another in Africa, in Europe, and in the United Kingdom.

QUESTION: *How have currency exchange rates affected your company?*

ANSWER: Currency fluctuations have huge implications. If the marketplace was used to buying something at $1 Canadian but now, due to an exchange rate change, it is $1.20 Canadian, that is a really tough situation to manage. Sometimes we hedge. We buy options on currency. We buy forwards on currency. We try to anticipate and protect ourselves by buying into the future. We never buy 100% into the future but we hedge 50 to 70% of our exposure.

QUESTION: *Are there any important international tax considerations you face?*

ANSWER: International tax rules affect where and how we do business. We are an Atlantic Canadian company. We form holding companies in various parts of the world depending upon the tax implications. In a specific instance in India, we determined that by manufacturing in China and exporting to India, we would face a huge import duty. The solution was to manufacture in India; by doing so, we saved about 27% in tax.

QUESTION: *Do you get involved in joint ventures, licensing agreements, etc., or do you access other countries directly?*

ANSWER: We do business in a variety of ways, including joint venture relationships, distribution relationships, and agency relationships. There are many countries that have such complex regulatory issues that a joint venture is the only practical way to go. In other situations, like the European Union, there is a common set of regulatory, tax, and deployment issues in terms of how people are hired, what your obligations are to them, and what their obligations are to you.

TABLE 31.4 SPREADSHEET Ityesi's Pound Free Cash Flows

	Year	0	1	2	3	4
Incremental Earnings Forecast (£ millions)						
1	Sales	—	37.500	37.500	37.500	37.500
2	Cost of Goods Sold	—	(5.625)	(5.625)	(5.625)	(5.625)
3	**Gross Profit**	—	31.875	31.875	31.875	31.875
4	Operating Expenses	(4.167)	(5.625)	(5.625)	(5.625)	(5.625)
5	Depreciation	—	(3.750)	(3.750)	(3.750)	(3.750)
6	**EBIT**	(4.167)	22.500	22.500	22.500	22.500
7	Income tax at 40%	1.667	(9.000)	(9.000)	(9.000)	(9.000)
8	**Unlevered Net Income**	(2.500)	13.500	13.500	13.500	13.500
Free Cash Flow						
9	Plus: Depreciation	—	3.750	3.750	3.750	3.750
10	Less: Capital Expenditures	(15.000)	—	—	—	—
11	Less: Increases in NWC	—	—	—	—	—
12	**Pound Free Cash Flow**	**(17.500)**	**17.250**	**17.250**	**17.250**	**17.250**

Whenever a project has cash flows that depend on the values of multiple currencies, the most convenient approach is to separate the cash flows by currency. For example, a fraction of Ityesi's manufacturing costs may be for inputs whose cost fluctuates with the value of the dollar. Specifically, suppose £5.625 million of the costs are denominated in pounds, and an additional $16 million (or £10 million at the current exchange rate of $1.60/£) is for inputs whose price fluctuates with the value of the dollar. Then we can calculate Ityesi's pound-denominated free cash flows excluding these dollar-based costs, as in Table 31.4.

If the revenues and costs in the spreadsheet in Table 31.4 are not affected by changes in the spot exchange rates, it makes sense to assume that changes in the free cash flows are uncorrelated with changes in the spot exchange rates. Hence, we can convert the pound-denominated free cash flows to equivalent dollar amounts using the forward exchange rate, as we did in Section 31.2. The spreadsheet in Table 31.5 performs this calculation, with the dollar value of the pound-denominated free cash flow shown in line 3.

Next, we add the dollar-based cash flows to determine the project's aggregate free cash flow in dollar terms. This calculation is done in lines 4 through 6 of Table 31.5. Note that we deduct Ityesi's dollar-denominated costs, and then add the tax shield associated with these costs. Even if the taxes will be paid in pounds in the U.K., they will fluctuate with the dollar cost of the inputs and so can be viewed as a dollar-denominated cash flow.

TABLE 31.5 SPREADSHEET Expected Dollar Free Cash Flows from Ityesi's U.K. Project

	Year	0	1	2	3	4
Dollar Free Cash Flow ($ millions)						
1	Pound FCF (£ millions)	(17.500)	17.250	17.250	17.250	17.250
2	Forward Exchange Rate ($/£)	1.600	1.555	1.512	1.469	1.428
3	**Dollar Value of Pound FCF** (1 × 2)	(28.000)	26.825	26.073	25.344	24.633
4	Dollar Costs	—	(16.000)	(16.000)	(16.000)	(16.000)
5	Income tax at 40%	—	6.400	6.400	6.400	6.400
6	**Free Cash Flow**	(28.000)	17.225	16.473	15.744	15.033

Given the dollar-denominated free cash flow in line 6 of Table 31.5, we can now compute the NPV of the investment using Ityesi's dollar WACC:[3]

$$\frac{17.225}{1.068} + \frac{16.473}{1.068^2} + \frac{15.744}{1.068^3} + \frac{15.033}{1.068^4} - 28.000 = \$27.05 \text{ million}$$

Notice that we would have gotten the same answer had we taken the dollar-based expected costs of $16 million and included them in Table 31.4 by first converting them to pounds at the forward exchange rate. But note that had we done so, these cash flows would no longer correspond to expected cash flows because the forward exchange rate is not an unbiased predictor of the future spot rate. Thus, another way to account for cash flows that are correlated with exchange rates is to convert the cash flows at the forward rate with the explicit understanding that the resulting numbers are not expectations.

The Ityesi example was simplified because we could easily isolate the cash flows that would vary perfectly with the dollar-pound exchange rate from those that would be uncorrelated with the exchange rate. In practice, determining these sensitivities may be difficult. If historical data is available, the tools of regression can be used to identify the exchange rate risk of project cash flows, in much the same way that we used regression to identify the market risk of security returns in Part 4.

In this chapter, we have endeavored to provide an introduction to international capital budgeting. This topic is sufficiently complicated that entire textbooks are devoted to it. Hence, it is difficult to do this issue justice in a single-chapter treatment. Although we have provided a basic framework for approaching the problem, a reader who is seriously considering undertaking a foreign venture should consult one of the books listed in the Further Readings section at the end of the chapter.

CONCEPT CHECK

1. What conditions cause the cash flows of a foreign project to be affected by exchange rate risk?
2. How do we make adjustments when a project has inputs and outputs in different currencies?

MyFinanceLab

Here is what you should know after reading this chapter. MyFinanceLab will help you identify what you know and where to go when you need to practice.

31.1 Internationally Integrated Capital Markets

- The condition necessary to ensure internationally integrated capital markets is that the value of a foreign investment does not depend on the currency (home or foreign) used in the analysis.

31.2 Valuation of Foreign Currency Cash Flows

- Two methods are used to value foreign currency cash flows when markets are internationally integrated and uncertainty in spot exchange rates is uncorrelated with the foreign currency cash flows:
  - Calculate the foreign currency value of a foreign project as the NPV of the expected foreign currency future cash flows discounted at the foreign cost of capital, and then convert the foreign currency NPV into the home currency using the current spot exchange rate.

[3]Again, we use the domestic WACC to discount the cash flows because we continue to assume, as in footnote 2, that the overall market risk of the project is unchanged.

- Compute the expected value of the foreign currency cash flows in the home currency by multiplying the expected value in the foreign currency by the forward exchange rates, and then compute the NPV of these home currency cash flows using the domestic cost of capital.

- When markets are internationally integrated and uncertainty in spot exchange rates is uncorrelated with the foreign currency cash flows, the foreign and domestic risk premia are approximately the same so the foreign WACC can be approximated as the foreign risk-free interest rate plus the domestic risk premium:

$$r_{£}^{*} = \frac{1 + r_{£}}{1 + r_{\$}}(1 + r_{\$}^{*}) - 1 \approx r_{£} + (r_{\$}^{*} - r_{\$}) \tag{31.7}$$

31.3 Valuation and International Taxation

- A U.S. corporation pays the higher of the foreign or domestic tax rate on its foreign project, so project valuation should use the higher of these two rates as well. The U.S. corporation may be able to reduce its tax liability by undertaking foreign projects in other countries whose earnings can be pooled with those of the new project, or by deferring the repatriation of earnings.

31.4 Internationally Segmented Capital Markets

- Capital markets might be internationally segmented. The implication is that one country or currency has a higher cost of capital than another country or currency, when the two are compared in the same currency. This segmentation may provide a firm with a comparative advantage based on its access to capital across markets.

31.5 Capital Budgeting with Exchange Risk

- When a project has inputs and outputs in different currencies, the foreign-denominated cash flows are likely to be correlated with changes in spot rates. To correctly value such projects, the foreign and domestic cash flows should be valued separately.

Key Terms

currency swaps *p. 1067*
internationally integrated capital markets *p. 1061*
repatriated *p. 1066*
segmented capital markets *p. 1067*

Further Reading

See the following textbooks devoted to international corporate finance: R. Click and J. Coval, *The Theory and Practice of International Financial Management* (Prentice Hall, 2001); M. Eaker, F. Fabozzi, and D. Grant, *International Corporate Finance* (The Dryden Press, 1996); D. Eiteman, A. Stonehill, and M. Moffett, *Multinational Business Finance* (Addison-Wesley, 2009); J. Grabbe, *International Financial Markets* (Prentice-Hall, 1995); M. Levi, *International Finance* (McGraw-Hill, 1996); J. Madura, *International Financial Management* (South-Western, 2003); P. Sercu and R. Uppal, *International Financial Markets and the Firm* (South-Western College Publishing, 1995); and A. Shapiro, *Multinational Financial Management* (John Wiley & Sons, 2009).

The effect that international operations have on the value of the firm and its cost of capital is studied in the following articles: V. Errunza and L. Senbet, "Market Segmentation and the Cost of Capital in International Equity Markets," *Journal of Financial and Quantitative Analysis* 35(4) (2000): 577–600; and R. Stulz, "Globalization, Corporate Finance, and the Cost of Capital," *Journal of Applied Corporate Finance* 12(3) (1999): 8–25.

Problems

All problems are available in MyFinanceLab. An asterisk (*) indicates problems with a higher level of difficulty.

Internationally Integrated Capital Markets

1. You are a U.S. investor who is trying to calculate the present value of a €5 million cash inflow that will occur one year in the future. The spot exchange rate is $S = \$1.25/€$ and the forward rate is $F_1 = \$1.215/€$. You estimate that the appropriate dollar discount rate for this cash flow is 4% and the appropriate euro discount rate is 7%.

a. What is the present value of the €5 million cash inflow computed by first discounting the euro and then converting it into dollars?

b. What is the present value of the €5 million cash inflow computed by first converting the cash flow into dollars and then discounting?

c. What can you conclude about whether these markets are internationally integrated, based on your answers to parts a and b?

2. Mia Caruso Enterprises, a U.S. manufacturer of children's toys, has made a sale in Bulgaria and is expecting a BGN4 million cash inflow in one year. The current spot rate is $S = \$1.80/\text{BGN}$ and the one-year forward rate is $F_1 = \$1.8857/\text{BGN}$

a. What is the present value of Mia Caruso's BGN4 million inflow computed by first discounting the cash flow at the appropriate Bulgarian Lev discount rate of 5%, and then converting the result into dollars?

b. What is the present value of Mia Caruso's BGN4 million inflow computed by first converting the cash flow into dollars, and then discounting at the appropriate dollar discount rate of 10%?

c. What can you conclude about whether these markets are internationally integrated, based on your answers to parts a and b?

Valuation of Foreign Currency Cash Flows

3. Etemadi Amalgamated, a U.S. manufacturing firm, is considering a new project in the euro area. You are in Etemadi's corporate finance department and are responsible for deciding whether to undertake the project. The expected free cash flows, in euros, are shown here:

Year	Free Cash Flow (€ million)
0	−15
1	9
2	10
3	11
4	12

You know that the spot exchange rate is $S = \$1.15/€$. In addition, the risk-free interest rate on dollars is 4% and the risk-free interest rate on euros is 6%.

Assume that these markets are internationally integrated and the uncertainty in the free cash flows is not correlated with uncertainty in the exchange rate. You determine that the dollar WACC for these cash flows is 8.5%. What is the dollar present value of the project? Should Etemadi Amalgamated undertake the project?

4. Etemadi Amalgamated, the U.S. manufacturing company in Problem 3, is still considering a new project in the euro area. All information presented in Problem 3 is still accurate, except the spot rate is now $S = \$0.85/€$, about 26% lower. What is the new present value of the project in dollars? Should Etemadi Amalgamated undertake the project?

5. You work for a U.S. firm, and your boss has asked you to estimate the cost of capital for countries using the euro. You know that $S = \$1.20/€$ and $F_1 = \$1.157/€$. Suppose the dollar

WACC for your company is known to be 8%. If these markets are internationally integrated, estimate the euro cost of capital for a project with free cash flows that are uncorrelated with spot exchange rates. Assume the firm pays the same tax rate no matter where the cash flows are earned.

6. Maryland Light, a U.S. light fixtures manufacturer, is considering an investment in Japan. The dollar cost of equity for Maryland Light is 11%. You are in the corporate treasury department, and you need to know the comparable cost of equity in Japanese yen for a project with free cash flows that are uncorrelated with spot exchange rates. The risk-free interest rates on dollars and yen are $r_{\$} = 5\%$ and $r_{¥} = 1\%$, respectively. Maryland Light is willing to assume that capital markets are internationally integrated. What is the yen cost of equity?

7. The dollar cost of debt for Coval Consulting, a U.S. research firm, is 7.5%. The firm faces a tax rate of 30% on all income, no matter where it is earned. Managers in the firm need to know its yen cost of debt because they are considering launching a new bond issue in Tokyo to raise money for a new investment there. The risk-free interest rates on dollars and yen are $r_{\$} = 5\%$ and $r_{¥} = 1\%$, respectively. Coval Consulting is willing to assume that capital markets are internationally integrated and that its free cash flows are uncorrelated with the yen-dollar spot rate. What is Coval Consulting's after-tax cost of debt in yen? (*Hint*: Start by finding the after-tax cost of debt in dollars and then find the yen equivalent.)

8. Manzetti Foods, a U.S. food processing and distribution company, is considering an investment in the euro area. You are in Manzetti's corporate finance department and are responsible for deciding whether to undertake the project. The expected free cash flows, in euros, are uncorrelated to the spot exchange rate and are shown here:

Year	Free Cash Flow (€ million)
0	−25
1	12
2	14
3	15
4	15

The new project has similar dollar risk to Manzetti's other projects. The company knows that its overall dollar WACC is 9.5%, so it feels comfortable using this WACC for the project. The risk-free interest rate on dollars is 4.5% and the risk-free interest rate on euros is 7%.

a. Manzetti is willing to assume that capital markets in the United States and the euro area are internationally integrated. What is the company's euro WACC?

b. What is the present value of the project in euros?

Valuation and International Taxation

9. Tailor Johnson, a U.S. maker of fine menswear, has a subsidiary in Ethiopia. This year, the subsidiary reported and repatriated earnings before interest and taxes (EBIT) of 100 million Ethiopian birrs. The current exchange rate is 8 birr/\$ or $S_1 = \$0.125/\text{birr}$. The Ethiopian tax rate on this activity is 25%. U.S. tax law requires Tailor Johnson to pay taxes on the Ethiopian earnings at the same rate as profits earned in the United States, which is currently 45%. However, the United States gives a full tax credit for foreign taxes paid up to the amount of the U.S. tax liability. What is Tailor Johnson's U.S. tax liability on its Ethiopian subsidiary?

***10.** Tailor Johnson, the menswear company with a subsidiary in Ethiopia described in Problem 9, is considering the tax benefits resulting from deferring repatriation of the earnings from the subsidiary. Under U.S. tax law, the U.S. tax liability is not incurred until the profits are brought back home. Tailor Johnson reasonably expects to defer repatriation for 10 years, at which point the birr earnings will be converted into dollars at the prevailing spot rate, S_{10}, and the tax credit for Ethiopian taxes paid will still be converted at the exchange rate $S_1 = \$0.125$/birr. Tailor Johnson's after-tax cost of debt is 5%.

a. Suppose the exchange rate in 10 years is identical to this year's exchange rate, so $S_{10} = \$0.125$/birr. What is the present value of deferring the U.S. tax liability on Tailor Johnson's Ethiopian earnings for 10 years?

b. How will the exchange rate in 10 years affect the actual amount of the U.S. tax liability? Write an equation for the U.S. tax liability as a function of the exchange rate S_{10}.

11. Peripatetic Enterprises, a U.S. import-export trading firm, is considering its international tax situation. U.S. tax law requires U.S. corporations to pay taxes on their foreign earnings at the same rate as profits earned in the United States; this rate is currently 45%. However, a full tax credit is given for the foreign taxes paid up to the amount of the U.S. tax liability. Peripatetic has major operations in Poland, where the tax rate is 20%, and in Sweden, where the tax rate is 60%. The profits, which are fully and immediately repatriated, and foreign taxes paid for the current year are shown here:

	Poland	Sweden
Earnings before interest and taxes (EBIT)	\$80 million	\$100 million
Host country taxes paid	\$16 million	\$60 million
Earnings before interest after taxes	\$64 million	\$40 million

a. What is the U.S. tax liability on the earnings from the Polish subsidiary assuming the Swedish subsidiary did not exist?

b. What is the U.S. tax liability on the earnings from the Swedish subsidiary assuming the Polish subsidiary did not exist?

c. Under U.S. tax law, Peripatetic is able to pool the earnings from its operations in Poland and Sweden when computing its U.S. tax liability on foreign earnings. Total EBIT is thus \$180 million and the total host country taxes paid is \$76 million. What is the total U.S. tax liability on foreign earnings? Show how this relates to the answers in parts a and b.

Internationally Segmented Capital Markets

***12.** Suppose the interest on Russian government bonds is 7.5%, and the current exchange rate is 28 rubles per dollar. If the forward exchange rate is 28.5 rubles per dollar, and the current U.S. risk-free interest rate is 4.5%, what is the implied credit spread for Russian government bonds?

Capital Budgeting with Exchange Risk

MFL ***13.** Assume that in the original Ityesi example in Table 31.1, all sales actually occur in the United States and are projected to be \$60 million per year for four years. Keeping the cost of sales, operating expenses, capital expenditures and depreciation expenses unchanged (and in pounds), and assuming the tax rate remains at 40%, calculate the NPV of the investment opportunity.

Data Case

You are a senior financial analyst with IBM in their capital budgeting division. IBM is considering expanding in Australia due to its positive business atmosphere and cultural similarities to the U.S.

The new facility would require an initial investment in fixed assets of \$5 billion Australian and an additional capital investment of 3% would be required each year in years 1–4. All capital investments would be depreciated straight-line over the five years that the facility operates. First-year revenues from the facility are expected to be \$6 billion Australian and grow at 10% per year. Cost of goods sold would be 40% of revenue; the other operating expenses would amount to 12% of revenue. Net working capital requirements would be 11% of sales and would be required the year prior to the actual revenues. All net working capital would be recovered at the end of the fifth year. Assume that the tax rates are the same in the two countries, that the two markets are internationally integrated, and that the cash flow uncertainty of the project is uncorrelated with changes in the exchange rate. Your team manager wants you to determine the NPV of the project in U.S. dollars using a cost of capital of 12%.

1. Go to the Yahoo! Finance Web site (www.finance.yahoo.com).
   a. Enter the stock symbol for IBM (IBM) in the box and click "Get Quotes."
   b. Click "Income Statement" under "Company Financials." Copy and paste the data to Excel, or if you have Internet Explorer, place the cursor inside the statement and right-click. Select "Export to Microsoft Excel" from the menu.
2. Obtain exchange rates and comparable interest rates for Australia at Bloomberg's Web site (www.bloomberg.com).
   a. Place the cursor on "Markets" and click "Currencies" from the drop-down menu. Copy the "AUD-USD" exchange rate (the U.S. dollars per Australian dollar) from the table and paste it into the same spreadsheet as the IBM Income Statement.
   b. Go to www.investing.com, click "Markets," then click "World Markets," and select Australia from the drop down menu. Click "Bonds" at the top of the "Australia Indices" panel to get the interest rates for Australia. Copy and paste the data into Excel.
   c. Go to www.investing.com, click "Markets," then click "United States." Click "Bonds" at the top of the "United States Indices" panel to get the interest rates for the United States. Copy and paste the data into Excel.
3. You may have noticed that the four-year rate is not available at www.investing.com for the U.S. Treasury. To find an estimate of the four-year yield, calculate the average of the three and five-year yields.
4. In your Excel spreadsheet, create a new worksheet with a timeline for the project expected cash flows.
   a. Compute the tax rate as the three-year average of IBM's annual income tax divided by annual earnings before tax.
   b. Determine the expected free cash flows of the project.
5. Note that the free cash flows you calculated in Question 4 are in Australian dollars. Use Eq. 30.3 to determine the forward exchange rates for each of the five years of the project. Then, use the forward rates to convert the cash flows to U.S. dollars.
6. Compute the NPV of the project in U.S. dollars using the 12% required return given by your team manager.

Note: Updates to this data case may be found at www.berkdemarzo.com.

Glossary

\$1.00 out lease A type of lease, also known as a finance lease, in which ownership of the asset transfers to the lessee at the end of the lease for a nominal cost of \$1.00.

10-K The annual form that U.S. companies use to file their financial statements with the U.S. Securities and Exchange Commission (SEC).

10-Q The quarterly reporting form that U.S. companies use to file their financial statements with the U.S. Securities and Exchange Commission (SEC).

95% confidence interval A confidence interval gives a range of values which is likely to include an unknown parameter. If independent samples are taken repeatedly from the same population, then the true parameter will lie outside the 95% confidence interval 5% of the time. For a normal distribution, the interval corresponds to approximately 2 standard deviations on both sides of the mean.

abandonment option An option for an investor to cease making investments in a project. Abandonment options can add value to a project because a firm can drop a project if it turns out to be unsuccessful.

ABS *See* asset-backed security.

absolute return *See* cash multiple.

accounts payable The amounts owed to creditors for products or services purchased with credit.

accounts payable days An expression of a firm's accounts payable in terms of the number of days' worth of cost of goods sold that the accounts payable represents.

accounts payable turnover The ratio of annual cost of sales to accounts payable. A measure of how quickly the firm is paying its suppliers.

accounts receivable Amounts owed to a firm by customers who have purchased goods or services on credit.

accounts receivable days An expression of a firm's accounts receivable in terms of the number of days' worth of sales that the accounts receivable represents.

accounts receivable turnover The ratio of annual sales to accounts receivable. A measure of how efficiently the firm is managing accounts receivable.

accumulated depreciation The cumulative depreciation of an asset up to a given point in its life; equal to last period's accumulated depreciation plus the current period's depreciation expense.

acquirer (or bidder) A firm that, in a takeover, buys another firm.

acquisition premium Paid by an acquirer in a takeover, it is the percentage difference between the acquisition price and the premerger price of a target firm.

actuarially fair When the NPV from selling insurance is zero because the price of insurance equals the present value of the expected payment.

adjustable rate mortgages (ARMs) Mortgages with interest rates that are not constant over the life of the mortgage. These were the most common type of "subprime" loans.

adjusted betas A beta that has been adjusted toward 1 to account for estimation error.

adjusted present value (APV) A valuation method to determine the levered value of an investment by first calculating its unlevered value (its value without any leverage) and then adding the value of the interest tax shield and deducting any costs that arise from other market imperfections.

adverse selection The idea that when the buyers and sellers have different information, the average quality of assets in the market will differ from the average quality overall.

after-tax interest rate Reflects the amount of interest an investor can keep after taxes have been deducted.

agency costs Costs that arise when there are conflicts of interest between a firm's stakeholders.

agency problem When decision makers, despite being hired as the agents of other stakeholders, put their own self-interest ahead of the interests of the stakeholders.

aggressive financing policy Financing part or all of a firm's permanent working capital with short-term debt.

aging schedule Categorizes a firm's accounts by the number of days they have been on the firm's books. It can be prepared using either the number of accounts or the dollar amount of the accounts receivable outstanding.

alpha The difference between a stock's expected return and its required return according to the security market line.

American options The most common kind of option, they allow their holders to exercise the option on any date up to, and including, the expiration date.

amortization A charge that captures the change in value of acquired assets. Like depreciation, amortization is not an actual cash expense.

amortizing loan A loan on which the borrower makes monthly payments that include interest on the loan plus some part of the loan balance.

angel group Group of angel investors who pool their money and decide as a group which investments to fund.

angel investors Individual investors who provide entrepreneurs with initial capital to start their business.

annual percentage rate (APR) Indicates the amount of interest earned in one year without the effect of compounding.

annual report The yearly summary of business sent by U.S. public companies to their shareholders that accompanies or includes the financial statement.

annuity A stream of equal periodic cash flows over a specified time period. These cash flows can be inflows of returns earned on investments or outflows of funds invested to earn future returns.

annuity spreadsheet An Excel spreadsheet that can compute any one of the five variables of *NPER, RATE, PV, PMT*, and *FV*. Given any four input variables the spreadsheet computes the fifth.

anti-dilution protection Provision which, in the event of a down round, lowers the price at which investors in an earlier round can convert their preferred shares to common stock, effectively increasing their ownership percentage at the expense of founders and employees.

APR *See* annual percentage rate.

APT *See* Arbitrage Pricing Theory.

APV *See* adjusted present value.

arbitrage The practice of buying and selling equivalent goods or portfolios to take advantage of a price difference.

arbitrage opportunity Any situation in which it is possible to make a profit without taking any risk or making any investment.

Arbitrage Pricing Theory (APT) A model that uses more than one portfolio to capture systematic risk. The portfolios themselves can be thought of as either the risk factor itself or a portfolio of stocks correlated with an unobservable risk factor. Also referred to as a multifactor model.

ARM *See* adjustable rate mortgages.

ask price The price at which a market maker or specialist is willing to sell a security.

asset-backed bonds A type of secured corporate debt. Specific assets are pledged as collateral that bondholders have a direct claim to in the event of bankruptcy. Asset-backed bonds can be secured by any kind of asset.

asset-backed security (ABS) A security whose cash flows come from an underlying pool of financial securities that "back" it.

asset beta *See* unlevered beta.

asset cost of capital The expected return required by the firm's investors to hold the firm's underlying assets; the weighted average of the firm's equity and debt costs of capital.

asset pool Security created by pooling together the cash flows from multiple underlying securities, such as mortgages.

asset securitization The process of creating an asset-backed security by packaging a portfolio of financial securities and issuing an asset-backed security backed by this portfolio.

asset substitution problem When a firm faces financial distress, shareholders can gain from decisions that increase the risk of the firm sufficiently, even if they have negative NPV.

asset turnover The ratio of sales to assets, a measure of how efficiently the firm is utilizing its assets to generate sales.

assets The cash, inventory, property, plant and equipment, and other investments a company has made.

asymmetric information A situation in which parties have different information. It can arise when, for example, managers have superior information to investors regarding the firm's future cash flows.

at-the-money Describes options whose exercise prices are equal to the current stock price.

auction IPO A method for selling new issues directly to the public. Rather than setting a price itself and then allocating shares to buyers, the underwriter in an auction IPO takes bids from investors and then sets the price to clear the market.

auditor A neutral third party that corporations are required to hire that checks the annual financial statements to ensure they are prepared according to GAAP, and to verify that the information is reliable.

availability float How long it takes a bank to give a firm credit for customer payments the firm has deposited in the bank.

average annual return The arithmetic average of an investment's realized returns for each year.

backdating The practice of choosing the grant date of a stock option retroactively, so that the date of the grant would coincide with a date when the stock price was lower than its price at the time the grant was actually awarded. By backdating the option in this way, the executive receives a stock option that is already in-the-money.

balance sheet A list of a firm's assets and liabilities that provides a snapshot of the firm's financial position at a given point in time.

balance sheet identity Total assets equals total liabilities plus stockholders' equity.

balloon payment A large payment that must be made on the maturity date of a bond.

basis risk The risk that the value of a security used to hedge an exposure will not track that exposure perfectly.

bearer bonds Similar to currency in that whoever physically holds this bond's certificate owns the bond. To receive a coupon payment, the holder of a bearer bond must provide explicit proof of ownership by literally clipping a coupon off the bond certificate and remitting it to the paying agent.

best-efforts IPO For smaller initial public offerings (IPOs), a situation in which the underwriter does not guarantee that the stock will be sold, but instead tries to sell the stock for the best possible price. Often such deals have an all-or-none clause: either all of the shares are sold in the IPO, or the deal is called off.

beta The expected percent change in the excess return of a security for a 1% change in the excess return of the market (or other benchmark) portfolio.

bid-ask spread The amount by which the ask price exceeds the bid price.

bid price The price at which a market maker or specialist is willing to buy a security.

bidder *See* acquirer.

Binomial Option Pricing Model A technique for pricing options based on the assumption that each period, the stock's return can take on only two values.

binomial tree A timeline with two branches at every date representing the possible events that could happen at those times.

bird in the hand hypothesis The thesis that firms choosing to pay higher current dividends will enjoy higher stock prices because shareholders prefer current dividends to future ones (with the same present value).

Black-Scholes Option Pricing Model A technique for pricing European-style options when the stock can be traded continuously. It can be derived from the Binomial Option Pricing Model by allowing the length of each period to shrink to zero.

blanket lien *See* floating lien.

board of directors A group elected by shareholders that has the ultimate decision-making authority in the corporation.

bond A security sold by governments and corporations to raise money from investors today in exchange for the promised future payment.

bond certificate States the terms of a bond as well as the amounts and dates of all payments to be made.

book building A process used by underwriters for coming up with an offer price based on customers' expressions of interest.

book enterprise value Book value of equity plus debt less cash. Equivalent to invested capital.

book-to-market ratio The ratio of the book value of equity to the market value of equity.

book value The acquisition cost of an asset less its accumulated depreciation.

book value of equity The difference between the book value of a firm's assets and its liabilities; also called stockholders' equity, it represents the net worth of a firm from an accounting perspective.

break-even The level for which an investment has an NPV of zero.

break-even analysis A calculation of the value of each parameter for which the NPV of the project is zero.

bridge loan A type of short-term bank loan that is often used to "bridge the gap" until a firm can arrange for long-term financing.

Bulldogs A term for foreign bonds in the United Kingdom.

business interruption insurance A type of insurance that protects a firm against the loss of earnings if the business is interrupted due to fire, accident, or some other insured peril.

business liability insurance A type of insurance that covers the costs that result if some aspect of a business causes harm to a third party or someone else's property.

butterfly spread An option portfolio that is long two calls with differing strike prices, and short two calls with a strike price equal to the average strike price of the first two calls.

buying stocks on margin (using leverage) Borrowing money to invest in stocks.

"C" corporations Corporations that have no restrictions on who owns their shares or the number of shareholders, and therefore cannot qualify for subchapter S treatment and are subject to direct taxation.

CAGR *See* compound annual growth rate.

call date The right (but not the obligation) of a bond issuer to retire outstanding bonds on (or after) a specific date.

call option A financial option that gives its owner the right to buy an asset.

call price A price specified at the issuance of a bond at which the issuer can redeem the bond.

callable annuity rate The rate on a risk-free annuity that can be repaid (or called) at any time.

callable bonds Bonds that contain a call provision that allows the issuer to repurchase the bonds at a predetermined price.

cannibalization When sales of a firm's new product displace sales of one of its existing products.

Capital Asset Pricing Model (CAPM) An equilibrium model of the relationship between risk and return that characterizes a security's expected return based on its beta with the market portfolio.

capital budget Lists all of the projects that a company plans to undertake during the next period.

capital budgeting The process of analyzing investment opportunities and deciding which ones to accept.

capital expenditures Purchases of new property, plant, and equipment.

capital gain The amount by which the sale price of an asset exceeds its initial purchase price.

capital gain rate An expression of a capital gain as a percentage of the initial price of the asset.

capital lease A lease viewed as an acquisition for accounting purposes. The asset acquired is listed on the lessee's balance sheet, and the lessee incurs depreciation expenses for the asset. In addition, the present value of the future lease payment is listed as a liability, and the interest portion of the lease payments is deducted as an interest expense. Also known as a *finance lease.*

capital market line (CML) When plotting expected returns versus volatility, the line from the risk-free investment through the efficient portfolio of risky stocks (the portfolio that has the highest possible Sharpe ratio). In the context of the CAPM, it is the line from the risk-free investment through the market portfolio. It shows the highest possible expected return that can be obtained for any given volatility.

capital structure The relative proportions of debt, equity, and other securities that a firm has outstanding.

CAPM *See* Capital Asset Pricing Model.

captured Describes a board of directors whose monitoring duties have been compromised by connections or perceived loyalties to management.

carried interest Fee representing general partners' share of any positive return generated by the fund.

carryback or carryforward *See* tax loss carryforwards and carrybacks.

cash-and-carry strategy A strategy used to lock in the future cost of an asset by buying the asset for cash today, and storing (or "carrying") it until a future date.

cash conversion cycle (CCC) A measure of the cash cycle calculated as the sum of a firm's inventory days and accounts receivable days, less its accounts payable days.

cash cycle The length of time between when a firm pays cash to purchase its initial inventory and when it receives cash from the sale of the output produced from that inventory.

cash multiple (multiple of money, absolute return) The ratio of the total cash received to the total cash invested.

cash offer A type of seasoned equity offering (SEO) in which a firm offers the new shares to investors at large.

cash ratio The ratio of cash to current liabilities. It is the most stringent liquidity ratio.

CCC *See* cash conversion cycle.

CDO *See* collaterized debt obligation.

CDS *See* credit default swap.

Chapter 7 liquidation A provision of the U.S. bankruptcy code in which a trustee is appointed to oversee the liquidation of a firm's assets through an auction. The proceeds from the liquidation are used to pay the firm's creditors, and the firm ceases to exist.

Chapter 11 reorganization A common form of bankruptcy for large corporations in which all pending collection attempts are automatically suspended, and the firm's existing management is given the opportunity to propose a reorganization plan. While developing the plan, management continues to operate the business as usual. The creditors must vote to accept the plan, and it must be approved by the bankruptcy court. If an acceptable plan is not put forth, the court may ultimately force a Chapter 7 liquidation of the firm.

Check 21 *See* Check Clearing for the 21st Century Act.

Check Clearing for the 21st Century Act (Check 21) Eliminates the disbursement float due to the check-clearing process. Under the act, banks can process check information electronically, and, in most cases, the funds are deducted from a firm's checking account on the same day that the firm's supplier deposits the check in its bank.

chief executive officer (CEO) The person charged with running the corporation by instituting the rules and policies set by the board of directors.

chief financial officer (CFO) The most senior financial manager, who often reports directly to the CEO.

classified board *See* staggered board.

clean expenses Expenses that do not include non-cash charges such as depreciation or amortization. While it differs from some accounting treatment, using clean expenses is preferred in financial models.

clean price A bond's cash price less an adjustment for accrued interest, the amount of the next coupon payment that has already accrued.

clientele effects When the dividend policy of a firm reflects the tax preference of its investor clientele.

CML *See* capital market line.

CMO *See* collateralized mortgage obligation.

collateralized debt obligation (CDO) The security that results when banks re-securitize other asset-backed securities.

collateralized mortgage obligation (CMO) A debt security where the cash flows are derived from large mortgage pools, and the payouts are divided into different tranches that have different priority claims on the underlying cash flows.

collection float The amount of time it takes for a firm to be able to use funds after a customer has paid for its goods.

commercial paper Short-term, unsecured debt issued by large corporations that is usually a cheaper source of funds than a short-term bank loan. Most commercial paper has a face value of at least $100,000. Like long-term debt, commercial paper is rated by credit rating agencies.

committed line of credit A legally binding agreement that obligates a bank to provide funds to a firm (up to a stated credit limit) as long as the firm satisfies any restrictions in the agreement.

common risk Perfectly correlated risk.

compensating balance An amount a firm's bank may require the firm to maintain in an account at the bank as compensation for services the bank may perform.

competitive market A market in which goods can be bought and sold at the same price.

compound annual growth rate (CAGR) Geometric average annual growth rate; year-over-year growth rate which, if applied to the initial value and compounded, will lead to the final value.

compound interest The effect of earning "interest on interest."

compounding The process of converting a cash flow to its future value, taking into to account the fact that interest is earned on prior interest payments.

conglomerate merger The type of merger when the target and acquirer operate in unrelated industries.

conservation of value principle With perfect capital markets, financial transactions neither add nor destroy value, but instead represent a repackaging of risk (and therefore return).

conservative financing policy When a firm finances its short-term needs with long-term debt.

consol A bond that promises its owner a fixed cash flow every year, forever.

constant dividend growth model A model for valuing a stock by viewing its dividends as a constant growth perpetuity.

constant interest coverage ratio When a firm keeps its interest payments equal to a target fraction of its free cash flows.

continuation value The current value of all future free cash flow from continuing a project or investment. *See also* terminal value.

continuous compounding The compounding of interest every instant (an infinite number of times per year).

conversion price The face value of a convertible bond divided by the number of shares received if the bond is converted.

conversion ratio The number of shares received upon conversion of a convertible bond, usually stated per $1000 face value.

convertible bonds Corporate bonds with a provision that gives the bondholder an option to convert each bond owned into a fixed number of shares of common stock.

convertible note Debt security or loan that can be converted to equity. Commonly used for angel financing, with note holders having the right to convert the note to preferred stock at a discount to the terms offered by new investors.

convertible preferred stock A preferred stock that gives the owner an option to convert it into common stock on some future date.

corporate bonds Bonds issued by a corporation.

corporate governance The system of controls, regulations, and incentives designed to minimize agency costs between managers and investors and prevent corporate fraud.

corporate investor, corporate partner, strategic partner, strategic investor A corporation that invests in private companies.

corporate partner *See* corporate investor.

corporation A legally defined, artificial being, separate from its owners.

correlation The covariance of the returns divided by the standard deviation of each return; a measure of the common risk shared by stocks that does not depend on their volatility.

cost of capital The expected return available on securities with equivalent risk and term to a particular investment.

coupon bonds Bonds that pay regular coupon interest payments up to maturity, when the face value is also paid.

coupon-paying yield curve A plot of the yield of coupon bonds of different maturities.

coupon rate Determines the amount of each coupon payment of a bond. The coupon rate, expressed as an APR, is set by the issuer and stated on the bond certificate.

coupons The promised interest payments of a bond.

covariance The expected product of the deviation of each return from its mean.

covenants Restrictive clauses in a bond contract that limit the issuers from undercutting their ability to repay bonds.

covered interest parity equation States that the difference between the forward and spot exchange rates is related to the interest rate differential between the currencies.

credibility principle The principle that claims in one's self-interest are credible only if they are supported by actions that would be too costly to take if the claims were untrue.

credit default swap (CDS) When a buyer pays a premium to the seller (often in the form of periodic payments) and receives a payment from the seller to make up for the loss if the underlying bond defaults.

credit rating A rating assigned by a rating agency that assesses the likelihood that a borrower will default.

credit risk The risk of default by the issuer of any bond that is not default free; it is an indication that the bond's cash flows are not known with certainty.

credit spread The difference between the risk-free interest rate on U.S. Treasury notes and the interest rates on all other loans. The magnitude of the credit spread will depend on investors' assessment of the likelihood that a particular firm will default. Also referred to as the *default spread*.

crowdfunding Raising very small amounts of money from a large number of people to fund start-up enterprises, usually over the internet.

cum-dividend When a stock trades before the ex-dividend date, entitling anyone who buys the stock to the dividend.

cumulative abnormal return Measure of a stock's cumulative return relative to that predicted based on its beta.

cumulative normal distribution The probability that an outcome from a standard normal distribution will be below a certain value.

currency forward contract A contract that sets a currency exchange rate, and an amount to exchange, in advance.

currency swaps A contract in which parties agree to exchange coupon payments and a final face value payment that are in different currencies.

currency timeline Indicates time horizontally by dates (as in a standard timeline) and currencies vertically (as in dollars and euros).

current assets Cash or assets that could be converted into cash within one year. This category includes marketable securities, accounts receivable, inventories, and pre-paid expenses such as rent and insurance.

current liabilities Liabilities that will be satisfied within one year. They include accounts payable, notes payable, short-term debt, current maturities of long-term debt, salary or taxes owed, and deferred or unearned revenue.

current ratio The ratio of current assets to current liabilities.

current yield Coupon amount expressed as a percentage of the current price of a bond.

daily settlement A procedure in which the margin used to secure a position in a financial contract is adjusted at the end of each day according to the change in the contract's market value.

dark pools Trading venues in which the size and price of orders are not disclosed to participants. Prices are within the best bid and ask prices available in public markets, but traders face the risk their orders may not be filled if an excess of either buy or sell orders is received.

data snooping bias The idea that given enough characteristics, it will always be possible to find some characteristic that by pure chance happens to be correlated with the estimation error of a regression.

Data Table An Excel function that allows the user to perform sensitivity analysis by computing updated output values (for example, NPV or IRR) by changing one or two assumptions or input variables (such as the discount rate or growth rate).

dealer paper Commercial paper that dealers sell to investors in exchange for a spread (or fee) for their services. The spread decreases the proceeds that the issuing firm receives, thereby increasing the effective cost of the paper.

debentures A type of unsecured corporate debt. Debentures typically have longer maturities (more than ten years) than notes, another type of unsecured corporate debt.

debt capacity The amount of debt at a particular date that is required to maintain the firm's target debt-to-value ratio.

debt ceiling A constraint imposed by the U.S. Congress limiting the overall amount of debt the government can incur.

debt cost of capital The cost of capital, or expected return, that a firm must pay on its debt.

debt covenants Conditions of making a loan in which creditors place restrictions on actions that a firm can take.

debt-equity ratio The ratio of a firm's total amount of short- and long-term debt (including current maturities) to the value of its equity, which may be calculated based on market or book values.

debt overhang When shareholders choose not to invest in a positive-NPV project because some of the gains from investment will accrue to debtholders.

debt-to-capital ratio The ratio of a firm's total amount of short- and long-term debt (including current maturities) to the sum of the value of its debt and the value of its equity, which may be calculated based on market or book values.

debt-to-enterprise-value ratio The fraction of a firm's enterprise value that corresponds to net debt.

debt-to-value ratio Ratio of debt to debt plus equity, in terms of market values. It is also common to use net debt in place of debt (the debt-to-enterprise value ratio).

debtor-in-possession (DIP) financing New debt issued by a bankrupt firm; this debt is senior to all existing creditors, providing renewed access to financing to allow a firm that has filed for bankruptcy to keep operating.

decision node A node on a decision tree at which a decision is made, and so corresponds to a real option.

decision tree A graphical representation of future decisions and uncertainty resolution.

declaration date The date on which a public company's board of directors authorizes the payment of a dividend.

deductible A provision of an insurance policy in which an initial amount of loss is not covered by the policy and must be paid by the insured.

deep in-the-money Describes options that are in-the-money and for which the strike price and stock price are very far apart.

deep out-of-the-money Describes options that are out-of-the-money and for which the strike price and the stock price are very far apart.

default When a firm fails to make the required interest or principal payments on its debt, or violates a debt covenant.

default spread *See* credit spread.

deferred taxes An asset or liability that results from the difference between a firm's tax expenses as reported for accounting purposes, and the actual amount paid to the taxing authority.

depreciation A yearly deduction a firm makes from the value of its fixed assets (other than land) over time according to a depreciation schedule that depends on an asset's life span.

depreciation expense Amount deducted, for accounting purposes, from an asset's value to reflect wear and tear over a given period.

depreciation tax shield The tax savings that result from the ability to deduct depreciation.

derivative security A security whose cash flows depend solely on the prices of other marketed assets.

diluted EPS A firm's disclosure of its potential for dilution from options it has awarded which shows the earnings per share the company would have if the stock options were exercised.

dilution An increase in the total number of shares that will divide a fixed amount of earnings; often occurs when stock options are exercised or convertible bonds are converted.

direct lease A type of lease in which the lessor is not the manufacturer, but is often an independent company that specializes in purchasing assets and leasing them to customers.

direct paper Commercial paper that a firm sells directly to investors.

dirty price A bond's actual cash price. Also referred to as the *invoice price.*

disbursement float The amount of time it takes before a firm's payments to its suppliers actually result in a cash outflow for the firm.

discount The amount by which a cash flow exceeds its present value. The process of converting a cash flow to its present value.

discount factor The value today of a dollar received in the future.

discount loan A type of bridge loan in which the borrower is required to pay the interest at the beginning of the loan period. The lender deducts interest from the loan proceeds when the loan is made.

discount rate The rate used to discount a stream of cash flows; the cost of capital of a stream of cash flows.

discounted free cash flow model A method for estimating a firm's enterprise value by discounting its future free cash flow.

discounting The process of converting a cash flow to its present value.

disposition effect The tendency to hold on to stocks that have lost value and sell stocks that have risen in value since the time of purchase.

distribution date *See* payable date.

diversifiable risk *See* firm-specific risk.

diversification The averaging of independent risks in a large portfolio.

dividend-capture theory The theory that absent transaction costs, investors can trade shares at the time of the dividend so that non-taxed investors receive the dividend.

dividend-discount model A model that values shares of a firm according to the present value of the future dividends the firm will pay.

dividend payments Payments made at the discretion of the corporation to its equity holders.

dividend payout rate The fraction of a firm's earnings that the firm pays as dividends each year.

dividend puzzle When firms continue to issue dividends despite their tax disadvantage.

dividend signaling hypothesis The idea that dividend changes reflect managers' views about a firm's future earnings prospects.

dividend smoothing The practice of maintaining relatively constant dividends.

dividend yield The expected annual dividend of a stock divided by its current price. The dividend yield is the percentage return an investor expects to earn from the dividend paid by the stock.

Dodd-Frank Act A 2010 Congressional act that sought to bring about financial stability by bringing about sweeping changes to the financial regulatory system in response to the 2008 financial crisis.

domestic bonds Bonds issued by a local entity and traded in a local market, but purchased by foreigners. They are denominated in the local currency.

double-barreled Describes municipal bonds for which the issuing local or state government has strengthened its promise to pay by committing itself to using general revenue to pay off the bonds.

down round Venture capital funding round in which the price per share paid by new investors is below the price paid by earlier investors.

dual class shares When one class of a firm's shares has superior voting rights over the other class.

DuPont Identity Expression of the ROE in terms of the firm's profitability, asset efficiency, and leverage.

duration The sensitivity of a bond's price to changes in interest rates. The value-weighted average maturity of a bond's cash flows.

duration mismatch When the durations of a firm's assets and liabilities are significantly different.

duration-neutral portfolio A portfolio with a zero duration.

Dutch auction A share repurchase method in which the firm lists different prices at which it is prepared to buy shares, and shareholders in turn indicate how many shares they are willing to sell at each price. The firm then pays the lowest price at which it can buy back its desired number of shares.

dynamic trading strategy A replication strategy based on the idea that an option payoff can be replicated by dynamically trading in a portfolio of the underlying stock and a risk-free bond.

EAB *See* equivalent annual benefit.

EAR *See* effective annual rate.

earnings per share (EPS) A firm's net income divided by the total number of shares outstanding.

earnings yield Ratio of expected earnings to share price; reciprocal of the forward P/E multiple.

EBIT A firm's earnings before interest and taxes are deducted.

EBIT break-even The level of sales for which a project's EBIT is zero.

EBIT margin The ratio of EBIT to sales.

EBITDA A computation of a firm's earnings before interest, taxes, depreciation, and amortization are deducted.

economic distress A significant decline in the value of a firm's assets, whether or not the firm experiences financial distress due to leverage.

economic value added Unlevered net income (EBIT after tax) less a charge for the required return on the firm's total invested capital (book enterprise value).

economies of scale The savings a large company can enjoy—that are not available to a small company—from producing goods in high volume.

economies of scope Savings large companies can realize that come from combining the marketing and distribution of different types of related products.

effective annual rate (EAR) The total amount of interest that will be earned at the end of one year.

effective dividend tax rate The effective dividend tax rate measures the additional tax paid by the investor per dollar of after-tax capital gain income that is instead received as a dividend.

efficient frontier The set of portfolios that can be formed from a given set of investments with the property that each portfolio has the highest possible expected return that can be attained without increasing its volatility.

efficient market When the cost of capital of an investment depends only on its systematic risk, and not its diversifiable risk.

efficient markets hypothesis The idea that competition among investors works to eliminate all positive-NPV trading opportunities. It implies that securities will be fairly priced, based on their future cash flows, given all information that is available to investors.

efficient portfolio A portfolio that contains only systematic risk. An efficient portfolio cannot be diversified further; there is no way to reduce the volatility of the portfolio without lowering its expected return. When risk-free borrowing and lending is available, the efficient portfolio is the tangent portfolio, the portfolio with the highest Sharpe ratio in the economy.

empirical distribution A plot showing the frequency of outcomes based on historical data.

enterprise value The total market value of a firm's equity and debt, less the value of its cash and marketable securities. It measures the value of the firm's underlying business.

EPS *See* earnings per share.

equal-ownership portfolio A portfolio containing an equal fraction of the total number of shares outstanding of each security in the portfolio. Equivalent to a value-weighted portfolio.

equally weighted portfolio A portfolio in which the same dollar amount is invested in each stock.

equity The collection of all the outstanding shares of a corporation.

equity cost of capital The expected rate of return available in the market on other investments with equivalent risk to the firm's shares.

equity holder (also shareholder or stockholder) An owner of a share of stock in a corporation.

equity multiplier Measure of leverage that indicates the value of assets held per dollar of shareholder equity.

equivalent annual benefit (EAB) The annual annuity payment over the life of an investment that has the same NPV as the investment.

equivalent annual benefit method A method of choosing between projects with different lives by selecting the project with the higher equivalent annual benefit. It ignores the value of any real options because it assumes that both projects will be replaced on their original terms.

equivalent annual cost Equal to the negative of the equivalent annual benefit.

error (or residual) term Represents the deviation from the best-fitting line in a regression. It is zero on average and uncorrelated with any regressors.

ESO *See* executive stock option.

ETF *See* exchange traded fund.

Eurobonds International bonds that are not denominated in the local currency of the country in which they are issued.

European options Options that allow their holders to exercise the option only on the expiration date; holders cannot exercise before the expiration date.

evergreen credit A revolving line of credit with no fixed maturity.

ex-dividend date A date, two days prior to a dividend's record date, on or after which anyone buying the stock will not be eligible for the dividend.

excess return The difference between the average return for an investment and the average return for a risk-free investment.

exchange ratio In a takeover, the number of bidder shares received in exchange for each target share.

exchange-traded fund (ETF) A security that trades directly on an exchange, like a stock, but represents ownership in a portfolio of stocks.

execution risk The risk that a misstep in the firm's execution may cause a project to fail to generate the forecasted cash flows.

executive stock options (ESOs) A common practice for compensating executives by granting them call options on their company's stock.

exercise price *See* strike price.

exercising (an option) When a holder of an option enforces the agreement and buys or sells a share of stock at the agreed-upon price

exit strategy An important consideration for investors in private companies, it details how they will eventually realize the return from their investment.

expected return A computation for the return of a security based on the average payoff expected.

expiration date The last date on which an option holder has the right to exercise the option.

face value The notional amount of a bond used to compute its interest payments. The face value of the bond is generally due at the bond's maturity. Also called par value or principal amount.

factor betas The sensitivity of the stock's excess return to the excess return of a factor portfolio, as computed in a multifactor regression.

factor portfolios Portfolios that can be combined to form an efficient portfolio.

factoring of accounts receivable An arrangement in which a firm sells receivables to the lender (i.e., the factor), and the lender agrees to pay the firm the amount due from its customers at the end of the firm's payment period.

factors Firms that purchase the receivables of other companies and are the most common sources for secured short-term loans.

failure cost index Used to rank the optimal sequence to pursue mutually dependent research projects; it is equal to one minus the present value of receiving $1 in the event of success, divided by the present value of the investment required.

fair market value (FMV) cap lease A type of lease in which the lessee can purchase the asset at the minimum of its fair market value and a fixed price or "cap."

fair market value (FMV) lease A type of lease that gives the lessee the option to purchase the asset at its fair market value at the termination of the lease.

Fama-French-Carhart (FFC) factor specification A multifactor model of risk and return in which the factor portfolios are the market, small-minus-big, high-minus-low, and PR1YR portfolios identified by Fama, French, and Carhart.

familiarity bias The tendency of investors to favor investments in companies with which they are familiar.

FCFE *See* free cash flow to equity.

federal funds rate The overnight loan rate charged by banks with excess reserves at a Federal Reserve bank (called federal funds) to banks that need additional funds to meet reserve requirements. The federal funds rate is influenced by the Federal Reserve's monetary policy, and itself influences other interest rates in the market.

FFC factor specification *See* Fama-French-Carhart factor specification.

field warehouse A warehouse arrangement that is operated by a third party, but is set up on the borrower's premises in a separate area. Inventory held in the field warehouse can be used as secure collateral for borrowing.

final prospectus Part of the final registration statement prepared by a company prior to an IPO that contains all the details of the offering, including the number of shares offered and the offer price.

finance lease *See* capital lease.

financial distress When a firm has difficulty meeting its debt obligations.

financial option A contract that gives its owner the right (but not the obligation) to purchase or sell an asset at a fixed price at some future date.

financial security An investment opportunity that trades in a financial market.

financial statements Firm-issued (usually quarterly and annually) accounting reports with past performance information.

firm commitment An agreement between an underwriter and an issuing firm in which the underwriter guarantees that it will sell all of the stock at the offer price.

firm-specific, idiosyncratic, unique, or diversifiable risk Fluctuations of a stock's return that are due to firm-specific news and are independent risks unrelated across stocks.

fixed price lease A type of lease in which the lessee has the option to purchase the asset at the end of the lease for a fixed price that is set upfront in the lease contract.

floating lien A financial arrangement in which all of a firm's inventory is used to secure a loan.

floating rate An interest rate or exchange rate that changes depending on supply and demand in the market.

floor planning *See* trust receipts loan.

flow-to-equity (FTE) A valuation method that calculates the free cash flow available to equity holders taking into account all payments to and from debt holders. The cash flows to equity holders are then discounted using the equity cost of capital.

FMV lease *See* fair market value lease.

foreign bonds Bonds issued by a foreign company in a local market and are intended for local investors. They are also denominated in the local currency.

forward earnings A firm's anticipated earnings over the coming 12 months.

forward exchange rate The exchange rate set in a currency forward contract, it applies to an exchange that will occur in the future.

forward interest rate (forward rate) An interest rate guaranteed today for a loan or investment that will occur in the future.

forward P/E A firm's price-earnings (P/E) ratio calculated using forward earnings.

forward rate agreement *See* interest rate forward contract.

free cash flow The incremental effect of a project on a firm's available cash.

free cash flow hypothesis The view that wasteful spending is more likely to occur when firms have high levels of cash flow in excess of what is needed after making all positive-NPV investments and payments to debt holders.

free cash flow to equity (FCFE) The free cash flow that remains after adjusting for interest payments, debt issuance, and debt repayment.

free float The number of shares actually available for public trading. Since 2005, this has been used to compute the value weights of the S&P 500 Index.

freezeout merger A situation in which the laws on tender offers allow an acquiring company to freeze existing shareholders out of the gains from merging by forcing non-tendering shareholders to sell their shares for the tender offer price.

friendly takeover When a target's board of directors supports a merger, negotiates with potential acquirers, and agrees on a price that is ultimately put to a shareholder vote.

FTE *See* flow to equity.

funding risk The risk of incurring financial distress costs should a firm not be able to refinance its debt in a timely manner or at a reasonable rate.

funding round Each occasion upon which a start-up firm raises additional capital by issuing new equity securities to investors.

future value The value of a cash flow that is moved forward in time.

futures contract A forward contract that is traded on an exchange.

GAAP *See* Generally Accepted Accounting Principles.

general lien *See* floating lien.

general obligation bonds Bonds backed by the full faith and credit of a local government.

Generally Accepted Accounting Principles (GAAP) A common set of rules and a standard format for public companies to use when they prepare their financial reports.

global bonds Bonds that are offered for sale in several different markets simultaneously. Unlike Eurobonds, global bonds can be offered for sale in the same currency as the country of issuance.

golden parachute An extremely lucrative severance package that is guaranteed to a firm's senior managers in the event that the firm is taken over and the managers are let go.

goodwill The difference between the price paid for a company and the book value assigned to its assets.

gray directors Members of a board of directors who are not as directly connected to the firm as insiders are, but who have existing or potential business relationships with the firm.

greenmail When a firm avoids a threat of takeover and removal of its management by a major shareholder by buying out the shareholder, often at a large premium over the current market price.

greenshoe provision *See* over-allotment allocation.

gross alpha Alpha before deducting fees.

gross margin The ratio of gross profit to revenues (sales).

gross profit The third line of an income statement that represents the difference between a firm's sales revenues and its costs.

growing annuity A stream of cash flows paid at regular intervals and growing at a constant rate, up to some final date.

growing perpetuity A stream of cash flows that occurs at regular intervals and grows at a constant rate forever.

growth option A real option to invest in the future. Because these options have value, they contribute to the value of any firm that has future possible investment opportunities.

growth stocks Firms with high market-to-book ratios.

hedge (or hedging) To reduce risk by holding contracts or securities whose payoffs are negatively correlated with some risk exposure.

herd behavior The tendency of investors to make similar trading errors by actively imitating other investors' actions.

high frequency traders (HFTs) Traders who place, update, cancel, and execute trades many times per second.

high-minus-low (HML) portfolio An annually updated portfolio that is long stocks with high book-to-market ratios and short stocks with low book-to-market ratios.

high-yield bonds Bonds below investment grade which trade with a high yield to maturity to compensate investors for their high risk of default.

HML portfolio *See* high-minus-low portfolio.

homemade dividend When an investor creates a cash payout from their holdings of a stock by simply selling some portion of their shares.

homemade leverage When investors use leverage in their own portfolios to adjust the leverage choice made by a firm.

homogeneous expectations A theoretical situation in which all investors have the same estimates concerning future investment returns.

horizontal merger The type of merger when the target and acquirer are in the same industry.

hostile takeover A situation in which an individual or organization, sometimes referred to as a corporate raider, purchases a large fraction of a target corporation's stock and in doing so gets enough votes to replace the target's board of directors and its CEO.

hurdle rate A higher discount rate created by the hurdle rate rule. If a project can jump the hurdle with a positive NPV at this higher discount rate, then it should be undertaken.

hurdle rate rule Raises the discount rate by using a higher discount rate than the cost of capital to compute the NPV, but then applies the regular NPV rule: Invest whenever the NPV calculated using this higher discount rate is positive.

idiosyncratic risk *See* firm-specific risk.

immunized portfolio *See* duration-neutral portfolio.

immunizing Adjusting a portfolio to make it duration neutral.

impairment charge Captures the change in value of the acquired assets; is not an actual cash expense.

implied volatility The volatility of an asset's return that is consistent with the quoted price of an option on the asset.

income statement A list of a firm's revenues and expenses over a period of time.

incremental earnings The amount by which a firm's earnings are expected to change as a result of an investment decision.

incremental IRR The IRR of the incremental cash flows associated with replacing one project with another, or changing from one decision to another.

incremental IRR investment rule Applies the IRR rule to the difference between the cash flows of two mutually exclusive alternatives (the *increment* to the cash flows of one investment over the other).

indenture Included in a prospectus, it is a formal contract between a bond issuer and a trust company. The trust company represents the bondholders and makes sure that the terms of the indenture are enforced. In the case of default, the trust company represents the bondholders' interests.

independent (outside) directors *See* outside directors.

independent risk Risks that bear no relation to each other. If risks are independent, then knowing the outcome of one provides no information about the other. Independent risks are always uncorrelated, but the reverse need not be true.

index funds Mutual funds that invest in stocks in proportion to their representation in a published index, such as the S&P 500 or Wilshire 5000.

inefficient portfolio Describes a portfolio for which it is possible to find another portfolio that has higher expected return and lower volatility.

information node A type of node on a decision tree indicating uncertainty that is out of the control of the decision maker.

informational cascade effect When traders ignore their own information hoping to profit from the information of others.

initial public offering (IPO) The process of selling stock to the public for the first time.

inside directors Members of a board of directors who are employees, former employees, or family members of employees.

insider trading Occurs when a person makes a trade based on privileged information.

insurance premium The fee a firm pays to an insurance company for the purchase of an insurance policy.

intangible assets Non-physical assets, such as intellectual property, brand names, trademarks, and goodwill. Intangible assets appear on the balance sheet as the difference between the price paid for an acquisiton and the book value assigned to its tangible assets.

interest coverage ratio An assessment by lenders of a firm's leverage. Common ratios consider operating income, EBIT, or EBITDA as a multiple of the firm's interest expenses.

interest rate factor One plus the interest rate, it is the rate of exchange between dollars today and dollars in the future.

interest rate forward contract A contract today that fixes the interest rate for a loan or investment in the future.

interest rate swap A contract in which two parties agree to exchange the coupons from two different types of loans.

interest tax shield The reduction in taxes paid due to the tax deductibility of interest payments.

internal rate of return (IRR) The interest rate that sets the net present value of the cash flows equal to zero.

internal rate of return (IRR) investment rule A decision rule that accepts any investment opportunity where IRR exceeds the opportunity cost of capital. This rule is only optimal in special circumstances, and often leads to errors if misapplied.

internationally integrated capital markets When any investor can exchange currencies in any amount at the spot or forward rates and is free to purchase or sell any security in any amount in any country at its current market prices.

in-the-money Describes an option whose value if immediately exercised would be positive.

intrinsic value The amount by which an option is in-the-money, or zero if the option is out-of-the-money.

inventories A firm's raw materials as well as its work-in-progress and finished goods.

inventory days An expression of a firm's inventory in terms of the number of days' worth or cost of goods sold that the inventory represents.

inventory turnover The ratio of the annual cost of sales to inventory. A measure of how efficiently a firm is managing its inventory.

invested capital Operating assets net of liabilities. Also calculated as the book value of equity plus debt less cash, see book enterprise value.

investment-grade bonds Bonds in the top four categories of creditworthiness with a low risk of default.

invoice price *See* dirty price.

IPO *See* initial public offering.

IRR *See* internal rate of return.

IRR investment rule *See* internal rate of return investment rule.

Jensen's alpha The constant term in a regression of a security's excess returns against those of the market portfolio. It can be interpreted as a risk-adjusted measure of the security's past performance.

JIT inventory management *See* "just-in-time" inventory management.

junk bonds Bonds in one of the bottom five categories of creditworthiness (below investment grade) that have a high risk of default.

"just-in-time" (JIT) inventory management When a firm acquires inventory precisely when needed so that its inventory balance is always zero, or very close to it.

key personnel insurance A type of insurance that compensates a firm for the loss or unavoidable absence of crucial employees in the firm.

Law of One Price In competitive markets, securities or portfolios with the same cash flows must have the same price.

LBO *See* leveraged buyout.

lead underwriter The primary banking firm responsible for managing a security issuance.

lease-equivalent loan A loan that is required on the purchase of an asset that leaves the purchaser with the same net future obligations as a lease would entail.

lemons principle When a seller has private information about the value of a good, buyers will discount the price they are willing to pay due to adverse selection.

lessee The party in a lease liable for periodic payments in exchange for the right to use the asset.

lessor The party in a lease who is entitled to the lease payments in exchange for lending the asset.

leverage The amount of debt held in a portfolio or issued by a firm. *See also* buying stocks on margin.

leverage ratchet effect Once existing debt is in place, shareholders may have an incentive to increase leverage even if it decreases the value of the firm, and shareholders may prefer not to decrease leverage by buying back debt even when it will increase the value of the firm.

leverage ratio (of an option) A measure of leverage obtained by looking at debt as a proportion of value, or interest payments as a proportion of cash flows.

leveraged buyout (LBO) When a group of private investors purchases all the equity of a public corporation and finances the purchase primarily with debt.

leveraged lease A lease in which the lessor borrows from a bank or other lender to obtain the initial capital to purchase an asset, using the lease payments to pay interest and principal on the loan.

leveraged recapitalization When a firm uses borrowed funds to pay a large special dividend or repurchase a significant amount of its outstanding shares.

levered equity Equity in a firm with outstanding debt.

liabilities A firm's obligations to its creditors.

LIBOR *See* London Inter-Bank Offered Rate.

limit order Order to buy or sell a set amount of a security at a fixed price.

limit order book Collection of all current limit orders for a given security.

limited liability When an investor's liability is limited to her initial investment.

limited liability company (LLC) A limited partnership without a general partner.

limited partnership A partnership with two kinds of owners, general partners and limited partners.

linear regression The statistical technique that identifies the best-fitting line through a set of points.

line of credit A bank loan arrangement in which a bank agrees to lend a firm any amount up to a stated maximum. This flexible agreement allows the firm to draw upon the line of credit whenever it chooses.

liquid Describes an investment that can easily be turned into cash because it can be sold immediately at a competitive market price.

liquidating dividend A return of capital to shareholders from a business operation that is being terminated.

liquidation Closing down a business and selling off all its assets; often the result of the business declaring bankruptcy.

liquidation preference Minimum amount that must be paid to holders of preferred shares before any payments can be made to common stockholders.

liquidity Extent to which the market for an asset is liquid. Limit orders provide liquidity by making available an immediate opportunity to trade.

liquidity risk The risk of being forced to liquidate an investment (at a loss) because the cash is required to satisfy another obligation (most often a margin requirement).

LLC *See* limited liability company.

loan origination fee A bank charge that a borrower must pay to initiate a loan.

lockup A restriction that prevents existing shareholders from selling their shares for some period (usually 180 days) after an IPO.

London Inter-Bank Offered Rate (LIBOR) The rate of interest at which banks borrow funds from each other in the London interbank market. It is quoted for maturities of one day to one year for ten major currencies.

long bonds Bonds issued by the U.S. Treasury with the longest outstanding maturities (30 years).

long position A positive investment in a security.

long-term assets Net property, plant, and equipment, as well as property not used in business operations, start-up costs in connection with a new business, investments in long-term securities, and property held for sale.

long-term debt Any loan or debt obligation with a maturity of more than a year.

long-term liabilities Liabilities that extend beyond one year.

MACRS depreciation The most accelerated cost recovery system allowed by the IRS. Based on the recovery period, MACRS depreciation tables assign a fraction of the purchase price that the firm can depreciate each year.

mail float How long it takes a firm to receive a customer's payment check after the customer has mailed it.

management buyout (MBO) A leveraged buyout in which the buyer is the firm's own management.

management discussion and analysis (MD&A) A preface to the financial statements in which a company's management discusses the recent year (or quarter), providing a background on the company and any significant events that may have occurred.

management entrenchment A situation arising as the result of the separation of ownership and control in which managers may make decisions that benefit themselves at investors' expense.

management entrenchment theory A theory that suggests managers choose a capital structure to avoid the discipline of debt and maintain their own job security.

margin Collateral that investors are required to post when buying or selling securities that could generate losses beyond the initial investment.

marginal corporate tax rate The tax rate a firm will pay on an incremental dollar of pretax income.

market capitalization The total market value of equity; equals the market price per share times the number of shares.

market index The market value of a broad-based portfolio of securities.

market makers Individuals on the trading floor of a stock exchange who match buyers with sellers.

market orders Orders to trade immediately at the best outstanding limit order available.

market portfolio A value-weighted portfolio of all shares of all stocks and securities in the market.

market proxy A portfolio whose return is believed to closely track the true market portfolio.

market risk *See* systematic risk.

market timing The strategy of buy or selling securities (or an asset class) based on a forecast of future price movements.

market timing view of capital structure The idea that capital structure decisions are made in part to exploit under or overpricing of the stock in the market.

market-to-book ratio (P/B) The ratio of a firm's market (equity) capitalization to the book value of its stockholders' equity. Also referred to as the *price-to-book* or *P/B ratio*.

market value balance sheet Similar to an accounting balance sheet, with two key distinctions: First, all assets and liabilities of the firm are included, even intangible assets such as reputation, brand name, or human capital that are missing from a standard accounting balance sheet; second, all values are current market values rather than historical costs.

marketable securities Short-term, low-risk investments that can be easily sold and converted to cash (such as money market investments, like government debt, that mature within a year).

marking to market Computing gains and losses each day based on the change in the market price of a futures contract.

martingale prices *See* risk-neutral probabilities.

matching principle States that a firm's short-term needs should be financed with short-term debt and long-term needs should be financed with long-term sources of funds.

maturity date The final repayment date of a bond.

MBO *See* management buyout.

MBS *See* mortgage-backed security.

MD&A *See* management discussion and analysis.

mean return See *expected return*.

merger-arbitrage spread In a takeover, the difference between a target stock's price and the implied offer price.

merger waves Peaks of heavy activity followed by quiet troughs of few transactions in the takeover market.

method of comparables An estimate of the value of a firm based on the value of other, comparable firms or other investments that are expected to generate very similar cash flows in the future.

mid-year convention A method of discounting in which cash flows that arrive continuously throughout the year are treated as though they arrive at the middle of the year. This mid-year convention is a reasonable approximation to continuous discounting.

momentum strategy Buying stocks that have had past high returns, and (short) selling stocks that have had past low returns.

money market Market for safe, short-term debt issued by high-quality borrowers, such as governments or high credit quality firms.

Monte Carlo simulation A common technique for pricing derivative assets in which the expected payoff of the derivative security is estimated by calculating its average payoff after simulating many random paths for the underlying stock price. In the randomization, the risk-neutral probabilities are used, so the average payoff can be discounted at the risk-free rate to estimate the derivative security's value.

moral hazard When purchasing insurance reduces a firm's incentive to avoid risk.

mortgage-backed security (MBS) An asset-backed security backed by home mortgages.

mortgage bonds A type of secured corporate debt. Real property is pledged as collateral that bondholders have a direct claim to in the event of bankruptcy.

multifactor model A model that uses more than one risk factor to capture risk. *See also* Arbitrage Pricing Theory (APT).

multiple of money *See* cash multiple.

multiple regression A regression with more than one independent variable.

municipal bonds Bonds issued by state and local governments. They are not taxable at the federal level (and sometimes not at the state or local level either) and so are sometimes also referred to as tax-exempt bonds.

mutually dependent investments Situation in which the value of one project depends upon the outcome of the others.

naked short sale Short sale in which the seller fails to locate shares to borrow before executing the sale.

natural hedge When a firm can pass on cost increases to its customers or revenue decreases to its suppliers.

net alpha Alpha after deducting fees.

net debt Total debt outstanding minus any cash balances.

net income or earnings The last or "bottom line" of a firm's income statement that is a measure of the firm's income over a given period of time.

net investment The firm's capital expenditures in excess of depreciation.

net operating profit after tax (NOPAT) *See* unlevered net income.

net present value (NPV) The difference between the present value of a project's or investment's benefits and the present value of its costs.

Net Present Value (NPV) Decision Rule When making an investment decision, take the alternative with the highest NPV. Choosing this alternative is equivalent to receiving its NPV in cash today. Also known as NPV Investment Rule.

net profit margin The ratio of net income to revenues, it shows the fraction of each dollar in revenues that is available to equity holders after the firm pays interest and taxes.

net working capital The difference between a firm's current assets and current liabilities that represents the capital available in the short-term to run the business.

no-arbitrage price In a normal market, when the price of a security equals the present value of the cash flows paid by the security.

nominal interest rate Interest rate quoted by banks and other financial institutions that indicates the rate at which money will grow if invested for a certain period of time.

non-tax lease A type of lease in which the lessee receives the depreciation deductions for tax purposes, and can also deduct the interest portion of the lease payments as an interest expense. The interest portion of the lease payment is interest income for the lessor.

NOPAT Net operating profit after tax; equivalent to unlevered net income.

normal market A competitive market in which there are no arbitrage opportunities.

notes A type of unsecured corporate debt. Notes typically are coupon bonds with maturities shorter than 10 years.

notional principal Used to calculate the coupon payments in an interest rate swap.

no-trade theorem The idea that when investors have rational expectations, prices will adjust to reflect new information before any trades can occur.

NPV *See* net present value.

NPV Decision Rule *See* Net Present Value (NPV) Decision Rule.

NPV Investment Rule *See* Net Present Value (NPV) Decision Rule.

NPV profile Graph that projects NPV over a range of discount rates.

off-balance sheet transactions Transactions or arrangements that can have a material impact on a firm's future performance yet do not appear on the balance sheet.

OID *See* original issue discount.

on-the-run bonds The most recently issued treasury security of a particular original maturity.

open interest The total number of contracts of a particular option that have been written.

open market repurchase When a firm repurchases shares by buying its shares in the open market.

operating cycle The average length of time between when a firm originally receives its inventory and when it receives the cash back from selling its product.

operating income A firm's gross profit less its operating expenses.

operating lease A type of lease, viewed as a rental for accounting purposes, in which the lessee reports the entire lease payment as an operating expense. The lessee does not deduct a depreciation expense for the asset and does not report the asset, or the lease payment liability, on its balance sheet.

operating leverage Relative proportion of fixed versus variable costs.

operating margin The ratio of operating income to revenues, it reveals how much a company has earned from each dollar of sales before interest and taxes are deducted.

opportunity cost The value a resource could have provided in its best alternative use.

opportunity cost of capital The best available expected return offered in the market on an investment of comparable risk and term to the cash flow being discounted; the return the investor forgoes on an alternative investment of equivalent riskiness and term when the investor takes on a new investment.

option delta The change in the price of an option given a $1 change in the price of the stock; the number of shares in the replicating portfolio for the option.

option premium The market price of the option.

option writer The seller of an option contract.

original issue discount (OID) Describes a coupon bond that is issued at a discount.

out-of-the-money Describes an option that if exercised immediately results in a loss of money.

outside (independent) directors Any member of a board of directors other than an inside or gray director.

over-allotment allocation (greenshoe provision) On an IPO, an option that allows the underwriter to issue more stock, usually amounting to 15% of the original offer size, at the IPO offer price.

overconfidence bias The tendency of individual investors to trade too much based on the mistaken belief that they can pick winners and losers better than investment professionals.

overhead expenses Those expenses associated with activities that are not directly attributable to a single business activity but instead affect many different areas of a corporation.

paid-in capital Capital contributed by stockholders through the purchase of stock from the corporation at a price in excess of its par value.

par A price at which coupon bonds trade that is equal to their face value.

pari passu Securities with equal priority.

participation rights Provision allowing preferred shareholders to receive payment as though they held common stock without converting their preferred stock. The amount that can be received in this way is often limited by a participation cap.

partnership A sole proprietorship with more than one owner.

passive portfolio A portfolio that is not rebalanced in response to price changes.

pass-through Describes securities whose payments derive directly from other assets like mortgages.

payable date (distribution date) A date, generally within a month after the record date, on which a firm mails dividend checks to its registered stockholders.

payback investment rule The simplest investment rule. Only projects that pay back their initial investment within the payback period are undertaken.

payback period A specified amount of time used in the payback investment rule. Only investments that pay back their initial investment within this amount of time are undertaken.

payments pattern Information on the percentage of monthly sales that the firm collects in each month after the sale.

payout policy The way a firm chooses between the alternative ways to pay cash out to equity holders.

P/E *See* price-earnings ratio.

pecking order hypothesis The idea that managers will prefer to fund investments by first using retained earnings, then debt and equity only as a last resort.

perfect capital markets A set of conditions in which investors and firms can trade the same set of securities at competitive market prices with no frictions such as taxes, transaction costs, issuance costs, asymmetric information, or agency costs.

permanent working capital The amount that a firm must keep invested in its short-term assets to support its continuing operations.

perpetuity A stream of equal cash flows that occurs at regular intervals and lasts forever.

pledging of accounts receivable An agreement in which a lender accepts accounts receivable as collateral for a loan. The lender typically lends a percentage of the value of the accepted invoices.

poison pill A defense against a hostile takeover. It is a rights offering that gives the target shareholders the right to buy shares in either the target or an acquirer at a deeply discounted price.

policy limits Those provisions of an insurance policy that limit the amount of loss that the policy covers regardless of the extent of the damage.

pool (of assets) *See* asset pool.

portfolio A collection of securities.

portfolio insurance A protective put written on a portfolio rather than a single stock. When the put does not itself trade, it is synthetically created by constructing a replicating portfolio.

portfolio weights The fraction of the total investment in a portfolio held in each individual investment in the portfolio.

post-money valuation At the issue of new equity, the value of the whole firm (old plus new shares) at the price the new equity is sold at.

PR1YR portfolio *See* prior one-year momentum portfolio.

pre-money valuation Value of the prior shares outstanding when evaluated at the price in the current funding round.

precautionary balance The amount of cash a firm holds to counter the uncertainty surrounding its future cash needs.

preferred stock Preferred stock issued by mature companies such as banks usually has a preferential dividend and seniority in any liquidation and sometimes special voting rights. Preferred stock issued by young companies has seniority in any liquidation but typically does not pay cash dividends and contains a right to convert to common stock.

preliminary prospectus (red herring) Part of the registration statement prepared by a company prior to an IPO that is circulated to investors before the stock is offered.

premium A price at which coupon bonds trade that is greater than their face value. Also, the price a firm pays to purchase insurance, allowing the firm to exchange a random future loss for a certain upfront expense.

prepackaged bankruptcy A method for avoiding many of the legal and other direct costs of bankruptcy in which a firm first develops a reorganization plan with the agreement of its main creditors, and then files Chapter 11 to implement the plan.

prepayment risk The risk faced by an investor in a callable bond or loan that the principal may be prepaid prior to maturity. This risk is the most important risk for holders of agency-backed mortgages.

present value (PV) The value of a cost or benefit computed in terms of cash today.

pretax WACC The weighted average cost of capital computed using the pretax cost of debt; it can be used to estimate the unlevered cost of capital for a firm that maintains a target leverage ratio.

price-earnings ratio (P/E) The ratio of the market value of equity to the firm's earnings, or its share price to its earnings per share.

price-to-book (PB) ratio *See* market-to-book ratio.

price-weighted portfolio A portfolio that holds an equal number of shares of each stock, independent of their size.

primary market Market used when a corporation itself issues new shares of stock and sells them to investors.

primary offering New shares available in a public offering that raise new capital.

primary shares New shares issued by a company in an equity offering.

prime rate The rate banks charge their most creditworthy customers.

prior one-year momentum (PR1YR) portfolio A self-financing portfolio that goes long on the top 30% of stocks with the highest prior year returns, and short on the 30% with the lowest prior year returns, each year.

private company A company whose shares do not trade on a public market.

private debt Debt that is not publicly traded.

private equity firm A firm organized very similarly to venture capital firms that invests in the equity of existing privately held firms rather than startup companies.

private placement A bond issue that is sold to a small group of investors rather than to the general public. Because a private placement does not need to be registered, it is less costly to issue.

pro forma Describes a statement that is not based on actual data but rather depicts a firm's financials under a given set of hypothetical assumptions.

probability distribution A graph that provides the probability of every possible discrete state.

processing float How long it takes a firm to process a customer's payment check and deposit it in the bank.

profitability index Measures the NPV per unit of resource consumed.

profitability index rule Recommends investment whenever the profitability index exceeds some predetermined number.

project externalities Indirect effects of a project that may increase or decrease the profits of other business activities of a firm.

promissory note A written statement that indicates the amount of a loan, the date payment is due, and the interest rate.

property insurance A type of insurance companies purchase to compensate them for losses to their assets due to fire, storm damage, vandalism, earthquakes, and other natural and environmental risks.

protective put A long position in a put option held on a stock you already own.

proxy fight In a hostile takeover, when the acquirer attempts to convince the target's shareholders to unseat the target's board by using their proxy votes to support the acquirers' candidates for election to the target's board.

public companies Those corporations whose stock is traded on a stock market or exchange, providing shareholders the ability to quickly and easily convert their investments into cash.

public warehouse A business that exists for the sole purpose of storing and tracking the inflow and outflow of inventory. If a lender extends a loan to a borrowing firm, based on the value of the inventory, this arrangement provides the lender with the tightest control over the inventory.

pure discount bond *See* zero-coupon bond.

put-call parity The relationship that gives the price of call option in terms of the price of put option plus the price of the underlying stock minus the present value of the strike price and the present value of any dividend payments.

put option A financial option that gives its owner the right to sell an asset for a fixed price up to (and on) a fixed date.

PV *See* present value.

pyramid structure A way for an investor to control a corporation without owning 50% of the equity whereby the investor first creates a company in which he has a controlling interest. This company then owns a controlling interest in another company. The investor controls both companies, but may own as little as 25% of the second company.

quick ratio The ratio of current assets other than inventory to current liabilities.

raider The acquirer in a hostile takeover.

rational expectations The idea that investors may have different information regarding expected returns, correlations, and volatilities, but they correctly interpret that information and the information contained in market prices and adjust their estimates of expected returns in a rational way.

real interest rate The rate of growth of purchasing power after adjusting for inflation.

real option The right to make a particular business decision, such as a capital investment. A key distinction between real options and financial options is that real options, and the underlying assets on which they are based, are often not traded in competitive markets.

realized return The return that actually occurs over a particular time period.

record date When a firm pays a dividend, only shareholders of record on this date receive the dividend.

red herring *See* preliminary prospectus.

refinance Repaying an existing loan and then taking out a new loan at a lower rate.

registered bonds The issuer of this type of bond maintains a list of all holders of its bonds. Coupon and principal payments are made only to people on this list.

registration statement A legal document that provides financial and other information about a company to investors, prior to a security issuance.

regression A statistical technique that estimates a linear relationship between two variables (the dependent and independent variable) by fitting a line that minimizes the squared distance between the data and the line.

relative wealth concerns When investors are concerned about the performance of their portfolio relative to that of their peers, rather than its absolute performance.

repatriated Refers to the profits from a foreign project that a firm brings back to its home country.

repatriation tax Additional corporate tax owed, based on the difference between the U.S. and foreign tax rates, if profits earned abroad are returned to the U.S.

replicating portfolio A portfolio consisting of a stock and a risk-free bond that has the same value and payoffs in one period as an option written on the same stock.

repurchase yield Amount spent on repurchases during the year divided by the firm's equity market capitalization at the start of the year. The repurchase yield plus the dividend yield provides a measure of the firm's total payouts.

required return The expected return of an investment that is necessary to compensate for the risk of undertaking the investment.

residual income Net income less an equity charge equal to the book value of equity times the equity cost of capital.

residual income method Valuation method based on discounting residual income; equivalent to the flow to equity method.

residual term *See* error term.

residual value An asset's market value at the end of a lease.

retained earnings The difference between a firm's net income and the amount it spends on dividends.

retention rate The fraction of a firm's current earnings that the firm retains.

return The difference between the selling price and purchasing price of an asset plus any cash distributions expressed as a percentage of the buying price.

return of capital When a firm, instead of paying dividends out of current earnings (or accumulated retained earnings), pays dividends from other sources, such as paid-in capital or the liquidation of assets.

return on assets (ROA) The ratio of net income plus interest expense to the total book value of the firm's assets. This measure of ROA includes the benefit of the interest tax shield associated with leverage. As a benchmark, ROA is most comparable to the firm's unlevered cost of capital.

return on equity (ROE) The ratio of a firm's net income to the book value of its equity. As a benchmark, ROE is most comparable to the firm's required return on equity.

return on invested capital (ROIC) The ratio of a firm's after-tax profit excluding any interest expense (or income) to the sum of the book value of its equity and net debt. As a benchmark, ROIC is most comparable to the firm's weighted average cost of capital.

revenue bonds Municipal bonds for which the local or state government can pledge as repayment revenues generated by specific projects.

reverse split When the price of a company's stock falls too low and the company reduces the number of outstanding shares.

revolving line of credit A credit commitment for a specific time period, typically two to three years, which a company can use as needed.

rights offer A type of seasoned equity offering (SEO) in which a firm offers the new shares only to existing shareholders.

risk-arbitrageurs Traders who, once a takeover offer is announced, speculate on the outcome of the deal.

risk aversion When investors prefer to have a safe future payment rather than an uncertain one of the same expected amount.

risk-free interest rate The interest rate at which money can be borrowed or lent without risk over a given period.

risk-neutral probabilities The probability of future states that are consistent with current prices of securities assuming all investors are risk neutral. Also known as state-contingent prices, state prices, or martingale prices.

risk premium Represents the additional return that investors expect to earn to compensate them for a security's risk.

ROA *See* return on assets.

road show During an IPO, when a company's senior management and its underwriters travel around the country (and sometimes around the world) promoting the company and explaining their rationale for an offer price to the underwriters' largest customers, mainly institutional investors such as mutual funds and pension funds.

ROE *See* return on equity.

ROIC *See* return on invested capital.

R-squared In the CAPM regression, the square of the correlation between the stock's and market's excess returns. More generally, the fraction of the variance of the independent variable that is explained in a regression.

"S" corporations Those corporations that elect subchapter S tax treatment and are allowed, by the U.S. Internal Revenue Tax code, an exemption from double taxation.

sale and leaseback Describes a type of lease in which a firm already owns an asset it would prefer to lease. The firm receives cash from the sale of the asset and then makes lease payments to retain the use of the asset.

sales-type lease A type of lease in which the lessor is the manufacturer (or a primary dealer) of the asset.

Samurai bonds A term for foreign bonds in Japan.

Sarbanes-Oxley Act (SOX) A 2002 Congressional act intended to improve the accuracy of information given to both boards and to shareholders.

scenario analysis An important capital budgeting tool that determines how the NPV varies as a number of the underlying assumptions are changed simultaneously.

seasoned equity offering (SEO) When a public company offers new shares for sale.

secondary market Market shares continue to trade on after the initial transaction between the corporation and investors.

secondary offering An equity offering of secondary shares.

secondary shares Shares sold by existing shareholders in an equity offering.

secured debt A type of corporate loan or debt security in which specific assets are pledged as a firm's collateral.

secured loans Loan collateralized with assets held by the firm, such as the firm's accounts receivables, inventory, or plant, property or equipment.

security *See* financial security.

security interest A classification of a lease in bankruptcy proceedings that assumes a firm has effective ownership of an asset and the asset is protected against seizure.

security market line (SML) The pricing implication of the CAPM, it specifies a linear relation between the risk premium of a security and its beta with the market portfolio.

segmented capital markets Capital markets that are not internationally integrated.

self-financing portfolio A portfolio that costs nothing to construct.

semi-strong form efficiency The theory that consistent profits should not be possible from trading on any public information, such as news announcements or analysts' recommendations.

seniority A bondholder's priority in claiming assets not already securing other debt.

sensation seeking The increase in trading activity due to an individual's desire for novel or intense risk-taking experiences.

sensitivity analysis An important capital budgeting tool that determines how the NPV varies as a single underlying assumption is changed.

SEO *See* seasoned equity offering.

Separate Trading of Registered Interest and Principal Securities (STRIPS) *See* STRIPS.

Separation Principle In a perfect market, the NPV of an investment decision can be evaluated separately from any financial transactions a firm is considering.

serial bonds A single issue of municipal bonds that are scheduled to mature serially over a period of years.

share repurchase A situation in which a firm uses cash to buy back its own stock.

shareholder (also stockholder or equity holder) An owner of a share of stock in a corporation.

Sharpe ratio The excess return of an asset divided by the volatility of the return of the asset; a measure of the reward per unit risk.

short interest The number of shares sold short.

short position A negative amount invested in a stock.

short sale Selling a security you do not own.

short-term debt Debt with a maturity of less than one year.

signaling theory of debt The use of leverage as a way to signal information to investors.

simple interest Interest earned without the effect of compounding.

single-factor model A model using an efficient portfolio, capturing all systemic risk alone.

sinking fund A method for repaying a bond in which a company makes regular payments into a fund administered by a trustee over the life of the bond. These payments are then used to repurchase bonds.

size effect The observation that small stocks (or stocks with a high book-to-market ratio) have higher returns.

small-minus-big (SMB) portfolio A portfolio resulting from a trading strategy that each year buys a small market value portfolio and finances that position by selling short a large market value portfolio.

SMB portfolio *See* small-minus-big portfolio.

SML *See* security market line.

sole proprietorship A business owned and run by one person.

sovereign bonds Bonds issued by national governments.

sovereign debt Debt issued by a national government.

SOX *See* Sarbanes-Oxley Act.

SPE *See* special-purpose entity.

special dividend A one-time dividend payment a firm makes that is usually much larger than a regular dividend.

special-purpose entity (SPE) A separate business partnership created by a lessee for the sole purpose of obtaining a lease.

specialists Individuals on the trading floor of the NYSE who match buyers with sellers; also called market makers.

speculate When investors use securities to place a bet on the direction in which they believe the market is likely to move.

speculative bonds Bonds in one of the bottom five categories of creditworthiness that have a high risk of default.

spin-off When a firm sells a subsidiary by selling shares in the subsidiary alone.

spot exchange rate The current foreign exchange rate.

spot interest rates Default-free, zero-coupon yields.

staggered (classified) board In many public companies, a board of directors whose three-year terms are staggered so that only one-third of the directors are up for election each year.

stakeholder model The explicit consideration most countries (other than the United States) give to other stakeholders besides equity holders, in particular, rank-and-file employees.

standard deviation A common method used to measure the risk of a probability distribution, it is the square root of the variance, the expected squared deviation from the mean.

standard error The standard deviation of the estimated value of the mean of the actual distribution around its true value; that is, it is the standard deviation of the average return.

state-contingent prices *See* risk-neutral probabilities.

state prices *See* risk-neutral probabilities.

statement of cash flows An accounting statement that shows how a firm has used the cash it earned during a set period.

statement of financial performance Statement showing the firm's revenues and expenses over a period of time. *See also* income statement.

statement of financial position List of the firm's assets and liabilities that provides a snapshot of the firm's financial position at a given point in time. *See also* balance sheet.

statement of stockholders' equity An accounting statement that breaks down the stockholders' equity computed on the balance sheet into the amount that came from issuing new shares versus retained earnings.

step up Refers to an increase in the book value of a target's assets to the purchase price when an acquirer purchases those assets directly instead of purchasing the target stock.

stock The ownership or equity of a corporation divided into shares.

stock dividend *See* stock split.

stock exchanges *See* stock markets.

stock market (also stock exchange) Organized market on which the shares of many corporations are publicly traded.

stock options A form of compensation a firm gives to its employees that gives them the right to buy a certain number of shares of stock by a specific date at a specific price.

stock-outs When a firm runs out of inventory, leading to lost sales.

stock split When a company issues a dividend in shares of stock rather than cash to its shareholders.

stock swap Merger deal when the target shareholders receive stock as payment for target shares.

stockholder (also shareholder or equity holder) An owner of a share of stock or equity in a corporation.

stockholders' equity An accounting measure of a firm's net worth that represents the difference between the firm's assets and its liabilities.

stop-out yield The highest yield competitive bid that will fund a particular U.S. Treasury security issue when all successful bidders (including the noncompetitive bidders) are awarded this yield.

straddle A portfolio that is long a call and a put on the same stock with the same exercise date and the strike price.

straight-line depreciation A method of depreciation in which an asset's cost is divided equally over its life.

strangle A portfolio that is long a call and a put with the same exercise date, but the strike price of the call exceeds the strike price of the put.

strategic investor *See* corporate investor.

strategic partner *See* corporate investor.

stream of cash flows A series of cash flows lasting several periods.

stretching the accounts payable When a firm ignores a payment due period and pays later.

strike (exercise) price The price at which an option holder buys or sells a share of stock when the option is exercised.

STRIPS (Separate Trading of Registered Interest and Principal Securities) Zero-coupon Treasury securities with maturities longer than one year that trade in the bond market.

strong form efficiency The theory that it should not be possible to consistently profit even by trading on private information.

subordinated debenture Debt that, in the event of a default, has a lower priority claim to the firm's assets than other outstanding debt.

subprime mortgages Mortgages for which borrowers do not meet typical credit standards, and thus have a high default probability.

sunk cost Any unrecoverable cost for which a firm is already liable.

sunk cost fallacy The idea that once a manager makes a large investment, he should not abandon a project.

sustainable growth rate Rate at which a firm can grow using only retained earnings.

syndicate A group of underwriters who jointly underwrite and distribute a security issuance.

syndicated bank loan A single loan that is funded by a group of banks rather than just a single bank.

synthetic lease A lease that commonly uses a special-purpose entity (SPE) and is designed to obtain specific accounting and tax treatment.

systematic, undiversifiable, or market risk Fluctuations of a stock's return that are due to market-wide news representing common risk.

tailing the hedge Adjusting the hedge position in a futures contract to account for interest earned on marked-to-market profits.

takeover Refers to two mechanisms, either a merger or an acquisition, by which ownership and control of a firm can change.

takeover synergies Value obtained from an acquisition that could not be obtained if the target remained an independent firm; i.e., value in excess of the firm's standalone value.

tangent portfolio A portfolio with the highest Sharpe ratio; the point of tangency to the efficient frontier of a line drawn from the risk-free asset; the market portfolio if the CAPM holds.

target The firm that is purchased in a merger or acquisition.

target firm A firm that is acquired by another in a merger or acquisition.

target leverage ratio When a firm adjusts its debt proportionally to a project's value or its cash flows (where the proportion need not remain constant). A constant market debt-equity ratio is a special case.

targeted repurchase When a firm purchases shares directly from a specific shareholder.

tax loss carryforwards and carrybacks Two features of the U.S. tax code that allow corporations to take losses during a current year and offset them against gains in nearby years. Since 1997, companies can "carry back" losses for two years and "carry forward" losses for 20 years.

TED (Treasury-Eurodollar) spread Difference in interest rates between the three-month London Inter-Bank Offered Rate (LIBOR) and three-month U.S. Treasury bills.

temporary working capital The difference between the actual level of short-term working capital needs and its permanent working capital requirements.

tender offer A public announcement of an offer to all existing security holders to buy back a specified amount of outstanding securities at a prespecified price over a prespecified period of time.

term Time remaining until the final repayment date of a bond.

term loan A bank loan that lasts for a specific term.

term sheet Summary of the structure of a merger transaction that includes details such as who will run the new company, the size and composition of the new board, the location of the headquarters, and the name of the new company.

term structure The relationship between the investment term and the interest rate.

terminal (continuation) value The value of a project's remaining free cash flows beyond the forecast horizon. This amount represents the market value (as of the last forecast period) of the free cash flow from the project at all future dates. *See also* continuation value.

TEV (total enterprise value) *See* enterprise value.

time value The difference between an option's price and its intrinsic value.

time value of money The difference in value between money today and money in the future; also, the observation that two cash flows at two different points in time have different values.

timeline A linear representation of the timing of (potential) cash flows.

TIPS (Treasury Inflation-Protected Securities) An inflation-indexed bond issued by the U.S. Treasury with maturities of 5, 10, and 20 years. They are standard coupon bonds with one difference: The outstanding principle is adjusted for inflation.

toehold An initial ownership stake in a firm that a corporate raider can use to initiate a takeover attempt.

tombstones Newspaper advertisements in which an underwriter advertises a security issuance.

total enterprise value (TEV) *See* enterprise value.

total payout model A firm's total payouts to equity holders (i.e., all the cash distributed as dividends and stock repurchases) are discounted and then divided by the current number of shares outstanding to determine the share price.

total return The sum of a stock's dividend yield and its capital gain rate.

trade credit The difference between receivables and payables that is the net amount of a firm's capital consumed as a result of those credit transactions; the credit that a firm extends to its customers.

trade-off theory The firm picks its capital structure by trading off the benefits of the tax shield from debt against the costs of financial distress and agency costs.

trailing earnings A firm's earnings over the prior 12 months.

trailing P/E The computation of a firm's P/E using its trailing earnings.

tranches Different classes of securities that comprise a single bond issuance. All classes of securities are paid from the same cash flow source.

transaction cost In most markets, an expense such as a broker commission and the bid-ask spread investors must pay in order to trade securities.

transactions balance The amount of cash a firm needs to be able to pay its bills.

Treasury bills Zero-coupon bonds, issued by the U.S. government, with a maturity of up to one year.

Treasury bonds A type of U.S. Treasury coupon securities, currently traded in financial markets, with original maturities of more than ten years.

Treasury Inflation-Protected Securities (TIPS) *See* TIPS.

Treasury notes A type of U.S. Treasury coupon securities, currently traded in financial markets, with original maturities from one to ten years.

treasury stock method Method of computing a firm's fully diluted share count by including the net new shares potentially created by unexercised in-the-money warrants and options. This method assumes any proceeds the company receives from the exercise are used to repurchase shares. It is equivalent to adding shares with the same market value as the intrinsic value of the options.

true lease A classification of a lease in bankruptcy proceedings in which the lessor retains ownership rights over an asset.

true tax lease A type of lease in which the lessor receives the depreciation deductions associated with the ownership of the asset. The lessee can deduct the full amount of the lease payments as an operating expense, and these lease payments are treated as revenue for the lessor.

trust receipts loan A type of loan in which distinguishable inventory items are held in a trust as security for the loan. As these items are sold, the firm remits the proceeds from their sale to the lender in repayment of the loan.

tunneling A conflict of interest that arises when a shareholder who has a controlling interest in multiple firms moves profits (and hence dividends) away from companies in which he has relatively less cash flow rights toward firms in which he has relatively more cash flow rights.

turnover ratios Measures of working capital computed by expressing annual revenues or costs as a multiple of the corresponding working capital account (accounts receivable, accounts payable, and inventory).

uncommitted line of credit A line of credit that does not legally bind a bank to provide the funds a borrower requests.

under-investment problem A situation in which equity holders choose not to invest in a postive NPV project because the firm is in financial distress and the value of undertaking the investment opportunity will accrue to bondholders rather than themselves.

underwriter An investment banking firm that manages a security issuance and designs its structure.

underwriting spread Company-paid fee to underwriters based on the issue price.

undiversifiable risk *See* systematic risk.

unicorn Pre-IPO start-up firms with valuations in excess of $1 billion.

unique risk *See* firm-specific risk.

unlevered beta Measures the risk of a firm were it unlevered; beta of the firm's assets; measures the market risk of the firm's business activities, ignoring any additional risk due to leverage.

unlevered cost of capital The cost of capital of a firm, were it unlevered; for a firm that maintains a target leverage ratio, it can be estimated as the weighted average cost of capital computed without taking into account taxes (pretax WACC).

unlevered equity Equity in a firm with no debt.

unlevered net income Net income plus after-tax interest expense; equivalently, after-tax EBIT. *See also* net operating profit after tax (NOPAT).

unlevered P/E ratio The enterprise value of a firm divided by its unlevered net income in a particular year.

unsecured debt A type of corporate debt that, in the event of a bankruptcy, gives bondholders a claim to only the assets of the firm that are not already pledged as collateral on other debt.

unsystematic risk *See* firm-specific risk.

valuation multiple A ratio of a firm's value to some measure of the firm's scale or cash flow.

Valuation Principle The value of an asset to the firm or its investors is determined by its competitive market price: The benefits and costs of a decision should be evaluated using these market prices, and when the value of the benefits exceeds the value of the costs, the decision will increase the market value of the firm.

value additivity A relationship determined by the Law of One Price, in which the price of an asset that consists of other assets must equal the sum of the prices of the other assets.

value stocks Firms with low market-to-book ratios.

value-weighted portfolio A portfolio in which each security is held in proportion to its market capitalization. Also called an equal-ownership portfolio, because it consists of the same fraction of the outstanding shares of each security.

variance A method to measure the risk of a probability distribution, it is the expected squared deviation from the mean.

venture capital firm A limited partnership that specializes in raising money to invest in the private equity of young firms.

venture capitalist One of the general partners who work for and run a venture capital firm.

vertical integration Refers to the merger of two companies in the same industry that make products required at different stages of the production cycle. Also, refers to the merger of a firm and its supplier or a firm and its customer.

vertical merger The type of merger when the target's industry buys or sells to the acquirer's industry.

VIX Index An index quoted in percent per annum that tracks the one-month implied volatility of options written on the S&P 500 Index. It is a popular measure of market volatility.

volatility The standard deviation of a return.

WACC *See* weighted average cost of capital.

warehouse arrangement When the inventory that serves as collateral for a loan is stored in a warehouse.

warrant A call option written by the company itself on new stock. When a holder of a warrant exercises it and thereby purchases stock, the company delivers this stock by issuing new stock.

weak form efficiency The theory that it should not be possible to profit by trading on information in past prices by, for example, selling winners and hanging on to losers or, conversely, by trading on momentum.

weighted average cost of capital (WACC) The average of a firm's equity and after-tax cost of capital, weighted by the fraction of the firm's enterprise value that corresponds to equity and debt, respectively. Discounting free cash flows using the WACC computes their value including the interest tax shield.

white knight A target company's defense against a hostile takeover attempt, in which it looks for another, friendlier company to acquire it.

white squire A variant of the white knight defense, in which a large, passive investor or firm agrees to purchase a substantial block of shares in a target with special voting rights.

winner's curse Refers to a situation in competitive bidding when the high bidder, by virtue of being the high bidder, has very likely overestimated the value of the item being bid on.

with recourse A loan or lease in which the lender can claim all the borrower's assets, not just explicitly pledged collateral, in the event of a default.

without recourse A loan or lease in which the lender's claim on the borrower's assets in the event of a default is limited to only explicitly pledged collateral.

workout A method for avoiding a declaration of bankruptcy in which a firm in financial distress negotiates directly with its creditors to reorganize.

Yankee bonds A term for foreign bonds in the United States.

yield curve A plot of bond yields as a function of the bonds' maturity date.

yield to call (YTC) The yield of a callable bond calculated under the assumption that the bond will be called on the earliest call date.

yield to maturity (YTM) The discount rate that sets the present value of the promised bond payments equal to the current market price of the bond. Equivalently, it is the IRR of an investment in a bond that is held to maturity and does not default.

YTC *See* yield to call.

YTM *See* yield to maturity.

zero-coupon bond A bond that makes only one payment at maturity.

zero-coupon yield curve A plot of the yield of risk-free zero-coupon bonds (STRIPS) as a function of the bond's maturity date.

Index

Note to reader: **Bold** page number indicates a key topic, which appears bold on the referenced page. Page number followed by *b, e, f,* or *t* indicates that the reference is within a box (*b*), example (*e*), figure (*f*), or table (*t*). Page number preceded by n. indicates that the reference is within a footnote.

C

E

G

Q

R

W

	COMMON MISTAKE boxes alert students to frequently made mistakes stemming from misunderstanding core concepts and calculations—in the classroom and in the field.	**GLOBAL FINANCIAL CRISIS** boxes reflect the reality of the recent financial crisis and ongoing sovereign debt crisis, noting lessons learned. 22 boxes across the book illustrate and analyze key details.	**USING EXCEL** boxes provide hands-on instruction of Excel techniques and include screenshots to serve as a guide for students.	**INTERVIEWS** with notable practitioners—19 in total—highlight leaders in the field and address the effect of the financial crisis.
CHAPTER 1 *The Corporation*		The Dodd-Frank Act The Dodd-Frank Act on Corporate Compensation and Governance		David Viniar, Goldman Sachs Frank Hatheway, Nasdaq
CHAPTER 2 *Introduction to Financial Statement Analysis*	Mismatched Ratios	Bernard Madoff's Ponzi Scheme		Ruth Porat, Google/Alphabet
CHAPTER 3 *Financial Decision Making and the Law of One Price*		Liquidity and the Informational Role of Prices		
CHAPTER 4 *The Time Value of Money*	Discounting One Too Many Times		Calculating Present Values in Excel Excel's IRR Function	
CHAPTER 5 *Interest Rates*	Using the Wrong Discount Rate in the Annuity Formula Using the Annuity Formula When Discount Rates Vary by Maturity States Dig a $3 Trillion Hole by Discounting at the Wrong Rate	Teaser Rates and Subprime Loans		Kevin M. Warsh, former Governor of the Federal Reserve Board
CHAPTER 6 *Valuing Bonds*		Negative Bond Yields The Credit Crisis and Bond Yields European Sovereign Debt Yields: A Puzzle		Carmen M. Reinhart, Harvard University
CHAPTER 7 *Investment Decision Rules*	IRR Versus the IRR Rule IRR and Project Financing			Dick Grannis, Qualcomm
CHAPTER 8 *Fundamentals of Capital Budgeting*	The Opportunity Cost of an Idle Asset The Sunk Cost Fallacy	The American Recovery and Reinvestment Act of 2009	Capital Budgeting Using a Spreadsheet Program Project Analysis Using Excel	David Holland, Cisco
CHAPTER 9 *Valuing Stocks*				Douglas Kehring, Oracle
CHAPTER 10 *Capital Markets and the Pricing of Risk*	A Fallacy of Long-Run Diversification Beta Versus Volatility	Diversification Benefits During Market Crashes		
CHAPTER 11 *Optimal Portfolio Choice and the Capital Asset Pricing Model*	Computing Variance, Covariance, and Correlation in Excel			John Powers, Stanford Management Company
CHAPTER 12 *Estimating the Cost of Capital*	Using the Debt Yield as Its Cost of Capital Adjusting for Execution Risk Using a Single Cost of Capital in Multi-Divisional Firms Changing the Index to Improve the Fit		Estimating Beta Using Excel	Shelagh Glaser, Intel
CHAPTER 13 *Investor Behavior and Capital Market Efficiency*				Jonathan Clements, author and personal finance columnist, *The Wall Street Journal*